MyMathLab®

www.mymathlab.com

Homework help, test prep, and tutoring—on your schedule

With MyMathLab, you have access to a personalized interactive learning environment, where you can learn at your own pace and measure your progress. MyMathLab includes learning tools such as videos, the complete ebook, and the Student's Solutions Manual.

Help when you need it

The exercises in MyMathLab correspond to the exercises in this textbook. Your instructor may assign them to you, or you can practice on your own.

Many exercises include guided solutions, sample problems, and learning aids.

Help Me Solve This — Breaks the problem down into steps that you complete to help build understanding.

View an Example — Reviews a worked-out problem similar to the one you are being asked to complete.

Textbook — Links to the section in the textbook where this problem is covered.

Video — Watch an instructor explain this concept.

Ask My Instructor

Print

Help Me Solve This
These guided solutions accompany the exercises and walk you through solving the problem step by step.

Study Plan ▸ Course Calendar
Legend 🖨 ⑦

Click a chapter below to start practicing, or follow these steps to create a personalized study plan.

① Take a sample test or an assigned test or quiz. Then return to this page.

② Practice the questions in the topics you need to study (🖊).

③ When you have answered all questions correctly (✓), take another sample test or an assigned ▸ **Learn More**
test or quiz to prove mastery (🎓).

[Show All 🖊 Show What I Need to Study]   ➡ **Jump to where I worked last**

Book Contents for All Topics		Correct	Worked	Questions	Time Spent
➕ Ch 0: Orientation Questions for Students				8	
➕ Ch 1: Linear Equations and Graphs				45	
➕ Ch 2: Functions and Graphs				104	
➕ Ch 3: Mathematics of Finance				67	
➖ Ch 4: Systems of Linear Equations; Matrices	🖊			117	
➕ 4.1 Review: Systems of Linear Equations in Two Variables	🖊			17	
➕ 4.2 Systems of Linear Equations and Augmented Matrices	🖊			18	
➕ 4.3 Gauss-Jordan Elimination	🖊			23	
➕ 4.4 Matrices; Basic Operations	🖊			19	
➕ 4.5 Inverse of a Square Matrix	🖊			17	
➕ 4.6 Matrix Equations and Systems of Linear Equations	🖊			14	
➕ 4.7 Leontief Input-Output Analysis	🖊			9	
➕ Ch 5: Linear Inequalities and Linear Programming				35	

Test prep when you need it

Take a practice test to gauge your readiness. MyMathLab then generates a personalized Study Plan with links to interactive tutorial exercises for those skills you need to review.

Pearson
Tutor Center

Tutors when you need them

MyMathLab users have access to tutoring from the Pearson Math Tutor Center.* The Tutor Center is staffed by qualified math instructors who provide one-on-one tutoring via toll-free phone, email, and real-time Web sessions. For more details, visit **www.pearsontutorservices.com**

Proven Success

Since 2001, more than 5 million students at more than 1,850 colleges have used MyMathLab and MathXL.® MyMathLab and MathXL provide you with a personalized, interactive learning environment where you can learn at your own pace, measure your progress, and improve your success in this course.

Student Purchasing Options

Talk to your instructor about using MyMathLab or MathXL for this course.

* Pearson Tutor Services are provided by Pearson Higher Education, a division of Pearson Education, Inc., for US and Canadian post-secondary students. Pearson's offer of tutoring service is subject to change without notice.

COLLEGE
MATHEMATICS

FOR BUSINESS, ECONOMICS, LIFE SCIENCES, AND SOCIAL SCIENCES

TWELFTH EDITION

RAYMOND A. BARNETT Merritt College

MICHAEL R. ZIEGLER Marquette University

KARL E BYLEEN Marquette University

Boston Columbs Indianapolis New York San Francisco Upper Saddle River
Amsterdam Ca Town Dubai London Madrid Milan Munich Paris Montréal Toronto
Delhi Mexico C São Paulo Sydney Hong Kong Seoul Singapore Taipei Tokyo

Dedicated to the memory of Michael R. Ziegler,
trusted author, colleague, and friend.

Editor in Chief: Deirdre Lynch
Executive Editor: Jennifer Crum
Executive Project Manager: Christine O'Brien
Editorial Assistant: Joanne Wendelken
Senior Managing Editor: Karen Wernholm
Senior Production Supervisor: Tracy Patruno
Cover Designer: Christina Gleason
Executive Manager, Course production: Peter Silvia
Media Producer: Shana Rosenthal
Associate Media Producer: Christina Maestri
Digital Assets Manager: Marianne Groth
Executive Marketing Manager: Jeff Weidenaar
Marketing Assistant: Kendra Bassi
Rights and Permissions Advisor: Michael Joyce
Senior Author Support/Technology Specialist: Joe Vetere
Senior Manufacturing Buyer: Carol Melville
Interior Design: Leslie Haimes
Illustrations: Scientific Illustrators and Laserwords Private Ltd.
Production Coordination and Composition: Prepare, Inc.

Photo credits p. 1 Liquidlibrary/Jupiter Unlimited; p. 43 Ingram Publishing/Alamy; p. 125 Photodisc/
Alamy; p. 169 luchschen/Shutterstock; p. 250 Gustavo Miguel Fernandes/Shutterstock;
p. 279 istockphoto.com; p. 334 Ryan Mcvay/Getty Images; p. 372 Thinkstock/Jupiter Unlimited;
p. 432 Anton Foltin/Shutterstock; p. 474 Lisa F. Young/Shutterstock; p. 558 Aron Brand/
Shutterstock; p. 614 Barry Austin Photography/Getty Images, Inc. - PhotoDisc; p. 697 Mike Cherim/
iStockphoto.com; p. 758 iStockphoto.com; p. 797 Vladimir Seliverstov/Dreamstime LLC -Royalty Free

1 2 3 4 5 6 7 8 9 10—EB—14 13 12 11 10

ISBN 10: 0-321-71082-7
ISBN 13: 978-0-321-71082-6

CONTENTS

Contents of Additional Calculus Topics to Accompany Calculus, 12e and College Mathematics, 12e (available separately)

Appendices A and B are found in the following publications:
Calculus for Business, Economics, Life Sciences and Social Sciences, 12e (0-321-61399-6) and *College Mathematics for Business, Economics, Life Sciences and Social Sciences,* 12e (0-321-61400-3).

Appendix C   Tables
Table III Area Under the Standard Normal Curve
Appendix D   Special Calculus Topic
D-1 Interpolating Polynomials and Divided Differences

Answers
Solutions to Odd-Numbered Exercises
Index
Applications Index

PREFACE

The twelfth edition of *College Mathematics for Business, Economics, Life Sciences, and Social Sciences* is designed for a two-term (or condensed one-term) course in finite mathematics and calculus for students who have had one to two years of high school algebra or the equivalent. The book's overall approach, refined by the authors' experience with large sections of college freshmen, addresses the challenges of teaching and learning when prerequisite knowledge varies greatly from student to student.

Our main goal was to write a text that students can easily comprehend.

Many elements play a role in determining a book's effectiveness for students. Not only is it critical that the text be accurate and readable but also, in order for a book to be effective, aspects such as the page design, the interactive nature of the presentation, and the ability to support and challenge all students have an incredible impact on how easily students comprehend the material. Here are some of the ways this text addresses the needs of students at all levels:

- Page layout is clean and free of potentially distracting elements.

- *Matched Problems* that accompany each of the completely worked examples help students gain solid knowledge of the basic topics and assess their own level of understanding before moving on.

- Review material (Appendix A and Chapters 1 and 2) can be used judiciously to help remedy gaps in prerequisite knowledge.

- A *Diagnostic Algebra Test* prior to Chapter 1 helps students assess their prerequisite skills, while the *Basic Algebra Review* in Appendix A provides students with the content they need to remediate those skills.

- *Explore & Discuss* problems lead the discussion into new concepts or build upon a current topic. They help students of all levels gain better insight into the mathematical concepts through thought-provoking questions that are effective in both small and large classroom settings.

- Exercise sets are very purposely and carefully broken down into three categories by level of difficulty: A, B, and C. This allows instructors to easily craft homework assignments that best meet the needs of their students.

- The MyMathLab course for this text is designed to help students help themselves and provide instructors with actionable information about their progress.

In addition to the above, all students get substantial experience in modeling and solving real-world problems through application exercises chosen from business and economics, life sciences, and social sciences. Great care has been taken to write a book that is mathematically correct, with its emphasis on computational skills, ideas, and problem solving rather than mathematical theory.

Finally, the choice and independence of topics make the text readily adaptable to a variety of courses (see the chapter dependencies chart on page xii). This text is one of three books in the authors' college mathematics series. The others are *Finite Mathematics for Business, Economics, Life Sciences, and Social Sciences*, and *Calculus for Business, Economics, Life Sciences, and Social Sciences*. *Additional Calculus Topics*, a supplement written to accompany the Barnett/Ziegler/Byleen series, can be used in conjunction with these books.

New to This Edition

Fundamental to a book's growth and effectiveness is classroom use and feedback. Now in its twelfth edition, *College Mathematics for Business, Economics, Life Sciences, and Social Sciences* has had the benefit of a substantial amount of both. Improvements in this edition evolved out of the generous response from a large number of users of the last and previous editions as well as survey results from instructors, mathematics departments, course outlines, and college catalogs. In this edition:

- Chapter 2 contains a new Section (2-4) on polynomial and rational functions to provide greater flexibility in the use of the review chapter.

- Continuous compound interest, which is given full treatment in Chapter 3, appears as a minor topic in Section 2-5.

- In Chapter 10, a discussion of vertical and horizontal asymptotes (Section 10-2) now precedes the treatment of continuity (Section 10-3).

- Examples and exercises have been given up-to-date contexts and data. (See pages 101, 104–5).

- Exposition has been simplified and clarified throughout the book.

- Answers to the *Matched Problems* are now included at the end of each section for easy student reference.

- The *Self-Test on Basic Algebra* has been renamed *Diagnostic Algebra Test* and has moved from Appendix A to the front of the book just prior to Chapter 1 to better encourage students to make use of this helpful assessment.

- Exercise coverage within MyMathLab has been expanded, including a complete chapter of prerequisite skills exercises labeled "Getting Ready."

Trusted Features

Emphasis and Style

As was stated earlier, this text is written for student comprehension. To that end, the focus has been on making the book both mathematically correct and accessible to students. Most derivations and proofs are omitted except where their inclusion adds significant insight into a particular concept as the emphasis is on computational skills, ideas, and problem solving rather than mathematical theory. General concepts and results are typically presented only after particular cases have been discussed.

Design

One of the hallmark features of this text is the **clean, straightforward design** of its pages. Navigation is made simple with an obvious hierarchy of key topics and a judicious use of call-outs and pedagogical features. We made the decision to maintain a 2-color design to help students stay focused on the mathematics and applications. Whether students start in the chapter opener or in the exercise sets, they can easily reference the content, examples, and *Conceptual Insights* they need to understand the topic at hand. Finally, a functional use of color improves the clarity of many illustrations, graphs, and explanations, and guides students through critical steps (see pages 27, 100, 107).

Examples and Matched Problems

More than **450** completely worked examples are used to introduce concepts and to demonstrate problem-solving techniques. Many examples have multiple parts, significantly increasing the total number of worked examples. The examples are annotated using blue text to the right of each step, and the problem-solving steps are clearly identified. **To give students extra help** in working through examples, dashed boxes are used to enclose steps that are usually performed mentally and rarely mentioned in other books (see Example 2 on page 4). Though some students may not need these additional steps, many will appreciate the fact that the authors do not assume too much in the way of prior knowledge.

EXAMPLE 5 Solving Logarithmic Equations   Find x so that

$$\tfrac{3}{2}\log_b 4 - \tfrac{2}{3}\log_b 8 + \log_b 2 = \log_b x$$

SOLUTION

$$\tfrac{3}{2}\log_b 4 - \tfrac{2}{3}\log_b 8 + \log_b 2 = \log_b x$$

$$\log_b 4^{3/2} - \log_b 8^{2/3} + \log_b 2 = \log_b x \qquad \textit{Property 7}$$

$$\log_b 8 - \log_b 4 + \log_b 2 = \log_b x$$

$$\log_b \frac{8 \cdot 2}{4} = \log_b x \qquad \textit{Properties 5 and 6}$$

$$\log_b 4 = \log_b x$$

$$x = 4 \qquad \textit{Property 8}$$

Matched Problem 5   Find x so that $3 \log_b 2 + \tfrac{1}{2}\log_b 25 - \log_b 20 = \log_b x$.

Each example is followed by a similar *Matched Problem* for the student to work while reading the material. This actively involves the student in the learning process. The answers to these matched problems are included at the end of each section for easy reference.

Explore & Discuss

Every section contains *Explore & Discuss* problems at appropriate places to encourage students to think about a relationship or process before a result is stated, or to investigate additional consequences of a development in the text. This serves to foster critical thinking and communication skills. The Explore & Discuss material can be used as in-class discussions or out-of-class group activities and is effective in both small and large class settings.

EXPLORE & DISCUSS 2   How many x intercepts can the graph of a quadratic function have? How many y intercepts? Explain your reasoning.

Exercise Sets

The book contains over 6,300 carefully selected and graded exercises. Many problems have multiple parts, significantly increasing the total number of exercises. Exercises are paired so that consecutive odd and even numbered exercises are of the same type and difficulty level. Each exercise set is designed to allow instructors to craft just the right assignment for students. Exercise sets are categorized as A (routine, easy mechanics), B (more difficult mechanics), and C (difficult mechanics and some theory) to make it easy for instructors to create assignments that are appropriate for their classes. The *writing exercises*, indicated by the icon ✎, provide students with an opportunity to express their understanding of the topic in writing. Answers to all odd-numbered problems are in the back of the book. Answers to application problems in linear programming include both the mathematical model and the numeric answer.

Applications

A major objective of this book is to give the student substantial experience in modeling and solving real-world problems. Enough applications are included to convince even the most skeptical student that mathematics is really useful (see the Index of Applications at the back of the book). Almost every exercise set contains application problems, including applications from business and economics, life sciences, and social sciences. An instructor with students from all three disciplines can let them choose applications from their own field of interest; if most students are from one of the three areas, then special emphasis can be placed there. Most of the applications are simplified versions of actual real world problems inspired by professional journals and books. No specialized experience is required to solve any of the application problems.

Technology

Although access to a graphing calculator or spreadsheets is not assumed, it is likely that many students will want to make use of this technology. To assist these students, optional graphing calculator and spreadsheet activities are included in appropriate places. These include brief discussions in the text, examples or portions of examples solved on a graphing calculator or spreadsheet, and exercises for the student to solve. For example, linear regression is introduced in Section 1-3, and regression techniques on a graphing calculator are used at appropriate points to illustrate mathematical modeling with real data. All the optional graphing calculator material is clearly identified with the icon ▱ and can be omitted without loss of continuity, if desired. Optional spreadsheet material is identified with the icon ▦. All graphs are computer-generated to ensure mathematical accuracy. Graphing calculator screens displayed in the text are actual output from a graphing calculator.

Additional Pedagogical Features

The following features, while helpful to any student, are particularly helpful to students enrolled in a large classroom setting where access to the instructor is more challenging or just less frequent. These features provide much-needed guidance for students as they tackle difficult concepts.

- **Call-out boxes** highlight important definitions, results, and step-by-step processes (see pages 90, 96–97).

- **Caution statements** appear throughout the text where student errors often occur.

> ⚠ **CAUTION** Note that in Example 11 we let $x = 0$ represent 1900. If we let $x = 0$ represent 1940, for example, we would obtain a different logarithmic regression equation, but the prediction for 2015 would be the same. We would *not* let $x = 0$ represent 1950 (the first year in Table 1) or any later year, because logarithmic functions are undefined at 0.

- **Conceptual Insights**, appearing in nearly every section, make explicit connections to students' previous knowledge.

> **CONCEPTUAL INSIGHT**
>
> The notation $(2, 7)$ has two common mathematical interpretations: the ordered pair with first coordinate 2 and second coordinate 7, and the open interval consisting of all real numbers between 2 and 7. The choice of interpretation is usually determined by the context in which the notation is used. The notation $(2, -7)$ could be interpreted as an ordered pair but not as an interval. In interval notation, the left endpoint is always written first. So, $(-7, 2)$ is correct interval notation, but $(2, -7)$ is not.

- **Boldface type** is used to introduce new terms and highlight important comments.
- The **Diagnostic Algebra Test**, now located at the front of the book, provides students with a tool to assess their prerequisite skills prior to taking the course. The **Basic Algebra Review**, in Appendix A, provides students with seven sections of content to help them remediate in specific areas of need. Answers to the Diagnostic Algebra Test are at the back of the book and reference specific sections in the Basic Algebra Review for students to use for remediation.

Chapter Reviews

Often it is during the preparation for a chapter exam that concepts gel for students, making the chapter review material particularly important. The chapter review sections in this text include a comprehensive summary of important terms, symbols, and concepts, keyed to completely worked examples, followed by a comprehensive set of review exercises. Answers to most review exercises are included at the back of the book; *each answer contains a reference to the section in which that type of problem is discussed* so students can remediate any deficiencies in their skills on their own.

Content

The text begins with the development of a library of elementary functions in **Chapters 1 and 2**, including their properties and uses. We encourage students to investigate mathematical ideas and processes graphically and numerically, as well as algebraically. This development lays a firm foundation for studying mathematics both in this book and in future endeavors. Depending on the course syllabus and the background of students, some or all of this material can be covered at the beginning of a course, or selected portions can be referenced as needed later in the course.

The material in Part Two (Finite Mathematics) can be thought of as four units:

1. Mathematics of finance (Chapter 3)
2. Linear algebra, including matrices, linear systems, and linear programming (Chapters 4, 5, and 6)
3. Probability (Chapters 7 and 8)
4. Applications of linear algebra and probability to Markov chains (Chapter 9)

The first three units are independent of each other, while Chapter 9 is dependent on some of the earlier chapters (see chart on next page).

- **Chapter 3** presents a thorough treatment of simple and compound interest and present and future value of ordinary annuities. Appendix B contains a section on arithmetic and geometric sequences that can be covered in conjunction with this chapter, if desired.

- **Chapter 4** covers linear systems and matrices with an emphasis on using row operations and Gauss–Jordan elimination to solve systems and to find matrix inverses. This chapter also contains numerous applications of mathematical modeling using systems and matrices. To assist students in formulating solutions, all answers at the back of the book for application problems in Exercises 4-3, 4-5, and the chapter Review Exercises contain both the mathematical model and its solution. The row operations discussed in Sections 4-2 and 4-3 are required for the simplex method in Chapter 6. Matrix multiplication, matrix inverses, and systems of equations are required for Markov chains in Chapter 9.

- **Chapters 5 and 6** provide a broad and flexible coverage of linear programming. Chapter 5 covers two-variable graphing techniques. Instructors who wish to emphasize linear programming techniques can cover the basic simplex method in Sections 6-1 and 6-2 and then discuss either or both of the following: the dual method (Section 6-3) and the big *M* method (Section 6-4). Those who want to emphasize modeling can discuss the formation of the mathematical model for any of the application examples in Sections 6-2, 6-3, and 6-4, and either omit the solution or use software to find the solution. To facilitate this approach, all answers at the back of the book for application problems in Exercises 6-2, 6-3, 6-4, and the chapter Review Exercises contain both the mathematical model and its solution.

- **Chapter 7** provides a foundation for probability with a treatment of logic, sets, and counting techniques.

STUDENT SUPPLEMENTS

Student's Solutions Manual

By Garret J. Etgen, University of Houston

This manual contains detailed, carefully worked-out solutions to all odd-numbered section exercises and all Chapter Review exercises. Each section begins with Things to Remember, a list of key material for review.

ISBN 13: 978-0-321-65497-7; ISBN 10: 0-321-65497-8

Graphing Calculator and Excel Spreadsheet Manual

By Dale R. Buske, St. Cloud State University and Karla V. Neal, Louisiana State University

This manual contains detailed instructions for using the TI-83/TI-83 Plus/TI-84 Plus, and Excel spreadsheets with this textbook. Instructions are organized by chapter and section.

ISBN 13: 978-0-321-64541-8; ISBN 10: 0-321-64541-3

Additional Calculus Topics to Accompany Calculus, 12e and College Mathematics, 12e

This separate book contains three unique chapters: Differential Equations, Taylor Polynomials and Infinite Series, and Probability and Calculus.

ISBN 13: 978-0-321-65509-7; ISBN 10: 0-321-65509-5

Worksheets for Classroom or Lab Practice

These Worksheets provide students with a structured place to take notes, define key concepts and terms, and work through unique examples to reinforce what is taught in the lecture.

ISBN 13: 978-0-321-69745-5; ISBN 10: 0-321-69745-6

Videos on DVD-ROM with Optional Captioning

The video lectures with optional captioning for this text make it easy and convenient for students to watch videos from a computer at home or on campus. The complete digitized set, affordable and portable for students, is ideal for distance learning or supplemental instruction. There is a video for every text example.

ISBN 13: 0-978-0-321-70869-4; ISBN 10: 0-321-70869-5

INSTRUCTOR SUPPLEMENTS

Instructor's Edition

This book contains answers to all exercises in the text.

ISBN 13: 978-0-321-64545-6; ISBN 10: 0-321-64545-6

Online Instructor's Solutions Manual (downloadable)

By Jason Aubrey, University of Missouri-Columbia

This manual contains detailed solutions to all even-numbered section problems.

Available in MyMathLab or through http://www.pearson highered.com.

Mini Lectures (downloadable)

Mini Lectures are provided for the teaching assistant, adjunct, part-time or even full-time instructor for lecture preparation by providing learning objectives, examples (and answers) not found in the text, and teaching notes.

Available in MyMathLab or through http://www.pearson highered.com.

TestGen®

TestGen® (www.pearsoned.com/testgen) enables instructors to build, edit, print, and administer tests using a computerized bank of questions developed to cover all the objectives of the text. TestGen is algorithmically based, allowing instructors to create multiple but equivalent versions of the same question or test with the click of a button. Instructors can also modify test bank questions or add new questions. The software and testbank are available for download from Pearson Education's online catalog.

PowerPoint® Lecture Slides

These slides present key concepts and definitions from the text. They are available in MyMathLab or at http://www.pearsonhighered.com/educator.

TECHNOLOGY RESOURCES

MyMathLab® Online Course (access code required)

MyMathLab is a text-specific, easily customizable online course that integrates interactive multimedia instruction with textbook content. MyMathLab gives you the tools you need to deliver all or a portion of your course online, whether your students are in a lab setting or working from home.

- **Interactive homework exercises**, correlated to your textbook at the objective level, are algorithmically generated for unlimited practice and mastery. Most exercises are free-response and provide guided solutions, sample problems, and tutorial learning aids for extra help.

- **Personalized Study Plan**, generated when students complete a test or quiz, indicates which topics have been mastered and links to tutorial exercises for topics students have not mastered. You can customize the Study Plan so that the topics available match your course contents or so that students' homework results also determine mastery.

- **Multimedia learning aids, such as videos for every example in the text**, provide help for students when they need it. Other student-help features include Help Me Solve This and Additional Examples. You can assign these multimedia learning aids as homework to help your students grasp the concepts.

- **Homework and Test Manager** lets you assign homework, quizzes, and tests that are automatically graded. Select just the right mix of questions from the MyMathLab exercise bank, instructor-created custom exercises, and/or TestGen® test items.

- **Gradebook,** designed specifically for mathematics and statistics, automatically tracks students' results, lets you stay on top of student performance, and gives you control over how to calculate final grades. You can also add offline (paper-and-pencil) grades to the gradebook.

- **MathXL Exercise Builder** allows you to create static and algorithmic exercises for your online assignments. You can use the library of sample exercises as an easy starting point, or you can edit any course-related exercise.

- **Pearson Tutor Center** (www.pearsontutorservices.com) access is automatically included with MyMathLab. The Tutor Center is staffed by qualified math instructors who provide textbook-specific tutoring for students via toll-free phone, fax, email, and interactive Web sessions.

Students do the assignments in the new Flash®-based MathXL Player, which is compatible with almost any browser (Firefox®, Safari™, or Internet Explorer®) on almost any platform (Macintosh® or Windows®). MyMathLab is powered by CourseCompass™, Pearson Education's online teaching and learning environment, and by MathXL®, our online homework, tutorial, and assessment system. MyMathLab is available to qualified adopters. For more information, visit www.mymathlab.com or contact your Pearson representative.

MathXL® Online Course (access code required)

MathXL® is an online homework, tutorial, and assessment system that accompanies Pearson's textbooks in mathematics or statistics.

- **Interactive homework exercises**, correlated to your textbook at the objective level, are algorithmically generated for unlimited practice and mastery. Most exercises are free-response and provide guided solutions, sample problems, and learning aids for extra help.

- **Personalized Study Plan,** generated when students complete a test or quiz, indicates which topics have been mastered and links to tutorial exercises for topics students have not mastered. Instructors can customize the available topics in the study plan to match their course concepts.

- **Multimedia learning aids, such as videos for every example in the text**, provide help for students when they need it. Other student-help features include Help Me Solve This and Additional Examples. These are assignable as homework, to further encourage their use.

- **Gradebook,** designed specifically for mathematics and statistics, automatically tracks students' results, lets you stay on top of student performance, and gives you control over how to calculate final grades.

- **MathXL Exercise Builder** allows you to create static and algorithmic exercises for your online assignments. You can use the library of sample exercises as an easy starting point or use the Exercise Builder to edit any of the course-related exercises.

- **Homework and Test Manager** lets you create online homework, quizzes, and tests that are automatically graded. Select just the right mix of questions from the MathXL exercise bank, instructor-created custom exercises, and/or TestGen test items.

The new Flash®-based MathXL Player is compatible with almost any browser (Firefox®, Safari™, or Internet Explorer®) on almost any platform (Macintosh® or Windows®). MathXL is available to qualified adopters. For more information, visit our website at www.mathxl.com, or contact your Pearson sales representative.

InterAct Math Tutorial Website:
www.interactmath.com

Get practice and tutorial help online! This interactive tutorial website provides algorithmically generated practice exercises that correlate directly to the exercises in the textbook. Students can retry an exercise as many times as they like with new values each time for unlimited practice and mastery. Every exercise is accompanied by an interactive guided solution that provides helpful feedback for incorrect answers, and students can also view a worked-out sample problem that steps them through an exercise similar to the one they're working on.

Acknowledgments

In addition to the authors many others are involved in the successful publication of a book. We wish to thank the following reviewers of the 11th and 12th editions:

Jason Aubrey, *University of Missouri—Columbia*
Christine Cosgrove, *Fitchburg State College*
Darryl Egley, *North Harris College*
Lauren Fern, *University of Montana*
Gregory Goeckel, *Presbyterian College*
Garland Guyton, *Montgomery College*
Virginia Hanning, *San Jacinto College*
Bruce Hedman, *University of Connecticut*
Celeste Hernandez, *Richland College*
Yvette Hester, *Texas A&M University*
Fritz Keinert, *Iowa State University*
Steven Klassen, *Missouri Western State University*
Donna Lynch, *Clinton Community College*
Wesley W. Maiers, *Valparaiso University*
James Martin, *Christopher Newport University*
Mari M. Peddycoart, *Lone Star College—Kingswood*
Gary R. Penner, *Richland College*
Jon Prewett, *University of Wyoming*
Cynthia Schultz, *Illinois Valley Community College*
Maria Terrell, *Cornell University*
Fred M. Wright, *Iowa State University*
Amy Ann Yielding, *Washington State University*

We also wish to thank our colleagues who have provided input on previous editions:

Chris Boldt, Bob Bradshaw, Bruce Chaffee, Robert Chaney, Dianne Clark, Charles E. Cleaver, Barbara Cohen, Richard L. Conlon, Catherine Cron, Lou D'Alotto, Madhu Deshpande, Kenneth A. Dodaro, Michael W. Ecker, Jerry R. Ehman, Lucina Gallagher, Martha M. Harvey, Sue Henderson, Lloyd R. Hicks, Louis F. Hoelzle, Paul Hutchins, K. Wayne James, Jeffrey Lynn Johnson, Robert H. Johnston, Robert Krystock, Inessa Levi, James T. Loats, Frank Lopez, Roy H. Luke, Wayne Miller, Mel Mitchell, Linda M. Neal, Ronald Persky, Kenneth A. Peters, Jr., Dix Petty, Tom Plavchak, Bob Prielipp, Thomas Riedel, Stephen Rodi, Arthur Rosenthal, Sheldon Rothman, Elaine Russell, John Ryan, Daniel E. Scanlon, George R. Schriro, Arnold L. Schroeder, Hari Shanker, Joan Smith, J. Sriskandarajah, Steven Terry, Beverly Vredevelt, Delores A. Williams, Caroline Woods, Charles W. Zimmerman, Pat Zrolka, and Cathleen A. Zucco-Tevelot.

We also express our thanks to:

Caroline Woods, Anthony Gagliardi, Damon Demas, John Samons, Theresa Schille, Blaise DeSesa, Debra McGivney, and Gary Williams for providing a careful and thorough accuracy check of the text, problems and answers.

Garret Etgen, Jason Aubrey, Dale R. Buske, and Karla Neal for developing the supplemental materials so important to the success of a text.

All the people at Pearson Education who contributed their efforts to the production of this book.

PART 1

A LIBRARY OF ELEMENTARY FUNCTIONS

Linear Equations
and Graphs

Introduction

We begin by discussing some algebraic methods for solving equations and inequalities. Next, we introduce coordinate systems that allow us to explore the relationship between algebra and geometry. Finally, we use this algebraic–geometric relationship to find equations that can be used to describe real-world data sets. For example, in Section 1-3 you will learn how to find the equation of a line that fits data on winning times in an Olympic swimming event (see Problems 27 and 28 on page 38). We also consider many applied problems that can be solved using the concepts discussed in this chapter.

1-1   Linear Equations and Inequalities

- Linear Equations
- Linear Inequalities
- Applications

The equation

$$3 - 2(x + 3) = \frac{x}{3} - 5$$

and the inequality

$$\frac{x}{2} + 2(3x - 1) \geq 5$$

are both first degree in one variable. In general, a **first-degree**, or **linear**, **equation** in one variable is any equation that can be written in the form

Standard form: $ax + b = 0$ $a \neq 0$ (1)

If the equality symbol, $=$, in (1) is replaced by $<, >, \leq$, or $\geq$, the resulting expression is called a **first-degree**, or **linear**, **inequality**.

A **solution** of an equation (or inequality) involving a single variable is a number that when substituted for the variable makes the equation (or inequality) true. The set of all solutions is called the **solution set**. When we say that we **solve an equation** (or inequality), we mean that we find its solution set.

Knowing what is meant by the solution set is one thing; finding it is another. We start by recalling the idea of equivalent equations and equivalent inequalities. If we perform an operation on an equation (or inequality) that produces another equation (or inequality) with the same solution set, then the two equations (or inequalities) are said to be **equivalent**. The basic idea in solving equations or inequalities is to perform operations that produce simpler equivalent equations or inequalities and to continue the process until we obtain an equation or inequality with an obvious solution.

Linear Equations

Linear equations are generally solved using the following equality properties.

THEOREM 1   Equality Properties

An equivalent equation will result if

1. The same quantity is added to or subtracted from each side of a given equation.
2. Each side of a given equation is multiplied by or divided by the same nonzero quantity.

EXAMPLE 1   **Solving a Linear Equation** Solve and check:

$$8x - 3(x - 4) = 3(x - 4) + 6$$

SOLUTION

$8x - 3(x - 4) = 3(x - 4) + 6$	Use the distributive property.
$8x - 3x + 12 = 3x - 12 + 6$	Combine like terms.
$5x + 12 = 3x - 6$	Subtract $3x$ from both sides.
$2x + 12 = -6$	Subtract 12 from both sides.
$2x = -18$	Divide both sides by 2.
$x = -9$	

CHECK

$$8x - 3(x - 4) = 3(x - 4) + 6$$
$$8(-9) - 3[(-9) - 4] \stackrel{?}{=} 3[(-9) - 4] + 6$$
$$-72 - 3(-13) \stackrel{?}{=} 3(-13) + 6$$
$$-33 \stackrel{\checkmark}{=} -33$$

Matched Problem 1   Solve and check: $3x - 2(2x - 5) = 2(x + 3) - 8$

EXPLORE & DISCUSS 1

According to equality property 2, multiplying both sides of an equation by a nonzero number always produces an equivalent equation. What is the smallest positive number that you could use to multiply both sides of the following equation to produce an equivalent equation without fractions?

$$\frac{x + 1}{3} - \frac{x}{4} = \frac{1}{2}$$

EXAMPLE 2   **Solving a Linear Equation**   Solve and check: $\dfrac{x + 2}{2} - \dfrac{x}{3} = 5$

SOLUTION   What operations can we perform on

$$\frac{x + 2}{2} - \frac{x}{3} = 5$$

to eliminate the denominators? If we can find a number that is exactly divisible by each denominator, we can use the multiplication property of equality to clear the denominators. The LCD (least common denominator) of the fractions, 6, is exactly what we are looking for! Actually, any common denominator will do, but the LCD results in a simpler equivalent equation. So, we multiply both sides of the equation by 6:

$$6\left(\frac{x + 2}{2} - \frac{x}{3}\right) = 6 \cdot 5 \quad {}^{*}$$

$$\overset{3}{6} \cdot \frac{(x + 2)}{2} - \overset{2}{6} \cdot \frac{x}{3} = 30$$
$$\phantom{6 \cdot \frac{(x+2)}{2}}_{1} \phantom{-6 \cdot \frac{x}{3}}_{1}$$

$$3(x + 2) - 2x = 30 \qquad \text{Use the distributive property.}$$
$$3x + 6 - 2x = 30 \qquad \text{Combine like terms.}$$
$$x + 6 = 30 \qquad \text{Subtract 6 from both sides.}$$
$$x = 24$$

CHECK

$$\frac{x + 2}{2} - \frac{x}{3} = 5$$

$$\frac{24 + 2}{2} - \frac{24}{3} \overset{?}{=} 5$$

$$13 - 8 \overset{?}{=} 5$$

$$5 \overset{\checkmark}{=} 5$$

Matched Problem 2   Solve and check: $\dfrac{x + 1}{3} - \dfrac{x}{4} = \dfrac{1}{2}$

In many applications of algebra, formulas or equations must be changed to alternative equivalent forms. The following example is typical.

EXAMPLE 3   **Solving a Formula for a Particular Variable**   If you deposit a principle P in an account that earns simple interest at an annual rate r, then the amount A in the account after t years is given by $A = P + Prt$. Solve for

(A) r in terms of $A, P,$ and t

(B) P in terms of $A, r,$ and t

---

*Dashed boxes are used throughout the book to denote steps that are usually performed mentally.

SOLUTION   (A)

$$A = P + Prt \qquad \text{Reverse equation.}$$
$$P + Prt = A \qquad \text{Subtract } P \text{ from both sides.}$$
$$Prt = A - P \qquad \text{Divide both members by } Pt.$$
$$r = \frac{A - P}{Pt}$$

(B)

$$A = P + Prt \qquad \text{Reverse equation.}$$
$$P + Prt = A \qquad \text{Factor out } P \text{ (note the use of the distributive property).}$$
$$P(1 + rt) = A \qquad \text{Divide by } (1 + rt).$$
$$P = \frac{A}{1 + rt}$$

Matched Problem 3   If a cardboard box has length L, width W, and height H, then its surface area is given by the formula $S = 2LW + 2LH + 2WH$. Solve the formula for

(A) L in terms of S, W, and H

(B) H in terms of S, L, and W

Linear Inequalities

Before we start solving linear inequalities, let us recall what we mean by $<$ (less than) and $>$ (greater than). If a and b are real numbers, we write

$$a < b \qquad a \text{ is less than } b$$

if there exists a positive number p such that $a + p = b$. Certainly, we would expect that if a positive number was added to any real number, the sum would be larger than the original. That is essentially what the definition states. If $a < b$, we may also write

$$b > a \qquad b \text{ is greater than } a.$$

EXAMPLE 4   Inequalities

(A) $3 < 5$ Since $3 + 2 = 5$

(B) $-6 < -2$ Since $-6 + 4 = -2$

(C) $0 > -10$ Since $-10 < 0$ (because $-10 + 10 = 0$)

Matched Problem 4   Replace each question mark with either $<$ or $>$.

(A) $2 ? 8$ (B) $-20 ? 0$ (C) $-3 ? -30$

Figure 1 $a < b, c > d$

The inequality symbols have a very clear geometric interpretation on the real number line. If $a < b$, then a is to the left of b on the number line; if $c > d$, then c is to the right of d on the number line (Fig. 1). Check this geometric property with the inequalities in Example 4.

EXPLORE & DISCUSS 2   Replace $?$ with $<$ or $>$ in each of the following:

(A) $-1 ? 3$ and $2(-1) ? 2(3)$

(B) $-1 ? 3$ and $-2(-1) ? -2(3)$

(C) $12 ? -8$ and $\dfrac{12}{4} ? \dfrac{-8}{4}$

(D) $12 ? -8$ and $\dfrac{12}{-4} ? \dfrac{-8}{-4}$

Based on these examples, describe verbally the effect of multiplying both sides of an inequality by a number.

The procedures used to solve linear inequalities in one variable are almost the same as those used to solve linear equations in one variable, but with one important exception, as noted in item 3 of Theorem 2.

THEOREM 2   Inequality Properties

An equivalent inequality will result, and the **sense or direction will remain the same** if each side of the original inequality

  1. has the same real number added to or subtracted from it.

  2. is multiplied or divided by the same *positive* number.

An equivalent inequality will result, and the **sense or direction will reverse** if each side of the original inequality

  3. is multiplied or divided by the same *negative* number.

NOTE: Multiplication by 0 and division by 0 are not permitted.

Therefore, we can perform essentially the same operations on inequalities that we perform on equations, with the exception that **the sense of the inequality reverses if we multiply or divide both sides by a negative number**. Otherwise, the sense of the inequality does not change. For example, if we start with the true statement

$$-3 > -7$$

and multiply both sides by 2, we obtain

$$-6 > -14$$

and the sense of the inequality stays the same. But if we multiply both sides of $-3 > -7$ by -2, the left side becomes 6 and the right side becomes 14, so we must write

$$6 < 14$$

to have a true statement. The sense of the inequality reverses.

If $a < b$, the **double inequality** $a < x < b$ means that $a < x$ **and** $x < b$; that is, x is between a and b. **Interval notation** is also used to describe sets defined by inequalities, as shown in Table 1.

The numbers a and b in Table 1 are called the **endpoints** of the interval. An interval is **closed** if it contains all its endpoints and **open** if it does not contain any of its endpoints. The intervals $[a, b]$, $(-\infty, a]$, and $[b, \infty)$ are closed, and the intervals (a, b), $(-\infty, a)$, and (b, ∞) are open. Note that the symbol ∞ (read infinity) is not a number. When we write $[b, \infty)$, we are simply referring to the interval that starts at b and continues indefinitely to the right. We never refer to ∞ as an endpoint, and we never write $[b, \infty]$. The interval $(-\infty, \infty)$ is the entire real number line.

Note that an endpoint of a line graph in Table 1 has a square bracket through it if the endpoint is included in the interval; a parenthesis through an endpoint indicates that it is not included.

CONCEPTUAL INSIGHT

The notation $(2, 7)$ has two common mathematical interpretations: the ordered pair with first coordinate 2 and second coordinate 7, and the open interval consisting of all real numbers between 2 and 7. The choice of interpretation is usually determined by the context in which the notation is used. The notation $(2, -7)$ could be interpreted as an ordered pair but not as an interval. In interval notation, the left endpoint is always written first. So, $(-7, 2)$ is correct interval notation, but $(2, -7)$ is not.

Table 1   Interval Notation

Interval Notation	Inequality Notation	Line Graph
$[a, b]$	$a \leq x \leq b$	
$[a, b)$	$a \leq x < b$	
$(a, b]$	$a < x \leq b$	
(a, b)	$a < x < b$	
$(-\infty, a]$	$x \leq a$	
$(-\infty, a)$	$x < a$	
$[b, \infty)$	$x \geq b$	
(b, ∞)	$x > b$	

EXAMPLE 5   **Interval and Inequality Notation, and Line Graphs**
(A) Write $[-2, 3)$ as a double inequality and graph.
(B) Write $x \geq -5$ in interval notation and graph.

SOLUTION   (A) $[-2, 3)$ is equivalent to $-2 \leq x < 3$.

(B) $x \geq -5$ is equivalent to $[-5, \infty)$.

Matched Problem 5   (A) Write $(-7, 4]$ as a double inequality and graph.
(B) Write $x < 3$ in interval notation and graph.

EXPLORE & DISCUSS 3   The solution to Example 5B shows the graph of the inequality $x \geq -5$. What is the graph of $x < -5$? What is the corresponding interval? Describe the relationship between these sets.

EXAMPLE 6   **Solving a Linear Inequality** Solve and graph:
$$2(2x + 3) < 6(x - 2) + 10$$

SOLUTION

$2(2x + 3) < 6(x - 2) + 10$	Remove parentheses.
$4x + 6 < 6x - 12 + 10$	Combine like terms.
$4x + 6 < 6x - 2$	Subtract 6x from both sides.
$-2x + 6 < -2$	Subtract 6 from both sides.
$-2x < -8$	Divide both sides by -2 and reverse the sense of the inequality.

$$x > 4 \quad \text{or} \quad (4, \infty)$$

Notice that in the graph of $x > 4$, we use a parenthesis through 4, since the point 4 is not included in the graph.

Matched Problem 6   Solve and graph: $3(x - 1) \le 5(x + 2) - 5$

EXAMPLE 7   **Solving a Double Inequality** Solve and graph: $-3 < 2x + 3 \le 9$

SOLUTION   We are looking for all numbers x such that $2x + 3$ is between -3 and 9, including 9 but not -3. We proceed as before except that we try to isolate x in the middle:

$$-3 < 2x + 3 \le 9$$
$$-3 - 3 < 2x + 3 - 3 \le 9 - 3$$
$$-6 < 2x \le 6$$
$$\frac{-6}{2} < \frac{2x}{2} \le \frac{6}{2}$$
$$-3 < x \le 3 \quad \text{or} \quad (-3, 3]$$

Matched Problem 7   Solve and graph: $-8 \le 3x - 5 < 7$

Note that a linear equation usually has exactly one solution, while a linear inequality usually has infinitely many solutions.

Applications

To realize the full potential of algebra, we must be able to translate real-world problems into mathematics. In short, we must be able to do word problems.

Here are some suggestions that will help you get started:

Procedure for Solving Word Problems

1. Read the problem carefully and introduce a variable to represent an unknown quantity in the problem. Often the question asked in a problem will indicate the best way to introduce this variable.
2. Identify other quantities in the problem (known or unknown), and whenever possible, express unknown quantities in terms of the variable you introduced in Step 1.
3. Write a verbal statement using the conditions stated in the problem and then write an equivalent mathematical statement (equation or inequality).
4. Solve the equation or inequality and answer the questions posed in the problem.
5. Check the solution(s) in the original problem.

EXAMPLE 8   **Purchase Price** John purchases a computer from an online store for $851.26, including a $57 shipping charge and 5.2% state sales tax. What is the purchase price of the computer?

SOLUTION   **Step 1** **Introduce a variable for the unknown quantity.** After reading the problem, we decide to let x represent the purchase price of the computer.

Step 2 **Identify quantities in the problem.**

Shipping charges: $57

Sales tax: $0.052x$

Total cost: $851.26

Step 3 **Write a verbal statement and an equation.**

Price + Shipping Charges + Sales Tax = Total Order Cost

$$x \quad + \quad\quad 57 \quad + \quad 0.052x \quad = 851.26$$

Step 4 **Solve the equation and answer the question.**

$$x + 57 + 0.052x = 851.26 \quad \text{Combine like terms.}$$
$$1.052x + 57 = 851.26 \quad \text{Subtract 57 from both sides.}$$
$$1.052x = 794.26 \quad \text{Divide both sides by 1.052.}$$
$$x = 755$$

The price of the computer is $755.

Step 5 **Check the answer in the original problem.**

$$\text{Price} = \$755.00$$
$$\text{Shipping charges} = \$57.00$$
$$\underline{\text{Tax } 0.052 \cdot 755 = \quad \$39.26}$$
$$\text{Total} = \$851.26$$

Matched Problem 8 Mary paid 8.5% sales tax and a $190 title and license fee when she bought a new car for a total of $28,400. What is the purchase price of the car?

The next example involves the important concept of **break-even analysis**, which is encountered in several places in this text. Any manufacturing company has **costs**, **C**, and **revenues**, **R**. The company will have a **loss** if $R < C$, will **break even** if $R = C$, and will have a **profit** if $R > C$. Costs involve **fixed costs**, such as plant over-head, product design, setup, and promotion, and **variable costs**, which are dependent on the number of items produced at a certain cost per item.

EXAMPLE 9 **Break-Even Analysis** A multimedia company produces DVDs. One-time fixed costs for a particular DVD are $48,000, which include costs such as filming, editing, and promotion. Variable costs amount to $12.40 per DVD and include manufacturing, packaging, and distribution costs for each DVD actually sold to a retailer. The DVD is sold to retail outlets at $17.40 each. How many DVDs must be manufactured and sold in order for the company to break even?

SOLUTION **Step 1** Let x = number of DVDs manufactured and sold.

Step 2
$$C = \text{cost of producing } x \text{ DVDs}$$
$$R = \text{revenue (return) on sales of } x \text{ DVDs}$$
$$\text{Fixed costs} = \$48,000$$
$$\text{Variable costs} = \$12.40x$$
$$C = \text{Fixed costs} + \text{variable costs}$$
$$= \$48,000 + \$12.40x$$
$$R = \$17.40x$$

Step 3 The company breaks even if $R = C$; that is, if

$$\$17.40x = \$48,000 + \$12.40x$$

Step 4 $17.4x = 48,000 + 12.4x \quad \text{Subtract 12.4x from both sides.}$
$$5x = 48,000 \quad\quad\quad \text{Divide both sides by 5.}$$
$$x = 9,600$$

The company must make and sell 9,600 DVDs to break even.

Step 5 Check:

	Costs	Revenue
	$48,000 + 12.4(9,600)$	$17.4(9,600)$
	$= \$167,040$	$= \$167,040$

Matched Problem 9   How many DVSs would a multimedia company have to make and sell to break even if the fixed costs are $36,000, variable costs are $10.40 per DVD, and the DVDs are sold to retailers for $15.20 each?

EXAMPLE 10   **Consumer Price Index** The Consumer Price Index (CPI) is a measure of the average change in prices over time from a designated reference period, which equals 100. The index is based on prices of basic consumer goods and services. Table 2 lists the CPI for several years from 1960 to 2005. What net annual salary in 2005 would have the same purchasing power as a net annual salary of $13,000 in 1960? Compute the answer to the nearest dollar. (*Source*: U.S. Bureau of Labor Statistics)

Table 2 CPI (1982–1984 = 100)

Year	Index
1960	29.6
1975	53.8
1990	130.7
2005	195.3

SOLUTION   **Step 1** Let $x =$ the purchasing power of an annual salary in 2005.

Step 2 Annual salary in 1960 = \$13,000

$$\text{CPI in } 1960 = 29.6$$
$$\text{CPI in } 2005 = 195.3$$

Step 3 The ratio of a salary in 2005 to a salary in 1960 is the same as the ratio of the CPI in 2005 to the CPI in 1960.

$$\frac{x}{13,000} = \frac{195.3}{29.6} \qquad \textit{Multiply both sides by 13,000.}$$

Step 4
$$x = 13,000 \cdot \frac{195.3}{29.6}$$
$$= \$85,774 \text{ per year}$$

Step 5

Salary Ratio	**CPI Ratio**
$\dfrac{85,774}{13,000} = 6.598$	$\dfrac{195.3}{29.6} = 6.59797$

Note: The slight difference in these ratios is due to rounding the 2005 salary to the nearest dollar.

Matched Problem 10   What net annual salary in 1975 would have had the same purchasing power as a net annual salary of $100,000 in 2005? Compute the answer to the nearest dollar.

Exercises 1-1

A

Solve Problems 1–6.

1. $2m + 9 = 5m - 6$

2. $3y - 4 = 6y - 19$

3. $2x + 3 < -4$

4. $5x + 2 > 1$

5. $-3x \geq -12$

6. $-4x \leq 8$

Solve Problems 7–10 and graph.

7. $-4x - 7 > 5$

8. $-2x + 8 < 4$

9. $2 \leq x + 3 \leq 5$

10. $-4 < 2y - 3 < 9$

Solve Problems 11–24.

11. $\dfrac{x}{4} + \dfrac{1}{2} = \dfrac{1}{8}$

12. $\dfrac{m}{3} - 4 = \dfrac{2}{3}$

13. $\dfrac{y}{-5} > \dfrac{3}{2}$ **14.** $\dfrac{x}{-4} < \dfrac{5}{6}$

15. $2u + 4 = 5u + 1 - 7u$ **16.** $-3y + 9 + y = 13 - 8y$

B

17. $10x + 25(x - 3) = 275$ **18.** $-3(4 - x) = 5 - (x + 1)$

19. $3 - y \le 4(y - 3)$ **20.** $x - 2 \ge 2(x - 5)$

21. $\dfrac{x}{5} - \dfrac{x}{6} = \dfrac{6}{5}$ **22.** $\dfrac{y}{4} - \dfrac{y}{3} = \dfrac{1}{2}$

23. $\dfrac{m}{5} - 3 < \dfrac{3}{5} - \dfrac{m}{2}$ **24.** $\dfrac{u}{2} - \dfrac{2}{3} < \dfrac{u}{3} + 2$

Solve Problems 25–28 and graph.

25. $2 \le 3x - 7 < 14$ **26.** $-4 \le 5x + 6 < 21$

27. $-4 \le \dfrac{9}{5}C + 32 \le 68$ **28.** $-1 \le \dfrac{2}{3}t + 5 \le 11$

C

Solve Problems 29–34 for the indicated variable.

29. $3x - 4y = 12$; for y **30.** $y = -\dfrac{2}{3}x + 8$; for x

31. $Ax + By = C$; for y ($B \ne 0$)

32. $y = mx + b$; for m **33.** $F = \dfrac{9}{5}C + 32$; for C

34. $C = \dfrac{5}{9}(F - 32)$; for F

Solve Problems 35 and 36 and graph.

35. $-3 \le 4 - 7x < 18$ **36.** $-10 \le 8 - 3u \le -6$

37. What can be said about the signs of the numbers a and b in each case?
  (A) $ab > 0$ (B) $ab < 0$
  (C) $\dfrac{a}{b} > 0$ (D) $\dfrac{a}{b} < 0$

38. What can be said about the signs of the numbers $a, b,$ and c in each case?
  (A) $abc > 0$ (B) $\dfrac{ab}{c} < 0$
  (C) $\dfrac{a}{bc} > 0$ (D) $\dfrac{a^2}{bc} < 0$

39. If both a and b are positive numbers and b/a is greater than 1, then is $a - b$ positive or negative?

40. If both a and b are negative numbers and b/a is greater than 1, then is $a - b$ positive or negative?

In Problems 41–46, discuss the validity of each statement. If the statement is true, explain why. If not, give a counterexample.

41. If the intersection of two open intervals is nonempty, then their intersection is an open interval.

42. If the intersection of two closed intervals is nonempty, then their intersection is a closed interval.

43. The union of any two open intervals is an open interval.

44. The union of any two closed intervals is a closed interval.

45. If the intersection of two open intervals is nonempty, then their union is an open interval.

46. If the intersection of two closed intervals is nonempty, then their union is a closed interval.

Applications

47. Ticket sales. A rock concert brought in $432,500 on the sale of 9,500 tickets. If the tickets sold for $35 and $55 each, how many of each type of ticket were sold?

48. Parking meter coins. An all-day parking meter takes only dimes and quarters. If it contains 100 coins with a total value of $14.50, how many of each type of coin are in the meter?

49. IRA. You have $500,000 in an IRA (Individual Retirement Account) at the time you retire. You have the option of investing this money in two funds: Fund A pays 5.2% annually and Fund B pays 7.7% annually. How should you divide your money between Fund A and Fund B to produce an annual interest income of $34,000?

50. IRA. Refer to Problem 49. How should you divide your money between Fund A and Fund B to produce an annual interest income of $30,000?

51. Car prices. If the price change of cars parallels the change in the CPI (see Table 2 in Example 10), what would a car sell for (to the nearest dollar) in 2005 if a comparable model sold for $10,000 in 1990?

52. Home values. If the price change in houses parallels the CPI (see Table 2 in Example 10), what would a house valued at $200,000 in 2005 be valued at (to the nearest dollar) in 1960?

53. Retail and wholesale prices. Retail prices in a department store are obtained by marking up the wholesale price by 40%. That is, retail price is obtained by adding 40% of the wholesale price to the wholesale price.
  (A) What is the retail price of a suit if the wholesale price is $300?
  (B) What is the wholesale price of a pair of jeans if the retail price is $77?

54. Retail and sale prices. Sale prices in a department store are obtained by marking down the retail price by 15%. That is, sale price is obtained by subtracting 15% of the retail price from the retail price.
  (A) What is the sale price of a hat that has a retail price of $60?
  (B) What is the retail price of a dress that has a sale price of $136?

55. Equipment rental. A golf course charges $52 for a round of golf using a set of their clubs, and $44 if you have your own clubs. If you buy a set of clubs for $270, how many rounds must you play to recover the cost of the clubs?

56. Equipment rental. The local supermarket rents carpet cleaners for $20 a day. These cleaners use shampoo in a special cartridge that sells for $16 and is available only from the supermarket. A home carpet cleaner can be purchased for $300. Shampoo for the home cleaner is readily available for $9 a bottle. Past experience has shown that it takes two shampoo cartridges to clean the 10-foot-by-12- foot carpet in your living room with the rented cleaner. Cleaning the same area with the home cleaner will consume three bottles of shampoo. If you buy the home cleaner, how many times must you clean the living-room carpet to make buying cheaper than renting?

57. Sales commissions. One employee of a computer store is paid a base salary of $2,000 a month plus an 8% commission on all sales over $7,000 during the month. How much must the employee sell in one month to earn a total of $4,000 for the month?

58. Sales commissions. A second employee of the computer store in Problem 57 is paid a base salary of $3,000 a month plus a 5% commission on all sales during the month.

(A) How much must this employee sell in one month to earn a total of $4,000 for the month?

(B) Determine the sales level at which both employees receive the same monthly income.

(C) If employees can select either of these payment methods, how would you advise an employee to make this selection?

59. Break-even analysis. A publisher for a promising new novel figures fixed costs (overhead, advances, promotion, copy editing, typesetting) at $55,000, and variable costs (printing, paper, binding, shipping) at $1.60 for each book produced. If the book is sold to distributors for $11 each, how many must be produced and sold for the publisher to break even?

60. Break-even analysis. The publisher of a new book figures fixed costs at $92,000 and variable costs at $2.10 for each book produced. If the book is sold to distributors for $15 each, how many must be sold for the publisher to break even?

61. Break-even analysis. The publisher in Problem 59 finds that rising prices for paper increase the variable costs to $2.10 per book.

(A) Discuss possible strategies the company might use to deal with this increase in costs.

(B) If the company continues to sell the books for $11, how many books must they sell now to make a profit?

(C) If the company wants to start making a profit at the same production level as before the cost increase, how much should they sell the book for now?

62. Break-even analysis. The publisher in Problem 60 finds that rising prices for paper increase the variable costs to $2.70 per book.

(A) Discuss possible strategies the company might use to deal with this increase in costs.

(B) If the company continues to sell the books for $15, how many books must they sell now to make a profit?

(C) If the company wants to start making a profit at the same production level as before the cost increase, how much should they sell the book for now?

63. Wildlife management. A naturalist estimated the total number of rainbow trout in a certain lake using the capture–mark–recapture technique. He netted, marked, and released 200 rainbow trout. A week later, allowing for thorough mixing, he again netted 200 trout, and found 8 marked ones among them. Assuming that the proportion of marked fish in the second sample was the same as the proportion of all marked fish in the total population, estimate the number of rainbow trout in the lake.

64. Temperature conversion. If the temperature for a 24-hour period at an Antarctic station ranged between $-49°F$ and $14°F$ (that is, $-49 \leq F \leq 14$), what was the range in degrees Celsius? [*Note:* $F = \frac{9}{5}C + 32$.]

65. Psychology. The IQ (intelligence quotient) is found by dividing the mental age (MA), as indicated on standard tests, by the chronological age (CA) and multiplying by 100. For example, if a child has a mental age of 12 and a chronological age of 8, the calculated IQ is 150. If a 9-year-old girl has an IQ of 140, compute her mental age.

66. Psychology. Refer to Problem 65. If the IQ of a group of 12-year-old children varies between 80 and 140, what is the range of their mental ages?

67. Anthropology. In their study of genetic groupings, anthropologists use a ratio called the **cephalic index**. This is the ratio of the breadth B of the head to its length L (looking down from above) expressed as a percentage. A study of the Gurung community of Nepal published in the *Kathmandu University Medical Journal* in 2005 found that the average head length of males was 18 cm, and their head breadths varied between 12 and 18 cm. Find the range of the cephalic index for males. Round endpoints to one decimal place.

Figure for 67–68

68. Anthropology. Refer to Problem 67. The same study found that the average head length of females was 17.4 cm, and their head breadths varied between 15 and 20 cm. Find the range of the cephalic index for females. Round endpoints to one decimal place.

Answers to Matched Problems

1. $x = 4$ **2.** $x = 2$

3. (A) $L = \dfrac{S - 2WH}{2W + 2H}$ (B) $H = \dfrac{S - 2LW}{2L + 2W}$

4. (A) $<$ (B) $<$ (C) $>$

5. (A) $-7 < x \leq 4$;

(B) $(-\infty, 3)$

6. $x \geq -4$ or $[-4, \infty)$

7. $-1 \leq x < 4$ or $[-1, 4)$

8. $26,000   **9.** 7,500 DVDs   **10.** $27,547

1-2   Graphs and Lines

In this section, we will consider one of the most basic geometric figures—a line. When we use the term *line* in this book, we mean *straight line*. We will learn how to recognize and graph a line, and how to use information concerning a line to find its equation. Examining the graph of any equation often results in additional insight into the nature of the equation's solutions.

Cartesian Coordinate System

Recall that to form a **Cartesian** or **rectangular coordinate system**, we select two real number lines—one horizontal and one vertical—and let them cross through their origins as indicated in Figure 1. Up and to the right are the usual choices for the positive directions. These two number lines are called the **horizontal axis** and the **vertical axis**, or, together, the **coordinate axes**. The horizontal axis is usually referred to as the *x* **axis** and the vertical axis as the *y* **axis**, and each is labeled accordingly. The coordinate axes divide the plane into four parts called **quadrants**, which are numbered counterclockwise from I to IV (see Fig. 1).

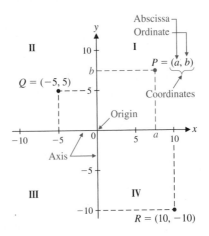

Figure 1 The Cartesian (rectangular) coordinate system

Now we want to assign *coordinates* to each point in the plane. Given an arbitrary point P in the plane, pass horizontal and vertical lines through the point (Fig. 1). The vertical line will intersect the horizontal axis at a point with coordinate a, and the horizontal line will intersect the vertical axis at a point with coordinate b. These two numbers, written as the **ordered pair** (a, b)* form the **coordinates** of the point P. The first coordinate, a, is called the **abscissa** of P; the second coordinate, b, is called the **ordinate** of P. The abscissa of Q in Figure 1 is -5, and the ordinate of Q is 5. The coordinates of a point can also be referenced in terms of the axis labels. The *x* **coordinate** of R in Figure 1 is 10, and the *y* **coordinate** of R is -10. The point with coordinates $(0, 0)$ is called the **origin**.

The procedure we have just described assigns to each point P in the plane a unique pair of real numbers (a, b). Conversely, if we are given an ordered pair of real numbers (a, b), then, reversing this procedure, we can determine a unique point P in the plane. Thus,

> **There is a one-to-one correspondence between the points in a plane and the elements in the set of all ordered pairs of real numbers.**

This is often referred to as the **fundamental theorem of analytic geometry**.

---

*Here we use (a, b) as the coordinates of a point in a plane. In Section 1-1, we used (a, b) to represent an interval on a real number line. These concepts are not the same. You must always interpret the symbol (a, b) in terms of the context in which it is used.

Graphs of $Ax + By = C$

In Section 1-1, we called an equation of the form $ax + b = 0$ $(a \neq 0)$ a linear equation in one variable. Now we want to consider linear equations in two variables:

DEFINITION **Linear Equations in Two Variables**

A **linear equation in two variables** is an equation that can be written in the **standard form**

$$Ax + By = C$$

where A, B, and C are constants (A and B not both 0), and x and y are variables.

A **solution** of an equation in two variables is an ordered pair of real numbers that satisfies the equation. For example, $(4, 3)$ is a solution of $3x - 2y = 6$. The **solution set** of an equation in two variables is the set of all solutions of the equation. The **graph** of an equation is the graph of its solution set.

EXPLORE & DISCUSS 1

(A) As noted earlier, $(4, 3)$ is a solution of the equation

$$3x - 2y = 6$$

Find three more solutions of this equation. Plot these solutions in a Cartesian coordinate system. What familiar geometric shape could be used to describe the solution set of this equation?

(B) Repeat part (A) for the equation $x = 2$.

(C) Repeat part (A) for the equation $y = -3$.

In Explore & Discuss 1, you may have recognized that the graph of each equation is a (straight) line. Theorem 1 confirms this fact.

THEOREM 1 **Graph of a Linear Equation in Two Variables**
The graph of any equation of the form

$$Ax + By = C \quad \text{(A and B not both O)} \tag{1}$$

is a line, and any line in a Cartesian coordinate system is the graph of an equation of this form.

If $A \neq 0$ and $B \neq 0$, then equation (1) can be written as

$$y = -\frac{A}{B}x + \frac{C}{B} = mx + b, m \neq 0$$

If $A = 0$ and $B \neq 0$, then equation (1) can be written as

$$y = \frac{C}{B}$$

and its graph is a **horizontal line**. If $A \neq 0$ and $B = 0$, then equation (1) can be written as

$$x = \frac{C}{A}$$

and its graph is a **vertical line**. To graph equation (1), or any of its special cases, plot any two points in the solution set and use a straightedge to draw the line through these two points. The points where the line crosses the axes are often the easiest to find. The *y* intercept* is the *y* coordinate of the point where the graph crosses the *y*

---

*If the *x* intercept is a and the *y* intercept is b, then the graph of the line passes through the points $(a, 0)$ and $(0, b)$. It is common practice to refer to both the numbers a and b and the points $(a, 0)$ and $(0, b)$ as the *x* and *y* intercepts of the line.

axis, and the x intercept is the x coordinate of the point where the graph crosses the x axis. To find the y intercept, let $x = 0$ and solve for y. To find the x intercept, let $y = 0$ and solve for x. It is a good idea to find a third point as a check point.

EXAMPLE 1   **Using Intercepts to Graph a Line**   Graph: $3x - 4y = 12$

SOLUTION

x	y	
0	–3	y intercept
4	0	x intercept
8	3	Check point

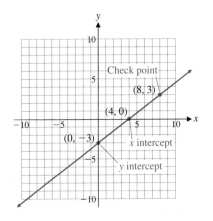

Matched Problem 1   Graph: $4x - 3y = 12$

   The icon in the margin is used throughout this book to identify optional graphing calculator activities that are intended to give you additional insight into the concepts under discussion. You may have to consult the manual for your calculator* for the details necessary to carry out these activities.

   EXAMPLE 2   **Using a Graphing Calculator**   Graph $3x - 4y = 12$ on a graphing calculator and find the intercepts.

SOLUTION   First, we solve $3x - 4y = 12$ for y.

$$3x - 4y = 12 \qquad \text{Add } -3x \text{ to both sides.}$$
$$-4y = -3x + 12 \qquad \text{Divide both sides by } -4.$$
$$y = \frac{-3x + 12}{-4} \qquad \text{Simplify.}$$
$$y = \frac{3}{4}x - 3 \tag{2}$$

Now we enter the right side of equation (2) in a calculator (Fig. 2A), enter values for the window variables (Fig. 2B), and graph the line (Fig. 2C). (The numerals to the left and right of the screen in Figure 2C are Xmin and Xmax, respectively. Similarly, the numerals below and above the screen are Ymin and Ymax.)

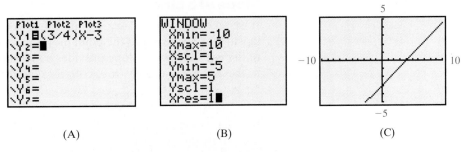

(A)   (B)   (C)

Figure 2 Graphing a line on a graphing calculator

---

*We used a Texas Instruments graphing calculator from the TI-83/84 family to produce the graphing calculator screens in the book. Manuals for most graphing calculators are readily available on the Internet.

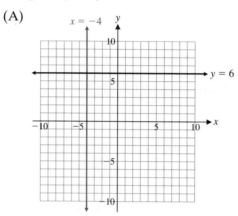

Figure 3 Using TRACE and zero on a graphing calculator

Next we use two calculator commands to find the intercepts: TRACE (Fig. 3A) and zero (Fig. 3B).

Matched Problem 2   Graph $4x - 3y = 12$ on a graphing calculator and find the intercepts.

EXAMPLE 3   **Horizontal and Vertical Lines**

(A) Graph $x = -4$ and $y = 6$ simultaneously in the same rectangular coordinate system.

(B) Write the equations of the vertical and horizontal lines that pass through the point $(7, -5)$.

SOLUTION   (A)

(B) Horizontal line through $(7, -5)$: $y = -5$
Vertical line through $(7, -5)$: $x = 7$

Matched Problem 3   (A) Graph $x = 5$ and $y = -3$ simultaneously in the same rectangular coordinate system.

(B) Write the equations of the vertical and horizontal lines that pass through the point $(-8, 2)$.

Slope of a Line

If we take two points, $P_1(x_1, y_1)$ and $P_2(x_2, y_2)$, on a line, then the ratio of the change in y to the change in x as the point moves from point P_1 to point P_2 is called the **slope** of the line. In a sense, slope provides a measure of the "steepness" of a line relative to the x axis. The change in x is often called the **run**, and the change in y is the **rise**.

DEFINITION Slope of a Line

If a line passes through two distinct points, $P_1(x_1, y_1)$ and $P_2(x_2, y_2)$, then its slope is given by the formula

$$m = \frac{y_2 - y_1}{x_2 - x_1} \qquad x_1 \neq x_2$$

$$= \frac{\text{vertical change (rise)}}{\text{horizontal change (run)}}$$

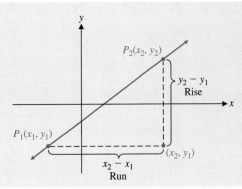

For a horizontal line, y does not change; its slope is 0. For a vertical line, x does not change; $x_1 = x_2$ so its slope is not defined. In general, the slope of a line may be positive, negative, 0, or not defined. Each case is illustrated geometrically in Table 1.

Table 1 Geometric Interpretation of Slope

Line	Rising as x moves from left to right	Falling as x moves from left to right	Horizontal	Vertical
Slope	Positive	Negative	0	Not defined
Example				

One property of real numbers discussed in Appendix A, Section A-1, is

$$\frac{-a}{-b} = -\frac{-a}{b} = -\frac{a}{-b} = \frac{a}{b}, \quad b \neq 0$$

This property implies that it does not matter which point we label as P_1 and which we label as P_2 in the slope formula. For example, if $A = (4, 3)$ and $B = (1, 2)$, then

$$B = P_2 = (1, 2) \qquad A = P_2 = (4, 3)$$
$$A = P_1 = (4, 3) \qquad B = P_1 = (1, 2)$$
$$m = \frac{2 - 3}{1 - 4} = \frac{-1}{-3} = \frac{1}{3} = \frac{3 - 2}{4 - 1}$$

A property of similar triangles (see Table I in Appendix C) ensures that the slope of a line is the same for any pair of distinct points on the line (Fig. 4).

$$m = \frac{b}{a} = \frac{b'}{a'}$$

Figure 4

EXAMPLE 4   **Finding Slopes** Sketch a line through each pair of points, and find the slope of each line.

(A) $(-3, -2), (3, 4)$ (B) $(-1, 3), (2, -3)$

(C) $(-2, -3), (3, -3)$ (D) $(-2, 4), (-2, -2)$

SOLUTION   (A)   (B)

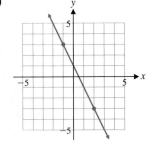

$$m = \frac{4 - (-2)}{3 - (-3)} = \frac{6}{6} = 1 \qquad\qquad m = \frac{-3 - 3}{2 - (-1)} = \frac{-6}{3} = -2$$

(C)

(D)

$$m = \frac{-3 - (-3)}{3 - (-2)} = \frac{0}{5} = 0$$

$$m = \frac{-2 - 4}{-2 - (-2)} = \frac{-6}{0}$$

Slope is not defined.

Matched Problem 4 Find the slope of the line through each pair of points.

(A) $(-2, 4), (3, 4)$ (B) $(-2, 4), (0, -4)$

(C) $(-1, 5), (-1, -2)$ (D) $(-1, -2), (2, 1)$

Equations of Lines: Special Forms

Let us start by investigating why $y = mx + b$ is called the *slope-intercept form* for a line.

EXPLORE & DISCUSS 2

(A) Graph $y = x + b$ for $b = -5, -3, 0, 3,$ and 5 simultaneously in the same coordinate system. Verbally describe the geometric significance of b.

(B) Graph $y = mx - 1$ for $m = -2, -1, 0, 1,$ and 2 simultaneously in the same coordinate system. Verbally describe the geometric significance of m.

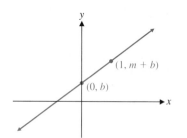

(C) Using a graphing calculator, explore the graph of $y = mx + b$ for different values of m and b.

As you may have deduced from Explore & Discuss 2, constants m and b in $y = mx + b$ have the following geometric interpretations.

If we let $x = 0$, then $y = b$. So the graph of $y = mx + b$ crosses the y axis at $(0, b)$. The constant b is the y *intercept*. For example, the y intercept of the graph of $y = -4x - 1$ is -1.

To determine the geometric significance of m, we proceed as follows: If $y = mx + b$, then by setting $x = 0$ and $x = 1$, we conclude that $(0, b)$ and $(1, m + b)$ lie on its graph (Fig. 5). The slope of this line is given by:

$$\text{Slope} = \frac{y_2 - y_1}{x_2 - x_1} = \frac{(m + b) - b}{1 - 0} = m$$

So m is the slope of the line given by $y = mx + b$.

Figure 5

DEFINITION Slope-Intercept Form

The equation

$$y = mx + b \quad m = \text{slope}, b = y \text{ intercept} \tag{3}$$

is called the **slope-intercept form** of an equation of a line.

EXAMPLE 5   Using the Slope-Intercept Form
(A) Find the slope and y intercept, and graph $y = -\frac{2}{3}x - 3$.
(B) Write the equation of the line with slope $\frac{2}{3}$ and y intercept -2.

SOLUTION
(A) Slope $= m = -\frac{2}{3}$
  y intercept $= b = -3$

(B) $m = \frac{2}{3}$ and $b = -2$;
  so, $y = \frac{2}{3}x - 2$

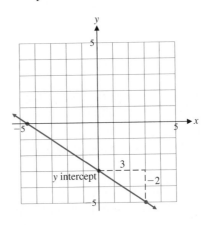

Matched Problem 5   Write the equation of the line with slope $\frac{1}{2}$ and y intercept -1. Graph.

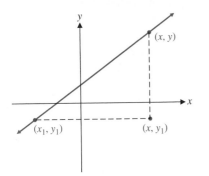

Figure 6

Suppose that a line has slope m and passes through a fixed point (x_1, y_1). If the point (x, y) is any other point on the line (Fig. 6), then

$$\frac{y - y_1}{x - x_1} = m$$

That is,

$$y - y_1 = m(x - x_1) \qquad (4)$$

We now observe that (x_1, y_1) also satisfies equation (4) and conclude that equation (4) is an equation of a line with slope m that passes through (x_1, y_1).

DEFINITION   Point-Slope Form
An equation of a line with slope m that passes through (x_1, y_1) is

$$y - y_1 = m(x - x_1) \qquad (4)$$

which is called the **point-slope form** of an equation of a line.

The point-slope form is extremely useful, since it enables us to find an equation for a line if we know its slope and the coordinates of a point on the line or if we know the coordinates of two points on the line.

EXAMPLE 6   Using the Point-Slope Form
(A) Find an equation for the line that has slope $\frac{1}{2}$ and passes through $(-4, 3)$. Write the final answer in the form $Ax + By = C$.
(B) Find an equation for the line that passes through the points $(-3, 2)$ and $(-4, 5)$. Write the resulting equation in the form $y = mx + b$.

SOLUTION
(A) Use $y - y_1 = m(x - x_1)$. Let $m = \frac{1}{2}$ and $(x_1, y_1) = (-4, 3)$. Then

$$y - 3 = \frac{1}{2}[x - (-4)]$$
$$y - 3 = \frac{1}{2}(x + 4) \qquad \text{Multiply both sides by 2.}$$
$$2y - 6 = x + 4$$
$$-x + 2y = 10 \quad \text{or} \quad x - 2y = -10$$

(B) First, find the slope of the line by using the slope formula:

$$m = \frac{y_2 - y_1}{x_2 - x_1} = \frac{5 - 2}{-4 - (-3)} = \frac{3}{-1} = -3$$

Now use $y - y_1 = m(x - x_1)$ with $m = -3$ and $(x_1, y_1) = (-3, 2)$:

$$y - 2 = -3[x - (-3)]$$
$$y - 2 = -3(x + 3)$$
$$y - 2 = -3x - 9$$
$$y = -3x - 7$$

Matched Problem 6   (A) Find an equation for the line that has slope $\frac{2}{3}$ and passes through $(6, -2)$. Write the resulting equation in the form $Ax + By = C, A > 0$.

(B) Find an equation for the line that passes through $(2, -3)$ and $(4, 3)$. Write the resulting equation in the form $y = mx + b$.

The various forms of the equation of a line that we have discussed are summarized in Table 2 for quick reference.

Table 2   Equations of a Line

Standard form	$Ax + By = C$	A and B not both 0
Slope-intercept form	$y = mx + b$	Slope: m; y intercept; b
Point-slope form	$y - y_1 = m(x - x_1)$	Slope: m; point: (x_1, y_1)
Horizontal line	$y = b$	Slope: 0
Vertical line	$x = a$	Slope: undefined

Applications

We will now see how equations of lines occur in certain applications.

EXAMPLE 7   **Cost Equation** The management of a company that manufactures skateboards has fixed costs (costs at 0 output) of \$300 per day and total costs of \$4,300 per day at an output of 100 skateboards per day. Assume that cost C is linearly related to output x.

(A) Find the slope of the line joining the points associated with outputs of 0 and 100; that is, the line passing through $(0, 300)$ and $(100, 4,300)$.

(B) Find an equation of the line relating output to cost. Write the final answer in the form $C = mx + b$.

(C) Graph the cost equation from part (B) for $0 \le x \le 200$.

SOLUTION   (A) $m = \dfrac{y_2 - y_1}{x_2 - x_1}$

$$= \frac{4,300 - 300}{100 - 0}$$

$$= \frac{4,000}{100} = 40$$

(B) We must find an equation of the line that passes through $(0, 300)$ with slope 40. We use the slope-intercept form:

$$C = mx + b$$
$$C = 40x + 300$$

(C)

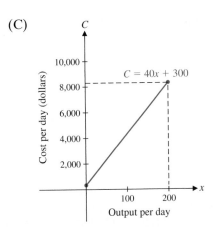

In Example 7, the *fixed cost* of $300 per day covers plant cost, insurance, and so on. This cost is incurred whether or not there is any production. The *variable cost* is $40x$, which depends on the day's output. Since increasing production from x to $x + 1$ will increase the cost by $40 (from $40x + 300$ to $40x + 340$), the slope 40 can be interpreted as the **rate of change** of the cost function with respect to production x.

Matched Problem 7   Answer parts (A) and (B) in Example 7 for fixed costs of $250 per day and total costs of $3,450 per day at an output of 80 skateboards per day.

In a free competitive market, the price of a product is determined by the relationship between supply and demand. If there is a surplus—that is, the supply is greater than the demand—the price tends to come down. If there is a shortage—that is, the demand is greater than the supply—the price tends to go up. The price tends to move toward an equilibrium price at which the supply and demand are equal. Example 8 introduces the basic concepts.

EXAMPLE 8   **Supply and Demand** At a price of $9.00 per box of oranges, the supply is 320,000 boxes and the demand is 200,000 boxes. At a price of $8.50 per box, the supply is 270,000 boxes and the demand is 300,000 boxes.

(A) Find a price–supply equation of the form $p = mx + b$, where p is the price in dollars and x is the corresponding supply in thousands of boxes.

(B) Find a price–demand equation of the form $p = mx + b$, where p is the price in dollars and x is the corresponding demand in thousands of boxes.

(C) Graph the price–supply and price–demand equations in the same coordinate system and find their point of intersection.

SOLUTION   (A) To find a price–supply equation of the form $p = mx + b$, we must find two points of the form (x, p) that are on the supply line. From the given supply data, $(320, 9)$ and $(270, 8.5)$ are two such points. First, find the slope of the line:

$$m = \frac{9 - 8.5}{320 - 270} = \frac{0.5}{50} = 0.01$$

Now use the point-slope form to find the equation of the line:

$$p - p_1 = m(x - x_1)$$
$$p - 9 = 0.01(x - 320) \qquad (x_1, p_1) = (320, 9)$$
$$p - 9 = 0.01x - 3.2$$
$$p = 0.01x + 5.8 \qquad \textit{Price–supply equation}$$

(B) From the given demand data, $(200, 9)$ and $(300, 8.5)$ are two points on the demand line.

$$m = \frac{8.5 - 9}{300 - 200} = \frac{-0.5}{100} = -0.005$$

$$p - p_1 = m(x - x_1)$$
$$p - 9 = -0.005(x - 200) \qquad (x_1, p_1) = (200, 9)$$
$$p - 9 = -0.005x + 1$$
$$p = -0.005x + 10 \qquad \textit{Price–demand equation}$$

(C) From part (A), we plot the points $(320, 9)$ and $(270, 8.5)$ and then draw the line through them. We do the same with the points $(200, 9)$ and $(300, 8.5)$ from part (B) (Fig. 7). (Note that we restricted the axes to intervals that contain these data points.) To find the intersection point of the two lines, we equate the right-hand sides of the price–supply and price–demand equations and solve for x:

$$\textbf{Price–supply} \quad \textbf{Price–demand}$$
$$0.01x + 5.8 = -0.005x + 10$$
$$0.015x = 4.2$$
$$x = 280$$

Figure 7 Graphs of price–supply and price–demand equations

Now use the price–supply equation to find p when $x = 280$:

$$p = 0.01x + 5.8$$
$$p = 0.01(280) + 5.8 = 8.6$$

As a check, we use the price–demand equation to find p when $x = 280$:

$$p = -0.005x + 10$$
$$p = -0.005(280) + 10 = 8.6$$

The lines intersect at $(280, 8.6)$. The intersection point of the price–supply and price–demand equations is called the **equilibrium point**, and its coordinates are the **equilibrium quantity** (280) and the **equilibrium price** ($8.60). These terms are illustrated in Figure 7. The intersection point can also be found by using the INTERSECT command on a graphing calculator (Fig. 8). To summarize, the price of a box of oranges tends toward the equilibrium price of $8.60, at which the supply and demand are both equal to 280,000 boxes.

Figure 8 Finding an intersection point

Matched Problem 8 At a price of $12.59 per box of grapefruit, the supply is 595,000 boxes and the demand is 650,000 boxes. At a price of $13.19 per box, the supply is 695,000 boxes and the demand is 590,000 boxes. Assume that the relationship between price and supply is linear and that the relationship between price and demand is linear.

(A) Find a price–supply equation of the form $p = mx + b$.

(B) Find a price–demand equation of the form $p = mx + b$.

(C) Find the equilibrium point.

Exercises 1-2

A

Problems 1–4 refer to graphs (A)–(D).

(A)   (B)

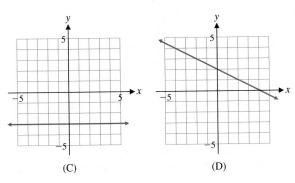

(C)   (D)

1. Identify the graph(s) of lines with a negative slope.

2. Identify the graph(s) of lines with a positive slope.

3. Identify the graph(s) of any lines with slope zero.

4. Identify the graph(s) of any lines with undefined slope.

In Problems 5–8, sketch a graph of each equation in a rectangular coordinate system.

5. $y = 2x - 3$

6. $y = \dfrac{x}{2} + 1$

7. $2x + 3y = 12$

8. $8x - 3y = 24$

In Problems 9–14, find the slope and y intercept of the graph of each equation.

9. $y = 5x - 7$

10. $y = 3x + 2$

11. $y = -\dfrac{5}{2}x - 9$

12. $y = -\dfrac{10}{3}x + 4$

13. $y = \dfrac{x}{4} + \dfrac{2}{3}$

14. $y = \dfrac{x}{5} - \dfrac{1}{2}$

In Problems 15–18, write an equation of the line with the indicated slope and y intercept.

15. Slope $= 2$
y intercept $= 1$

16. Slope $= 1$
y intercept $= 5$

17. Slope $= -\dfrac{1}{3}$
y intercept $= 6$

18. Slope $= \dfrac{6}{7}$
y intercept $= -\dfrac{9}{2}$

In Problems 19–22, use the graph of each line to find the x intercept, y intercept, and slope. Write the slope-intercept form of the equation of the line.

19.

20.

21.

22.

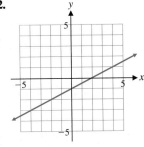

Sketch a graph of each equation or pair of equations in Problems 23–28 in a rectangular coordinate system.

23. $y = -\dfrac{2}{3}x - 2$

24. $y = -\dfrac{3}{2}x + 1$

25. $3x - 2y = 10$

26. $5x - 6y = 15$

27. $x = 3; y = -2$

28. $x = -3; y = 2$

In Problems 29–34, find the slope of the graph of each equation.

29. $4x + y = 3$

30. $5x - y = -2$

31. $3x + 5y = 15$

32. $2x - 3y = 18$

33. $-4x + 2y = 9$

34. $-x + 8y = 4$

35. Given $Ax + By = 12$, graph each of the following three cases in the same coordinate system.

(A) $A = 2$ and $B = 0$

(B) $A = 0$ and $B = 3$

(C) $A = 3$ and $B = 4$

36. Given $Ax + By = 24$, graph each of the following three cases in the same coordinate system.

(A) $A = 6$ and $B = 0$

(B) $A = 0$ and $B = 8$

(C) $A = 2$ and $B = 3$

37. Graph $y = 25x + 200, x \geq 0$.

38. Graph $y = 40x + 160, x \geq 0$.

39. (A) Graph $y = 1.2x - 4.2$ in a rectangular coordinate system.

(B) Find the x and y intercepts algebraically to one decimal place.

(C) Graph $y = 1.2x - 4.2$ in a graphing calculator.

(D) Find the x and y intercepts to one decimal place using TRACE and the zero command.

40. (A) Graph $y = -0.8x + 5.2$ in a rectangular coordinate system.

(B) Find the x and y intercepts algebraically to one decimal place.

(C) Graph $y = -0.8x + 5.2$ in a graphing calculator.

(D) Find the x and y intercepts to one decimal place using TRACE and the zero command.

(E) Using the results of parts (A) and (B), or (C) and (D), find the solution set for the linear inequality

$$-0.8x + 5.2 < 0$$

In Problems 41–44, write the equations of the vertical and horizontal lines through each point.

41. $(4, -3)$

42. $(-5, 6)$

43. $(-1.5, -3.5)$

44. $(2.6, 3.8)$

In Problems 45–50, write the equation of the line through each indicated point with the indicated slope. Write the final answer in the form $y = mx + b$.

45. $m = -4; (2, -3)$

46. $m = -6; (-4, 1)$

47. $m = \frac{3}{2}; (-4, -5)$

48. $m = \frac{4}{3}; (-6, 2)$

49. $m = 0; (-1.5, 4.6)$

50. $m = 0; (3.1, -2.7)$

In Problems 51–58,

(A) *Find the slope of the line that passes through the given points.*

(B) *Find the standard form of the equation of the line.*

(C) *Find the slope-intercept form of the equation of the line.*

51. $(2, 5)$ and $(5, 7)$

52. $(1, 2)$ and $(3, 5)$

53. $(-2, -1)$ and $(2, -6)$

54. $(2, 3)$ and $(-3, 7)$

55. $(5, 3)$ and $(5, -3)$

56. $(1, 4)$ and $(0, 4)$

57. $(-2, 5)$ and $(3, 5)$

58. $(2, 0)$ and $(2, -3)$

59. Discuss the relationship among the graphs of the lines with equation $y = mx + 2$, where m is any real number.

60. Discuss the relationship among the graphs of the lines with equation $y = -0.5x + b$, where b is any real number.

Applications

61. Cost analysis. A donut shop has a fixed cost of $124 per day and a variable cost of $0.12 per donut. Find the total daily cost of producing x donuts. How many donuts can be produced for a total daily cost of $250?

62. Cost analysis. A small company manufactures picnic tables. The weekly fixed cost is $1,200 and the variable cost is $45 per table. Find the total weekly cost of producing x picnic tables. How many picnic tables can be produced for a total weekly cost of $4,800?

63. Cost analysis. A plant can manufacture 80 golf clubs per day for a total daily cost of $7,647 and 100 golf clubs per day for a total daily cost of $9,147.

(A) Assuming that daily cost and production are linearly related, find the total daily cost of producing x golf clubs.

(B) Graph the total daily cost for $0 \leq x \leq 200$.

(C) Interpret the slope and y intercept of this cost equation.

64. Cost analysis. A plant can manufacture 50 tennis rackets per day for a total daily cost of $3,855 and 60 tennis rackets per day for a total daily cost of $4,245.

(A) Assuming that daily cost and production are linearly related, find the total daily cost of producing x tennis rackets.

(B) Graph the total daily cost for $0 \leq x \leq 100$.

(C) Interpret the slope and y intercept of this cost equation.

65. Business—Markup policy. A drugstore sells a drug costing $85 for $112 and a drug costing $175 for $238.

(A) If the markup policy of the drugstore is assumed to be linear, write an equation that expresses retail price *R* in terms of cost *C* (wholesale price).

(B) What does a store pay (to the nearest dollar) for a drug that retails for $185?

66. **Business—Markup policy.** A clothing store sells a shirt costing $20 for $33 and a jacket costing $60 for $93.

   (A) If the markup policy of the store is assumed to be linear, write an equation that expresses retail price *R* in terms of cost *C* (wholesale price).

   (B) What does a store pay for a suit that retails for $240?

67. **Business—Depreciation.** A farmer buys a new tractor for $157,000 and assumes that it will have a trade-in value of $82,000 after 10 years. The farmer uses a constant rate of depreciation (commonly called **straight-line depreciation**— one of several methods permitted by the IRS) to determine the annual value of the tractor.

   (A) Find a linear model for the depreciated value *V* of the tractor *t* years after it was purchased.

   (B) What is the depreciated value of the tractor after 6 years?

   (C) When will the depreciated value fall below $70,000?

   (D) Graph *V* for $0 \leq t \leq 20$ and illustrate the answers from parts (A) and (B) on the graph.

68. **Business—Depreciation.** A charter fishing company buys a new boat for $224,000 and assumes that it will have a trade-in value of $115,200 after 16 years.

   (A) Find a linear model for the depreciated value *V* of the boat *t* years after it was purchased.

   (B) What is the depreciated value of the tractor after 10 years?

   (C) When will the depreciated value fall below $100,000?

   (D) Graph *V* for $0 \leq t \leq 30$ and illustrate the answers from (A) and (B) on the graph.

69. **Boiling point.** The temperature at which water starts to boil is called its **boiling point** and is linearly related to the altitude. Water boils at 212°F at sea level and at 193.6°F at an altitude of 10,000 feet. (*Source*: biggreenegg.com)

   (A) Find a relationship of the form $T = mx + b$ where *T* is degrees Fahrenheit and *x* is altitude in thousands of feet.

   (B) Find the boiling point at an altitude of 3,500 feet.

   (C) Find the altitude if the boiling point is 200°F.

   (D) Graph *T* and illustrate the answers to (B) and (C) on the graph.

70. **Boiling point.** The temperature at which water starts to boil is also linearly related to barometric pressure. Water boils at 212°F at a pressure of 29.9 inHg (inches of mercury) and at 191°F at a pressure of 28.4 inHg. (*Source*: biggreenegg.com)

   (A) Find a relationship of the form $T = mx + b$, where *T* is degrees Fahrenheit and *x* is pressure in inches of mercury.

   (B) Find the boiling point at a pressure of 31 inHg.

   (C) Find the pressure if the boiling point is 199°F.

(D) Graph *T* and illustrate the answers to (B) and (C) on the graph.

71. **Flight conditions.** In stable air, the air temperature drops about 3.6°F for each 1,000-foot rise in altitude. (*Source*: Federal Aviation Administration)

   (A) If the temperature at sea level is 70°F, write a linear equation that expresses temperature *T* in terms of altitude *A* in thousands of feet.

   (B) At what altitude is the temperature 34°F?

72. **Flight navigation.** The airspeed indicator on some aircraft is affected by the changes in atmospheric pressure at different altitudes. A pilot can estimate the true airspeed by observing the indicated airspeed and adding to it about 1.6% for every 1,000 feet of altitude. (*Source:* Megginson Technologies Ltd.)

   (A) A pilot maintains a constant reading of 200 miles per hour on the airspeed indicator as the aircraft climbs from sea level to an altitude of 10,000 feet. Write a linear equation that expresses true airspeed *T* (in miles per hour) in terms of altitude *A* (in thousands of feet).

   (B) What would be the true airspeed of the aircraft at 6,500 feet?

73. **Demographics.** The average number of persons per household in the United States has been shrinking steadily for as long as statistics have been kept and is approximately linear with respect to time. In 1980 there were about 2.76 persons per household, and in 2008 about 2.55. (*Source:* U.S. Census Bureau)

   (A) If *N* represents the average number of persons per household and *t* represents the number of years since 1980, write a linear equation that expresses *N* in terms of *t*.

   (B) Use this equation to estimate household size in the year 2020.

74. **Demographics.** The **median** household income divides the households into two groups: the half whose income is less than or equal to the median, and the half whose income is greater than the median. The median household income in the United States grew from about $30,000 in 1990 to about $48,000 in 2006. (*Source*: U.S. Census Bureau)

   (A) If *I* represents the median household income and *t* represents the number of years since 1990, write a linear equation that expresses *I* in terms of *t*.

   (B) Use this equation to estimate median household income in the year 2030.

75. **Cigarette smoking.** The percentage of female cigarette smokers in the United States declined from 21% in 2000 to 18% in 2006. (*Source*: Centers for Disease Control)

   (A) Find a linear equation relating percentage of female smokers (*f*) to years since 2000 (*t*).

   (B) Find the year in which the percentage of female smokers falls below 10%.

76. **Cigarette smoking.** The percentage of male cigarette smokers in the United States declined from 25.2% in 2001 to 23.9% in 2006. (*Source:* Centers for Disease Control)

   (A) Find a linear equation relating percentage of male smokers (*m*) to years since 2000 (*t*).

   (B) Find the year in which the percentage of male smokers falls below 20%.

77. Supply and demand. At a price of $2.28 per bushel, the supply of barley is 7,500 million bushels and the demand is 7,900 million bushels. At a price of $2.37 per bushel, the supply is 7,900 million bushels and the demand is 7,800 million bushels.

(A) Find a price–supply equation of the form $p = mx + b$.

(B) Find a price–demand equation of the form $p = mx + b$.

(C) Find the equilibrium point.

(D) Graph the price–supply equation, price–demand equation, and equilibrium point in the same coordinate system.

78. Supply and demand. At a price of $1.94 per bushel, the supply of corn is 9,800 million bushels and the demand is 9,300 million bushels. At a price of $1.82 per bushel, the supply is 9,400 million bushels and the demand is 9,500 million bushels.

(A) Find a price–supply equation of the form $p = mx + b$.

(B) Find a price–demand equation of the form $p = mx + b$.

(C) Find the equilibrium point.

(D) Graph the price–supply equation, price–demand equation, and equilibrium point in the same coordinate system.

79. Physics. Hooke's law states that the relationship between the stretch s of a spring and the weight w causing the stretch is linear. For a particular spring, a 5-pound weight causes a stretch of 2 inches, while with no weight, the stretch of the spring is 0.

(A) Find a linear equation that expresses s in terms of w.

(B) What is the stretch for a weight of 20 pounds?

(C) What weight will cause a stretch of 3.6 inches?

80. Physics. The distance d between a fixed spring and the floor is a linear function of the weight w attached to the bottom of the spring. The bottom of the spring is 18 inches from the floor when the weight is 3 pounds, and 10 inches from the floor when the weight is 5 pounds.

(A) Find a linear equation that expresses d in terms of w.

(B) Find the distance from the bottom of the spring to the floor if no weight is attached.

(C) Find the smallest weight that will make the bottom of the spring touch the floor. (Ignore the height of the weight.)

81. Energy consumption. Table 3 lists U.S. oil imports as a percentage* of total energy consumption for selected years. Let x represent years since 1960 and y represent the corresponding percentage of oil imports.

(A) Find the equation of the line through $(0, 9)$ and $(40, 29)$, the first and last data points in Table 3.

(B) Find the equation of the line through $(0, 9)$ and $(10, 12)$, the first and second data points in Table 3.

(C) Graph the lines from parts (A) and (B) and the data points (x, y) from Table 3 in the same coordinate system.

*We use percentage because energy is measured in quadrillion BTUs (British Thermal Units) and one quadrillion is 1,000,000,000,000,000. Percentages are easier to comprehend.

Table 3

Year	Oil Imports (%)
1960	9
1970	12
1980	21
1990	24
2000	29

Source: Energy Information Administration

(D) Use each equation to predict oil imports as a percentage of total consumption in 2020.

(E) Which of the two lines seems to better represent the data in Table 3? Discuss.

82. Energy production. Table 4 lists U.S. crude oil production as a percentage of total U.S. energy production for selected years. Let x represent years since 1960 and y represent the corresponding percentage of oil production.

(A) Find the equation of the line through $(0, 35)$ and $(40, 17)$, the first and last data points in Table 4.

(B) Find the equation of the line through $(0, 35)$ and $(10, 32)$, the first and second data points in Table 4.

(C) Graph the lines from parts (A) and (B) and the data points (x, y) from Table 4 in the same coordinate system.

(D) Use each equation to predict oil imports as a percentage of total consumption in 2020.

(E) Which of the two lines better represents the data in Table 4? Discuss.

Table 4

Year	Oil Production (%)
1960	35
1970	32
1980	27
1990	22
2000	17

Source: Energy Information Administration

Answers to Matched Problems

1.

2. y intercept $= -4$, x intercept $= 3$

3. (A)

(B) Horizontal line: $y = 2$;
   vertical line: $= -8$

4. (A) 0   (B) -4
   (C) Not defined   (D) 1

5. $y = \frac{1}{2}x - 1$

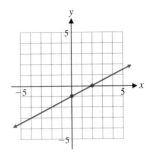

6. (A) $2x - 3y = 18$ (B) $y = 3x - 9$

7. (A) $m = 40$ (B) $C = 40x + 250$

8. (A) $p = 0.006x + 9.02$ (B) $p = -0.01x + 19.09$
   (C) $(629, 12.80)$

1-3   Linear Regression

- Slope as a Rate of Change
- Linear Regression

Mathematical modeling is the process of using mathematics to solve real-world problems. This process can be broken down into three steps (Fig. 1):

Step 1   *Construct* the **mathematical model** (that is, a mathematics problem that, when solved, will provide information about the real-world problem).

Step 2   *Solve* the mathematical model.

Step 3   *Interpret* the solution to the mathematical model in terms of the original real-world problem.

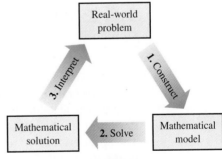

Figure 1

In more complex problems, this cycle may have to be repeated several times to obtain the required information about the real-world problem. In this section, we will discuss one of the simplest mathematical models, a linear equation. With the aid of a graphing calculator or computer, we also will learn how to analyze a linear model based on real-world data.

Slope as a Rate of Change

If x and y are related by the equation $y = mx + b$, where m and b are constants with $m \neq 0$, then x and y are **linearly related**. If (x_1, y_1) and (x_2, y_2) are two distinct points on this line, then the slope of the line is

$$m = \frac{y_2 - y_1}{x_2 - x_1} = \frac{\text{Change in } y}{\text{Change in } x} \tag{1}$$

In applications, ratio (1) is called the **rate of change** of y with respect to x. Since the slope of a line is unique, **the rate of change of two linearly related variables is constant**. Here are some examples of familiar rates of change: miles per hour, revolutions per minute, price per pound, passengers per plane, and so on. If the relationship between x and y is not linear, ratio (1) is called the **average rate of change** of y with respect to x.

EXAMPLE 1 **Estimating Body Surface Area** Appropriate doses of medicine for both animals and humans are often based on body surface area (BSA). Since weight is much easier to determine than BSA, veterinarians use the weight of an animal to estimate BSA. The following linear equation expresses BSA for canines in terms of weight:

$$a = 16.12w + 375.6$$

where a is BSA in square inches and w is weight in pounds. (*Source*: Veterinary Oncology Consultants, PTY LTD)

(A) Interpret the slope of the BSA equation.

(B) What is the effect of a one-pound increase in weight?

SOLUTION (A) The rate-of-change BSA with respect to weight is 16.12 square inches per pound.

(B) Since slope is the ratio of rise to run, increasing w by 1 pound (run) increases a by 16.12 square inches (rise).

Matched Problem 1 The equation $a = 28.55w + 118.7$ expresses BSA for felines in terms of weight, where a is BSA in square inches and w is weight in pounds.

(A) Interpret the slope of the BSA equation.

(B) What is the effect of a one-pound increase in weight?

EXPLORE & DISCUSS 1 As illustrated in Example 1A, the slope m of a line with equation $y = mx + b$ has two interpretations:

  1. m is the rate of change of y with respect to x.
  2. Increasing x by one unit will change y by m units.

How are these two interpretations related?

Parachutes are used to deliver cargo to areas that cannot be reached by other means. The **rate of descent** of the cargo is the rate of change of altitude with respect to time. The absolute value of the rate of descent is called the **speed** of the cargo. At low altitudes, the altitude of the cargo and the time in the air are linearly related. The appropriate rate of descent varies widely with the item. Bulk food (rice, flour, beans, etc.) and clothing can tolerate nearly any rate of descent under 40 ft/sec. Machinery and electronics (pumps, generators, radios, etc.) should generally be dropped at 15 ft/sec or less. Butler Tactical Parachute Systems in Roanoke, Virginia, manufactures a variety of canopies for dropping cargo. The following example uses information taken from the company's brochures.

EXAMPLE 2 **Finding the Rate of Descent** A 100-pound cargo of delicate electronic equipment is dropped from an altitude of 2,880 feet and lands 200 seconds later. (*Source*: Butler Tactical Parachute Systems)

(A) Find a linear model relating altitude a (in feet) and time in the air t (in seconds).

(B) How fast is the cargo moving when it lands?

SOLUTION (A) If $a = mt + b$ is the linear equation relating altitude a and time in air t, then the graph of this equation must pass through the following points:

$$(t_1, a_1) = (0, 2{,}880) \qquad \text{Cargo is dropped from plane.}$$
$$(t_2, a_2) = (200, 0) \qquad \text{Cargo lands.}$$

The slope of this line is

$$m = \frac{a_2 - a_1}{t_2 - t_1} = \frac{0 - 2{,}880}{200 - 0} = -14.4$$

and the equation of this line is

$$a - 0 = -14.4(t - 200)$$
$$a = -14.4t + 2{,}880$$

(B) The rate of descent is the slope $m = -14.4$, so the speed of the cargo at landing is $|-14.4| = 14.4$ ft/sec.

Matched Problem 2   A 400-pound load of grain is dropped from an altitude of 2,880 feet and lands 80 seconds later.

(A) Find a linear model relating altitude a (in feet) and time in the air t (in seconds).

(B) How fast is the cargo moving when it lands?

Linear Regression

In real-world applications, we often encounter numerical data in the form of a table. **Regression analysis** is a process for finding a function that provides a useful model for a set of data points. Graphs of equations are often called **curves**, and regression analysis is also referred to as **curve fitting**. In the next example, we use a linear model obtained by using **linear regression** on a graphing calculator.

EXAMPLE 3   **Diamond Prices** Prices for round-shaped diamonds taken from an online trader are given in Table 1.

(A) A linear model for the data in Table 1 is given by

$$p = 6{,}140c - 480 \qquad (2)$$

where p is the price of a diamond weighing c carats. (We will discuss the source of models like this later in this section.) Plot the points in Table 1 on a Cartesian coordinate system, producing a *scatter plot*, and graph the model on the same axes.

(B) Interpret the slope of the model in (2).

(C) Use the model to estimate the cost of a 0.85-carat diamond and the cost of a 1.2-carat diamond. Round answers to the nearest dollar.

(D) Use the model to estimate the weight of a diamond (to two decimal places) that sells for $4,000.

Table 1 Round-Shaped Diamond Prices

Weight (carats)	Price
0.5	$2,790
0.6	$3,191
0.7	$3,694
0.8	$4,154
0.9	$5,018
1.0	$5,898

Source: www.tradeshop.com

SOLUTION   (A) A **scatter plot** is simply a graph of the points in Table 1 (Fig. 2A). To add the graph of the model to the scatter plot, we find any two points that satisfy equation (2) [we choose $(0.4, 1{,}976)$ and $(1.1, 6{,}274)$]. Plotting these points and drawing a line through them gives us Figure 2B.

(A) Scatter plot

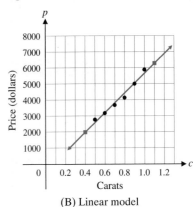

(B) Linear model

Figure 2

(B) The rate of change of the price of a diamond with respect to its weight is 6,140. Increasing the weight by one carat will increase the price by about $6,140.

(C) The graph of the model (Fig. 2B) does not pass through any of the points in the scatter plot, but it comes close to all of them. [Verify this by evaluating equation (2) at $c = 0.5, 0.6, \dots, 1$.] So we can use equation (2) to approximate points not in Table 1.

$$c = 0.85 \qquad\qquad c = 1.2$$
$$p \approx 6{,}140(0.85) - 480 \qquad p \approx 6{,}140(1.2) - 480$$
$$= \$4{,}739 \qquad\qquad = \$6{,}888$$

A 0.85-carat diamond will cost about $4,739, and a 1.2-carat diamond will cost about $6,888.

(D) To find the weight of a $4,000 diamond, we solve the following equation for c:

$$6{,}140c - 480 = 4{,}000 \qquad \text{Add 480 to both sides.}$$
$$6{,}140c = 4{,}480 \qquad \text{Divide both sides by 6,140.}$$
$$c = \frac{4{,}480}{6{,}140} \approx 0.73 \qquad \text{Rounded to two decimal places.}$$

A $4,000 diamond will weigh about 0.73 carats.

Matched Problem 3

Prices for emerald-shaped diamonds from an online trader are given in Table 2. Repeat Example 3 for this data with the linear model

$$p = 5{,}600c - 1{,}100$$

where p is the price of an emerald-shaped diamond weighing c carats.

Table 2 Emerald-Shaped Diamond Prices

Weight (carats)	Price
0.5	$1,677
0.6	$2,353
0.7	$2,718
0.8	$3,218
0.9	$3,982
1.0	$4,510

Source: www.tradeshop.com

The model we used in Example 3 was obtained using a technique called **linear regression**, and the model is called the **regression line**. This technique produces a line that is the **best fit** for a given data set. Although you can find a linear regression line by hand, we prefer to leave the calculations to a graphing calculator or a computer. Don't be concerned if you don't have either of these electronic devices. We will supply the regression model in most of the applications we discuss, as we did in Example 3.

EXPLORE & DISCUSS 2

As stated above, we used linear regression to produce the model in Example 3. If you have a graphing calculator that supports linear regression, then you can find this model. The linear regression process varies greatly from one calculator to another. Consult the user's manual* for the details of linear regression. The screens in Figure 3 are related to the construction of the model in Example 3 on a Texas Instruments TI-84 Plus.

(A) Produce similar screens on your graphing calculator.

(B) Do the same for Matched Problem 3.

(A) Entering the data

(B) Finding the model

(C) Graphing the data and the model

Figure 3 Linear regression on a graphing calculator

*Manuals for most graphing calculators are readily available on the Internet.

In Example 3, we used the regression model to approximate points that were not given in Table 1 but would fit between points in the table. This process is called **interpolation**. In the next example, we use a regression model to approximate points outside the given data set. This process is called **extrapolation**, and the approximations are often referred to as **predictions**.

EXAMPLE 4

Carbon Monoxide Emissions Table 3 contains information about U.S. carbon monoxide emissions. The linear regression model for carbon monoxide emissions from all sources (after rounding) is

$$C = 188 - 3.6t$$

where C is the carbon monoxide emissions (in millions of short tons*) and t is time in years with $t = 0$ corresponding to 1980.

(A) Interpret the slope of the regression line as a rate of change.

(B) Use the regression model to predict carbon monoxide emissions from all sources in 2018.

Table 3 U.S. Carbon Monoxide Emissions (millions of short tons)

	1980	1985	1990	1995	2000	2005
All sources	185	177	154	129	114	103
Highway vehicles	144	134	110	84	68	56

Source: U.S. Bureau of Transportation Statistics

SOLUTION

(A) The slope $m = -3.6$ is the rate of change of emissions with respect to time. Since the slope is negative and the emissions are given in millions of tons, the emissions are decreasing at a rate of $3.6(1{,}000{,}000) = 3{,}600{,}000$ tons per year.

(B) If $t = 36$, then

$$C = 188 - 3.6(38) = 51.2 \quad \text{or} \quad 51{,}200{,}000 \text{ tons}$$

So approximately 51,200,000 tons of carbon monoxide will be emitted in 2018.

Matched Problem 4

Repeat Example 4 using the linear regression model

$$C = -3.8t + 147$$

where C is the carbon monoxide emissions from highway vehicles (in millions of short tons) and t is time in years with $t = 0$ corresponding to 1980.

Forest managers estimate growth, volume, yield, and forest potential. One common measure is the diameter of a tree at breast height (Dbh), which is defined as the diameter of the tree at a point 4.5 feet above the ground on the uphill side of the tree. Example 5 uses Dbh to estimate the height of balsam fir trees.

 EXAMPLE 5

Forestry A linear regression model for the height of balsam fir trees is

$$h = 3.8d + 18.73$$

where d is Dbh in inches and h is the height in feet.

(A) Interpret the slope of this model.

(B) What is the effect of a 1-inch increase in Dbh?

(C) Estimate the height of a balsam fir with a Dbh of 8 inches. Round your answer to the nearest foot.

---

*A short ton (or a U.S. ton) is 2,000 pounds, a long ton (or a U.K. ton) is 2,240 pounds, and a metric tonne is 1,000 kilograms, or 2204.6 pounds.

(D) Estimate the Dbh of a balsam fir that is 30 feet tall. Round your answer to the nearest inch.

SOLUTION

(A) The rate of change of height with respect to breast height diameter is 3.8 feet per inch.

(B) Height increases by 3.8 feet.

(C) We must find h when $d = 8$:

$$h = 3.8d + 18.73 \qquad \text{Substitute } d = 8.$$
$$h = 3.8(8) + 18.73 \qquad \text{Evaluate.}$$
$$h = 49.13 \approx 49 \text{ ft}$$

(D) We must find d when $h = 30$:

$$h = 3.8d + 18.73 \qquad \text{Substitute } h = 30.$$
$$30 = 3.8d + 18.73 \qquad \text{Subtract 18.73 from both sides.}$$
$$11.27 = 3.8d \qquad \text{Divide both sides by 3.8.}$$
$$d = \frac{11.27}{3.8} \approx 3 \text{ in}$$

The data used to produce the regression model in Example 5 are from the Jack Haggerty Forest at Lakehead University in Canada (Table 4). We used the popular spreadsheet Excel to produce a scatter plot of the data in Table 4 and to find the regression model (Fig. 4).

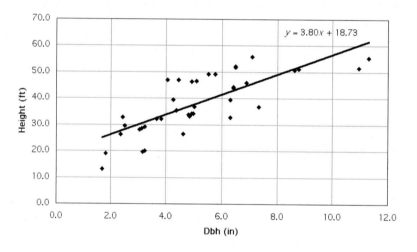

Figure 4 Linear regression with a spreadsheet

Table 4 Height and Diameter of the Balsam Fir

Dbh (in)	Height (ft)	Dbh (in)	Height (ft)	Dbh (in)	Height (ft)	Dbh (in)	Height (ft)
6.5	51.8	6.4	44.0	3.1	19.7	4.6	26.6
8.6	50.9	4.4	46.9	7.1	55.8	4.8	33.1
5.7	49.2	6.5	52.2	6.3	32.8	3.1	28.5
4.9	46.3	4.1	46.9	2.4	26.2	3.2	29.2
6.4	44.3	8.8	51.2	2.5	29.5	5.0	34.1
4.1	46.9	5.0	36.7	6.9	45.9	3.0	28.2
1.7	13.1	4.9	34.1	2.4	32.8	4.8	33.8
1.8	19.0	3.8	32.2	4.3	39.4	4.4	35.4
3.2	20.0	5.5	49.2	7.3	36.7	11.3	55.4
5.1	46.6	6.3	39.4	10.9	51.5	3.7	32.2

(*Source*: Jack Haggerty Forest, Lakehead University, Canada)

Figure 5 Linear regression for white spruce trees

Matched Problem 5   Figure 5 shows the scatter plot for white spruce trees in the Jack Haggerty Forest at Lakehead University in Canada. A regression model produced by a spreadsheet (Fig. 5), after rounding, is

$$h = 1.8d + 34$$

where d is Dbh in inches and h is the height in feet.

(A) Interpret the slope of this model.

(B) What is the effect of a 1-inch increase in Dbh?

(C) Estimate the height of a white spruce with a Dbh of 10 inches. Round your answer to the nearest foot.

(D) Estimate the Dbh of a white spruce that is 65 feet tall. Round your answer to the nearest inch.

Exercises 1-3

Applications

1. **Ideal weight.** In 1983, Dr. J. D. Robinson published the following estimate of the ideal body weight of a woman:

   49 kg + 1.7 kg for each inch over 5 ft

   (A) Find a linear model for Robinson's estimate of the ideal weight of a woman using w for ideal body weight (in kilograms) and h for height over 5 ft (in inches).

   (B) Interpret the slope of the model.

   (C) If a woman is 5′4″ tall, what does the model predict her weight to be?

   (D) If a woman weighs 60 kg, what does the model predict her height to be?

2. **Ideal weight.** Dr. J. D. Robinson also published the following estimate of the ideal body weight of a man:

   52 kg + 1.9 kg for each inch over 5 ft

   (A) Find a linear model for Robinson's estimate of the ideal weight of a man using w for ideal body weight (in kilograms) and h for height over 5 ft (in inches).

   (B) Interpret the slope of the model.

   (C) If a man is 5′8″ tall, what does the model predict his weight to be?

   (D) If a man weighs 70 kg, what does the model predict his height to be?

3. **Underwater pressure.** At sea level, the weight of the atmosphere exerts a pressure of 14.7 pounds per square inch, commonly referred to as 1 **atmosphere of pressure**. As an object descends in water, pressure P and depth d are linearly related. In salt water, the pressure at a depth of 33 ft is 2 atms, or 29.4 pounds per square inch.

   (A) Find a linear model that relates pressure P (in pounds per square inch) to depth d (in feet).

   (B) Interpret the slope of the model.

   (C) Find the pressure at a depth of 50 ft.

   (D) Find the depth at which the pressure is 4 atms.

4. **Underwater pressure.** Refer to Problem 3. In fresh water, the pressure at a depth of 34 ft is 2 atms, or 29.4 pounds per square inch.

   (A) Find a linear model that relates pressure P (in pounds per square inch) to depth d (in feet).

(B) Interpret the slope of the model.

(C) Find the pressure at a depth of 50 ft.

(D) Find the depth at which the pressure is 4 atms.

5. **Rate of descent — Parachutes.** At low altitudes, the altitude of a parachutist and time in the air are linearly related. A jump at 2,880 ft using the U.S. Army's T-10 parachute system lasts 120 secs.

(A) Find a linear model relating altitude a (in feet) and time in the air t (in seconds).

(B) Find the rate of descent for a T-10 system.

(C) Find the speed of the parachutist at landing.

6. **Rate of descent — Parachutes.** The U.S Army is considering a new parachute, the Advanced Tactical Parachute System (ATPS). A jump at 2,880 ft using the ATPS system lasts 180 secs.

(A) Find a linear model relating altitude a (in feet) and time in the air t (in seconds).

(B) Find the rate of descent for an ATPS system parachute.

(C) Find the speed of the parachutist at landing.

7. **Speed of sound.** The speed of sound through air is linearly related to the temperature of the air. If sound travels at 331 m/sec at 0°C and at 343 m/sec at 20°C, construct a linear model relating the speed of sound (s) and the air temperature (t). Interpret the slope of this model. (*Source:* Engineering Toolbox)

8. **Speed of sound.** The speed of sound through sea water is linearly related to the temperature of the water. If sound travels at 1,403 m/sec at 0°C and at 1,481 m/sec at 20°C, construct a linear model relating the speed of sound (s) and the air temperature (t). Interpret the slope of this model. (*Source:* Engineering Toolbox)

9. **Energy production.** Table 5 lists U.S. fossil fuel production as a percentage of total energy production for selected years. A linear regression model for this data is

$$y = -0.3x + 84.6$$

where x represents years since 1985 and y represents the corresponding percentage of total energy production.

Table 5 U.S. Fossil Fuel Production

Year	Production (%)
1985	85
1990	83
1995	81
2000	80
2005	79

Source: Energy Information Administration

(A) Draw a scatter plot of the data and a graph of the model on the same axes.

(B) Interpret the slope of the model.

(C) Use the model to predict fossil fuel production in 2020.

(D) Use the model to estimate the first year for which fossil fuel production is less than 70% of total energy production.

10. **Energy consumption.** Table 6 lists U.S. fossil fuel consumption as a percentage of total energy consumption for selected years. A linear regression model for this data is

$$y = -0.06x + 85.6$$

where x represents years since 1985 and y represents the corresponding percentage of fossil fuel consumption.

Table 6 U.S. Fossil Fuel Consumption

Year	Consumption (%)
1985	86
1990	85
1995	85
2000	84
2005	85

Source: Energy Information Administration

(A) Draw a scatter plot of the data and a graph of the model on the same axes.

(B) Interpret the slope of the model.

(C) Use the model to predict fossil fuel consumption in 2020.

(D) Use the model to estimate the first year for which fossil fuel consumption is less than 80% of total energy consumption.

11. **Cigarette smoking.** The data in Table 7 shows that the percentage of female cigarette smokers in the U.S. declined from 22.1% in 1997 to 18.0% in 2006.

Table 7 Percentage of Smoking Prevalence among U.S. Adults

Year	Males (%)	Females (%)
1997	27.6	22.1
2000	25.7	21.0
2003	24.1	19.2
2006	23.9	18.0

Source: Centers for Disease Control

(A) Applying linear regression to the data for females in Table 7 produces the model

$$f = -0.47t + 22.19$$

where f is percentage of female smokers and t is time in years since 1997. Draw a scatter plot of the female smoker data and a graph of the regression model on the same axes for $0 \le t \le 30$.

(B) Estimate the first year in which the percentage of female smokers is less than 10%.

12. **Cigarette smoking.** The data in Table 7 shows that the percentage of male cigarette smokers in the U.S. declined from 27.6% in 1997 to 23.9% in 2006.

(A) Applying linear regression to the data for males in Table 7 produces the model

$$m = -0.42t + 27.23$$

where m is percentage of male smokers and t is time in years since 1997. Draw a scatter plot of the male smoker data and a graph of the regression model for $0 \le t \le 30$.

(B) Estimate the first year in which the percentage of male smokers is less than 15%.

13. Undergraduate enrollment. Table 8 lists enrollment in U.S. degree-granting institutions for both undergraduate and graduate students. A linear regression model for undergraduate enrollment is

$$y = 0.17x + 10.1$$

where x represents years since 1980 and y is undergraduate enrollment in millions of students.

Table 8 Fall Undergraduate and Graduate Enrollment (millions of students)

Year	Undergraduate	Graduate
1980	10.48	1.34
1985	10.60	1.38
1990	11.96	1.59
1995	12.23	1.73
2000	13.16	1.85
2005	14.96	2.19

Source: National Center for Education Statistics

(A) Draw a scatter plot of the undergraduate enrollment data and a graph of the model on the same axes.

(B) Predict the undergraduate student enrollment in 2016 (to the nearest 100,000).

(C) Interpret the slope of the model.

14. Graduate student enrollment. A linear regression model for the graduate student enrollment in Table 8 is

$$y = 0.033x + 1.27$$

where x represents years since 1980 and y is graduate enrollment in millions of students.

(A) Draw a scatter plot of the graduate enrollment data and a graph of the model on the same axes.

(B) Predict the graduate student enrollment in 2016 (to the nearest 100,000).

(C) Interpret the slope of the model.

15. Licensed drivers. Table 9 contains the state population and the number of licensed drivers in the state (both in millions) for the states with population under 1 million in 2006. The regression model for this data is

$$y = 0.72x + 0.03$$

where x is the state population and y is the number of licensed drivers in the state.

Table 9 Licensed Drivers in 2006

State	Population	Licensed Drivers
Alaska	0.67	0.49
Delaware	0.85	0.62
Montana	0.94	0.72
North Dakota	0.64	0.47
South Dakota	0.78	0.58
Vermont	0.62	0.53
Wyoming	0.52	0.39

Source: Bureau of Transportation Statistics

(A) Draw a scatter plot of the data and a graph of the model on the same axes.

(B) If the population of Idaho in 2006 was about 1.5 million, use the model to estimate the number of licensed drivers in Idaho in 2006 to the nearest thousand.

(C) If the number of licensed drivers in Rhode Island in 2006 was about 0.74 million, use the model to estimate the population of Rhode Island in 2006 to the nearest thousand.

16. Licensed drivers. Table 10 contains the state population and the number of licensed drivers in the state (both in millions) for the states with population over 10 million in 2006. The regression model for this data is

$$y = 0.60x + 1.15$$

where x is the state population and y is the number of licensed drivers in the state.

Table 10 Licensed Drivers in 2006

State	Population	Licensed Drivers
California	36	23
Florida	18	14
Illinois	13	8
Michigan	10	7
New York	19	11
Ohio	11	8
Pennsylvania	12	9
Texas	24	15

Source: Bureau of Transportation Statistics

(A) Draw a scatter plot of the data and a graph of the model on the same axes.

(B) If the population of Minnesota in 2006 was about 5 million, use the model to estimate the number of licensed drivers in Minnesota in 2006 to the nearest thousand.

(C) If the number of licensed drivers in Wisconsin in 2006 was about 4 million, use the model to estimate the population of Wisconsin in 2006 to the nearest thousand.

17. Net sales. A linear regression model for the net sales data in Table 11 is

$$S = 30.7t + 128$$

where S is net sales and t is time since 2000 in years.

Table 11 Wal-Mart Stores, Inc.

Billions of U.S. Dollars	2004	2005	2006	2007	2008
Net sales	253	282	304	345	375
Operating income	15.3	17.3	18.7	20.5	22.0

Source: Wal-Mart Stores, Inc.

(A) Draw a scatter plot of the data and a graph of the model on the same axes.

(B) Predict Wal-Mart's net sales for 2017.

EXAMPLE 7 **Price–Demand and Revenue Modeling** A manufacturer of a popular digital camera wholesales the camera to retail outlets throughout the United States. Using statistical methods, the financial department in the company produced the price–demand data in Table 4, where p is the wholesale price per camera at which x million cameras are sold. Notice that as the price goes down, the number sold goes up.

Table 4 Price–Demand

x (Millions)	p ($)
2	87
5	68
8	53
12	37

Table 5 Revenue

x (Millions)	$R(x)$ (Million $)
1	90
3	
6	
9	
12	
15	

Using special analytical techniques (regression analysis), an analyst obtained the following price–demand function to model the Table 4 data:

$$p(x) = 94.8 - 5x \qquad 1 \le x \le 15 \tag{4}$$

(A) Plot the data in Table 4. Then sketch a graph of the price–demand function in the same coordinate system.

(B) What is the company's revenue function for this camera, and what is its domain?

(C) Complete Table 5, computing revenues to the nearest million dollars.

(D) Plot the data in Table 5. Then sketch a graph of the revenue function using these points.

(E) Plot the revenue function on a graphing calculator.

SOLUTION (A)

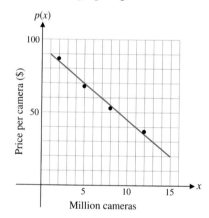

Figure 7 Price–demand

In Figure 7, notice that the model approximates the actual data in Table 4, and it is assumed that it gives realistic and useful results for all other values of x between 1 million and 15 million.

(B) $R(x) = xp(x) = x(94.8 - 5x)$ million dollars

Domain: $1 \le x \le 15$

[Same domain as the price–demand function, equation (4).]

(C)

Table 5 Revenue

x (Millions)	$R(x)$ (Million $)
1	90
3	239
6	389
9	448
12	418
15	297

(D)

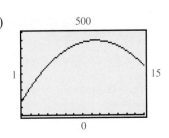 (E)

Matched Problem 7

The financial department in Example 7, using statistical techniques, produced the data in Table 6, where $C(x)$ is the cost in millions of dollars for manufacturing and selling x million cameras.

Table 6 Cost Data

x (Millions)	$C(x)$ (Million $)
1	175
5	260
8	305
12	395

Using special analytical techniques (regression analysis), an analyst produced the following cost function to model the Table 6 data:

$$C(x) = 156 + 19.7x \qquad 1 \le x \le 15 \qquad (5)$$

(A) Plot the data in Table 6. Then sketch a graph of equation (5) in the same coordinate system.

(B) What is the company's profit function for this camera, and what is its domain?

(C) Complete Table 7, computing profits to the nearest million dollars.

Table 7 Profit

x (Millions)	$P(x)$ (Million $)
1	−86
3	
6	
9	
12	
15	

(D) Plot the data in Table 7. Then sketch a graph of the profit function using these points.

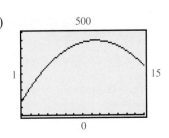 (E) Plot the profit function on a graphing calculator.

Exercises 2-1

A

In Problems 1–8, use point-by-point plotting to sketch the graph of each equation.

1. $y = x + 1$

2. $x = y + 1$

3. $x = y^2$

4. $y = x^2$

5. $y = x^3$

6. $x = y^3$

7. $xy = -6$

8. $xy = 12$

Indicate whether each table in Problems 9–14 specifies a function.

9.

10.

Domain		Range
-1	→	5
-2	→	7
-3	→	9

11.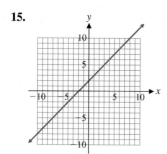

12.

Domain		Range
8	→	0
9	→	1
		2
10	→	3

13.

14.

Domain		Range
-2		
-1	→	6
0		
1		

Indicate whether each graph in Problems 15–20 specifies a function.

15.

16.

17.

18.

19.

20.

In Problems 21–28, each equation specifies a function with independent variable x. Determine whether the function is linear, constant, or neither.

21. $y - 2x = 7$

22. $y = 10 - 3x$

23. $xy - 4 = 0$

24. $x^2 - y = 8$

25. $y = 5x + \frac{1}{2}(7 - 10x)$

26. $y = \frac{2 + x}{3} + \frac{2 - x}{3}$

27. $3x + 4y = 5$

28. $9x - 2y + 6 = 0$

In Problems 29–36, use point-by-point plotting to sketch the graph of each function.

29. $f(x) = 1 - x$

30. $f(x) = \frac{x}{2} - 3$

31. $f(x) = x^2 - 1$

32. $f(x) = 3 - x^2$

33. $f(x) = 4 - x^3$

34. $f(x) = x^3 - 2$

35. $f(x) = \frac{8}{x}$

36. $f(x) = \frac{-6}{x}$

In Problems 37 and 38, the three points in the table are on the graph of the indicated function f. Do these three points provide sufficient information for you to sketch the graph of $y = f(x)$? Add more points to the table until you are satisfied that your sketch is a good representation of the graph of $y = f(x)$ on the interval $[-5, 5]$.

37.

x	-1	0	1
$f(x)$	-1	0	1

$f(x) = \frac{2x}{x^2 + 1}$

38.

x	0	1	2
$f(x)$	0	1	2

$f(x) = \frac{3x^2}{x^2 + 2}$

In Problems 39–46, use the following graph of a function f to determine x or y to the nearest integer, as indicated. Some problems may have more than one answer.

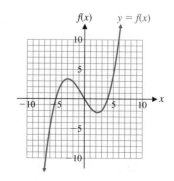

39. $y = f(-5)$ **40.** $y = f(4)$

41. $y = f(5)$ **42.** $y = f(-2)$

43. $0 = f(x)$ **44.** $3 = f(x), x < 0$

45. $-4 = f(x)$ **46.** $4 = f(x)$

In Problems 47–54, find each expression if $f(x) = 2x - 3$ and $g(x) = x^2 + 2x$.

47. $f(5)$ **48.** $f(-6)$

49. $g(-8)$ **50.** $f(9)$

51. $f(10 + 4)$ **52.** $g(3 + 7)$

53. $f(10) + f(4)$ **54.** $g(3) + g(7)$

B

In Problems 55–60, find the domain of each function.

55. $F(x) = 2x^3 - x^2 + 3$ **56.** $H(x) = 7 - 2x^2 - x^4$

57. $f(x) = \dfrac{x - 2}{x + 4}$ **58.** $g(x) = \dfrac{x + 1}{x - 2}$

59. $g(x) = \sqrt{7 - x}$ **60.** $F(x) = \dfrac{1}{\sqrt{5 + x}}$

In Problems 61–68, determine which of the equations specify functions with independent variable x. For those that do, find the domain. For those that do not, find a value of x to which there corresponds more than one value of y.

61. $x^2 - y = 1$ **62.** $x - y^2 = 1$

63. $x + y^2 = 10$ **64.** $x^2 + y = 10$

65. $xy - 4y = 1$ **66.** $xy + y - x = 5$

67. $x^2 + y^2 = 25$ **68.** $x^2 - y^2 = 16$

In Problems 69–76, find and simplify each expression if $f(x) = x^2 - 1$.

69. $f(2x)$ **70.** $f(-3x)$

71. $f(x - 3)$ **72.** $f(x + 2)$

73. $f(4 + h)$ **74.** $f(5 + h)$

75. $f(4 + h) - f(4)$ **76.** $f(5 + h) - f(5)$

C

In Problems 77–82, find and simplify each of the following, assuming $h \neq 0$ in (C).

(A) $f(x + h)$

(B) $f(x + h) - f(x)$

(C) $\dfrac{f(x + h) - f(x)}{h}$

77. $f(x) = 4x - 3$ **78.** $f(x) = -3x + 9$

79. $f(x) = 4x^2 - 7x + 6$ **80.** $f(x) = 3x^2 + 5x - 8$

81. $f(x) = x(20 - x)$ **82.** $f(x) = x(x + 40)$

Problems 83–86 refer to the area A and perimeter P of a rectangle with length l and width w (see the figure).

$A = lw$

$P = 2l + 2w$

w

l

83. The area of a rectangle is 25 sq/in. Express the perimeter $P(w)$ as a function of the width w, and state the domain of this function.

84. The area of a rectangle is 81 sq/in. Express the perimeter $P(l)$ as a function of the length l, and state the domain of this function.

85. The perimeter of a rectangle is 100 m. Express the area $A(l)$ as a function of the length l, and state the domain of this function.

86. The perimeter of a rectangle is 160 m. Express the area $A(w)$ as a function of the width w, and state the domain of this function.

Applications

87. Price–demand. A company manufactures memory chips for microcomputers. Its marketing research department, using statistical techniques, collected the data shown in Table 8, where p is the wholesale price per chip at which x million chips can be sold. Using special analytical techniques (regression analysis), an analyst produced the following price–demand function to model the data:

$$p(x) = 75 - 3x \qquad 1 \leq x \leq 20$$

Table 8	Price–Demand
x (Millions)	**p ($)**
1	72
4	63
9	48
14	33
20	15

(A) Plot the data points in Table 8, and sketch a graph of the price–demand function in the same coordinate system.

(B) What would be the estimated price per chip for a demand of 7 million chips? For a demand of 11 million chips?

88. Price–demand. A company manufactures notebook computers. Its marketing research department, using statistical techniques, collected the data shown in Table 9, where p is the wholesale price per computer at which x thousand computers can be sold. Using special analytical techniques (regression analysis), an analyst produced the following price–demand function to model the data:

$$p(x) = 2{,}000 - 60x \qquad 1 \le x \le 25$$

Table 9 Price–Demand

x (Thousands)	p ($)
1	1,940
8	1,520
16	1,040
21	740
25	500

(A) Plot the data points in Table 9, and sketch a graph of the price–demand function in the same coordinate system.

(B) What would be the estimated price per computer for a demand of 11,000 computers? For a demand of 18,000 computers?

89. Revenue.

(A) Using the price–demand function

$$p(x) = 75 - 3x \qquad 1 \le x \le 20$$

from Problem 87, write the company's revenue function and indicate its domain.

(B) Complete Table 10, computing revenues to the nearest million dollars.

Table 10 Revenue

x (Millions)	R(x) (Million $)
1	72
4	
8	
12	
16	
20	

(C) Plot the points from part (B) and sketch a graph of the revenue function using these points. Choose millions for the units on the horizontal and vertical axes.

90. Revenue.

(A) Using the price–demand function

$$p(x) = 2{,}000 - 60x \qquad 1 \le x \le 25$$

from Problem 88, write the company's revenue function and indicate its domain.

(B) Complete Table 11, computing revenues to the nearest thousand dollars.

Table 11 Revenue

x (Thousands)	R(x) (Thousand $)
1	1,940
5	
10	
15	
20	
25	

(C) Plot the points from part (B) and sketch a graph of the revenue function using these points. Choose thousands for the units on the horizontal and vertical axes.

91. Profit. The financial department for the company in Problems 87 and 89 established the following cost function for producing and selling x million memory chips:

$$C(x) = 125 + 16x \text{ million dollars}$$

(A) Write a profit function for producing and selling x million memory chips and indicate its domain.

(B) Complete Table 12, computing profits to the nearest million dollars.

Table 12 Profit

x (Millions)	P(x) (Million $)
1	−69
4	
8	
12	
16	
20	

(C) Plot the points in part (B) and sketch a graph of the profit function using these points.

92. Profit. The financial department for the company in Problems 88 and 90 established the following cost function for producing and selling x thousand notebook computers:

$$C(x) = 4{,}000 + 500x \text{ thousand dollars}$$

(A) Write a profit function for producing and selling x thousand notebook computers and indicate its domain.

(B) Complete Table 13, computing profits to the nearest thousand dollars.

Table 13 Profit

x (Thousands)	P(x) (Thousand $)
1	−2,560
5	
10	
15	
20	
25	

(C) Plot the points in part (B) and sketch a graph of the profit function using these points.

93. Packaging. A candy box will be made out of a piece of cardboard that measures 8 by 12 in. Equal-sized squares x inches on a side will be cut out of each corner, and then the ends and sides will be folded up to form a rectangular box.

(A) Express the volume of the box $V(x)$ in terms of x.

(B) What is the domain of the function V (determined by the physical restrictions)?

(C) Complete Table 14.

Table 14 Volume

x	$V(x)$
1	
2	
3	

(D) Plot the points in part (C) and sketch a graph of the volume function using these points.

94. Packaging. Refer to Problem 93.

(A) Table 15 shows the volume of the box for some values of x between 1 and 2. Use these values to estimate to one decimal place the value of x between 1 and 2 that would produce a box with a volume of 65 cu/in.

Table 15 Volume

x	$V(x)$
1.1	62.524
1.2	64.512
1.3	65.988
1.4	66.976
1.5	67.5
1.6	67.584
1.7	67.252

(B) Describe how you could refine this table to estimate x to two decimal places.

(C) Carry out the refinement you described in part (B) and approximate x to two decimal places.

95. Packaging. Refer to Problems 93 and 94.

(A) Examine the graph of $V(x)$ from Problem 93D and discuss the possible locations of other values of x that would produce a box with a volume of 65 cu/in.

(B) Construct a table like Table 15 to estimate any such value to one decimal place.

(C) Refine the table you constructed in part (B) to provide an approximation to two decimal places.

96. Packaging. A parcel delivery service will only deliver packages with length plus girth (distance around) not exceeding 108 in. A rectangular shipping box with square ends x inches on a side is to be used.

(A) If the full 108 in. is to be used, express the volume of the box $V(x)$ in terms of x.

(B) What is the domain of the function V (determined by the physical restrictions)?

(C) Complete Table 16.

Table 16 Volume

x	$V(x)$
5	
10	
15	
20	
25	

(D) Plot the points in part (C) and sketch a graph of the volume function using these points.

97. Muscle contraction. In a study of the speed of muscle contraction in frogs under various loads, British biophysicist A. W. Hill determined that the weight w (in grams) placed on the muscle and the speed of contraction v (in centimeters per second) are approximately related by an equation of the form

$$(w + a)(v + b) = c$$

where a, b, and c are constants. Suppose that for a certain muscle, $a = 15$, $b = 1$, and $c = 90$. Express v as a function of w. Find the speed of contraction if a weight of 16 g is placed on the muscle.

98. Politics. The percentage s of seats in the House of Representatives won by Democrats and the percentage v of votes cast for Democrats (when expressed as decimal fractions) are related by the equation

$$5v - 2s = 1.4 \qquad 0 < s < 1, \quad 0.28 < v < 0.68$$

(A) Express v as a function of s and find the percentage of votes required for the Democrats to win 51% of the seats.

(B) Express s as a function of v and find the percentage of seats won if Democrats receive 51% of the votes.

Answers to Matched Problems

1. (A)

(B)

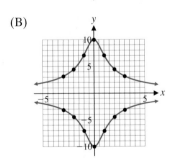

2. (A) Does not specify a function

(B) Specifies a function

3. $x \geq 2$ (inequality notation) or $[2, \infty)$ (interval notation)

4. (A) -3 (B) 0   (C) Does not exist   (D) 6

5. Domain of F: R; domain of G: all real numbers except -3; domain of H: $x \leq 2$ (inequality notation) or $(-\infty, 2]$ (interval notation)

6. (A) $a^2 - 4a + 9$ (B) $a^2 + 2ah + h^2 - 4a - 4h + 9$
(C) $2ah + h^2 - 4h$ (D) $2a + h - 4$

7. (A)

(D)

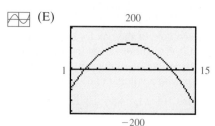 (E)

(B) $P(x) = R(x) - C(x) = x(94.8 - 5x) - (156 + 19.7x)$; domain: $1 \leq x \leq 15$

(C)

Table 7   Profit

x (Millions)	$P(x)$ (Million $)
1	-86
3	24
6	115
9	115
12	25
15	-155

2-2   Elementary Functions: Graphs and Transformations

- A Beginning Library of Elementary Functions
- Vertical and Horizontal Shifts
- Reflections, Stretches, and Shrinks
- Piecewise-Defined Functions

Each of the functions

$$g(x) = x^2 - 4 \qquad h(x) = (x - 4)^2 \qquad k(x) = -4x^2$$

can be expressed in terms of the function $f(x) = x^2$:

$$g(x) = f(x) - 4 \qquad h(x) = f(x - 4) \qquad k(x) = -4f(x)$$

In this section, we will see that the graphs of functions $g, h,$ and k are closely related to the graph of function f. Insight gained by understanding these relationships will help us analyze and interpret the graphs of many different functions.

A Beginning Library of Elementary Functions

As you progress through this book, you will repeatedly encounter a small number of elementary functions. We will identify these functions, study their basic properties, and include them in a library of elementary functions (see the inside front cover).

This library will become an important addition to your mathematical toolbox and can be used in any course or activity where mathematics is applied.

We begin by placing six basic functions in our library.

DEFINITION Basic Elementary Functions

$$f(x) = x \qquad \text{Identity function}$$
$$h(x) = x^2 \qquad \text{Square function}$$
$$m(x) = x^3 \qquad \text{Cube function}$$
$$n(x) = \sqrt{x} \qquad \text{Square root function}$$
$$p(x) = \sqrt[3]{x} \qquad \text{Cube root function}$$
$$g(x) = |x| \qquad \text{Absolute value function}$$

These elementary functions can be evaluated by hand for certain values of x and with a calculator for all values of x for which they are defined.

EXAMPLE 1 **Evaluating Basic Elementary Functions** Evaluate each basic elementary function at

(A) $x = 64$ (B) $x = -12.75$

Round any approximate values to four decimal places.

SOLUTION
(A) $f(64) = 64$
$h(64) = 64^2 = 4,096$ *Use a calculator.*
$m(64) = 64^3 = 262,144$ *Use a calculator.*
$n(64) = \sqrt{64} = 8$
$p(64) = \sqrt[3]{64} = 4$
$g(64) = |64| = 64$

(B) $f(-12.75) = -12.75$
$h(-12.75) = (-12.75)^2 = 162.5625$ *Use a calculator.*
$m(-12.75) = (-12.75)^3 \approx -2{,}072.6719$ *Use a calculator.*
$n(-12.75) = \sqrt{-12.75}$ *Not a real number.*
$p(-12.75) = \sqrt[3]{-12.75} \approx -2.3362$ *Use a calculator.*
$g(-12.75) = |-12.75| = 12.75$

Matched Problem 1 Evaluate each basic elementary function at

(A) $x = 729$ (B) $x = -5.25$

Round any approximate values to four decimal places.

 Remark—Most computers and graphing calculators use ABS(x) to represent the absolute value function. The following representation can also be useful:

$$|x| = \sqrt{x^2}$$

Figure 1 shows the graph, range, and domain of each of the basic elementary functions.

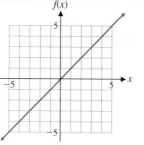

(A) **Identity function**
$f(x) = x$
Domain: R
Range: R

(B) **Square function**
$h(x) = x^2$
Domain: R
Range: $[0, \infty)$

(C) **Cube function**
$m(x) = x^3$
Domain: R
Range: R

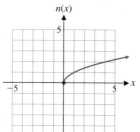

(D) **Square root function**
$n(x) = \sqrt{x}$
Domain: $[0, \infty)$
Range: $[0, \infty)$

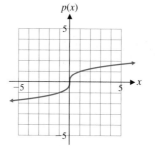

(E) **Cube root function**
$p(x) = \sqrt[3]{x}$
Domain: R
Range: R

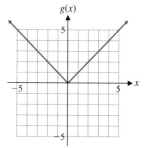

(F) **Absolute value function**
$g(x) = |x|$
Domain: R
Range: $[0, \infty)$

Figure 1 Some basic functions and their graphs*

CONCEPTUAL INSIGHT

Absolute Value In beginning algebra, absolute value is often interpreted as distance from the origin on a real number line (see Appendix A, Section A-1).

distance = 6 = −(−6)   distance = 5

If $x < 0$, then $-x$ is the *positive* distance from the origin to x, and if $x > 0$, then x is the positive distance from the origin to x. Thus,

$$|x| = \begin{cases} -x & \text{if } x < 0 \\ x & \text{if } x \geq 0 \end{cases}$$

Vertical and Horizontal Shifts

If a new function is formed by performing an operation on a given function, then the graph of the new function is called a **transformation** of the graph of the original function. For example, graphs of $y = f(x) + k$ and $y = f(x + h)$ are transformations of the graph of $y = f(x)$.

---

*Note: Letters used to designate these functions may vary from context to context; R is the set of all real numbers.

EXPLORE & DISCUSS 1

Let $f(x) = x^2$.

(A) Graph $y = f(x) + k$ for $k = -4, 0$, and 2 simultaneously in the same coordinate system. Describe the relationship between the graph of $y = f(x)$ and the graph of $y = f(x) + k$ for any real number k.

(B) Graph $y = f(x + h)$ for $h = -4, 0$, and 2 simultaneously in the same coordinate system. Describe the relationship between the graph of $y = f(x)$ and the graph of $y = f(x + h)$ for any real number h.

EXAMPLE 2   **Vertical and Horizontal Shifts**

(A) How are the graphs of $y = |x| + 4$ and $y = |x| - 5$ related to the graph of $y = |x|$? Confirm your answer by graphing all three functions simultaneously in the same coordinate system.

(B) How are the graphs of $y = |x + 4|$ and $y = |x - 5|$ related to the graph of $y = |x|$? Confirm your answer by graphing all three functions simultaneously in the same coordinate system.

SOLUTION

(A) The graph of $y = |x| + 4$ is the same as the graph of $y = |x|$ shifted upward 4 units, and the graph of $y = |x| - 5$ is the same as the graph of $y = |x|$ shifted downward 5 units. Figure 2 confirms these conclusions. [It appears that the graph of $y = f(x) + k$ is the graph of $y = f(x)$ shifted up if k is positive and down if k is negative.]

(B) The graph of $y = |x + 4|$ is the same as the graph of $y = |x|$ shifted to the left 4 units, and the graph of $y = |x - 5|$ is the same as the graph of $y = |x|$ shifted to the right 5 units. Figure 3 confirms these conclusions. [It appears that the graph of $y = f(x + h)$ is the graph of $y = f(x)$ shifted right if h is negative and left if h is positive—the opposite of what you might expect.]

Figure 2 Vertical shifts

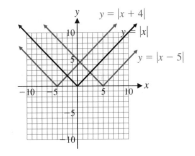

Figure 3 Horizontal shifts

Matched Problem 2

(A) How are the graphs of $y = \sqrt{x} + 5$ and $y = \sqrt{x} - 4$ related to the graph of $y = \sqrt{x}$? Confirm your answer by graphing all three functions simultaneously in the same coordinate system.

(B) How are the graphs of $y = \sqrt{x + 5}$ and $y = \sqrt{x - 4}$ related to the graph of $y = \sqrt{x}$? Confirm your answer by graphing all three functions simultaneously in the same coordinate system.

Comparing the graphs of $y = f(x) + k$ with the graph of $y = f(x)$, we see that the graph of $y = f(x) + k$ can be obtained from the graph of $y = f(x)$ by **vertically translating** (shifting) the graph of the latter upward k units if k is positive and downward $|k|$ units if k is negative. Comparing the graphs of $y = f(x + h)$ with the graph of $y = f(x)$, we see that the graph of $y = f(x + h)$ can be obtained from the graph of $y = f(x)$ by **horizontally translating** (shifting) the graph of the latter h units to the left if h is positive and $|h|$ units to the right if h is negative.

EXAMPLE 3 **Vertical and Horizontal Translations (Shifts)** The graphs in Figure 4 are either horizontal or vertical shifts of the graph of $f(x) = x^2$. Write appropriate equations for functions H, G, M, and N in terms of f.

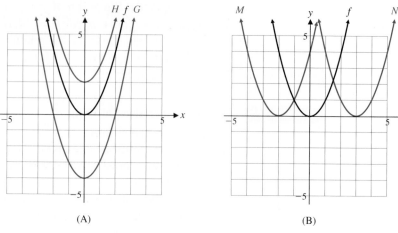

(A)   (B)

Figure 4 Vertical and horizontal shifts

SOLUTION Functions H and G are vertical shifts given by

$$H(x) = x^2 + 2 \qquad G(x) = x^2 - 4$$

Functions M and N are horizontal shifts given by

$$M(x) = (x + 2)^2 \qquad N(x) = (x - 3)^2$$

Matched Problem 3 The graphs in Figure 5 are either horizontal or vertical shifts of the graph of $f(x) = \sqrt[3]{x}$. Write appropriate equations for functions $H, G, M,$ and N in terms of f.

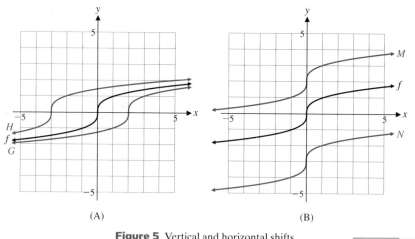

(A)   (B)

Figure 5 Vertical and horizontal shifts

Reflections, Stretches, and Shrinks

We now investigate how the graph of $y = Af(x)$ is related to the graph of $y = f(x)$ for different real numbers A.

EXPLORE & DISCUSS 2

(A) Graph $y = Ax^2$ for $A = 1, 4$, and $\frac{1}{4}$ simultaneously in the same coordinate system.

(B) Graph $y = Ax^2$ for $A = -1, -4$, and $-\frac{1}{4}$ simultaneously in the same coordinate system.

(C) Describe the relationship between the graph of $h(x) = x^2$ and the graph of $G(x) = Ax^2$ for any real number A.

Comparing $y = Af(x)$ to $y = f(x)$, we see that the graph of $y = Af(x)$ can be obtained from the graph of $y = f(x)$ by multiplying each ordinate value of the latter by A. The result is a **vertical stretch** of the graph of $y = f(x)$ if $A > 1$, a **vertical shrink** of the graph of $y = f(x)$ if $0 < A < 1$, and a **reflection in the x axis** if $A = -1$. If A is a negative number other than -1, then the result is a combination of a reflection in the x axis and either a vertical stretch or a vertical shrink.

EXAMPLE 4 **Reflections, Stretches, and Shrinks**

(A) How are the graphs of $y = 2|x|$ and $y = 0.5|x|$ related to the graph of $y = |x|$? Confirm your answer by graphing all three functions simultaneously in the same coordinate system.

(B) How is the graph of $y = -2|x|$ related to the graph of $y = |x|$? Confirm your answer by graphing both functions simultaneously in the same coordinate system.

SOLUTION (A) The graph of $y = 2|x|$ is a vertical stretch of the graph of $y = |x|$ by a factor of 2, and the graph of $y = 0.5|x|$ is a vertical shrink of the graph of $y = |x|$ by a factor of 0.5. Figure 6 confirms this conclusion.

(B) The graph of $y = -2|x|$ is a reflection in the x axis and a vertical stretch of the graph of $y = |x|$. Figure 7 confirms this conclusion.

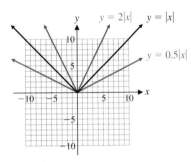

Figure 6 Vertical stretch and shrink

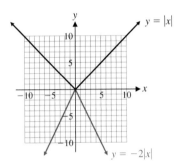

Figure 7 Reflection and vertical stretch

Matched Problem 4 (A) How are the graphs of $y = 2x$ and $y = 0.5x$ related to the graph of $y = x$? Confirm your answer by graphing all three functions simultaneously in the same coordinate system.

(B) How is the graph of $y = -0.5x$ related to the graph of $y = x$? Confirm your answer by graphing both functions in the same coordinate system.

The various transformations considered above are summarized in the following box for easy reference:

SUMMARY Graph Transformations

Vertical Translation:

$$y = f(x) + k \quad \begin{cases} k > 0 & \text{Shift graph of } y = f(x) \text{ up } k \text{ units.} \\ k < 0 & \text{Shift graph of } y = f(x) \text{ down } |k| \text{ units.} \end{cases}$$

Horizontal Translation:

$$y = f(x + h) \quad \begin{cases} h > 0 & \text{Shift graph of } y = f(x) \text{ left } h \text{ units.} \\ h < 0 & \text{Shift graph of } y = f(x) \text{ right } |h| \text{ units.} \end{cases}$$

Reflection:

$$y = -f(x) \quad \text{Reflect the graph of } y = f(x) \text{ in the } x \text{ axis.}$$

Vertical Stretch and Shrink:

$$y = Af(x) \begin{cases} A > 1 & \text{Stretch graph of } y = f(x) \text{ vertically} \\ & \text{by multiplying each ordinate value by } A. \\ 0 < A < 1 & \text{Shrink graph of } y = f(x) \text{ vertically} \\ & \text{by multiplying each ordinate value by } A. \end{cases}$$

EXPLORE & DISCUSS 3   Use a graphing calculator to explore the graph of $y = A(x + h)^2 + k$ for various values of the constants $A, h,$ and k. Discuss how the graph of $y = A(x + h)^2 + k$ is related to the graph of $y = x^2$.

EXAMPLE 5   **Combining Graph Transformations** Discuss the relationship between the graphs of $y = -|x - 3| + 1$ and $y = |x|$. Confirm your answer by graphing both functions simultaneously in the same coordinate system.

SOLUTION   The graph of $y = -|x - 3| + 1$ is a reflection in the x axis, a horizontal translation of 3 units to the right, and a vertical translation of 1 unit upward of the graph of $y = |x|$. Figure 8 confirms this description.

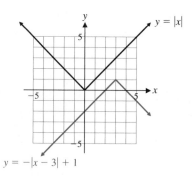

Figure 8 Combined transformations

Matched Problem 5   The graph of $y = G(x)$ in Figure 9 involves a reflection and a translation of the graph of $y = x^3$. Describe how the graph of function G is related to the graph of $y = x^3$ and find an equation of the function G.

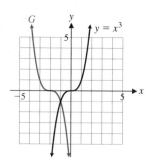

Figure 9 Combined transformations

Piecewise-Defined Functions

Earlier we noted that the absolute value of a real number x can be defined as

$$|x| = \begin{cases} -x & \text{if } x < 0 \\ x & \text{if } x \geq 0 \end{cases}$$

Notice that this function is defined by different rules for different parts of its domain. Functions whose definitions involve more than one rule are called **piecewise-defined functions**. Graphing one of these functions involves graphing each rule over the appropriate portion of the domain (Fig. 10). In Figure 10C, notice that an open dot is used to show that the point $(0, -2)$ is not part of the graph and a solid dot is used to show that $(0, 2)$ is part of the graph.

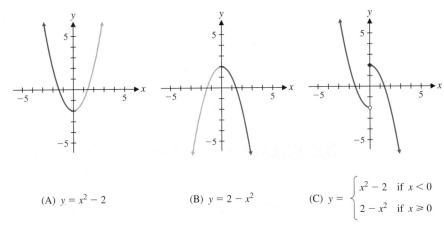

(A) $y = x^2 - 2$

(B) $y = 2 - x^2$

(C) $y = \begin{cases} x^2 - 2 & \text{if } x < 0 \\ 2 - x^2 & \text{if } x \geqslant 0 \end{cases}$

Figure 10 Graphing a piecewise-defined function

As the next example illustrates, piecewise-defined functions occur naturally in many applications.

EXAMPLE 6 **Natural Gas Rates** Easton Utilities uses the rates shown in Table 1 to compute the monthly cost of natural gas for each customer. Write a piecewise definition for the cost of consuming x CCF (cubic hundred feet) of natural gas and graph the function.

Table 1 Charges per Month

$0.7866 per CCF for the first 5 CCF
$0.4601 per CCF for the next 35 CCF
$0.2508 per CCF for all over 40 CCF

SOLUTION If $C(x)$ is the cost, in dollars, of using x CCF of natural gas in one month, then the first line of Table 1 implies that

$$C(x) = 0.7866x \quad \text{if } 0 \leq x \leq 5$$

Note that $C(5) = 3.933$ is the cost of 5 CCF. If $5 < x \leq 40$, then $x - 5$ represents the amount of gas that cost $0.4601 per CCF, $0.4601(x - 5)$ represents the cost of this gas, and the total cost is

$$C(x) = 3.933 + 0.4601(x - 5)$$

If $x > 40$, then

$$C(x) = 20.0365 + 0.2508(x - 40)$$

where $20.0365 = C(40)$, the cost of the first 40 CCF. Combining all these equations, we have the following piecewise definition for $C(x)$:

$$C(x) = \begin{cases} 0.7866x & \text{if } 0 \leq x \leq 5 \\ 3.933 + 0.46501(x - 5) & \text{if } 5 < x \leq 40 \\ 20.0365 + 0.2508(x - 40) & \text{if } x > 40 \end{cases}$$

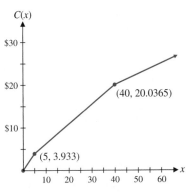

$C(x)$

Figure 11 Cost of purchasing x CCF of natural gas

To graph C, first note that each rule in the definition of C represents a transformation of the identity function $f(x) = x$. Graphing each transformation over the indicated interval produces the graph of C shown in Figure 11.

Matched Problem 6   Trussville Utilities uses the rates shown in Table 2 to compute the monthly cost of natural gas for residential customers. Write a piecewise definition for the cost of consuming x CCF of natural gas and graph the function.

Table 2   Charges per Month

$0.7675 per CCF for the first 50 CCF
$0.6400 per CCF for the next 150 CCF
$0.6130 per CCF for all over 200 CCF

Exercise 2-2

A

In Problems 1–8, give the domain and range of each function.

1. $f(x) = x^2 + 3$

2. $g(x) = x^2 - 4$

3. $h(x) = -5|x|$

4. $k(x) = -2|x|$

5. $m(x) = \sqrt{x} - 10$

6. $n(x) = -6\sqrt{x}$

7. $r(x) = -\sqrt[3]{8x}$

8. $s(x) = 1 + \sqrt[3]{x}$

In Problems 9–20, graph each of the functions using the graphs of functions f and g below.

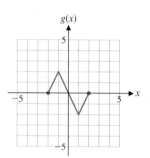

9. $y = f(x) + 2$

10. $y = g(x) - 1$

11. $y = f(x + 2)$

12. $y = g(x - 1)$

13. $y = g(x - 3)$

14. $y = f(x + 3)$

15. $y = g(x) - 3$

16. $y = f(x) + 3$

17. $y = -f(x)$

18. $y = -g(x)$

19. $y = 0.5g(x)$

20. $y = 2f(x)$

B

In Problems 21–28, indicate verbally how the graph of each function is related to the graph of one of the six basic functions in Figure 1 on page 60. Sketch a graph of each function.

21. $g(x) = -|x + 3|$

22. $h(x) = -|x - 5|$

23. $f(x) = (x - 4)^2 - 3$

24. $m(x) = (x + 3)^2 + 4$

25. $f(x) = 7 - \sqrt{x}$

26. $g(x) = -6 + \sqrt[3]{x}$

27. $h(x) = -3|x|$

28. $m(x) = -0.4x^2$

Each graph in Problems 29–36 is the result of applying a sequence of transformations to the graph of one of the six basic functions in Figure 1 on page 60. Identify the basic function and describe the transformation verbally. Write an equation for the given graph.

29.

30.

31.

32.

33.

34.

35.

36.
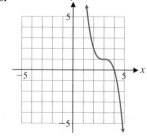

In Problems 37–42, the graph of the function g is formed by applying the indicated sequence of transformations to the given function f. Find an equation for the function g and graph g using $-5 \leq x \leq 5$ *and* $-5 \leq y \leq 5$.

37. The graph of $f(x) = \sqrt{x}$ is shifted 2 units to the right and 3 units down.

38. The graph of $f(x) = \sqrt[3]{x}$ is shifted 3 units to the left and 2 units up.

39. The graph of $f(x) = |x|$ is reflected in the x axis and shifted to the left 3 units.

40. The graph of $f(x) = |x|$ is reflected in the x axis and shifted to the right 1 unit.

41. The graph of $f(x) = x^3$ is reflected in the x axis and shifted 2 units to the right and down 1 unit.

42. The graph of $f(x) = x^2$ is reflected in the x axis and shifted to the left 2 units and up 4 units.

Graph each function in Problems 43–48.

43. $f(x) = \begin{cases} 2 - 2x & \text{if } x < 2 \\ x - 2 & \text{if } x \geq 2 \end{cases}$

44. $g(x) = \begin{cases} x + 1 & \text{if } x < -1 \\ 2 + 2x & \text{if } x \geq -1 \end{cases}$

45. $h(x) = \begin{cases} 5 + 0.5x & \text{if } 0 \leq x \leq 10 \\ -10 + 2x & \text{if } x > 10 \end{cases}$

46. $h(x) = \begin{cases} 10 + 2x & \text{if } 0 \leq x \leq 20 \\ 40 + 0.5x & \text{if } x > 20 \end{cases}$

47. $h(x) = \begin{cases} 2x & \text{if } 0 \leq x \leq 20 \\ x + 20 & \text{if } 20 < x \leq 40 \\ 0.5x + 40 & \text{if } x > 40 \end{cases}$

48. $h(x) = \begin{cases} 4x + 20 & \text{if } 0 \leq x \leq 20 \\ 2x + 60 & \text{if } 20 < x \leq 100 \\ -x + 360 & \text{if } x > 100 \end{cases}$

C

✎ *Each of the graphs in Problems 49–54 involves a reflection in the x axis and/or a vertical stretch or shrink of one of the basic functions in Figure 1 on page 60. Identify the basic function, and describe the transformation verbally. Write an equation for the given graph.*

49.

50.

51.

52.

53.

54.

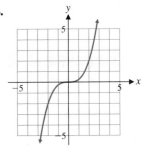

✎ *Changing the order in a sequence of transformations may change the final result. Investigate each pair of transformations in Problems 55–60 to determine if reversing their order can produce a different result. Support your conclusions with specific examples and/or mathematical arguments.*

55. Vertical shift; horizontal shift

56. Vertical shift; reflection in y axis

57. Vertical shift; reflection in x axis

58. Vertical shift; vertical stretch

59. Horizontal shift; reflection in y axis

60. Horizontal shift; vertical shrink

Applications

61. Price–demand. A retail chain sells DVD players. The retail price $p(x)$ (in dollars) and the weekly demand x for a particular model are related by

$$p(x) = 115 - 4\sqrt{x} \qquad 9 \leq x \leq 289$$

(A) Describe how the graph of function p can be obtained from the graph of one of the basic functions in Figure 1 on page 60.

(B) Sketch a graph of function p using part (A) as an aid.

62. Price–supply. The manufacturers of the DVD players in Problem 61 are willing to supply x players at a price of $p(x)$ as given by the equation

$$p(x) = 4\sqrt{x} \qquad 9 \leq x \leq 289$$

(A) Describe how the graph of function p can be obtained from the graph of one of the basic functions in Figure 1 on page 60.

(B) Sketch a graph of function p using part (A) as an aid.

63. Hospital costs. Using statistical methods, the financial department of a hospital arrived at the cost equation

$$C(x) = 0.00048(x - 500)^3 + 60{,}000 \qquad 100 \le x \le 1{,}000$$

where $C(x)$ is the cost in dollars for handling x cases per month.

(A) Describe how the graph of function C can be obtained from the graph of one of the basic functions in Figure 1 on page 60.

(B) Sketch a graph of function C using part (A) and a graphing calculator as aids.

64. Price–demand. A company manufactures and sells in-line skates. Its financial department has established the price–demand function

$$p(x) = 190 - 0.013(x - 10)^2 \quad 10 \le x \le 100$$

where $p(x)$ is the price at which x thousand pairs of in-line skates can be sold.

(A) Describe how the graph of function p can be obtained from the graph of one of the basic functions in Figure 1 on page 60.

(B) Sketch a graph of function p using part (A) and a graphing calculator as aids.

65. Electricity rates. Table 3 shows the electricity rates charged by Monroe Utilities in the summer months. The base is a fixed monthly charge, independent of the kWh (kilowatt-hours) used during the month.

(A) Write a piecewise definition of the monthly charge $S(x)$ for a customer who uses x kWh in a summer month.

(B) Graph $S(x)$.

Table 3 Summer (July–October)
Base charge, $8.50
First 700 kWh or less at 0.0650/kWh
Over 700 kWh at 0.0900/kWh

66. Electricity rates. Table 4 shows the electricity rates charged by Monroe Utilities in the winter months.

(A) Write a piecewise definition of the monthly charge $W(x)$ for a customer who uses x kWh in a winter month.

Table 4 Winter (November–June)
Base charge, $8.50
First 700 kWh or less at 0.0650/kWh
Over 700 kWh at 0.0530/kWh

(B) Graph $W(x)$.

67. State income tax. Table 5 shows a recent state income tax schedule for married couples filing a joint return in Kansas.

(A) Write a piecewise definition for the tax due $T(x)$ on an income of x dollars.

(B) Graph $T(x)$.

(C) Find the tax due on a taxable income of $40,000. Of $70,000.

Table 5   Kansas State Income Tax

SCHEDULE I—MARRIED FILING JOINT

If taxable income is

Over	But Not Over	Tax Due Is
$0	$30,000	3.50% of taxable income
$30,000	$60,000	$1,050 plus 6.25% of excess over $30,000
$60,000		$2,925 plus 6.45% of excess over $60,000

68. State income tax. Table 6 shows a recent state income tax schedule for individuals filing a return in Kansas.

Table 6   Kansas State Income Tax

SCHEDULE II—SINGLE, HEAD OF HOUSEHOLD, OR MARRIED FILING SEPARATE

If taxable income is

Over	But Not Over	Tax Due Is
$0	$15,000	3.50% of taxable income
$15,000	$30,000	$525 plus 6.25% of excess over $15,000
$30,000		$1,462.50 plus 6.45% of excess over $30,000

(A) Write a piecewise definition for the tax due $T(x)$ on an income of x dollars.

(B) Graph $T(x)$.

(C) Find the tax due on a taxable income of $20,000. Of $35,000.

(D) Would it be better for a married couple in Kansas with two equal incomes to file jointly or separately? Discuss.

69. Human weight. A good approximation of the normal weight of a person 60 inches or taller but not taller than 80 inches is given by $w(x) = 5.5x - 220$, where x is height in inches and $w(x)$ is weight in pounds.

(A) Describe how the graph of function w can be obtained from the graph of one of the basic functions in Figure 1, page 60.

(B) Sketch a graph of function w using part (A) as an aid.

70. Herpetology. The average weight of a particular species of snake is given by $w(x) = 463x^3$, $0.2 \le x \le 0.8$, where x is length in meters and $w(x)$ is weight in grams.

✎ (A) Describe how the graph of function w can be obtained from the graph of one of the basic functions in Figure 1, page 60.

(B) Sketch a graph of function w using part (A) as an aid.

71. Safety research. Under ideal conditions, if a person driving a vehicle slams on the brakes and skids to a stop, the speed of the vehicle $v(x)$ (in miles per hour) is given approximately by $v(x) = C\sqrt{x}$, where x is the length of skid marks (in feet) and C is a constant that depends on the road conditions and the weight of the vehicle. For a particular vehicle, $v(x) = 7.08\sqrt{x}$ and $4 \le x \le 144$.

✎ (A) Describe how the graph of function v can be obtained from the graph of one of the basic functions in Figure 1, page 60.

(B) Sketch a graph of function v using part (A) as an aid.

72. Learning. A production analyst has found that on average it takes a new person $T(x)$ minutes to perform a particular assembly operation after x performances of the operation, where $T(x) = 10 - \sqrt[3]{x}$, $0 \le x \le 125$.

✎ (A) Describe how the graph of function T can be obtained from the graph of one of the basic functions in Figure 1, page 60.

(B) Sketch a graph of function T using part (A) as an aid.

Answers to Matched Problems

1. (A) $f(729) = 729$, $h(729) = 531{,}441$,
$m(729) = 387{,}420{,}489$, $n(729) = 27$, $p(729) = 9$,
$g(729) = 729$

(B) $f(-5.25) = -5.25$, $h(-5.25) = 27.5625$,
$m(-5.25) = -144.7031$, $n(-5.25)$ is not a real number,
$p(-5.25) = -1.7380$, $g(-5.25) = 5.25$

2. (A) The graph of $y = \sqrt{x} + 5$ is the same as the graph of $y = \sqrt{x}$ shifted upward 5 units, and the graph of $y = \sqrt{x} - 4$ is the same as the graph of $y = \sqrt{x}$ shifted downward 4 units. The figure confirms these conclusions.

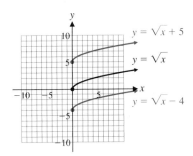

(B) The graph of $y = \sqrt{x + 5}$ is the same as the graph of $y = \sqrt{x}$ shifted to the left 5 units, and the graph of $y = \sqrt{x - 4}$ is the same as the graph of $y = \sqrt{x}$ shifted to the right 4 units. The figure confirms these conclusions.

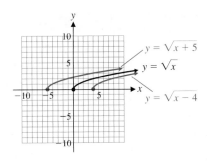

3. $H(x) = \sqrt[3]{x + 3}$, $G(x) = \sqrt[3]{x - 2}$, $M(x) = \sqrt[3]{x} + 2$, $N(x) = \sqrt[3]{x} - 3$

4. (A) The graph of $y = 2x$ is a vertical stretch of the graph of $y = x$, and the graph of $y = 0.5x$ is a vertical shrink of the graph of $y = x$. The figure confirms these conclusions.

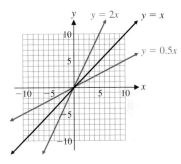

(B) The graph of $y = -0.5x$ is a vertical shrink and a reflection in the x axis of the graph of $y = x$. The figure confirms this conclusion.

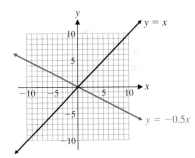

5. The graph of function G is a reflection in the x axis and a horizontal translation of 2 units to the left of the graph of $y = x^3$. An equation for G is $G(x) = -(x + 2)^3$.

6. $C(x) = \begin{cases} 0.7675x & \text{if } 0 \le x \le 50 \\ 38.375 + 0.64(x - 50) & \text{if } 50 < x \le 200 \\ 134.375 + 0.613(x - 200) & \text{if } 200 < x \end{cases}$

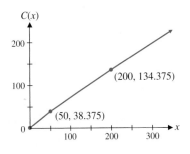

2-3 Quadratic Functions

- Quadratic Functions, Equations, and Inequalities
- Properties of Quadratic Functions and Their Graphs
- Applications

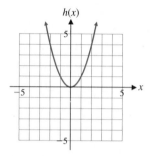

Figure 1 Square function $h(x) = x^2$

If the degree of a linear function is increased by one, we obtain a *second-degree function,* usually called a *quadratic function,* another basic function that we will need in our library of elementary functions. We will investigate relationships between quadratic functions and the solutions to quadratic equations and inequalities. Other important properties of quadratic functions will also be investigated, including maxima and minima. We will then be in a position to solve important practical problems such as finding production levels that will generate maximum revenue or maximum profit.

Quadratic Functions, Equations, and Inequalities

The graph of the square function $h(x) = x^2$ is shown in Figure 1. Notice that the graph is symmetric with respect to the y axis and that $(0, 0)$ is the lowest point on the graph. Let's explore the effect of applying a sequence of basic transformations to the graph of h.

EXPLORE & DISCUSS 1

Indicate how the graph of each function is related to the graph of the function $h(x) = x^2$. Find the highest or lowest point, whichever exists, on each graph.

(A) $f(x) = (x - 3)^2 - 7 = x^2 - 6x + 2$

(B) $g(x) = 0.5(x + 2)^2 + 3 = 0.5x^2 + 2x + 5$

(C) $m(x) = -(x - 4)^2 + 8 = -x^2 + 8x - 8$

(D) $n(x) = -3(x + 1)^2 - 1 = -3x^2 - 6x - 4$

Graphing the functions in Explore & Discuss 1 produces figures similar in shape to the graph of the square function in Figure 1. These figures are called *parabolas.* The functions that produce these parabolas are examples of the important class of *quadratic functions.*

DEFINITION Quadratic Functions

If $a, b,$ and c are real numbers with $a \neq 0$, then the function

$$f(x) = ax^2 + bx + c \quad \text{Standard form}$$

is a **quadratic function** and its graph is a **parabola**.

CONCEPTUAL INSIGHT

If x is any real number, then $ax^2 + bx + c$ is also a real number. According to the agreement on domain and range in Section 2-1, the domain of a quadratic function is R, the set of real numbers.

We will discuss methods for determining the range of a quadratic function later in this section. Typical graphs of quadratic functions are illustrated in Figure 2.

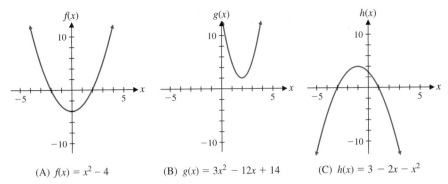

Figure 2 Graphs of quadratic functions

CONCEPTUAL INSIGHT

An x intercept of a function is also called a **zero** of the function. The x intercepts of a linear function can be found by solving the linear equation $y = mx + b = 0$ for $x, m \neq 0$ (see Section 1-2). Similarly, the x intercepts of a quadratic function can be found by solving the quadratic equation $y = ax^2 + bx + c = 0$ for $x, a \neq 0$. Several methods for solving quadratic equations are discussed in Appendix A, Section A-7. The most popular of these is the **quadratic formula**.

If $ax^2 + bx + c = 0, a \neq 0$, then

$$x = \frac{-b \pm \sqrt{b^2 - 4ac}}{2a}, \text{ provided } b^2 - 4ac \geq 0$$

EXAMPLE 1   **Intercepts, Equations, and Inequalities**

(A) Sketch a graph of $f(x) = -x^2 + 5x + 3$ in a rectangular coordinate system.

(B) Find x and y intercepts algebraically to four decimal places.

(C) Graph $f(x) = -x^2 + 5x + 3$ in a standard viewing window.

(D) Find the x and y intercepts to four decimal places using TRACE and ZERO on your graphing calculator.

(E) Solve the quadratic inequality $-x^2 + 5x + 3 \geq 0$ graphically to four decimal places using the results of parts (A) and (B) or (C) and (D).

(F) Solve the equation $-x^2 + 5x + 3 = 4$ graphically to four decimal places using INTERSECT on your graphing calculator.

SOLUTION   (A) Hand-sketching a graph of f:

x	y
-1	-3
0	3
1	7
2	9
3	9
4	7
5	3
6	-3

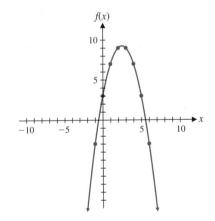

(B) Finding intercepts algebraically:

$$y \text{ intercept:} \quad f(0) = -(0)^2 + 5(0) + 3 = 3$$

x intercepts: $f(x) = 0$

$$-x^2 + 5x + 3 = 0 \qquad \textit{Quadratic equation}$$

$$x = \frac{-b \pm \sqrt{b^2 - 4ac}}{2a} \qquad \textit{Quadratic formula (see Appendix A-7)}$$

$$x = \frac{-(5) \pm \sqrt{5^2 - 4(-1)(3)}}{2(-1)}$$

$$= \frac{-5 \pm \sqrt{37}}{-2} = -0.5414 \quad \text{or} \quad 5.5414$$

(C) Graphing in a graphing calculator:

(D) Finding intercepts graphically using a graphing calculator:

x intercept: -0.5414 x intercept: 5.5414 y intercept: 3

(E) Solving $-x^2 + 5x + 3 \geq 0$ graphically: The quadratic inequality

$$-x^2 + 5x + 3 \geq 0$$

holds for those values of x for which the graph of $f(x) = -x^2 + 5x + 3$ in the figures in parts (A) and (C) is at or above the x axis. This happens for x between the two x intercepts [found in part (B) or (D)], including the two x intercepts. The solution set for the quadratic inequality is $-0.5414 \leq x \leq 5.5414$ or $[-0.5414, 5.5414]$.

(F) Solving the equation $-x^2 + 5x + 3 = 4$ using a graphing calculator:

$-x^2 + 5x + 3 = 4$ at $x = 0.2087$ $-x^2 + 5x + 3 = 4$ at $x = 4.7913$

Matched Problem 1

(A) Sketch a graph of $g(x) = 2x^2 - 5x - 5$ in a rectangular coordinate system.

(B) Find x and y intercepts algebraically to four decimal places.

(C) Graph $g(x) = 2x^2 - 5x - 5$ in a standard viewing window.

(D) Find the x and y intercepts to four decimal places using TRACE and the ZERO command on your graphing calculator.

(E) Solve $2x^2 - 5x - 5 \geq 0$ graphically to four decimal places using the results of parts (A) and (B) or (C) and (D).

(F) Solve the equation $2x^2 - 5x - 5 = -3$ graphically to four decimal places using INTERSECT on your graphing calculator.

EXPLORE & DISCUSS 2

How many x intercepts can the graph of a quadratic function have? How many y intercepts? Explain your reasoning.

Properties of Quadratic Functions and Their Graphs

Many useful properties of the quadratic function can be uncovered by transforming

$$f(x) = ax^2 + bx + c \qquad a \neq 0$$

into the **vertex form**

$$f(x) = a(x - h)^2 + k$$

The process of *completing the square* (see Appendix A-7) is central to the transformation. We illustrate the process through a specific example and then generalize the results.

Consider the quadratic function given by

$$f(x) = -2x^2 + 16x - 24 \tag{1}$$

We use completing the square to transform this function into vertex form:

$$f(x) = -2x^2 + 16x - 24 \qquad \text{Factor the coefficient of } x^2$$
$$= -2(x^2 - 8x) - 24 \qquad \text{out of the first two terms.}$$
$$= -2(x^2 - 8x + ?) - 24$$

$$= -2(x^2 - 8x + \mathbf{16}) - 24 + \mathbf{32}$$

Add 16 to complete the square inside the parentheses. Because of the -2 outside the parentheses, we have actually added -32, so we must add 32 to the outside.

$$= -2(x - 4)^2 + 8$$

The transformation is complete and can be checked by multiplying out.

Therefore,

$$f(x) = -2(x - 4)^2 + 8 \tag{2}$$

If $x = 4$, then $-2(x - 4)^2 = 0$ and $f(4) = 8$. For any other value of x, the negative number $-2(x - 4)^2$ is added to 8, making it smaller. Therefore,

$$f(4) = 8$$

is the *maximum value* of $f(x)$ for all x. Furthermore, if we choose any two x values that are the same distance from 4, we will obtain the same function value. For example, $x = 3$ and $x = 5$ are each one unit from $x = 4$ and their function values are

$$f(3) = -2(3 - 4)^2 + 8 = 6$$
$$f(5) = -2(5 - 4)^2 + 8 = 6$$

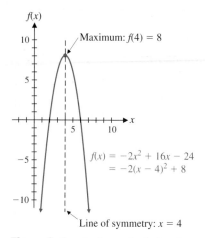

Figure 3 Graph of a quadratic function

Therefore, the vertical line $x = 4$ is a line of symmetry. That is, if the graph of equation (1) is drawn on a piece of paper and the paper is folded along the line $x = 4$, then the two sides of the parabola will match exactly. All these results are illustrated by graphing equations (1) and (2) and the line $x = 4$ simultaneously in the same coordinate system (Fig. 3).

From the preceding discussion, we see that as x moves from left to right, $f(x)$ is increasing on $(-\infty, 4]$, and decreasing on $[4, \infty)$, and that $f(x)$ can assume no value greater than 8. Thus,

$$\text{Range of } f: \quad y \le 8 \quad \text{or} \quad (-\infty, 8]$$

In general, the graph of a quadratic function is a parabola with line of symmetry parallel to the vertical axis. The lowest or highest point on the parabola, whichever exists, is called the **vertex**. The maximum or minimum value of a quadratic function always occurs at the vertex of the parabola. The line of symmetry through the vertex is called the **axis** of the parabola. In the example above, $x = 4$ is the axis of the parabola and $(4, 8)$ is its vertex.

CONCEPTUAL INSIGHT

Applying the graph transformation properties discussed in Section 2-2 to the transformed equation,

$$f(x) = -2x^2 + 16x - 24$$
$$= -2(x - 4)^2 + 8$$

we see that the graph of $f(x) = -2x^2 + 16x - 24$ is the graph of $g(x) = x^2$ vertically stretched by a factor of 2, reflected in the x axis, and shifted to the right 4 units and up 8 units, as shown in Figure 4.

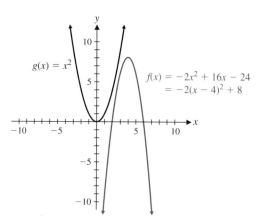

Figure 4 Graph of f is the graph of g transformed

Note the important results we have obtained from the vertex form of the quadratic function f:

- The vertex of the parabola
- The axis of the parabola
- The maximum value of $f(x)$
- The range of the function f
- The relationship between the graph of $g(x) = x^2$ and the graph of $f(x) = -2x^2 + 16x - 24$

The preceding discussion is generalized to all quadratic functions in the following summary:

SUMMARY Properties of a Quadratic Function and Its Graph

Given a quadratic function and the vertex form obtained by completing the square

$$f(x) = ax^2 + bx + c \qquad a \neq 0 \qquad \text{Standard form}$$
$$= a(x - h)^2 + k \qquad\qquad \text{Vertex form}$$

we summarize general properties as follows:

1. The graph of f is a parabola:

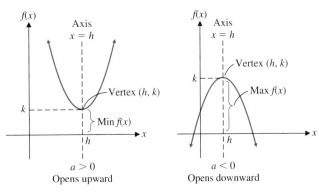

2. Vertex: (h, k) (parabola increases on one side of the vertex and decreases on the other)

3. Axis (of symmetry): $x = h$ (parallel to y axis)

4. $f(h) = k$ is the minimum if $a > 0$ and the maximum if $a < 0$

5. Domain: All real numbers.   Range: $(-\infty, k]$ if $a < 0$ or $[k, \infty)$ if $a > 0$

6. The graph of f is the graph of $g(x) = ax^2$ translated horizontally h units and vertically k units.

EXAMPLE 2   **Analyzing a Quadratic Function**   Given the quadratic function

$$f(x) = 0.5x^2 - 6x + 21$$

(A) Find the vertex form for f.

(B) Find the vertex and the maximum or minimum. State the range of f.

(C) Describe how the graph of function f can be obtained from the graph of $g(x) = x^2$ using transformations.

(D) Sketch a graph of function f in a rectangular coordinate system.

(E) Graph function f using a suitable viewing window.

(F) Find the vertex and the maximum or minimum using the appropriate graphing calculator command.

SOLUTION   (A) Complete the square to find the vertex form:

$$f(x) = 0.5x^2 - 6x + 21$$
$$= 0.5(x^2 - 12x + ?) + 21$$
$$= 0.5(x^2 - 12x + 36) + 21 - 18$$
$$= 0.5(x - 6)^2 + 3$$

(B) From the vertex form, we see that $h = 6$ and $k = 3$. Thus, vertex: $(6, 3)$; minimum: $f(6) = 3$; range: $y \geq 3$ or $[3, \infty)$.

(C) The graph of $f(x) = 0.5(x - 6)^2 + 3$ is the same as the graph of $g(x) = x^2$ vertically shrunk by a factor of 0.5, and shifted to the right 6 units and up 3 units.

45. $f(x) = -0.4x(x - 10)$
$g(x) = 0.3x + 5$
$0 \le x \le 10$

46. $f(x) = -0.7x(x - 7)$
$g(x) = 0.5x + 3.5$
$0 \le x \le 7$

47. $f(x) = -0.9x^2 + 7.2x$
$g(x) = 1.2x + 5.5$
$0 \le x \le 8$

48. $f(x) = -0.7x^2 + 6.3x$
$g(x) = 1.1x + 4.8$
$0 \le x \le 9$

49. How can you tell from the graph of a quadratic function whether it has exactly one real zero?

50. How can you tell from the graph of a quadratic function whether it has no real zeros?

51. How can you tell from the standard form $y = ax^2 + bx + c$ whether a quadratic function has two real zeros?

52. How can you tell from the standard form $y = ax^2 + bx + c$ whether a quadratic function has exactly one real zero?

53. How can you tell from the vertex form $y = a(x - h)^2 + k$ whether a quadratic function has no real zeros?

54. How can you tell from the vertex form $y = a(x - h)^2 + k$ whether a quadratic function has two real zeros?

In Problems 55 and 56, assume that a, b, c, h, and k are constants with a ≠ 0 such that

$$ax^2 + bx + c = a(x - h)^2 + k$$

for all real numbers x.

55. Show that $h = -\dfrac{b}{2a}$.

56. Show that $k = \dfrac{4ac - b^2}{4a}$.

Applications

57. Tire mileage. An automobile tire manufacturer collected the data in the table relating tire pressure x (in pounds per square inch) and mileage (in thousands of miles):

x	Mileage
28	45
30	52
32	55
34	51
36	47

A mathematical model for the data is given by

$$f(x) = -0.518x^2 + 33.3x - 481$$

(A) Complete the following table. Round values of $f(x)$ to one decimal place.

x	Mileage	f(x)
28	45	
30	52	
32	55	
34	51	
36	47	

(B) Sketch the graph of f and the mileage data in the same coordinate system.

(C) Use values of the modeling function rounded to two decimal places to estimate the mileage for a tire pressure of 31 lbs/sq in. and for 35 lbs/sq in.

(D) Write a brief description of the relationship between tire pressure and mileage.

58. Automobile production. The table shows the retail market share of passenger cars from Ford Motor Company as a percentage of the U.S. market.

Year	Market Share
1980	17.2%
1985	18.8%
1990	20.0%
1995	20.7%
2000	20.2%
2005	17.4%

A mathematical model for this data is given by

$$f(x) = -0.0206x^2 + 0.548x + 16.9$$

where $x = 0$ corresponds to 1980.

(A) Complete the following table. Round values of $f(x)$ to one decimal place.

x	Market Share	f(x)
0	17.2	
5	18.8	
10	20.0	
15	20.7	
20	20.2	
25	17.4	

(B) Sketch the graph of f and the market share data in the same coordinate system.

(C) Use values of the modeling function f to estimate Ford's market share in 2015 and in 2020.

(D) Write a brief verbal description of Ford's market share from 1980 to 2005.

59. Tire mileage. Using quadratic regression on a graphing calculator, show that the quadratic function that best fits the data on tire mileage in Problem 57 is

$$f(x) = -0.518x^2 + 33.3x - 481$$

60. Automobile production. Using quadratic regression on a graphing calculator, show that the quadratic function that best fits the data on market share in Problem 58 is

$$f(x) = -0.0206x^2 + 0.548x + 16.9$$

61. Revenue. The marketing research department for a company that manufactures and sells memory chips for microcomputers established the following price–demand and revenue functions:

$$p(x) = 75 - 3x \qquad \textit{Price–demand function}$$
$$R(x) = xp(x) = x(75 - 3x) \qquad \textit{Revenue function}$$

where $p(x)$ is the wholesale price in dollars at which x million chips can be sold, and $R(x)$ is in millions of dollars. Both functions have domain $1 \le x \le 20$.

(A) Sketch a graph of the revenue function in a rectangular coordinate system.

(B) Find the value of x that will produce the maximum revenue. What is the maximum revenue?

(C) What is the wholesale price per chip that produces the maximum revenue?

62. Revenue. The marketing research department for a company that manufactures and sells notebook computers established the following price–demand and revenue functions:

$$p(x) = 2{,}000 - 60x \qquad \textit{Price–demand function}$$
$$R(x) = xp(x) \qquad \textit{Revenue function}$$
$$\quad = x(2{,}000 - 60x)$$

where $p(x)$ is the wholesale price in dollars at which x thousand computers can be sold, and $R(x)$ is in thousands of dollars. Both functions have domain $1 \le x \le 25$.

(A) Sketch a graph of the revenue function in a rectangular coordinate system.

(B) Find the value of x that will produce the maximum revenue. What is the maximum revenue to the nearest thousand dollars?

(C) What is the wholesale price per computer (to the nearest dollar) that produces the maximum revenue?

63. Break-even analysis. Use the revenue function from Problem 61 in this exercise and the given cost function:

$$R(x) = x(75 - 3x) \qquad \textit{Revenue function}$$
$$C(x) = 125 + 16x \qquad \textit{Cost function}$$

where x is in millions of chips, and $R(x)$ and $C(x)$ are in millions of dollars. Both functions have domain $1 \le x \le 20$.

(A) Sketch a graph of both functions in the same rectangular coordinate system.

(B) Find the break-even points to the nearest thousand chips.

(C) For what values of x will a loss occur? A profit?

64. Break-even analysis. Use the revenue function from Problem 62, in this exercise and the given cost function:

$$R(x) = x(2{,}000 - 60x) \qquad \textit{Revenue function}$$
$$C(x) = 4{,}000 + 500x \qquad \textit{Cost function}$$

where x is thousands of computers, and $C(x)$ and $R(x)$ are in thousands of dollars. Both functions have domain $1 \le x \le 25$.

(A) Sketch a graph of both functions in the same rectangular coordinate system.

(B) Find the break-even points.

(C) For what values of x will a loss occur? A profit?

65. Profit–loss analysis. Use the revenue and cost functions from Problem 63 in this exercise:

$$R(x) = x(75 - 3x) \qquad \textit{Revenue function}$$
$$C(x) = 125 + 16x \qquad \textit{Cost function}$$

where x is in millions of chips, and $R(x)$ and $C(x)$ are in millions of dollars. Both functions have domain $1 \le x \le 20$.

(A) Form a profit function P, and graph R, C, and P in the same rectangular coordinate system.

(B) Discuss the relationship between the intersection points of the graphs of R and C and the x intercepts of P.

(C) Find the x intercepts of P and the break-even points to the nearest thousand chips.

(D) Refer to the graph drawn in part (A). Does the maximum profit appear to occur at the same value of x as the maximum revenue? Are the maximum profit and the maximum revenue equal? Explain.

(E) Verify your conclusion in part (D) by finding the value of x (to the nearest thousand chips) that produces the maximum profit. Find the maximum profit (to the nearest thousand dollars), and compare with Problem 61B.

66. Profit–loss analysis. Use the revenue and cost functions from Problem 64 in this exercise:

$$R(x) = x(2{,}000 - 60x) \qquad \textit{Revenue function}$$
$$C(x) = 4{,}000 + 500x \qquad \textit{Cost function}$$

where x is thousands of computers, and $R(x)$ and $C(x)$ are in thousands of dollars. Both functions have domain $1 \le x \le 25$.

(A) Form a profit function P, and graph R, C, and P in the same rectangular coordinate system.

(B) Discuss the relationship between the intersection points of the graphs of R and C and the x intercepts of P.

(C) Find the x intercepts of P and the break-even points.

(D) Refer to the graph drawn in part (A). Does the maximum profit appear to occur at the same value of x as the maximum revenue? Are the maximum profit and the maximum revenue equal? Explain.

(E) Verify your conclusion in part (D) by finding the value of x that produces the maximum profit. Find the maximum profit and compare with Problem 62B.

67. Medicine. The French physician Poiseuille was the first to discover that blood flows faster near the center of an artery than near the edge. Experimental evidence has shown that the rate of flow v (in centimeters per second) at a point x centimeters from the center of an artery (see the figure) is given by

$$v = f(x) = 1{,}000(0.04 - x^2) \qquad 0 \le x \le 0.2$$

Find the distance from the center that the rate of flow is 20 centimeters per second. Round answer to two decimal places.

Figure for 67 and 68

68. Medicine. Refer to Problem 67. Find the distance from the center that the rate of flow is 30 centimeters per second. Round answer to two decimal places.

69. Outboard motors. The table gives performance data for a boat powered by an Evinrude outboard motor. Find a quadratic regression model ($y = ax^2 + bx + c$) for boat speed y (in miles per hour) as a function of engine speed (in revolutions per minute). Estimate the boat speed at an engine speed of 3,100 revolutions per minute.

Table for 69 and 70

rpm	mph	mpg
1,500	4.5	8.2
2,000	5.7	6.9
2,500	7.8	4.8
3,000	9.6	4.1
3,500	13.4	3.7

70. Outboard motors. The table gives performance data for a boat powered by an Evinrude outboard motor. Find a quadratic regression model ($y = ax^2 + bx + c$) for fuel consumption y (in miles per gallon) as a function of engine speed (in revolutions per minute). Estimate the fuel consumption at an engine speed of 2,300 revolutions per minute.

Answers to Matched Problems

1. (A)

(B) x intercepts: $-0.7656, 3.2656$; y intercept: -5

(C)

(D) x intercepts: $-0.7656, 3.2656$; y intercept: -5

(E) $x \le -0.7656$ or $x \ge 3.2656$; or $(-\infty, -0.7656]$ or $[3.2656, \infty)$

(F) $x = -0.3508, 2.8508$

2. (A) $f(x) = -0.25(x + 4)^2 + 6$.

(B) Vertex: $(-4, 6)$; maximum: $f(-4) = 6$; range: $y \le 6$ or $(-\infty, 6]$

(C) The graph of $f(x) = -0.25(x + 4)^2 + 6$ is the same as the graph of $g(x) = x^2$ vertically shrunk by a factor of 0.25, reflected in the x axis, and shifted 4 units to the left and 6 units up.

(D)

(E)

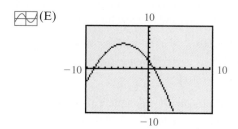

(F) Vertex: $(-4, 6)$; maximum: $f(-4) = 6$

3. (A) $P(x) = R(x) - C(x) = -5x^2 + 75.1x - 156$

(B) $P(x) = R(x) - C(x) = -5(x - 7.51)^2 + 126.0005$; the manufacture and sale of 7,510,000 million cameras will produce a maximum profit of $126,001,000.

(C) $p(7.510) = \$57$

(D)

(E)

The manufacture and sale of 7,510,000 million cameras will produce a maximum profit of $126,001,000. (Notice that maximum profit does not occur at the same value of x where maximum revenue occurs.)

4. (A)

$P(x)$

(B) $x = 2.490$ million cameras (2,490,000 cameras) and $x = 12.530$ million cameras. (12,530,000 cameras)

(C)

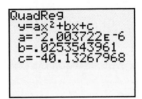(D) $x = 2.490$ million cameras (2,490,000 cameras) and $x = 12.530$ million cameras (12,530,000 cameras)

(E) Loss: $1 \leq x < 2.490$ or $12.530 < x \leq 15$; profit: $2.490 < x < 12.530$

5. 22.9 mph

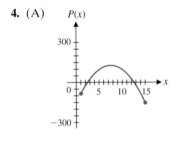

2-4 Polynomial and Rational Functions

- Polynomial Functions
- Regression Polynomials
- Rational Functions
- Applications

Linear and quadratic functions are special cases of the more general class of *polynomial functions*. Polynomial functions are a special case of an even larger class of functions, the *rational functions*. We will describe the basic features of the graphs of polynomial and rational functions. We will use these functions to solve real-world problems where linear or quadratic models are inadequate; for example, to determine the relationship between length and weight of a species of fish, or to model the training of new employees.

Polynomial Functions

A linear function has the form $f(x) = mx + b$ (where $m \neq 0$) and is a polynomial function of degree 1. A quadratic function has the form $f(x) = ax^2 + bx + c$ (where $a \neq 0$) and is a polynomial function of degree 2. Here is the general definition of a polynomial function.

DEFINITION Polynomial Function

A **polynomial function** is a function that can be written in the form

$$f(x) = a_n x^n + a_{n-1} x^{n-1} + \cdots + a_1 x + a_0$$

for n a nonnegative integer, called the **degree** of the polynomial. The coefficients $a_0, a_1, \ldots, a_n$ are real numbers with $a_n \neq 0$. The **domain** of a polynomial function is the set of all real numbers.

Figure 1 shows graphs of representative polynomial functions of degrees 1 through 6. The figure suggests some general properties of graphs of polynomial functions.

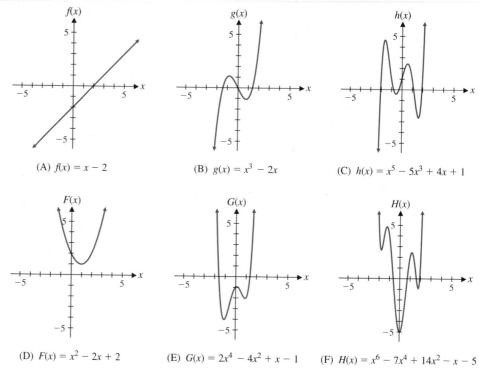

(A) $f(x) = x - 2$ (B) $g(x) = x^3 - 2x$ (C) $h(x) = x^5 - 5x^3 + 4x + 1$

(D) $F(x) = x^2 - 2x + 2$ (E) $G(x) = 2x^4 - 4x^2 + x - 1$ (F) $H(x) = x^6 - 7x^4 + 14x^2 - x - 5$

Figure 1 Graphs of polynomial functions

Notice that the odd-degree polynomial graphs start negative, end positive, and cross the x axis at least once. The even-degree polynomial graphs start positive, end positive, and may not cross the x axis at all. In all cases in Figure 1, the **leading coefficient**—that is, the coefficient of the highest-degree term—was chosen positive. If any leading coefficient had been chosen negative, then we would have a similar graph but reflected in the x axis.

A polynomial of degree n can have, at most, n linear factors. Therefore, the graph of a polynomial function of positive degree n can intersect the x axis at most n times. Note from Figure 1 that a polynomial of degree n may intersect the x axis fewer than n times. An x intercept of a function is also called a **zero*** or **root** of the function.

The graph of a polynomial function is **continuous**, with no holes or breaks. That is, the graph can be drawn without removing a pen from the paper. Also, the graph of a polynomial has no sharp corners. Figure 2 shows the graphs of two functions—one that is not continuous, and the other that is continuous but with a sharp corner. Neither function is a polynomial.

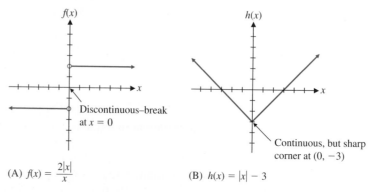

(A) $f(x) = \dfrac{2|x|}{x}$ (B) $h(x) = |x| - 3$

Figure 2 Discontinuous and sharp-corner functions

*Only real numbers can be x intercepts. Functions may have complex zeros that are not real numbers, but such zeros, which are not x intercepts, will not be discussed in this book.

Regression Polynomials

In Chapter 1, we saw that regression techniques can be used to fit a straight line to a set of data. Linear functions are not the only ones that can be applied in this manner. Most graphing calculators have the ability to fit a variety of curves to a given set of data. We will discuss polynomial regression models in this section and other types of regression models in later sections.

 EXAMPLE 1

Estimating the Weight of a Fish Using the length of a fish to estimate its weight is of interest to both scientists and sport anglers. The data in Table 1 give the average weights of lake trout for certain lengths. Use the data and regression techniques to find a polynomial model that can be used to estimate the weight of a lake trout for any length. Estimate (to the nearest ounce) the weights of lake trout of lengths 39, 40, 41, 42, and 43 inches, respectively.

Table 1 Lake Trout

Length (in.)	Weight (oz)	Length (in.)	Weight (oz)
x	y	x	y
10	5	30	152
14	12	34	226
18	26	38	326
22	56	44	536
26	96		

SOLUTION The graph of the data in Table 1 (Fig. 3A) indicates that a linear regression model would not be appropriate in this case. And, in fact, we would not expect a linear relationship between length and weight. Instead, it is more likely that the weight would be related to the cube of the length. We use a cubic regression polynomial to model the data (Fig. 3B). (Consult your manual for the details of calculating regression polynomials on your graphing utility.) Figure 3C adds the graph of the polynomial model to the graph of the data. The graph in Figure 3C shows that this cubic polynomial does provide a good fit for the data. (We will have more to say about the choice of functions and the accuracy of the fit provided by regression analysis later in the book.) Figure 3D shows the estimated weights for the lengths requested.

(A)

(B)

(C)

(D)

Figure 3

 Matched Problem 1 The data in Table 2 give the average weights of pike for certain lengths. Use a cubic regression polynomial to model the data. Estimate (to the nearest ounce) the weights of pike of lengths 39, 40, 41, 42, and 43 inches, respectively.

Table 2 Pike

Length (in.)	Weight (oz)	Length (in.)	Weight (oz)
x	y	x	y
10	5	30	108
14	12	34	154
18	26	38	210
22	44	44	326
26	72	52	522

Rational Functions

Just as rational numbers are defined in terms of quotients of integers, *rational functions* are defined in terms of quotients of polynomials. The following equations specify rational functions:

$$f(x) = \frac{1}{x} \quad g(x) = \frac{x-2}{x^2 - x - 6} \quad h(x) = \frac{x^3 - 8}{x}$$

$$p(x) = 3x^2 - 5x \quad q(x) = 7 \quad r(x) = 0$$

DEFINITION Rational Function

A **rational function** is any function that can be written in the form

$$f(x) = \frac{n(x)}{d(x)} \qquad d(x) \neq 0$$

where $n(x)$ and $d(x)$ are polynomials. The **domain** is the set of all real numbers such that $d(x) \neq 0$.

Figure 4 shows the graphs of representative rational functions. Note, for example, that in Figure 4A the line $x = 2$ is a *vertical asymptote* for the function. The graph of f gets closer to this line as x gets closer to 2. The line $y = 1$ in Figure 4A is a *horizontal asymptote* for the function. The graph of f gets closer to this line as x increases or decreases without bound.

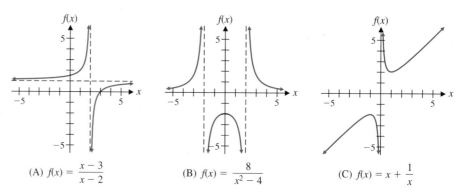

$$(A) \; f(x) = \frac{x-3}{x-2} \qquad (B) \; f(x) = \frac{8}{x^2 - 4} \qquad (C) \; f(x) = x + \frac{1}{x}$$

Figure 4 Graphs of rational functions

The number of vertical asymptotes of a rational function $f(x) = n(x)/d(x)$ is at most equal to the degree of $d(x)$. A rational function has at most one horizontal asymptote (note that the graph in Fig. 4C does not have a horizontal asymptote). Moreover, the graph of a rational function approaches the horizontal asymptote (when one exists) both as x increases and decreases without bound.

EXAMPLE 2   **Graphing Rational Functions** Given the rational function:

$$f(x) = \frac{3x}{x^2 - 4}$$

(A) Find the domain.

(B) Find the x and y intercepts.

(C) Find the equations of all vertical asymptotes.

(D) If there is a horizontal asymptote, find its equation.

(E) Using the information from (A)–(D) and additional points as necessary, sketch a graph of f for $-7 \leq x \leq 7$.

SOLUTION   (A) $x^2 - 4 = (x - 2)(x + 2)$, so the denominator is 0 if $x = -2$ or $x = 2$. Therefore the domain is the set of all real numbers except -2 and 2.

(B) *x intercepts:* $f(x) = 0$ only if $3x = 0$, or $x = 0$. So the only x intercept is 0.

y intercept:

$$f(0) = \frac{3 \cdot 0}{0^2 - 4} = \frac{0}{-4} = 0$$

So the *y* intercept is 0.

(C) Consider individually the values of x for which the denominator is 0, namely, 2 and -2, found in part (A).

(i) If $x = 2$, the numerator is 6, and the denominator is 0, so $f(2)$ is undefined. But for numbers just to the right of 2 (like 2.1, 2.01, 2.001), the numerator is close to 6, and the denominator is a positive number close to 0, so the fraction $f(x)$ is large and positive. For numbers just to the left of 2 (like 1.9, 1.99, 1.999), the numerator is close to 6, and the denominator is a negative number close to 0, so the fraction $f(x)$ is large (in absolute value) and negative. Therefore, the line $x = 2$ is a vertical asymptote, and $f(x)$ is positive to the right of the asymptote, and negative to the left.

(ii) If $x = -2$, the numerator is -6, and the denominator is 0, so $f(2)$ is undefined. But for numbers just to the right of -2 (like $-1.9, -1.99, -1.999$), the numerator is close to -6, and the denominator is a negative number close to 0, so the fraction $f(x)$ is large and positive. For numbers just to the left of 2 (like $-2.1, -2.01, -2.001$), the numerator is close to -6, and the denominator is a positive number close to 0, so the fraction $f(x)$ is large (in absolute value) and negative. Therefore, the line $x = -2$ is a vertical asymptote, and $f(x)$ is positive to the right of the asymptote and negative to the left.

(D) Rewrite $f(x)$ by dividing each term in the numerator and denominator by the highest power of x in $f(x)$.

$$f(x) = \frac{3x}{x^2 - 4} = \frac{\dfrac{3x}{x^2}}{\dfrac{x^2}{x^2} - \dfrac{4}{x^2}} = \frac{\dfrac{3}{x}}{1 - \dfrac{4}{x^2}}$$

As x increases or decreases without bound, the numerator tends to 0 and the denominator tends to 1; so, $f(x)$ tends to 0. The line $y = 0$ is a horizontal asymptote.

(E) Use the information from parts (A)–(D) and plot additional points as necessary to complete the graph, as shown in Figure 5.

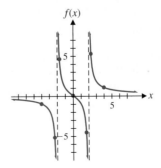

x	$f(x)$
-4	-1
-2.3	-5.3
-1.7	4.6
0	0
1.7	-4.6
2.3	5.3
4	1

Figure 5

Matched Problem 2   Given the rational function $g(x) = \dfrac{3x + 3}{x^2 - 9}$,

(A) Find the domain.

(B) Find the x and y intercepts.

(C) Find the equations of all vertical asymptotes.

(D) If there is a horizontal asymptote, find its equation.

(E) Using the information from parts (A)–(D) and additional points as necessary, sketch a graph of g for $-10 \le x \le 10$.

CONCEPTUAL INSIGHT

Consider the rational function

$$g(x) = \frac{3x^2 - 12x}{x^3 - 4x^2 - 4x + 16} = \frac{3x(x - 4)}{(x^2 - 4)(x - 4)}$$

The numerator and denominator of g have a common zero, $x = 4$. If $x \ne 4$, then we can cancel the factor $x - 4$ from the numerator and denominator, leaving the function $f(x)$ of Example 2. So the graph of g (Fig. 6) is identical to the graph of f (Fig. 5), except that the graph of g has an open dot at $(4, 1)$, indicating that 4 is not in the domain of g. In particular, f and g have the same asymptotes. Note that the line $x = 4$ is *not* a vertical asymptote of g, even though 4 is a zero of its denominator.

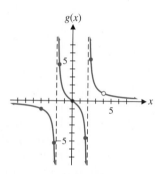

Figure 6

Graphing rational functions is aided by locating vertical and horizontal asymptotes first, if they exist. The following general procedure is suggested by Example 2 and the Conceptual Insight above.

PROCEDURE   Vertical and Horizontal Asymptotes of Rational Functions

Consider the rational function

$$f(x) = \frac{n(x)}{d(x)}$$

where $n(x)$ and $d(x)$ are polynomials.

Vertical asymptotes:

Case 1. Suppose $n(x)$ and $d(x)$ have no real zero in common. If c is a real number such that $d(c) = 0$, then the line $x = c$ is a vertical asymptote of the graph of f.

Case 2. If $n(x)$ and $d(x)$ have one or more real zeros in common, cancel common linear factors, as in Example 2, and apply Case 1 to the reduced function. (The reduced function has the same asymptotes as f.)

Horizontal asymptote:

Case 1. If degree $n(x) <$ degree $d(x)$, then $y = 0$ is the horizontal asymptote.

Case 2. If degree $n(x) =$ degree $d(x)$, then $y = a/b$ is the horizontal asymptote, where a is the leading coefficient of $n(x)$, and b is the leading coefficient of $d(x)$.

Case 3. If degree $n(x) >$ degree $d(x)$, there is no horizontal asymptote.

EXAMPLE 3 **Finding Asymptotes** Find the vertical and horizontal asymptotes of the rational function

$$f(x) = \frac{3x^2 + 3x - 6}{2x^2 - 2}$$

SOLUTION **Vertical asymptotes** We factor the numerator $n(x)$ and the denominator $d(x)$:

$$n(x) = 3(x^2 + x - 2) = 3(x - 1)(x + 2)$$
$$d(x) = 2(x^2 - 1) = 2(x - 1)(x + 1)$$

The reduced function is

$$\frac{3(x + 2)}{2(x + 1)}$$

which, by the procedure, has the vertical asymptote $x = -1$. Therefore, $x = -1$ is the only vertical asymptote of f.

Horizontal asymptote Both $n(x)$ and $d(x)$ have degree 2 (Case 2 of the procedure for horizontal asymptotes). The leading coefficient of the numerator $n(x)$ is 3, and the leading coefficient of the denominator $d(x)$ is 2. So $y = 3/2$ is the horizontal asymptote.

Matched Problem 3 Find the vertical and horizontal asymptotes of the rational function

$$f(x) = \frac{x^3 - 4x}{x^2 + 5x}$$

EXPLORE & DISCUSS 1 A function f is **bounded** if the entire graph of f lies between two horizontal lines. The only polynomials that are bounded are the constant functions, but there are many rational functions that are bounded. Give an example of a bounded rational function, with domain the set of all real numbers, that is not a constant function.

Applications

Rational functions occur naturally in many types of applications.

EXAMPLE 4 **Employee Training** A company that manufactures computers has established that, on the average, a new employee can assemble $N(t)$ components per day after t days of on-the-job training, as given by

$$N(t) = \frac{50t}{t + 4} \quad t \geq 0$$

Sketch a graph of N, $0 \leq t \leq 100$, including any vertical or horizontal asymptotes. What does $N(t)$ approach as t increases without bound?

SOLUTION **Vertical asymptotes** None for $t \geq 0$

Horizontal asymptote

$$N(t) = \frac{50t}{t + 4} = \frac{50}{1 + \dfrac{4}{t}}$$

$N(t)$ approaches 50 (the leading coefficient of $50t$ divided by the leading coefficient of $t + 4$) as t increases without bound. So $y = 50$ is a horizontal asymptote.

Sketch of graph The graph is shown in the margin.

$N(t)$ approaches 50 as t increases without bound. It appears that 50 components per day would be the upper limit that an employee would be expected to assemble.

Matched Problem 4 Repeat Example 4 for $N(t) = \dfrac{25t + 5}{t + 5}$ $t \geq 0$.

Exercises 2-4

A

In Problems 1–10, for each polynomial function find the following:

(A) *Degree of the polynomial*

(B) *All x intercepts*

(C) *The y intercept*

1. $f(x) = 5x + 3$ **2.** $f(x) = 4 - 3x$

3. $f(x) = x^2 - 9$ **4.** $f(x) = 5x - x^2 - 6$

5. $f(x) = (x - 2)(x + 3)(x - 5)$

6. $f(x) = (x + 7)(x - 4)$

7. $f(x) = (2x - 9)(3x + 4)$

8. $f(x) = (2 - 5x)(x - 6)(x + 1)$

9. $f(x) = x^6 + 1$

10. $f(x) = (x^8 + 5)(x^{12} + 7)$

Each graph in Problems 11–18 is the graph of a polynomial function. Answer the following questions for each graph:

(A) *What is the minimum degree of a polynomial function that could have the graph?*

(B) *Is the leading coefficient of the polynomial negative or positive?*

11.   **12.**

13.   **14.**

15.   **16.**

17.   **18.**

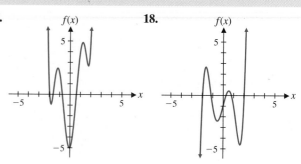

19. What is the maximum number of x intercepts that a polynomial of degree 10 can have?

20. What is the maximum number of x intercepts that a polynomial of degree 7 can have?

21. What is the minimum number of x intercepts that a polynomial of degree 9 can have? Explain.

22. What is the minimum number of x intercepts that a polynomial of degree 6 can have? Explain.

B

For each rational function in Problems 23–28,

(A) *Find the intercepts for the graph.*

(B) *Determine the domain.*

(C) *Find any vertical or horizontal asymptotes for the graph.*

(D) *Sketch any asymptotes as dashed lines. Then sketch a graph of $y = f(x)$ for $-10 \le x \le 10$ and $-10 \le y \le 10$.*

(E) *Graph $y = f(x)$ in a standard viewing window using a graphing calculator.*

23. $f(x) = \dfrac{x + 2}{x - 2}$ **24.** $f(x) = \dfrac{x - 3}{x + 3}$

25. $f(x) = \dfrac{3x}{x + 2}$ **26.** $f(x) = \dfrac{2x}{x - 3}$

27. $f(x) = \dfrac{4 - 2x}{x - 4}$ **28.** $f(x) = \dfrac{3 - 3x}{x - 2}$

29. Compare the graph of $y = 2x^4$ to the graph of $y = 2x^4 - 5x^2 + x + 2$ in the following two viewing windows:

(A) $-5 \le x \le 5, -5 \le y \le 5$

(B) $-5 \le x \le 5, -500 \le y \le 500$

30. Compare the graph of $y = x^3$ to the graph of $y = x^3 - 2x + 2$ in the following two viewing windows:

(A) $-5 \le x \le 5, -5 \le y \le 5$

(B) $-5 \le x \le 5, -500 \le y \le 500$

31. Compare the graph of $y = -x^5$ to the graph of $y = -x^5 + 4x^3 - 4x + 1$ in the following two viewing windows:

(A) $-5 \le x \le 5, -5 \le y \le 5$

(B) $-5 \le x \le 5, -500 \le y \le 500$

32. Compare the graph of $y = -x^5$ to the graph of $y = -x^5 + 5x^3 - 5x + 2$ in the following two viewing windows:

(A) $-5 \le x \le 5, -5 \le y \le 5$

(B) $-5 \le x \le 5, -500 \le y \le 500$

In Problems 33–40, find the equation of any horizontal asymptote.

33. $f(x) = \dfrac{5x^3 + 2x - 3}{6x^3 - 7x + 1}$

34. $f(x) = \dfrac{6x^4 - x^3 + 2}{4x^4 + 10x + 5}$

35. $f(x) = \dfrac{1 - 5x + x^2}{2 + 3x + 4x^2}$

36. $f(x) = \dfrac{8 - x^3}{1 + 2x^3}$

37. $f(x) = \dfrac{x^4 + 2x^2 + 1}{1 - x^5}$

38. $f(x) = \dfrac{3 + 5x}{x^2 + x + 3}$

39. $f(x) = \dfrac{x^2 + 6x + 1}{x - 5}$

40. $f(x) = \dfrac{x^2 + x^4 + 1}{x^3 + 2x - 4}$

In Problems 41–46, find the equations of any vertical asymptotes.

41. $f(x) = \dfrac{x^2 + 1}{(x^2 - 1)(x^2 - 9)}$

42. $f(x) = \dfrac{2x + 5}{(x^2 - 4)(x^2 - 16)}$

43. $f(x) = \dfrac{x^2 - x - 6}{x^2 - 3x - 10}$

44. $f(x) = \dfrac{x^2 - 8x + 7}{x^2 + 7x - 8}$

45. $f(x) = \dfrac{x^2 + 3x}{x^3 - 36x}$

46. $f(x) = \dfrac{x^2 + x - 2}{x^3 - 3x^2 + 2x}$

C

For each rational function in Problems 47–52,

(A) *Find any intercepts for the graph.*

(B) *Find any vertical and horizontal asymptotes for the graph.*

(C) *Sketch any asymptotes as dashed lines. Then sketch a graph of f for $-10 \le x \le 10$ and $-10 \le y \le 10$.*

 (D) *Graph the function in a standard viewing window using a graphing calculator.*

47. $f(x) = \dfrac{2x^2}{x^2 - x - 6}$

48. $f(x) = \dfrac{3x^2}{x^2 + x - 6}$

49. $f(x) = \dfrac{6 - 2x^2}{x^2 - 9}$

50. $f(x) = \dfrac{3 - 3x^2}{x^2 - 4}$

51. $f(x) = \dfrac{-4x}{x^2 + x - 6}$

52. $f(x) = \dfrac{5x}{x^2 + x - 12}$

53. Write an equation for the lowest-degree polynomial function with the graph and intercepts shown in the figure.

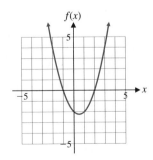

Figure for 53

54. Write an equation for the lowest-degree polynomial function with the graph and intercepts shown in the figure.

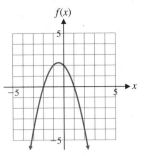

Figure for 54

55. Write an equation for the lowest-degree polynomial function with the graph and intercepts shown in the figure.

Figure for 55

56. Write an equation for the lowest-degree polynomial function with the graph and intercepts shown in the figure.

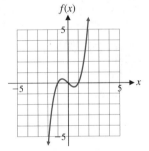

Figure for 56

Applications

57. Average cost. A company manufacturing snowboards has fixed costs of $200 per day and total costs of $3,800 per day at a daily output of 20 boards.

(A) Assuming that the total cost per day, $C(x)$, is linearly related to the total output per day, x, write an equation for the cost function.

(B) The average cost per board for an output of x boards is given by $\overline{C}(x) = C(x)/x$. Find the average cost function.

(C) Sketch a graph of the average cost function, including any asymptotes, for $1 \le x \le 30$.

(D) What does the average cost per board tend to as production increases?

58. Average cost. A company manufacturing surfboards has fixed costs of $300 per day and total costs of $5,100 per day at a daily output of 20 boards.

(A) Assuming that the total cost per day, $C(x)$, is linearly related to the total output per day, x, write an equation for the cost function.

(B) The average cost per board for an output of x boards is given by $\overline{C}(x) = C(x)/x$. Find the average cost function.

(C) Sketch a graph of the average cost function, including any asymptotes, for $1 \le x \le 30$.

(D) What does the average cost per board tend to as production increases?

59. Replacement time. An office copier has an initial price of $2,500. A service contract costs $200 for the first year and increases $50 per year thereafter. It can be shown that the total cost of the copier after n years is given by

$$C(n) = 2,500 + 175n + 25n^2$$

The average cost per year for n years is given by $\overline{C}(n) = C(n)/n$.

(A) Find the rational function $\overline{C}$.

(B) Sketch a graph of $\overline{C}$ for $2 \le n \le 20$.

(C) When is the average cost per year at a minimum, and what is the minimum average annual cost? [*Hint:* Refer to the sketch in part (B) and evaluate $\overline{C}(n)$ at appropriate integer values until a minimum value is found.] The time when the average cost is minimum is frequently referred to as the **replacement time** for the piece of equipment.

 (D) Graph the average cost function $\overline{C}$ on a graphing calculator and use an appropriate command to find when the average annual cost is at a minimum.

60. Minimum average cost. Financial analysts in a company that manufactures DVD players arrived at the following daily cost equation for manufacturing x DVD players per day:

$$C(x) = x^2 + 2x + 2,000$$

The average cost per unit at a production level of x players per day is $\overline{C}(x) = C(x)/x$.

(A) Find the rational function $\overline{C}$.

(B) Sketch a graph of $\overline{C}$ for $5 \le x \le 150$.

(C) For what daily production level (to the nearest integer) is the average cost per unit at a minimum, and what is the minimum average cost per player (to the nearest cent)? [*Hint:* Refer to the sketch in part (B) and evaluate $\overline{C}(x)$ at appropriate integer values until a minimum value is found.]

 (D) Graph the average cost function $\overline{C}$ on a graphing calculator and use an appropriate command to find the daily production level (to the nearest integer) at which the average cost per player is at a minimum. What is the minimum average cost to the nearest cent?

61. Minimum average cost. A consulting firm, using statistical methods, provided a veterinary clinic with the cost equation

$$C(x) = 0.00048(x - 500)^3 + 60,000$$
$$100 \le x \le 1,000$$

where $C(x)$ is the cost in dollars for handling x cases per month. The average cost per case is given by $\overline{C}(x) = C(x)/x$.

(A) Write the equation for the average cost function $\overline{C}$.

(B) Graph $\overline{C}$ on a graphing calculator.

(C) Use an appropriate command to find the monthly caseload for the minimum average cost per case. What is the minimum average cost per case?

62. Minimum average cost. The financial department of a hospital, using statistical methods, arrived at the cost equation

$$C(x) = 20x^3 - 360x^2 + 2,300x - 1,000$$
$$1 \le x \le 12$$

where $C(x)$ is the cost in thousands of dollars for handling x thousand cases per month. The average cost per case is given by $\overline{C}(x) = C(x)/x$.

(A) Write the equation for the average cost function $\overline{C}$.

(B) Graph $\overline{C}$ on a graphing calculator.

(C) Use an appropriate command to find the monthly caseload for the minimum average cost per case. What is the minimum average cost per case to the nearest dollar?

63. Diet. Table 3 shows the per capita consumption of ice cream and eggs in the United States for selected years since 1980.

(A) Let x represent the number of years since 1980 and find a cubic regression polynomial for the per capita consumption of ice cream.

(B) Use the polynomial model from part (A) to estimate (to the nearest tenth of a pound) the per capita consumption of ice cream in 2020.

64. Diet. Refer to Table 3.

(A) Let x represent the number of years since 1980 and find a cubic regression polynomial for the per capita consumption of eggs.

(B) Use the polynomial model from part (A) to estimate (to the nearest integer) the per capita consumption of eggs in 2020.

Table 3	Per Capita Consumption of Ice Cream and Eggs	
Year	Ice Cream (pounds)	Eggs (number)
1980	17.5	266
1985	18.1	251
1990	15.8	231
1995	15.5	229
2000	16.5	247
2005	14.4	255

65. Physiology. In a study on the speed of muscle contraction in frogs under various loads, researchers W. O. Fems and J. Marsh found that the speed of contraction decreases with increasing loads. In particular, they found that the relationship between speed of contraction v (in centimeters per second) and load x (in grams) is given approximately by

$$v(x) = \frac{26 + 0.06x}{x} \quad x \ge 5$$

(A) What does $v(x)$ approach as x increases?

(B) Sketch a graph of function v.

66. Learning theory. In 1917, L. L. Thurstone, a pioneer in quantitative learning theory, proposed the rational function

$$f(x) = \frac{a(x + c)}{(x + c) + b}$$

to model the number of successful acts per unit time that a person could accomplish after x practice sessions. Suppose that for a particular person enrolled in a typing class,

$$f(x) = \frac{55(x + 1)}{(x + 8)} \quad x \geq 0$$

where $f(x)$ is the number of words per minute the person is able to type after x weeks of lessons.

(A) What does $f(x)$ approach as x increases?

(B) Sketch a graph of function f, including any vertical or horizontal asymptotes.

 67. Marriage. Table 4 shows the marriage and divorce rates per 1,000 population for selected years since 1960.

(A) Let x represent the number of years since 1960 and find a cubic regression polynomial for the marriage rate.

(B) Use the polynomial model from part (A) to estimate the marriage rate (to one decimal place) for 2020.

Table 4 Marriages and Divorces (per 1,000 Population)

Date	Marriages	Divorces
1960	8.5	2.2
1970	10.6	3.5
1980	10.6	5.2
1990	9.8	4.7
2000	8.5	4.1

68. Divorce. Refer to Table 4.

 (A) Let x represent the number of years since 1950 and find a cubic regression polynomial for the divorce rate.

(B) Use the polynomial model from part (A) to estimate the divorce rate (to one decimal place) for 2020.

Answers to Matched Problems

1.

2. (A) Domain: all real numbers except -3 and 3

(B) x intercept: -1; y intercept: $-\dfrac{1}{3}$

(C) Vertical asymptotes: $x = -3$ and $x = 3$;

(D) Horizontal asymptote: $y = 0$

(E)

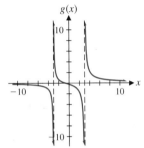

3. Vertical asymptote: $x = -5$

Horizontal asymptote: none

4. No vertical asymptotes for $t \leq 0$; $y = 25$ is a horizontal asymptote. $N(t)$ approaches 25 as t increases without bound. It appears that 25 components per day would be the upper limit that an employee would be expected to assemble.

2-5 Exponential Functions

- Exponential Functions
- Base e Exponential Functions
- Growth and Decay Applications
- Compound Interest

This section introduces an important class of functions called *exponential functions*. These functions are used extensively in modeling and solving a wide variety of real-world problems, including growth of money at compound interest, growth of populations, radioactive decay and learning associated with the mastery of such devices as a new computer or an assembly process in a manufacturing plant.

N

10,000

5

0

Time (hours)

Figure 4

SOLUTION Substituting $N_0 = 25$ into the preceding equation, we obtain

$$N = 25e^{1.386t}$$ *The graph is shown in Figure 4.*

(A) Solve for N when $t = 0.6$:

$$N = 25e^{1.386(0.6)}$$ *Use a calculator.*

$$= 57 \text{ bacteria}$$

(B) Solve for N when $t = 3.5$:

$$N = 25e^{1.386(3.5)}$$ *Use a calculator.*

$$= 3{,}197 \text{ bacteria}$$

Matched Problem 2 Refer to the exponential growth model for cholera in Example 2. If we start with 55 bacteria, how many bacteria (to the nearest unit) will be present
(A) In 0.85 hour?   (B) In 7.25 hours?

EXAMPLE 3 **Exponential Decay** Cosmic-ray bombardment of the atmosphere produces neutrons, which in turn react with nitrogen to produce radioactive carbon-14 (^{14}C). Radioactive ^{14}C enters all living tissues through carbon dioxide, which is first absorbed by plants. As long as a plant or animal is alive, ^{14}C is maintained in the living organism at a constant level. Once the organism dies, however, ^{14}C decays according to the equation

$$A = A_0 e^{-0.000124t}$$

where A is the amount present after t years and A_0 is the amount present at time $t = 0$. If 500 milligrams of ^{14}C is present in a sample from a skull at the time of death, how many milligrams will be present in the sample in
(A) 15,000 years?   (B) 45,000 years?
Compute answers to two decimal places.

A

500
400
300
200
100

Milligrams

0
50,000

Years

Figure 5

SOLUTION Substituting $A_0 = 500$ in the decay equation, we have

$$A = 500e^{-0.000124t}$$ *See the graph in Figure 5.*

(A) Solve for A when $t = 15{,}000$:

$$A = 500e^{-0.000124(15{,}000)}$$ *Use a calculator.*

$$= 77.84 \text{ milligrams}$$

(B) Solve for A when $t = 45{,}000$:

$$A = 500e^{-0.000124(45{,}000)}$$ *Use a calculator.*

$$= 1.89 \text{ milligrams}$$

Matched Problem 3 Refer to the exponential decay model in Example 3. How many milligrams of ^{14}C would have to be present at the beginning in order to have 25 milligrams present after 18,000 years? Compute the answer to the nearest milligram.

If you buy a new car, it is likely to depreciate in value by several thousand dollars during the first year you own it. You would expect the value of the car to decrease in each subsequent year, but not by as much as in the previous year. If you drive the car long enough, its resale value will get close to zero. An exponential decay function will often be a good model of depreciation; a linear or quadratic function would not be suitable (why?). We can use **exponential regression** on a graphing calculator to find the function of the form $y = ab^x$ that best fits a data set.

EXAMPLE 4

Depreciation Table 2 gives the market value of a hybrid sedan (in dollars) x years after its purchase. Find an exponential regression model of the form $y = ab^x$ for this data set. Estimate the purchase price of the hybrid. Estimate the value of the hybrid 10 years after its purchase. Round answers to the nearest dollar.

Table 2

x	Value ($)
1	12,575
2	9,455
3	8,115
4	6,845
5	5,225
6	4,485

SOLUTION

Enter the data into a graphing calculator (Fig. 6A) and find the exponential regression equation (Fig. 6B). The estimated purchase price is $y_1(0) = \$14,910$. The data set and the regression equation are graphed in Figure 6C. Using TRACE, we see that the estimated value after 10 years is $1,959.

Figure 6

Matched Problem 4

Table 3 gives the market value of a midsize sedan (in dollars) x years after its purchase. Find an exponential regression model of the form $y = ab^x$ for this data set. Estimate the purchase price of the sedan. Estimate the value of the sedan 10 years after its purchase. Round answers to the nearest dollar.

Table 3

x	Value ($)
1	23,125
2	19,050
3	15,625
4	11,875
5	9,450
6	7,125

Compound Interest

The fee paid to use another's money is called **interest**. It is usually computed as a percent (called **interest rate**) of the principal over a given period of time. If, at the end of a payment period, the interest due is reinvested at the same rate, then the interest earned as well as the principal will earn interest during the next payment period. Interest paid on interest reinvested is called **compound interest** and may be calculated using the following compound interest formula:

If a **principal P (present value)** is invested at an annual **rate r** (expressed as a decimal) compounded m times a year, then the **amount A (future value)** in the account at the end of t years is given by

$$A = P\left(1 + \frac{r}{m}\right)^{mt} \qquad \textit{Compound interest formula}$$

For given r and m, the amount A is equal to the principal P multiplied by the exponential function b^t, where $b = (1 + r/m)^m$.

EXAMPLE 5 **Compound Growth** If $1,000 is invested in an account paying 10% compounded monthly, how much will be in the account at the end of 10 years? Compute the answer to the nearest cent.

SOLUTION We use the compound interest formula as follows:

Figure 7

$$A = P\left(1 + \frac{r}{m}\right)^{mt}$$

$$= 1,000\left(1 + \frac{0.10}{12}\right)^{(12)(10)} \quad \text{Use a calculator.}$$

$$= \$2,707.04$$

The graph of

$$A = 1,000\left(1 + \frac{0.10}{12}\right)^{12t}$$

for $0 \le t \le 20$ is shown in Figure 7.

Matched Problem 5 If you deposit $5,000 in an account paying 9% compounded daily, how much will you have in the account in 5 years? Compute the answer to the nearest cent.

EXPLORE & DISCUSS 2 Suppose that $1,000 is deposited in a savings account at an annual rate of 5%. Guess the amount in the account at the end of 1 year if interest is compounded (1) quarterly, (2) monthly, (3) daily, (4) hourly. Use the compound interest formula to compute the amounts at the end of 1 year to the nearest cent. Discuss the accuracy of your initial guesses.

Explore & Discuss 2 suggests that if $1,000 were deposited in a savings account at an annual interest rate of 5%, then the amount at the end of 1 year would be less than $1,051.28, even if interest were compounded every minute or every second. The limiting value, approximately $1,051.271096, is said to be the amount in the account if interest were compounded continuously.

If a principal, P, is invested at an annual rate, r, and compounded continuously, then the amount in the account at the end of t years is given by

$$A = Pe^{rt} \quad \text{Continuous compound interest formula}$$

where the constant $e \approx 2.71828$ is the base of the exponential function.

EXAMPLE 6 **Continuous Compound Interest** If $1,000 is invested in an account paying 10% compounded continuously, how much will be in the account at the end of 10 years? Compute the answer to the nearest cent.

SOLUTION We use the continuous compound interest formula:

$$A = Pe^{rt} = 1000e^{0.10(10)} = 1000e = \$2,718.28$$

Compare with the answer to Example 5.

Matched Problem 6 If you deposit $5,000 in an account paying 9% compounded continuously, how much will you have in the account in 5 years? Compute the answer to the nearest cent.

The formulas for compound interest and continuous compound interest are summarized below for convenient reference.

> **SUMMARY**
>
> Compound Interest: $A = P\left(1 + \dfrac{r}{m}\right)^{mt}$
>
> Continuous Compound Interest: $A = Pe^{rt}$
>
> where A = amount (future value) at the end of t years
> P = principal (present value)
> r = annual rate (expressed as a decimal)
> m = number of compounding periods per year
> t = time in years

Exercises 2-5

A

1. Match each equation with the graph of f, g, h, or k in the figure.

 (A) $y = 2^x$ (B) $y = (0.2)^x$

 (C) $y = 4^x$ (D) $y = \left(\frac{1}{3}\right)^x$

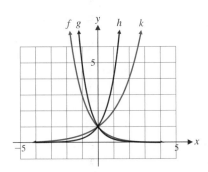

2. Match each equation with the graph of f, g, h, or k in the figure.

 (A) $y = \left(\frac{1}{4}\right)^x$ (B) $y = (0.5)^x$

 (C) $y = 5^x$ (D) $y = 3^x$

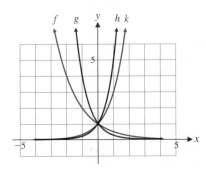

Graph each function in Problems 3–10 over the indicated interval.

3. $y = 5^x$; $[-2, 2]$ **4.** $y = 3^x$; $[-3, 3]$

5. $y = \left(\frac{1}{5}\right)^x = 5^{-x}$; $[-2, 2]$ **6.** $y = \left(\frac{1}{3}\right)^x = 3^{-x}$; $[-3, 3]$

7. $f(x) = -5^x$; $[-2, 2]$ **8.** $g(x) = -3^{-x}$; $[-3, 3]$

9. $y = -e^{-x}$; $[-3, 3]$ **10.** $y = -e^x$; $[-3, 3]$

B

In Problems 11–18, describe verbally the transformations that can be used to obtain the graph of g from the graph of f (see Section 2-2).

11. $g(x) = -2^x$; $f(x) = 2^x$ **12.** $g(x) = 2^{x-2}$; $f(x) = 2^x$

13. $g(x) = 3^{x+1}$; $f(x) = 3^x$ **14.** $g(x) = -3^x$; $f(x) = 3^x$

15. $g(x) = e^x + 1$; $f(x) = e^x$ **16.** $g(x) = e^x - 2$; $f(x) = e^x$

17. $g(x) = 2e^{-(x+2)}$; $f(x) = e^{-x}$

18. $g(x) = 0.5e^{-(x-1)}$; $f(x) = e^{-x}$

19. Use the graph of f shown in the figure to sketch the graph of each of the following.

 (A) $y = f(x) - 1$ (B) $y = f(x + 2)$

 (C) $y = 3f(x) - 2$ (D) $y = 2 - f(x - 3)$

20. Use the graph of f shown in the figure to sketch the graph of each of the following.

 (A) $y = f(x) + 2$ (B) $y = f(x - 3)$

 (C) $y = 2f(x) - 4$ (D) $y = 4 - f(x + 2)$

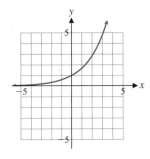

Figure for 19 and 20

In Problems 21–26, graph each function over the indicated interval.

21. $f(t) = 2^{t/10}$; $[-30, 30]$ **22.** $G(t) = 3^{t/100}$; $[-200, 200]$

23. $y = -3 + e^{1+x}$; $[-4, 2]$ **24.** $y = 2 + e^{x-2}$; $[-1, 5]$

25. $y = e^{|x|}$; $[-3, 3]$ **26.** $y = e^{-|x|}$; $[-3, 3]$

27. Find all real numbers a such that $a^2 = a^{-2}$. Explain why this does not violate the second exponential function property in Theorem 2 on page 98.

28. Find real numbers a and b such that $a \neq b$ but $a^4 = b^4$. Explain why this does not violate the third exponential function property in Theorem 2 on page 98.

Solve each equation in Problems 29–34 for x.

29. $10^{2-3x} = 10^{5x-6}$

30. $5^{3x} = 5^{4x-2}$

31. $4^{5x-x^2} = 4^{-6}$

32. $7^{x^2} = 7^{2x+3}$

33. $5^3 = (x + 2)^3$

34. $(1 - x)^5 = (2x - 1)^5$

C

Solve each equation in Problems 35–38 for x. (Remember: $e^x \neq 0$ and $e^{-x} \neq 0$.)

35. $(x - 3)e^x = 0$

36. $2xe^{-x} = 0$

37. $3xe^{-x} + x^2e^{-x} = 0$

38. $x^2e^x - 5xe^x = 0$

Graph each function in Problems 39–42 over the indicated interval.

39. $h(x) = x(2^x)$; $[-5, 0]$

40. $m(x) = x(3^{-x})$; $[0, 3]$

41. $N = \dfrac{100}{1 + e^{-t}}$; $[0, 5]$

42. $N = \dfrac{200}{1 + 3e^{-t}}$; $[0, 5]$

Applications

In all problems involving days, a 365-day year is assumed.

43. Continuous compound interest. Find the value of an investment of $10,000 in 12 years if it earns an annual rate of 3.95% compounded continuously.

44. Continuous compound interest. Find the value of an investment of $24,000 in 7 years if it earns an annual rate of 4.35% compounded continuously.

45. Compound growth. Suppose that $2,500 is invested at 7% compounded quarterly. How much money will be in the account in

(A) $\frac{3}{4}$ year?

(B) 15 years?

Compute answers to the nearest cent.

46. Compound growth. Suppose that $4,000 is invested at 6% compounded weekly. How much money will be in the account in

(A) $\frac{1}{2}$ year?

(B) 10 years?

Compute answers to the nearest cent.

47. Finance. A person wishes to have $15,000 cash for a new car 5 years from now. How much should be placed in an account now, if the account pays 6.75% compounded weekly? Compute the answer to the nearest dollar.

48. Finance. A couple just had a baby. How much should they invest now at 5.5% compounded daily in order to have $40,000 for the child's education 17 years from now? Compute the answer to the nearest dollar.

49. Money growth. BanxQuote operates a network of Web sites providing real-time market data from leading financial providers. The following rates for 12-month certificates of deposit were taken from the Web sites:

(A) Stonebridge Bank, 5.40% compounded monthly

(B) DeepGreen Bank, 4.95% compounded daily

(C) Provident Bank, 5.15% compounded quarterly

Compute the value of $10,000 invested in each account at the end of 1 year.

50. Money growth. Refer to Problem 49. The following rates for 60-month certificates of deposit were also taken from BanxQuote Web sites:

(A) Oriental Bank & Trust, 5.50% compounded quarterly

(B) BMW Bank of North America, 5.12% compounded monthly

(C) BankFirst Corporation, 4.86% compounded daily

Compute the value of $10,000 invested in each account at the end of 5 years.

51. Advertising. A company is trying to introduce a new product to as many people as possible through television advertising in a large metropolitan area with 2 million possible viewers. A model for the number of people N (in millions) who are aware of the product after t days of advertising was found to be

$$N = 2(1 - e^{-0.037t})$$

Graph this function for $0 \leq t \leq 50$. What value does N approach as t increases without bound?

52. Learning curve. People assigned to assemble circuit boards for a computer manufacturing company undergo on-the-job training. From past experience, the learning curve for the average employee is given by

$$N = 40(1 - e^{-0.12t})$$

where N is the number of boards assembled per day after t days of training. Graph this function for $0 \leq t \leq 30$. What is the maximum number of boards an average employee can be expected to produce in 1 day?

53. Sports salaries. Table 4 shows the average salaries for players in Major League Baseball (MLB) and the National Basketball Association (NBA) in selected years since 1990.

(A) Let x represent the number of years since 1990 and find an exponential regression model ($y = ab^x$) for the average salary in MLB. Use the model to estimate the average salary (to the nearest thousand dollars) in 2020.

(B) The average salary in MLB in 2000 was 1.984 million. How does this compare with the value given by the model of part (A)? How would the inclusion of the year 2000 data affect the estimated average salary in 2020? Explain.

Table 4	Average Salary (thousand $)	
Year	MLB	NBA
1990	589	750
1993	1,062	1,300
1996	1,101	2,000
1999	1,724	2,400
2002	2,300	4,500
2005	2,633	5,000
2008	3,155	5,585

54. **Sports salaries.** Refer to Table 4.

    (A) Let x represent the number of years since 1990 and find an exponential regression model ($y = ab^x$) for the average salary in the NBA. Use the model to estimate the average salary (to the nearest thousand dollars) in 2020.

    (B) The average salary in the NBA in 1997 was $2.2 million. How does this compare with the value given by the model of part (A)? How would the inclusion of the year 1997 data affect the estimated average salary in 2020? Explain.

55. **Marine biology.** Marine life depends on the microscopic plant life that exists in the photic zone, a zone that goes to a depth where only 1% of surface light remains. In some waters with a great deal of sediment, the photic zone may go down only 15 to 20 feet. In some murky harbors, the intensity of light d feet below the surface is given approximately by

    $$I = I_0 e^{-0.23d}$$

    What percentage of the surface light will reach a depth of

    (A) 10 feet?   (B) 20 feet?

56. **Marine biology.** Refer to Problem 55. Light intensity I relative to depth d (in feet) for one of the clearest bodies of water in the world, the Sargasso Sea, can be approximated by

    $$I = I_0 e^{-0.00942d}$$

    where I_0 is the intensity of light at the surface. What percentage of the surface light will reach a depth of

    (A) 50 feet?   (B) 100 feet?

57. **World population growth.** From the dawn of humanity to 1830, world population grew to one billion people. In 100 more years (by 1930) it grew to two billion, and 3 billion more were added in only 60 years (by 1990). In 2009, the estimated world population was 6.8 billion with a relative growth rate of 1.14%.

    (A) Write an equation that models the world population growth, letting 2009 be year 0.

    (B) Based on the model, what is the expected world population (to the nearest hundred million) in 2020? In 2030?

58. **Population growth in Ethiopia.** In 2008, the estimated population in Ethiopia was 83 million people with a relative growth rate of 3.2%.

    (A) Write an equation that models the population growth in Ethiopia, letting 2008 be year 0.

    (B) Based on the model, what is the expected population in Ethiopia (to the nearest million) in 2020? In 2030?

59. **Internet growth.** The number of Internet hosts grew very rapidly from 1994 to 2009 (Table 5).

    (A) Let x represent the number of years since 1994. Find an exponential regression model ($y = ab^x$) for this data set and estimate the number of hosts in 2018 (to the nearest million).

    (B) Discuss the implications of this model if the number of Internet hosts continues to grow at this rate.

Table 5 Internet Hosts (Millions)

Year	Hosts
1994	2.4
1997	16.1
2000	72.4
2003	171.6
2006	394.0
2009	625.2

Source: Internet Software Consortium

60. **Life expectancy.** Table 6 shows the life expectancy (in years) at birth for residents of the United States from 1970 to 2005. Let x represent years since 1970. Find an exponential regression model for this data and use it to estimate the life expectancy for a person born in 2015.

Table 6

Year of Birth	Life Expectancy
1970	70.8
1975	72.6
1980	73.7
1985	74.7
1990	75.4
1995	75.9
2000	76.9
2005	77.7

Answers to Matched Problems

1.

2. (A) 179 bacteria   (B) 1,271,659 bacteria

3. 233 mg

4. Purchase price: $30,363; value after 10 yr: $2,864

5. $7,841.13   6. $7,841.56

2-6   Logarithmic Functions

Find the exponential function keys $\boxed{10^x}$ and $\boxed{e^x}$ on your calculator. Close to these keys you will find the $\boxed{\text{LOG}}$ and $\boxed{\text{LN}}$ keys. The latter two keys represent *logarithmic functions,* and each is closely related to its nearby exponential function. In fact, the exponential function and the corresponding logarithmic function are said to be *inverses* of each other. In this section we will develop the concept of inverse functions and use it to define a logarithmic function as the inverse of an exponential function. We will then investigate basic properties of logarithmic functions, use a calculator to evaluate them for particular values of x, and apply them to real-world problems.

Logarithmic functions are used in modeling and solving many types of problems. For example, the decibel scale is a logarithmic scale used to measure sound intensity, and the Richter scale is a logarithmic scale used to measure the strength of the force of an earthquake. An important business application has to do with finding the time it takes money to double if it is invested at a certain rate compounded a given number of times a year or compounded continuously. This requires the solution of an exponential equation, and logarithms play a central role in the process.

Inverse Functions

Look at the graphs of $f(x) = \dfrac{x}{2}$ and $g(x) = \dfrac{|x|}{2}$ in Figure 1:

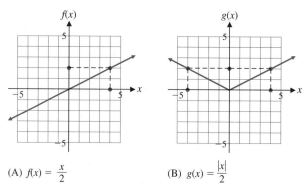

(A) $f(x) = \dfrac{x}{2}$ (B) $g(x) = \dfrac{|x|}{2}$

Figure 1

Because both f and g are functions, each domain value corresponds to exactly one range value. For which function does each range value correspond to exactly one domain value? This is the case only for function f. Note that for function f, the range value 2 corresponds to the domain value 4. For function g the range value 2 corresponds to both -4 and 4. Function f is said to be *one-to-one.*

DEFINITION One-to-One Functions

A function f is said to be **one-to-one** if each range value corresponds to exactly one domain value.

It can be shown that any continuous function that is either increasing* or decreasing for all domain values is one-to-one. If a continuous function increases for some domain values and decreases for others, then it cannot be one-to-one. Figure 1 shows an example of each case.

---

*Formally, we say that the function f is **increasing** on an interval (a, b) if $f(x_2) > f(x_1)$ whenever $a < x_1 < x_2 < b$; and f is **decreasing** on (a, b) if $f(x_2) < f(x_1)$ whenever $a < x_1 < x_2 < b$.

EXPLORE & DISCUSS 1

Graph $f(x) = 2^x$ and $g(x) = x^2$. For a range value of 4, what are the corresponding domain values for each function? Which of the two functions is one-to-one? Explain why.

Starting with a one-to-one function f, we can obtain a new function called the *inverse* of f.

DEFINITION Inverse of a Function

If f is a one-to-one function, then the **inverse** of f is the function formed by interchanging the independent and dependent variables for f. Thus, if (a, b) is a point on the graph of f, then (b, a) is a point on the graph of the inverse of f.

Note: If f is not one-to-one, then f **does not have an inverse**.

In this course, we are interested in the inverses of exponential functions, called *logarithmic functions*.

Logarithmic Functions

If we start with the exponential function f defined by

$$y = 2^x \qquad (1)$$

and interchange the variables, we obtain the inverse of f:

$$x = 2^y \qquad (2)$$

We call the inverse the **logarithmic function with base 2**, and write

$$y = \log_2 x \quad \text{if and only if} \quad x = 2^y$$

We can graph $y = \log_2 x$ by graphing $x = 2^y$ since they are equivalent. Any ordered pair of numbers on the graph of the exponential function will be on the graph of the logarithmic function if we interchange the order of the components. For example, $(3, 8)$ satisfies equation (1) and $(8, 3)$ satisfies equation (2). The graphs of $y = 2^x$ and $y = \log_2 x$ are shown in Figure 2. Note that if we fold the paper along the dashed line $y = x$ in Figure 2, the two graphs match exactly. The line $y = x$ is a line of symmetry for the two graphs.

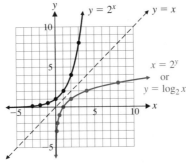

Figure 2

Exponential Function		Logarithmic Function	
x	$y = 2^x$	$x = 2^y$	y
-3	$\frac{1}{8}$	$\frac{1}{8}$	-3
-2	$\frac{1}{4}$	$\frac{1}{4}$	-2
-1	$\frac{1}{2}$	$\frac{1}{2}$	-1
0	1	1	0
1	2	2	1
2	4	4	2
3	8	8	3

$$\left[\begin{array}{c} \text{Ordered} \\ \text{pairs} \\ \text{reversed} \end{array}\right]$$

In general, since the graphs of all exponential functions of the form $f(x) = b^x, b \neq 1, b > 0$, are either increasing or decreasing, exponential functions have inverses.

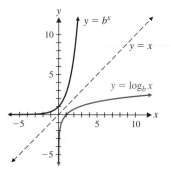

Figure 3

DEFINITION Logarithmic Functions

The inverse of an exponential function is called a **logarithmic function**. For $b > 0$ and $b \neq 1$,

Logarithmic form		Exponential form
$y = \log_b x$	is equivalent to	$x = b^y$

The **log to the base b of x** is the exponent to which b must be raised to obtain x. [*Remember*: A logarithm is an exponent.] The **domain** of the logarithmic function is the set of all positive real numbers, which is also the range of the corresponding exponential function; and the **range** of the logarithmic function is the set of all real numbers, which is also the domain of the corresponding exponential function. Typical graphs of an exponential function and its inverse, a logarithmic function, are shown in Figure 3.

CONCEPTUAL INSIGHT

Because the domain of a logarithmic function consists of the positive real numbers, the entire graph of a logarithmic function lies to the right of the y axis. In contrast, the graphs of polynomial and exponential functions intersect every vertical line, and the graphs of rational functions intersect all but a finite number of vertical lines.

The following examples involve converting logarithmic forms to equivalent exponential forms, and vice versa.

EXAMPLE 1   **Logarithmic–Exponential Conversions** Change each logarithmic form to an equivalent exponential form:

(A) $\log_5 25 = 2$ (B) $\log_9 3 = \frac{1}{2}$ (C) $\log_2 \left(\frac{1}{4}\right) = -2$

SOLUTION   (A) $\log_5 25 = 2$ is equivalent to $25 = 5^2$
(B) $\log_9 3 = \frac{1}{2}$ is equivalent to $3 = 9^{1/2}$
(C) $\log_2 \left(\frac{1}{4}\right) = -2$ is equivalent to $\frac{1}{4} = 2^{-2}$

Matched Problem 1   Change each logarithmic form to an equivalent exponential form:

(A) $\log_3 9 = 2$ (B) $\log_4 2 = \frac{1}{2}$ (C) $\log_3 \left(\frac{1}{9}\right) = -2$

EXAMPLE 2   **Exponential–Logarithmic Conversions** Change each exponential form to an equivalent logarithmic form:

(A) $64 = 4^3$ (B) $6 = \sqrt{36}$ (C) $\frac{1}{8} = 2^{-3}$

SOLUTION   (A) $64 = 4^3$ is equivalent to $\log_4 64 = 3$
(B) $6 = \sqrt{36}$ is equivalent to $\log_{36} 6 = \frac{1}{2}$
(C) $\frac{1}{8} = 2^{-3}$ is equivalent to $\log_2 \left(\frac{1}{8}\right) = -3$

Matched Problem 2   Change each exponential form to an equivalent logarithmic form:

(A) $49 = 7^2$ (B) $3 = \sqrt{9}$ (C) $\frac{1}{3} = 3^{-1}$

To gain a deeper understanding of logarithmic functions and their relationship to exponential functions, we consider a few problems where we want to find x, b, or y in $y = \log_b x$, given the other two values. All values are chosen so that the problems can be solved exactly without a calculator.

EXAMPLE 3 **Solutions of the Equation** $y = \log_b x$ Find $y, b,$ or $x,$ as indicated.

(A) Find y: $y = \log_4 16$ (B) Find x: $\log_2 x = -3$
(C) Find b: $\log_b 100 = 2$

SOLUTION (A) $y = \log_4 16$ is equivalent to $16 = 4^y$. So,
$$y = 2$$

(B) $\log_2 x = -3$ is equivalent to $x = 2^{-3}$. So,
$$x = \frac{1}{2^3} = \frac{1}{8}$$

(C) $\log_b 100 = 2$ is equivalent to $100 = b^2$. So,
$$b = 10 \quad \text{Recall that } b \text{ cannot be negative.}$$

Matched Problem 3 Find $y, b,$ or $x,$ as indicated.

(A) Find y: $y = \log_9 27$ (B) Find x: $\log_3 x = -1$
(C) Find b: $\log_b 1{,}000 = 3$

Properties of Logarithmic Functions

Logarithmic functions have many powerful and useful properties. We list eight basic properties in Theorem 1.

THEOREM 1   Properties of Logarithmic Functions
If $b, M,$ and N are positive real numbers, $b \neq 1,$ and p and x are real numbers, then

1. $\log_b 1 = 0$
2. $\log_b b = 1$
3. $\log_b b^x = x$
4. $b^{\log_b x} = x, \quad x > 0$
5. $\log_b MN = \log_b M + \log_b N$
6. $\log_b \dfrac{M}{N} = \log_b M - \log_b N$
7. $\log_b M^p = p \log_b M$
8. $\log_b M = \log_b N$ if and only if $M = N$

EXAMPLE 4 **Using Logarithmic Properties**

(A) $\log_b \dfrac{wx}{yz}$ $= \log_b wx - \log_b yz$
$= \log_b w + \log_b x - (\log_b y + \log_b z)$
$= \log_b w + \log_b x - \log_b y - \log_b z$

(B) $\log_b (wx)^{3/5} = \frac{3}{5}\log_b wx = \frac{3}{5}(\log_b w + \log_b x)$

(C) $e^{x \log_e b} = e^{\log_e b^x} = b^x$

(D) $\dfrac{\log_e x}{\log_e b} = \dfrac{\log_e(b^{\log_b x})}{\log_e b} = \dfrac{(\log_b x)(\log_e b)}{\log_e b} = \log_b x$

Matched Problem 4 Write in simpler forms, as in Example 4.

(A) $\log_b \dfrac{R}{ST}$ (B) $\log_b \left(\dfrac{R}{S}\right)^{2/3}$ (C) $2^{u \log_2 b}$ (D) $\dfrac{\log_2 x}{\log_2 b}$

The following examples and problems will give you additional practice in using basic logarithmic properties.

EXAMPLE 5 **Solving Logarithmic Equations** Find x so that

$$\tfrac{3}{2}\log_b 4 - \tfrac{2}{3}\log_b 8 + \log_b 2 = \log_b x$$

SOLUTION

$$\tfrac{3}{2}\log_b 4 - \tfrac{2}{3}\log_b 8 + \log_b 2 = \log_b x$$

$$\log_b 4^{3/2} - \log_b 8^{2/3} + \log_b 2 = \log_b x \qquad \text{Property 7}$$

$$\log_b 8 - \log_b 4 + \log_b 2 = \log_b x$$

$$\log_b \frac{8 \cdot 2}{4} = \log_b x \qquad \text{Properties 5 and 6}$$

$$\log_b 4 = \log_b x$$

$$x = 4 \qquad \text{Property 8}$$

Matched Problem 5 Find x so that $3\log_b 2 + \tfrac{1}{2}\log_b 25 - \log_b 20 = \log_b x$.

EXAMPLE 6 **Solving Logarithmic Equations** Solve: $\log_{10} x + \log_{10}(x + 1) = \log_{10} 6$.

SOLUTION

$$\log_{10} x + \log_{10}(x + 1) = \log_{10} 6$$

$$\log_{10}[x(x + 1)] = \log_{10} 6 \qquad \text{Property 5}$$

$$x(x + 1) = 6 \qquad \text{Property 8}$$

$$x^2 + x - 6 = 0 \qquad \text{Solve by factoring.}$$

$$(x + 3)(x - 2) = 0$$

$$x = -3, 2$$

We must exclude $x = -3$, since the domain of the function $\log_{10}(x + 1)$ is $x > -1$ or $(-1, \infty)$; so $x = 2$ is the only solution.

Matched Problem 6 Solve: $\log_3 x + \log_3(x - 3) = \log_3 10$.

Calculator Evaluation of Logarithms

Of all possible logarithmic bases, e and 10 are used almost exclusively. Before we can use logarithms in certain practical problems, we need to be able to approximate the logarithm of any positive number either to base 10 or to base e. And conversely, if we are given the logarithm of a number to base 10 or base e, we need to be able to approximate the number. Historically, tables were used for this purpose, but now calculators make computations faster and far more accurate.

Common logarithms are logarithms with base 10. **Natural logarithms** are logarithms with base e. Most calculators have a key labeled "log" (or "LOG") and a key labeled "ln" (or "LN"). The former represents a common (base 10) logarithm and the latter a natural (base e) logarithm. In fact, "log" and "ln" are both used extensively in mathematical literature, and whenever you see either used in this book without a base indicated, they will be interpreted as follows:

> **Common logarithm:** $\log x$ means $\log_{10} x$
>
> **Natural logarithm:** $\ln x$ means $\log_e x$

Finding the common or natural logarithm using a calculator is very easy. On some calculators, you simply enter a number from the domain of the function and press LOG or LN. On other calculators, you press either LOG or LN, enter a number from the domain, and then press ENTER. Check the user's manual for your calculator.

EXAMPLE 7   **Calculator Evaluation of Logarithms**   Use a calculator to evaluate each to six decimal places:

(A) log 3,184   (B) ln 0.000 349   (C) log(−3.24)

SOLUTION   (A) log 3,184 = 3.502 973
(B) ln 0.000 349 = −7.960 439
(C) log(−3.24) = Error*   *−3.24 is not in the domain of the log function.*

Matched Problem 7   Use a calculator to evaluate each to six decimal places:

(A) log 0.013 529

(B) ln 28.693 28

(C) ln(−0.438)

Given the logarithm of a number, how do you find the number? We make direct use of the logarithmic–exponential relationships, which follow from the definition of logarithmic function given at the beginning of this section.

$$\log x = y \quad \text{is equivalent to} \quad x = 10^{y}$$
$$\ln x = y \quad \text{is equivalent to} \quad x = e^{y}$$

EXAMPLE 8   **Solving $\log_b x = y$ for x**   Find x to four decimal places, given the indicated logarithm:

(A) log x = −2.315   (B) ln x = 2.386

SOLUTION   (A) log x = −2.315   *Change to equivalent exponential form.*
$x = 10^{-2.315}$ *Evaluate with a calculator.*
= 0.0048

(B)   ln x = 2.386   *Change to equivalent exponential form.*
$x = e^{2.386}$ *Evaluate with a calculator.*
= 10.8699

Matched Problem 8   Find x to four decimal places, given the indicated logarithm:

(A) ln x = −5.062   (B) log x = 2.0821

We can use logarithms to solve exponential equations.

EXAMPLE 9   **Solving Exponential Equations**   Solve for x to four decimal places:

(A) $10^x = 2$ (B) $e^x = 3$ (C) $3^x = 4$

SOLUTION   (A) $10^x = 2$ *Take common logarithms of both sides.*
$\log 10^x = \log 2$ *Property 3*
$x = \log 2$ *Use a calculator.*
= 0.3010   *To four decimal places*

---

*Some calculators use a more advanced definition of logarithms involving complex numbers and will display an ordered pair of real numbers as the value of log(−3.24). You should interpret such a result as an indication that the number entered is not in the domain of the logarithm function as we have defined it.

Mathematics of Finance

3

Introduction

How do I choose the right loan for college? Would it be better to take the dealer's financing or the rebate for my new car? Should my parents refinance their home mortgage? To make wise decisions in such matters, you need a basic understanding of the mathematics of finance.

In Chapter 3 we study the mathematics of simple and compound interest, ordinary annuities, auto loans, and home mortgage loans (see Problems 27–30 in Section 3-4). You will need a calculator with logarithmic and exponential keys. A graphing calculator would be even better: It can help you visualize the rate at which an investment grows or the rate at which principal on a loan is amortized.

You may wish to review arithmetic and geometric sequences, discussed in Appendix B-2, before beginning this chapter.

Finally, to avoid repeating the following reminder many times, we emphasize it here: Throughout the chapter, **interest rates are to be converted to decimal form before they are used in a formula**.

3-1 Simple Interest

The Simple Interest Formula

Simple interest is used on short-term notes—often of duration less than 1 year. The concept of simple interest, however, forms the basis of much of the rest of the material developed in this chapter, for which time periods may be much longer than a year.

If you deposit a sum of money P in a savings account or if you borrow a sum of money P from a lender, then P is referred to as the **principal**. When money is borrowed—whether it is a savings institution borrowing from you when you deposit money in your account, or you borrowing from a lender—a fee is charged for the money borrowed. This fee is rent paid for the use of another's money, just as rent is paid for the use of another's house. The fee is called **interest**. It is usually computed as a percentage (called the **interest rate**)* of the principal over a given period of time. The interest rate, unless otherwise stated, is an annual rate. **Simple interest** is given by the following formula:

> **DEFINITION Simple Interest**
>
> $$I = Prt \tag{1}$$
>
> where I = interest
> P = principal
> r = annual simple interest rate (written as a decimal)
> t = time in years

For example, the interest on a loan of $100 at 12% for 9 months would be

$$I = Prt$$
$$= (100)(0.12)(0.75)$$
$$= \$9$$

Convert 12% to a decimal (0.12) and 9 months to years $\left(\frac{9}{12} = 0.75\right)$.

At the end of 9 months, the borrower would repay the principal ($100) plus the interest ($9), or a total of $109.

In general, if a principal P is borrowed at a rate r, then after t years, the borrower will owe the lender an amount A that will include the principal P plus the interest I. Since P is the amount that is borrowed now and A is the amount that must be paid back in the future, P is often referred to as the **present value** and A as the **future value**. The formula relating A and P follows:

> **THEOREM 1 Simple Interest**
>
> $$A = P + Prt$$
> $$= P(1 + rt) \tag{2}$$
>
> where A = amount, or future value
> P = principal, or present value
> r = annual simple interest rate (written as a decimal)
> t = time in years

Given any three of the four variables A, P, r, and t in (2), we can solve for the fourth. The following examples illustrate several types of common problems that can be solved by using formula (2).

---

*If r is the interest rate written as a decimal, then $100r\%$ is the rate using %. For example, if $r = 0.12$, then $100r\% = 100(0.12)\% = 12\%$. The expressions 0.12 and 12% are equivalent.

EXAMPLE 1 **Total Amount Due on a Loan** Find the total amount due on a loan of $800 at 9% simple interest at the end of 4 months.

SOLUTION To find the amount A (future value) due in 4 months, we use formula (2) with $P = 800$, $r = 0.09$, and $t = \frac{4}{12} = \frac{1}{3}$ year. Thus,

$$
\begin{aligned}
A &= P(1 + rt) \\
&= 800\left[1 + 0.09\left(\tfrac{1}{3}\right)\right] \\
&= 800(1.03) \\
&= \$824
\end{aligned}
$$

Matched Problem 1 Find the total amount due on a loan of $500 at 12% simple interest at the end of 30 months.

EXPLORE & DISCUSS 1

(A) Your sister has loaned you $1,000 with the understanding that you will repay the principal plus 4% simple interest when you can. How much would you owe her if you repaid the loan after 1 year? After 2 years? After 5 years? After 10 years?

(B) How is the interest after 10 years related to the interest after 1 year? After 2 years? After 5 years?

(C) Explain why your answers are consistent with the fact that for simple interest, the graph of future value as a function of time is a straight line (Fig. 1).

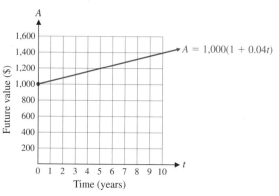

Figure 1

EXAMPLE 2 **Present Value of an Investment** If you want to earn an annual rate of 10% on your investments, how much (to the nearest cent) should you pay for a note that will be worth $5,000 in 9 months?

SOLUTION We again use formula (2), but now we are interested in finding the principal P (present value), given $A = \$5,000$, $r = 0.1$, and $t = \frac{9}{12} = 0.75$ year. Thus,

$$
\begin{aligned}
A &= P(1 + rt) \\
5,000 &= P[1 + 0.1(0.75)] \qquad \text{\small Replace A, r, and t with the given} \\
5,000 &= (1.075)P \qquad\qquad\quad\ \text{\small values, and solve for P.} \\
P &= \$4,651.16
\end{aligned}
$$

Matched Problem 2 Repeat Example 2 with a time period of 6 months.

CONCEPTUAL INSIGHT

If we consider future value A as a function of time t with the present value P and the annual rate r being fixed, then $A = P + Prt$ is a linear function of t with y intercept P and slope Pr. For example, if $P = 1,000$ and $r = 0.04$ (Fig. 1), then

$$A = 1,000(1 + 0.04t) = 1,000 + 40t$$

is a linear function with y intercept 1,000 and slope 40.

Simple Interest and Investments

EXAMPLE 3 **Interest Rate Earned on a Note** T-bills (Treasury bills) are one of the instruments that the U.S. Treasury Department uses to finance the public debt. If you buy a 180-day T-bill with a maturity value of $10,000 for $9,893.78, what annual simple interest rate will you earn? (Express answer as a percentage, correct to three decimal places.)

SOLUTION Again we use formula (2), but this time we are interested in finding r, given $P = \$9{,}893.78$, $A = \$10{,}000$, and $t = 180/360 = 0.5$ year.*

$$A = P(1 + rt)$$ *Replace P, A, and t with the*
$$10{,}000 = 9{,}893.78(1 + 0.5r)$$ *given values, and solve for r.*
$$10{,}000 = 9{,}893.78 + 4{,}946.89r$$
$$106.22 = 4{,}946.89r$$
$$r = \frac{106.22}{4{,}946.89} \approx 0.02147 \quad \text{or} \quad 2.147\%$$

Matched Problem 3 Repeat Example 3, assuming that you pay $9,828.74 for the T-bill.

EXAMPLE 4 **Interest Rate Earned on an Investment** Suppose that after buying a new car you decide to sell your old car to a friend. You accept a 270-day note for $3,500 at 10% simple interest as payment. (Both principal and interest are paid at the end of 270 days.) Sixty days later you find that you need the money and sell the note to a third party for $3,550. What annual interest rate will the third party receive for the investment? Express the answer as a percentage, correct to three decimal places.

SOLUTION **Step 1** Find the amount that will be paid at the end of 270 days to the holder of the note.

$$A = P(1 + rt)$$
$$= \$3{,}500\left[1 + (0.1)\left(\tfrac{270}{360}\right)\right]$$
$$= \$3{,}762.50$$

Step 2 For the third party, we are to find the annual rate of interest r required to make $3,550 grow to $3,762.50 in 210 days $(270 - 60)$; that is, we are to find r (which is to be converted to $100\,r\%$), given $A = \$3{,}762.50$, $P = \$3{,}550$, and $t = \frac{210}{360}$.

$$A = P + Prt \quad \text{Solve for r.}$$
$$r = \frac{A - P}{Pt}$$
$$r = \frac{3{,}762.50 - 3{,}550}{(3{,}550)\left(\tfrac{210}{360}\right)} \approx 0.102\,62 \quad \text{or} \quad 10.262\%$$

Matched Problem 4 Repeat Example 4 assuming that 90 days after it was initially signed, the note was sold to a third party for $3,500.

---

*In situations that involve days, some institutions use a 360-day year, called a banker's year, to simplify calculations. In this section, we will use a 360-day year. In other sections, we will use a 365-day year. The choice will always be clearly stated.

Some online discount brokerage firms offer flat rates for trading stock, but many still charge commissions based on the transaction amount (principal). Table 1 shows the commission schedule for one of these firms.

Table 1 Commission Schedule	
Principal	**Commission**
$0–$2,499	$29 + 1.6% of principal
$2,500–$9,999	$49 + 0.8% of principal
$10,000+	$99 + 0.3% of principal

EXAMPLE 5　**Interest on an Investment**　An investor purchases 50 shares of a stock at $47.52 per share. After 200 days, the investor sells the stock for $52.19 per share. Using Table 1, find the annual rate of interest earned by this investment. Express the answer as a percentage, correct to three decimal places.

SOLUTION　The principal referred to in Table 1 is the value of the stock. The total cost for the investor is the cost of the stock plus the commission:

$$47.52(50) = \$2,376 \qquad \text{Principal}$$
$$29 + 0.016(2,376) = \$67.02 \qquad \text{Commission, using line 1 of Table 1}$$
$$2,376 + 67.02 = \$2,443.02 \qquad \text{Total investment}$$

When the stock is sold, the commission is subtracted from the proceeds of the sale and the remainder is returned to the investor:

$$52.19(50) = \$2,609.50 \qquad \text{Principal}$$
$$49 + 0.008(2,609.50) = \$69.88 \qquad \text{Commission, using line 2 of Table 1}$$
$$2,609.50 - 69.88 = \$2,539.62 \qquad \text{Total return}$$

Now using formula (2) with $A = 2,539.62, P = 2,443.02,$ and $t = \dfrac{200}{360} = \dfrac{5}{9}$, we have

$$A = P(1 + rt)$$
$$2,539.62 = 2,443.02\left(1 + \frac{5}{9}r\right)$$
$$= 2,443.02 + 1,357.23r$$
$$96.60 = 1,357.23r$$
$$r = \frac{96.60}{1,357.23} \approx 0.07117 \quad \text{or} \quad 7.117\%$$

Matched Problem 5　Repeat Example 5 if 500 shares of stock were purchased for $17.64 per share and sold 270 days later for $22.36 per share.

> **CONCEPTUAL INSIGHT**
>
> The commission schedule in Table 1 specifies a piecewise defined function C with independent variable p, the principal (see Section 2-2).
>
> $$C = \begin{cases} 29 + 0.016p & \text{if } 0 \le p < 2,500 \\ 49 + 0.008p & \text{if } 2,500 \le p < 10,000 \\ 99 + 0.003p & \text{if } 10,000 \le p \end{cases}$$

Exercises 3-1

A

In Problems 1–8, convert the given interest rate to decimal form if it is given as a percentage, and to a percentage if it is given in decimal form.

1. 3%   **2.** 5.25%

3. 0.105   **4.** 0.08

5. 4.75%   **6.** 16%

7. 0.21   **8.** 0.005

In Problems 9–16, convert the given time period to years, in fraction form, assuming a 360-day year [this assumption does not affect the number of quarters (4), months (12), or weeks (52) in a year].

9. 4 months   **10.** 39 weeks

11. 240 days   **12.** 6 quarters

13. 12 weeks   **14.** 10 months

15. 2 quarters   **16.** 30 days

In Problems 17–24, use formula (1) for simple interest to find each of the indicated quantities.

17. $P = \$300; r = 7\%; t = 2$ years; $I = $?

18. $P = \$950; r = 9\%; t = 1$ year; $I = $?

19. $I = \$36; r = 4\%; t = 6$ months; $P = $?

20. $I = \$15; r = 8\%; t = 3$ quarters; $P = $?

21. $I = \$48; P = \$600; t = 240$ days; $r = $?

22. $I = \$28; P = \$700; t = 13$ weeks; $r = $?

23. $I = \$60; P = \$2,400; r = 5\%; t = $?

24. $I = \$96; P = \$3,200; r = 4\%; t = $?

B

In Problems 25–32, use formula (2) for the amount to find each of the indicated quantities.

25. $P = \$4,500; r = 10\%; t = 1$ quarter; $A = $?

26. $P = \$3,000; r = 4.5\%; t = 30$ days; $A = $?

27. $A = \$910; r = 16\%; t = 13$ weeks; $P = $?

28. $A = \$6,608; r = 24\%; t = 3$ quarters; $P = $?

29. $A = \$14,560; P = \$13,000; t = 4$ months; $r = $?

30. $A = \$22,135; P = \$19,000; t = 39$ weeks; $r = $?

31. $A = \$736; P = \$640; r = 15\%; t = $?

32. $A = \$410; P = \$400; r = 10\%; t = $?

C

In Problems 33–38, solve each formula for the indicated variable.

33. $I = Prt$; for r **34.** $I = Prt$; for P

35. $A = P + Prt$; for P **36.** $A = P + Prt$; for r

37. $A = P(1 + rt)$; for t **38.** $I = Prt$; for t

39. Discuss the similarities and differences in the graphs of future value A as a function of time t if $1,000 is invested at simple interest at rates of 4%, 8%, and 12%, respectively (see the figure).

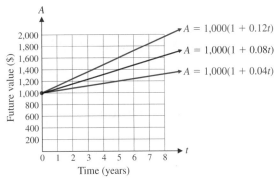

Figure for 39

40. Discuss the similarities and differences in the graphs of future value A as a function of time t for loans of $400, $800, and $1,200, respectively, each at 7.5% simple interest (see the figure).

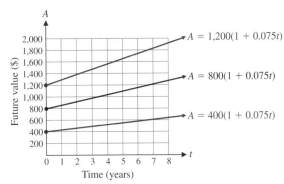

Figure for 40

Applications*

In all problems involving days, a 360-day year is assumed. When annual rates are requested as an answer, express the rate as a percentage, correct to three decimal places. Round dollar amounts to the nearest cent.

41. If $3,000 is loaned for 4 months at a 4.5% annual rate, how much interest is earned?

42. If $5,000 is loaned for 9 months at a 6.2% annual rate, how much interest is earned?

43. How much interest will you have to pay for a credit card balance of $554 that is 1 month overdue, if a 20% annual rate is charged?

---

*The authors wish to thank Professor Roy Luke of Pierce College and Professor Dennis Pence of Western Michigan University for their many useful suggestions of applications for this chapter.

44. A department store charges an 18% annual rate for overdue accounts. How much interest will be owed on an $835 account that is 2 months overdue?

45. A loan of $7,260 was repaid at the end of 8 months. What size repayment check (principal and interest) was written, if an 8% annual rate of interest was charged?

46. A loan of $10,000 was repaid at the end of 6 months. What amount (principal and interest) was repaid, if a 6.5% annual rate of interest was charged?

47. A loan of $4,000 was repaid at the end of 10 months with a check for $4,270. What annual rate of interest was charged?

48. A check for $3,097.50 was used to retire a 5-month $3,000 loan. What annual rate of interest was charged?

49. If you paid $30 to a loan company for the use of $1,000 for 60 days, what annual rate of interest did they charge?

50. If you paid $120 to a loan company for the use of $2,000 for 90 days, what annual rate of interest did they charge?

51. A radio commercial for a loan company states: "You only pay 29¢ a day for each $500 borrowed." If you borrow $1,500 for 120 days, what amount will you repay, and what annual interest rate is the company charging?

52. George finds a company that charges 59¢ per day for each $1,000 borrowed. If he borrows $3,000 for 60 days, what amount will he repay, and what annual interest rate will he pay the company?

53. What annual interest rate is earned by a 13-week T-bill with a maturity value of $1,000 that sells for $989.37?

54. What annual interest rate is earned by a 33-day T-bill with a maturity value of $1,000 that sells for $996.16?

55. What is the purchase price of a 50-day T-bill with a maturity value of $1,000 that earns an annual interest rate of 5.53%?

56. What is the purchase price of a 26-week T-bill with a maturity value of $1,000 that earns an annual interest rate of 4.903%?

57. For services rendered, an attorney accepts a 90-day note for $5,500 at 8% simple interest from a client. (Both interest and principal are repaid at the end of 90 days.) Wishing to use her money sooner, the attorney sells the note to a third party for $5,560 after 30 days. What annual interest rate will the third party receive for the investment?

58. To complete the sale of a house, the seller accepts a 180-day note for $10,000 at 7% simple interest. (Both interest and principal are repaid at the end of 180 days.) Wishing to use the money sooner for the purchase of another house, the seller sells the note to a third party for $10,124 after 60 days. What annual interest rate will the third party receive for the investment?

Use the commission schedule from Company A shown in Table 2 to find the annual rate of interest earned by each investment in Problems 59 and 60.

Table 2 Company A

Principal	Commission
Under $3,000	$25 + 1.8% of principal
$3,000–$10,000	$37 + 1.4% of principal
Over $10,000	$107 + 0.7% of principal

59. An investor purchases 200 shares at $14.20 a share, holds the stock for 39 weeks, and then sells the stock for $15.75 a share.

60. An investor purchases 450 shares at $21.40 a share, holds the stock for 26 weeks, and then sells the stock for $24.60 a share.

Use the commission schedule from Company B shown in Table 3 to find the annual rate of interest earned by each investment in Problems 61 and 62.

Table 3 Company B

Principal	Commission
Under $3,000	$32 + 1.8% of principal
$3,000–$10,000	$56 + 1% of principal
Over $10,000	$106 + 0.5% of principal

61. An investor purchases 215 shares at $45.75 a share, holds the stock for 300 days, and then sells the stock for $51.90 a share.

62. An investor purchases 75 shares at $37.90 a share, holds the stock for 150 days, and then sells the stock for $41.20 a share.

Many tax preparation firms offer their clients a refund anticipation loan (RAL). For a fee, the firm will give a client his refund when the return is filed. The loan is repaid when the IRS refund is sent to the firm. The RAL fee is equivalent to the interest charge for a loan. The schedule in Table 4 is from a major RAL lender. Use this schedule to find the annual rate of interest for the RALs in Problems 63–66.

Table 4

RAL Amount	RAL Fee
$0–$500	$29.00
$501–$1,000	$39.00
$1,001–$1,500	$49.00
$1,501–$2,000	$69.00
$2,001–$5,000	$89.00

63. A client receives a $475 RAL, which is paid back in 20 days.

64. A client receives a $1,100 RAL, which is paid back in 30 days.

65. A client receives a $1,900 RAL, which is paid back in 15 days.

66. A client receives a $3,000 RAL, which is paid back in 25 days.

Answers to Matched Problems

1. $650

2. $4,761.90

3. 3.485%

4. 15.0%

5. 31.439%

3-2   Compound and Continuous Compound Interest

Compound Interest

If at the end of a payment period the interest due is reinvested at the same rate, then the interest as well as the original principal will earn interest during the next payment period. Interest paid on interest reinvested is called **compound interest**.

For example, suppose you deposit $1,000 in a bank that pays 8% compounded quarterly. How much will the bank owe you at the end of a year? *Compounding quarterly* means that earned interest is paid to your account at the end of each 3-month period and that interest as well as the principal earns interest for the next quarter. Using the simple interest formula (2) from the preceding section, we compute the amount in the account at the end of the first quarter after interest has been paid:

$$A = P(1 + rt)$$
$$= 1,000\left[1 + 0.08\left(\tfrac{1}{4}\right)\right]$$
$$= 1,000(1.02) = \$1,020$$

Now, $1,020 is your new principal for the second quarter. At the end of the second quarter, after interest is paid, the account will have

$$A = \$1,020\left[1 + 0.08\left(\tfrac{1}{4}\right)\right]$$
$$= \$1,020(1.02) = \$1,040.40$$

Similarly, at the end of the third quarter, you will have

$$A = \$1,040.40\left[1 + 0.08\left(\tfrac{1}{4}\right)\right]$$
$$= \$1,040.40(1.02) = \$1,061.21$$

Finally, at the end of the fourth quarter, the account will have

$$A = \$1,061.21\left[1 + 0.08\left(\tfrac{1}{4}\right)\right]$$
$$= \$1,061.21(1.02) = \$1,082.43$$

How does this compounded amount compare with simple interest? The amount with simple interest would be

$$A = P(1 + rt)$$
$$= \$1,000[1 + 0.08(1)]$$
$$= \$1,000(1.08) = \$1,080$$

We see that compounding quarterly yields $2.43 more than simple interest would provide.

Let's look over the calculations for compound interest above to see if we can uncover a pattern that might lead to a general formula for computing compound interest:

$$A = 1,000(1.02) \qquad \text{End of first quarter}$$
$$A = [1,000(1.02)](1.02) = 1,000(1.02)^2 \qquad \text{End of second quarter}$$
$$A = [1,000(1.02)^2](1.02) = 1,000(1.02)^3 \qquad \text{End of third quarter}$$
$$A = [1,000(1.02)^3](1.02) = 1,000(1.02)^4 \qquad \text{End of fourth quarter}$$

It appears that at the end of n quarters, we would have

$$A = 1,000(1.02)^n \qquad \text{End of nth quarter}$$

or

$$A = 1,000\left[1 + 0.08\left(\tfrac{1}{4}\right)\right]^n$$
$$= 1,000\left[1 + \tfrac{0.08}{4}\right]^n$$

where $\frac{0.08}{4} = 0.02$ is the interest rate per quarter. Since interest rates are generally quoted as *annual nominal rates*, the **rate per compounding period** is found by dividing the annual nominal rate by the number of compounding periods per year.

> **THEOREM 2   Continuous Compound Interest Formula**
> If a principal P is invested at an annual rate r (expressed as a decimal) compounded continuously, then the amount A in the account at the end of t years is given by
> $$A = Pe^{rt} \qquad\qquad (2)$$

EXAMPLE 2   **Compounding Daily and Continuously** What amount will an account have after 2 years if $5,000 is invested at an annual rate of 8%

(A) compounded daily?   (B) compounded continuously?

Compute answers to the nearest cent.

SOLUTION   (A) Use the compounded interest formula

$$A = P\left(1 + \frac{r}{m}\right)^{mt}$$

with $P = 5{,}000$, $r = 0.08$, $m = 365$, and $t = 2$:

$$A = 5{,}000\left(1 + \frac{0.08}{365}\right)^{(365)(2)} \qquad \textit{Use a calculator.}$$

$$= \$5{,}867.45$$

(B) Use the continuous compound interest formula

$$A = Pe^{rt}$$

with $P = 5{,}000$, $r = 0.08$, and $t = 2$:

$$A = 5{,}000e^{(0.08)(2)} \qquad \textit{Use a calculator.}$$

$$= \$5{,}867.55$$

⚠ **CAUTION** In Example 2B, do not use the approximation 2.7183 for e; it is not accurate enough to compute the correct amount to the nearest cent. Instead, use your calculator's built-in e. Avoid any rounding off until the end of the calculation, when you round the amount to the nearest cent.

Matched Problem 2   What amount will an account have after 1.5 years if $8,000 is invested at an annual rate of 9%

(A) compounded weekly?   (B) compounded continuously?

Compute answers to the nearest cent.

CONCEPTUAL INSIGHT

The continuous compound interest formula $A = Pe^{rt}$ is identical, except for the names of the variables, to the equation $y = ce^{kt}$ that we used to model population growth in Section 2-4. Like the growth of an investment that earns continuous compound interest, we usually consider the population growth of a country to be continuous: Births and deaths occur all the time, not just at the end of a month or quarter.

Growth and Time

How much should you invest now to have a given amount at a future date? What annual rate of return have your investments earned? How long will it take your investment to double in value? The formulas for compound interest and continuous compound interest can be used to answer such questions. If the values of all but one of the variables in the formula are known, then we can solve for the remaining variable.

EXAMPLE 3   **Finding Present Value** How much should you invest now at 10% to have $8,000 toward the purchase of a car in 5 years if interest is

(A) compounded quarterly?   (B) compounded continuously?

SOLUTION   (A) We are given a future value $A = \$8{,}000$ for a compound interest investment, and we need to find the present value P given $i = \frac{0.10}{4} = 0.025$ and $n = 4(5) = 20$.

$$A = P(1 + i)^n$$

$$8{,}000 = P(1 + 0.025)^{20}$$

$$P = \frac{8{,}000}{(1 + 0.025)^{20}} \qquad \text{Use a calculator.}$$

$$= \frac{8{,}000}{1.638\,616}$$

$$= \$4{,}882.17$$

Your initial investment of $4,882.17 will grow to $8,000 in 5 years.

(B) We are given $A = \$8{,}000$ for an investment at continuous compound interest, and we need to find the present value P given $r = 0.10$ and $t = 5$.

$$A = Pe^{rt}$$

$$8{,}000 = Pe^{0.10(5)}$$

$$P = \frac{8{,}000}{e^{0.10(5)}} \qquad \text{Use a calculator.}$$

$$P = \$4{,}852.25$$

Your initial investment of $4,852.25 will grow to $8,000 in 5 years.

Matched Problem 3   How much should new parents invest at 8% to have $80,000 toward their child's college education in 17 years if interest is

(A) compounded semiannually?   (B) compounded continuously?

A graphing calculator is a useful tool for studying compound interest. In Figure 2, we use a spreadsheet to illustrate the growth of the investment in Example 3A both numerically and graphically. Similar results can be obtained from most graphing calculators.

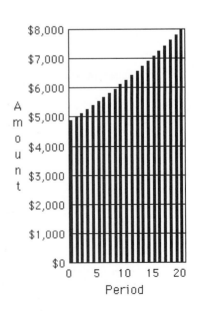

	A	B	C
	Period	Interest	Amount
1			
2	0		$4,882.17
3	1	$122.05	$5,004.22
4	2	$125.11	$5,129.33
5	3	$128.23	$5,257.56
6	4	$131.44	$5,389.00
7	5	$134.73	$5,523.73
8	6	$138.09	$5,661.82
9	7	$141.55	$5,803.37
10	8	$145.08	$5,948.45
11	9	$148.71	$6,097.16
12	10	$152.43	$6,249.59
13	11	$156.24	$6,405.83
14	12	$160.15	$6,565.98
15	13	$164.15	$6,730.13
16	14	$168.25	$6,898.38
17	15	$172.46	$7,070.84
18	16	$176.77	$7,247.61
19	17	$181.19	$7,428.80
20	18	$185.72	$7,614.52
21	19	$190.36	$7,804.88
22	20	$195.12	$8,000.00

Figure 2 Growth of $4,882.17 at 10% compounded quarterly for 5 years

Solving the compound interest formula or the continuous compound interest formula for r enables us to determine the rate of growth of an investment.

EXAMPLE 4   **Computing Growth Rate** Figure 3 shows that a $10,000 investment in a growth-oriented mutual fund over a recent 10-year period would have grown to $126,000. What annual nominal rate would produce the same growth if interest was:

(A) compounded annually?   (B) compounded continuously?

Express answers as percentages, rounded to three decimal places.

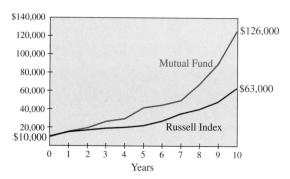

Figure 3 Growth of a $10,000 investment

SOLUTION   (A) $126,000 = 10,000 (1 + r)^{10}$

$$12.6 = (1 + r)^{10}$$

$$\sqrt[10]{12.6} = 1 + r$$

$$r = \sqrt[10]{12.6} - 1 = 0.28836 \quad \text{or} \quad 28.836\%$$

(B) $126,000 = 10,000e^{r(10)}$

$$12.6 = e^{10r} \qquad\qquad\qquad \textit{Take ln of both sides.}$$

$$\ln 12.6 = 10r$$

$$r = \frac{\ln 12.6}{10} = 0.25337 \quad \text{or} \quad 25.337\%$$

Matched Problem 4   The Russell Index tracks the average performance of various groups of stocks. Figure 3 shows that, on average, a $10,000 investment in midcap growth funds over a recent 10-year period would have grown to $63,000. What annual nominal rate would produce the same growth if interest were

(A) compounded annually?   (B) compounded continuously?

Express answers as percentages, rounded to three decimal places.

CONCEPTUAL INSIGHT

We can solve $A = P(1 + i)^n$ for n using a property of logarithms:

$$\log_b M^p = p \log_b M$$

Theoretically, any base can be used for the logarithm, but most calculators only evaluate logarithms with base 10 (denoted log) or base e (denoted ln).

Finally, if we solve the compound interest formula for n (or the continuous compound interest formula for t), we can determine the **growth time** of an investment — the time it takes a given principal to grow to a particular value (the shorter the time, the greater the return on the investment).

Example 5 illustrates three methods for solving for growth time.

EXAMPLE 5   **Computing Growth Time** How long will it take $10,000 to grow to $12,000 if it is invested at 9% compounded monthly?

SOLUTION   **Method 1.** Use logarithms and a calculator:

$$A = P(1 + i)^n$$

$$12,000 = 10,000\left(1 + \frac{0.09}{12}\right)^n$$

$$1.2 = 1.0075^n$$

Now, solve for n by taking logarithms of both sides:

$\ln 1.2 = \ln 1.0075^n$ *We choose the natural logarithm (base e)*

$\ln 1.2 = n \ln 1.0075$ *and use the property $\ln M^p = p \ln M$.*

$$n = \frac{\ln 1.2}{\ln 1.0075}$$

$$\approx 24.40 \approx 25 \text{ months}\quad\text{or}\quad 2 \text{ years and 1 month}$$

Note: 24.40 is rounded up to 25 to guarantee reaching $12,000 since interest is paid at the end of each month.

14000

0 ⟍⟍⟍ 50

Intersection
X=24.400588 Y=12000

10000

$y_1 = 10000(1.0075)^x$
$y_2 = 12000$

Figure 4

Method 2. Use a graphing calculator: To solve this problem using graphical approximation techniques, we graph both sides of the equation $12,000 = 10,000(1.0075)^n$ and find that the graphs intersect at $x = n = 24.40$ months (Fig. 4). So, the growth time is 25 months.

A-P(1+I)^N=0
 A=12000
 P=10000
 I=.0075
■N=24.400588158...
 bound={-1E99,1...
■left-rt=0

(B)

Figure 5 TI-84 equation solver

Method 3. Most graphing calculators have an approximation process that is referred to as **equation solver**. Figure 5 shows the equation solver on a TI-84. Notice that this solver requires that one side of the equation is equal to zero (see the first line in Fig. 5). After entering values for three of the four variables, the solver will approximate the value of the remaining variable. Once again, we see that the growth time is 25 months (Fig. 5).

Matched Problem 5   How long will it take $10,000 to grow to $25,000 if it is invested at 8% compounded quarterly?

Annual Percentage Yield

Table 1 lists the rate and compounding period for certificates of deposit (CDs) recently offered by three banks. How can we tell which of these CDs has the best return?

Table 1   Certificates of Deposit (CDs)

Bank	Rate	Compounded
Advanta	4.93%	monthly
DeepGreen	4.95%	daily
Charter One	4.97%	quarterly
Liberty	4.94%	continuously

EXPLORE & DISCUSS 1

Determine the value after 1 year of a $1,000 CD purchased from each of the banks in Table 1. Which CD offers the greatest return? Which offers the least return?

If a principal P is invested at an annual rate r compounded m times a year, then the amount after 1 year is

$$A = P\left(1 + \frac{r}{m}\right)^m$$

The simple interest rate that will produce the same amount A in 1 year is called the **annual percentage yield** (APY). To find the APY, we proceed as follows:

$$\begin{pmatrix} \text{amount at} \\ \text{simple interest} \\ \text{after 1 year} \end{pmatrix} = \begin{pmatrix} \text{amount at} \\ \text{compound interest} \\ \text{after 1 year} \end{pmatrix}$$

$$P(1 + \text{APY}) = P\left(1 + \frac{r}{m}\right)^m \qquad \textit{Divide both sides by P.}$$

$$1 + \text{APY} = \left(1 + \frac{r}{m}\right)^m \qquad \textit{Isolate APY on the left side.}$$

$$\text{APY} = \left(1 + \frac{r}{m}\right)^m - 1$$

If interest is compounded continuously, then the amount after 1 year is $A = Pe^r$. So to find the annual percentage yield, we solve the equation

$$P(1 + \text{APY}) = Pe^r$$

for APY, obtaining $\text{APY} = e^r - 1$. We summarize our results in Theorem 3.

THEOREM 3 Annual Percentage Yield

If a principal is invested at the annual (nominal) rate r compounded m times a year, then the annual percentage yield is

$$\text{APY} = \left(1 + \frac{r}{m}\right)^m - 1$$

If a principal is invested at the annual (nominal) rate r compounded continuously, then the annual percentage yield is

$$\text{APY} = e^r - 1$$

The annual percentage yield is also referred to as the **effective rate** or **true interest rate**.

Compound rates with different compounding periods cannot be compared directly (see Explore & Discuss 1). But since the annual percentage yield is a simple interest rate, the annual percentage yields for two different compound rates can be compared.

EXAMPLE 6

Using APY to Compare Investments Find the APYs (expressed as a percentage, correct to three decimal places) for each of the banks in Table 1 and compare these CDs.

SOLUTION

$$\text{Advanta: APY} = \left(1 + \frac{0.0493}{12}\right)^{12} - 1 = 0.05043 \quad \text{or} \quad 5.043\%$$

$$\text{DeepGreen: APY} = \left(1 + \frac{0.0495}{365}\right)^{365} - 1 = 0.05074 \quad \text{or} \quad 5.074\%$$

$$\text{Charter One: APY} = \left(1 + \frac{0.0497}{4}\right)^{4} - 1 = 0.05063 \quad \text{or} \quad 5.063\%$$

$$\text{Liberty: APY} = e^{0.0494} - 1 = 0.05064 \quad \text{or} \quad 5.064\%$$

Comparing these APYs, we conclude that the DeepGreen CD will have the largest return and the Advanta CD will have the smallest.

Matched Problem 6 Southern Pacific Bank recently offered a 1-year CD that paid 4.8% compounded daily and Washington Savings Bank offered one that paid 4.85% compounded quarterly. Find the APY (expressed as a percentage, correct to three decimal places) for each CD. Which has the higher return?

EXAMPLE 7 **Computing the Annual Nominal Rate Given the APY** A savings and loan wants to offer a CD with a monthly compounding rate that has an APY of 7.5%. What annual nominal rate compounded monthly should they use?

 Check with a graphing calculator.

SOLUTION

$$\text{APY} = \left(1 + \frac{r}{m}\right)^m - 1$$

$$0.075 = \left(1 + \frac{r}{12}\right)^{12} - 1$$

$$1.075 = \left(1 + \frac{r}{12}\right)^{12}$$

$$\sqrt[12]{1.075} = 1 + \frac{r}{12}$$

$$\sqrt[12]{1.075} - 1 = \frac{r}{12}$$

$$r = 12(\sqrt[12]{1.075} - 1) \qquad \textit{Use a calculator.}$$

$$= 0.072\,539 \quad \text{or} \quad 7.254\%$$

So, an annual nominal rate of 7.254% compounded monthly is equivalent to an APY of 7.5%.

```
A-(1+R/M)^M+1=0
 A=.075
■R=.07253902829…
 M=12
 bound={-1E99,1…
■left-rt=0
```

Figure 6 TI-84 equation solver

 CHECK We use an equation solver on a graphing calculator to check this result (Fig. 6).

Matched Problem 7 What is the annual nominal rate compounded quarterly for a bond that has an APY of 5.8%?

⚠ **CAUTION** Each compound interest problem involves two interest rates. Referring to Example 5, $r = 0.09$ or 9% is the annual nominal compounding rate, and $i = r/12 = 0.0075$ or 0.75% is the interest rate per month. Do not confuse these two rates by using r in place of i in the compound interest formula. If interest is compounded annually, then $i = r/1 = r$. In all other cases, r and i are not the same.

EXPLORE & DISCUSS 2

(A) Which would be the better way to invest $1,000: at 9% simple interest for 10 years, or at 7% compounded monthly for 10 years?

(B) Explain why the graph of future value as a function of time is a straight line for simple interest, but for compound interest the graph curves upward (see Fig. 7).

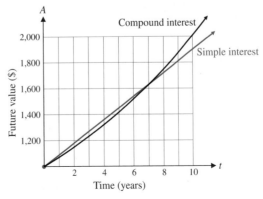

Figure 7

CONCEPTUAL INSIGHT

The two curves in Figure 7 intersect at $t = 0$ and again near $t = 7$. The t coordinate of each intersection point is a solution of the equation

$$1,000(1 + 0.09t) = 1,000(1 + 0.07/12)^{12t}$$

Don't try to use algebra to solve this equation. It can't be done. But the solutions are easily approximated on a graphing calculator (Fig. 8).

Figure 8

Exercises 3-2

Find all dollar amounts to the nearest cent. When an interest rate is requested as an answer, express the rate as a percentage correct to two decimal places, unless directed otherwise. In all problems involving days, use a 365-day year.

A

In Problems 1–4, use compound interest formula (1) to find each of the indicated values.

1. $P = \$5,000$; $i = 0.005$; $n = 36$; $A = ?$

2. $P = \$2,800$; $i = 0.003$; $n = 24$; $A = ?$

3. $A = \$8,000$; $i = 0.02$; $n = 32$; $P = ?$

4. $A = \$15,000$; $i = 0.01$; $n = 28$; $P = ?$

In Problems 5–12, use the continuous compound interest formula (2) to find each of the indicated values.

5. $P = \$2,450$; $r = 8.12\%$; $t = 3$ years; $A = ?$

6. $P = \$995$; $r = 22\%$; $t = 2$ years; $A = ?$

7. $A = \$6,300$; $r = 9.45\%$; $t = 8$ years; $P = ?$

8. $A = \$19,000$; $r = 7.69\%$; $t = 5$ years; $P = ?$

9. $A = \$88,000$; $P = \$71,153$; $r = 8.5\%$; $t = ?$

10. $A = \$32,982$; $P = \$27,200$; $r = 5.93\%$; $t = ?$

11. $A = \$15,875$; $P = \$12,100$; $t = 48$ months; $r = ?$

12. $A = \$23,600$; $P = \$19,150$; $t = 60$ months; $r = ?$

In Problems 13–18, use the given annual interest rate r and the compounding period to find i, the interest rate per compounding period.

13. 9% compounded monthly

14. 6% compounded quarterly

15. 14.6% compounded daily

16. 15% compounded monthly

17. 4.8% compounded quarterly

18. 3.2% compounded semiannually

In Problems 19–24, use the given interest rate i per compounding period to find r, the annual rate.

19. 0.395% per month

20. 0.012% per day

21. 0.9% per quarter

22. 0.175% per month

23. 2.1% per half year

24. 1.4% per quarter

B

25. If \$100 is invested at 6% compounded
(A) annually   (B) quarterly   (C) monthly
what is the amount after 4 years? How much interest is earned?

26. If \$2,000 is invested at 7% compounded
(A) annually   (B) quarterly   (C) monthly
what is the amount after 5 years? How much interest is earned?

27. If \$5,000 is invested at 5% compounded monthly, what is the amount after
(A) 2 years?   (B) 4 years?

28. If \$20,000 is invested at 4% compounded monthly, what is the amount after
(A) 5 years?   (B) 8 years?

29. If \$8,000 is invested at 7% compounded continuously, what is the amount after 6 years?

30. If \$23,000 is invested at 13.5% compounded continuously, what is the amount after 15 years?

31. Discuss the similarities and the differences in the graphs of future value A as a function of time t if \$1,000 is invested for 8 years and interest is compounded monthly at annual rates of 4%, 8%, and 12%, respectively (see the figure).

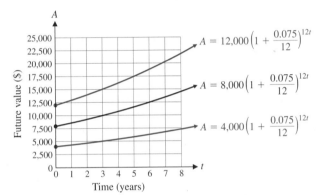

Figure for 31

✎ **32.** Discuss the similarities and differences in the graphs of future value A as a function of time t for loans of $4,000, $8,000, and $12,000, respectively, each at 7.5% compounded monthly for 8 years (see the figure).

Figure for 32

33. If $1,000 is invested in an account that earns 9.75% compounded annually for 6 years, find the interest earned during each year and the amount in the account at the end of each year. Organize your results in a table.

34. If $2,000 is invested in an account that earns 8.25% compounded annually for 5 years, find the interest earned during each year and the amount in the account at the end of each year. Organize your results in a table.

35. If an investment company pays 6% compounded semiannually, how much should you deposit now to have $10,000

(A) 5 years from now?   (B) 10 years from now?

36. If an investment company pays 8% compounded quarterly, how much should you deposit now to have $6,000

(A) 3 years from now?   (B) 6 years from now?

37. If an investment earns 9% compounded continuously, how much should you deposit now to have $25,000

(A) 36 months from now?   (B) 9 years from now?

38. If an investment earns 12% compounded continuously, how much should you deposit now to have $4,800

(A) 48 months from now?   (B) 7 years from now?

39. What is the annual percentage yield (APY) for money invested at an annual rate of

(A) 3.9% compounded monthly?

(B) 2.3% compounded quarterly?

40. What is the annual percentage yield (APY) for money invested at an annual rate of

(A) 4.32% compounded monthly?

(B) 4.31% compounded daily?

41. What is the annual percentage yield (APY) for money invested at an annual rate of

(A) 5.15% compounded continuously?

(B) 5.20% compounded semiannually?

42. What is the annual percentage yield (APY) for money invested at an annual rate of

(A) 3.05% compounded quarterly?

(B) 2.95% compounded continuously?

43. How long will it take $4,000 to grow to $9,000 if it is invested at 7% compounded monthly?

44. How long will it take $5,000 to grow to $7,000 if it is invested at 6% compounded quarterly?

45. How long will it take $6,000 to grow to $8,600 if it is invested at 9.6% compounded continuously?

46. How long will it take $42,000 to grow to $60,276 if it is invested at 4.25% compounded continuously?

C

In Problems 47 and 48, use the compound interest formula (1) to find n to the nearest larger integer value.

47. $A = 2P; i = 0.06; n = ?$

48. $A = 2P; i = 0.05; n = ?$

49. How long will it take money to double if it is invested at

(A) 10% compounded quarterly?

(B) 12% compounded quarterly?

50. How long will it take money to double if it is invested at

(A) 8% compounded semiannually?

(B) 7% compounded semiannually?

51. How long will it take money to double if it is invested at

(A) 9% compounded continuously?

(B) 11% compounded continuously?

52. How long will it take money to double if it is invested at

(A) 21% compounded continuously?

(B) 33% compounded continuously?

Applications

53. A newborn child receives a $20,000 gift toward college from her grandparents. How much will the $20,000 be worth in 17 years if it is invested at 7% compounded quarterly?

54. A person with $14,000 is trying to decide whether to purchase a car now, or to invest the money at 6.5% compounded semiannually and then buy a more expensive car. How much will be available for the purchase of a car at the end of 3 years?

55. What will a $210,000 house cost 10 years from now if the inflation rate over that period averages 3% compounded annually?

56. If the inflation rate averages 4% per year compounded annually for the next 5 years, what will a car that costs $17,000 now cost 5 years from now?

57. Rental costs for office space have been going up at 4.8% per year compounded annually for the past 5 years. If office space rent is now $25 per square foot per month, what were the rental rates 5 years ago?

58. In a suburb, housing costs have been increasing at 5.2% per year compounded annually for the past 8 years. A house worth $260,000 now would have had what value 8 years ago?

59. If the population in a particular country is growing at 1.7% compounded continuously, how long will it take the population to double? (Round up to the next-higher year if not exact.)

60. If the world population is now about 6.5 billion people and is growing at 1.14% compounded continuously, how long will it take the population to grow to 10 billion people? (Round up to the next-higher year if not exact.)

61. Which is the better investment and why: 9% compounded monthly or 9.3% compounded annually?

62. Which is the better investment and why: 8% compounded quarterly or 8.3% compounded annually?

63. (A) If an investment of $100 were made in 1776, and if it earned 3% compounded quarterly, how much would it be worth in 2016?

(B) Discuss the effect of compounding interest monthly, daily, and continuously (rather than quarterly) on the $100 investment.

(C) Use a graphing calculator to graph the growth of the investment of part (A).

64. (A) Starting with formula (1), derive each of the following formulas:

$$P = \frac{A}{(1 + i)^n}, \quad i = \left(\frac{A}{P}\right)^{1/n} - 1, \quad n = \frac{\ln A - \ln P}{\ln(1 + i)}$$

(B) Explain why it is unnecessary to memorize the formulas above for $P, i,$ and n if you know formula (1).

65. A promissory note will pay $50,000 at maturity 6 years from now. If you pay $28,000 for the note now, what rate compounded continuously would you earn?

66. If you deposit $10,000 in a savings account now, what rate compounded continuously would be required for you to withdraw $12,500 at the end of 4 years?

67. You have saved $7,000 toward the purchase of a car costing $9,000. How long will the $7,000 have to be invested at 9% compounded monthly to grow to $9,000? (Round up to the next-higher month if not exact.)

68. A married couple has $15,000 toward the purchase of a house. For the house that the couple wants to buy, a down payment of $20,000 is required. How long will the money have to be invested at 7% compounded quarterly to grow to $20,000? (Round up to the next-higher quarter if not exact.)

69. An Individual Retirement Account (IRA) has $20,000 in it, and the owner decides not to add any more money to the account other than interest earned at 6% compounded daily. How much will be in the account 35 years from now when the owner reaches retirement age?

70. If $1 had been placed in a bank account in the year 1066 and forgotten until now, how much would be in the account at the end of 2016 if the money earned 2% interest compounded annually? 2% simple interest? (Now you can see the power of compounding and why inactive accounts are closed after a relatively short period of time.)

71. How long will it take money to double if it is invested at 7% compounded daily? 8.2% compounded continuously?

72. How long will it take money to triple if it is invested at 5% compounded daily? 6% compounded continuously?

73. In a conversation with a friend, you note that you have two real estate investments, one that has doubled in value in the past 9 years and another that has doubled in value in the past 12 years. Your friend says that the first investment has been growing at approximately 8% compounded annually and the second at 6% compounded annually. How did your friend make these estimates? The **rule of 72** states that the annual compound rate of growth r of an investment that doubles in n years can be approximated by $r = 72/n$. Construct a table comparing the exact rate of growth and the approximate rate provided by the rule of 72 for doubling times of $n = 6, 7, \ldots, 12$ years. Round both rates to one decimal place.

74. Refer to Problem 73. Show that the exact annual compound rate of growth of an investment that doubles in n years is given by $r = 100(2^{1/n} - 1)$. Graph this equation and the rule of 72 on a graphing calculator for $5 \leq n \leq 20$.

Solve Problems 75–78 using graphical approximation techniques on a graphing calculator.

75. How long does it take for a $2,400 investment at 13% compounded quarterly to be worth more than a $3,000 investment at 6% compounded quarterly?

76. How long does it take for a $4,800 investment at 8% compounded monthly to be worth more than a $5,000 investment at 5% compounded monthly?

77. One investment pays 10% simple interest and another pays 7% compounded annually. Which investment would you choose? Why?

78. One investment pays 9% simple interest and another pays 6% compounded monthly. Which investment would you choose? Why?

79. What is the annual nominal rate compounded daily for a bond that has an annual percentage yield of 6.8%?

80. What is the annual nominal rate compounded monthly for a CD that has an annual percentage yield of 5.9%?

81. What annual nominal rate compounded monthly has the same annual percentage yield as 7% compounded continuously?

82. What annual nominal rate compounded continuously has the same annual percentage yield as 6% compounded monthly?

*Problems 83–86 refer to zero coupon bonds. A **zero coupon bond** is a bond that is sold now at a discount and will pay its **face value** at some time in the future when it matures—no interest payments are made.*

83. A zero coupon bond with a face value of $30,000 matures in 15 years. What should the bond be sold for now if its rate of return is to be 4.348% compounded annually?

84. A zero coupon bond with a face value of $20,000 matures in 10 years. What should the bond be sold for now if its rate of return is to be 4.194% compounded annually?

85. If you pay $4,126 for a 20-year zero coupon bond with a face value of $10,000, what is your annual compound rate of return?

86. If you pay $32,000 for a 5-year zero coupon bond with a face value of $40,000, what is your annual compound rate of return?

87. An online financial service listed the following money market accounts:

(A) Republic Bank: 4.31% compounded continuously

(B) Chase Bank: 4.35% compounded daily

(C) BankFirst: 4.36% compounded monthly

What is the annual percentage yield of each?

88. An online financial service listed the following 1-year CD accounts:

(A) Banking for CDs: 4.5% compounded quarterly

(B) Wingspan Bank: 4.6% compounded monthly

(C) Discover Bank: 4.6% compounded continuously

What is the annual percentage yield of each?

The buying and selling commission schedule shown at the top of the next column is from an online discount brokerage firm. Taking into consideration the buying and selling commissions in this schedule, find the annual compound rate of interest earned by each investment in Problems 89–92.

Transaction Size	Commission Rate
$0–$1,500	$29 + 2.5% of principal
$1,501–$6,000	$57 + 0.6% of principal
$6,001–$22,000	$75 + 0.30% of principal
$22,001–$50,000	$97 + 0.20% of principal
$50,001–$500,000	$147 + 0.10% of principal
$500,001+	$247 + 0.08% of principal

89. An investor purchases 100 shares of stock at $65 per share, holds the stock for 5 years, and then sells the stock for $125 a share.

90. An investor purchases 300 shares of stock at $95 per share, holds the stock for 3 years, and then sells the stock for $156 a share.

91. An investor purchases 200 shares of stock at $28 per share, holds the stock for 4 years, and then sells the stock for $55 a share.

92. An investor purchases 400 shares of stock at $48 per share, holds the stock for 6 years, and then sells the stock for $147 a share.

Answers to Matched Problems

1. (A) $1,593.85 (C) $1,610.32

(B) $1,604.71 (D) $1,614.14

2. (A) $9,155.23 **3.** (A) $21,084.17

(B) $9,156.29 (B) $20,532.86

4. (A) 20.208%

(B) 18.405%

5. 47 quarters, or 11 years and 3 quarters

6. Southern Pacific Bank: 4.917%
Washington Savings Bank: 4.939%
Washington Savings Bank has the higher return.

7. 5.678%

3-3 Future Value of an Annuity; Sinking Funds

- Future Value of an Annuity
- Sinking Funds
- Approximating Interest Rates

Future Value of an Annuity

An **annuity** is any sequence of equal periodic payments. If payments are made at the end of each time interval, then the annuity is called an **ordinary annuity**. We consider only ordinary annuities in this book. The amount, or **future value**, of an annuity is the sum of all payments plus all interest earned.

Suppose you decide to deposit $100 every 6 months into an account that pays 6% compounded semiannually. If you make six deposits, one at the end of each interest payment period, over 3 years, how much money will be in the account after the last deposit is made? To solve this problem, let's look at it in terms of a time line. Using the compound amount formula $A = P(1 + i)^n$, we can find the value of each deposit after it has earned compound interest up through the sixth deposit, as shown in Figure 1.

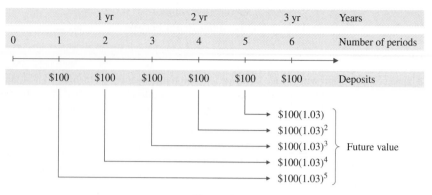

Figure 1

We could, of course, evaluate each of the future values in Figure 1 using a calculator and then add the results to find the amount in the account at the time of the sixth deposit—a tedious project at best. Instead, we take another approach, which leads directly to a formula that will produce the same result in a few steps (even when the number of deposits is very large). We start by writing the total amount in the account after the sixth deposit in the form

$$S = 100 + 100(1.03) + 100(1.03)^2 + 100(1.03)^3 + 100(1.03)^4 + 100(1.03)^5 \quad (1)$$

We would like a simple way to sum these terms. Let us multiply each side of (1) by 1.03 to obtain

$$1.03S = 100(1.03) + 100(1.03)^2 + 100(1.03)^3 + 100(1.03)^4 + 100(1.03)^5 + 100(1.03)^6 \quad (2)$$

Subtracting equation (1) from equation (2), left side from left side and right side from right side, we obtain

$$1.03S - S = 100(1.03)^6 - 100 \qquad \text{Notice how many terms drop out.}$$
$$0.03S = 100[(1.03)^6 - 1]$$
$$S = 100\frac{(1 + 0.03)^6 - 1}{0.03} \qquad \begin{array}{l}\text{We write } S \text{ in this form to} \\ \text{observe a general pattern.}\end{array} \quad (3)$$

In general, if R is the periodic deposit, i the rate per period, and n the number of periods, then the future value is given by

$$S = R + R(1 + i) + R(1 + i)^2 + \cdots + R(1 + i)^{n-1} \qquad \begin{array}{l}\text{Note how this} \\ \text{compares to (1).}\end{array} \quad (4)$$

and proceeding as in the above example, we obtain the general formula for the future value of an ordinary annuity:

$$S = R\frac{(1 + i)^n - 1}{i} \qquad \text{Note how this compares to (3).} \quad (5)$$

Returning to the example above, we use a calculator to complete the problem:

$$S = 100\frac{(1.03)^6 - 1}{0.03} \qquad \begin{array}{l}\text{For improved accuracy, keep all values in the} \\ \text{calculator until the end; round to the} \\ \text{required number of decimal places.}\end{array}$$

$$= \$646.84$$

An alternative to the preceding computation of S is provided by the use of tables of values of certain functions of the mathematics of finance. One such function is the fractional factor of formula (5), denoted by the symbol $s_{\overline{n}|i}$ (read "s angle n at i"):

$$s_{\overline{n}|i} = \frac{(1 + i)^n - 1}{i}$$

CONCEPTUAL INSIGHT

In general, an expression of the form

$$a + ar + ar^2 + \cdots + ar^{n-1}$$

is called a finite geometric series (each term is obtained from the preceding term by multiplying by r). The sum of the terms of a finite geometric series is (see Section B-2)

$$a + ar + ar^2 + \cdots + ar^{n-1} = a\frac{r^n - 1}{r - 1}$$

If $a = R$ and $r = 1 + i$, then equation (4) is the sum of the terms of a finite geometric series and, using the preceding formula, we have

$$S = R + R(1 + i) + R(1 + i)^2 + \cdots + R(1 + i)^{n-1}$$

$$= R\frac{(1 + i)^n - 1}{1 + i - 1} \qquad a = R, r = 1 + i$$

$$= R\frac{(1 + i)^n - 1}{i} \qquad\qquad\qquad (5)$$

So formula (5) is really a direct consequence of the sum formula for a finite geometric series.

Tables found in books on finance and mathematical handbooks list values of $s_{\overline{n}|i}$ for various values of n and i. To complete the computation of S, R is multiplied by $s_{\overline{n}|i}$ as indicated by formula (5). (A main advantage of using a calculator rather than tables is that a calculator can handle many more situations than a table, no matter how large the table.)

It is common to use FV (future value) for S and PMT (payment) for R in formula (5). Making these changes, we have the formula in Theorem 1.

THEOREM 1 Future Value of an Ordinary Annuity

$$FV = PMT\frac{(1 + i)^n - 1}{i} = PMT\,s_{\overline{n}|i} \qquad\qquad (6)$$

where FV = future value (amount)
PMT = periodic payment
i = rate per period
n = number of payments (periods)

Note: Payments are made at the end of each period.

EXAMPLE 1 **Future Value of an Ordinary Annuity** What is the value of an annuity at the end of 20 years if $2,000 is deposited each year into an account earning 8.5% compounded annually? How much of this value is interest?

SOLUTION To find the value of the annuity, use formula (6) with $PMT = \$2,000$, $i = r = 0.085$, and $n = 20$.

$$FV = PMT\frac{(1 + i)^n - 1}{i}$$

$$= 2,000\frac{(1.085)^{20} - 1}{0.085} = \$96,754.03 \qquad \textit{Use a calculator.}$$

To find the amount of interest earned, subtract the total amount deposited in the annuity (20 payments of $2,000) from the total value of the annuity after the 20th payment.

Deposits = 20(2,000) = \$40,000

Interest = value − deposits = 96,754.03 − 40,000 = \$56,754.03

Figure 2 on the next page, which was generated using a spreadsheet, illustrates the growth of this account over 20 years.

	A	B	C	D
1	Period	Payment	Interest	Balance
2	1	$2,000.00	$0.00	$2,000.00
3	2	$2,000.00	$170.00	$4,170.00
4	3	$2,000.00	$354.45	$6,524.45
5	4	$2,000.00	$554.58	$9,079.03
6	5	$2,000.00	$771.72	$11,850.75
7	6	$2,000.00	$1,007.31	$14,858.06
8	7	$2,000.00	$1,262.94	$18,120.99
9	8	$2,000.00	$1,540.28	$21,661.28
10	9	$2,000.00	$1,841.21	$25,502.49
11	10	$2,000.00	$2,167.71	$29,670.20
12	11	$2,000.00	$2,521.97	$34,192.17
13	12	$2,000.00	$2,906.33	$39,098.50
14	13	$2,000.00	$3,323.37	$44,421.87
15	14	$2,000.00	$3,775.86	$50,197.73
16	15	$2,000.00	$4,266.81	$56,464.54
17	16	$2,000.00	$4,799.49	$63,264.02
18	17	$2,000.00	$5,377.44	$70,641.47
19	18	$2,000.00	$6,004.52	$78,645.99
20	19	$2,000.00	$6,684.91	$87,330.90
21	20	$2,000.00	$7,423.13	$96,754.03
22	Totals	$40,000.00	$56,754.03	

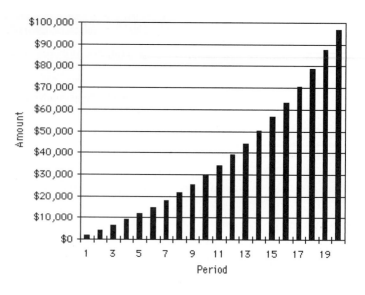

Figure 2 Ordinary annuity at 8.5% compounded annually for 20 years

Matched Problem 1   What is the value of an annuity at the end of 10 years if $1,000 is deposited every 6 months into an account earning 8% compounded semiannually? How much of this value is interest?

The table in Figure 2 is called a **balance sheet**. Let's take a closer look at the construction of this table. The first line is a special case because the payment is made at the end of the period and no interest is earned. Each subsequent line of the table is computed as follows:

payment + interest   + old balance = new balance

2,000   + 0.085(2,000) + 2,000   = 4,170   *Period 2*

2,000   + 0.085(4,170) + 4,170   = 6,524.45   *Period 3*

And so on. The amounts at the bottom of each column in the balance sheet agree with the results we obtained by using formula (6), as you would expect. Although balance sheets are appropriate for certain situations, we will concentrate on applications of formula (6). There are many important problems that can be solved only by using this formula.

EXPLORE & DISCUSS 1   (A) Discuss the similarities and differences in the graphs of future value *FV* as a function of time *t* for ordinary annuities in which $100 is deposited each month for 8 years and interest is compounded monthly at annual rates of 4%, 8%, and 12%, respectively (Fig. 3).

Figure 3

(B) Discuss the connections between the graph of the equation $y = 100t$, where *t* is time in months, and the graphs of part (A).

Sinking Funds

The formula for the future value of an ordinary annuity has another important application. Suppose the parents of a newborn child decide that on each of the child's birthdays up to the 17th year, they will deposit $$PMT$ in an account that pays 6% compounded annually. The money is to be used for college expenses. What should the annual deposit ($$PMT$) be in order for the amount in the account to be $80,000 after the 17th deposit?

We are given FV, i, and n in formula (6), and we must find PMT:

$$FV = PMT \frac{(1 + i)^n - 1}{i}$$

$$80{,}000 = PMT \frac{(1.06)^{17} - 1}{0.06} \qquad \text{Solve for PMT.}$$

$$PMT = 80{,}000 \frac{0.06}{(1.06)^{17} - 1} \qquad \text{Use a calculator.}$$

$$= \$2{,}835.58 \text{ per year}$$

An annuity of 17 annual deposits of $2,835.58 at 6% compounded annually will amount to $80,000 in 17 years.

This is an example of a *sinking fund problem*. In general, any account that is established for accumulating funds to meet future obligations or debts is called a **sinking fund**. If the payments are to be made in the form of an ordinary annuity, then we have only to solve formula (6) for the **sinking fund payment** PMT:

$$PMT = FV \frac{i}{(1 + i)^n - 1} \qquad (7)$$

It is important to understand that formula (7), which is convenient to use, is simply a variation of formula (6). You can always find the sinking fund payment by first substituting the appropriate values into formula (6) and then solving for PMT, as we did in the college fund example discussed above. Or you can substitute directly into formula (7), as we do in the next example. Use whichever method is easier for you.

EXAMPLE 2   **Computing the Payment for a Sinking Fund**   A company estimates that it will have to replace a piece of equipment at a cost of $800,000 in 5 years. To have this money available in 5 years, a sinking fund is established by making equal monthly payments into an account paying 6.6% compounded monthly.

(A) How much should each payment be?

(B) How much interest is earned during the last year?

SOLUTION   (A) To find PMT, we can use either formula (6) or (7). We choose formula (7) with $FV = \$800{,}000$, $i = \frac{0.066}{12} = 0.0055$, and $n = 12 \cdot 5 = 60$:

$$PMT = FV \frac{i}{(1 + i)^n - 1}$$

$$= 800{,}000 \frac{0.0055}{(1.0055)^{60} - 1}$$

$$= \$11{,}290.42 \text{ per month}$$

(B) To find the interest earned during the fifth year, we first use formula (6) with $PMT = \$11{,}290.42$, $i = 0.0055$, and $n = 12 \cdot 4 = 48$ to find the amount in the account after 4 years:

$$FV = PMT \frac{(1 + i)^n - 1}{i}$$

$$= 11{,}290.42 \frac{(1.0055)^{48} - 1}{0.0055}$$

$$= \$618{,}277.04 \qquad \text{Amount after 4 years}$$

During the 5th year, the amount in the account grew from \$618,277.04 to \$800,000. A portion of this growth was due to the 12 monthly payments of \$11,290.42. The remainder of the growth was interest. Thus,

$$800,000 - 618,277.04 = 181,722.96 \qquad \textit{Growth in the 5th year}$$
$$12 \cdot 11,290.42 = 135,485.04 \qquad \textit{Payments during the 5th year}$$
$$181,722.96 - 135,485.04 = \$46,237.92 \qquad \textit{Interest during the 5th year}$$

Matched Problem 2   A bond issue is approved for building a marina in a city. The city is required to make regular payments every 3 months into a sinking fund paying 5.4% compounded quarterly. At the end of 10 years, the bond obligation will be retired with a cost of \$5,000,000.

(A) What should each payment be?

(B) How much interest is earned during the 10th year?

EXAMPLE 3   **Growth in an IRA** Jane deposits \$2,000 annually into a Roth IRA that earns 6.85% compounded annually. (The interest earned by a Roth IRA is tax free.) Due to a change in employment, these deposits stop after 10 years, but the account continues to earn interest until Jane retires 25 years after the last deposit was made. How much is in the account when Jane retires?

SOLUTION   First, we use the future value formula with $PMT = \$2,000, i = 0.0685$, and $n = 10$ to find the amount in the account after 10 years:

$$FV = PMT \frac{(1 + i)^n - 1}{i}$$

$$= 2,000 \frac{(1.0685)^{10} - 1}{0.0685}$$

$$= \$27,437.89$$

Now we use the compound interest formula from Section 3-2 with $P = \$27,437.89, i = 0.0685$, and $n = 25$ to find the amount in the account when Jane retires:

$$A = P(1 + i)^n$$

$$= 27,437.89(1.0685)^{25}$$

$$= \$143,785.10$$

Matched Problem 3   Refer to Example 3. Mary starts a Roth IRA earning the same rate of interest at the time Jane stops making payments into her IRA. How much must Mary deposit each year for the next 25 years in order to have the same amount at retirement as Jane?

EXPLORE & DISCUSS 2   Refer to Example 3 and Matched Problem 3. What was the total amount Jane deposited in order to have \$143,785.10 at retirement? What was the total amount Mary deposited in order to have the same amount at retirement? Do you think it is advisable to start saving for retirement as early as possible?

Approximating Interest Rates

Algebra can be used to solve the future value formula (6) for *PMT* or *n* but not for *i*. However, graphical techniques or equation solvers can be used to approximate *i* to as many decimal places as desired.

EXAMPLE 4   **Approximating an Interest Rate**   A person makes monthly deposits of $100 into an ordinary annuity. After 30 years, the annuity is worth $160,000. What annual rate compounded monthly has this annuity earned during this 30-year period? Express the answer as a percentage, correct to two decimal places.

SOLUTION   Substituting $FV = \$160{,}000$, $PMT = \$100$, and $n = 30(12) = 360$ in (6) produces the following equation:

$$160{,}000 = 100\frac{(1 + i)^{360} - 1}{i}$$

We can approximate the solution to this equation by using graphical techniques (Figs. 4A, 4B) or an equation solver (Fig. 4C). From Figure 4B or 4C, we see that $i = 0.006\,956\,7$ and $12(i) = 0.083\,480\,4$. So the annual rate (to two decimal places) is $r = 8.35\%$.

(A)   (B)   (C)

Figure 4

Matched Problem 4   A person makes annual deposits of $1,000 into an ordinary annuity. After 20 years, the annuity is worth $55,000. What annual compound rate has this annuity earned during this 20-year period? Express the answer as a percentage, correct to two decimal places.

Exercises 3-3

A

In Problems 1–8, find i (the rate per period) and n (the number of periods) for each annuity.

1. Quarterly deposits of $500 are made for 20 years into an annuity that pays 8% compounded quarterly.

2. Monthly deposits of $350 are made for 6 years into an annuity that pays 6% compounded monthly.

3. Semiannual deposits of $900 are made for 12 years into an annuity that pays 7.5% compounded semiannually.

4. Annual deposits of $2,500 are made for 15 years into an annuity that pays 6.25% compounded annually.

5. Monthly deposits of $235 are made for 4 years into an annuity that pays 9% compounded monthly.

6. Semiannual deposits of $1,900 are made for 7 years into an annuity that pays 8.5% compounded semiannually.

7. Annual deposits of $3,100 are made for 12 years into an annuity that pays 5.95% compounded annually.

8. Quarterly deposits of $1,200 are made for 18 years into an annuity that pays 7.6% compounded quarterly.

In Problems 9–16, use the future value formula (6) to find each of the indicated values.

9. $n = 20; i = 0.03; PMT = \$500; FV = ?$

10. $n = 25; i = 0.04; PMT = \$100; FV = ?$

11. $FV = \$5{,}000; n = 15; i = 0.01; PMT = ?$

12. $FV = \$2{,}500; n = 10; i = 0.08; PMT = ?$

B

13. $FV = \$4{,}000; i = 0.02; PMT = 200; n = ?$

14. $FV = \$8{,}000; i = 0.04; PMT = 500; n = ?$

15. $FV = \$7{,}600; PMT = \$500; n = 10; i = ?$
    (Round answer to two decimal places.)

16. $FV = \$4{,}100; PMT = \$100; n = 20; i = ?$
    (Round answer to two decimal places.)

C

17. Explain what is meant by an ordinary annuity.

18. Explain why no interest is credited to an ordinary annuity at the end of the first period.

19. Solve the future value formula (6) for n.

20. Solve the future value formula (6) for i if $n = 2$.

Applications

21. Guaranty Income Life offered an annuity that pays 6.65% compounded monthly. If $500 is deposited into this annuity every month, how much is in the account after 10 years? How much of this is interest?

22. USG Annuity and Life offered an annuity that pays 7.25% compounded monthly. If $1,000 is deposited into this annuity every month, how much is in the account after 15 years? How much of this is interest?

23. In order to accumulate enough money for a down payment on a house, a couple deposits $300 per month into an account paying 6% compounded monthly. If payments are made at the end of each period, how much money will be in the account in 5 years?

24. A self-employed person has a Keogh retirement plan. (This type of plan is free of taxes until money is withdrawn.) If deposits of $7,500 are made each year into an account paying 8% compounded annually, how much will be in the account after 20 years?

25. Sun America recently offered an annuity that pays 6.35% compounded monthly. What equal monthly deposit should be made into this annuity in order to have $200,000 in 15 years?

26. Recently, The Hartford offered an annuity that pays 5.5% compounded monthly. What equal monthly deposit should be made into this annuity in order to have $100,000 in 10 years?

27. A company estimates that it will need $100,000 in 8 years to replace a computer. If it establishes a sinking fund by making fixed monthly payments into an account paying 7.5% compounded monthly, how much should each payment be?

28. Parents have set up a sinking fund in order to have $120,000 in 15 years for their children's college education. How much should be paid semiannually into an account paying 6.8% compounded semiannually?

29. If $1,000 is deposited at the end of each year for 5 years into an ordinary annuity earning 8.32% compounded annually, construct a balance sheet showing the interest earned during each year and the balance at the end of each year.

30. If $2,000 is deposited at the end of each quarter for 2 years into an ordinary annuity earning 7.9% compounded quarterly, construct a balance sheet showing the interest earned during each quarter and the balance at the end of each quarter.

31. Beginning in January, a person plans to deposit $100 at the end of each month into an account earning 6% compounded monthly. Each year taxes must be paid on the interest earned during that year. Find the interest earned during each year for the first 3 years.

32. If $500 is deposited each quarter into an account paying 8% compounded quarterly for 3 years, find the interest earned during each of the 3 years.

33. Bob makes his first $1,000 deposit into an IRA earning 6.4% compounded annually on his 24th birthday and his last $1,000 deposit on his 35th birthday (12 equal deposits in all). With no additional deposits, the money in the IRA continues to earn 6.4% interest compounded annually until Bob retires on his 65th birthday. How much is in the IRA when Bob retires?

34. Refer to Problem 33. John procrastinates and does not make his first $1,000 deposit into an IRA until he is 36, but then he continues to deposit $1,000 each year until he is 65 (30 deposits in all). If John's IRA also earns 6.4% compounded annually, how much is in his IRA when he makes his last deposit on his 65th birthday?

35. Refer to Problems 33 and 34. How much would John have to deposit each year in order to have the same amount at retirement as Bob has?

36. Refer to Problems 33 and 34. Suppose that Bob decides to continue to make $1,000 deposits into his IRA every year until his 65th birthday. If John still waits until he is 36 to start his IRA, how much must he deposit each year in order to have the same amount at age 65 as Bob has?

37. Compubank, an online banking service, offered a money market account with an APY of 4.86%.

   (A) If interest is compounded monthly, what is the equivalent annual nominal rate?

   (B) If you wish to have $10,000 in this account after 4 years, what equal deposit should you make each month?

38. American Express's online banking division offered a money market account with an APY of 5.65%.

   (A) If interest is compounded monthly, what is the equivalent annual nominal rate?

   (B) If a company wishes to have $1,000,000 in this account after 8 years, what equal deposit should be made each month?

39. You can afford monthly deposits of $200 into an account that pays 5.7% compounded monthly. How long will it be until you have $7,000? (Round to the next-higher month if not exact.)

40. A company establishes a sinking fund for upgrading office equipment with monthly payments of $2,000 into an account paying 6.6% compounded monthly. How long will it be before the account has $100,000? (Round up to the next-higher month if not exact.)

In Problems 41–44, use graphical approximation techniques or an equation solver to approximate the desired interest rate. Express each answer as a percentage, correct to two decimal places.

41. A person makes annual payments of $1,000 into an ordinary annuity. At the end of 5 years, the amount in the annuity is $5,840. What annual nominal compounding rate has this annuity earned?

42. A person invests $2,000 annually in an IRA. At the end of 6 years, the amount in the fund is $14,000. What annual nominal compounding rate has this fund earned?

43. At the end of each month, an employee deposits $50 into a Christmas club fund. At the end of the year, the fund contains $620. What annual nominal rate compounded monthly has this fund earned?

44. At the end of each month, an employee deposits $80 into a credit union account. At the end of 2 years, the account contains $2,100. What annual nominal rate compounded monthly has this account earned?

In Problems 45 and 46, use graphical approximation techniques to answer the questions.

45. When would an ordinary annuity consisting of quarterly payments of $500 at 6% compounded quarterly be worth more than a principal of $5,000 invested at 4% simple interest?

46. When would an ordinary annuity consisting of monthly payments of $200 at 5% compounded monthly be worth more than a principal of $10,000 invested at 7.5% compounded monthly?

Answers to Matched Problems

1. Value: $29,778.08; interest: $9,778.08

2. (A) $95,094.67   (B) $248,628.89

3. $2,322.73   **4.** 9.64%

3-4   Present Value of an Annuity; Amortization

- Present Value of an Annuity
- Amortization
- Amortization Schedules
- General Problem-Solving Strategy

Present Value of an Annuity

How much should you deposit in an account paying 6% compounded semiannually in order to be able to withdraw $1,000 every 6 months for the next 3 years? (After the last payment is made, no money is to be left in the account.)

Actually, we are interested in finding the present value of each $1,000 that is paid out during the 3 years. We can do this by solving for P in the compound interest formula:

$$A = P(1 + i)^n$$

$$P = \frac{A}{(1 + i)^n} = A(1 + i)^{-n}$$

The rate per period is $i = \frac{0.06}{2} = 0.03$. The present value P of the first payment is $1,000(1.03)^{-1}$, the present value of the second payment is $1,000(1.03)^{-2}$, and so on. Figure 1 shows this in terms of a time line.

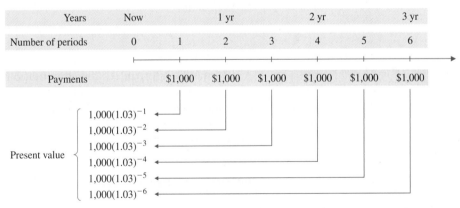

Figure 1

We could evaluate each of the present values in Figure 1 using a calculator and add the results to find the total present values of all the payments (which will be the amount needed now to buy the annuity). Since this is a tedious process, particularly when the number of payments is large, we will use the same device we used in the preceding section to produce a formula that will accomplish the same result in a couple of steps. We start by writing the sum of the present values in the form

$$P = 1,000(1.03)^{-1} + 1,000(1.03)^{-2} + \cdots + 1,000(1.03)^{-6} \tag{1}$$

Multiplying both sides of equation (1) by 1.03, we obtain

$$1.03P = 1,000 + 1,000(1.03)^{-1} + \cdots + 1,000(1.03)^{-5} \qquad (2)$$

Now subtract equation (1) from equation (2):

$$1.03P - P = 1,000 - 1,000(1.03)^{-6} \qquad \text{Notice how many terms drop out.}$$

$$0.03P = 1,000[1 - (1 + 0.03)^{-6}]$$

$$P = 1,000\frac{1 - (1 + 0.03)^{-6}}{0.03} \qquad \begin{array}{l}\text{We write } P \text{ in this form to} \\ \text{observe a general pattern.}\end{array} \qquad (3)$$

In general, if R is the periodic payment, i the rate per period, and n the number of periods, then the present value of all payments is given by

$$P = R(1 + i)^{-1} + R(1 + i)^{-2} + \cdots + R(1 + i)^{-n} \qquad \begin{array}{l}\text{Note how this} \\ \text{compares to (1).}\end{array}$$

Proceeding as in the above example, we obtain the general formula for the present value of an ordinary annuity:

$$P = R\frac{1 - (1 + i)^{-n}}{i} \qquad \text{Note how this compares to (3).} \qquad (4)$$

Returning to the preceding example, we use a calculator to complete the problem:

$$P = 1,000\frac{1 - (1.03)^{-6}}{0.03}$$

$$= \$5,417.19$$

CONCEPTUAL INSIGHT

Formulas (3) and (4) can also be established by using the sum formula for a finite geometric series (see Section B-2):

$$a + ar + ar^2 + \cdots + ar^{n-1} = a\frac{r^n - 1}{r - 1}$$

The fractional factor of formula (4) may be denoted by the symbol $a_{\overline{n}|i}$, read as "a angle n at i":

$$a_{\overline{n}|i} = \frac{1 - (1 + i)^{-n}}{i}$$

An alternative approach to the computation of P is to use a table that gives values of $a_{\overline{n}|i}$ for various values of n and i. The computation of P is then completed by multiplying R by $a_{\overline{n}|i}$ as indicated by formula (4).

It is common to use PV (present value) for P and PMT (payment) for R in formula (4). Making these changes, we have the following:

THEOREM 1   Present Value of an Ordinary Annuity

$$PV = PMT\frac{1 - (1 + i)^{-n}}{i} = PMT\,a_{\overline{n}|i} \qquad (5)$$

where PV = present value of all payments

PMT = periodic payment

i = rate per period

n = number of periods

Note: Payments are made at the end of each period.

EXAMPLE 1   **Present Value of an Annuity** What is the present value of an annuity that pays $200 per month for 5 years if money is worth 6% compounded monthly?

SOLUTION   To solve this problem, use formula (5) with $PMT = \$200$, $i = \frac{0.06}{12} = 0.005$, and $n = 12(5) = 60$:

$$PV = PMT\frac{1 - (1 + i)^{-n}}{i}$$

$$= 200\frac{1 - (1.005)^{-60}}{0.005} \qquad \textit{Use a calculator.}$$

$$= \$10,345.11$$

Matched Problem 1   How much should you deposit in an account paying 8% compounded quarterly in order to receive quarterly payments of $1,000 for the next 4 years?

EXAMPLE 2   **Retirement Planning** Lincoln Benefit Life offered an ordinary annuity that earned 6.5% compounded annually. A person plans to make equal annual deposits into this account for 25 years and then make 20 equal annual withdrawals of $25,000, reducing the balance in the account to zero. How much must be deposited annually to accumulate sufficient funds to provide for these payments? How much total interest is earned during this entire 45-year process?

SOLUTION   This problem involves both future and present values. Figure 2 illustrates the flow of money into and out of the annuity.

Figure 2

Since we are given the required withdrawals, we begin by finding the present value necessary to provide for these withdrawals. Using formula (5) with $PMT = \$25,000$, $i = 0.065$, and $n = 20$, we have

$$PV = PMT\frac{1 - (1 + i)^{-n}}{i}$$

$$= 25,000\frac{1 - (1.065)^{-20}}{0.065} \qquad \textit{Use a calculator.}$$

$$= \$275,462.68$$

Now we find the deposits that will produce a future value of $275,462.68 in 25 years. Using formula (7) from Section 3-3 with $FV = \$275,462.68$, $i = 0.065$, and $n = 25$, we have

$$PMT = FV\frac{i}{(1 + i)^{n} - 1}$$

$$= 275,462.68\frac{0.065}{(1.065)^{25} - 1} \qquad \textit{Use a calculator.}$$

$$= \$4,677.76$$

Thus, depositing $4,677.76 annually for 25 years will provide for 20 annual withdrawals of $25,000. The interest earned during the entire 45-year process is

$$\text{interest} = (\text{total withdrawals}) - (\text{total deposits})$$

$$= 20(25,000) - 25(\$4,677.76)$$

$$= \$383,056$$

Matched Problem 2 Refer to Example 2. If $2,000 is deposited annually for the first 25 years, how much can be withdrawn annually for the next 20 years?

Amortization

The present value formula for an ordinary annuity, formula (5), has another important use. Suppose that you borrow $5,000 from a bank to buy a car and agree to repay the loan in 36 equal monthly payments, including all interest due. If the bank charges 1% per month on the unpaid balance (12% per year compounded monthly), how much should each payment be to retire the total debt, including interest in 36 months?

Actually, the bank has bought an annuity from you. The question is: If the bank pays you $5,000 (present value) for an annuity paying them $PMT per month for 36 months at 12% interest compounded monthly, what are the monthly payments (PMT)? (Note that the value of the annuity at the end of 36 months is zero.) To find PMT, we have only to use formula (5) with $PV = \$5,000$, $i = 0.01$, and $n = 36$:

$$PV = PMT\frac{1 - (1 + i)^{-n}}{i}$$

$$5,000 = PMT\frac{1 - (1.01)^{-36}}{0.01} \qquad \textit{Solve for PMT and use a calculator.}$$

$$PMT = \$166.07 \text{ per month}$$

At $166.07 per month, the car will be yours after 36 months. That is, you have *amortized* the debt in 36 equal monthly payments. (*Mort* means "death"; you have "killed" the loan in 36 months.) In general, **amortizing a debt** means that the debt is retired in a given length of time by equal periodic payments that include compound interest. We are interested in computing the equal periodic payments. Solving the present value formula (5) for *PMT* in terms of the other variables, we obtain the following **amortization formula**:

$$PMT = PV\frac{i}{1 - (1 + i)^{-n}} \tag{6}$$

Formula (6) is simply a variation of formula (5), and either formula can be used to find the periodic payment *PMT*.

EXAMPLE 3 **Monthly Payment and Total Interest on an Amortized Debt** Assume that you buy a television set for $800 and agree to pay for it in 18 equal monthly payments at $1\frac{1}{2}\%$ interest per month on the unpaid balance.

(A) How much are your payments?

(B) How much interest will you pay?

SOLUTION (A) Use formula (6) with $PV = \$800$, $i = 0.015$, and $n = 18$:

$$PMT = PV\frac{i}{1 - (1 + i)^{-n}}$$

$$= 800\frac{0.015}{1 - (1.015)^{-18}} \qquad \textit{Use a calculator.}$$

$$= \$51.04 \text{ per month}$$

(B) Total interest paid = (amount of all payments) − (initial loan)

$$= 18(\$51.04) - \$800$$

$$= \$118.72$$

Matched Problem 3 If you sell your car to someone for $2,400 and agree to finance it at 1% per month on the unpaid balance, how much should you receive each month to amortize the loan in 24 months? How much interest will you receive?

EXPLORE & DISCUSS 1

To purchase a home, a family plans to sign a mortgage of $70,000 at 8% on the unpaid balance. Discuss the advantages and disadvantages of a 20-year mortgage as opposed to a 30-year mortgage. Include a comparison of monthly payments and total interest paid.

Amortization Schedules

What happens if you are amortizing a debt with equal periodic payments and later decide to pay off the remainder of the debt in one lump-sum payment? This occurs each time a home with an outstanding mortgage is sold. In order to understand what happens in this situation, we must take a closer look at the amortization process. We begin with an example that allows us to examine the effect each payment has on the debt.

EXAMPLE 4   **Constructing an Amortization Schedule** If you borrow $500 that you agree to repay in six equal monthly payments at 1% interest per month on the unpaid balance, how much of each monthly payment is used for interest and how much is used to reduce the unpaid balance?

SOLUTION   First, we compute the required monthly payment using formula (5) or (6). We choose formula (6) with $PV = \$500$, $i = 0.01$, and $n = 6$:

$$PMT = PV\frac{i}{1 - (1 + i)^{-n}}$$

$$= 500\frac{0.01}{1 - (1.01)^{-6}} \qquad \textit{Use a calculator.}$$

$$= \$86.27 \text{ per month}$$

At the end of the first month, the interest due is

$$\$500(0.01) = \$5.00$$

The amortization payment is divided into two parts, payment of the interest due and reduction of the unpaid balance (repayment of principal):

Monthly payment		Interest due		Unpaid balance: reduction
$86.27	=	$5.00	+	$81.27

The unpaid balance for the next month is

Previous unpaid balance		Unpaid balance reduction		New unpaid balance
$500.00	−	$81.27	=	$418.73

At the end of the second month, the interest due on the unpaid balance of $418.73 is

$$\$418.73(0.01) = \$4.19$$

Thus, at the end of the second month, the monthly payment of $86.27 covers interest and unpaid balance reduction as follows:

$$\$86.27 = \$4.19 + \$82.08$$

and the unpaid balance for the third month is

$$\$418.73 - \$82.08 = \$336.65$$

This process continues until all payments have been made and the unpaid balance is reduced to zero. The calculations for each month are listed in Table 1, often referred to as an **amortization schedule**.

In Table 1, notice that the last payment had to be increased by $0.03 in order to reduce the unpaid balance to zero. This small discrepancy is due to rounding the monthly payment and the entries in the interest column to two decimal places.

Table 1   Amortization Schedule

Payment Number	Payment	Interest	Unpaid Balance Reduction	Unpaid Balance
0				$500.00
1	$86.27	$5.00	$81.27	418.73
2	86.27	4.19	82.08	336.65
3	86.27	3.37	82.90	253.75
4	86.27	2.54	83.73	170.02
5	86.27	1.70	84.57	85.45
6	86.30	0.85	85.45	0.00
Totals	$517.65	$17.65	$500.00	

Matched Problem 4   Construct the amortization schedule for a $1,000 debt that is to be amortized in six equal monthly payments at 1.25% interest per month on the unpaid balance.

EXAMPLE 5   **Equity in a Home**   A family purchased a home 10 years ago for $80,000. The home was financed by paying 20% down and signing a 30-year mortgage at 9% on the unpaid balance. The net market value of the house (amount received after subtracting all costs involved in selling the house) is now $120,000, and the family wishes to sell the house. How much equity (to the nearest dollar) does the family have in the house now after making 120 monthly payments?

[**Equity** = (current net market value) − (unpaid loan balance).]*

SOLUTION   How can we find the unpaid loan balance after 10 years or 120 monthly payments? One way to proceed would be to construct an amortization schedule, but this would require a table with 120 lines. Fortunately, there is an easier way. The unpaid balance after 120 payments is the amount of the loan that can be paid off with the remaining 240 monthly payments (20 remaining years on the loan). Since the lending institution views a loan as an annuity that they bought from the family, **the unpaid balance of a loan with n remaining payments is the present value of that annuity and can be computed by using formula (5)**. Since formula (5) requires knowledge of the monthly payment, we compute PMT first using formula (6).

Step 1   Find the monthly payment:

$$PMT = PV \frac{i}{1 - (1 + i)^{-n}}$$

$PV = (0.80)(\$80,000) = \$64,000$

$i = \frac{0.09}{12} = 0.0075$

$$= 64,000 \frac{0.0075}{1 - (1.0075)^{-360}}$$

$n = 12(30) = 360$

$$= \$514.96 \text{ per month}$$ Use a calculator.

Step 2   Find the present value of a $514.96 per month, 20-year annuity:

$$PV = PMT \frac{1 - (1 + i)^{-n}}{i}$$

$PMT = \$514.96$

$n = 12(20) = 240$

$$= 514.96 \frac{1 - (1.0075)^{-240}}{0.0075}$$

$i = \frac{0.09}{12} = 0.0075$

Use a calculator.

$$= \$57,235$$ Unpaid loan balance

---

*If a family wants to sell a house and buy another, more expensive house, then the price of a new house that the family can afford to buy will often depend on the family's *equity* in the first house, where equity is defined by the equation given here. In refinancing a house or taking out an "equity loan," the new mortgage (or second mortgage) often will be based on the equity in the house.

Step 3 Find the equity:

$$\text{equity} = (\text{current net market value}) - (\text{unpaid loan balance})$$
$$= \$120{,}000 - \$57{,}235$$
$$= \$62{,}765$$

If the family sells the house for $120,000 net, the family will have $62,765 after paying off the unpaid loan balance of $57,235.

Matched Problem 5 A couple purchased a home 20 years ago for $65,000. The home was financed by paying 20% down and signing a 30-year mortgage at 8% on the unpaid balance. The net market value of the house is now $130,000, and the couple wishes to sell the house. How much equity (to the nearest dollar) does the couple have in the house now after making 240 monthly payments?

The unpaid loan balance in Example 5 may seem a surprisingly large amount to owe after having made payments for 10 years, but long-term amortizations start out with very small reductions in the unpaid balance. For example, the interest due at the end of the very first period of the loan in Example 5 was

$$\$64{,}000(0.0075) = \$480.00$$

The first monthly payment was divided as follows:

		Unpaid
Monthly	Interest	balance
payment	due	reduction

$$\$514.96 - \$480.00 = \$34.96$$

Only $34.96 was applied to the unpaid balance.

Exerci

A

In Problems 1 *of periods) for*

1. Monthly a loan at

2. Semiannu repay a l

3. Quarterly a loan at

4. Annual p a loan at

5. Semiannu repay a l

6. Quarterly loan at 8.

7. Annual p a loan at

8. Monthly a loan at

In Problems 9

9. $n = 30; i$

10. $n = 40; i$

B

11. $PV = \$4$

12. $PV = \$1$

C

13. $PV = \$5$

14. $PV = \$2$

15. $PV = \$9$ (Round

EXPLORE & DISCUSS 2

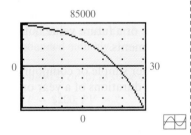

85000

0 ┤─────────┤ 30

0

Figure 3

(A) A family has an $85,000, 30-year mortgage at 9.6% compounded monthly. Show that the monthly payments are $720.94.

(B) Explain why the equation

$$y = 720.94\frac{1 - (1.008)^{-12(30-x)}}{0.008}$$

gives the unpaid balance of the loan after x years.

(C) Find the unpaid balance after 5 years, after 10 years, and after 15 years.

(D) When is the unpaid balance exactly half of the original $85,000?

(E) Solve part (D) using graphical approximation techniques on a graphing calculator (see Fig. 3).

EXAMPLE 6 **Automobile Financing** You have negotiated a price of $25,200 for a new Bison pickup truck. Now you must choose between 0% financing for 48 months or a $3,000 rebate. If you choose the rebate, you can obtain a credit union loan for the balance at 4.5% compounded monthly for 48 months. Which option should you choose?

- **Amortizing** a debt means that the debt is retired in a given length of time by equal periodic payments that include compound interest. Solving the present value formula for the payment gives us the **amortization formula**:   Ex. 3, p. 156   Ex. 6, p. 159

$$PMT = PV \frac{i}{1 - (1 + i)^{-n}}$$

- An **amortization schedule** is a table that shows the interest due and the balance reduction for each payment of a loan.   Ex. 4, p. 157

- The **equity** in a property is the difference between the current net market value and the unpaid loan balance. The unpaid balance of a loan with n **remaining payments** is given by the present value formula.   Ex. 5, p. 158

- A strategy for solving problems in the mathematics of finance is presented on page 160.

ALL 2
$3,(
or 0% A

Review Exercises

Work through all the problems in this chapter review and check your answers in the back of the book. Answers to all review problems are there along with section numbers in italics to indicate where each type of problem is discussed. Where weaknesses show up, review appropriate sections in the text.

A

In Problems 1–4, find the indicated quantity, given
$A = P(1 + rt).$

1. $A = ?; P = \$100; r = 9\%; t = 6\,\text{months}$

2. $A = \$808; P = ?; r = 12\%; t = 1\,\text{month}$

3. $A = \$212; P = \$200; r = 8\%; t = ?$

4. $A = \$4,120; P = \$4,000; r = ?; t = 6\,\text{months}$

B

In Problems 5 and 6, find the indicated quantity, given
$A = P(1 + i)^n.$

5. $A = ?; P = \$1,200; i = 0.005; n = 30$

6. $A = \$5,000; P = ?; i = 0.0075; n = 60$

In Problems 7 and 8, find the indicated quantity, given $A = Pe^{rt}$.

7. $A = ?; P = \$4,750; r = 6.8\%; t = 3\,\text{years}$

8. $A = \$36,000; P = ?; r = 9.3\%; t = 60\,\text{months}$

In Problems 9 and 10, find the indicated quantity, given

$$FV = PMT \frac{(1 + i)^n - 1}{i}$$

9. $FV = ?; PMT = \$1,000; i = 0.005; n = 60$

10. $FV = \$8,000; PMT = ?; i = 0.015; n = 48$

In Problems 11 and 12, find the indicated quantity, given

$$PV = PMT \frac{1 - (1 + i)^{-n}}{i}$$

11. $PV = ?; PMT = \$2,500; i = 0.02; n = 16$

12. $PV = \$8,000; PMT = ?; i = 0.0075; n = 60$

C

13. Solve the equation $2,500 = 1,000(1.06)^n$ for n to the nearest integer using:

    (A) Logarithms

    (B) Graphical approximation techniques or an equation solver on a graphing calculator

14. Solve the equation

$$5,000 = 100\frac{(1.01)^n - 1}{0.01}$$

    for n to the nearest integer using:

    (A) Logarithms

    (B) Graphical approximation techniques or an equation solver on a graphing calculator.

Applications

Find all dollar amounts correct to the nearest cent. When an interest rate is requested as an answer, express the rate as a percentage, correct to two decimal places.

15. If you borrow \$3,000 at 14% simple interest for 10 months, how much will you owe in 10 months? How much interest will you pay?

16. Grandparents deposited \$6,000 into a grandchild's account toward a college education. How much money (to the nearest dollar) will be in the account 17 years from now if the account earns 7% compounded monthly?

17. How much should you pay for a corporate bond paying 6.6% compounded monthly in order to have \$25,000 in 10 years?

18. A savings account pays 5.4% compounded annually. Construct a balance sheet showing the interest earned during each year and the balance at the end of each year for 4 years if

    (A) A single deposit of \$400 is made at the beginning of the first year.

    (B) Four deposits of \$100 are made at the end of each year.

19. One investment pays 13% simple interest and another 9% compounded annually. Which investment would you choose? Why?

20. A $10,000 retirement account is left to earn interest at 7% compounded daily. How much money will be in the account 40 years from now when the owner reaches 65? (Use a 365-day year and round answer to the nearest dollar.)

21. A couple wishes to have $40,000 in 6 years for the down payment on a house. At what rate of interest compounded continuously must $25,000 be invested now to accomplish this goal?

22. Which is the better investment and why: 9% compounded quarterly or 9.25% compounded annually?

23. What is the value of an ordinary annuity at the end of 8 years if $200 per month is deposited into an account earning 7.2% compounded monthly? How much of this value is interest?

24. A credit card company charges a 22% annual rate for overdue accounts. How much interest will be owed on a $635 account 1 month overdue?

25. What will a $23,000 car cost (to the nearest dollar) 5 years from now if the inflation rate over that period averages 5% compounded annually?

26. What would the $23,000 car in Problem 25 have cost (to the nearest dollar) 5 years ago if the inflation rate over that period had averaged 5% compounded annually?

27. A loan of $2,500 was repaid at the end of 10 months with a check for $2,812.50. What annual rate of interest was charged?

28. You want to purchase an automobile for $21,600. The dealer offers you 0% financing for 48 months or a $3,000 rebate. You can obtain 4.8% financing for 48 months at the local bank. Which option should you choose? Explain.

29. Find the annual percentage yield on a CD earning 6.25% if interest is compounded

(A) monthly.

(B) continuously.

30. You have $5,000 toward the purchase of a boat that will cost $6,000. How long will it take the $5,000 to grow to $6,000 if it is invested at 9% compounded quarterly? (Round up to the next-higher quarter if not exact.)

31. How long will it take money to double if it is invested at 6% compounded monthly? 9% compounded monthly? (Round up to the next-higher month if not exact.)

32. Starting on his 21st birthday, and continuing on every birthday up to and including his 65th, John deposits $2,000 a year into an IRA. How much (to the nearest dollar) will be in the account on John's 65th birthday, if the account earns:

(A) 7% compounded annually?

(B) 11% compounded annually?

33. If you just sold a stock for $17,388.17 (net) that cost you $12,903.28 (net) 3 years ago, what annual compound rate of return did you make on your investment?

34. The table shows the fees for refund anticipation loans (RALs) offered by an online tax preparation firm. Find the annual rate of interest for each of the following loans.

(A) A $400 RAL paid back in 15 days

(B) A $1,800 RAL paid back in 21 days

RAL Amount	RAL Fee
$10–$500	$29.00
$501–$1,000	$39.00
$1,001–$1,500	$49.00
$1,501–$2,000	$69.00
$2,001–$5,000	$82.00

35. Lincoln Benefit Life offered an annuity that pays 5.5% compounded monthly. What equal monthly deposit should be made into this annuity in order to have $50,000 in 5 years?

36. A person wants to establish an annuity for retirement purposes. He wants to make quarterly deposits for 20 years so that he can then make quarterly withdrawals of $5,000 for 10 years. The annuity earns 7.32% interest compounded quarterly.

(A) How much will have to be in the account at the time he retires?

(B) How much should be deposited each quarter for 20 years in order to accumulate the required amount?

(C) What is the total amount of interest earned during the 30-year period?

37. If you borrow $4,000 from an online lending firm for the purchase of a computer and agree to repay it in 48 equal installments at 0.9% interest per month on the unpaid balance, how much are your monthly payments? How much total interest will be paid?

38. A company decides to establish a sinking fund to replace a piece of equipment in 6 years at an estimated cost of $50,000. To accomplish this, they decide to make fixed monthly payments into an account that pays 6.12% compounded monthly. How much should each payment be?

39. How long will it take money to double if it is invested at 7.5% compounded daily? 7.5% compounded annually?

40. A student receives a student loan for $8,000 at 5.5% interest compounded monthly to help her finish the last 1.5 years of college. Starting 1 year after finishing college, the student must amortize the loan in the next 5 years by making equal monthly payments. What will the payments be and what total interest will the student pay?

41. If you invest $5,650 in an account paying 8.65% compounded continuously, how much money will be in the account at the end of 10 years?

42. A company makes a payment of $1,200 each month into a sinking fund that earns 6% compounded monthly. Use graphical approximation techniques on a graphing calculator to determine when the fund will be worth $100,000.

43. A couple has a $50,000, 20-year mortgage at 9% compounded monthly. Use graphical approximation techniques on a graphing calculator to determine when the unpaid balance will drop below $10,000.

44. A loan company advertises in the paper that you will pay only 8¢ a day for each $100 borrowed. What annual rate of interest are they charging? (Use a 360-day year.)

45. Construct the amortization schedule for a $1,000 debt that is to be amortized in four equal quarterly payments at 2.5% interest per quarter on the unpaid balance.

46. You can afford monthly deposits of only $300 into an account that pays 7.98% compounded monthly. How long will it be until you will have $9,000 to purchase a used car? (Round to the next-higher month if not exact.)

47. A company establishes a sinking fund for plant retooling in 6 years at an estimated cost of $850,000. How much should be invested semiannually into an account paying 8.76% compounded semiannually? How much interest will the account earn in the 6 years?

48. What is the annual nominal rate compounded monthly for a CD that has an annual percentage yield of 6.48%?

49. If you buy a 13-week T-bill with a maturity value of $5,000 for $4,922.15 from the U.S. Treasury Department, what annual interest rate will you earn?

50. In order to save enough money for the down payment on a condominium, a young couple deposits $200 each month into an account that pays 7.02% interest compounded monthly. If the couple needs $10,000 for a down payment, how many deposits will the couple have to make?

51. A business borrows $80,000 at 9.42% interest compounded monthly for 8 years.

(A) What is the monthly payment?

(B) What is the unpaid balance at the end of the first year?

(C) How much interest was paid during the first year?

52. You unexpectedly inherit $10,000 just after you have made the 72nd monthly payment on a 30-year mortgage of $60,000 at 8.2% compounded monthly. Discuss the relative merits of using the inheritance to reduce the principal of the loan or to buy a certificate of deposit paying 7% compounded monthly.

53. Your parents are considering a $75,000, 30-year mortgage to purchase a new home. The bank at which they have done business for many years offers a rate of 7.54% compounded monthly. A competitor is offering 6.87% compounded monthly. Would it be worthwhile for your parents to switch banks? Explain.

54. How much should a $5,000 face value zero coupon bond, maturing in 5 years, be sold for now, if its rate of return is to be 5.6% compounded annually?

55. If you pay $5,695 for a $10,000 face value zero coupon bond that matures in 10 years, what is your annual compound rate of return?

56. If an investor wants to earn an annual interest rate of 6.4% on a 26-week T-bill with a maturity value of $5,000, how much should the investor pay for the T-bill?

57. Two years ago you borrowed $10,000 at 12% interest compounded monthly, which was to be amortized over 5 years.

Now you have acquired some additional funds and decide that you want to pay off this loan. What is the unpaid balance after making equal monthly payments for 2 years?

58. What annual nominal rate compounded monthly has the same annual percentage yield as 7.28% compounded quarterly?

59. (A) A man deposits $2,000 in an IRA on his 21st birthday and on each subsequent birthday up to, and including, his 29th (nine deposits in all). The account earns 8% compounded annually. If he leaves the money in the account without making any more deposits, how much will he have on his 65th birthday, assuming the account continues to earn the same rate of interest?

(B) How much would be in the account (to the nearest dollar) on his 65th birthday if he had started the deposits on his 30th birthday and continued making deposits on each birthday until (and including) his 65th birthday?

60. A promissory note will pay $27,000 at maturity 10 years from now. How much money should you be willing to pay now if money is worth 5.5% compounded continuously?

61. In a new housing development, the houses are selling for $100,000 and require a 20% down payment. The buyer is given a choice of 30-year or 15-year financing, both at 7.68% compounded monthly.

(A) What is the monthly payment for the 30-year choice? For the 15-year choice?

(B) What is the unpaid balance after 10 years for the 30-year choice? For the 15-year choice?

62. A loan company will loan up to 60% of the equity in a home. A family purchased their home 8 years ago for $83,000. The home was financed by paying 20% down and signing a 30-year mortgage at 8.4% for the balance. Equal monthly payments were made to amortize the loan over the 30-year period. The market value of the house is now $95,000. After making the 96th payment, the family applied to the loan company for the maximum loan. How much (to the nearest dollar) will the family receive?

63. A $600 stereo is financed for 6 months by making monthly payments of $110. What is the annual nominal compounding rate for this loan?

64. A person deposits $2,000 each year for 25 years into an IRA. When she retires immediately after making the 25th deposit, the IRA is worth $220,000.

(A) Find the interest rate earned by the IRA over the 25-year period leading up to retirement.

(B) Assume that the IRA continues to earn the interest rate found in part (A). How long can the retiree withdraw $30,000 per year? How long can she withdraw $24,000 per year?

Systems of Linear Equations; Matrices

4

Introduction

Systems of linear equations can be used to solve resource allocation problems in business and economics (see Problems 65 and 68 in Section 4-3 on production schedules for boats and leases for airplanes). Such systems can involve many equations in many variables. So after reviewing methods for solving two linear equations in two variables, we use matrices and matrix operations to develop procedures that are suitable for solving linear systems of any size. We also discuss Wassily Leontief's Nobel prizewinning application of matrices to economic planning for industrialized countries.

4-1   Review: Systems of Linear Equations in Two Variables

- Systems of Linear Equations in Two Variables
- Graphing
- Substitution
- Elimination by Addition
- Applications

Systems of Linear Equations in Two Variables

To establish basic concepts, let's consider the following simple example: If 2 adult tickets and 1 child ticket cost $8, and if 1 adult ticket and 3 child tickets cost $9, what is the price of each?

$$\text{Let:} \quad x = \text{price of adult ticket}$$
$$y = \text{price of child ticket}$$
$$\text{Then:} \quad 2x + y = 8$$
$$x + 3y = 9$$

Now we have a system of two linear equations in two variables. It is easy to find ordered pairs (x, y) that satisfy one or the other of these equations. For example, the ordered pair $(4, 0)$ satisfies the first equation but not the second, and the ordered pair $(6, 1)$ satisfies the second but not the first. To solve this system, we must find all ordered pairs of real numbers that satisfy both equations at the same time. In general, we have the following definition:

DEFINITION   Systems of Two Linear Equations in Two Variables

Given the **linear system**

$$ax + by = h$$
$$cx + dy = k$$

where $a, b, c, d, h,$ and k are real constants, a pair of numbers $x = x_0$ and $y = y_0$ [also written as an ordered pair (x_0, y_0)] is a **solution** of this system if each equation is satisfied by the pair. The set of all such ordered pairs is called the **solution set** for the system. To **solve** a system is to find its solution set.

We will consider three methods of solving such systems: *graphing, substitution,* and *elimination by addition.* Each method has its advantages, depending on the situation.

Graphing

Recall that the graph of a line is a graph of all the ordered pairs that satisfy the equation of the line. To solve the ticket problem by graphing, we graph both equations in the same coordinate system. The coordinates of any points that the graphs have in common must be solutions to the system since they satisfy both equations.

EXAMPLE 1   **Solving a System by Graphing**   Solve the ticket problem by graphing:

$$2x + y = 8$$
$$x + 3y = 9$$

SOLUTION   An easy way to find two distinct points on the first line is to find the x and y intercepts. Substitute $y = 0$ to find the x intercept ($2x = 8$, so $x = 4$), and substitute $x = 0$ to find the y intercept ($y = 8$). Then draw the line through $(4, 0)$ and $(0, 8)$. After graphing both lines in the same coordinate system (Fig. 1), estimate the coordinates of the intersection point:

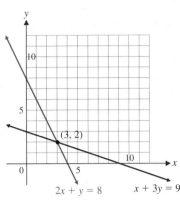

$x = \$3$ Adult ticket

$y = \$2$ Child ticket

Figure 1

CHECK

$$2x + y = 8 \qquad\qquad x + 3y = 9$$
$$2(3) + 2 \stackrel{?}{=} 8 \qquad 3 + 3(2) \stackrel{?}{=} 9$$
$$8 \stackrel{\checkmark}{=} 8 \qquad\qquad 9 \stackrel{\checkmark}{=} 9$$

Check that (3, 2) satisfies each of the original equations.

Matched Problem 1   Solve by graphing and check:

$$2x - y = -3$$
$$x + 2y = -4$$

It is clear that Example 1 has exactly one solution since the lines have exactly one point in common. In general, lines in a rectangular coordinate system are related to each other in one of the three ways illustrated in the next example.

EXAMPLE 2   **Solving a System by Graphing** Solve each of the following systems by graphing:

(A) $x - 2y = 2$ (B) $x + 2y = -4$ (C) $2x + 4y = 8$
    $x + y = 5$ $2x + 4y = 8$ $x + 2y = 4$

SOLUTION   (A)   (B)   (C)

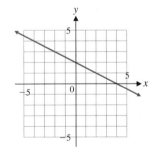

Intersection at one point only—exactly one solution

Lines are parallel (each has slope $-\frac{1}{2}$)—no solutions

Lines coincide—infinite number of solutions

Matched Problem 2   Solve each of the following systems by graphing:

(A) $x + y = 4$ (B) $6x - 3y = 9$ (C) $2x - y = 4$
    $2x - y = 2$ $2x - y = 3$ $6x - 3y = -18$

We introduce some terms that describe the different types of solutions to systems of equations.

DEFINITION Systems of Linear Equations: Basic Terms

A system of linear equations is **consistent** if it has one or more solutions and **inconsistent** if no solutions exist. Furthermore, a consistent system is said to be **independent** if it has exactly one solution (often referred to as the **unique solution**) and **dependent** if it has more than one solution. Two systems of equations are **equivalent** if they have the same solution set.

Referring to the three systems in Example 2, the system in part (A) is consistent and independent with the unique solution $x = 4$, $y = 1$. The system in part (B) is inconsistent. And the system in part (C) is consistent and dependent with an infinite number of solutions (all points on the two coinciding lines).

EXPLORE & DISCUSS 1

Can a consistent and dependent system have exactly two solutions? Exactly three solutions? Explain.

By graphing a system of two linear equations in two variables, we gain useful information about the solution set of the system. In general, any two lines in a coordinate plane must intersect in exactly one point, be parallel, or coincide (have identical graphs). So the systems in Example 2 illustrate the only three possible types of solutions for systems of two linear equations in two variables. These ideas are summarized in Theorem 1.

THEOREM 1 Possible Solutions to a Linear System
The linear system

$$ax + by = h$$
$$cx + dy = k$$

must have

(A) Exactly one solution   Consistent and independent

or

(B) No solution   Inconsistent

or

(C) Infinitely many solutions   Consistent and dependent

There are no other possibilities.

In the past, one drawback to solving systems by graphing was the inaccuracy of hand-drawn graphs. Graphing calculators have changed that. Graphical solutions on a graphing calculator provide an accurate approximation of the solution to a system of linear equations in two variables. Example 3 demonstrates this.

EXAMPLE 3 **Solving a System Using a Graphing Calculator** Solve to two decimal places using graphical approximation techniques on a graphing calculator:

$$5x + 2y = 15$$
$$2x - 3y = 16$$

SOLUTION First, solve each equation for y:

$$5x + 2y = 15$$
$$2y = -5x + 15$$
$$y = -2.5x + 7.5$$

$$2x - 3y = 16$$
$$-3y = -2x + 16$$
$$y = \frac{2}{3}x - \frac{16}{3}$$

Next, enter each equation in the graphing calculator (Fig. 2A), graph in an appropriate viewing window, and approximate the intersection point (Fig. 2B).

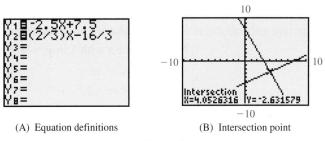

(A) Equation definitions   (B) Intersection point

Figure 2

Rounding the values in Figure 2B to two decimal places, we see that the solution is $x = 4.05$ and $y = -2.63$, or $(4.05, -2.63)$.

CHECK

$$5x + 2y = 15 \qquad\qquad 2x - 3y = 16$$
$$5(4.05) + 2(-2.63) \overset{?}{=} 15 \qquad 2(4.05) - 3(-2.63) \overset{?}{=} 16$$
$$14.99 \overset{\checkmark}{\approx} 15 \qquad\qquad 15.99 \overset{\checkmark}{\approx} 16$$

The checks are sufficiently close but, due to rounding, not exact.

Matched Problem 3

Solve to two decimal places using graphical approximation techniques on a graphing calculator:

$$2x - 5y = -25$$
$$4x + 3y = 5$$

Graphical methods help us to visualize a system and its solutions, reveal relationships that might otherwise be hidden, and, with the assistance of a graphing calculator, provide accurate approximations to solutions.

Substitution

Now we review an algebraic method that is easy to use and provides exact solutions to a system of two equations in two variables, provided that solutions exist. In this method, first we choose one of two equations in a system and solve for one variable in terms of the other. (We make a choice that avoids fractions, if possible.) Then we **substitute** the result into the other equation and solve the resulting linear equation in one variable. Finally, we substitute this result back into the results of the first step to find the second variable.

EXAMPLE 4 **Solving a System by Substitution** Solve by substitution:

$$5x + y = 4$$
$$2x - 3y = 5$$

SOLUTION Solve either equation for one variable in terms of the other; then substitute into the remaining equation. In this problem, we avoid fractions by choosing the first equation and solving for y in terms of x:

$$5x + y = 4 \qquad\qquad \textit{Solve the first equation for y in terms of x.}$$
$$y = 4 - 5x \qquad \textit{Substitute into the second equation.}$$

$$2x - 3y = 5 \qquad\qquad \textit{Second equation}$$

EXAMPLE 7 **Supply and Demand** The price–supply and price–demand equations for the sale of cherries in a large city are

$$p = 0.07x + 0.76 \quad \text{Price–supply equation}$$
$$p = -0.2x + 4 \quad \text{Price–demand equation}$$

where p is the price per pound of cherries and x is the quantity of cherries in thousands of pounds.

(A) Find the supply and demand at a price of $2.09 per pound.

(B) Find the supply and demand at a price of $1.32 per pound.

(C) Use the substitution method to find the equilibrium price and equilibrium quantity.

SOLUTION (A) Substitute $p = 2.09$ into the price–supply equation, and also into the price–demand equation, and solve for x:

Price–supply equation	Price–demand equation
$p = 0.07x + 0.76$	$p = -0.2x + 4$
$2.09 = 0.07x + 0.76$	$2.09 = -0.2x + 4$
$x = 19$	$x = 9.55$

At a price of $2.09 per pound, the supply is 19,000 pounds of cherries and the demand is 9,550 pounds. (The supply is greater than the demand, so the price will tend to come down.)

(B) Substitute $p = 1.32$ in each equation and solve for x:

Price–supply equation	Price–demand equation
$p = 0.07x + 0.76$	$p = -0.2x + 4$
$1.32 = 0.07x + 0.76$	$1.32 = -0.2x + 4$
$x = 8$	$x = 13.4$

At a price of $1.32 per pound, the supply is 8,000 pounds of cherries, and the demand is 13,400 pounds. (The demand is greater than the supply, so the price will tend to go up.)

(C) We solve the linear system

$$p = 0.07x + 0.76 \quad \text{Price–supply equation}$$
$$p = -0.2x + 4 \quad \text{Price–demand equation}$$

using substitution (substitute $p = -0.2x + 4$ in the first equation):

$$-0.2x + 4 = 0.07x + 0.76$$
$$-0.27x = -3.24 \qquad \text{Equilibrium quantity}$$
$$x = 12 \text{ thousand pounds}$$

Now substitute $x = 12$ into the price–demand equation:

$$p = -0.2(12) + 4$$
$$p = \$1.60 \text{ per pound} \qquad \text{Equilibrium price}$$

The results are interpreted graphically in Figure 4 (it is customary to refer to the graphs of price–supply and price–demand equations as "curves" even when they are lines). Note that if the price is above the equilibrium price of $1.60 per pound, the supply will exceed the demand and the price will come down. If the price is below the equilibrium price of $1.60 per pound, the demand will exceed the supply and the price will go up. So the price will stabilize at $1.60 per pound. At this equilibrium price, suppliers will supply 12,000 pounds of cherries and consumers will purchase 12,000 pounds.

Figure 4

Matched Problem 7   Repeat Example 7 (including drawing the graph) given:

$$p = -0.1q + 3 \qquad \text{Price–demand equation}$$
$$p = 0.08q + 0.66 \qquad \text{Price–supply equation}$$

Exercises 4-1

A

Match each system in Problems 1–4 with one of the following graphs, and use the graph to solve the system.

(A)

(B)

(C)

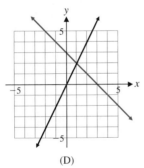

(D)

1. $-4x + 2y = 8$
    $2x - y = 0$

2. $x + y = 3$
    $2x - y = 0$

3. $-x + 2y = 5$
    $2x + 3y = -3$

4. $2x - 4y = -10$
    $-x + 2y = 5$

Solve Problems 5–8 by graphing.

5. $3x - y = 2$
    $x + 2y = 10$

6. $3x - 2y = 12$
    $7x + 2y = 8$

7. $m + 2n = 4$
    $2m + 4n = -8$

8. $3u + 5v = 15$
    $6u + 10v = -30$

Solve Problems 9–12 using substitution.

9. $y = 2x - 3$
    $x + 2y = 14$

10. $y = x - 4$
    $x + 3y = 12$

11. $2x + y = 6$
    $x - y = -3$

12. $3x - y = 7$
    $2x + 3y = 1$

Solve Problems 13–16 using elimination by addition.

13. $3u - 2v = 12$
    $7u + 2v = 8$

14. $2x - 3y = -8$
    $5x + 3y = 1$

15. $2m - n = 10$
    $m - 2n = -4$

16. $2x + 3y = 1$
    $3x - y = 7$

B

Solve Problems 17–26 using substitution or elimination by addition.

17. $9x - 3y = 24$
    $11x + 2y = 1$

18. $4x + 3y = 26$
    $3x - 11y = -7$

19. $2x - 3y = -2$
    $-4x + 6y = 7$

20. $3x - 6y = -9$
    $-2x + 4y = 12$

21. $3x + 8y = 4$
    $15x + 10y = -10$

22. $7m + 12n = -1$
    $5m - 3n = 7$

23. $-6x + 10y = -30$
    $3x - 5y = 15$

24. $2x + 4y = -8$
    $x + 2y = 4$

25. $x + y = 1$
    $0.3x - 0.4y = 0$

26. $x + y = 1$
    $0.5x - 0.4y = 0$

In Problems 27–34, solve the system. Note that each solution can be found mentally, without the use of a calculator or pencil-and-paper calculation; try to visualize the graphs of both lines.

27. $x + 0y = 7$
    $0x + y = 3$

28. $x + 0y = -4$
    $0x + y = 9$

29. $5x + 0y = 4$
    $0x + 3y = -2$

30. $6x + 0y = 7$
    $0x + 4y = 9$

31. $x + y = 0$
    $x - y = 0$

32. $-2x + y = 0$
    $5x - y = 0$

33. $x - 2y = 4$
    $0x + y = 5$

34. $x + 3y = 9$
    $0x + y = -2$

35. In a free competitive market, if the supply of a good is greater than the demand, will the price tend to go up or come down?

36. In a free competitive market, if the demand for a good is greater than the supply, will the price tend to go up or come down?

✏️ *Problems 37–40 are concerned with the linear system*

$$y = mx + b$$
$$y = nx + c$$

where m, b, n, and c are nonzero constants.

37. If the system has a unique solution, discuss the relationships among the four constants.

38. If the system has no solution, discuss the relationships among the four constants.

39. If the system has an infinite number of solutions, discuss the relationships among the four constants.

40. If $m = 0$, how many solutions does the system have?

📉 *In Problems 41–48, use a graphing calculator to find the solution to each system. Round any approximate solutions to three decimal places.*

41. $y = 2x - 9$
$y = 3x + 5$

42. $y = -3x + 3$
$y = 5x + 8$

43. $y = 2x + 1$
$y = 2x + 7$

44. $y = -3x + 6$
$y = -3x + 9$

45. $3x - 2y = 15$
$4x + 3y = 13$

46. $3x - 7y = -20$
$2x + 5y = 8$

47. $-2.4x + 3.5y = 0.1$
$-1.7x + 2.6y = -0.2$

48. $4.2x + 5.4y = -12.9$
$6.4x + 3.7y = -4.5$

C

✏️*In Problems 49–54, graph the equations in the same coordinate system. Find the coordinates of any points where two or more lines intersect and discuss the nature of the solution set.*

49. $x - 2y = -6$
$2x + y = 8$
$x + 2y = -2$

50. $x + y = 3$
$x + 3y = 15$
$3x - y = 5$

51. $x + y = 1$
$x - 2y = -8$
$3x + y = -3$

52. $x - y = 6$
$x - 2y = 8$
$x + 4y = -4$

53. $4x - 3y = -24$
$2x + 3y = 12$
$8x - 6y = 24$

54. $2x + 3y = 18$
$2x - 6y = -6$
$4x + 6y = -24$

✏️ **55.** The coefficients of the three systems given below are similar. One might guess that the solution sets to the three systems would be nearly identical. Develop evidence for or against this guess by considering graphs of the systems and solutions obtained using substitution or elimination by addition.

(A) $5x + 4y = 4$
$11x + 9y = 4$

(B) $5x + 4y = 4$
$11x + 8y = 4$

(C) $5x + 4y = 4$
$10x + 8y = 4$

✏️ **56.** Repeat Problem 55 for the following systems:

(A) $6x - 5y = 10$
$-13x + 11y = -20$

(B) $6x - 5y = 10$
$-13x + 10y = -20$

(C) $6x - 5y = 10$
$-12x + 10y = -20$

Applications

57. Supply and demand for T-shirts. Suppose that the supply and demand equations for printed T-shirts for a particular week are

$$p = 0.7q + 3 \quad \text{Price–supply equation}$$
$$p = -1.7q + 15 \quad \text{Price–demand equation}$$

where p is the price in dollars and q is the quantity in hundreds.

🖊️ (A) Find the supply and demand (to the nearest unit) if T-shirts are $4 each. Discuss the stability of the T-shirt market at this price level.

🖊️ (B) Find the supply and demand (to the nearest unit) if T-shirts are $9 each. Discuss the stability of the T-shirt market at this price level.

(C) Find the equilibrium price and quantity.

(D) Graph the two equations in the same coordinate system and identify the equilibrium point, supply curve, and demand curve.

58. Supply and demand for baseball caps. Suppose that the supply and demand for printed baseball caps for a particular week are

$$p = 0.4q + 3.2 \quad \text{Price–supply equation}$$
$$p = -1.9q + 17 \quad \text{Price–demand equation}$$

where p is the price in dollars and q is the quantity in hundreds.

✏️ (A) Find the supply and demand (to the nearest unit) if baseball caps are $4 each. Discuss the stability of the baseball cap market at this price level.

✏️ (B) Find the supply and demand (to the nearest unit) if baseball caps are $9 each. Discuss the stability of the baseball cap market at this price level.

(C) Find the equilibrium price and quantity.

(D) Graph the two equations in the same coordinate system and identify the equilibrium point, supply curve, and demand curve.

59. Supply and demand for soybeans. At $4.80 per bushel, the annual supply for soybeans in the Midwest is 1.9 billion bushels, and the annual demand is 2.0 billion bushels. When the price increases to $5.10 per bushel, the annual supply increases to 2.1 billion bushels, and the annual demand decreases to 1.8 billion bushels. Assume that the price–supply and price–demand equations are linear. (*Source:* U.S. Census Bureau)

(A) Find the price–supply equation.

(B) Find the price–demand equation.

(C) Find the equilibrium price and quantity.

(D) Graph the two equations in the same coordinate system and identify the equilibrium point, supply curve, and demand curve.

60. Supply and demand for corn. At $2.13 per bushel, the annual supply for corn in the Midwest is 8.9 billion bushels and the annual demand is 6.5 billion bushels. When the price falls to $1.50 per bushel, the annual supply decreases to 8.2 billion bushels and the annual demand increases to 7.4 billion bushels. Assume that the price–supply and price–demand equations are linear. (*Source:* U.S. Census Bureau)

(A) Find the price–supply equation.

(B) Find the price–demand equation.

(C) Find the equilibrium price and quantity.

(D) Graph the two equations in the same coordinate system and identify the equilibrium point, supply curve, and demand curve.

61. Break-even analysis. A small plant manufactures riding lawn mowers. The plant has fixed costs (leases, insurance, etc.) of $48,000 per day and variable costs (labor, materials, etc.) of $1,400 per unit produced. The mowers are sold for $1,800 each. So the cost and revenue equations are

$$y = 48,000 + 1,400x \quad \text{Cost equation}$$
$$y = 1,800x \quad \text{Revenue equation}$$

where x is the total number of mowers produced and sold each day. The daily costs and revenue are in dollars.

(A) How many units must be manufactured and sold each day for the company to break even?

(B) Graph both equations in the same coordinate system and show the break-even point. Interpret the regions between the lines to the left and to the right of the break-even point.

62. Break-even analysis. Repeat Problem 61 with the cost and revenue equations

$$y = 65,000 + 1,100x \quad \text{Cost equation}$$
$$y = 1,600x \quad \text{Revenue equation}$$

63. Break-even analysis. A company markets exercise DVDs that sell for $19.95, including shipping and handling. The monthly fixed costs (advertising, rent, etc.) are $24,000 and the variable costs (materials, shipping, etc) are $7.45 per DVD.

(A) Find the cost equation and the revenue equation.

(B) How many DVDs must be sold each month for the company to break even?

(C) Graph the cost and revenue equations in the same coordinate system and show the break-even point. Interpret the regions between the lines to the left and to the right of the break-even point.

64. Break-even analysis. Repeat Problem 63 if the monthly fixed costs increase to $27,200, the variable costs increase to $9.15, and the company raises the selling price of the DVDs to $21.95.

65. Delivery charges. United Express, a national package delivery service, charges a base price for overnight delivery of packages weighing 1 pound or less and a surcharge for each additional pound (or fraction thereof). A customer is billed $27.75 for shipping a 5-pound package and $64.50 for a 20-pound package. Find the base price and the surcharge for each additional pound.

66. Delivery charges. Refer to Problem 65. Federated Shipping, a competing overnight delivery service, informs the customer in Problem 65 that they would ship the 5-pound package for $29.95 and the 20-pound package for $59.20.

(A) If Federated Shipping computes its cost in the same manner as United Express, find the base price and the surcharge for Federated Shipping.

(B) Devise a simple rule that the customer can use to choose the cheaper of the two services for each package shipped. Justify your answer.

67. Coffee blends. A coffee company uses Colombian and Brazilian coffee beans to produce two blends, robust and mild. A pound of the robust blend requires 12 ounces of Colombian beans and 4 ounces of Brazilian beans. A pound of the mild blend requires 6 ounces of Colombian beans and 10 ounces of Brazilian beans. Coffee is shipped in 132-pound burlap bags. The company has 50 bags of Colombian beans and 40 bags of Brazilian beans on hand. How many pounds of each blend should the company produce in order to use all the available beans?

68. Coffee blends. Refer to Problem 67.

(A) If the company decides to discontinue production of the robust blend and produce only the mild blend, how many pounds of the mild blend can the company produce? How many beans of each type will the company use? Are there any beans that are not used?

(B) Repeat part (A) if the company decides to discontinue production of the mild blend and produce only the robust blend.

69. Animal diet. Animals in an experiment are to be kept under a strict diet. Each animal should receive 20 grams of protein and 6 grams of fat. The laboratory technician is able to purchase two food mixes: Mix A has 10% protein and 6% fat; mix B has 20% protein and 2% fat. How many grams of each mix should be used to obtain the right diet for one animal?

70. Fertilizer. A fruit grower uses two types of fertilizer in an orange grove, brand *A* and brand *B*. Each bag of brand *A* contains 8 pounds of nitrogen and 4 pounds of phosphoric acid. Each bag of brand *B* contains 7 pounds of nitrogen and 6 pounds of phosphoric acid. Tests indicate that the grove needs 720 pounds of nitrogen and 500 pounds of phosphoric acid. How many bags of each brand should be used to provide the required amounts of nitrogen and phosphoric acid?

71. Electronics. A supplier for the electronics industry manufactures keyboards and screens for graphing calculators at plants in Mexico and Taiwan. The hourly production rates at each plant are given in the table. How many hours should each plant be operated to exactly fill an order for 4,000 keyboards and 4,000 screens?

Plant	Keyboards	Screens
Mexico	40	32
Taiwan	20	32

72. Sausage. A company produces Italian sausages and bratwursts at plants in Green Bay and Sheboygan. The hourly production rates at each plant are given in the table. How many hours should each plant operate to exactly fill an order for 62,250 Italian sausages and 76,500 bratwursts?

Plant	Italian Sausage	Bratwurst
Green Bay	800	800
Sheboygan	500	1,000

73. Physics. An object dropped off the top of a tall building falls vertically with constant acceleration. If *s* is the distance of the object above the ground (in feet) *t* seconds after its release, then *s* and *t* are related by an equation of the form $s = a + bt^2$, where *a* and *b* are constants. Suppose the object is 180 feet above the ground 1 second after its release and 132 feet above the ground 2 seconds after its release.

(A) Find the constants *a* and *b*.

(B) How high is the building?

(C) How long does the object fall?

74. Physics. Repeat Problem 73 if the object is 240 feet above the ground after 1 second and 192 feet above the ground after 2 seconds.

75. Earthquakes. An earthquake emits a primary wave and a secondary wave. Near the surface of the Earth the primary wave travels at 5 miles per second and the secondary wave at 3 miles per second. From the time lag between the two waves arriving at a given receiving station, it is possible to estimate the distance to the quake. Suppose a station measured a time difference of 16 seconds between the arrival of the two waves. How long did each wave travel, and how far was the earthquake from the station?

76. Sound waves. A ship using sound-sensing devices above and below water recorded a surface explosion 6 seconds sooner by its underwater device than its above-water device. Sound travels in air at 1,100 feet per second and in seawater at 5,000 feet per second. How long did it take each sound wave to reach the ship? How far was the explosion from the ship?

77. Psychology. People approach certain situations with "mixed emotions." For example, public speaking often brings forth the positive response of recognition and the negative response of

failure. Which dominates? J. S. Brown, in an experiment on approach and avoidance, trained rats by feeding them from a goal box. The rats received mild electric shocks from the same goal box. This established an approach—avoidance conflict relative to the goal box. Using an appropriate apparatus, Brown arrived at the following relationships:

$$p = -\tfrac{1}{5}d + 70 \quad \textit{Approach equation}$$
$$p = -\tfrac{4}{3}d + 230 \quad \textit{Avoidance equation}$$

where $30 \le d \le 172.5$. The approach equation gives the pull (in grams) toward the food goal box when the rat is placed *d* centimeters away from it. The avoidance equation gives the pull (in grams) away from the shock goal box when the rat is placed *d* centimeters from it.

(A) Graph the approach equation and the avoidance equation in the same coordinate system.

(B) Find the value of *d* for the point of intersection of these two equations.

(C) What do you think the rat would do when placed the distance *d* from the box found in part (B)?

(*Source: Journal of Comparative and Physiological Psychology*, 41:450–465.)

Answers to Matched Problems

1. $x = -2, y = -1$

$$2x - \quad y = -3$$
$$2(-2) - (-1) \stackrel{?}{=} -3$$
$$-3 \stackrel{\checkmark}{=} -3$$
$$x + \quad 2y = -4$$
$$(-2) + 2(-1) \stackrel{?}{=} -4$$
$$-4 \stackrel{\checkmark}{=} -4$$

2. (A) $x = 2, y = 2$
(B) Infinitely many solutions
(C) No solution

3. $x = -1.92, y = 4.23$

4. $x = -2, y = 2$

5. $x = 2, y = -1$

6. 16.5 oz of cottage cheese, 12.5 oz of yogurt

7. Equilibrium quantity = 13 thousand pounds; equilibrium price = $1.70 per pound

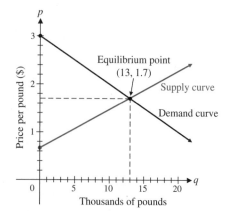

4-2 Systems of Linear Equations and Augmented Matrices

Most linear systems of any consequence involve large numbers of equations and variables. It is impractical to try to solve such systems by hand. In the past, these complex systems could be solved only on large computers. Now there are a wide array of approaches to solving linear systems, ranging from graphing calculators to software and spreadsheets. In the rest of this chapter, we develop several *matrix methods* for solving systems with the understanding that these methods are generally used with a graphing calculator. It is important to keep in mind that we are not presenting these techniques as efficient methods for solving linear systems by hand. Instead, we emphasize formulation of mathematical models and interpretation of the results—two activities that graphing calculators cannot perform for you.

Matrices

In solving systems of equations using elimination by addition, the coefficients of the variables and the constant terms played a central role. The process can be made more efficient for generalization and computer work by the introduction of a mathematical form called a *matrix*. A **matrix** is a rectangular array of numbers written within brackets. Two examples are

$$A = \begin{bmatrix} 1 & -4 & 5 \\ 7 & 0 & -2 \end{bmatrix} \qquad B = \begin{bmatrix} -4 & 5 & 12 \\ 0 & 1 & 8 \\ -3 & 10 & 9 \\ -6 & 0 & -1 \end{bmatrix} \qquad (1)$$

Each number in a matrix is called an **element** of the matrix. Matrix A has 6 elements arranged in 2 rows and 3 columns. Matrix B has 12 elements arranged in 4 rows and 3 columns. If a matrix has m rows and n columns, it is called an **$m \times n$ matrix** (read "m by n matrix"). The expression $m \times n$ is called the **size** of the matrix, and the numbers m and n are called the **dimensions** of the matrix. It is important to note that the number of rows is always given first. Referring to equations (1), A is a 2×3 matrix and B is a 4×3 matrix. A matrix with n rows and n columns is called a **square matrix of order n**. A matrix with only 1 column is called a **column matrix**, and a matrix with only 1 row is called a **row matrix**.

$$
\begin{array}{ccc}
3 \times 3 & 4 \times 1 & 1 \times 4
\end{array}
$$

$$
\begin{bmatrix} 0.5 & 0.2 & 1.0 \\ 0.0 & 0.3 & 0.5 \\ 0.7 & 0.0 & 0.2 \end{bmatrix}
\qquad
\begin{bmatrix} 3 \\ -2 \\ 1 \\ 0 \end{bmatrix}
\qquad
\begin{bmatrix} 2 & \frac{1}{2} & 0 & -\frac{2}{3} \end{bmatrix}
$$

Square matrix of order 3   Column matrix   Row matrix

The **position** of an element in a matrix is given by the row and column containing the element. This is usually denoted using **double subscript notation** a_{ij}, where i is the row and j is the column containing the element a_{ij}, as illustrated below:

$$A = \begin{bmatrix} 1 & -4 & 5 \\ 7 & 0 & -2 \end{bmatrix} \qquad \begin{array}{lll} a_{11} = 1, & a_{12} = -4, & a_{13} = 5 \\ a_{21} = 7, & a_{22} = 0, & a_{23} = -2 \end{array}$$

Note that a_{12} is read "a sub one two" (*not* "a sub twelve"). The elements $a_{11} = 1$ and $a_{22} = 0$ make up the *principal diagonal* of A. In general, the **principal diagonal** of a matrix A consists of the elements $a_{11}, a_{22}, a_{33}, \ldots$.

Remark—Most graphing calculators are capable of storing and manipulating matrices. Figure 1 shows matrix A displayed in the editing screen of a graphing calculator. The size of the matrix is given at the top of the screen. The position and value of the currently selected element is given at the bottom. Note that a comma is used in the notation for the position. This is common practice on many graphing calculators but not in mathematical literature. In

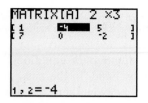

Figure 1 Matrix notation on a graphing calculator

a spreadsheet, matrices are referred to by their location (upper left corner to lower right corner), using either row and column numbers (Fig. 2A) or row numbers and column letters (Fig. 2B).

	1	2	3
1	1	-4	5
2	7	0	-2

	A	B	C	D	E	F
1						
2						
3						
4						
5					1	-4	5
6					7	0	-2

(A) Location of matrix A:
R1C1:R2C3

(B) Location of matrix A:
D5:F6

Figure 2 Matrix notation in a spreadsheet

The coefficients and constant terms in a system of linear equations can be used to form several matrices of interest. Related to the system

$$2x - 3y = 5$$
$$x + 2y = -3 \tag{2}$$

are the following matrices:

Coefficient matrix
$$\begin{bmatrix} 2 & -3 \\ 1 & 2 \end{bmatrix}$$

Constant matrix
$$\begin{bmatrix} 5 \\ -3 \end{bmatrix}$$

Augmented coefficient matrix
$$\begin{bmatrix} 2 & -3 & | & 5 \\ 1 & 2 & | & -3 \end{bmatrix}$$

The augmented coefficient matrix contains all the essential parts of the system—both the coefficients and the constants. The vertical bar is included only as a visual aid to help us separate the coefficients from the constant terms. (Matrices entered and displayed on a graphing calculator or computer will not display this line.) Later in this chapter we use coefficient and constant matrices. For now, we will use just the augmented coefficient matrix.

For ease of generalization to the larger systems in later sections, we will change the notation for the variables in system (2) to a subscript form. That is, in place of x and y, we use x_1 and x_2, respectively, and system (2) is rewritten as

$$2x_1 - 3x_2 = 5$$
$$x_1 + 2x_2 = -3$$

In general, associated with each linear system of the form

$$a_{11}x_1 + a_{12}x_2 = k_1$$
$$a_{21}x_1 + a_{22}x_2 = k_2 \tag{3}$$

where x_1 and x_2 are variables, is the **augmented matrix** of the system:

$$\begin{bmatrix} a_{11} & a_{12} & | & k_1 \\ a_{21} & a_{22} & | & k_2 \end{bmatrix} \begin{array}{l} \leftarrow \text{Row 1 } (R_1) \\ \leftarrow \text{Row 2 } (R_2) \end{array}$$

Column 1 (C_1)
Column 2 (C_2)
Column 3 (C_3)

This matrix contains the essential parts of system (3). Our objective is to learn how to manipulate augmented matrices in order to solve system (3), if a solution exists. The manipulative process is closely related to the elimination process discussed in Section 4-1.

Recall that two linear systems are said to be equivalent if they have the same solution set. In Theorem 2, Section 4-1, we used the operations listed below to transform linear systems into equivalent systems:

(A) Two equations are interchanged.

(B) An equation is multiplied by a nonzero constant.

(C) A constant multiple of one equation is added to another equation.

Paralleling the earlier discussion, we say that two augmented matrices are **row equivalent**, denoted by the symbol $\sim$ placed between the two matrices, if they are augmented matrices of equivalent systems of equations. How do we transform augmented matrices into row-equivalent matrices? We use Theorem 1, which is a direct consequence of the operations listed in Section 4-1.

THEOREM 1   Operations That Produce Row-Equivalent Matrices

An augmented matrix is transformed into a row-equivalent matrix by performing any of the following **row operations**:

(A) Two rows are interchanged ($R_i \leftrightarrow R_j$).

(B) A row is multiplied by a nonzero constant ($kR_i \rightarrow R_i$).

(C) A constant multiple of one row is added to another row
$(kR_j + R_i \rightarrow R_i)$.

Note: The arrow $\rightarrow$ means "replaces."

Solving Linear Systems Using Augmented Matrices

We illustrate the use of Theorem 1 by several examples.

EXAMPLE 1   **Solving a System Using Augmented Matrix Methods** Solve using augmented matrix methods:

$$3x_1 + 4x_2 = 1$$
$$x_1 - 2x_2 = 7 \tag{4}$$

SOLUTION   We start by writing the augmented matrix corresponding to system (4):

$$\begin{bmatrix} 3 & 4 & | & 1 \\ 1 & -2 & | & 7 \end{bmatrix} \tag{5}$$

Our objective is to use row operations from Theorem 1 to try to transform matrix (5) into the form

$$\begin{bmatrix} 1 & 0 & | & m \\ 0 & 1 & | & n \end{bmatrix} \tag{6}$$

where m and n are real numbers. Then the solution to system (4) will be obvious, since matrix (6) will be the augmented matrix of the following system (a row in an augmented matrix always corresponds to an equation in a linear system):

$$\begin{array}{ll} x_1 = m & x_1 + 0x_2 = m \\ x_2 = n & 0x_1 + x_2 = n \end{array}$$

Now we use row operations to transform matrix (5) into form (6).

Step 1   To get a 1 in the upper left corner, we interchange R_1 and R_2 (Theorem 1A):

$$\begin{bmatrix} 3 & 4 & | & 1 \\ 1 & -2 & | & 7 \end{bmatrix} \begin{array}{c} R_1 \leftrightarrow R_2 \\ \sim \end{array} \begin{bmatrix} 1 & -2 & | & 7 \\ 3 & 4 & | & 1 \end{bmatrix}$$

Step 2 To get a 0 in the lower left corner, we multiply R_1 by (-3) and add to R_2 (Theorem 1C)—this changes R_2 but not R_1. Some people find it useful to write $(-3R_1)$ outside the matrix to help reduce errors in arithmetic, as shown:

$$\begin{bmatrix} 1 & -2 & | & 7 \\ 3 & 4 & | & 1 \end{bmatrix} \quad (-3)R_1 + R_2 \rightarrow R_2 \quad \begin{bmatrix} 1 & -2 & | & 7 \\ 0 & 10 & | & -20 \end{bmatrix}$$
$$\begin{array}{ccc} -3 & 6 & -21 \end{array}$$

Step 3 To get a 1 in the second row, second column, we multiply R_2 by $\frac{1}{10}$ (Theorem 1B):

$$\begin{bmatrix} 1 & -2 & | & 7 \\ 0 & 10 & | & -20 \end{bmatrix} \quad \tfrac{1}{10}R_2 \rightarrow R_2 \quad \begin{bmatrix} 1 & -2 & | & 7 \\ 0 & 1 & | & -2 \end{bmatrix}$$

Step 4 To get a 0 in the first row, second column, we multiply R_2 by 2 and add the result to R_1 (Theorem 1C)—this changes R_1 but not R_2:

$$\begin{array}{ccc} 0 & 2 & -4 \end{array}$$
$$\begin{bmatrix} 1 & -2 & | & 7 \\ 0 & 1 & | & -2 \end{bmatrix} \quad 2R_2 + R_1 \rightarrow R_1 \quad \begin{bmatrix} 1 & 0 & | & 3 \\ 0 & 1 & | & -2 \end{bmatrix}$$

We have accomplished our objective! The last matrix is the augmented matrix for the system

$$\begin{aligned} x_1 &= 3 & x_1 + 0x_2 &= 3 \\ x_2 &= -2 & 0x_1 + x_2 &= -2 \end{aligned} \tag{7}$$

Since system (7) is equivalent to system (4), our starting system, we have solved system (4); that is, $x_1 = 3$ and $x_2 = -2$.

CHECK

$$\begin{aligned} 3x_1 + 4x_2 &= 1 & x_1 - 2x_2 &= 7 \\ 3(3) + 4(-2) &\overset{?}{=} 1 & 3 - 2(-2) &\overset{?}{=} 7 \\ 1 &\overset{\checkmark}{=} 1 & 7 &\overset{\checkmark}{=} 7 \end{aligned}$$

The preceding process may be written more compactly as follows:

Step 1:
Need a 1 here.
$$\begin{bmatrix} 3 & 4 & | & 1 \\ 1 & -2 & | & 7 \end{bmatrix} \quad R_1 \leftrightarrow R_2$$

Step 2:
Need a 0 here.
$$\sim \begin{bmatrix} 1 & -2 & | & 7 \\ 3 & 4 & | & 1 \end{bmatrix} \quad (-3)R_1 + R_2 \rightarrow R_2$$
$$\begin{array}{ccc} -3 & 6 & -21 \end{array}$$

Step 3:
Need a 1 here.
$$\sim \begin{bmatrix} 1 & -2 & | & 7 \\ 0 & 10 & | & -20 \end{bmatrix} \quad \tfrac{1}{10}R_2 \rightarrow R_2$$

Step 4:
Need a 0 here.
$$\begin{array}{ccc} 0 & 2 & -4 \end{array}$$
$$\sim \begin{bmatrix} 1 & -2 & | & 7 \\ 0 & 1 & | & -2 \end{bmatrix} \quad 2R_2 + R_1 \rightarrow R_1$$

$$\sim \begin{bmatrix} 1 & 0 & | & 3 \\ 0 & 1 & | & -2 \end{bmatrix}$$

Therefore, $x_1 = 3$ and $x_2 = -2$.

Matched Problem 1   Solve using augmented matrix methods:

$$2x_1 - x_2 = -7$$
$$x_1 + 2x_2 = 4$$

Many graphing calculators can perform row operations. Figure 3 shows the results of performing the row operations used in the solution of Example 1. Consult your manual for the details of performing row operations on your graphing calculator.

(A) $R_1 \leftrightarrow R_2$

(B) $(-3)R_1 + R_2 \to R_2$

(C) $\frac{1}{10}R_2 \to R_2$

[A]
[[1 -2 7]
 [0 1 -2]]
*row+(2,[A],2,1)

[[1 0 3]
 [0 1 -2]]

(D) $2R_2 + R_1 \to R_1$

Figure 3 Row operations on a graphing calculator

EXPLORE & DISCUSS 1   The summary following the solution of Example 1 shows five augmented coefficient matrices. Write the linear system that each matrix represents, solve each system graphically, and discuss the relationships among these solutions.

EXAMPLE 2   **Solving a System Using Augmented Matrix Methods** Solve using augmented matrix methods:

$$2x_1 - 3x_2 = 6$$
$$3x_1 + 4x_2 = \frac{1}{2}$$

SOLUTION

Step 1:
Need a 1 here.
$$\begin{bmatrix} 2 & -3 \\ 3 & 4 \end{bmatrix} \begin{array}{|c} 6 \\ \frac{1}{2} \end{array} \quad \tfrac{1}{2}R_1 \to R_1$$

Step 2:
Need a 0 here.
$$\sim \begin{bmatrix} 1 & -\frac{3}{2} \\ 3 & 4 \end{bmatrix} \begin{array}{|c} 3 \\ \frac{1}{2} \end{array} \quad (-3)R_1 + R_2 \to R_2$$
$$-3 \quad \frac{9}{2} \qquad -9$$

Step 3:
Need a 1 here.
$$\sim \begin{bmatrix} 1 & -\frac{3}{2} \\ 0 & \frac{17}{2} \end{bmatrix} \begin{array}{|c} 3 \\ -\frac{17}{2} \end{array} \quad \tfrac{2}{17}R_2 \to R_2$$
$$0 \quad \frac{3}{2} \qquad -\frac{3}{2}$$

Step 4:
Need a 0 here.
$$\sim \begin{bmatrix} 1 & -\frac{3}{2} \\ 0 & 1 \end{bmatrix} \begin{array}{|c} 3 \\ -1 \end{array} \quad \tfrac{3}{2}R_2 + R_1 \to R_1$$

$$\sim \begin{bmatrix} 1 & 0 \\ 0 & 1 \end{bmatrix} \begin{array}{|c} \frac{3}{2} \\ -1 \end{array}$$

So, $x_1 = \frac{3}{2}$ and $x_2 = -1$. The check is left for you.

Matched Problem 2 Solve using augmented matrix methods:

$$2x_1 - 2x_2 = 11$$

$$5x_1 - 2x_2 = 11$$
$$2x_1 + 3x_2 = \frac{5}{2}$$

EXAMPLE 3 **Solving a System Using Augmented Matrix Methods** Solve using augmented matrix methods:

$$\begin{matrix} 2x_1 - x_2 = 4 \\ -6x_1 + 3x_2 = -12 \end{matrix} \qquad (8)$$

SOLUTION

$$\begin{bmatrix} 2 & -1 & \bigm| & 4 \\ -6 & 3 & \bigm| & -12 \end{bmatrix} \quad \begin{matrix} \frac{1}{2}R_1 \to R_1 \text{ (to get a 1 in the upper left corner)} \\ \frac{1}{3}R_2 \to R_2 \text{ (this simplifies } R_2) \end{matrix}$$

$$\sim \begin{bmatrix} 1 & -\frac{1}{2} & \bigm| & 2 \\ -2 & 1 & \bigm| & -4 \end{bmatrix} \quad 2R_1 + R_2 \to R_2 \text{ (to get a 0 in the lower left corner)}$$

$$\begin{matrix} 2 & -1 & & 4 \end{matrix}$$

$$\sim \begin{bmatrix} 1 & -\frac{1}{2} & \bigm| & 2 \\ 0 & 0 & \bigm| & 0 \end{bmatrix}$$

The last matrix corresponds to the system

$$x_1 - \frac{1}{2}x_2 = 2 \qquad x_1 - \frac{1}{2}x_2 = 2 \qquad (9)$$
$$0 = 0 \qquad 0x_1 + 0x_2 = 0$$

This system is equivalent to the original system. Geometrically, the graphs of the two original equations coincide, and there are infinitely many solutions. In general, if we end up with a row of zeros in an augmented matrix for a two-equation, two-variable system, the system is dependent, and there are infinitely many solutions.

We represent the infinitely many solutions using the same method that was used in Section 4-1; that is, by introducing a parameter. We start by solving $x_1 - \frac{1}{2}x_2 = 2$, the first equation in system (9), for either variable in terms of the other. We choose to solve for x_1 in terms of x_2 because it is easier:

$$x_1 = \frac{1}{2}x_2 + 2 \qquad (10)$$

Now we introduce a parameter t (we can use other letters, such as k, s, p, q, and so on, to represent a parameter also). If we let $x_2 = t$, then for any real number t,

$$x_1 = \frac{1}{2}t + 2 \qquad (11)$$
$$x_2 = t$$

represents a solution of system (8). Using ordered-pair notation, we write: For any real number t,

$$\left(\frac{1}{2}t + 2, t \right) \qquad (12)$$

is a solution of system (8). More formally, we write

$$\text{solution set} = \left\{ \left(\frac{1}{2}t + 2, t \right) \,\middle|\, t \in R \right\} \qquad (13)$$

Typically we use the less formal notations (11) or (12) to represent the solution set for problems of this type.

CHECK   The following is a check that system (11) provides a solution to system (8) for any real number t:

$$2x_1 - x_2 = 4 \qquad\qquad -6x_1 + 3x_2 = -12$$

$$2\left(\frac{1}{2}t + 2\right) - t \overset{?}{=} 4 \qquad\qquad -6\left(\frac{1}{2}t + 2\right) + 3t \overset{?}{=} -12$$

$$t + 4 - t \overset{?}{=} 4 \qquad\qquad -3t - 12 + 3t \overset{?}{=} -12$$

$$4 \overset{\checkmark}{=} 4 \qquad\qquad -12 \overset{\checkmark}{=} -12$$

Matched Problem 3   Solve using augmented matrix methods:

$$-2x_1 + 6x_2 = 6$$
$$3x_1 - 9x_2 = -9$$

EXPLORE & DISCUSS 2   The solution of Example 3 involved three augmented coefficient matrices. Write the linear system that each matrix represents, solve each system graphically, and discuss the relationships among these solutions.

EXAMPLE 4   **Solving a System Using Augmented Matrix Methods** Solve using augmented matrix methods:

$$2x_1 + 6x_2 = -3$$
$$x_1 + 3x_2 = 2$$

SOLUTION

$$\begin{bmatrix} 2 & 6 & | & -3 \\ 1 & 3 & | & 2 \end{bmatrix} \quad R_1 \leftrightarrow R_2$$

$$\sim \begin{bmatrix} 1 & 3 & | & 2 \\ 2 & 6 & | & -3 \end{bmatrix} \quad (-2)R_1 + R_2 \to R_2$$
$$\quad\, -2\ -6 \qquad -4 \leftarrow$$

$$\sim \begin{bmatrix} 1 & 3 & | & 2 \\ 0 & 0 & | & -7 \end{bmatrix} \quad R_2 \text{ implies the contradiction } 0 = -7.$$

This is the augmented matrix of the system

$$x_1 + 3x_2 = 2 \qquad x_1 + 3x_2 = 2$$
$$0 = -7 \qquad 0x_1 + 0x_2 = -7$$

The second equation is not satisfied by any ordered pair of real numbers. As we saw in Section 4-1, the original system is inconsistent and has no solution. If in a row of an augmented matrix we obtain all zeros to the left of the vertical bar and a nonzero number to the right, the system is inconsistent and there are no solutions.

Matched Problem 4   Solve using augmented matrix methods:

$$2x_1 - x_2 = 3$$
$$4x_1 - 2x_2 = -1$$

Summary

Examples 2, 3, and 4 illustrate the three possible solution types for a system of two linear equations in two variables, as discussed in Theorem 1, Section 4-1. Examining the final matrix form in each of these solutions leads to the following summary.

SUMMARY **Possible Final Matrix Forms for a System of Two Linear Equations in Two Variables**

Form 1: Exactly one solution (consistent and independent)

$$\left[\begin{array}{cc|c} 1 & 0 & m \\ 0 & 1 & n \end{array}\right]$$

Form 2: Infinitely many solutions (consistent and dependent)

$$\left[\begin{array}{cc|c} 1 & m & n \\ 0 & 0 & 0 \end{array}\right]$$

Form 3: No solution (inconsistent)

$$\left[\begin{array}{cc|c} 1 & m & n \\ 0 & 0 & p \end{array}\right]$$

m, n, p are real numbers; $p \neq 0$

The process of solving systems of equations described in this section is referred to as **Gauss–Jordan elimination.** We formalize this method in the next section so that it will apply to systems of any size, including systems where the number of equations and the number of variables are not the same.

Exercises 4-2

A

Problems 1–10 refer to the following matrices:

$$A = \begin{bmatrix} 2 & -4 & 0 \\ 6 & 1 & -5 \end{bmatrix} \qquad B = \begin{bmatrix} -1 & 9 & 0 \\ -4 & 8 & 7 \\ 2 & 4 & 0 \end{bmatrix}$$

$$C = \begin{bmatrix} 2 & -3 & 0 \end{bmatrix} \qquad D = \begin{bmatrix} -5 \\ 8 \end{bmatrix}$$

1. What is the size of A? Of C?

2. What is the size of B? Of D?

3. Identify all row matrices.

4. Identify all column matrices.

5. Identify all square matrices.

6. For matrix B, find b_{21} and b_{13}.

7. For matrix A, find a_{12} and a_{23}.

8. For matrices C and D, find c_{13} and d_{21}.

9. Find the elements on the principal diagonal of matrix B.

10. Find the elements on the principal diagonal of matrix A.

Problems 11 and 12 refer to the matrices shown below.

$$E = \begin{bmatrix} 1 & -2 & 3 & 9 \\ -5 & 0 & 7 & -8 \end{bmatrix} \qquad F = \begin{bmatrix} 4 & -6 \\ 2 & 3 \\ -5 & 7 \end{bmatrix}$$

11. (A) What is the size of E?

   (B) How many additional columns would F have to have to be a square matrix?

   (C) Find e_{23} and f_{12}.

12. (A) What is the size of F?

   (B) How many additional rows would E have to have to be a square matrix?

   (C) Find e_{14} and f_{31}.

Perform the row operations indicated in Problems 13–24 on the following matrix:

$$\left[\begin{array}{cc|c} 1 & -3 & 2 \\ 4 & -6 & -8 \end{array}\right]$$

13. $R_1 \leftrightarrow R_2$

14. $\frac{1}{2}R_2 \rightarrow R_2$

15. $-4R_1 \rightarrow R_1$

16. $-2R_1 \rightarrow R_1$

17. $2R_2 \rightarrow R_2$

18. $-1R_2 \rightarrow R_2$

19. $(-4)R_1 + R_2 \rightarrow R_2$

20. $\left(-\frac{1}{2}\right)R_2 + R_1 \rightarrow R_1$

21. $(-2)R_1 + R_2 \rightarrow R_2$

22. $(-3)R_1 + R_2 \rightarrow R_2$

23. $(-1)R_1 + R_2 \rightarrow R_2$

24. $R_1 + R_2 \rightarrow R_2$

Each of the matrices in Problems 25–32 is the result of performing a single row operation on the matrix A shown below. Identify the row operation.

$$A = \left[\begin{array}{cc|c} -1 & 2 & -3 \\ 6 & -3 & 12 \end{array}\right]$$

25. $\left[\begin{array}{cc|c} -1 & 2 & -3 \\ 2 & -1 & 4 \end{array}\right]$

26. $\left[\begin{array}{cc|c} -2 & 4 & -6 \\ 6 & -3 & 12 \end{array}\right]$

27. $\left[\begin{array}{cc|c} -1 & 2 & -3 \\ 0 & 9 & -6 \end{array}\right]$

28. $\left[\begin{array}{cc|c} 3 & 0 & 5 \\ 6 & -3 & 12 \end{array}\right]$

29. $\left[\begin{array}{cc|c} 1 & 1 & 1 \\ 6 & -3 & 12 \end{array}\right]$

30. $\left[\begin{array}{cc|c} -1 & 2 & -3 \\ 2 & 5 & 0 \end{array}\right]$

31. $\left[\begin{array}{cc|c} 6 & -3 & 12 \\ -1 & 2 & -3 \end{array}\right]$

32. $\left[\begin{array}{cc|c} -1 & 2 & -3 \\ 0 & 9 & -6 \end{array}\right]$

✎ *Solve Problems 33–36 using augmented matrix methods. Graph each solution set. Discuss the differences between the graph of an equation in the system and the graph of the system's solution set.*

33. $3x_1 - 2x_2 = 6$
$\quad 4x_1 - 3x_2 = 6$

34. $x_1 - 2x_2 = 5$
$\quad -2x_1 + 4x_2 = -10$

35. $3x_1 - 2x_2 = -3$
$\quad -6x_1 + 4x_2 = 6$

36. $x_1 - 2x_2 = 1$
$\quad -2x_1 + 5x_2 = 2$

✎ *Solve Problems 37 and 38 using augmented matrix methods. Write the linear system represented by each augmented matrix in your solution, and solve each of these systems graphically. Discuss the relationships among the solutions of these systems.*

37. $x_1 + x_2 = 5$
$\quad x_1 - x_2 = 1$

38. $x_1 - x_2 = 2$
$\quad x_1 + x_2 = 6$

Each of the matrices in Problems 39–44 is the final matrix form for a system of two linear equations in the variables x_1 and x_2. Write the solution of the system.

39. $\begin{bmatrix} 1 & 0 & | & -4 \\ 0 & 1 & | & 6 \end{bmatrix}$

40. $\begin{bmatrix} 1 & 0 & | & 3 \\ 0 & 1 & | & -5 \end{bmatrix}$

41. $\begin{bmatrix} 1 & 3 & | & 2 \\ 0 & 0 & | & 4 \end{bmatrix}$

42. $\begin{bmatrix} 1 & -2 & | & 7 \\ 0 & 0 & | & -9 \end{bmatrix}$

43. $\begin{bmatrix} 1 & -2 & | & 15 \\ 0 & 0 & | & 0 \end{bmatrix}$

44. $\begin{bmatrix} 1 & 5 & | & 10 \\ 0 & 0 & | & 0 \end{bmatrix}$

B

Solve Problems 45–64 using augmented matrix methods.

45. $x_1 - 2x_2 = 1$
$\quad 2x_1 - x_2 = 5$

46. $x_1 + 3x_2 = 1$
$\quad 3x_1 - 2x_2 = 14$

47. $x_1 - 4x_2 = -2$
$\quad -2x_1 + x_2 = -3$

48. $x_1 - 3x_2 = -5$
$\quad -3x_1 - x_2 = 5$

49. $3x_1 - x_2 = 2$
$\quad x_1 + 2x_2 = 10$

50. $2x_1 + x_2 = 0$
$\quad x_1 - 2x_2 = -5$

51. $x_1 + 2x_2 = 4$
$\quad 2x_1 + 4x_2 = -8$

52. $2x_1 - 3x_2 = -2$
$\quad -4x_1 + 6x_2 = 7$

53. $2x_1 + x_2 = 6$
$\quad x_1 - x_2 = -3$

54. $3x_1 - x_2 = -5$
$\quad x_1 + 3x_2 = 5$

55. $3x_1 - 6x_2 = -9$
$\quad -2x_1 + 4x_2 = 6$

56. $2x_1 - 4x_2 = -2$
$\quad -3x_1 + 6x_2 = 3$

57. $4x_1 - 2x_2 = 2$
$\quad -6x_1 + 3x_2 = -3$

58. $-6x_1 + 2x_2 = 4$
$\quad 3x_1 - x_2 = -2$

59. $2x_1 + x_2 = 1$
$\quad 4x_1 - x_2 = -7$

60. $2x_1 - x_2 = -8$
$\quad 2x_1 + x_2 = 8$

61. $4x_1 - 6x_2 = 8$
$\quad -6x_1 + 9x_2 = -10$

62. $2x_1 - 4x_2 = -4$
$\quad -3x_1 + 6x_2 = 4$

63. $-4x_1 + 6x_2 = -8$
$\quad 6x_1 - 9x_2 = 12$

64. $-2x_1 + 4x_2 = 4$
$\quad 3x_1 - 6x_2 = -6$

C

Solve Problems 61–66 using augmented matrix methods.

65. $3x_1 - x_2 = 7$
$\quad 2x_1 + 3x_2 = 1$

66. $2x_1 - 3x_2 = -8$
$\quad 5x_1 + 3x_2 = 1$

67. $3x_1 + 2x_2 = 4$
$\quad 2x_1 - x_2 = 5$

68. $4x_1 + 3x_2 = 26$
$\quad 3x_1 - 11x_2 = -7$

69. $0.2x_1 - 0.5x_2 = 0.07$
$\quad 0.8x_1 - 0.3x_2 = 0.79$

70. $0.3x_1 - 0.6x_2 = 0.18$
$\quad 0.5x_1 - 0.2x_2 = 0.54$

 Solve Problems 71–74 using augmented matrix methods. Use a graphing calculator to perform the row operations.

71. $0.8x_1 + 2.88x_2 = 4$
$\quad 1.25x_1 + 4.34x_2 = 5$

72. $2.7x_1 - 15.12x_2 = 27$
$\quad 3.25x_1 - 18.52x_2 = 33$

73. $4.8x_1 - 40.32x_2 = 295.2$
$\quad -3.75x_1 + 28.7x_2 = -211.2$

74. $5.7x_1 - 8.55x_2 = -35.91$
$\quad 4.5x_1 + 5.73x_2 = 76.17$

Answers to Matched Problems

1. $x_1 = -2, x_2 = 3$

2. $x_1 = 2, x_2 = -\frac{1}{2}$

3. The system is dependent. For t any real number, a solution is $x_1 = 3t - 3, x_2 = t$.

4. Inconsistent—no solution

4-3 Gauss–Jordan Elimination

- Reduced Matrices
- Solving Systems by Gauss–Jordan Elimination
- Application

Now that you have had some experience with row operations on simple augmented matrices, we consider systems involving more than two variables. We will not require a system to have the same number of equations as variables. Just as for systems of two linear equations in two variables, any linear system, regardless of the number of equations or number of variables, has either

1. Exactly one solution (consistent and independent), or
2. Infinitely many solutions (consistent and dependent), or
3. No solution (inconsistent).

Reduced Matrices

In the preceding section we used row operations to transform the augmented coefficient matrix for a system of two equations in two variables,

$$\begin{bmatrix} a_{11} & a_{12} & k_1 \\ a_{21} & a_{22} & k_2 \end{bmatrix} \qquad \begin{matrix} a_{11}x_1 + a_{12}x_2 = k_1 \\ a_{21}x_1 + a_{22}x_2 = k_2 \end{matrix}$$

into one of the following simplified forms:

Form 1   Form 2   Form 3

$$\begin{bmatrix} 1 & 0 & m \\ 0 & 1 & n \end{bmatrix} \begin{bmatrix} 1 & m & n \\ 0 & 0 & 0 \end{bmatrix} \begin{bmatrix} 1 & m & n \\ 0 & 0 & p \end{bmatrix} \qquad (1)$$

where m, n, and p are real numbers, $p \neq 0$. Each of these reduced forms represents a system that has a different type of solution set, and no two of these forms are row equivalent.

For large linear systems, it is not practical to list all such simplified forms; there are too many of them. Instead, we give a general definition of a simplified form called a **reduced matrix**, which can be applied to all matrices and systems, regardless of size.

DEFINITION   Reduced Form

A matrix is said to be in **reduced row echelon form**, or, more simply, in **reduced form**, if

1. Each row consisting entirely of zeros is below any row having at least one nonzero element.
2. The leftmost nonzero element in each row is 1.
3. All other elements in the column containing the leftmost 1 of a given row are zeros.
4. The leftmost 1 in any row is to the right of the leftmost 1 in the row above.

The following matrices are in reduced form. Check each one carefully to convince yourself that the conditions in the definition are met.

$$\begin{bmatrix} 1 & 0 & 2 \\ 0 & 1 & -3 \end{bmatrix} \begin{bmatrix} 1 & 0 & 0 & 2 \\ 0 & 1 & 0 & -1 \\ 0 & 0 & 1 & 3 \end{bmatrix} \begin{bmatrix} 1 & 0 & 3 \\ 0 & 1 & -1 \\ 0 & 0 & 0 \end{bmatrix}$$

$$\begin{bmatrix} 1 & 4 & 0 & 0 & -3 \\ 0 & 0 & 1 & 0 & 2 \\ 0 & 0 & 0 & 1 & 6 \end{bmatrix} \begin{bmatrix} 1 & 0 & 4 & 0 \\ 0 & 1 & 3 & 0 \\ 0 & 0 & 0 & 1 \end{bmatrix}$$

EXAMPLE 1   **Reduced Forms** The following matrices are not in reduced form. Indicate which condition in the definition is violated for each matrix. State the row operation(s) required to transform the matrix into reduced form, and find the reduced form.

(A) $\begin{bmatrix} 0 & 1 & -2 \\ 1 & 0 & 3 \end{bmatrix}$ (B) $\begin{bmatrix} 1 & 2 & -2 & 3 \\ 0 & 0 & 1 & -1 \end{bmatrix}$

$$(C) \begin{bmatrix} 1 & 0 & | & -3 \\ 0 & 0 & | & 0 \\ 0 & 1 & | & -2 \end{bmatrix} \qquad (D) \begin{bmatrix} 1 & 0 & 0 & | & -1 \\ 0 & 2 & 0 & | & 3 \\ 0 & 0 & 1 & | & -5 \end{bmatrix}$$

SOLUTION (A) Condition 4 is violated: The leftmost 1 in row 2 is not to the right of the leftmost 1 in row 1. Perform the row operation $R_1 \leftrightarrow R_2$ to obtain

$$\begin{bmatrix} 1 & 0 & | & 3 \\ 0 & 1 & | & -2 \end{bmatrix}$$

(B) Condition 3 is violated: The column containing the leftmost 1 in row 2 has a nonzero element above the 1. Perform the row operation $2R_2 + R_1 \rightarrow R_1$ to obtain

$$\begin{bmatrix} 1 & 2 & 0 & | & 1 \\ 0 & 0 & 1 & | & -1 \end{bmatrix}$$

(C) Condition 1 is violated: The second row contains all zeros and is not below any row having at least one nonzero element. Perform the row operation $R_2 \leftrightarrow R_3$ to obtain

$$\begin{bmatrix} 1 & 0 & | & -3 \\ 0 & 1 & | & -2 \\ 0 & 0 & | & 0 \end{bmatrix}$$

(D) Condition 2 is violated: The leftmost nonzero element in row 2 is not a 1. Perform the row operation $\frac{1}{2}R_2 \rightarrow R_2$ to obtain

$$\begin{bmatrix} 1 & 0 & 0 & | & -1 \\ 0 & 1 & 0 & | & \frac{3}{2} \\ 0 & 0 & 1 & | & -5 \end{bmatrix}$$

Matched Problem 1 The matrices below are not in reduced form. Indicate which condition in the definition is violated for each matrix. State the row operation(s) required to transform the matrix into reduced form, and find the reduced form.

$$(A) \begin{bmatrix} 1 & 0 & | & 2 \\ 0 & 3 & | & -6 \end{bmatrix} \qquad (B) \begin{bmatrix} 1 & 5 & 4 & | & 3 \\ 0 & 1 & 2 & | & -1 \\ 0 & 0 & 0 & | & 0 \end{bmatrix}$$

$$(C) \begin{bmatrix} 0 & 1 & 0 & | & -3 \\ 1 & 0 & 0 & | & 0 \\ 0 & 0 & 1 & | & 2 \end{bmatrix} \qquad (D) \begin{bmatrix} 1 & 2 & 0 & | & 3 \\ 0 & 0 & 0 & | & 0 \\ 0 & 0 & 1 & | & 4 \end{bmatrix}$$

Solving Systems by Gauss–Jordan Elimination

We are now ready to outline the Gauss–Jordan method for solving systems of linear equations. The method systematically transforms an augmented matrix into a reduced form. The system corresponding to a reduced augmented coefficient matrix is called a **reduced system**. As we shall see, reduced systems are easy to solve.

The Gauss–Jordan elimination method is named after the German mathematician Carl Friedrich Gauss (1777–1885) and the German geodesist Wilhelm Jordan

(1842–1899). Gauss, one of the greatest mathematicians of all time, used a method of solving systems of equations in his astronomical work that was later generalized by Jordan to solve problems in large-scale surveying.

EXAMPLE 2 **Solving a System Using Gauss–Jordan Elimination** Solve by Gauss–Jordan elimination:

$$2x_1 - 2x_2 + x_3 = 3$$
$$3x_1 + x_2 - x_3 = 7$$
$$x_1 - 3x_2 + 2x_3 = 0$$

SOLUTION Write the augmented matrix and follow the steps indicated at the right.

Need a 1 here.

$$\begin{bmatrix} 2 & -2 & 1 & | & 3 \\ 3 & 1 & -1 & | & 7 \\ 1 & -3 & 2 & | & 0 \end{bmatrix} \quad R_1 \leftrightarrow R_3$$

Step 1 Choose the leftmost nonzero column and get a 1 at the top.

Need O's here.

$$\sim \begin{bmatrix} 1 & -3 & 2 & | & 0 \\ 3 & 1 & -1 & | & 7 \\ 2 & -2 & 1 & | & 3 \end{bmatrix} \quad \begin{matrix} \\ (-3)R_1 + R_2 \to R_2 \\ (-2)R_1 + R_3 \to R_3 \end{matrix}$$

Step 2 Use multiples of the row containing the 1 from step 1 to get zeros in all remaining places in the column containing this 1.

Need a 1 here.

$$\sim \begin{bmatrix} 1 & -3 & 2 & | & 0 \\ 0 & 10 & -7 & | & 7 \\ 0 & 4 & -3 & | & 3 \end{bmatrix} \quad 0.1R_2 \to R_2$$

Step 3 Repeat step 1 with the *submatrix* formed by (mentally) deleting the top row.

Need O's here.

$$\sim \begin{bmatrix} 1 & -3 & 2 & | & 0 \\ 0 & 1 & -0.7 & | & 0.7 \\ 0 & 4 & -3 & | & 3 \end{bmatrix} \quad \begin{matrix} 3R_2 + R_1 \to R_1 \\ \\ (-4)R_2 + R_3 \to R_3 \end{matrix}$$

Step 4 Repeat step 2 with the *entire matrix*.

Need a 1 here.

$$\sim \begin{bmatrix} 1 & 0 & -0.1 & | & 2.1 \\ 0 & 1 & -0.7 & | & 0.7 \\ 0 & 0 & -0.2 & | & 0.2 \end{bmatrix} \quad (-5)R_3 \to R_3$$

Step 3 Repeat step 1 with the *submatrix* formed by (mentally) deleting the top rows.

Need O's here.

$$\sim \begin{bmatrix} 1 & 0 & -0.1 & | & 2.1 \\ 0 & 1 & -0.7 & | & 0.7 \\ 0 & 0 & 1 & | & -1 \end{bmatrix} \quad \begin{matrix} 0.1R_3 + R_1 \to R_1 \\ 0.7R_3 + R_2 \to R_2 \end{matrix}$$

Step 4 Repeat step 2 with the *entire matrix*.

$$\sim \begin{bmatrix} 1 & 0 & 0 & | & 2 \\ 0 & 1 & 0 & | & 0 \\ 0 & 0 & 1 & | & -1 \end{bmatrix}$$

The matrix is now in reduced form, and we can solve the corresponding reduced system.

$$\begin{matrix} x_1 & & & = & 2 \\ & x_2 & & = & 0 \\ & & x_3 & = & -1 \end{matrix}$$

The solution to this system is $x_1 = 2$, $x_2 = 0$, $x_3 = -1$. You should check this solution in the original system.

PROCEDURE Gauss–Jordan Elimination

Step 1 Choose the leftmost nonzero column and use appropriate row operations to get a 1 at the top.

Step 2 Use multiples of the row containing the 1 from step 1 to get zeros in all remaining places in the column containing this 1.

Step 3 Repeat step 1 with the **submatrix** formed by (mentally) deleting the row used in step 2 and all rows above this row.

Step 4 Repeat step 2 with the **entire matrix,** including the rows deleted mentally. Continue this process until the entire matrix is in reduced form.

Note: If at any point in this process we obtain a row with all zeros to the left of the vertical line and a nonzero number to the right, we can stop before we find the reduced form since we will have a contradiction: $0 = n, n \neq 0$. We can then conclude that the system has no solution.

Remarks

1. Even though each matrix has a unique reduced form, the sequence of steps presented here for transforming a matrix into a reduced form is not unique. For example, it is possible to use row operations in such a way that computations involving fractions are minimized. But we emphasize again that we are not interested in the most efficient hand methods for transforming small matrices into reduced forms. Our main interest is in giving you a little experience with a method that is suitable for solving large-scale systems on a graphing calculator or computer.

2. Most graphing calculators have the ability to find reduced forms. Figure 1 illustrates the solution of Example 2 on a TI-86 graphing calculator using the rref command (rref is an acronym for reduced row echelon form). Notice that in row 2 and column 4 of the reduced form the graphing calculator has displayed the very small number $-3.5\text{E}-13$, instead of the exact value 0. This is a common occurrence on a graphing calculator and causes no problems. Just replace any very small numbers displayed in scientific notation with 0.

Figure 1 Gauss–Jordan elimination on a graphing calculator

Matched Problem 2   Solve by Gauss–Jordan elimination:

$$
\begin{aligned}
3x_1 + \ x_2 - 2x_3 &= 2 \\
x_1 - 2x_2 + \ x_3 &= 3 \\
2x_1 - \ x_2 - 3x_3 &= 3
\end{aligned}
$$

EXAMPLE 3   Solving a System Using Gauss–Jordan Elimination   Solve by Gauss–Jordan elimination:

$$2x_1 - 4x_2 + \ x_3 = -4$$
$$4x_1 - 8x_2 + 7x_3 = \ \ 2$$
$$-2x_1 + 4x_2 - 3x_3 = \ \ 5$$

SOLUTION

$$\begin{bmatrix} 2 & -4 & 1 & | & -4 \\ 4 & -8 & 7 & | & 2 \\ -2 & 4 & -3 & | & 5 \end{bmatrix} \quad 0.5R_1 \to R_1$$

$$\sim \begin{bmatrix} 1 & -2 & 0.5 & | & -2 \\ 4 & -8 & 7 & | & 2 \\ -2 & 4 & -3 & | & 5 \end{bmatrix} \quad \begin{matrix} (-4)R_1 + R_2 \to R_2 \\ 2R_1 + R_3 \to R_3 \end{matrix}$$

$$\sim \begin{bmatrix} 1 & -2 & 0.5 & | & -2 \\ 0 & 0 & 5 & | & 10 \\ 0 & 0 & -2 & | & 1 \end{bmatrix} \quad \begin{matrix} 0.2R_2 \to R_2 \quad \text{Note that column 3 is the} \\ \text{leftmost nonzero column in} \\ \text{this submatrix.} \end{matrix}$$

$$\sim \begin{bmatrix} 1 & -2 & 0.5 & | & -2 \\ 0 & 0 & 1 & | & 2 \\ 0 & 0 & -2 & | & 1 \end{bmatrix} \quad \begin{matrix} (-0.5)R_2 + R_1 \to R_1 \\ \\ 2R_2 + R_3 \to R_3 \end{matrix}$$

$$\sim \begin{bmatrix} 1 & -2 & 0 & | & -3 \\ 0 & 0 & 1 & | & 2 \\ 0 & 0 & 0 & | & 5 \end{bmatrix} \quad \begin{matrix} \text{We stop the Gauss–Jordan elimination, even} \\ \text{though the matrix is not in reduced form,} \\ \text{since the last row produces a contradiction.} \end{matrix}$$

The system has no solution.

Matched Problem 3   Solve by Gauss–Jordan elimination:

$$2x_1 - 4x_2 - \ x_3 = -8$$
$$4x_1 - 8x_2 + 3x_3 = \ \ 4$$
$$-2x_1 + 4x_2 + \ x_3 = \ 11$$

⚠ **CAUTION** Figure 2 shows the solution to Example 3 on a graphing calculator with a built-in reduced-form routine. Notice that the graphing calculator does not stop when a contradiction first occurs, but continues on to find the reduced form. Nevertheless, the last row in the reduced form still produces a contradiction. Do not confuse this type of reduced form with one that represents a consistent system (see Fig. 1).

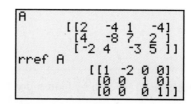

Figure 2 Recognizing contradictions on a graphing calculator

EXAMPLE 4   **Solving a System Using Gauss–Jordan Elimination** Solve by Gauss–Jordan elimination:

$$3x_1 + 6x_2 - 9x_3 = 15$$
$$2x_1 + 4x_2 - 6x_3 = 10$$
$$-2x_1 - 3x_2 + 4x_3 = -6$$

SOLUTION

$$\begin{bmatrix} 3 & 6 & -9 & | & 15 \\ 2 & 4 & -6 & | & 10 \\ -2 & -3 & 4 & | & -6 \end{bmatrix} \quad \tfrac{1}{3}R_1 \to R_1$$

$$\sim \begin{bmatrix} 1 & 2 & -3 & | & 5 \\ 2 & 4 & -6 & | & 10 \\ -2 & -3 & 4 & | & -6 \end{bmatrix} \quad \begin{array}{l} (-2)R_1 + R_2 \to R_2 \\ 2R_1 + R_3 \to R_3 \end{array}$$

$$\sim \begin{bmatrix} 1 & 2 & -3 & | & 5 \\ 0 & 0 & 0 & | & 0 \\ 0 & 1 & -2 & | & 4 \end{bmatrix} \quad R_2 \leftrightarrow R_3$$

Note that we must interchange rows 2 and 3 to obtain a nonzero entry at the top of the second column of this submatrix.

$$\sim \begin{bmatrix} 1 & 2 & -3 & | & 5 \\ 0 & 1 & -2 & | & 4 \\ 0 & 0 & 0 & | & 0 \end{bmatrix} \quad (-2)R_2 + R_1 \to R_1$$

$$\sim \begin{bmatrix} 1 & 0 & 1 & | & -3 \\ 0 & 1 & -2 & | & 4 \\ 0 & 0 & 0 & | & 0 \end{bmatrix}$$

The matrix is now in reduced form. Write the corresponding reduced system and solve.

$$x_1 + x_3 = -3$$
$$x_2 - 2x_3 = 4$$

We discard the equation corresponding to the third (all zero) row in the reduced form, since it is satisfied by all values of x_1, x_2, and x_3.

Note that the leftmost variable in each equation appears in one and only one equation. We solve for the leftmost variables x_1 and x_2 in terms of the remaining variable, x_3 :

$$x_1 = -x_3 - 3$$
$$x_2 = 2x_3 + 4$$

If we let $x_3 = t$, then for any real number t,

$$x_1 = -t - 3$$
$$x_2 = 2t + 4$$
$$x_3 = t$$

You should check that $(-t - 3, 2t + 4, t)$ is a solution of the original system for any real number t. Some particular solutions are

$$\begin{array}{ccc} t = 0 & t = -2 & t = 3.5 \\ (-3, 4, 0) & (-1, 0, -2) & (-6.5, 11, 3.5) \end{array}$$

In general,

> **If the number of leftmost 1's in a reduced augmented coefficient matrix is less than the number of variables in the system and there are no contradictions, then the system is dependent and has infinitely many solutions.**

Describing the solution set to this type of system is not difficult. In a reduced system, the **leftmost variables** correspond to the leftmost 1's in the corresponding reduced augmented matrix. The definition of reduced form for an augmented matrix ensures that each leftmost variable in the corresponding reduced system appears in one and only one equation of the system. Solving for each leftmost variable in terms of the remaining variables and writing a general solution to the system is usually easy. Example 5 illustrates a slightly more involved case.

Matched Problem 4   Solve by Gauss–Jordan elimination:

$$2x_1 - 2x_2 - 4x_3 = -2$$
$$3x_1 - 3x_2 - 6x_3 = -3$$
$$-2x_1 + 3x_2 + x_3 = 7$$

EXPLORE & DISCUSS 1   Explain why the definition of reduced form ensures that each leftmost variable in a reduced system appears in one and only one equation and no equation contains more than one leftmost variable. Discuss methods for determining whether a consistent system is independent or dependent by examining the reduced form.

EXAMPLE 5   **Solving a System Using Gauss–Jordan Elimination** Solve by Gauss–Jordan elimination:

$$x_1 + 2x_2 + 4x_3 + x_4 - x_5 = 1$$
$$2x_1 + 4x_2 + 8x_3 + 3x_4 - 4x_5 = 2$$
$$x_1 + 3x_2 + 7x_3 + 3x_5 = -2$$

SOLUTION

$$\begin{bmatrix} 1 & 2 & 4 & 1 & -1 & | & 1 \\ 2 & 4 & 8 & 3 & -4 & | & 2 \\ 1 & 3 & 7 & 0 & 3 & | & -2 \end{bmatrix} \quad \begin{matrix} (-2)R_1 + R_2 \rightarrow R_2 \\ (-1)R_1 + R_3 \rightarrow R_3 \end{matrix}$$

$$\sim \begin{bmatrix} 1 & 2 & 4 & 1 & -1 & | & 1 \\ 0 & 0 & 0 & 1 & -2 & | & 0 \\ 0 & 1 & 3 & -1 & 4 & | & -3 \end{bmatrix} \quad R_2 \leftrightarrow R_3$$

$$\sim \begin{bmatrix} 1 & 2 & 4 & 1 & -1 & | & 1 \\ 0 & 1 & 3 & -1 & 4 & | & -3 \\ 0 & 0 & 0 & 1 & -2 & | & 0 \end{bmatrix} \quad (-2)R_2 + R_1 \rightarrow R_1$$

$$\sim \begin{bmatrix} 1 & 0 & -2 & 3 & -9 & | & 7 \\ 0 & 1 & 3 & -1 & 4 & | & -3 \\ 0 & 0 & 0 & 1 & -2 & | & 0 \end{bmatrix} \quad \begin{matrix} (-3)R_3 + R_1 \rightarrow R_1 \\ R_3 + R_2 \rightarrow R_2 \end{matrix}$$

$$\sim \begin{bmatrix} 1 & 0 & -2 & 0 & -3 & | & 7 \\ 0 & 1 & 3 & 0 & 2 & | & -3 \\ 0 & 0 & 0 & 1 & -2 & | & 0 \end{bmatrix} \quad \text{Matrix is in reduced form.}$$

$$x_1 - 2x_3 - 3x_5 = 7$$
$$x_2 + 3x_3 + 2x_5 = -3$$
$$x_4 - 2x_5 = 0$$

Solve for the leftmost variables $x_1, x_2,$ and x_4 in terms of the remaining variables x_3 and x_5 :

$$x_1 = 2x_3 + 3x_5 + 7$$
$$x_2 = -3x_3 - 2x_5 - 3$$
$$x_4 = 2x_5$$

If we let $x_3 = s$ and $x_5 = t$, then for any real numbers s and t,

$$x_1 = 2s + 3t + 7$$
$$x_2 = -3s - 2t - 3$$
$$x_3 = s$$
$$x_4 = 2t$$
$$x_5 = t$$

is a solution. The check is left for you.

Matched Problem 5   Solve by Gauss–Jordan elimination:

$$\begin{aligned} x_1 - \ x_2 + 2x_3 \quad\quad - 2x_5 &= \ \ 3 \\ -2x_1 + 2x_2 - 4x_3 - x_4 + \ x_5 &= -5 \\ 3x_1 - 3x_2 + 7x_3 + x_4 - 4x_5 &= \ \ 6 \end{aligned}$$

Application

Dependent systems of linear equations provide an excellent opportunity to discuss mathematical modeling in more detail. The process of using mathematics to solve real-world problems can be broken down into three steps (Fig. 3):

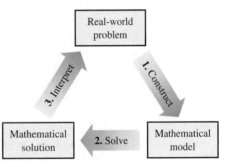

Figure 3

Step 1   *Construct* a mathematical model whose solution will provide information about the real-world problem.

Step 2   *Solve* the mathematical model.

Step 3   *Interpret* the solution to the mathematical model in terms of the original real-world problem.

In more complex problems, this cycle may have to be repeated several times to obtain the required information about the real-world problem.

EXAMPLE 6   **Purchasing** A company that rents small moving trucks wants to purchase 25 trucks with a combined capacity of 28,000 cubic feet. Three different types of trucks are available: a 10-foot truck with a capacity of 350 cubic feet, a 14-foot truck with a capacity of 700 cubic feet, and a 24-foot truck with a capacity of 1,400 cubic feet. How many of each type of truck should the company purchase?

SOLUTION   The question in this example indicates that the relevant variables are the number of each type of truck:

$$x_1 = \text{number of 10-foot trucks}$$
$$x_2 = \text{number of 14-foot trucks}$$
$$x_3 = \text{number of 24-foot trucks}$$

Next we form the mathematical model:

$$x_1 + x_2 + x_3 = 25 \qquad \text{Total number of trucks}$$
$$350x_1 + 700x_2 + 1{,}400x_3 = 28{,}000 \qquad \text{Total capacity} \tag{2}$$

Now we form the augmented coefficient matrix of the system and solve by Gauss–Jordan elimination:

$$\begin{bmatrix} 1 & 1 & 1 & 25 \\ 350 & 700 & 1{,}400 & 28{,}000 \end{bmatrix} \quad \tfrac{1}{350}R_2 \to R_2$$

$$\sim \begin{bmatrix} 1 & 1 & 1 & 25 \\ 1 & 2 & 4 & 80 \end{bmatrix} \quad -R_1 + R_2 \to R_2$$

$$\sim \begin{bmatrix} 1 & 1 & 1 & 25 \\ 0 & 1 & 3 & 55 \end{bmatrix} \quad -R_2 + R_1 \to R_1$$

$$\sim \begin{bmatrix} 1 & 0 & -2 & -30 \\ 0 & 1 & 3 & 55 \end{bmatrix} \quad \text{Matrix is in reduced form.}$$

$$x_1 - 2x_3 = -30 \qquad \text{or} \qquad x_1 = 2x_3 - 30$$
$$x_2 + 3x_3 = 55 \qquad \text{or} \qquad x_2 = -3x_3 + 55$$

Let $x_3 = t$. Then for t any real number,

$$x_1 = 2t - 30$$
$$x_2 = -3t + 55 \tag{3}$$
$$x_3 = t$$

is a solution to mathematical model (2).

Now we must interpret this solution in terms of the original problem. Since the variables x_1, x_2, and x_3 represent numbers of trucks, they must be nonnegative real numbers. And since we can't purchase a fractional number of trucks, each must be a nonnegative whole number. Since $t = x_3$, it follows that t must also be a nonnegative whole number. The first and second equations in model (3) place additional restrictions on the values that t can assume:

$$x_1 = 2t - 30 \geq 0 \qquad \text{implies that} \qquad t \geq 15$$

$$x_2 = -3t + 55 \geq 0 \qquad \text{implies that} \qquad t \leq \frac{55}{3} = 18\tfrac{1}{3}$$

So the only possible values of t that will produce meaningful solutions to the original problem are 15, 16, 17, and 18. That is, the only combinations of 25 trucks that will result in a combined capacity of 28,000 cubic feet are $x_1 = 2t - 30$ 10-foot trucks, $x_2 = -3t + 55$ 14-foot trucks, and $x_3 = t$ 24-foot trucks, where $t = 15, 16, 17$, or 18. A table is a convenient way to display these solutions:

t	10-Foot Truck x_1	14-Foot Truck x_2	24-Foot Truck x_3
15	0	10	15
16	2	7	16
17	4	4	17
18	6	1	18

Matched Problem 6   A company that rents small moving trucks wants to purchase 16 trucks with a combined capacity of 19,200 cubic feet. Three different types of trucks are available: a cargo van with a capacity of 300 cubic feet, a 15-foot truck with a capacity of 900 cubic feet, and a 24-foot truck with a capacity of 1,500 cubic feet. How many of each type of truck should the company purchase?

EXPLORE & DISCUSS 2	Refer to Example 6. The rental company charges $19.95 per day for a 10-foot truck, $29.95 per day for a 14-foot truck, and $39.95 per day for a 24-foot truck. Which of the four possible choices in the table would produce the largest daily income from truck rentals?

Exercises 4-3

A

In Problems 1–10, if a matrix is in reduced form, say so. If not, explain why and indicate the row operation(s) necessary to transform the matrix into reduced form.

1. $\begin{bmatrix} 1 & 0 & | & 2 \\ 0 & 1 & | & -1 \end{bmatrix}$

2. $\begin{bmatrix} 0 & 1 & | & 2 \\ 1 & 0 & | & -1 \end{bmatrix}$

3. $\begin{bmatrix} 1 & 0 & 2 & | & 3 \\ 0 & 0 & 0 & | & 0 \\ 0 & 1 & -1 & | & 4 \end{bmatrix}$

4. $\begin{bmatrix} 1 & 0 & 0 & | & -2 \\ 0 & 1 & 0 & | & 0 \\ 0 & 0 & 1 & | & 1 \end{bmatrix}$

5. $\begin{bmatrix} 0 & 1 & 0 & | & 2 \\ 0 & 0 & 3 & | & -1 \\ 0 & 0 & 0 & | & 0 \end{bmatrix}$

6. $\begin{bmatrix} 1 & 2 & -3 & | & 1 \\ 0 & 0 & 1 & | & 4 \\ 0 & 0 & 0 & | & 0 \end{bmatrix}$

7. $\begin{bmatrix} 1 & 1 & 0 & | & 1 \\ 0 & 0 & 1 & | & 1 \\ 0 & 0 & 0 & | & 0 \end{bmatrix}$

8. $\begin{bmatrix} 1 & 0 & -1 & | & 3 \\ 0 & 2 & 1 & | & 1 \\ 0 & 0 & 0 & | & 0 \end{bmatrix}$

9. $\begin{bmatrix} 1 & 0 & -2 & 0 & | & 1 \\ 0 & 0 & 1 & 1 & | & 0 \end{bmatrix}$

10. $\begin{bmatrix} 1 & -2 & 0 & 0 & | & 1 \\ 0 & 0 & 1 & 1 & | & 0 \end{bmatrix}$

Write the linear system corresponding to each reduced augmented matrix in Problems 11–20 and write the solution of the system.

11. $\begin{bmatrix} 1 & 0 & 0 & | & -2 \\ 0 & 1 & 0 & | & 3 \\ 0 & 0 & 1 & | & 0 \end{bmatrix}$

12. $\begin{bmatrix} 1 & 0 & 0 & 0 & | & -2 \\ 0 & 1 & 0 & 0 & | & 0 \\ 0 & 0 & 1 & 0 & | & 1 \\ 0 & 0 & 0 & 1 & | & 3 \end{bmatrix}$

13. $\begin{bmatrix} 1 & 0 & -2 & | & 3 \\ 0 & 1 & 1 & | & -5 \\ 0 & 0 & 0 & | & 0 \end{bmatrix}$

14. $\begin{bmatrix} 1 & -2 & 0 & | & -3 \\ 0 & 0 & 1 & | & 5 \\ 0 & 0 & 0 & | & 0 \end{bmatrix}$

15. $\begin{bmatrix} 1 & 0 & | & 0 \\ 0 & 1 & | & 0 \\ 0 & 0 & | & 1 \end{bmatrix}$

16. $\begin{bmatrix} 1 & 0 & | & 5 \\ 0 & 1 & | & -3 \\ 0 & 0 & | & 0 \end{bmatrix}$

17. $\begin{bmatrix} 1 & 0 & -3 & | & 5 \\ 0 & 1 & 2 & | & -7 \end{bmatrix}$

18. $\begin{bmatrix} 1 & 0 & 1 & | & -4 \\ 0 & 1 & -1 & | & 6 \end{bmatrix}$

19. $\begin{bmatrix} 1 & -2 & 0 & -3 & | & -5 \\ 0 & 0 & 1 & 3 & | & 2 \end{bmatrix}$

20. $\begin{bmatrix} 1 & 0 & -2 & 3 & | & 4 \\ 0 & 1 & -1 & 2 & | & -1 \end{bmatrix}$

21. In which of Problems 11, 13, 15, 17, and 19 is the number of leftmost ones equal to the number of variables?

22. In which of Problems 12, 14, 16, 18, and 20 is the number of leftmost ones equal to the number of variables?

23. In which of Problems 11, 13, 15, 17, and 19 is the number of leftmost ones less than the number of variables?

24. In which of Problems 12, 14, 16, 18, and 20 is the number of leftmost ones less than the number of variables?

In Problems 25–30, discuss the validity of each statement about linear systems. If the statement is always true, explain why. If not, give a counterexample.

25. If the number of leftmost ones is equal to the number of variables, then the system has exactly one solution.

26. If the number of leftmost ones is less than the number of variables, then the system has infinitely many solutions.

27. If the number of leftmost ones is equal to the number of variables and the system is consistent, then the system has exactly one solution.

28. If the number of leftmost ones is less than the number of variables and the system is consistent, then the system has infinitely many solutions.

29. The number of equations is less than or equal to the number of variables.

30. The number of leftmost ones is less than or equal to the number of equations.

Use row operations to change each matrix in Problems 31–38 to reduced form.

31. $\begin{bmatrix} 1 & 2 & | & -1 \\ 0 & 1 & | & 3 \end{bmatrix}$

32. $\begin{bmatrix} 1 & 3 & | & 1 \\ 0 & 2 & | & -4 \end{bmatrix}$

33. $\begin{bmatrix} 1 & 1 & 1 & | & 16 \\ 2 & 3 & 4 & | & 25 \end{bmatrix}$

34. $\begin{bmatrix} 1 & 1 & 1 & | & 8 \\ 3 & 5 & 7 & | & 30 \end{bmatrix}$

35. $\begin{bmatrix} 1 & 0 & -3 & | & 1 \\ 0 & 1 & 2 & | & 0 \\ 0 & 0 & 3 & | & -6 \end{bmatrix}$

36. $\begin{bmatrix} 1 & 0 & 4 & | & 0 \\ 0 & 1 & -3 & | & -1 \\ 0 & 0 & -2 & | & 2 \end{bmatrix}$

37. $\begin{bmatrix} 1 & 2 & -2 & | & -1 \\ 0 & 3 & -6 & | & 1 \\ 0 & -1 & 2 & | & -\frac{1}{3} \end{bmatrix}$

38. $\begin{bmatrix} 0 & -2 & 8 & | & 1 \\ 2 & -2 & 6 & | & -4 \\ 0 & -1 & 4 & | & \frac{1}{2} \end{bmatrix}$

Solve Problems 39–54 using Gauss–Jordan elimination.

39. $2x_1 + 4x_2 - 10x_3 = -2$
$3x_1 + 9x_2 - 21x_3 = 0$
$x_1 + 5x_2 - 12x_3 = 1$

40. $3x_1 + 5x_2 - x_3 = -7$
$x_1 + x_2 + x_3 = -1$
$2x_1 + 11x_3 = 7$

41. $3x_1 + 8x_2 - x_3 = -18$
$2x_1 + x_2 + 5x_3 = 8$
$2x_1 + 4x_2 + 2x_3 = -4$

42. $2x_1 + 6x_2 + 15x_3 = -12$
$4x_1 + 7x_2 + 13x_3 = -10$
$3x_1 + 6x_2 + 12x_3 = -9$

43. $2x_1 - x_2 - 3x_3 = 8$
$x_1 - 2x_2 = 7$

44. $2x_1 + 4x_2 - 6x_3 = 10$
$3x_1 + 3x_2 - 3x_3 = 6$

45. $2x_1 - x_2 = 0$
$3x_1 + 2x_2 = 7$
$x_1 - x_2 = -1$

46. $2x_1 - x_2 = 0$
$3x_1 + 2x_2 = 7$
$x_1 - x_2 = -2$

47. $3x_1 - 4x_2 - x_3 = 1$
$2x_1 - 3x_2 + x_3 = 1$
$x_1 - 2x_2 + 3x_3 = 2$

48. $3x_1 + 7x_2 - x_3 = 11$
$x_1 + 2x_2 - x_3 = 3$
$2x_1 + 4x_2 - 2x_3 = 10$

49. $3x_1 - 2x_2 + x_3 = -7$
$2x_1 + x_2 - 4x_3 = 0$
$x_1 + x_2 - 3x_3 = 1$

50. $2x_1 + 3x_2 + 5x_3 = 21$
$x_1 - x_2 - 5x_3 = -2$
$2x_1 + x_2 - x_3 = 11$

51. $2x_1 + 4x_2 - 2x_3 = 2$
$-3x_1 - 6x_2 + 3x_3 = -3$

52. $3x_1 - 9x_2 + 12x_3 = 6$
$-2x_1 + 6x_2 - 8x_3 = -4$

53. $4x_1 - x_2 + 2x_3 = 3$
$-4x_1 + x_2 - 3x_3 = -10$
$8x_1 - 2x_2 + 9x_3 = -1$

54. $4x_1 - 2x_2 + 2x_3 = 5$
$-6x_1 + 3x_2 - 3x_3 = -2$
$10x_1 - 5x_2 + 9x_3 = 4$

55. Consider a consistent system of three linear equations in three variables. Discuss the nature of the system and its solution set if the reduced form of the augmented coefficient matrix has

(A) One leftmost 1

(B) Two leftmost 1's

(C) Three leftmost 1's

(D) Four leftmost 1's

56. Consider a system of three linear equations in three variables. Give examples of two reduced forms that are not row-equivalent if the system is

(A) Consistent and dependent

(B) Inconsistent

Solve Problems 57–62 using Gauss–Jordan elimination.

57. $x_1 + 2x_2 - 4x_3 - x_4 = 7$
$2x_1 + 5x_2 - 9x_3 - 4x_4 = 16$
$x_1 + 5x_2 - 7x_3 - 7x_4 = 13$

58. $2x_1 + 4x_2 + 5x_3 + 4x_4 = 8$
$x_1 + 2x_2 + 2x_3 + x_4 = 3$

59. $x_1 - x_2 + 3x_3 - 2x_4 = 1$
$-2x_1 + 4x_2 - 3x_3 + x_4 = 0.5$
$3x_1 - x_2 + 10x_3 - 4x_4 = 2.9$
$4x_1 - 3x_2 + 8x_3 - 2x_4 = 0.6$

60.
$$x_1 + x_2 + 4x_3 + x_4 = 1.3$$
$$-x_1 + x_2 - x_3 = 1.1$$
$$2x_1 + x_3 + 3x_4 = -4.4$$
$$2x_1 + 5x_2 + 11x_3 + 3x_4 = 5.6$$

61.
$$x_1 - 2x_2 + x_3 + x_4 + 2x_5 = 2$$
$$-2x_1 + 4x_2 + 2x_3 + 2x_4 - 2x_5 = 0$$
$$3x_1 - 6x_2 + x_3 + x_4 + 5x_5 = 4$$
$$-x_1 + 2x_2 + 3x_3 + x_4 + x_5 = 3$$

62.
$$x_1 - 3x_2 + x_3 + x_4 + 2x_5 = 2$$
$$-x_1 + 5x_2 + 2x_3 + 2x_4 - 2x_5 = 0$$
$$2x_1 - 6x_2 + 2x_3 + 2x_4 + 4x_5 = 4$$
$$-x_1 + 3x_2 - x_3 + x_5 = -3$$

63. Find $a, b,$ and c so that the graph of the quadratic equation $y = ax^2 + bx + c$ passes through the points $(-2, 9)$, $(1, -9)$, and $(4, 9)$.

64. Find $a, b,$ and c so that the graph of the quadratic equation $y = ax^2 + bx + c$ passes through the points $(-1, -5)$, $(2, 7)$, and $(5, 1)$.

Applications

Construct a mathematical model for each of the following problems. (The answers in the back of the book include both the mathematical model and the interpretation of its solution.) Use Gauss–Jordan elimination to solve the model and then interpret the solution.

65. Boat production. A small manufacturing plant makes three types of inflatable boats: one-person, two-person, and four-person models. Each boat requires the services of three departments, as listed in the table. The cutting, assembly, and packaging departments have available a maximum of 380, 330, and 120 labor-hours per week, respectively.

Department	One-Person Boat	Two-Person Boat	Four-Person Boat
Cutting	0.5 hr	1.0 hr	1.5 hr
Assembly	0.6 hr	0.9 hr	1.2 hr
Packaging	0.2 hr	0.3 hr	0.5 hr

(A) How many boats of each type must be produced each week for the plant to operate at full capacity?

(B) How is the production schedule in part (A) affected if the packaging department is no longer used?

(C) How is the production schedule in part (A) affected if the four-person boat is no longer produced?

66. Production scheduling. Repeat Problem 65 assuming that the cutting, assembly, and packaging departments have available a maximum of 350, 330, and 115 labor-hours per week, respectively.

67. Tank car leases. A chemical manufacturer wants to lease a fleet of 24 railroad tank cars with a combined carrying ca-

pacity of 520,000 gallons. Tank cars with three different carrying capacities are available: 8,000 gallons, 16,000 gallons, and 24,000 gallons. How many of each type of tank car should be leased?

68. Airplane leases. A corporation wants to lease a fleet of 12 airplanes with a combined carrying capacity of 220 passengers. The three available types of planes carry 10, 15, and 20 passengers, respectively. How many of each type of plane should be leased?

69. Tank car leases. Refer to Problem 67. The cost of leasing an 8,000-gallon tank car is $450 per month, a 16,000-gallon tank car is $650 per month, and a 24,000-gallon tank car is $1,150 per month. Which of the solutions to Problem 67 would minimize the monthly leasing cost?

70. Airplane leases. Refer to Problem 68. The cost of leasing a 10-passenger airplane is $8,000 per month, a 15-passenger airplane is $14,000 per month, and a 20-passenger airplane is $16,000 per month. Which of the solutions to Problem 68 would minimize the monthly leasing cost?

71. Income tax. A corporation has a taxable income of $7,650,000. At this income level, the federal income tax rate is 50%, the state tax rate is 20%, and the local tax rate is 10%. If each tax rate is applied to the total taxable income, the resulting tax liability for the corporation would be 80% of taxable income. However, it is customary to deduct taxes paid to one agency before computing taxes for the other agencies. Assume that the federal taxes are based on the income that remains after the state and local taxes are deducted, and that state and local taxes are computed in a similar manner. What is the tax liability of the corporation (as a percentage of taxable income) if these deductions are taken into consideration?

72. Income tax. Repeat Problem 71 if local taxes are not allowed as a deduction for federal and state taxes.

73. Taxable income. As a result of several mergers and acquisitions, stock in four companies has been distributed among the companies. Each row of the following table gives the percentage of stock in the four companies that a particular company owns and the annual net income of each company (in millions of dollars):

Company	Percentage of Stock Owned in Company				Annual Net Income Million $
	A	B	C	D	
A	71	8	3	7	3.2
B	12	81	11	13	2.6
C	11	9	72	8	3.8
D	6	2	14	72	4.4

So company A holds 71% of its own stock, 8% of the stock in company B, 3% of the stock in company C, etc. For the purpose of assessing a state tax on corporate income, the taxable income of each company is defined to be its share of its own annual net income plus its share of the taxable income of each of the other companies, as determined by the percentages in the table. What is the taxable income of each company (to the nearest thousand dollars)?

74. Taxable income. Repeat Problem 73 if tax law is changed so that the taxable income of a company is defined to be all of its own annual net income plus its share of the taxable income of each of the other companies.

75. Nutrition. A dietitian in a hospital is to arrange a special diet composed of three basic foods. The diet is to include exactly 340 units of calcium, 180 units of iron, and 220 units of vitamin A. The number of units per ounce of each special ingredient for each of the foods is indicated in the table.

	Units per Ounce		
	Food A	**Food B**	**Food C**
Calcium	30	10	20
Iron	10	10	20
Vitamin A	10	30	20

(A) How many ounces of each food must be used to meet the diet requirements?

(B) How is the diet in part (A) affected if food C is not used?

(C) How is the diet in part (A) affected if the vitamin A requirement is dropped?

76. Nutrition. Repeat Problem 75 if the diet is to include exactly 400 units of calcium, 160 units of iron, and 240 units of vitamin A.

77. Plant food. A farmer can buy four types of plant food. Each barrel of mix A contains 30 pounds of phosphoric acid, 50 pounds of nitrogen, and 30 pounds of potash; each barrel of mix B contains 30 pounds of phosphoric acid, 75 pounds of nitrogen, and 20 pounds of potash; each barrel of mix C contains 30 pounds of phosphoric acid, 25 pounds of nitrogen, and 20 pounds of potash; and each barrel of mix D contains 60 pounds of phosphoric acid, 25 pounds of nitrogen, and 50 pounds of potash. Soil tests indicate that a particular field needs 900 pounds of phosphoric acid, 750 pounds of nitrogen, and 700 pounds of potash. How many barrels of each type of food should the farmer mix together to supply the necessary nutrients for the field?

78. Animal feed. In a laboratory experiment, rats are to be fed 5 packets of food containing a total of 80 units of vitamin E. There are four different brands of food packets that can be used. A packet of brand A contains 5 units of vitamin E, a packet of brand B contains 10 units of vitamin E, a packet of brand C contains 15 units of vitamin E, and a packet of brand D contains 20 units of vitamin E. How many packets of each brand should be mixed and fed to the rats?

79. Plant food. Refer to Problem 77. The costs of the four mixes are Mix A, $46; Mix B, $72; Mix C, $57; and Mix D, $63. Which of the solutions to Problem 77 would minimize the cost of the plant food?

80. Animal feed. Refer to Problem 78. The costs of the four brands are Brand A, $1.50; Brand B, $3.00; Brand C, $3.75; and Brand D, $2.25. Which of the solutions to Problem 78 would minimize the cost of the rat food?

81. Population growth. The U.S. population was approximately 75 million in 1900, 150 million in 1950, and 275 million in 2000. Construct a model for this data by finding a quadratic equation whose graph passes through the points $(0, 75)$,

$(50, 150)$, and $(100, 275)$. Use this model to estimate the population in 2050.

82. Population growth. The population of California was approximately 24 million in 1980, 30 million in 1990, and 34 million in 2000. Construct a model for this data by finding a quadratic equation whose graph passes through the points $(0, 24)$, $(10, 30)$, and $(20, 34)$. Use this model to estimate the population in 2020. Do you think the estimate is plausible? Explain.

83. Female life expectancy. The life expectancy for females born during 1980–1985 was approximately 77.6 years. This grew to 78 years during 1985–1990 and to 78.6 years during 1990–1995. Construct a model for this data by finding a quadratic equation whose graph passes through the points $(0, 77.6)$, $(5, 78)$, and $(10, 78.6)$. Use this model to estimate the life expectancy for females born between 1995 and 2000 and for those born between 2000 and 2005.

84. Male life expectancy. The life expectancy for males born during 1980–1985 was approximately 70.7 years. This grew to 71.1 years during 1985–1990 and to 71.8 years during 1990–1995. Construct a model for this data by finding a quadratic equation whose graph passes through the points $(0, 70.7)$, $(5, 71.1)$, and $(10, 71.8)$. Use this model to estimate the life expectancy for males born between 1995 and 2000 and for those born between 2000 and 2005.

85. Female life expectancy. Refer to Problem 83. Subsequent data indicated that life expectancy grew to 79.1 years for females born during 1995–2000 and to 79.7 years for females born during 2000–2005. Add the points $(15, 79.1)$ and $(20, 79.7)$ to the data set in Problem 83. Use a graphing calculator to find a quadratic regression model for all five data points. Graph the data and the model in the same viewing window.

86. Male life expectancy. Refer to Problem 84. Subsequent data indicated that life expectancy grew to 73.2 years for males born during 1995–2000 and to 74.3 years for males born during 2000–2005. Add the points $(15, 73.2)$ and $(20, 74.3)$ to the data set in Problem 84. Use a graphing calculator to find a quadratic regression model for all five data points. Graph the data and the model in the same viewing window.

87. Sociology. Two sociologists have grant money to study school busing in a particular city. They wish to conduct an opinion survey using 600 telephone contacts and 400 house contacts. Survey company A has personnel to do 30 telephone and 10 house contacts per hour; survey company B can handle 20 telephone and 20 house contacts per hour. How many hours should be scheduled for each firm to produce exactly the number of contacts needed?

88. Sociology. Repeat Problem 87 if 650 telephone contacts and 350 house contacts are needed.

89. Traffic flow. The rush-hour traffic flow for a network of four one-way streets in a city is shown in the figure. The numbers next to each street indicate the number of vehicles per hour that enter and leave the network on that street. The variables x_1, x_2, x_3, and x_4 represent the flow of traffic between the four intersections in the network.

(A) For a smooth traffic flow, the number of vehicles entering each intersection should always equal the number leaving. For example, since 1,500 vehicles enter the intersection of 5th Street and Washington Avenue each hour and $x_1 + x_4$ vehicles leave this intersection, we see that $x_1 + x_4 = 1,500$. Find the equations determined by the traffic flow at each of the other three intersections.

Figure for 89

(B) Find the solution to the system in part (A).

(C) What is the maximum number of vehicles that can travel from Washington Avenue to Lincoln Avenue on 5th Street? What is the minimum number?

(D) If traffic lights are adjusted so that 1,000 vehicles per hour travel from Washington Avenue to Lincoln Avenue on 5th Street, determine the flow around the rest of the network.

90. **Traffic flow.** Refer to Problem 89. Closing Washington Avenue east of 6th Street for construction changes the traffic flow for the network as indicated in the figure. Repeat parts (A)–(D) of Problem 89 for this traffic flow.

Figure for 90

Answers to Matched Problems

1. (A) Condition 2 is violated: The 3 in row 2 and column 2 should be a 1. Perform the operation $\frac{1}{3}R_2 \rightarrow R_2$ to obtain

$$\begin{bmatrix} 1 & 0 & | & 2 \\ 0 & 1 & | & -2 \end{bmatrix}$$

(B) Condition 3 is violated: The 5 in row 1 and column 2 should be a 0. Perform the operation $(-5)R_2 + R_1 \rightarrow R_1$ to obtain

$$\begin{bmatrix} 1 & 0 & -6 & | & 8 \\ 0 & 1 & 2 & | & -1 \\ 0 & 0 & 0 & | & 0 \end{bmatrix}$$

(C) Condition 4 is violated. The leftmost 1 in the second row is not to the right of the leftmost 1 in the first row. Perform the operation $R_1 \leftrightarrow R_2$ to obtain

$$\begin{bmatrix} 1 & 0 & 0 & | & 0 \\ 0 & 1 & 0 & | & -3 \\ 0 & 0 & 1 & | & 2 \end{bmatrix}$$

(D) Condition 1 is violated: The all-zero second row should be at the bottom. Perform the operation $R_2 \leftrightarrow R_3$ to obtain

$$\begin{bmatrix} 1 & 2 & 0 & | & 3 \\ 0 & 0 & 1 & | & 4 \\ 0 & 0 & 0 & | & 0 \end{bmatrix}$$

2. $x_1 = 1, x_2 = -1, x_3 = 0$

3. Inconsistent; no solution

4. $x_1 = 5t + 4, x_2 = 3t + 5, x_3 = t, t$ any real number

5. $x_1 = s + 7, x_2 = s, x_3 = t - 2, x_4 = -3t - 1, x_5 = t, s$ and t any real numbers

6. $t - 8$ cargo vans, $-2t + 24$ 15-foot trucks, and t 24-foot trucks, where $t = 8, 9, 10, 11,$ or 12

4-4 Matrices: Basic Operations

- Addition and Subtraction
- Product of a Number k and a Matrix M
- Matrix Product

In the two preceding sections we introduced the important idea of matrices. In this and following sections, we develop this concept further. Matrices are both an ancient and a current mathematical concept. References to matrices and systems of equations can be found in Chinese manuscripts dating back to about 200 B.C. More recently, computers have made matrices a useful tool for a wide variety of applications. Most graphing calculators and computers are capable of performing calculations with matrices.

As we will see, matrix addition and multiplication are similar to real number addition and multiplication in many respects, but there are some important differences. A brief review of Appendix A, Section A-1, where real number operations are discussed, will help you understand the similarities and the differences.

Addition and Subtraction

Before we can discuss arithmetic operations for matrices, we have to define equality for matrices. Two matrices are **equal** if they have the same size and their corresponding elements are equal. For example,

$$
\underset{2 \times 3}{\begin{bmatrix} a & b & c \\ d & e & f \end{bmatrix}} = \underset{2 \times 3}{\begin{bmatrix} u & v & w \\ x & y & z \end{bmatrix}} \quad \text{if and only if} \quad \begin{array}{ccc} a = u & b = v & c = w \\ d = x & e = y & f = z \end{array}
$$

The **sum of two matrices of the same size** is the matrix with elements that are the sum of the corresponding elements of the two given matrices. Addition is not defined for matrices of different sizes.

EXAMPLE 1   Matrix Addition

(A) $\begin{bmatrix} a & b \\ c & d \end{bmatrix} + \begin{bmatrix} w & x \\ y & z \end{bmatrix} = \begin{bmatrix} (a + w) & (b + x) \\ (c + y) & (d + z) \end{bmatrix}$

(B) $\begin{bmatrix} 2 & -3 & 0 \\ 1 & 2 & -5 \end{bmatrix} + \begin{bmatrix} 3 & 1 & 2 \\ -3 & 2 & 5 \end{bmatrix} = \begin{bmatrix} 5 & -2 & 2 \\ -2 & 4 & 0 \end{bmatrix}$

(C) $\begin{bmatrix} 5 & 0 & -2 \\ 1 & -3 & 8 \end{bmatrix} + \begin{bmatrix} -1 & 7 \\ 0 & 6 \\ -2 & 8 \end{bmatrix}$ *Not defined*

Matched Problem 1

Add: $\begin{bmatrix} 3 & 2 \\ -1 & -1 \\ 0 & 3 \end{bmatrix} + \begin{bmatrix} -2 & 3 \\ 1 & -1 \\ 2 & -2 \end{bmatrix}$

Figure 1 Addition on a graphing calculator

Graphing calculators can be used to solve problems involving matrix operations. Figure 1 illustrates the solution to Example 1B on a TI-84.

Because we add two matrices by adding their corresponding elements, it follows from the properties of real numbers that matrices of the same size are commutative and associative relative to addition. That is, if A, B, and C are matrices of the same size, then

Commutative: $A + B = B + A$

Associative: $(A + B) + C = A + (B + C)$

A matrix with elements that are all zeros is called a **zero matrix**. For example,

$$
\begin{bmatrix} 0 & 0 & 0 \end{bmatrix} \quad \begin{bmatrix} 0 & 0 \\ 0 & 0 \end{bmatrix} \quad \begin{bmatrix} 0 \\ 0 \\ 0 \\ 0 \end{bmatrix} \quad \begin{bmatrix} 0 & 0 & 0 & 0 \\ 0 & 0 & 0 & 0 \\ 0 & 0 & 0 & 0 \end{bmatrix}
$$

are zero matrices of different sizes. [*Note:* The simpler notation "0" is often used to denote the zero matrix of an arbitrary size.] The **negative of a matrix M**, denoted by $-M$ is a matrix with elements that are the negatives of the elements in M. Thus, if

$$
M = \begin{bmatrix} a & b \\ c & d \end{bmatrix} \quad \text{then} \quad -M = \begin{bmatrix} -a & -b \\ -c & -d \end{bmatrix}
$$

Note that $M + (-M) = 0$ (a zero matrix).

If A and B are matrices of the same size, we define **subtraction** as follows:

$$A - B = A + (-B)$$

So to subtract matrix B from matrix A, we simply add the negative of B to A.

EXAMPLE 2   **Matrix Subtraction**

$$\begin{bmatrix} 3 & -2 \\ 5 & 0 \end{bmatrix} - \begin{bmatrix} -2 & 2 \\ 3 & 4 \end{bmatrix} = \begin{bmatrix} 3 & -2 \\ 5 & 0 \end{bmatrix} + \begin{bmatrix} 2 & -2 \\ -3 & -4 \end{bmatrix} = \begin{bmatrix} 5 & -4 \\ 2 & -4 \end{bmatrix}$$

Matched Problem 2   Subtract: $[2 \quad -3 \quad 5] - [3 \quad -2 \quad 1]$

EXAMPLE 3   **Matrix Equations**   Find $a, b, c,$ and d so that

$$\begin{bmatrix} a & b \\ c & d \end{bmatrix} - \begin{bmatrix} 2 & -1 \\ -5 & 6 \end{bmatrix} = \begin{bmatrix} 4 & 3 \\ -2 & 4 \end{bmatrix}$$

SOLUTION

$$\begin{bmatrix} a & b \\ c & d \end{bmatrix} - \begin{bmatrix} 2 & -1 \\ -5 & 6 \end{bmatrix} = \begin{bmatrix} 4 & 3 \\ -2 & 4 \end{bmatrix} \qquad \textit{Subtract the matrices on the left side.}$$

$$\begin{bmatrix} a - 2 & b - (-1) \\ c - (-5) & d - 6 \end{bmatrix} = \begin{bmatrix} 4 & 3 \\ -2 & 4 \end{bmatrix} \qquad \textit{Remove parentheses.}$$

$$\begin{bmatrix} a - 2 & b + 1 \\ c + 5 & d - 6 \end{bmatrix} = \begin{bmatrix} 4 & 3 \\ -2 & 4 \end{bmatrix} \qquad \textit{Use the definition of equality to change this matrix equation into four real number equations.}$$

$$
\begin{array}{cccc}
a - 2 = 4 & b + 1 = 3 & c + 5 = -2 & d - 6 = 4 \\
a = 6 & b = 2 & c = -7 & d = 10
\end{array}
$$

Matched Problem 3   Find $a, b, c,$ and d so that

$$\begin{bmatrix} a & b \\ c & d \end{bmatrix} - \begin{bmatrix} -4 & 2 \\ 1 & -3 \end{bmatrix} = \begin{bmatrix} -2 & 5 \\ 8 & 2 \end{bmatrix}$$

Product of a Number k and a Matrix M

The **product of a number k and a matrix M**, denoted by kM, is a matrix formed by multiplying each element of M by k.

EXAMPLE 4   **Multiplication of a Matrix by a Number**

$$-2 \begin{bmatrix} 3 & -1 & 0 \\ -2 & 1 & 3 \\ 0 & -1 & -2 \end{bmatrix} = \begin{bmatrix} -6 & 2 & 0 \\ 4 & -2 & -6 \\ 0 & 2 & 4 \end{bmatrix}$$

Matched Problem 4   Find: $10 \begin{bmatrix} 1.3 \\ 0.2 \\ 3.5 \end{bmatrix}$

The next example illustrates the use of matrix operations in an applied setting.

We now try to perform row operations on matrix (1) until we obtain a row-equivalent matrix of the form

$$\begin{array}{cc} I & B \\ \begin{bmatrix} 1 & 0 & 0 \\ 0 & 1 & 0 \\ 0 & 0 & 1 \end{bmatrix} & \left.\begin{array}{ccc} a & d & g \\ b & e & h \\ c & f & i \end{array}\right] = [I \,|\, B] \end{array} \qquad (2)$$

If this can be done, the new matrix B to the right of the vertical bar will be M^{-1}. Now let's try to transform matrix (1) into a form like matrix (2). We follow the same sequence of steps as we did in the solution of linear systems by Gauss–Jordan elimination (see Section 4-3).

$$\begin{array}{cc} M & I \\ \left[\begin{array}{ccc|ccc} 1 & -1 & 1 & 1 & 0 & 0 \\ 0 & 2 & -1 & 0 & 1 & 0 \\ 2 & 3 & 0 & 0 & 0 & 1 \end{array}\right] & (-2)R_1 + R_3 \rightarrow R_3 \end{array}$$

$$\sim \left[\begin{array}{ccc|ccc} 1 & -1 & 1 & 1 & 0 & 0 \\ 0 & 2 & -1 & 0 & 1 & 0 \\ 0 & 5 & -2 & -2 & 0 & 1 \end{array}\right] \quad \tfrac{1}{2}R_2 \rightarrow R_2$$

$$\sim \left[\begin{array}{ccc|ccc} 1 & -1 & 1 & 1 & 0 & 0 \\ 0 & 1 & -\tfrac{1}{2} & 0 & \tfrac{1}{2} & 0 \\ 0 & 5 & -2 & -2 & 0 & 1 \end{array}\right] \quad \begin{array}{l} R_2 + R_1 \rightarrow R_1 \\ \\ (-5)R_2 + R_3 \rightarrow R_3 \end{array}$$

$$\sim \left[\begin{array}{ccc|ccc} 1 & 0 & \tfrac{1}{2} & 1 & \tfrac{1}{2} & 0 \\ 0 & 1 & -\tfrac{1}{2} & 0 & \tfrac{1}{2} & 0 \\ 0 & 0 & \tfrac{1}{2} & -2 & -\tfrac{5}{2} & 1 \end{array}\right] \quad 2R_3 \rightarrow R_3$$

$$\sim \left[\begin{array}{ccc|ccc} 1 & 0 & \tfrac{1}{2} & 1 & \tfrac{1}{2} & 0 \\ 0 & 1 & -\tfrac{1}{2} & 0 & \tfrac{1}{2} & 0 \\ 0 & 0 & 1 & -4 & -5 & 2 \end{array}\right] \quad \begin{array}{l} \left(-\tfrac{1}{2}\right)R_3 + R_1 \rightarrow R_1 \\ \tfrac{1}{2}R_3 + R_2 \rightarrow R_2 \end{array}$$

$$\sim \left[\begin{array}{ccc|ccc} 1 & 0 & 0 & 3 & 3 & -1 \\ 0 & 1 & 0 & -2 & -2 & 1 \\ 0 & 0 & 1 & -4 & -5 & 2 \end{array}\right] = [I \,|\, B]$$

Converting back to systems of equations equivalent to our three original systems, we have

$$\begin{array}{lll} a = & 3 & d = & 3 & g = -1 \\ b = -2 & e = -2 & h = & 1 \\ c = -4 & f = -5 & i = & 2 \end{array}$$

And these are just the elements of M^{-1} that we are looking for!

$$M^{-1} = \begin{bmatrix} 3 & 3 & -1 \\ -2 & -2 & 1 \\ -4 & -5 & 2 \end{bmatrix}$$

Note that this is the matrix to the right of the vertical line in the last augmented matrix. That is, $M^{-1} = B$.

Since the definition of matrix inverse requires that

$$M^{-1}M = I \qquad \text{and} \qquad MM^{-1} = I \qquad (3)$$

it appears that we must compute both $M^{-1}M$ and MM^{-1} to check our work. However, it can be shown that if one of the equations in (3) is satisfied, the other is also satisfied. So to check our answer it is sufficient to compute either $M^{-1}M$ or MM^{-1}; we do not need to do both.

CHECK

$$M^{-1}M = \begin{bmatrix} 3 & 3 & -1 \\ -2 & -2 & 1 \\ -4 & -5 & 2 \end{bmatrix} \begin{bmatrix} 1 & -1 & 1 \\ 0 & 2 & -1 \\ 2 & 3 & 0 \end{bmatrix} = \begin{bmatrix} 1 & 0 & 0 \\ 0 & 1 & 0 \\ 0 & 0 & 1 \end{bmatrix} = I$$

Matched Problem 2

Let $M = \begin{bmatrix} 3 & -1 & 1 \\ -1 & 1 & 0 \\ 1 & 0 & 1 \end{bmatrix}$.

(A) Form the augmented matrix $[M\,|\,I]$.

(B) Use row operations to transform $[M\,|\,I]$ into $[I\,|\,B]$.

(C) Verify by multiplication that $B = M^{-1}$ (that is, show that $BM = I$).

The procedure shown in Example 2 can be used to find the inverse of any square matrix, if the inverse exists, and will also indicate when the inverse does not exist. These ideas are summarized in Theorem 1.

THEOREM 1   Inverse of a Square Matrix M

If $[M\,|\,I]$ is transformed by row operations into $[I\,|\,B]$, then the resulting matrix B is M^{-1}. However, if we obtain all 0's in one or more rows to the left of the vertical line, then M^{-1} does not exist.

EXPLORE & DISCUSS 2

(A) Suppose that the square matrix M has a row of all zeros. Explain why M has no inverse.

(B) Suppose that the square matrix M has a column of all zeros. Explain why M has no inverse.

EXAMPLE 3   **Finding a Matrix Inverse** Find M^{-1}, given $M = \begin{bmatrix} 4 & -1 \\ -6 & 2 \end{bmatrix}$.

SOLUTION

$$\begin{bmatrix} 4 & -1 & | & 1 & 0 \\ -6 & 2 & | & 0 & 1 \end{bmatrix} \quad \tfrac{1}{4}R_1 \rightarrow R_1$$

$$\sim \begin{bmatrix} 1 & -\tfrac{1}{4} & | & \tfrac{1}{4} & 0 \\ -6 & 2 & | & 0 & 1 \end{bmatrix} \quad 6R_1 + R_2 \rightarrow R_2$$

$$\sim \begin{bmatrix} 1 & -\tfrac{1}{4} & | & \tfrac{1}{4} & 0 \\ 0 & \tfrac{1}{2} & | & \tfrac{3}{2} & 1 \end{bmatrix} \quad 2R_2 \rightarrow R_2$$

$$\sim \begin{bmatrix} 1 & -\tfrac{1}{4} & | & \tfrac{1}{4} & 0 \\ 0 & 1 & | & 3 & 2 \end{bmatrix} \quad \tfrac{1}{4}R_2 + R_1 \rightarrow R_1$$

$$\sim \begin{bmatrix} 1 & 0 & | & 1 & \tfrac{1}{2} \\ 0 & 1 & | & 3 & 2 \end{bmatrix}$$

Therefore,

$$M^{-1} = \begin{bmatrix} 1 & \frac{1}{2} \\ 3 & 2 \end{bmatrix}$$

Check by showing that $M^{-1}M = I$.

Matched Problem 3   Find M^{-1}, given $M = \begin{bmatrix} 2 & -6 \\ 1 & -2 \end{bmatrix}$.

Most graphing calculators and spreadsheets can compute matrix inverses, as illustrated in Figure 4 for the solution to Example 3.

(A) The command M^{-1} produces the inverse on this graphing calculator

(B) The command MINVERSE (B2:C3) produces the inverse in this spreadsheet

Figure 4 Finding a matrix inverse

EXPLORE & DISCUSS 3   The inverse of

$$A = \begin{bmatrix} a & b \\ c & d \end{bmatrix}$$

is

$$A^{-1} = \begin{bmatrix} \dfrac{d}{ad-bc} & \dfrac{-b}{ad-bc} \\ \dfrac{-c}{ad-bc} & \dfrac{a}{ad-bc} \end{bmatrix} = \frac{1}{D} \begin{bmatrix} d & -b \\ -c & a \end{bmatrix} \qquad D = ad - bc$$

provided that $D \neq 0$.

(A) Use matrix multiplication to verify this formula. What can you conclude about A^{-1} if $D = 0$?

(B) Use this formula to find the inverse of matrix A in Example 3.

EXAMPLE 4   **Finding a Matrix Inverse**   Find M^{-1}, given $M = \begin{bmatrix} 2 & -4 \\ -3 & 6 \end{bmatrix}$.

SOLUTION

$$\begin{bmatrix} 2 & -4 & | & 1 & 0 \\ -3 & 6 & | & 0 & 1 \end{bmatrix} \quad \tfrac{1}{2} R_1 \rightarrow R_1$$

$$\sim \begin{bmatrix} 1 & -2 & | & \tfrac{1}{2} & 0 \\ -3 & 6 & | & 0 & 1 \end{bmatrix} \quad 3R_1 + R_2 \rightarrow R_2$$

$$\sim \begin{bmatrix} 1 & -2 & | & \tfrac{1}{2} & 0 \\ 0 & 0 & | & \tfrac{3}{2} & 1 \end{bmatrix}$$

We have all 0's in the second row to the left of the vertical bar; therefore, the inverse does not exist.

Matched Problem 4 Find N^{-1}, given $N = \begin{bmatrix} 3 & 1 \\ 6 & 2 \end{bmatrix}$.

Square matrices that do not have inverses are called **singular matrices.** Graphing calculators and spreadsheets recognize singular matrices and generally respond with some type of error message, as illustrated in Figure 5 for the solution to Example 4.

(A) A graphing calculator displays
    a clear error message

(B) A spreadsheet displays a more cryptic error message

Figure 5

Application: Cryptography

Matrix inverses can provide a simple and effective procedure for encoding and decoding messages. To begin, assign the numbers 1–26 to the letters in the alphabet, as shown below. Also assign the number 0 to a blank to provide for space between words. (A more sophisticated code could include both capital and lowercase letters and punctuation symbols.)

Blank A B C D E F G H I J K L M N O P Q R S T U V W X Y Z
0   1 2 3 4 5 6 7 8 9 10 11 12 13 14 15 16 17 18 19 20 21 22 23 24 25 26

The message "SECRET CODE" corresponds to the sequence

19 5 3 18 5 20 0 3 15 4 5

Any matrix whose elements are positive integers and whose inverse exists can be used as an **encoding matrix**. For example, to use the 2 × 2 matrix

$$A = \begin{bmatrix} 4 & 3 \\ 1 & 1 \end{bmatrix}$$

to encode the preceding message, first we divide the numbers in the sequence into groups of 2 and use these groups as the columns of a matrix B with 2 rows:

$$B = \begin{bmatrix} 19 & 3 & 5 & 0 & 15 & 5 \\ 5 & 18 & 20 & 3 & 4 & 0 \end{bmatrix}$$ *Proceed down the columns, not across the rows.*

Notice that we added an extra blank at the end of the message to make the columns come out even. Then we multiply this matrix on the left by A:

$$AB = \begin{bmatrix} 4 & 3 \\ 1 & 1 \end{bmatrix}\begin{bmatrix} 19 & 3 & 5 & 0 & 15 & 5 \\ 5 & 18 & 20 & 3 & 4 & 0 \end{bmatrix}$$

$$= \begin{bmatrix} 91 & 66 & 80 & 9 & 72 & 20 \\ 24 & 21 & 25 & 3 & 19 & 5 \end{bmatrix}$$

The coded message is

91 24 66 21 80 25 9 3 72 19 20 5

This message can be decoded simply by putting it back into matrix form and multiplying on the left by the **decoding matrix** A^{-1}. Since A^{-1} is easily determined if A is known, the encoding matrix A is the only key needed to decode messages that are encoded in this manner.

EXAMPLE 5   **Cryptography**   The message

$$46 \quad 84 \quad 85 \quad 28 \quad 47 \quad 46 \quad 4 \quad 5 \quad 10 \quad 30 \quad 48 \quad 72 \quad 29 \quad 57 \quad 38 \quad 38 \quad 57 \quad 95$$

was encoded with the matrix A shown next. Decode this message.

$$A = \begin{bmatrix} 1 & 1 & 1 \\ 2 & 1 & 2 \\ 2 & 3 & 1 \end{bmatrix}$$

SOLUTION   Since the encoding matrix A is 3×3, we begin by entering the coded message in the columns of a matrix C with three rows:

$$C = \begin{bmatrix} 46 & 28 & 4 & 30 & 29 & 38 \\ 84 & 47 & 5 & 48 & 57 & 57 \\ 85 & 46 & 10 & 72 & 38 & 95 \end{bmatrix}$$

If B is the matrix containing the uncoded message, then B and C are related by $C = AB$. To recover B, we find A^{-1} (details omitted) and multiply both sides of the equation $C = AB$ by A^{-1}:

$$B = A^{-1}C$$

$$= \begin{bmatrix} -5 & 2 & 1 \\ 2 & -1 & 0 \\ 4 & -1 & -1 \end{bmatrix} \begin{bmatrix} 46 & 28 & 4 & 30 & 29 & 38 \\ 84 & 47 & 5 & 48 & 57 & 57 \\ 85 & 46 & 10 & 72 & 38 & 95 \end{bmatrix}$$

$$= \begin{bmatrix} 23 & 0 & 0 & 18 & 7 & 19 \\ 8 & 9 & 3 & 12 & 1 & 19 \\ 15 & 19 & 1 & 0 & 21 & 0 \end{bmatrix}$$

Writing the numbers in the columns of this matrix in sequence and using the correspondence between numbers and letters noted earlier produces the decoded message:

23	8	15	0	9	19	0	3	1	18	12	0	7	1	21	19	19	0
W	H	O		I	S		C	A	R	L		G	A	U	S	S	

The answer to this question can be found earlier in this chapter.

Matched Problem 5   The message below was also encoded with the matrix A in Example 5. Decode this message:

$$46 \quad 84 \quad 85 \quad 28 \quad 47 \quad 46 \quad 32 \quad 41 \quad 78 \quad 25 \quad 42 \quad 53 \quad 25 \quad 37 \quad 63 \quad 43 \quad 71 \quad 83 \quad 19 \quad 37 \quad 25$$

Exercises 4-5

A

In Problems 1–10, find the matrix products. Note that each product can be found mentally, without the use of a calculator or pencil-and-paper calculations.

1. (A) $\begin{bmatrix} 1 & 0 \\ 0 & 0 \end{bmatrix} \begin{bmatrix} 2 & -3 \\ 4 & 5 \end{bmatrix}$ (B) $\begin{bmatrix} 2 & -3 \\ 4 & 5 \end{bmatrix} \begin{bmatrix} 1 & 0 \\ 0 & 0 \end{bmatrix}$

2. (A) $\begin{bmatrix} 1 & 0 \\ 0 & 0 \end{bmatrix} \begin{bmatrix} -1 & 6 \\ 5 & 2 \end{bmatrix}$ (B) $\begin{bmatrix} -1 & 6 \\ 5 & 2 \end{bmatrix} \begin{bmatrix} 1 & 0 \\ 0 & 0 \end{bmatrix}$

3. (A) $\begin{bmatrix} 0 & 0 \\ 0 & 1 \end{bmatrix} \begin{bmatrix} 2 & -3 \\ 4 & 5 \end{bmatrix}$ (B) $\begin{bmatrix} 2 & -3 \\ 4 & 5 \end{bmatrix} \begin{bmatrix} 0 & 0 \\ 0 & 1 \end{bmatrix}$

4. (A) $\begin{bmatrix} 0 & 0 \\ 0 & 1 \end{bmatrix} \begin{bmatrix} -1 & 6 \\ 5 & 2 \end{bmatrix}$ (B) $\begin{bmatrix} -1 & 6 \\ 5 & 2 \end{bmatrix} \begin{bmatrix} 0 & 0 \\ 0 & 1 \end{bmatrix}$

5. (A) $\begin{bmatrix} 1 & 0 \\ 0 & 1 \end{bmatrix} \begin{bmatrix} 2 & -3 \\ 4 & 5 \end{bmatrix}$ (B) $\begin{bmatrix} 2 & -3 \\ 4 & 5 \end{bmatrix} \begin{bmatrix} 1 & 0 \\ 0 & 1 \end{bmatrix}$

6. (A) $\begin{bmatrix} 1 & 0 \\ 0 & 1 \end{bmatrix} \begin{bmatrix} -1 & 6 \\ 5 & 2 \end{bmatrix}$ (B) $\begin{bmatrix} -1 & 6 \\ 5 & 2 \end{bmatrix} \begin{bmatrix} 1 & 0 \\ 0 & 1 \end{bmatrix}$

7. $\begin{bmatrix} 1 & 0 & 0 \\ 0 & 1 & 0 \\ 0 & 0 & 1 \end{bmatrix} \begin{bmatrix} -2 & 1 & 3 \\ 2 & 4 & -2 \\ 5 & 1 & 0 \end{bmatrix}$

8. $\begin{bmatrix} 1 & 0 & 0 \\ 0 & 1 & 0 \\ 0 & 0 & 1 \end{bmatrix} \begin{bmatrix} 3 & -4 & 0 \\ 1 & 2 & -5 \\ 6 & -3 & -1 \end{bmatrix}$

9. $\begin{bmatrix} -2 & 1 & 3 \\ 2 & 4 & -2 \\ 5 & 1 & 0 \end{bmatrix} \begin{bmatrix} 1 & 0 & 0 \\ 0 & 1 & 0 \\ 0 & 0 & 1 \end{bmatrix}$

10. $\begin{bmatrix} 3 & -4 & 0 \\ 1 & 2 & -5 \\ 6 & -3 & -1 \end{bmatrix} \begin{bmatrix} 1 & 0 & 0 \\ 0 & 1 & 0 \\ 0 & 0 & 1 \end{bmatrix}$

In Problems 11–20, examine the product of the two matrices to determine if each is the inverse of the other.

11. $\begin{bmatrix} 3 & -4 \\ -2 & 3 \end{bmatrix}$; $\begin{bmatrix} 3 & 4 \\ 2 & 3 \end{bmatrix}$

12. $\begin{bmatrix} -2 & -1 \\ -4 & 2 \end{bmatrix}$; $\begin{bmatrix} 1 & -1 \\ 2 & -2 \end{bmatrix}$

13. $\begin{bmatrix} 2 & 2 \\ -1 & -1 \end{bmatrix}$; $\begin{bmatrix} 1 & 1 \\ -1 & -1 \end{bmatrix}$

14. $\begin{bmatrix} 5 & -7 \\ -2 & 3 \end{bmatrix}$; $\begin{bmatrix} 3 & 7 \\ 2 & 5 \end{bmatrix}$

15. $\begin{bmatrix} -5 & 2 \\ -8 & 3 \end{bmatrix}$; $\begin{bmatrix} 3 & -2 \\ 8 & -5 \end{bmatrix}$

16. $\begin{bmatrix} 7 & 4 \\ -5 & -3 \end{bmatrix}$; $\begin{bmatrix} 3 & 4 \\ -5 & -7 \end{bmatrix}$

17. $\begin{bmatrix} 1 & 2 & 0 \\ 0 & 1 & 0 \\ -1 & -1 & 1 \end{bmatrix}$; $\begin{bmatrix} 1 & -2 & 0 \\ 0 & 1 & 0 \\ 1 & -1 & 0 \end{bmatrix}$

18. $\begin{bmatrix} 1 & 0 & 1 \\ -3 & 1 & -2 \\ 0 & 0 & 1 \end{bmatrix}$; $\begin{bmatrix} 1 & 0 & -1 \\ 3 & 1 & -1 \\ 0 & 0 & 1 \end{bmatrix}$

19. $\begin{bmatrix} 1 & -1 & 1 \\ 0 & 2 & -1 \\ 2 & 3 & 0 \end{bmatrix}$; $\begin{bmatrix} 3 & 3 & -1 \\ -2 & -2 & 1 \\ -4 & -5 & 2 \end{bmatrix}$

20. $\begin{bmatrix} 1 & 0 & -1 \\ 3 & 1 & -1 \\ 0 & 0 & 0 \end{bmatrix}$; $\begin{bmatrix} 1 & 0 & -1 \\ -3 & 1 & -2 \\ 0 & 0 & 1 \end{bmatrix}$

✎ *Without performing any row operations, explain why each of the matrices in Problems 21–30 does not have an inverse.*

21. $\begin{bmatrix} 1 & 2 & 0 \\ -3 & 2 & -1 \end{bmatrix}$

22. $\begin{bmatrix} -2 & 3 & -1 \\ 4 & 0 & 1 \end{bmatrix}$

23. $\begin{bmatrix} 1 & -2 \\ 3 & 0 \\ 2 & -1 \end{bmatrix}$

24. $\begin{bmatrix} 0 & -1 \\ 2 & -2 \\ 1 & -3 \end{bmatrix}$

25. $\begin{bmatrix} -1 & 2 \\ 0 & 0 \end{bmatrix}$

26. $\begin{bmatrix} 0 & 0 \\ 1 & 2 \end{bmatrix}$

27. $\begin{bmatrix} 0 & 2 \\ 0 & -1 \end{bmatrix}$

28. $\begin{bmatrix} 1 & 0 \\ 3 & 0 \end{bmatrix}$

29. $\begin{bmatrix} 1 & 2 \\ 3 & 6 \end{bmatrix}$

30. $\begin{bmatrix} -2 & -3 \\ 4 & 6 \end{bmatrix}$

B

Given M in Problems 31–40, find M^{-1} and show that $M^{-1}M = I$.

31. $\begin{bmatrix} -1 & 0 \\ -3 & 1 \end{bmatrix}$

32. $\begin{bmatrix} 1 & -5 \\ 0 & -1 \end{bmatrix}$

33. $\begin{bmatrix} 1 & 2 \\ 1 & 3 \end{bmatrix}$

34. $\begin{bmatrix} 2 & 1 \\ 5 & 3 \end{bmatrix}$

35. $\begin{bmatrix} 1 & 3 \\ 2 & 7 \end{bmatrix}$

36. $\begin{bmatrix} 2 & 1 \\ 1 & 1 \end{bmatrix}$

37. $\begin{bmatrix} 1 & -3 & 0 \\ 0 & 1 & 1 \\ 2 & -1 & 4 \end{bmatrix}$

38. $\begin{bmatrix} 2 & 3 & 0 \\ 1 & 2 & 3 \\ 0 & -1 & -5 \end{bmatrix}$

39. $\begin{bmatrix} 1 & 1 & 0 \\ 2 & 3 & -1 \\ 1 & 0 & 2 \end{bmatrix}$

40. $\begin{bmatrix} 1 & 0 & -1 \\ 2 & -1 & 0 \\ 1 & 1 & -2 \end{bmatrix}$

Find the inverse of each matrix in Problems 41–46, if it exists.

41. $\begin{bmatrix} 4 & 3 \\ -3 & -2 \end{bmatrix}$

42. $\begin{bmatrix} -4 & 3 \\ -5 & 4 \end{bmatrix}$

43. $\begin{bmatrix} 2 & 6 \\ 3 & 9 \end{bmatrix}$

44. $\begin{bmatrix} 2 & -4 \\ -3 & 6 \end{bmatrix}$

45. $\begin{bmatrix} 2 & 1 \\ 4 & 3 \end{bmatrix}$

46. $\begin{bmatrix} -5 & 3 \\ 2 & -2 \end{bmatrix}$

In problems 47–52, find the inverse. Note that each inverse can be found mentally, without the use of a calculator or pencil-and-paper calculations.

47. $\begin{bmatrix} 2 & 0 \\ 0 & 2 \end{bmatrix}$

48. $\begin{bmatrix} 4 & 0 \\ 0 & 4 \end{bmatrix}$

49. $\begin{bmatrix} 3 & 0 \\ 0 & -5 \end{bmatrix}$

50. $\begin{bmatrix} -2 & 0 \\ 0 & \frac{1}{2} \end{bmatrix}$

51. $\begin{bmatrix} 4 & 0 & 0 \\ 0 & 2 & 0 \\ 0 & 0 & -8 \end{bmatrix}$

52. $\begin{bmatrix} 3 & 0 & 0 \\ 0 & -6 & 0 \\ 0 & 0 & -5 \end{bmatrix}$

C

Find the inverse of each matrix in Problems 53–60, if it exists.

53. $\begin{bmatrix} -5 & -2 & -2 \\ 2 & 1 & 0 \\ 1 & 0 & 1 \end{bmatrix}$

54. $\begin{bmatrix} 2 & -2 & 4 \\ 1 & 1 & 1 \\ 1 & 0 & 1 \end{bmatrix}$

55. $\begin{bmatrix} 2 & 1 & 1 \\ 1 & 1 & 0 \\ -1 & -1 & 0 \end{bmatrix}$

56. $\begin{bmatrix} 1 & -1 & 0 \\ 2 & -1 & 1 \\ 0 & 1 & 1 \end{bmatrix}$

57. $\begin{bmatrix} -1 & -2 & 2 \\ 4 & 3 & 0 \\ 4 & 0 & 4 \end{bmatrix}$

58. $\begin{bmatrix} 4 & 2 & 2 \\ 4 & 2 & 0 \\ 5 & 0 & 5 \end{bmatrix}$

59. $\begin{bmatrix} 2 & -1 & -2 \\ -4 & 2 & 8 \\ 6 & -2 & -1 \end{bmatrix}$

60. $\begin{bmatrix} -1 & -1 & 4 \\ 3 & 3 & -22 \\ -2 & -1 & 19 \end{bmatrix}$

61. Show that $(A^{-1})^{-1} = A$ for: $A = \begin{bmatrix} 4 & 3 \\ 3 & 2 \end{bmatrix}$

62. Show that $(AB)^{-1} = B^{-1}A^{-1}$ for

$$A = \begin{bmatrix} 4 & 3 \\ 3 & 2 \end{bmatrix} \quad \text{and} \quad B = \begin{bmatrix} 2 & 5 \\ 3 & 7 \end{bmatrix}$$

63. Discuss the existence of M^{-1} for 2×2 diagonal matrices of the form

$$M = \begin{bmatrix} a & 0 \\ 0 & d \end{bmatrix}$$

Generalize your conclusions to $n \times n$ diagonal matrices.

64. Discuss the existence of M^{-1} for 2×2 upper triangular matrices of the form

$$M = \begin{bmatrix} a & b \\ 0 & d \end{bmatrix}$$

Generalize your conclusions to $n \times n$ upper triangular matrices.

In Problems 65–67, find A^{-1} and A^2.

65. $A = \begin{bmatrix} 3 & 2 \\ -4 & -3 \end{bmatrix}$ **66.** $A = \begin{bmatrix} -2 & -1 \\ 3 & 2 \end{bmatrix}$

67. $A = \begin{bmatrix} 4 & 3 \\ -5 & -4 \end{bmatrix}$

68. Based on your observations in Problems 65–67, if $A = A^{-1}$ for a square matrix A, what is A^2? Give a mathematical argument to support your conclusion.

Applications

Problems 69–72 refer to the encoding matrix

$$A = \begin{bmatrix} 1 & 2 \\ 1 & 3 \end{bmatrix}$$

69. Cryptography. Encode the message "THE SUN ALSO RISES" using matrix A.

70. Cryptography. Encode the message "THE GRAPES OF WRATH" using matrix A.

71. Cryptography. The following message was encoded with matrix A. Decode this message:

37 52 24 29 46 69 49 69 8 8 36 44 5 5 41
50 22 26

72. Cryptography. The following message was encoded with matrix A. Decode this message:

9 13 40 49 29 34 2 3 22 26 6 9 43 57 29
34 54 74

Problems 73–76 require the use of a graphing calculator or a computer. To use the 5×5 encoding matrix B given below, form a matrix with 5 rows and as many columns as necessary to accommodate each message.

$$B = \begin{bmatrix} 1 & 0 & 1 & 0 & 1 \\ 0 & 1 & 1 & 0 & 3 \\ 2 & 1 & 1 & 1 & 1 \\ 0 & 0 & 1 & 0 & 2 \\ 1 & 1 & 1 & 2 & 1 \end{bmatrix}$$

73. Cryptography. Encode the message "THE BEST YEARS OF OUR LIVES" using matrix B.

74. Cryptography. Encode the message "THE BRIDGE ON THE RIVER KWAI" using matrix B.

75. Cryptography. The following message was encoded with matrix B. Decode this message:

32 34 60 19 40 24 21 67 11 69
27 44 85 16 85 29 65 82 28 82
21 66 44 41 62 8 0 16 0 8

76. Cryptography. The following message was encoded with matrix B. Decode this message:

28 22 56 11 36 30 27 75 15 78
30 51 64 30 62 39 30 58 25 44

Answers to Matched Problems

1. (A) $\begin{bmatrix} 2 & -3 \\ 5 & 7 \end{bmatrix}$ (B) $\begin{bmatrix} 4 & 2 \\ 3 & -5 \\ 6 & 8 \end{bmatrix}$

2. (A) $\left[\begin{array}{ccc|ccc} 3 & -1 & 1 & 1 & 0 & 0 \\ -1 & 1 & 0 & 0 & 1 & 0 \\ 1 & 0 & 1 & 0 & 0 & 1 \end{array}\right]$

(B) $\left[\begin{array}{ccc|ccc} 1 & 0 & 0 & 1 & 1 & -1 \\ 0 & 1 & 0 & 1 & 2 & -1 \\ 0 & 0 & 1 & -1 & -1 & 2 \end{array}\right]$

(C) $\begin{bmatrix} 1 & 1 & -1 \\ 1 & 2 & -1 \\ -1 & -1 & 2 \end{bmatrix}\begin{bmatrix} 3 & -1 & 1 \\ -1 & 1 & 0 \\ 1 & 0 & 1 \end{bmatrix} = \begin{bmatrix} 1 & 0 & 0 \\ 0 & 1 & 0 \\ 0 & 0 & 1 \end{bmatrix}$

3. $\begin{bmatrix} -1 & 3 \\ -\frac{1}{2} & 1 \end{bmatrix}$

4. Does not exist

5. WHO IS WILHELM JORDAN

4-6 Matrix Equations and Systems of Linear Equations

- Matrix Equations
- Matrix Equations and Systems of Linear Equations
- Application

The identity matrix and inverse matrix discussed in the preceding section can be put to immediate use in the solution of certain simple matrix equations. Being able to solve a matrix equation gives us another important method of solving systems of equations, provided that the system is independent and has the same number of variables as equations. If the system is dependent or if it has either fewer or more variables than equations, we must return to the Gauss–Jordan method of elimination.

Matrix Equations

Solving simple matrix equations follows very much the same procedures as those used in solving real number equations. We have, however, less freedom with matrix equations because matrix multiplication is not commutative. In solving matrix equations, we will be guided by the properties of matrices summarized in Theorem 1.

THEOREM 1   Basic Properties of Matrices

Assuming that all products and sums are defined for the indicated matrices A, B, C, I, and 0, then

Addition Properties

Associative:	$(A + B) + C = A + (B + C)$
Commutative:	$A + B = B + A$
Additive identity:	$A + 0 = 0 + A = A$
Additive inverse:	$A + (-A) = (-A) + A = 0$

Multiplication Properties

Associative property:	$A(BC) = (AB)C$
Multiplicative identity:	$AI = IA = A$
Multiplicative inverse:	If A is a square matrix and A^{-1} exists, then $AA^{-1} = A^{-1}A = I$.

Combined Properties

Left distributive:	$A(B + C) = AB + AC$
Right distributive:	$(B + C)A = BA + CA$

Equality

Addition:	If $A = B$, then $A + C = B + C$.
Left multiplication:	If $A = B$, then $CA = CB$.
Right multiplication:	If $A = B$, then $AC = BC$.

EXAMPLE 1   **Solving a Matrix Equation** Given an $n \times n$ matrix A and $n \times 1$ column matrices B and X, solve $AX = B$ for X. Assume that all necessary inverses exist.

SOLUTION   We are interested in finding a column matrix X that satisfies the matrix equation $AX = B$. To solve this equation, we multiply both sides on the left by A^{-1} to isolate X on the left side.

$$AX = B \qquad \text{Use the left multiplication property.}$$
$$A^{-1}(AX) = A^{-1}B \qquad \text{Use the associative property.}$$
$$(A^{-1}A)X = A^{-1}B \qquad A^{-1}A = I$$
$$IX = A^{-1}B \qquad IX = X$$
$$X = A^{-1}B$$

Matched Problem 1   Given an $n \times n$ matrix A and $n \times 1$ column matrices B, C, and X, solve $AX + C = B$ for X. Assume that all necessary inverses exist.

⚠ **CAUTION** Do not mix the left multiplication property and the right multiplication property. If $AX = B$, then

$$A^{-1}(AX) \neq BA^{-1}$$

Matrix Equations and Systems of Linear Equations

Now we show how independent systems of linear equations with the same number of variables as equations can be solved. First, convert the system into a matrix equation of the form $AX = B$, and then use $X = A^{-1}B$ as obtained in Example 1.

EXAMPLE 2   **Using Inverses to Solve Systems of Equations**   Use matrix inverse methods to solve the system:

$$
\begin{aligned}
x_1 &- x_2 + x_3 = 1 \\
&2x_2 - x_3 = 1 \\
2x_1 &+ 3x_2 \qquad\;\; = 1
\end{aligned}
\tag{1}
$$

SOLUTION   The inverse of the coefficient matrix

$$
A = \begin{bmatrix} 1 & -1 & 1 \\ 0 & 2 & -1 \\ 2 & 3 & 0 \end{bmatrix}
$$

provides an efficient method for solving this system. To see how, we convert system (1) into a matrix equation:

$$
\overset{A}{\begin{bmatrix} 1 & -1 & 1 \\ 0 & 2 & -1 \\ 2 & 3 & 0 \end{bmatrix}}
\overset{X}{\begin{bmatrix} x_1 \\ x_2 \\ x_3 \end{bmatrix}}
=
\overset{B}{\begin{bmatrix} 1 \\ 1 \\ 1 \end{bmatrix}}
\tag{2}
$$

Check that matrix equation (2) is equivalent to system (1) by finding the product of the left side and then equating corresponding elements on the left with those on the right.

We are interested in finding a column matrix X that satisfies the matrix equation $AX = B$. In Example 1 we found that if A^{-1} exists, then

$$X = A^{-1}B$$

The inverse of A was found in Example 2, Section 4-5, to be

$$
A^{-1} = \begin{bmatrix} 3 & 3 & -1 \\ -2 & -2 & 1 \\ -4 & -5 & 2 \end{bmatrix}
$$

Therefore,

$$
\overset{X}{\begin{bmatrix} x_1 \\ x_2 \\ x_3 \end{bmatrix}}
=
\overset{A^{-1}}{\begin{bmatrix} 3 & 3 & -1 \\ -2 & -2 & 1 \\ -4 & -5 & 2 \end{bmatrix}}
\overset{B}{\begin{bmatrix} 1 \\ 1 \\ 1 \end{bmatrix}}
=
\begin{bmatrix} 5 \\ -3 \\ -7 \end{bmatrix}
$$

and we can conclude that $x_1 = 5$, $x_2 = -3$, and $x_3 = -7$. Check this result in system (1).

Matched Problem 2   Use matrix inverse methods to solve the system:

$$3x_1 - x_2 + x_3 = 1$$
$$-x_1 + x_2 \qquad = 3$$
$$x_1 \qquad + x_3 = 2$$

[*Note:* The inverse of the coefficient matrix was found in Matched Problem 2, Section 4-5.]

At first glance, using matrix inverse methods seems to require the same amount of effort as using Gauss–Jordan elimination. In either case, row operations must be applied to an augmented matrix involving the coefficients of the system. The advantage of the inverse matrix method becomes readily apparent when solving a number of systems with a common coefficient matrix and different constant terms.

EXAMPLE 3   **Using Inverses to Solve Systems of Equations**   Use matrix inverse methods to solve each of the following systems:

(A) $x_1 - x_2 + x_3 = 3$
$\qquad 2x_2 - x_3 = 1$
$\quad 2x_1 + 3x_2 \qquad = 4$

(B) $x_1 - x_2 + x_3 = -5$
$\qquad 2x_2 - x_3 = 2$
$\quad 2x_1 + 3x_2 \qquad = -3$

SOLUTION   Notice that both systems have the same coefficient matrix A as system (1) in Example 2. Only the constant terms have changed. We can use A^{-1} to solve these systems just as we did in Example 2.

(A)
$$\begin{matrix} X & A^{-1} & B \end{matrix}$$
$$\begin{bmatrix} x_1 \\ x_2 \\ x_3 \end{bmatrix} = \begin{bmatrix} 3 & 3 & -1 \\ -2 & -2 & 1 \\ -4 & -5 & 2 \end{bmatrix} \begin{bmatrix} 3 \\ 1 \\ 4 \end{bmatrix} = \begin{bmatrix} 8 \\ -4 \\ -9 \end{bmatrix}$$

$x_1 = 8, x_2 = -4$, and $x_3 = -9$.

(B)
$$\begin{matrix} X & A^{-1} & B \end{matrix}$$
$$\begin{bmatrix} x_1 \\ x_2 \\ x_3 \end{bmatrix} = \begin{bmatrix} 3 & 3 & -1 \\ -2 & -2 & 1 \\ -4 & -5 & 2 \end{bmatrix} \begin{bmatrix} -5 \\ 2 \\ -3 \end{bmatrix} = \begin{bmatrix} -6 \\ 3 \\ 4 \end{bmatrix}$$

$x_1 = -6, x_2 = 3$, and $x_3 = 4$.

Matched Problem 3   Use matrix inverse methods to solve each of the following systems (see Matched Problem 2):

(A) $3x_1 - x_2 + x_3 = 3$
$\quad -x_1 + x_2 \qquad = -3$
$\quad x_1 + \qquad x_3 = 2$

(B) $3x_1 - x_2 + x_3 = -5$
$\quad -x_1 + x_2 \qquad = 1$
$\quad x_1 \qquad + x_3 = -4$

   As Examples 2 and 3 illustrate, inverse methods are very convenient for hand calculations because once the inverse is found, it can be used to solve any new system formed by changing only the constant terms. Since most graphing calculators and computers can compute the inverse of a matrix, this method also adapts readily

	A	B	C	D	E	F	G	H	I	J
1		A				B	X		B	X
2		1	-1	1		3	8		-5	-6
3		0	2	-1		1	-4		2	3
4		2	3	0		4	-9		-3	4

Figure 1 Using inverse methods on a spreadsheet: The values in G2:G4 are produced by the command MMULT (MINVERSE(B2:D4),F2:F4)

to graphing calculator and spreadsheet solutions (Fig. 1). However, if your graphing calculator (or spreadsheet) also has a built-in procedure for finding the reduced form of an augmented coefficient matrix, it is just as convenient to use Gauss–Jordan elimination. Furthermore, Gauss–Jordan elimination can be used in all cases and, as noted below, matrix inverse methods cannot always be used.

SUMMARY Using Inverse Methods to Solve Systems of Equations

If the number of equations in a system equals the number of variables and the coefficient matrix has an inverse, then the system will always have a unique solution that can be found by using the inverse of the coefficient matrix to solve the corresponding matrix equation.

Matrix equation   Solution

$$AX = B \qquad X = A^{-1}B$$

CONCEPTUAL INSIGHT

There are two cases where inverse methods will not work:

Case 1. The coefficient matrix is singular.
Case 2. The number of variables is not the same as the number of equations.

In either case, use Gauss–Jordan elimination.

Application

The following application illustrates the usefulness of the inverse matrix method for solving systems of equations.

EXAMPLE 4   **Investment Analysis** An investment advisor currently has two types of investments available for clients: a conservative investment A that pays 10% per year and a higher risk investment B that pays 20% per year. Clients may divide their investments between the two to achieve any total return desired between 10% and 20%. However, the higher the desired return, the higher the risk. How should each client invest to achieve the indicated return?

	Client			
	1	**2**	**3**	k
Total investment	$20,000	$50,000	$10,000	k_1
Annual return desired	$ 2,400	$ 7,500	$ 1,300	k_2
	(12%)	(15%)	(13%)	

SOLUTION   The answer to this problem involves six quantities, two for each client. Utilizing inverse matrices provides an efficient way to find these quantities. We will solve the problem for an arbitrary client k with unspecified amounts k_1 for the total investment and k_2 for the annual return. (Do not confuse k_1 and k_2 with variables. Their values are known—they just differ for each client.)

Let x_1 = amount invested in A by a given client
x_2 = amount invested in B by a given client

Then we have the following mathematical model:

$$x_1 + x_2 = k_1 \quad \text{Total invested}$$
$$0.1x_1 + 0.2x_2 = k_2 \quad \text{Total annual return desired}$$

Write as a matrix equation:

$$\underset{A}{\begin{bmatrix} 1 & 1 \\ 0.1 & 0.2 \end{bmatrix}} \underset{X}{\begin{bmatrix} x_1 \\ x_2 \end{bmatrix}} = \underset{B}{\begin{bmatrix} k_1 \\ k_2 \end{bmatrix}}$$

If A^{-1} exists, then

$$X = A^{-1}B$$

We now find A^{-1} by starting with the augmented matrix $[A|I]$ and proceeding as discussed in Section 4-5:

$$\begin{bmatrix} 1 & 1 & | & 1 & 0 \\ 0.1 & 0.2 & | & 0 & 1 \end{bmatrix} \quad 10R_2 \to R_2$$

$$\sim \begin{bmatrix} 1 & 1 & | & 1 & 0 \\ 1 & 2 & | & 0 & 10 \end{bmatrix} \quad (-1)R_1 + R_2 \to R_2$$

$$\sim \begin{bmatrix} 1 & 1 & | & 1 & 0 \\ 0 & 1 & | & -1 & 10 \end{bmatrix} \quad (-1)R_2 + R_1 \to R_1$$

$$\sim \begin{bmatrix} 1 & 0 & | & 2 & -10 \\ 0 & 1 & | & -1 & 10 \end{bmatrix}$$

Therefore,

$$A^{-1} = \begin{bmatrix} 2 & -10 \\ -1 & 10 \end{bmatrix} \quad \text{Check:} \quad \underset{A^{-1}}{\begin{bmatrix} 2 & -10 \\ -1 & 10 \end{bmatrix}} \underset{A}{\begin{bmatrix} 1 & 1 \\ 0.1 & 0.2 \end{bmatrix}} = \underset{I}{\begin{bmatrix} 1 & 0 \\ 0 & 1 \end{bmatrix}}$$

and

$$\underset{X}{\begin{bmatrix} x_1 \\ x_2 \end{bmatrix}} = \underset{A^{-1}}{\begin{bmatrix} 2 & -10 \\ -1 & 10 \end{bmatrix}} \underset{B}{\begin{bmatrix} k_1 \\ k_2 \end{bmatrix}}$$

To solve each client's investment problem, we replace k_1 and k_2 with appropriate values from the table and multiply by A^{-1}:

Client 1

$$\begin{bmatrix} x_1 \\ x_2 \end{bmatrix} = \begin{bmatrix} 2 & -10 \\ -1 & 10 \end{bmatrix} \begin{bmatrix} 20,000 \\ 2,400 \end{bmatrix} = \begin{bmatrix} 16,000 \\ 4,000 \end{bmatrix}$$

Solution: $x_1 = \$16,000$ in investment A, $x_2 = \$4,000$ in investment B

Client 2

$$\begin{bmatrix} x_1 \\ x_2 \end{bmatrix} = \begin{bmatrix} 2 & -10 \\ -1 & 10 \end{bmatrix} \begin{bmatrix} 50,000 \\ 7,500 \end{bmatrix} = \begin{bmatrix} 25,000 \\ 25,000 \end{bmatrix}$$

Solution: $x_1 = \$25,000$ in investment A, $x_2 = \$25,000$ in investment B

Client 3

$$\begin{bmatrix} x_1 \\ x_2 \end{bmatrix} = \begin{bmatrix} 2 & -10 \\ -1 & 10 \end{bmatrix} \begin{bmatrix} 10{,}000 \\ 1{,}300 \end{bmatrix} = \begin{bmatrix} 7{,}000 \\ 3{,}000 \end{bmatrix}$$

Solution: $x_1 = \$7{,}000$ in investment A, $x_2 = \$3{,}000$ in investment B

Matched Problem 4   Repeat Example 4 with investment A paying 8% and investment B paying 24%.

Figure 2 illustrates a solution to Example 4 on a spreadsheet.

	A	B	C	D	E	F	G
1			Clients				
2		1	2	3		A	
3	Total Investment	$20,000	$50,000	$10,000		1	1
4	Annual Return	$2,400	$7,500	$1,300		0.1	0.2
5	Amount Invested in A	$16,000	$25,000	$7,000			
6	Amount Invested in B	$4,000	$25,000	$3,000			

Figure 2

EXPLORE & DISCUSS 1

Refer to the mathematical model in Example 4:

$$\overset{A}{\begin{bmatrix} 1 & 1 \\ 0.1 & 0.2 \end{bmatrix}} \overset{X}{\begin{bmatrix} x_1 \\ x_2 \end{bmatrix}} = \overset{B}{\begin{bmatrix} k_1 \\ k_2 \end{bmatrix}} \tag{3}$$

(A) Does matrix equation (3) always have a solution for any constant matrix B?

(B) Do all these solutions make sense for the original problem? If not, give examples.

(C) If the total investment is $k_1 = \$10{,}000$, describe all possible annual returns k_2.

Exercises 4-6

A

Write Problems 1–4 as systems of linear equations without matrices.

1. $\begin{bmatrix} 3 & 1 \\ 2 & -1 \end{bmatrix} \begin{bmatrix} x_1 \\ x_2 \end{bmatrix} = \begin{bmatrix} 5 \\ -4 \end{bmatrix}$

2. $\begin{bmatrix} -2 & 1 \\ -3 & 4 \end{bmatrix} \begin{bmatrix} x_1 \\ x_2 \end{bmatrix} = \begin{bmatrix} -5 \\ 7 \end{bmatrix}$

3. $\begin{bmatrix} -3 & 1 & 0 \\ 2 & 0 & 1 \\ -1 & 3 & -2 \end{bmatrix} \begin{bmatrix} x_1 \\ x_2 \\ x_3 \end{bmatrix} = \begin{bmatrix} 3 \\ -4 \\ 2 \end{bmatrix}$

4. $\begin{bmatrix} 2 & -1 & 0 \\ -2 & 3 & -1 \\ 4 & 0 & 3 \end{bmatrix} \begin{bmatrix} x_1 \\ x_2 \\ x_3 \end{bmatrix} = \begin{bmatrix} 6 \\ -4 \\ 7 \end{bmatrix}$

Write each system in Problems 5–8 as a matrix equation of the form $AX = B$.

5. $\begin{aligned} 3x_1 - 4x_2 &= 1 \\ 2x_1 + x_2 &= 5 \end{aligned}$

6. $\begin{aligned} 2x_1 + x_2 &= 8 \\ -5x_1 + 3x_2 &= -4 \end{aligned}$

7. $\begin{aligned} x_1 - 3x_2 + 2x_3 &= -3 \\ -2x_1 + 3x_2 &= 1 \\ x_1 + x_2 + 4x_3 &= -2 \end{aligned}$

8. $\begin{aligned} 3x_1 + 2x_3 &= 9 \\ -x_1 + 4x_2 + x_3 &= -7 \\ -2x_1 + 3x_2 &= 6 \end{aligned}$

Find x_1 and x_2 in Problems 9–12.

9. $\begin{bmatrix} x_1 \\ x_2 \end{bmatrix} = \begin{bmatrix} 3 & -2 \\ 1 & 4 \end{bmatrix} \begin{bmatrix} -2 \\ 1 \end{bmatrix}$

10. $\begin{bmatrix} x_1 \\ x_2 \end{bmatrix} = \begin{bmatrix} -2 & 1 \\ -1 & 2 \end{bmatrix} \begin{bmatrix} 3 \\ -2 \end{bmatrix}$

11. $\begin{bmatrix} x_1 \\ x_2 \end{bmatrix} = \begin{bmatrix} -2 & 3 \\ 2 & -1 \end{bmatrix} \begin{bmatrix} 3 \\ 2 \end{bmatrix}$

12. $\begin{bmatrix} x_1 \\ x_2 \end{bmatrix} = \begin{bmatrix} 3 & -1 \\ 0 & 2 \end{bmatrix} \begin{bmatrix} -2 \\ 1 \end{bmatrix}$

In Problems 13–16, find x_1 and x_2.

13. $\begin{bmatrix} 1 & -1 \\ 1 & -2 \end{bmatrix} \begin{bmatrix} x_1 \\ x_2 \end{bmatrix} = \begin{bmatrix} 5 \\ 7 \end{bmatrix}$

14. $\begin{bmatrix} 1 & 3 \\ 1 & 4 \end{bmatrix} \begin{bmatrix} x_1 \\ x_2 \end{bmatrix} = \begin{bmatrix} 9 \\ 6 \end{bmatrix}$

15. $\begin{bmatrix} 1 & 1 \\ 2 & -3 \end{bmatrix} \begin{bmatrix} x_1 \\ x_2 \end{bmatrix} = \begin{bmatrix} 15 \\ 10 \end{bmatrix}$

16. $\begin{bmatrix} 1 & 1 \\ 3 & -2 \end{bmatrix} \begin{bmatrix} x_1 \\ x_2 \end{bmatrix} = \begin{bmatrix} 10 \\ 20 \end{bmatrix}$

In Problems 17–22, solve for x_1 and x_2.

17. $\begin{bmatrix} 1 & 2 \\ 1 & 1 \end{bmatrix} \begin{bmatrix} x_1 \\ x_2 \end{bmatrix} + \begin{bmatrix} 3 \\ 4 \end{bmatrix} = \begin{bmatrix} 9 \\ 9 \end{bmatrix}$

18. $\begin{bmatrix} 3 & 1 \\ 2 & 1 \end{bmatrix}\begin{bmatrix} x_1 \\ x_2 \end{bmatrix} + \begin{bmatrix} 4 \\ 1 \end{bmatrix} = \begin{bmatrix} 7 \\ 8 \end{bmatrix}$

19. $\begin{bmatrix} 2 & 2 \\ 2 & 3 \end{bmatrix}\begin{bmatrix} x_1 \\ x_2 \end{bmatrix} + \begin{bmatrix} -5 \\ 2 \end{bmatrix} = \begin{bmatrix} 2 \\ 3 \end{bmatrix}$

20. $\begin{bmatrix} 3 & -4 \\ -6 & 8 \end{bmatrix}\begin{bmatrix} x_1 \\ x_2 \end{bmatrix} + \begin{bmatrix} 1 \\ 0 \end{bmatrix} = \begin{bmatrix} 2 \\ 1 \end{bmatrix}$

21. $\begin{bmatrix} 3 & -2 \\ 6 & -4 \end{bmatrix}\begin{bmatrix} x_1 \\ x_2 \end{bmatrix} + \begin{bmatrix} 0 \\ -3 \end{bmatrix} = \begin{bmatrix} 1 \\ -2 \end{bmatrix}$

22. $\begin{bmatrix} 3 & -1 \\ 6 & -4 \end{bmatrix}\begin{bmatrix} x_1 \\ x_2 \end{bmatrix} + \begin{bmatrix} -2 \\ -3 \end{bmatrix} = \begin{bmatrix} -2 \\ -3 \end{bmatrix}$

B

In Problems 23–30, write each system as a matrix equation and solve using inverses. [Note: The inverses were found in Problems 33–40, Exercise 4-5.]

23. $x_1 + 2x_2 = k_1$
$x_1 + 3x_2 = k_2$
(A) $k_1 = 1, k_2 = 3$
(B) $k_1 = 3, k_2 = 5$
(C) $k_1 = -2, k_2 = 1$

24. $2x_1 + x_2 = k_1$
$5x_1 + 3x_2 = k_2$
(A) $k_1 = 2, k_2 = 13$
(B) $k_1 = 2, k_2 = 4$
(C) $k_1 = 1, k_2 = -3$

25. $x_1 + 3x_2 = k_1$
$2x_1 + 7x_2 = k_2$
(A) $k_1 = 2, k_2 = -1$
(B) $k_1 = 1, k_2 = 0$
(C) $k_1 = 3, k_2 = -1$

26. $2x_1 + x_2 = k_1$
$x_1 + x_2 = k_2$
(A) $k_1 = -1, k_2 = -2$
(B) $k_1 = 2, k_2 = 3$
(C) $k_1 = 2, k_2 = 0$

27. $x_1 - 3x_2 \qquad = k_1$
$x_2 + x_3 = k_2$
$2x_1 - x_2 + 4x_3 = k_3$
(A) $k_1 = 1, k_2 = 0, k_3 = 2$
(B) $k_1 = -1, k_2 = 1, k_3 = 0$
(C) $k_1 = 2, k_2 = -2, k_3 = 1$

28. $2x_1 + 3x_2 \qquad = k_1$
$x_1 + 2x_2 + 3x_3 = k_2$
$-x_2 - 5x_3 = k_3$
(A) $k_1 = 0, k_2 = 2, k_3 = 1$
(B) $k_1 = -2, k_2 = 0, k_3 = 1$
(C) $k_1 = 3, k_2 = 1, k_3 = 0$

29. $x_1 + x_2 \qquad = k_1$
$2x_1 + 3x_2 - x_3 = k_2$
$x_1 \qquad + 2x_3 = k_3$
(A) $k_1 = 2, k_2 = 0, k_3 = 4$
(B) $k_1 = 0, k_2 = 4, k_3 = -2$
(C) $k_1 = 4, k_2 = 2, k_3 = 0$

30. $x_1 \qquad - x_3 = k_1$
$2x_1 - x_2 \qquad = k_2$
$x_1 + x_2 - 2x_3 = k_3$
(A) $k_1 = 4, k_2 = 8, k_3 = 0$
(B) $k_1 = 4, k_2 = 0, k_3 = -4$
(C) $k_1 = 0, k_2 = 8, k_3 = -8$

In Problems 31–36, the matrix equation is not solved correctly. Explain the mistake and find the correct solution. Assume that the indicated inverses exist.

31. $AX = B, X = \dfrac{B}{A}$

32. $XA = B, X = \dfrac{B}{A}$

33. $XA = B, X = A^{-1}B$

34. $AX = B, X = BA^{-1}$

35. $AX = BA, X = A^{-1}BA, X = B$

36. $XA = AB, X = ABA^{-1}, X = B$

In Problems 37–42, explain why the system cannot be solved by matrix inverse methods. Discuss methods that could be used and then solve the system.

37. $-2x_1 + 4x_2 = -5$
$6x_1 - 12x_2 = 15$

38. $-2x_1 + 4x_2 = 5$
$6x_1 - 12x_2 = 15$

39. $x_1 - 3x_2 - 2x_3 = -1$
$-2x_1 + 6x_2 + 4x_3 = 3$

40. $x_1 - 3x_2 - 2x_3 = -1$
$-2x_1 + 7x_2 + 3x_3 = 3$

41. $x_1 - 2x_2 + 3x_3 = 1$
$2x_1 - 3x_2 - 2x_3 = 3$
$x_1 - x_2 - 5x_3 = 2$

42. $x_1 - 2x_2 + 3x_3 = 1$
$2x_1 - 3x_2 - 2x_3 = 3$
$x_1 - x_2 - 5x_3 = 4$

C

For $n \times n$ matrices A and B, and $n \times 1$ column matrices C, D, and X, solve each matrix equation in Problems 43–48 for X. Assume that all necessary inverses exist.

43. $AX - BX = C$ **44.** $AX + BX = C$

45. $AX + X = C$ **46.** $AX - X = C$

47. $AX - C = D - BX$ **48.** $AX + C = BX + D$

49. Use matrix inverse methods to solve the following system for the indicated values of k_1 and k_2.

$$x_1 + 2.001x_2 = k_1$$
$$x_1 + 2x_2 = k_2$$

(A) $k_1 = 1, k_2 = 1$
(B) $k_1 = 1, k_2 = 0$
(C) $k_1 = 0, k_2 = 1$

Discuss the effect of small changes in the constant terms on the solution set of this system.

50. Repeat Problem 49 for the following system:

$$x_1 - 3.001x_2 = k_1$$
$$x_1 - 3x_2 = k_2$$

In Problems 51–54, write each system as a matrix equation and solve using the inverse coefficient matrix. Use a graphing calculator or computer to perform the necessary calculations.

51. $x_1 + 8x_2 + 7x_3 = 135$
$6x_1 + 6x_2 + 8x_3 = 155$
$3x_1 + 4x_2 + 6x_3 = 75$

52. $5x_1 + 3x_2 - 2x_3 = 112$
$7x_1 + 5x_2 = 70$
$3x_1 + x_2 - 9x_3 = 96$

53. $6x_1 + 9x_2 + 7x_3 + 5x_4 = 250$
$6x_1 + 4x_2 + 7x_3 + 3x_4 = 195$
$4x_1 + 5x_2 + 3x_3 + 2x_4 = 145$
$4x_1 + 3x_2 + 8x_3 + 2x_4 = 125$

54. $3x_1 + 3x_2 + 6x_3 + 5x_4 = 10$
$4x_1 + 5x_2 + 8x_3 + 2x_4 = 15$
$3x_1 + 6x_2 + 7x_3 + 4x_4 = 30$
$4x_1 + x_2 + 6x_3 + 3x_4 = 25$

Applications

Construct a mathematical model for each of the following problems. (The answers in the back of the book include both the mathematical model and the interpretation of its solution.) Use matrix inverse methods to solve the model and then interpret the solution.

55. Concert tickets. A concert hall has 10,000 seats and two categories of ticket prices, $25 and $35. Assume that all seats in each category can be sold.

	Concert		
	1	2	3
Tickets sold	10,000	10,000	10,000
Return required	$275,000	$300,000	$325,000

(A) How many tickets of each category should be sold to bring in each of the returns indicated in the table?

(B) Is it possible to bring in a return of $200,000? Of $400,000? Explain.

(C) Describe all the possible returns.

56. Parking receipts. Parking fees at a zoo are $5.00 for local residents and $7.50 for all others. At the end of each day, the total number of vehicles parked that day and the gross receipts for the day are recorded, but the number of vehicles in each category is not. The following table contains the relevant information for a recent 4-day period:

	Day			
	1	2	3	4
Vehicles parked	1,200	1,550	1,740	1,400
Gross receipts	$7,125	$9,825	$11,100	$8,650

(A) How many vehicles in each category used the zoo's parking facilities each day?

(B) If 1,200 vehicles are parked in one day, is it possible to take in gross receipts of $5,000? Of $10,000? Explain.

(C) Describe all possible gross receipts on a day when 1,200 vehicles are parked.

57. Production scheduling. A supplier manufactures car and truck frames at two different plants. The production rates (in frames per hour) for each plant are given in the table:

Plant	Car Frames	Truck Frames
A	10	5
B	8	8

How many hours should each plant be scheduled to operate to exactly fill each of the orders in the following table?

	Orders		
	1	2	3
Car frames	3,000	2,800	2,600
Truck frames	1,600	2,000	2,200

58. Production scheduling. Labor and material costs for manufacturing two guitar models are given in the table:

Guitar Model	Labor Cost	Material Cost
A	$30	$20
B	$40	$30

(A) If a total of $3,000 a week is allowed for labor and material, how many of each model should be produced each week to use exactly each of the allocations of the $3,000 indicated in the following table?

	Weekly Allocation		
	1	2	3
Labor	$1,800	$1,750	$1,720
Material	$1,200	$1,250	$1,280

(B) Is it possible to use an allocation of $1,600 for labor and $1,400 for material? Of $2,000 for labor and $1,000 for material? Explain.

59. Incentive plan. A small company provides an incentive plan for its top executives. Each executive receives as a bonus a percentage of the portion of the annual profit that remains after the bonuses for the other executives have been deducted (see the table). If the company has an annual profit of $2 million, find the bonus for each executive. Round each bonus to the nearest hundred dollars.

Officer	Bonus
President	3%
Executive vice-president	2.5%
Associate vice-president	2%
Assistant vice-president	1.5%

60. Incentive plan. Repeat Problem 59 if the company decides to include a 1% bonus for the sales manager in the incentive plan.

61. Diets. A biologist has available two commercial food mixes containing the percentage of protein and fat given in the table.

Mix	Protein (%)	Fat (%)
A	20	4
B	14	3

(A) How many ounces of each mix should be used to prepare each of the diets listed in the following table?

	Diet		
	1	2	3
Protein	80 oz	90 oz	100 oz
Fat	17 oz	18 oz	21 oz

(B) Is it possible to prepare a diet consisting of 100 ounces of protein and 22 ounces of fat? Of 80 ounces of protein and 15 ounces of fat? Explain.

62. Education. A state university system is planning to hire new faculty at the rank of lecturer or instructor for several of its two-year community colleges. The number of sections taught and the annual salary (in thousands of dollars) for each rank are given in the table.

	Rank	
	Lecturer	Instructor
Sections taught	3	4
Annual salary (thousand $)	20	25

The number of sections taught by new faculty and the amount budgeted for salaries (in thousands of dollars) at each of the colleges are given in the following table. How many faculty of each rank should be hired at each college to exactly meet the demand for sections and completely exhaust the salary budget?

	Community College		
	1	2	3
Demand for sections	30	33	35
Salary budget (thousand $)	200	210	220

Answers to Matched Problems

1.
$$AX + C = B$$
$$(AX + C) - C = B - C$$
$$AX + (C - C) = B - C$$
$$AX + 0 = B - C$$
$$AX = B - C$$
$$A^{-1}(AX) = A^{-1}(B - C)$$
$$(A^{-1}A)X = A^{-1}(B - C)$$
$$IX = A^{-1}(B - C)$$
$$X = A^{-1}(B - C)$$

2. $x_1 = 2, x_2 = 5, x_3 = 0$

3. (A) $x_1 = -2, x_2 = -5, x_3 = 4$ (B) $x_1 = 0, x_2 = 1, x_3 = -4$

4. $A^{-1} = \begin{bmatrix} 1.5 & -6.25 \\ -0.5 & 6.25 \end{bmatrix}$; client 1: $15,000 in A and $5,000 in B; client 2: $28,125 in A and $21,875 in B; client 3: $6,875 in A and $3,125 in B

4-7 Leontief Input–Output Analysis

- Two-Industry Model
- Three-Industry Model

An important application of matrices and their inverses is **input–output analysis**. Wassily Leontief (1905–1999), the primary force behind this subject, was awarded the Nobel Prize in economics in 1973 because of the significant impact his work had on economic planning for industrialized countries. Among other things, he conducted a comprehensive study of how 500 sectors of the U.S. economy interacted with each other. Of course, large-scale computers played a crucial role in this analysis.

Our investigation will be more modest. In fact, we start with an economy comprised of only two industries. From these humble beginnings, ideas and definitions will evolve that can be readily generalized for more realistic economies. Input–output analysis attempts to establish equilibrium conditions under which industries in an economy have just enough output to satisfy each other's demands in addition to final (outside) demands.

Two-Industry Model

We start with an economy comprised of only two industries, electric company E and water company W. Output for both companies is measured in dollars. The electric company uses both electricity and water (inputs) in the production of electricity (output), and the water company uses both electricity and water (inputs) in the production of water (output). Suppose that the production of each dollar's worth of electricity requires \$0.30 worth of electricity and \$0.10 worth of water, and the production of each dollar's worth of water requires \$0.20 worth of electricity and \$0.40 worth of water. If the final demand (the demand from all other users of electricity and water) is

$$d_1 = \$12 \text{ million for electricity}$$
$$d_2 = \$8 \text{ million for water}$$

how much electricity and water should be produced to meet this final demand?

To begin, suppose that the electric company produces \$12 million worth of electricity and the water company produces \$8 million worth of water. Then the production processes of the companies would require

Electricity required to produce electricity	Electricity required to produce water

$$0.3(12) + 0.2(8) = \$5.2 \text{ million of electricity}$$

and

Water required to produce electricity	Water required to produce water

$$0.1(12) + 0.4(8) = \$4.4 \text{ million of water}$$

leaving only \$6.8 million of electricity and \$3.6 million of water to satisfy the final demand. To meet the internal demands of both companies and to end up with enough electricity for the final outside demand, both companies must produce more than just the final demand. In fact, they must produce exactly enough to meet their own internal demands plus the final demand. To determine the total output that each company must produce, we set up a system of equations.

If

$$x_1 = \text{total output from electric company}$$
$$x_2 = \text{total output from water company}$$

then, reasoning as before, the internal demands are

$$0.3x_1 + 0.2x_2 \qquad \text{Internal demand for electricity}$$
$$0.1x_1 + 0.4x_2 \qquad \text{Internal demand for water}$$

Combining the internal demand with the final demand produces the following system of equations:

Total output	Internal demand	Final demand

$$x_1 = 0.3x_1 + 0.2x_2 + d_1$$
$$x_2 = 0.1x_1 + 0.4x_2 + d_2 \qquad \qquad (1)$$

or, in matrix form,

$$\begin{bmatrix} x_1 \\ x_2 \end{bmatrix} = \begin{bmatrix} 0.3 & 0.2 \\ 0.1 & 0.4 \end{bmatrix} \begin{bmatrix} x_1 \\ x_2 \end{bmatrix} + \begin{bmatrix} d_1 \\ d_2 \end{bmatrix}$$

or

$$X = MX + D \qquad (2)$$

where

$$D = \begin{bmatrix} d_1 \\ d_2 \end{bmatrix} \qquad \text{Final demand matrix}$$

$$X = \begin{bmatrix} x_1 \\ x_2 \end{bmatrix} \qquad \text{Output matrix}$$

$$\begin{array}{cc} & \hspace{0.5em} E \hspace{1em} W \end{array}$$
$$M = \begin{array}{c} E \\ W \end{array} \begin{bmatrix} 0.3 & 0.2 \\ 0.1 & 0.4 \end{bmatrix} \qquad \text{Technology matrix}$$

The **technology matrix** is the heart of input–output analysis. The elements in the technology matrix are determined as follows (read from left to right and then up):

> ### CONCEPTUAL INSIGHT
>
> Labeling the rows and columns of the technology matrix with the first letter of each industry is an important part of the process. The same order must be used for columns as for rows, and that same order must be used for the entries of D (the final demand matrix) and the entries of X (the output matrix). In this book we normally label the rows and columns in alphabetical order.

Now we solve equation (2) for X. We proceed as in Section 4-6:

$$X = MX + D$$
$$X - MX = D$$
$$IX - MX = D \qquad \qquad I = \begin{bmatrix} 1 & 0 \\ 0 & 1 \end{bmatrix}$$
$$(I - M)X = D$$
$$X = (I - M)^{-1}D \qquad \text{Assuming } I - M \text{ has an inverse} \qquad (3)$$

Omitting the details of the calculations, we find

$$I - M = \begin{bmatrix} 0.7 & -0.2 \\ -0.1 & 0.6 \end{bmatrix} \qquad \text{and} \qquad (I - M)^{-1} = \begin{bmatrix} 1.5 & 0.5 \\ 0.25 & 1.75 \end{bmatrix}$$

Then we have

$$\begin{bmatrix} x_1 \\ x_2 \end{bmatrix} = \begin{bmatrix} 1.5 & 0.5 \\ 0.25 & 1.75 \end{bmatrix}\begin{bmatrix} d_1 \\ d_2 \end{bmatrix} = \begin{bmatrix} 1.5 & 0.5 \\ 0.25 & 1.75 \end{bmatrix}\begin{bmatrix} 12 \\ 8 \end{bmatrix} = \begin{bmatrix} 22 \\ 17 \end{bmatrix} \qquad (4)$$

Therefore, the electric company must produce an output of $22 million and the water company must produce an output of $17 million so that each company can meet both internal and final demands.

CHECK   We use equation (2) to check our work:

$$X = MX + D$$

$$\begin{bmatrix} 22 \\ 17 \end{bmatrix} \overset{?}{=} \begin{bmatrix} 0.3 & 0.2 \\ 0.1 & 0.4 \end{bmatrix} \begin{bmatrix} 22 \\ 17 \end{bmatrix} + \begin{bmatrix} 12 \\ 8 \end{bmatrix}$$

$$\begin{bmatrix} 22 \\ 17 \end{bmatrix} \overset{?}{=} \begin{bmatrix} 10 \\ 9 \end{bmatrix} + \begin{bmatrix} 12 \\ 8 \end{bmatrix}$$

$$\begin{bmatrix} 22 \\ 17 \end{bmatrix} \overset{\checkmark}{=} \begin{bmatrix} 22 \\ 17 \end{bmatrix}$$

To solve this input–output problem on a graphing calculator, simply store matrices $M, D,$ and I in memory; then use equation (3) to find X and equation (2) to check your results. Figure 1 illustrates this process on a graphing calculator.

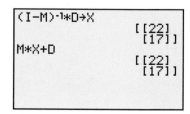

(A) Store $M, D,$ and I in the graphing calculator's memory

(B) Compute X and check in equation (2)

Figure 1

Actually, equation (4) solves the original problem for arbitrary final demands d_1 and d_2. This is very useful, since equation (4) gives a quick solution not only for the final demands stated in the original problem, but also for various other projected final demands. If we had solved system (1) by Gauss–Jordan elimination, then we would have to start over for each new set of final demands.

Suppose that in the original problem the projected final demands 5 years from now are $d_1 = 24$ and $d_2 = 16$. To determine each company's output for this projection, we simply substitute these values into equation (4) and multiply:

$$\begin{bmatrix} x_1 \\ x_2 \end{bmatrix} = \begin{bmatrix} 1.5 & 0.5 \\ 0.25 & 1.75 \end{bmatrix} \begin{bmatrix} 24 \\ 16 \end{bmatrix} = \begin{bmatrix} 44 \\ 34 \end{bmatrix}$$

We summarize these results for convenient reference.

SUMMARY   Solution to a Two-Industry Input–Output Problem

Given two industries, C_1 and C_2, with

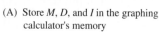

$$M = \begin{array}{c} \\ C_1 \\ C_2 \end{array} \begin{array}{c} \overset{C_1 \quad\ C_2}{\begin{bmatrix} a_{11} & a_{12} \\ a_{21} & a_{22} \end{bmatrix}} \end{array} \qquad X = \begin{bmatrix} x_1 \\ x_2 \end{bmatrix} \qquad D = \begin{bmatrix} d_1 \\ d_2 \end{bmatrix}$$

where a_{ij} is the input required from C_i to produce a dollar's worth of output for C_j, the solution to the input–output matrix equation

$$
\begin{array}{ccccc}
\text{Total} & & \text{Internal} & & \text{Final} \\
\text{output} & & \text{demand} & & \text{demand} \\
X & = & MX & + & D
\end{array}
$$

is

$$X = (I - M)^{-1}D \tag{3}$$

assuming that $I - M$ has an inverse.

Three-Industry Model

Equations (2) and (3) in the solution to a two-industry input–output problem are the same for a three-industry economy, a four-industry economy, or an economy with n industries (where n is any natural number). The steps we took going from equation (2) to equation (3) hold for arbitrary matrices as long as the matrices have the correct sizes and $(I - M)^{-1}$ exists.

EXPLORE & DISCUSS 1   If equations (2) and (3) are valid for an economy with n industries, discuss the size of all the matrices in each equation.

The next example illustrates the application of equations (2) and (3) to a three-industry economy.

EXAMPLE 1   **Input–Output Analysis** An economy is based on three sectors, agriculture (A), energy (E), and manufacturing (M). Production of a dollar's worth of agriculture requires an input of $0.20 from the agriculture sector and $0.40 from the energy sector. Production of a dollar's worth of energy requires an input of $0.20 from the energy sector and $0.40 from the manufacturing sector. Production of a dollar's worth of manufacturing requires an input of $0.10 from the agriculture sector, $0.10 from the energy sector, and $0.30 from the manufacturing sector. Find the output from each sector that is needed to satisfy a final demand of $20 billion for agriculture, $10 billion for energy, and $30 billion for manufacturing.

SOLUTION   Since this is a three-industry problem, the technology matrix will be a 3×3 matrix, and the output and final demand matrices will be 3×1 column matrices.

To begin, we form a blank 3×3 technology matrix and label the rows and columns in alphabetical order.

$$
\begin{array}{c}
\textit{Technology matrix} \\
\textit{Output} \\
\begin{array}{ccc} A & E & M \end{array} \\
\textit{Input}\ \begin{array}{c} A \\ E \\ M \end{array}
\begin{bmatrix} & & \\ & & \\ & & \end{bmatrix} = M
\end{array}
$$

Now we analyze the production information given in the problem, beginning with agriculture.

"Production of a dollar's worth of agriculture requires an input of $0.20 from the agriculture sector and $0.40 from the energy sector."

We organize this information in a table and then insert it in the technology matrix. Since manufacturing is not mentioned in the agriculture production information, the input from manufacturing is $0.

$$
\begin{array}{c}
\textit{Agriculture} \\
\begin{array}{cc} \textit{Input} & \textit{Output} \end{array}
\end{array}
\qquad
\begin{array}{ccc} A & E & M \end{array}
$$

$$
\begin{array}{cc}
A \xrightarrow{0.2} A \\
E \xrightarrow{0.4} A \\
M \xrightarrow{0} A
\end{array}
\qquad
\begin{array}{c} A \\ E \\ M \end{array}
\begin{bmatrix} 0.2 & & \\ 0.4 & & \\ 0 & & \end{bmatrix}
$$

"Production of a dollar's worth of energy requires an input of $0.20 from the energy sector and $0.40 from the manufacturing sector."

$$
\begin{array}{c}
\textit{Energy} \\
\begin{array}{cc} \textit{Input} & \textit{Output} \end{array}
\end{array}
\qquad
\begin{array}{ccc} A & E & M \end{array}
$$

$$
\begin{array}{cc}
A \xrightarrow{0} E \\
E \xrightarrow{0.2} E \\
M \xrightarrow{0.4} E
\end{array}
\qquad
\begin{array}{c} A \\ E \\ M \end{array}
\begin{bmatrix} 0.2 & 0 & \\ 0.4 & 0.2 & \\ 0 & 0.4 & \end{bmatrix}
$$

(A) Find the output for each sector that is needed to satisfy a final demand of $40 million for agriculture and $40 million for manufacturing.

(B) Discuss the effect on the final demand if the agriculture output in part (A) is increased by $20 million and manufacturing output remains unchanged.

20. The technology matrix for an economy based on energy (E) and transportation (T) is

$$M = \begin{array}{c} \\ E \\ T \end{array} \begin{array}{c} E \qquad T \\ \begin{bmatrix} 0.25 & 0.25 \\ 0.4 & 0.2 \end{bmatrix} \end{array}$$

(A) Find the output for each sector that is needed to satisfy a final demand of $50 million for energy and $50 million for transportation.

(B) Discuss the effect on the final demand if the transportation output in part (A) is increased by $40 million and the energy output remains unchanged.

21. Refer to Problem 19. Fill in the elements in the following technology matrix.

$$T = \begin{array}{c} \\ M \\ A \end{array} \begin{array}{c} M \qquad A \\ \begin{bmatrix} \qquad \\ \qquad \end{bmatrix} \end{array}$$

Use this matrix to solve Problem 19. Discuss any differences in your calculations and in your answers.

22. Refer to Problem 20. Fill in the elements in the following technology matrix.

$$T = \begin{array}{c} \\ T \\ E \end{array} \begin{array}{c} T \qquad E \\ \begin{bmatrix} \qquad \\ \qquad \end{bmatrix} \end{array}$$

Use this matrix to solve Problem 20. Discuss any differences in your calculations and in your answers.

23. The technology matrix for an economy based on energy (E) and mining (M) is

$$M = \begin{array}{c} \\ E \\ M \end{array} \begin{array}{c} E \qquad M \\ \begin{bmatrix} 0.2 & 0.3 \\ 0.4 & 0.3 \end{bmatrix} \end{array}$$

The management of these two sectors would like to set the total output level so that the final demand is always 40% of the total output. Discuss methods that could be used to accomplish this objective.

24. The technology matrix for an economy based on automobiles (A) and construction (C) is

$$M = \begin{array}{c} \\ A \\ C \end{array} \begin{array}{c} A \qquad C \\ \begin{bmatrix} 0.1 & 0.4 \\ 0.1 & 0.1 \end{bmatrix} \end{array}$$

The management of these two sectors would like to set the total output level so that the final demand is always 70% of the total output. Discuss methods that could be used to accomplish this objective.

25. All the technology matrices in the text have elements between 0 and 1. Why is this the case? Would you ever expect to find an element in a technology matrix that is negative? That is equal to 0? That is equal to 1? That is greater than 1?

26. The sum of the elements in a column of any of the technology matrices in the text is less than 1. Why is this the case? Would you ever expect to find a column with a sum equal to 1? Greater than 1? How would you describe an economic system where the sum of the elements in every column of the technology matrix is 1?

Applications

27. Coal, steel. An economy is based on two industrial sectors, coal and steel. Production of a dollar's worth of coal requires an input of $0.10 from the coal sector and $0.20 from the steel sector. Production of a dollar's worth of steel requires an input of $0.20 from the coal sector and $0.40 from the steel sector. Find the output for each sector that is needed to satisfy a final demand of $20 billion for coal and $10 billion for steel.

28. Transportation, manufacturing. An economy is based on two sectors, transportation and manufacturing. Production of a dollar's worth of transportation requires an input of $0.10 from each sector and production of a dollar's worth of manufacturing requires an input of $0.40 from each sector. Find the output for each sector that is needed to satisfy a final demand of $5 billion for transportation and $20 billion for manufacturing.

29. Agriculture, tourism. The economy of a small island nation is based on two sectors, agriculture and tourism. Production of a dollar's worth of agriculture requires an input of $0.20 from agriculture and $0.15 from tourism. Production of a dollar's worth of tourism requires an input of $0.40 from agriculture and $0.30 from tourism. Find the output from each sector that is needed to satisfy a final demand of $60 million for agriculture and $80 million for tourism.

30. Agriculture, oil. The economy of a country is based on two sectors, agriculture and oil. Production of a dollar's worth of agriculture requires an input of $0.40 from agriculture and $0.35 from oil. Production of a dollar's worth of oil requires an input of $0.20 from agriculture and $0.05 from oil. Find the output from each sector that is needed to satisfy a final demand of $40 million for agriculture and $250 million for oil.

31. Agriculture, manufacturing, energy. An economy is based on three sectors, agriculture, manufacturing, and energy. Production of a dollar's worth of agriculture requires inputs of $0.20 from agriculture, $0.20 from manufacturing, and $0.20 from energy. Production of a dollar's worth of manufacturing requires inputs of $0.40 from agriculture, $0.10 from manufacturing, and $0.10 from energy. Production of a dollar's worth of energy requires inputs of $0.30 from agriculture, $0.10 from manufacturing, and $0.10 from energy. Find the output for each sector that is needed to satisfy a final demand of $10 billion for agriculture, $15 billion for manufacturing, and $20 billion for energy.

32. Electricity, natural gas, oil. A large energy company produces electricity, natural gas, and oil. The production of a dollar's worth of electricity requires inputs of $0.30 from electricity, $0.10 from natural gas, and $0.20 from oil. Production of a dollar's worth of natural gas requires inputs of $0.30 from electricity, $0.10 from natural gas, and $0.20 from oil. Production of a dollar's worth of oil requires inputs of $0.10 from each sector. Find the output for each sector that is needed to satisfy a final demand of $25 billion for electricity, $15 billion for natural gas, and $20 billion for oil.

33. Four sectors. An economy is based on four sectors, agriculture (A), energy (E), labor (L), and manufacturing (M). The table gives the input requirements for a dollar's worth of output for each sector, along with the projected final demand (in billions of dollars) for a 3-year period. Find the output for each sector that is needed to satisfy each of these final demands. Round answers to the nearest billion dollars.

		Output				Final Demand		
		A	E	L	M	1	2	3
Input	A	0.05	0.17	0.23	0.09	23	32	55
	E	0.07	0.12	0.15	0.19	41	48	62
	L	0.25	0.08	0.03	0.32	18	21	25
	M	0.11	0.19	0.28	0.16	31	33	35

34. Repeat Problem 33 with the following table:

		Output				Final Demand		
		A	E	L	M	1	2	3
Input	A	0.07	0.09	0.27	0.12	18	22	37
	E	0.14	0.07	0.21	0.24	26	31	42
	L	0.17	0.06	0.02	0.21	12	19	28
	M	0.15	0.13	0.31	0.19	41	45	49

Answers to Matched Problems

1. (A) $\begin{bmatrix} 0.2 & 0 & 0.4 \\ 0 & 0.1 & 0.2 \\ 0.4 & 0.2 & 0.2 \end{bmatrix}$ (B) $\begin{bmatrix} 1.7 & 0.2 & 0.9 \\ 0.2 & 1.2 & 0.4 \\ 0.9 & 0.4 & 1.8 \end{bmatrix}$

(C) $71 billion for coal, $26 billion for oil, and $67 billion for transportation

Chapter 4   Review

Important Terms, Symbols, and Concepts

4-1 Review: Systems of Linear Equations in Two Variables

EXAMPLES

- The **solution** of a system is an ordered pair of real numbers that satisfies each equation in the system. Solution by **graphing** is one method that can be used to find a solution.

Ex. 1, p. 170
Ex. 2, p. 171

- A linear system is **consistent** if it has a unique solution, **dependent** if it has an infinite number of solutions, and **inconsistent** if it has no solutions.

- A **graphing calculator** provides accurate solutions to a linear system.

Ex. 3, p. 172

- The **substitution** method can also be used to solve linear systems.

Ex. 4, p. 173

- The **method of elimination by addition** is easily extended to larger systems.

Ex. 5, p. 175

4-2 Systems of Linear Equations and Augmented Matrices

- A **matrix** is a rectangular array of real numbers. **Row operations** performed on an **augmented coefficient matrix** produce equivalent systems (Theorem 1, page 185).

Ex. 1, p. 185
Ex. 2, p. 187
Ex. 3, p. 188
Ex. 4, p. 189

- There are only three possible final forms for the augmented coefficient matrix for a linear system of two equations in two variables (p. 190).

4-3 Gauss–Jordan Elimination

- There are many possibilities for the final **reduced form** of the augmented matrix of a larger system of linear equations. Reduced form is defined on page 192.

Ex. 1, p. 192
Ex. 2, p. 194
Ex. 3, p. 196
Ex. 4, p. 197
Ex. 5, p. 198

- The **Gauss–Jordan elimination procedure** is described on page 195.

4-4 Matrices: Basic Operations

- Two matrices are **equal** if they are the same size and their corresponding elements are equal. The **sum** of two matrices of the same size is the matrix with elements that are the sum of the corresponding elements of the two given matrices.

Ex. 1, p. 206

- The **negative of a matrix** is the matrix with elements that are the negatives of the given matrix. If A and B are matrices of the same size, then B can subtracted from A by adding the negative of B to A.

Ex. 2, p. 207

- Matrix equations involving addition and subtraction are solved much like real number equations.

Ex. 3, p. 207

- The product of a real number k and a matrix M is the matrix formed by multiplying each element of M by k.

Ex. 4, p. 207
Ex. 6, p. 209
Ex. 8, p. 210

- The product of a row matrix and a column matrix is defined on page 209.

- The matrix product of an $m \times p$ matrix with a $p \times n$ is defined on page 209.

4-5 Inverse of a Square Matrix

- The **identity matrix** for multiplication is defined on page 218.
- The **inverse** of a square matrix is defined on page 219.

Ex. 1, p. 218
Ex. 2, p. 221
Ex. 3, p. 223
Ex. 4, p. 224

4-6 Matrix Equations and Systems of Linear Equations

- Basic properties of matrices are summarized in Theorem 1 on page 229.
- **Matrix inverse methods** for solving systems of equations are described in the Summary on page 232.

Ex. 1, p. 229
Ex. 2, p. 230
Ex. 3, p. 231

4-7 Leontief Input–Output Analysis

- Leontief **input–output** analysis is summarized on page 240.

Ex. 1, p. 241

Review Exercises

Work through all the problems in this chapter review and check your answers in the back of the book. Answers to all problems are there along with section numbers in italics to indicate where each type of problem is discussed. Where weaknesses show up, review appropriate sections in the text.

A

1. Solve the following system by graphing:

$$2x - y = 4$$
$$x - 2y = -4$$

2. Solve the system in Problem 1 by substitution.

3. If a matrix is in reduced form, say so. If not, explain why and state the row operation(s) necessary to transform the matrix into reduced form.

(A) $\begin{bmatrix} 0 & 1 & | & 2 \\ 1 & 0 & | & 3 \end{bmatrix}$ (B) $\begin{bmatrix} 1 & 0 & | & 2 \\ 0 & 3 & | & 3 \end{bmatrix}$

(C) $\begin{bmatrix} 1 & 0 & 1 & | & 2 \\ 0 & 1 & 1 & | & 3 \end{bmatrix}$ (D) $\begin{bmatrix} 1 & 1 & 0 & | & 2 \\ 0 & 1 & 1 & | & 3 \end{bmatrix}$

4. Given matrices A and B,

$$A = \begin{bmatrix} 5 & 3 & -1 & 0 & 2 \\ -4 & 8 & 1 & 3 & 0 \end{bmatrix} \quad B = \begin{bmatrix} -3 & 2 \\ 0 & 4 \\ -1 & 7 \end{bmatrix}$$

(A) What is the size of A? Of B?

(B) Find a_{24}, a_{15}, b_{31}, and b_{22}.

(C) Is AB defined? Is BA defined?

5. Find x_1 and x_2:

(A) $\begin{bmatrix} 1 & -2 \\ 1 & -3 \end{bmatrix} \begin{bmatrix} x_1 \\ x_2 \end{bmatrix} = \begin{bmatrix} 4 \\ 2 \end{bmatrix}$

(B) $\begin{bmatrix} 5 & 3 \\ 1 & 1 \end{bmatrix} \begin{bmatrix} x_1 \\ x_2 \end{bmatrix} + \begin{bmatrix} 25 \\ 14 \end{bmatrix} = \begin{bmatrix} 18 \\ 22 \end{bmatrix}$

In Problems 6–14, perform the operations that are defined, given the following matrices:

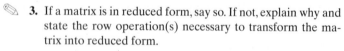

$$A = \begin{bmatrix} 1 & 2 \\ 3 & 1 \end{bmatrix} \quad B = \begin{bmatrix} 2 & 1 \\ 1 & 1 \end{bmatrix} \quad C = [2 \quad 3] \quad D = \begin{bmatrix} 1 \\ 2 \end{bmatrix}$$

6. $A + B$ **7.** $B + D$

8. $A - 2B$ **9.** AB

10. AC **11.** AD

12. DC **13.** CD

14. $C + D$

15. Find the inverse of the matrix A given below by appropriate row operations on $[A|I]$. Show that $A^{-1}A = I$.

$$A = \begin{bmatrix} 4 & 3 \\ 3 & 2 \end{bmatrix}$$

16. Solve the following system using elimination by addition:

$$4x_1 + 3x_2 = 3$$
$$3x_1 + 2x_2 = 5$$

17. Solve the system in Problem 16 by performing appropriate row operations on the augmented matrix of the system.

18. Solve the system in Problem 16 by writing the system as a matrix equation and using the inverse of the coefficient matrix (see Problem 15). Also, solve the system if the constants 3 and 5 are replaced by 7 and 10, respectively. By 4 and 2, respectively.

B

In Problems 19–24, perform the operations that are defined, given the following matrices:

$$A = \begin{bmatrix} 2 & -2 \\ 1 & 0 \\ 3 & 2 \end{bmatrix} \quad B = \begin{bmatrix} -1 \\ 2 \\ 3 \end{bmatrix} \quad C = [2 \quad 1 \quad 3]$$

$$D = \begin{bmatrix} 3 & -2 & 1 \\ -1 & 1 & 2 \end{bmatrix} \quad E = \begin{bmatrix} 3 & -4 \\ -1 & 0 \end{bmatrix}$$

19. $A + D$ **20.** $E + DA$

21. $DA - 3E$ **22.** BC

23. CB **24.** $AD - BC$

25. Find the inverse of the matrix A given below by appropriate row operations on $[A|I]$. Show that $A^{-1}A = I$.

$$A = \begin{bmatrix} 1 & 2 & 3 \\ 2 & 3 & 4 \\ 1 & 2 & 1 \end{bmatrix}$$

26. Solve by Gauss–Jordan elimination:

(A) $x_1 + 2x_2 + 3x_3 = 1$
$2x_1 + 3x_2 + 4x_3 = 3$
$x_1 + 2x_2 + x_3 = 3$

(B) $x_1 + 2x_2 - x_3 = 2$
$2x_1 + 3x_2 + x_3 = -3$
$3x_1 + 5x_2 = -1$

(C) $x_1 + x_2 + x_3 = 8$
$3x_1 + 2x_2 + 4x_3 = 21$

27. Solve the system in Problem 26A by writing the system as a matrix equation and using the inverse of the coefficient matrix (see Problem 25). Also, solve the system if the constants 1, 3, and 3 are replaced by 0, 0, and −2, respectively. By −3, −4, and 1, respectively.

28. Discuss the relationship between the number of solutions of the following system and the constant k.

$$2x_1 - 6x_2 = 4$$
$$-x_1 + kx_2 = -2$$

29. An economy is based on two sectors, agriculture and energy. Given the technology matrix M and the final demand matrix D (in billions of dollars), find $(I - M)^{-1}$ and the output matrix X:

$$M = \begin{array}{c} A \\ E \end{array} \begin{bmatrix} 0.2 & 0.15 \\ 0.4 & 0.3 \end{bmatrix} \qquad D = \begin{array}{c} A \\ E \end{array} \begin{bmatrix} 30 \\ 20 \end{bmatrix}$$

with column labels $\begin{array}{cc} A & E \end{array}$

30. Use the matrix M in Problem 29 to fill in the elements in the following technology matrix.

$$T = \begin{array}{c} E \\ A \end{array} \begin{bmatrix} & \\ & \end{bmatrix}$$

with column labels $\begin{array}{cc} E & A \end{array}$

Use this matrix to solve Problem 29. Discuss any differences in your calculations and in your answers.

31. An economy is based on two sectors, coal and steel. Given the technology matrix M and the final demand matrix D (in billions of dollars), find $(I - M)^{-1}$ and the output matrix X:

$$M = \begin{array}{c} C \\ S \end{array} \begin{bmatrix} 0.45 & 0.65 \\ 0.55 & 0.35 \end{bmatrix} \qquad D = \begin{array}{c} C \\ S \end{array} \begin{bmatrix} 40 \\ 10 \end{bmatrix}$$

with column labels $\begin{array}{cc} C & S \end{array}$

32. Use graphical approximation techniques on a graphing calculator to find the solution of the following system to two decimal places:

$$x - 5y = -5$$
$$2x + 3y = 12$$

C

33. Find the inverse of the matrix A given below. Show that $A^{-1}A = I$.

$$A = \begin{bmatrix} 4 & 5 & 6 \\ 4 & 5 & -4 \\ 1 & 1 & 1 \end{bmatrix}$$

34. Solve the system

$$0.04x_1 + 0.05x_2 + 0.06x_3 = 360$$
$$0.04x_1 + 0.05x_2 - 0.04x_3 = 120$$
$$x_1 + x_2 + x_3 = 7{,}000$$

by writing it as a matrix equation and using the inverse of the coefficient matrix. (Before starting, multiply the first two equations by 100 to eliminate decimals. Also, see Problem 33.)

35. Solve Problem 34 by Gauss–Jordan elimination.

36. Given the technology matrix M and the final demand matrix D (in billions of dollars), find $(I - M)^{-1}$ and the output matrix X:

$$M = \begin{bmatrix} 0.2 & 0 & 0.4 \\ 0.1 & 0.3 & 0.1 \\ 0 & 0.4 & 0.2 \end{bmatrix} \qquad D = \begin{bmatrix} 40 \\ 20 \\ 30 \end{bmatrix}$$

37. Discuss the number of solutions for a system of n equations in n variables if the coefficient matrix

(A) Has an inverse.

(B) Does not have an inverse.

38. Discuss the number of solutions for the system corresponding to the reduced form shown below if

(A) $m \neq 0$

(B) $m = 0$ and $n \neq 0$

(C) $m = 0$ and $n = 0$

$$\begin{bmatrix} 1 & 0 & -2 & | & 5 \\ 0 & 1 & 3 & | & 3 \\ 0 & 0 & m & | & n \end{bmatrix}$$

39. One solution to the input–output equation $X = MX + D$ is given by $X = (I - M)^{-1}D$. Discuss the validity of each step in the following solutions of this equation. (Assume that all necessary inverses exist.) Are both solutions correct?

(A) $\qquad X = MX + D$
$\qquad X - MX = D$
$\qquad X(I - M) = D$
$\qquad\qquad X = D(I - M)^{-1}$

(B) $\quad X = MX + D$
$\quad -D = MX - X$
$\quad -D = (M - I)X$
$\qquad X = (M - I)^{-1}(-D)$

Applications

40. Break-even analysis. A cookware manufacturer is preparing to market a new pasta machine. The company's fixed costs for research, development, tooling, etc., are $243,000 and the variable costs are $22.45 per machine. The company sells the pasta machine for $59.95.

(A) Find the cost and revenue equations.

(B) Find the break-even point.

(C) Graph both equations in the same coordinate system and show the break-even point. Use the graph to determine the production levels that will result in a profit and in a loss.

41. Resource allocation. An international mining company has two mines in Voisey's Bay and Hawk Ridge. The composition of the ore from each field is given in the table. How many tons of ore from each mine should be used to obtain exactly 6 tons of nickel and 8 tons of copper?

Mine	Nickel (%)	Copper (%)
Voisey's Bay	2	4
Hawk Ridge	3	2

42. Resource allocation.

(A) Set up Problem 41 as a matrix equation and solve using the inverse of the coefficient matrix.

(B) Solve Problem 41 as in part (A) if 7.5 tons of nickel and 7 tons of copper are needed.

43. Business leases. A grain company wants to lease a fleet of 20 covered hopper railcars with a combined capacity of 108,000 cubic feet. Hoppers with three different carrying capacities are available: 3,000 cubic feet, 4,500 cubic feet, and 6,000 cubic feet.

(A) How many of each type of hopper should they lease?

(B) The monthly rates for leasing these hoppers are $180 for 3,000 cubic feet, $225 for 4,500 cubic feet, and $325 for 6,000 cubic feet. Which of the solutions in part (A) would minimize the monthly leasing costs?

44. Material costs. A manufacturer wishes to make two different bronze alloys in a metal foundry. The quantities of copper, tin, and zinc needed are indicated in matrix M. The costs for these materials (in dollars per pound) from two suppliers are summarized in matrix N. The company must choose one supplier or the other.

$$M = \begin{bmatrix} 4,800\,\text{lb} & 600\,\text{lb} & 300\,\text{lb} \\ 6,000\,\text{lb} & 1,400\,\text{lb} & 700\,\text{lb} \end{bmatrix} \begin{matrix} \text{Alloy 1} \\ \text{Alloy 2} \end{matrix}$$

with column headings *Copper*, *Tin*, *Zinc*

$$N = \begin{bmatrix} \$0.75 & \$0.70 \\ \$6.50 & \$6.70 \\ \$0.40 & \$0.50 \end{bmatrix} \begin{matrix} \text{Copper} \\ \text{Tin} \\ \text{Zinc} \end{matrix}$$

with column headings *Supplier A*, *Supplier B*

(A) Discuss possible interpretations of the elements in the matrix products MN and NM.

(B) If either product MN or NM has a meaningful interpretation, find the product and label its rows and columns.

(C) Discuss methods of matrix multiplication that can be used to determine the supplier that will provide the necessary materials at the lowest cost.

45. Labor costs. A company with manufacturing plants in California and Texas has labor-hour and wage requirements for the manufacture of two inexpensive calculators as given in matrices M and N below:

Labor-hours per calculator

$$M = \begin{bmatrix} 0.15\,\text{hr} & 0.10\,\text{hr} & 0.05\,\text{hr} \\ 0.25\,\text{hr} & 0.20\,\text{hr} & 0.05\,\text{hr} \end{bmatrix} \begin{matrix} \text{Model A} \\ \text{Model B} \end{matrix}$$

with column headings *Fabricating department*, *Assembly department*, *Packaging department*

Hourly wages

$$N = \begin{bmatrix} \$12 & \$10 \\ \$15 & \$12 \\ \$7 & \$6 \end{bmatrix} \begin{matrix} \text{Fabricating department} \\ \text{Assembly department} \\ \text{Packaging department} \end{matrix}$$

with column headings *California plant*, *Texas plant*

(A) Find the labor cost for producing one model B calculator at the California plant.

(B) Discuss possible interpretations of the elements in the matrix products MN and NM.

(C) If either product MN or NM has a meaningful interpretation, find the product and label its rows and columns.

46. Investment analysis. A person has $5,000 to invest, part at 5% and the rest at 10%. How much should be invested at each rate to yield $400 per year? Solve using augmented matrix methods.

47. Investment analysis. Solve Problem 46 by using a matrix equation and the inverse of the coefficient matrix.

48. Investment analysis. In Problem 46, is it possible to have an annual yield of $200? Of $600? Describe all possible annual yields.

49. Ticket prices. An outdoor amphitheater has 25,000 seats. Ticket prices are $8, $12, and $20, and the number of tickets priced at $8 must equal the number priced at $20. How many tickets of each type should be sold (assuming that all seats can be sold) to bring in each of the returns indicated in the table? Solve using the inverse of the coefficient matrix.

	Concert		
	1	2	3
Tickets sold	25,000	25,000	25,000
Return required	$320,000	$330,000	$340,000

50. Ticket prices. Discuss the effect on the solutions to Problem 49 if it is no longer required to have an equal number of $8 tickets and $20 tickets.

51. Input–output analysis. An economy is based on two industrial sectors, agriculture and fabrication. Production of a dollar's worth of agriculture requires an input of $0.30 from the agriculture sector and $0.20 from the fabrication sector. Production of a dollar's worth of fabrication requires $0.10 from the agriculture sector and $0.40 from the fabrication sector.

(A) Find the output for each sector that is needed to satisfy a final demand of $50 billion for agriculture and $20 billion for fabrication.

(B) Find the output for each sector that is needed to satisfy a final demand of $80 billion for agriculture and $60 billion for fabrication.

52. Cryptography. The following message was encoded with the matrix B shown below. Decode the message.

25 8 26 24 25 33 21 14 21 41 30 50
21 32 41 25 25 25

$$B = \begin{bmatrix} 1 & 1 & 0 \\ 1 & 0 & 1 \\ 1 & 1 & 1 \end{bmatrix}$$

53. Traffic flow. The rush-hour traffic flow (in vehicles per hour) for a network of four one-way streets is shown in the figure.

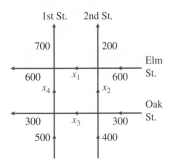

Figure for 53

(A) Write the system of equations determined by the flow of traffic through the four intersections.

(B) Find the solution of the system in part (A).

(C) What is the maximum number of vehicles per hour that can travel from Oak Street to Elm Street on 1st Street? What is the minimum number?

(D) If traffic lights are adjusted so that 500 vehicles per hour travel from Oak Street to Elm Street on 1st Street, determine the flow around the rest of the network.

Linear Inequalities and Linear Programming

5

Introduction

Real-world problems often involve limitations on materials, time, and money. To express such constraints mathematically, we formulate systems of inequalities. In Chapter 5 we discuss systems of inequalities in two variables and introduce a relatively new mathematical tool called linear programming. Linear programming can be used to determine how resources should be allocated in order to maximize profit (see Problem 31 in Section 5-3 on manufacturing water skis).

5-1 Linear Inequalities in Two Variables

Graphing Linear Inequalities in Two Variables

We know how to graph first-degree equations such as

$$y = 2x - 3 \quad \text{and} \quad 2x - 3y = 5$$

but how do we graph first-degree inequalities such as the following?

$$y \le 2x - 3 \quad \text{and} \quad 2x - 3y > 5$$

We will find that graphing these inequalities is similar to graphing the equations, but first we must discuss some important subsets of a plane in a rectangular coordinate system.

A line divides the plane into two regions called **half-planes**. A vertical line divides it into **left** and **right half-planes**; a nonvertical line divides it into **upper** and **lower half-planes**. In either case, the dividing line is called the **boundary line** of each half-plane, as indicated in Figure 1.

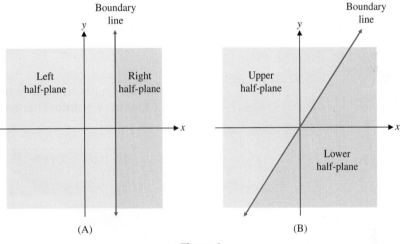

Figure 1

To find the half-planes determined by a linear equation such as $y - x = -2$, we rewrite the equation as $y = x - 2$. For any given value of x, there is exactly one value for y such that (x, y) lies on the line. For example, for $x = 4$, we have $y = 4 - 2 = 2$. For the same x and smaller values of y, the point (x, y) will lie below the line since $y < x - 2$. So the lower half-plane corresponds to the solution of the inequality $y < x - 2$. Similarly, the upper half-plane corresponds to $y > x - 2$, as shown in Figure 2.

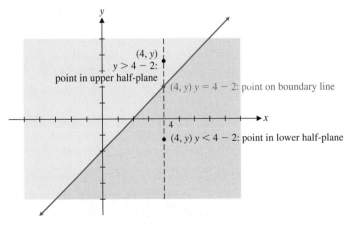

Figure 2

The four inequalities formed from $y = x - 2$, replacing the $=$ sign by $>$, $\geq$, $<$, and $\leq$, respectively, are

$$y > x - 2 \qquad y \geq x - 2 \qquad y < x - 2 \qquad y \leq x - 2$$

The graph of each is a half-plane, excluding the boundary line for $<$ and $>$ and including the boundary line for $\leq$ and $\geq$. In Figure 3, the half-planes are indicated with small arrows on the graph of $y = x - 2$ and then graphed as shaded regions. Excluded boundary lines are shown as dashed lines, and included boundary lines are shown as solid lines.

(A)

(B)

(C)

(D)

Figure 3

Figure 4 shows the graphs of Figures 3B and 3D on a graphing calculator. Note that it is impossible to show a dotted boundary line when using shading on a calculator.

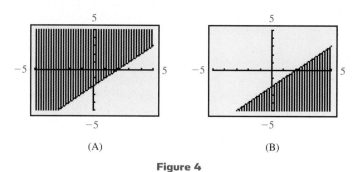
(A)   (B)

Figure 4

The preceding discussion suggests the following theorem, which is stated without proof:

THEOREM 1   Graphs of Linear Inequalities

The graph of the linear inequality

$$Ax + By < C \qquad \text{or} \qquad Ax + By > C$$

with $B \neq 0$, is either the upper half-plane or the lower half-plane (but not both) determined by the line $Ax + By = C$.

If $B = 0$ and $A \neq 0$, the graph of

$$Ax < C \qquad \text{or} \qquad Ax > C$$

is either the left half-plane or the right half-plane (but not both) determined by the line $Ax = C$.

As a consequence of this theorem, we state a simple and fast mechanical procedure for graphing linear inequalities.

PROCEDURE   Graphing Linear Inequalities

Step 1 First graph $Ax + By = C$ as a dashed line if equality is not included in the original statement, or as a solid line if equality is included.

Step 2 Choose a test point anywhere in the plane not on the line [the origin $(0, 0)$ usually requires the least computation], and substitute the coordinates into the inequality.

Step 3 Does the test point satisfy the original inequality? If so, shade the half-plane that contains the test point. If not, shade the opposite half-plane.

EXAMPLE 1   **Graphing a Linear Inequality** Graph $2x - 3y \leq 6$.

SOLUTION   **Step 1** Graph $2x - 3y = 6$ as a solid line, since equality is included in the original statement (Fig. 5).

CONCEPTUAL INSIGHT

Recall that the line $2x - 3y = 6$ can be graphed by finding any two points on the line. The x and y intercepts are usually a good choice (see Fig. 5).

x	y
0	-2
3	0

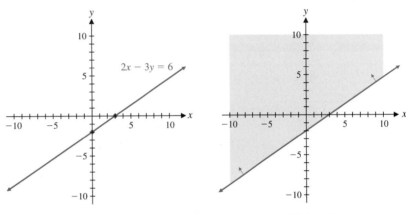

Figure 5   Figure 6

Step 2 Pick a convenient test point above or below the line. The origin $(0, 0)$ requires the least computation, so substituting $(0, 0)$ into the inequality, we get

$$2x - 3y \leq 6$$
$$2(0) - 3(0) = 0 \leq 6$$

This is a true statement; therefore, the point $(0, 0)$ is in the solution set.

Step 3 The line $2x - 3y = 6$ and the half-plane containing the origin form the graph of $2x - 3y \leq 6$, as shown in Figure 6.

Matched Problem 1   Graph $6x - 3y > 18$.

EXAMPLE 2   **Graphing Inequalities** Graph

(A) $y > -3$ (B) $2x \leq 5$ (C) $x \leq 3y$

SOLUTION   (A) **Step 1** Graph the horizontal line $y = -3$ as a dotted line, since equality is not included in the original statement (Fig. 7).

Step 2 Substituting $x = 0$ and $y = 0$ in the inequality produces a true statement, so the point $(0, 0)$ is in the solution set.

Step 3 The graph of the solution set is the upper half-plane, excluding the boundary line (Fig. 8).

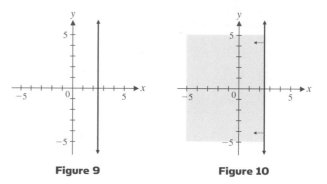

Figure 7   **Figure 8**

(B) **Step 1** Graph the vertical line $2x = 5$ as a solid line, since equality is included in the original statement (Fig. 9).

   Step 2 Substituting $x = 0$ and $y = 0$ in the inequality produces a true statement, so the point $(0, 0)$ is in the solution set.

   Step 3 The graph of the solution set is the left half-plane, including the boundary line (Fig. 10).

Figure 9   **Figure 10**

(C) **Step 1** Graph the line $x = 3y$ as a solid line, since equality is included in the original statement (Fig. 11).

   Step 2 Since the line passes through the origin, we must use a different test point. We choose $(0, 2)$ for a test point and conclude that this point is in the solution set.

   Step 3 The graph of the solution set is the upper half-plane, including the boundary line (Fig. 12).

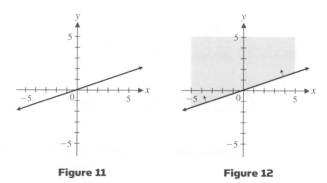

Figure 11   **Figure 12**

Matched Problem 2   Graph

(A) $y < 4$ (B) $4x \geq -9$ (C) $3x \geq 2y$

EXAMPLE 3   **Interpreting a Graph** Find the linear inequality whose graph is given in Figure 13. Write the boundary line equation in the form $Ax + By = C$, where A, B, and C are integers, before stating the inequality.

SOLUTION   The boundary line (Fig. 13) passes through the points $(0, 6)$ and $(8, 0)$. We use the slope-intercept form to find the equation of this line:

$$\text{Slope: } m = \frac{0 - 6}{8 - 0} = -\frac{6}{8} = -\frac{3}{4}$$

$$y \text{ intercept: } b = 6$$

$$\text{Boundary line equation: } y = -\frac{3}{4}x + 6 \qquad \text{Multiply both sides by 4.}$$

$$4y = -3x + 24 \qquad \text{Add 3x to both sides.}$$

$$3x + 4y = 24 \qquad \text{Form: } Ax + By = C$$

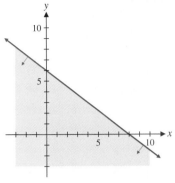

Figure 13

Since $(0, 0)$ is in the shaded region in Figure 13 and the boundary line is solid, the graph in Figure 13 is the graph of $3x + 4y \leq 24$.

Matched Problem 3   Find the linear inequality whose graph is given in Figure 14. Write the boundary line equation in the form $Ax + By = C$, where A, B, and C are integers, before stating the inequality.

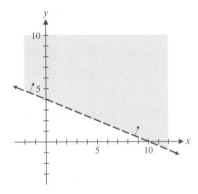

Figure 14

Application

EXAMPLE 4   **Sales** A concert promoter wants to book a rock group for a stadium concert. A ticket for admission to the stadium playing field will cost $125, and a ticket for a seat in the stands will cost $175. The group wants to be guaranteed total ticket sales of at least $700,000. How many tickets of each type must be sold to satisfy the group's guarantee? Express the answer as a linear inequality and draw its graph.

SOLUTION   Let x = Number of tickets sold for the playing field

y = Number of tickets sold for seats in the stands

We use these variables to translate the following statement from the problem into a mathematical statement:

The group wants to be guaranteed total ticket sales of at least $700,000.

$$\begin{pmatrix} \text{Sales for the} \\ \text{playing field} \end{pmatrix} + \begin{pmatrix} \text{Sales for seats} \\ \text{in the stands} \end{pmatrix} \begin{pmatrix} \text{At} \\ \text{least} \end{pmatrix} \begin{pmatrix} \text{Total Sales} \\ \text{guarantee} \end{pmatrix}$$

$$125x \qquad + \qquad 175y \qquad \geq \qquad 700,000$$

Dividing both sides of this inequality by 25, x and y must satisfy

$$5x + 7y \geq 28,000$$

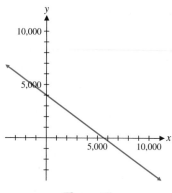

Figure 15

We use the three-step procedure to graph this inequality.

Step 1 Graph $5x + 7y = 28{,}000$ as a solid line (Fig. 15).

Step 2 Substituting $x = 0$ and $y = 0$ in the inequality produces a false statement, so the point $(0, 0)$ is not in the solution set.

Step 3 The graph of the inequality is the upper half-plane including the boundary line (Fig. 16), but does this graph really represent ticket sales?

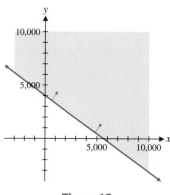

Figure 16   **Figure 17**

The shaded region in Figure 16 contains points in the second quadrant (where $x < 0$) and the fourth quadrant (where $y < 0$). It is not possible to sell a negative number of tickets, so we must restrict both x and y to the first quadrant. With this restriction, the solution becomes

$$5x + 7y \geq 28{,}000$$
$$x \geq 0, \ y \geq 0$$

and the final graph is shown in Figure 17.

Matched Problem 4   A food vendor at a rock concert sells hot dogs for $4 and hamburgers for $5. How many of these sandwiches must be sold to produce sales of at least $1,000? Express the answer as a linear inequality and draw its graph.

Requiring variables to be non-negative is a common occurrence in applications. Be sure to consider the possibility of non-negative restrictions in any application you solve.

Exercises 5-1

A

Graph each inequality in Problems 1–10.

1. $y \leq x - 1$

2. $y > x + 1$

3. $3x - 2y > 6$

4. $2x - 5y \leq 10$

5. $x \geq -4$

6. $y < 5$

7. $6x + 4y \geq 24$

8. $4x + 8y \geq 32$

9. $5x \leq -2y$

10. $6x \geq 4y$

In Problems 11–14,
(A) graph the set of points that satisfy the inequality.
(B) graph the set of points that do not satisfy the inequality.

11. $2x + 3y < 18$

12. $3x + 4y > 24$

13. $5x - 2y \geq 20$

14. $3x - 5y \leq 30$

In Problems 15–20, define the variable and translate the sentence into an inequality.

15. The number of overtime hours is less than 20.

16. Fixed costs are less than $8,000.

17. The annual salary is at least $65,000.

18. Full-time status requires at least 12 credit hours.

19. No more than 1,700 freshmen are admitted.

20. The annual deficit exceeds $600 billion.

B

In Exercises 21–26, state the linear inequality whose graph is given in the figure. Write the boundary-line equation in the form $Ax + By = C$, where A, B, and C are integers, before stating the inequality.

21.

22.

23.

24.

25.

26.

In Problems 27–32, define two variables and translate the sentence into an inequality.

27. Enrollment in finite mathematics plus enrollment in calculus is less than 300.

28. New-car sales and used-car sales combined are at most $500,000.

29. Revenue is at least $20,000 under the cost.

30. The Democratic candidate beat the Republican by at least seven percentage points.

31. The number of grams of saturated fat is more than three times the number of grams of unsaturated fat.

32. The plane is at least 500 miles closer to Chicago than to Denver.

C

In Problems 33–42, graph each inequality subject to the non-negative restrictions.

33. $25x + 40y \leq 3,000$, $x \geq 0$, $y \geq 0$

34. $24x + 30y > 7,200$, $x \geq 0$, $y \geq 0$

35. $15x - 50y < 1,500$, $x \geq 0$, $y \geq 0$

36. $16x - 12y \geq 4,800$, $x \geq 0$, $y \geq 0$

37. $-18x + 30y \geq 2,700$, $x \geq 0$, $y \geq 0$

38. $-14x + 22y < 1,540$, $x \geq 0$, $y \geq 0$

39. $40x - 55y > 0$, $x \geq 0$, $y \geq 0$

40. $-35x + 75y \leq 0$, $x \geq 0$, $y \geq 0$

41. $25x + 75y < -600$, $x \geq 0$, $y \geq 0$

42. $75x + 25y > -600$, $x \geq 0$, $y \geq 0$

Applications

In Problems 43–54, express your answer as a linear inequality with appropriate non-negative restrictions and draw its graph.

43. Seed costs. Seed costs for a farmer are $40 per acre for corn and $32 per acre for soybeans. How many acres of each crop should the farmer plant if he wants to spend no more than $5,000 on seed?

44. Labor costs. Labor costs for a farmer are $55 per acre for corn and $45 per acre for soybeans. How many acres of each crop should the farmer plant if he wants to spend no more than $6,900 on labor?

45. Fertilizer. A farmer wants to use two brands of fertilizer for his corn crop. Brand *A* contains 26% nitrogen, 3% phosphate, and 3% potash. Brand *B* contains 16% nitrogen, 8% phosphate, and 8% potash.
(*Source:* Spectrum Analytic, Inc.)

(A) How many pounds of each brand of fertilizer should he add to each acre if he wants to add at least 120 pounds of nitrogen to each acre?

(B) How many pounds of each brand of fertilizer should he add to each acre if he wants to add at most 28 pounds of phosphate to each acre?

46. Fertilizer. A farmer wants to use two brands of fertilizer for his soybean crop. Brand *A* contains 18% nitrogen, 24% phosphate, and 12% potash. Brand *B* contains 5% nitrogen, 10% phosphate, and 15% potash.
(*Source:* Spectrum Analytic, Inc.)

(A) How many pounds of each brand of fertilizer should he add to each acre if he wants to add at least 50 pounds of phosphate to each acre?

(B) How many pounds of each brand of fertilizer should he add to each acre if he wants to add at most 60 pounds of potash to each acre?

47. Textiles. A textile mill uses two blended yarns—a standard blend that is 30% acrylic, 30% wool, and 40% nylon and a deluxe blend that is 9% acrylic, 39% wool, and 52% nylon—to produce various fabrics. How many pounds of each yarn should the mill use to produce a fabric that is at least 20% acrylic?

48. Textiles. Refer to Exercise 47. How many pounds of each yarn should the mill use to produce a fabric that is at least 45% nylon?

49. Customized vehicles. A company uses sedans and minivans to produce custom vehicles for transporting hotel guests to and from airports. Plant *A* can produce 10 sedans and 8 minivans per week, and Plant *B* can produce 8 sedans and 6 minivans per week. How many weeks should each plant operate in order to produce at least 400 sedans?

50. Customized vehicles. Refer to Exercise 49. How many weeks should each plant operate in order to produce at least 480 minivans?

51. Political advertising. A candidate has budgeted $10,000 to spend on radio and television advertising. A radio ad costs $200 per 30-second spot, and a television ad costs $800 per 30-second spot. How many radio and television spots can the candidate purchase without exceeding the budget?

52. Political advertising. Refer to Problem 51. The candidate decides to replace the television ads with newspaper ads that cost $500 per ad. How many radio spots and newspaper ads can the candidate purchase without exceeding the budget?

53. Mattresses. A company produces foam mattresses in two sizes: regular and king. It takes 5 minutes to cut the foam for a regular mattress and 6 minutes for a king mattress. If the cutting department has 50 labor-hours available each day, how many regular and king mattresses can be cut in one day?

54. Mattresses. Refer to Problem 53. It takes 15 minutes to cover a regular mattress and 20 minutes to cover a king mattress. If the covering department has 160 labor-hours available each day, how many regular and king mattresses can be covered in one day?

(B)

(C)

3. $2x + 5y > 20$

4. Let x = Number of hot dogs sold

y = Number of hamburgers sold

$$4x + 5y \geq 1,000 \qquad x \geq 0, y \geq 0$$

Answers to Matched Problems

1.

2. (A)

5-2 Systems of Linear Inequalities in Two Variables

- Solving Systems of Linear Inequalities Graphically
- Applications

Solving Systems of Linear Inequalities Graphically

We now consider systems of linear inequalities such as

$$
\begin{array}{ll}
x + y \geq 6 \quad \text{and} & 2x + y \leq 22 \\
2x - y \geq 0 & x + y \leq 13 \\
 & 2x + 5y \leq 50 \\
 & x \geq 0 \\
 & y \geq 0
\end{array}
$$

We wish to **solve** such systems **graphically**—that is, to find the graph of all ordered pairs of real numbers (x, y) that simultaneously satisfy all the inequalities in the system. The graph is called the **solution region** for the system (the solution region is also known as the **feasible region**). To find the solution region, we graph each inequality in the system and then take the intersection of all the graphs. To simplify the discussion that follows, *we consider only systems of linear inequalities where equality is included in each statement in the system.*

EXAMPLE 1   **Solving a System of Linear Inequalities Graphically** Solve the following system of linear inequalities graphically:

$$x + y \geq 6$$
$$2x - y \geq 0$$

SOLUTION   Graph the line $x + y = 6$ and shade the region that satisfies the linear inequality $x + y \geq 6$. This region is shaded with gray lines in Figure 1A. Next, graph the line $2x - y = 0$ and shade the region that satisfies the inequality $2x - y \geq 0$. This region is shaded with blue lines in Figure 1A. The solution region for the system of inequalities is the intersection of these two regions. This is the region shaded in both gray and blue (crosshatched) in Figure 1A and redrawn in Figure 1B with only the solution region shaded. The coordinates of any point in the shaded region of Figure 1B specify a solution to the system. For example, the points $(2, 4)$, $(6, 3)$, and $(7.43, 8.56)$ are three of infinitely many solutions, as can be easily checked. The intersection point $(2, 4)$ is obtained by solving the equations $x + y = 6$ and $2x - y = 0$ simultaneously using any of the techniques discussed in Chapter 4.

CONCEPTUAL INSIGHT

To check that you have shaded a solution region correctly, choose a test point in the region and check that it satisfies each inequality in the system. For example, choosing the point $(5, 5)$ in the shaded region in Figure 1B, we have

$$x + y \geq 6 \quad 2x + y \geq 0$$
$$5 + 5 \overset{?}{\geq} 6 \quad 10 - 5 \overset{?}{\geq} 0$$
$$10 \overset{\checkmark}{\geq} 6 \quad 5 \overset{\checkmark}{\geq} 0$$

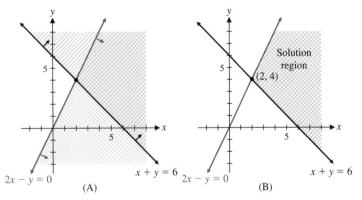

Figure 1

Matched Problem 1   Solve the following system of linear inequalities graphically:

$$3x + y \leq 21$$
$$x - 2y \leq 0$$

The points of intersection of the lines that form the boundary of a solution region will play a fundamental role in the solution of linear programming problems, which are discussed in the next section.

DEFINITION **Corner Point**

A **corner point** of a solution region is a point in the solution region that is the intersection of two boundary lines.

For example, the point $(2, 4)$ is the only corner point of the solution region in Example 1 (Fig. 1B).

EXAMPLE 2 **Solving a System of Linear Inequalities Graphically** Solve the following system of linear inequalities graphically and find the corner points:

$$2x + \ y \le 22$$
$$x + \ y \le 13$$
$$2x + 5y \le 50$$
$$x \ge 0$$
$$y \ge 0$$

SOLUTION The inequalities $x \ge 0$ and $y \ge 0$ indicate that the solution region will lie in the first quadrant. So we can restrict our attention to that portion of the plane. First, we graph the lines

$$2x + \ y = 22$$ *Find the x and y intercepts of each line; then sketch*
$$x + \ y = 13$$ *the line through these points.*
$$2x + 5y = 50$$

Next, choosing $(0, 0)$ as a test point, we see that the graph of each of the first three inequalities in the system consists of its corresponding line and the half-plane lying below the line, as indicated by the small arrows in Figure 2. The solution region of the system consists of the points in the first quadrant that simultaneously lie on or below all three of these lines (see the shaded region in Fig. 2).

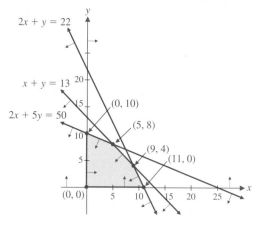

Figure 2

The corner points $(0, 0)$, $(0, 10)$, and $(11, 0)$ can be determined from the graph. The other two corner points are determined as follows:

Solve the system   Solve the system
$$2x + 5y = 50$$ $$2x + \ y = 22$$
$$x + \ \ y = 13$$ $$x + y = 13$$
to obtain $(5, 8)$.   to obtain $(9, 4)$.

Note that the lines $2x + 5y = 50$ and $2x + y = 22$ also intersect, but the intersection point is not part of the solution region and so is not a corner point.

Matched Problem 2   Solve the following system of linear inequalities graphically and find the corner points:

$$5x + y \geq 20$$
$$x + y \geq 12$$
$$x + 3y \geq 18$$
$$x \geq 0$$
$$y \geq 0$$

If we compare the solution regions of Examples 1 and 2, we see that there is a fundamental difference between these two regions. We can draw a circle around the solution region in Example 2; however, it is impossible to include all the points in the solution region in Example 1 in any circle, no matter how large we draw it. This leads to the following definition:

DEFINITION   Bounded and Unbounded Solution Regions

A solution region of a system of linear inequalities is **bounded** if it can be enclosed within a circle. If it cannot be enclosed within a circle, it is **unbounded**.

The solution region for Example 2 is bounded, and the solution region for Example 1 is unbounded. This definition will be important in the next section.

Applications

EXAMPLE 3   **Medication**   A hospital patient is required to have at least 84 units of drug A and 120 units of drug B each day (assume that an overdose of either drug is harmless). Each gram of substance M contains 10 units of drug A and 8 units of drug B, and each gram of substance N contains 2 units of drug A and 4 units of drug B. How many grams of substances M and N can be mixed to meet the minimum daily requirements?

SOLUTION   The question posed in the example indicates that the relevant variables are

$$x = \text{number of grams of substance } M \text{ used}$$
$$y = \text{number of grams of substance } N \text{ used}$$

Next, we arrange the information in the problem in a table with the variables x and y related to columns of the table.

	Amount of Drug per Gram		Minimum Daily
	Substance M	Substance N	Requirement
Drug A	10 units/gram	2 units/gram	84 units
Drug B	8 units/gram	4 units/gram	120 units

Since there are 10 units per gram of drug A substance M and x grams of substance M in the daily dose of medication, there are $10x$ units of drug A in the daily dose. Using similar reasoning, we can list all the components of the daily dose.

$$10x = \text{number of units of drug } A \text{ in } x \text{ grams of substance } M$$
$$2y = \text{number of units of drug } A \text{ in } y \text{ grams of substance } N$$
$$8x = \text{number of units of drug } B \text{ in } x \text{ grams of substance } M$$
$$4y = \text{number of units of drug } B \text{ in } y \text{ grams of substance } N$$

EXAMPLE 2   **Solving a Linear Programming Problem**

(A) Minimize and maximize

subject to

$$z = 3x + y$$
$$2x + \ y \le 20$$
$$10x + \ y \ge 36$$
$$2x + 5y \ge 36$$
$$x, y \ge 0$$

(B) Minimize and maximize

subject to

$$z = 10x + 20y$$
$$6x + 2y \ge 36$$
$$2x + 4y \ge 32$$
$$y \le 20$$
$$x, y \ge 0$$

SOLUTION   (A) **Step 1** Graph the feasible region S (Fig. 4). Then, after checking Theorem 2 to determine whether an optimal solution exists, find the coordinates of each corner point. Since S is bounded, z will have both a maximum and a minimum value on S (Theorem 2A) and these will both occur at corner points (Theorem 1).

Step 2 Evaluate the objective function at each corner point, as shown in the table.

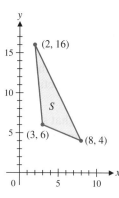

Figure 4

Corner Point

(x, y)	$z = 3x + y$
$(3, 6)$	15
$(2, 16)$	22
$(8, 4)$	28

Step 3 Determine the optimal solutions from Step 2. Examining the values in the table, we see that the minimum value of z is 15 at $(3, 6)$ and the maximum value of z is 28 at $(8, 4)$.

(B) **Step 1** Graph the feasible region S (Fig. 5). Then, after checking Theorem 2 to determine whether an optimal solution exists, find the coordinates of each corner point. Since S is unbounded and the coefficients of the objective function are positive, z has a minimum value on S but no maximum value (Theorem 2B).

Step 2 Evaluate the objective function at each corner point, as shown in the table.

Figure 5

Corner Point

(x, y)	$z = 10x + 20y$
$(0, 20)$	400
$(0, 18)$	360
$(4, 6)$	160
$(16, 0)$	160

Step 3 Determine the optimal solution from Step 2. The minimum value of z is 160 at $(4, 6)$ and at $(16, 0)$.

The solution to Example 2 is a **multiple optimal solution**. In general, if two corner points are both optimal solutions to a linear programming problem, then any point on the line segment joining them is also an optimal solution. This is the only way that optimal solutions can occur at non-corner points.

Matched Problem 2   (A) Maximize and minimize $z = 4x + 2y$ subject to the constraints given in Example 2A.

(B) Maximize and minimize $z = 20x + 5y$ subject to the constraints given in Example 2B.

CONCEPTUAL INSIGHT

Determining that an optimal solution exists is a critical step in the solution of a linear programming problem. If you skip this step, you may examine a corner point table like the one in the solution of Example 2B and erroneously conclude that the maximum value of the objective function is 400.

EXPLORE & DISCUSS 2

In Example 2B we saw that there was no optimal solution for the problem of maximizing the objective function z over the feasible region S. We want to add an additional constraint to modify the feasible region so that an optimal solution for the maximization problem does exist. Which of the following constraints will accomplish this objective?

(A) $x \le 20$ (B) $y \ge 4$ (C) $x \le y$ (D) $y \le x$

For an illustration of Theorem 2C, consider the following:

$$\text{Maximize} \quad P = 2x + 3y$$
$$\text{subject to} \quad x + y \ge 8$$
$$x + 2y \le 8$$
$$2x + y \le 10$$
$$x, y \ge 0$$

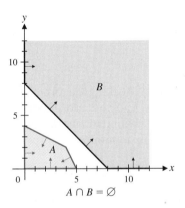

$A \cap B = \varnothing$

Figure 6

The intersection of the graphs of the constraint inequalities is the empty set (Fig. 6); so the *feasible region is empty*. If this happens, the problem should be reexamined to see if it has been formulated properly. If it has, the management may have to reconsider items such as labor-hours, overtime, budget, and supplies allocated to the project in order to obtain a nonempty feasible region and a solution to the original problem.

Applications

EXAMPLE 3   **Medication** A hospital patient is required to have at least 84 units of drug A and 120 units of drug B each day (assume that an overdose of either drug is harmless). Each gram of substance M contains 10 units of drug A and 8 units of drug B, and each gram of substance N contains 2 units of drug A and 4 units of drug B (compare Example 3 in Section 5-2). Now, suppose that both M and N contain an undesirable drug D: 3 units per gram in M and 1 unit per gram in N. How many grams of each of substances M and N should be mixed to meet the minimum daily requirements and simultaneously minimize the intake of drug D? How many units of the undesirable drug D will be in this mixture?

SOLUTION   First we construct the mathematical model.

Step 1   Introduce decision variables. According to the questions asked, we must decide how many grams of substances M and N should be mixed to form the daily dose of medication. These two quantities are the decision variables:

$$x = \text{number of grams of substance } M \text{ used}$$
$$y = \text{number of grams of substance } N \text{ used}$$

Step 2 Summarize relevant material in a table, relating the columns to substances M and N.

	Amount of Drug per Gram		Minimum Daily Requirement
	Substance M	Substance N	
Drug A	10 units/gram	2 units/gram	84 units
Drug B	8 units/gram	4 units/gram	120 units
Drug D	3 units/gram	1 unit/gram	

Step 3 Determine the objective and the objective function. The objective is to minimize the amount of drug D in the daily dose of medication. Using the decision variables and the information in the table, we form the linear objective function

$$C = 3x + y$$

Step 4 Write the problem constraints. The constraints in this problem involve minimum requirements, so the inequalities will take a different form:

$$10x + 2y \geq 84 \quad \text{Drug A constraint}$$
$$8x + 4y \geq 120 \quad \text{Drug B constraint}$$

Step 5 Add the non-negative constraints and summarize the model.

Minimize $C = 3x + y$ *Objective function*
subject to $10x + 2y \geq 84$ *Drug A constraint*
$8x + 4y \geq 120$ *Drug B constraint*
$x, y \geq 0$ *Non-negative constraints*

Now we use the geometric method to solve the problem.

Step 1 Graph the feasible region (Fig. 7). Then, after checking Theorem 2 to determine whether an optimal solution exists, find the coordinates of each corner point. Since the feasible region is unbounded and the coefficients of the objective function are positive, this minimization problem has a solution.

Step 2 Evaluate the objective function at each corner point, as shown in the table.

Step 3 Determine the optimal solution from Step 2. The optimal solution is $C = 34$ at the corner point $(4, 22)$.

Step 4 Interpret the optimal solution in terms of the original problem. If we use 4 grams of substance M and 22 grams of substance N, we will supply the minimum daily requirements for drugs A and B and minimize the intake of the undesirable drug D at 34 units. (Any other combination of M and N from the feasible region will result in a larger amount of the undesirable drug D.)

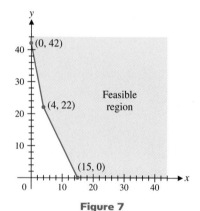

Figure 7

Corner Point

(x, y)	$C = 3x + y$
$(0, 42)$	42
$(4, 22)$	34
$(15, 0)$	45

Matched Problem 3   A chicken farmer can buy a special food mix A at 20¢ per pound and a special food mix B at 40¢ per pound. Each pound of mix A contains 3,000 units of nutrient N_1 and 1,000 units of nutrient N_2; each pound of mix B contains 4,000 units of nutrient N_1 and 4,000 units of nutrient N_2. If the minimum daily requirements for the chickens collectively are 36,000 units of nutrient N_1 and 20,000 units of nutrient N_2, how many pounds of each food mix should be used each day to minimize daily food costs while meeting (or exceeding) the minimum daily nutrient requirements? What is the minimum daily cost? Construct a mathematical model and solve using the geometric method.

> **CONCEPTUAL INSIGHT**
>
> Refer to Example 3. If we change the minimum requirement for drug B from 120 to 125, the optimal solution changes to 3.6 grams of substance M and 24.1 grams of substance N, correct to one decimal place.
>
> Now refer to Example 1. If we change the maximum labor-hours available per day in the assembly department from 84 to 79, the solution changes to 15 standard tents and 8.5 expedition tents.
>
> We can measure 3.6 grams of substance M and 24.1 grams of substance N, but how can we make 8.5 tents? Should we make 8 tents? Or 9 tents? If the solutions to a problem must be integers and the optimal solution found graphically involves decimals, then rounding the decimal value to the nearest integer does not always produce the *optimal integer solution* (see Problem 36, Exercise 5-3). Finding optimal integer solutions to a linear programming problem is called *integer programming* and requires special techniques that are beyond the scope of this book. As mentioned earlier, if we encounter a solution like 8.5 tents per day, we will interpret this as an *average* value over many days of production.

Exercises 5-3

A

In Problems 1–4, graph the constant-profit lines through (3, 3) and (6, 6). Use a straightedge to identify the corner point where the maximum profit occurs (see Explore & Discuss 1). Confirm your answer by constructing a corner-point table.

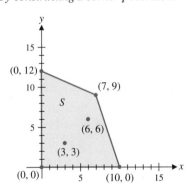

1. $P = x + y$ **2.** $P = 4x + y$

3. $P = 3x + 7y$ **4.** $P = 9x + 3y$

In Problems 5–8, graph the constant-cost lines through (9, 9) and (12, 12). Use a straightedge to identify the corner point where the minimum cost occurs. Confirm your answer by constructing a corner-point table.

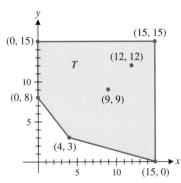

5. $C = 7x + 4y$ **6.** $C = 7x + 9y$

7. $C = 3x + 8y$ **8.** $C = 2x + 11y$

B

Solve the linear programming problems stated in Problems 9–26.

9. Maximize $P = 5x + 5y$
    subject to $2x + y \le 10$
                 $x + 2y \le 8$
                    $x, y \ge 0$

10. Maximize $P = 3x + 2y$
    subject to $6x + 3y \le 24$
                 $3x + 6y \le 30$
                   $x, y \ge 0$

11. Minimize and maximize
     $z = 2x + 3y$
    subject to $2x + y \ge 10$
                  $x + 2y \ge 8$
                    $x, y \ge 0$

12. Minimize and maximize
     $z = 8x + 7y$
    subject to $4x + 3y \ge 24$
                 $3x + 4y \ge 8$
                   $x, y \ge 0$

13. Maximize $P = 30x + 40y$
    subject to $2x + y \le 10$
                  $x + y \le 7$
                  $x + 2y \le 12$
                   $x, y \ge 0$

14. Maximize $P = 20x + 10y$
    subject to $3x + y \le 21$
                  $x + y \le 9$
                  $x + 3y \le 21$
                   $x, y \ge 0$

15. Minimize and maximize
     $z = 10x + 30y$
    subject to $2x + y \ge 16$
                  $x + y \ge 12$
                  $x + 2y \ge 14$
                   $x, y \ge 0$

16. Minimize and maximize

$z = 400x + 100y$

subject to $\quad 3x + y \geq 24$

$\qquad\qquad x + y \geq 16$

$\qquad\qquad x + 3y \geq 30$

$\qquad\qquad x, y \geq 0$

17. Minimize and maximize

$P = 30x + 10y$

subject to $\quad 2x + 2y \geq 4$

$\qquad\qquad 6x + 4y \leq 36$

$\qquad\qquad 2x + y \leq 10$

$\qquad\qquad x, y \geq 0$

18. Minimize and maximize

$P = 2x + y$

subject to $\quad x + y \geq 2$

$\qquad\qquad 6x + 4y \leq 36$

$\qquad\qquad 4x + 2y \leq 20$

$\qquad\qquad x, y \geq 0$

19. Minimize and maximize

$P = 3x + 5y$

subject to $\quad x + 2y \leq 6$

$\qquad\qquad x + y \leq 4$

$\qquad\qquad 2x + 3y \geq 12$

$\qquad\qquad x, y \geq 0$

20. Minimize and maximize

$P = -x + 3y$

subject to $\quad 2x - y \geq 4$

$\qquad\qquad -x + 2y \leq 4$

$\qquad\qquad\qquad y \leq 6$

$\qquad\qquad x, y \geq 0$

21. Minimize and maximize

$P = 20x + 10y$

subject to $\quad 2x + 3y \geq 30$

$\qquad\qquad 2x + y \leq 26$

$\qquad\qquad -2x + 5y \leq 34$

$\qquad\qquad x, y \geq 0$

22. Minimize and maximize

$P = 12x + 14y$

subject to $\quad -2x + y \geq 6$

$\qquad\qquad x + y \leq 15$

$\qquad\qquad 3x - y \geq 0$

$\qquad\qquad x, y \geq 0$

23. Maximize $\quad P = 20x + 30y$

subject to $\quad 0.6x + 1.2y \leq 960$

$\qquad\qquad 0.03x + 0.04y \leq 36$

$\qquad\qquad 0.3x + 0.2y \leq 270$

$\qquad\qquad x, y \geq 0$

24. Minimize $\quad C = 30x + 10y$

subject to $\quad 1.8x + 0.9y \geq 270$

$\qquad\qquad 0.3x + 0.2y \geq 54$

$\qquad\qquad 0.01x + 0.03y \geq 3.9$

$\qquad\qquad x, y \geq 0$

25. Maximize $\quad P = 525x + 478y$

subject to $\quad 275x + 322y \leq 3,381$

$\qquad\qquad 350x + 340y \leq 3,762$

$\qquad\qquad 425x + 306y \leq 4,114$

$\qquad\qquad x, y \geq 0$

26. Maximize $\quad P = 300x + 460y$

subject to $\quad 245x + 452y \leq 4,181$

$\qquad\qquad 290x + 379y \leq 3,888$

$\qquad\qquad 390x + 299y \leq 4,407$

$\qquad\qquad x, y \geq 0$

In Problems 27 and 28, explain why Theorem 2 cannot be used to conclude that a maximum or minimum value exists. Graph the feasible regions and use graphs of the objective function $z = x - y$ for various values of z to discuss the existence of a maximum value and a minimum value.

27. Minimize and maximize

$z = x - y$

subject to $\quad x - 2y \leq 0$

$\qquad\qquad 2x - y \leq 6$

$\qquad\qquad x, y \geq 0$

28. Minimize and maximize

$z = x - y$

subject to $\quad x - 2y \geq -6$

$\qquad\qquad 2x - y \geq 0$

$\qquad\qquad x, y \geq 0$

C

29. The corner points for the bounded feasible region determined by the system of linear inequalities

$$x + 2y \leq 10$$
$$3x + y \leq 15$$
$$x, y \geq 0$$

are $O = (0, 0)$, $A = (0, 5)$, $B = (4, 3)$, and $C = (5, 0)$. If $P = ax + by$ and $a, b > 0$, determine conditions on a and b that will ensure that the maximum value of P occurs

(A) only at A

(B) only at B

(C) only at C

(D) at both A and B

(E) at both B and C

30. The corner points for the feasible region determined by the system of linear inequalities

$$x + 4y \geq 30$$
$$3x + y \geq 24$$
$$x, y \geq 0$$

are $A = (0, 24)$, $B = (6, 6)$, and $D = (30, 0)$. If $C = ax + by$ and $a, b > 0$, determine conditions on a and b that will ensure that the minimum value of C occurs

(A) only at A

(B) only at B

(C) only at D

(D) at both A and B

(E) at both B and D

Applications

In Problems 31–46, construct a mathematical model in the form of a linear programming problem. (The answers in the back of the book for these application problems include the model.) Then solve by the geometric method.

31. Water skis. A manufacturing company makes two types of water skis—a trick ski and a slalom ski. The relevant manufacturing data are given in the table below.

Department	Labor-Hours per Ski		Maximum Labor-Hours Available per Day
	Trick Ski	Slalom Ski	
Fabricating	6	4	108
Finishing	1	1	24

(A) If the profit on a trick ski is $40 and the profit on a slalom ski is $30, how many of each type of ski should be manufactured each day to realize a maximum profit? What is the maximum profit?

(B) Discuss the effect on the production schedule and the maximum profit if the profit on a slalom ski decreases to $25.

(C) Discuss the effect on the production schedule and the maximum profit if the profit on a slalom ski increases to $45.

32. Furniture. A furniture manufacturing company manufactures dining-room tables and chairs. The relevant manufacturing data are given in the table below.

Department	Labor-Hours per Unit		Maximum Labor-Hours Available per Day
	Table	Chair	
Assembly	8	2	400
Finishing	2	1	120
Profit per unit	$90	$25	

(A) How many tables and chairs should be manufactured each day to realize a maximum profit? What is the maximum profit?

(B) Discuss the effect on the production schedule and the maximum profit if the marketing department of the company decides that the number of chairs produced should be at least four times the number of tables produced.

33. Production scheduling. A furniture company has two plants that produce the lumber used in manufacturing tables and chairs. In 1 day of operation, plant *A* can produce the lumber required to manufacture 20 tables and 60 chairs, and plant *B* can produce the lumber required to manufacture 25 tables and 50 chairs. The company needs enough lumber to manufacture at least 200 tables and 500 chairs.

(A) If it costs $1,000 to operate plant *A* for 1 day and $900 to operate plant *B* for 1 day, how many days should each plant be operated to produce a sufficient amount of lumber at a minimum cost? What is the minimum cost?

(B) Discuss the effect on the operating schedule and the minimum cost if the daily cost of operating plant *A* is reduced to $600 and all other data in part (A) remain the same.

(C) Discuss the effect on the operating schedule and the minimum cost if the daily cost of operating plant *B* is reduced to $800 and all other data in part (A) remain the same.

34. Computers. An electronics firm manufactures two types of personal computers—a standard model and a portable model. The production of a standard computer requires a capital expenditure of $400 and 40 hours of labor. The production of a portable computer requires a capital expenditure of $250 and 30 hours of labor. The firm has $20,000 capital and 2,160 labor-hours available for production of standard and portable computers.

(A) What is the maximum number of computers the company is capable of producing?

(B) If each standard computer contributes a profit of $320 and each portable model contributes a profit of $220, how much profit will the company make by producing the maximum number of computers determined in part (A)? Is this the maximum profit? If not, what is the maximum profit?

35. Transportation. The officers of a high school senior class are planning to rent buses and vans for a class trip. Each bus can transport 40 students, requires 3 chaperones, and costs $1,200 to rent. Each van can transport 8 students, requires 1 chaperone, and costs $100 to rent. Since there are 400 students in the senior class that may be eligible to go on the trip, the officers must plan to accommodate at least 400 students. Since only 36 parents have volunteered to serve as chaperones, the officers must plan to use at most 36 chaperones. How many vehicles of each type should the officers rent in order to minimize the transportation costs? What are the minimal transportation costs?

36. Transportation. Refer to Problem 35. If each van can transport 7 people and there are 35 available chaperones, show that the optimal solution found graphically involves decimals. Find all feasible solutions with integer coordinates and identify the one that minimizes the transportation costs. Can this optimal integer solution be obtained by rounding the optimal decimal solution? Explain.

37. Investment. An investor has $60,000 to invest in a CD and a mutual fund. The CD yields 5% and the mutual fund yields an average of 9%. The mutual fund requires a minimum investment of $10,000, and the investor requires that twice as much should be invested in CDs as in the mutual fund. How much should be invested in CDs and how much in the mutual fund to maximize the return? What is the maximum return?

38. Investment. An investor has $24,000 to invest in bonds of AAA and B qualities. The AAA bonds yield an average of 6%, and the B bonds yield 10%. The investor requires that at least three times as much money should be invested in AAA bonds as in B bonds. How much should be invested in each type of bond to maximize the return? What is the maximum return?

39. Pollution control. Because of new federal regulations on pollution, a chemical plant introduced a new, more expensive process to supplement or replace an older process used in the production of a particular chemical. The older process emitted 20 grams of sulfur dioxide and 40 grams of particulate matter into the atmosphere for each gallon of chemical produced. The new process emits 5 grams of sulfur dioxide and 20 grams of particulate matter for each gallon produced. The company makes a profit of 60¢ per gallon and 20¢ per gallon on the old and new processes, respectively.

(A) If the government allows the plant to emit no more than 16,000 grams of sulfur dioxide and 30,000 grams of particulate matter daily, how many gallons of the chemical should be produced by each process to maximize daily profit? What is the maximum daily profit?

(B) Discuss the effect on the production schedule and the maximum profit if the government decides to restrict emissions of sulfur dioxide to 11,500 grams daily and all other data remain unchanged.

(C) Discuss the effect on the production schedule and the maximum profit if the government decides to restrict emissions of sulfur dioxide to 7,200 grams daily and all other data remain unchanged.

40. Capital expansion. A fast-food chain plans to expand by opening several new restaurants. The chain operates two types of restaurants, drive-through and full-service. A drive-through restaurant costs $100,000 to construct, requires 5 employees, and has an expected annual revenue of $200,000. A full-service restaurant costs $150,000 to construct, requires 15 employees, and has an expected annual revenue of $500,000. The chain has $2,400,000 in capital available for expansion. Labor contracts require that they hire no more than 210 employees, and licensing restrictions require that they open no more than 20 new restaurants. How many restaurants of each type should the chain open in order to maximize the expected revenue? What is the maximum expected revenue? How much of their capital will they use and how many employees will they hire?

41. Fertilizer. A fruit grower can use two types of fertilizer in his orange grove, brand A and brand B. The amounts (in pounds) of nitrogen, phosphoric acid, and chloride in a bag of each brand are given in the table. Tests indicate that the grove needs at least 1,000 pounds of phosphoric acid and at most 400 pounds of chloride.

	Pounds per Bag	
	Brand A	Brand B
Nitrogen	8	3
Phosphoric acid	4	4
Chloride	2	1

(A) If the grower wants to maximize the amount of nitrogen added to the grove, how many bags of each mix should be used? How much nitrogen will be added?

(B) If the grower wants to minimize the amount of nitrogen added to the grove, how many bags of each mix should be used? How much nitrogen will be added?

42. Nutrition. A dietitian is to arrange a special diet composed of two foods, M and N. Each ounce of food M contains 30 units of calcium, 10 units of iron, 10 units of vitamin A, and 8 units of cholesterol. Each ounce of food N contains 10 units of calcium, 10 units of iron, 30 units of vitamin A, and 4 units of cholesterol. If the minimum daily requirements are 360 units of calcium, 160 units of iron, and 240 units of vitamin A, how many ounces of each food should be used to meet the minimum requirements and at the same time minimize the cholesterol intake? What is the minimum cholesterol intake?

43. Plant food. A farmer can buy two types of plant food, mix A and mix B. Each cubic yard of mix A contains 20 pounds of phosphoric acid, 30 pounds of nitrogen, and 5 pounds of potash. Each cubic yard of mix B contains 10 pounds of phosphoric acid, 30 pounds of nitrogen, and 10 pounds of potash. The minimum monthly requirements are 460 pounds of phosphoric acid, 960 pounds of nitrogen, and 220 pounds of potash. If mix A costs $30 per cubic yard and mix B costs $35 per cubic yard, how many cubic yards of each mix should the farmer blend to meet the minimum monthly requirements at a minimal cost? What is this cost?

44. Animal food. A laboratory technician in a medical research center is asked to formulate a diet from two commercially packaged foods, food A and food B, for a group of animals. Each ounce of food A contains 8 units of fat, 16 units of carbohydrate, and 2 units of protein. Each ounce of food B contains 4 units of fat, 32 units of carbohydrate, and 8 units of protein. The minimum daily requirements are 176 units of fat, 1,024 units of carbohydrate, and 384 units of protein. If food A costs 5¢ per ounce and food B costs 5¢ per ounce, how many ounces of each food should be used to meet the minimum daily requirements at the least cost? What is the cost for this amount of food?

45. Psychology. A psychologist uses two types of boxes with mice and rats. The amount of time (in minutes) that each mouse and each rat spends in each box per day is given in the table. What is the maximum number of mice and rats that can be used in this experiment? How many mice and how many rats produce this maximum?

	Time		Maximum Time
	Mice	Rats	Available per Day
Box A	10 min	20 min	800 min
Box B	20 min	10 min	640 min

46. Sociology. A city council voted to conduct a study on inner-city community problems using sociologists and research assistants from a nearby university. Allocation of time and costs per week are given in the table. How many sociologists and how many research assistants should be hired to minimize the cost and meet the weekly labor-hour requirements? What is the minimum weekly cost?

	Labor-Hours		Minimum Labor-Hours
		Research	Needed per
	Sociologist	Assistant	Week
Fieldwork	10	30	180
Research center	30	10	140
Costs per week	$500	$300	

Answers to Matched Problems

1. (A) x = number of two-person boats produced each month

y = number of four-person boats produced each month

(B)

	Labor-Hours Required		Maximum Labor-Hours
	Two-Person Boat	Four-Person Boat	Available per Month
Cutting department	0.9	1.8	864
Assembly department	0.8	1.2	672
Profit per boat	$25	$40	

(C) $P = 25x + 40y$

(D) $0.9x + 1.8y \leq 864$

$0.8x + 1.2y \leq 672$

$x, y \geq 0$

(E)

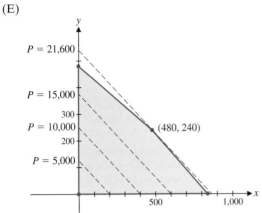

(F) 480 two-person boats, 240 four-person boats;
Max $P = \$21,600$ per month

2. (A) Min $z = 24$ at $(3, 6)$; Max $z = 40$ at $(2, 16)$ and $(8, 4)$ (multiple optimal solution)

(B) Min $z = 90$ at $(0, 18)$; no maximum value

3. Min $C = 0.2x + 0.4y$

subject to $3{,}000x + 4{,}000y \geq 36{,}000$

$1{,}000x + 4{,}000y \geq 20{,}000$

$x, y \geq 0$

8 lb of mix A, 3 lb of mix B; Min $C = \$2.80$ per day

Chapter 5   Review

Important Terms, Symbols, and Concepts

5-1 Linear Inequalities in Two Variables

EXAMPLES

- A line divides the plane into two regions called **half-planes**. A vertical line divides the plane into **left** and **right half-planes**; a nonvertical line divides it into **upper** and **lower half-planes**. In either case, the dividing line is called the **boundary line** of each half-plane.
- The **graph of a linear inequality** is the half-plane obtained by following the procedure on page 253.
Ex. 1, p. 253
Ex. 2, p. 253
Ex. 3, p. 255
Ex. 4, p. 255
- The variables in an applied problem are often required to be nonnegative.

5-2 System of Linear Inequalities in Two Variables

- The **solution region** (also called the **feasible region**) of a system of linear inequalities is the graph of all ordered pairs that simultaneously satisfy all the inequalities in the system.
Ex. 1, p. 259
- A **corner point** of a solution region is a point in the region that is the intersection of two boundary lines.
Ex. 2, p. 260
- A solution region is **bounded** if it can be enclosed in a circle and **unbounded** if it cannot.
Ex. 1, p. 259
Ex. 2, p. 260

5-3 Linear Programming in Two Dimensions: A Geometric Approach

- The problem of finding the optimal (maximum or minimum) value of a linear objective function on a feasible region is called a **linear programming problem**.
Ex. 1, p. 265
- The optimal value (if it exists) of the objective function in a linear programming problem must occur at one (or more) of the corner points of the feasible region (Theorem 1, page 269). Existence criteria are described in Theorem 2, page 269, and a solution procedure is listed on page 269.
Ex. 2, p. 270
Ex. 3, p. 271

Review Exercises

Work through all the problems in this chapter review and check answers in the back of the book. Answers to all review problems are there, and following each answer is a number in italics indicating the section in which that type of problem is discussed. Where weaknesses show up, review appropriate sections in the text.

Graph each inequality.

1. $x > 2y - 3$

2. $3y - 5x \leq 30$

Graph the systems in Problems 3–6 and indicate whether each solution region is bounded or unbounded. Find the coordinates of each corner point.

3. $5x + 9y \le 90$
     $x, y \ge 0$

4. $15x + 16y \ge 1{,}200$
     $x, y \ge 0$

5. $2x + y \le 8$
     $3x + 9y \le 27$
     $x, y \ge 0$

6. $3x + y \ge 9$
     $2x + 4y \ge 16$
     $x, y \ge 0$

In Exercises 7 and 8, state the linear inequality whose graph is given in the figure. Write the boundary line equation in the form $Ax + By = C$, with A, B, and C integers, before stating the inequality.

7.   **8.**

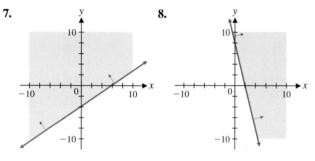

B

Solve the linear programming problems in Problems 9–13.

9. Maximize $P = 2x + 6y$
    subject to $x + 2y \le 8$
                      $2x + y \le 10$
                      $x, y \ge 0$

10. Minimize $C = 5x + 2y$
     subject to $x + 3y \ge 15$
                       $2x + y \ge 20$
                       $x, y \ge 0$

11. Maximize $P = 3x + 4y$
     subject to $x + 2y \le 12$
                       $x + y \le 7$
                       $2x + y \le 10$
                       $x, y \ge 0$

12. Maximize $C = 8x + 3y$
     subject to $x + y \ge 10$
                       $2x + y \ge 15$
                       $x \ge 3$
                       $x, y \ge 0$

C

13. Maximize $P = 3x + 2y$
     subject to $2x + y \le 22$
                       $x + 3y \le 26$
                       $x \le 10$
                       $y \le 10$
                       $x, y \ge 0$

Applications

14. Electronics. A company uses two machines to solder circuit boards, an oven and a wave soldering machine. A circuit board for a calculator needs 4 minutes in the oven and 2 minutes on the wave machine, while a circuit board for a toaster requires 3 minutes in the oven and 1 minute on the wave machine. (*Source*: Universal Electronics)

(A) How many circuit boards for calculators and toasters can be produced if the oven is available for 5 hours? Express your answer as a linear inequality with appropriate non-negative restrictions and draw its graph.

(B) How many circuit boards for calculators and toasters can be produced if the wave machine is available for 2 hours? Express your answer as a linear inequality with appropriate non-negative restrictions and draw its graph.

In Problems 15 and 16, construct a mathematical model in the form of a linear programming problem. (The answers in the back of the book for these application problems include the model.) Then solve the problem by the indicated method.

15. Sail manufacture. South Shore Sail Loft manufactures regular and competition sails. Each regular sail takes 2 hours to cut and 4 hours to sew. Each competition sail takes 3 hours to cut and 10 hours to sew. There are 150 hours available in the cutting department and 380 hours available in the sewing department.

(A) If the Loft makes a profit of $100 on each regular sail and $200 on each competition sail, how many sails of each type should the company manufacture to maximize their profit? What is the maximum profit?

(B) An increase in the demand for competition sails causes the profit on a competition sail to rise to $260. Discuss the effect of this change on the number of sails manufactured and on the maximum profit.

(C) A decrease in the demand for competition sails causes the profit on a competition sail to drop to $140. Discuss the effect of this change on the number of sails manufactured and on the maximum profit.

16. Animal food. A special diet for laboratory animals is to contain at least 850 units of vitamins, 800 units of minerals, and 1,150 calories. There are two feed mixes available, mix *A* and mix *B*. A gram of mix *A* contains 2 units of vitamins, 2 units of minerals, and 4 calories. A gram of mix *B* contains 5 units of vitamins, 4 units of minerals, and 5 calories.

(A) If mix *A* costs $0.04 per gram and mix *B* costs $0.09 per gram, how many grams of each mix should be used to satisfy the requirements of the diet at minimal cost? What is the minimum cost?

(B) If the price of mix *B* decreases to $0.06 per gram, discuss the effect of this change on the solution in part (A).

(C) If the price of mix *B* increases to $0.12 per gram, discuss the effect of this change on the solution in part (A).

Linear Programming: The Simplex Method

Introduction

The geometric method of solving linear programming problems (presented in Chapter 5) provides an overview of linear programming. But, practically speaking, the geometric method is useful only for problems involving two decision variables and relatively few problem constraints. What happens when we need more decision variables and more problem constraints? We use an algebraic method called the *simplex method*, developed by George B. Dantzig (1914–2005) in 1947. Ideally suited to computer use, the simplex method is used routinely on applied problems involving thousands of variables and problem constraints. In this chapter, we move from a geometric introduction of the simplex method to the *big M method*, which can be used to solve linear programming problems with a large number of variables and constraints. We also explore many applications. For example, we determine allocations of resources that maximize profit, and we determine production schedules that minimize cost (see Problem 44 in Section 6-2 on bicycle manufacturing and Problem 45 in Section 6-3 on ice-cream production).

6-1   A Geometric Introduction to the Simplex Method

In Chapter 5, we denoted variables with single letters such as x and y. In this chapter, we will denote variables with subscript forms such as x_1 and x_2. This change is essential to computer implementation of the simplex method. The algebraic procedures utilized in the simplex method require the problem constraints to be written as equations rather than inequalities. This new form of the linear programming problem also prompts the use of new terminology. We introduce this new terminology through a simple example and an appropriate geometric interpretation. From this example, we can illustrate what the simplex method does geometrically before immersing ourselves in the algebraic details.

Standard Maximization Problems in Standard Form

We now return to the tent production problem in Example 1, Section 5-3, and restate the model using subscript notation.

$$\begin{aligned}
\text{Maximize} \quad & P = 50x_1 + 80x_2 && \text{Objective function} \\
\text{subject to} \quad & x_1 + 2x_2 \le 32 && \text{Cutting department constraint} \\
& 3x_1 + 4x_2 \le 84 && \text{Assembly department constraint} \\
& x_1, x_2 \ge 0 && \text{Non-negative constraints}
\end{aligned} \tag{1}$$

The decision variables x_1 and x_2 are the number of standard and expedition tents, respectively, produced each day.

Notice that the problem constraints involve $\le$ inequalities with positive constants to the right of the inequality. Maximization problems that satisfy this condition are called *standard maximization problems*. In this and the next section, we restrict our attention to standard maximization problems.

DEFINITION **Standard Maximization Problem in Standard Form**

A linear programming problem is said to be a **standard maximization problem in standard form** if its mathematical model is of the following form:

Maximize the objective function

$$P = c_1x_1 + c_2x_2 + \cdots + c_nx_n$$

subject to problem constraints of the form

$$a_1x_1 + a_2x_2 + \cdots + a_nx_n \le b \quad b \ge 0$$

with non-negative constraints

$$x_1, x_2, \ldots, x_n \ge 0$$

Note: Mathematical model (1) is a standard maximization problem in standard form. The coefficients of the objective function can be any real numbers.

EXPLORE & DISCUSS 1

Find an example of a standard maximization problem in standard form involving two variables and one problem constraint such that

(A) The feasible region is bounded.

(B) The feasible region is unbounded.

Is it possible for a standard maximization problem to have no solution? Explain.

Slack Variables

To adapt a linear programming problem to the matrix methods used in the simplex process (as discussed in the next section), we convert the problem constraint inequalities into a system of linear equations using *slack variables*.

In particular, to convert the system of problem constraint inequalities from model (1),

$$x_1 + 2x_2 \leq 32 \quad \textit{Cutting department constraint}$$
$$3x_1 + 4x_2 \leq 84 \quad \textit{Assembly department constraint}$$

(2)

into a system of equations, we add variables s_1 and s_2 to the left sides of inequalities (2) to obtain

$$x_1 + 2x_2 + s_1 \qquad = 32$$
$$3x_1 + 4x_2 \qquad + s_2 = 84$$

(3)

The variables s_1 and s_2 are called **slack variables** because each makes up the difference (takes up the slack) between the left and right sides of an inequality in system (2). For example, if we produced 20 standard tents ($x_1 = 20$) and 5 expedition tents ($x_2 = 5$), then the number of labor-hours used in the cutting department would be $20 + 2(5) = 30$, leaving a slack of 2 unused labor-hours out of the 32 available. So s_1 would have the value of 2.

Notice that if the decision variables x_1 and x_2 satisfy the system of constraint inequalities (2), then the slack variables s_1 and s_2 are non-negative.

Basic and Nonbasic Variables: Basic Solutions and Basic Feasible Solutions

Observe that system (3) has infinitely many solutions—just solve for s_1 and s_2 in terms of x_1 and x_2, and then assign x_1 and x_2 arbitrary values. Certain solutions of system (3), called *basic solutions*, are related to the intersection points of the (extended) boundary lines of the feasible region in Figure 1.

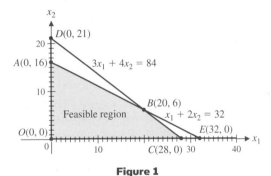

Figure 1

How are basic solutions to system (3) determined? System (3) involves four variables and two equations. We divide the four variables into two groups, called *basic variables* and *nonbasic variables,* as follows: Basic variables are selected arbitrarily with the restriction that there are as many basic variables as there are equations. The remaining variables are nonbasic variables.

Since system (3) has two equations, we can select any two of the four variables as basic variables. The remaining two variables are then nonbasic variables. A solution found by setting the two nonbasic variables equal to 0 and solving for the two basic variables is called a *basic solution*. [Note that setting two variables equal to 0 in system (3) results in a system of two equations with two variables, which has exactly one solution, infinitely many solutions, or no solution.]

EXAMPLE 1   **Basic Solutions and the Feasible Region**

(A) Find two basic solutions for system (3) by first selecting s_1 and s_2 as basic variables, and then by selecting x_2 and s_1 as basic variables.

(B) Associate each basic solution found in part (A) with an intersection point of the (extended) boundary lines of the feasible region in Figure 1, and indicate which boundary lines produce each intersection point.

(C) Indicate which of the intersection points found in part (B) are in the feasible region.

SOLUTION

(A) With s_1 and s_2 selected as basic variables, x_1 and x_2 are nonbasic variables. A basic solution is found by setting the nonbasic variables equal to 0 and solving for the basic variables. If $x_1 = 0$ and $x_2 = 0$, then system (3) becomes

$$s_1 = 32 \qquad \overset{0}{x_1} + 2\overset{0}{x_2} + s_1 \qquad = 32$$
$$s_2 = 84 \qquad 3x_1 + 4x_2 \qquad + s_2 = 84$$

and the basic solution is

$$x_1 = 0, \quad x_2 = 0, \quad s_1 = 32, \quad s_2 = 84 \tag{4}$$

If we select x_2 and s_1 as basic variables, then x_1 and s_2 are nonbasic variables. Setting the nonbasic variables equal to 0, system (3) becomes

$$2x_2 + s_1 = 32 \qquad \overset{0}{x_1} + 2x_2 + s_1 \qquad = 32$$
$$4x_2 \quad = 84 \qquad 3x_1 + 4x_2 \qquad + \overset{0}{s_2} = 84$$

Solving, we see that $x_2 = 21$ and $s_1 = -10$, and the basic solution is

$$x_1 = 0, \quad x_2 = 21, \quad s_1 = -10, \quad s_2 = 0 \tag{5}$$

(B) Basic solution (4)—since $x_1 = 0$ and $x_2 = 0$—corresponds to the origin $O(0, 0)$ in Figure 1, which is the intersection of the boundary lines $x_1 = 0$ and $x_2 = 0$. Basic solution (5)—since $x_1 = 0$ and $x_2 = 21$—corresponds to the intersection point $D(0, 21)$, which is the intersection of the boundary lines $x_1 = 0$ and $3x_1 + 4x_2 = 84$.

(C) The intersection point $O(0, 0)$ is in the feasible region; so it is natural to call the corresponding basic solution a *basic feasible solution*. The intersection point $D(0, 21)$ is not in the feasible region; so the corresponding basic solution is not feasible.

Matched Problem 1

(A) Find two basic solutions for system (3) by first selecting x_1 and s_1 as basic variables, and then by selecting x_1 and s_2 as basic variables.

(B) Associate each basic solution found in part (A) with an intersection point of the (extended) boundary lines of the feasible region in Figure 1, and indicate which boundary lines produce each intersection point.

(C) Indicate which of the intersection points found in part (B) are in the feasible region.

Proceeding systematically as in Example 1 and Matched Problem 1, we can obtain all basic solutions to system (3). The results are summarized in Table 1, which also includes geometric interpretations of the basic solutions. Figure 2 summarizes these interpretations. A careful study of Table 1 and Figure 2 is very worthwhile. (Note that to be sure we have listed all possible basic solutions in Table 1, it is convenient to organize the table in terms of the zero values of the nonbasic variables.)

> **CONCEPTUAL INSIGHT**
>
> In Table 1, observe that a basic solution that is not feasible includes at least one negative value and that a basic feasible solution does not include any negative values. That is, we can determine the feasibility of a basic solution simply by examining the signs of all the variables in the solution.
>
> In Table 1 and Figure 2, observe that basic feasible solutions are associated with the corner points of the feasible region, which include the optimal solution to the original linear programming problem.

Table 1 Basic Solutions

Basic Solutions						
x_1	x_2	s_1	s_2	Intersection Point	Intersecting Boundary Lines	Feasible
0	0	32	84	$O(0,0)$	$x_1 = 0$ $x_2 = 0$	Yes
0	16	0	20	$A(0,16)$	$x_1 = 0$ $x_1 + 2x_2 = 32$	Yes
0	21	−10	0	$D(0,21)$	$x_1 = 0$ $3x_1 + 4x_2 = 84$	No
32	0	0	−12	$E(32,0)$	$x_2 = 0$ $x_1 + 2x_2 = 32$	No
28	0	4	0	$C(28,0)$	$x_2 = 0$ $3x_1 + 4x_2 = 84$	Yes
20	6	0	0	$B(20,6)$	$x_1 + 2x_2 = 32$ $3x_1 + 4x_2 = 84$	Yes

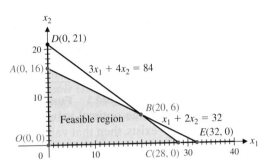

Figure 2 Basic feasible solutions: O, A, B, C
Basic solutions that are not feasible: D, E

Before proceeding further, let us formalize the definitions alluded to in the discussion above so that they apply to standard maximization problems in general, without any reference to geometric interpretation.

DEFINITION Basic Variables and Nonbasic Variables; Basic Solutions and Basic Feasible Solutions

Given a system of linear equations associated with a linear programming problem (such a system will always have more variables than equations),

The variables are divided into two (mutually exclusive) groups as follows: **Basic variables** are selected arbitrarily with the one restriction that there are as many basic variables as there are equations. The remaining variables are called **nonbasic variables**.

A solution found by setting the nonbasic variables equal to 0 and solving for the basic variables is called a **basic solution**. If a basic solution has no negative values, it is a **basic feasible solution**.

EXAMPLE 2   **Basic Variables and Basic Solutions** Suppose that there is a system of three problem constraint equations with eight (slack and decision) variables associated with a standard maximization problem.

(A) How many basic variables and how many nonbasic variables are associated with the system?

(B) Setting the nonbasic variables equal to 0 will result in a system of how many linear equations with how many variables?

(C) If a basic solution has all non-negative elements, is it feasible or not feasible?

SOLUTION   (A) Since there are three equations in the system, there should be three basic variables and five nonbasic variables.

(B) Three equations with three variables

(C) Feasible

Matched Problem 2   Suppose that there is a system of five problem constraint equations with eleven (slack and decision) variables associated with a standard maximization problem.

(A) How many basic variables and how many nonbasic variables are associated with the system?

(B) Setting the nonbasic variables equal to 0 will result in a system of how many linear equations with how many variables?

(C) If a basic solution has one or more negative elements, is it feasible or not feasible?

Matched Problem 1   Form the dual problem:

$$\text{Minimize} \quad C = 16x_1 + 9x_2 + 21x_3$$
$$\text{subject to} \quad x_1 + x_2 + 3x_3 \geq 12$$
$$2x_1 + x_2 + x_3 \geq 16$$
$$x_1, x_2, x_3 \geq 0$$

Solution of Minimization Problems

The following theorem establishes the relationship between the solution of a minimization problem and the solution of its dual problem:

> **THEOREM 1   Fundamental Principle of Duality**
> A minimization problem has a solution if and only if its dual problem has a solution. If a solution exists, then the optimal value of the minimization problem is the same as the optimal value of the dual problem.

The proof of Theorem 1 is beyond the scope of this text. However, we can illustrate Theorem 1 by solving minimization problem (1) and its dual maximization problem (2) geometrically. (Note that Theorem 2, Section 5-3, guarantees that both problems have solutions.)

ORIGINAL PROBLEM (1)	*DUAL PROBLEM* (2)
Minimize $\quad C = 16x_1 + 45x_2$	Maximize $\quad P = 50y_1 + 27y_2$
subject to $\quad 2x_1 + 5x_2 \geq 50$	subject to $\quad 2y_1 + y_2 \leq 16$
$x_1 + 3x_2 \geq 27$	$5y_1 + 3y_2 \leq 45$
$x_1, x_2 \geq 0$	$y_1, y_2 \geq 0$

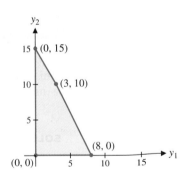

Corner Point

(x_1, x_2)	$C = 16x_1 + 45x_2$
$(0, 10)$	450
$(15, 4)$	420
$(27, 0)$	432

Min $C = 420$ at $(15, 4)$

Corner Point

(y_1, y_2)	$P = 50y_1 + 27y_2$
$(0, 0)$	0
$(0, 15)$	405
$(3, 10)$	420
$(8, 0)$	400

Max $P = 420$ at $(3, 10)$

Note that the minimum value of C in problem (1) is the same as the maximum value of P in problem (2). The optimal solutions producing this optimal value are different: $(15, 4)$ is the optimal solution for problem (1), and $(3, 10)$ is the optimal solution for problem (2). Theorem 1 only guarantees that the optimal values of a minimization problem and its dual are equal, not that the optimal solutions are the same. In general, it is not possible to determine an optimal solution for a minimization problem by examining the feasible set for the dual problem. However, it is possible to apply the simplex method to the dual problem and find both the optimal value and an optimal solution to the original minimization problem. To see how this is done, we will solve problem (2) using the simplex method.

DEFINITION Tautology, Contradiction, and Contingency

A proposition is a **tautology** if each entry in its column of the truth table is T, a **contradiction** if each entry is F, and a **contingency** if at least one entry is T and at least one entry is F.

EXAMPLE 5 **Constructing a Truth Table** Construct the truth table for $p \wedge \neg(p \vee q)$.

SOLUTION It is helpful to insert a third column labeled $p \vee q$ and a fourth labeled $\neg(p \vee q)$. We complete the first three columns. Then we use the third column to complete the fourth, and we use the first and fourth columns to complete the last column.

p	q	$p \vee q$	$\neg(p \vee q)$	$p \wedge \neg(p \vee q)$
T	T	T	F	F
T	F	T	F	F
F	T	T	F	F
F	F	F	T	F

Note that $p \wedge \neg(p \vee q)$ is a contradiction; it is always false, regardless of the truth values of p and q.

Matched Problem 5 Construct the truth table for $(p \rightarrow q) \wedge (p \wedge \neg q)$.

EXPLORE & DISCUSS 1 The LOGIC menu on the TI-84 Plus contains the operators "and," "or," "xor," and "not." The truth table for $p \wedge q$, for example, can be displayed by entering all combinations of truth values for p and q in lists L_1 and L_2 (using 1 to represent T and 0 to represent F), and then, for L_3, entering "L_1 and L_2" (see Figure 1).

Figure 1

(A) Use a calculator to display the truth table for the exclusive or operator "xor."

(B) Show that the truth table for "xor" is identical to the truth table for the proposition $(p \vee q) \wedge \neg(p \wedge q)$.

Logical Implications and Equivalences

At the beginning of the section, we noted that the notation $[(p \rightarrow q) \wedge p] \Rightarrow q$ could be used to represent the form of a familiar logical deduction. The notion of such a deduction can be defined in terms of truth tables. Consider the truth tables for the propositions $(p \rightarrow q) \wedge p$ and q:

Table 1			
p	q	$p \rightarrow q$	$(p \rightarrow q) \wedge p$
T	T	T	T
T	F	F	F
F	T	T	F
F	F	T	F

Whenever the proposition $(p \rightarrow q) \wedge p$ is true (in this case, in the first row only), the proposition q is also true. We say that $(p \rightarrow q) \wedge p$ *implies* q, or that $[(p \rightarrow q) \wedge p] \Rightarrow q$ is a *logical implication*.

DEFINITION Logical Implication

Consider the rows of the truth tables for the compound propositions P and Q. If whenever P is true, Q is also true, we say that P **logically implies** Q and write $P \Rightarrow Q$. We call $P \Rightarrow Q$ a **logical implication**.

CONCEPTUAL INSIGHT

If $P \Rightarrow Q$, then whenever P is true, so is Q. So to say that P implies Q is the same as saying that the proposition $P \rightarrow Q$ is a tautology. This gives us two methods of verifying that P implies Q: We can check the rows of the truth tables for P and Q as we did previously, or we can construct the truth table for $P \rightarrow Q$ to check that it is a tautology. Compare the truth tables in Table 1 with the truth table of Example 4 to decide which of the two methods you prefer.

EXAMPLE 6   **Verifying a Logical Implication** Show that $[(p \rightarrow q) \wedge \neg q] \Rightarrow \neg p$.

SOLUTION   To construct the truth table for $(p \rightarrow q) \wedge \neg q$, it is helpful to insert a third column labeled $p \rightarrow q$ and a fourth labeled $\neg q$. We complete the first three columns. Then we use the second column to complete the fourth, and we use the third and fourth columns to complete the fifth column.

p	q	$p \rightarrow q$	$\neg q$	$(p \rightarrow q) \wedge \neg q$	$\neg p$
T	T	T	F	F	F
T	F	F	T	F	F
F	T	T	F	F	T
F	F	T	T	T	T

Now we compare the fifth column to the sixth: Whenever $(p \rightarrow q) \wedge \neg q$ is true (in the fourth row only), $\neg p$ is also true. We conclude that $[(p \rightarrow q) \wedge \neg q] \Rightarrow \neg p$.

Matched Problem 6   Show that $[(p \rightarrow q) \rightarrow p)] \Rightarrow (q \rightarrow p)$.

If the compound propositions P and Q have identical truth tables, then $P \Rightarrow Q$ and $Q \Rightarrow P$. In this case, we say that P and Q are *logically equivalent*.

DEFINITION Logical Equivalence

If the compound propositions P and Q have identical truth tables, we say that P and Q are **logically equivalent** and write $P \equiv Q$. We call $P \equiv Q$ a **logical equivalence**.

CONCEPTUAL INSIGHT

Formulas (5) and (6) in Table 2 are known as **De Morgan's laws**. They may remind you of the way a negative sign is distributed over a binomial in algebra:

$$-(a + b) = (-a) + (-b)$$

But there is an important difference: Formula (5) has a disjunction ($\vee$) on the left side but a conjunction ($\wedge$) on the right side. Similarly, formula (6) has a conjunction on the left side but a disjunction on the right side.

In Example 3, we noted that $p \rightarrow q$ and $\neg p \vee q$ have identical truth tables. Therefore, $p \rightarrow q \equiv \neg p \vee q$. This is formula (4) in Table 2, which lists several logical equivalences. The first three equivalences of Table 2 are obvious, and the last three equivalences are established in Example 7, Matched Problem 7, and Example 8, respectively.

Table 2 Some Logical Equivalences	
$\neg(\neg p) \equiv p$	(1)
$p \vee q \equiv q \vee p$	(2)
$p \wedge q \equiv q \wedge p$	(3)
$p \rightarrow q \equiv \neg p \vee q$	(4)
$\neg(p \vee q) \equiv \neg p \wedge \neg q$	(5)
$\neg(p \wedge q) \equiv \neg p \vee \neg q$	(6)
$p \rightarrow q \equiv \neg q \rightarrow \neg p$	(7)

EXAMPLE 7   **Verifying a Logical Equivalence** Show that $\neg(p \lor q) \equiv \neg p \land \neg q$.

SOLUTION   We construct truth tables for $\neg(p \lor q)$ and $\neg p \land \neg q$.

p	q	$p \lor q$	$\neg p \lor q$	$\neg p$	$\neg q$	$\neg p \land \neg q$
T	T	T	F	F	F	F
T	F	T	F	F	T	F
F	T	T	F	T	F	F
F	F	F	T	T	T	T

The fourth and seventh columns are identical, so $\neg(p \lor q) \equiv \neg p \land \neg q$.

Matched Problem 7   Show that $\neg(p \land q) \equiv \neg p \lor \neg q$.

One way to show that two propositions are logically equivalent is to check that their truth tables are identical (as in Example 7). Another way is to convert one to the other by a sequence of steps, where a known logical equivalence is used at each step to replace part or all of the proposition by an equivalent proposition. This procedure, analogous to simplifying an algebraic expression, is illustrated in Example 8 to show that **any conditional proposition is logically equivalent to its contrapositive**.

EXAMPLE 8   **Any Conditional and Its Contrapositive Are Logically Equivalent** Show that $p \to q \equiv \neg q \to \neg p$.

SOLUTION   Each step is justified by a reference to one of the formulas in Table 2:

$$p \to q \equiv \neg p \lor q \qquad \text{By (4)}$$
$$\equiv q \lor \neg p \qquad \text{By (2)}$$
$$\equiv \neg(\neg q) \lor \neg p \qquad \text{By (1)}$$
$$\equiv \neg q \to \neg p \qquad \text{By (4)}$$

Therefore, $p \to q \equiv \neg q \to \neg p$.

Matched Problem 8   Use equivalences from Table 2 to show that $p \to q \equiv \neg(\neg q \land p)$.

EXPLORE & DISCUSS 2   If a compound proposition contains three variables p, q, and r, then its truth table will have eight rows, one for each of the eight ways of assigning truth values to p, q, and r (TTT, TTF, TFT, TFF, FTT, FTF, FFT, FFF). Construct truth tables to verify the following logical implication and equivalences:

(A) $(p \to q) \land (q \to r) \Rightarrow (p \to r)$

(B) $p \land (q \lor r) \equiv (p \land q) \lor (p \land r)$

(C) $p \lor (q \land r) \equiv (p \lor q) \land (p \lor r)$

Exercises 7-1

A

In Problems 1–6, express each proposition as an English sentence and determine whether it is true or false, where p and q are the propositions

p: "$11 \cdot 11 = 121$" q: "$10 \cdot 12 < 9 \cdot 13$"

1. $\neg q$

2. $p \lor q$

3. $p \land q$

4. $p \to q$

5. The converse of $p \to q$

6. The contrapositive of $p \to q$

In Problems 7–12, express each proposition as an English sentence and determine whether it is true or false, where r and s are the propositions

r: "$2^9 + 2^8 + 2^7 > 987$"

s: "$9 \cdot 10^2 + 8 \cdot 10 + 7 = 987$"

7. $r \to s$ **8.** $r \land s$

9. $r \lor s$ **10.** $\neg r$

11. The contrapositive of $r \to s$

12. The converse of $r \to s$

In Problems 13–20, describe each proposition as a negation, disjunction, conjunction, or conditional, and determine whether the proposition is true or false.

13. $-3 < 0$ or $-3 > 0$ **14.** $-3 < 0$ and $-3 > 0$

15. If $-3 < 0$, then $(-3)^2 < 0$ **16.** -3 is not greater than 0

17. 11 is not prime*   **18.** 9 is even or 9 is prime

19. 7 is odd and 7 is prime   **20.** If 4 is even, then 4 is prime

In Problems 21–26, state the converse and the contrapositive of the given proposition.

21. If triangle ABC is equilateral, then triangle ABC is equiangular.

22. If triangle ABC is isosceles, then the base angles of triangle ABC are congruent.

23. If $f(x)$ is a linear function with positive slope, then $f(x)$ is an increasing function.

24. If $g(x)$ is a quadratic function, then $g(x)$ is a function that is neither increasing nor decreasing.

25. If n is an integer that is a multiple of 8, then n is an integer that is a multiple of 2 and a multiple of 4.

26. If n is an integer that is a multiple of 6, then n is an integer that is a multiple of 2 and a multiple of 3.

B

In Problems 27–44, construct a truth table for the proposition and determine whether the proposition is a contingency, tautology, or contradiction.

27. $\neg p \land q$ **28.** $p \lor \neg q$

29. $\neg p \to q$ **30.** $p \to \neg q$

31. $q \land (p \lor q)$ **32.** $q \lor (p \land q)$

33. $p \lor (p \to q)$ **34.** $p \land (p \to q)$

35. $p \to (p \land q)$ **36.** $p \to (p \lor q)$

37. $(p \to q) \to \neg p$ **38.** $(p \to q) \to \neg q$

39. $\neg p \to (p \lor q)$ **40.** $\neg p \to (p \land q)$

41. $q \to (\neg p \land q)$ **42.** $q \to (p \lor \neg q)$

43. $(\neg p \land q) \land (q \to p)$ **44.** $(p \to \neg q) \land (p \land q)$

C

In Problems 45–50, construct a truth table to verify each implication.

45. $p \Rightarrow p \lor q$ **46.** $\neg p \Rightarrow p \to q$

47. $\neg p \land q \Rightarrow p \lor q$ **48.** $p \land q \Rightarrow p \to q$

49. $\neg p \to (q \land \neg q) \Rightarrow p$ **50.** $(p \land \neg p) \Rightarrow q$

In Problems 51–56, construct a truth table to verify each equivalence.

51. $\neg p \to (p \lor q) \equiv p \lor q$

52. $q \to (\neg p \land q) \equiv \neg (p \land q)$

53. $q \land (p \lor q) \equiv q \lor (p \land q)$

54. $p \land (p \to q) \equiv p \land q$

55. $p \lor (p \to q) \equiv p \to (p \lor q)$

56. $p \to (p \land q) \equiv p \to q$

In Problems 57–60, verify each equivalence using formulas from Table 2.

57. $p \to \neg q \equiv \neg (p \land q)$ **58.** $\neg p \to q \equiv p \lor q$

59. $\neg (p \to q) \equiv p \land \neg q$ **60.** $\neg (\neg p \to \neg q) \equiv q \land \neg p$

61. If the conditional proposition p is a contingency, is $\neg p$ also a contingency? Explain.

62. If the conditional proposition p is a contradiction, is $\neg p$ also a contradiction? Explain.

63. Can a conditional proposition be false if its contrapositive is true? Explain.

64. Can a conditional proposition be false if its converse is true? Explain.

Answers to Matched Problems

1. (A) "14^2 is not less than 200"; False
   (B) "23^2 is not less than 500"; True
   (C) "14^2 is less than 200 or 23^2 is less than 500"; True
   (D) "14^2 is less than 200 and 23^2 is less than 500"; False
   (E) "If 14^2 is less than 200, then 23^2 is less than 500"; False

2. (A) "If $5^2 + 12^2 = 13^2$, then $7^2 + 24^2 = 25^2$"; True
   (B) "If $7^2 + 24^2 = 25^2$, then $5^2 + 12^2 = 13^2$"; True
   (C) "If $7^2 + 24^2 \neq 25^2$, then $5^2 + 12^2 \neq 13^2$"; True

3.

p	q	$p \land \neg q$
T	T	F
T	F	T
F	T	F
F	F	F

4.

p	q	$[(p \to q) \land \neg q] \to \neg p$
T	T	T
T	F	T
F	T	T
F	F	T

5.

p	q	$(p \to q) \land (p \land \neg q)$
T	T	F
T	F	F
F	T	F
F	F	F

---

*Recall that an integer d is a **divisor** of an integer n if $n = dk$ for some integer k. An integer n is **even** if 2 is a divisor of n; otherwise n is **odd**. A positive integer $p > 1$ is **prime** if its only positive divisors are 1 and p.

6.

p	q	$(p \rightarrow q) \rightarrow p$	$q \rightarrow p$
T	T	T	T
T	F	T	T
F	T	F	F
F	F	F	T

Whenever $(p \rightarrow q) \rightarrow p$ is true, so is $q \rightarrow p$, so $[(p \rightarrow q) \rightarrow p)] \Rightarrow (q \rightarrow p)$.

7.

p	q	$\neg (p \wedge q)$	$\neg p \vee \neg q$
T	T	F	F
T	F	T	T
F	T	T	T
F	F	T	T

The third and fourth columns are identical, so $\neg(p \wedge q) \equiv \neg p \vee \neg q$.

8.
$$
\begin{aligned}
p \rightarrow q &\equiv \neg p \vee q && \text{By (4)} \\
&\equiv q \vee \neg p && \text{By (2)} \\
&\equiv \neg(\neg q) \vee \neg p && \text{By (1)} \\
&\equiv \neg(\neg q \wedge p) && \text{By (6)}
\end{aligned}
$$

7-2 Sets

- Set Properties and Set Notation
- Set Operations
- Application

In this section, we review a few key ideas about sets. Set concepts and notation help us talk about certain mathematical ideas with greater clarity and precision, and they are indispensable to a clear understanding of probability.

Set Properties and Set Notation

We can think of a **set** as any collection of objects specified in such a way that we can tell whether any given object is or is not in the collection. Capital letters, such as A, B, and C, are often used to designate particular sets. Each object in a set is called a **member**, or **element**, of the set. Symbolically,

$$a \in A \qquad \text{means} \qquad \text{"}a \text{ is an element of set } A\text{"}$$
$$a \notin A \qquad \text{means} \qquad \text{"}a \text{ is not an element of set } A\text{"}$$

A set without any elements is called the **empty**, or **null**, **set**. For example, the set of all people over 20 feet tall is an empty set. Symbolically,

$$\varnothing \text{ denotes the empty set}$$

A set is described either by listing all its elements between braces { } (the listing method) or by enclosing a rule within braces that determines the elements of the set (the rule method). So if $P(x)$ is a statement about x, then

$$S = \{x \mid P(x)\} \qquad \text{means} \qquad \text{"}S \text{ is the set of all } x \text{ such that } P(x) \text{ is true"}$$

Recall that the vertical bar within the braces is read "such that." The following example illustrates the rule and listing methods of representing sets.

EXAMPLE 1 **Representing Sets**

Rule method	Listing method

$$\{x \mid x \text{ is a weekend day}\} = \{\text{Saturday, Sunday}\}$$
$$\{x \mid x^2 = 4\} = \{-2, 2\}$$
$$\{x \mid x \text{ is an odd positive counting number}\} = \{1, 3, 5, \ldots\}$$

The three dots ($\ldots$) in the last set of Example 1 indicate that the pattern established by the first three entries continues indefinitely. The first two sets in Example 1 are **finite sets** (the elements can be counted, and there is an end); the last set is an **infinite set** (there is no end when counting the elements). When listing the elements in a set, we do not list an element more than once, and the order in which the elements are listed does not matter.

Matched Problem 1 Let G be the set of all numbers such that $x^2 = 9$.

(A) Denote G by the rule method.

(B) Denote G by the listing method.

(C) Indicate whether the following are true or false: $3 \in G, 9 \notin G$.

CONCEPTUAL INSIGHT

To conclude that $\varnothing$ is a subset of any set A, we must show that the conditional proposition "if $x \in \varnothing$, then $x \in A$" is true. But the set $\varnothing$ has no element, so the hypothesis of the conditional is false, and therefore the conditional itself is vacuously true (see Section 7-1). We correctly conclude that $\varnothing$ is a subset of every set. Note, however, that $\varnothing$ is *not* an *element* of every set.

If each element of a set A is also an element of set B, we say that A is a **subset** of B. For example, the set of all women students in a class is a subset of the whole class. Note that the definition implies that every set is a subset of itself. If set A and set B have exactly the same elements, then the two sets are said to be **equal**. Symbolically,

$A \subset B$	means	"A is a subset of B"
$A = B$	means	"A and B have exactly the same elements"
$A \not\subset B$	means	"A is not a subset of B"
$A \neq B$	means	"A and B do not have exactly the same elements"

From the definition of subset, we conclude that

$\varnothing$ **is a subset of every set, and**

if $A \subset B$ **and** $B \subset A$, **then** $A = B.$

EXAMPLE 2 Set Notation If $A = \{-3, -1, 1, 3\}$, $B = \{3, -3, 1, -1\}$, and $C = \{-3, -2, -1, 0, 1, 2, 3\}$, then each of the following statements is true:

$$A = B \qquad A \subset C \qquad A \subset B$$
$$C \neq A \qquad C \not\subset A \qquad B \subset A$$
$$\varnothing \subset A \qquad \varnothing \subset C \qquad \varnothing \notin A$$

Matched Problem 2 Given $A = \{0, 2, 4, 6\}$, $B = \{0, 1, 2, 3, 4, 5, 6\}$, and $C = \{2, 6, 0, 4\}$, indicate whether the following relationships are true (T) or false (F):

(A) $A \subset B$ (B) $A \subset C$ (C) $A = C$

(D) $C \subset B$ (E) $B \not\subset A$ (F) $\varnothing \subset B$

EXAMPLE 3 Subsets List all subsets of the set $\{a, b, c\}$.

SOLUTION $\{a, b, c\}, \qquad \{a, b\}, \qquad \{a, c\}, \qquad \{b, c\}, \qquad \{a\}, \qquad \{b\}, \qquad \{c\}, \qquad \varnothing$

Matched Problem 3 List all subsets of the set $\{1, 2\}$.

EXPLORE & DISCUSS 1 Which of the following statements are true?

(A) $\varnothing \subset \varnothing$ (B) $\varnothing \in \varnothing$

(C) $\varnothing = \{0\}$ (D) $\varnothing \subset \{0\}$

Set Operations

The **union** of sets A and B, denoted by $A \cup B$, is the set of all elements formed by combining all the elements of A and all the elements of B into one set.

DEFINITION Union

$$A \cup B = \{x \mid x \in A \text{ **or** } x \in B\}$$

Here we use the word **or** in the way it is always used in mathematics; that is, x may be an element of set A or set B or both.

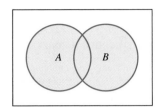

Figure 1 $A \cup B$ is the shaded region.

Venn diagrams are useful in visualizing set relationships. The union of two sets can be illustrated as shown in Figure 1. Note that

$$A \subset A \cup B \quad \text{and} \quad B \subset A \cup B$$

The **intersection** of sets A and B, denoted by $A \cap B$, is the set of elements in set A that are also in set B.

DEFINITION Intersection

$$A \cap B = \{x \,|\, x \in A \text{ and } x \in B\}$$

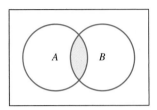

Figure 2 $A \cap B$ is the shaded region.

This relationship is easily visualized in the Venn diagram shown in Figure 2. Note that

$$A \cap B \subset A \quad \text{and} \quad A \cap B \subset B$$

If $A \cap B = \varnothing$, then the sets A and B are said to be **disjoint**, as shown in Figure 3.

The set of all elements under consideration is called the **universal set U**. Once the universal set is determined for a particular case, all other sets under discussion must be subsets of U.

We now define an operation on sets called the *complement*. The **complement** of A (relative to U), denoted by A', is the set of elements in U that are not in A (Fig. 4).

DEFINITION Complement

$$A' = \{x \in U \,|\, x \notin A\}$$

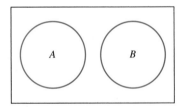

Figure 3 $A \cap B = \varnothing$; A and B are disjoint.

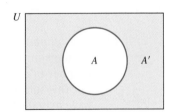

Figure 4 The complement of A is A'.

EXAMPLE 4   **Union, Intersection, and Complement** If $A = \{3, 6, 9\}$, $B = \{3, 4, 5, 6, 7\}$, $C = \{4, 5, 7\}$, and $U = \{1, 2, 3, 4, 5, 6, 7, 8, 9\}$, then

$$A \cup B = \{3, 4, 5, 6, 7, 9\}$$
$$A \cap B = \{3, 6\}$$
$$A \cap C = \varnothing \qquad \textit{A and C are disjoint.}$$
$$B' = \{1, 2, 8, 9\}$$

Matched Problem 4   If $R = \{1, 2, 3, 4\}$, $S = \{1, 3, 5, 7\}$, $T = \{2, 4\}$, and $U = \{1, 2, 3, 4, 5, 6, 7, 8, 9\}$, find

(A) $R \cup S$ (B) $R \cap S$ (C) $S \cap T$ (D) S'

Application

EXAMPLE 5   **Marketing Survey** In a survey of 100 randomly chosen students, a marketing questionnaire included the following three questions:

1. Do you own a TV?

2. Do you own a car?

3. Do you own a TV and a car?

Seventy-five answered yes to question 1, 45 answered yes to question 2, and 35 answered yes to question 3.

(A) How many students owned either a car or a TV?

(B) How many students did not own either a car or a TV?

SOLUTION   Venn diagrams are very useful for this type of problem. If we let

$$U = \text{set of students in sample (100)}$$
$$T = \text{set of students who own TV sets (75)}$$
$$C = \text{set of students who own cars (45)}$$
$$T \cap C = \text{set of students who own cars and TV sets (35)}$$

then

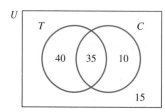

First place the number 35 in the intersection; then work outward to obtain 40, 10, and 15:

$$75 - 35 = 40$$
$$45 - 35 = 10$$
$$100 - (40 + 35 + 10) = 15$$

(A) The number of students who own either a car or a TV is the number of students in the set $T \cup C$. You might be tempted to say that this is just the number of students in T plus the number of students in C, $75 + 45 = 120$, but this sum is larger than the sample we started with! What is wrong? We have actually counted the number in the intersection (35) twice. The correct answer, as seen in the Venn diagram, is

$$40 + 35 + 10 = 85$$

(B) The number of students who do not own either a car or a TV is the number of students in the set $(T \cup C)'$, that is, 15.

Matched Problem 5   Referring to Example 5,

(A) How many students owned a car but not a TV set?

(B) How many students did not own both a car and a TV set?

Note in Example 5 and Matched Problem 5 that the word **and** is associated with intersection and the word **or** is associated with union.

EXPLORE & DISCUSS 2   In Example 5, find the number of students in the set $(T \cup C) \cap C'$. Describe this set verbally and with a Venn diagram.

Exercises 7-2

A

In Problems 1–8, indicate true (T) or false (F).

1. $\{1, 2\} \subset \{2, 1\}$

2. $\{3, 2, 1\} \subset \{1, 2, 3, 4\}$

3. $\{5, 10\} = \{10, 5\}$

4. $1 \in \{10, 11\}$

5. $\{0\} \in \{0, \{0\}\}$

6. $\{0, 6\} = \{6\}$

7. $8 \in \{1, 2, 4\}$

8. $\varnothing \subset \{1, 2, 3\}$

In Problems 9–22, write the resulting set using the listing method.

9. $\{1, 2, 3\} \cap \{2, 3, 4\}$

10. $\{1, 2, 4\} \cup \{4, 8, 16\}$

11. $\{1, 2, 3\} \cup \{2, 3, 4\}$

12. $\{1, 2, 4\} \cap \{4, 8, 16\}$

13. $\{1, 4, 7\} \cup \{10, 13\}$

14. $\{-3, -1\} \cap \{1, 3\}$

15. $\{1, 4, 7\} \cap \{10, 13\}$

16. $\{-3, -1\} \cap \{1, 3\}$

B

17. $\{x \mid x^2 = 25\}$

18. $\{x \mid x^2 = 36\}$

19. $\{x \mid x^3 = -27\}$

20. $\{x \mid x^4 = 16\}$

21. $\{x \mid x$ is an odd number between 1 and 9, inclusive$\}$

22. $\{x \mid x$ is a month starting with $M\}$

23. For $U = \{1, 2, 3, 4, 5\}$ and $A = \{2, 3, 4\}$, find A'.

24. For $U = \{7, 8, 9, 10, 11\}$ and $A = \{7, 11\}$, find A'.

Problems 25–36 refer to the Venn diagram below. How many elements are in each of the indicated sets?

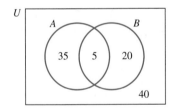

25. A

26. U

27. A'

28. B'

29. $A \cup B$

30. $A \cap B$

31. $A' \cap B$

32. $A \cap B'$

33. $(A \cap B)'$

34. $(A \cup B)'$

35. $A' \cap B'$

36. U'

37. If $R = \{1, 2, 3, 4\}$ and $T = \{2, 4, 6\}$, find
(A) $\{x \mid x \in R$ **or** $x \in T\}$ (B) $R \cup T$

38. If $R = \{1, 3, 4\}$ and $T = \{2, 4, 6\}$, find
(A) $\{x \mid x \in R$ **and** $x \in T\}$ (B) $R \cap T$

39. For $P = \{1, 2, 3, 4\}$, $Q = \{2, 4, 6\}$, and $R = \{3, 4, 5, 6\}$, find $P \cup (Q \cap R)$.

40. For P, Q, and R in Problem 39, find $P \cap (Q \cup R)$.

C

In Problems 41–50, determine whether the given set is finite or infinite. Consider the set N of positive integers to be the universal set, and let

$$H = \{n \in N \mid \quad n > 100\}$$
$$T = \{n \in N \mid \quad n < 1{,}000\}$$
$$E = \{n \in N \mid \quad n \text{ is even}\}$$
$$P = \{n \in N \mid \quad n \text{ is prime}\}$$

41. H'

42. T'

43. $E \cup P$

44. $H \cap T$

45. $E \cap P$

46. $H \cup T$

47. E'

48. P'

49. $H' \cup T$

50. $(E \cup P)'$

In Problems 51–54, are the given sets disjoint? For the definitions of H, T, E, and P, refer to the instructions for Problems 41–50.

51. H' and T'

52. E and P

53. P' and H

54. E and E'

In Problems 55–64, discuss the validity of each statement. Venn diagrams may be helpful. If the statement is true, explain why. If not, give a counterexample.

55. If $A \subset B$, then $A \cap B = A$.

56. If $A \subset B$, then $A \cup B = A$.

57. If $A \cup B = A$, then $A \subset B$.

58. If $A \cap B = A$, then $A \subset B$.

59. If $A \cap B = \varnothing$, then $A = \varnothing$.

60. If $A = \varnothing$, then $A \cap B = \varnothing$.

61. If $A \subset B$, then $A' \subset B'$.

62. If $A \subset B$, then $B' \subset A'$.

63. The empty set is an element of every set.

64. The empty set is a subset of the empty set.

65. How many subsets does each of the following sets contain?
(A) $\{a\}$
(B) $\{a, b\}$
(C) $\{a, b, c\}$
(D) $\{a, b, c, d\}$

66. Let A be a set that contains exactly n elements. Find a formula in terms of n for the number of subsets of A.

Applications

Marketing survey. *A marketing survey of 1,000 car commuters found that 600 listen to the news, 500 listen to music, and 300 listening to both. Let*

N = set of commuters in the sample who listen to news

M = set of commuters in the sample who listen to music

In Problems 67–78, follow the procedures in Example 5 to find the number of commuters in each set.

67. $N \cup M$ **68.** $N \cap M$

69. $(N \cup M)'$ **70.** $(N \cap M)'$

71. $N' \cap M$ **72.** $N \cap M'$

73. Set of commuters who listen to either news or music

74. Set of commuters who listen to both news and music

75. Set of commuters who do not listen to either news or music

76. Set of commuters who do not listen to both news and music

77. Set of commuters who listen to music but not news

78. Set of commuters who listen to news but not music

79. Committee selection. A company president and three vice-presidents, denoted by the set $\{P, V_1, V_2, V_3\}$, wish to select a committee of 2 people from among themselves. How many ways can this committee be formed? That is, how many 2-person subsets can be formed from a set of 4 people?

80. Voting coalition. The company's leaders in Problem 79 decide for or against certain measures as follows: The president has 2 votes and each vice-president has 1 vote. Three favorable votes are needed to pass a measure. List all minimal winning coalitions; that is, list all subsets of $\{P, V_1, V_2, V_3\}$ that represent exactly 3 votes.

Blood types. *When receiving a blood transfusion, a recipient must have all the antigens of the donor. A person may have one or more of the three antigens A, B, and Rh, or none at all. Eight blood types are possible, as indicated in the following Venn diagram, where U is the set of all people under consideration:*

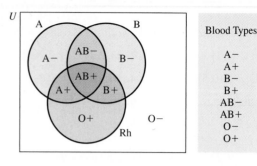

Blood Types
A−
A+
B−
B+
AB−
AB+
O−
O+

An A− person has A antigens but no B or Rh antigens; an O+ person has Rh but neither A nor B; an AB− person has A and B but no Rh; and so on.

In Problems 81–88, use the Venn diagram to indicate which of the eight blood types are included in each set.

81. $A \cap Rh$ **82.** $A \cap B$

83. $A \cup Rh$ **84.** $A \cup B$

85. $(A \cup B)'$ **86.** $(A \cup B \cup Rh)'$

87. $A' \cap B$ **88.** $Rh' \cap A$

Answers to Matched Problems

1. (A) $\{x \,|\, x^2 = 9\}$ (B) $\{-3, 3\}$ (C) True; true

2. All are true.

3. $\{1, 2\}, \{1\}, \{2\}, \varnothing$

4. (A) $\{1, 2, 3, 4, 5, 7\}$ (B) $\{1, 3\}$
    (C) $\varnothing$ (D) $\{2, 4, 6, 8, 9\}$

5. (A) 10, the number in $T' \cap C$
    (B) 65, the number in $(T \cap C)'$

7-3   Basic Counting Principles

- Addition Principle
- Venn Diagrams
- Multiplication Principle

Addition Principle

If the enrollment in a college chemistry class consists of 13 males and 15 females, then there are a total of 28 students enrolled in the class. This is a simple example of a **counting technique**, a method for determining the number of elements in a set without actually enumerating the elements one by one. Set operations play a fundamental role in many counting techniques. For example, if M is the set of male students in the chemistry class and F is the set of female students, then the *union* of sets M and F, denoted $M \cup F$, is the set of all students in the class. Since these sets have no elements in common, the *intersection* of sets M and F, denoted $M \cap F$, is the *empty set* $\varnothing$; we then say that M and F are *disjoint sets*. The total number of students enrolled in the class is the **number of elements** in $M \cup F$, denoted by $n(M \cup F)$ and given by

$$n(M \cup F) = n(M) + n(F)$$
$$= 13 + 15 = 28 \tag{1}$$

In this example, the number of elements in the union of sets M and F is the sum of the number of elements in M and in F. However, this does not work for all pairs of sets. To see why, consider another example. Suppose that the enrollment in a mathematics class consists of 22 math majors and 16 physics majors, and that 7 of these students have majors in both subjects. If M represents the set of math majors and P represents the set of physics majors, then $M \cap P$ represents the set of double majors. It is tempting to proceed as before and conclude that there are $22 + 16 = 38$ students in the class, but this is incorrect. We have counted the double majors twice, once as math majors and again as physics majors. To correct for this double counting, we subtract the number of double majors from this sum. Thus, the total number of students enrolled in this class is given by

$$n(M \cup P) = n(M) + n(P) - n(M \cap P)$$
$$= 22 + 16 - 7 = 31 \tag{2}$$

Equation (1) for the chemistry class and equation (2) for the math class are illustrations of the *addition principle* for counting the elements in the union of two sets.

THEOREM 1 Addition Principle (for Counting)

For any two sets A and B,

$$n(A \cup B) = n(A) + n(B) - n(A \cap B) \tag{3}$$

If A and B are disjoint, then

$$n(A \cup B) = n(A) + n(B) \tag{4}$$

EXAMPLE 1   **Employee Benefits** According to a survey of business firms in a certain city, 750 firms offer their employees health insurance, 640 offer dental insurance, and 280 offer health insurance and dental insurance. How many firms offer their employees health insurance or dental insurance?

SOLUTION   If H is the set of firms that offer their employees health insurance and D is the set that offer dental insurance, then

$$H \cap D = \text{set of firms that offer health insurance \textbf{and} dental insurance}$$
$$H \cup D = \text{set of firms that offer health insurance \textbf{or} dental insurance}$$

So

$$n(H) = 750 \qquad n(D) = 640 \qquad n(H \cap D) = 280$$

and

$$n(H \cup D) = n(H) + n(D) - n(H \cap D)$$
$$= 750 + 640 - 280 = 1{,}110$$

Therefore, 1,110 firms offer their employees health insurance or dental insurance.

Matched Problem 1   The survey in Example 1 also indicated that 345 firms offer their employees group life insurance, 285 offer long-term disability insurance, and 115 offer group life insurance and long-term disability insurance. How many firms offer their employees group life insurance or long-term disability insurance?

Venn Diagrams

The next example introduces some additional concepts that provide useful counting techniques.

EXAMPLE 2 **Market Research** A city has two daily newspapers, the *Sentinel* and the *Journal*. The following information was obtained from a survey of 100 city residents: 35 people subscribe to the *Sentinel*, 60 subscribe to the *Journal*, and 20 subscribe to both newspapers.

(A) How many people subscribe to the *Sentinel* but not to the *Journal*?

(B) How many subscribe to the *Journal* but not to the *Sentinel*?

(C) How many do not subscribe to either paper?

(D) Organize this information in a table.

SOLUTION Let U be the group of people surveyed. Let S be the set of people who subscribe to the *Sentinel*, and let J be the set of people who subscribe to the *Journal*. Since U contains all the elements under consideration, it is the *universal set* for this problem. The *complement* of S, denoted by S', is the set of people in the survey group U who do not subscribe to the *Sentinel*. Similarly, J' is the set of people in the group who do not subscribe to the *Journal*. Using the sets S and J, their complements, and set intersection, we can divide U into the four disjoint subsets defined below and illustrated as a *Venn diagram* in Figure 1.

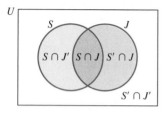

Figure 1 Venn diagram for the newspaper survey

$S \cap J$ = set of people who subscribe to both papers

$S \cap J'$ = set of people who subscribe to the *Sentinel* but not the *Journal*

$S' \cap J$ = set of people who subscribe to the *Journal* but not the *Sentinel*

$S' \cap J'$ = set of people who do not subscribe to either paper

The given survey information can be expressed in terms of set notation as

$$n(U) = 100 \qquad n(S) = 35 \qquad n(J) = 60 \qquad n(S \cap J) = 20$$

We can use this information and a Venn diagram to answer parts (A)–(C). First, we place 20 in $S \cap J$ in the diagram (see Fig. 2). As we proceed with parts (A) through (C), we add each answer to the diagram.

(A) Since 35 people subscribe to the *Sentinel* and 20 subscribe to both papers, the number of people who subscribe to the *Sentinel* but not to the *Journal* is

$$n(S \cap J') = 35 - 20 = 15$$

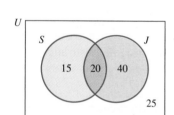

Figure 2 Newspaper survey results

(B) In a similar manner, the number of people who subscribe to the *Journal* but not to the *Sentinel* is

$$n(S' \cap J) = 60 - 20 = 40$$

(C) The total number of newspaper subscribers is $20 + 15 + 40 = 75$. So the number of people who do not subscribe to either paper is

$$n(S' \cap J') = 100 - 75 = 25$$

CONCEPTUAL INSIGHT

Carefully compare Table 1 and Figure 2 of Example 2, and note that we do *not* include any of the totals in Table 1 in the Venn diagram. Instead, the numbers in the Venn diagram give the numbers of elements in the four disjoint sets $S \cap J$, $S \cap J'$, $S' \cap J$, and $S' \cap J'$. From Figure 2, it is easy to construct Table 1 (the totals are easily calculated from the Venn diagram). And from Table 1, it is easy to construct the Venn diagram of Figure 2 (simply disregard the totals).

(D) Venn diagrams are useful tools for determining the number of elements in the various sets of a survey, but often the results must be presented in the form of a table, rather than a diagram. Table 1 contains the information of Figure 2 and also includes totals that give the numbers of elements in the sets S, S', J, J', and U.

Table 1

		Journal		
		Subscriber, J	**Nonsubscriber, J'**	**Totals**
	Subscriber, S	20	15	35
Sentinel	**Nonsubscriber, S'**	40	25	65
	Totals	60	40	100

Matched Problem 2 A small town has two radio stations: an AM station and an FM station. A survey of 100 town residents produced the following results: In the last 30 days, 65 people have listened to the AM station, 45 have listened to the FM station, and 30 have listened to both stations.

(A) During this 30-day period, how many people in the survey have listened to the AM station but not to the FM station?

(B) How many have listened to the FM station but not to the AM station?

(C) How many have not listened to either station?

(D) Organize this information in a table.

EXPLORE & DISCUSS 1 Let A, B, and C be three sets. Use a Venn diagram (Fig. 3) to explain the following equation:

$$n(A \cup B \cup C) = n(A) + n(B) + n(C) - n(A \cap B) - n(A \cap C) \\ - n(B \cap C) + n(A \cap B \cap C)$$

Figure 3

Multiplication Principle

As we have just seen, if the elements of a set are determined by the union operation, addition and subtraction are used to count the number of elements in the set. Now we want to consider sets whose elements are determined by a sequence of operations. We will see that multiplication is used to count the number of elements in sets formed this way.

EXAMPLE 3 **Product Mix** A retail store stocks windbreaker jackets in small, medium, large, and extra large. All are available in blue or red. What are the combined choices, and how many combined choices are there?

SOLUTION To solve the problem, we use a tree diagram:

SIZE CHOICES (OUTCOMES)	COLOR CHOICES (OUTCOMES)	COMBINED CHOICES (OUTCOMES)
S	B	(S, B)
	R	(S, R)
M	B	(M, B)
	R	(M, R)
L	B	(L, B)
	R	(L, R)
XL	B	(XL, B)
	R	(XL, R)

There are 8 possible combined choices (outcomes). There are 4 ways that a size can be chosen and 2 ways that a color can be chosen. The first element in the ordered pair represents a size choice, and the second element represents a color choice.

Matched Problem 3 A company offers its employees health plans from three different companies: R, S, and T. Each company offers two levels of coverage, A and B, with one level requiring additional employee contributions. What are the combined choices, and how many choices are there? Solve using a tree diagram.

Suppose that you asked, "From the 26 letters in the alphabet, how many ways can 3 letters appear in a row on a license plate if no letter is repeated?" To try to count the possibilities using a tree diagram would be extremely tedious. The following **multiplication principle** will enable us to solve this problem easily. In addition, it forms the basis for developing other counting devices in the next section.

> **THEOREM 2   Multiplication Principle (for Counting)**
>
> 1. If two operations O_1 and O_2 are performed in order, with N_1 possible outcomes for the first operation and N_2 possible outcomes for the second operation, then there are
>
> $$N_1 \cdot N_2$$
>
> possible combined outcomes of the first operation followed by the second.
>
> 2. In general, if n operations $O_1, O_2, \ldots, O_n$ are performed in order, with possible number of outcomes $N_1, N_2, \ldots, N_n$, respectively, then there are
>
> $$N_1 \cdot N_2 \cdot \cdots \cdot N_n$$
>
> possible combined outcomes of the operations performed in the given order.

In Example 3, we see that there are 4 possible outcomes in choosing a size (the first operation) and 2 possible outcomes in choosing a color (the second operation). So by the multiplication principle, there are $4 \cdot 2 = 8$ possible combined outcomes. Use the multiplication principle to solve Matched Problem 3. [*Answer:* $3 \cdot 2 = 6$]

To answer the license plate question: There are 26 ways the first letter can be chosen; after a first letter is chosen, there are 25 ways a second letter can be chosen; and after 2 letters are chosen, there are 24 ways a third letter can be chosen. Hence, using the multiplication principle, there are $26 \cdot 25 \cdot 24 = 15,600$ possible ways that 3 letters can be chosen from the alphabet without repeats.

EXAMPLE 4   **Computer-Assisted Testing**   Many colleges and universities use computer-assisted testing. Suppose that a screening test is to consist of 5 questions, and a computer stores 5 comparable questions for the first test question, 8 for the second, 6 for the third, 5 for the fourth, and 10 for the fifth. How many different 5-question tests can the computer select? (Two tests are considered different if they differ in one or more questions.)

SOLUTION

O_1:	Selecting the first question	N_1:	5 ways
O_2:	Selecting the second question	N_2:	8 ways
O_3:	Selecting the third question	N_3:	6 ways
O_4:	Selecting the fourth question	N_4:	5 ways
O_5:	Selecting the fifth question	N_5:	10 ways

The computer can generate

$$5 \cdot 8 \cdot 6 \cdot 5 \cdot 10 = 12,000 \text{ different tests}$$

Matched Problem 4   Each question on a multiple-choice test has 5 choices. If there are 5 such questions on a test, how many different responses are possible if only 1 choice is marked for each question?

EXAMPLE 5   **Code Words**   How many 3-letter code words are possible using the first 8 letters of the alphabet if

(A) No letter can be repeated?

(B) Letters can be repeated?

(C) Adjacent letters cannot be alike?

SOLUTION   To form 3-letter code words from the 8 letters available, we select a letter for the first position, one for the second position, and one for the third position. Altogether, there are three operations.

(A) No letter can be repeated:

O_1: Selecting the first letter N_1: 8 ways

O_2: Selecting the second letter N_2: 7 ways   *Since 1 letter has been used*

O_3: Selecting the third letter N_3: 6 ways   *Since 2 letters have been used*

There are

$$8 \cdot 7 \cdot 6 = 336 \text{ possible code words}$$ *Possible combined operations*

(B) Letters can be repeated:

O_1: Selecting the first letter N_1: 8 ways

O_2: Selecting the second letter N_2: 8 ways   *Repeats allowed*

O_3: Selecting the third letter N_3: 8 ways   *Repeats allowed*

There are

$$8 \cdot 8 \cdot 8 = 8^3 = 512 \text{ possible code words}$$

(C) Adjacent letters cannot be alike:

O_1: Selecting the first letter N_1: 8 ways

O_2: Selecting the second letter N_2: 7 ways   *Cannot be the same as the first*

O_3: Selecting the third letter N_3: 7 ways   *Cannot be the same as the second, but can be the same as the first*

There are

$$8 \cdot 7 \cdot 7 = 392 \text{ possible code words}$$

Matched Problem 5   How many 4-letter code words are possible using the first 10 letters of the alphabet under the three different conditions stated in Example 5?

Exercises 7-3

A

Problems 1–12 refer to the following Venn diagram. Find the number of elements in each of the indicated sets.

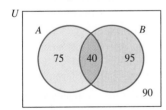

1. A **2.** B **3.** U

4. A' **5.** B' **6.** $A \cap B$

7. $A \cup B$ **8.** $A \cap B'$ **9.** $A' \cap B$

10. $A' \cap B'$ **11.** $(A \cap B)'$ **12.** $(A \cup B)'$

Solve Problems 13–16 two ways: (A) using a tree diagram, and (B) using the multiplication principle.

13. How many ways can 2 coins turn up—heads, H, or tails, T—if the combined outcome (H, T) is to be distinguished from the outcome (T, H)?

14. How many 2-letter code words can be formed from the first 3 letters of the alphabet if no letter can be used more than once?

15. A coin is tossed with possible outcomes of heads H, or tails T. Then a single die is tossed with possible outcomes 1, 2, 3, 4, 5, or 6. How many combined outcomes are there?

16. In how many ways can 3 coins turn up—heads H, or tails T—if combined outcomes such as (H, T, H), (H, H, T), and (T, H, H) are considered as different?

17. An entertainment guide recommends 6 restaurants and 3 plays that appeal to a couple.

(A) If the couple goes to dinner or a play, how many selections are possible?

(B) If the couple goes to dinner and then to a play, how many combined selections are possible?

18. A college offers 2 introductory courses in history, 3 in science, 2 in mathematics, 2 in philosophy, and 1 in English.

(A) If a freshman takes one course in each area during her first semester, how many course selections are possible?

(B) If a part-time student can afford to take only one introductory course, how many selections are possible?

B

19. A county park system rates its 20 golf courses in increasing order of difficulty as bronze, silver, or gold. There are only two gold courses and twice as many bronze as silver courses.

(A) If a golfer decides to play a round at a silver or gold course, how many selections are possible?

(B) If a golfer decides to play one round per week for 3 weeks, first on a bronze course, then silver, then gold, how many combined selections are possible?

20. The 14 colleges of interest to a high school senior include 6 that are expensive (tuition more than $30,000 per year), 7 that are far from home (more than 200 miles away), and 2 that are both expensive and far from home.

(A) If the student decides to select a college that is not expensive and within 200 miles of home, how many selections are possible?

(B) If the student decides to attend a college that is not expensive and within 200 miles from home during his first two years of college, and then will transfer to a college that is not expensive but is far from home, how many selections of two colleges are possible?

In Problems 21–26, use the given information to determine the number of elements in each of the four disjoint subsets in the following Venn diagram.

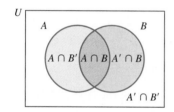

21. $n(A) = 80$, $n(B) = 50$,
$n(A \cap B) = 20$, $n(U) = 200$

22. $n(A) = 45$, $n(B) = 35$,
$n(A \cap B) = 15$, $n(U) = 100$

23. $n(A) = 25$, $n(B) = 55$,
$n(A \cup B) = 60$, $n(U) = 100$

24. $n(A) = 70$, $n(B) = 90$,
$n(A \cup B) = 120$, $n(U) = 200$

25. $n(A') = 65$, $n(B') = 40$,
$n(A' \cap B') = 25$, $n(U) = 150$

26. $n(A') = 35$, $n(B') = 75$,
$n(A' \cup B') = 95$, $n(U) = 120$

In Problems 27–32, use the given information to complete the following table.

	A	A'	Totals
B	?	?	?
B'	?	?	?
Totals	?	?	?

27. $n(A) = 70$, $n(B) = 90$,
$n(A \cap B) = 30$, $n(U) = 200$

28. $n(A) = 55$, $n(B) = 65$,
$n(A \cap B) = 35$, $n(U) = 100$

29. $n(A) = 45$, $n(B) = 55$,
$n(A \cup B) = 80$, $n(U) = 100$

30. $n(A) = 80$, $n(B) = 70$,
$n(A \cup B) = 110$, $n(U) = 200$

31. $n(A') = 15$, $n(B') = 24$,
$n(A' \cup B') = 32$, $n(U) = 90$

32. $n(A') = 81$, $n(B') = 90$,
$n(A' \cap B') = 63$, $n(U) = 180$

In Problems 33 and 34, discuss the validity of each statement. If the statement is always true, explain why. If not, give a counterexample.

33. (A) If A or B is the empty set, then A and B are disjoint.

(B) If A and B are disjoint, then A or B is the empty set.

34. (A) If A and B are disjoint, then $n(A \cap B) = n(A) + n(B)$.

(B) If $n(A \cup B) = n(A) + n(B)$, then A and B are disjoint.

35. A particular new car model is available with 5 choices of color, 3 choices of transmission, 4 types of interior, and 2 types of engine. How many different variations of this model are possible?

36. A delicatessen serves meat sandwiches with the following options: 3 kinds of bread, 5 kinds of meat, and lettuce or sprouts. How many different sandwiches are possible, assuming that one item is used out of each category?

37. How many 4-letter code words are possible from the first 6 letters of the alphabet if no letter is repeated? If letters can be repeated? If adjacent letters must be different?

38. How many 5-letter code words are possible from the first 7 letters of the alphabet if no letter is repeated? If letters can be repeated? If adjacent letters must be different?

39. A combination lock has 5 wheels, each labeled with the 10 digits from 0 to 9. How many 5-digit opening combinations are possible if no digit is repeated? If digits can be repeated? If successive digits must be different?

40. A small combination lock has 3 wheels, each labeled with the 10 digits from 0 to 9. How many 3-digit combinations are possible if no digit is repeated? If digits can be repeated? If successive digits must be different?

41. How many different license plates are possible if each contains 3 letters (out of the alphabet's 26 letters) followed by 3 digits (from 0 to 9)? How many of these license plates contain no repeated letters and no repeated digits?

42. How many 5-digit ZIP code numbers are possible? How many of these numbers contain no repeated digits?

43. In Example 3, does it make any difference in which order the selection operations are performed? That is, if we select a jacket color first and then select a size, are there as many combined choices available as selecting a size first and then a color? Justify your answer using tree diagrams and the multiplication principle.

44. Explain how three sets, A, B, and C, can be related to each other in order for the following equation to hold true (Venn diagrams may be helpful):

$$n(A \cup B \cup C) = n(A) + n(B) + n(C)$$
$$- n(A \cap C) - n(B \cap C)$$

C

Problems 45–48 refer to the following Venn diagram.

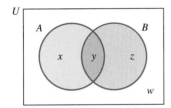

45. Which of the numbers x, y, z, or w must equal 0 if $B \subset A$?

46. Which of the numbers x, y, z, or w must equal 0 if A and B are disjoint?

47. Which of the numbers x, y, z, or w must equal 0 if $A \cup B = A \cap B$?

48. Which of the numbers x, y, z, or w must equal 0 if $A \cup B = U$?

49. A group of 75 people includes 32 who play tennis, 37 who play golf, and 8 who play both tennis and golf. How many people in the group play neither sport?

50. A class of 30 music students includes 13 who play the piano, 16 who play the guitar, and 5 who play both the piano and the guitar. How many students in the class play neither instrument?

51. A group of 100 people touring Europe includes 42 people who speak French, 55 who speak German, and 17 who speak neither language. How many people in the group speak both French and German?

52. A high school football team with 40 players includes 16 players who played offense last year, 17 who played defense, and 12 who were not on last year's team. How many players from last year played both offense and defense?

Applications

53. Management. A management selection service classifies its applicants (using tests and interviews) as high-IQ, middle-IQ, or low-IQ and as aggressive or passive. How many combined classifications are possible?

(A) Solve using a tree diagram.

(B) Solve using the multiplication principle.

54. Management. A corporation plans to fill 2 different positions for vice-president, V_1 and V_2, from administrative officers in 2 of its manufacturing plants. Plant A has 6 officers and plant B has 8. How many ways can these 2 positions be filled if the V_1 position is to be filled from plant A and the V_2 position from plant B? How many ways can the 2 positions be filled if the selection is made without regard to plant?

55. Transportation. A sales representative who lives in city A wishes to start from home and fly to 3 different cities: B, C, and D. If there are 2 choices of local transportation (drive her own car or use a taxi), and if all cities are interconnected by airlines, how many travel plans can be constructed to visit each city exactly once and return home?

56. Transportation. A manufacturing company in city A wishes to truck its product to 4 different cities: B, C, D, and E. If roads interconnect all 4 cities, how many different route plans can be constructed so that a single truck, starting from A, will visit each city exactly once, then return home?

57. Market research. A survey of 1,200 people indicates that 850 own HDTV's, 740 own DVD players, and 580 own HDTV's and DVD players.

(A) How many people in the survey own either an HDTV or a DVD player?

(B) How many own neither an HDTV nor a DVD player?

(C) How many own an HDTV and do not own a DVD player?

58. Market research. A survey of 800 small businesses indicates that 250 own a video conferencing system, 420 own projection equipment, and 180 own a video conferencing system and projection equipment.

(A) How many businesses in the survey own either a video conferencing system or projection equipment?

(B) How many own neither a video conferencing system nor projection equipment?

(C) How many own projection equipment and do not own a video conferencing system?

59. Communications. A cable television company has 8,000 subscribers in a suburban community. The company offers two premium channels: HBO and Showtime. If 2,450 subscribers receive HBO, 1,940 receive Showtime, and 5,180 do not receive any premium channel, how many subscribers receive both HBO and Showtime?

60. Communications. A cable company offers its 10,000 customers two special services: high-speed internet and digital phone. If 3,770 customers use high-speed internet, 3,250 use digital phone, and 4,530 do not use either of these services, how many customers use both high-speed internet and digital phone?

61. Minimum wage. The table below gives the number of male and female workers earning at or below the minimum wage for several age categories.

(A) How many males are of age 20–24 and earn below minimum wage?

	Workers per Age Group (Thousands)			
	16–19	20–24	25+	Totals
Males at Minimum Wage	343	154	237	734
Males below Minimum Wage	118	102	159	379
Females at Minimum Wage	367	186	503	1,056
Females below Minimum Wage	251	202	540	993
Totals	1,079	644	1,439	3,162

(B) How many females are of age 20 or older and earn minimum wage?

(C) How many workers are of age 16–19 or males earning minimum wage?

(D) How many workers earn below minimum wage?

62. Minimum wage. Refer to the table in Problem 61.

(A) How many females are of age 16–19 and earn minimum wage?

(B) How many males are of age 16–24 and earn below minimum wage?

(C) How many workers are of age 20–24 or females earning below minimum wage?

(D) How many workers earn minimum wage?

63. Medicine. A medical researcher classifies subjects according to male or female; smoker or nonsmoker; and underweight, average weight, or overweight. How many combined classifications are possible?

(A) Solve using a tree diagram.

(B) Solve using the multiplication principle.

64. Family planning. A couple is planning to have 3 children. How many boy–girl combinations are possible? Distinguish between combined outcomes such as (B, B, G), (B, G, B), and (G, B, B).

(A) Solve using a tree diagram.

(B) Solve using the multiplication principle.

65. Politics. A politician running for a third term is planning to contact all contributors to her first two campaigns. If 1,475 individuals contributed to the first campaign, 2,350 contributed to the second campaign, and 920 contributed to the first and second campaigns, how many individuals have contributed to the first or second campaign?

66. Politics. If 12,457 people voted for a politician in his first election, 15,322 voted for him in his second election, and 9,345 voted for him in the first and second elections, how many people voted for this politician in the first or second election?

Answers to Matched Problems

1. 515

2. (A) 35
(B) 15
(C) 20
(D)

		FM		
		Listener	Nonlistener	Totals
	Listener	30	35	65
AM	Nonlistener	15	20	35
	Totals	45	55	100

3. There are 6 combined choices:

COMPANY CHOICES (OUTCOMES)	COVERAGE CHOICES (OUTCOMES)	COMBINED CHOICES (OUTCOMES)
R	A	(R, A)
	B	(R, B)
S	A	(S, A)
	B	(S, B)
T	A	(T, A)
	B	(T, B)

Start

4. 5^5, or 3,125

5. (A) $10 \cdot 9 \cdot 8 \cdot 7 = 5,040$
(B) $10 \cdot 10 \cdot 10 \cdot 10 = 10,000$
(C) $10 \cdot 9 \cdot 9 \cdot 9 = 7,290$

7-4 Permutations and Combinations

- Factorials
- Permutations
- Combinations
- Applications

The multiplication principle discussed in the preceding section can be used to develop two additional counting devices that are extremely useful in more complicated counting problems. Both of these devices use *factorials*.

Factorials

When using the multiplication principle, we encountered expressions such as

$$26 \cdot 25 \cdot 24 \quad \text{or} \quad 8 \cdot 7 \cdot 6$$

where each natural number factor is decreased by 1 as we move from left to right. The factors in the following product continue to decrease by 1 until a factor of 1 is reached:

$$5 \cdot 4 \cdot 3 \cdot 2 \cdot 1$$

Products like this are encountered so frequently in counting problems that it is useful to express them in a concise notation. The product of the first n natural numbers is called n **factorial** and is denoted by $n!$. Also, we define **zero factorial, 0!,** to be 1.

> **DEFINITION Factorial***
>
> For a natural number n,
>
> $$n! = n(n - 1)(n - 2) \cdot \cdots \cdot 2 \cdot 1 \qquad 4! = 4 \cdot 3 \cdot 2 \cdot 1$$
> $$0! = 1$$
> $$n! = n \cdot (n - 1)!$$

EXAMPLE 1 **Computing Factorials**

(A) $5! = 5 \cdot 4 \cdot 3 \cdot 2 \cdot 1 = 120$

(B) $\dfrac{7!}{6!} = \dfrac{7 \cdot \cancel{6!}}{\cancel{6!}} = 7$

(C) $\dfrac{8!}{5!} = \dfrac{8 \cdot 7 \cdot 6 \cdot \cancel{5!}}{\cancel{5!}} = 8 \cdot 7 \cdot 6 = 336$

(D) $\dfrac{52!}{5!47!} = \dfrac{52 \cdot 51 \cdot 50 \cdot 49 \cdot 48 \cdot \cancel{47!}}{5 \cdot 4 \cdot 3 \cdot 2 \cdot 1 \cdot \cancel{47!}} = 2{,}598{,}960$

Matched Problem 1 Find

(A) $6!$ (B) $\dfrac{10!}{9!}$ (C) $\dfrac{10!}{7!}$ (D) $\dfrac{5!}{0!3!}$ (E) $\dfrac{20!}{3!17!}$

It is interesting and useful to note that $n!$ grows very rapidly. Compare the following:

$$5! = 120 \qquad 10! = 3{,}628{,}800 \qquad 15! = 1{,}307{,}674{,}368{,}000$$

Try $69!, 70!,$ and $71!$ on your calculator.

Permutations

A particular (horizontal or vertical) arrangement of a set of paintings on a wall is called a *permutation* of the set of paintings.

DEFINITION Permutation of a Set of Objects

A **permutation** of a set of distinct objects is an arrangement of the objects in a specific order without repetition.

Suppose that 4 pictures are to be arranged from left to right on one wall of an art gallery. How many permutations (ordered arrangements) are possible? Using the multiplication principle, there are 4 ways of selecting the first picture; after the first picture is selected, there are 3 ways of selecting the second picture. After the first 2 pictures are selected, there are 2 ways of selecting the third picture, and after the first 3 pictures are selected, there is only 1 way to select the fourth. So the number of permutations (ordered arrangements) of the set of 4 pictures is

$$4 \cdot 3 \cdot 2 \cdot 1 = 4! = 24$$

In general, how many permutations of a set of n distinct objects are possible? Reasoning as above, there are n ways in which the first object can be chosen; there are $n - 1$ ways in which the second object can be chosen, and so on. Using the multiplication principle, we have the following:

THEOREM 1   Number of Permutations of n Objects

The number of permutations of n distinct objects without repetition, denoted by $P_{n,n}$, is

$$P_{n,n} = n(n - 1) \cdot \cdots \cdot 2 \cdot 1 = n! \qquad \textit{n factors}$$

Example: The number of permutations of 7 objects is

$$P_{7,7} = 7 \cdot 6 \cdot 5 \cdot 4 \cdot 3 \cdot 2 \cdot 1 = 7! \qquad \textit{7 factors}$$

---

*Many calculators have an n! key or its equivalent.

Now suppose that the director of the art gallery decides to use only 2 of the 4 available paintings, and they will be arranged on the wall from left to right. We are now talking about a particular arrangement of 2 paintings out of the 4, which is called a *permutation of 4 objects taken 2 at a time*. In general,

---

DEFINITION Permutation of n Objects Taken r at a Time

A permutation of a set of n distinct objects taken r at a time without repetition is an arrangement of r of the n objects in a specific order.

How many ordered arrangements of 2 pictures can be formed from the 4? That is, how many permutations of 4 objects taken 2 at a time are there? There are 4 ways that the first picture can be selected; after selecting the first picture, there are 3 ways that the second picture can be selected. So the number of permutations of a set of 4 objects taken 2 at a time, which is denoted by $P_{4,2}$, is given by

$$P_{4,2} = 4 \cdot 3$$

In terms of factorials, we have

$$P_{4,2} = 4 \cdot 3 = \frac{4 \cdot 3 \cdot 2!}{2!} = \frac{4!}{2!} \qquad \text{Multiplying } 4 \cdot 3 \text{ by 1 in the form } 2!/2!$$

Reasoning in the same way as in the example, we find that the number of permutations of n distinct objects taken r at a time without repetition ($0 \leq r \leq n$) is given by

$$P_{n,r} = n(n - 1)(n - 2) \cdot \cdots \cdot (n - r + 1) \qquad r \text{ factors}$$
$$P_{9,6} = 9(9 - 1)(9 - 2) \cdot \cdots \cdot (9 - 6 + 1) \qquad 6 \text{ factors}$$
$$= 9 \cdot 8 \cdot 7 \cdot 6 \cdot 5 \cdot 4$$

Multiplying the right side of the equation for $P_{n,r}$ by 1 in the form $(n - r)!/(n - r)!$, we obtain a factorial form for $P_{n,r}$:

$$P_{n,r} = n(n - 1)(n - 2) \cdot \cdots \cdot (n - r + 1)\frac{(n - r)!}{(n - r)!}$$

But, since

$$n(n - 1)(n - 2) \cdot \cdots \cdot (n - r + 1)(n - r)! = n!$$

the expression above simplifies to

$$P_{n,r} = \frac{n!}{(n - r)!}$$

We summarize these results in Theorem 2.

THEOREM 2   Number of Permutations of n Objects Taken r at a Time

The number of permutations of n distinct objects taken r at a time without repetition is given by*

$$P_{n,r} = n(n - 1)(n - 2) \cdot \cdots \cdot (n - r + 1) \qquad r \text{ factors}$$
$$P_{5,2} = 5 \cdot 4 \quad 2 \text{ factors}$$

or

$$P_{n,r} = \frac{n!}{(n - r)!} \qquad 0 \leq r \leq n \qquad P_{5,2} = \frac{5!}{(5 - 2)!} = \frac{5!}{3!}$$

Note: $P_{n,n} = \dfrac{n!}{(n - n)!} = \dfrac{n!}{0!} = n!$ permutations of n objects taken n at a time.

Remember, by definition, $0! = 1$.

---

*In place of the symbol $P_{n,r}$, the symbols P_r^n, $_nP_r$, and $P(n, r)$ are often used.

EXAMPLE 2   **Permutations** Given the set $\{A, B, C\}$, how many permutations are possible for this set of 3 objects taken 2 at a time? Answer the question

(A) Using a tree diagram

(B) Using the multiplication principle

(C) Using the two formulas for $P_{n,r}$

SOLUTION   (A) Using a tree diagram:

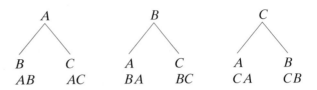

There are 6 permutations of 3 objects taken 2 at a time.

(B) Using the multiplication principle:

O_1:   Fill the first position N_1:   3 ways

O_2:   Fill the second position N_2:   2 ways

There are

$$3 \cdot 2 = 6 \text{ permutations of 3 objects taken 2 at a time}$$

(C) Using the two formulas for $P_{n,r}$:

2 factors
↓

$$P_{3,2} = 3 \cdot 2 = 6 \quad \text{or} \quad P_{3,2} = \frac{3!}{(3-2)!} = \frac{3 \cdot 2 \cdot 1}{1} = 6$$

There are 6 permutations of 3 objects taken 2 at a time. Of course, all three methods produce the same answer.

Matched Problem 2   Given the set $\{A, B, C, D\}$, how many permutations are possible for this set of 4 objects taken 2 at a time? Answer the question

(A) Using a tree diagram

(B) Using the multiplication principle

(C) Using the two formulas for $P_{n,r}$

In Example 2 you probably found the multiplication principle to be the easiest method to use. But for large values of n and r, you will find that the factorial formula is more convenient. In fact, many calculators have functions that compute $n!$ and $P_{n,r}$ directly.

EXAMPLE 3   **Permutations** Find the number of permutations of 13 objects taken 8 at a time. Compute the answer using a calculator.

SOLUTION   We use the factorial formula for $P_{n,r}$:

$$P_{13,8} = \frac{13!}{(13-8)!} = \frac{13!}{5!} = 51,891,840$$

```
13!
       6227020800
13!/5!
         51891840
13 nPr 8
         51891840
```

Figure 1

Using a tree diagram to solve this problem would involve a monumental effort. Using the multiplication principle would mean multiplying $13 \cdot 12 \cdot 11 \cdot 10 \cdot 9 \cdot 8 \cdot 7 \cdot 6$ (8 factors), which is not too bad. However, a calculator can provide instant results (see Fig. 1).

choosing a 3-person subcommittee. In part (A), we are interested in the number of *permutations* of 10 objects taken 3 at a time; and in part (B), we are interested in the number of *combinations* of 10 objects taken 3 at a time. These quantities are computed as follows (and since the numbers are not large, we do not need to use a calculator):

$$\text{(A)} \quad P_{10,3} = \frac{10!}{(10-3)!} = \frac{10!}{7!} = \boxed{\frac{10 \cdot 9 \cdot 8 \cdot 7!}{7!}} = 720 \text{ ways}$$

$$\text{(B)} \quad C_{10,3} = \frac{10!}{3!(10-3)!} = \frac{10!}{3!7!} = \boxed{\frac{10 \cdot 9 \cdot 8 \cdot 7!}{3 \cdot 2 \cdot 1 \cdot 7!}} = 120 \text{ ways}$$

Matched Problem 4 From a committee of 12 people,

(A) In how many ways can we choose a chairperson, a vice-chairperson, a secretary, and a treasurer, assuming that one person cannot hold more than one position?

(B) In how many ways can we choose a subcommittee of 4 people?

If n and r are large numbers, a calculator is useful in evaluating expressions involving factorials. Many calculators have a function that computes $C_{n,r}$ directly (see Fig. 3).

```
13 nCr 8
            1287
13 nPr 8
        51891840
13 nPr 8/8!
            1287
```

Figure 3

EXAMPLE 5 **Combinations** Find the number of combinations of 13 objects taken 8 at a time. Compute the answer using a calculator.

SOLUTION $C_{13,8} = \begin{pmatrix} 13 \\ 8 \end{pmatrix} = \dfrac{13!}{8!(13-8)!} = \dfrac{13!}{8!5!} = 1,287$

Compare the result in Example 5 with that obtained in Example 3, and note that $C_{13,8}$ is substantially smaller than $P_{13,8}$ (see Fig. 3).

Matched Problem 5 Find the number of combinations of 30 objects taken 4 at a time. Compute the answer using a calculator.

CONCEPTUAL INSIGHT

Permutations and combinations are similar in that both are selections in which repetition is *not* allowed. But there is a crucial distinction between the two:

In a permutation, order is vital.

In a combination, order is irrelevant.

To determine whether a given selection is a permutation or combination, see if rearranging the elements of the selection would produce a different object. If so, the selection is a permutation; if not, the selection is a combination.

EXPLORE & DISCUSS 1
(A) List alphabetically by the first letter, all 3-letter license plate codes consisting of 3 different letters chosen from M, A, T, H. Discuss how this list relates to $P_{n,r}$.

(B) Reorganize the list from part (A) so that all codes without M come first, then all codes without A, then all codes without T, and finally all codes without H. Discuss how this list illustrates the formula $P_{n,r} = r! C_{n,r}$.

Applications

We now consider some applications of permutations and combinations. Several applications in this section involve a standard 52-card deck of playing cards.

Standard 52-Card Deck of Playing Cards

A standard deck of 52 cards (see Fig. 4) has four 13-card suits: diamonds, hearts, clubs, and spades. The diamonds and hearts are red, and the clubs and spades are black. Each 13-card suit contains cards numbered from 2 to 10, a jack, a queen, a king, and an ace. The jack, queen, and king are called *face cards*. Depending on the game, the ace may be counted as the lowest and/or the highest card in the suit.

Figure 4

EXAMPLE 6 **Counting Techniques** How many 5-card hands have 3 aces and 2 kings?

SOLUTION The solution involves both the multiplication principle and combinations. Think of selecting the 5-card hand in terms of the following two operations:

O_1: Choosing 3 aces out of 4 possible $\qquad N_1$: $C_{4,3}$
(order is not important)

O_2: Choosing 2 kings out of 4 possible $\qquad N_2$: $C_{4,2}$
(order is not important)

Using the multiplication principle, we have

$$\text{number of hands} = C_{4,3} \cdot C_{4,2}$$
$$= \frac{4!}{3!(4-3)!} \cdot \frac{4!}{2!(4-2)!}$$
$$= 4 \cdot 6 = 24$$

Matched Problem 6 How many 5-card hands have 3 hearts and 2 spades?

EXAMPLE 7 **Counting Techniques** Serial numbers for a product are made using 2 letters followed by 3 numbers. If the letters are taken from the first 8 letters of the alphabet with no repeats and the numbers are taken from the 10 digits (0–9) with no repeats, how many serial numbers are possible?

SOLUTION The solution involves both the multiplication principle and permutations. Think of selecting a serial number in terms of the following two operations:

O_1: Choosing 2 letters out of 8 available $\qquad N_1$: $P_{8,2}$
(order is important)

O_2: Choosing 3 numbers out of 10 available $\qquad N_2$: $P_{10,3}$
(order is important)

Using the multiplication principle, we have

$$\text{number of serial numbers} = P_{8,2} \cdot P_{10,3}$$

$$= \frac{8!}{(8-2)!} \cdot \frac{10!}{(10-3)!}$$

$$= 56 \cdot 720 = 40{,}320$$

Matched Problem 7   Repeat Example 7 under the same conditions, except that the serial numbers will now have 3 letters followed by 2 digits (no repeats).

EXAMPLE 8   **Counting Techniques**   A company has 7 senior and 5 junior officers. It wants to form an ad hoc legislative committee. In how many ways can a 4-officer committee be formed so that it is composed of

(A) Any 4 officers?

(B) 4 senior officers?

(C) 3 senior officers and 1 junior officer?

(D) 2 senior and 2 junior officers?

(E) At least 2 senior officers?

SOLUTION   (A) Since there are a total of 12 officers in the company, the number of different 4-member committees is

$$C_{12,4} = \frac{12!}{4!(12-4)!} = \frac{12!}{4!8!} = 495$$

(B) If only senior officers can be on the committee, the number of different committees is

$$C_{7,4} = \frac{7!}{4!(7-4)!} = \frac{7!}{4!3!} = 35$$

(C) The 3 senior officers can be selected in $C_{7,3}$ ways, and the 1 junior officer can be selected in $C_{5,1}$ ways. Applying the multiplication principle, the number of ways that 3 senior officers and 1 junior officer can be selected is

$$C_{7,3} \cdot C_{5,1} = \frac{7!}{3!(7-3)!} \cdot \frac{5!}{1!(5-1)!} = \frac{7!5!}{3!4!1!4!} = 175$$

(D) $C_{7,2} \cdot C_{5,2} = \dfrac{7!}{2!(7-2)!} \cdot \dfrac{5!}{2!(5-2)!} = \dfrac{7!5!}{2!5!2!3!} = 210$

(E) The committees with *at least* 2 senior officers can be divided into three disjoint collections:

1. Committees with 4 senior officers and 0 junior officers

2. Committees with 3 senior officers and 1 junior officer

3. Committees with 2 senior officers and 2 junior officers

The number of committees of types 1, 2, and 3 is computed in parts (B), (C), and (D), respectively. The total number of committees of all three types is the sum of these quantities:

Type 1   Type 2   Type 3

$$C_{7,4} + C_{7,3} \cdot C_{5,1} + C_{7,2} \cdot C_{5,2} = 35 + 175 + 210 = 420$$

Matched Problem 8   Given the information in Example 8, answer the following questions:

(A) How many 4-officer committees with 1 senior officer and 3 junior officers can be formed?

(B) How many 4-officer committees with 4 junior officers can be formed?

(C) How many 4-officer committees with at least 2 junior officers can be formed?

EXAMPLE 9   **Counting Techniques** From a standard 52-card deck, how many 3-card hands have all cards from the same suit?

SOLUTION   There are 13 cards in each suit, so the number of 3-card hands having all hearts, for example, is

$$C_{13,3} = \frac{13!}{3!(13-3)!} = \frac{13!}{3!10!} = 286$$

Similarly, there are 286 3-card hands having all diamonds, 286 having all clubs, and 286 having all spades. So the total number of 3-card hands having all cards from the same suit is

$$4C_{13,3} = 1{,}144$$

Matched Problem 9   From a standard 52-card deck, how many 5-card hands have all cards from the same suit?

Exercises 7-4

A

In Problems 1–20, evaluate the expression. If the answer is not an integer, round to four decimal places.

1. $7!$

2. $10!$

3. $(5 + 6)!$

4. $(7 + 2)!$

5. $5! + 6!$

6. $7! + 2!$

7. $\dfrac{8!}{4!}$

8. $\dfrac{10!}{5!}$

9. $\dfrac{8!}{4!(8-4)!}$

10. $\dfrac{10!}{5!(10-5)!}$

11. $\dfrac{500!}{498!}$

12. $\dfrac{601!}{599!}$

13. $P_{12,7}$

14. $P_{11,6}$

15. $C_{12,7}$

16. $C_{11,6}$

17. $\dfrac{C_{13,4}}{C_{52,4}}$

18. $\dfrac{C_{26,3}}{C_{52,3}}$

19. $\dfrac{P_{12,6}}{12^6}$

20. $\dfrac{P_{365,30}}{365^{30}}$

In Problems 21–24, simplify each expression assuming that n is an integer and $n \geq 2$.

21. $\dfrac{n!}{(n-2)!}$

22. $\dfrac{(n+1)!}{3!(n-2)!}$

23. $\dfrac{(n+1)!}{2!(n-1)!}$

24. $\dfrac{(n+3)!}{(n+1)!}$

In Problems 25–30, would you consider the selection to be a permutation, a combination, or neither? Explain your reasoning.

25. The university president named 3 new officers: a vice-president of finance, a vice-president of academic affairs, and a vice-president of student affairs.

26. The university president selected 2 of her vice-presidents to attend the dedication ceremony of a new branch campus.

27. A student checked out 4 novels from the library.

28. A student bought 4 books: 1 for his father, 1 for his mother, 1 for his younger sister, and 1 for his older brother.

29. A father ordered an ice cream cone (chocolate, vanilla, or strawberry) for each of his 4 children.

30. A book club meets monthly at the home of one of its 10 members. In December, the club selects a host for each meeting of the next year.

31. In a horse race, how many different finishes among the first 3 places are possible if 10 horses are running? (Exclude ties.)

32. In a long-distance foot race, how many different finishes among the first 5 places are possible if 50 people are running? (Exclude ties.)

33. How many ways can a 3-person subcommittee be selected from a committee of 7 people? How many ways can a president, vice-president, and secretary be chosen from a committee of 7 people?

34. Nine cards are numbered with the digits from 1 to 9. A 3-card hand is dealt, 1 card at a time. How many hands are possible in which

(A) Order is taken into consideration?

(B) Order is not taken into consideration?

B

35. Discuss the relative growth rates of $x!$, 3^x, and x^3.

36. Discuss the relative growth rates of $x!$, 2^x, and x^2.

37. From a standard 52-card deck, how many 5-card hands have all hearts?

38. From a standard 52-card deck, how many 5-card hands have all face cards? All face cards, but no kings?

39. From a standard 52-card deck, how many 7-card hands have 5 spades and 2 hearts?

40. From a standard 52-card deck, how many 5-card hands have 2 clubs and 3 hearts?

41. A catering service offers 8 appetizers, 10 main courses, and 7 desserts. A banquet committee selects 3 appetizers, 4 main courses, and 2 desserts. How many ways can this be done?

42. Three departments have 12, 15, and 18 members, respectively. If each department selects a delegate and an alternate to represent the department at a conference, how many ways can this be done?

In Problems 43 and 44, refer to the table in the graphing calculator display below, which shows $y_1 = P_{n,r}$ and $y_2 = C_{n,r}$ for $n = 6$.

X	Y1	Y2
0	1	1
1	6	6
2	30	15
3	120	20
4	360	15
5	720	6
6	720	1

Y2■6 nCr X

43. Discuss and explain the symmetry of the numbers in the y_2 column of the table.

44. Explain how the table illustrates the formula

$$P_{n,r} = r! C_{n,r}$$

In Problems 45–50, discuss the validity of each statement. If the statement is true, explain why. If not, give a counterexample.

45. If n is a positive integer, then $n! < (n + 1)!$.

46. If n is a positive integer greater than 3, then $n! > 2^n$.

47. If n and r are positive integers and $1 < r < n$, then $P_{n,r} < P_{n,r+1}$.

48. If n and r are positive integers and $1 < r < n$, then $C_{n,r} < C_{n,r+1}$.

49. If n and r are positive integers and $1 < r < n$, then $C_{n,r} = C_{n,n-r}$.

50. If n and r are positive integers and $1 < r < n$, then $P_{n,r} = P_{n,n-r}$.

C

51. Eight distinct points are selected on the circumference of a circle.

(A) How many line segments can be drawn by joining the points in all possible ways?

(B) How many triangles can be drawn using these 8 points as vertices?

(C) How many quadrilaterals can be drawn using these 8 points as vertices?

52. Five distinct points are selected on the circumference of a circle.

(A) How many line segments can be drawn by joining the points in all possible ways?

(B) How many triangles can be drawn using these 5 points as vertices?

53. How many ways can 2 people be seated in a row of 5 chairs? 3 people? 4 people? 5 people?

54. Each of 2 countries sends 5 delegates to a negotiating conference. A rectangular table is used with 5 chairs on each long side. If each country is assigned a long side of the table (operation 1), how many seating arrangements are possible?

55. A basketball team has 5 distinct positions. Out of 8 players, how many starting teams are possible if

(A) The distinct positions are taken into consideration?

(B) The distinct positions are not taken into consideration?

(C) The distinct positions are not taken into consideration, but either Mike or Ken (but not both) must start?

56. How many 4-person committees are possible from a group of 9 people if

(A) There are no restrictions?

(B) Both Jim and Mary must be on the committee?

(C) Either Jim or Mary (but not both) must be on the committee?

57. Find the largest integer k such that your calculator can compute $k!$ without an overflow error.

58. Find the largest integer k such that your calculator can compute $C_{2k,k}$ without an overflow error.

59. Note from the table in the graphing calculator display below that the largest value of $C_{n,r}$ when $n = 20$ is $C_{20,10} = 184,756$. Use a similar table to find the largest value of $C_{n,r}$ when $n = 24$.

X	Y1
7	77520
8	125970
9	167960
10	184756
11	167960
12	125970
13	77520

Y1■20 nCr X

60. Note from the table in the graphing calculator display that the largest value of $C_{n,r}$ when $n = 21$ is $C_{21,10} = C_{21,11} = 352,716$. Use a similar table to find the largest value of $C_{n,r}$ when $n = 17$.

X	Y1
7	116280
8	203490
9	293930
10	352716
11	352716
12	293930
13	203490

Y1■21 nCr X

Applications

61. Quality control. An office supply store receives a shipment of 24 high speed printers, including 5 that are defective. Three of these printers are selected for a store display.

(A) How many selections can be made?

(B) How many of these selections will contain no defective printers?

62. Quality control. An electronics store receives a shipment of 30 graphing calculators, including 6 that are defective. Four of these calculators are selected for a local high school.

(A) How many selections can be made?

(B) How many of these selections will contain no defective calculators?

63. Business closings. A jewelry store chain with 8 stores in Georgia, 12 in Florida, and 10 in Alabama is planning to close 10 of these stores.

(A) How many ways can this be done?

(B) The company decides to close 2 stores in Georgia, 5 in Florida, and 3 in Alabama. In how many ways can this be done?

64. Employee layoffs. A real estate company with 14 employees in their central office, 8 in their north office, and 6 in their south office is planning to lay off 12 employees.

(A) How many ways can this be done?

(B) The company decides to lay off 5 employees from the central office, 4 from the north office, and 3 from the south office. In how many ways can this be done?

65. Personnel selection. Suppose that 6 female and 5 male applicants have been successfully screened for 5 positions. In how many ways can the following compositions be selected?

(A) 3 females and 2 males

(B) 4 females and 1 male

(C) 5 females

(D) 5 people regardless of sex

(E) At least 4 females

66. Committee selection. A 4-person grievance committee is selected out of 2 departments A and B, with 15 and 20 people, respectively. In how many ways can the following committees be selected?

(A) 3 from A and 1 from B

(B) 2 from A and 2 from B

(C) All from A

(D) 4 people regardless of department

(E) At least 3 from department A

67. Medicine. There are 8 standard classifications of blood type. An examination for prospective laboratory technicians consists of having each candidate determine the type for 3 blood samples. How many different examinations can be given if no 2 of the samples provided for the candidate have the same type? If 2 or more samples have the same type?

68. Medical research. Because of limited funds, 5 research centers are chosen out of 8 suitable ones for a study on heart disease. How many choices are possible?

69. Politics. A nominating convention will select a president and vice-president from among 4 candidates. Campaign buttons, listing a president and a vice-president, will be designed for each possible outcome before the convention. How many different kinds of buttons should be designed?

70. Politics. In how many different ways can 6 candidates for an office be listed on a ballot?

Answers to Matched Problems

1. (A) 720 (B) 10
(C) 720 (D) 20
(E) 1,140

2. (A)

12 *permutations of 4 objects taken 2 at a time*

(B) O_1: Fill first position N_1: 4 ways
O_2: Fill second position N_2: 3 ways
$4 \cdot 3 = 12$

(C) $P_{4,2} = 4 \cdot 3 = 12$; $P_{4,2} = \dfrac{4!}{(4-2)!} = 12$

3. $P_{30,4} = \dfrac{30!}{(30-4)!} = 657,720$

4. (A) $P_{12,4} = \dfrac{12!}{(12-4)!} = 11,880$ ways

(B) $C_{12,4} = \dfrac{12!}{4!(12-4)!} = 495$ ways

5. $C_{30,4} = \dfrac{30!}{4!(30-4)!} = 27,405$

6. $C_{13,3} \cdot C_{13,2} = 22,308$

7. $P_{8,3} \cdot P_{10,2} = 30,240$

8. (A) $C_{7,1} \cdot C_{5,3} = 70$

(B) $C_{5,4} = 5$

(C) $C_{7,2} \cdot C_{5,2} + C_{7,1} \cdot C_{5,3} + C_{5,4} = 285$

9. $4C_{13,5} = 5,148$

Chapter 7   Review

Important Terms, Symbols, and Concepts

7-1 Logic

- A **proposition** is a statement (not a question or command) that is either true or false.

- If p and q are propositions, then the compound propositions,

  Ex. 1, p. 337

$$\neg p, p \vee q, p \wedge q, \text{ and } p \rightarrow q$$

  can be formed using the negation symbol $\neg$ and the connectives $\vee$, $\wedge$, and $\rightarrow$. These propositions are called **not p, p or q, p and q**, and **if p then q**, respectively (or **negation, disjunction, conjunction**, and **conditional**, respectively). Each of these compound propositions is specified by a truth table (see pages 335–336).

- Given any conditional proposition $p \rightarrow q$, the proposition $q \rightarrow p$ is called the **converse** of $p \rightarrow q$, and the   Ex. 2, p. 337
  proposition $\neg q \rightarrow \neg p$, is called the **contrapositive** of $p \rightarrow q$.

- A **truth table** for a compound proposition specifies whether it is true or false for any assignment of truth   Ex. 3, p. 338
  values to its variables. A proposition is a **tautology** if each entry in its column of the truth table is T; a   Ex. 4, p. 338
  contradiction if each entry is F, and a **contingency** if at least one entry is T and at least one entry is F.   Ex. 5, p. 339

- Consider the rows of the truth tables for the compound propositions P and Q. If whenever P is true, Q is   Ex. 6, p. 340
  also true, we say that P **logically implies** Q and write $P \Rightarrow Q$. We call $P \Rightarrow Q$ a **logical implication**. If the com-   Ex. 7, p. 341
  pound propositions P and Q have identical truth tables, we say that P and Q are **logically equivalent** and write
  $P \equiv Q$. We call $P \equiv Q$ a **logical equivalence**.

- Several logical equivalences are given in Table 2 on page 340. The last of these implies that **any conditional proposition is logically equivalent to its contrapositive.**

7-2 Sets

- A **set** is a collection of objects specified in such a way that we can tell whether any given object is or is not in the collection.

- Each object in a set is called a **member**, or **element**, of the set. If a is an element of the set A, we write $a \in A$.

- A set without any elements is called the **empty**, or **null**, set, denoted by $\varnothing$.

- A set can be described by listing its elements, or by giving a rule that determines the elements of the set. If   Ex. 1, p. 343
  $P(x)$ is a statement about x, then $\{x \,|\, P(x)\}$ denotes the set of all x such that $P(x)$ is true.

- A set is **finite** if its elements can be counted and there is an end; a set such as the positive integers, in which there is no end in counting its elements, is **infinite**.

- We write $A \subset B$, and say that A is a **subset** of B, if each element of A is an element of B. We write $A = B$,   Ex. 2, p. 344
  and say that sets A and B are equal, if they have exactly the same elements. The empty set $\varnothing$ is a subset of   Ex. 3, p. 344
  every set.

- If A and B are sets, then   Ex. 4, p. 345

$$A \cup B = \{x \,|\, x \in A \text{ or } x \in B\}$$

  is called the **union** of A and B, and

$$A \cap B = \{x \,|\, x \in A \text{ and } x \in B\}$$

  is called the **intersection** of A and B.

- **Venn diagrams** are useful in visualizing set relationships.   Ex. 5, p. 346

- If $A \cap B = \varnothing$, the sets A and B are said to be **disjoint**.

- The set of all elements under consideration in a given discussion is called the **universal set** U. The set
  $A' = \{x \in U \,|\, x \notin A\}$ is called the **complement** of A (relative to U).

7-3 Basic Counting Principles

- If A and B are sets, then the number of elements in the union of A and B is given by the **addition principle** for counting (Theorem 1, page 349).

Ex. 1, p. 349
Ex. 2, p. 350

- If the elements of a set are determined by a sequence of operations, tree diagrams can be used to list all combined outcomes. To count the number of combined outcomes without using a tree diagram, use the **multiplication principle** for counting (Theorem 2, page 352).

Ex. 3, p. 351
Ex. 4, p. 352
Ex. 5, p. 352

7-4 Permutations and Combinations

- The product of the first n natural numbers, denoted $n!$, is called n **factorial**:

Ex. 1, p. 357

$$n! = n(n - 1)(n - 2) \cdot \cdots \cdot 2 \cdot 1$$
$$0! = 1$$
$$n! = n \cdot (n - 1)!$$

- A **permutation** of a set of distinct objects is an arrangement of the objects in a specific order without repetition. The number of permutations of a set of n distinct objects is given by $P_{n,n} = n!$. A permutation of a set of n distinct objects taken r at a time without repetition is an arrangement of r of the n objects in a specific order. The number of permutations of n distinct objects taken r at a time without repetition is given by

Ex. 2, p. 359
Ex. 3, p. 359

$$P_{n,r} = \frac{n!}{(n - r)!} \qquad 0 \le r \le n$$

- A **combination** of a set of n distinct objects taken r at a time without repetition is an r-element subset of the set of n objects. The arrangement of the elements in the subset is irrelevant. The number of combinations of n distinct objects taken r at a time without repetition is given by

Ex. 4, p. 361
Ex. 5, p. 362
Ex. 6, p. 363
Ex. 7, p. 363
Ex. 8, p. 364

$$C_{n,r} = \binom{n}{r} = \frac{P_{n,r}}{r!} = \frac{n!}{r!(n - r)!} \qquad 0 \le r \le n$$

Review Exercises

Work through all the problems in this chapter review and check your answers in the back of the book. Answers to all problems are there along with section numbers in italics to indicate where each type of problem is discussed. Where weaknesses show up, review appropriate sections in the text.

A

In Problems 1–6, express each proposition in an English sentence and determine whether it is true or false, where p and q are the propositions

$$p: \text{ "}2^3 < 3^2\text{"} \qquad q: \text{ "}3^4 < 4^3\text{"}$$

1. $\neg q$

2. $p \vee q$

3. $p \wedge q$

4. $p \to q$

5. The converse of $p \to q$

6. The contrapositive of $p \to q$

In Problems 7–10, indicate true (T) or false (F).

7. $\{5, 6, 7\} = \{6, 7, 5\}$

8. $5 \in \{55, 555\}$

9. $\{9, 27\} \subset \{3, 9, 27, 81\}$

10. $\{1, 2\} \subset \{1, \{1, 2\}\}$

In Problems 11–14, describe each proposition as a negation, disjunction, conjunction, or conditional, and determine whether the proposition is true or false.

11. If 9 is prime, then 10 is odd.

12. 7 is even or 8 is odd.

13. 53 is prime and 57 is prime.

14. 51 is not prime.

In Problems 15–16, state the converse and the contrapositive of the given proposition.

15. If the square matrix A has a row of zeros, then the square matrix A has no inverse.

16. If the square matrix A is an identity matrix, then the square matrix A has an inverse.

In Problems 17–19, write the resulting set using the listing method.

17. $\{1, 2, 3, 4\} \cup \{2, 3, 4, 5\}$

18. $\{1, 2, 3, 4\} \cap \{2, 3, 4, 5\}$

19. $\{1, 2, 3, 4\} \cap \{5, 6\}$

20. A single die is rolled, and a coin is flipped. How many combined outcomes are possible? Solve:

(A) Using a tree diagram

(B) Using the multiplication principle

21. Use the Venn diagram to find the number of elements in each of the following sets:

(A) A (B) B

(C) $A \cap B$ (D) $A \cup B$

(E) U (F) A'

(G) $(A \cap B)'$ (H) $(A \cup B)'$

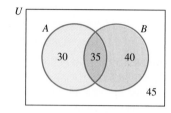

Evaluate the expressions in Problems 22–28.

22. $11!$ **23.** $(10 - 6)!$

24. $10! - 6!$ **25.** $\dfrac{15!}{10!}$

26. $\dfrac{15!}{10!5!}$ **27.** $C_{8,5}$

28. $P_{8,5}$

29. How many seating arrangements are possible with 6 people and 6 chairs in a row? Solve using the multiplication principle.

30. Solve Problem 29 using permutations or combinations, whichever is applicable.

B

In Problems 31–36, construct a truth table for the proposition and determine whether the proposition is a contingency, tautology, or contradiction.

31. $(p \to q) \land (q \to p)$

32. $p \lor (q \to p)$

33. $(p \lor \neg p) \to (q \land \neg q)$

34. $\neg q \land (p \to q)$

35. $\neg p \to (p \to q)$

36. $\neg(p \lor \neg q)$

In Problems 37–40, determine whether the given set is finite or infinite. Consider the set Z of integers to be the universal set, and let

$$M = \{n \in Z \mid n < 10^6\}$$
$$K = \{n \in Z \mid n > 10^3\}$$
$$E = \{n \in Z \mid n \text{ is even}\}$$

37. $E \cup K$ **38.** $M \cap K$

39. K' **40.** $E \cap M$

In Problems 41–43, determine whether or not the given sets are disjoint. For the definitions of M, K, and E, refer to the instructions for Problems 37–40.

41. M' and K'

42. M and E'

43. K and K'

 44. A man has 5 children. Each of those children has 3 children, who in turn each have 2 children. Discuss the number of descendants that the man has.

45. How many 3-letter code words are possible using the first 8 letters of the alphabet if no letter can be repeated? If letters can be repeated? If adjacent letters cannot be alike?

46. Solve the following problems using $P_{n,r}$ or $C_{n,r}$:

(A) How many 3-digit opening combinations are possible on a combination lock with 6 digits if the digits cannot be repeated?

(B) Five tennis players have made the finals. If each of the 5 players is to play every other player exactly once, how many games must be scheduled?

 47. Use graphical techniques on a graphing calculator to find the largest value of $C_{n,r}$ when $n = 25$.

48. If 3 operations O_1, O_2, O_3 are performed in order, with possible number of outcomes N_1, N_2, N_3, respectively, determine the number of branches in the corresponding tree diagram.

In Problems 49–51, write the resulting set using the listing method.

49. $\{x \mid x^3 - x = 0\}$

50. $\{x \mid x \text{ is a positive integer and } x! < 100\}$

51. $\{x \mid x \text{ is a positive integer that is a perfect square and } x < 50\}$

C

52. A software development department consists of 6 women and 4 men.

(A) How many ways can the department select a chief programmer, a backup programmer, and a programming librarian?

(B) How many of the selections in part (A) consist entirely of women?

(C) How many ways can the department select a team of 3 programmers to work on a particular project?

53. A group of 150 people includes 52 who play chess, 93 who play checkers, and 28 who play both chess and checkers. How many people in the group play neither game?

Problems 54 and 55 refer to the following Venn diagram.

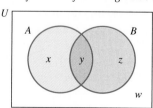

54. Which of the numbers x, y, z, or w must equal 0 if $A \subset B$?

55. Which of the numbers x, y, z, or w must equal 0 if $A \cap B = U$?

In Problems 56–58, discuss the validity of each statement. If the statement is true, explain why. If not, give a counterexample.

56. If n and r are positive integers and $1 < r < n$, then $C_{n,r} < P_{n,r}$.

57. If n and r are positive integers and $1 < r < n$, then $P_{n,r} < n!$.

58. If n and r are positive integers and $1 < r < n$, then $C_{n,r} < n!$.

In Problems 59–64, construct a truth table to verify the implication or equivalence.

59. $p \wedge q \Rightarrow p$

60. $q \Rightarrow p \rightarrow q$

61. $\neg p \rightarrow (q \wedge \neg q) \equiv p$

62. $p \vee q \equiv \neg p \rightarrow q$

63. $p \wedge (p \rightarrow q) \Rightarrow q$

64. $\neg(p \wedge \neg q) \equiv p \rightarrow q$

65. How many different 5-child families are possible where the gender of the children in the order of their births is taken into consideration [that is, birth sequences such as (B, G, G, B, B) and (G, B, G, B, B) produce different families]? How many families are possible if the order pattern is not taken into account?

66. Can a selection of r objects from a set of n distinct objects, where n is a positive integer, be a combination and a permutation simultaneously? Explain.

Applications

67. Transportation. A distribution center A wishes to send its products to five different retail stores: B, C, D, E, and F. How many different route plans can be constructed so that a single truck, starting from A, will deliver to each store exactly once, and then return to the center?

68. Market research. A survey of 1,000 people indicates that 340 have invested in stocks, 480 have invested in bonds, and 210 have invested in stocks and bonds.

(A) How many people in the survey have invested in stocks or bonds?

(B) How many have invested in neither stocks nor bonds?

(C) How many have invested in bonds and not stocks?

69. Medical research. In a study of twins, a sample of 6 pairs of identical twins will be selected for medical tests from a group of 40 pairs of identical twins. In how many ways can this be done?

70. Elections. In an unusual recall election, there are 67 candidates to replace the governor of a state. To negate the advantage that might accrue to candidates whose names appear near the top of the ballot, it is proposed that equal numbers of ballots be printed for each possible order in which the candidates' names can be listed.

(A) In how many ways can the candidates' names be listed?

(B) Explain why the proposal is not feasible, and discuss possible alternatives.

Probability

8

Introduction

Like other branches of mathematics, probability evolved out of practical considerations. Girolamo Cardano (1501–1576), a gambler and physician, produced some of the best mathematics of his time, including a systematic analysis of gambling problems. In 1654, another gambler, Chevalier de Méré, approached the well-known French philosopher and mathematician Blaise Pascal (1623–1662) regarding certain dice problems. Pascal became interested in these problems, studied them, and discussed them with Pierre de Fermat (1601–1665), another French mathematician. So out of the gaming rooms of western Europe, the study of probability was born.

Despite this lowly birth, probability has matured into a highly respected and immensely useful branch of mathematics. It is used in practically every field. In this chapter, we use the counting techniques developed in Chapter 7 to assign probabilities to events. Then we consider many situations in which probability is used to measure and manage risk (see, for instance, Example 5 in Section 8-5 on decision making related to insurance).

8-1 Sample Spaces, Events, and Probability

This section provides a brief and relatively informal introduction to probability. It assumes a familiarity with the basics of set theory as presented in Chapter 7, including the union, intersection, and complement of sets, as well as various techniques for counting the number of elements in a set. Probability studies involve many subtle ideas, and care must be taken at the beginning to understand the fundamental concepts.

Experiments

Our first step in constructing a mathematical model for probability studies is to describe the type of experiments on which probability studies are based. Some experiments do not yield the same results each time that they are performed, no matter how carefully they are repeated under the same conditions. These experiments are called **random experiments**. Familiar examples of random experiments are flipping coins, rolling dice, observing the frequency of defective items from an assembly line, or observing the frequency of deaths in a certain age group.

Probability theory is a branch of mathematics that has been developed to deal with outcomes of random experiments, both real and conceptual. In the work that follows, we simply use the word **experiment** to mean a random experiment.

Figure 1

Sample Spaces and Events

Associated with outcomes of experiments are *sample spaces* and *events*. Our second step in constructing a mathematical model for probability studies is to define these two terms.

Consider the experiment, "A wheel with 18 numbers on the perimeter (Fig. 1) spins and comes to rest so that a pointer points within a numbered sector."

What outcomes might we observe? When the wheel stops, we might be interested in which number is next to the pointer, or whether that number is an odd number, or whether that number is divisible by 5, or whether that number is prime, or whether the pointer is in a shaded or white sector, and so on. The list of possible outcomes appears endless. In general, there is no unique method of analyzing all possible outcomes of an experiment. Therefore, before conducting an experiment, it is important to decide just what outcomes are of interest.

Suppose we limit our interest to the set of numbers on the wheel and to various subsets of these numbers, such as the set of prime numbers or the set of odd numbers on the wheel. Having decided what to observe, we make a list of outcomes of the experiment, called *simple outcomes* or *simple events*, such that in each trial of the experiment (each spin of the wheel), one and only one of the outcomes on the list will occur. For our stated interests, we choose each number on the wheel as a simple event and form the set

$$S = \{1, 2, 3, \ldots, 17, 18\}$$

The set of simple events S for the experiment is called a *sample space* for the experiment.

Now consider the outcome, "When the wheel comes to rest, the number next to the pointer is divisible by 4." This outcome is not a simple outcome (or simple event) since it is not associated with one and only one element in the sample space S. The outcome will occur whenever any one of the simple events 4, 8, 12, or 16 occurs, that is, whenever an element in the subset

$$E = \{4, 8, 12, 16\}$$

occurs. Subset E is called a *compound event* (and the outcome, a *compound outcome*).

DEFINITION Sample Spaces and Events

If we formulate a set S of outcomes (events) of an experiment in such a way that in each trial of the experiment one and only one of the outcomes (events) in the set will occur, we call the set S a **sample space** for the experiment. Each element in S is called a **simple outcome**, or **simple event**.

An **event** E is defined to be any subset of S (including the empty set $\varnothing$ and the sample space S). Event E is a **simple event** if it contains only one element and a **compound event** if it contains more than one element. We say that **an event E occurs** if any of the simple events in E occurs.

We use the terms *event* and *outcome of an experiment* interchangeably. Technically, an event is the mathematical counterpart of an outcome of an experiment, but we will not insist on strict adherence to this distinction in our development of probability.

Real World	Mathematical Model
Experiment (real or conceptual)	Sample space (set S)
Outcome (simple or compound)	Event (subset of S; simple or compound)

EXAMPLE 1 **Simple and Compound Events** Relative to the number wheel experiment (Fig. 1) and the sample space

$$S = \{1, 2, 3, \ldots, 17, 18\}$$

what is the event E (subset of the sample space S) that corresponds to each of the following outcomes? Indicate whether the event is a simple event or a compound event.

(A) The outcome is a prime number.   (B) The outcome is the square of 4.

SOLUTION (A) The outcome is a prime number if any of the simple events 2, 3, 5, 7, 11, 13, or 17 occurs.* To say "A prime number occurs" is the same as saying that the experiment has an outcome in the set

$$E = \{2, 3, 5, 7, 11, 13, 17\}$$

Since event E has more than one element, it is a compound event.

(B) The outcome is the square of 4 if 16 occurs. To say "The square of 4 occurs" is the same as saying that the experiment has an outcome in the set

$$E = \{16\}$$

Since E has only one element, it is a simple event.

Matched Problem 1 Repeat Example 1 for

(A) The outcome is a number divisible by 12.

(B) The outcome is an even number greater than 15.

---

*Technically, we should write {2}, {3}, {5}, {7}, {11}, {13}, and {17} for the simple events since there is a logical distinction between an element of a set and a subset consisting of only that element. But we will keep this in mind and drop the braces for simple events to simplify the notation.

EXAMPLE 2

Sample Spaces A nickel and a dime are tossed. How do we identify a sample space for this experiment? There are a number of possibilities, depending on our interest. We will consider three.

(A) If we are interested in whether each coin falls heads (H) or tails (T), then, using a tree diagram, we can easily determine an appropriate sample space for the experiment:

$$S_1 = \{HH, HT, TH, TT\}$$

and there are 4 simple events in the sample space.

(B) If we are interested only in the number of heads that appear on a single toss of the two coins, we can let

$$S_2 = \{0, 1, 2\}$$

and there are 3 simple events in the sample space.

(C) If we are interested in whether the coins match (*M*) or do not match (*D*), we can let

$$S_3 = \{M, D\}$$

and there are only 2 simple events in the sample space.

CONCEPTUAL INSIGHT

There is no single correct sample space for a given experiment. When specifying a sample space for an experiment, we include as much detail as necessary to answer all questions of interest regarding the outcomes of the experiment. If in doubt, we choose a sample space that contains more elements rather than fewer.

In Example 2, which sample space would be appropriate for all three interests? Sample space S_1 contains more information than either S_2 or S_3. If we know which outcome has occurred in S_1, then we know which outcome has occurred in S_2 and S_3. However, the reverse is not true. (Note that the simple events in S_2 and S_3 are compound events in S_1.) In this sense, we say that S_1 is a more **fundamental sample space** than either S_2 or S_3. Thus, we would choose S_1 as an appropriate sample space for all three expressed interests.

Matched Problem 2

An experiment consists of recording the boy–girl composition of a two-child family. What would be an appropriate sample space.

(A) If we are interested in the genders of the children in the order of their births? Draw a tree diagram.

(B) If we are interested only in the number of girls in a family?

(C) If we are interested only in whether the genders are alike (*A*) or different (*D*)?

(D) For all three interests expressed in parts (*A*) to (*C*)?

EXAMPLE 3

Sample Spaces and Events Consider an experiment of rolling two dice. Figure 2 shows a convenient sample space that will enable us to answer many questions about interesting events. Let *S* be the set of all ordered pairs in the figure. The simple event (3, 2) is distinguished from the simple event (2, 3). The former indicates that a 3 turned up on the first die and a 2 on the second, while the latter indicates that a 2 turned up on the first die and a 3 on the second.

Second Die

	⚀	⚁	⚂	⚃	⚄	⚅
⚀	(1, 1)	(1, 2)	(1, 3)	(1, 4)	(1, 5)	(1, 6)
⚁	(2, 1)	(2, 2)	(2, 3)	(2, 4)	(2, 5)	(2, 6)
⚂	(3, 1)	(3, 2)	(3, 3)	(3, 4)	(3, 5)	(3, 6)
⚃	(4, 1)	(4, 2)	(4, 3)	(4, 4)	(4, 5)	(4, 6)
⚄	(5, 1)	(5, 2)	(5, 3)	(5, 4)	(5, 5)	(5, 6)
⚅	(6, 1)	(6, 2)	(6, 3)	(6, 4)	(6, 5)	(6, 6)

First Die

Figure 2

What is the event (subset of the sample space S) that corresponds to each of the following outcomes?

(A) A sum of 7 turns up.   (B) A sum of 11 turns up.

(C) A sum less than 4 turns up.   (D) A sum of 12 turns up.

SOLUTION   (A) By "A sum of 7 turns up," we mean that the sum of all dots on both turned-up faces is 7. This outcome corresponds to the event

$$\{(6, 1), (5, 2), (4, 3), (3, 4), (2, 5), (1, 6)\}$$

(B) "A sum of 11 turns up" corresponds to the event

$$\{(6, 5), (5, 6)\}$$

(C) "A sum less than 4 turns up" corresponds to the event

$$\{(1, 1), (2, 1), (1, 2)\}$$

(D) "A sum of 12 turns up" corresponds to the event

$$\{(6, 6)\}$$

Matched Problem 3   Refer to the sample space shown in Figure 2. What is the event that corresponds to each of the following outcomes?

(A) A sum of 5 turns up.

(B) A sum that is a prime number greater than 7 turns up.

As indicated earlier, we often use the terms *event* and *outcome of an experiment* interchangeably. In Example 3, we might say "the event, 'A sum of 11 turns up'" in place of "the outcome, 'A sum of 11 turns up,'" or even write

$$E = \text{a sum of 11 turns up} = \{(6, 5), (5, 6)\}$$

Probability of an Event

The next step in developing our mathematical model for probability studies is the introduction of a *probability function*. This is a function that assigns to an arbitrary event associated with a sample space a real number between 0 and 1, inclusive. We start by discussing ways in which probabilities are assigned to simple events in the sample space S.

DEFINITION Probabilities for Simple Events

Given a sample space

$$S = \{e_1, e_2, \ldots, e_n\}$$

with n simple events, to each simple event e_i we assign a real number, denoted by $P(e_i)$, called the **probability of the event** e_i. These numbers can be assigned in an arbitrary manner as long as the following two conditions are satisfied:

Condition 1. The probability of a simple event is a number between 0 and 1, inclusive. That is,

$$0 \le P(e_i) \le 1$$

Condition 2. The sum of the probabilities of all simple events in the sample space is 1. That is,

$$P(e_1) + P(e_2) + \cdots + P(e_n) = 1$$

Any probability assignment that satisfies Conditions 1 and 2 is said to be an **acceptable probability assignment**.

Our mathematical theory does not explain how acceptable probabilities are assigned to simple events. These assignments are generally based on the expected or actual percentage of times that a simple event occurs when an experiment is repeated a large number of times. Assignments based on this principle are called **reasonable**.

Let an experiment be the flipping of a single coin, and let us choose a sample space S to be

$$S = \{H, T\}$$

If a coin appears to be fair, we are inclined to assign probabilities to the simple events in S as follows:

$$P(H) = \tfrac{1}{2} \qquad \text{and} \qquad P(T) = \tfrac{1}{2}$$

These assignments are based on reasoning that, since there are 2 ways a coin can land, in the long run, a head will turn up half the time and a tail will turn up half the time. These probability assignments are acceptable since both conditions for acceptable probability assignments stated in the preceding box are satisfied:

1. $0 \le P(H) \le 1, \qquad 0 \le P(T) \le 1$

2. $P(H) + P(T) = \tfrac{1}{2} + \tfrac{1}{2} = 1$

If we were to flip a coin 1,000 times, we would expect a head to turn up approximately, but not exactly, 500 times. The random number feature on a graphing calculator can be used to simulate 1,000 flips of a coin. Figure 3 shows the results of 3 such simulations: 497 heads the first time, 495 heads the second, and 504 heads the third.

If, however, we get only 376 heads in 1,000 flips of a coin, we might suspect that the coin is not fair. Then we might assign the simple events in the sample space S the following probabilities, based on our experimental results:

$$P(H) = .376 \qquad \text{and} \qquad P(T) = .624$$

This is also an acceptable assignment. However, the probability assignment

$$P(H) = 1 \qquad \text{and} \qquad P(T) = 0$$

although acceptable, is not reasonable (unless the coin has 2 heads). And the assignment

$$P(H) = .6 \qquad \text{and} \qquad P(T) = .8$$

```
randBin(1000,.5,
3)
        {497 495 504}
```

Figure 3

is not acceptable, since .6 + .8 = 1.4, which violates Condition 2 in the box on page 377.*

It is important to keep in mind that out of the infinitely many possible acceptable probability assignments to simple events in a sample space, we are generally inclined to choose one assignment over another based on reasoning or experimental results.

Given an acceptable probability assignment for simple events in a sample space S, how do we define the probability of an arbitrary event E associated with S?

DEFINITION Probability of an Event E

Given an acceptable probability assignment for the simple events in a sample space S, we define the **probability of an arbitrary event E**, denoted by $P(E)$, as follows:

(A) If E is the empty set, then $P(E) = 0$.

(B) If E is a simple event, then $P(E)$ has already been assigned.

(C) If E is a compound event, then $P(E)$ is the sum of the probabilities of all the simple events in E.

(D) If E is the sample space S, then $P(E) = P(S) = 1$ [this is a special case of part (C)].

EXAMPLE 4   **Probabilities of Events** Let us return to Example 2, the tossing of a nickel and a dime, and the sample space

$$S = \{HH, HT, TH, TT\}$$

Since there are 4 simple outcomes and the coins are assumed to be fair, it would appear that each outcome would occur 25% of the time, in the long run. Let us assign the same probability of $\frac{1}{4}$ to each simple event in S:

Simple Event				
e_i	**HH**	**HT**	**TH**	**TT**
$P(e_i)$	$\frac{1}{4}$	$\frac{1}{4}$	$\frac{1}{4}$	$\frac{1}{4}$

This is an acceptable assignment according to Conditions 1 and 2, and it is a reasonable assignment for ideal (perfectly balanced) coins or coins close to ideal.

(A) What is the probability of getting 1 head (and 1 tail)?

(B) What is the probability of getting at least 1 head?

(C) What is the probability of getting at least 1 head or at least 1 tail?

(D) What is the probability of getting 3 heads?

SOLUTION   (A) E_1 = getting 1 head = $\{HT, TH\}$

Since E_1 is a compound event, we use part (C) in the box and find $P(E_1)$ by adding the probabilities of the simple events in E_1:

$$P(E_1) = P(HT) + P(TH) = \tfrac{1}{4} + \tfrac{1}{4} = \tfrac{1}{2}$$

(B) E_2 = getting at least 1 head = $\{HH, HT, TH\}$

$$P(E_2) = P(HH) + P(HT) + P(TH) = \tfrac{1}{4} + \tfrac{1}{4} + \tfrac{1}{4} = \tfrac{3}{4}$$

(C) $E_3 = \{HH, HT, TH, TT\} = S$

$$P(E_3) = P(S) = 1 \qquad \tfrac{1}{4} + \tfrac{1}{4} + \tfrac{1}{4} + \tfrac{1}{4} = 1$$

(D) E_4 = getting 3 heads = $\varnothing$ *Empty set*

$$P(\varnothing) = 0$$

---

*In probability studies, the 0 to the left of the decimal is usually omitted. So we write .6 and .8 instead of 0.6 and 0.8.

> **PROCEDURE Steps for Finding the Probability of an Event E**
>
> **Step 1** Set up an appropriate sample space S for the experiment.
>
> **Step 2** Assign acceptable probabilities to the simple events in S.
>
> **Step 3** To obtain the probability of an arbitrary event E, add the probabilities of the simple events in E.

The function P defined in Steps 2 and 3 is a **probability function** whose domain is all possible events (subsets) in the sample space S and whose range is a set of real numbers between 0 and 1, inclusive.

Matched Problem 4   Suppose in Example 4 that after flipping the nickel and dime 1,000 times, we find that HH turns up 273 times, HT turns up 206 times, TH turns up 312 times, and TT turns up 209 times. On the basis of this evidence, we assign probabilities to the simple events in S as follows:

Simple Event				
e_i	HH	HT	TH	TT
$P(e_i)$	.273	.206	.312	.209

This is an acceptable and reasonable probability assignment for the simple events in S. What are the probabilities of the following events?

(A) $E_1 =$ getting at least 1 tail

(B) $E_2 =$ getting 2 tails

(C) $E_3 =$ getting at least 1 head or at least 1 tail

Example 4 and Matched Problem 4 illustrate two important ways in which acceptable and reasonable probability assignments are made for simple events in a sample space S. Each approach has its advantage in certain situations:

1. *Theoretical Approach.* We use assumptions and a deductive reasoning process to assign probabilities to simple events. No experiments are actually conducted. This is what we did in Example 4.

2. *Empirical Approach.* We assign probabilities to simple events based on the results of actual experiments. This is what we did in Matched Problem 4.

Empirical probability concepts are stated more precisely as follows: If we conduct an experiment n times and event E occurs with **frequency $f(E)$**, then the ratio $f(E)/n$ is called the **relative frequency** of the occurrence of event E in n trials. We define the **empirical probability** of E, denoted by $P(E)$, by the number (if it exists) that the relative frequency $f(E)/n$ approaches as n gets larger and larger. Therefore,

$$P(E) \approx \frac{\text{frequency of occurrence of } E}{\text{total number of trials}} = \frac{f(E)}{n}$$

For any particular n, the relative frequency $f(E)/n$ is also called the **approximate empirical probability** of event E.

For most of this section, we emphasize the theoretical approach. In the next section, we return to the empirical approach.

Equally Likely Assumption

In tossing a nickel and a dime (Example 4), we assigned the same probability, $\frac{1}{4}$, to each simple event in the sample space $S = \{HH, HT, TH, TT\}$. By assigning the same probability to each simple event in S, we are actually making the assumption that each simple event is as likely to occur as any other. We refer to this as an **equally likely assumption**. If, in a sample space

$$S = \{e_1, e_2, \ldots, e_n\}$$

with n elements, we assume that each simple event e_i is as likely to occur as any other, then we assign the probability $1/n$ to each. That is,

$$P(e_i) = \frac{1}{n}$$

Under an equally likely assumption, we can develop a very useful formula for finding probabilities of arbitrary events associated with a sample space S. Consider the following example:

If a single die is rolled and we assume that each face is as likely to come up as any other, then for the sample space

$$S = \{1, 2, 3, 4, 5, 6\}$$

we assign a probability of $\frac{1}{6}$ to each simple event since there are 6 simple events. The probability of

$$E = \text{rolling a prime number} = \{2, 3, 5\}$$

is

Number of elements in E
↓

$$P(E) = P(2) + P(3) + P(5) = \tfrac{1}{6} + \tfrac{1}{6} + \tfrac{1}{6} = \tfrac{3}{6} = \tfrac{1}{2}$$

↑
Number of elements in S

Under the assumption that each simple event is as likely to occur as any other, the computation of the probability of the occurrence of any event E in a sample space S is the number of elements in E divided by the number of elements in S.

THEOREM 1 Probability of an Arbitrary Event under an Equally Likely Assumption

If we assume that each simple event in sample space S is as likely to occur as any other, then the probability of an arbitrary event E in S is given by

$$P(E) = \frac{\text{number of elements in } E}{\text{number of elements in } S} = \frac{n(E)}{n(S)}$$

EXAMPLE 5 **Probabilities and Equally Likely Assumptions** Let us again consider rolling two dice, and assume that each simple event in the sample space shown in Figure 2 (page 376) is as likely as any other. Find the probabilities of the following events:

(A) E_1 = a sum of 7 turns up

(B) E_2 = a sum of 11 turns up

(C) E_3 = a sum less than 4 turns up

(D) E_4 = a sum of 12 turns up

SOLUTION Referring to Figure 2 (page 376) and the results found in Example 3, we find

(A) $P(E_1) = \dfrac{n(E_1)}{n(S)} = \dfrac{6}{36} = \dfrac{1}{6}$ $E_1 = \{(6, 1), (5, 2), (4, 3), (3, 4), (2, 5), (1, 6)\}$

(B) $P(E_2) = \dfrac{n(E_2)}{n(S)} = \dfrac{2}{36} = \dfrac{1}{18}$ $E_2 = \{(6, 5), (5, 6)\}$

(C) $P(E_3) = \dfrac{n(E_3)}{n(S)} = \dfrac{3}{36} = \dfrac{1}{12}$ $E_3 = \{(1, 1), (2, 1), (1, 2)\}$

(D) $P(E_4) = \dfrac{n(E_4)}{n(S)} = \dfrac{1}{36}$ $E_4 = \{(6, 6)\}$

Matched Problem 5   Under the conditions in Example 5, find the probabilities of the following events (each event refers to the sum of the dots facing up on both dice):

(A) E_5 = a sum of 5 turns up

(B) E_6 = a sum that is a prime number greater than 7 turns up

EXAMPLE 6   **Simulation and Empirical Probabilities** Use output from the random number feature of a graphing calculator to simulate 100 rolls of two dice. Determine the empirical probabilities of the following events, and compare with the theoretical probabilities:

(A) E_1 = a sum of 7 turns up

(B) E_2 = a sum of 11 turns up

SOLUTION   A graphing calculator can be used to select a random integer from 1 to 6. Each of the six integers in the given range is equally likely to be selected. Therefore, by selecting a random integer from 1 to 6 and adding it to a second random integer from 1 to 6, we simulate rolling two dice and recording the sum (see the first command in Figure 4A). The second command in Figure 4A simulates 100 rolls of two dice; the sums are stored in list L_1. From the statistical plot of L_1 in Figure 4B we obtain the empirical probabilities.*

(A) The empirical probability of E_1 is $\frac{15}{100}$ = .15; the theoretical probability of E_1 (see Example 5A) is $\frac{6}{36}$ = .167.

(B) The empirical probability of E_2 is $\frac{6}{100}$ = .06; the theoretical probability of E_2 (see Example 5B) is $\frac{2}{36}$ = .056.

(A)   (B)

Figure 4

Matched Problem 6   Use the graphing calculator output in Figure 4B to determine the empirical probabilities of the following events, and compare with the theoretical probabilities:

(A) E_3 = a sum less than 4 turns up   (B) E_4 = a sum of 12 turns up

EXPLORE & DISCUSS 1   A shipment box contains 12 graphing calculators, out of which 2 are defective. A calculator is drawn at random from the box and then, without replacement, a second calculator is drawn. Discuss whether the equally likely assumption would be appropriate for the sample space $S = \{GG, GD, DG, DD\}$, where G is a good calculator and D is a defective one.

---

*If you simulate this experiment on your graphing calculator, you should not expect to get the same empirical probabilities.

We now turn to some examples that make use of the counting techniques developed in Chapter 7.

EXAMPLE 7 **Probability and Equally Likely Assumption** In drawing 5 cards from a 52-card deck without replacement, what is the probability of getting 5 spades?

SOLUTION Let the sample space S be the set of all 5-card hands from a 52-card deck. Since the order in a hand does not matter, $n(S) = C_{52,5}$. Let event E be the set of all 5-card hands from 13 spades. Again, the order does not matter and $n(E) = C_{13,5}$. Assuming that each 5-card hand is as likely as any other,

$$P(E) = \frac{n(E)}{n(S)} = \frac{C_{13,5}}{C_{52,5}} = \frac{1{,}287}{2{,}598{,}960} \approx .0005$$

Matched Problem 7 In drawing 7 cards from a 52-card deck without replacement, what is the probability of getting 7 hearts?

EXAMPLE 8 **Probability and Equally Likely Assumption** The board of regents of a university is made up of 12 men and 16 women. If a committee of 6 is chosen at random, what is the probability that it will contain 3 men and 3 women?

SOLUTION Let S be the set of all 6-person committees out of 28 people. Then

$$n(S) = C_{28,6}$$

Let E be the set of all 6-person committees with 3 men and 3 women. To find $n(E)$, we use the multiplication principle and the following two operations:

O_1: Select 3 men out of the 12 available N_1: $C_{12,3}$

O_2: Select 3 women out of the 16 available N_2: $C_{16,3}$

Therefore,

$$n(E) = N_1 \cdot N_2 = C_{12,3} \cdot C_{16,3}$$

and

$$P(E) = \frac{n(E)}{n(S)} = \frac{C_{12,3} \cdot C_{16,3}}{C_{28,6}} \approx .327$$

Matched Problem 8 What is the probability that the committee in Example 8 will have 4 men and 2 women?

There are many counting problems for which it is not possible to produce a simple formula that will yield the number of possible cases. In situations of this type, we often revert back to tree diagrams and counting branches.

Exercises 8-1

A

 1. How would you interpret $P(E) = 1$?

 2. How would you interpret $P(E) = 0$?

A circular spinner is divided into 12 sectors of equal area: 5 red sectors, 4 blue, 2 yellow, and 1 green. In Problems 3–10, consider the experiment of spinning the spinner once. Find the probability that the spinner lands on:

3. Blue

4. Yellow

5. Yellow or green

6. Red or blue

7. Orange

8. Yellow, red, or green

9. Blue, red, yellow, or green

10. Purple

Refer to the description of a standard deck of 52 cards and Figure 4 on page 363. An experiment consists of drawing 1 card from a standard 52-card deck. In Problems 11–20, what is the probability of drawing

11. A club

12. A black card

13. A heart or diamond

14. A numbered card

15. The jack of clubs

16. An ace

17. A king or spade

18. A red queen

19. A black diamond

20. A six or club

21. In a family with 2 children, excluding multiple births, what is the probability of having 2 children of the opposite gender? Assume that a girl is as likely as a boy at each birth.

22. In a family with 2 children, excluding multiple births, what is the probability of having 2 girls? Assume that a girl is as likely as a boy at each birth.

23. A store carries four brands of DVD players: J, G, P, and S. From past records, the manager found that the relative frequency of brand choice among customers varied. Which of the following probability assignments for a particular customer choosing a particular brand of DVD player would have to be rejected? Why?

(A) $P(J) = .15$, $P(G) = -.35$, $P(P) = .50$, $P(S) = .70$

(B) $P(J) = .32$, $P(G) = .28$, $P(P) = .24$, $P(S) = .30$

(C) $P(J) = .26$, $P(G) = .14$, $P(P) = .30$, $P(S) = .30$

24. Using the probability assignments in Problem 23C, what is the probability that a random customer will not choose brand S?

25. Using the probability assignments in Problem 23C, what is the probability that a random customer will choose brand J or brand P?

26. Using the probability assignments in Problem 23C, what is the probability that a random customer will not choose brand J or brand P?

B

27. In a family with 3 children, excluding multiple births, what is the probability of having 2 boys and 1 girl, in that order? Assume that a boy is as likely as a girl at each birth.

28. In a family with 3 children, excluding multiple births, what is the probability of having 2 boys and 1 girl, in any order? Assume that a boy is as likely as a girl at each birth.

29. A small combination lock has 3 wheels, each labeled with the 10 digits from 0 to 9. If an opening combination is a particular sequence of 3 digits with no repeats, what is the probability of a person guessing the right combination?

30. A combination lock has 5 wheels, each labeled with the 10 digits from 0 to 9. If an opening combination is a particular sequence of 5 digits with no repeats, what is the probability of a person guessing the right combination?

Refer to the description of a standard deck of 52 cards and Figure 4 on page 363. An experiment consists of dealing 5 cards from a standard 52-card deck. In Problems 31–34, what is the probability of being dealt

31. 5 black cards?

32. 5 hearts?

33. 5 face cards?

34. 5 nonface cards?

35. Twenty thousand students are enrolled at a state university. A student is selected at random, and his or her birthday (month and day, not year) is recorded. Describe an appropriate sample space for this experiment and assign acceptable probabilities to the simple events. What are your assumptions in making this assignment?

36. In a three-way race for the U.S. Senate, polls indicate that the two leading candidates are running neck-and-neck, while the third candidate is receiving half the support of either of the others. Registered voters are chosen at random and asked which of the three will get their vote. Describe an appropriate sample space for this random survey experiment and assign acceptable probabilities to the simple events.

37. Suppose that 5 thank-you notes are written and 5 envelopes are addressed. Accidentally, the notes are randomly inserted into the envelopes and mailed without checking the addresses. What is the probability that all the notes will be inserted into the correct envelopes?

38. Suppose that 6 people check their coats in a checkroom. If all claim checks are lost and the 6 coats are randomly returned, what is the probability that all the people will get their own coats back?

An experiment consists of rolling two fair dice and adding the dots on the two sides facing up. Using the sample space shown in Figure 2 (page 376) and assuming each simple event is as likely as any other, find the probability of the sum of the dots indicated in Problems 39–54.

39. Sum is 2.

40. Sum is 10.

41. Sum is 6.

42. Sum is 8.

43. Sum is less than 5.

44. Sum is greater than 8.

45. Sum is not 7 or 11.

46. Sum is not 2, 4, or 6.

47. Sum is 1.

48. Sum is 13.

49. Sum is divisible by 3.

50. Sum is divisible by 4.

51. Sum is 7 or 11 (a "natural").

52. Sum is 2, 3, or 12 ("craps").

53. Sum is divisible by 2 or 3.

54. Sum is divisible by 2 and 3.

An experiment consists of tossing three fair (not weighted) coins, except that one of the three coins has a head on both sides. Compute the probability of obtaining the indicated results in Problems 55–60.

55. 1 head

56. 2 heads

57. 3 heads

58. 0 heads

59. More than 1 head

60. More than 1 tail

In Problems 61–66, a sample space S is described. Would it be reasonable to make the equally likely assumption? Explain.

61. A single card is drawn from a standard deck. We are interested in whether or not the card drawn is a heart, so an appropriate sample space is $S = \{H, N\}$.

62. A single fair coin is tossed. We are interested in whether the coin falls heads or tails, so an appropriate sample space is $S = \{H, T\}$.

63. A single fair die is rolled. We are interested in whether or not the number rolled is even or odd, so an appropriate sample space is $S = \{E, O\}$.

64. A nickel and dime are tossed. We are interested in the number of heads that appear, so an appropriate sample space is $S = \{0, 1, 2\}$.

65. A wheel of fortune has seven sectors of equal area colored red, orange, yellow, green, blue, indigo, and violet. We are interested in the color that the pointer indicates when the wheel stops, so an appropriate sample space is $S = \{R, O, Y, G, B, I, V\}$.

66. A wheel of fortune has seven sectors of equal area colored red, orange, yellow, red, orange, yellow, and red. We are interested in the color that the pointer indicates when the wheel stops, so an appropriate sample space is $S = \{R, O, Y\}$.

67. (A) Is it possible to get 19 heads in 20 flips of a fair coin? Explain.

(B) If you flipped a coin 40 times and got 37 heads, would you suspect that the coin was unfair? Why or why not? If you suspect an unfair coin, what empirical probabilities would you assign to the simple events of the sample space?

68. (A) Is it possible to get 7 double 6's in 10 rolls of a pair of fair dice? Explain.

(B) If you rolled a pair of dice 36 times and got 11 double 6's, would you suspect that the dice were unfair? Why or why not? If you suspect loaded dice, what empirical probability would you assign to the event of rolling a double 6?

C

An experiment consists of rolling two fair (not weighted) dice and adding the dots on the two sides facing up. Each die has the number 1 on two opposite faces, the number 2 on two opposite faces, and the number 3 on two opposite faces. Compute the probability of obtaining the indicated sums in Problems 69–76.

69. 2   **70.** 3

71. 4   **72.** 5

73. 6   **74.** 7

75. An odd sum   **76.** An even sum

Refer to the description of a standard deck of 52 cards on page 363. An experiment consists of dealing 5 cards from a standard 52-card deck. In Problems 77–84, what is the probability of being dealt

77. 5 cards, each of which is either a face card or an ace?

78. 5 numbered cards (2 through 10)?

79. 4 aces?

80. Four of a kind (4 queens, 4 kings, and so on)?

81. A 10, jack, queen, king, and ace, all in the same suit?

82. A 2, 3, 4, 5, and 6, all in the same suit?

83. 2 aces and 3 queens?

84. 2 kings and 3 aces?

In Problems 85–88, several experiments are simulated using the random number feature on a graphing calculator. For example, the roll of a fair die can be simulated by selecting a random inte- ger from 1 to 6, and 50 rolls of a fair die by selecting 50 random integers from 1 to 6 (see Fig. A for Problem 85 and your user's manual).

85. From the statistical plot of the outcomes of rolling a fair die 50 times (see Fig. B), we see, for example, that the number 4 was rolled exactly 11 times.

(A)   (B)

Figure for 85

(A) What is the empirical probability that the number 6 was rolled?

(B) What is the probability that a 6 is rolled under the equally likely assumption?

(C) Use a graphing calculator to simulate 100 rolls of a fair die and determine the empirical probabilities of the six outcomes.

86. Use a graphing calculator to simulate 200 tosses of a nickel and dime, representing the outcomes HH, HT, TH, and TT by 1, 2, 3, and 4, respectively.

(A) Find the empirical probabilities of the four outcomes.

(B) What is the probability of each outcome under the equally likely assumption?

87. (A) Explain how a graphing calculator can be used to simulate 500 tosses of a coin.

(B) Carry out the simulation and find the empirical probabilities of the two outcomes.

(C) What is the probability of each outcome under the equally likely assumption?

88. From a box containing 12 balls numbered 1 through 12, one ball is drawn at random.

(A) Explain how a graphing calculator can be used to simulate 400 repetitions of this experiment.

(B) Carry out the simulation and find the empirical probability of drawing the 8 ball.

(C) What is the probability of drawing the 8 ball under the equally likely assumption?

Applications

89. Consumer testing. Twelve popular brands of beer are used in a blind taste study for consumer recognition.

(A) If 4 distinct brands are chosen at random from the 12 and if a consumer is not allowed to repeat any answers, what is the probability that all 4 brands could be identified by just guessing?

(B) If repeats are allowed in the 4 brands chosen at random from the 12 and if a consumer is allowed to repeat answers, what is the probability that all 4 brands are identified correctly by just guessing?

90. Consumer testing. Six popular brands of cola are to be used in a blind taste study for consumer recognition.

(A) If 3 distinct brands are chosen at random from the 6 and if a consumer is not allowed to repeat any answers, what is the probability that all 3 brands could be identified by just guessing?

(B) If repeats are allowed in the 3 brands chosen at random from the 6 and if a consumer is allowed to repeat answers, what is the probability that all 3 brands are identified correctly by just guessing?

91. Personnel selection. Suppose that 6 female and 5 male applicants have been successfully screened for 5 positions. If the 5 positions are filled at random from the 11 finalists, what is the probability of selecting

(A) 3 females and 2 males?

(B) 4 females and 1 male?

(C) 5 females?

(D) At least 4 females?

92. Committee selection. A 4-person grievance committee is to include employees in 2 departments, *A* and *B*, with 15 and 20 employees, respectively. If the 4 people are selected at random from the 35 employees, what is the probability of selecting

(A) 3 from *A* and 1 from *B*?

(B) 2 from *A* and 2 from *B*?

(C) All 4 from *A*?

(D) At least 3 from *A*?

93. Medicine. A laboratory technician is to be tested on identifying blood types from 8 standard classifications.

(A) If 3 distinct samples are chosen at random from the 8 types and if the technician is not allowed to repeat any answers, what is the probability that all 3 could be correctly identified by just guessing?

(B) If repeats are allowed in the 3 blood types chosen at random from the 8 and if the technician is allowed to repeat answers, what is the probability that all 3 are identified correctly by just guessing?

94. Medical research. Because of limited funds, 5 research centers are to be chosen out of 8 suitable ones for a study on heart disease. If the selection is made at random, what is the probability that 5 particular research centers will be chosen?

95. Membership selection. A town council has 11 members: 6 Democrats and 5 Republicans.

(A) If the president and vice-president are selected at random, what is the probability that both are Democrats?

(B) If a 3-person committee is selected at random, what is the probability that Republicans make up the majority?

Answers to Matched Problems

1. (A) $E = \{12\}$; simple event
   (B) $E = \{16, 18\}$; compound event

2. (A) $S_1 = \{BB, BG, GB, GG\}$;

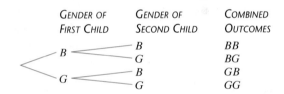

GENDER OF FIRST CHILD	GENDER OF SECOND CHILD	COMBINED OUTCOMES
B	B	BB
	G	BG
G	B	GB
	G	GG

   (B) $S_2 = \{0, 1, 2\}$ (C) $S_3 = \{A, D\}$ (D) S_1

3. (A) $\{(4, 1), (3, 2), (2, 3), (1, 4)\}$ (B) $\{(6, 5), (5, 6)\}$

4. (A) .727   (B) .209   (C) 1

5. (A) $P(E_5) = \frac{1}{9}$ (B) $P(E_6) = \frac{1}{18}$

6. (A) $\frac{9}{100} = .09$ (empirical); $\frac{3}{36} = .083$ (theoretical)
   (B) $\frac{1}{100} = .01$ (empirical); $\frac{1}{36} = .028$ (theoretical)

7. $C_{13,7}/C_{52,7} \approx 1.3 \times 10^{-5}$ 8. $C_{12,4}C_{16,2}/C_{28,6} \approx .158$

8-2   Union, Intersection, and Complement of Events; Odds

- Union and Intersection
- Complement of an Event
- Odds
- Applications to Empirical Probability

Recall from Section 8-1 that given a sample space

$$S = \{e_1, e_2, \ldots, e_n\}$$

any function P defined on S such that

$$0 \le P(e_i) \le 1 \qquad i = 1, 2, \ldots, n$$

and

$$P(e_1) + P(e_2) + \cdots + P(e_n) = 1$$

is called a *probability function*. In addition, any subset of S is called an *event E*, and the probability of E is the sum of the probabilities of the simple events in E.

Union and Intersection

Since events are subsets of a sample space, the union and intersection of events are simply the union and intersection of sets as defined in the following box. In this section, we concentrate on the union of events and consider only simple cases of intersection. The latter will be investigated in more detail in the next section.

DEFINITION Union and Intersection of Events*

If A and B are two events in a sample space S, then the **union** of A and B, denoted by $A \cup B$, and the **intersection** of A and B, denoted by $A \cap B$, are defined as follows:

$$A \cup B = \{e \in S \mid e \in A \text{ or } e \in B\} \qquad A \cap B = \{e \in S \mid e \in A \text{ and } e \in B\}$$

      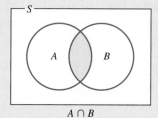

$$A \cup B \qquad\qquad\qquad A \cap B$$

Furthermore, we define

The **event A or B** to be $A \cup B$
The **event A and B** to be $A \cap B$

---

*See Section 7-2 for a discussion of set notation.

EXAMPLE 1   **Probability Involving Union and Intersection**   Consider the sample space of equally likely events for the rolling of a single fair die:

$$S = \{1, 2, 3, 4, 5, 6\}$$

(A) What is the probability of rolling a number that is odd **and** exactly divisible by 3?

(B) What is the probability of rolling a number that is odd **or** exactly divisible by 3?

SOLUTION   (A) Let A be the event of rolling an odd number, B the event of rolling a number divisible by 3, and F the event of rolling a number that is odd **and** divisible by 3. Then

$$A = \{1, 3, 5\} \qquad B = \{3, 6\} \qquad F = A \cap B = \{3\}$$

The probability of rolling a number that is odd **and** exactly divisible by 3 is

$$P(F) = P(A \cap B) = \frac{n(A \cap B)}{n(S)} = \frac{1}{6}$$

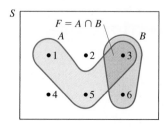

(B) Let A and B be the same events as in part (A), and let E be the event of rolling a number that is odd **or** divisible by 3. Then

$$A = \{1, 3, 5\} \qquad B = \{3, 6\} \qquad E = A \cup B = \{1, 3, 5, 6\}$$

The probability of rolling a number that is odd **or** exactly divisible by 3 is

$$P(E) = P(A \cup B) = \frac{n(A \cup B)}{n(S)} = \frac{4}{6} = \frac{2}{3}$$

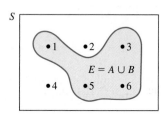

Matched Problem 1 Use the sample space in Example 1 to answer the following:

(A) What is the probability of rolling an odd number **and** a prime number?

(B) What is the probability of rolling an odd number **or** a prime number?

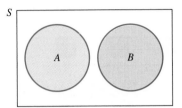

Figure 1 Mutually exclusive:
$A \cap B = \varnothing$

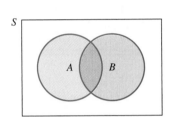

Figure 2 Not mutually exclusive:
$A \cap B = \varnothing$

Suppose that

$$E = A \cup B$$

Can we find $P(E)$ in terms of A and B? The answer is almost yes, but we must be careful. It would be nice if

$$P(A \cup B) = P(A) + P(B) \qquad (1)$$

This turns out to be true if events A and B are **mutually exclusive (disjoint)**, that is, if $A \cap B = \varnothing$ (Fig. 1). In this case, $P(A \cup B)$ is the sum of all the probabilities of simple events in A added to the sum of all the probabilities of simple events in B. But what happens if events A and B are not mutually exclusive, that is, if $A \cap B \neq \varnothing$ (Fig. 2)? If we simply add the probabilities of the elements in A to the probabilities of the elements in B, we are including some of the probabilities twice, namely those for elements that are in both A and B. To compensate for this double counting, we subtract $P(A \cap B)$ from equation (1) to obtain

$$P(A \cup B) = P(A) + P(B) - P(A \cap B) \qquad (2)$$

We notice that equation (2) holds for both cases, $A \cap B \neq \varnothing$ and $A \cap B = \varnothing$, since equation (2) reduces to equation (1) for the latter case $[P(A \cap B) = P(\varnothing) = 0]$. It is better to use equation (2) if there is any doubt that A and B are mutually exclusive. We summarize this discussion in Theorem 1.

THEOREM 1 Probability of a Union of Two Events

For any events A and B,
$$P(A \cup B) = P(A) + P(B) - P(A \cap B) \qquad (2)$$
If A and B are mutually exclusive, then
$$P(A \cup B) = P(A) + P(B) \qquad (1)$$

CONCEPTUAL INSIGHT

To count the number of elements in the union of sets A and B, we can count the number of elements in A, then count the number of elements in B, and subtract from the sum the number of elements that have been counted twice. Expressed algebraically, we have

$$n(A \cup B) = n(A) + n(B) - n(A \cap B)$$

Similarly, to find the total weight of the objects in the union of sets A and B, we can weigh all the objects in A, then weigh all the objects in B, and subtract from the sum the weight of all the objects that have been weighed twice. If we consider the probability of each simple event of a sample space to be its "weight," we have

$$P(A \cup B) = P(A) + P(B) - P(A \cap B)$$

EXAMPLE 2 **Probability Involving Union and Intersection** Suppose that two fair dice are rolled.

(A) What is the probability that a sum of 7 or 11 turns up?

(B) What is the probability that both dice turn up the same or that a sum less than 5 turns up?

SOLUTION (A) If A is the event that a sum of 7 turns up and B is the event that a sum of 11 turns up, then (Fig. 3) the event that a sum of 7 or 11 turns up is $A \cup B$, where

$$A = \{(1, 6), (2, 5), (3, 4), (4, 3), (5, 2), (6, 1)\}$$
$$B = \{(5, 6), (6, 5)\}$$

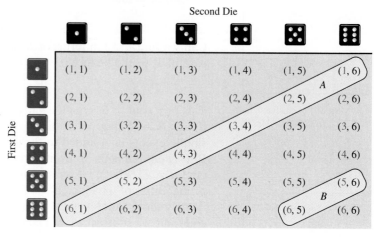

Figure 3

Since events A and B are mutually exclusive, we can use equation (1) to calculate $P(A \cup B)$:

$$P(A \cup B) = P(A) + P(B)$$
$$= \frac{6}{36} + \frac{2}{36}$$
$$= \frac{8}{36} = \frac{2}{9}$$

In this equally likely sample space, $n(A) = 6$, $n(B) = 2$, and $n(S) = 36$.

(B) If A is the event that both dice turn up the same and B is the event that the sum is less than 5, then (Fig. 4) the event that both dice turn up the same or the sum is less than 5 is $A \cup B$, where

$$A = \{(1, 1), (2, 2), (3, 3), (4, 4), (5, 5), (6, 6)\}$$
$$B = \{(1, 1), (1, 2), (1, 3), (2, 1), (2, 2), (3, 1)\}$$

Since $A \cap B = \{(1, 1), (2, 2)\}$, A and B are not mutually exclusive, and we use equation (2) to calculate $P(A \cup B)$:

$$P(A \cup B) = P(A) + P(B) - P(A \cap B)$$
$$= \frac{6}{36} + \frac{6}{36} - \frac{2}{36}$$
$$= \frac{10}{36} = \frac{5}{18}$$

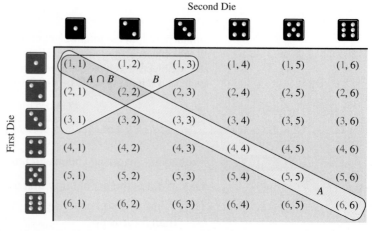

Figure 4

Matched Problem 2   Use the sample space in Example 2 to answer the following:

(A) What is the probability that a sum of 2 or 3 turns up?

(B) What is the probability that both dice turn up the same or that a sum greater than 8 turns up?

You no doubt noticed in Example 2 that we actually did not have to use either formula (1) or (2). We could have proceeded as in Example 1 and simply counted sample points in $A \cup B$. The following example illustrates the use of formula (2) in a situation where visual representation of sample points is not practical.

EXAMPLE 3   **Probability Involving Union and Intersection**   What is the probability that a number selected at random from the first 500 positive integers is (exactly) divisible by 3 or 4?

SOLUTION   Let A be the event that a drawn integer is divisible by 3 and B the event that a drawn integer is divisible by 4. Note that events A and B are not mutually exclusive because multiples of 12 are divisible by both 3 and 4. Since each of the positive integers from 1 to 500 is as likely to be drawn as any other, we can use $n(A)$, $n(B)$, and $n(A \cap B)$ to determine $P(A \cup B)$, where

$$n(A) = \text{the largest integer less than or equal to } \tfrac{500}{3} = 166$$
$$n(B) = \text{the largest integer less than or equal to } \tfrac{500}{4} = 125$$
$$n(A \cap B) = \text{the largest integer less than or equal to } \tfrac{500}{12} = 41$$

Now we can compute $P(A \cup B)$:

$$P(A \cup B) = P(A) + P(B) - P(A \cap B)$$
$$= \frac{n(A)}{n(S)} + \frac{n(B)}{n(S)} - \frac{n(A \cap B)}{n(S)}$$
$$= \frac{166}{500} + \frac{125}{500} - \frac{41}{500} = \frac{250}{500} = .5$$

Matched Problem 3   What is the probability that a number selected at random from the first 140 positive integers is (exactly) divisible by 4 or 6?

Complement of an Event

Suppose that we divide a finite sample space

$$S = \{e_1, \dots, e_n\}$$

into two subsets E and E' such that

$$E \cap E' = \varnothing$$

that is, E and E' are mutually exclusive and

$$E \cup E' = S$$

Then E' is called the **complement of E** relative to S. Note that E' contains all the elements of S that are not in E (Fig. 5). Furthermore,

$$P(S) = P(E \cup E')$$
$$= P(E) + P(E') = 1$$

Therefore,

$$P(E) = 1 - P(E') \qquad P(E') = 1 - P(E) \tag{3}$$

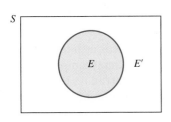

S

E E'

Figure 5

If the probability of rain is .67, then the probability of no rain is $1 - .67 = .33$; if the probability of striking oil is .01, then the probability of not striking oil is .99. If the probability of having at least 1 boy in a 2-child family is .75, what is the probability of having 2 girls? [*Answer:* .25.]

EXPLORE & DISCUSS 1

(A) Suppose that E and F are complementary events. Are E and F necessarily mutually exclusive? Explain why or why not.

(B) Suppose that E and F are mutually exclusive events. Are E and F necessarily complementary? Explain why or why not.

In looking for $P(E)$, there are situations in which it is easier to find $P(E')$ first, and then use equations (3) to find $P(E)$. The next two examples illustrate two such situations.

EXAMPLE 4   **Quality Control** A shipment of 45 precision parts, including 9 that are defective, is sent to an assembly plant. The quality control division selects 10 at random for testing and rejects the entire shipment if 1 or more in the sample are found to be defective. What is the probability that the shipment will be rejected?

SOLUTION   If E is the event that 1 or more parts in a random sample of 10 are defective, then E', the complement of E, is the event that no parts in a random sample of 10 are defective. It is easier to compute $P(E')$ than to compute $P(E)$ directly. Once $P(E')$ is found, we will use $P(E) = 1 - P(E')$ to find $P(E)$.

The sample space S for this experiment is the set of all subsets of 10 elements from the set of 45 parts shipped. Thus, since there are $45 - 9 = 36$ non-defective parts,

$$P(E') = \frac{n(E')}{n(S)} = \frac{C_{36,10}}{C_{45,10}} \approx .08$$

and

$$P(E) = 1 - P(E') \approx 1 - .08 = .92$$

Matched Problem 4   A shipment of 40 precision parts, including 8 that are defective, is sent to an assembly plant. The quality control division selects 10 at random for testing and rejects the entire shipment if 1 or more in the sample are found to be defective. What is the probability that the shipment will be rejected?

EXAMPLE 5   **Birthday Problem** In a group of n people, what is the probability that at least 2 people have the same birthday (same month and day, excluding February 29)? Make a guess for a class of 40 people, and check your guess with the conclusion of this example.

SOLUTION   If we form a list of the birthdays of all the people in the group, we have a simple event in the sample space

$$S = \text{set of all lists of } n \text{ birthdays}$$

For any person in the group, we will assume that any birthday is as likely as any other, so that the simple events in S are equally likely. How many simple events are in the set S? Since any person could have any one of 365 birthdays (excluding February 29), the multiplication principle implies that the number of simple events in S is

$$
\begin{array}{cccccc}
& \text{1st} & \text{2nd} & \text{3rd} & & \text{nth} \\
& \text{person} & \text{person} & \text{person} & & \text{person} \\
n(S) = & 365 & \cdot\ 365 & \cdot\ 365 & \cdot\ \cdots\ \cdot & 365 \\
= & 365^n
\end{array}
$$

Now, let E be the event that at least 2 people in the group have the same birthday. Then E' is the event that no 2 people have the same birthday. The multiplication principle can be used to determine the number of simple events in E':

$$
\begin{array}{ccccc}
\text{1st} & \text{2nd} & \text{3rd} & & \text{nth} \\
\text{person} & \text{person} & \text{person} & & \text{person}
\end{array}
$$

$$n(E') = 365 \cdot 364 \cdot 363 \cdots (366 - n)$$

$$= \frac{[365 \cdot 364 \cdot 363 \cdots (366 - n)](365 - n)!}{(365 - n)!}$$

Multiply numerator and denominator by $(365 - n)!$.

$$= \frac{365!}{(365 - n)!}$$

Since we have assumed that S is an equally likely sample space,

$$P(E') = \frac{n(E')}{n(S)} = \frac{\dfrac{365!}{(365 - n)!}}{365^n} = \frac{365!}{365^n(365 - n)!}$$

Therefore,

$$P(E) = 1 - P(E')$$

$$= 1 - \frac{365!}{365^n(365 - n)!} \qquad (4)$$

Equation (4) is valid for any n satisfying $1 \le n \le 365$. [What is $P(E)$ if $n > 365$?] For example, in a group of 6 people,

$$P(E) = 1 - \frac{365!}{(365)^6\, 359!}$$

$$= 1 - \frac{365 \cdot 364 \cdot 363 \cdot 362 \cdot 361 \cdot 360 \cdot \cancel{359!}}{365 \cdot 365 \cdot 365 \cdot 365 \cdot 365 \cdot 365 \cdot \cancel{359!}}$$

$$= .04$$

It is interesting to note that as the size of the group increases, $P(E)$ increases more rapidly than you might expect. Figure 6* shows the graph of $P(E)$ for $1 \le n \le 39$. Table 1 gives the value of $P(E)$ for selected values of n. Notice that for a group of only 23 people, the probability that 2 or more have the same birthday is greater than $\frac{1}{2}$.

Figure 6

Table 1 Birthday Problem

Number of People in Group	Probability That 2 or More Have Same Birthday
n	$P(E)$
5	.027
10	.117
15	.253
20	.411
23	.507
30	.706
40	.891
50	.970
60	.994
70	.999

Matched Problem 5 Use equation (4) to evaluate $P(E)$ for $n = 4$.

EXPLORE & DISCUSS 2 Determine the smallest number n such that in a group of n people, the probability that 2 or more have a birthday in the same month is greater than .5. Discuss the assumptions underlying your computation.

Odds

When the probability of an event E is known, it is often customary (especially in gaming situations) to speak of odds for or against E rather than the probability of E. For example, if you roll a fair die once, then the *odds for* rolling a 2 are 1 to 5 (also written $1:5$), and the *odds against* rolling a 2 are 5 to 1 (or $5:1$). This is consistent with the following instructions for converting probabilities to odds.

---

*See Problem 63 in Exercise 8-2 for a discussion of the form of equation (4) used to produce the graph in Figure 6.

DEFINITION From Probabilities to Odds

If $P(E)$ is the probability of the event E, then

(A) **Odds for E** $= \dfrac{P(E)}{1 - P(E)} = \dfrac{P(E)}{P(E')}$ $P(E) \neq 1$

(B) **Odds against E** $= \dfrac{P(E')}{P(E)}$ $P(E) \neq 0$

The ratio $\dfrac{P(E)}{P(E')}$, giving odds for E, is usually expressed as an equivalent ratio $\dfrac{a}{b}$ of whole numbers (by multiplying numerator and denominator by the same number), and written "a to b" or "$a : b$." In this case, the odds against E are written "b to a" or "$b : a$."

Odds have a natural interpretation in terms of **fair games**. Let's return to the experiment of rolling a fair die once. Recall that the odds for rolling a 2 are 1 to 5. Turn the experiment into a fair game as follows: If you bet $1 on rolling a 2, then the house pays you $5 (and returns your $1 bet) if you roll a 2; otherwise, you lose the $1 bet.

More generally, consider any experiment and an associated event E. If the odds for E are a to b, then the experiment can be turned into a fair game as follows: If you bet a on event E, then the house pays you b (and returns your a bet) if E occurs; otherwise, you lose the a bet.

EXAMPLE 6   **Probability and Odds**

(A) What are the odds for rolling a sum of 7 in a single roll of two fair dice?

(B) If you bet $1 on rolling a sum of 7, what should the house pay (plus returning your $1 bet) if you roll a sum of 7 in order for the game to be fair?

SOLUTION   (A) Let E denote the event of rolling a sum of 7. Then $P(E) = \frac{6}{36} = \frac{1}{6}$. So the odds for E are

$$\frac{P(E)}{P(E')} = \frac{\frac{1}{6}}{\frac{5}{6}} = \frac{1}{5} \qquad \text{Also written as "1 to 5" or "1:5."}$$

(B) The odds for rolling a sum of 7 are 1 to 5. The house should pay $5 (and return your $1 bet) if you roll a sum of 7 for the game to be fair.

Matched Problem 6   (A) What are the odds for rolling a sum of 8 in a single roll of two fair dice?

(B) If you bet $5 that a sum of 8 will turn up, what should the house pay (plus returning your $5 bet) if a sum of 8 does turn up in order for the game to be fair?

Now we will go in the other direction: If we are given the odds for an event, what is the probability of the event? (The verification of the following formula is left to Problem 67 in Exercise 8-2.)

If the odds for event E are a/b, then the probability of E is

$$P(E) = \frac{a}{a + b}$$

EXAMPLE 7   **Odds and Probability** If in repeated rolls of two fair dice, the odds for rolling a 5 before rolling a 7 are 2 to 3, then the probability of rolling a 5 before rolling a 7 is

$$P(E) = \frac{a}{a + b} = \frac{2}{2 + 3} = \frac{2}{5}$$

Matched Problem 7   If in repeated rolls of two fair dice, the odds against rolling a 6 before rolling a 7 are 6 to 5, then what is the probability of rolling a 6 before rolling a 7?

Applications to Empirical Probability

In the following discussions, the term *empirical probability* will mean the probability of an event determined by a sample that is used to approximate the probability of the corresponding event in the total population. How does the approximate empirical probability of an event determined from a sample relate to the actual probability of an event relative to the total population? In mathematical statistics an important theorem called the **law of large numbers** (or the **law of averages**) is proved. Informally, it states that the approximate empirical probability can be made as close to the actual probability as we please by making the sample sufficiently large.

EXAMPLE 8   **Market Research**   From a survey of 1,000 people in Springfield, it was found that 500 people had tried a certain brand of diet cola, 600 had tried a certain brand of regular cola, and 200 had tried both types of cola. If a person from Springfield is selected at random, what is the (empirical) probability that

(A) He or she has tried the diet cola or the regular cola? What are the (empirical) odds for this event?

(B) He or she has tried one of the colas but not both? What are the (empirical) odds against this event?

SOLUTION   Let D be the event that a person has tried the diet cola and R the event that a person has tried the regular cola. The events D and R can be used to partition the population of Springfield into four mutually exclusive subsets (a collection of subsets is mutually exclusive if the intersection of any two of them is the empty set):

$D \cap R$ = set of people who have tried both colas

$D \cap R'$ = set of people who have tried the diet cola but not the regular cola

$D' \cap R$ = set of people who have tried the regular cola but not the diet cola

$D' \cap R'$ = set of people who have not tried either cola

These sets are displayed in the Venn diagram in Figure 7.

The sample population of 1,000 persons is also partitioned into four mutually exclusive sets, with $n(D) = 500$, $n(R) = 600$, and $n(D \cap R) = 200$. By using a Venn diagram (Fig. 8), we can determine the number of sample points in the sets $D \cap R'$, $D' \cap R$, and $D' \cap R'$ (see Example 2, Section 7-3).

Figure 7 Total population

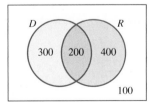

Figure 8 Sample population

These numbers are displayed in a table:

	Regular R	No Regular R'	Totals
Diet D	200	300	500
No Diet D'	400	100	500
Totals	600	400	1,000

Assuming that each sample point is equally likely, we form a probability table by dividing each entry in this table by 1,000, the total number surveyed. These are empirical probabilities for the sample population, which we can use to approximate the corresponding probabilities for the total population.

		Regular R	No Regular R'	Totals
Diet	D	.2	.3	.5
No Diet	D'	.4	.1	.5
Totals		.6	.4	1.0

Now we are ready to compute the required probabilities.

(A) The event that a person has tried the diet cola or the regular cola is $E = D \cup R$. We compute $P(E)$ two ways:

Method 1. Directly:

$$P(E) = P(D \cup R)$$
$$= P(D) + P(R) - P(D \cap R)$$
$$= .5 + .6 - .2 = .9$$

Method 2. Using the complement of E:

$$P(E) = 1 - P(E')$$
$$= 1 - P(D' \cap R') \qquad E' = (D \cup R)' = D' \cap R' \text{ (see Fig. 7)}$$
$$= 1 - .1 = .9$$

In either case,

$$\text{odds for } E = \frac{P(E)}{P(E')} = \frac{.9}{.1} = \frac{9}{1} \quad \text{or} \quad 9:1$$

(B) The event that a person has tried one cola but not both is the event that the person has tried diet cola and not regular cola or has tried regular cola and not diet cola. In terms of sets, this is event $E = (D \cap R') \cup (D' \cap R)$. Since $D \cap R'$ and $D' \cap R$ are mutually exclusive (Fig. 7),

$$P(E) = P[(D \cap R') \cup (D' \cap R)]$$
$$= P(D \cap R') + P(D' \cap R)$$
$$= .3 + .4 = .7$$

$$\text{odds against } E = \frac{P(E')}{P(E)} = \frac{.3}{.7} = \frac{3}{7} \quad \text{or} \quad 3:7$$

Matched Problem 8   Refer to Example 8. If a person from Springfield is selected at random, what is the (empirical) probability that

(A) He or she has not tried either cola? What are the (empirical) odds for this event?

(B) He or she has tried the diet cola or has not tried the regular cola? What are the (empirical) odds against this event?

Exercises 8-2

Problems 1–6 refer to the Venn diagram below for events A and B in an equally likely sample space S. Find each of the indicated probabilities.

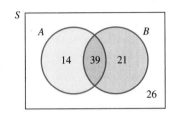

1. $P(A \cap B)$ **2.** $P(A \cup B)$

3. $P(A' \cup B)$ **4.** $P(A \cap B')$

5. $P((A \cup B)')$ **6.** $P((A \cap B)')$

A single card is drawn from a standard 52-card deck. Let D be the event that the card drawn is a diamond, and let F be the event that the card drawn is a face card. In Problems 7–18, find the indicated probabilities.

7. $P(D)$ **8.** $P(F)$

9. $P(F')$ **10.** $P(D')$

11. $P(D \cap F)$ **12.** $P(D' \cap F)$

13. $P(D \cup F)$ **14.** $P(D' \cup F)$

15. $P(D \cap F')$ **16.** $P(D' \cap F')$

17. $P(D \cup F')$ **18.** $P(D' \cup F')$

In a lottery game, a single ball is drawn at random from a container that contains 25 identical balls numbered from 1 through 25. In Problems 19–24, use equation (1) or (2), indicating which is used, to compute the probability that the number drawn is:

19. Less than 6 or greater than 19

20. Divisible by 4 or divisible by 7

21. Divisible by 3 or divisible by 4

22. Odd or greater than 15

23. Even or divisible by 5

24. Less than 12 or greater than 13

25. If the probability is .51 that a candidate wins the election, what is the probability that he loses?

26. If the probability is .03 that an automobile tire fails in less than 50,000 miles, what is the probability that the tire does not fail in 50,000 miles?

In Problems 27–30, use the equally likely sample space in Example 2 to compute the probability of the following events:

27. A sum that is less than or equal to 5

28. A sum that is greater than 9

29. The number on the first die is a 6 or the number on the second die is a 3.

30. The number on the first die is even or the number on the second die is even.

31. Given the following probabilities for an event E, find the odds for and against E:

(A) $\frac{3}{8}$ (B) $\frac{1}{4}$ (C) .4   (D) .55

32. Given the following probabilities for an event E, find the odds for and against E:

(A) $\frac{3}{5}$ (B) $\frac{1}{7}$ (C) .6   (D) .35

33. Compute the probability of event E if the odds in favor of E are

(A) $\frac{3}{8}$ (B) $\frac{11}{7}$ (C) $\frac{4}{1}$ (D) $\frac{49}{51}$

34. Compute the probability of event E if the odds in favor of E are

(A) $\frac{5}{9}$ (B) $\frac{4}{3}$ (C) $\frac{3}{7}$ (D) $\frac{23}{77}$

In Problems 35–40, discuss the validity of each statement. If the statement is always true, explain why. If not, give a counterexample.

35. If the odds for E equal the odds against E', then $P(E) = \frac{1}{2}$.

36. If the odds for E are $a:b$, then the odds against E are $b:a$.

37. If $P(E) + P(F) = P(E \cup F) + P(E \cap F)$, then E and F are mutually exclusive events.

38. The theoretical probability of an event is less than or equal to its empirical probability.

39. If E and F are complementary events, then E and F are mutually exclusive.

40. If E and F are mutually exclusive events, then E and F are complementary.

In Problems 41–44, compute the odds in favor of obtaining

41. A head in a single toss of a coin

42. A number divisible by 3 in a single roll of a die

43. At least 1 head when a single coin is tossed 3 times

44. 1 head when a single coin is tossed twice

In Problems 45–48, compute the odds against obtaining

45. A number greater than 4 in a single roll of a die

46. 2 heads when a single coin is tossed twice

47. A 3 or an even number in a single roll of a die

48. An odd number or a number divisible by 3 in a single roll of a die

49. (A) What are the odds for rolling a sum of 5 in a single roll of two fair dice?

(B) If you bet \$1 that a sum of 5 will turn up, what should the house pay (plus returning your \$1 bet) if a sum of 5 turns up in order for the game to be fair?

50. (A) What are the odds for rolling a sum of 10 in a single roll of two fair dice?

(B) If you bet \$1 that a sum of 10 will turn up, what should the house pay (plus returning your \$1 bet) if a sum of 10 turns up in order for the game to be fair?

A pair of dice are rolled 1,000 times with the following frequencies of outcomes:

Sum	2	3	4	5	6	7	8	9	10	11	12
Frequency	10	30	50	70	110	150	170	140	120	80	70

Use these frequencies to calculate the approximate empirical probabilities and odds for the events in Problems 51 and 52.

51. (A) The sum is less than 4 or greater than 9.

(B) The sum is even or exactly divisible by 5.

52. (A) The sum is a prime number or is exactly divisible by 4.

(B) The sum is an odd number or exactly divisible by 3.

In Problems 53–56, a single card is drawn from a standard 52-card deck. Calculate the probability of and odds for each event.

53. A face card or a club is drawn.

54. A king or a heart is drawn.

55. A black card or an ace is drawn.

56. A heart or a number less than 7 (count an ace as 1) is drawn.

57. What is the probability of getting at least 1 diamond in a 5-card hand dealt from a standard 52-card deck?

58. What is the probability of getting at least 1 black card in a 7-card hand dealt from a standard 52-card deck?

59. What is the probability that a number selected at random from the first 1,000 positive integers is (exactly) divisible by 6 or 8?

60. What is the probability that a number selected at random from the first 600 positive integers is (exactly) divisible by 6 or 9?

61. Explain how the three events A, B, and C from a sample space S are related to each other in order for the following equation to hold true:

$$P(A \cup B \cup C) = P(A) + P(B) + P(C) - P(A \cap B)$$

62. Explain how the three events A, B, and C from a sample space S are related to each other in order for the following equation to hold true:

$$P(A \cup B \cup C) = P(A) + P(B) + P(C)$$

63. Show that the solution to the birthday problem in Example 5 can be written in the form

$$P(E) = 1 - \frac{P_{365,n}}{365^n}$$

For a calculator that has a $P_{n,r}$ function, explain why this form may be better for direct evaluation than the other form used in the solution to Example 5. Try direct evaluation of both forms on a calculator for $n = 25$.

64. Many (but not all) calculators experience an overflow error when computing $P_{365,n}$ for $n > 39$ and when computing 365^n. Explain how you would evaluate $P(E)$ for any $n > 39$ on such a calculator.

65. In a group of n people ($n \le 12$), what is the probability that at least 2 of them have the same birth month? (Assume that any birth month is as likely as any other.)

66. In a group of n people ($n \le 100$), each person is asked to select a number between 1 and 100, write the number on a slip of paper and place the slip in a hat. What is the probability that at least 2 of the slips in the hat have the same number written on them?

67. If the odds in favor of an event E occurring are a to b, show that

$$P(E) = \frac{a}{a + b}$$

[*Hint:* Solve the equation $P(E)/P(E') = a/b$ for $P(E)$.]

68. If $P(E) = c/d$, show that odds in favor of E occurring are c to $d - c$.

69. The command in Figure A was used on a graphing calculator to simulate 50 repetitions of rolling a pair of dice and recording their sum. A statistical plot of the results is shown in Figure B.

(A) Use Figure B to find the empirical probability of rolling a 7 or 8.

(B) What is the theoretical probability of rolling a 7 or 8?

(C) Use a graphing calculator to simulate 200 repetitions of rolling a pair of dice and recording their sum, and find the empirical probability of rolling a 7 or 8.

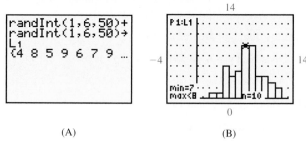

(A)   (B)

Figure for 69

70. Consider the command in Figure A and the associated statistical plot in Figure B.

(A) Explain why the command does not simulate 50 repetitions of rolling a pair of dice and recording their sum.

(B) Describe an experiment that is simulated by this command.

(C) Simulate 200 repetitions of the experiment you described in part (B), and find the empirical probability of recording a 7 or 8.

(D) What is the theoretical probability of recording a 7 or 8?

(A)   (B)

Figure for 70

Applications

71. **Market research.** From a survey involving 1,000 university students, a market research company found that 750 students owned laptops, 450 owned cars, and 350 owned cars and laptops. If a university student is selected at random, what is the (empirical) probability that

(A) The student owns either a car or a laptop?

(B) The student owns neither a car nor a laptop?

72. **Market research.** Refer to Problem 71. If a university student is selected at random, what is the (empirical) probability that

(A) The student does not own a car?

(B) The student owns a car but not a laptop?

73. **Insurance.** By examining the past driving records of city drivers, an insurance company has determined the following (empirical) probabilities:

	Miles Driven per Year			
	Less than 10,000, M_1	10,000–15,000, inclusive, M_2	More than 15,000, M_3	Totals
Accident A	.05	.1	.15	.3
No Accident A'	.15	.2	.35	.7
Totals	.2	.3	.5	1.0

If a city driver is selected at random, what is the probability that

(A) He or she drives less than 10,000 miles per year or has an accident?

(B) He or she drives 10,000 or more miles per year and has no accidents?

74. **Insurance.** Use the (empirical) probabilities in Problem 73 to find the probability that a city driver selected at random:

(A) Drives more than 15,000 miles per year or has an accident

(B) Drives 15,000 or fewer miles per year and has an accident

75. **Quality control.** A shipment of 60 game players, including 9 that are defective, is sent to a retail store. The receiving department selects 10 at random for testing and rejects the whole shipment if 1 or more in the sample are found to be defective. What is the probability that the shipment will be rejected?

76. **Quality control.** An assembly plant produces 40 outboard motors, including 7 that are defective. The quality control department selects 10 at random (from the 40 produced) for testing and will shut down the plant for trouble shooting if 1 or more in the sample are found to be defective. What is the probability that the plant will be shut down?

77. **Medicine.** In order to test a new drug for adverse reactions, the drug was administered to 1,000 test subjects with the following results: 60 subjects reported that their only adverse reaction was a loss of appetite, 90 subjects reported that their only adverse reaction was a loss of sleep, and 800 subjects reported no adverse reactions at all. If this drug is released for general use, what is the (empirical) probability that a person using the drug will suffer both a loss of appetite and a loss of sleep?

78. **Product testing.** To test a new car, an automobile manufacturer wants to select 4 employees to test drive the car for 1 year. If 12 management and 8 union employees volunteer to be test drivers and the selection is made at random, what is the probability that at least 1 union employee is selected?

Problems 79 and 80 refer to the data in the following table, obtained from a random survey of 1,000 residents of a state. The participants were asked their political affiliations and their preferences in an upcoming election. (In the table, D = Democrat, R = Republican, and U = Unaffiliated.)

		D	R	U	Totals
Candidate A	A	200	100	85	385
Candidate B	B	250	230	50	530
No Preference	N	50	20	15	85
Totals		500	350	150	1,000

79. **Politics.** If a state resident is selected at random, what is the (empirical) probability that the resident is

(A) Not affiliated with a political party or has no preference? What are the odds for this event?

(B) Affiliated with a political party and prefers candidate A? What are the odds against this event?

80. **Politics.** If a state resident is selected at random, what is the (empirical) probability that the resident is

(A) A Democrat or prefers candidate B? What are the odds for this event?

(B) Not a Democrat and has no preference? What are the odds against this event?

Answers to Matched Problems

1. (A) $\frac{1}{3}$ (B) $\frac{2}{3}$

2. (A) $\frac{1}{12}$ (B) $\frac{7}{18}$

3. $\frac{47}{140} \approx .336$ 4. .92   5. .016

6. (A) $5:31$ (B) \$31

7. $\frac{5}{11} \approx .455$

8. (A) $P(D' \cap R') = .1$; odds for $D' \cap R' = \frac{1}{9}$ or $1:9$

    (B) $P(D \cup R') = .6$; odds against $D \cup R' = \frac{2}{3}$ or $2:3$

8-3   Conditional Probability, Intersection, and Independence

In the preceding section, we asked if the probability of the union of two events could be expressed in terms of the probabilities of the individual events, and we found the answer to be a qualified yes (see page 387). Now we ask the same question for the intersection of two events; that is, can the probability of the intersection of two events be represented in terms of the probabilities of the individual events? The answer again is a qualified yes. But before we find out how and under what conditions, we must investigate a related concept called *conditional probability*.

Conditional Probability

The probability of an event may change if we are told of the occurrence of another event. For example, if an adult (21 years or older) is selected at random from all adults in the United States, the probability of that person having lung cancer would not be high. However, if we are told that the person is also a heavy smoker, we would want to revise the probability upward.

In general, the probability of the occurrence of an event A, given the occurrence of another event B, is called a **conditional probability** and is denoted by $P(A|B)$.

In the preceding situation, events A and B would be

$$A = \text{adult has lung cancer}$$

$$B = \text{adult is a heavy smoker}$$

and $P(A|B)$ would represent the probability of an adult having lung cancer, given that he or she is a heavy smoker.

Our objective now is to try to formulate a precise definition of $P(A|B)$. It is helpful to start with a relatively simple problem, solve it intuitively, and then generalize from this experience.

What is the probability of rolling a prime number (2, 3, or 5) in a single roll of a fair die? Let

$$S = \{1, 2, 3, 4, 5, 6\}$$

Then the event of rolling a prime number is (Fig. 1)

$$A = \{2, 3, 5\}$$

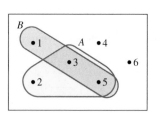

Figure 1

Thus, since we assume that each simple event in the sample space is equally likely,

$$P(A) = \frac{n(A)}{n(S)} = \frac{3}{6} = \frac{1}{2}$$

Now suppose you are asked, "In a single roll of a fair die, what is the probability that a prime number has turned up if we are given the additional information that an odd number has turned up?" The additional knowledge that another event has occurred, namely,

$$B = \text{odd number turns up}$$

Figure 2 B is the new sample space.

puts the problem in a new light. We are now interested only in the part of event A (rolling a prime number) that is in event B (rolling an odd number). Event B, since we know it has occurred, becomes the new sample space. The Venn diagrams in Figure 2 illustrate the various relationships. Thus, the probability of A given B is the number of A elements in B divided by the total number of elements in B. Symbolically,

$$P(A|B) = \frac{n(A \cap B)}{n(B)} = \frac{2}{3}$$

Dividing the numerator and denominator of $n(A \cap B)/n(B)$ by $n(S)$, the number of elements in the original sample space, we can express $P(A|B)$ in terms of $P(A \cap B)$ and $P(B)$:*

$$P(A|B) = \frac{n(A \cap B)}{n(B)} = \frac{\dfrac{n(A \cap B)}{n(S)}}{\dfrac{n(B)}{n(S)}} = \frac{P(A \cap B)}{P(B)}$$

Using the right side to compute $P(A|B)$ for the preceding example, we obtain the same result:

$$P(A|B) = \frac{P(A \cap B)}{P(B)} = \frac{\frac{2}{6}}{\frac{3}{6}} = \frac{2}{3}$$

We use the formula above to motivate the following definition of *conditional probability*, which applies to any sample space, including those having simple events that are not equally likely (see Example 1).

DEFINITION   Conditional Probability

For events A and B in an arbitrary sample space S, we define the **conditional probability of A given B** by

$$P(A|B) = \frac{P(A \cap B)}{P(B)} \qquad P(B) \neq 0 \tag{1}$$

EXAMPLE 1   **Conditional Probability**   A pointer is spun once on a circular spinner (Fig. 3). The probability assigned to the pointer landing on a given integer (from 1 to 6) is the ratio of the area of the corresponding circular sector to the area of the whole circle, as given in the table:

e_i	1	2	3	4	5	6
$P(e_i)$	.1	.2	.1	.1	.3	.2

$S = \{1, 2, 3, 4, 5, 6\}$

(A) What is the probability of the pointer landing on a prime number?

(B) What is the probability of the pointer landing on a prime number, given that it landed on an odd number?

Figure 3

SOLUTION   Let the events E and F be defined as follows:

$$E = \text{pointer lands on a prime number} = \{2, 3, 5\}$$

$$F = \text{pointer lands on an odd number} = \{1, 3, 5\}$$

(A) $P(E) = P(2) + P(3) + P(5)$

$$= .2 + .1 + .3 = .6$$

(B) First note that $E \cap F = \{3, 5\}$.

$$P(E|F) = \frac{P(E \cap F)}{P(F)} = \frac{P(3) + P(5)}{P(1) + P(3) + P(5)}$$

$$= \frac{.1 + .3}{.1 + .1 + .3} = \frac{.4}{.5} = .8$$

---

*Note that $P(A|B)$ is a probability based on the new sample space B, while $P(A \cap B)$ and $P(B)$ are both probabilities based on the original sample space S.

Matched Problem 1 Refer to Example 1.

(A) What is the probability of the pointer landing on a number greater than 4?

(B) What is the probability of the pointer landing on a number greater than 4, given that it landed on an even number?

EXAMPLE 2 **Safety Research** Suppose that city records produced the following probability data on a driver being in an accident on the last day of a Memorial Day weekend:

		Accident A	No Accident A'	Totals
Rain	R	.025	.335	.360
No Rain	R'	.015	.625	.640
Totals		.040	.960	1.000

$S = \{RA, RA', R'A, R'A'\}$

(A) Find the probability of an accident, rain or no rain.

(B) Find the probability of rain, accident or no accident.

(C) Find the probability of an accident and rain.

(D) Find the probability of an accident, given rain.

SOLUTION (A) Let $A = \{RA, R'A\}$ Event: "accident"

$$P(A) = P(RA) + P(R'A) = .025 + .015 = .040$$

(B) Let $R = \{RA, RA'\}$ Event: "rain"

$$P(R) = P(RA) + P(RA') = .025 + .335 = .360$$

(C) $A \cap R = \{RA\}$ Event: "accident and rain"

$$P(A \cap R) = P(RA) = .025$$

(D) $P(A|R) = \dfrac{P(A \cap R)}{P(R)} = \dfrac{.025}{.360} = .069$ Event: "accident, given rain"

Compare the result in part (D) with that in part (A). Note that $P(A|R) \neq P(A)$, and the probability of an accident, given rain, is higher than the probability of an accident without the knowledge of rain.

Matched Problem 2 Referring to the table in Example 2, determine the following:

(A) Probability of no rain

(B) Probability of an accident and no rain

(C) Probability of an accident, given no rain [Use formula (1) and the results of parts (A) and (B).]

Intersection of Events: Product Rule

Let's return to the original problem of this section, that is, representing the probability of an intersection of two events in terms of the probabilities of the individual events. If $P(A) \neq 0$ and $P(B) \neq 0$, then using formula (1), we can write

$$P(A|B) = \frac{P(A \cap B)}{P(B)} \quad \text{and} \quad P(B|A) = \frac{P(B \cap A)}{P(A)}$$

Solving the first equation for $P(A \cap B)$ and the second equation for $P(B \cap A)$, we have

$$P(A \cap B) = P(B)P(A|B) \quad \text{and} \quad P(B \cap A) = P(A)P(B|A)$$

Since $A \cap B = B \cap A$ for any sets A and B, it follows that

$$P(A \cap B) = P(B)P(A|B) = P(A)P(B|A)$$

and we have the **product rule:**

> **THEOREM 1 Product Rule**
> For events A and B with nonzero probabilities in a sample space S,
> $$P(A \cap B) = P(A)P(B|A) = P(B)P(A|B) \qquad (2)$$
> and we can use either $P(A)P(B|A)$ or $P(B)P(A|B)$ to compute $P(A \cap B)$.

EXAMPLE 3   **Consumer Survey** If 60% of a department store's customers are female and 75% of the female customers have credit cards at the store, what is the probability that a customer selected at random is a female and has a store credit card?

SOLUTION   Let

$$S = \text{all store customers}$$
$$F = \text{female customers}$$
$$C = \text{customers with a store credit card}$$

If 60% of the customers are female, then the probability that a customer selected at random is a female is

$$P(F) = .60$$

Since 75% of the female customers have store credit cards, the probability that a customer has a store credit card, given that the customer is a female, is

$$P(C|F) = .75$$

Using equation (2), the probability that a customer is a female and has a store credit card is

$$P(F \cap C) = P(F)P(C|F) = (.60)(.75) = .45$$

Matched Problem 3   If 80% of the male customers of the department store in Example 3 have store credit cards, what is the probability that a customer selected at random is a male and has a store credit card?

Probability Trees

We used tree diagrams in Section 7-3 to help us count the number of combined outcomes in a sequence of experiments. In a similar way, we will use probability trees to help us compute the probabilities of combined outcomes in a sequence of experiments.

EXAMPLE 4   **Probability Tree** Two balls are drawn in succession, without replacement, from a box containing 3 blue and 2 white balls (Fig. 4). What is the probability of drawing a white ball on the second draw?

SOLUTION   We start with a tree diagram (Fig. 5) showing the combined outcomes of the two experiments (first draw and second draw). Then we assign a probability to each branch of the tree (Fig. 6). For example, we assign the probability $\frac{2}{5}$ to the branch Sw_1, since this is the probability of drawing a white ball on the first draw (there are 2 white balls and 3 blue balls in the box). What probability should be assigned to the branch w_1w_2? This is the conditional probability $P(w_2|w_1)$, that is, the probability of drawing a white ball on the second draw given that a white ball was drawn on the first draw and not replaced. Since the box now contains 1 white ball and 3 blue balls, the probability is $\frac{1}{4}$. Continuing in the same way, we assign probabilities to the other branches of the tree and obtain Figure 6.

Figure 4

Figure 5

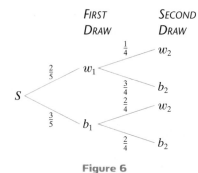

Figure 6

What is the probability of the combined outcome $w_1 \cap w_2$, that is, the probability of drawing a white ball on the first draw and a white ball on the second draw?* Using the product rule (2), we have

$$P(w_1 \cap w_2) = P(w_1)P(w_2|w_1)$$
$$= \left(\tfrac{2}{5}\right)\left(\tfrac{1}{4}\right) = \tfrac{1}{10}$$

The combined outcome $w_1 \cap w_2$ corresponds to the unique path Sw_1w_2 in the tree diagram, and we see that the probability of reaching w_2 along this path is the product of the probabilities assigned to the branches on the path. Reasoning in this way, we obtain the probability of each remaining combined outcome by multiplying the probabilities assigned to the branches on the path corresponding to the given combined outcomes. These probabilities are often written at the ends of the paths to which they correspond (Fig. 7).

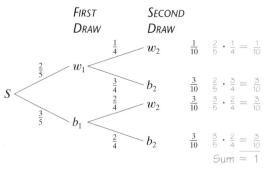

Figure 7

Now we can complete the problem. A white ball drawn on the second draw corresponds to either the combined outcome $w_1 \cap w_2$ or $b_1 \cap w_2$ occurring. Thus, since these combined outcomes are mutually exclusive,

$$P(w_2) = P(w_1 \cap w_2) + P(b_1 \cap w_2)$$
$$= \tfrac{1}{10} + \tfrac{3}{10} = \tfrac{4}{10} = \tfrac{2}{5}$$

which is the sum of the probabilities listed at the ends of the two paths terminating in w_2.

Matched Problem 4   Two balls are drawn in succession without replacement from a box containing 4 red and 2 white balls. What is the probability of drawing a red ball on the second draw?

The sequence of two experiments in Example 4 is an example of a *stochastic process*. In general, a **stochastic process** involves a sequence of experiments where the outcome of each experiment is not certain. Our interest is in making predictions about the process as a whole. The analysis in Example 4 generalizes to stochastic processes involving any finite sequence of experiments. We summarize the procedures used in Example 4 for general application:

---

*The sample space for the combined outcomes is $S = \{w_1w_2, w_1b_2, b_1w_2, b_1b_2\}$. If we let $w_1 = \{w_1w_2, w_1b_2\}$ and $w_2 = \{w_1w_2, b_1w_2\}$, then $w_1 \cap w_2 = \{w_1w_2\}$.

PROCEDURE   Constructing Probability Trees

Step 1   Draw a tree diagram corresponding to all combined outcomes of the sequence of experiments.

Step 2   Assign a probability to each tree branch. (This is the probability of the occurrence of the event on the right end of the branch subject to the occurrence of all events on the path leading to the event on the right end of the branch. The probability of the occurrence of a combined outcome that corresponds to a path through the tree is the product of all branch probabilities on the path.*)

Step 3   Use the results in Steps 1 and 2 to answer various questions related to the sequence of experiments as a whole.

---

*If we form a sample space S such that each simple event in S corresponds to one path through the tree, and if the probability assigned to each simple event in S is the product of the branch probabilities on the corresponding path, then it can be shown that this is not only an acceptable assignment (all probabilities for the simple events in S are nonnegative and their sum is 1), but it is the only assignment consistent with the method used to assign branch probabilities within the tree.

EXPLORE & DISCUSS 1

Refer to the table on rain and accidents in Example 2 and use formula (1), where appropriate, to complete the following probability tree:

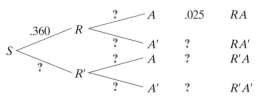

Discuss the difference between $P(R \cap A)$ and $P(A|R)$.

EXAMPLE 5   **Product Defects** An auto company A subcontracts the manufacturing of its onboard computers to two companies: 40% to company B and 60% to company C. Company B in turn subcontracts 70% of the orders it receives from company A to company D and the remaining 30% to company E, both subsidiaries of company B. When the onboard computers are completed by companies D, E, and C, they are shipped to company A to be used in various car models. It has been found that 1.5%, 1%, and .5% of the boards from D, E, and C, respectively, prove defective during the 3-year warranty period after a car is first sold. What is the probability that a given onboard computer will be defective during the 3-year warranty period?

SOLUTION   Draw a tree diagram and assign probabilities to each branch (Fig. 8):

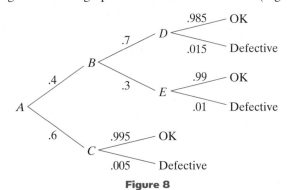

Figure 8

There are three paths leading to defective (the onboard computer will be defective within the 3-year warranty period). We multiply the branch probabilities on each path and add the three products:

$$P(\text{defective}) = (.4)(.7)(.015) + (.4)(.3)(.01) + (.6)(.005)$$

$$= .0084$$

Matched Problem 5   In Example 5, what is the probability that a given onboard computer came from company E or C?

Independent Events

We return to Example 4, which involved drawing two balls in succession without replacement from a box of 3 blue and 2 white balls. What difference does "without replacement" and "with replacement" make? Figure 9 shows probability trees corresponding to each case. Go over the probability assignments for the branches in Figure 9B to convince yourself of their correctness.

| | | | | |
| FIRST DRAW | SECOND DRAW | COMBINED OUTCOMES | SECOND DRAW | FIRST DRAW |

(A) Without replacement   (B) With replacement

Figure 9 $S = \{w_1w_2, w_1b_2, b_1w_2, b_1b_2\}$

Let

$$A = \text{white ball on second draw} = \{w_1w_2, b_1w_2\}$$
$$B = \text{white ball on first draw} = \{w_1w_2, w_1b_2\}$$

We now compute $P(A|B)$ and $P(A)$ for each case in Figure 9.

Case 1. *Without replacement:*

$$P(A|B) = \frac{P(A \cap B)}{P(B)} = \frac{P\{w_1w_2\}}{P\{w_1w_2, w_1b_2\}} = \frac{.10}{.10 + .30} = .25$$

(This is the assignment to branch w_1w_2 that we made by looking in the box and counting.)

$$P(A) = P\{w_1w_2, b_1w_2\} = .10 + .30 = .40$$

Note that $P(A|B) \neq P(A)$, and we conclude that the probability of A is affected by the occurrence of B.

Case 2. *With replacement:*

$$P(A|B) = \frac{P(A \cap B)}{P(B)} = \frac{P\{w_1w_2\}}{P\{w_1w_2, w_1b_2\}} = \frac{.16}{.16 + .24} = .40$$

(This is the assignment to branch w_1w_2 that we made by looking in the box and counting.)

$$P(A) = P\{w_1w_2, b_1w_2\} = .16 + .24 = .40$$

Note that $P(A|B) = P(A)$, and we conclude that the probability of A is not affected by the occurrence of B.

Intuitively, if $P(A|B) = P(A)$, then it appears that event A is "independent" of B. Let us pursue this further. If events A and B are such that

$$P(A|B) = P(A)$$

then replacing the left side by its equivalent from formula (1), we obtain

$$\frac{P(A \cap B)}{P(B)} = P(A)$$

After multiplying both sides by $P(B)$, the last equation becomes

$$P(A \cap B) = P(A)P(B)$$

This result motivates the following definition of *independence:*

DEFINITION Independence

If A and B are any events in a sample space S, we say that **A and B are independent** if and only if

$$P(A \cap B) = P(A)P(B) \tag{3}$$

Otherwise, A and B are said to be **dependent**.

From the definition of independence one can prove (see Problems 53 and 54, Exercise 8-3) the following theorem:

THEOREM 2   On Independence

If A and B are independent events with nonzero probabilities in a sample space S, then

$$P(A|B) = P(A) \qquad \text{and} \qquad P(B|A) = P(B) \tag{4}$$

If either equation in (4) holds, then A and B are independent.

CONCEPTUAL INSIGHT

Sometimes intuitive reasoning can be helpful in deciding whether or not two events are independent. Suppose that a fair coin is tossed five times. What is the probability of a head on the fifth toss, given that the first four tosses are all heads? Our intuition tells us that a coin has no memory, so the probability of a head on the fifth toss given four previous heads should be equal to the probability of a head on the fifth toss, namely, 1/2. In other words, the first equation of Theorem 2 holds intuitively, so "heads on the fifth toss" and "heads on the first four tosses" are independent events.

Often, unfortunately, intuition is *not* a reliable guide to the notion of independence. Independence is a technical concept. So in all cases, an appropriate sample space should be chosen, and either equation (3) or equation (4) should be tested, to confirm that two events are (or are not) independent.

EXAMPLE 6 **Testing for Independence** In two tosses of a single fair coin, show that the events "A head on the first toss" and "A head on the second toss" are independent.

SOLUTION Consider the sample space of equally likely outcomes for the tossing of a fair coin twice,

$$S = \{HH, HT, TH, TT\}$$

and the two events,

$$A = \text{a head on the first toss} = \{HH, HT\}$$
$$B = \text{a head on the second toss} = \{HH, TH\}$$

Then

$$P(A) = \tfrac{2}{4} = \tfrac{1}{2} \qquad P(B) = \tfrac{2}{4} = \tfrac{1}{2} \qquad P(A \cap B) = \tfrac{1}{4}$$

Thus,

$$P(A \cap B) = \tfrac{1}{4} = \tfrac{1}{2} \cdot \tfrac{1}{2} = P(A)P(B)$$

and the two events are independent. (The theory agrees with our intuition—a coin has no memory.)

Matched Problem 6   In Example 6, compute $P(B|A)$ and compare with $P(B)$.

EXAMPLE 7   **Testing for Independence** A single card is drawn from a standard 52-card deck. Test the following events for independence (try guessing the answer to each part before looking at the solution):

(A) E = the drawn card is a spade.
F = the drawn card is a face card.

(B) G = the drawn card is a club.
H = the drawn card is a heart.

SOLUTION   (A) To test E and F for independence, we compute $P(E \cap F)$ and $P(E)P(F)$. If they are equal, then events E and F are independent; if they are not equal, then events E and F are dependent.

$$P(E \cap F) = \tfrac{3}{52} \qquad P(E)P(F) = \left(\tfrac{13}{52}\right)\left(\tfrac{12}{52}\right) = \tfrac{3}{52}$$

Events E and F are independent. (Did you guess this?)

(B) Proceeding as in part (A), we see that

$$P(G \cap H) = P(\varnothing) = 0 \qquad P(G)P(H) = \left(\tfrac{13}{52}\right)\left(\tfrac{13}{52}\right) = \tfrac{1}{16}$$

Events G and H are dependent. (Did you guess this?)

⚠ **CAUTION** Students often confuse *mutually exclusive (disjoint) events* with *independent events*. One does not necessarily imply the other. In fact, it is not difficult to show (see Problem 57, Exercise 8-3) that any two mutually exclusive events A and B, with nonzero probabilities, are always dependent.

Matched Problem 7   A single card is drawn from a standard 52-card deck. Test the following events for independence:

(A) E = the drawn card is a red card
F = the drawn card's number is divisible by 5 (face cards are not assigned values)

(B) G = the drawn card is a king
H = the drawn card is a queen

EXPLORE & DISCUSS 2   In college basketball, would it be reasonable to assume that the following events are independent? Explain why or why not.

A = the Golden Eagles win in the first round of the NCAA tournament.

B = the Golden Eagles win in the second round of the NCAA tournament.

The notion of independence can be extended to more than two events:

DEFINITION Independent Set of Events

A set of events is said to be **independent** if for each finite subset $\{E_1, E_2, \ldots, E_k\}$

$$P(E_1 \cap E_2 \cap \cdots \cap E_k) = P(E_1)P(E_2) \cdot \cdots \cdot P(E_k) \tag{5}$$

The next example makes direct use of this definition.

EXAMPLE 8 **Computer Control Systems** A space shuttle has four independent computer control systems. If the probability of failure (during flight) of any one system is .001, what is the probability of failure of all four systems?

SOLUTION Let

$$E_1 = \text{failure of system 1} \qquad E_3 = \text{failure of system 3}$$
$$E_2 = \text{failure of system 2} \qquad E_4 = \text{failure of system 4}$$

Then, since events E_1, E_2, E_3, and E_4 are given to be independent,

$$P(E_1 \cap E_2 \cap E_3 \cap E_4) = P(E_1)P(E_2)P(E_3)P(E_4)$$
$$= (.001)^4$$
$$= .000\ 000\ 000\ 001$$

Matched Problem 8 A single die is rolled 6 times. What is the probability of getting the sequence 1, 2, 3, 4, 5, 6?

Summary

The key results in this section are summarized in the following box:

SUMMARY Key Concepts

Conditional Probability

$$P(A|B) = \frac{P(A \cap B)}{P(B)} \qquad P(B|A) = \frac{P(B \cap A)}{P(A)}$$

Note: $P(A|B)$ is a probability based on the new sample space B, while $P(A \cap B)$ and $P(B)$ are probabilities based on the original sample space S.

Product Rule

$$P(A \cap B) = P(A)P(B|A) = P(B)P(A|B)$$

Independent Events

- A and B are independent if and only if
$$P(A \cap B) = P(A)P(B)$$
- If A and B are independent events with nonzero probabilities, then
$$P(A|B) = P(A) \quad \text{and} \quad P(B|A) = P(B)$$
- If A and B are events with nonzero probabilities and either $P(A|B) = P(A)$ or $P(B|A) = P(B)$, then A and B are independent.
- If $E_1, E_2, \ldots, E_n$ are independent, then
$$P(E_1 \cap E_2 \cap \cdots \cap E_n) = P(E_1)P(E_2) \cdot \cdots \cdot P(E_n)$$

Exercises 8-3

A

In Problems 1–20, use the table below. Events A, B, and C are mutually exclusive; so are D, E, and F.

	A	B	C	Totals
D	.20	.03	.07	.30
E	.28	.05	.07	.40
F	.22	.02	.06	.30
Totals	.70	.10	.20	1.00

In Problems 1–4, find each probability directly from the table.

1. $P(B)$ **2.** $P(E)$

3. $P(B \cap D)$ **4.** $P(C \cap E)$

In Problems 5–12, compute each probability using formula (1) on page 399 and appropriate table values.

5. $P(D|B)$ **6.** $P(C|E)$

7. $P(B|D)$ **8.** $P(E|C)$

(A) Convert this table to a probability table by dividing each entry by 1,000.

(B) What is the probability of an employee voting to strike, given that the person is paid hourly?

(C) What is the probability of an employee voting to strike, given that the person receives a salary plus bonus?

(D) What is the probability of an employee being on straight salary (S)? Of being on straight salary given that he or she voted in favor of striking?

(E) What is the probability of an employee being paid hourly? Of being paid hourly given that he or she voted in favor of striking?

(F) What is the probability of an employee being in a salary plus bonus position and voting against striking?

(G) Are events S and Y independent?

(H) Are events H and Y independent?

(I) Are events B and N independent?

60. Quality control. An automobile manufacturer produces 37% of its cars at plant A. If 5% of the cars manufactured at plant A have defective emission control devices, what is the probability that one of this manufacturer's cars was manufactured at plant A and has a defective emission control device?

61. Bonus incentives. If a salesperson has gross sales of over $600,000 in a year, then he or she is eligible to play the company's bonus game: A black box contains 1 twenty-dollar bill, 2 five-dollar bills, and 1 one-dollar bill. Bills are drawn out of the box one at a time without replacement until a twenty-dollar bill is drawn. Then the game stops. The salesperson's bonus is 1,000 times the value of the bills drawn.

(A) What is the probability of winning a $26,000 bonus?

(B) What is the probability of winning the maximum bonus, $31,000, by drawing out all bills in the box?

(C) What is the probability of the game stopping at the third draw?

62. Personnel selection. To transfer into a particular technical department, a company requires an employee to pass a screening test. A maximum of 3 attempts are allowed at 6-month intervals between trials. From past records it is found that 40% pass on the first trial; of those that fail the first trial and take the test a second time, 60% pass; and of those that fail on the second trial and take the test a third time, 20% pass. For an employee wishing to transfer:

(A) What is the probability of passing the test on the first or second try?

(B) What is the probability of failing on the first 2 trials and passing on the third?

(C) What is the probability of failing on all 3 attempts?

63. U.S. Food and Drug Administration. An ice cream company wishes to use a red dye to enhance the color in its strawberry ice cream. The U.S. Food and Drug Administration (FDA) requires the dye to be tested for cancer-producing potential using laboratory rats. The results of one test on 1,000 rats are summarized in the following table:

		Cancer C	No Cancer C'	Totals
Ate Red Dye	R	60	440	500
No Red Dye	R'	20	480	500
Totals		80	920	1,000

(A) Convert the table into a probability table by dividing each entry by 1,000.

(B) Are "developing cancer" and "eating red dye" independent events?

(C) Should the FDA approve or ban the use of the dye? Explain why or why not using $P(C|R)$ and $P(C)$.

(D) Suppose the number of rats that ate red dye and developed cancer was 20, but the number that developed cancer was still 80 and the number that ate red dye was still 500. What should the FDA do based on these results? Explain why.

64. Genetics. In a study to determine frequency and dependency of color-blindness relative to females and males, 1,000 people were chosen at random, and the following results were recorded:

		Female F	Male F'	Totals
Color-Blind	C	2	24	26
Normal	C'	518	456	974
Totals		520	480	1,000

(A) Convert this table to a probability table by dividing each entry by 1,000.

(B) What is the probability that a person is a woman, given that the person is color-blind?

(C) What is the probability that a person is color-blind, given that the person is a male?

(D) Are the events color-blindness and male independent?

(E) Are the events color-blindness and female independent?

65. Psychology. In a study to determine the frequency and dependency of IQ ranges relative to males and females, 1,000 people were chosen at random and the following results were recorded:

		IQ Below 90 (A)	90–120 (B)	Above 120 (C)	Totals
Female	F	130	286	104	520
Male	F'	120	264	96	480
Totals		250	550	200	1,000

(A) Convert this table to a probability table by dividing each entry by 1,000.

(B) What is the probability of a person having an IQ below 90, given that the person is a female? A male?

(C) What is the probability of a person having an IQ above 120, given that the person is a female? A male?

(D) What is the probability of a person having an IQ below 90?

(E) What is the probability of a person having an IQ between 90 and 120? Of a person having an IQ between 90 and 120, given that the person is a male?

(F) What is the probability of a person being female and having an IQ above 120?

(G) Are any of the events A, B, or C dependent relative to F or F'?

66. Voting patterns. A survey of a precinct's residents revealed that 55% of the residents were members of the Democratic party and 60% of the Democratic party members voted in the last election. What is the probability that a person selected at random from this precinct is a member of the Democratic party and voted in the last election?

Answers to Matched Problems

1. (A) .5   (B) .4

2. (A) $P(R') = .640$

(B) $P(A \cap R') = .015$

(C) $P(A|R') = \dfrac{P(A \cap R')}{P(R')} = .023$

3. $P(M \cap C) = P(M)P(C|M) = .32$

4. $\frac{2}{3}$ **5.** .72

6. $P(B|A) = \dfrac{P(A \cap B)}{P(A)} = \dfrac{\frac{1}{4}}{\frac{1}{2}} = \dfrac{1}{2} = P(B)$

7. (A) E and F are independent.

(B) G and H are dependent.

8. $\left(\frac{1}{6}\right)^6 \approx .000\ 021\ 4$

8-4 Bayes' Formula

In the preceding section, we discussed the conditional probability of the occurrence of an event, given the occurrence of an earlier event. Now we will reverse the problem and try to find the probability of an earlier event conditioned on the occurrence of a later event. As you will see, a number of practical problems have this form. First, let us consider a relatively simple problem that will provide the basis for a generalization.

EXAMPLE 1   **Probability of an Earlier Event Given a Later Event** One urn has 3 blue and 2 white balls; a second urn has 1 blue and 3 white balls (Fig. 1). A single fair die is rolled and if 1 or 2 comes up, a ball is drawn out of the first urn; otherwise, a ball is drawn out of the second urn. If the drawn ball is blue, what is the probability that it came out of the first urn? Out of the second urn?

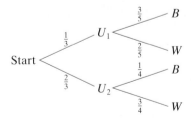

Figure 1

SOLUTION   We form a probability tree, letting U_1 represent urn 1, U_2 urn 2, B a blue ball, and W a white ball. Then, on the various outcome branches, we assign appropriate probabilities. For example, $P(U_1) = \frac{1}{3}$, $P(B|U_1) = \frac{3}{5}$, and so on:

Now we are interested in finding $P(U_1|B)$; that is, the probability that the ball came out of urn 1, given that the drawn ball is blue. Using equation (1) from Section 8-3, we can write

$$P(U_1|B) = \frac{P(U_1 \cap B)}{P(B)} \qquad (1)$$

If we look at the tree diagram, we can see that B is at the end of two different branches; thus,

$$P(B) = P(U_1 \cap B) + P(U_2 \cap B) \qquad (2)$$

After substituting equation (2) into equation (1), we get

$$P(U_1|B) = \frac{P(U_1 \cap B)}{P(U_1 \cap B) + P(U_2 \cap B)} \qquad P(A \cap B) = P(A)P(B|A)$$

$$= \frac{P(U_1)P(B|U_1)}{P(U_1)P(B|U_1) + P(U_2)P(B|U_2)}$$

$$= \frac{P(B|U_1)P(U_1)}{P(B|U_1)P(U_1) + P(B|U_2)P(U_2)} \qquad (3)$$

Equation (3) is really a lot simpler to use than it looks. You do not need to memorize it; you simply need to understand its form relative to the probability tree above. Referring to the probability tree, we see that

$$P(B|U_1)P(U_1) = \text{product of branch probabilities leading to } B \text{ through } U_1$$
$$= \left(\tfrac{3}{5}\right)\left(\tfrac{1}{3}\right) \qquad \text{We usually start at } B \text{ and work back through } U_1.$$

$$P(B|U_2)P(U_2) = \text{product of branch probabilities leading to } B \text{ through } U_2$$
$$= \left(\tfrac{1}{4}\right)\left(\tfrac{2}{3}\right) \qquad \text{We usually start at } B \text{ and work back through } U_2.$$

Equation (3) now can be interpreted in terms of the probability tree as follows:

$$P(U_1|B) = \frac{\text{product of branch probabilities leading to } B \text{ through } U_1}{\text{sum of all branch products leading to } B}$$

$$= \frac{\left(\tfrac{3}{5}\right)\left(\tfrac{1}{3}\right)}{\left(\tfrac{3}{5}\right)\left(\tfrac{1}{3}\right) + \left(\tfrac{1}{4}\right)\left(\tfrac{2}{3}\right)} = \frac{6}{11} \approx .55$$

Similarly,

$$P(U_2|B) = \frac{\text{product of branch probabilities leading to } B \text{ through } U_2}{\text{sum of all branch products leading to } B}$$

$$= \frac{\left(\tfrac{1}{4}\right)\left(\tfrac{2}{3}\right)}{\left(\tfrac{3}{5}\right)\left(\tfrac{1}{3}\right) + \left(\tfrac{1}{4}\right)\left(\tfrac{2}{3}\right)} = \frac{5}{11} \approx .45$$

Note: We could have obtained $P(U_2|B)$ by subtracting $P(U_1|B)$ from 1. Why?

Matched Problem 1 Repeat Example 1, but find $P(U_1|W)$ and $P(U_2|W)$.

EXPLORE & DISCUSS 1 Study the probability tree below:

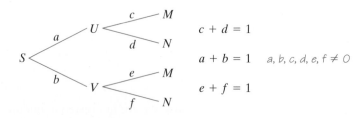

$c + d = 1$

$a + b = 1 \qquad a, b, c, d, e, f \neq 0$

$e + f = 1$

(A) Discuss the difference between $P(M|U)$ and $P(U|M)$, and between $P(N|V)$ and $P(V|N)$, in terms of $a, b, c, d, e,$ and f.

(B) Show that $ac + ad + be + bf = 1$. What is the significance of this result?

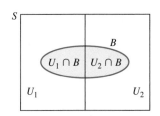

Figure 2

In generalizing the results in Example 1, it is helpful to look at its structure in terms of the Venn diagram shown in Figure 2. We note that U_1 and U_2 are mutually exclusive (disjoint), and their union forms S. The following two equations can now be interpreted in terms of this diagram:

$$P(U_1|B) = \frac{P(U_1 \cap B)}{P(B)} = \frac{P(U_1 \cap B)}{P(U_1 \cap B) + P(U_2 \cap B)}$$

$$P(U_2|B) = \frac{P(U_2 \cap B)}{P(B)} = \frac{P(U_2 \cap B)}{P(U_1 \cap B) + P(U_2 \cap B)}$$

Look over the equations and the diagram carefully.

Of course, there is no reason to stop here. Suppose that U_1, U_2, and U_3 are three mutually exclusive events whose union is the whole sample space S. Then, for an arbitrary event E in S, with $P(E) \neq 0$, the corresponding Venn diagram looks like Figure 3, and

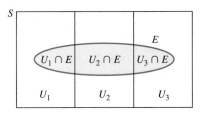

Figure 3

$$P(U_1|E) = \frac{P(U_1 \cap E)}{P(E)} = \frac{P(U_1 \cap E)}{P(U_1 \cap E) + P(U_2 \cap E) + P(U_3 \cap E)}$$

Similar results hold for U_2 and U_3.

Using the same reasoning, we arrive at the following famous theorem, which was first stated by Thomas Bayes (1702–1763):

THEOREM 1 Bayes' Formula

Let $U_1, U_2, \ldots, U_n$ be n mutually exclusive events whose union is the sample space S. Let E be an arbitrary event in S such that $P(E) \neq 0$. Then,

$$P(U_1|E) = \frac{P(U_1 \cap E)}{P(E)} = \frac{P(U_1 \cap E)}{P(U_1 \cap E) + P(U_2 \cap E) + \cdots + P(U_n \cap E)}$$

$$= \frac{P(E|U_1)P(U_1)}{P(E|U_1)P(U_1) + P(E|U_2)P(U_2) + \cdots + P(E|U_n)P(U_n)}$$

Similar results hold for $U_2, U_3, \ldots, U_n$.

You do not need to memorize Bayes' formula. In practice, it is often easier to draw a probability tree and use the following:

$$P(U_1|E) = \frac{\text{product of branch probabilities leading to } E \text{ through } U_1}{\text{sum of all branch products leading to } E}$$

Similar results hold for $U_2, U_3, \ldots, U_n$.

EXAMPLE 2 **Tuberculosis Screening** A new, inexpensive skin test is devised for detecting tuberculosis. To evaluate the test before it is used, a medical researcher randomly selects 1,000 people. Using precise but more expensive methods, it is found that 8% of the 1,000 people tested have tuberculosis. Now each of the 1,000 subjects is given the new skin test, and the following results are recorded: The test indicates tuberculosis in 96% of those who have it and in 2% of those who do not. Based on these results, what is the probability of a randomly chosen person having tuberculosis given that the skin test indicates the disease? What is the probability of a person not having tuberculosis given that the skin test indicates the disease? (That is, what is the probability of the skin test giving a *false positive result?*)

SOLUTION To start, we form a tree diagram and place appropriate probabilities on each branch:

$$T = \text{tuberculosis}$$
$$T' = \text{no tuberculosis}$$
$$S = \text{skin test indicates tuberculosis}$$
$$S' = \text{skin test indicates no tuberculosis}$$

We are interested in finding $P(T|S)$, that is, the probability of a person having tuberculosis given that the skin test indicates the disease. Bayes' formula for this case is

$$P(T|S) = \frac{\text{product of branch probabilities leading to } S \text{ through } T}{\text{sum of all branch products leading to } S}$$

Substituting appropriate values from the probability tree, we obtain

$$P(T|S) = \frac{(.08)(.96)}{(.08)(.96) + (.92)(.02)} = .81$$

The probability of a person not having tuberculosis given that the skin test indicates the disease, denoted by $P(T'|S)$, is

$$P(T'|S) = 1 - P(T|S) = 1 - .81 = .19 \qquad P(T|S) + P(T'|S) = 1$$

Matched Problem 2 What is the probability that a person has tuberculosis given that the test indicates no tuberculosis is present? (That is, what is the probability of the skin test giving a *false negative result*?) What is the probability that a person does not have tuberculosis given that the test indicates no tuberculosis is present?

CONCEPTUAL INSIGHT

From a public health standpoint, which is the more serious error in Example 2 and Matched Problem 2: a false positive result or a false negative result? A false positive result will certainly be unsettling to the subject, who might lose sleep thinking that she has tuberculosis. But she will be sent for further testing and will be relieved to learn it was a false alarm; she does not have the disease. A false negative result, on the other hand, is more serious. A person who has tuberculosis will be unaware that he has a communicable disease and so may pose a considerable risk to public health.

In designing an inexpensive skin test, we would expect a tradeoff between cost and false results. We might be willing to tolerate a moderate number of false positives if we could keep the number of false negatives at a minimum.

EXAMPLE 3 **Product Defects** A company produces 1,000 refrigerators a week at three plants. Plant *A* produces 350 refrigerators a week, plant *B* produces 250 refrigerators a week, and plant *C* produces 400 refrigerators a week. Production records indicate that 5% of the refrigerators produced at plant *A* will be defective, 3% of those produced at plant *B* will be defective, and 7% of those produced at plant *C* will be defective. All the refrigerators are shipped to a central warehouse. If a refrigerator at the warehouse is found to be defective, what is the probability that it was produced at plant *A*?

SOLUTION   We begin by constructing a tree diagram:

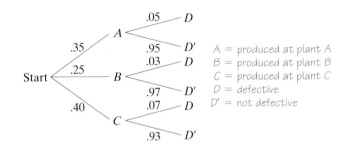

The probability that a defective refrigerator was produced at plant A is $P(A|D)$. Bayes' formula for this case is

$$P(A|D) = \frac{\text{product of branch probabilities leading to } D \text{ through } A}{\text{sum of all branch products leading to } D}$$

Using the values from the probability tree, we have

$$P(A|D) = \frac{(.35)(.05)}{(.35)(.05) + (.25)(.03) + (.40)(.07)}$$

$$\approx .33$$

Matched Problem 3   In Example 3, what is the probability that a defective refrigerator in the warehouse was produced at plant B? At plant C?

Exercises 8-4

Find the probabilities in Problems 1–6 by referring to the tree diagram below.

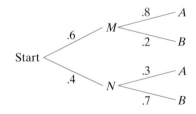

1. $P(M \cap A) = P(M)P(A|M)$

2. $P(N \cap B) = P(N)P(B|N)$

3. $P(A) = P(M \cap A) + P(N \cap A)$

4. $P(B) = P(M \cap B) + P(N \cap B)$

5. $P(M|A) = \dfrac{P(M \cap A)}{P(M \cap A) + P(N \cap A)}$

6. $P(N|B) = \dfrac{P(N \cap B)}{P(N \cap B) + P(M \cap B)}$

Find the probabilities in Problems 7–10 by referring to the following Venn diagram and using Bayes' formula (assume that the simple events in S are equally likely):

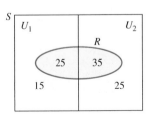

7. $P(U_1|R)$ **8.** $P(U_2|R)$

9. $P(U_1|R')$ **10.** $P(U_2|R')$

B

Find the probabilities in Problems 11–16 by referring to the following tree diagram and using Bayes' formula. Round answers to three decimal places.

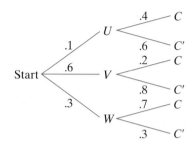

11. $P(U|C)$ **12.** $P(V|C')$

13. $P(W|C)$ **14.** $P(U|C')$

15. $P(V|C)$ **16.** $P(W|C')$

Find the probabilities in Problems 17–22 by referring to the following Venn diagram and using Bayes' formula (assume that the simple events in S are equally likely):

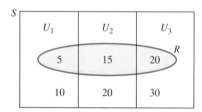

17. $P(U_1|R)$ **18.** $P(U_2|R')$

19. $P(U_3|R)$ **20.** $P(U_1|R')$

21. $P(U_2|R)$ **22.** $P(U_3|R')$

In Problems 23 and 24, use the probabilities in the first tree diagram to find the probability of each branch of the second tree diagram.

23.

24.

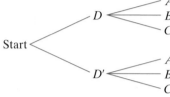

In Problems 25–28, one of two urns is chosen at random with one as likely to be chosen as the other. Then a ball is withdrawn from the chosen urn. Urn 1 contains 1 white and 4 red balls, and urn 2 has 3 white and 2 red balls.

25. If a white ball is drawn, what is the probability that it came from urn 1?

26. If a white ball is drawn, what is the probability that it came from urn 2?

27. If a red ball is drawn, what is the probability that it came from urn 2?

28. If a red ball is drawn, what is the probability that it came from urn 1?

In Problems 29 and 30, an urn contains 4 red and 5 white balls. Two balls are drawn in succession without replacement.

29. If the second ball is white, what is the probability that the first ball was white?

30. If the second ball is red, what is the probability that the first ball was red?

In Problems 31 and 32, urn 1 contains 7 red and 3 white balls. Urn 2 contains 4 red and 5 white balls. A ball is drawn from urn 1 and placed in urn 2. Then a ball is drawn from urn 2.

31. If the ball drawn from urn 2 is red, what is the probability that the ball drawn from urn 1 was red?

32. If the ball drawn from urn 2 is white, what is the probability that the ball drawn from urn 1 was white?

✎ In Problems 33 and 34, refer to the following probability tree:

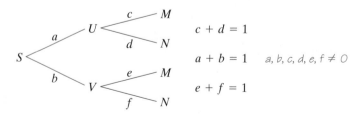

33. Suppose that $c = e$. Discuss the dependence or independence of events U and M.

34. Suppose that $c = d = e = f$. Discuss the dependence or independence of events M and N.

✎ *In Problems 35 and 36, two balls are drawn in succession from an urn containing m blue balls and n white balls ($m \geq 2$ and $n \geq 2$). Discuss the validity of each statement. If the statement is always true, explain why. If not, give a counterexample.*

35. (A) If the two balls are drawn with replacement, then $P(B_1|B_2) = P(B_2|B_1)$.

    (B) If the two balls are drawn without replacement, then $P(B_1|B_2) = P(B_2|B_1)$.

36. (A) If the two balls are drawn with replacement, then $P(B_1|W_2) = P(W_2|B_1)$.

    (B) If the two balls are drawn without replacement, then $P(B_1|W_2) = P(W_2|B_1)$.

C

37. If 2 cards are drawn in succession from a standard 52-card deck without replacement and the second card is a heart, what is the probability that the first card is a heart?

38. A box contains 10 balls numbered 1 through 10. Two balls are drawn in succession without replacement. If the second ball drawn has the number 4 on it, what is the probability that the first ball had a smaller number on it? An even number on it?

In Problems 39–44, a 3-card hand is dealt from a standard 52-card deck, and then one of the 3 cards is chosen at random.

39. If only one of the cards in the hand is a club, what is the probability that the chosen card is a club?

40. If only two of the cards in the hand are clubs, what is the probability that the chosen card is a club?

41. If the chosen card is a club, what is the probability that it is the only club in the hand?

42. If the chosen card is a club, what is the probability that exactly two of the cards in the hand are clubs?

43. If the chosen card is a club, what is the probability that all of the cards in the hand are clubs?

44. If the chosen card is not a club, what is the probability that none of the cards in the hand is a club?

45. Show that $P(U_1|R) + P(U_1'|R) = 1$.

46. If U_1 and U_2 are two mutually exclusive events whose union is the equally likely sample space S and if E is an arbitrary event in S such that $P(E) \neq 0$, show that

$$P(U_1|E) = \frac{n(U_1 \cap E)}{n(U_1 \cap E) + n(U_2 \cap E)}$$

Applications

In the following applications, the word "probability" is often understood to mean "approximate empirical probability."

47. Employee screening. The management of a company finds that 30% of the administrative assistants hired are unsatisfactory. The personnel director is instructed to devise a test that will improve the situation. One hundred employed administrative assistants are chosen at random and are given the newly constructed test. Out of these, 90% of the satisfactory administrative assistants pass the test and 20% of the unsatisfactory administrative assistants pass. Based on these results, if a person applies for a job, takes the test, and passes it, what is the probability that he or she is a satisfactory administrative assistant? If the applicant fails the test, what is the probability that he or she is a satisfactory administrative assistant?

48. Employee rating. A company has rated 75% of its employees as satisfactory and 25% as unsatisfactory. Personnel records indicate that 80% of the satisfactory workers had previous work experience, while only 40% of the unsatisfactory workers had any previous work experience. If a person with previous work experience is hired, what is the probability that this person will be a satisfactory employee? If a person with no previous work experience is hired, what is the probability that this person will be a satisfactory employee?

49. Product defects. A manufacturer obtains GPS systems from three different subcontractors: 20% from A, 40% from B, and 40% from C. The defective rates for these subcontractors are 1%, 3%, and 2%, respectively. If a defective GPS system is returned by a customer, what is the probability that it came from subcontractor A? From B? From C?

50. Product defects. A store sells three types of flash drives: brand A, brand B, and brand C. Of the flash drives it sells, 60% are brand A, 25% are brand B, and 15% are brand C. The store has found that 20% of the brand A flash drives, 15% of the brand B flash drives, and 5% of the brand C flash drives are returned as defective. If a flash drive is returned as defective, what is the probability that it is a brand A flash drive? A brand B flash drive? A brand C flash drive?

51. Cancer screening. A new, simple test has been developed to detect a particular type of cancer. The test must be evaluated before it is used. A medical researcher selects a random sample of 1,000 adults and finds (by other means) that 2% have this type of cancer. Each of the 1,000 adults is given the test, and it is found that the test indicates cancer in 98% of those who have it and in 1% of those who do not. Based on these results, what is the probability of a randomly chosen person having cancer given that the test indicates cancer? Of a person having cancer given that the test does not indicate cancer?

52. Pregnancy testing. In a random sample of 200 women who suspect that they are pregnant, 100 turn out to be pregnant. A new pregnancy test given to these women indicated pregnancy in 92 of the 100 pregnant women and in 12 of the 100 nonpregnant women. If a woman suspects she is pregnant and this test indicates that she is pregnant, what is the probability that she is pregnant? If the test indicates that she is not pregnant, what is the probability that she is not pregnant?

53. Medical research. In a random sample of 1,000 people, it is found that 7% have a liver ailment. Of those who have a liver ailment, 40% are heavy drinkers, 50% are moderate drinkers, and 10% are nondrinkers. Of those who do not have a liver ailment, 10% are heavy drinkers, 70% are moderate drinkers, and 20% are nondrinkers. If a person is chosen at random and he or she is a heavy drinker, what is the probability of that person having a liver ailment? What is the probability for a nondrinker?

54. Tuberculosis screening. A test for tuberculosis was given to 1,000 subjects, 8% of whom were known to have tuberculosis. For the subjects who had tuberculosis, the test indicated tuberculosis in 90% of the subjects, was inconclusive for 7%, and indicated no tuberculosis in 3%. For the subjects who did not have tuberculosis, the test indicated tuberculosis in 5% of the subjects, was inconclusive for 10%, and indicated no tuberculosis in the remaining 85%. What is the probability of a randomly selected person having tuberculosis given that the test indicates tuberculosis? Of not having tuberculosis given that the test was inconclusive?

55. Police science. A new lie-detector test has been devised and must be tested before it is used. One hundred people are selected at random, and each person draws a card from a box of 100 cards. Half the cards instruct the person to lie, and the others instruct the person to tell the truth. Of those who lied, 80% fail the new lie-detector test (that is, the test indicates lying). Of those who told the truth, 5% failed the test. What is the probability that a randomly chosen subject will have lied given that the subject failed the test? That the subject will not have lied given that the subject failed the test?

56. Politics. In a given county, records show that of the registered voters, 45% are Democrats, 35% are Republicans, and 20% are independents. In an election, 70% of the Democrats, 40% of the Republicans, and 80% of the independents voted in favor of a parks and recreation bond proposal. If a registered voter chosen at random is found to have voted in favor of the bond, what is the probability that the voter is a Republican? An independent? A Democrat?

Answers to Matched Problems

1. $P(U_1|W) = \frac{4}{19} \approx .21$; $P(U_2|W) = \frac{15}{19} \approx .79$

2. $P(T|S') = .004$; $P(T'|S') = .996$

3. $P(B|D) \approx .14$; $P(C|D) \approx .53$

8-5   Random Variable, Probability Distribution, and Expected Value

- Random Variable and Probability Distribution
- Expected Value of a Random Variable
- Decision Making and Expected Value

Random Variable and Probability Distribution

When performing a random experiment, a sample space S is selected in such a way that all probability problems of interest relative to the experiment can be solved. In many situations we may not be interested in each simple event in the sample space S but in some numerical value associated with the event. For example, if 3 coins are tossed, we may be interested in the number of heads that turn up rather than in the particular pattern that turns up. Or, in selecting a random sample of students, we may be interested in the proportion that are women rather than which particular students are women. In the same way, a "craps" player is usually interested in the sum of the dots on the showing faces of the dice rather than the pattern of dots on each face.

In each of these examples, there is a rule that assigns to each simple event in S a single real number. Mathematically speaking, we are dealing with a function (see Section 2-1). Historically, this particular type of function has been called a "random variable."

DEFINITION Random Variable

A **random variable** is a function that assigns a numerical value to each simple event in a sample space S.

Table 1   Number of Heads in the Toss of 3 Coins

Sample Space S		Number of Heads $X(e_i)$
e_1:	TTT	0
e_2:	TTH	1
e_3:	THT	1
e_4:	HTT	1
e_5:	THH	2
e_6:	HTH	2
e_7:	HHT	2
e_8:	HHH	3

The term *random variable* is an unfortunate choice, since it is neither random nor a variable—it is a function with a numerical value, and it is defined on a sample space. But the terminology has stuck and is now standard. Capital letters, such as X, are used to represent random variables.

Let us return to the experiment of tossing 3 coins. A sample space S of equally likely simple events is indicated in Table 1. Suppose that we are interested in the number of heads (0, 1, 2, or 3) appearing on each toss of the 3 coins and the probability of each of these events. We introduce a random variable X (a function) that indicates the number of heads for each simple event in S (see the second column in Table 1). For example, $X(e_1) = 0$, $X(e_2) = 1$, and so on. The random variable X assigns a numerical value to each simple event in the sample space S.

We are interested in the probability of the occurrence of each image or range value of X; that is, in the probability of the occurrence of 0 heads, 1 head, 2 heads, or 3 heads in the single toss of 3 coins. We indicate this probability by

$$p(x) \qquad \text{where} \quad x \in \{0, 1, 2, 3\}$$

The function p is called the **probability distribution* of the random variable X.**

What is $p(2)$, the probability of getting exactly 2 heads on the single toss of 3 coins? "Exactly 2 heads occur" is the event

$$E = \{\text{THH, HTH, HHT}\}$$

Thus,

$$p(2) = \frac{n(E)}{n(S)} = \frac{3}{8}$$

Table 2   Probability Distribution

Number of Heads x	0	1	2	3
Probability $p(x)$	$\frac{1}{8}$	$\frac{3}{8}$	$\frac{3}{8}$	$\frac{1}{8}$

Proceeding similarly for $p(0)$, $p(1)$, and $p(3)$, we obtain the probability distribution of the random variable X presented in Table 2. Probability distributions are also represented graphically, as shown in Figure 1. The graph of a probability distribution is often called a **histogram**.

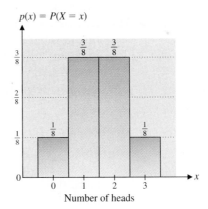

$p(x) = P(X = x)$

Number of heads

Figure 1 Histogram for a probability distribution

Note from Table 2 or Figure 1 that

1. $0 \le p(x) \le 1$, $x \in \{0, 1, 2, 3\}$

2. $p(0) + p(1) + p(2) + p(3) = \frac{1}{8} + \frac{3}{8} + \frac{3}{8} + \frac{1}{8} = 1$

These are general properties that any probability distribution of a random variable X associated with a finite sample space must have.

---

*The probability distribution p of the random variable X is defined by $p(x) = P(\{e_i \in S \mid X(e_i) = x\})$, which, because of its cumbersome nature, is usually simplified to $p(x) = P(X = x)$ or simply $p(x)$. We will use the simplified notation.

> **THEOREM 1   Probability Distribution of a Random Variable** X
> The **probability distribution of a random variable** X, denoted by $P(X = x) = p(x)$, satisfies
>
> **1.** $0 \leq p(x) \leq 1$, $\quad x \in \{x_1, x_2, \ldots, x_n\}$
> **2.** $p(x_1) + p(x_2) + \cdots + p(x_n) = 1$
>
> where $\{x_1, x_2, \ldots, x_n\}$ are the (range) values of X (see Fig. 2).

Figure 2 illustrates the process of forming a probability distribution of a random variable.

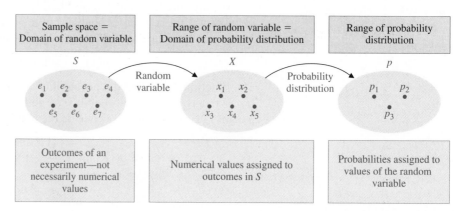

Figure 2 Probability distribution of a random variable for a finite sample space

Expected Value of a Random Variable

Suppose that the experiment of tossing 3 coins was repeated many times. What would be the average number of heads per toss (the total number of heads in all tosses divided by the total number of tosses)? Consulting the probability distribution in Table 2 or Figure 1, we would expect to toss 0 heads $\frac{1}{8}$ of the time, 1 head $\frac{3}{8}$ of the time, 2 heads $\frac{3}{8}$ of the time, and 3 heads $\frac{1}{8}$ of the time. In the long run, we would expect the average number of heads per toss of the 3 coins, or the *expected value* $E(X)$, to be given by

$$E(X) = 0\left(\tfrac{1}{8}\right) + 1\left(\tfrac{3}{8}\right) + 2\left(\tfrac{3}{8}\right) + 3\left(\tfrac{1}{8}\right) = \tfrac{12}{8} = 1.5$$

It is important to note that the expected value is not a value that will necessarily occur in a single experiment (1.5 heads cannot occur in the toss of 3 coins), but it is an average of what occurs over a large number of experiments. Sometimes we will toss more than 1.5 heads and sometimes less, but if the experiment is repeated many times, the average number of heads per experiment should be close to 1.5.

We now make the preceding discussion more precise through the following definition of expected value:

> **DEFINITION   Expected Value of a Random Variable** X
> Given the probability distribution for the random variable X,
>
> | x_i | x_1 | x_2 | $\cdots$ | x_n |
> |---|---|---|---|---|
> | p_i | p_1 | p_2 | $\cdots$ | p_n |
>
> where $p_i = p(x_i)$, we define the **expected value of** X, denoted $E(X)$, by the formula
>
> $$E(X) = x_1 p_1 + x_2 p_2 + \cdots + x_n p_n$$

As you might guess, we can get the second-state matrix S_2 (for the second purchase) by multiplying the first-state matrix by the transition matrix:

$$S_1P = \begin{matrix} A & A' \\ [.62 & .38] \end{matrix} \begin{bmatrix} .8 & .2 \\ .6 & .4 \end{bmatrix} = \begin{matrix} A & A' \\ [.724 & .276] \end{matrix} = S_2$$

$$\underset{\substack{\text{First} \\ \text{state}}}{} \qquad\qquad \underset{\substack{\text{Second} \\ \text{state}}}{}$$

The third-state matrix S_3 is computed in a similar manner:

$$S_2P = \begin{matrix} A & A' \\ [.724 & .276] \end{matrix} \begin{bmatrix} .8 & .2 \\ .6 & .4 \end{bmatrix} = \begin{matrix} A & A' \\ [.7448 & .2552] \end{matrix} = S_3$$

$$\underset{\substack{\text{Second} \\ \text{state}}}{} \qquad\qquad \underset{\substack{\text{Third} \\ \text{state}}}{}$$

Examining the values in the first three state matrices, we see that brand A's market share increases after each toothpaste purchase. Will the market share for brand A continue to increase until it approaches 100%, or will it level off at some value less than 100%? These questions are answered in Section 9-2 when we develop techniques for determining the long-run behavior of state matrices.

Transition and State Matrices

The sequence of trials (toothpaste purchases) with the constant transition matrix P is a special kind of stochastic process called a *Markov chain*. In general, a **Markov chain** is a sequence of experiments, trials, or observations such that the transition probability matrix from one state to the next is constant. A Markov chain has no memory. The various matrices associated with a Markov chain are defined in the next box.

DEFINITION Markov Chains

Given a Markov chain with n states, a **kth-state matrix** is a matrix of the form

$$S_k = [s_{k1} \quad s_{k2} \quad \cdots \quad s_{kn}]$$

Each entry s_{ki} is the proportion of the population that is in state i after the kth trial, or, equivalently, the probability of a randomly selected element of the population being in state i after the kth trial. The sum of all the entries in the kth state matrix S_k must be 1.

A **transition matrix** is a constant square matrix P of order n such that the entry in the ith row and jth column indicates the probability of the system moving from the ith state to the jth state on the next observation or trial. The sum of the entries in each row must be 1.

CONCEPTUAL INSIGHT

1. Since the entries in a kth-state matrix or transition matrix are probabilities, they must be real numbers between 0 and 1, inclusive.
2. Rearranging the various states and corresponding transition probabilities in a transition matrix will produce a different, but equivalent, transition matrix. For example, both of the following matrices are transition matrices for the toothpaste company discussed earlier:

$$P = \begin{matrix} & A & A' \\ A & \\ A' \end{matrix}\begin{bmatrix} .8 & .2 \\ .6 & .4 \end{bmatrix} \qquad P' = \begin{matrix} & A' & A \\ A' & \\ A \end{matrix}\begin{bmatrix} .4 & .6 \\ .2 & .8 \end{bmatrix}$$

Such rearrangements will affect the form of the matrices used in the solution of a problem but will not affect any of the information obtained from these matrices. In Section 9-3, we encounter situations where it will be helpful to select a transition matrix that has a special form. For now, you can choose any order for the states in a transition matrix.

As we indicated in the preceding discussion, matrix multiplication can be used to compute the various state matrices of a Markov chain:

If S_0 is the initial-state matrix and P is the transition matrix for a Markov chain, then the subsequent state matrices are given by

$$S_1 = S_0 P \qquad \text{First-state matrix}$$
$$S_2 = S_1 P \qquad \text{Second-state matrix}$$
$$S_3 = S_2 P \qquad \text{Third-state matrix}$$
$$\vdots$$
$$S_k = S_{k-1} P \qquad \text{kth-state matrix}$$

EXAMPLE 1

Insurance An insurance company found that on average, over a period of 10 years, 23% of the drivers in a particular community who were involved in an accident one year were also involved in an accident the following year. They also found that only 11% of the drivers who were not involved in an accident one year were involved in an accident the following year. Use these percentages as approximate empirical probabilities for the following:

(A) Draw a transition diagram.

(B) Find the transition matrix P.

(C) If 5% of the drivers in the community are involved in an accident this year, what is the probability that a driver chosen at random from the community will be involved in an accident next year? Year after next?

SOLUTION   (A)

.77
.23 ◯ _A_ ⟶ _A'_ ◯ .89 A = accident
.11 A' = no accident

(B)

$$
\begin{array}{c}
 \\
\text{This} \\
\text{year}
\end{array}
\begin{array}{cc}
 & \text{Next year} \\
\begin{array}{c} A \\ A' \end{array} &
\begin{array}{cc} A & A' \end{array}
\end{array}
\left[\begin{array}{cc} .23 & .77 \\ .11 & .89 \end{array}\right] = P \qquad \text{Transition matrix}
$$

(C) The initial-state matrix S_0 is

$$
\begin{array}{cc} A & A' \end{array}
$$
$$S_0 = [.05 \quad .95] \qquad \text{Initial-state matrix}$$

Thus,

$$
S_0 P = [.05 \quad .95]\left[\begin{array}{cc} .23 & .77 \\ .11 & .89 \end{array}\right] = [.116 \quad .884] = S_1
$$

This year   Next year
(initial state)   (first state)

$$
S_1 P = [.116 \quad .884]\left[\begin{array}{cc} .23 & .77 \\ .11 & .89 \end{array}\right] = [.12392 \quad .87608] = S_2
$$

Next year   Year after next
(first state)   (second state)

The probability that a driver chosen at random from the community will have an accident next year is .116, and the year after next is .12392. That is, it is expected that 11.6% of the drivers in the community will have an accident next year and 12.392% the year after.

Matched Problem 1   An insurance company classifies drivers as low-risk if they are accident-free for one year. Past records indicate that 98% of the drivers in the low-risk category (L) one year will remain in that category the next year, and 78% of the drivers who are not in the low-risk category (L') one year will be in the low-risk category the next year.

(A) Draw a transition diagram.

(B) Find the transition matrix P.

(C) If 90% of the drivers in the community are in the low-risk category this year, what is the probability that a driver chosen at random from the community will be in the low-risk category next year? Year after next?

Powers of Transition Matrices

Next we investigate the powers of a transition matrix.

The state matrices for a Markov chain are defined **recursively**; that is, each state matrix is defined in terms of the preceding state matrix. For example, to find the fourth-state matrix S_4, it is necessary to compute the preceding three state matrices:

$$S_1 = S_0P \qquad S_2 = S_1P \qquad S_3 = S_2P \qquad S_4 = S_3P$$

Is there any way to compute a given state matrix directly without first computing all the preceding state matrices? If we substitute the equation for S_1 into the equation for S_2, substitute this new equation for S_2 into the equation for S_3, and so on, a definite pattern emerges:

$$S_1 = S_0P$$
$$S_2 = S_1P = (S_0P)P = S_0P^2$$
$$S_3 = S_2P = (S_0P^2)P = S_0P^3$$
$$S_4 = S_3P = (S_0P^3)P = S_0P^4$$
$$\vdots$$

In general, it can be shown that the kth-state matrix is given by $S_k = S_0P^k$. We summarize this important result in Theorem 1.

THEOREM 1   Powers of a Transition Matrix

If P is the transition matrix and S_0 is an initial-state matrix for a Markov chain, then the kth-state matrix is given by

$$S_k = S_0P^k$$

The entry in the ith row and jth column of P^k indicates the probability of the system moving from the ith state to the jth state in k observations or trials. The sum of the entries in each row of P^k is 1.

EXAMPLE 2   Using P^k to Compute S_k Find P^4 and use it to find S_4 for

$$P = \begin{array}{c} \\ A \\ A' \end{array}\begin{array}{cc} A & A' \\ \begin{bmatrix} .1 & .9 \\ .6 & .4 \end{bmatrix} \end{array} \qquad \text{and} \qquad S_0 = \begin{array}{c} A \quad\ A' \\ [.2 \quad .8] \end{array}$$

SOLUTION

$$P^2 = PP = \begin{bmatrix} .1 & .9 \\ .6 & .4 \end{bmatrix}\begin{bmatrix} .1 & .9 \\ .6 & .4 \end{bmatrix} = \begin{bmatrix} .55 & .45 \\ .3 & .7 \end{bmatrix}$$

$$P^4 = P^2P^2 = \begin{bmatrix} .55 & .45 \\ .3 & .7 \end{bmatrix}\begin{bmatrix} .55 & .45 \\ .3 & .7 \end{bmatrix} = \begin{bmatrix} .4375 & .5625 \\ .375 & .625 \end{bmatrix}$$

$$S_4 = S_0P^4 = [.2 \quad .8]\begin{bmatrix} .4375 & .5625 \\ .375 & .625 \end{bmatrix} = [.3875 \quad .6125]$$

Matched Problem 2 Find P^4 and use it to find S_4 for

$$P = \begin{array}{cc} & \begin{array}{cc} A & A' \end{array} \\ \begin{array}{c} A \\ A' \end{array} & \begin{bmatrix} .8 & .2 \\ .3 & .7 \end{bmatrix} \end{array} \quad \text{and} \quad S_0 = \begin{array}{cc} \begin{array}{cc} A & A' \end{array} \\ [.8 \quad .2] \end{array}$$

If a graphing calculator or a computer is available for computing matrix products and powers of a matrix, finding state matrices for any number of trials becomes a routine calculation.

EXAMPLE 3 **Using a Graphing Calculator and P^k to Compute S_k** Use P^8 and a graphing calculator to find S_8 for P and S_0 as given in Example 2. Round values in S_8 to six decimal places.

SOLUTION After storing the matrices P and S_0 in the graphing calculator's memory, we use the equation

$$S_8 = S_0 P^8$$

```
P
          [[.1 .9]
           [.6 .4]]
S0
          [[.2 .8]]
S0*P^8
  [[.399219 .600781]]
```
Figure 2

to compute S_8. Figure 2 shows the result on a typical graphing calculator. We see that (to six decimal places)

$$S_8 = [.399219 \quad .600781]$$

Matched Problem 3 Use P^8 and a graphing calculator to find S_8 for P and S_0 as given in Matched Problem 2. Round values in S_8 to six decimal places.

Application

The next example illustrates the use of Theorem 1 in an application.

EXAMPLE 4 **University Enrollment** Part-time students in a university MBA program are considered to be first-year students until they complete 15 credits successfully. Then they are classified as second-year students and can take more advanced courses and work on the thesis required for graduation. Past records indicate that at the end of each year, 10% of the first-year students (F) drop out of the program (D) and 30% become second-year students (S). Also, 10% of the second-year students drop out of the program and 40% graduate (G) each year. Students that graduate or drop out never return to the program.

(A) Draw a transition diagram.

(B) Find the transition matrix P.

(C) What is the probability that a first-year student graduates within 4 years? Drops out within 4 years?

SOLUTION (A) If 10% of first-year students drop out and 30% become second-year students, then the remaining 60% must continue as first-year students for another year (see the diagram). Similarly, 50% of second-year students must continue as second-year students for another year. Since students who drop out never return, all students in state D in one year will continue in that state the next year. We indicate this by placing a 1 on the arrow from D back to D. State G is labeled in the same manner.

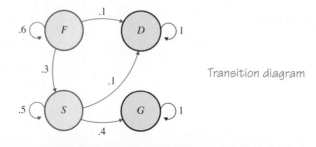

Transition diagram

(B)

$$P = \begin{array}{c} \\ F \\ D \\ S \\ G \end{array} \begin{array}{cccc} F & D & S & G \\ \begin{bmatrix} .6 & .1 & .3 & 0 \\ 0 & 1 & 0 & 0 \\ 0 & .1 & .5 & .4 \\ 0 & 0 & 0 & 1 \end{bmatrix} \end{array} \qquad \text{Transition matrix}$$

(C)   The probability that a first-year student moves from state F to state G within 4 years is the entry in row 1 and column 4 of P^4 (Theorem 1). Hand computation of P^4 requires two multiplications:

$$P^2 = \begin{bmatrix} .6 & .1 & .3 & 0 \\ 0 & 1 & 0 & 0 \\ 0 & .1 & .5 & .4 \\ 0 & 0 & 0 & 1 \end{bmatrix} \begin{bmatrix} .6 & .1 & .3 & 0 \\ 0 & 1 & 0 & 0 \\ 0 & .1 & .5 & .4 \\ 0 & 0 & 0 & 1 \end{bmatrix} = \begin{bmatrix} .36 & .19 & .33 & .12 \\ 0 & 1 & 0 & 0 \\ 0 & .15 & .25 & .6 \\ 0 & 0 & 0 & 1 \end{bmatrix}$$

$$P^4 = P^2 P^2 = \begin{bmatrix} .36 & .19 & .33 & .12 \\ 0 & 1 & 0 & 0 \\ 0 & .15 & .25 & .6 \\ 0 & 0 & 0 & 1 \end{bmatrix} \begin{bmatrix} .36 & .19 & .33 & .12 \\ 0 & 1 & 0 & 0 \\ 0 & .15 & .25 & .6 \\ 0 & 0 & 0 & 1 \end{bmatrix}$$

$$= \begin{bmatrix} .1296 & .3079 & .2013 & .3612 \\ 0 & 1 & 0 & 0 \\ 0 & .1875 & .0625 & .75 \\ 0 & 0 & 0 & 1 \end{bmatrix}$$

The probability that a first-year student has graduated within 4 years is .3612. Similarly, the probability that a first-year student has dropped out within 4 years is .3079 (the entry in row 1 and column 2 of P^4).

Matched Problem 4   Refer to Example 4. At the end of each year the faculty examines the progress that each second-year student has made on the required thesis. Past records indicate that 30% of second-year students (S) have their theses approved (A) and 10% are dropped from the program for insufficient progress (D), never to return. The remaining students continue to work on their theses.

(A)   Draw a transition diagram.

(B)   Find the transition matrix P.

(C)   What is the probability that a second-year student completes the thesis requirement within 4 years? Is dropped from the program for insufficient progress within 4 years?

Explore & Discuss 2   Refer to Example 4. States D and G are referred to as *absorbing states,* because a student who enters either one of these states never leaves it. Absorbing states are discussed in detail in Section 9-3.

(A)   How can absorbing states be recognized from a transition diagram? Draw a transition diagram with two states, one that is absorbing and one that is not, to illustrate.

(B)   How can absorbing states be recognized from a transition matrix? Write the transition matrix for the diagram you drew in part (A) to illustrate.

Exercises 9-1

A

Problems 1–8 refer to the following transition matrix:

$$P = \begin{array}{c} A \\ B \end{array} \begin{bmatrix} .8 & .2 \\ .4 & .6 \end{bmatrix} \begin{array}{c} A \quad B \end{array}$$

In Problems 1–4, find S_1 for the indicated initial-state matrix S_0 and interpret with a tree diagram.

1. $S_0 = [1 \quad 0]$ **2.** $S_0 = [0 \quad 1]$

3. $S_0 = [.5 \quad .5]$ **4.** $S_0 = [.3 \quad .7]$

In Problems 5–8, find S_2 for the indicated initial-state matrix S_0, and explain what it represents.

5. $S_0 = [1 \quad 0]$ **6.** $S_0 = [0 \quad 1]$

7. $S_0 = [.5 \quad .5]$ **8.** $S_0 = [.3 \quad .7]$

In Problems 9–12, use the transition diagram to find S_1 for the indicated initial state matrix S_0.

9. $S_0 = [.2 \quad .8]$ **10.** $S_0 = [.6 \quad .4]$

11. $S_0 = [.9 \quad .1]$ **12.** $S_0 = [.7 \quad .3]$

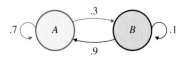

Figure for Problems 9–16

In Problems 13–16, use the transition diagram to find S_2 for the indicated initial state matrix S_0.

13. $S_0 = [.2 \quad .8]$ **14.** $S_0 = [.6 \quad .4]$

15. $S_0 = [.9 \quad .1]$ **16.** $S_0 = [.7 \quad .3]$

In Problems 17–24, could the given matrix be the transition matrix of a Markov chain?

17. $\begin{bmatrix} .3 & .7 \\ 1 & 0 \end{bmatrix}$ **18.** $\begin{bmatrix} .9 & .1 \\ .4 & .8 \end{bmatrix}$

19. $\begin{bmatrix} .5 & .5 \\ .7 & -.3 \end{bmatrix}$ **20.** $\begin{bmatrix} 0 & 1 \\ 1 & 0 \end{bmatrix}$

21. $\begin{bmatrix} .1 & .3 & .6 \\ .2 & .4 & .4 \end{bmatrix}$ **22.** $\begin{bmatrix} .2 & .8 \\ .5 & .5 \\ .9 & .1 \end{bmatrix}$

23. $\begin{bmatrix} .5 & .1 & .4 \\ 0 & .5 & .5 \\ .2 & .1 & .7 \end{bmatrix}$ **24.** $\begin{bmatrix} .3 & .3 & .4 \\ .7 & .2 & .2 \\ .1 & .8 & .1 \end{bmatrix}$

In Problems 25–30, is there a unique way of filling in the missing probabilities in the transition diagram? If so, complete the transition diagram and write the corresponding transition matrix. If not, explain why.

25.

26.

27.

28.

29.

30.

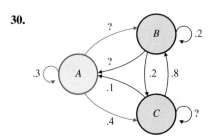

In Problems 31–36, are there unique values of a, b, and c that make P a transition matrix? If so, complete the transition matrix and draw the corresponding transition diagram. If not, explain why.

31. $P = \begin{array}{c} A \\ B \\ C \end{array} \begin{bmatrix} 0 & .5 & a \\ b & 0 & .4 \\ .2 & c & .1 \end{bmatrix} \begin{array}{c} A \quad B \quad C \end{array}$ **32.** $P = \begin{array}{c} A \\ B \\ C \end{array} \begin{bmatrix} a & 0 & .9 \\ .2 & .3 & b \\ .6 & c & 0 \end{bmatrix} \begin{array}{c} A \quad B \quad C \end{array}$

33. $P = \begin{array}{c} A \\ B \\ C \end{array} \begin{bmatrix} 0 & a & .3 \\ 0 & b & 0 \\ c & .8 & 0 \end{bmatrix} \begin{array}{c} A \quad B \quad C \end{array}$ **34.** $P = \begin{array}{c} A \\ B \\ C \end{array} \begin{bmatrix} 0 & 1 & a \\ 0 & 0 & b \\ c & .5 & 0 \end{bmatrix} \begin{array}{c} A \quad B \quad C \end{array}$

35. $P = \begin{array}{c} A \\ B \\ C \end{array} \begin{bmatrix} .2 & .1 & .7 \\ a & .4 & c \\ .5 & b & .4 \end{bmatrix} \begin{array}{c} A \quad B \quad C \end{array}$ **36.** $P = \begin{array}{c} A \\ B \\ C \end{array} \begin{bmatrix} a & .8 & .1 \\ .3 & b & .4 \\ .6 & .5 & c \end{bmatrix} \begin{array}{c} A \quad B \quad C \end{array}$

B

In Problems 37–40, use the given information to draw the transition diagram and find the transition matrix.

37. A Markov chain has two states, A and B. The probability of going from state A to state B in one trial is .7, and the probability of going from state B to state A in one trial is .9.

Limiting Matrix

We will now discuss the long-run behavior of absorbing Markov chains.

EXAMPLE 3   **Real Estate Development** Two competing real estate companies are trying to buy all the farms in a particular area for future housing development. Each year, 20% of the farmers decide to sell to company A, 30% decide to sell to company B, and the rest continue to farm their land. Neither company ever sells any of the farms they purchase.

(A) Draw a transition diagram and determine whether or not the Markov chain is absorbing.

(B) Write a transition matrix that is in standard form.

(C) If neither company owns any farms at the beginning of this competitive buying process, estimate the percentage of farms that each company will purchase in the long run.

(D) If company A buys 50% of the farms before company B enters the competitive buying process, estimate the percentage of farms that each company will purchase in the long run.

SOLUTION   (A)

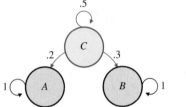

A = sells to company A
B = sells to company B
C = continues farming

The associated Markov chain is absorbing since there are two absorbing states, A and B. It is possible to go from the nonabsorbing state C to either A or B in one step.

(B) We use the transition diagram to write a transition matrix that is in standard form:

$$P = \begin{array}{c} \\ A \\ B \\ C \end{array} \begin{array}{c} \begin{array}{ccc} A & B & C \end{array} \\ \left[\begin{array}{ccc} 1 & 0 & 0 \\ 0 & 1 & 0 \\ .2 & .3 & .5 \end{array} \right] \end{array} \qquad \text{Standard form}$$

(C) At the beginning of the competitive buying process all the farmers are in state C (own a farm). Thus, $S_0 = [0 \quad 0 \quad 1]$. The successive state matrices are (multiplication details omitted):

$$S_1 = S_0P = [.2 \quad .3 \quad .5]$$
$$S_2 = S_1P = [.3 \quad .45 \quad .25]$$
$$S_3 = S_2P = [.35 \quad .525 \quad .125]$$
$$S_4 = S_3P = [.375 \quad .5625 \quad .0625]$$
$$S_5 = S_4P = [.3875 \quad .58125 \quad .03125]$$
$$S_6 = S_5P = [.39375 \quad .590625 \quad .015625]$$
$$S_7 = S_6P = [.396875 \quad .5953125 \quad .0078125]$$
$$S_8 = S_7P = [.3984375 \quad .59765625 \quad .00390625]$$
$$S_9 = S_8P = [.39921875 \quad .598828125 \quad .001953125]$$

It appears that these state matrices are approaching the matrix

$$S = \begin{array}{c} \begin{array}{ccc} A & B & C \end{array} \\ [.4 \quad .6 \quad 0] \end{array}$$

This indicates that in the long run, company A will acquire approximately 40% of the farms and company B will acquire the remaining 60%.

(D) This time, at the beginning of the competitive buying process 50% of farmers are already in state A and the rest are in state C. So $S_0 = [.5 \quad 0 \quad .5]$. The successive state matrices are (multiplication details omitted):

$$S_1 = S_0 P = [.6 \quad .15 \quad .25]$$

$$S_2 = S_1 P = [.65 \quad .225 \quad .125]$$

$$S_3 = S_2 P = [.675 \quad .2625 \quad .0625]$$

$$S_4 = S_3 P = [.6875 \quad .28125 \quad .03125]$$

$$S_5 = S_4 P = [.69375 \quad .290625 \quad .015625]$$

$$S_6 = S_5 P = [.696875 \quad .2953125 \quad .0078125]$$

$$S_7 = S_6 P = [.6984375 \quad .29765625 \quad .00390625]$$

$$S_8 = S_7 P = [.69921875 \quad .298828125 \quad .001953125]$$

These state matrices approach a matrix different from the one in part (C):

$$\begin{matrix} A & B & C \\ S' = [.7 & .3 & 0] \end{matrix}$$

Because of its head start, company A will now acquire approximately 70% of the farms and company B will acquire the remaining 30%.

Matched Problem 3 Repeat Example 3 if 10% of farmers sell to company A each year, 40% sell to company B, and the remainder continue farming.

Recall from Theorem 1, Section 9-2, that the successive state matrices of a regular Markov chain always approach a stationary matrix. Furthermore, this stationary matrix is unique. That is, changing the initial-state matrix does not change the stationary matrix. The successive state matrices for an absorbing Markov chain also approach a stationary matrix, but this matrix is not unique. To confirm this, consider the transition matrix P and the state matrices S and S' from Example 3:

$$P = \begin{matrix} & \begin{matrix} A & B & C \end{matrix} \\ \begin{matrix} A \\ B \\ C \end{matrix} & \begin{bmatrix} 1 & 0 & 0 \\ 0 & 1 & 0 \\ .2 & .3 & .5 \end{bmatrix} \end{matrix} \qquad \begin{matrix} A & B & C \\ S = [.4 & .6 & 0] \end{matrix} \qquad \begin{matrix} A & B & C \\ S' = [.7 & .3 & 0] \end{matrix}$$

It turns out that S and S' are both stationary matrices, as the following multiplications verify:

$$SP = [.4 \quad .6 \quad 0] \begin{bmatrix} 1 & 0 & 0 \\ 0 & 1 & 0 \\ .2 & .3 & .5 \end{bmatrix} = [.4 \quad .6 \quad 0] = S$$

$$S'P = [.7 \quad .3 \quad 0] \begin{bmatrix} 1 & 0 & 0 \\ 0 & 1 & 0 \\ .2 & .3 & .5 \end{bmatrix} = [.7 \quad .3 \quad 0] = S'$$

In fact, this absorbing Markov chain has an infinite number of stationary matrices (see Problems 41–48, Exercise 9-3).

Changing the initial-state matrix for an absorbing Markov chain can cause the successive state matrices to approach a different stationary matrix.

In Section 9-2, we used the unique stationary matrix for a regular Markov chain to find the limiting matrix $\overline{P}$. Since an absorbing Markov chain can have many different stationary matrices, we cannot expect this approach to work for absorbing chains. However, it turns out that transition matrices for absorbing chains do have limiting matrices, and they are not very difficult to find. Theorem 2 gives us the necessary tools. The proof of this theorem is left for more advanced courses.

> **THEOREM 2   Limiting Matrices for Absorbing Markov Chains**
> If a standard form P for an absorbing Markov chain is partitioned as
>
> $$P = \begin{bmatrix} I & 0 \\ \hline R & Q \end{bmatrix}$$
>
> then P^k approaches a limiting matrix $\overline{P}$ as k increases, where
>
> $$\overline{P} = \begin{bmatrix} I & 0 \\ \hline FR & 0 \end{bmatrix}$$
>
> The matrix F is given by $F = (I - Q)^{-1}$ and is called the **fundamental matrix** for P.
> The identity matrix used to form the fundamental matrix F must be the same size as the matrix Q.

EXAMPLE 4   **Finding the Limiting Matrix**

(A) Find the limiting matrix $\overline{P}$ for the standard form P found in Example 3.

(B) Use $\overline{P}$ to find the limit of the successive state matrices for $S_0 = [0 \quad 0 \quad 1]$.

(C) Use $\overline{P}$ to find the limit of the successive state matrices for $S_0 = [.5 \quad 0 \quad .5]$.

SOLUTION   (A) From Example 3, we have

$$P = \begin{bmatrix} 1 & 0 & 0 \\ 0 & 1 & 0 \\ \hline .2 & .3 & .5 \end{bmatrix} \qquad \begin{bmatrix} I & 0 \\ \hline R & Q \end{bmatrix}$$

where

$$I = \begin{bmatrix} 1 & 0 \\ 0 & 1 \end{bmatrix} \qquad 0 = \begin{bmatrix} 0 \\ 0 \end{bmatrix} \qquad R = [.2 \quad .3] \qquad Q = [.5]$$

If $I = [1]$ is the 1×1 identity matrix, then $I - Q$ is also a 1×1 matrix; $F = (I - Q)^{-1}$ is simply the multiplicative inverse of the single entry in $I - Q$. So

$$F = ([1] - [.5])^{-1} = [.5]^{-1} = [2]$$

$$FR = [2][.2 \quad .3] = [.4 \quad .6]$$

and the limiting matrix is

$$\overline{P} = \begin{array}{c} \\ A \\ B \\ C \end{array} \begin{array}{ccc} A & B & C \\ \begin{bmatrix} 1 & 0 & 0 \\ 0 & 1 & 0 \\ .4 & .6 & 0 \end{bmatrix} \end{array} \qquad \begin{bmatrix} I & 0 \\ \hline FR & 0 \end{bmatrix}$$

(B) Since the successive state matrices are given by $S_k = S_0 P^k$ (Theorem 1, Section 9-1) and P^k approaches $\overline{P}$, it follows that S_k approaches

$$S_0 \overline{P} = [0 \quad 0 \quad 1] \begin{bmatrix} 1 & 0 & 0 \\ 0 & 1 & 0 \\ .4 & .6 & 0 \end{bmatrix} = [.4 \quad .6 \quad 0]$$

which agrees with the results in part (C) of Example 3.

(C) This time, the successive state matrices approach

$$S_0 \overline{P} = [.5 \quad 0 \quad .5] \begin{bmatrix} 1 & 0 & 0 \\ 0 & 1 & 0 \\ .4 & .6 & 0 \end{bmatrix} = [.7 \quad .3 \quad 0]$$

which agrees with the results in part (D) of Example 3.

Matched Problem 4   Repeat Example 4 for the standard form P found in Matched Problem 3.

Recall that the limiting matrix for a regular Markov chain contains the long-run probabilities of going from any state to any other state. This is also true for the limiting matrix of an absorbing Markov chain. Let's compare the transition matrix P and its limiting matrix $\overline{P}$ from Example 4:

$$P = \begin{array}{c} \\ A \\ B \\ C \end{array}\begin{array}{ccc} A & B & C \\ \left[\begin{array}{ccc} 1 & 0 & 0 \\ 0 & 1 & 0 \\ .2 & .3 & .5 \end{array}\right] \end{array} \quad \text{approaches} \quad \overline{P} = \begin{array}{c} \\ A \\ B \\ C \end{array}\begin{array}{ccc} A & B & C \\ \left[\begin{array}{ccc} 1 & 0 & 0 \\ 0 & 1 & 0 \\ .4 & .6 & 0 \end{array}\right] \end{array}$$

The rows of P and $\overline{P}$ corresponding to the absorbing states A and B are identical. That is, if the probability of going from state A to state A is 1 at the beginning of the chain, then this probability will remain 1 for all trials in the chain and for the limiting matrix. The entries in the third row of $\overline{P}$ give the long-run probabilities of going from the nonabsorbing state C to states A, B, or C.

The fundamental matrix F provides some additional information about an absorbing chain. Recall from Example 4 that $F = [2]$. It can be shown that the entries in F determine the average number of trials that it takes to go from a given nonabsorbing state to an absorbing state. In the case of Example 4, the single entry 2 in F indicates that it will take an average of 2 years for a farmer to go from state C (owns a farm) to one of the absorbing states (sells the farm). Some will reach an absorbing state in 1 year, and some will take more than 2 years. But the average will be 2 years. These observations are summarized in Theorem 3, which we state without proof.

THEOREM 3   Properties of the Limiting Matrix $\overline{P}$

If P is a transition matrix in standard form for an absorbing Markov chain, F is the fundamental matrix, and $\overline{P}$ is the limiting matrix, then

(A) The entry in row i and column j of $\overline{P}$ is the long-run probability of going from state i to state j. For the nonabsorbing states, these probabilities are also the entries in the matrix FR used to form $\overline{P}$.

(B) The sum of the entries in each row of the fundamental matrix F is the average number of trials it will take to go from each nonabsorbing state to some absorbing state.

(Note that the rows of both F and FR correspond to the nonabsorbing states in the order given in the standard form P.)

CONCEPTUAL INSIGHT

1. The zero matrix in the lower right corner of the limiting matrix $\overline{P}$ in Theorem 2 indicates that the long-run probability of going from any nonabsorbing state to any other nonabsorbing state is always 0. That is, in the long run, all elements in an absorbing Markov chain end up in one of the absorbing states.

2. If the transition matrix for an absorbing Markov chain is not in standard form, it is still possible to find a limiting matrix (see Problems 47 and 48, Exercises 9-3). However, it is customary to use standard form when investigating the limiting behavior of an absorbing chain.

Now that we have developed the necessary tools for analyzing the long-run behavior of an absorbing Markov chain, we apply these tools to an earlier application (see Example 4, Section 9-1).

EXAMPLE 5   **University Enrollment** The following transition diagram is for part-time students enrolled in a university MBA program:

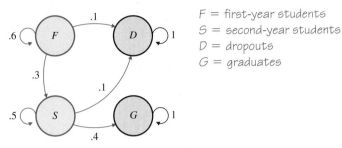

F = first-year students
S = second-year students
D = dropouts
G = graduates

(A) In the long run, what percentage of first-year students will graduate? What percentage of second-year students will not graduate?

(B) What is the average number of years that a first-year student will remain in this program? A second-year student?

SOLUTION   (A) First, notice that this is an absorbing Markov chain with two absorbing states, state D and state G. A standard form for this absorbing chain is

$$
P = \begin{array}{c} \\ D \\ G \\ F \\ S \end{array}
\begin{array}{c} \begin{array}{cccc} D & G & F & S \end{array} \\
\left[\begin{array}{cc|cc}
1 & 0 & 0 & 0 \\
0 & 1 & 0 & 0 \\ \hline
.1 & 0 & .6 & .3 \\
.1 & .4 & 0 & .5
\end{array}\right]
\end{array}
\qquad
\left[\begin{array}{c|c} I & O \\ \hline R & Q \end{array}\right]
$$

The submatrices in this partition are

$$
I = \begin{bmatrix} 1 & 0 \\ 0 & 1 \end{bmatrix} \qquad
O = \begin{bmatrix} 0 & 0 \\ 0 & 0 \end{bmatrix} \qquad
R = \begin{bmatrix} .1 & 0 \\ .1 & .4 \end{bmatrix} \qquad
Q = \begin{bmatrix} .6 & .3 \\ 0 & .5 \end{bmatrix}
$$

Therefore,

$$
\begin{aligned}
F = (I - Q)^{-1} &= \left(\begin{bmatrix} 1 & 0 \\ 0 & 1 \end{bmatrix} - \begin{bmatrix} .6 & .3 \\ 0 & .5 \end{bmatrix} \right)^{-1} \\
&= \begin{bmatrix} .4 & -.3 \\ 0 & .5 \end{bmatrix}^{-1} \qquad \text{Use row operations to find this matrix inverse.} \\
&= \begin{bmatrix} 2.5 & 1.5 \\ 0 & 2 \end{bmatrix}
\end{aligned}
$$

and

$$
FR = \begin{bmatrix} 2.5 & 1.5 \\ 0 & 2 \end{bmatrix} \begin{bmatrix} .1 & 0 \\ .1 & .4 \end{bmatrix} = \begin{bmatrix} .4 & .6 \\ .2 & .8 \end{bmatrix}
$$

The limiting matrix is

$$
\overline{P} = \begin{array}{c} \\ D \\ G \\ F \\ S \end{array}
\begin{array}{c} \begin{array}{cccc} D & G & F & S \end{array} \\
\left[\begin{array}{cc|cc}
1 & 0 & 0 & 0 \\
0 & 1 & 0 & 0 \\ \hline
.4 & .6 & 0 & 0 \\
.2 & .8 & 0 & 0
\end{array}\right]
\end{array}
\qquad
\left[\begin{array}{c|c} I & O \\ \hline FR & O \end{array}\right]
$$

From this limiting form, we see that in the long run 60% of the first-year students will graduate and 20% of the second-year students will not graduate.

(B) The sum of the first-row entries of the fundamental matrix F is $2.5 + 1.5 = 4$. According to Theorem 3, this indicates that a first-year student will spend an average of 4 years in the transient states F and S before reaching one of the absorbing states, D or G. The sum of the second-row entries of F is $0 + 2 = 2$. So a second-year student spends an average of 2 years in the program before either graduating or dropping out.

Matched Problem 5   Repeat Example 5 for the following transition diagram:

F = first-year students
S = second-year students
D = dropouts
G = graduates

Graphing Calculator Approximations

Just as was the case for regular Markov chains, the limiting matrix $\overline{P}$ for an absorbing Markov chain with transition matrix P can be approximated by computing P^k on a graphing calculator for sufficiently large values of k. For example, computing P^{50} for the standard form P in Example 5 produces the following results:

$$P^{50} = \begin{bmatrix} 1 & 0 & 0 & 0 \\ 0 & 1 & 0 & 0 \\ .1 & 0 & .6 & .3 \\ .1 & .4 & 0 & .5 \end{bmatrix}^{50} = \begin{bmatrix} 1 & 0 & 0 & 0 \\ 0 & 1 & 0 & 0 \\ .4 & .6 & 0 & 0 \\ .2 & .8 & 0 & 0 \end{bmatrix} = \overline{P}$$

where we have replaced very small numbers displayed in scientific notation with 0 (see the Conceptual Insight on page 449, Section 9-2).

⚠️ **CAUTION** Before you use P^k to approximate $\overline{P}$, be certain to determine that $\overline{P}$ exists. If you attempt to approximate a limiting matrix when none exists, the results can be misleading. For example, consider the transition matrix

$$P = \begin{bmatrix} 1 & 0 & 0 & 0 & 0 \\ .2 & .2 & 0 & .3 & .3 \\ 0 & 0 & 0 & .5 & .5 \\ 0 & 0 & 1 & 0 & 0 \\ 0 & 0 & 1 & 0 & 0 \end{bmatrix}$$

Computing P^{50} on a graphing calculator produces the following matrix:

$$P^{50} = \begin{bmatrix} 1 & 0 & 0 & 0 & 0 \\ .25 & 0 & .625 & .0625 & .0625 \\ 0 & 0 & 1 & 0 & 0 \\ 0 & 0 & 0 & .5 & .5 \\ 0 & 0 & 0 & .5 & .5 \end{bmatrix} \quad (2)$$

It is tempting to stop at this point and conclude that the matrix in (2) must be a good approximation for $\overline{P}$. But to do so would be incorrect! If P^{50} approximates a limiting matrix $\overline{P}$, then P^{51} should also approximate the same matrix. However, computing P^{51} produces quite a different matrix:

$$P^{51} = \begin{bmatrix} 1 & 0 & 0 & 0 & 0 \\ .25 & 0 & .125 & .3125 & .3125 \\ 0 & 0 & 0 & .5 & .5 \\ 0 & 0 & 1 & 0 & 0 \\ 0 & 0 & 1 & 0 & 0 \end{bmatrix} \quad (3)$$

Computing additional powers of P shows that the even powers of P approach matrix (2) while the odd powers approach matrix (3). The transition matrix P does not have a limiting matrix.

A graphing calculator can be used to perform the matrix calculations necessary to find $\overline{P}$ exactly, as illustrated in Figure 4 for the transition matrix P from Example 5. This approach has the advantage of producing the fundamental matrix F, whose row sums provide additional information about the long-run behavior of the chain.

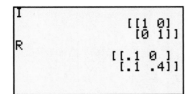

(A) Store I and R in the graphing calculator memory

(B) Store Q in the graphing calculator memory

(C) Compute F and FR

Figure 4 Matrix calculations

Exercises 9-3

A

In Problems 1–6, identify the absorbing states in the indicated transition matrix.

1. $P = \begin{array}{c} \\ A \\ B \\ C \end{array} \begin{array}{ccc} A & B & C \\ \left[\begin{array}{ccc} .6 & .3 & .1 \\ 0 & 1 & 0 \\ 0 & 0 & 1 \end{array}\right] \end{array}$

2. $P = \begin{array}{c} \\ A \\ B \\ C \end{array} \begin{array}{ccc} A & B & C \\ \left[\begin{array}{ccc} 0 & 1 & 0 \\ .3 & .2 & .5 \\ 0 & 0 & 1 \end{array}\right] \end{array}$

3. $P = \begin{array}{c} \\ A \\ B \\ C \end{array} \begin{array}{ccc} A & B & C \\ \left[\begin{array}{ccc} 0 & 0 & 1 \\ 1 & 0 & 0 \\ 0 & 1 & 0 \end{array}\right] \end{array}$

4. $P = \begin{array}{c} \\ A \\ B \\ C \end{array} \begin{array}{ccc} A & B & C \\ \left[\begin{array}{ccc} 1 & 0 & 0 \\ .3 & .4 & .3 \\ 0 & 0 & 1 \end{array}\right] \end{array}$

5. $P = \begin{array}{c} \\ A \\ B \\ C \\ D \end{array} \begin{array}{cccc} A & B & C & D \\ \left[\begin{array}{cccc} 1 & 0 & 0 & 0 \\ 0 & 0 & 1 & 0 \\ .1 & .1 & .5 & .3 \\ 0 & 0 & 0 & 1 \end{array}\right] \end{array}$

6. $P = \begin{array}{c} \\ A \\ B \\ C \\ D \end{array} \begin{array}{cccc} A & B & C & D \\ \left[\begin{array}{cccc} 0 & 1 & 0 & 0 \\ 1 & 0 & 0 & 0 \\ .1 & .2 & .3 & .4 \\ .7 & .1 & .1 & .1 \end{array}\right] \end{array}$

In Problems 7–10, identify the absorbing states for each transition diagram, and determine whether or not the diagram represents an absorbing Markov chain.

7.

8.

9.

10.

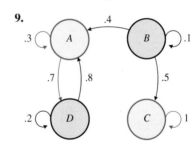

In Problems 11–20, could the given matrix be the transition matrix of an absorbing Markov chain?

11. $\begin{bmatrix} 0 & 1 \\ 1 & 0 \end{bmatrix}$

12. $\begin{bmatrix} 1 & 0 \\ 0 & 1 \end{bmatrix}$

13. $\begin{bmatrix} .3 & .7 \\ 0 & 1 \end{bmatrix}$

14. $\begin{bmatrix} .6 & .4 \\ 1 & 0 \end{bmatrix}$

15. $\begin{bmatrix} 1 & 0 & 0 \\ 0 & 1 & 0 \\ 0 & 0 & 1 \end{bmatrix}$

16. $\begin{bmatrix} 0 & 1 & 0 \\ 0 & 0 & 1 \\ 1 & 0 & 0 \end{bmatrix}$

17. $\begin{bmatrix} .9 & .1 & 0 \\ .1 & .9 & 0 \\ 0 & 0 & 1 \end{bmatrix}$ **18.** $\begin{bmatrix} .5 & .5 & 0 \\ .4 & .3 & .3 \\ 0 & 0 & 1 \end{bmatrix}$

19. $\begin{bmatrix} .9 & 0 & .1 \\ 0 & 1 & 0 \\ 0 & .2 & .8 \end{bmatrix}$ **20.** $\begin{bmatrix} 1 & 0 & 0 \\ 0 & 0 & 1 \\ 0 & .7 & .3 \end{bmatrix}$

B

In Problems 21–24, find a standard form for the absorbing Markov chain with the indicated transition diagram.

21.

22.

23.

24.

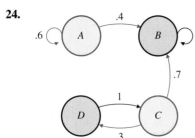

In Problems 25–28, find a standard form for the absorbing Markov chain with the indicated transition matrix.

25. $P = \begin{array}{c} A \\ B \\ C \end{array} \begin{array}{ccc} A & B & C \\ \begin{bmatrix} .2 & .3 & .5 \\ 1 & 0 & 0 \\ 0 & 0 & 1 \end{bmatrix} \end{array}$

26. $P = \begin{array}{c} A \\ B \\ C \end{array} \begin{array}{ccc} A & B & C \\ \begin{bmatrix} 0 & 0 & 1 \\ 0 & 1 & 0 \\ .7 & .2 & .1 \end{bmatrix} \end{array}$

27. $P = \begin{array}{c} A \\ B \\ C \\ D \end{array} \begin{array}{cccc} A & B & C & D \\ \begin{bmatrix} .1 & .2 & .3 & .4 \\ 0 & 1 & 0 & 0 \\ .5 & .2 & .2 & .1 \\ 0 & 0 & 0 & 1 \end{bmatrix} \end{array}$

28. $P = \begin{array}{c} A \\ B \\ C \\ D \end{array} \begin{array}{cccc} A & B & C & D \\ \begin{bmatrix} 0 & .3 & .3 & .4 \\ 0 & 1 & 0 & 0 \\ 0 & 0 & 1 & 0 \\ .8 & .1 & .1 & 0 \end{bmatrix} \end{array}$

In Problems 29–34, find the limiting matrix for the indicated standard form. Find the long-run probability of going from each nonabsorbing state to each absorbing state and the average number of trials needed to go from each nonabsorbing state to an absorbing state.

29. $P = \begin{array}{c} A \\ B \\ C \end{array} \begin{array}{ccc} A & B & C \\ \begin{bmatrix} 1 & 0 & 0 \\ 0 & 1 & 0 \\ .1 & .4 & .5 \end{bmatrix} \end{array}$

30. $P = \begin{array}{c} A \\ B \\ C \end{array} \begin{array}{ccc} A & B & C \\ \begin{bmatrix} 1 & 0 & 0 \\ 0 & 1 & 0 \\ .3 & .2 & .5 \end{bmatrix} \end{array}$

31. $P = \begin{array}{c} A \\ B \\ C \end{array} \begin{array}{ccc} A & B & C \\ \begin{bmatrix} 1 & 0 & 0 \\ .2 & .6 & .2 \\ .4 & .2 & .4 \end{bmatrix} \end{array}$

32. $P = \begin{array}{c} A \\ B \\ C \end{array} \begin{array}{ccc} A & B & C \\ \begin{bmatrix} 1 & 0 & 0 \\ .1 & .6 & .3 \\ .2 & .2 & .6 \end{bmatrix} \end{array}$

33. $P = \begin{array}{c} A \\ B \\ C \\ D \end{array} \begin{array}{cccc} A & B & C & D \\ \begin{bmatrix} 1 & 0 & 0 & 0 \\ 0 & 1 & 0 & 0 \\ .1 & .2 & .6 & .1 \\ .2 & .2 & .3 & .3 \end{bmatrix} \end{array}$

34. $P = \begin{array}{c} A \\ B \\ C \\ D \end{array} \begin{array}{cccc} A & B & C & D \\ \begin{bmatrix} 1 & 0 & 0 & 0 \\ 0 & 1 & 0 & 0 \\ .1 & .1 & .7 & .1 \\ .3 & .1 & .4 & .2 \end{bmatrix} \end{array}$

Problems 35–40 refer to the matrices in Problems 29–34. Use the limiting matrix $\overline{P}$ found for each transition matrix P in Problems 29–34 to determine the long-run behavior of the successive state matrices for the indicated initial-state matrices.

35. For matrix P from Problem 29 with
  (A) $S_0 = [0 \quad 0 \quad 1]$ (B) $S_0 = [.2 \quad .5 \quad .3]$

36. For matrix P from Problem 30 with
  (A) $S_0 = [0 \quad 0 \quad 1]$ (B) $S_0 = [.2 \quad .5 \quad .3]$

37. For matrix P from Problem 31 with

    (A) $S_0 = [0 \quad 0 \quad 1]$ (B) $S_0 = [.2 \quad .5 \quad .3]$

38. For matrix P from Problem 32 with

    (A) $S_0 = [0 \quad 0 \quad 1]$ (B) $S_0 = [.2 \quad .5 \quad .3]$

39. For matrix P from Problem 33 with

    (A) $S_0 = [0 \quad 0 \quad 0 \quad 1]$

    (B) $S_0 = [0 \quad 0 \quad 1 \quad 0]$

    (C) $S_0 = [0 \quad 0 \quad .4 \quad .6]$

    (D) $S_0 = [.1 \quad .2 \quad .3 \quad .4]$

40. For matrix P from Problem 34 with

    (A) $S_0 = [0 \quad 0 \quad 0 \quad 1]$

    (B) $S_0 = [0 \quad 0 \quad 1 \quad 0]$

    (C) $S_0 = [0 \quad 0 \quad .4 \quad .6]$

    (D) $S_0 = [.1 \quad .2 \quad .3 \quad .4]$

In Problems 41–48, discuss the validity of each statement. If the statement is always true, explain why. If not, give a counterexample.

41. If a Markov chain has an absorbing state, then it is an absorbing chain.

42. If a Markov chain has exactly two states and at least one absorbing state, then it is an absorbing chain.

43. If a Markov chain has exactly three states, one absorbing and two nonabsorbing, then it is an absorbing chain.

44. If a Markov chain has exactly three states, one nonabsorbing and two absorbing, then it is an absorbing chain.

45. If every state of a Markov chain is an absorbing state, then it is an absorbing chain.

46. If a Markov chain is absorbing, then it has a unique stationary matrix.

47. If a Markov chain is absorbing, then it is regular.

48. If a Markov chain is regular, then it is absorbing.

In Problems 49–52, use a graphing calculator to approximate the limiting matrix for the indicated standard form.

49. $P = \begin{array}{c} \\ A \\ B \\ C \\ D \end{array} \begin{array}{c} \begin{array}{cccc} A & B & C & D \end{array} \\ \left[\begin{array}{cccc} 1 & 0 & 0 & 0 \\ 0 & 1 & 0 & 0 \\ .5 & .3 & .1 & .1 \\ .6 & .2 & .1 & .1 \end{array} \right] \end{array}$

50. $P = \begin{array}{c} \\ A \\ B \\ C \\ D \end{array} \begin{array}{c} \begin{array}{cccc} A & B & C & D \end{array} \\ \left[\begin{array}{cccc} 1 & 0 & 0 & 0 \\ 0 & 1 & 0 & 0 \\ .1 & .1 & .5 & .3 \\ 0 & .2 & .3 & .5 \end{array} \right] \end{array}$

51. $P = \begin{array}{c} \\ A \\ B \\ C \\ D \\ E \end{array} \begin{array}{c} \begin{array}{ccccc} A & B & C & D & E \end{array} \\ \left[\begin{array}{ccccc} 1 & 0 & 0 & 0 & 0 \\ 0 & 1 & 0 & 0 & 0 \\ 0 & .4 & .5 & 0 & .1 \\ 0 & .4 & 0 & .3 & .3 \\ .4 & .4 & 0 & .2 & 0 \end{array} \right] \end{array}$

52. $P = \begin{array}{c} \\ A \\ B \\ C \\ D \\ E \end{array} \begin{array}{c} \begin{array}{ccccc} A & B & C & D & E \end{array} \\ \left[\begin{array}{ccccc} 1 & 0 & 0 & 0 & 0 \\ 0 & 1 & 0 & 0 & 0 \\ .5 & 0 & 0 & 0 & .5 \\ 0 & .4 & 0 & .2 & .4 \\ 0 & 0 & .1 & .7 & .2 \end{array} \right] \end{array}$

C

53. The following matrix P is a nonstandard transition matrix for an absorbing Markov chain:

$$P = \begin{array}{c} \\ A \\ B \\ C \\ D \end{array} \begin{array}{c} \begin{array}{cccc} A & B & C & D \end{array} \\ \left[\begin{array}{cccc} .2 & .2 & .6 & 0 \\ 0 & 1 & 0 & 0 \\ .5 & .1 & 0 & .4 \\ 0 & 0 & 0 & 1 \end{array} \right] \end{array}$$

To find a limiting matrix for P, follow the steps outlined below.

    Step 1 Using a transition diagram, rearrange the columns and rows of P to produce a standard form for this chain.

    Step 2 Find the limiting matrix for this standard form.

    Step 3 Using a transition diagram, reverse the process used in Step 1 to produce a limiting matrix for the original matrix P.

54. Repeat Problem 53 for

$$P = \begin{array}{c} \\ A \\ B \\ C \\ D \end{array} \begin{array}{c} \begin{array}{cccc} A & B & C & D \end{array} \\ \left[\begin{array}{cccc} 1 & 0 & 0 & 0 \\ .3 & .6 & 0 & .1 \\ .2 & .3 & .5 & 0 \\ 0 & 0 & 0 & 1 \end{array} \right] \end{array}$$

55. Verify the results in Problem 53 by computing P^k on a graphing calculator for large values of k.

56. Verify the results in Problem 54 by computing P^k on a graphing calculator for large values of k.

57. Show that $S = [x \quad 1 - x \quad 0], 0 \leq x \leq 1$, is a stationary matrix for the transition matrix

$$P = \begin{array}{c} \\ A \\ B \\ C \end{array} \begin{array}{c} \begin{array}{ccc} A & B & C \end{array} \\ \left[\begin{array}{ccc} 1 & 0 & 0 \\ 0 & 1 & 0 \\ .1 & .5 & .4 \end{array} \right] \end{array}$$

Discuss the generalization of this result to any absorbing Markov chain with two absorbing states and one nonabsorbing state.

58. Show that $S = [x \quad 1 - x \quad 0 \quad 0], 0 \leq x \leq 1$, is a stationary matrix for the transition matrix

$$P = \begin{array}{c} \\ A \\ B \\ C \\ D \end{array} \begin{array}{c} \begin{array}{cccc} A & B & C & D \end{array} \\ \left[\begin{array}{cccc} 1 & 0 & 0 & 0 \\ 0 & 1 & 0 & 0 \\ .1 & .2 & .3 & .4 \\ .6 & .2 & .1 & .1 \end{array} \right] \end{array}$$

Discuss the generalization of this result to any absorbing Markov chain with two absorbing states and two nonabsorbing states.

59. An absorbing Markov chain has the following matrix P as a standard form:

$$P = \begin{array}{c} \\ A \\ B \\ C \\ D \end{array} \begin{array}{cccc} A & B & C & D \\ \left[\begin{array}{cccc} 1 & 0 & 0 & 0 \\ .2 & .3 & .1 & .4 \\ 0 & .5 & .3 & .2 \\ 0 & .1 & .6 & .3 \end{array}\right] \end{array} \qquad \left[\begin{array}{c|c} I & O \\ \hline R & Q \end{array}\right]$$

Let w_k denote the maximum entry in Q^k. Note that $w_1 = .6$

(A) Find w_2, w_4, w_8, w_{16}, and w_{32} to three decimal places.

(B) Describe Q^k when k is large.

60. Refer to the matrices P and Q of Problem 59. For k a positive integer, let $T_k = I + Q + Q^2 + \cdots + Q^k$.

(A) Explain why $T_{k+1} = T_k Q + I$.

(B) Using a graphing calculator and part (A) to quickly compute the matrices T_k, discover and describe the connection between $(I - Q)^{-1}$ and T_k when k is large.

Applications

61. Loans. A credit union classifies car loans into one of four categories: the loan has been paid in full (F), the account is in good standing (G) with all payments up to date, the account is in arrears (A) with one or more missing payments, or the account has been classified as a bad debt (B) and sold to a collection agency. Past records indicate that each month 10% of the accounts in good standing pay the loan in full, 80% remain in good standing, and 10% become in arrears. Furthermore, 10% of the accounts in arrears are paid in full, 40% become accounts in good standing, 40% remain in arrears, and 10% are classified as bad debts.

(A) In the long run, what percentage of the accounts in arrears will pay their loan in full?

(B) In the long run, what percentage of the accounts in good standing will become bad debts?

(C) What is the average number of months that an account in arrears will remain in this system before it is either paid in full or classified as a bad debt?

62. Employee training. A chain of car muffler and brake repair shops maintains a training program for its mechanics. All new mechanics begin training in muffler repairs. Every 3 months, the performance of each mechanic is reviewed. Past records indicate that after each quarterly review, 30% of the muffler repair trainees are rated as qualified to repair mufflers and begin training in brake repairs, 20% are terminated for unsatisfactory performance, and the remainder continue as muffler repair trainees. Also, 30% of the brake repair trainees are rated as fully qualified mechanics requiring no further training, 10% are terminated for unsatisfactory performance, and the remainder continue as brake repair trainees.

(A) In the long run, what percentage of muffler repair trainees will become fully qualified mechanics?

(B) In the long run, what percentage of brake repair trainees will be terminated?

(C) What is the average number of quarters that a muffler repair trainee will remain in the training program before being either terminated or promoted to fully qualified mechanic?

63. Marketing. Three electronics firms are aggressively marketing their graphing calculators to high school and college mathematics departments by offering volume discounts, complimentary display equipment, and assistance with curriculum development. Due to the amount of equipment involved and the necessary curriculum changes, once a department decides to use a particular calculator in their courses, they never switch to another brand or stop using calculators. Each year, 6% of the departments decide to use calculators from company A, 3% decide to use calculators from company B, 11% decide to use calculators from company C, and the remainder decide not to use any calculators in their courses.

(A) In the long run, what is the market share of each company?

(B) On average, how many years will it take a department to decide to use calculators from one of these companies in their courses?

64. Pensions. Once a year company employees are given the opportunity to join one of three pension plans: A, B, or C. Once an employee decides to join one of these plans, the employee cannot drop the plan or switch to another plan. Past records indicate that each year 4% of employees elect to join plan A, 14% elect to join plan B, 7% elect to join plan C, and the remainder do not join any plan.

(A) In the long run, what percentage of the employees will elect to join plan A? Plan B? Plan C?

(B) On average, how many years will it take an employee to decide to join a plan?

65. Medicine. After bypass surgery, patients are placed in an intensive care unit (ICU) until their condition stabilizes. Then they are transferred to a cardiac care ward (CCW), where they remain until they are released from the hospital. In a particular metropolitan area, a study of hospital records produced the following data: each day 2% of the patients in the ICU died, 52% were transferred to the CCW, and the remainder stayed in the ICU. Furthermore, each day 4% of the patients in the CCW developed complications and were returned to the ICU, 1% died while in the CCW, 22% were released from the hospital, and the remainder stayed in the CCW.

(A) In the long run, what percentage of the patients in the ICU are released from the hospital?

(B) In the long run, what percentage of the patients in the CCW die without ever being released from the hospital?

(C) What is the average number of days that a patient in the ICU will stay in the hospital?

66. Medicine. The study discussed in Problem 65 also produced the following data for patients who underwent aortic valve replacements: each day 2% of the patients in the ICU died, 60% were transferred to the CCW, and the remainder stayed in the ICU. Furthermore, each day 5% of the patients in the CCW developed complications and were returned to the ICU, 1% died while in the CCW, 19% were released from the hospital, and the remainder stayed in the CCW.

(A) In the long run, what percentage of the patients in the CCW are released from the hospital?

(B) In the long run, what percentage of the patients in the ICU die without ever being released from the hospital?

(C) What is the average number of days a patient in the CCW will stay in the hospital?

67. Psychology. A rat is placed in room F or room B of the maze shown in the figure. The rat wanders from room to room until it enters one of the rooms containing food, L or R. Assume that the rat chooses an exit from a room at random and that once it enters a room with food it never leaves.

(A) What is the long-run probability that a rat placed in room B ends up in room R?

(B) What is the average number of exits that a rat placed in room B will choose until it finds food?

Figure for 67 and 68

68. Psychology. Repeat Problem 67 if the exit from room B to room R is blocked.

___

Answers to Matched Problems

1. (A) State B is absorbing.

(B) State C is absorbing.

2. (A) Absorbing Markov chain

(B) Not an absorbing Markov chain

3. (A)

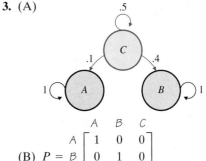

(B) $P = \begin{matrix} & A & B & C \\ A & \begin{bmatrix} 1 & 0 & 0 \\ B \\ C \end{bmatrix} \end{matrix}$

$$P = \begin{array}{c} A \\ B \\ C \end{array}\begin{array}{ccc} A & B & C \\ \begin{bmatrix} 1 & 0 & 0 \\ 0 & 1 & 0 \\ .1 & .4 & .5 \end{bmatrix} \end{array}$$

(C) Company A will purchase 20% of the farms, and company B will purchase 80%.

(D) Company A will purchase 60% of the farms, and company B will purchase 40%.

4. (A) $$\overline{P} = \begin{array}{c} A \\ B \\ C \end{array}\begin{array}{ccc} A & B & C \\ \begin{bmatrix} 1 & 0 & 0 \\ 0 & 1 & 0 \\ .2 & .8 & 0 \end{bmatrix} \end{array}$$

(B) $[.2 \quad .8 \quad 0]$

(C) $[.6 \quad .4 \quad 0]$

5. (A) 30% of first-year students will graduate; 50% of second-year students will not graduate.

(B) A first-year student will spend an average of 3.5 years in the program; a second-year student will spend an average of 2.5 years in the program.

Chapter 9 Review

Important Terms, Symbols, and Concepts

9-1 Properties of Markov Chains

EXAMPLES

- The progression of a system through a sequence of states is called a **stochastic process** if chance elements are involved in the transition from one state to the next.

- A **transition diagram** or **transition probability matrix** can be used to represent the probabilities of moving from one state to another. If those probabilities do not change with time, the stochastic process is called a **Markov chain**.

- If a Markov chain has n states, then the entry S_{ki} of the **kth-state matrix**

$$S_k = [S_{k1} \quad S_{k2} \cdots \quad S_{kn}]$$

gives the probability of being in state i after the kth trial. The sum of the entries in S_k is 1.

- The entry $p_{i,j}$ of the $n \times n$ **transition matrix** P gives the probability of moving from state i to state j on the next trial. The sum of the entries in each row of P is 1.

- If S_0 is an initial-state matrix for a Markov chain, then $S_k = S_0 P^k$ (Theorem 1, page 437).

Ex. 1, p. 436
Ex. 2, p. 437
Ex. 3, p. 438
Ex. 4, p. 438

9-2 Regular Markov Chains

- A transition matrix P is **regular** if some power of P has only positive entries.

Ex. 1, p. 445

- A Markov chain is a **regular Markov chain** if its transition matrix is regular.

- A state matrix S is **stationary** if $SP = S$.

Ex. 2, p. 446

- The state matrices for a regular Markov chain approach a unique stationary matrix S (Theorem 1, page 446).

Ex. 3, p. 447

- If P is the transition matrix for a regular Markov chain, then the matrices P^k approach a **limiting matrix** $\overline{P}$, where each row of $\overline{P}$ is equal to the unique stationary matrix S (Theorem 1, page 446).

Ex. 4, p. 447
Ex. 5, p. 448

9-3 Absorbing Markov Chains

- A state in a Markov chain is an **absorbing state** if once the state is entered it is impossible to leave. A state is absorbing if and only if its row in the transition matrix has a 1 on the main diagonal and 0's elsewhere.

Ex. 1, p. 454

- A Markov chain is an **absorbing Markov chain** if there is at least one absorbing state and it is possible to go from each nonabsorbing state to at least one absorbing state in a finite number of steps.

Ex. 2, p. 455

- A transition matrix for an absorbing Markov chain is in **standard form** if the rows and columns are labeled so that all the absorbing states precede all the nonabsorbing states.

- If a standard form P for an absorbing Markov chain is partitioned as

Ex. 3, p. 457
Ex. 4, p. 459

$$P = \begin{bmatrix} I & 0 \\ \hline R & Q \end{bmatrix}$$

then P^k approaches a limiting matrix $\overline{P}$ as k increases, where

$$\overline{P} = \begin{bmatrix} I & 0 \\ \hline FR & 0 \end{bmatrix}$$

The matrix $F = (I - Q)^{-1}$, where I is the identity matrix of the same size as Q, is called the **fundamental matrix** for P (Theorem 2, page 459).

- The entry in row i and column j of $\overline{P}$ is the long-run probability of going from state i to state j. The sum of the entries in each row of F is the average number of trials that it will take to go from each nonabsorbing state to some absorbing state (Theorem 3, page 460).

Ex. 5. p. 461

Review Exercises

Work through all the problems in this chapter review and check your answers in the back of the book. Answers to all review problems are there along with section numbers in italics to indicate where each type of problem is discussed. Where weaknesses show up, review appropriate sections in the text.

A

1. Given the transition matrix P and initial-state matrix S_0 shown below, find S_1 and S_2 and explain what each represents:

$$P = \begin{array}{c} \\ A \\ B \end{array} \begin{array}{c} A \quad B \\ \begin{bmatrix} .6 & .4 \\ .2 & .8 \end{bmatrix} \end{array} \qquad S_0 = [.3 \quad .7]$$

In Problems 2–6, P is a transition matrix for a Markov chain. Identify any absorbing states and classify the chain as regular, absorbing, or neither.

2. $P = \begin{array}{c} A \\ B \end{array} \begin{array}{c} A \quad B \\ \begin{bmatrix} 1 & 0 \\ .7 & .3 \end{bmatrix} \end{array}$

3. $P = \begin{array}{c} A \\ B \end{array} \begin{array}{c} A \quad B \\ \begin{bmatrix} 0 & 1 \\ .7 & .3 \end{bmatrix} \end{array}$

4. $P = \begin{array}{c} A \\ B \end{array} \begin{array}{c} A \quad B \\ \begin{bmatrix} 0 & 1 \\ 1 & 0 \end{bmatrix} \end{array}$

5. $P = \begin{array}{c} A \\ B \\ C \end{array} \begin{array}{c} A \quad B \quad C \\ \begin{bmatrix} .8 & 0 & .2 \\ 0 & 1 & 0 \\ 0 & 0 & 1 \end{bmatrix} \end{array}$

6. $P = \begin{array}{c} A \\ B \\ C \\ D \end{array} \begin{array}{c} A \quad B \quad C \quad D \\ \begin{bmatrix} 1 & 0 & 0 & 0 \\ 0 & 1 & 0 & 0 \\ 0 & 0 & .3 & .7 \\ 0 & 0 & .6 & .4 \end{bmatrix} \end{array}$

In Problems 7–10, write a transition matrix for the transition diagram indicated, identify any absorbing states, and classify each Markov chain as regular, absorbing, or neither.

7.

8.

9.

10.

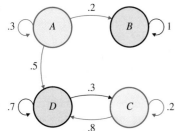

11. A Markov chain has three states, A, B, and C. The probability of going from state A to state B in one trial is .2, the probability of going from state A to state C in one trial is .5, the probability of going from state B to state A in one trial is .8, the probability of going from state B to state C in one trial is .2, the probability of going from state C to state A in one trial is .1, and the probability of going from state C to state B in one trial is .3. Draw a transition diagram and write a transition matrix for this chain.

12. Given the transition matrix

$$P = \begin{array}{c} \\ A \\ B \end{array} \begin{array}{c} A \quad B \\ \begin{bmatrix} .4 & .6 \\ .9 & .1 \end{bmatrix} \end{array}$$

find the probability of

(A) Going from state A to state B in two trials

(B) Going from state B to state A in three trials

In Problems 13 and 14, solve the equation $SP = S$ to find the stationary matrix S and the limiting matrix $\overline{P}$.

13. $P = \begin{array}{c} A \\ B \end{array} \begin{array}{c} A \quad B \\ \begin{bmatrix} .4 & .6 \\ .2 & .8 \end{bmatrix} \end{array}$

14. $P = \begin{array}{c} A \\ B \\ C \end{array} \begin{array}{c} A \quad B \quad C \\ \begin{bmatrix} .4 & .6 & 0 \\ .5 & .3 & .2 \\ 0 & .8 & .2 \end{bmatrix} \end{array}$

In Problems 15 and 16, find the limiting matrix for the indicated standard form. Find the long-run probability of going from each nonabsorbing state to each absorbing state and the average number of trials needed to go from each nonabsorbing state to an absorbing state.

15. $P = \begin{array}{c} A \\ B \\ C \end{array} \begin{array}{c} A \quad B \quad C \\ \begin{bmatrix} 1 & 0 & 0 \\ 0 & 1 & 0 \\ .3 & .1 & .6 \end{bmatrix} \end{array}$

16. $P = \begin{array}{c} A \\ B \\ C \\ D \end{array} \begin{array}{c} A \quad B \quad C \quad D \\ \begin{bmatrix} 1 & 0 & 0 & 0 \\ 0 & 1 & 0 & 0 \\ .1 & .5 & .2 & .2 \\ .1 & .1 & .4 & .4 \end{bmatrix} \end{array}$

In Problems 17–20, use a graphing calculator to approximate the limiting matrix for the indicated transition matrix.

17. Matrix P from Problem 13

18. Matrix P from Problem 14

19. Matrix P from Problem 15

20. Matrix P from Problem 16

21. Find a standard form for the absorbing Markov chain with transition matrix

$$P = \begin{array}{c} A \\ B \\ C \\ D \end{array} \begin{array}{c} A \quad B \quad C \quad D \\ \begin{bmatrix} .6 & .1 & .2 & .1 \\ 0 & 1 & 0 & 0 \\ .3 & .2 & .3 & .2 \\ 0 & 0 & 0 & 1 \end{bmatrix} \end{array}$$

In Problems 22 and 23, determine the long-run behavior of the successive state matrices for the indicated transition matrix and initial-state matrices.

22. $P = \begin{array}{c} A \\ B \\ C \end{array} \begin{array}{c} A \quad B \quad C \\ \begin{bmatrix} 0 & 1 & 0 \\ 0 & 0 & 1 \\ .2 & .6 & .2 \end{bmatrix} \end{array}$

(A) $S_0 = [0 \quad 0 \quad 1]$

(B) $S_0 = [.5 \quad .3 \quad .2]$

23. $P = \begin{array}{c} A \\ B \\ C \end{array} \begin{array}{c} A \quad B \quad C \\ \begin{bmatrix} 1 & 0 & 0 \\ 0 & 1 & 0 \\ .2 & .6 & .2 \end{bmatrix} \end{array}$

(A) $S_0 = [0 \quad 0 \quad 1]$

(B) $S_0 = [.5 \quad .3 \quad .2]$

24. Let P be a 2×2 transition matrix for a Markov chain. Can P be regular if two of its entries are 0? Explain.

25. Let P be a 3×3 transition matrix for a Markov chain. Can P be regular if three of its entries are 0? If four of its entries are 0? Explain.

C

26. A red urn contains 2 red marbles, 1 blue marble, and 1 green marble. A blue urn contains 1 red marble, 3 blue marbles, and 1 green marble. A green urn contains 6 red marbles, 3 blue marbles, and 1 green marble. A marble is selected from an urn, the color is noted, and the marble is returned to the urn from which it was drawn. The next marble is drawn from the urn whose color is the same as the marble just drawn. Thus, this is a Markov process with three states: draw from the red urn, draw from the blue urn, or draw from the green urn.

(A) Draw a transition diagram for this process.

(B) Write the transition matrix P.

(C) Determine whether this chain is regular, absorbing, or neither.

(D) Find the limiting matrix $\overline{P}$, if it exists, and describe the long-run behavior of this process.

27. Repeat Problem 26 if the blue and green marbles are removed from the red urn.

28. Show that $S = [x \quad y \quad z \quad 0]$, where $0 \le x \le 1$, $0 \le y \le 1$, $0 \le z \le 1$, and $x + y + z = 1$, is a stationary matrix for the transition matrix

$$P = \begin{array}{c} A \\ B \\ C \\ D \end{array} \begin{array}{c} A \quad B \quad C \quad D \\ \begin{bmatrix} 1 & 0 & 0 & 0 \\ 0 & 1 & 0 & 0 \\ 0 & 0 & 1 & 0 \\ .1 & .3 & .4 & .2 \end{bmatrix} \end{array}$$

Discuss the generalization of this result to any absorbing chain with three absorbing states and one nonabsorbing state.

In Problems 29–35, either give an example of a Markov chain with the indicated properties or explain why no such chain can exist.

29. A regular Markov chain with an absorbing state

30. An absorbing Markov chain that is regular

31. A regular Markov chain with two different stationary matrices

32. An absorbing Markov chain with two different stationary matrices

33. A Markov chain with no limiting matrix

34. A regular Markov chain with no limiting matrix

35. An absorbing Markov chain with no limiting matrix

In Problems 36 and 37, use a graphing calculator to approximate the entries (to three decimal places) of the limiting matrix, if it exists, of the indicated transition matrix.

36.
$$P = \begin{array}{c} \\ A \\ B \\ C \\ D \end{array} \begin{array}{cccc} A & B & C & D \\ \left[\begin{array}{cccc} .2 & .3 & .1 & .4 \\ 0 & 0 & 1 & 0 \\ 0 & .8 & 0 & .2 \\ 0 & 0 & 1 & 0 \end{array}\right] \end{array}$$

37.
$$P = \begin{array}{c} \\ A \\ B \\ C \\ D \end{array} \begin{array}{cccc} A & B & C & D \\ \left[\begin{array}{cccc} .1 & 0 & .3 & .6 \\ .2 & .4 & .1 & .3 \\ .3 & .5 & 0 & .2 \\ .9 & .1 & 0 & 0 \end{array}\right] \end{array}$$

Applications

38. Product switching. A company's brand (X) has 20% of the market. A market research firm finds that if a person uses brand X, the probability is .7 that he or she will buy it next time. On the other hand, if a person does not use brand X (represented by X'), the probability is .5 that he or she will switch to brand X next time.

(A) Draw a transition diagram.

(B) Write a transition matrix.

(C) Write the initial-state matrix.

(D) Find the first-state matrix and explain what it represents.

(E) Find the stationary matrix.

(F) What percentage of the market will brand X have in the long run if the transition matrix does not change?

39. Marketing. Recent technological advances have led to the development of three new milling machines: brand A, brand B, and brand C. Due to the extensive retooling and startup costs, once a company converts its machine shop to one of these new machines, it never switches to another

brand. Each year, 6% of the machine shops convert to brand A machines, 8% convert to brand B machines, 11% convert to brand C machines, and the remainder continue to use their old machines.

(A) In the long run, what is the market share of each brand?

(B) What is the average number of years that a company waits before converting to one of the new milling machines?

40. Internet. Table 1 gives the percentage of U.S. adults who at least occasionally used the Internet in the given year.

Table 1

Year	Percent
1995	14
2000	49
2005	68

Source: Pew Internet & American Life Project Surveys

The following transition matrix P is proposed as a model for the data, where I represents the population of Internet users.

$$\begin{array}{c} \\ \text{Current} \\ \text{Year} \end{array} \begin{array}{c} \\ I \\ I' \end{array} \overset{\begin{array}{cc} \text{Five years later} \\ I \qquad\quad I' \end{array}}{\left[\begin{array}{cc} .95 & .05 \\ .40 & .60 \end{array}\right]} = P$$

(A) Let $S_0 = \begin{bmatrix} .14 & .86 \end{bmatrix}$ and find S_1 and S_2. Compute both matrices exactly and then round entries to two decimal places.

(B) Construct a new table comparing the results from part (A) with the data in Table 1.

(C) According to this transition matrix, what percentage of the adult U.S. population will use the Internet in the long run?

41. Employee training. In order to become a fellow of the Society of Actuaries, a person must pass a series of ten examinations. Passage of the first two preliminary exams is a prerequisite for employment as a trainee in the actuarial department of a large insurance company. Each year, 15% of the trainees complete the next three exams and become associates of the Society of Actuaries, 5% leave the company, never to return, and the remainder continue as trainees. Furthermore, each year, 17% of the associates complete the remaining five exams and become fellows of the Society of Actuaries, 3% leave the company, never to return, and the remainder continue as associates.

(A) In the long run, what percentage of the trainees will become fellows?

(B) In the long run, what percentage of the associates will leave the company?

(C) What is the average number of years that a trainee remains in this program before either becoming a fellow or being discharged?

42. Genetics. A given plant species has red, pink, or white flowers according to the genotypes RR, RW, and WW, respectively. If each of these genotypes is crossed with a red-flowering plant, the transition matrix is

$$
\begin{array}{c}
\text{Next generation} \\
\text{Red} \quad \text{Pink} \quad \text{White}
\end{array}
$$

This generation
$$
\begin{array}{c}
\text{Red} \\
\text{Pink} \\
\text{White}
\end{array}
\begin{bmatrix}
1 & 0 & 0 \\
.5 & .5 & 0 \\
0 & 1 & 0
\end{bmatrix}
$$

If each generation of the plant is crossed only with red plants to produce the next generation, show that eventually all the flowers produced by the plants will be red. (Find the limiting matrix.)

43. **Smoking.** Table 2 gives the percentage of U.S. adults who were smokers in the given year.

Table 2

Year	Percent
1985	30.1
1995	24.7
2005	20.9

Source: American Lung Association

The following transition matrix P is proposed as a model for the data, where S represents the population of U.S. adult smokers.

$$
\begin{array}{c}
\text{Five years later} \\
\quad S \qquad S'
\end{array}
$$

$$
\begin{array}{cc}
\text{Current} & S \\
\text{year} & S'
\end{array}
\begin{bmatrix}
.74 & .26 \\
.03 & .97
\end{bmatrix} = P
$$

(A) Let $S_0 = [.301 \quad .699]$, and find S_1 and S_2. Compute the matrices exactly and then round entries to three decimal places.

(B) Construct a new table comparing the results from part (A) with the data in Table 2.

(C) According to this transition matrix, what percentage of the adult U.S. population will be smokers in the long run?

PART 3

CALCULUS

Limits and the Derivative

Introduction

How do algebra and calculus differ? The two words *static* and *dynamic* probably come as close as any to expressing the difference between the two disciplines. In algebra, we solve equations for a particular value of a variable—a static notion. In calculus, we are interested in how a change in one variable affects another variable—a dynamic notion.

Isaac Newton (1642–1727) of England and Gottfried Wilhelm von Leibniz (1646–1716) of Germany developed calculus independently to solve problems concerning motion. Today calculus is used not just in the physical sciences, but also in business, economics, life sciences, and social sciences—any discipline that seeks to understand dynamic phenomena.

In Chapter 10 we introduce the *derivative*, one of the two key concepts of calculus. The second, the *integral*, is the subject of Chapter 13. Both key concepts depend on the notion of *limit*, which is explained in Sections 10–1 and 10–2. We consider many applications of limits and derivatives. See, for example, Problems 69 and 70 in Section 10–3 on the concentration of a drug in the bloodstream.

10-1   Introduction to Limits

Basic to the study of calculus is the concept of a *limit*. This concept helps us to describe, in a precise way, the behavior of $f(x)$ when x is close, but not equal, to a particular value c. In this section, we develop an intuitive and informal approach to evaluating limits.

Functions and Graphs: Brief Review

The graph of the function $y = f(x) = x + 2$ is the graph of the set of all ordered pairs $(x, f(x))$. For example, if $x = 2$, then $f(2) = 4$ and $(2, f(2)) = (2, 4)$ is a point on the graph of f. Figure 1 shows $(-1, f(-1))$, $(1, f(1))$, and $(2, f(2))$ plotted on the graph of f. Notice that the domain values $-1, 1$, and 2 are associated with the x axis and the range values $f(-1) = 1$, $f(1) = 3$, and $f(2) = 4$ are associated with the y axis.

Given x, it is sometimes useful to read $f(x)$ directly from the graph of f. Example 1 reviews this process.

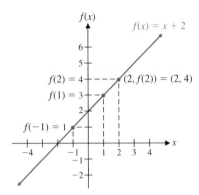

Figure 1

EXAMPLE 1   **Finding Values of a Function from Its Graph**   Complete the following table, using the given graph of the function g.

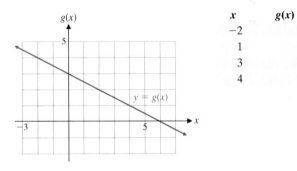

x	$g(x)$
-2	
1	
3	
4	

SOLUTION   To determine $g(x)$, proceed vertically from the x value on the x axis to the graph of g and then horizontally to the corresponding y value $g(x)$ on the y axis (as indicated by the dashed lines).

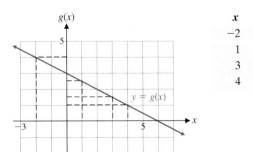

x	$g(x)$
-2	4.0
1	2.5
3	1.5
4	1.0

Matched Problem 3   Graph

$$h(x) = \frac{x - 2}{|x - 2|}$$

and find $\lim_{x \to 2} h(x)$ if it exists.

In Example 3, we see that the values of the function $h(x)$ approach two different numbers, depending on the direction of approach, and it is natural to refer to these values as "the limit from the left" and "the limit from the right." These experiences suggest that the notion of **one-sided limits** will be very useful in discussing basic limit concepts.

DEFINITION **One-Sided Limits**

We write

$$\lim_{x \to c^-} f(x) = K \qquad x \to c^- \text{ is read "x approaches c from}$$
$$\text{the left" and means } x \to c \text{ and } x < c.$$

and call K the **limit from the left** or the **left-hand limit** if $f(x)$ is close to K whenever x is close to, but to the left of, c on the real number line. We write

$$\lim_{x \to c^+} f(x) = L \qquad x \to c^+ \text{ is read "x approaches c from}$$
$$\text{the right" and means } x \to c \text{ and } x > c.$$

and call L the **limit from the right** or the **right-hand limit** if $f(x)$ is close to L whenever x is close to, but to the right of, c on the real number line.

If no direction is specified in a limit statement, we will always assume that the limit is **two-sided** or **unrestricted**. Theorem 1 states an important relationship between one-sided limits and unrestricted limits.

THEOREM 1   On the Existence of a Limit

For a (two-sided) limit to exist, the limit from the left and the limit from the right must exist and be equal. That is,

$$\lim_{x \to c} f(x) = L \text{ if and only if } \lim_{x \to c^-} f(x) = \lim_{x \to c^+} f(x) = L$$

In Example 3,

$$\lim_{x \to 0^-} \frac{|x|}{x} = -1 \qquad \text{and} \qquad \lim_{x \to 0^+} \frac{|x|}{x} = 1$$

Since the left- and right-hand limits are *not* the same,

$$\lim_{x \to 0} \frac{|x|}{x} \text{ does not exist}$$

EXAMPLE 4   **Analyzing Limits Graphically** Given the graph of the function f in Figure 5, discuss the behavior of $f(x)$ for x near (A) -1, (B) 1, and (C) 2.

SOLUTION   (A) Since we have only a graph to work with, we use vertical and horizontal lines to relate the values of x and the corresponding values of $f(x)$. For any x near -1 on either side of -1, we see that the corresponding value of $f(x)$, determined by a horizontal line, is close to 1.

Figure 5

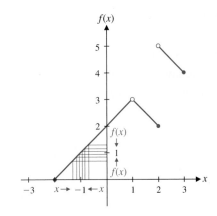

$$\lim_{x \to -1^-} f(x) = 1$$

$$\lim_{x \to -1^+} f(x) = 1$$

$$\lim_{x \to -1} f(x) = 1$$

$$f(-1) = 1$$

(B) Again, for any x near, but not equal to, 1, the vertical and horizontal lines indicate that the corresponding value of $f(x)$ is close to 3. The open dot at $(1, 3)$, together with the absence of a solid dot anywhere on the vertical line through $x = 1$, indicates that $f(1)$ is not defined.

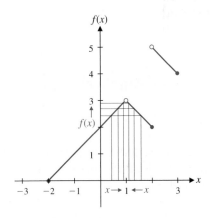

$$\lim_{x \to 1^-} f(x) = 3$$

$$\lim_{x \to 1^+} f(x) = 3$$

$$\lim_{x \to 1} f(x) = 3$$

$$f(1) \text{ not defined}$$

(C) The abrupt break in the graph at $x = 2$ indicates that the behavior of the graph near $x = 2$ is more complicated than in the two preceding cases. If x is close to 2 on the left side of 2, the corresponding horizontal line intersects the y axis at a point close to 2. If x is close to 2 on the right side of 2, the corresponding horizontal line intersects the y axis at a point close to 5. This is a case where the one-sided limits are different.

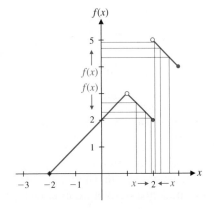

$$\lim_{x \to 2^-} f(x) = 2$$

$$\lim_{x \to 2^+} f(x) = 5$$

$$\lim_{x \to 2} f(x) \text{ does not exist}$$

$$f(2) = 2$$

Matched Problem 4   Given the graph of the function f shown in Figure 6, discuss the following, as we did in Example 4:

(A) Behavior of $f(x)$ for x near 0

(B) Behavior of $f(x)$ for x near 1

(C) Behavior of $f(x)$ for x near 3

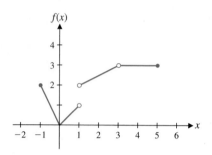

Figure 6

CONCEPTUAL INSIGHT

In Example 4B, note that $\lim\limits_{x \to 1} f(x)$ exists even though f is not defined at $x = 1$ and the graph has a hole at $x = 1$. In general, the value of a function at $x = c$ has no effect on the limit of the function as x approaches c.

Limits: An Algebraic Approach

Graphs are very useful tools for investigating limits, especially if something unusual happens at the point in question. However, many of the limits encountered in calculus are routine and can be evaluated quickly with a little algebraic simplification, some intuition, and basic properties of limits. The following list of properties of limits forms the basis for this approach:

THEOREM 2   Properties of Limits
Let f and g be two functions, and assume that
$$\lim_{x \to c} f(x) = L \qquad \lim_{x \to c} g(x) = M$$
where L and M are real numbers (both limits exist). Then

1. $\lim\limits_{x \to c} k = k$ for any constant k

2. $\lim\limits_{x \to c} x = c$

3. $\lim\limits_{x \to c} [f(x) + g(x)] = \lim\limits_{x \to c} f(x) + \lim\limits_{x \to c} g(x) = L + M$

4. $\lim\limits_{x \to c} [f(x) - g(x)] = \lim\limits_{x \to c} f(x) - \lim\limits_{x \to c} g(x) = L - M$

5. $\lim\limits_{x \to c} kf(x) = k \lim\limits_{x \to c} f(x) = kL$ for any constant k

6. $\lim\limits_{x \to c} [f(x) \cdot g(x)] = \left[\lim\limits_{x \to c} f(x)\right]\left[\lim\limits_{x \to c} g(x)\right] = LM$

7. $\lim\limits_{x \to c} \dfrac{f(x)}{g(x)} = \dfrac{\lim\limits_{x \to c} f(x)}{\lim\limits_{x \to c} g(x)} = \dfrac{L}{M}$ if $M \neq 0$

8. $\lim\limits_{x \to c} \sqrt[n]{f(x)} = \sqrt[n]{\lim\limits_{x \to c} f(x)} = \sqrt[n]{L}$ $L > 0$ for n even

Each property in Theorem 2 is also valid if $x \to c$ is replaced everywhere by $x \to c^-$ or replaced everywhere by $x \to c^+$.

EXPLORE & DISCUSS 1

The properties listed in Theorem 2 can be paraphrased in brief verbal statements. For example, property 3 simply states that *the limit of a sum is equal to the sum of the limits*. Write brief verbal statements for the remaining properties in Theorem 2.

EXAMPLE 5 **Using Limit Properties** Find $\lim_{x \to 3}(x^2 - 4x)$.

SOLUTION

$$\lim_{x \to 3}(x^2 - 4x) = \lim_{x \to 3} x^2 - \lim_{x \to 3} 4x \qquad \text{Property 4}$$

$$= \left(\lim_{x \to 3} x\right) \cdot \left(\lim_{x \to 3} x\right) - 4 \lim_{x \to 3} x \qquad \text{Properties 5 and 6}$$

$$= 3 \cdot 3 - 4 \cdot 3 = -3 \qquad \text{Property 2}$$

With a little practice, you will soon be able to omit the steps in the dashed boxes and simply write

$$\lim_{x \to 3}(x^2 - 4x) = 3 \cdot 3 - 4 \cdot 3 = -3$$

Matched Problem 5 Find $\lim_{x \to -2}(x^2 + 5x)$.

What happens if we try to evaluate a limit like the one in Example 5, but with x approaching an unspecified number, such as c? Proceeding as we did in Example 5, we have

$$\lim_{x \to c}(x^2 - 4x) = c \cdot c - 4 \cdot c = c^2 - 4c$$

If we let $f(x) = x^2 - 4x$, we have

$$\lim_{x \to c} f(x) = \lim_{x \to c}(x^2 - 4x) = c^2 - 4c = f(c)$$

That is, this limit can be evaluated simply by evaluating the function f at c. It would certainly simplify the process of evaluating limits if we could identify the functions for which

$$\lim_{x \to c} f(x) = f(c) \tag{1}$$

since we could use this fact to evaluate the limit. It turns out that there are many functions that satisfy equation (1). We postpone a detailed discussion of these functions until the next section. For now, we note that if

$$f(x) = a_n x^n + a_{n-1} x^{n-1} + \cdots + a_0$$

is a polynomial function, then, by the properties in Theorem 1,

$$\lim_{x \to c} f(x) = \lim_{x \to c}(a_n x^n + a_{n-1} x^{n-1} + \cdots + a_0)$$

$$= a_n c^n + a_{n-1} c^{n-1} + \cdots + a_0 = f(c)$$

and if

$$r(x) = \frac{n(x)}{d(x)}$$

is a rational function, where $n(x)$ and $d(x)$ are polynomials with $d(c) \neq 0$, then by property 7 and the fact that polynomials $n(x)$ and $d(x)$ satisfy equation (1),

$$\lim_{x \to c} r(x) = \lim_{x \to c} \frac{n(x)}{d(x)} = \frac{\lim_{x \to c} n(x)}{\lim_{x \to c} d(x)} = \frac{n(c)}{d(c)} = r(c)$$

These results are summarized in Theorem 3.

> **THEOREM 3   Limits of Polynomial and Rational Functions**
>
> 1. $\lim\limits_{x \to c} f(x) = f(c)$ for f any polynomial function.
> 2. $\lim\limits_{x \to c} r(x) = r(c)$ for r any rational function with a nonzero denominator at $x = c$.

EXAMPLE 6   **Evaluating Limits** Find each limit.

(A) $\lim\limits_{x \to 2}(x^3 - 5x - 1)$ (B) $\lim\limits_{x \to -1} \sqrt{2x^2 + 3}$ (C) $\lim\limits_{x \to 4}\dfrac{2x}{3x + 1}$

SOLUTION   (A) $\lim\limits_{x \to 2}(x^3 - 5x - 1) = 2^3 - 5 \cdot 2 - 1 = -3$ Theorem 3

(B) $\lim\limits_{x \to -1} \sqrt{2x^2 + 3} = \sqrt{\lim\limits_{x \to -1}(2x^2 + 3)}$ Property 8

$\qquad\qquad\qquad = \sqrt{2(-1)^2 + 3}$ Theorem 3

$\qquad\qquad\qquad = \sqrt{5}$

(C) $\lim\limits_{x \to 4}\dfrac{2x}{3x + 1} = \dfrac{2 \cdot 4}{3 \cdot 4 + 1}$ Theorem 3

$\qquad\qquad\qquad = \dfrac{8}{13}$

Matched Problem 6   Find each limit.

(A) $\lim\limits_{x \to -1}(x^4 - 2x + 3)$ (B) $\lim\limits_{x \to 2} \sqrt{3x^2 - 6}$ (C) $\lim\limits_{x \to -2}\dfrac{x^2}{x^2 + 1}$

EXAMPLE 7   **Evaluating Limits** Let

$$f(x) = \begin{cases} x^2 + 1 & \text{if } x < 2 \\ x - 1 & \text{if } x > 2 \end{cases}$$

Find each limit.

(A) $\lim\limits_{x \to 2^-} f(x)$ (B) $\lim\limits_{x \to 2^+} f(x)$ (C) $\lim\limits_{x \to 2} f(x)$ (D) $f(2)$

SOLUTION   (A) $\lim\limits_{x \to 2^-} f(x) = \lim\limits_{x \to 2^-}(x^2 + 1)$ If $x < 2$, $f(x) = x^2 + 1$.

$\qquad\qquad\qquad = 2^2 + 1 = 5$

(B) $\lim\limits_{x \to 2^+} f(x) = \lim\limits_{x \to 2^+}(x - 1)$ If $x > 2$, $f(x) = x - 1$.

$\qquad\qquad\qquad = 2 - 1 = 1$

(C) Since the one-sided limits are not equal, $\lim\limits_{x \to 2} f(x)$ does not exist.

(D) Because the definition of f does not assign a value to f for $x = 2$, only for $x < 2$ and $x > 2$, $f(2)$ does not exist.

Matched Problem 7   Let

$$f(x) = \begin{cases} 2x + 3 & \text{if } x < 5 \\ -x + 12 & \text{if } x > 5 \end{cases}$$

Find each limit.

(A) $\lim\limits_{x \to 5^-} f(x)$ (B) $\lim\limits_{x \to 5^+} f(x)$ (C) $\lim\limits_{x \to 5} f(x)$ (D) $f(5)$

It is important to note that there are restrictions on some of the limit properties. In particular, if

$$\lim_{x\to c} f(x) = 0 \quad \text{and} \quad \lim_{x\to c} g(x) = 0, \quad \text{then finding } \lim_{x\to c} \frac{f(x)}{g(x)}$$

may present some difficulties, since limit property 7 (the limit of a quotient) does not apply when $\lim_{x\to c} g(x) = 0$. The next example illustrates some techniques that can be useful in this situation.

EXAMPLE 8   **Evaluating Limits** Find each limit.

(A) $\lim\limits_{x\to 2} \dfrac{x^2 - 4}{x - 2}$

(B) $\lim\limits_{x\to -1} \dfrac{x|x + 1|}{x + 1}$

SOLUTION   (A) Algebraic simplification is often useful when the numerator and denominator are both approaching 0.

$$\lim_{x\to 2} \frac{x^2 - 4}{x - 2} = \lim_{x\to 2} \frac{(x - 2)(x + 2)}{x - 2} = \lim_{x\to 2}(x + 2) = 4$$

(B) One-sided limits are helpful for limits involving the absolute value function.

$$\lim_{x\to -1^+} \frac{x|x + 1|}{x + 1} = \lim_{x\to -1^+}(x) = -1 \quad \text{If } x > -1, \text{ then } \frac{|x + 1|}{x + 1} = 1.$$

$$\lim_{x\to -1^-} \frac{x|x + 1|}{x + 1} = \lim_{x\to -1^-}(-x) = 1 \quad \text{If } x < -1, \text{ then } \frac{|x + 1|}{x + 1} = -1.$$

Since the limit from the left and the limit from the right are not the same, we conclude that

$$\lim_{x\to -1} \frac{x|x + 1|}{x + 1} \quad \text{does not exist}$$

Matched Problem 8   Find each limit.

(A) $\lim\limits_{x\to -3} \dfrac{x^2 + 4x + 3}{x + 3}$

(B) $\lim\limits_{x\to 4} \dfrac{x^2 - 16}{|x - 4|}$

CONCEPTUAL INSIGHT

In the solution to Example 8A we used the following algebraic identity:

$$\frac{x^2 - 4}{x - 2} = \frac{(x - 2)(x + 2)}{x - 2} = x + 2, \quad x \neq 2$$

The restriction $x \neq 2$ is necessary here because the first two expressions are not defined at $x = 2$. Why didn't we include this restriction in the solution? When x approaches 2 in a limit problem, it is assumed that x is close, but not equal, to 2. It is important that you understand that both of the following statements are valid:

$$\lim_{x\to 2} \frac{x^2 - 4}{x - 2} = \lim_{x\to 2}(x + 2) \quad \text{and} \quad \frac{x^2 - 4}{x - 2} = x + 2, \, x \neq 2$$

Limits like those in Example 8 occur so frequently in calculus that they are given a special name.

DEFINITION Indeterminate Form

If $\lim\limits_{x\to c} f(x) = 0$ and $\lim\limits_{x\to c} g(x) = 0$, then $\lim\limits_{x\to c} \dfrac{f(x)}{g(x)}$ is said to be **indeterminate**, or, more specifically, a **0/0 indeterminate form**.

The term *indeterminate* is used because the limit of an indeterminate form may or may not exist (see Example 8A and 8B).

⚠ **CAUTION** The expression 0/0 does not represent a real number and should never be used as the value of a limit. If a limit is a 0/0 indeterminate form, further investigation is always required to determine whether the limit exists and to find its value if it does exist.

If the denominator of a quotient approaches 0 and the numerator approaches a nonzero number, then the limit of the quotient is not an indeterminate form. In fact, a limit of this form never exists.

THEOREM 4 **Limit of a Quotient**
If $\lim\limits_{x\to c} f(x) = L$, $L \neq 0$, and $\lim\limits_{x\to c} g(x) = 0$,

then

$$\lim\limits_{x\to c} \frac{f(x)}{g(x)} \qquad \text{does not exist}$$

EXPLORE & DISCUSS 2

Use algebraic and/or graphical techniques to analyze each of the following indeterminate forms.

(A) $\lim\limits_{x\to 1} \dfrac{x-1}{x^2-1}$ 　　　(B) $\lim\limits_{x\to 1} \dfrac{(x-1)^2}{x^2-1}$ 　　　(C) $\lim\limits_{x\to 1} \dfrac{x^2-1}{(x-1)^2}$

Limits of Difference Quotients

Let the function f be defined in an open interval containing the number a. One of the most important limits in calculus is the limit of the **difference quotient**,

$$\lim\limits_{h\to 0} \frac{f(a+h) - f(a)}{h} \tag{2}$$

If

$$\lim\limits_{h\to 0} [f(a+h) - f(a)] = 0$$

as it often does, then limit (2) is an indeterminate form.

EXAMPLE 9 **Limit of a Difference Quotient** Find the following limit for $f(x) = 4x - 5$:

$$\lim\limits_{h\to 0} \frac{f(3+h) - f(3)}{h}$$

SOLUTION
$$\lim\limits_{h\to 0} \frac{f(3+h) - f(3)}{h} = \lim\limits_{h\to 0} \frac{[4(3+h) - 5] - [4(3) - 5]}{h}$$

Since this is a 0/0 indeterminate form and property 7 in Theorem 2 does not apply, we proceed with algebraic simplification.

$$= \lim\limits_{h\to 0} \frac{12 + 4h - 5 - 12 + 5}{h}$$

$$= \lim\limits_{h\to 0} \frac{4h}{h} = \lim\limits_{h\to 0} 4 = 4$$

Matched Problem 9   Find the following limit for $f(x) = 7 - 2x$: $\displaystyle\lim_{h \to 0} \frac{f(4 + h) - f(4)}{h}$.

EXAMPLE 10   **Limit of a Difference Quotient**   Find the following limit for $f(x) = |x + 5|$:

$$\lim_{h \to 0} \frac{f(-5 + h) - f(-5)}{h}$$

SOLUTION

$$\lim_{h \to 0} \frac{f(-5 + h) - f(-5)}{h} = \lim_{h \to 0} \frac{|(\mathbf{-5 + h}) + 5| - |\mathbf{-5} + 5|}{h}$$

$$= \lim_{h \to 0} \frac{|h|}{h} \text{ does not exist}$$

Since this is a 0/0 indeterminate form and property 7 in Theorem 2 does not apply, we proceed with algebraic simplification.

Matched Problem 10   Find the following limit for $f(x) = |x - 1|$: $\displaystyle\lim_{h \to 0} \frac{f(1 + h) - f(1)}{h}$.

EXAMPLE 11   **Limit of a Difference Quotient**   Find the following limit for $f(x) = \sqrt{x}$:

$$\lim_{h \to 0} \frac{f(2 + h) - f(2)}{h}$$

SOLUTION

$$\lim_{h \to 0} \frac{f(2 + h) - f(2)}{h} = \lim_{h \to 0} \frac{\sqrt{2 + h} - \sqrt{2}}{h}$$

$$= \lim_{h \to 0} \frac{\sqrt{2 + h} - \sqrt{2}}{h} \cdot \frac{\sqrt{2 + h} + \sqrt{2}}{\sqrt{2 + h} + \sqrt{2}}$$

$$= \lim_{h \to 0} \frac{2 + h - 2}{h(\sqrt{2 + h} + \sqrt{2})}$$

$$= \lim_{h \to 0} \frac{1}{\sqrt{2 + h} + \sqrt{2}}$$

$$= \frac{1}{\sqrt{2} + \sqrt{2}} = \frac{1}{2\sqrt{2}}$$

This is a 0/0 indeterminate form, so property 7 in Theorem 2 does not apply. Rationalizing the numerator will help.

$$(A - B)(A + B) = A^2 - B^2$$

Matched Problem 11   Find the following limit for $f(x) = \sqrt{x}$: $\displaystyle\lim_{h \to 0} \frac{f(3 + h) - f(3)}{h}$.

Exercises 10-1

A

In Problems 1–8, use the graph of the function f shown to estimate the indicated limits and function values.

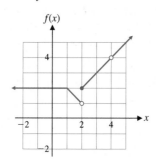

Figure for 1–8

1. $f(-0.5)$ **2.** $f(-1.5)$

3. $f(1.75)$ **4.** $f(1.25)$

5. (A) $\lim\limits_{x\to 0^-} f(x)$ (B) $\lim\limits_{x\to 0^+} f(x)$
(C) $\lim\limits_{x\to 0} f(x)$ (D) $f(0)$

6. (A) $\lim\limits_{x\to 1^-} f(x)$ (B) $\lim\limits_{x\to 1^+} f(x)$
(C) $\lim\limits_{x\to 1} f(x)$ (D) $f(1)$

7. (A) $\lim\limits_{x\to 2^-} f(x)$ (B) $\lim\limits_{x\to 2^+} f(x)$
(C) $\lim\limits_{x\to 2} f(x)$ (D) $f(2)$

 (E) Is it possible to redefine $f(2)$ so that $\lim\limits_{x\to 2} f(x) = f(2)$? Explain.

8. (A) $\lim\limits_{x\to 4^-} f(x)$ (B) $\lim\limits_{x\to 4^+} f(x)$
(C) $\lim\limits_{x\to 4} f(x)$ (D) $f(4)$

(E) Is it possible to define $f(4)$ so that $\lim\limits_{x\to 4} f(x) = f(4)$? Explain.

In Problems 9–16, use the graph of the function g shown to estimate the indicated limits and function values.

Figure for 9–16

9. $g(1.9)$ **10.** $g(0.1)$

11. $g(3.5)$ **12.** $g(2.5)$

13. (A) $\lim\limits_{x\to 1^-} g(x)$ (B) $\lim\limits_{x\to 1^+} g(x)$
(C) $\lim\limits_{x\to 1} g(x)$ (D) $g(1)$

(E) Is it possible to define $g(1)$ so that $\lim\limits_{x\to 1} g(x) = g(1)$? Explain.

14. (A) $\lim\limits_{x\to 2^-} g(x)$ (B) $\lim\limits_{x\to 2^+} g(x)$
(C) $\lim\limits_{x\to 2} g(x)$ (D) $g(2)$

15. (A) $\lim\limits_{x\to 3^-} g(x)$ (B) $\lim\limits_{x\to 3^+} g(x)$
(C) $\lim\limits_{x\to 3} g(x)$ (D) $g(3)$

(E) Is it possible to redefine $g(3)$ so that $\lim\limits_{x\to 3} g(x) = g(3)$? Explain.

16. (A) $\lim\limits_{x\to 4^-} g(x)$ (B) $\lim\limits_{x\to 4^+} g(x)$
(C) $\lim\limits_{x\to 4} g(x)$ (D) $g(4)$

In Problems 17–20, use the graph of the function f shown to estimate the indicated limits and function values.

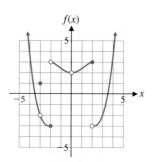

Figure for 17–20

17. (A) $\lim\limits_{x\to -3^+} f(x)$ (B) $\lim\limits_{x\to -3^-} f(x)$
(C) $\lim\limits_{x\to -3} f(x)$ (D) $f(-3)$

(E) Is it possible to redefine $f(-3)$ so that $\lim\limits_{x\to -3} f(x) = f(-3)$? Explain.

18. (A) $\lim\limits_{x\to -2^+} f(x)$ (B) $\lim\limits_{x\to -2^-} f(x)$
(C) $\lim\limits_{x\to -2} f(x)$ (D) $f(-2)$

(E) Is it possible to define $f(-2)$ so that $\lim\limits_{x\to -2} f(x) = f(-2)$? Explain.

19. (A) $\lim\limits_{x\to 0^+} f(x)$ (B) $\lim\limits_{x\to 0^-} f(x)$
(C) $\lim\limits_{x\to 0} f(x)$ (D) $f(0)$

(E) Is it possible to redefine $f(0)$ so that $\lim\limits_{x\to 0} f(x) = f(0)$? Explain.

20. (A) $\lim\limits_{x\to 2^+} f(x)$ (B) $\lim\limits_{x\to 2^-} f(x)$
(C) $\lim\limits_{x\to 2} f(x)$ (D) $f(2)$

(E) Is it possible to redefine $f(2)$ so that $\lim\limits_{x\to 2} f(x) = f(2)$? Explain.

In Problems 21–30, find each limit if it exists.

21. $\lim\limits_{x\to 3} 4x$ **22.** $\lim\limits_{x\to -2} 3x$

23. $\lim\limits_{x\to -4} (x + 5)$ **24.** $\lim\limits_{x\to 5}(x - 3)$

25. $\lim\limits_{x\to 2} x(x - 4)$ **26.** $\lim\limits_{x\to -1} x(x + 3)$

27. $\lim\limits_{x\to -3} \dfrac{x}{x + 5}$ **28.** $\lim\limits_{x\to 4} \dfrac{x - 2}{x}$

29. $\lim\limits_{x\to 1} \sqrt{5x + 4}$ **30.** $\lim\limits_{x\to 0} \sqrt{16 - 7x}$

Given that $\lim_{x \to 1} f(x) = -5$ *and* $\lim_{x \to 1} g(x) = 4$, *find the indicated limits in Problems 31–38.*

31. $\lim_{x \to 1}(-3)f(x)$

32. $\lim_{x \to 1} 2g(x)$

33. $\lim_{x \to 1}[2f(x) + g(x)]$

34. $\lim_{x \to 1}[g(x) - 3f(x)]$

35. $\lim_{x \to 1}\dfrac{2 - f(x)}{x + g(x)}$

36. $\lim_{x \to 1}\dfrac{3 - f(x)}{1 - 4g(x)}$

37. $\lim_{x \to 1}\sqrt{g(x) - f(x)}$

38. $\lim_{x \to 1}\sqrt[3]{2x + 2f(x)}$

In Problems 39–42, sketch a possible graph of a function that satisfies the given conditions.

39. $f(0) = 1;\ \lim_{x \to 0^-} f(x) = 3;\ \lim_{x \to 0^+} f(x) = 1$

40. $f(1) = -2;\ \lim_{x \to 1^-} f(x) = 2;\ \lim_{x \to 1^+} f(x) = -2$

41. $f(-2) = 2;\ \lim_{x \to -2^-} f(x) = 1;\ \lim_{x \to -2^+} f(x) = 1$

42. $f(0) = -1;\ \lim_{x \to 0^-} f(x) = 2;\ \lim_{x \to 0^+} f(x) = 2$

B

In Problems 43–58, find each indicated quantity if it exists.

43. Let $f(x) = \begin{cases} 1 - x^2 & \text{if } x \le 0 \\ 1 + x^2 & \text{if } x > 0 \end{cases}$. Find

(A) $\lim_{x \to 0^+} f(x)$ (B) $\lim_{x \to 0^-} f(x)$

(C) $\lim_{x \to 0} f(x)$ (D) $f(0)$

44. Let $f(x) = \begin{cases} 2 + x & \text{if } x \le 0 \\ 2 - x & \text{if } x > 0 \end{cases}$. Find

(A) $\lim_{x \to 0^+} f(x)$ (B) $\lim_{x \to 0^-} f(x)$

(C) $\lim_{x \to 0} f(x)$ (D) $f(0)$

45. Let $f(x) = \begin{cases} x^2 & \text{if } x < 1 \\ 2x & \text{if } x > 1 \end{cases}$. Find

(A) $\lim_{x \to 1^+} f(x)$ (B) $\lim_{x \to 1^-} f(x)$

(C) $\lim_{x \to 1} f(x)$ (D) $f(1)$

46. Let $f(x) = \begin{cases} x + 3 & \text{if } x < -2 \\ \sqrt{x + 2} & \text{if } x > -2 \end{cases}$. Find

(A) $\lim_{x \to -2^+} f(x)$ (B) $\lim_{x \to -2^-} f(x)$

(C) $\lim_{x \to -2} f(x)$ (D) $f(-2)$

47. Let $f(x) = \begin{cases} \dfrac{x^2 - 9}{x + 3} & \text{if } x < 0 \\ \dfrac{x^2 - 9}{x - 3} & \text{if } x > 0 \end{cases}$. Find

(A) $\lim_{x \to -3} f(x)$ (B) $\lim_{x \to 0} f(x)$

(C) $\lim_{x \to 3} f(x)$

48. Let $f(x) = \begin{cases} \dfrac{x}{x + 3} & \text{if } x < 0 \\ \dfrac{x}{x - 3} & \text{if } x > 0 \end{cases}$. Find

(A) $\lim_{x \to -3} f(x)$ (B) $\lim_{x \to 0} f(x)$

(C) $\lim_{x \to 3} f(x)$

49. Let $f(x) = \dfrac{|x - 1|}{x - 1}$. Find

(A) $\lim_{x \to 1^+} f(x)$ (B) $\lim_{x \to 1^-} f(x)$

(C) $\lim_{x \to 1} f(x)$ (D) $f(1)$

50. Let $f(x) = \dfrac{x - 3}{|x - 3|}$. Find

(A) $\lim_{x \to 3^+} f(x)$ (B) $\lim_{x \to 3^-} f(x)$

(C) $\lim_{x \to 3} f(x)$ (D) $f(3)$

51. Let $f(x) = \dfrac{x - 2}{x^2 - 2x}$. Find

(A) $\lim_{x \to 0} f(x)$ (B) $\lim_{x \to 2} f(x)$

(C) $\lim_{x \to 4} f(x)$

52. Let $f(x) = \dfrac{x + 3}{x^2 + 3x}$. Find

(A) $\lim_{x \to -3} f(x)$ (B) $\lim_{x \to 0} f(x)$

(C) $\lim_{x \to 3} f(x)$

53. Let $f(x) = \dfrac{x^2 - x - 6}{x + 2}$. Find

(A) $\lim_{x \to -2} f(x)$ (B) $\lim_{x \to 0} f(x)$

(C) $\lim_{x \to 3} f(x)$

54. Let $f(x) = \dfrac{x^2 + x - 6}{x + 3}$. Find

(A) $\lim_{x \to -3} f(x)$ (B) $\lim_{x \to 0} f(x)$

(C) $\lim_{x \to 2} f(x)$

55. Let $f(x) = \dfrac{(x + 2)^2}{x^2 - 4}$. Find

(A) $\lim_{x \to -2} f(x)$ (B) $\lim_{x \to 0} f(x)$

(C) $\lim_{x \to 2} f(x)$

56. Let $f(x) = \dfrac{x^2 - 1}{(x + 1)^2}$. Find

(A) $\lim_{x \to -1} f(x)$ (B) $\lim_{x \to 0} f(x)$

(C) $\lim_{x \to 1} f(x)$

57. Let $f(x) = \dfrac{2x^2 - 3x - 2}{x^2 + x - 6}$. Find

(A) $\lim_{x \to 2} f(x)$ (B) $\lim_{x \to 0} f(x)$

(C) $\lim_{x \to 1} f(x)$

58. Let $f(x) = \dfrac{3x^2 + 2x - 1}{x^2 + 3x + 2}$. Find

(A) $\lim_{x \to -3} f(x)$ (B) $\lim_{x \to -1} f(x)$

(C) $\lim_{x \to 2} f(x)$

In Problems 59–64, discuss the validity of each statement. If the statement is always true, explain why. If not, give a counterexample.

59. If $\lim_{x \to 1} f(x) = 0$ and $\lim_{x \to 1} g(x) = 0$, then $\lim_{x \to 1}\dfrac{f(x)}{g(x)} = 0$.

60. If $\lim_{x \to 1} f(x) = 1$ and $\lim_{x \to 1} g(x) = 1$, then $\lim_{x \to 1}\dfrac{f(x)}{g(x)} = 1$.

61. If f is a polynomial, then, as x approaches 0, the right-hand limit exists and is equal to the left-hand limit.

62. If f is a rational function, then, as x approaches 0, the right-hand limit exists and is equal to the left-hand limit.

63. If f is a function such that $\lim_{x \to 0} f(x)$ exists, then $f(0)$ exists.

64. If f is a function such that $f(0)$ exists, then $\lim_{x \to 0} f(x)$ exists.

Compute the following limit for each function in Problems 65–68.

$$\lim_{h \to 0} \frac{f(2 + h) - f(2)}{h}$$

65. $f(x) = 3x + 1$ **66.** $f(x) = 5x - 1$

67. $f(x) = x^2 + 1$ **68.** $f(x) = x^2 - 2$

C

69. Let f be defined by

$$f(x) = \begin{cases} 1 + mx & \text{if } x \leq 1 \\ 4 - mx & \text{if } x > 1 \end{cases}$$

where m is a constant.

(A) Graph f for $m = 1$, and find

$$\lim_{x \to 1^-} f(x) \quad \text{and} \quad \lim_{x \to 1^+} f(x)$$

(B) Graph f for $m = 2$, and find

$$\lim_{x \to 1^-} f(x) \quad \text{and} \quad \lim_{x \to 1^+} f(x)$$

(C) Find m so that

$$\lim_{x \to 1^-} f(x) = \lim_{x \to 1^+} f(x)$$

and graph f for this value of m.

(D) Write a brief verbal description of each graph. How does the graph in part (C) differ from the graphs in parts (A) and (B)?

70. Let f be defined by

$$f(x) = \begin{cases} -3m + 0.5x & \text{if } x \leq 2 \\ 3m - x & \text{if } x > 2 \end{cases}$$

where m is a constant.

(A) Graph f for $m = 0$, and find

$$\lim_{x \to 2^-} f(x) \quad \text{and} \quad \lim_{x \to 2^+} f(x)$$

(B) Graph f for $m = 1$, and find

$$\lim_{x \to 2^-} f(x) \quad \text{and} \quad \lim_{x \to 2^+} f(x)$$

(C) Find m so that

$$\lim_{x \to 2^-} f(x) = \lim_{x \to 2^+} f(x)$$

and graph f for this value of m.

(D) Write a brief verbal description of each graph. How does the graph in part (C) differ from the graphs in parts (A) and (B)?

Find each limit in Problems 71–74, where a is a real constant.

71. $\lim\limits_{h \to 0} \dfrac{(a + h)^2 - a^2}{h}$

72. $\lim\limits_{h \to 0} \dfrac{[3(a + h) - 2] - (3a - 2)}{h}$

73. $\lim\limits_{h \to 0} \dfrac{\sqrt{a + h} - \sqrt{a}}{h}, \quad a > 0$

74. $\lim\limits_{h \to 0} \dfrac{\dfrac{1}{a + h} - \dfrac{1}{a}}{h}, \quad a \neq 0$

Applications

75. Telephone rates. A long-distance telephone service charges $0.99 for the first 20 minutes or less of a call and $0.07 per minute for each additional minute or fraction thereof.

(A) Write a piecewise definition of the charge $F(x)$ for a long-distance call lasting x minutes.

(B) Graph $F(x)$ for $0 < x \leq 40$.

(C) Find $\lim\limits_{x \to 20^-} F(x)$, $\lim\limits_{x \to 20^+} F(x)$, and $\lim\limits_{x \to 20} F(x)$, whichever exist.

76. Telephone rates. A second long-distance telephone service charges $0.09 per minute or fraction thereof for calls lasting 10 minutes or more and $0.18 per minute or fraction thereof for calls lasting less than 10 minutes.

(A) Write a piecewise definition of the charge $G(x)$ for a long-distance call lasting x minutes.

(B) Graph $G(x)$ for $0 < x \leq 40$.

(C) Find $\lim\limits_{x \to 10^-} G(x)$, $\lim\limits_{x \to 10^+} G(x)$, and $\lim\limits_{x \to 10} G(x)$, whichever exist.

77. Telephone rates. Refer to Problems 75 and 76. Write a brief verbal comparison of the two services described for calls lasting 20 minutes or less.

78. Telephone rates. Refer to Problems 75 and 76. Write a brief verbal comparison of the two services described for calls lasting more than 20 minutes.

A company sells custom embroidered apparel and promotional products. Table 1 shows the volume discounts offered by the company, where x is the volume of a purchase in dollars. Problems 79 and 80 deal with two different interpretations of this discount method.

Table 1

Volume Discount (Excluding Tax)

Volume (x)	Discount Amount
$300 \leq x < $1,000	3%
$1,000 \leq x < $3,000	5%
$3,000 \leq x < $5,000	7%
$5,000 \leq x	10%

79. Volume discount. Assume that the volume discounts in Table 1 apply to the entire purchase. That is, if the volume x satisfies $300 \leq x < $1,000, then the entire purchase is discounted 3%. If the volume x satisfies $1,000 \leq x < $3,000, the entire purchase is discounted 5%, and so on.

(A) If x is the volume of a purchase before the discount is applied, then write a piecewise definition for the discounted price $D(x)$ of this purchase.

(B) Use one-sided limits to investigate the limit of $D(x)$ as x approaches $1,000. As x approaches $3,000.

80. Volume discount. Assume that the volume discounts in Table 1 apply only to that portion of the volume in each interval. That is, the discounted price for a $4,000 purchase would be computed as follows:

$$300 + 0.97(700) + 0.95(2,000) + 0.93(1,000) = 3,809$$

(A) If x is the volume of a purchase before the discount is applied, then write a piecewise definition for the discounted price $P(x)$ of this purchase.

(B) Use one-sided limits to investigate the limit of $P(x)$ as x approaches \$1,000. As x approaches \$3,000.

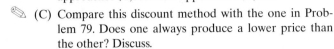 (C) Compare this discount method with the one in Problem 79. Does one always produce a lower price than the other? Discuss.

81. Pollution. A state charges polluters an annual fee of \$20 per ton for each ton of pollutant emitted into the atmosphere, up to a maximum of 4,000 tons. No fees are charged for emissions beyond the 4,000-ton limit. Write a piecewise definition of the fees $F(x)$ charged for the emission of x tons of pollutant in a year. What is the limit of $F(x)$ as x approaches 4,000 tons? As x approaches 8,000 tons?

82. Pollution. Refer to Problem 81. The fee per ton of pollution is given by $A(x) = F(x)/x$. Write a piecewise definition of $A(x)$. What is the limit of $A(x)$ as x approaches 4,000 tons? As x approaches 8,000 tons?

83. Voter turnout. Statisticians often use piecewise-defined functions to predict outcomes of elections. For the following functions f and g, find the limit of each function as x approaches 5 and as x approaches 10.

$$f(x) = \begin{cases} 0 & \text{if } x \le 5 \\ 0.8 - 0.08x & \text{if } 5 < x < 10 \\ 0 & \text{if } 10 \le x \end{cases}$$

$$g(x) = \begin{cases} 0 & \text{if } x \le 5 \\ 0.8x - 0.04x^2 - 3 & \text{if } 5 < x < 10 \\ 1 & \text{if } 10 \le x \end{cases}$$

Answers to Matched Problems

1.

x	-2	-1	0	1	2	3	4
$h(x)$	1.0	1.5	2.0	2.5	3.0	3.5	4.0

2. $\lim\limits_{x \to 1^-} f(x) = 2$

3.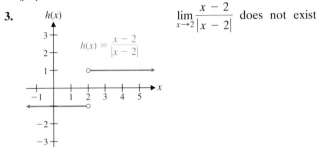
$\lim\limits_{x \to 2} \dfrac{x-2}{|x-2|}$ does not exist

4. (A) $\lim\limits_{x \to 0^-} f(x) = 0$
$\lim\limits_{x \to 0^+} f(x) = 0$
$\lim\limits_{x \to 0} f(x) = 0$
$f(0) = 0$

(B) $\lim\limits_{x \to 1^-} f(x) = 1$
$\lim\limits_{x \to 1^+} f(x) = 2$
$\lim\limits_{x \to 1} f(x)$ does not exist
$f(1)$ not defined

(C) $\lim\limits_{x \to 3^-} f(x) = 3$
$\lim\limits_{x \to 3^+} f(x) = 3$
$\lim\limits_{x \to 3} f(x) = 3$
$f(3)$ not defined

5. -6

6. (A) 6
(B) $\sqrt{6}$
(C) $\frac{4}{5}$

7. (A) 13
(B) 7
(C) Does not exist
(D) Not defined

8. (A) -2
(B) Does not exist

9. -2 **10.** Does not exist   **11.** $1/(2\sqrt{3})$

10-2 Infinite Limits and Limits at Infinity

- Infinite Limits
- Locating Vertical Asymptotes
- Limits at Infinity
- Finding Horizontal Asymptotes

In this section, we consider two new types of limits: infinite limits and limits at infinity. Infinite limits and vertical asymptotes are used to describe the behavior of functions that are unbounded near $x = a$. Limits at infinity and horizontal asymptotes are used to describe the behavior of functions as x assumes arbitrarily large positive values or arbitrarily large negative values. Although we will include graphs to illustrate basic concepts, we postpone a discussion of graphing techniques until Chapter 12.

Infinite Limits

The graph of $f(x) = \dfrac{1}{x-1}$ (Fig. 1) indicates that

$$\lim_{x \to 1^+} \frac{1}{x-1}$$

does not exist. There does not exist a real number L that the values of $f(x)$ approach as x approaches 1 from the right. Instead, as x approaches 1 from the right, the values of $f(x)$ are positive and become larger and larger; that is, $f(x)$ increases without bound (Table 1). We express this behavior symbolically as

$$\lim_{x \to 1^+} \frac{1}{x-1} = \infty \quad \text{or} \quad f(x) = \frac{1}{x-1} \to \infty \quad \text{as} \quad x \to 1^+ \qquad (1)$$

Since ∞ is a not a real number, *the limit in (1) does not exist.* We are using the symbol ∞ to describe the manner in which the limit fails to exist, and we call this situation an **infinite limit**. If x approaches 1 from the left, the values of $f(x)$ are negative and become larger and larger in absolute value; that is, $f(x)$ decreases through negative values without bound (Table 2). We express this behavior symbolically as

$$\lim_{x \to 1^-} \frac{1}{x-1} = -\infty \quad \text{or} \quad f(x) = \frac{1}{x-1} \to -\infty \quad \text{as} \quad x \to 1^- \qquad (2)$$

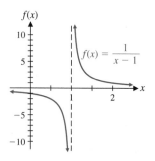

$f(x)$

$f(x) = \dfrac{1}{x-1}$

Figure 1

Table 1	
x	$f(x) = \dfrac{1}{x-1}$
1.1	10
1.01	100
1.001	1,000
1.0001	10,000
1.00001	100,000
1.000001	1,000,000

Table 2	
x	$f(x) = \dfrac{1}{x-1}$
0.9	−10
0.99	−100
0.999	−1,000
0.9999	−10,000
0.99999	−100,000
0.999999	−1,000,000

The one-sided limits in (1) and (2) describe the behavior of the graph as $x \to 1$ (Fig. 1). Does the two-sided limit of $f(x)$ as $x = 1$ exist? No, because neither of the one-sided limits exists. Also, there is no reasonable way to use the symbol ∞ to describe the behavior of $f(x)$ as $x \to 1$ on both sides of 1. We say that

$$\lim_{x \to 1} \frac{1}{x-1} \text{ does not exist}$$

EXPLORE & DISCUSS 1

Let $g(x) = \dfrac{1}{(x-1)^2}$

Construct tables for $g(x)$ as $x \to 1^+$ and as $x \to 1^-$. Use these tables and infinite limits to discuss the behavior of $g(x)$ near $x = 1$.

We used the dashed vertical line $x = 1$ in Figure 1 to illustrate the infinite limits as x approaches 1 from the right and from the left. We call this line a *vertical asymptote.*

> **DEFINITION Infinite Limits and Vertical Asymptotes**
>
> The vertical line $x = a$ is a **vertical asymptote** for the graph of $y = f(x)$ if
>
> $$f(x) \to \infty \quad \text{or} \quad f(x) \to -\infty \quad \text{as} \quad x \to a^+ \quad \text{or} \quad x \to a^-$$
>
> [That is, if $f(x)$ either increases or decreases without bound as x approaches a from the right or from the left].

Locating Vertical Asymptotes

How do we locate vertical asymptotes? If f is a polynomial function, then $\lim_{x \to a} f(x)$ is equal to the real number $f(a)$ [Theorem 3, Section 10-1]. So *a polynomial function has no vertical asymptotes.* Similarly (again by Theorem 3, Section 10-1), *a vertical asymptote of a rational function can occur only at a zero of its denominator.* Theorem 1 provides a simple procedure for locating the vertical asymptotes of a rational function.

> **THEOREM 1   Locating Vertical Asymptotes of Rational Functions**
> If $f(x) = n(x)/d(x)$ is a rational function, $d(c) = 0$ and $n(c) \neq 0$, then the line $x = c$ is a vertical asymptote of the graph of f.

If $f(x) = n(x)/d(x)$ and both $n(c) = 0$ and $d(c) = 0$, then the limit of $f(x)$ as x approaches c involves an indeterminate form and Theorem 1 does not apply:

$$\lim_{x \to c} f(x) = \lim_{x \to c} \frac{n(x)}{d(x)} \quad \frac{0}{0} \text{ indeterminate form}$$

Algebraic simplification is often useful in this situation.

EXAMPLE 1   **Locating Vertical Asymptotes** Let $f(x) = \dfrac{x^2 + x - 2}{x^2 - 1}$.

Describe the behavior of f at each zero of the denominator. Use ∞ and $-\infty$ when appropriate. Identify all vertical asymptotes.

SOLUTION   Let $n(x) = x^2 + x - 2$ and $d(x) = x^2 - 1$. Factoring the denominator, we see that

$$d(x) = x^2 - 1 = (x - 1)(x + 1)$$

has two zeros: $x = -1$ and $x = 1$.

First, we consider $x = -1$. Since $d(-1) = 0$ and $n(-1) = -2 \neq 0$, Theorem 1 tells us that the line $x = -1$ is a vertical asymptote. So at least one of the one-sided limits at $x = -1$ must be either ∞ or $-\infty$. Examining tables of values of f for x near -1 or a graph on a graphing calculator will show which is the case. From Tables 3 and 4, we see that

$$\lim_{x \to -1^-} \frac{x^2 + x - 2}{x^2 - 1} = -\infty \quad \text{and} \quad \lim_{x \to -1^+} \frac{x^2 + x - 2}{x^2 - 1} = \infty$$

Table 3	
x	$f(x) = \dfrac{x^2 + x - 2}{x^2 - 1}$
-1.1	-9
-1.01	-99
-1.001	-999
-1.0001	$-9{,}999$
-1.00001	$-99{,}999$

Table 4	
x	$f(x) = \dfrac{x^2 + x - 2}{x^2 - 1}$
-0.9	11
-0.99	101
-0.999	$1{,}001$
-0.9999	$10{,}001$
-0.99999	$100{,}001$

Now we consider the other zero of $d(x)$, $x = 1$. This time $n(1) = 0$ and Theorem 1 does not apply. We use algebraic simplification to investigate the behavior of the function at $x = 1$:

$$\lim_{x \to 1} f(x) = \lim_{x \to 1} \frac{x^2 + x - 2}{x^2 - 1} \qquad \frac{0}{0} \text{ indeterminate form}$$

$$= \lim_{x \to 1} \frac{(x - 1)(x + 2)}{(x - 1)(x + 1)}$$

$$= \lim_{x \to 1} \frac{x + 2}{x + 1} \qquad \text{Reduced to lowest terms (see Appendix A-4)}$$

$$= \frac{3}{2}$$

Figure 2 $f(x) = \dfrac{x^2 + x - 2}{x^2 - 1}$

Since the limit exists as x approaches 1, f does not have a vertical asymptote at $x = 1$. The graph of f (Fig. 2) shows the behavior at the vertical asymptote $x = -1$ and also at $x = 1$.

Matched Problem 1   Let $f(x) = \dfrac{x - 3}{x^2 - 4x + 3}$.

Describe the behavior of f at each zero of the denominator. Use ∞ and $-\infty$ when appropriate. Identify all vertical asymptotes.

EXAMPLE 2 **Locating Vertical Asymptotes** Let $f(x) = \dfrac{x^2 + 20}{5(x - 2)^2}$

Describe the behavior of f at each zero of the denominator. Use ∞ and $-\infty$ when appropriate. Identify all vertical asymptotes.

SOLUTION Let $n(x) = x^2 + 20$ and $d(x) = 5(x - 2)^2$. The only zero of $d(x)$ is $x = 2$. Since $n(2) = 24 \neq 0$, f has a vertical asymptote at $x = 2$ (Theorem 1). Tables 5 and 6 show that $f(x) \to \infty$ as $x \to 2$ from either side, and we have

$$\lim_{x \to 2^+} \frac{x^2 + 20}{5(x - 2)^2} = \infty \quad \text{and} \quad \lim_{x \to 2^-} \frac{x^2 + 20}{5(x - 2)^2} = \infty$$

Table 5

x	$f(x) = \dfrac{x^2 + 20}{5(x - 2)^2}$
2.1	488.2
2.01	48,080.02
2.001	4,800,800.2

Table 6

x	$f(x) = \dfrac{x^2 + 20}{5(x - 2)^2}$
1.9	472.2
1.99	47,920.02
1.999	4,799,200.2

$f(x) = \dfrac{x^2 + 20}{5(x - 2)^2}$

Figure 3

The denominator d has no other zeros, so f does not have any other vertical asymptotes. The graph of f (Fig. 3) shows the behavior at the vertical asymptote $x = 2$. Because the left- and right-hand limits are both infinite, we write

$$\lim_{x \to 2} \frac{x^2 + 20}{5(x - 2)^2} = \infty$$

Matched Problem 2 Let $f(x) = \dfrac{x - 1}{(x + 3)^2}$.

Describe the behavior of f at each zero of the denominator. Use ∞ and $-\infty$ when appropriate. Identify all vertical asymptotes.

CONCEPTUAL INSIGHT

When is it correct to say that a limit does not exist, and when is it correct to use $\pm\infty$? It depends on the situation. Table 7 lists the infinite limits that we discussed in Examples 1 and 2.

Table 7

Right-Hand Limit	Left-Hand Limit	Two-Sided Limit
$\lim\limits_{x \to -1^+} \dfrac{x^2 + x - 2}{x^2 - 1} = \infty$	$\lim\limits_{x \to -1^-} \dfrac{x^2 + x - 2}{x^2 - 1} = -\infty$	$\lim\limits_{x \to -1} \dfrac{x^2 + x - 2}{x^2 - 1}$ does not exist
$\lim\limits_{x \to 2^+} \dfrac{x^2 + 20}{5(x - 2)^2} = \infty$	$\lim\limits_{x \to 2^-} \dfrac{x^2 + 20}{5(x - 2)^2} = \infty$	$\lim\limits_{x \to 2} \dfrac{x^2 + 20}{5(x - 2)^2} = \infty$

The instructions in Examples 1 and 2 said that we should use infinite limits to describe the behavior at vertical asymptotes. If we had been asked to *evaluate* the limits, with no mention of ∞ or asymptotes, then the correct answer would be that **all of these limits do not exist**. Remember, ∞ is a symbol used to describe the behavior of functions at vertical asymptotes.

Limits at Infinity

The symbol ∞ can also be used to indicate that an independent variable is increasing or decreasing without bound. We write $x \to \infty$ to indicate that x is increasing without bound through positive values and $x \to -\infty$ to indicate that x is decreasing without bound through negative values. We begin by considering power functions of the form x^p and $1/x^p$ where p is a positive real number.

If p is a positive real number, then x^p increases as x increases. There is no upper bound on the values of x^p. We indicate this behavior by writing

$$\lim_{x \to \infty} x^p = \infty \quad \text{or} \quad x^p \to \infty \quad \text{as} \quad x \to \infty$$

Since the reciprocals of very large numbers are very small numbers, it follows that $1/x^p$ approaches 0 as x increases without bound. We indicate this behavior by writing

$$\lim_{x \to \infty} \frac{1}{x^p} = 0 \quad \text{or} \quad \frac{1}{x^p} \to 0 \quad \text{as} \quad x \to \infty$$

Figure 4 illustrates the preceding behavior for $f(x) = x^2$ and $g(x) = 1/x^2$, and we write

$$\lim_{x \to \infty} f(x) = \infty \quad \text{and} \quad \lim_{x \to \infty} g(x) = 0$$

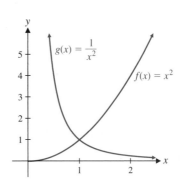

Figure 4

Limits of power forms as x decreases without bound behave in a similar manner, with two important differences. First, if x is negative, then x^p is not defined for all values of p. For example, $x^{1/2} = \sqrt{x}$ is not defined for negative values of x. Second, if x^p is defined, then it may approach ∞ or $-\infty$, depending on the value of p. For example,

$$\lim_{x \to -\infty} x^2 = \infty \quad \text{but} \quad \lim_{x \to -\infty} x^3 = -\infty$$

For the function g in Figure 4, the line $y = 0$ (the x axis) is called a *horizontal asymptote*. In general, a line $y = b$ is a **horizontal asymptote** of the graph of $y = f(x)$ if $f(x)$ approaches b as either x increases without bound or x decreases without bound. Symbolically, $y = b$ is a horizontal asymptote if either

$$\lim_{x \to -\infty} f(x) = b \quad \text{or} \quad \lim_{x \to \infty} f(x) = b$$

In the first case, the graph of f will be close to the horizontal line $y = b$ for large (in absolute value) negative x. In the second case, the graph will be close to the horizontal line $y = b$ for large positive x. Figure 5 shows the graph of a function with two horizontal asymptotes: $y = 1$ and $y = -1$.

Theorem 2 summarizes the various possibilities for limits of power functions as x increases or decreases without bound.

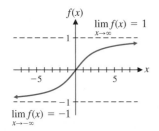

Figure 5

THEOREM 2   Limits of Power Functions at Infinity

If p is a positive real number and k is any real number except 0, then

1. $\lim\limits_{x \to -\infty} \dfrac{k}{x^p} = 0$ 2. $\lim\limits_{x \to \infty} \dfrac{k}{x^p} = 0$

3. $\lim\limits_{x \to -\infty} kx^p = \pm\infty$ 4. $\lim\limits_{x \to \infty} kx^p = \pm\infty$

provided that x^p is a real number for negative values of x. The limits in 3 and 4 will be either $-\infty$ or ∞, depending on k and p.

How can we use Theorem 2 to evaluate limits at infinity? It turns out that the limit properties listed in Theorem 2, Section 10-1, are also valid if we replace the statement $x \to c$ with $x \to \infty$ or $x \to -\infty$.

EXAMPLE 3   **Limit of a Polynomial Function at Infinity** Let $p(x) = 2x^3 - x^2 - 7x + 3$. Find the limit of $p(x)$ as x approaches ∞ and as x approaches $-\infty$.

SOLUTION   Since limits of power functions of the form $1/x^p$ approach 0 as x approaches ∞ or $-\infty$, it is convenient to work with these reciprocal forms whenever possible. If we factor out the term involving the highest power of x, then we can write $p(x)$ as

$$p(x) = 2x^3\left(1 - \frac{1}{2x} - \frac{7}{2x^2} + \frac{3}{2x^3}\right)$$

Using Theorem 2 in Section 10-3 and Theorem 2 in Section 10-1, we write

$$\lim\limits_{x \to \infty}\left(1 - \frac{1}{2x} - \frac{7}{2x^2} + \frac{3}{2x^3}\right) = 1 - 0 - 0 + 0 = 1$$

For large values of x,

$$\left(1 - \frac{1}{2x} - \frac{7}{2x^2} + \frac{3}{2x^3}\right) \approx 1$$

and

$$p(x) = 2x^3\left(1 - \frac{1}{2x} - \frac{7}{2x^2} + \frac{3}{2x^3}\right) \approx 2x^3$$

Since $2x^3 \to \infty$ as $x \to \infty$, it follows that

$$\lim\limits_{x \to \infty} p(x) = \lim\limits_{x \to \infty} 2x^3 = \infty$$

Similarly, $2x^3 \to -\infty$ as $x \to -\infty$ implies that

$$\lim\limits_{x \to -\infty} p(x) = \lim\limits_{x \to -\infty} 2x^3 = -\infty$$

So the behavior of $p(x)$ for large values is the same as the behavior of the highest-degree term, $2x^3$.

Matched Problem 3   Let $p(x) = -4x^4 + 2x^3 + 3x$. Find the limit of $p(x)$ as x approaches ∞ and as x approaches $-\infty$.

The term with highest degree in a polynomial is called the **leading term**. In the solution to Example 3, the limits at infinity of $p(x) = 2x^3 - x^2 - 7x + 3$ were the same as the limits of the leading term $2x^3$. Theorem 3 states that this is true for any polynomial of degree greater than or equal to 1.

> **THEOREM 3   Limits of Polynomial Functions at Infinity**
> If
> $$p(x) = a_n x^n + a_{n-1} x^{n-1} + \cdots + a_1 x + a_0, a_n \neq 0, n \geq 1$$
> then
> $$\lim_{x \to \infty} p(x) = \lim_{x \to \infty} a_n x^n = \pm\infty$$
> and
> $$\lim_{x \to -\infty} p(x) = \lim_{x \to -\infty} a_n x^n = \pm\infty$$
> Each limit will be either $-\infty$ or ∞, depending on a_n and n.

A polynomial of degree 0 is a constant function $p(x) = a_0$, and its limit as x approaches ∞ or $-\infty$ is the number a_0. For any polynomial of degree 1 or greater, Theorem 3 states that the limit as x approaches ∞ or $-\infty$ cannot be equal to a number. This means that **polynomials of degree 1 or greater never have horizontal asymptotes**.

A description of the behavior of the limits of any function f at infinity is called the **end behavior** of f. $\lim_{x \to \infty} f(x)$ determines the right end behavior, and $\lim_{x \to -\infty} f(x)$ determines the left end behavior. According to Theorem 3, the right and left end behavior of a nonconstant polynomial $p(x)$ is always an infinite limit.

EXAMPLE 4   **End Behavior of a Polynomial** Describe the end behavior of each polynomial.

(A) $p(x) = 3x^3 - 500x^2$ (B) $p(x) = 3x^3 - 500x^4$

SOLUTION   (A) According to Theorem 3, as x increases without bound to the right, the right end behavior is

$$\lim_{x \to \infty} (3x^3 - 500x^2) = \lim_{x \to \infty} 3x^3 = \infty$$

and as x increases without bound to the left, the end behavior is

$$\lim_{x \to -\infty} (3x^3 - 500x^2) = \lim_{x \to -\infty} 3x^3 = -\infty$$

(B) As x increases without bound to the right, the end behavior is

$$\lim_{x \to \infty} (3x^3 - 500x^4) = \lim_{x \to \infty} (-500x^4) = -\infty$$

and as x increases without bound to the left, the end behavior is

$$\lim_{x \to -\infty} (3x^3 - 500x^4) = \lim_{x \to -\infty} (-500x^4) = -\infty$$

Matched Problem 4   Describe the end behavior of each polynomial.

(A) $p(x) = 300x^2 - 4x^5$ (B) $p(x) = 300x^6 - 4x^5$

Finding Horizontal Asymptotes

Since a rational function is the ratio of two polynomials, it is not surprising that reciprocals of powers of x can be used to analyze limits of rational functions at infinity. For example, consider the rational function

$$f(x) = \frac{3x^2 - 5x + 9}{2x^2 + 7}$$

Factoring the highest-degree term out of the numerator and the denominator, we write

$$f(x) = \frac{3x^2}{2x^2} \cdot \frac{1 - \dfrac{5}{3x} + \dfrac{3}{x^2}}{1 + \dfrac{7}{2x^2}}$$

$$\lim_{x \to \infty} f(x) = \lim_{x \to \infty} \frac{3x^2}{2x^2} \cdot \lim_{x \to \infty} \frac{1 - \dfrac{5}{3x} + \dfrac{3}{x^2}}{1 + \dfrac{7}{2x^2}} \quad \boxed{= \frac{3}{2} \cdot \frac{1 - 0 + 0}{1 + 0}} = \frac{3}{2}$$

The behavior of this rational function as x approaches infinity is determined by the ratio of the highest-degree term in the numerator $(3x^2)$ to the highest-degree term in the denominator $(2x^2)$. Theorem 4 generalizes this result to any rational function and lists the three possible outcomes.

THEOREM 4   Limits of Rational Functions at Infinity and Horizontal Asymptotes of Rational Functions

(A) If $f(x) = \dfrac{a_m x^m + a_{m-1} x^{m-1} + \cdots + a_1 x + a_0}{b_n x^n + b_{n-1} x^{n-1} + \cdots + b_1 x + b_0}, \ a_m \ne 0, b_n \ne 0$

then $\displaystyle\lim_{x \to \infty} f(x) = \lim_{x \to \infty} \frac{a_m x^m}{b_n x^n}$ and $\displaystyle\lim_{x \to -\infty} f(x) = \lim_{x \to -\infty} \frac{a_m x^m}{b_n x^n}$

(B) There are three possible cases for these limits:

1. If $m < n$, then $\displaystyle\lim_{x \to \infty} f(x) = \lim_{x \to -\infty} f(x) = 0$, and the line $y = 0$ (the x axis) is a horizontal asymptote of $f(x)$.

2. If $m = n$, then $\displaystyle\lim_{x \to \infty} f(x) = \lim_{x \to -\infty} f(x) = \frac{a_m}{b_n}$, and the line $y = \dfrac{a_m}{b_n}$ is a horizontal asymptote of $f(x)$.

3. If $m > n$, then each limit will be ∞ or $-\infty$, depending on m, n, a_m, and b_n, and $f(x)$ does not have a horizontal asymptote.

Notice that in cases 1 and 2 of Theorem 4, the limit is the same if x approaches ∞ or $-\infty$. So, **a rational function can have at most one horizontal asymptote** (see Fig. 6).

Figure 6 $f(x) = \dfrac{3x^2 - 5x + 9}{2x^2 + 7}$

CONCEPTUAL INSIGHT

The graph of f in Figure 6 dispels the misconception that the graph of a function cannot cross a horizontal asymptote. Horizontal asymptotes give us information about the graph of a function only as $x \to \infty$ and $x \to -\infty$, not at any specific value of x.

EXAMPLE 5 **Finding Horizontal Asymptotes** Find all horizontal asymptotes, if any, of each function.

(A) $f(x) = \dfrac{5x^3 - 2x^2 + 1}{4x^3 + 2x - 7}$ (B) $f(x) = \dfrac{3x^4 - x^2 + 1}{8x^6 - 10}$

(C) $f(x) = \dfrac{2x^5 - x^3 - 1}{6x^3 + 2x^2 - 7}$

SOLUTION We will make use of part A of Theorem 4.

(A) $\displaystyle\lim_{x\to\infty} f(x) = \lim_{x\to\infty}\dfrac{5x^3 - 2x^2 + 1}{4x^3 + 2x - 7} = \lim_{x\to\infty}\dfrac{5x^3}{4x^3} = \dfrac{5}{4}$

The line $y = 5/4$ is a horizontal asymptote of $f(x)$.

(B) $\displaystyle\lim_{x\to\infty} f(x) = \lim_{x\to\infty}\dfrac{3x^4 - x^2 + 1}{8x^6 - 10} = \lim_{x\to\infty}\dfrac{3x^4}{8x^6} = \lim_{x\to\infty}\dfrac{3}{8x^2} = 0$

The line $y = 0$ (the x axis) is a horizontal asymptote of $f(x)$.

(C) $\displaystyle\lim_{x\to\infty} f(x) = \lim_{x\to\infty}\dfrac{2x^5 - x^3 - 1}{6x^3 + 2x^2 - 7} = \lim_{x\to\infty}\dfrac{2x^5}{6x^3} = \lim_{x\to\infty}\dfrac{x^2}{3} = \infty$

The function $f(x)$ has no horizontal asymptotes.

Matched Problem 5 Find all horizontal asymptotes, if any, of each function.

(A) $f(x) = \dfrac{4x^3 - 5x + 8}{2x^4 - 7}$ (B) $f(x) = \dfrac{5x^6 + 3x}{2x^5 - x - 5}$

(C) $f(x) = \dfrac{2x^3 - x + 7}{4x^3 + 3x^2 - 100}$

An accurate sketch of the graph of a rational function requires knowledge of both vertical and horizontal asymptotes. As we mentioned earlier, we are postponing a detailed discussion of graphing techniques until Section 12-4.

EXAMPLE 6 **Finding the Asymptotes of a Rational Function** Find all the asymptotes of the function

$$f(x) = \frac{2x^2 - 5}{x^2 + 4x + 4}$$

SOLUTION Let $n(x) = 2x^2 - 5$ and $d(x) = x^2 + 4x + 4 = (x + 2)^2$. Since $d(x) = 0$ only at $x = -2$ and $n(-2) = 3$, the only vertical asymptote of f is the line $x = -2$ (Theorem 1). Since

$$\lim_{x\to\infty} f(x) = \lim_{x\to\infty}\frac{2x^2 - 5}{x^2 + 4x + 4} = \lim_{x\to\infty}\frac{2x^2}{x^2} = 2$$

the horizontal asymptote is the line $y = 2$ (Theorem 3).

Matched Problem 6 Find all the asymptotes of the function $f(x) = \dfrac{x^2 - 9}{x^2 - 4}$.

Exercises 10-2

A

Problems 1–8 refer to the following graph of $y = f(x)$.

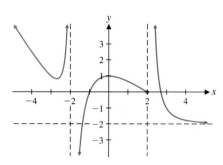

Figure for 1–8

1. $\lim\limits_{x \to \infty} f(x) = ?$ **2.** $\lim\limits_{x \to -\infty} f(x) = ?$

3. $\lim\limits_{x \to -2^+} f(x) = ?$ **4.** $\lim\limits_{x \to -2^-} f(x) = ?$

5. $\lim\limits_{x \to -2} f(x) = ?$ **6.** $\lim\limits_{x \to 2^+} f(x) = ?$

7. $\lim\limits_{x \to 2^-} f(x) = ?$ **8.** $\lim\limits_{x \to 2} f(x) = ?$

In Problems 9–16, find each limit. Use $-\infty$ and ∞ when appropriate.

9. $f(x) = \dfrac{x}{x - 5}$

(A) $\lim\limits_{x \to 5^-} f(x)$ (B) $\lim\limits_{x \to 5^+} f(x)$ (C) $\lim\limits_{x \to 5} f(x)$

10. $f(x) = \dfrac{x^2}{x + 3}$

(A) $\lim\limits_{x \to -3^-} f(x)$ (B) $\lim\limits_{x \to -3^+} f(x)$ (C) $\lim\limits_{x \to -3} f(x)$

11. $f(x) = \dfrac{2x - 4}{(x - 4)^2}$

(A) $\lim\limits_{x \to 4^-} f(x)$ (B) $\lim\limits_{x \to 4^+} f(x)$ (C) $\lim\limits_{x \to 4} f(x)$

12. $f(x) = \dfrac{2x + 2}{(x + 2)^2}$

(A) $\lim\limits_{x \to -2^-} f(x)$ (B) $\lim\limits_{x \to -2^+} f(x)$ (C) $\lim\limits_{x \to -2} f(x)$

13. $f(x) = \dfrac{x^2 + x - 2}{x - 1}$

(A) $\lim\limits_{x \to 1^-} f(x)$ (B) $\lim\limits_{x \to 1^+} f(x)$ (C) $\lim\limits_{x \to 1} f(x)$

14. $f(x) = \dfrac{x^2 + x + 2}{x - 1}$

(A) $\lim\limits_{x \to 1^-} f(x)$ (B) $\lim\limits_{x \to 1^+} f(x)$ (C) $\lim\limits_{x \to 1} f(x)$

15. $f(x) = \dfrac{x^2 - 3x + 2}{x + 2}$

(A) $\lim\limits_{x \to -2^-} f(x)$ (B) $\lim\limits_{x \to -2^+} f(x)$ (C) $\lim\limits_{x \to -2} f(x)$

16. $f(x) = \dfrac{x^2 + x - 2}{x + 2}$

(A) $\lim\limits_{x \to -2^-} f(x)$ (B) $\lim\limits_{x \to -2^+} f(x)$ (C) $\lim\limits_{x \to -2} f(x)$

In Problems 17–20, find the limit of each polynomial $p(x)$ (A) as x approaches ∞ (B) as x approaches $-\infty$

17. $p(x) = 4x^5 - 3x^4 + 1$ **18.** $p(x) = 4x^3 - 3x^4 + x^2$

19. $p(x) = 2x^5 - 2x^6 - 11$ **20.** $p(x) = 2x^4 - 2x^3 + 9x$

B

In Problems 21–30, use $-\infty$ or ∞ where appropriate to describe the behavior at each zero of the denominator and identify all vertical asymptotes.

21. $f(x) = \dfrac{1}{x + 3}$ **22.** $g(x) = \dfrac{x}{4 - x}$

23. $h(x) = \dfrac{x^2 + 4}{x^2 - 4}$ **24.** $k(x) = \dfrac{x^2 - 9}{x^2 + 9}$

25. $F(x) = \dfrac{x^2 - 4}{x^2 + 4}$ **26.** $G(x) = \dfrac{x^2 + 9}{9 - x^2}$

27. $H(x) = \dfrac{x^2 - 2x - 3}{x^2 - 4x + 3}$ **28.** $K(x) = \dfrac{x^2 + 2x - 3}{x^2 - 4x + 3}$

29. $T(x) = \dfrac{8x - 16}{x^4 - 8x^3 + 16x^2}$ **30.** $S(x) = \dfrac{6x + 9}{x^4 + 6x^3 + 9x^2}$

In Problems 31–38, find each function value and limit. Use $-\infty$ or ∞ where appropriate.

31. $f(x) = \dfrac{4x + 7}{5x - 9}$

(A) $f(10)$ (B) $f(100)$ (C) $\lim\limits_{x \to \infty} f(x)$

32. $f(x) = \dfrac{2 - 3x^3}{7 + 4x^3}$

(A) $f(5)$ (B) $f(10)$ (C) $\lim\limits_{x \to \infty} f(x)$

33. $f(x) = \dfrac{5x^2 + 11}{7x - 2}$

(A) $f(20)$ (B) $f(50)$ (C) $\lim\limits_{x \to \infty} f(x)$

34. $f(x) = \dfrac{5x + 11}{7x^3 - 2}$

(A) $f(8)$ (B) $f(16)$ (C) $\lim\limits_{x \to -\infty} f(x)$

35. $f(x) = \dfrac{7x^4 - 14x^2}{6x^5 + 3}$

(A) $f(-6)$ (B) $f(-12)$ (C) $\lim\limits_{x \to -\infty} f(x)$

36. $f(x) = \dfrac{4x^7 - 8x}{6x^4 + 9x^2}$

(A) $f(-3)$ (B) $f(-6)$ (C) $\lim\limits_{x \to -\infty} f(x)$

37. $f(x) = \dfrac{10 - 7x^3}{4 + x^3}$

(A) $f(-10)$ (B) $f(-20)$ (C) $\lim\limits_{x \to -\infty} f(x)$

38. $f(x) = \dfrac{3 + x}{5 + 4x}$

(A) $f(-50)$ (B) $f(-100)$ (C) $\lim\limits_{x \to -\infty} f(x)$

In Problems 39–52, find all horizontal and vertical asymptotes.

39. $f(x) = \dfrac{2x}{x + 2}$

40. $f(x) = \dfrac{3x + 2}{x - 4}$

41. $f(x) = \dfrac{x^2 + 1}{x^2 - 1}$

42. $f(x) = \dfrac{x^2 - 1}{x^2 + 2}$

43. $f(x) = \dfrac{x^3}{x^2 + 6}$

44. $f(x) = \dfrac{x}{x^2 - 4}$

45. $f(x) = \dfrac{x}{x^2 + 4}$

46. $f(x) = \dfrac{x^2 + 9}{x}$

47. $f(x) = \dfrac{x^2}{x - 3}$

48. $f(x) = \dfrac{x + 5}{x^2}$

49. $f(x) = \dfrac{2x^2 + 3x - 2}{x^2 - x - 2}$

50. $f(x) = \dfrac{2x^2 + 7x + 12}{2x^2 + 5x - 12}$

51. $f(x) = \dfrac{2x^2 - 5x + 2}{x^2 - x - 2}$

52. $f(x) = \dfrac{x^2 - x - 12}{2x^2 + 5x - 12}$

 In Problems 53–58, discuss the validity of each statement. If the statement is always true, explain why. If not, give a counterexample.

53. A rational function has at least one vertical asymptote.

54. A rational function has at most one vertical asymptote.

55. A rational function has at least one horizontal asymptote.

56. A rational function has at most one horizontal asymptote.

57. A polynomial function of degree ≥ 1 has neither horizontal nor vertical asymptotes.

58. The graph of a rational function cannot cross a horizontal asymptote.

C

59. Theorem 3 states that

$$\lim_{x \to \infty} (a_n x^n + a_{n-1} x^{n-1} + \cdots + a_0) = \pm\infty.$$

What conditions must n and a_n satisfy for the limit to be ∞? For the limit to be $-\infty$?

60. Theorem 3 also states that

$$\lim_{x \to -\infty} (a_n x^n + a_{n-1} x^{n-1} + \cdots + a_0) = \pm\infty.$$

What conditions must n and a_n satisfy for the limit to be ∞? For the limit to be $-\infty$?

Describe the end behavior of each function in Problems 61–68.

61. $f(x) = 2x^4 - 5x + 11$

62. $f(x) = 3x - 7x^5 - 2$

63. $f(x) = 7x^2 + 9x^3 + 5x$

64. $f(x) = 4x^3 - 5x^2 - 6x^6$

65. $f(x) = \dfrac{x^2 - 5x - 7}{x + 11}$

66. $f(x) = \dfrac{5x^4 + 7x^7 - 10}{x^2 + 6x^4 + 3}$

67. $f(x) = \dfrac{5x^5 + 7x^4 - 10}{-x^3 + 6x^2 + 3}$

68. $f(x) = \dfrac{-3x^6 + 4x^4 + 2}{2x^2 - 2x - 3}$

Applications

69. Average cost. A company manufacturing snowboards has fixed costs of \$200 per day and total costs of \$3,800 per day for a daily output of 20 boards.

(A) Assuming that the total cost per day $C(x)$ is linearly related to the total output per day x, write an equation for the cost function.

(B) The average cost per board for an output of x boards is given by $\overline{C}(x) = C(x)/x$. Find the average cost function.

(C) Sketch a graph of the average cost function, including any asymptotes, for $1 \leq x \leq 30$.

(D) What does the average cost per board tend to as production increases?

70. Average cost. A company manufacturing surfboards has fixed costs of \$300 per day and total costs of \$5,100 per day for a daily output of 20 boards.

(A) Assuming that the total cost per day $C(x)$ is linearly related to the total output per day x, write an equation for the cost function.

(B) The average cost per board for an output of x boards is given by $\overline{C}(x) = C(x)/x$. Find the average cost function.

(C) Sketch a graph of the average cost function, including any asymptotes, for $1 \leq x \leq 30$.

(D) What does the average cost per board tend to as production increases?

71. Energy costs. Most appliance manufacturers produce conventional and energy-efficient models. The energy-efficient models are more expensive to make but cheaper to operate. The costs of purchasing and operating a 23-cubic-foot refrigerator of each type are given in Table 8. These costs do not include maintenance charges or changes in electricity prices.

Table 8 23-ft³ Refrigerators	Energy-Efficient Model	Conventional Model
Initial cost	\$950	\$900
Total volume	23 ft³	23 ft³
Annual cost of electricity	\$56	\$66

(A) Express the total cost $C_e(x)$ and the average cost $\overline{C}_e(x) = C_e(x)/x$ of purchasing and operating an energy-efficient model for x years.

(B) Express the total cost $C_c(x)$ and the average cost $\overline{C}_c(x) = C_c(x)/x$ of purchasing and operating a conventional model for x years.

(C) Are the total costs for an energy-efficient model and for a conventional model ever the same? If so, when?

(D) Are the average costs for an energy-efficient model and for a conventional model ever the same? If so, when?

(E) Find the limit of each average cost function as $x \to \infty$ and discuss the implications of the results.

72. Energy costs. Most appliance manufacturers produce conventional and energy-efficient models. The energy-efficient models are more expensive to make but cheaper to operate. The costs of purchasing and operating a 36,000-Btu central air conditioner of each type are given in Table 9. These costs do not include maintenance charges or changes in electricity prices.

Table 9   36,000 Btu Central Air Conditioner

	Energy-Efficient Model	Conventional Model
Initial cost	$4,000	$2,700
Total capacity	36,000 Btu	36,000 Btu
Annual cost of electricity	$932	$1,332

(A) Express the total cost $C_e(x)$ and the average cost $\overline{C}_e(x) = C_e(x)/x$ of purchasing and operating an energy-efficient model for x years.

(B) Express the total cost $C_c(x)$ and the average cost $\overline{C}_c(x) = C_c(x)/x$ of purchasing and operating a conventional model for x years.

(C) Are the total costs for an energy-efficient model and for a conventional model ever the same? If so, when?

(D) Are the average costs for an energy-efficient model and for a conventional model ever the same? If so, when?

(E) Find the limit of each average cost function as $x \to \infty$ and discuss the implications of the results.

73. Drug concentration. A drug is administered to a patient through an injection. The drug concentration (in milligrams/milliliter) in the bloodstream t hours after the injection is given by $C(t) = \dfrac{5t^2(t + 50)}{t^3 + 100}$. Find and interpret $\lim_{t \to \infty} C(t)$.

74. Drug concentration. A drug is administered to a patient through an IV drip. The drug concentration (in milligrams/milliliter) in the bloodstream t hours after the drip was started is given by $C(t) = \dfrac{5t(t + 50)}{t^3 + 100}$. Find and interpret $\lim_{t \to \infty} C(t)$.

75. Pollution. In Silicon Valley, a number of computer-related manufacturing firms were contaminating underground water supplies with toxic chemicals stored in leaking underground containers. A water quality control agency ordered the companies to take immediate corrective action and contribute to a monetary pool for the testing and cleanup of the underground contamination. Suppose that the monetary pool (in millions of dollars) for the testing and cleanup is given by

$$P(x) = \frac{2x}{1 - x} \qquad 0 \le x < 1$$

where x is the percentage (expressed as a decimal) of the total contaminant removed.

(A) How much must be in the pool to remove 90% of the contaminant?

(B) How much must be in the pool to remove 95% of the contaminant?

(C) Find $\lim_{x \to 1^-} P(x)$ and discuss the implications of this limit.

76. Employee training. A company producing computer components has established that, on average, a new employee can assemble $N(t)$ components per day after t days of on-the-job training, as given by

$$N(t) = \frac{100t}{t + 9} \qquad t \ge 0$$

(A) How many components per day can a new employee assemble after 6 days of on-the-job training?

(B) How many days of on-the-job training will a new employee need to reach the level of 70 components per day?

(C) Find $\lim_{t \to \infty} N(t)$ and discuss the implications of this limit.

77. Biochemistry. In 1913, biochemists Leonor Michaelis and Maude Menten proposed the rational function model (see figure)

$$v(s) = \frac{V_{\max}\, s}{K_M + s}$$

for the velocity of the enzymatic reaction v, where s is the substrate concentration. The constants $V_{\max}$ and K_M are determined from experimental data.

Figure for 77

(A) Show that $\lim_{s \to \infty} v(s) = V_{\max}$.

(B) Show that $v(K_M) = \dfrac{V_{\max}}{2}$.

(C) Table 10* lists data for an enzyme treated with the substrate saccharose.
Plot the preceding points on graph paper and estimate $V_{\max}$ to the nearest integer. To estimate K_M, add the

Table 10

s	v
5.2	0.866
10.4	1.466
20.8	2.114
41.6	2.666
83.3	3.236
167	3.636
333	3.636

*Michaelis and Menten (1913) *Biochem. Z.* 49, 333–369.

horizontal line $v = \dfrac{V_{\max}}{2}$ to your graph, connect successive points on the graph with straight-line segments, and estimate the value of s (to the nearest multiple of 10) that satisfies $v(s) = \dfrac{V_{\max}}{2}$.

(D) Use the constants $V_{\max}$ and K_M from part C to form a Michaelis–Menten function for the data in Table 10.

(E) Use the function from part D to estimate the velocity of the enzyme reaction when the saccharose is 15 and to estimate the saccharose when the velocity is 3.

78. Biochemistry. Table 11* lists data for the enzyme invertase treated with the substrate sucrose. We want to model these data with a Michaelis–Menten function.

Table 11

s	v
2.92	18.2
5.84	26.5
8.76	31.1
11.7	33
14.6	34.9
17.5	37.2
23.4	37.1

(A) Plot the points in Table 11 on graph paper and estimate $V_{\max}$ to the nearest integer. To estimate K_M, add the horizontal line $v = \dfrac{V_{\max}}{2}$ to your graph, connect successive points on the graph with straight-line segments, and estimate the value of s (to the nearest integer) that satisfies $v(s) = \dfrac{V_{\max}}{2}$.

(B) Use the constants $V_{\max}$ and K_M from part (A) to form a Michaelis–Menten function for the data in Table 11.

(C) Use the function from part (B) to estimate the velocity of the enzyme reaction when the sucrose is 9 and to estimate the sucrose when the velocity is 32.

79. Physics. The coefficient of thermal expansion (CTE) is a measure of the expansion of an object subjected to extreme temperatures. To model this coefficient, we use a Michaelis–Menten function of the form

$$C(T) = \frac{C_{\max} T}{M + T} \qquad \text{(Problem 77)}$$

where $C = $ CTE, T is temperature in K (degrees Kelvin), and $C_{\max}$ and M are constants. Table 12† lists the coeffi-

cients of thermal expansion for nickel and for copper at various temperatures.

Table 12 Coefficients of Thermal Expansion

T (K)	Nickel	Copper
100	6.6	10.3
200	11.3	15.2
293	13.4	16.5
500	15.3	18.3
800	16.8	20.3
1,100	17.8	23.7

(A) Plot the points in columns 1 and 2 of Table 12 on graph paper and estimate $C_{\max}$ to the nearest integer. To estimate M, add the horizontal line CTE $= \dfrac{C_{\max}}{2}$ to your graph, connect successive points on the graph with straight-line segments, and estimate the value of T (to the nearest multiple of fifty) that satisfies $C(T) = \dfrac{C_{\max}}{2}$.

(B) Use the constants $\dfrac{C_{\max}}{2}$ and M from part (A) to form a Michaelis–Menten function for the CTE of nickel.

(C) Use the function from part (B) to estimate the CTE of nickel at 600 K and to estimate the temperature when the CTE of nickel is 12.

80. Physics. Repeat Problem 79 for the CTE of copper (column 3 of Table 12).

Answers to Matched Problems

1. Vertical asymptote: $x = 1$; $\displaystyle\lim_{x \to 1^+} f(x) = \infty$, $\displaystyle\lim_{x \to 1^-} f(x) = -\infty$
   $\displaystyle\lim_{x \to 3} f(x) = 1/2$ so f does not have a vertical asymptote at $x = 3$

2. Vertical asymptote: $x = -3$; $\displaystyle\lim_{x \to -3^+} f(x) = \displaystyle\lim_{x \to -3^-} f(x) = -\infty$

3. $\displaystyle\lim_{x \to \infty} p(x) = \displaystyle\lim_{x \to -\infty} p(x) = -\infty$

4. (A) $\displaystyle\lim_{x \to \infty} p(x) = -\infty$, $\displaystyle\lim_{x \to -\infty} p(x) = \infty$
   (B) $\displaystyle\lim_{x \to \infty} p(x) = \infty$, $\displaystyle\lim_{x \to -\infty} p(x) = \infty$

5. (A) $y = 0$ \qquad (B) No horizontal asymptotes
   (C) $y = 1/2$

6. Vertical asymptotes: $x = -2$, $x = 2$; horizontal asymptote: $y = 1$

---

*Institute of Chemistry, Macedonia.

†National Physical Laboratory

10-3 Continuity

Theorem 3 in Section 10-1 states that if f is a polynomial function or a rational function with a nonzero denominator at $x = c$, then

$$\lim_{x \to c} f(x) = f(c) \qquad (1)$$

Functions that satisfy equation (1) are said to be *continuous* at $x = c$. A firm understanding of continuous functions is essential for sketching and analyzing graphs. We will also see that continuity properties provide a simple and efficient method for solving inequalities—a tool that we will use extensively in later sections.

Continuity

Compare the graphs shown in Figure 1. Notice that two of the graphs are broken; that is, they cannot be drawn without lifting a pen off the paper. Informally, a function is *continuous over an interval* if its graph over the interval can be drawn without removing a pen from the paper. A function whose graph is broken (disconnected) at $x = c$ is said to be *discontinuous* at $x = c$. Function f (Fig. 1A) is continuous for all x. Function g (Fig. 1B) is discontinuous at $x = 2$ but is continuous over any interval that does not include 2. Function h (Fig. 1C) is discontinuous at $x = 0$ but is continuous over any interval that does not include 0.

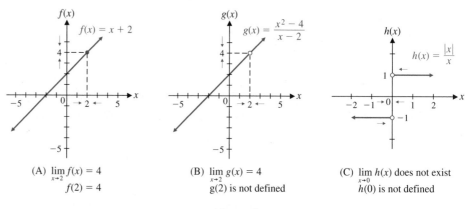

(A) $\lim_{x \to 2} f(x) = 4$
$f(2) = 4$

(B) $\lim_{x \to 2} g(x) = 4$
$g(2)$ is not defined

(C) $\lim_{x \to 0} h(x)$ does not exist
$h(0)$ is not defined

Figure 1

Most graphs of natural phenomena are continuous, whereas many graphs in business and economics applications have discontinuities. Figure 2A illustrates temperature variation over a 24-hour period—a continuous phenomenon. Figure 2B illustrates warehouse inventory over a 1-week period—a discontinuous phenomenon.

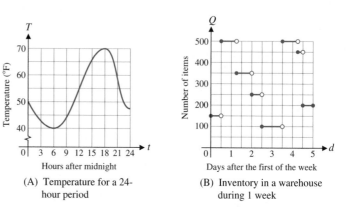

(A) Temperature for a 24-hour period

(B) Inventory in a warehouse during 1 week

Figure 2

EXPLORE & DISCUSS 1

(A) Write a brief verbal description of the temperature variation illustrated in Figure 2A, including estimates of the high and low temperatures during the period shown and the times at which they occurred.

(B) Write a brief verbal description of the changes in inventory illustrated in Figure 2B, including estimates of the changes in inventory and the times at which those changes occurred.

The preceding discussion leads to the following formal definition of continuity:

DEFINITION Continuity

A function f is **continuous at the point $x = c$ if**

1. $\lim\limits_{x \to c} f(x)$ exists   **2.** $f(c)$ exists   **3.** $\lim\limits_{x \to c} f(x) = f(c)$

A function is **continuous on the open interval*** **(a, b)** if it is continuous at each point on the interval.

---

*See Section 1-1 for a review of interval notation.

If one or more of the three conditions in the definition fails, then the function is **discontinuous** at $x = c$.

EXAMPLE 1   **Continuity of a Function Defined by a Graph** Use the definition of continuity to discuss the continuity of the function whose graph is shown in Figure 3.

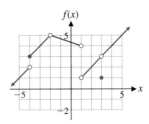

Figure 3

SOLUTION   We begin by identifying the points of discontinuity. Examining the graph, we see breaks or holes at $x = -4, -2, 1$, and 3. Now we must determine which conditions in the definition of continuity are not satisfied at each of these points. In each case, we find the value of the function and the limit of the function at the point in question.

Discontinuity at $x = -4$:

$$\lim\limits_{x \to -4^-} f(x) = 2$$ Since the one-sided limits are different,
the limit does not exist (Section 10-1).
$$\lim\limits_{x \to -4^+} f(x) = 3$$

$$\lim\limits_{x \to -4} f(x) \text{ does not exist}$$

$$f(-4) = 3$$

So, f is not continuous at $x = -4$ because condition 1 is not satisfied.

Discontinuity at $x = -2$:

$$\lim\limits_{x \to -2^-} f(x) = 5$$ The hole at $(-2, 5)$ indicates that 5 is not the value of f
at -2. Since there is no solid dot elsewhere on the verti-
$$\lim\limits_{x \to -2^+} f(x) = 5$$ cal line $x = -2$, $f(-2)$ is not defined.

$$\lim\limits_{x \to -2} f(x) = 5$$

$$f(-2) \text{ does not exist}$$

From the sign chart, we can easily write the solution of the given nonlinear inequality:

$$f(x) > 0 \quad \text{for} \quad \begin{array}{ll} x < -1 \quad \text{or} \quad x > 2 & \textit{Inequality notation} \\ (-\infty, -1) \cup (2, \infty) & \textit{Interval notation} \end{array}$$

Matched Problem 4   Solve $\dfrac{x^2 - 1}{x - 3} < 0$.

Most of the inequalities we encounter will involve strict inequalities ($>$ or $<$). If it is necessary to solve inequalities of the form $\geq$ or $\leq$, we simply include the endpoint x of any interval if f is defined at x and $f(x)$ satisfies the given inequality. For example, from the sign chart in Figure 8, the solution of the inequality

$$\dfrac{x + 1}{x - 2} \geq 0 \quad \text{is} \quad \begin{array}{ll} x \leq -1 \quad \text{or} \quad x > 2 & \textit{Inequality notation} \\ (-\infty, -1] \cup (2, \infty) & \textit{Interval notation} \end{array}$$

In general, given a function f, a **partition number** is a value of x such that f is discontinuous at x or $f(x) = 0$. **Partition numbers determine open intervals in which $f(x)$ does not change sign.** By using a test number from each interval, we can construct a sign chart for $f(x)$ on the real-number line. It is then easy to solve the inequality $f(x) < 0$ or $f(x) > 0$.

We summarize the procedure for constructing sign charts in the following box:

PROCEDURE Constructing Sign Charts

Given a function f,

Step 1   Find all partition numbers:

    (A) Find all numbers such that f is discontinuous. (Rational functions are discontinuous for values of x that make a denominator 0.)

    (B) Find all numbers such that $f(x) = 0$. (For a rational function, this occurs where the numerator is 0 and the denominator is not 0.)

Step 2   Plot the numbers found in step 1 on a real-number line, dividing the number line into intervals.

Step 3   Select a test number in each open interval determined in step 2 and evaluate $f(x)$ at each test number to determine whether $f(x)$ is positive ($+$) or negative ($-$) in each interval.

Step 4   Construct a sign chart, using the real-number line in step 2. This will show the sign of $f(x)$ on each open interval.

Exercises 10-3

A

In Problems 1–6, sketch a possible graph of a function that satisfies the given conditions at $x = 1$ and discuss the continuity of f at $x = 1$.

1. $f(1) = 2$ and $\lim\limits_{x \to 1} f(x) = 2$

2. $f(1) = -2$ and $\lim\limits_{x \to 1} f(x) = 2$

3. $f(1) = 2$ and $\lim\limits_{x \to 1} f(x) = -2$

4. $f(1) = -2$ and $\lim\limits_{x \to 1} f(x) = -2$

5. $f(1) = -2$, $\lim\limits_{x \to 1^-} f(x) = 2$, and $\lim\limits_{x \to 1^+} f(x) = -2$

6. $f(1) = 2$, $\lim\limits_{x \to 1^-} f(x) = 2$, and $\lim\limits_{x \to 1^+} f(x) = -2$

Problems 7–14 refer to the function f shown in the figure. Use the graph to estimate the indicated function values and limits.

$f(x)$

Figure for 7–14

7. $f(0.9)$ **8.** $f(0.1)$

9. $f(-1.9)$ **10.** $f(-0.9)$

11. (A) $\lim\limits_{x \to 1^-} f(x)$ (B) $\lim\limits_{x \to 1^+} f(x)$
     (C) $\lim\limits_{x \to 1} f(x)$ (D) $f(1)$
     (E) Is f continuous at $x = 1$? Explain.

12. (A) $\lim\limits_{x \to 2^-} f(x)$ (B) $\lim\limits_{x \to 2^+} f(x)$
     (C) $\lim\limits_{x \to 2} f(x)$ (D) $f(2)$
     (E) Is f continuous at $x = 2$? Explain.

13. (A) $\lim\limits_{x \to -2^-} f(x)$ (B) $\lim\limits_{x \to -2^+} f(x)$
     (C) $\lim\limits_{x \to -2} f(x)$ (D) $f(-2)$
     (E) Is f continuous at $x = -2$? Explain.

14. (A) $\lim\limits_{x \to -1^-} f(x)$ (B) $\lim\limits_{x \to -1^+} f(x)$
     (C) $\lim\limits_{x \to -1} f(x)$ (D) $f(-1)$
     (E) Is f continuous at $x = -1$? Explain.

Problems 15–22 refer to the function g shown in the figure. Use the graph to estimate the indicated function values and limits.

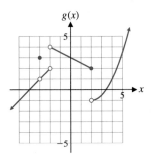

$g(x)$

Figure for 15–22

15. $g(-3.1)$ **16.** $g(-2.1)$

17. $g(1.9)$ **18.** $g(-1.9)$

19. (A) $\lim\limits_{x \to -3^-} g(x)$ (B) $\lim\limits_{x \to -3^+} g(x)$
     (C) $\lim\limits_{x \to -3} g(x)$ (D) $g(-3)$
     (E) Is g continuous at $x = -3$? Explain.

20. (A) $\lim\limits_{x \to -2^-} g(x)$ (B) $\lim\limits_{x \to -2^+} g(x)$
     (C) $\lim\limits_{x \to -2} g(x)$ (D) $g(-2)$
     (E) Is g continuous at $x = -2$? Explain.

21. (A) $\lim\limits_{x \to 2^-} g(x)$ (B) $\lim\limits_{x \to 2^+} g(x)$
     (C) $\lim\limits_{x \to 2} g(x)$ (D) $g(2)$
     (E) Is g continuous at $x = 2$? Explain.

22. (A) $\lim\limits_{x \to 4^-} g(x)$ (B) $\lim\limits_{x \to 4^+} g(x)$
     (C) $\lim\limits_{x \to 4} g(x)$ (D) $g(4)$
     (E) Is g continuous at $x = 4$? Explain.

Use Theorem 1 to determine where each function in Problems 23–32 is continuous.

23. $f(x) = 3x - 4$ **24.** $h(x) = 4 - 2x$

25. $g(x) = \dfrac{3x}{x + 2}$ **26.** $k(x) = \dfrac{2x}{x - 4}$

27. $m(x) = \dfrac{x + 1}{(x - 1)(x + 4)}$ **28.** $n(x) = \dfrac{x - 2}{(x - 3)(x + 1)}$

29. $F(x) = \dfrac{2x}{x^2 + 9}$ **30.** $G(x) = \dfrac{1 - x^2}{x^2 + 1}$

31. $M(x) = \dfrac{x - 1}{4x^2 - 9}$ **32.** $N(x) = \dfrac{x^2 + 4}{4 - 25x^2}$

B

33. Given the function

$$f(x) = \begin{cases} 2 & \text{if } x \text{ is an integer} \\ 1 & \text{if } x \text{ is not an integer} \end{cases}$$

(A) Graph f.

(B) $\lim\limits_{x \to 2} f(x) = ?$

(C) $f(2) = ?$

(D) Is f continuous at $x = 2$?

(E) Where is f discontinuous?

34. Given the function

$$g(x) = \begin{cases} -1 & \text{if } x \text{ is an even integer} \\ 1 & \text{if } x \text{ is not an even integer} \end{cases}$$

(A) Graph g.

(B) $\lim\limits_{x \to 1} g(x) = ?$

(C) $g(1) = ?$

(D) Is g continuous at $x = 1$?

(E) Where is g discontinuous?

In Problems 35–42, use a sign chart to solve each inequality. Express answers in inequality and interval notation.

35. $x^2 - x - 12 < 0$

36. $x^2 - 2x - 8 < 0$

37. $x^2 + 21 > 10x$

38. $x^2 + 7x > -10$

39. $x^3 < 4x$

40. $x^4 - 9x^2 > 0$

41. $\dfrac{x^2 + 5x}{x - 3} > 0$

42. $\dfrac{x - 4}{x^2 + 2x} < 0$

43. Use the graph of f to determine where

    (A) $f(x) > 0$ (B) $f(x) < 0$

Express answers in interval notation.

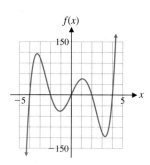

Figure for 43

44. Use the graph of g to determine where

    (A) $g(x) > 0$ (B) $g(x) < 0$

Express answers in interval notation.

Figure for 44

 In Problems 45–48, use a graphing calculator to approximate the partition numbers of each function $f(x)$ to four decimal places. Then solve the following inequalities:

(A) $f(x) > 0$ (B) $f(x) < 0$

Express answers in interval notation.

45. $f(x) = x^4 - 6x^2 + 3x + 5$

46. $f(x) = x^4 - 4x^2 - 2x + 2$

47. $f(x) = \dfrac{3 + 6x - x^3}{x^2 - 1}$ **48.** $f(x) = \dfrac{x^3 - 5x + 1}{x^2 - 1}$

Use Theorem 1 to determine where each function in Problems 49–56 is continuous. Express the answer in interval notation.

49. $\sqrt{x - 6}$ **50.** $\sqrt{7 - x}$

51. $\sqrt[3]{5 - x}$ **52.** $\sqrt[3]{x - 8}$

53. $\sqrt{x^2 - 9}$ **54.** $\sqrt{4 - x^2}$

55. $\sqrt{x^2 + 1}$ **56.** $\sqrt[3]{x^2 + 2}$

In Problems 57–62, graph f, locate all points of discontinuity, and discuss the behavior of f at these points.

57. $f(x) = \begin{cases} 1 + x & \text{if } x < 1 \\ 5 - x & \text{if } x \geq 1 \end{cases}$

58. $f(x) = \begin{cases} x^2 & \text{if } x \leq 1 \\ 2x & \text{if } x > 1 \end{cases}$

59. $f(x) = \begin{cases} 1 + x & \text{if } x \leq 2 \\ 5 - x & \text{if } x > 2 \end{cases}$

60. $f(x) = \begin{cases} x^2 & \text{if } x \leq 2 \\ 2x & \text{if } x > 2 \end{cases}$

61. $f(x) = \begin{cases} -x & \text{if } x < 0 \\ 1 & \text{if } x = 0 \\ x & \text{if } x > 0 \end{cases}$

62. $f(x) = \begin{cases} 1 & \text{if } x < 0 \\ 0 & \text{if } x = 0 \\ 1 + x & \text{if } x > 0 \end{cases}$

C

*Problems 63 and 64 refer to the **greatest integer function**, which is denoted by $[\![x]\!]$ and is defined as*

$$[\![x]\!] = \text{greatest integer} \leq x$$

For example,

$$[\![-3.6]\!] = \text{greatest integer} \leq -3.6 = -4$$

$$[\![2]\!] = \text{greatest integer} \leq 2 = 2$$

$$[\![2.5]\!] = \text{greatest integer} \leq 2.5 = 2$$

The graph of $f(x) = [\![x]\!]$ is shown. There, we can see that

$$[\![x]\!] = -2 \quad for \quad -2 \leq x < -1$$

$$[\![x]\!] = -1 \quad for \quad -1 \leq x < 0$$

$$[\![x]\!] = 0 \quad for \quad 0 \leq x < 1$$

$$[\![x]\!] = 1 \quad for \quad 1 \leq x < 2$$

$$[\![x]\!] = 2 \quad for \quad 2 \leq x < 3$$

and so on.

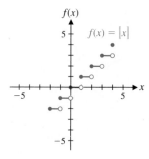

Figure for 63 and 64

63. (A) Is *f* continuous from the right at *x* = 0?

(B) Is *f* continuous from the left at *x* = 0?

(C) Is *f* continuous on the open interval (0, 1)?

(D) Is *f* continuous on the closed interval [0, 1]?

(E) Is *f* continuous on the half-closed interval [0, 1)?

64. (A) Is *f* continuous from the right at *x* = 2?

(B) Is *f* continuous from the left at *x* = 2?

(C) Is *f* continuous on the open interval (1, 2)?

(D) Is *f* continuous on the closed interval [1, 2]?

(E) Is *f* continuous on the half-closed interval [1, 2)?

 In Problems 65–70, discuss the validity of each statement. If the statement is always true, explain why. If not, give a counterexample.

65. A polynomial function is continuous for all real numbers.

66. A rational function is continuous for all but finitely many real numbers.

67. If *f* is a function that is continuous at *x* = 0 and *x* = 2, then *f* is continuous at *x* = 1.

68. If *f* is a function that is continuous on the open interval (0, 2), then *f* is continuous at *x* = 1.

69. If *f* is a function that has no partition numbers in the interval (*a*, *b*), then *f* is continuous on (*a*, *b*).

70. The greatest integer function (see Problem 61) is a rational function.

In Problems 71–74, sketch a possible graph of a function f that is continuous for all real numbers and satisfies the given conditions. Find the x intercepts of f.

71. $f(x) < 0$ on $(-\infty, -5)$ and $(2, \infty)$; $f(x) > 0$ on $(-5, 2)$

72. $f(x) > 0$ on $(-\infty, -4)$ and $(3, \infty)$; $f(x) < 0$ on $(-4, 3)$

73. $f(x) < 0$ on $(-\infty, -6)$ and $(-1, 4)$; $f(x) > 0$ on $(-6, -1)$ and $(4, \infty)$

74. $f(x) > 0$ on $(-\infty, -3)$ and $(2, 7)$; $f(x) < 0$ on $(-3, 2)$ and $(7, \infty)$

75. The function $f(x) = 2/(1 - x)$ satisfies $f(0) = 2$ and $f(2) = -2$. Is *f* equal to 0 anywhere on the interval $(-1, 3)$? Does this contradict Theorem 2? Explain.

76. The function $f(x) = 6/(x - 4)$ satisfies $f(2) = -3$ and $f(7) = 2$. Is *f* equal to 0 anywhere on the interval $(0, 9)$? Does this contradict Theorem 2? Explain.

Applications

77. Postal rates. First-class postage in 2009 was $0.44 for the first ounce (or any fraction thereof) and $0.17 for each additional ounce (or fraction thereof) up to a maximum weight of 3.5 ounces.

(A) Write a piecewise definition of the first-class postage *P*(*x*) for a letter weighing *x* ounces.

(B) Graph *P*(*x*) for 0 < *x* ≤ 3.5.

(C) Is *P*(*x*) continuous at *x* = 2.5? At *x* = 3? Explain.

78. Telephone rates. A long-distance telephone service charges $0.07 for the first minute (or any fraction thereof) and $0.05 for each additional minute (or fraction thereof).

(A) Write a piecewise definition of the charge *R*(*x*) for a long-distance call lasting *x* minutes.

(B) Graph *R*(*x*) for 0 < *x* ≤ 6.

(C) Is *R*(*x*) continuous at *x* = 3.5? At *x* = 3? Explain.

79. Postal rates. Discuss the differences between the function $Q(x) = 0.44 + 0.17[\![x]\!]$ and the function *P*(*x*) defined in Problem 77.

80. Telephone rates. Discuss the differences between the function $S(x) = 0.07 + 0.05[\![x]\!]$ and the function *R*(*x*) defined in Problem 78.

81. Natural-gas rates. Table 1 shows the rates for natural gas charged by the Middle Tennessee Natural Gas Utility District during summer months. The customer charge is a fixed monthly charge, independent of the amount of gas used per month.

Table 1 Summer (May–September)	
Base charge	$5.00
First 50 therms	0.63 per therm
Over 50 therms	0.45 per therm

(A) Write a piecewise definition of the monthly charge *S*(*x*) for a customer who uses *x* therms* in a summer month.

(B) Graph *S*(*x*).

(C) Is *S*(*x*) continuous at *x* = 50? Explain.

82. Natural-gas rates. Table 2 shows the rates for natural gas charged by the Middle Tennessee Natural Gas Utility District during winter months. The customer charge is a fixed monthly charge, independent of the amount of gas used per month.

Table 2 Winter (October–April)	
Base charge	$5.00
First 5 therms	0.69 per therm
Next 45 therms	0.65 per therm
Over 50 therms	0.63 per therm

*A British thermal unit (Btu) is the amount of heat required to raise the temperature of 1 pound of water 1 degree Fahrenheit, and a therm is 100,000 Btu.

(A) Write a piecewise definition of the monthly charge $S(x)$ for a customer who uses x therms in a winter month.

(B) Graph $S(x)$.

✎ (C) Is $S(x)$ continuous at $x = 5$? At $x = 50$? Explain.

83. Income. A personal-computer salesperson receives a base salary of $1,000 per month and a commission of 5% of all sales over $10,000 during the month. If the monthly sales are $20,000 or more, then the salesperson is given an additional $500 bonus. Let $E(s)$ represent the person's earnings per month as a function of the monthly sales s.

(A) Graph $E(s)$ for $0 \le s \le 30,000$.

(B) Find $\lim_{s \to 10,000} E(s)$ and $E(10,000)$.

(C) Find $\lim_{s \to 20,000} E(s)$ and $E(20,000)$.

(D) Is E continuous at $s = 10,000$? At $s = 20,000$?

84. Equipment rental. An office equipment rental and leasing company rents copiers for $10 per day (and any fraction thereof) or for $50 per 7-day week. Let $C(x)$ be the cost of renting a copier for x days.

(A) Graph $C(x)$ for $0 \le x \le 10$.

(B) Find $\lim_{x \to 4.5} C(x)$ and $C(4.5)$.

(C) Find $\lim_{x \to 8} C(x)$ and $C(8)$.

(D) Is C continuous at $x = 4.5$? At $x = 8$?

85. Animal supply. A medical laboratory raises its own rabbits. The number of rabbits $N(t)$ available at any time t depends on the number of births and deaths. When a birth or death occurs, the function N generally has a discontinuity, as shown in the figure.

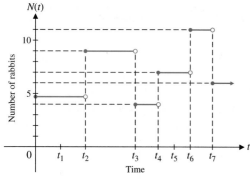

Figure for 85

(A) Where is the function N discontinuous?

(B) $\lim_{t \to t_5} N(t) = ?$; $N(t_5) = ?$

(C) $\lim_{t \to t_3} N(t) = ?$; $N(t_3) = ?$

86. Learning. The graph shown represents the history of a person learning the material on limits and continuity in this book. At time t_2, the student's mind goes blank during a quiz. At time t_4, the instructor explains a concept particularly well, then suddenly a big jump in understanding takes place.

(A) Where is the function p discontinuous?

(B) $\lim_{t \to t_1} p(t) = ?$; $p(t_1) = ?$

(C) $\lim_{t \to t_2} p(t) = ?$; $p(t_2) = ?$

(D) $\lim_{t \to t_4} p(t) = ?$; $p(t_4) = ?$

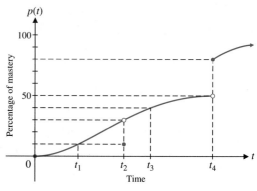

Figure for 86

Answers to Matched Problems

1. f is not continuous at $x = -3, -1, 2,$ and 4.

$x = -3$: $\lim_{x \to -3} f(x) = 3$, but $f(-3)$ does not exist

$x = -1$: $f(-1) = 1$, but $\lim_{x \to -1} f(x)$ does not exist

$x = 2$: $\lim_{x \to 2} f(x) = 5$, but $f(2) = 3$

$x = 4$: $\lim_{x \to 4} f(x)$ does not exist, and $f(4)$ does not exist

2. (A) f is continuous at $x = 1$, since $\lim_{x \to 1} f(x) = 2 = f(1)$.

(B) g is not continuous at $x = 1$, since $g(1)$ is not defined.

(C) h is not continuous at $x = 2$ for two reasons: $h(2)$ does not exist and $\lim_{x \to 2} h(x)$ does not exist.
h is continuous at $x = 0$, since $\lim_{x \to 0} h(x) = -1 = h(0)$.

3. (A) Since f is a polynomial function, f is continuous for all x.

(B) Since f is a rational function, f is continuous for all x except -1 and 4 (values that make the denominator 0).

(C) The polynomial function $x - 4$ is continuous for all x and nonnegative for $x \ge 4$. Since $n = 2$ is even, f is continuous for $x \ge 4$, or on the interval $[4, \infty)$.

(D) The polynomial function $x^3 + 1$ is continuous for all x. Since $n = 3$ is odd, f is continuous for all x.

4. $-\infty < x < -1$ or $1 < x < 3$; $(-\infty, -1) \cup (1, 3)$

10-4   The Derivative

- Rate of Change
- Slope of the Tangent Line
- The Derivative
- Nonexistence of the Derivative

We will now make use of the limit concepts developed in Sections 10-1, 10-2, and 10-3 to solve the two important problems illustrated in Figure 1. The solution of each of these apparently unrelated problems involves a common concept called the *derivative*.

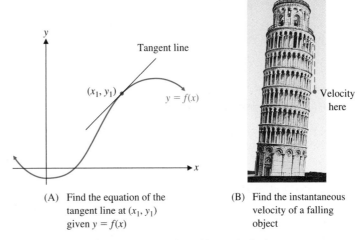

(A) Find the equation of the tangent line at (x_1, y_1) given $y = f(x)$

(B) Find the instantaneous velocity of a falling object

Figure 1 Two basic problems of calculus

Rate of Change

Let us start by considering a simple example.

EXAMPLE 1   **Revenue Analysis** The revenue (in dollars) from the sale of x plastic planter boxes is given by

$$R(x) = 20x - 0.02x^2 \qquad 0 \le x \le 1,000$$

and is graphed in Figure 2.

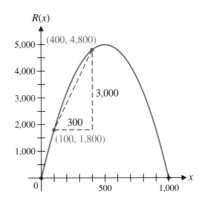

Figure 2 $R(x) = 20x - 0.02x^2$

(A) What is the change in revenue if production is changed from 100 planters to 400 planters?

(B) What is the average change in revenue for this change in production?

SOLUTION   (A) The change in revenue is given by

$$R(400) - R(100) = 20(400) - 0.02(400)^2 - [20(100) - 0.02(100)^2]$$
$$= 4,800 - 1,800 = \$3,000$$

Increasing production from 100 planters to 400 planters will increase revenue by \$3,000.

(B) To find the average change in revenue, we divide the change in revenue by the change in production:

$$\frac{R(400) - R(100)}{400 - 100} = \frac{3,000}{300} = \$10$$

The average change in revenue is \$10 per planter when production is increased from 100 to 400 planters.

Matched Problem 1   Refer to the revenue function in Example 1.

(A) What is the change in revenue if production is changed from 600 planters to 800 planters?

(B) What is the average change in revenue for this change in production?

In general, if we are given a function $y = f(x)$ and if x is changed from a to $a + h$, then y will change from $f(a)$ to $f(a + h)$. The *average rate of change is the ratio of the change in y to the change in x.*

> **DEFINITION Average Rate of Change**
>
> For $y = f(x)$, the **average rate of change from $x = a$ to $x = a + h$** is
>
> $$\frac{f(a + h) - f(a)}{(a + h) - a} = \frac{f(a + h) - f(a)}{h} \qquad h \neq 0 \qquad (1)$$

As we noted in Section 10-1, equation (1) is called the **difference quotient**. The preceding discussion shows that the difference quotient can be interpreted as an average rate of change. The next example illustrates another interpretation of this quotient: the velocity of a moving object.

EXAMPLE 2   **Velocity** A small steel ball dropped from a tower will fall a distance of y feet in x seconds, as given approximately by the formula

$$y = f(x) = 16x^2$$

Figure 3 shows the position of the ball on a coordinate line (positive direction down) at the end of 0, 1, 2, and 3 seconds.

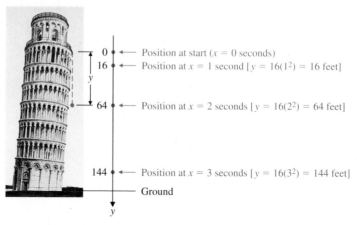

Figure 3 Note: Positive y direction is down.

(A) Find the average velocity from $x = 2$ seconds to $x = 3$ seconds.

(B) Find and simplify the average velocity from $x = 2$ seconds to $x = 2 + h$ seconds, $h \neq 0$.

(C) Find the limit of the expression from part B as $h \to 0$ if that limit exists.

(D) Discuss possible interpretations of the limit from part C.

SOLUTION (A) Recall the formula $d = rt$, which can be written in the form

$$r = \frac{d}{t} = \frac{\text{Distance covered}}{\text{Elapsed time}} = \text{Average velocity}$$

For example, if a person drives from San Francisco to Los Angeles (a distance of about 420 miles) in 7 hours, then the average velocity is

$$r = \frac{d}{t} = \frac{420}{7} = 60 \text{ miles per hour}$$

Sometimes the person will be traveling faster and sometimes slower, but the average velocity is 60 miles per hour. In our present problem, the average velocity of the steel ball from $x = 2$ seconds to $x = 3$ seconds is

$$\begin{aligned}
\text{Average velocity} &= \frac{\text{Distance covered}}{\text{Elapsed time}} \\
&= \frac{f(3) - f(2)}{3 - 2} \\
&= \frac{16(3)^2 - 16(2)^2}{1} = 80 \text{ feet per second}
\end{aligned}$$

We see that if $y = f(x)$ is the position of the falling ball, then the average velocity is simply the average rate of change of $f(x)$ with respect to time x, and we have another interpretation of the difference quotient (1).

(B) Proceeding as in part A, we have

$$\begin{aligned}
\text{Average velocity} &= \frac{\text{Distance covered}}{\text{Elapsed time}} \\
&= \frac{f(2 + h) - f(2)}{h} && \text{\textit{Difference quotient}} \\
&= \frac{16(2 + h)^2 - 16(2)^2}{h} && \text{\textit{Simplify this 0/0}} \\
& && \text{\textit{indeterminate form.}} \\
&= \frac{64 + 64h + 16h^2 - 64}{h} \\
&= \frac{h(64 + 16h)}{h} = 64 + 16h && h \neq 0
\end{aligned}$$

Notice that if $h = 1$, the average velocity is 80 feet per second, which is the result in part A.

(C) The limit of the average velocity expression from part B as $h \to 0$ is

$$\lim_{h \to 0} \frac{f(2 + h) - f(2)}{h} = \lim_{h \to 0} (64 + 16h)$$

$$= 64 \text{ feet per second}$$

(D) The average velocity over smaller and smaller time intervals approaches 64 feet per second. This limit can be interpreted as the velocity of the ball at the *instant* that the ball has been falling for exactly 2 seconds. Therefore, 64 feet per second is referred to as the **instantaneous velocity** at $x = 2$ seconds, and we have solved one of the basic problems of calculus (see Fig. 1B).

Matched Problem 2   For the falling steel ball in Example 2, find

(A) The average velocity from $x = 1$ second to $x = 2$ seconds

(B) The average velocity (in simplified form) from $x = 1$ second to $x = 1 + h$ seconds, $h \neq 0$

(C) The instantaneous velocity at $x = 1$ second

The ideas introduced in Example 2 are not confined to average velocity, but can be applied to the average rate of change of any function.

DEFINITION   Instantaneous Rate of Change

For $y = f(x)$, the **instantaneous rate of change at $x = a$** is

$$\lim_{h \to 0} \frac{f(a + h) - f(a)}{h} \qquad (2)$$

if the limit exists.

The adjective *instantaneous* is often omitted with the understanding that the phrase **rate of change** always refers to the instantaneous rate of change and not the average rate of change. Similarly, **velocity** always refers to the instantaneous rate of change of distance with respect to time.

Slope of the Tangent Line

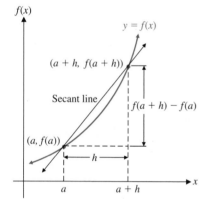

Figure 4 Secant line

So far, our interpretations of the difference quotient have been numerical in nature. Now we want to consider a geometric interpretation. A line through two points on the graph of a function is called a **secant line**. If $(a, f(a))$ and $(a + h, f(a + h))$ are two points on the graph of $y = f(x)$, then we can use the slope formula from Section 1-2 to find the slope of the secant line through these points (Fig. 4).

$$\begin{aligned}
\textbf{Slope of secant line } &= \frac{f(a + h) - f(a)}{(a + h) - a} \\
&= \frac{f(a + h) - f(a)}{h} \qquad \text{Difference quotient}
\end{aligned}$$

The difference quotient can be interpreted as both the average rate of change and the slope of the secant line.

CONCEPTUAL INSIGHT

If (x_1, y_1) and (x_2, y_2) are two points in the plane with $x_1 \neq x_2$ and L is the line passing through these two points (see Section 1-2), then

$$\underbrace{m = \frac{y_2 - y_1}{x_2 - x_1}}_{\text{Slope of } L} \qquad \underbrace{y - y_1 = m(x - x_1)}_{\text{Point–slope form for } L}$$

These formulas will be used extensively in the remainder of this chapter.

EXAMPLE 3   **Slope of a Secant Line**   Given $f(x) = x^2$,

(A) Find the slope of the secant line for $a = 1$ and $h = 2$ and 1, respectively. Graph $y = f(x)$ and the two secant lines.

(B) Find and simplify the slope of the secant line for $a = 1$ and h any nonzero number.

(C) Find the limit of the expression in part B.

(D) Discuss possible interpretations of the limit in part C.

SOLUTION   (A) For $a = 1$ and $h = 2$, the secant line goes through $(1, f(1)) = (1, 1)$ and $(3, f(3)) = (3, 9)$, and its slope is

$$\frac{f(1 + 2) - f(1)}{2} = \frac{3^2 - 1^2}{2} = 4$$

For $a = 1$ and $h = 1$, the secant line goes through $(1, f(1)) = (1, 1)$ and $(2, f(2)) = (2, 4)$, and its slope is

$$\frac{f(1 + 1) - f(1)}{1} = \frac{2^2 - 1^2}{1} = 3$$

The graphs of $y = f(x)$ and the two secant lines are shown in Figure 5.

(B) For $a = 1$ and h any nonzero number, the secant line goes through $(1, f(1)) = (1, 1)$ and $(1 + h, f(1 + h)) = (1 + h, (1 + h)^2)$, and its slope is

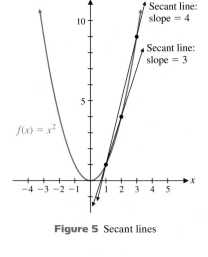

Figure 5 Secant lines

$$\frac{f(1 + h) - f(1)}{h} = \frac{(1 + h)^2 - 1^2}{h} \qquad \textit{Square the binomial.}$$

$$= \frac{1 + 2h + h^2 - 1}{h} \qquad \textit{Combine like terms and factor the numerator.}$$

$$= \frac{h(2 + h)}{h} \qquad \textit{Cancel.}$$

$$= 2 + h \qquad h \neq 0$$

(C) The limit of the secant line slope from part B is

$$\lim_{h \to 0} \frac{f(1 + h) - f(1)}{h} = \lim_{h \to 0} (2 + h)$$
$$= 2$$

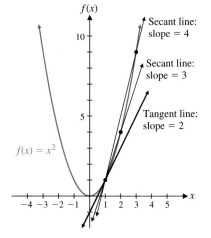

Figure 6 Tangent line

(D) In part C, we saw that the limit of the slopes of the secant lines through the point $(1, f(1))$ is 2. If we graph the line through $(1, f(1))$ with slope 2 (Fig. 6), then this line is the limit of the secant lines. The slope obtained from the limit of slopes of secant lines is called the *slope of the graph* at $x = 1$. The line through the point $(1, f(1))$ with this slope is called the *tangent line*. We have solved another basic problem of calculus (see Fig. 1A on page 165).

Matched Problem 3   Given $f(x) = x^2$,

(A) Find the slope of the secant line for $a = 2$ and $h = 2$ and 1, respectively.

(B) Find and simplify the slope of the secant line for $a = 2$ and h any nonzero number.

(C) Find the limit of the expression in part B.

(D) Find the slope of the graph and the slope of the tangent line at $a = 2$.

The ideas introduced in the preceding example are summarized next:

> **DEFINITION   Slope of a Graph**
> Given $y = f(x)$, the **slope of the graph** at the point $(a, f(a))$ is given by
> $$\lim_{h \to 0} \frac{f(a + h) - f(a)}{h} \tag{3}$$
> provided that the limit exists. The slope of the graph is also the **slope of the tangent line** at the point $(a, f(a))$.

CONCEPTUAL INSIGHT

If the function f is continuous at a, then

$$\lim_{h \to 0} f(a + h) = f(a)$$

and limit (3) will be a 0/0 indeterminate form. As we saw in Examples 2 and 3, evaluating this type of limit typically involves algebraic simplification.

From plane geometry, we know that a line tangent to a circle is a line that passes through one and only one point of the circle (Fig. 7A). Although this definition cannot be extended to graphs of functions in general, the visual relationship between graphs of functions and their tangent lines (Fig. 7B) is similar to the circle case. Limit (3) provides both a mathematically sound definition of a tangent line and a method for approximating the slope of the tangent line.

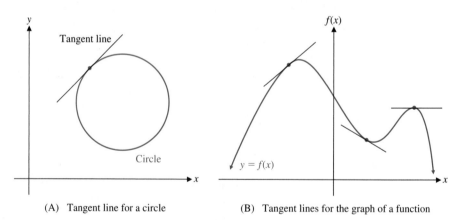

(A) Tangent line for a circle   (B) Tangent lines for the graph of a function

Figure 7

The Derivative

We have seen that the limit of a difference quotient can be interpreted as a rate of change, as a velocity, or as the slope of a tangent line. In addition, this limit provides solutions to two of the three basic problems stated at the beginning of the chapter. We are now ready to introduce some terms that refer to that limit. To follow customary practice, we use x in place of a and think of the difference quotient

$$\frac{f(x + h) - f(x)}{h}$$

as a function of h, with x held fixed as h tends to 0.

> **DEFINITION** The Derivative
>
> For $y = f(x)$, we define the **derivative of f at x**, denoted by $f'(x)$, to be
>
> $$f'(x) = \lim_{h \to 0} \frac{f(x + h) - f(x)}{h} \text{ if the limit exists}$$
>
> If $f'(x)$ exists for each x in the open interval (a, b), then f is said to be **differentiable** over (a, b).

(Differentiability from the left or from the right is defined by using $h \to 0^-$ or $h \to 0^+$, respectively, in place of $h \to 0$ in the preceding definition.)

The process of finding the derivative of a function is called **differentiation**. The derivative of a function is obtained by **differentiating** the function.

SUMMARY Interpretations of the Derivative

The derivative of a function f is a new function f'. The domain of f' is a subset of the domain of f. The derivative has various applications and interpretations, including the following:

1. *Slope of the tangent line.* For each x in the domain of f', $f'(x)$ is the slope of the line tangent to the graph of f at the point $(x, f(x))$.
2. *Instantaneous rate of change.* For each x in the domain of f', $f'(x)$ is the instantaneous rate of change of $y = f(x)$ with respect to x.
3. *Velocity.* If $f(x)$ is the position of a moving object at time x, then $v = f'(x)$ is the velocity of the object at that time.

Example 4 illustrates the **four-step process** that we use to find derivatives in this section. In subsequent sections, we develop rules for finding derivatives that do not involve limits. However, it is important that you master the limit process in order to fully comprehend and appreciate the various applications we will consider.

EXAMPLE 4 **Finding a Derivative** Find $f'(x)$, the derivative of f at x, for $f(x) = 4x - x^2$.

SOLUTION To find $f'(x)$, we use a four-step process.

Step 1 Find $f(x + h)$.
$$f(x + h) = 4(x + h) - (x + h)^2$$
$$= 4x + 4h - x^2 - 2xh - h^2$$

Step 2 Find $f(x + h) - f(x)$.
$$f(x + h) - f(x) = 4x + 4h - x^2 - 2xh - h^2 - (4x - x^2)$$
$$= 4h - 2xh - h^2$$

Step 3 Find $\dfrac{f(x + h) - f(x)}{h}$.
$$\frac{f(x + h) - f(x)}{h} = \frac{4h - 2xh - h^2}{h} = \frac{h(4 - 2x - h)}{h}$$
$$= 4 - 2x - h, \quad h \neq 0$$

Step 4 Find $f'(x) = \lim_{h \to 0} \dfrac{f(x + h) - f(x)}{h}$.
$$f'(x) = \lim_{h \to 0} \frac{f(x + h) - f(x)}{h} = \lim_{h \to 0}(4 - 2x - h) = 4 - 2x$$

So if $f(x) = 4x - x^2$, then $f'(x) = 4 - 2x$. The function f' is a new function derived from the function f.

Matched Problem 4   Find $f'(x)$, the derivative of f at x, for $f(x) = 8x - 2x^2$.

The four-step process used in Example 4 is summarized as follows for easy reference:

PROCEDURE The four-step process for finding the derivative of a function f:

Step 1   Find $f(x + h)$.

Step 2   Find $f(x + h) - f(x)$.

Step 3   Find $\dfrac{f(x + h) - f(x)}{h}$.

Step 4   Find $\displaystyle\lim_{h \to 0} \dfrac{f(x + h) - f(x)}{h}$.

EXAMPLE 5   **Finding Tangent Line Slopes** In Example 4, we started with the function $f(x) = 4x - x^2$ and found the derivative of f at x to be $f'(x) = 4 - 2x$. So the slope of a line tangent to the graph of f at any point $(x, f(x))$ on the graph is

$$m = f'(x) = 4 - 2x$$

(A) Find the slope of the graph of f at $x = 0$, $x = 2$, and $x = 3$.

(B) Graph $y = f(x) = 4x - x^2$ and use the slopes found in part (A) to make a rough sketch of the lines tangent to the graph at $x = 0$, $x = 2$, and $x = 3$.

SOLUTION   (A) Using $f'(x) = 4 - 2x$, we have

$$f'(0) = 4 - 2(0) = 4 \qquad \textit{Slope at } x = 0$$
$$f'(2) = 4 - 2(2) = 0 \qquad \textit{Slope at } x = 2$$
$$f'(3) = 4 - 2(3) = -2 \quad \textit{Slope at } x = 3$$

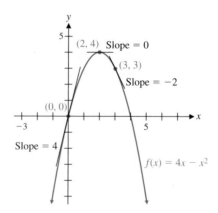

Matched Problem 5   In Matched Problem 4, we started with the function $f(x) = 8x - 2x^2$. Using the derivative found there,

(A) Find the slope of the graph of f at $x = 1$, $x = 2$, and $x = 4$.

(B) Graph $y = f(x) = 8x - 2x^2$, and use the slopes from part (A) to make a rough sketch of the lines tangent to the graph at $x = 1$, $x = 2$, and $x = 4$.

EXPLORE & DISCUSS 1

In Example 4, we found that the derivative of $f(x) = 4x - x^2$ is $f'(x) = 4 - 2x$. In Example 5, we graphed $f(x)$ and several tangent lines.

(A) Graph f and f' on the same set of axes.

(B) The graph of f' is a straight line. Is it a tangent line for the graph of f? Explain.

(C) Find the x intercept for the graph of f'. What is the slope of the line tangent to the graph of f for this value of x? Write a verbal description of the relationship between the slopes of the tangent lines of a function and the x intercepts of the derivative of the function.

EXAMPLE 6   **Finding a Derivative** Find $f'(x)$, the derivative of f at x, for $f(x) = \sqrt{x} + 2$.

SOLUTION   We use the four-step process to find $f'(x)$.

Step 1 Find $f(x + h)$.

$$f(x + h) = \sqrt{x + h} + 2$$

Step 2 Find $f(x + h) - f(x)$.

$$f(x + h) - f(x) = \sqrt{x + h} + 2 - (\sqrt{x} + 2) \quad \text{Combine like terms.}$$
$$= \sqrt{x + h} - \sqrt{x}$$

Step 3 Find $\dfrac{f(x + h) - f(x)}{h}$.

$$\frac{f(x + h) - f(x)}{h} = \frac{\sqrt{x + h} - \sqrt{x}}{h}$$

$$= \frac{\sqrt{x + h} - \sqrt{x}}{h} \cdot \frac{\sqrt{x + h} + \sqrt{x}}{\sqrt{x + h} + \sqrt{x}}$$

$$= \frac{x + h - x}{h(\sqrt{x + h} + \sqrt{x})}$$

$$= \frac{h}{h(\sqrt{x + h} + \sqrt{x})}$$

$$= \frac{1}{\sqrt{x + h} + \sqrt{x}} \quad h \neq 0$$

We rationalize the numerator (Appendix A, Section A-6) to change the form of this fraction.
Combine like terms.
Cancel.

Step 4 Find $f'(x) = \lim\limits_{h \to 0} \dfrac{f(x + h) - f(x)}{h}$.

$$\lim_{h \to 0} \frac{f(x + h) - f(x)}{h} = \lim_{h \to 0} \frac{1}{\sqrt{x + h} + \sqrt{x}}$$

$$= \frac{1}{\sqrt{x} + \sqrt{x}} = \frac{1}{2\sqrt{x}} \quad x > 0$$

So the derivative of $f(x) = \sqrt{x} + 2$ is $f'(x) = 1/(2\sqrt{x})$, a new function. The domain of f is $[0, \infty)$. Since $f'(0)$ is not defined, the domain of f' is $(0, \infty)$, a subset of the domain of f.

Matched Problem 6   Find $f'(x)$ for $f(x) = \sqrt{x} + 4$.

EXAMPLE 7   **Sales Analysis** A company's total sales (in millions of dollars) t months from now are given by $S(t) = \sqrt{t} + 2$. Find and interpret $S(25)$ and $S'(25)$. Use these results to estimate the total sales after 26 months and after 27 months.

SOLUTION   The total sales function S has the same form as the function f in Example 6. Only the letters used to represent the function and the independent variable have been changed. It follows that S' and f' also have the same form:

$$S(t) = \sqrt{t} + 2 \qquad f(x) = \sqrt{x} + 2$$

$$S'(t) = \frac{1}{2\sqrt{t}} \qquad f'(x) = \frac{1}{2\sqrt{x}}$$

Evaluating S and S' at $t = 25$, we have

$$S(25) = \sqrt{25} + 2 = 7 \qquad S'(25) = \frac{1}{2\sqrt{25}} = 0.1$$

So 25 months from now, the total sales will be $7 million and will be increasing at the rate of $0.1 million ($100,000) per month. If this instantaneous rate of change of sales remained constant, the sales would grow to $7.1 million after 26 months, $7.2 million after 27 months, and so on. Even though $S'(t)$ is not a constant function in this case, these values provide useful estimates of the total sales.

Matched Problem 7   A company's total sales (in millions of dollars) t months from now are given by $S(t) = \sqrt{t + 4}$. Find and interpret $S(12)$ and $S'(12)$. Use these results to estimate the total sales after 13 months and after 14 months. (Use the derivative found in Matched Problem 6.)

In Example 7, we can compare the estimates of total sales by using the derivative with the corresponding exact values of $S(t)$:

Exact values	Estimated values

$$S(26) = \sqrt{26} + 2 = 7.099\ldots \approx 7.1$$
$$S(27) = \sqrt{27} + 2 = 7.196\ldots \approx 7.2$$

For this function, the estimated values provide very good approximations to the exact values of $S(t)$. For other functions, the approximation might not be as accurate.

Using the instantaneous rate of change of a function at a point to estimate values of the function at nearby points is an important application of the derivative.

Nonexistence of the Derivative

The existence of a derivative at $x = a$ depends on the existence of a limit at $x = a$, that is, on the existence of

$$f'(a) = \lim_{h \to 0} \frac{f(a + h) - f(a)}{h} \tag{4}$$

If the limit does not exist at $x = a$, we say that the function f is **nondifferentiable at $x = a$**, or **$f'(a)$ does not exist.**

EXPLORE & DISCUSS 2   Let $f(x) = |x - 1|$.

(A) Graph f.

(B) Complete the following table:

h	-0.1	-0.01	-0.001	$\to 0 \leftarrow$	0.001	0.01	0.1
$\dfrac{f(1 + h) - f(1)}{h}$	?	?	?	$\to ? \leftarrow$	?	?	?

(C) Find the following limit if it exists:

$$\lim_{h \to 0} \frac{f(1 + h) - f(1)}{h}$$

(D) Use the results of parts (A)–(C) to discuss the existence of $f'(1)$.

(E) Repeat parts (A)–(D) for $\sqrt[3]{x-1}$.

How can we recognize the points on the graph of f where $f'(a)$ does not exist? It is impossible to describe all the ways that the limit of a difference quotient can fail to exist. However, we can illustrate some common situations where $f'(a)$ fails to exist (see Fig. 8):

   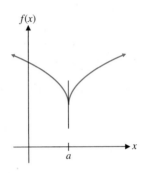

(A) Not continuous at
$x = a$

(B) Graph has sharp
corner at $x = a$

(C) Vertical tangent
at $x = a$

(D) Vertical tangent
at $x = a$

Figure 8 The function f is nondifferentiable at $x = a$.

1. If the graph of f has a hole or a break at $x = a$, then $f'(a)$ does not exist (Fig. 8A).

2. If the graph of f has a sharp corner at $x = a$, then $f'(a)$ does not exist, and the graph has no tangent line at $x = a$ (Fig. 8B). (In Fig. 8B, the left- and right-hand derivatives exist but are not equal.)

3. If the graph of f has a vertical tangent line at $x = a$, then $f'(a)$ does not exist (Fig. 8C and D).

Exercises 10-4

A

In Problems 1 and 2, find the indicated quantity for $y = f(x) = 5 - x^2$ and interpret that quantity in terms of the following graph.

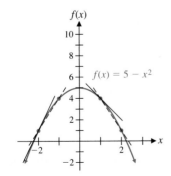

1. (A) $\dfrac{f(2) - f(1)}{2 - 1}$ (B) $\dfrac{f(1 + h) - f(1)}{h}$

(C) $\lim\limits_{h \to 0} \dfrac{f(1 + h) - f(1)}{h}$

2. (A) $\dfrac{f(-1) - f(-2)}{-1 - (-2)}$

(B) $\dfrac{f(-2 + h) - f(-2)}{h}$

(C) $\lim\limits_{h \to 0} \dfrac{f(-2 + h) - f(-2)}{h}$

3. Find the indicated quantities for $f(x) = 3x^2$.

(A) The average rate of change of $f(x)$ if x changes from 1 to 4.

(B) The slope of the secant line through the points $(1, f(1))$ and $(4, f(4))$ on the graph of $y = f(x)$.

(C) The slope of the secant line through the points $(1, f(1))$ and $(1 + h, f(1 + h))$, $h \neq 0$. Simplify your answer.

(D) The slope of the graph at $(1, f(1))$.

(E) The instantaneous rate of change of $y = f(x)$ with respect to x at $x = 1$.

(F) The slope of the tangent line at $(1, f(1))$.

(G) The equation of the tangent line at $(1, f(1))$.

4. Find the indicated quantities for $f(x) = 3x^2$.

(A) The average rate of change of $f(x)$ if x changes from 2 to 5.

(B) The slope of the secant line through the points $(2, f(2))$ and $(5, f(5))$ on the graph of $y = f(x)$.

(C) The slope of the secant line through the points $(2, f(2))$ and $(2 + h, f(2 + h))$, $h \neq 0$. Simplify your answer.

(D) The slope of the graph at $(2, f(2))$.

(E) The instantaneous rate of change of $y = f(x)$ with respect to x at $x = 2$.

(F) The slope of the tangent line at $(2, f(2))$.

(G) The equation of the tangent line at $(2, f(2))$.

In Problems 5–26, use the four-step process to find $f'(x)$ and then find $f'(1)$, $f'(2)$, and $f'(3)$.

5. $f(x) = -5$

6. $f(x) = 9$

7. $f(x) = 3x - 7$

8. $f(x) = 4 - 6x$

9. $f(x) = 2 - 3x^2$

10. $f(x) = 2x^2 + 8$

11. $f(x) = x^2 + 6x - 10$

12. $f(x) = x^2 + 4x + 7$

13. $f(x) = 2x^2 - 7x + 3$

14. $f(x) = 2x^2 + 5x + 1$

15. $f(x) = -x^2 + 4x - 9$

16. $f(x) = -x^2 + 9x - 2$

17. $f(x) = 2x^3 + 1$

18. $f(x) = -2x^3 + 5$

19. $f(x) = 4 + \dfrac{4}{x}$

20. $f(x) = \dfrac{6}{x} - 2$

21. $f(x) = 5 + 3\sqrt{x}$

22. $f(x) = 3 - 7\sqrt{x}$

23. $f(x) = 10\sqrt{x + 5}$

24. $f(x) = 16\sqrt{x + 9}$

25. $f(x) = \dfrac{3x}{x + 2}$

26. $f(x) = \dfrac{5x}{3 + x}$

B

Problems 27 and 28 refer to the graph of $y = f(x) = x^2 + x$ shown.

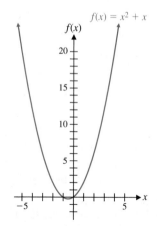

27. (A) Find the slope of the secant line joining $(1, f(1))$ and $(3, f(3))$.

(B) Find the slope of the secant line joining $(1, f(1))$ and $(1 + h, f(1 + h))$.

(C) Find the slope of the tangent line at $(1, f(1))$.

(D) Find the equation of the tangent line at $(1, f(1))$.

28. (A) Find the slope of the secant line joining $(2, f(2))$ and $(4, f(4))$.

(B) Find the slope of the secant line joining $(2, f(2))$ and $(2 + h, f(2 + h))$.

(C) Find the slope of the tangent line at $(2, f(2))$.

(D) Find the equation of the tangent line at $(2, f(2))$.

In Problems 29 and 30, suppose an object moves along the y axis so that its location is $y = f(x) = x^2 + x$ at time x (y is in meters and x is in seconds). Find

29. (A) The average velocity (the average rate of change of y with respect to x) for x changing from 1 to 3 seconds

(B) The average velocity for x changing from 1 to $1 + h$ seconds

(C) The instantaneous velocity at $x = 1$ second

30. (A) The average velocity (the average rate of change of y with respect to x) for x changing from 2 to 4 seconds

(B) The average velocity for x changing from 2 to $2 + h$ seconds

(C) The instantaneous velocity at $x = 2$ seconds

Problems 31–38 refer to the function F in the graph shown. Use the graph to determine whether $F'(x)$ exists at each indicated value of x.

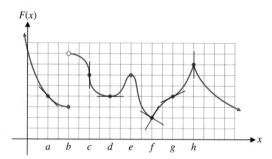

31. $x = a$

32. $x = b$

33. $x = c$

34. $x = d$

35. $x = e$

36. $x = f$

37. $x = g$

38. $x = h$

39. Given $f(x) = x^2 - 4x$,

(A) Find $f'(x)$.

(B) Find the slopes of the lines tangent to the graph of f at $x = 0, 2,$ and 4.

(C) Graph f and sketch in the tangent lines at $x = 0, 2,$ and 4.

40. Given $f(x) = x^2 + 2x$,

(A) Find $f'(x)$.

(B) Find the slopes of the lines tangent to the graph of f at $x = -2, -1,$ and 1.

(C) Graph f and sketch in the tangent lines at $x = -2, -1,$ and 1.

41. If an object moves along a line so that it is at $y = f(x) = 4x^2 - 2x$ at time x (in seconds), find the instantaneous velocity function $v = f'(x)$ and find the velocity at times $x = 1, 3,$ and 5 seconds (y is measured in feet).

42. Repeat Problem 41 with $f(x) = 8x^2 - 4x$.

43. Let $f(x) = x^2$, $g(x) = x^2 - 1$, and $h(x) = x^2 + 2$.

(A) How are the graphs of these functions related? How would you expect the derivatives of these functions to be related?

(B) Use the four-step process to find the derivative of $m(x) = x^2 + C$, where C is any real constant.

44. Let $f(x) = -x^2$, $g(x) = -x^2 - 1$, and $h(x) = -x^2 + 2$.

(A) How are the graphs of these functions related? How would you expect the derivatives of these functions to be related?

(B) Use the four-step process to find the derivative of $m(x) = -x^2 + C$, where C is any real constant.

In Problems 45–50, discuss the validity of each statement. If the statement is always true, explain why. If not, give a counterexample.

45. If $f(x) = C$ is a constant function, then $f'(x) = 0$.

46. If $f(x) = mx + b$ is a linear function, then $f'(x) = m$.

47. If a function f is continuous on the interval (a, b), then f is differentiable on (a, b).

48. If a function f is differentiable on the interval (a, b), then f is continuous on (a, b).

49. The average rate of change of a function f from $x = a$ to $x = a + h$ is less than the instantaneous rate of change at $x = a + \dfrac{h}{2}$.

50. If the graph of f has a sharp corner at $x = a$, then f is not continuous at $x = a$.

C

In Problems 51–54, sketch the graph of f and determine where f is nondifferentiable.

51. $f(x) = \begin{cases} 2x & \text{if } x < 1 \\ 2 & \text{if } x \geq 1 \end{cases}$
52. $f(x) = \begin{cases} 2x & \text{if } x < 2 \\ 6 - x & \text{if } x \geq 2 \end{cases}$

53. $f(x) = \begin{cases} x^2 + 1 & \text{if } x < 0 \\ 1 & \text{if } x \geq 0 \end{cases}$

54. $f(x) = \begin{cases} 2 - x^2 & \text{if } x \leq 0 \\ 2 & \text{if } x > 0 \end{cases}$

In Problems 55–60, determine whether f is differentiable at $x = 0$ by considering

$$\lim_{h \to 0} \frac{f(0 + h) - f(0)}{h}$$

55. $f(x) = |x|$
56. $f(x) = 1 - |x|$

57. $f(x) = x^{1/3}$
58. $f(x) = x^{2/3}$

59. $f(x) = \sqrt{1 - x^2}$
60. $f(x) = \sqrt{1 + x^2}$

61. A ball dropped from a balloon falls $y = 16x^2$ feet in x seconds. If the balloon is 576 feet above the ground when the ball is dropped, when does the ball hit the ground? What is the velocity of the ball at the instant it hits the ground?

62. Repeat Problem 61 if the balloon is 1,024 feet above the ground when the ball is dropped.

Applications

63. Revenue. The revenue (in dollars) from the sale of x infant car seats is given by

$$R(x) = 60x - 0.025x^2 \qquad 0 \leq x \leq 2,400$$

(A) Find the average change in revenue if production is changed from 1,000 car seats to 1,050 car seats.

(B) Use the four-step process to find $R'(x)$.

(C) Find the revenue and the instantaneous rate of change of revenue at a production level of 1,000 car seats, and write a brief verbal interpretation of these results.

64. Profit. The profit (in dollars) from the sale of x infant car seats is given by

$$P(x) = 45x - 0.025x^2 - 5,000 \qquad 0 \leq x \leq 2,400$$

(A) Find the average change in profit if production is changed from 800 car seats to 850 car seats.

(B) Use the four-step process to find $P'(x)$.

(C) Find the profit and the instantaneous rate of change of profit at a production level of 800 car seats, and write a brief verbal interpretation of these results.

65. Sales analysis. A company's total sales (in millions of dollars) t months from now are given by

$$S(t) = 2\sqrt{t} + 10$$

(A) Use the four-step process to find $S'(t)$.

(B) Find $S(15)$ and $S'(15)$. Write a brief verbal interpretation of these results.

(C) Use the results in part (B) to estimate the total sales after 16 months and after 17 months.

66. Sales analysis. A company's total sales (in millions of dollars) t months from now are given by

$$S(t) = 2\sqrt{t} + 6$$

(A) Use the four-step process to find $S'(t)$.

(B) Find $S(10)$ and $S'(10)$. Write a brief verbal interpretation of these results.

(C) Use the results in part (B) to estimate the total sales after 11 months and after 12 months.

67. Mineral consumption. The U.S. consumption of tungsten (in metric tons) is given approximately by

$$p(t) = 164t^2 + 161t + 12,326$$

where t is time in years and $t = 0$ corresponds to 2005.

(A) Use the four-step process to find $p'(t)$.

(B) Find the annual production in 2015 and the instantaneous rate of change of production in 2015, and write a brief verbal interpretation of these results.

68. Mineral consumption. The U.S. consumption of copper (in thousands of metric tons) is given approximately by

$$p(t) = 29t^2 - 258t + 4,658$$

where t is time in years and $t = 0$ corresponds to 2005.

(A) Use the four-step process to find $p'(t)$.

(B) Find the annual production in 2017 and the instantaneous rate of change of production in 2017, and write a brief verbal interpretation of these results.

69. Electricity consumption. Table 1 gives the retail sales of electricity (in billions of kilowatt-hours) for the residential and commercial sectors in the United States. (*Source:* Energy Information Administration)

Table 1   Electricity Sales

Year	Residential	Commercial
2000	1,192	1,055
2002	1,265	1,104
2004	1,292	1,230
2006	1,352	1,300
2008	1,379	1,352

(A) Let x represent time (in years) with $x = 0$ corresponding to 2000, and let y represent the corresponding residential sales. Enter the appropriate data set in a graphing calculator and find a quadratic regression equation for the data.

(B) If $y = R(x)$ denotes the regression equation found in part (A), find $R(20)$ and $R'(20)$, and write a brief verbal interpretation of these results. Round answers to the nearest tenth of a billion.

70. Electricity consumption. Refer to the data in Table 1.

(A) Let x represent time (in years) with $x = 0$ corresponding to 2000, and let y represent the corresponding commercial sales. Enter the appropriate data set in a graphing calculator and find a quadratic regression equation for the data.

(B) If $y = C(x)$ denotes the regression equation found in part (A), find $C(20)$ and $C'(20)$, and write a brief verbal interpretation of these results. Round answers to the nearest tenth of a billion.

71. Air pollution. The ozone level (in parts per billion) on a summer day in a metropolitan area is given by

$$P(t) = 80 + 12t - t^2$$

where t is time in hours and $t = 0$ corresponds to 9 A.M.

(A) Use the four-step process to find $P'(t)$.

(B) Find $P(3)$ and $P'(3)$. Write a brief verbal interpretation of these results.

72. Medicine. The body temperature (in degrees Fahrenheit) of a patient t hours after taking a fever-reducing drug is given by

$$F(t) = 98 + \frac{4}{t + 1}$$

(A) Use the four-step process to find $F'(t)$.

(B) Find $F(3)$ and $F'(3)$. Write a brief verbal interpretation of these results.

Answers to Matched Problems

1. (A) −$1,600 (B) −$8 per planter

2. (A) 48 ft/s
   (B) 32 + 16h
   (C) 32 ft/s

3. (A) 6, 5 (B) 4 + h
   (C) 4 (D) Both are 4

4. $f'(x) = 8 - 4x$

5. (A) $f'(1) = 4, f'(2) = 0, f'(4) = -8$

   (B)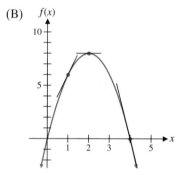

6. $f'(x) = 1/(2\sqrt{x + 4})$

7. $S(12) = 4, S'(12) = 0.125$; 12 months from now, the total sales will be $4 million and will be increasing at the rate of $0.125 million ($125,000) per month. The estimated total sales are $4.125 million after 13 months and $4.25 million after 14 months.

10-5   Basic Differentiation Properties

- Constant Function Rule
- Power Rule
- Constant Multiple Property
- Sum and Difference Properties
- Applications

In Section 10-4, we defined the derivative of f at x as

$$f'(x) = \lim_{h \to 0} \frac{f(x + h) - f(x)}{h}$$

if the limit exists, and we used this definition and a four-step process to find the derivatives of several functions. Now we want to develop some rules of differentiation. These rules will enable us to find the derivative of many functions without using the four-step process.

Before exploring these rules, we list some symbols that are often used to represent derivatives.

NOTATION   The Derivative

If $y = f(x)$, then

$$f'(x) \qquad y' \qquad \frac{dy}{dx}$$

all represent the derivative of f at x.

Each of these derivative symbols has its particular advantage in certain situations. All of them will become familiar to you after a little experience.

Constant Function Rule

If $f(x) = C$ is a constant function, then the four-step process can be used to show that $f'(x) = 0$. Therefore,

> The derivative of any constant function is 0.

THEOREM 1   Constant Function Rule

If $y = f(x) = C$, then

$$f'(x) = 0$$

Also, $y' = 0$ and $dy/dx = 0$.

Note: When we write $C' = 0$ or $\dfrac{d}{dx}C = 0$, we mean that $y' = \dfrac{dy}{dx} = 0$ when $y = C$.

CONCEPTUAL INSIGHT

The graph of $f(x) = C$ is a horizontal line with slope 0 (Fig. 1), so we would expect that $f'(x) = 0$.

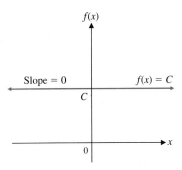

Figure 1

EXAMPLE 1   **Differentiating Constant Functions**

(A) If $f(x) = 3$,   then $f'(x) = 0$.   (B) If $y = -1.4$,   then $y' = 0$.

(C) If $y = \pi$,   then $\dfrac{dy}{dx} = 0$.   (D) $\dfrac{d}{dx}23 = 0$

Matched Problem 1   Find

(A) $f'(x)$ for $f(x) = -24$ (B) y' for $y = 12$

(C) $\dfrac{dy}{dx}$ for $y = -\sqrt{7}$ (D) $\dfrac{d}{dx}(-\pi)$

Power Rule

A function of the form $f(x) = x^k$, where k is a real number, is called a **power function**. The following elementary functions are examples of power functions:

$$f(x) = x \qquad h(x) = x^2 \qquad m(x) = x^3$$
$$n(x) = \sqrt{x} \qquad p(x) = \sqrt[3]{x} \tag{1}$$

EXPLORE & DISCUSS 1

(A) It is clear that the functions f, h, and m in (1) are power functions. Explain why the functions n and p are also power functions.

(B) The domain of a power function depends on the power. Discuss the domain of each of the following power functions:

$$r(x) = x^4 \qquad s(x) = x^{-4} \qquad t(x) = x^{1/4}$$
$$u(x) = x^{-1/4} \qquad v(x) = x^{1/5} \qquad w(x) = x^{-1/5}$$

The definition of the derivative and the four-step process introduced in Section 10-4 can be used to find the derivatives of many power functions. For example, it can be shown that

$$\text{If} \qquad f(x) = x^2, \qquad \text{then} \qquad f'(x) = 2x.$$
$$\text{If} \qquad f(x) = x^3, \qquad \text{then} \qquad f'(x) = 3x^2.$$
$$\text{If} \qquad f(x) = x^4, \qquad \text{then} \qquad f'(x) = 4x^3.$$
$$\text{If} \qquad f(x) = x^5, \qquad \text{then} \qquad f'(x) = 5x^4.$$

Notice the pattern in these derivatives. In each case, the power in f becomes the coefficient in f' and the power in f' is 1 less than the power in f. In general, for any positive integer n,

$$\text{If} \qquad f(x) = x^n, \qquad \text{then} \qquad f'(x) = nx^{n-1}. \tag{2}$$

In fact, more advanced techniques can be used to show that (2) holds for *any* real number n. We will assume this general result for the remainder of the book.

THEOREM 2   Power Rule

If $y = f(x) = x^n$, where n is a real number, then

$$f'(x) = nx^{n-1}$$

Also, $y' = nx^{n-1}$ and $dy/dx = nx^{n-1}$.

EXAMPLE 2   **Differentiating Power Functions**

(A) If $f(x) = x^5$, then $f'(x) = 5x^{5-1} = 5x^4$.

(B) If $y = x^{25}$, then $y' = 25x^{25-1} = 25x^{24}$.

(C) If $y = t^{-3}$, then $\dfrac{dy}{dt} = -3t^{-3-1} = -3t^{-4} = -\dfrac{3}{t^4}$.

(D) $\dfrac{d}{dx}x^{5/3} = \dfrac{5}{3}x^{(5/3)-1} = \dfrac{5}{3}x^{2/3}$.

Matched Problem 2   Find

(A) $f'(x)$ for $f(x) = x^6$

(B) y' for $y = x^{30}$

(C) $\dfrac{dy}{dt}$ for $y = t^{-2}$

(D) $\dfrac{d}{dx}x^{3/2}$

In some cases, properties of exponents must be used to rewrite an expression before the power rule is applied.

EXAMPLE 3 **Differentiating Power Functions**

(A) If $f(x) = 1/x^4$, we can write $f(x) = x^{-4}$ and

$$f'(x) = -4x^{-4-1} = -4x^{-5}, \quad \text{or} \quad \frac{-4}{x^5}$$

(B) If $y = \sqrt{u}$, we can write $y = u^{1/2}$ and

$$y' = \frac{1}{2}u^{(1/2)-1} = \frac{1}{2}u^{-1/2}, \quad \text{or} \quad \frac{1}{2\sqrt{u}}$$

(C) $\dfrac{d}{dx}\dfrac{1}{\sqrt[3]{x}} = \dfrac{d}{dx}x^{-1/3} = -\dfrac{1}{3}x^{(-1/3)-1} = -\dfrac{1}{3}x^{-4/3}, \text{or} \dfrac{-1}{3\sqrt[3]{x^4}}$

Matched Problem 3 Find

(A) $f'(x)$ for $f(x) = \dfrac{1}{x}$ (B) y' for $y = \sqrt[3]{u^2}$ (C) $\dfrac{d}{dx}\dfrac{1}{\sqrt{x}}$

Constant Multiple Property

Let $f(x) = ku(x)$, where k is a constant and u is differentiable at x. Using the four-step process, we have the following:

Step 1 $f(x + h) = ku(x + h)$

Step 2 $f(x + h) - f(x) = ku(x + h) - ku(x) = k[u(x + h) - u(x)]$

Step 3 $\dfrac{f(x + h) - f(x)}{h} = \dfrac{k[u(x + h) - u(x)]}{h} = k\left[\dfrac{u(x + h) - u(x)}{h}\right]$

Step 4 $f'(x) = \lim\limits_{h \to 0} \dfrac{f(x + h) - f(x)}{h}$

$= \lim\limits_{h \to 0} k\left[\dfrac{u(x + h) - u(x)}{h}\right]$ $\quad \lim\limits_{x \to c} kg(x) = k \lim\limits_{x \to c} g(x)$

$= k \lim\limits_{h \to 0}\left[\dfrac{u(x + h) - u(x)}{h}\right]$ $\quad$ Definition of $u'(x)$

$= ku'(x)$

Therefore,

The derivative of a constant times a differentiable function is the constant times the derivative of the function.

THEOREM 3 Constant Multiple Property

If $y = f(x) = ku(x)$, then

$$f'(x) = ku'(x)$$

Also,

$$y' = ku' \qquad \frac{dy}{dx} = k\frac{du}{dx}$$

EXAMPLE 4 **Differentiating a Constant Times a Function**

(A) If $f(x) = 3x^2$, then $f'(x) = 3 \cdot 2x^{2-1} = 6x$.

(B) If $y = \dfrac{t^3}{6} = \dfrac{1}{6}t^3$, then $\dfrac{dy}{dt} = \dfrac{1}{6} \cdot 3t^{3-1} = \dfrac{1}{2}t^2$.

(C) If $y = \dfrac{1}{2x^4} = \dfrac{1}{2}x^{-4}$, then $y' = \dfrac{1}{2}(-4x^{-4-1}) = -2x^{-5}$, or $\dfrac{-2}{x^5}$.

(D) $\dfrac{d}{dx}\dfrac{0.4}{\sqrt{x^3}} = \dfrac{d}{dx}\dfrac{0.4}{x^{3/2}} = \dfrac{d}{dx}0.4x^{-3/2} = 0.4\left[-\dfrac{3}{2}x^{(-3/2)-1}\right]$

$$= -0.6x^{-5/2}, \quad \text{or} \quad -\dfrac{0.6}{\sqrt{x^5}}$$

Matched Problem 4 Find

(A) $f'(x)$ for $f(x) = 4x^5$

(B) $\dfrac{dy}{dt}$ for $y = \dfrac{t^4}{12}$

(C) y' for $y = \dfrac{1}{3x^3}$

(D) $\dfrac{d}{dx}\dfrac{0.9}{\sqrt[3]{x}}$

Sum and Difference Properties

Let $f(x) = u(x) + v(x)$, where $u'(x)$ and $v'(x)$ exist. Using the four-step process, we have the following:

Step 1 $f(x + h) = u(x + h) + v(x + h)$

Step 2 $f(x + h) - f(x) = u(x + h) + v(x + h) - [u(x) + v(x)]$

$$= u(x + h) - u(x) + v(x + h) - v(x)$$

Step 3 $\dfrac{f(x + h) - f(x)}{h} = \dfrac{u(x + h) - u(x) + v(x + h) - v(x)}{h}$

$$= \dfrac{u(x + h) - u(x)}{h} + \dfrac{v(x + h) - v(x)}{h}$$

Step 4 $f'(x) = \lim\limits_{h \to 0} \dfrac{f(x + h) - f(x)}{h}$

$$= \lim\limits_{h \to 0}\left[\dfrac{u(x + h) - u(x)}{h} + \dfrac{v(x + h) - v(x)}{h}\right]$$

$$\lim\limits_{x \to c}[g(x) + h(x)] = \lim\limits_{x \to c}g(x) + \lim\limits_{x \to c}h(x)$$

$$= \lim\limits_{h \to 0}\dfrac{u(x + h) - u(x)}{h} + \lim\limits_{h \to 0}\dfrac{v(x + h) - v(x)}{h}$$

$$= u'(x) + v'(x)$$

Therefore,

> The derivative of the sum of two differentiable functions is the sum of the derivatives of the functions.

Similarly, we can show that

> The derivative of the difference of two differentiable functions is the difference of the derivatives of the functions.

Together, we have the **sum and difference property** for differentiation:

THEOREM 4   Sum and Difference Property

If $y = f(x) = u(x) \pm v(x)$, then

$$f'(x) = u'(x) \pm v'(x)$$

Also,

$$y' = u' \pm v' \qquad \frac{dy}{dx} = \frac{du}{dx} \pm \frac{dv}{dx}$$

Note: This rule generalizes to the sum and difference of any given number of functions.

With Theorems 1 through 4, we can compute the derivatives of all polynomials and a variety of other functions.

EXAMPLE 5   **Differentiating Sums and Differences**

(A) If $f(x) = 3x^2 + 2x$, then

$$f'(x) = (3x^2)' + (2x)' = 3(2x) + 2(1) = 6x + 2$$

(B) If $y = 4 + 2x^3 - 3x^{-1}$, then

$$y' = (4)' + (2x^3)' - (3x^{-1})' = 0 + 2(3x^2) - 3(-1)x^{-2} = 6x^2 + 3x^{-2}$$

(C) If $y = \sqrt[3]{w} - 3w$, then

$$\frac{dy}{dw} = \frac{d}{dw}w^{1/3} - \frac{d}{dw}3w = \frac{1}{3}w^{-2/3} - 3 = \frac{1}{3w^{2/3}} - 3$$

(D) $\dfrac{d}{dx}\left(\dfrac{5}{3x^2} - \dfrac{2}{x^4} + \dfrac{x^3}{9}\right) = \dfrac{d}{dx}\dfrac{5}{3}x^{-2} - \dfrac{d}{dx}2x^{-4} + \dfrac{d}{dx}\dfrac{1}{9}x^3$

$$= \frac{5}{3}(-2)x^{-3} - 2(-4)x^{-5} + \frac{1}{9}\cdot 3x^2$$

$$= -\frac{10}{3x^3} + \frac{8}{x^5} + \frac{1}{3}x^2$$

Matched Problem 5   Find

(A) $f'(x)$ for $f(x) = 3x^4 - 2x^3 + x^2 - 5x + 7$

(B) y' for $y = 3 - 7x^{-2}$

(C) $\dfrac{dy}{dv}$ for $y = 5v^3 - \sqrt[4]{v}$

(D) $\dfrac{d}{dx}\left(-\dfrac{3}{4x} + \dfrac{4}{x^3} - \dfrac{x^4}{8}\right)$

Applications

EXAMPLE 6   **Instantaneous Velocity** An object moves along the y axis (marked in feet) so that its position at time x (in seconds) is

$$f(x) = x^3 - 6x^2 + 9x$$

(A) Find the instantaneous velocity function v.

(B) Find the velocity at $x = 2$ and $x = 5$ seconds.

(C) Find the time(s) when the velocity is 0.

SOLUTION

(A) $v = f'(x) = (x^3)' - (6x^2)' + (9x)' = 3x^2 - 12x + 9$

(B) $f'(2) = 3(2)^2 - 12(2) + 9 = -3$ feet per second

$f'(5) = 3(5)^2 - 12(5) + 9 = 24$ feet per second

(C) $v = f'(x) = 3x^2 - 12x + 9 = 0$ Factor 3 out of each term.

$3(x^2 - 4x + 3) = 0$ Factor the quadratic term.

$3(x - 1)(x - 3) = 0$ Use the zero property.

$x = 1, 3$

So, $v = 0$ at $x = 1$ and $x = 3$ seconds.

Matched Problem 6   Repeat Example 6 for $f(x) = x^3 - 15x^2 + 72x.$

EXAMPLE 7   **Tangents** Let $f(x) = x^4 - 6x^2 + 10.$

(A) Find $f'(x)$.

(B) Find the equation of the tangent line at $x = 1$.

(C) Find the values of x where the tangent line is horizontal.

SOLUTION

(A) $f'(x) = (x^4)' - (6x^2)' + (10)'$

$= 4x^3 - 12x$

(B) $y - y_1 = m(x - x_1)$ $y_1 = f(x_1) = f(1) = (1)^4 - 6(1)^2 + 10 = 5$

$y - 5 = -8(x - 1)$ $m = f'(x_1) = f'(1) = 4(1)^3 - 12(1) = -8$

$y = -8x + 13$ Tangent line at $x = 1$

(C) Since a horizontal line has 0 slope, we must solve $f'(x) = 0$ for x:

$f'(x) = 4x^3 - 12x = 0$ Factor 4x out of each term.

$4x(x^2 - 3) = 0$ Factor the difference of two squares.

$4x(x + \sqrt{3})(x - \sqrt{3}) = 0$ Use the zero property.

$x = 0, -\sqrt{3}, \sqrt{3}$

Matched Problem 7   Repeat Example 7 for $f(x) = x^4 - 8x^3 + 7.$

Exercises 10-5

A

Find the indicated derivatives in Problems 1–18.

1. $f'(x)$ for $f(x) = 7$

2. $\dfrac{d}{dx} 3$

3. $\dfrac{dy}{dx}$ for $y = x^9$

4. y' for $y = x^6$

5. $\dfrac{d}{dx} x^3$

6. $g'(x)$ for $g(x) = x^5$

7. y' for $y = x^{-4}$

8. $\dfrac{dy}{dx}$ for $y = x^{-8}$

9. $g'(x)$ for $g(x) = x^{8/3}$

10. $f'(x)$ for $f(x) = x^{9/2}$

11. $\dfrac{dy}{dx}$ for $y = \dfrac{1}{x^{10}}$

12. y' for $y = \dfrac{1}{x^{12}}$

13. $f'(x)$ for $f(x) = 5x^2$

14. $\dfrac{d}{dx}(-2x^3)$

15. y' for $y = 0.4x^7$

16. $f'(x)$ for $f(x) = 0.8x^4$

17. $\dfrac{d}{dx}\left(\dfrac{x^3}{18}\right)$

18. $\dfrac{dy}{dx}$ for $y = \dfrac{x^5}{25}$

Problems 19–24 refer to functions f and g that satisfy $f'(2) = 3$ and $g'(2) = -1$. In each problem, find $h'(2)$ for the indicated function h.

19. $h(x) = 4f(x)$

20. $h(x) = 5g(x)$

21. $h(x) = f(x) + g(x)$

22. $h(x) = g(x) - f(x)$

23. $h(x) = 2f(x) - 3g(x) + 7$

24. $h(x) = -4f(x) + 5g(x) - 9$

B

Find the indicated derivatives in Problems 25–48.

25. $\dfrac{d}{dx}(2x - 5)$

26. $\dfrac{d}{dx}(-4x + 9)$

27. $f'(t)$ if $f(t) = 2t^2 - 3t + 1$

28. $\dfrac{dy}{dt}$ if $y = 2 + 5t - 8t^3$

29. y' for $y = 5x^{-2} + 9x^{-1}$

30. $g'(x)$ if $g(x) = 5x^{-7} - 2x^{-4}$

31. $\dfrac{d}{du}(5u^{0.3} - 4u^{2.2})$

32. $\dfrac{d}{du}(2u^{4.5} - 3.1u + 13.2)$

33. $h'(t)$ if $h(t) = 2.1 + 0.5t - 1.1t^3$

34. $F'(t)$ if $F(t) = 0.2t^3 - 3.1t + 13.2$

35. y' if $y = \dfrac{2}{5x^4}$

36. w' if $w = \dfrac{7}{5u^2}$

37. $\dfrac{d}{dx}\left(\dfrac{3x^2}{2} - \dfrac{7}{5x^2}\right)$

38. $\dfrac{d}{dx}\left(\dfrac{5x^3}{4} - \dfrac{2}{5x^3}\right)$

39. $G'(w)$ if $G(w) = \dfrac{5}{9w^4} + 5\sqrt[3]{w}$

40. $H'(w)$ if $H(w) = \dfrac{5}{w^6} - 2\sqrt{w}$

41. $\dfrac{d}{du}(3u^{2/3} - 5u^{1/3})$

42. $\dfrac{d}{du}(8u^{3/4} + 4u^{-1/4})$

43. $h'(t)$ if $h(t) = \dfrac{3}{t^{3/5}} - \dfrac{6}{t^{1/2}}$

44. $F'(t)$ if $F(t) = \dfrac{5}{t^{1/5}} - \dfrac{8}{t^{3/2}}$

45. y' if $y = \dfrac{1}{\sqrt[3]{x}}$

46. w' if $w = \dfrac{10}{\sqrt[5]{u}}$

47. $\dfrac{d}{dx}\left(\dfrac{1.2}{\sqrt{x}} - 3.2x^{-2} + x\right)$

48. $\dfrac{d}{dx}\left(2.8x^{-3} - \dfrac{0.6}{\sqrt[3]{x^2}} + 7\right)$

For Problems 49–52, find

(A) $f'(x)$

(B) The slope of the graph of f at $x = 2$ and $x = 4$

(C) The equations of the tangent lines at $x = 2$ and $x = 4$

(D) The value(s) of x where the tangent line is horizontal

49. $f(x) = 6x - x^2$

50. $f(x) = 2x^2 + 8x$

51. $f(x) = 3x^4 - 6x^2 - 7$

52. $f(x) = x^4 - 32x^2 + 10$

If an object moves along the y axis (marked in feet) so that its position at time x (in seconds) is given by the indicated functions in Problems 53–56, find

(A) The instantaneous velocity function $v = f'(x)$

(B) The velocity when $x = 0$ and $x = 3$ seconds

(C) The time(s) when $v = 0$

53. $f(x) = 176x - 16x^2$

54. $f(x) = 80x - 10x^2$

55. $f(x) = x^3 - 9x^2 + 15x$

56. $f(x) = x^3 - 9x^2 + 24x$

Problems 57–64 require the use of a graphing calculator. For each problem, find $f'(x)$ and approximate (to four decimal places) the value(s) of x where the graph of f has a horizontal tangent line.

57. $f(x) = x^2 - 3x - 4\sqrt{x}$

58. $f(x) = x^2 + x - 10\sqrt{x}$

59. $f(x) = 3\sqrt[3]{x^4} - 1.5x^2 - 3x$

60. $f(x) = 3\sqrt[3]{x^4} - 2x^2 + 4x$

61. $f(x) = 0.05x^4 + 0.1x^3 - 1.5x^2 - 1.6x + 3$

62. $f(x) = 0.02x^4 - 0.06x^3 - 0.78x^2 + 0.94x + 2.2$

63. $f(x) = 0.2x^4 - 3.12x^3 + 16.25x^2 - 28.25x + 7.5$

64. $f(x) = 0.25x^4 - 2.6x^3 + 8.1x^2 - 10x + 9$

65. Let $f(x) = ax^2 + bx + c$, $a \neq 0$. Recall that the graph of $y = f(x)$ is a parabola. Use the derivative $f'(x)$ to derive a formula for the x coordinate of the vertex of this parabola.

66. Now that you know how to find derivatives, explain why it is no longer necessary for you to memorize the formula for the x coordinate of the vertex of a parabola.

67. Give an example of a cubic polynomial function that has

(A) No horizontal tangents

(B) One horizontal tangent

(C) Two horizontal tangents

68. Can a cubic polynomial function have more than two horizontal tangents? Explain.

C

Find the indicated derivatives in Problems 69–76.

69. $f'(x)$ if $f(x) = (2x - 1)^2$

70. y' if $y = (2x - 5)^2$

71. $\dfrac{d}{dx} \dfrac{10x + 20}{x}$

72. $\dfrac{dy}{dx}$ if $y = \dfrac{x^2 + 25}{x^2}$

73. $\dfrac{dy}{dx}$ if $y = \dfrac{3x - 4}{12x^2}$

74. $f'(x)$ if $f(x) = \dfrac{2x^5 - 4x^3 + 2x}{x^3}$

In Problems 75-80, discuss the validity of each statement. If the statement is always true, explain why. If not, give a counterexample.

75. The derivative of a sum is the sum of the derivatives.

76. The derivative of a difference is the difference of the derivatives.

77. The derivative of a product is the product of the derivatives.

78. The derivative of a quotient is the quotient of the derivatives.

79. The derivative of a constant is 0.

80. The derivative of a constant times a function is 0.

Applications

81. Sales analysis. A company's total sales (in millions of dollars) t months from now are given by

$$S(t) = 0.03t^3 + 0.5t^2 + 2t + 3$$

(A) Find $S'(t)$.

(B) Find $S(5)$ and $S'(5)$ (to two decimal places). Write a brief verbal interpretation of these results.

(C) Find $S(10)$ and $S'(10)$ (to two decimal places). Write a brief verbal interpretation of these results.

82. Sales analysis. A company's total sales (in millions of dollars) t months from now are given by

$$S(t) = 0.015t^4 + 0.4t^3 + 3.4t^2 + 10t - 3$$

(A) Find $S'(t)$.

(B) Find $S(4)$ and $S'(4)$ (to two decimal places). Write a brief verbal interpretation of these results.

(C) Find $S(8)$ and $S'(8)$ (to two decimal places). Write a brief verbal interpretation of these results.

83. Advertising. A marine manufacturer will sell $N(x)$ power boats after spending $\$x$ thousand on advertising, as given by

$$N(x) = 1{,}000 - \frac{3{,}780}{x} \qquad 5 \le x \le 30$$

(see figure).

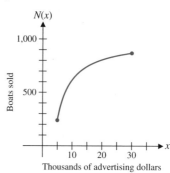

Figure for 83

(A) Find $N'(x)$.

(B) Find $N'(10)$ and $N'(20)$. Write a brief verbal interpretation of these results.

84. Price–demand equation. Suppose that, in a given gourmet food store, people are willing to buy x pounds of chocolate candy per day at $\$p$ per quarter pound, as given by the price–demand equation

$$x = 10 + \frac{180}{p} \qquad 2 \le p \le 10$$

This function is graphed in the figure. Find the demand and the instantaneous rate of change of demand with respect to price when the price is $5. Write a brief verbal interpretation of these results.

Figure for 84

85. College enrollment. The percentages of male high-school graduates who enrolled in college are given in the second column of Table 1.

Table 1   College enrollment percentages

Year	Male	Female
1970	55.2	48.5
1980	46.7	51.8
1990	58.0	62.2
2000	59.9	66.2
2006	65.8	66.1

(A) Let x represent time (in years) since 1970, and let y represent the corresponding percentage of male high-school graduates who enrolled in college. Enter the data in a graphing calculator and find a cubic regression equation for the data.

(B) If $y = M(x)$ denotes the regression equation found in part A, find $M(46)$ and $M'(46)$ (to the nearest tenth), and write a brief verbal interpretation of these results.

86. College enrollment. The percentages of female high-school graduates who enrolled in college are given in the third column of Table 1.

(A) Let x represent time (in years) since 1970, and let y represent the corresponding percentage of female high-school graduates who enrolled in college. Enter the data in a graphing calculator and find a cubic regression equation for the data.

(B) If $y = F(x)$ denotes the regression equation found in part A, find $F(46)$ and $F'(46)$ (to the nearest tenth), and write a brief verbal interpretation of these results.

87. Medicine. A person x inches tall has a pulse rate of y beats per minute, as given approximately by

$$y = 590x^{-1/2} \qquad 30 \le x \le 75$$

What is the instantaneous rate of change of pulse rate at the

(A) 36-inch level?

(B) 64-inch level?

88. Ecology. A coal-burning electrical generating plant emits sulfur dioxide into the surrounding air. The concentration $C(x)$, in parts per million, is given approximately by

$$C(x) = \frac{0.1}{x^2}$$

where x is the distance from the plant in miles. Find the instantaneous rate of change of concentration at

(A) $x = 1$ mile

(B) $x = 2$ miles

89. Learning. Suppose that a person learns y items in x hours, as given by

$$y = 50\sqrt{x} \qquad 0 \le x \le 9$$

(see figure). Find the rate of learning at the end of

(A) 1 hour

(B) 9 hours

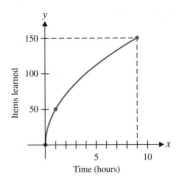

Figure for 89

90. Learning. If a person learns y items in x hours, as given by

$$y = 21\sqrt[3]{x^2} \qquad 0 \le x \le 8$$

find the rate of learning at the end of

(A) 1 hour

(B) 8 hours

Answers to Matched Problems

1. All are 0.

2. (A) $6x^5$ (B) $30x^{29}$
   (C) $-2t^{-3} = -2/t^3$ (D) $\frac{3}{2}x^{1/2}$

3. (A) $-x^{-2}$, or $-1/x^2$ (B) $\frac{2}{3}u^{-1/3}$, or $2/(3\sqrt[3]{u})$
   (C) $-\frac{1}{2}x^{-3/2}$, or $-1/(2\sqrt{x^3})$

4. (A) $20x^4$ (B) $t^3/3$
   (C) $-x^{-4}$, or $-1/x^4$ (D) $-0.3x^{-4/3}$, or $-0.3/\sqrt[3]{x^4}$

5. (A) $12x^3 - 6x^2 + 2x - 5$
   (B) $14x^{-3}$, or $14/x^3$
   (C) $15v^2 - \frac{1}{4}v^{-3/4}$, or $15v^2 - 1/(4v^{3/4})$
   (D) $3/(4x^2) - (12/x^4) - (x^3/2)$

6. (A) $v = 3x^2 - 30x + 72$
   (B) $f'(2) = 24$ ft/s; $f'(5) = -3$ ft/s
   (C) $x = 4$ and $x = 6$ seconds

7. (A) $f'(x) = 4x^3 - 24x^2$
   (B) $y = -20x + 20$
   (C) $x = 0$ and $x = 6$

10-6 Differentials

- Increments
- Differentials
- Approximations Using Differentials

In this section, we introduce increments and differentials. Increments are useful and they provide an alternative notation for defining the derivative. Differentials are often easier to compute than increments and can be used to approximate increments.

Increments

In Section 10-4, we defined the derivative of f at x as the limit of the difference quotient

$$f'(x) = \lim_{h \to 0} \frac{f(x + h) - f(x)}{h}$$

We considered various interpretations of this limit, including slope, velocity, and instantaneous rate of change. Increment notation enables us to interpret the numerator and denominator of the difference quotient separately.

Given $y = f(x) = x^3$, if x changes from 2 to 2.1, then y will change from $y = f(2) = 2^3 = 8$ to $y = f(2.1) = 2.1^3 = 9.261$. The change in x is called the *increment in x* and is denoted by Δx (read as "delta x").* Similarly, the change in y is called the *increment in y* and is denoted by Δy. In terms of the given example, we write

$$\Delta x = 2.1 - 2 = 0.1 \qquad \text{\textit{Change in x}}$$

$$\Delta y = f(2.1) - f(2) \qquad \text{\textit{f(x) = x}}^3$$

$$= 2.1^3 - 2^3 \qquad \text{\textit{Use a calculator.}}$$

$$= 9.261 - 8$$

$$= 1.261 \qquad \text{\textit{Corresponding change in y}}$$

CONCEPTUAL INSIGHT

The symbol Δx does not represent the product of Δ and x but is the symbol for a single quantity: the *change in x*. Likewise, the symbol Δy represents a single quantity: the *change in y*.

DEFINITION Increments

For $y = f(x)$, $\Delta x = x_2 - x_1$, so $x_2 = x_1 + \Delta x$, and

$$\Delta y = y_2 - y_1$$

$$= f(x_2) - f(x_1)$$

$$= f(x_1 + \Delta x) - f(x_1)$$

Δy represents the change in y corresponding to a change Δx in x.
Δx can be either positive or negative.

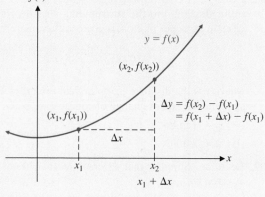

[**Note:** Δy depends on the function f, the input x_1, and the increment Δx.]

EXAMPLE 1   **Increments** Given the function $y = f(x) = \dfrac{x^2}{2}$,

(A) Find Δx, Δy, and $\Delta y / \Delta x$ for $x_1 = 1$ and $x_2 = 2$.

(B) Find $\dfrac{f(x_1 + \Delta x) - f(x_1)}{\Delta x}$ for $x_1 = 1$ and $\Delta x = 2$.

SOLUTION   (A) $\Delta x = x_2 - x_1 = 2 - 1 = 1$

$$\Delta y = f(x_2) - f(x_1)$$

$$= f(2) - f(1) = \frac{4}{2} - \frac{1}{2} = \frac{3}{2}$$

$$\frac{\Delta y}{\Delta x} = \frac{f(x_2) - f(x_1)}{x_2 - x_1} = \frac{\frac{3}{2}}{1} = \frac{3}{2}$$

*Δ is the symbol for the Greek letter delta.

(B) $\dfrac{f(x_1 + \Delta x) - f(x_1)}{\Delta x} = \dfrac{f(1 + 2) - f(1)}{2}$

$= \dfrac{f(3) - f(1)}{2} = \dfrac{\frac{9}{2} - \frac{1}{2}}{2} = \dfrac{4}{2} = 2$

Matched Problem 1 Given the function $y = f(x) = x^2 + 1$,

(A) Find Δx, Δy, and $\Delta y / \Delta x$ for $x_1 = 2$ and $x_2 = 3$.

(B) Find $\dfrac{f(x_1 + \Delta x) - f(x_1)}{\Delta x}$ for $x_1 = 1$ and $\Delta x = 2$.

In Example 1, we observe another notation for the difference quotient

$$\dfrac{f(x + h) - f(x)}{h} \tag{1}$$

It is common to refer to h, the change in x, as Δx. Then the difference quotient (1) takes on the form

$$\dfrac{f(x + \Delta x) - f(x)}{\Delta x} \quad \text{or} \quad \dfrac{\Delta y}{\Delta x} \qquad \Delta y = f(x + \Delta x) - f(x)$$

and the derivative is defined by

$$f'(x) = \lim_{\Delta x \to 0} \dfrac{f(x + \Delta x) - f(x)}{\Delta x}$$

or

$$f'(x) = \lim_{\Delta x \to 0} \dfrac{\Delta y}{\Delta x} \tag{2}$$

if the limit exists.

EXPLORE & DISCUSS 1 Suppose that $y = f(x)$ defines a function whose domain is the set of all real numbers. If every increment Δy is equal to 0, then what is the range of f?

Differentials

Assume that the limit in equation (2) exists. Then, for small Δx, the difference quotient $\Delta y / \Delta x$ provides a good approximation for $f'(x)$. Also, $f'(x)$ provides a good approximation for $\Delta y / \Delta x$. We write

$$\dfrac{\Delta y}{\Delta x} \approx f'(x) \qquad \text{Δx is small, but $\neq 0$} \tag{3}$$

Multiplying both sides of (3) by Δx gives us

$$\Delta y \approx f'(x)\, \Delta x \qquad \text{Δx is small, but $\neq 0$} \tag{4}$$

From equation (4), we see that $f'(x)\Delta x$ provides a good approximation for Δy when Δx is small.

Because of the practical and theoretical importance of $f'(x)\, \Delta x$, we give it the special name **differential** and represent it with the special symbol **dy** or **df**:

$$dy = f'(x)\Delta x \qquad \text{or} \qquad df = f'(x)\Delta x$$

For example,

$$d(2x^3) = (2x^3)'\, \Delta x = 6x^2\, \Delta x$$

$$d(x) = (x)'\, \Delta x = 1\, \Delta x = \Delta x$$

In the second example, we usually drop the parentheses in $d(x)$ and simply write

$$dx = \Delta x$$

In summary, we have the following:

> **DEFINITION Differentials**
>
> If $y = f(x)$ defines a differentiable function, then the **differential dy, or df**, is defined as the product of $f'(x)$ and dx, where $dx = \Delta x$. Symbolically,
>
> $$dy = f'(x)\,dx, \qquad \text{or} \qquad df = f'(x)\,dx$$
>
> where
>
> $$dx = \Delta x$$
>
> **Note:** The differential dy (or df) is actually a function involving two independent variables, x and dx. A change in either one or both will affect dy (or df).

EXAMPLE 2   **Differentials** Find dy for $f(x) = x^2 + 3x$. Evaluate dy for

(A) $x = 2$ and $dx = 0.1$

(B) $x = 3$ and $dx = 0.1$

(C) $x = 1$ and $dx = 0.02$

SOLUTION $dy = f'(x)\,dx$

$\qquad = (2x + 3)\,dx$

(A) When $x = 2$ and $dx = 0.1$, $\qquad\qquad$ (B) When $x = 3$ and $dx = 0.1$,

$\qquad dy = [2(2) + 3]0.1 = 0.7$ $\qquad\qquad\qquad dy = [2(3) + 3]0.1 = 0.9$

(C) When $x = 1$ and $dx = 0.02$,

$\qquad dy = [2(1) + 3]0.02 = 0.1$

Matched Problem 2   Find dy for $f(x) = \sqrt{x} + 3$. Evaluate dy for

(A) $x = 4$ and $dx = 0.1$

(B) $x = 9$ and $dx = 0.12$

(C) $x = 1$ and $dx = 0.01$

We now have two interpretations of the symbol dy/dx. Referring to the function $y = f(x) = x^2 + 3x$ in Example 2 with $x = 2$ and $dx = 0.1$, we have

$$\frac{dy}{dx} = f'(2) = 7 \qquad \text{Derivative}$$

and

$$\frac{dy}{dx} = \frac{0.7}{0.1} = 7 \qquad \text{Ratio of differentials}$$

Approximations Using Differentials

Earlier, we noted that for small Δx,

$$\frac{\Delta y}{\Delta x} \approx f'(x) \qquad \text{and} \qquad \Delta y \approx f'(x)\Delta x$$

Also, since

$$dy = f'(x)\,dx$$

it follows that

$$\Delta y \approx dy$$

and dy can be used to approximate Δy.

To interpret this result geometrically, we need to recall a basic property of the slope. The vertical change in a line is equal to the product of the slope and the horizontal change, as shown in Figure 1.

Now consider the line tangent to the graph of $y = f(x)$, as shown in Figure 2. Since $f'(x)$ is the slope of the tangent line and dx is the horizontal change in the tangent line, it follows that the vertical change in the tangent line is given by $dy = f'(x)\,dx$, as indicated in Figure 2.

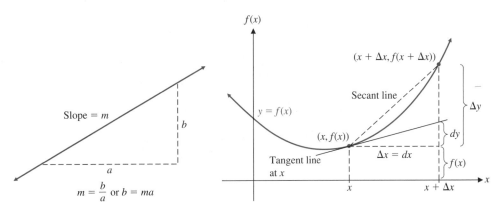

Figure 1   **Figure 2**

EXAMPLE 3   **Comparing Increments and Differentials** Let $y = f(x) = 6x - x^2$.

(A) Find Δy and dy when $x = 2$.

(B) Graph Δy and dy from part A for $-1 \le \Delta x \le 1$.

(C) Compare Δy and dy from part A for $\Delta x = 0.1, 0.2,$ and 0.3.

SOLUTION   (A) $\Delta y = f(2 + \Delta x) - f(2)$

$\qquad = 6(2 + \Delta x) - (2 + \Delta x)^2 - (6 \cdot 2 - 2^2)$ *Remove parentheses.*

$\qquad = 12 + 6\Delta x - 4 - 4\Delta x - \Delta x^2 - 12 + 4$ *Collect like terms.*

$\qquad = 2\Delta x - \Delta x^2$

Since $f'(x) = 6 - 2x$, $f'(2) = 2$, and $dx = \Delta x$, $dy = f'(2)\,dx = 2\Delta x$

(B) The graphs of $\Delta y = 2\Delta x - \Delta x^2$ and $dy = 2\Delta x$ are shown in Figure 3. Examining the graphs, we conclude that the differential provides a linear approximation of the increments and that the approximation is better for values of $\Delta x = dx$ close to 0.

(C) Table 1 compares the values of Δx and dy for the indicated values of Δx.

Figure 3 $\Delta y = 2\Delta x - \Delta x^2$, $dy = 2\Delta x$

Table 1		
Δx	Δy	dy
0.1	0.19	0.2
0.2	0.36	0.4
0.3	0.51	0.6

Matched Problem 3   Repeat Example 3 for $x = 4$ and $\Delta x = dx = -0.1, -0.2,$ and -0.3.

CONCEPTUAL INSIGHT

The error in the approximation $\Delta y \approx dy$ is usually small when $\Delta x = dx$ is small (see Example 3C), but it can be quite substantial in some cases.

EXAMPLE 4   **Cost–Revenue** A company manufactures and sells x transistor radios per week. If the weekly cost and revenue equations are

$$C(x) = 5,000 + 2x \qquad R(x) = 10x - \frac{x^2}{1,000} \qquad 0 \le x \le 8,000$$

then find the approximate changes in revenue and profit if production is increased from 2,000 to 2,010 units per week.

SOLUTION   We will approximate ΔR and ΔP with dR and dP, respectively, using $x = 2,000$ and $dx = 2,010 - 2,000 = 10$.

$$R(x) = 10x - \frac{x^2}{1,000} \qquad\qquad P(x) = R(x) - C(x) = 10x - \frac{x^2}{1,000} - 5,000 - 2x$$

$$dR = R'(x)\, dx \qquad\qquad\qquad = 8x - \frac{x^2}{1,000} - 5,000$$

$$= \left(10 - \frac{x}{500}\right) dx \qquad\qquad dP = P'(x)\, dx$$

$$= \left(10 - \frac{2,000}{500}\right) 10 \qquad\qquad = \left(8 - \frac{x}{500}\right) dx$$

$$= \$60 \text{ per week} \qquad\qquad\qquad = \left(8 - \frac{2,000}{500}\right) 10$$

$$\qquad\qquad\qquad\qquad\qquad\qquad = \$40 \text{ per week}$$

Matched Problem 4   Repeat Example 4 with production increasing from 6,000 to 6,010.

Comparing the results in Example 4 and Matched Problem 4, we see that an increase in production results in a revenue and profit increase at the 2,000 production level but a revenue and profit loss at the 6,000 production level.

Exercises 10-6

A

In Problems 1–6, find the indicated quantities for $y = f(x) = 3x^2$.

1. Δx, Δy, and $\Delta y / \Delta x$; given $x_1 = 1$ and $x_2 = 4$

2. Δx, Δy, and $\Delta y / \Delta x$; given $x_1 = 2$ and $x_2 = 5$

3. $\dfrac{f(x_1 + \Delta x) - f(x_1)}{\Delta x}$; given $x_1 = 1$ and $\Delta x = 2$

4. $\dfrac{f(x_1 + \Delta x) - f(x_1)}{\Delta x}$; given $x_1 = 2$ and $\Delta x = 1$

5. $\Delta y / \Delta x$; given $x_1 = 1$ and $x_2 = 3$

6. $\Delta y / \Delta x$; given $x_1 = 2$ and $x_2 = 3$

In Problems 7–12, find dy for each function.

7. $y = 30 + 12x^2 - x^3$

8. $y = 200x - \dfrac{x^2}{30}$

9. $y = x^2\left(1 - \dfrac{x}{9}\right)$

10. $y = x^3(60 - x)$

11. $y = \dfrac{590}{\sqrt{x}}$

12. $y = 52\sqrt{x}$

B

In Problems 13 and 14, find the indicated quantities for $y = f(x) = 3x^2$.

13. (A) $\dfrac{f(2 + \Delta x) - f(2)}{\Delta x}$ (simplify)

   (B) What does the quantity in part (A) approach as Δx approaches 0?

14. (A) $\dfrac{f(3 + \Delta x) - f(3)}{\Delta x}$ (simplify)

   (B) What does the quantity in part (A) approach as Δx approaches 0?

In Problems 15–18, find dy for each function.

15. $y = (2x + 1)^2$

16. $y = (3x + 5)^2$

17. $y = \dfrac{x^2 + 9}{x}$

18. $y = \dfrac{(x - 1)^2}{x^2}$

In Problems 19–22, evaluate dy and Δy for each function for the indicated values.

19. $y = f(x) = x^2 - 3x + 2; x = 5, dx = \Delta x = 0.2$

20. $y = f(x) = 30 + 12x^2 - x^3; x = 2, dx = \Delta x = 0.1$

21. $y = f(x) = 75\left(1 - \dfrac{2}{x}\right); x = 5, dx = \Delta x = -0.5$

22. $y = f(x) = 100\left(x - \dfrac{4}{x^2}\right); x = 2, dx = \Delta x = -0.1$

23. A cube with 10-inch sides is covered with a coat of fiberglass 0.2 inch thick. Use differentials to estimate the volume of the fiberglass shell.

24. A sphere with a radius of 5 centimeters is coated with ice 0.1 centimeter thick. Use differentials to estimate the volume of the ice. [Recall that $V = \frac{4}{3}\pi r^3$.]

C

In Problems 25–28,

(A) Find Δy and dy for the function f at the indicated value of x.

(B) Graph Δy and dy from part A.

(C) Compare the values of Δy and dy from part A at the indicated values of Δx.

25. $f(x) = x^2 + 2x + 3; x = -0.5, \Delta x = dx = 0.1, 0.2, 0.3$

26. $f(x) = x^2 + 2x + 3; x = -2, \Delta x = dx = -0.1, -0.2, -0.3$

27. $f(x) = x^3 - 2x^2; x = 1, \Delta x = dx = 0.05, 0.10, 0.15$

28. $f(x) = x^3 - 2x^2; x = 2, \Delta x = dx = -0.05, -0.10, -0.15$

In Problems 29–32, discuss the validity of each statement. If the statement is always true, explain why. If not, give a counterexample.

29. If the graph of the function $y = f(x)$ is a line, then the functions Δy and dy (of the independent variable $\Delta x = dx$) for $f(x)$ at $x = 3$ are identical.

30. If the graph of the function $y = f(x)$ is a parabola, then the functions Δy and dy (of the independent variable $\Delta x = dx$) for $f(x)$ at $x = 0$ are identical.

31. Suppose that $y = f(x)$ defines a differentiable function whose domain is the set of all real numbers. If every differential dy at $x = 2$ is equal to 0, then $f(x)$ is a constant function.

32. Suppose that $y = f(x)$ defines a function whose domain is the set of all real numbers. If every increment at $x = 2$ is equal to 0, then $f(x)$ is a constant function.

33. Find dy if $y = (1 - 2x)\sqrt[3]{x^2}$.

34. Find dy if $y = (2x^2 - 4)\sqrt{x}$.

35. Find dy and Δy for $y = 52\sqrt{x}$, $x = 4$, and $\Delta x = dx = 0.3$.

36. Find dy and Δy for $y = 590/\sqrt{x}$, $x = 64$, and $\Delta x = dx = 1$.

Applications

Use differential approximations in the following problems.

37. Advertising. A company will sell N units of a product after spending x thousand in advertising, as given by

$$N = 60x - x^2 \qquad 5 \le x \le 30$$

Approximately what increase in sales will result by increasing the advertising budget from $10,000 to $11,000? From $20,000 to $21,000?

38. Price–demand. Suppose that the daily demand (in pounds) for chocolate candy at $x per pound is given by

$$D = 1,000 - 40x^2 \qquad 1 \le x \le 5$$

If the price is increased from $3.00 per pound to $3.20 per pound, what is the approximate change in demand?

39. Average cost. For a company that manufactures tennis rackets, the average cost per racket $\overline{C}$ is

$$\overline{C} = \frac{400}{x} + 5 + \frac{1}{2}x \qquad x \ge 1$$

where x is the number of rackets produced per hour. What will the approximate change in average cost per racket be if production is increased from 20 per hour to 25 per hour? From 40 per hour to 45 per hour?

40. Revenue and profit. A company manufactures and sells x televisions per month. If the cost and revenue equations are

$$C(x) = 72,000 + 60x$$

$$R(x) = 200x - \frac{x^2}{30} \qquad 0 \le x \le 6,000$$

what will the approximate changes in revenue and profit be if production is increased from 1,500 to 1,510? From 4,500 to 4,510?

41. Pulse rate. The average pulse rate y (in beats per minute) of a healthy person x inches tall is given approximately by

$$y = \frac{590}{\sqrt{x}} \qquad 30 \le x \le 75$$

Approximately how will the pulse rate change for a change in height from 36 to 37 inches? From 64 to 65 inches?

42. Measurement. An egg of a particular bird is nearly spherical. If the radius to the inside of the shell is 5 millimeters and the radius to the outside of the shell is 5.3 millimeters, approximately what is the volume of the shell? [Remember that $V = \frac{4}{3}\pi r^3$.]

43. Medicine. A drug is given to a patient to dilate her arteries. If the radius of an artery is increased from 2 to 2.1 millimeters, approximately how much is the cross-sectional area increased? [Assume that the cross section of the artery is circular; that is, $A = \pi r^2$.]

44. Drug sensitivity. One hour after x milligrams of a particular drug are given to a person, the change in body temperature T (in degrees Fahrenheit) is given by

$$T = x^2\left(1 - \frac{x}{9}\right) \qquad 0 \le x \le 6$$

Approximate the changes in body temperature produced by the following changes in drug dosages:

(A) From 2 to 2.1 milligrams

(B) From 3 to 3.1 milligrams

(C) From 4 to 4.1 milligrams

45. Learning. A particular person learning to type has an achievement record given approximately by

$$N = 75\left(1 - \frac{2}{t}\right) \qquad 3 \le t \le 20$$

where N is the number of words per minute typed after t weeks of practice. What is the approximate improvement from 5 to 5.5 weeks of practice?

46. Learning. If a person learns y items in x hours, as given approximately by

$$y = 52\sqrt{x} \qquad 0 \le x \le 9$$

what is the approximate increase in the number of items learned when x changes from 1 to 1.1 hours? From 4 to 4.1 hours?

47. Politics. In a new city, the voting population (in thousands) is given by

$$N(t) = 30 + 12t^2 - t^3 \qquad 0 \le t \le 8$$

where t is time in years. Find the approximate change in votes for the following changes in time:

(A) From 1 to 1.1 years

(B) From 4 to 4.1 years

(C) From 7 to 7.1 years

Answers to Matched Problems

1. (A) $\Delta x = 1, \Delta y = 5, \Delta y/\Delta x = 5$

   (B) 4

2. $dy = \dfrac{1}{2\sqrt{x}}\,dx$

   (A) 0.025

   (B) 0.02

   (C) 0.005

3. (A) $\Delta y = -2\Delta x - \Delta x^2; dy = -2\Delta x$

   (B)

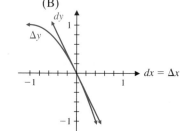

   (C)

Δx	Δy	dy
-0.1	0.19	0.2
-0.2	0.36	0.4
-0.3	0.51	0.6

4. $dR = -\$20/\text{wk}; dP = -\$40/\text{wk}$

10-7   Marginal Analysis in Business and Economics

- Marginal Cost, Revenue, and Profit
- Application
- Marginal Average Cost, Revenue, and Profit

Marginal Cost, Revenue, and Profit

One important application of calculus to business and economics involves *marginal analysis*. In economics, the word *marginal* refers to a rate of change—that is, to a derivative. Thus, if $C(x)$ is the total cost of producing x items, then $C'(x)$ is called the *marginal cost* and represents the instantaneous rate of change of total cost with respect to the number of items produced. Similarly, the *marginal revenue* is the derivative of the total revenue function, and the *marginal profit* is the derivative of the total profit function.

> **DEFINITION Marginal Cost, Revenue, and Profit**
>
> If x is the number of units of a product produced in some time interval, then
>
> $$\text{total cost} = C(x)$$
> $$\textbf{marginal cost} = C'(x)$$
> $$\text{total revenue} = R(x)$$
> $$\textbf{marginal revenue} = R'(x)$$
> $$\text{total profit} = P(x) = R(x) - C(x)$$
> $$\textbf{marginal profit} = P'(x) = R'(x) - C'(x)$$
> $$= (\text{marginal revenue}) - (\text{marginal cost})$$
>
> Marginal cost (or revenue or profit) is the instantaneous rate of change of cost (or revenue or profit) relative to production at a given production level.

To begin our discussion, we consider a cost function $C(x)$. It is important to remember that $C(x)$ represents the *total* cost of producing x items, not the cost of producing a *single* item. To find the cost of producing a single item, we use the difference of two successive values of $C(x)$:

$$\text{Total cost of producing } x + 1 \text{ items} = C(x + 1)$$
$$\text{Total cost of producing } x \text{ items} = C(x)$$
$$\text{Exact cost of producing the } (x + 1)\text{st item} = C(x + 1) - C(x)$$

EXAMPLE 1   **Cost Analysis** A company manufactures fuel tanks for cars. The total weekly cost (in dollars) of producing x tanks is given by

$$C(x) = 10,000 + 90x - 0.05x^2$$

(A) Find the marginal cost function.

(B) Find the marginal cost at a production level of 500 tanks per week.

(C) Interpret the results of part B.

(D) Find the exact cost of producing the 501st item.

SOLUTION   (A) $C'(x) = 90 - 0.1x$

(B) $C'(500) = 90 - 0.1(500) = \$40$ Marginal cost

(C) At a production level of 500 tanks per week, the total production costs are increasing at the rate of \$40 per tank.

(D)
$$C(501) = 10,000 + 90(501) - 0.05(501)^2$$
$$= \$42,539.95 \quad \text{Total cost of producing 501 tanks per week}$$
$$C(500) = 10,000 + 90(500) - 0.05(500)^2$$
$$= \$42,500.00 \quad \text{Total cost of producing 500 tanks per week}$$
$$C(501) - C(500) = 42,539.95 - 42,500.00$$
$$= \$39.95 \quad \text{Exact cost of producing the 501st tank}$$

Matched Problem 1   A company manufactures automatic transmissions for cars. The total weekly cost (in dollars) of producing x transmissions is given by

$$C(x) = 50,000 + 600x - 0.75x^2$$

(A) Find the marginal cost function.

(B) Find the marginal cost at a production level of 200 transmissions per week.

(C) Interpret the results of part B.

(D) Find the exact cost of producing the 201st transmission.

In Example 1, we found that the cost of the 501st tank and the marginal cost at a production level of 500 tanks differ by only a nickel. Increments and differentials will help us understand the relationship between marginal cost and the cost of a single item. If $C(x)$ is any total cost function, then

$$C'(x) \approx \frac{C(x + \Delta x) - C(x)}{\Delta x} \quad \text{See Section 10-6}$$

$$C'(x) \approx C(x + 1) - C(x) \quad \Delta x = 1$$

We see that the marginal cost $C'(x)$ approximates $C(x + 1) - C(x)$, the exact cost of producing the $(x + 1)$st item. These observations are summarized next and are illustrated in Figure 1.

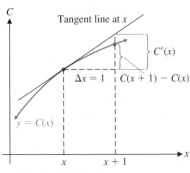

Figure 1 $C'(x) \approx C(x + 1) - C(x)$

> **THEOREM 1   Marginal Cost and Exact Cost**
>
> If $C(x)$ is the total cost of producing x items, then the marginal cost function approximates the exact cost of producing the $(x + 1)$st item:
>
> Marginal cost   Exact cost
>
> $$C'(x) \approx C(x + 1) - C(x)$$
>
> Similar statements can be made for total revenue functions and total profit functions.

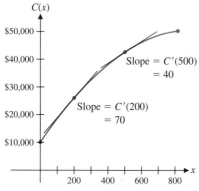

Figure 2 $C(x) = 10,000 + 90x - 0.05x^2$

> **CONCEPTUAL INSIGHT**
>
> Theorem 1 states that the marginal cost at a given production level x approximates the cost of producing the $(x + 1)$st, or *next,* item. In practice, the marginal cost is used more frequently than the exact cost. One reason for this is that the marginal cost is easily visualized when one is examining the graph of the total cost function. Figure 2 shows the graph of the cost function discussed in Example 1, with tangent lines added at $x = 200$ and $x = 500$. The graph clearly shows that as production increases, the slope of the tangent line decreases. Thus, the cost of producing the next tank also decreases, a desirable characteristic of a total cost function. We will have much more to say about graphical analysis in Chapter 12.

Application

Now we discuss how price, demand, revenue, cost, and profit are tied together in typical applications. Although either price or demand can be used as the independent variable in a price–demand equation, it is common to use demand as the independent variable when marginal revenue, cost, and profit are also involved.

EXAMPLE 2   **Production Strategy**   A company's market research department recommends the manufacture and marketing of a new headphone set for MP3 players. After suitable test marketing, the research department presents the following **price–demand equation**:

$$x = 10,000 - 1,000p \qquad \text{x is demand at price p.} \qquad (1)$$

Solving (1) for p gives

$$p = 10 - 0.001x \qquad (2)$$

where x is the number of headphones that retailers are likely to buy at $\$p$ per set. The financial department provides the **cost function**

$$C(x) = 7,000 + 2x \qquad (3)$$

where $\$7,000$ is the estimate of fixed costs (tooling and overhead) and $\$2$ is the estimate of variable costs per headphone set (materials, labor, marketing, transportation, storage, etc.).

(A) Find the domain of the function defined by the price–demand equation (2).

(B) Find and interpret the marginal cost function $C'(x)$.

(C) Find the revenue function as a function of x and find its domain.

(D) Find the marginal revenue at $x = 2,000$, $5,000$, and $7,000$. Interpret these results.

(E) Graph the cost function and the revenue function in the same coordinate system. Find the intersection points of these two graphs and interpret the results.

(F) Find the profit function and its domain and sketch the graph of the function.

(G) Find the marginal profit at $x = 1,000$, $4,000$, and $6,000$. Interpret these results.

SOLUTION (A) Since price p and demand x must be non-negative, we have $x \geq 0$ and

$$p = 10 - 0.001x \geq 0$$
$$10 \geq 0.001x$$
$$10,000 \geq x$$

Thus, the permissible values of x are $0 \leq x \leq 10,000$.

(B) The marginal cost is $C'(x) = 2$. Since this is a constant, it costs an additional $2 to produce one more headphone set at any production level.

(C) The **revenue** is the amount of money R received by the company for manufacturing and selling x headphone sets at $\$p$ per set and is given by

$$R = (\text{number of headphone sets sold})(\text{price per headphone set}) = xp$$

In general, the revenue R can be expressed as a function of p using equation (1) or as a function of x using equation (2). As we mentioned earlier, when using marginal functions, we will always use the number of items x as the independent variable. Thus, the **revenue function** is

$$R(x) = xp = x(10 - 0.001x) \quad \text{Using equation (2)} \quad (4)$$
$$= 10x - 0.001x^2$$

Since equation (2) is defined only for $0 \leq x \leq 10,000$, it follows that the domain of the revenue function is $0 \leq x \leq 10,000$.

(D) The **marginal revenue** is

$$R'(x) = 10 - 0.002x$$

For production levels of $x = 2,000, 5,000$, and $7,000$, we have

$$R'(2,000) = 6 \qquad R'(5,000) = 0 \qquad R'(7,000) = -4$$

This means that at production levels of $2,000, 5,000$, and $7,000$, the respective approximate changes in revenue per unit change in production are $6, $0, and $-\$4$. That is, at the 2,000 output level, revenue increases as production increases; at the 5,000 output level, revenue does not change with a "small" change in production; and at the 7,000 output level, revenue decreases with an increase in production.

(E) Graphing $R(x)$ and $C(x)$ in the same coordinate system results in Figure 3. The intersection points are called the **break-even points**, because revenue equals cost at these production levels. The company neither makes nor loses money, but just breaks even. The break-even points are obtained as follows:

$$C(x) = R(x)$$
$$7,000 + 2x = 10x - 0.001x^2$$
$$0.001x^2 - 8x + 7,000 = 0 \quad \text{Solve by the quadratic formula}$$
$$x^2 - 8,000x + 7,000,000 = 0 \quad \text{(see Appendix A-7).}$$

$$x = \frac{8,000 \pm \sqrt{8,000^2 - 4(7,000,000)}}{2}$$
$$= \frac{8,000 \pm \sqrt{36,000,000}}{2}$$
$$= \frac{8,000 \pm 6,000}{2}$$
$$= 1,000, \quad 7,000$$

$$R(1,000) = 10(1,000) - 0.001(1,000)^2 = 9,000$$
$$C(1,000) = 7,000 + 2(1,000) = 9,000$$
$$R(7,000) = 10(7,000) - 0.001(7,000)^2 = 21,000$$
$$C(7,000) = 7,000 + 2(7,000) = 21,000$$

The break-even points are (1,000, 9,000) and (7,000, 21,000), as shown in Figure 3. Further examination of the figure shows that cost is greater than revenue for production levels between 0 and 1,000 and also between 7,000 and 10,000. Consequently, the company incurs a loss at these levels. By contrast, for production levels between 1,000 and 7,000, revenue is greater than cost, and the company makes a profit.

(F) The **profit function** is

$$P(x) = R(x) - C(x)$$
$$= (10x - 0.001x^2) - (7,000 + 2x)$$
$$= -0.001x^2 + 8x - 7,000$$

The domain of the cost function is $x \geq 0$, and the domain of the revenue function is $0 \leq x \leq 10,000$. The domain of the profit function is the set of x values for which both functions are defined—that is, $0 \leq x \leq 10,000$. The graph of the profit function is shown in Figure 4. Notice that the x coordinates of the break-even points in Figure 3 are the x intercepts of the profit function. Furthermore, the intervals on which cost is greater than revenue and on which revenue is greater than cost correspond, respectively, to the intervals on which profit is negative and on which profit is positive.

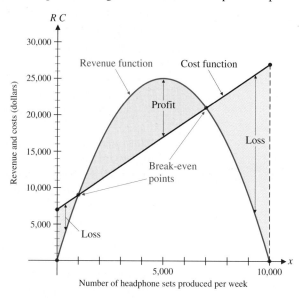

Figure 3

(G) The **marginal profit** is

$$P'(x) = -0.002x + 8$$

For production levels of 1,000, 4,000, and 6,000, we have

$$P'(1,000) = 6 \qquad P'(4,000) = 0 \qquad P'(6,000) = -4$$

This means that at production levels of 1,000, 4,000, and 6,000, the respective approximate changes in profit per unit change in production are $6, $0, and −$4. That is, at the 1,000 output level, profit will be increased if production is increased; at the 4,000 output level, profit does not change for "small" changes in production; and at the 6,000 output level, profits will decrease if production is increased. It seems that the best production level to produce a maximum profit is 4,000.

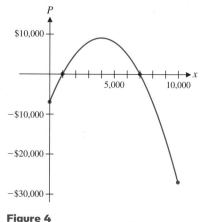

Figure 4

Example 2 requires careful study since a number of important ideas in economics and calculus are involved. In the next chapter, we will develop a systematic procedure for finding the production level (and, using the demand equation, the selling price) that will maximize profit.

Matched Problem 2

Refer to the revenue and profit functions in Example 2.

(A) Find $R'(3,000)$ and $R'(6,000)$. Interpret the results.

(B) Find $P'(2,000)$ and $P'(7,000)$. Interpret the results.

Marginal Average Cost, Revenue, and Profit

Sometimes it is desirable to carry out marginal analysis relative to **average cost (cost per unit)**, **average revenue (revenue per unit)**, and **average profit (profit per unit)**.

DEFINITION Marginal Average Cost, Revenue, and Profit

If x is the number of units of a product produced in some time interval, then

Cost per unit: average cost $= \overline{C}(x) = \dfrac{C(x)}{x}$

marginal average cost $= \overline{C}'(x) = \dfrac{d}{dx}\overline{C}(x)$

Revenue per unit: average revenue $= \overline{R}(x) = \dfrac{R(x)}{x}$

marginal average revenue $= \overline{R}'(x) = \dfrac{d}{dx}\overline{R}(x)$

Profit per unit: average profit $= \overline{P}(x) = \dfrac{P(x)}{x}$

marginal average profit $= \overline{P}'(x) = \dfrac{d}{dx}\overline{P}(x)$

EXAMPLE 3

Cost Analysis A small machine shop manufactures drill bits used in the petroleum industry. The manager estimates that the total daily cost (in dollars) of producing x bits is

$$C(x) = 1,000 + 25x - 0.1x^2$$

(A) Find $\overline{C}(x)$ and $\overline{C}'(x)$.

(B) Find $\overline{C}(10)$ and $\overline{C}'(10)$. Interpret these quantities.

(C) Use the results in part (B) to estimate the average cost per bit at a production level of 11 bits per day.

SOLUTION (A) $\overline{C}(x) = \dfrac{C(x)}{x} = \dfrac{1,000 + 25x - 0.1x^2}{x}$

$= \dfrac{1,000}{x} + 25 - 0.1x$ *Average cost function*

$\overline{C}'(x) = \dfrac{d}{dx}\overline{C}(x) = -\dfrac{1,000}{x^2} - 0.1$ *Marginal average cost function*

(B) $\overline{C}(10) = \dfrac{1,000}{10} + 25 - 0.1(10) = \$124$

$\overline{C}'(10) = -\dfrac{1,000}{10^2} - 0.1 = -\$10.10$

At a production level of 10 bits per day, the average cost of producing a bit is $124. This cost is decreasing at the rate of $10.10 per bit.

(C) If production is increased by 1 bit, then the average cost per bit will decrease by approximately $10.10. So, the average cost per bit at a production level of 11 bits per day is approximately $124 − $10.10 = $113.90.

Matched Problem 3   Consider the cost function for the production of headphone sets from Example 2:

$$C(x) = 7,000 + 2x$$

(A) Find $\overline{C}(x)$ and $\overline{C}'(x)$.

(B) Find $\overline{C}(100)$ and $\overline{C}'(100)$. Interpret these quantities.

(C) Use the results in part (B) to estimate the average cost per headphone set at a production level of 101 headphone sets.

EXPLORE & DISCUSS 1   A student produced the following solution to Matched Problem 3:

$$C(x) = 7,000 + 2x \quad \text{Cost}$$

$$C'(x) = 2 \qquad\qquad \text{Marginal cost}$$

$$\frac{C'(x)}{x} = \frac{2}{x} \qquad \text{"Average" of the marginal cost}$$

Explain why the last function is not the same as the marginal average cost function.

 CAUTION

1. The marginal average cost function is computed by first finding the average cost function and then finding its derivative. As Explore & Discuss 1 illustrates, reversing the order of these two steps produces a different function that does not have any useful economic interpretations.

2. Recall that the marginal cost function has two interpretations: the usual interpretation of any derivative as an instantaneous rate of change and the special interpretation as an approximation to the exact cost of the $(x + 1)$st item. This special interpretation does not apply to the marginal average cost function. Referring to Example 3, we would be incorrect to interpret $\overline{C}'(10) = -\$10.10$ to mean that the average cost of the next bit is approximately $-\$10.10$. In fact, the phrase "average cost of the next bit" does not even make sense. Averaging is a concept applied to a collection of items, not to a single item.

These remarks also apply to revenue and profit functions.

Exercises 10-7

A

In Problems 1–4, find the marginal cost function.

1. $C(x) = 175 + 0.8x$

2. $C(x) = 4,500 + 9.5x$

3. $C(x) = 210 + 4.6x - 0.01x^2$

4. $C(x) = 790 + 13x - 0.2x^2$

In Problems 5–8, find the marginal revenue function.

5. $R(x) = 4x - 0.01x^2$

6. $R(x) = 36x - 0.03x^2$

7. $R(x) = x(12 - 0.04x)$

8. $R(x) = x(25 - 0.05x)$

In Problems 9-12, find the marginal profit function if the cost and revenue, respectively, are those in the indicated problems.

9. Problem 1 and Problem 5

10. Problem 2 and Problem 6

11. Problem 3 and Problem 7

12. Problem 4 and Problem 8

B

In Problems 13–20, find the indicated function if cost and revenue are given by $C(x) = 145 + 1.1x$ and $R(x) = 5x - 0.02x^2$, respectively.

13. Average cost function

14. Average revenue function

91. Employee training. A company producing computer components has established that, on average, a new employee can assemble $N(t)$ components per day after t days of on-the-job training, as given by

$$N(t) = \frac{40t - 80}{t}, t \geq 2$$

(A) Find the average rate of change of $N(t)$ from 2 days to 5 days.

(B) Find the instantaneous rate of change of $N(t)$ at 2 days.

92. Sales analysis. The total number of swimming pools, N (in thousands), sold during a year is given by

$$N(t) = 2t + \frac{1}{3}t^{3/2}$$

where t is the number of months since the beginning of the year. Find $N(9)$ and $N'(9)$, and interpret these quantities.

93. Natural-gas consumption. The data in Table 2 give the U.S. consumption of natural gas in trillions of cubic feet.

Table 2

Year	Natural-Gas Consumption
1960	12.0
1970	21.1
1980	19.9
1990	18.7
2000	21.9

(A) Let x represent time (in years), with $x = 0$ corresponding to 1960, and let y represent the corresponding U.S. consumption of natural gas. Enter the data set in a graphing calculator and find a cubic regression equation for the data.

(B) If $y = N(x)$ denotes the regression equation found in part (A), find $N(50)$ and $N'(50)$, and write a brief verbal interpretation of these results.

94. Break-even analysis. Table 3 contains price–demand and total cost data from a bakery for the production of kringles (a Danish pastry), where p is the price (in dollars) of a kringle for a daily demand of x kringles and C is the total cost (in dollars) of producing x kringles.

Table 3

x	$p(\$)$	$C(\$)$
125	9	740
140	8	785
170	7	850
200	6	900

(A) Find a linear regression equation for the price–demand data, using x as the independent variable.

(B) Find a linear regression equation for the cost data, using x as the independent variable. Use this equation to estimate the fixed costs and variable costs per kringle.

(C) Find the break-even points.

(D) Find the price range for which the bakery will make a profit.

95. Pollution. A sewage treatment plant uses a pipeline that extends 1 mile toward the center of a large lake. The concentration of effluent $C(x)$ in parts per million, x meters from the end of the pipe is given approximately by

$$C(x) = \frac{500}{x^2}, x \geq 1$$

What is the instantaneous rate of change of concentration at 10 meters? At 100 meters?

96. Medicine. The body temperature (in degrees Fahrenheit) of a patient t hours after taking a fever-reducing drug is given by

$$F(t) = 0.16t^2 - 1.6t + 102$$

Find $F(4)$ and $F'(4)$. Write a brief verbal interpretation of these quantities.

97. Learning. If a person learns N items in t hours, as given by

$$N(t) = 20\sqrt{t}$$

find the rate of learning after

(A) 1 hour   (B) 4 hours

98. Physics: The coefficient of thermal expansion (CTE) is a measure of the expansion of an object subjected to extreme temperatures. We want to use a Michaelis–Menten function of the form

$$C(T) = \frac{C_{\max}T}{M + T}$$

where C = CTE, T is temperature in K (degrees Kelvin), and $C_{\max}$ and M are constants. Table 4 lists the coefficients of thermal expansion for titanium at various temperatures.

Table 4   Coefficients of Thermal Expansion

T (K)	Titanium
100	4.5
200	7.4
293	8.6
500	9.9
800	11.1
1100	11.7

(A) Plot the points in columns 1 and 2 of Table 4 on graph paper and estimate $C_{\max}$ to the nearest integer. To estimate M, add the horizontal line CTE $= \frac{C_{\max}}{2}$ to your graph, connect successive points on the graph with straight-line segments, and estimate the value of T (to the nearest multiple of fifty) that satisfies

$$C(T) = \frac{C_{\max}}{2}.$$

(B) Use the constants $\frac{C_{\max}}{2}$ and M from part (A) to form a Michaelis–Menten function for the CTE of titanium.

(C) Use the function from part (B) to estimate the CTE of titanium at 600 K and to estimate the temperature when the CTE of titanium is 10.

Additional Derivative Topics

Introduction

In this chapter, we develop techniques for finding derivatives of a wide variety of functions, including exponential and logarithmic functions. There are straightforward procedures—the product rule, quotient rule, and chain rule—for writing down the derivative of any function that is the product, quotient, or composite of functions whose derivatives are known. With the ability to calculate derivatives easily, we consider a wealth of applications involving rates of change. For example, we apply the derivative to study population growth, radioactive decay, elasticity of demand, and environmental crises (see Problem 31 in Section 11-6 or Problem 71 in Section 11-7). Before starting this chapter, you may find it helpful to review the basic properties of exponential and logarithmic functions in Sections 2-5 and 2-6.

11-1 The Constant e and Continuous Compound Interest

- The Constant e
- Continuous Compound Interest

In Chapter 2, both the exponential function with base e and continuous compound interest were introduced informally. Now, with an understanding of limit concepts, we can give precise definitions of e and continuous compound interest.

The Constant e

The irrational number e is a particularly suitable base for both exponential and logarithmic functions. The reasons for choosing this number as a base will become clear as we develop differentiation formulas for the exponential function e^x and the natural logarithmic function $\ln x$.

In precalculus treatments (Chapter 2), the number e is defined informally as the irrational number that can be approximated by the expression $[1 + (1/n)]^n$ for n sufficiently large. Now we will use the limit concept to formally define e as either of the following two limits. [*Note:* If $s = 1/n$, then as $n \to \infty$, $s \to 0$.]

> **DEFINITION The Number e**
>
> $$e = \lim_{n \to \infty} \left(1 + \frac{1}{n}\right)^n \qquad \text{or, alternatively,} \qquad e = \lim_{s \to 0}(1 + s)^{1/s}$$

Both limits are equal to $e = 2.718\ 281\ 828\ 459 \ldots$

Proof that the indicated limits exist and represent an irrational number between 2 and 3 is not easy and is omitted.

> **CONCEPTUAL INSIGHT**
>
> The two limits used to define e are unlike any we have encountered so far. Some people reason (incorrectly) that both limits are 1, since $1 + s \to 1$ as $s \to 0$ and 1 to any power is 1. An ordinary scientific calculator with a y^x key can convince you otherwise. Consider the following table of values for s and $f(s) = (1 + s)^{1/s}$ and Figure 1 for s close to 0. Compute the table values with a calculator yourself, and try several values of s even closer to 0. Note that the function is discontinuous at $s = 0$.
>
>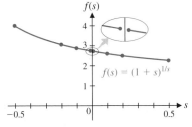
>
> **Figure 1**
>
> s approaches 0 from the left $\to 0 \leftarrow$ s approaches 0 from the right
>
> | s | -0.5 | -0.2 | -0.1 | $-0.01 \to 0 \leftarrow 0.01$ | 0.1 | 0.2 | 0.5 |
> |---|---|---|---|---|---|---|---|
> | $(1 + s)^{1/s}$ | 4.0000 | 3.0518 | 2.8680 | $2.7320 \to e \leftarrow 2.7048$ | 2.5937 | 2.4883 | 2.2500 |

Continuous Compound Interest

Now we can see how e appears quite naturally in the important application of compound interest. Let us start with simple interest, move on to compound interest, and then proceed on to continuous compound interest.

On one hand, if a principal P is borrowed at an annual rate r,* then after t years at simple interest, the borrower will owe the lender an amount A given by

$$A = P + Prt = P(1 + rt) \quad \text{Simple interest} \tag{1}$$

On the other hand, if interest is compounded n times a year, then the borrower will owe the lender an amount A given by

$$A = P\left(1 + \frac{r}{n}\right)^{nt} \quad \text{Compound interest} \tag{2}$$

where r/n is the interest rate per compounding period and nt is the number of compounding periods. Suppose that P, r, and t in equation (2) are held fixed and n is increased. Will the amount A increase without bound, or will it tend to approach some limiting value?

Let us perform a calculator experiment before we attack the general limit problem. If $P = \$100$, $r = 0.06$, and $t = 2$ years, then

$$A = 100\left(1 + \frac{0.06}{n}\right)^{2n}$$

We compute A for several values of n in Table 1. The biggest gain appears in the first step, then the gains slow down as n increases. The amount A appears to approach \$112.75 as n gets larger and larger.

Table 1

Compounding Frequency	n	$A = 100\left(1 + \dfrac{0.06}{n}\right)^{2n}$
Annually	1	\$112.3600
Semiannually	2	112.5509
Quarterly	4	112.6493
Monthly	12	112.7160
Weekly	52	112.7419
Daily	365	112.7486
Hourly	8,760	112.7496

Keeping P, r, and t fixed in equation (2), we compute the following limit and observe an interesting and useful result:

$$\lim_{n \to \infty} P\left(1 + \frac{r}{n}\right)^{nt} = P \lim_{n \to \infty} \left(1 + \frac{r}{n}\right)^{(n/r)rt} \quad \begin{array}{l}\text{Insert } r/r \text{ in the exponent and} \\ \text{let } s = r/n. \text{ Note that} \\ n \to \infty \text{ implies } s \to 0.\end{array}$$

$$= P \lim_{s \to 0} [(1 + s)^{1/s}]^{rt} \quad \text{Use a limit property.}^\dagger$$

$$= P[\lim_{s \to 0} (1 + s)^{1/s}]^{rt} \quad \lim_{s \to 0} (1 + s)^{1/s} = e$$

$$= Pe^{rt}$$

The resulting formula is called the **continuous compound interest formula**, a widely used formula in business and economics.

THEOREM 1 Continuous Compound Interest Formula

If a principal P is invested at an annual rate r (expressed as a decimal) compounded continuously, then the amount A in the account at the end of t years is given by

$$A = Pe^{rt}$$

---

*If r is the interest rate written as a decimal, then $100r\%$ is the rate in percent. For example, if $r = 0.12$, then $100r\% = 100(0.12)\% = 12\%$. The expressions 0.12 and 12% are equivalent. Unless stated otherwise, all formulas in this book use r in decimal form.

†The following new limit property is used: If $\lim_{x \to c} f(x)$ exists, then $\lim_{x \to c}[f(x)]^p = [\lim_{x \to c} f(x)]^p$, provided that the last expression names a real number.

EXAMPLE 1   **Computing Continuously Compounded Interest** If $100 is invested at 6% compounded continuously,[*] what amount will be in the account after 2 years? How much interest will be earned?

SOLUTION

$$A = Pe^{rt}$$
$$= 100e^{(0.06)(2)} \qquad 6\% \text{ is equivalent to } r = 0.06.$$
$$\approx \$112.7497$$

Compare this result with the values calculated in Table 1. The interest earned is $112.7497 − $100 = $12.7497.

Matched Problem 1   What amount (to the nearest cent) will be in an account after 5 years if $100 is invested at an annual nominal rate of 8% compounded annually? Semiannually? Continuously?

EXAMPLE 2   **Graphing the Growth of an Investment** Union Savings Bank offers a 5-year certificate of deposit (CD) that earns 5.75% compounded continuously. If $1,000 is invested in one of these CDs, graph the amount in the account as a function of time for a period of 5 years.

SOLUTION   We want to graph

$$A = 1,000e^{0.0575t} \qquad 0 \le t \le 5$$

Using a calculator, we construct a table of values (Table 2). Then we graph the points from the table and join the points with a smooth curve (Fig. 2).

Table 2	
t	*A*($)
0	1,000
1	1,059
2	1,122
3	1,188
4	1,259
5	1,333

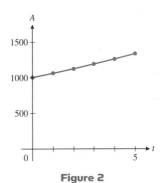

Figure 2

CONCEPTUAL INSIGHT

Depending on the domain, the graph of an exponential function can appear to be linear. Table 2 shows that the graph in Figure 2 is *not* linear. The slope determined by the first two points (for *t* = 0 and *t* = 1) is 59 but the slope determined by the first and third points (for *t* = 0 and *t* = 2) is 61. For a linear graph, the slope determined by any two points is constant.

Matched Problem 2   If $5,000 is invested in a Union Savings Bank 4-year CD that earns 5.61% compounded continuously, graph the amount in the account as a function of time for a period of 4 years.

---

[*]Following common usage, we will often write "at 6% compounded continuously," understanding that this means "at an annual nominal rate of 6% compounded continuously."

EXAMPLE 3   **Computing Growth Time**   How long will it take an investment of $5,000 to grow to $8,000 if it is invested at 5% compounded continuously?

SOLUTION   Starting with the continous compound interest formula $A = Pe^{rt}$, we must solve for t:

$$A = Pe^{rt}$$
$$8,000 = 5,000e^{0.05t}$$
$$e^{0.05t} = 1.6$$
$$\ln e^{0.05t} = \ln 1.6$$
$$0.05t = \ln 1.6$$
$$t = \frac{\ln 1.6}{0.05}$$
$$t \approx 9.4 \text{ years}$$

Divide both sides by 5,000 and reverse the equation.

Take the natural logarithm of both sides—recall that $\log_b b^x = x$.

Figure 3
$y_1 = 5,000e^{0.05x}$
$y_2 = 8,000$

   Figure 3 shows an alternative method for solving Example 3 on a graphing calculator.

Matched Problem 3   How long will it take an investment of $10,000 to grow to $15,000 if it is invested at 9% compounded continuously?

EXAMPLE 4   **Computing Doubling Time**   How long will it take money to double if it is invested at 6.5% compounded continuously?

SOLUTION   Starting with the continuous compound interest formula $A = Pe^{rt}$, we solve for t, given $A = 2P$ and $R = 0.065$:

$$2P = Pe^{0.065t}$$
$$e^{0.065t} = 2$$
$$\ln e^{0.065t} = \ln 2$$
$$0.065t = \ln 2$$
$$t = \frac{\ln 2}{0.065}$$
$$t \approx 10.66 \text{ years}$$

Divide both sides by P and reverse the equation.

Take the natural logarithm of both sides.

Matched Problem 4   How long will it take money to triple if it is invested at 5.5% compounded continuously?

EXPLORE & DISCUSS 1   You are considering three options for investing $10,000: at 7% compounded annually, at 6% compounded monthly, and at 5% compounded continuously.
(A) Which option would be the best for investing $10,000 for 8 years?
(B) How long would you need to invest your money for the third option to be the best?

Exercises 11-1

A

Use a calculator to evaluate A to the nearest cent in Problems 1 and 2.

1. $A = \$1,000e^{0.1t}$ for $t = 2, 5$, and 8

2. $A = \$5,000e^{0.08t}$ for $t = 1, 4$, and 10

3. If \$6,000 is invested at 10% compounded continuously, graph the amount in the account as a function of time for a period of 8 years.

4. If \$4,000 is invested at 8% compounded continuously, graph the amount in the account as a function of time for a period of 6 years.

B

In Problems 5–10, solve for t or r to two decimal places.

5. $2 = e^{0.06t}$

6. $2 = e^{0.03t}$

7. $3 = e^{0.1r}$

8. $3 = e^{0.25t}$

9. $2 = e^{5r}$

10. $3 = e^{10r}$

C

In Problems 11 and 12, use a calculator to complete each table to five decimal places.

11.

n	$[1 + (1/n)]^n$
10	2.593 74
100	
1,000	
10,000	
100,000	
1,000,000	
10,000,000	
↓	↓
∞	$e = 2.718\ 281\ 828\ 459\ldots$

12.

s	$(1 + s)^{1/s}$
0.01	2.704 81
−0.01	
0.001	
−0.001	
0.000 1	
−0.000 1	
0.000 01	
−0.000 01	
↓	↓
0	$e = 2.718\ 281\ 828\ 459\ldots$

13. Use a calculator and a table of values to investigate
$$\lim_{n \to \infty} (1 + n)^{1/n}$$
Do you think this limit exists? If so, what do you think it is?

14. Use a calculator and a table of values to investigate
$$\lim_{s \to 0^+} \left(1 + \frac{1}{s}\right)^s$$
Do you think this limit exists? If so, what do you think it is?

15. It can be shown that the number e satisfies the inequality
$$\left(1 + \frac{1}{n}\right)^n < e < \left(1 + \frac{1}{n}\right)^{n+1} \qquad n \geq 1$$
Illustrate this condition by graphing
$$y_1 = (1 + 1/n)^n$$
$$y_2 = 2.718\ 281\ 828 \approx e$$
$$y_3 = (1 + 1/n)^{n+1}$$
in the same viewing window, for $1 \leq n \leq 20$.

16. It can be shown that
$$e^s = \lim_{n \to \infty} \left(1 + \frac{s}{n}\right)^n$$
for any real number s. Illustrate this equation graphically for $s = 2$ by graphing
$$y_1 = (1 + 2/n)^n$$
$$y_2 = 7.389\ 056\ 099 \approx e^2$$
in the same viewing window, for $1 \leq n \leq 50$.

Applications

17. **Continuous compound interest.** Provident Bank offers a 10-year CD that earns 4.15% compounded continuously.
    (A) If \$10,000 is invested in this CD, how much will it be worth in 10 years?
    (B) How long will it take for the account to be worth \$18,000?

18. **Continuous compound interest.** Provident Bank also offers a 3-year CD that earns 3.64% compounded continuously.
    (A) If \$10,000 is invested in this CD, how much will it be worth in 3 years?
    (B) How long will it take for the account to be worth \$11,000?

19. **Present value.** A note will pay \$20,000 at maturity 10 years from now. How much should you be willing to pay for the note now if money is worth 5.2% compounded continuously?

20. **Present value.** A note will pay \$50,000 at maturity 5 years from now. How much should you be willing to pay for the note now if money is worth 6.4% compounded continuously?

21. **Continuous compound interest.** An investor bought stock for \$20,000. Five years later, the stock was sold for \$30,000. If interest is compounded continuously, what annual nominal rate of interest did the original \$20,000 investment earn?

22. Continuous compound interest. A family paid $99,000 cash for a house. Fifteen years later, the house was sold for $195,000. If interest is compounded continuously, what annual nominal rate of interest did the original $99,000 investment earn?

23. Present value. Solving $A = Pe^{rt}$ for P, we obtain

$$P = Ae^{-rt}$$

which is the present value of the amount A due in t years if money earns interest at an annual nominal rate r compounded continuously.

(A) Graph $P = 10,000e^{-0.08t}, 0 \le t \le 50$.

(B) $\lim_{t \to \infty} 10,000e^{-0.08t} = $? [Guess, using part (A).]

[*Conclusion:* The longer the time until the amount A is due, the smaller is its present value, as we would expect.]

24. Present value. Referring to Problem 23, in how many years will the $10,000 be due in order for its present value to be $5,000?

25. Doubling time. How long will it take money to double if it is invested at 4% compounded continuously?

26. Doubling time. How long will it take money to double if it is invested at 5% compounded continuously?

27. Doubling rate. At what nominal rate compounded continuously must money be invested to double in 8 years?

28. Doubling rate. At what nominal rate compounded continuously must money be invested to double in 10 years?

29. Growth time. A man with $20,000 to invest decides to diversify his investments by placing $10,000 in an account that earns 7.2% compounded continuously and $10,000 in an account that earns 8.4% compounded annually. Use graphical approximation methods to determine how long it will take for his total investment in the two accounts to grow to $35,000.

30. Growth time. A woman invests $5,000 in an account that earns 8.8% compounded continuously and $7,000 in an account that earns 9.6% compounded annually. Use graphical approximation methods to determine how long it will take for her total investment in the two accounts to grow to $20,000.

31. Doubling times

(A) Show that the doubling time t (in years) at an annual rate r compounded continuously is given by

$$t = \frac{\ln 2}{r}$$

(B) Graph the doubling-time equation from part (A) for $0.02 \le r \le 0.30$. Is this restriction on r reasonable? Explain.

(C) Determine the doubling times (in years, to two decimal places) for $r = 5\%, 10\%, 15\%, 20\%, 25\%$, and 30%.

32. Doubling rates

(A) Show that the rate r that doubles an investment at continuously compounded interest in t years is given by

$$r = \frac{\ln 2}{t}$$

(B) Graph the doubling-rate equation from part (A) for $1 \le t \le 20$. Is this restriction on t reasonable? Explain.

(C) Determine the doubling rates for $t = 2, 4, 6, 8, 10$, and 12 years.

33. Radioactive decay. A mathematical model for the decay of radioactive substances is given by

$$Q = Q_0e^{rt}$$

where

$Q_0 = $ amount of the substance at time $t = 0$
$r = $ continuous compound rate of decay
$t = $ time in years
$Q = $ amount of the substance at time t

If the continuous compound rate of decay of radium per year is $r = -0.000\,433\,2$, how long will it take a certain amount of radium to decay to half the original amount? (This period is the *half-life* of the substance.)

34. Radioactive decay. The continuous compound rate of decay of carbon-14 per year is $r = -0.000\,123\,8$. How long will it take a certain amount of carbon-14 to decay to half the original amount? (Use the radioactive decay model in Problem 33.)

35. Radioactive decay. A cesium isotope has a half-life of 30 years. What is the continuous compound rate of decay? (Use the radioactive decay model in Problem 33.)

36. Radioactive decay. A strontium isotope has a half-life of 90 years. What is the continuous compound rate of decay? (Use the radioactive decay model in Problem 33.)

37. World population. A mathematical model for world population growth over short intervals is given by

$$P = P_0e^{rt}$$

where

$P_0 = $ population at time $t = 0$
$r = $ continuous compound rate of growth
$t = $ time in years
$P = $ population at time t

How long will it take world population to double if it continues to grow at its current continuous compound rate of 1.3% per year?

38. U.S. population. How long will it take for the U.S. population to double if it continues to grow at a rate of 0.975% per year?

39. Population growth. Some underdeveloped nations have population doubling times of 50 years. At what continuous compound rate is the population growing? (Use the population growth model in Problem 37.)

40. Population growth. Some developed nations have population doubling times of 200 years. At what continuous compound rate is the population growing? (Use the population growth model in Problem 37.)

3. 4.51 yr

4. 19.97 yr

Answers to Matched Problems

1. $146.93; $148.02; $149.18

2. $A = 5{,}000e^{0.0561t}$

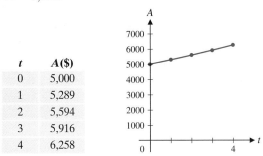

t	A($)
0	5,000
1	5,289
2	5,594
3	5,916
4	6,258

11-2 Derivatives of Exponential and Logarithmic Functions

- The Derivative of e^x
- The Derivative of $\ln x$
- Other Logarithmic and Exponential Functions
- Exponential and Logarithmic Models

In this section, we find formulas for the derivatives of logarithmic and exponential functions. A review of Sections 2–5 and 2–6 may prove helpful. In particular, recall that $f(x) = e^x$ is the exponential function with base $e \approx 2.718$, and the inverse of the function e^x is the natural logarithm function $\ln x$. More generally, if b is a positive real number, $b \neq 1$, then the exponential function b^x with base b, and the logarithmic function $\log_b x$ with base b, are inverses of each other.

The Derivative of e^x

In the process of finding the derivative of e^x, we use (without proof) the fact that

$$\lim_{h \to 0} \frac{e^h - 1}{h} = 1 \tag{1}$$

EXPLORE & DISCUSS 1

Complete Table 1.

Table 1

h	−0.1	−0.01	−0.001	→ 0 ←	0.001	0.01	0.1
$\dfrac{e^h - 1}{h}$							

Do your calculations make it reasonable to conclude that

$$\lim_{h \to 0} \frac{e^h - 1}{h} = 1?$$

Discuss.

We now apply the four-step process (Section 10-4) to the exponential function $f(x) = e^x$.

Step 1 Find $f(x + h)$.

$$f(x + h) = e^{x+h} = e^x e^h \qquad \textit{See Section 2-4.}$$

Step 2 Find $f(x + h) - f(x)$.

$$f(x + h) - f(x) = e^x e^h - e^x \qquad \textit{Factor out } e^x.$$

$$= e^x(e^h - 1)$$

Step 3 Find $\dfrac{f(x + h) - f(x)}{h}$.

$$\frac{f(x + h) - f(x)}{h} = \frac{e^x(e^h - 1)}{h} = e^x\left(\frac{e^h - 1}{h}\right)$$

Step 4 Find $f'(x) = \lim\limits_{h \to 0} \dfrac{f(x + h) - f(x)}{h}$.

$$\begin{aligned}
f'(x) &= \lim_{h \to 0} \frac{f(x + h) - f(x)}{h} \\
&= \lim_{h \to 0} e^x\left(\frac{e^h - 1}{h}\right) \\
&= e^x \lim_{h \to 0} \left(\frac{e^h - 1}{h}\right) \qquad \text{Use the limit in (1).} \\
&= e^x \cdot 1 = e^x
\end{aligned}$$

Therefore,

$$\frac{d}{dx}e^x = e^x \qquad \begin{array}{l}\text{The derivative of the exponential function}\\ \text{is the exponential function.}\end{array}$$

EXAMPLE 1 **Finding Derivatives** Find $f'(x)$ for

(A) $f(x) = 5e^x - 3x^4 + 9x + 16$ (B) $f(x) = -7x^e + 2e^x + e^2$

SOLUTIONS (A) $f'(x) = 5e^x - 12x^3 + 9$ (B) $f'(x) = -7ex^{e-1} + 2e^x$

Remember that e is a real number, so the power rule (Section 10-5) is used to find the derivative of x^e. The derivative of the exponential function e^x, however, is e^x. Note that $e^2 \approx 7.389$ is a constant, so its derivative is 0.

Matched Problem 1 Find $f'(x)$ for

(A) $f(x) = 4e^x + 8x^2 + 7x - 14$ (B) $f(x) = x^7 - x^5 + e^3 - x + e^x$

⚠️ **CAUTION**

$$\frac{d}{dx}e^x \neq xe^{x-1} \qquad \frac{d}{dx}e^x = e^x$$

The power rule cannot be used to differentiate the exponential function. The power rule applies to exponential forms x^n, where the exponent is a constant and the base is a variable. In the exponential form e^x, the base is a constant and the exponent is a variable.

The Derivative of $\ln x$

We summarize some important facts about logarithmic functions from Section 2–6:

SUMMARY

Recall that the inverse of an exponential function is called a **logarithmic function**. For $b > 0$ and $b \neq 1$,

Logarithmic form		Exponential form
$y = \log_b x$	is equivalent to	$x = b^y$
Domain: $(0, \infty)$		Domain: $(-\infty, \infty)$
Range: $(-\infty, \infty)$		Range: $(0, \infty)$

The graphs of $y = \log_b x$ and $y = b^x$ are symmetric with respect to the line $y = x$. (See Figure 1.)

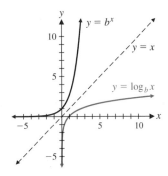

Figure 1

Of all the possible bases for logarithmic functions, the two most widely used are

$$\log x = \log_{10} x \quad \text{Common logarithm (base 10)}$$

$$\ln x = \log_e x \quad \text{Natural logarithm (base } e\text{)}$$

We are now ready to use the definition of the derivative and the four-step process discussed in Section 10-4 to find a formula for the derivative of $\ln x$. Later we will extend this formula to include $\log_b x$ for any base b.

Let $f(x) = \ln x, x > 0$.

Step 1 Find $f(x + h)$.

$$f(x + h) = \ln(x + h) \quad \ln(x + h) \text{ cannot be simplified.}$$

Step 2 Find $f(x + h) - f(x)$.

$$f(x + h) - f(x) = \ln(x + h) - \ln x \qquad \text{Use } \ln A - \ln B = \ln \frac{A}{B}.$$

$$= \ln \frac{x + h}{x}$$

Step 3 Find $\dfrac{f(x + h) - f(x)}{h}$.

$$\frac{f(x + h) - f(x)}{h} = \frac{\ln(x + h) - \ln x}{h}$$

$$= \frac{1}{h} \ln \frac{x + h}{x}$$

$$= \frac{x}{x} \cdot \frac{1}{h} \ln \frac{x + h}{x} \qquad \text{Multiply by } 1 = x/x \text{ to change form.}$$

$$= \frac{1}{x}\left[\frac{x}{h}\ln\left(1 + \frac{h}{x}\right)\right] \qquad \text{Use } p \ln A = \ln A^p.$$

$$= \frac{1}{x}\ln\left(1 + \frac{h}{x}\right)^{x/h}$$

Step 4 Find $f'(x) = \lim\limits_{h\to 0}\dfrac{f(x + h) - f(x)}{h}$.

$$f'(x) = \lim_{h\to 0}\frac{f(x + h) - f(x)}{h}$$

$$= \lim_{h\to 0}\left[\frac{1}{x}\ln\left(1 + \frac{h}{x}\right)^{x/h}\right] \qquad \begin{array}{l}\text{Let } s = h/x.\text{ Note that } h \to 0 \\ \text{implies } s \to 0.\end{array}$$

$$= \frac{1}{x}\lim_{s\to 0}\left[\ln(1 + s)^{1/s}\right] \qquad \text{Use a new limit property.*}$$

$$= \frac{1}{x}\ln\left[\lim_{s\to 0}(1 + s)^{1/s}\right] \qquad \text{Use the definition of } e.$$

$$= \frac{1}{x}\ln e \qquad \ln e = \log_e e = 1$$

$$= \frac{1}{x}$$

Therefore,

$$\frac{d}{dx}\ln x = \frac{1}{x}$$

CONCEPTUAL INSIGHT

In finding the derivative of $\ln x$, we used the following properties of logarithms:

$$\ln\frac{A}{B} = \ln A - \ln B \qquad \ln A^p = p \ln A$$

We also noted that there is no property that simplifies $\ln(A + B)$. (See Theorem 1 in Section 2-6 for a list of properties of logarithms.)

EXAMPLE 2 **Finding Derivatives** Find y' for

(A) $y = 3e^x + 5 \ln x$ \qquad (B) $y = x^4 - \ln x^4$

SOLUTIONS (A) $y' = 3e^x + \dfrac{5}{x}$

(B) Before taking the derivative, we use a property of logarithms (see Theorem 1, Section 2-6) to rewrite y.

$$y = x^4 - \ln x^4 \qquad \text{Use } \ln M^p = p \ln M.$$

$$y = x^4 - 4 \ln x \qquad \text{Now take the derivative of both sides.}$$

$$y' = 4x^3 - \frac{4}{x}$$

Matched Problem 2 Find y' for

(A) $y = 10x^3 - 100 \ln x$ \qquad (B) $y = \ln x^5 + e^x - \ln e^2$

---

*The following new limit property is used: If $\lim_{x\to c} f(x)$ exists and is positive, then $\lim_{x\to c}[\ln f(x)] = \ln[\lim_{x\to c} f(x)]$.

Other Logarithmic and Exponential Functions

In most applications involving logarithmic or exponential functions, the number e is the preferred base. However, in some situations it is convenient to use a base other than e. Derivatives of $y = \log_b x$ and $y = b^x$ can be obtained by expressing these functions in terms of the natural logarithmic and exponential functions.

We begin by finding a relationship between $\log_b x$ and $\ln x$ for any base b such that $b > 0$ and $b \neq 1$.

$$y = \log_b x \qquad \text{Change to exponential form.}$$
$$b^y = x \qquad \text{Take the natural logarithm of both sides.}$$
$$\ln b^y = \ln x \qquad \text{Recall that } \ln b^y = y \ln b.$$
$$y \ln b = \ln x \qquad \text{Solve for } y.$$
$$y = \frac{1}{\ln b} \ln x$$

Therefore,

$$\log_b x = \frac{1}{\ln b} \ln x \qquad \text{Change-of-base formula for logarithms}^* \qquad (2)$$

Similarly, we can find a relationship between b^x and e^x for any base b such that $b > 0, b \neq 1$.

$$y = b^x \qquad \text{Take the natural logarithm of both sides.}$$
$$\ln y = \ln b^x \qquad \text{Recall that } \ln b^x = x \ln b.$$
$$\ln y = x \ln b \qquad \text{Take the exponential function of both sides.}$$
$$y = e^{x \ln b}$$

Therefore,

$$b^x = e^{x \ln b} \qquad \text{Change-of-base formula for exponential functions} \qquad (3)$$

Differentiating both sides of equation (2) gives

$$\frac{d}{dx} \log_b x = \frac{1}{\ln b} \frac{d}{dx} \ln x = \frac{1}{\ln b} \left(\frac{1}{x} \right)$$

It can be shown that the derivative of the function e^{cx}, where c is a constant, is the function ce^{cx} (see Problems 49–50 in Exercise 11-2 or the more general results of Section 11–4). Therefore, differentiating both sides of equation (3), we have

$$\frac{d}{dx} b^x = e^{x \ln b} \ln b = b^x \ln b$$

For convenience, we list the derivative formulas for exponential and logarithmic functions:

Derivatives of Exponential and Logarithmic Functions
For $b > 0, b \neq 1$,

$$\frac{d}{dx} e^x = e^x \qquad\qquad \frac{d}{dx} b^x = b^x \ln b$$

$$\frac{d}{dx} \ln x = \frac{1}{x} \qquad \frac{d}{dx} \log_b x = \frac{1}{\ln b} \left(\frac{1}{x} \right)$$

*Equation (2) is a special case of the **general change-of-base formula** for logarithms (which can be derived in the same way): $\log_b x = (\log_a x)/(\log_a b)$.

EXAMPLE 3 **Finding Derivatives** Find $g'(x)$ for

(A) $g(x) = 2^x - 3^x$ (B) $g(x) = \log_4 x^5$

SOLUTIONS (A) $g'(x) = 2^x \ln 2 - 3^x \ln 3$

(B) First, use a property of logarithms to rewrite $g(x)$.

$$g(x) = \log_4 x^5 \qquad \text{Use } \log_b M^p = p \log_b M.$$
$$g(x) = 5 \log_4 x \qquad \text{Take the derivative of both sides.}$$
$$g'(x) = \frac{5}{\ln 4}\left(\frac{1}{x}\right)$$

Matched Problem 3 Find $g'(x)$ for

(A) $g(x) = x^{10} + 10^x$ (B) $g(x) = \log_2 x - 6 \log_5 x$

EXPLORE & DISCUSS 2 (A) The graphs of $f(x) = \log_2 x$ and $g(x) = \log_4 x$ are shown in Figure 2. Which graph belongs to which function?

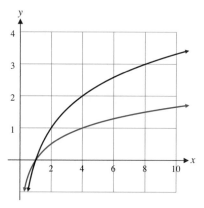

Figure 2

(B) Sketch graphs of $f'(x)$ and $g'(x)$.

(C) The function $f(x)$ is related to $g(x)$ in the same way that $f'(x)$ is related to $g'(x)$. What is that relationship?

Exponential and Logarithmic Models

EXAMPLE 4 **Price–Demand Model** An Internet store sells Australian wool blankets. If the store sells x blankets at a price of $\$p$ per blanket, then the price–demand equation is $p = 350(0.999)^x$. Find the rate of change of price with respect to demand when the demand is 800 blankets and interpret the result.

SOLUTION $\dfrac{dp}{dx} = 350(0.999)^x \ln 0.999$

If $x = 800$, then

$$\frac{dp}{dx} = 350(0.999)^{800} \ln 0.999 \approx -0.157, \text{ or } -\$0.16$$

When the demand is 800 blankets, the price is decreasing by $\$0.16$ per blanket.

Matched Problem 4   The store in Example 4 also sells a reversible fleece blanket. If the price–demand equation for reversible fleece blankets is $p = 200(0.998)^x$, find the rate of change of price with respect to demand when the demand is 400 blankets and interpret the result.

EXAMPLE 5   **Cable TV Subscribers**   A statistician used data from the U.S. Census Bureau to construct the model

$$S(t) = 21 \ln t + 2$$

where $S(t)$ is the number of cable TV subscribers (in millions) in year t ($t = 0$ corresponds to 1980). Use this model to estimate the number of cable TV subscribers in 2015 and the rate of change of the number of subscribers in 2015. Round both to the nearest tenth of a million. Interpret these results.

SOLUTION   Since 2015 corresponds to $t = 35$, we must find $S(35)$ and $S'(35)$.

$$S(35) = 21 \ln 35 + 2 = 76.7 \text{ million}$$

$$S'(t) = 21\frac{1}{t} = \frac{21}{t}$$

$$S'(35) = \frac{21}{35} = 0.6 \text{ million}$$

In 2015 there will be approximately 76.7 million subscribers, and this number is growing at the rate of 0.6 million subscribers per year.

Matched Problem 5   A model for newspaper circulation is

$$C(t) = 83 - 9 \ln t$$

where $C(t)$ is newspaper circulation (in millions) in year t ($t = 0$ corresponds to 1980). Use this model to estimate the circulation and the rate of change of circulation in 2015. Round both to the nearest tenth of a million. Interpret these results.

CONCEPTUAL INSIGHT

On most graphing calculators, exponential regression produces a function of the form $y = a \cdot b^x$. Formula (3) on page 569 allows you to change the base b (chosen by the graphing calculator) to the more familiar base e:

$$y = a \cdot b^x = a \cdot e^{x \ln b}$$

On most graphing calculators, logarithmic regression produces a function of the form $y = a + b \ln x$. Formula (2) on page 569 allows you to write the function in terms of logarithms to any base d that you may prefer:

$$y = a + b \ln x = a + b(\ln d) \log_d x$$

Exercises 11-2

A

In Problems 1–14, find $f'(x)$.

1. $f(x) = 5e^x + 3x + 1$

2. $f(x) = -7e^x - 2x + 5$

3. $f(x) = -2 \ln x + x^2 - 4$

4. $f(x) = 6 \ln x - x^3 + 2$

5. $f(x) = x^3 - 6e^x$

6. $f(x) = 9e^x + 2x^2$

7. $f(x) = e^x + x - \ln x$

8. $f(x) = \ln x + 2e^x - 3x^2$

9. $f(x) = \ln x^3$

10. $f(x) = \ln x^8$

11. $f(x) = 5x - \ln x^5$

12. $f(x) = 4 + \ln x^9$

13. $f(x) = \ln x^2 + 4e^x$

14. $f(x) = \ln x^{10} + 2 \ln x$

B

In Problems 15–22, find the equation of the line tangent to the graph of f at the indicated value of x.

15. $f(x) = 3 + \ln x; x = 1$

16. $f(x) = 2 \ln x; x = 1$

17. $f(x) = 3e^x; x = 0$

18. $f(x) = e^x + 1; x = 0$

19. $f(x) = \ln x^3; x = e$

20. $f(x) = 1 + \ln x^4; x = e$

21. $f(x) = 2 + e^x; x = 1$

22. $f(x) = 5e^x; x = 1$

23. A student claims that the line tangent to the graph of $f(x) = e^x$ at $x = 3$ passes through the point $(2, 0)$ (see the figure). Is she correct? Will the line tangent at $x = 4$ pass through $(3, 0)$? Explain.

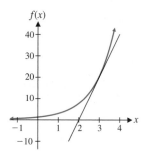

Figure for 23

24. Refer to Problem 23. Does the line tangent to the graph of $f(x) = e^x$ at $x = 1$ pass through the origin? Are there any other lines tangent to the graph of f that pass through the origin? Explain.

25. A student claims that the line tangent to the graph of $g(x) = \ln x$ at $x = 3$ passes through the origin (see the figure). Is he correct? Will the line tangent at $x = 4$ pass through the origin? Explain.

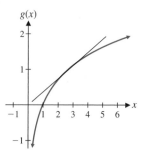

Figure for 25

26. Refer to Problem 25. Does the line tangent to the graph of $f(x) = \ln x$ at $x = e$ pass through the origin? Are there any other lines tangent to the graph of f that pass through the origin? Explain.

In Problems 27–30, first use appropriate properties of logarithms to rewrite f(x), and then find $f'(x)$.

27. $f(x) = 10x + \ln 10x$

28. $f(x) = 2 + 3 \ln \dfrac{1}{x}$

29. $f(x) = \ln \dfrac{4}{x^3}$

30. $f(x) = x + 5 \ln 6x$

C

In Problems 31–42, find $\dfrac{dy}{dx}$ for the indicated function y.

31. $y = \log_2 x$

32. $y = 3 \log_5 x$

33. $y = 3^x$

34. $y = 4^x$

35. $y = 2x - \log x$

36. $y = \log x + 4x^2 + 1$

37. $y = 10 + x + 10^x$

38. $y = x^5 - 5^x$

39. $y = 3 \ln x + 2 \log_3 x$

40. $y = -\log_2 x + 10 \ln x$

41. $y = 2^x + e^2$

42. $y = e^3 - 3^x$

In Problems 43–48, use graphical approximation methods to find the points of intersection of f(x) and g(x) (to two decimal places).

43. $f(x) = e^x; g(x) = x^4$

[Note that there are three points of intersection and that e^x is greater than x^4 for large values of x.]

44. $f(x) = e^x; g(x) = x^5$

[Note that there are two points of intersection and that e^x is greater than x^5 for large values of x.]

45. $f(x) = (\ln x)^2$; $g(x) = x$

46. $f(x) = (\ln x)^3$; $g(x) = \sqrt{x}$

47. $f(x) = \ln x$; $g(x) = x^{1/5}$

48. $f(x) = \ln x$; $g(x) = x^{1/4}$

49. Explain why $\lim\limits_{h \to 0} \dfrac{e^{ch} - 1}{h} = c$.

50. Use the result of Problem 49 and the four-step process to show that if $f(x) = e^{cx}$, then $f'(x) = ce^{cx}$.

Applications

51. Salvage value. The estimated salvage value S (in dollars) of a company airplane after t years is given by

$$S(t) = 300{,}000(0.9)^t$$

What is the rate of depreciation (in dollars per year) after 1 year? 5 years? 10 years?

52. Resale value. The estimated resale value R (in dollars) of a company car after t years is given by

$$R(t) = 20{,}000(0.86)^t$$

What is the rate of depreciation (in dollars per year) after 1 year? 2 years? 3 years?

53. Bacterial growth. A single cholera bacterium divides every 0.5 hour to produce two complete cholera bacteria. If we start with a colony of 5,000 bacteria, then after t hours, there will be

$$A(t) = 5{,}000 \cdot 2^{2t} = 5{,}000 \cdot 4^t$$

bacteria. Find $A'(t)$, $A'(1)$, and $A'(5)$, and interpret the results.

54. Bacterial growth. Repeat Problem 53 for a starting colony of 1,000 bacteria such that a single bacterium divides every 0.25 hour.

55. Blood pressure. An experiment was set up to find a relationship between weight and systolic blood pressure in children. Using hospital records for 5,000 children, the experimenters found that the systolic blood pressure was given approximately by

$$P(x) = 17.5(1 + \ln x) \qquad 10 \le x \le 100$$

where $P(x)$ is measured in millimeters of mercury and x is measured in pounds. What is the rate of change of blood pressure with respect to weight at the 40-pound weight level? At the 90-pound weight level?

56. Blood pressure. Refer to Problem 55. Find the weight (to the nearest pound) at which the rate of change of blood pressure with respect to weight is 0.3 millimeter of mercury per pound.

57. Psychology: stimulus/response. In psychology, the Weber–Fechner law for the response to a stimulus is

$$R = k \ln \frac{S}{S_0}$$

where R is the response, S is the stimulus, and S_0 is the lowest level of stimulus that can be detected. Find dR/dS.

58. Psychology: learning. A mathematical model for the average of a group of people learning to type is given by

$$N(t) = 10 + 6 \ln t \qquad t \ge 1$$

where $N(t)$ is the number of words per minute typed after t hours of instruction and practice (2 hours per day, 5 days per week). What is the rate of learning after 10 hours of instruction and practice? After 100 hours?

Answers to Matched Problems

1. (A) $4e^x + 16x + 7$
  (B) $7x^6 - 5x^4 - 1 + e^x$

2. (A) $30x^2 - \dfrac{100}{x}$
  (B) $\dfrac{5}{x} + e^x$

3. (A) $10x^9 + 10^x \ln 10$
  (B) $\left(\dfrac{1}{\ln 2} - \dfrac{6}{\ln 5} \right) \dfrac{1}{x}$

4. The price is decreasing at the rate of $0.18 per blanket.

5. The circulation in 2015 is approximately 51.0 million and is decreasing at the rate of 0.3 million per year.

11-3 Derivatives of Products and Quotients

- Derivatives of Products
- Derivatives of Quotients

The derivative properties discussed in Section 10-5 add substantially to our ability to compute and apply derivatives to many practical problems. In this and the next two sections, we add a few more properties that will increase this ability even further.

Derivatives of Products

In Section 10-5, we found that the derivative of a sum is the sum of the derivatives. Is the derivative of a product the product of the derivatives?

Let $F(x) = x^2$, $S(x) = x^3$, and $f(x) = F(x)S(x) = x^5$. Which of the following is $f'(x)$?

(A) $F'(x)S'(x)$ (B) $F(x)S'(x)$

(C) $F'(x)S(x)$ (D) $F(x)S'(x) + F'(x)S(x)$

Comparing the various expressions computed in Explore & Discuss 1, we see that the derivative of a product is not the product of the derivatives.

Using the definition of the derivative and the four-step process, we can show that

The derivative of the product of two functions is the first function times the derivative of the second function, plus the second function times the derivative of the first function.

THEOREM 1   **Product Rule**

If

$$y = f(x) = F(x)S(x)$$

and if $F'(x)$ and $S'(x)$ exist, then

$$f'(x) = F(x)S'(x) + S(x)F'(x)$$

Using simplified notation,

$$y' = FS' + SF' \qquad \text{or} \qquad \frac{dy}{dx} = F\frac{dS}{dx} + S\frac{dF}{dx}$$

EXAMPLE 1   **Differentiating a Product**   Use two different methods to find $f'(x)$ for

$$f(x) = 2x^2(3x^4 - 2).$$

SOLUTION   **Method 1.** Use the product rule:

$$f'(x) = 2x^2(3x^4 - 2)' + (3x^4 - 2)(2x^2)' \qquad \text{\small First times derivative of}$$
$$= 2x^2(12x^3) + (3x^4 - 2)(4x) \qquad \text{\small second, plus second times}$$
$$\qquad\qquad\qquad\qquad\qquad\qquad\qquad \text{\small derivative of first}$$
$$= 24x^5 + 12x^5 - 8x$$
$$= 36x^5 - 8x$$

Method 2. Multiply first; then take derivatives:

$$f(x) = 2x^2(3x^4 - 2) = 6x^6 - 4x^2$$
$$f'(x) = 36x^5 - 8x$$

Matched Problem 1   Use two different methods to find $f'(x)$ for $f(x) = 3x^3(2x^2 - 3x + 1)$.

Some products we encounter can be differentiated by either method illustrated in Example 1. In other situations, the product rule *must* be used. Unless instructed otherwise, you should use the product rule to differentiate all products in this section in order to gain experience with this important differentiation rule.

EXAMPLE 2   **Tangent Lines**   Let $f(x) = (2x - 9)(x^2 + 6)$.

(A) Find the equation of the line tangent to the graph of $f(x)$ at $x = 3$.

(B) Find the value(s) of x where the tangent line is horizontal.

SOLUTION   (A) First, find $f'(x)$:

$$f'(x) = (2x - 9)(x^2 + 6)' + (x^2 + 6)(2x - 9)'$$
$$= (2x - 9)(2x) + (x^2 + 6)(2)$$

Then, find $f(3)$ and $f'(3)$:

$$f(3) = [2(3) - 9](3^2 + 6) = (-3)(15) = -45$$
$$f'(3) = [2(3) - 9]2(3) + (3^2 + 6)(2) = -18 + 30 = 12$$

Now, find the equation of the tangent line at $x = 3$:

$$y - y_1 = m(x - x_1) \qquad y_1 = f(x_1) = f(3) = -45$$
$$y - (-45) = 12(x - 3) \qquad m = f'(x_1) = f'(3) = 12$$
$$y = 12x - 81 \qquad \text{Tangent line at } x = 3$$

(B) The tangent line is horizontal at any value of x such that $f'(x) = 0$, so

$$f'(x) = (2x - 9)2x + (x^2 + 6)2 = 0$$
$$6x^2 - 18x + 12 = 0$$
$$x^2 - 3x + 2 = 0$$
$$(x - 1)(x - 2) = 0$$
$$x = 1, 2$$

The tangent line is horizontal at $x = 1$ and at $x = 2$.

Matched Problem 2   Repeat Example 2 for $f(x) = (2x + 9)(x^2 - 12)$.

CONCEPTUAL INSIGHT

As Example 2 illustrates, the way we write $f'(x)$ depends on what we want to do. If we are interested only in evaluating $f'(x)$ at specified values of x, then the form in part (A) is sufficient. However, if we want to solve $f'(x) = 0$, we must multiply and collect like terms, as we did in part (B).

EXAMPLE 3   **Finding Derivatives**   Find $f'(x)$ for

(A) $f(x) = 2x^3 e^x$ (B) $f(x) = 6x^4 \ln x$

SOLUTIONS   (A) $f'(x) = 2x^3(e^x)' + e^x(2x^3)'$ (B) $f'(x) = 6x^4 (\ln x)' + (\ln x) (6x^4)'$

$\qquad = 2x^3 e^x + e^x(6x^2)$ $\qquad = 6x^4 \dfrac{1}{x} + (\ln x)(24x^3)$

$\qquad = 2x^2 e^x(x + 3)$ $\qquad = 6x^3 + 24x^3 \ln x$

$\qquad\qquad\qquad\qquad\qquad\qquad = 6x^3 (1 + 4 \ln x)$

Matched Problem 3   Find $f'(x)$ for

(A) $f(x) = 5x^8 e^x$ (B) $f(x) = x^7 \ln x$

Derivatives of Quotients

The derivative of a quotient of two functions is not the quotient of the derivatives of the two functions.

EXPLORE & DISCUSS 2

Let $T(x) = x^5$, $B(x) = x^2$, and

$$f(x) = \frac{T(x)}{B(x)} = \frac{x^5}{x^2} = x^3$$

Which of the following is $f'(x)$?

(A) $\dfrac{T'(x)}{B'(x)}$ (B) $\dfrac{T'(x)B(x)}{[B(x)]^2}$ (C) $\dfrac{T(x)B'(x)}{[B(x)]^2}$

(D) $\dfrac{T'(x)B(x)}{[B(x)]^2} - \dfrac{T(x)B'(x)}{[B(x)]^2} = \dfrac{T'(x)B(x) - T(x)B'(x)}{[B(x)]^2}$

The expressions in Explore & Discuss 2 suggest that the derivative of a quotient leads to a more complicated quotient than expected.

If $T(x)$ and $B(x)$ are any two differentiable functions and

$$f(x) = \frac{T(x)}{B(x)}$$

then

$$f'(x) = \frac{B(x)T'(x) - T(x)B'(x)}{[B(x)]^2}$$

Therefore,

The derivative of the quotient of two functions is the denominator function times the derivative of the numerator function, minus the numerator function times the derivative of the denominator function, divided by the denominator function squared.

THEOREM 2   Quotient Rule

If

$$y = f(x) = \frac{T(x)}{B(x)}$$

and if $T'(x)$ and $B'(x)$ exist, then

$$f'(x) = \frac{B(x)T'(x) - T(x)B'(x)}{[B(x)]^2}$$

Using simplified notation,

$$y' = \frac{BT' - TB'}{B^2} \quad \text{or} \quad \frac{dy}{dx} = \frac{B\dfrac{dT}{dx} - T\dfrac{dB}{dx}}{B^2}$$

EXAMPLE 4 **Differentiating Quotients**

(A) If $f(x) = \dfrac{x^2}{2x - 1}$, find $f'(x)$.   (B) If $y = \dfrac{t^2 - t}{t^3 + 1}$, find y'.

(C) Find $\dfrac{d}{dx} \dfrac{x^2 - 3}{x^2}$ by using the quotient rule and also by splitting the fraction into two fractions.

SOLUTION (A) $f'(x) = \dfrac{(2x - 1)(x^2)' - x^2(2x - 1)'}{(2x - 1)^2}$

The denominator times the derivative of the numerator, minus the numerator times the derivative of the denominator, divided by the square of the denominator

$= \dfrac{(2x - 1)(2x) - x^2(2)}{(2x - 1)^2}$

$= \dfrac{4x^2 - 2x - 2x^2}{(2x - 1)^2}$

$= \dfrac{2x^2 - 2x}{(2x - 1)^2}$

(B) $y' = \dfrac{(t^3 + 1)(t^2 - t)' - (t^2 - t)(t^3 + 1)'}{(t^3 + 1)^2}$

$= \dfrac{(t^3 + 1)(2t - 1) - (t^2 - t)(3t^2)}{(t^3 + 1)^2}$

$= \dfrac{2t^4 - t^3 + 2t - 1 - 3t^4 + 3t^3}{(t^3 + 1)^2}$

$= \dfrac{-t^4 + 2t^3 + 2t - 1}{(t^3 + 1)^2}$

(C) **Method 1.** Use the quotient rule:

$$\frac{d}{dx} \frac{x^2 - 3}{x^2} = \frac{x^2 \dfrac{d}{dx}(x^2 - 3) - (x^2 - 3)\dfrac{d}{dx}x^2}{(x^2)^2}$$

$$= \frac{x^2(2x) - (x^2 - 3)2x}{x^4}$$

$$= \frac{2x^3 - 2x^3 + 6x}{x^4} = \frac{6x}{x^4} = \frac{6}{x^3}$$

Method 2. Split into two fractions:

$$\frac{x^2 - 3}{x^2} = \frac{x^2}{x^2} - \frac{3}{x^2} = 1 - 3x^{-2}$$

$$\frac{d}{dx}(1 - 3x^{-2}) = 0 - 3(-2)x^{-3} = \frac{6}{x^3}$$

Comparing methods 1 and 2, we see that it often pays to change an expression algebraically before choosing a differentiation formula.

Matched Problem 4 Find

(A) $f'(x)$ for $f(x) = \dfrac{2x}{x^2 + 3}$ (B) y' for $y = \dfrac{t^3 - 3t}{t^2 - 4}$

(C) $\dfrac{d}{dx} \dfrac{2 + x^3}{x^3}$ in two ways

EXAMPLE 5   **Finding Derivatives** Find $f'(x)$ for

(A) $f(x) = \dfrac{3e^x}{1 + e^x}$

(B) $f(x) = \dfrac{\ln x}{2x + 5}$

SOLUTIONS   (A) $f'(x) = \dfrac{(1 + e^x)(3e^x)' - 3e^x(1 + e^x)'}{(1 + e^x)^2}$

$\qquad = \dfrac{(1 + e^x)3e^x - 3e^x e^x}{(1 + e^x)^2}$

$\qquad = \dfrac{3e^x}{(1 + e^x)^2}$

(B) $f'(x) = \dfrac{(2x + 5)(\ln x)' - (\ln x)(2x + 5)'}{(2x + 5)^2}$

$\qquad = \dfrac{(2x + 5) \cdot \dfrac{1}{x} - (\ln x)(2)}{(2x + 5)^2}$ Multiply by $\dfrac{x}{x}$

$\qquad = \dfrac{2x + 5 - 2x \ln x}{x(2x + 5)^2}$

Matched Problem 5   Find $f'(x)$ for

(A) $f(x) = \dfrac{x^3}{e^x + 2}$

(B) $f(x) = \dfrac{4x}{1 + \ln x}$

EXAMPLE 6   **Sales Analysis** The total sales S (in thousands of games) of a video game t months after the game is introduced are given by

$$S(t) = \frac{125t^2}{t^2 + 100}$$

(A) Find $S'(t)$.

(B) Find $S(10)$ and $S'(10)$. Write a brief interpretation of these results.

(C) Use the results from part (B) to estimate the total sales after 11 months.

SOLUTION   (A) $S'(t) = \dfrac{(t^2 + 100)(125t^2)' - 125t^2(t^2 + 100)'}{(t^2 + 100)^2}$

$\qquad = \dfrac{(t^2 + 100)(250t) - 125t^2(2t)}{(t^2 + 100)^2}$

$\qquad = \dfrac{250t^3 + 25{,}000t - 250t^3}{(t^2 + 100)^2}$

$\qquad = \dfrac{25{,}000t}{(t^2 + 100)^2}$

(B) $S(10) = \dfrac{125(10)^2}{10^2 + 100} = 62.5$ and $S'(10) = \dfrac{25{,}000(10)}{(10^2 + 100)^2} = 6.25.$

Total sales after 10 months are 62,500 games, and sales are increasing at the rate of 6,250 games per month.

(C) Total sales will increase by approximately 6,250 games during the next month, so the estimated total sales after 11 months are 62,500 + 6,250 = 68,750 games.

Matched Problem 6 Refer to Example 6. Suppose that the total sales S (in thousands of games) t months after the game is introduced are given by

$$S(t) = \frac{150t}{t + 3}$$

(A) Find $S'(t)$.

(B) Find $S(12)$ and $S'(12)$. Write a brief interpretation of these results.

(C) Use the results from part (B) to estimate the total sales after 13 months.

Exercises 11-3

Answers to most of the problems in this exercise set contain both an unsimplified form and a simplified form of the derivative. When checking your work, first check that you applied the rules correctly and then check that you performed the algebraic simplification correctly. Unless instructed otherwise, when differentiating a product, use the product rule rather than performing the multiplication first.

A

In Problems 1–26, find $f'(x)$ and simplify.

1. $f(x) = 2x^3(x^2 - 2)$ 2. $f(x) = 5x^2(x^3 + 2)$

3. $f(x) = (x - 3)(2x - 1)$

4. $f(x) = (3x + 2)(4x - 5)$

5. $f(x) = \dfrac{x}{x - 3}$

6. $f(x) = \dfrac{3x}{2x + 1}$ 7. $f(x) = \dfrac{2x + 3}{x - 2}$

8. $f(x) = \dfrac{3x - 4}{2x + 3}$ 9. $f(x) = 3xe^x$

10. $f(x) = x^2 e^x$ 11. $f(x) = x^3 \ln x$

12. $f(x) = 5x \ln x$

13. $f(x) = (x^2 + 1)(2x - 3)$

14. $f(x) = (3x + 5)(x^2 - 3)$

15. $f(x) = (0.4x + 2)(0.5x - 5)$

16. $f(x) = (0.5x - 4)(0.2x + 1)$

17. $f(x) = \dfrac{x^2 + 1}{2x - 3}$ 18. $f(x) = \dfrac{3x + 5}{x^2 - 3}$

19. $f(x) = (x^2 + 2)(x^2 - 3)$

20. $f(x) = (x^2 - 4)(x^2 + 5)$

21. $f(x) = \dfrac{x^2 + 2}{x^2 - 3}$ 22. $f(x) = \dfrac{x^2 - 4}{x^2 + 5}$

23. $f(x) = \dfrac{e^x}{x^2 + 1}$ 24. $f(x) = \dfrac{1 - e^x}{1 + e^x}$

25. $f(x) = \dfrac{\ln x}{1 + x}$ 26. $f(x) = \dfrac{2x}{1 + \ln x}$

In Problems 27–38, find $h'(x)$, where $f(x)$ is an unspecified differentiable function.

27. $h(x) = xf(x)$ 28. $h(x) = x^2 f(x)$

29. $h(x) = x^3 f(x)$ 30. $h(x) = \dfrac{f(x)}{x}$

31. $h(x) = \dfrac{f(x)}{x^2}$ 32. $h(x) = \dfrac{f(x)}{x^3}$

33. $h(x) = \dfrac{x}{f(x)}$ 34. $h(x) = \dfrac{x^2}{f(x)}$

35. $h(x) = e^x f(x)$ 36. $h(x) = \dfrac{e^x}{f(x)}$

37. $h(x) = \dfrac{\ln x}{f(x)}$ 38. $h(x) = \dfrac{f(x)}{\ln x}$

B

In Problems 39–48, find the indicated derivatives and simplify.

39. $f'(x)$ for $f(x) = (2x + 1)(x^2 - 3x)$

40. y' for $y = (x^3 + 2x^2)(3x - 1)$

41. $\dfrac{dy}{dt}$ for $y = (2.5t - t^2)(4t + 1.4)$

42. $\dfrac{d}{dt}[(3 - 0.4t^3)(0.5t^2 - 2t)]$

43. y' for $y = \dfrac{5x - 3}{x^2 + 2x}$

44. $f'(x)$ for $f(x) = \dfrac{3x^2}{2x - 1}$

45. $\dfrac{d}{dw}\dfrac{w^2 - 3w + 1}{w^2 - 1}$

46. $\dfrac{dy}{dw}$ for $y = \dfrac{w^4 - w^3}{3w - 1}$

47. y' for $y = (1 + x - x^2)e^x$

48. $\dfrac{dy}{dt}$ for $y = (1 + e^t)\ln t$

In Problems 49–54, find $f'(x)$ and find the equation of the line tangent to the graph of f at $x = 2$.

49. $f(x) = (1 + 3x)(5 - 2x)$

50. $f(x) = (7 - 3x)(1 + 2x)$

51. $f(x) = \dfrac{x-8}{3x-4}$

52. $f(x) = \dfrac{2x-5}{2x-3}$

53. $f(x) = \dfrac{x}{2^x}$

54. $f(x) = (x-2)\ln x$

In Problems 55–58, find $f'(x)$ and find the value(s) of x where $f'(x) = 0$.

55. $f(x) = (2x - 15)(x^2 + 18)$

56. $f(x) = (2x - 3)(x^2 - 6)$

57. $f(x) = \dfrac{x}{x^2 + 1}$

58. $f(x) = \dfrac{x}{x^2 + 9}$

In Problems 59–62, find $f'(x)$ in two ways: (1) using the product or quotient rule and (2) simplifying first.

59. $f(x) = x^3(x^4 - 1)$

60. $f(x) = x^4(x^3 - 1)$

61. $f(x) = \dfrac{x^3 + 9}{x^3}$

62. $f(x) = \dfrac{x^4 + 4}{x^4}$

C

In Problems 63–82, find each indicated derivative and simplify.

63. $f(w) = (w + 1)2^w$

64. $g(w) = (w - 5)\log_3 w$

65. $\dfrac{d}{dx}\dfrac{3x^2 - 2x + 3}{4x^2 + 5x - 1}$

66. y' for $y = \dfrac{x^3 - 3x + 4}{2x^2 + 3x - 2}$

67. $\dfrac{dy}{dx}$ for $y = 9x^{1/3}(x^3 + 5)$

68. $\dfrac{d}{dx}[(4x^{1/2} - 1)(3x^{1/3} + 2)]$

69. y' for $y = \dfrac{\log_2 x}{1 + x^2}$

70. $\dfrac{dy}{dx}$ for $y = \dfrac{10^x}{1 + x^4}$

71. $f'(x)$ for $f(x) = \dfrac{6\sqrt[3]{x}}{x^2 - 3}$

72. y' for $y = \dfrac{2\sqrt{x}}{x^2 - 3x + 1}$

73. $g'(t)$ if $g(t) = \dfrac{0.2t}{3t^2 - 1}$

74. $h'(t)$ if $h(t) = \dfrac{-0.05t^2}{2t + 1}$

75. $\dfrac{d}{dx}[4x \log x^5]$

76. $\dfrac{d}{dt}[10^t \log t]$

77. $\dfrac{d}{dx}\dfrac{x^3 - 2x^2}{\sqrt[3]{x^2}}$

78. $\dfrac{dy}{dx}$ for $y = \dfrac{x^2 - 3x + 1}{\sqrt[4]{x}}$

79. $f'(x)$ for $f(x) = \dfrac{(2x^2 - 1)(x^2 + 3)}{x^2 + 1}$

80. y' for $y = \dfrac{2x - 1}{(x^3 + 2)(x^2 - 3)}$

81. $\dfrac{dy}{dt}$ for $y = \dfrac{t \ln t}{e^t}$

82. $\dfrac{dy}{du}$ for $y = \dfrac{u^2 e^u}{1 + \ln u}$

Applications

83. Sales analysis. The total sales S (in thousands of DVDs) of a DVD are given by

$$S(t) = \dfrac{90t^2}{t^2 + 50}$$

where t is the number of months since the release of the DVD.

(A) Find $S'(t)$.

(B) Find $S(10)$ and $S'(10)$. Write a brief interpretation of these results.

(C) Use the results from part (B) to estimate the total sales after 11 months.

84. Sales analysis. A communications company has installed a new cable television system in a city. The total number N (in thousands) of subscribers t months after the installation of the system is given by

$$N(t) = \dfrac{180t}{t + 4}$$

(A) Find $N'(t)$.

(B) Find $N(16)$ and $N'(16)$. Write a brief interpretation of these results.

(C) Use the results from part (B) to estimate the total number of subscribers after 17 months.

85. Price–demand equation. According to economic theory, the demand x for a quantity in a free market decreases as the price p increases (see the figure). Suppose that the number x of DVD players people are willing to buy per week from a retail chain at a price of \$$p$ is given by

$$x = \dfrac{4,000}{0.1p + 1} \qquad 10 \le p \le 70$$

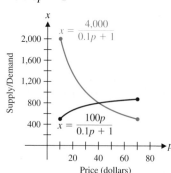

Figure for 85 and 86

(A) Find dx/dp.

(B) Find the demand and the instantaneous rate of change of demand with respect to price when the price is \$40. Write a brief interpretation of these results.

(C) Use the results from part (B) to estimate the demand if the price is increased to \$41.

86. Price–supply equation. According to economic theory, the supply x of a quantity in a free market increases as the price p increases (see the figure). Suppose that the number x of DVD players a retail chain is willing to sell per week at a price of $\$p$ is given by

$$x = \frac{100p}{0.1p + 1} \qquad 10 \le p \le 70$$

(A) Find dx/dp.

✎ (B) Find the supply and the instantaneous rate of change of supply with respect to price when the price is $40. Write a brief verbal interpretation of these results.

(C) Use the results from part (B) to estimate the supply if the price is increased to $41.

87. Medicine. A drug is injected into a patient's bloodstream through her right arm. The drug concentration (in milligrams per cubic centimeter) in the bloodstream of the left arm t hours after the injection is given by

$$C(t) = \frac{0.14t}{t^2 + 1}$$

(A) Find $C'(t)$.

(B) Find $C'(0.5)$ and $C'(3)$, and interpret the results.

88. Drug sensitivity. One hour after a dose of x milligrams of a particular drug is administered to a person, the change in body temperature $T(x)$, in degrees Fahrenheit, is given approximately by

$$T(x) = x^2\left(1 - \frac{x}{9}\right) \qquad 0 \le x \le 7$$

The rate $T'(x)$ at which T changes with respect to the size of the dosage x is called the *sensitivity* of the body to the dosage.

(A) Use the product rule to find $T'(x)$.

(B) Find $T'(1), T'(3)$, and $T'(6)$.

89. Learning. In the early twentieth century, L. L. Thurstone found that a given person successfully accomplished $N(x)$ acts after x practice acts, as given by

$$N(x) = \frac{100x + 200}{x + 32}$$

(A) Find the instantaneous rate of change of learning, $N'(x)$, with respect to the number of practice acts, x.

(B) Find $N'(4)$ and $N'(68)$.

Answers to Matched Problems

1. $30x^4 - 36x^3 + 9x^2$
2. (A) $y = 84x - 297$
   (B) $x = -4, x = 1$
3. (A) $5x^8e^x + e^x(40x^7) = 5x^7(x + 8)e^x$
   (B) $x^7 \cdot \dfrac{1}{x} + \ln x\,(7x^6) = x^6\,(1 + 7\ln x)$
4. (A) $\dfrac{(x^2 + 3)2 - (2x)(2x)}{(x^2 + 3)^2} = \dfrac{6 - 2x^2}{(x^2 + 3)^2}$
   (B) $\dfrac{(t^2 - 4)(3t^2 - 3) - (t^3 - 3t)(2t)}{(t^2 - 4)^2} = \dfrac{t^4 - 9t^2 + 12}{(t^2 - 4)^2}$
   (C) $-\dfrac{6}{x^4}$
5. (A) $\dfrac{(e^x + 2)\,3x^2 - x^3 e^x}{(e^x + 2)^2}$
   (B) $\dfrac{(1 + \ln x)\,4 - 4x\,\dfrac{1}{x}}{(1 + \ln x)^2} = \dfrac{4\ln x}{(1 + \ln x)^2}$
6. (A) $S'(t) = \dfrac{450}{(t + 3)^2}$
   (B) $S(12) = 120; S'(12) = 2$. After 12 months, the total sales are 120,000 games, and sales are increasing at the rate of 2,000 games per month.
   (C) 122,000 games

11-4 The Chain Rule

- Composite Functions
- General Power Rule
- The Chain Rule

The word *chain* in the name "chain rule" comes from the fact that a function formed by composition involves a chain of functions—that is, a function of a function. The *chain rule* enables us to compute the derivative of a composite function in terms of the derivatives of the functions making up the composition. In this section, we review composite functions, introduce the chain rule by means of a special case known as the *general power rule,* and then discuss the chain rule itself.

Composite Functions

The function $m(x) = (x^2 + 4)^3$ is a combination of a quadratic function and a cubic function. To see this more clearly, let

$$y = f(u) = u^3 \qquad \text{and} \qquad u = g(x) = x^2 + 4$$

We can express y as a function of x:

$$y = f(u) = f[g(x)] = [x^2 + 4]^3 = m(x)$$

The function m is the *composite* of the two functions f and g.

DEFINITION **Composite Functions**

A function m is a **composite** of functions f and g if

$$m(x) = f[g(x)]$$

The domain of m is the set of all numbers x such that x is in the domain of g, and $g(x)$ is in the domain of f.

EXAMPLE 1 **Composite Functions** Let $f(u) = e^u$ and $g(x) = -3x$. Find $f[g(x)]$ and $g[f(u)]$.

SOLUTION
$$f[g(x)] = f(-3x) = e^{-3x}$$
$$g[f(u)] = g(e^u) = -3e^u$$

Matched Problem 1 Let $f(u) = 2u$ and $g(x) = e^x$. Find $f[g(x)]$ and $g[f(u)]$.

EXAMPLE 2 **Composite Functions** Write each function as a composition of two simpler functions.

(A) $y = 100e^{0.04x}$ (B) $y = \sqrt{4 - x^2}$

SOLUTION (A) Let

$$y = f(u) = 100e^u$$
$$u = g(x) = 0.04x$$

Check: $y = f[g(x)] = 100e^{g(x)} = 100e^{0.04x}$

(B) Let

$$y = f(u) = \sqrt{u}$$
$$u = g(x) = 4 - x^2$$

Check: $y = f[g(x)] = \sqrt{g(x)} = \sqrt{4 - x^2}$

Matched Problem 2 Write each function as a composition of two simpler functions.

(A) $y = 50e^{-2x}$ (B) $y = \sqrt[3]{1 + x^3}$

CONCEPTUAL INSIGHT

There can be more than one way to express a function as a composition of simpler functions. Choosing $y = f(u) = 100u$ and $u = g(x) = e^{0.04x}$ in Example 2A produces the same result:

$$y = f[g(x)] = 100g(x) = 100e^{0.04x}$$

Since we will be using composition as a means to an end (finding a derivative), usually it will not matter what functions you choose for the composition.

General Power Rule

We have already made extensive use of the power rule,

$$\frac{d}{dx}x^n = nx^{n-1} \tag{1}$$

Now we can generalize this rule in order to differentiate composite functions of the form $[u(x)]^n$, where $u(x)$ is a differentiable function. Is rule (1) still valid if we replace x with a function $u(x)$?

EXPLORE & DISCUSS 1

Let $u(x) = 2x^2$ and $f(x) = [u(x)]^3 = 8x^6$. Which of the following is $f'(x)$?

(A) $3[u(x)]^2$ (B) $3[u'(x)]^2$ (C) $3[u(x)]^2u'(x)$

The calculations in Explore & Discuss 1 show that we cannot generalize the power rule simply by replacing x with $u(x)$ in equation (1).

How can we find a formula for the derivative of $[u(x)]^n$, where $u(x)$ is an arbitrary differentiable function? Let's begin by considering the derivatives of $[u(x)]^2$ and $[u(x)]^3$ to see if a general pattern emerges. Since $[u(x)]^2 = u(x)u(x)$, we use the product rule to write

$$\frac{d}{dx}[u(x)]^2 = \frac{d}{dx}[u(x)u(x)]$$

$$= u(x)u'(x) + u(x)u'(x)$$

$$= 2u(x)u'(x) \tag{2}$$

Because $[u(x)]^3 = [u(x)]^2u(x)$, we use the product rule and the result in equation (2) to write

$$\frac{d}{dx}[u(x)]^3 = \frac{d}{dx}\{[u(x)]^2u(x)\}$$

$$= [u(x)]^2\frac{d}{dx}u(x) + u(x)\frac{d}{dx}[u(x)]^2$$

$$= [u(x)]^2u'(x) + u(x)[2u(x)u'(x)]$$

$$= 3[u(x)]^2u'(x)$$

Use equation (2) to substitute for $\frac{d}{dx}[u(x)]^2.$

Continuing in this fashion, we can show that

$$\frac{d}{dx}[u(x)]^n = n[u(x)]^{n-1}u'(x) \qquad n \text{ a positive integer} \tag{3}$$

Using more advanced techniques, we can establish formula (3) for all real numbers n, obtaining the **general power rule**.

THEOREM 1   General Power Rule

If $u(x)$ is a differentiable function, n is any real number, and

$$y = f(x) = [u(x)]^n$$

then

$$f'(x) = n[u(x)]^{n-1}u'(x)$$

Using simplified notation,

$$y' = nu^{n-1}u' \qquad \text{or} \qquad \frac{d}{dx}u^n = nu^{n-1}\frac{du}{dx} \qquad \text{where } u = u(x)$$

EXAMPLE 3 **Using the General Power Rule** Find the indicated derivatives:

(A) $f'(x)$ if $f(x) = (3x + 1)^4$ (B) y' if $y = (x^3 + 4)^7$

(C) $\dfrac{d}{dt}\dfrac{1}{(t^2 + t + 4)^3}$ (D) $\dfrac{dh}{dw}$ if $h(w) = \sqrt{3 - w}$

SOLUTION

(A) $f(x) = (3x + 1)^4$ Let $u = 3x + 1$, $n = 4$.

$f'(x) = 4(3x + 1)^3(3x + 1)'$ $nu^{n-1}\dfrac{du}{dx}$

$= 4(3x + 1)^3\, 3$ $\dfrac{du}{dx} = 3$

$= 12(3x + 1)^3$

(B) $y = (x^3 + 4)^7$ Let $u = (x^3 + 4)$, $n = 7$.

$y' = 7(x^3 + 4)^6(x^3 + 4)'$ $nu^{n-1}\dfrac{du}{dx}$

$= 7(x^3 + 4)^6\, 3x^2$ $\dfrac{du}{dx} = 3x^2$

$= 21x^2(x^3 + 4)^6$

(C) $\dfrac{d}{dt}\dfrac{1}{(t^2 + t + 4)^3}$

$= \dfrac{d}{dt}(t^2 + t + 4)^{-3}$ Let $u = t^2 + t + 4$, $n = -3$.

$= -3(t^2 + t + 4)^{-4}(t^2 + t + 4)'$ $nu^{n-1}\dfrac{du}{dt}$

$= -3(t^2 + t + 4)^{-4}(2t + 1)$ $\dfrac{du}{dt} = 2t + 1$

$= \dfrac{-3(2t + 1)}{(t^2 + t + 4)^4}$

(D) $h(w) = \sqrt{3 - w} = (3 - w)^{1/2}$ Let $u = 3 - w$, $n = \dfrac{1}{2}$.

$\dfrac{dh}{dw} = \dfrac{1}{2}(3 - w)^{-1/2}(3 - w)'$ $nu^{n-1}\dfrac{du}{dw}$

$= \dfrac{1}{2}(3 - w)^{-1/2}(-1)$ $\dfrac{du}{dw} = -1$

$= -\dfrac{1}{2(3 - w)^{1/2}}$ or $-\dfrac{1}{2\sqrt{3 - w}}$

Matched Problem 3 Find the indicated derivatives:

(A) $h'(x)$ if $h(x) = (5x + 2)^3$ (B) y' if $y = (x^4 - 5)^5$

(C) $\dfrac{d}{dt}\dfrac{1}{(t^2 + 4)^2}$ (D) $\dfrac{dg}{dw}$ if $g(w) = \sqrt{4 - w}$

Notice that we used two steps to differentiate each function in Example 3. First, we applied the general power rule, and then we found du/dx. As you gain experience with the general power rule, you may want to combine these two steps. If you do this, be certain to multiply by du/dx. For example,

$\dfrac{d}{dx}(x^5 + 1)^4 = 4(x^5 + 1)^3 5x^4$ Correct

$\dfrac{d}{dx}(x^5 + 1)^4 \neq 4(x^5 + 1)^3$ $du/dx = 5x^4$ is missing

CONCEPTUAL INSIGHT

If we let $u(x) = x$, then $du/dx = 1$, and the general power rule reduces to the (ordinary) power rule discussed in Section 10-5. Compare the following:

$$\frac{d}{dx}x^n = nx^{n-1} \qquad \text{Yes—power rule}$$

$$\frac{d}{dx}u^n = nu^{n-1}\frac{du}{dx} \qquad \text{Yes—general power rule}$$

$$\frac{d}{dx}u^n \neq nu^{n-1} \qquad \text{Unless } u(x) = x + k, \text{ so that } du/dx = 1$$

The Chain Rule

We have used the general power rule to find derivatives of composite functions of the form $f(g(x))$, where $f(u) = u^n$ is a power function. But what if f is not a power function? Then a more general rule, the *chain rule,* enables us to compute the derivatives of many composite functions of the form $f(g(x))$.

Suppose that

$$y = m(x) = f[g(x)]$$

is a composite of f and g, where

$$y = f(u) \qquad \text{and} \qquad u = g(x)$$

To express the derivative dy/dx in terms of the derivatives of f and g, we use the definition of a derivative (see Section 10-4).

$$\frac{dy}{dx} = \lim_{h \to 0} \frac{m(x + h) - m(x)}{h} \qquad \begin{array}{l}\text{Substitute } m(x + h) = f[g(x + h)] \\ \text{and } m(x) = f[g(x)].\end{array}$$

$$= \lim_{h \to 0} \frac{f[g(x + h)] - f[g(x)]}{h} \qquad \text{Multiply by } 1 = \frac{g(x + h) - g(x)}{g(x + h) - g(x)}.$$

$$= \lim_{h \to 0} \left[\frac{f[g(x + h)] - f[g(x)]}{h} \cdot \frac{g(x + h) - g(x)}{g(x + h) - g(x)} \right]$$

$$= \lim_{h \to 0} \left[\frac{f[g(x + h)] - f[g(x)]}{g(x + h) - g(x)} \cdot \frac{g(x + h) - g(x)}{h} \right] \qquad (4)$$

We recognize the second factor in equation (4) as the difference quotient for $g(x)$. To interpret the first factor as the difference quotient for $f(u)$, we let $k = g(x + h) - g(x)$. Since $u = g(x)$, we write

$$u + k = g(x) + g(x + h) - g(x) = g(x + h)$$

Substituting in equation (1), we have

$$\frac{dy}{dx} = \lim_{h \to 0} \left[\frac{f(u + k) - f(u)}{k} \cdot \frac{g(x + h) - g(x)}{h} \right] \qquad (5)$$

If we assume that $k = [g(x + h) - g(x)] \to 0$ as $h \to 0$, we can find the limit of each difference quotient in equation (5):

$$\frac{dy}{dx} = \left[\lim_{k \to 0} \frac{f(u + k) - f(u)}{k} \right] \left[\lim_{h \to 0} \frac{g(x + h) - g(x)}{h} \right]$$

$$= f'(u)g'(x)$$

$$= \frac{dy}{du}\frac{du}{dx}$$

This result is correct under general conditions and is called the *chain rule,* but our "derivation" is superficial because it ignores some hidden problems. Since a formal proof of the chain rule is beyond the scope of this book, we simply state it as follows:

THEOREM 2   Chain Rule

If $y = f(u)$ and $u = g(x)$ define the composite function

$$y = m(x) = f[g(x)]$$

then

$$\frac{dy}{dx} = \frac{dy}{du}\frac{du}{dx} \qquad \text{provided that } \frac{dy}{du} \text{ and } \frac{du}{dx} \text{ exist}$$

or, equivalently,

$$m'(x) = f'[g(x)]g'(x) \qquad \text{provided that } f'[g(x)] \text{ and } g'(x) \text{ exist}$$

EXAMPLE 4   **Using the Chain Rule** Find dy/du, du/dx, and dy/dx (express dy/dx as a function of x) for

(A) $y = u^{3/2}$ and $u = 3x^2 + 1$
(B) $y = e^u$ and $u = 2x^3 + 5$
(C) $y = \ln u$ and $u = x^2 - 4x + 2$

SOLUTION   (A) $\dfrac{dy}{du} = \dfrac{3}{2}u^{1/2}$ and $\dfrac{du}{dx} = 6x$ *Basic derivative rules*

$$\frac{dy}{dx} = \frac{dy}{du}\frac{du}{dx} \qquad\qquad\qquad \textit{Chain rule}$$

$$= \frac{3}{2}u^{1/2}(6x) = 9x(3x^2 + 1)^{1/2} \quad \textit{Since } u = 3x^2 + 1$$

(B) $\dfrac{dy}{du} = e^u$ and $\dfrac{du}{dx} = 6x^2$ *Basic derivative rules*

$$\frac{dy}{dx} = \frac{dy}{du}\frac{du}{dx} \qquad\qquad\qquad \textit{Chain rule}$$

$$= e^u(6x^2) = 6x^2 e^{2x^3 + 5} \qquad \textit{Since } u = 2x^3 + 5$$

(C) $\dfrac{dy}{du} = \dfrac{1}{u}$ and $\dfrac{du}{dx} = 2x - 4$ *Basic derivative rules*

$$\frac{dy}{dx} = \frac{dy}{du}\frac{du}{dx} \qquad\qquad\qquad \textit{Chain rule}$$

$$= \frac{1}{u}(2x - 4) = \frac{2x - 4}{x^2 - 4x + 2} \quad \textit{Since } u = x^2 - 4x + 2$$

Matched Problem 4   Find dy/du, du/dx, and dy/dx (express dy/dx as a function of x) for
(A) $y = u^{-5}$ and $u = 2x^3 + 4$
(B) $y = e^u$ and $u = 3x^4 + 6$
(C) $y = \ln u$ and $u = x^2 + 9x + 4$

EXPLORE & DISCUSS 2

Let $m(x) = f[g(x)]$. Use the chain rule and Figures 1 and 2 to find

(A) $f(4)$ (B) $g(6)$ (C) $m(6)$

(D) $f'(4)$ (E) $g'(6)$ (F) $m'(6)$

Figure 1

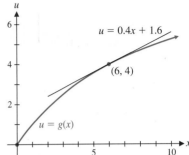

Figure 2

The chain rule can be extended to compositions of three or more functions. For example, if $y = f(w)$, $w = g(u)$, and $u = h(x)$, then

$$\frac{dy}{dx} = \frac{dy}{dw} \frac{dw}{du} \frac{du}{dx}$$

EXAMPLE 5   **Using the Chain Rule**   For $y = h(x) = e^{1+(\ln x)^2}$, find dy/dx.

SOLUTION   Note that h is of the form $y = e^w$, where $w = 1 + u^2$ and $u = \ln x$.

$$\frac{dy}{dx} = \frac{dy}{dw} \frac{dw}{du} \frac{du}{dx}$$

$$= e^w (2u) \left(\frac{1}{x}\right)$$

$$= e^{1+u^2} (2u) \left(\frac{1}{x}\right) \qquad \text{Since } w = 1 + u^2$$

$$= e^{1+(\ln x)^2} (2 \ln x) \left(\frac{1}{x}\right) \qquad \text{Since } u = \ln x$$

$$= \frac{2}{x} (\ln x) e^{1+(\ln x)^2}$$

Matched Problem 5   For $y = h(x) = [\ln(1 + e^x)]^3$, find dy/dx.

The chain rule generalizes basic derivative rules. We list three general derivative rules here for convenient reference [the first, equation (6), is the general power rule of Theorem 1].

General Derivative Rules

$$\frac{d}{dx}[f(x)]^n = n[f(x)]^{n-1} f'(x) \qquad (6)$$

$$\frac{d}{dx} \ln[f(x)] = \frac{1}{f(x)} f'(x) \qquad (7)$$

$$\frac{d}{dx} e^{f(x)} = e^{f(x)} f'(x) \qquad (8)$$

Unless directed otherwise, you now have a choice between the chain rule and the general derivative rules. However, practicing with the chain rule will help prepare you for concepts that appear later in the text. Examples 4 and 5 illustrate the chain rule method, and the next example illustrates the general derivative rules method.

EXAMPLE 6 **Using General Derivative Rules**

(A) $\dfrac{d}{dx}e^{2x} = e^{2x}\dfrac{d}{dx}2x$ *Using equation (5)*

$\qquad\qquad = e^{2x}(2) = 2e^{2x}$

(B) $\dfrac{d}{dx}\ln(x^2 + 9) = \dfrac{1}{x^2 + 9}\dfrac{d}{dx}(x^2 + 9)$ *Using equation (4)*

$\qquad\qquad\qquad = \dfrac{1}{x^2 + 9}2x = \dfrac{2x}{x^2 + 9}$

(C) $\dfrac{d}{dx}(1 + e^{x^2})^3 = 3(1 + e^{x^2})^2\dfrac{d}{dx}(1 + e^{x^2})$ *Using equation (3)*

$\qquad\qquad\qquad = 3(1 + e^{x^2})^2 e^{x^2}\dfrac{d}{dx}x^2$ *Using equation (5)*

$\qquad\qquad\qquad = 3(1 + e^{x^2})^2 e^{x^2}(2x)$

$\qquad\qquad\qquad = 6xe^{x^2}(1 + e^{x^2})^2$

Matched Problem 6 Find

(A) $\dfrac{d}{dx}\ln(x^3 + 2x)$ (B) $\dfrac{d}{dx}e^{3x^2+2}$ (C) $\dfrac{d}{dx}(2 + e^{-x^2})^4$

Exercises 11-4

For many of the problems in this exercise set, the answers in the back of the book include both an unsimplified form and a simplified form. When checking your work, first check that you applied the rules correctly, and then check that you performed the algebraic simplification correctly.

A

In Problems 1–4, find f[g(x)].

1. $f(u) = u^3$; $g(x) = 3x^2 + 2$

2. $f(u) = u^4$; $g(x) = 1 - 4x^3$

3. $f(u) = e^u$; $g(x) = -x^2$

4. $g(u) = e^u$; $g(x) = 3x^3$

In Problems 5–8, write each composite function in the form y = f(u) and u = g(x).

5. $y = (3x^2 - x + 5)^4$

6. $y = (2x^3 + x + 3)^5$

7. $y = e^{1+x+x^2}$

8. $y = e^{x^4+2x^2+5}$

In Problems 9–16, replace ? with an expression that will make the indicated equation valid.

9. $\dfrac{d}{dx}(3x + 4)^4 = 4(3x + 4)^3\underline{\ ?\ }$

10. $\dfrac{d}{dx}(5 - 2x)^6 = 6(5 - 2x)^5\underline{\ ?\ }$

11. $\dfrac{d}{dx}(4 - 2x^2)^3 = 3(4 - 2x^2)^2\underline{\ ?\ }$

12. $\dfrac{d}{dx}(3x^2 + 7)^5 = 5(3x^2 + 7)^4\underline{\ ?\ }$

13. $\dfrac{d}{dx}e^{x^2+1} = e^{x^2+1}\underline{\ ?\ }$

14. $\dfrac{d}{dx}e^{4x-2} = e^{4x-2}\underline{\ ?\ }$

15. $\dfrac{d}{dx}\ln(x^4 + 1) = \dfrac{1}{x^4 + 1}\underline{\ ?\ }$

16. $\dfrac{d}{dx}\ln(x - x^3) = \dfrac{1}{x - x^3}\underline{\ ?\ }$

In Problems 17–42, find f'(x) and simplify.

17. $f(x) = (x + 3)^2$

18. $f(x) = (x - 6)^3$

19. $f(x) = (2x + 5)^3$

20. $f(x) = (3x - 7)^5$

21. $f(x) = (5 - 2x)^4$

22. $f(x) = (9 - 5x)^2$

23. $f(x) = (4 + 0.2x)^5$

24. $f(x) = (6 - 0.5x)^4$

25. $f(x) = (3x^2 + 5)^5$

26. $f(x) = (5x^2 - 3)^6$

27. $f(x) = 5e^x$

28. $f(x) = 10 - 4e^x$

29. $f(x) = e^{5x}$

30. $f(x) = 6e^{-2x}$

31. $f(x) = 3e^{-6x}$

32. $f(x) = e^{x^2 + 3x + 1}$

33. $f(x) = (2x - 5)^{1/2}$

34. $f(x) = (4x + 3)^{1/2}$

35. $f(x) = (x^4 + 1)^{-2}$

36. $f(x) = (x^5 + 2)^{-3}$

37. $f(x) = 4 - 2 \ln x$

38. $f(x) = 8 \ln x$

39. $f(x) = 3 \ln(1 + x^2)$

40. $f(x) = 2 \ln(x^2 - 3x + 4)$

41. $f(x) = (1 + \ln x)^3$

42. $f(x) = (x - 2 \ln x)^4$

In Problems 43–48, find f'(x) and the equation of the line tangent to the graph of f at the indicated value of x. Find the value(s) of x where the tangent line is horizontal.

43. $f(x) = (2x - 1)^3$; $x = 1$

44. $f(x) = (3x - 1)^4$; $x = 1$

45. $f(x) = (4x - 3)^{1/2}$; $x = 3$

46. $f(x) = (2x + 8)^{1/2}$; $x = 4$

47. $f(x) = 5e^{x^2 - 4x + 1}$; $x = 0$

48. $f(x) = \ln(1 - x^2 + 2x^4)$; $x = 1$

B

In Problems 49–64, find the indicated derivative and simplify.

49. y' if $y = 3(x^2 - 2)^4$

50. y' if $y = 2(x^3 + 6)^5$

51. $\dfrac{d}{dt} 2(t^2 + 3t)^{-3}$

52. $\dfrac{d}{dt} 3(t^3 + t^2)^{-2}$

53. $\dfrac{dh}{dw}$ if $h(w) = \sqrt{w^2 + 8}$

54. $\dfrac{dg}{dw}$ if $g(w) = \sqrt[3]{3w - 7}$

55. $g'(x)$ if $g(x) = 4xe^{3x}$

56. $h'(x)$ if $h(x) = \dfrac{e^{2x}}{x^2 + 9}$

57. $\dfrac{d}{dx} \dfrac{\ln(1 + x)}{x^3}$

58. $\dfrac{d}{dx} [x^4 \ln(1 + x^4)]$

59. $F'(t)$ if $F(t) = (e^{t^2 + 1})^3$

60. $G'(t)$ if $G(t) = (1 - e^{2t})^2$

61. y' if $y = \ln(x^2 + 3)^{3/2}$

62. y' if $y = [\ln(x^2 + 3)]^{3/2}$

63. $\dfrac{d}{dw} \dfrac{1}{(w^3 + 4)^5}$

64. $\dfrac{d}{dw} \dfrac{1}{(w^2 - 2)^6}$

In Problems 65–70, find f'(x) and find the equation of the line tangent to the graph of f at the indicated value of x.

65. $f(x) = x(4 - x)^3$; $x = 2$

66. $f(x) = x^2(1 - x)^4$; $x = 2$

67. $f(x) = \dfrac{x}{(2x - 5)^3}$; $x = 3$

68. $f(x) = \dfrac{x^4}{(3x - 8)^2}$; $x = 4$

69. $f(x) = \sqrt{\ln x}$; $x = e$

70. $f(x) = e\sqrt{x}$; $x = 1$

In Problems 71–76, find f'(x) and find the value(s) of x where the tangent line is horizontal.

71. $f(x) = x^2(x - 5)^3$

72. $f(x) = x^3(x - 7)^4$

73. $f(x) = \dfrac{x}{(2x + 5)^2}$

74. $f(x) = \dfrac{x - 1}{(x - 3)^3}$

75. $f(x) = \sqrt{x^2 - 8x + 20}$

76. $f(x) = \sqrt{x^2 + 4x + 5}$

77. A student reasons that the functions $f(x) = \ln[5(x^2 + 3)^4]$ and $g(x) = 4 \ln(x^2 + 3)$ must have the same derivative since he has entered $f(x)$, $g(x)$, $f'(x)$, and $g'(x)$ into a graphing calculator, but only three graphs appear (see the figure). Is his reasoning correct? Are $f'(x)$ and $g'(x)$ the same function? Explain.

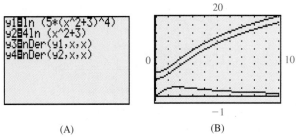

(A)   (B)

Figure for 77

78. A student reasons that the functions $f(x) = (x + 1) \ln(x + 1) - x$ and $g(x) = (x + 1)^{1/3}$ must have the same derivative since she has entered $f(x)$, $g(x)$, $f'(x)$, and $g'(x)$ into a graphing calculator, but only three graphs appear (see the figure). Is her reasoning correct? Are $f'(x)$ and $g'(x)$ the same function? Explain.

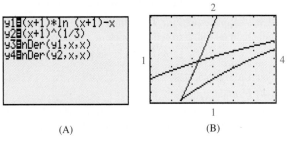

(A)   (B)

Figure for 78

C

In Problems 79–90, find each derivative and simplify.

79. $\dfrac{d}{dx}[3x(x^2 + 1)^3]$

80. $\dfrac{d}{dx}[2x^2(x^3 - 3)^4]$

81. $\dfrac{d}{dx}\dfrac{(x^3 - 7)^4}{2x^3}$

82. $\dfrac{d}{dx}\dfrac{3x^2}{(x^2 + 5)^3}$

83. $\dfrac{d}{dx}\log_2(3x^2 - 1)$

84. $\dfrac{d}{dx}\log(x^3 - 1)$

85. $\dfrac{d}{dx}10^{x^2+x}$

86. $\dfrac{d}{dx}8^{1-2x^2}$

87. $\dfrac{d}{dx}\log_3(4x^3 + 5x + 7)$

88. $\dfrac{d}{dx}\log_5(5^{x^2-1})$

89. $\dfrac{d}{dx}2^{x^3-x^2+4x+1}$

90. $\dfrac{d}{dx}10^{\ln x}$

Applications

91. Cost function. The total cost (in hundreds of dollars) of producing x cell phones per day is

$$C(x) = 10 + \sqrt{2x + 16} \qquad 0 \le x \le 50$$

(see the figure).

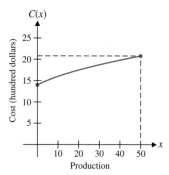

Figure for 91

(A) Find $C'(x)$.

(B) Find $C'(24)$ and $C'(42)$. Interpret the results.

92. Cost function. The total cost (in hundreds of dollars) of producing x cameras per week is

$$C(x) = 6 + \sqrt{4x + 4} \qquad 0 \le x \le 30$$

(A) Find $C'(x)$.

(B) Find $C'(15)$ and $C'(24)$. Interpret the results.

93. Price–supply equation. The number x of bicycle helmets a retail chain is willing to sell per week at a price of p is given by

$$x = 80\sqrt{p + 25} - 400 \qquad 20 \le p \le 100$$

(see the figure).

(A) Find dx/dp.

(B) Find the supply and the instantaneous rate of change of supply with respect to price when the price is $75. Write a brief interpretation of these results.

Figure for 93 and 94

94. Price–demand equation. The number x of bicycle helmets people are willing to buy per week from a retail chain at a price of p is given by

$$x = 1,000 - 60\sqrt{p + 25} \qquad 20 \le p \le 100$$

(see the figure).

(A) Find dx/dp.

(B) Find the demand and the instantaneous rate of change of demand with respect to price when the price is $75. Write a brief interpretation of these results.

95. Drug concentration. The drug concentration in the bloodstream t hours after injection is given approximately by

$$C(t) = 4.35e^{-t} \qquad 0 \le t \le 5$$

where $C(t)$ is concentration in milligrams per milliliter.

(A) What is the rate of change of concentration after 1 hour? After 4 hours?

(B) Graph C.

96. Water pollution. The use of iodine crystals is a popular way of making small quantities of water safe to drink. Crystals placed in a 1-ounce bottle of water will dissolve until the solution is saturated. After saturation, half of the solution is poured into a quart container of water, and after about an hour, the water is usually safe to drink. The half-empty 1-ounce bottle is then refilled, to be used again in the same way. Suppose that the concentration of iodine in the 1-ounce bottle t minutes after the crystals are introduced can be approximated by

$$C(t) = 250(1 - e^{-t}) \qquad t \ge 0$$

where $C(t)$ is the concentration of iodine in micrograms per milliliter.

(A) What is the rate of change of the concentration after 1 minute? After 4 minutes?

(B) Graph C for $0 \le t \le 5$.

97. Blood pressure and age. A research group using hospital records developed the following mathematical model relating systolic blood pressure and age:

$$P(x) = 40 + 25\ln(x + 1) \qquad 0 \le x \le 65$$

$P(x)$ is pressure, measured in millimeters of mercury, and x is age in years. What is the rate of change of pressure at the end of 10 years? At the end of 30 years? At the end of 60 years?

98. Biology. A yeast culture at room temperature (68°F) is placed in a refrigerator set at a constant temperature of 38°F. After t hours, the temperature T of the culture is given approximately by

$$T = 30e^{-0.58t} + 38 \qquad t \geq 0$$

What is the rate of change of temperature of the culture at the end of 1 hour? At the end of 4 hours?

99. Learning. In 1930, L. L. Thurstone developed the following formula to indicate how learning time T depends on the length of a list n:

$$T = f(n) = \frac{c}{k} n \sqrt{n - a}$$

Here, a, c, and k are empirical constants. Suppose that, for a particular person, the time T (in minutes) required to learn a list of length n is

$$T = f(n) = 2n\sqrt{n - 2}$$

(A) Find dT/dn.

✎ (B) Find $f'(11)$ and $f'(27)$. Interpret the results.

Answers to Matched Problems

1. $f[g(x)] = 2e^x, \quad g[f(u)] = e^{2u}$

2. (A) $f(u) = 50e^u, \quad u = -2x$

  (B) $f(u) = \sqrt[3]{u}, \quad u = 1 + x^3$

  [*Note:* There are other correct answers.]

3. (A) $15(5x + 2)^2$

  (B) $20x^3(x^4 - 5)^4$

  (C) $-4t/(t^2 + 4)^3$

  (D) $-1/(2\sqrt{4 - w})$

4. (A) $\dfrac{dy}{dx} = -5u^{-4}, \dfrac{du}{dx} = 6x^2, \dfrac{dy}{dx} = -30x^2(2x^3 + 4)^{-6}$

  (B) $\dfrac{dy}{du} = e^u, \dfrac{du}{dx} = 12x^3, \dfrac{dy}{dx} = 12x^3 e^{3x^4 + 6}$

  (C) $\dfrac{dy}{du} = \dfrac{1}{u}, \dfrac{du}{dx} = 2x + 9, \dfrac{dy}{dx} = \dfrac{2x + 9}{x^2 + 9x + 4}$

5. $\dfrac{3e^x[\ln(1 + e^x)]^2}{1 + e^x}$

6. (A) $\dfrac{3x^2 + 2}{x^3 + 2x}$ (B) $6xe^{3x^2 + 2}$ (C) $-8xe^{-x^2}(2 + e^{-x^2})^3$

11-5   Implicit Differentiation

- Special Function Notation
- Implicit Differentiation

Special Function Notation

The equation

$$y = 2 - 3x^2 \tag{1}$$

defines a function f with y as a dependent variable and x as an independent variable. Using function notation, we would write

$$y = f(x) \qquad \text{or} \qquad f(x) = 2 - 3x^2$$

In order to minimize the number of symbols, we will often write equation (1) in the form

$$y = 2 - 3x^2 = y(x)$$

where y is *both* a dependent variable and a function symbol. This is a convenient notation, and no harm is done as long as one is aware of the double role of y. Other examples are

$$x = 2t^2 - 3t + 1 = x(t)$$

$$z = \sqrt{u^2 - 3u} = z(u)$$

$$r = \frac{1}{(s^2 - 3s)^{2/3}} = r(s)$$

Until now, we have considered functions involving only one independent variable. There is no reason to stop there: The concept can be generalized to functions involving two or more independent variables, and this will be done in detail in

Chapter 15. For now, we will "borrow" the notation for a function involving two independent variables. For example,

$$F(x, y) = x^2 - 2xy + 3y^2 - 5$$

specifies a function F involving two independent variables.

Implicit Differentiation

Consider the equation

$$3x^2 + y - 2 = 0 \tag{2}$$

and the equation obtained by solving equation (2) for y in terms of x,

$$y = 2 - 3x^2 \tag{3}$$

Both equations define the same function with x as the independent variable and y as the dependent variable. For equation (3), we write

$$y = f(x)$$

where

$$f(x) = 2 - 3x^2 \tag{4}$$

and we have an **explicit** (directly stated) rule that enables us to determine y for each value of x. On the other hand, the y in equation (2) is the same y as in equation (3), and equation (2) **implicitly** gives (implies, though does not directly express) y as a function of x. We say that equations (3) and (4) define the function f explicitly and equation (2) defines f implicitly.

The direct use of an equation that defines a function implicitly to find the derivative of the dependent variable with respect to the independent variable is called **implicit differentiation**. Let's differentiate equation (2) implicitly and equation (3) directly, and compare results.

Starting with

$$3x^2 + y - 2 = 0$$

we think of y as a function of x and write

$$3x^2 + y(x) - 2 = 0$$

Then we differentiate both sides with respect to x:

$$\frac{d}{dx}[(3x^2 + y(x) - 2)] = \frac{d}{dx}0$$

$$\frac{d}{dx}3x^2 + \frac{d}{dx}y(x) - \frac{d}{dx}2 = 0$$

$$6x + y' - 0 = 0$$

Since y is a function of x, but is not explicitly given, we simply write $\frac{d}{dx}y(x) = y'$ to indicate its derivative.

Now we solve for y':

$$y' = -6x$$

Note that we get the same result if we start with equation (3) and differentiate directly:

$$y = 2 - 3x^2$$
$$y' = -6x$$

Why are we interested in implicit differentiation? Why not solve for y in terms of x and differentiate directly? The answer is that there are many equations of the form

$$F(x, y) = 0 \tag{5}$$

that are either difficult or impossible to solve for y explicitly in terms of x (try it for $x^2y^5 - 3xy + 5 = 0$ or for $e^y - y = 3x$, for example). But it can be shown that, under fairly general conditions on F, equation (5) will define one or more functions in which y is a dependent variable and x is an independent variable. To find y' under these conditions, we differentiate equation (5) implicitly.

EXPLORE & DISCUSS 1

(A) How many tangent lines are there to the graph in Figure 1 when $x = 0$? When $x = 1$? When $x = 2$? When $x = 4$? When $x = 6$?

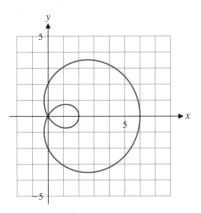

Figure 1

(B) Sketch the tangent lines referred to in part (A), and estimate each of their slopes.

(C) Explain why the graph in Figure 1 is not the graph of a function.

EXAMPLE 1   **Differentiating Implicitly** Given

$$F(x, y) = x^2 + y^2 - 25 = 0 \qquad (6)$$

find y' and the slope of the graph at $x = 3$.

SOLUTION   We start with the graph of $x^2 + y^2 - 25 = 0$ (a circle, as shown in Fig. 2) so that we can interpret our results geometrically. From the graph, it is clear that equation (6) does not define a function. But with a suitable restriction on the variables, equation (6) can define two or more functions. For example, the upper half and the lower half of the circle each define a function. On each half-circle, a point that corresponds to $x = 3$ is found by substituting $x = 3$ into equation (6) and solving for y:

$$x^2 + y^2 - 25 = 0$$
$$(3)^2 + y^2 = 25$$
$$y^2 = 16$$
$$y = \pm 4$$

The point $(3, 4)$ is on the upper half-circle, and the point $(3, -4)$ is on the lower half-circle. We will use these results in a moment. We now differentiate equation (6) implicitly, treating y as a function of x [i.e., $y = y(x)$]:

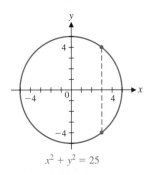

$$x^2 + y^2 = 25$$

Figure 2

$$x^2 + y^2 - 25 = 0$$

$$x^2 + [y(x)]^2 - 25 = 0$$

$$\frac{d}{dx}\{x^2 + [y(x)]^2 - 25\} = \frac{d}{dx}0$$

$$\frac{d}{dx}x^2 + \frac{d}{dx}[y(x)]^2 - \frac{d}{dx}25 = 0 \qquad \text{Use the chain rule.}$$

$$2x + 2[y(x)]^{2-1}y'(x) - 0 = 0$$

$$2x + 2yy' = 0 \qquad \text{Solve for } y' \text{ in terms of x and y.}$$

$$y' = -\frac{2x}{2y}$$

$$y' = -\frac{x}{y} \qquad \text{Leave the answer in terms of x and y.}$$

We have found y' without first solving $x^2 + y^2 - 25 = 0$ for y in terms of x. And by leaving y' in terms of x and y, we can use $y' = -x/y$ to find y' for *any* point on the graph of $x^2 + y^2 - 25 = 0$ (except where $y = 0$). In particular, for $x = 3$, we found that $(3, 4)$ and $(3, -4)$ are on the graph. The slope of the graph at $(3, 4)$ is

$$y'\big|_{(3,4)} = -\tfrac{3}{4} \qquad \text{The slope of the graph at } (3, 4)$$

and the slope at $(3, -4)$ is

$$y'\big|_{(3,-4)} = -\tfrac{3}{-4} = \tfrac{3}{4} \qquad \text{The slope of the graph at } (3, -4)$$

The symbol

$$y'\big|_{(a,b)}$$

is used to indicate that we are evaluating y' at $x = a$ and $y = b$.

The results are interpreted geometrically in Figure 3 on the original graph.

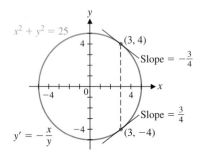

Figure 3

Matched Problem 1 Graph $x^2 + y^2 - 169 = 0$, find y' by implicit differentiation, and find the slope of the graph when $x = 5$.

CONCEPTUAL INSIGHT

When differentiating implicitly, the derivative of y^2 is $2yy'$, not just $2y$. This is because y represents a function of x, so the chain rule applies. Suppose, for example, that y represents the function $y = 5x + 4$. Then

$$(y^2)' = [(5x + 4)^2]' = 2(5x + 4) \cdot 5 = 2yy'$$

So, when differenting implicitly, the derivative of y is y', the derivative of y^2 is $2yy'$, the derivative of y^3 is $3y^2y'$, and so on.

EXAMPLE 2 **Differentiating Implicitly** Find the equation(s) of the tangent line(s) to the graph of

$$y - xy^2 + x^2 + 1 = 0 \qquad (7)$$

at the point(s) where $x = 1$.

SOLUTION   We first find y when $x = 1$:

$$y - xy^2 + x^2 + 1 = 0$$
$$y - (1)y^2 + (1)^2 + 1 = 0$$
$$y - y^2 + 2 = 0$$
$$y^2 - y - 2 = 0$$
$$(y - 2)(y + 1) = 0$$
$$y = -1, 2$$

So there are two points on the graph of (7) where $x = 1$, namely, $(1, -1)$and $(1, 2)$. We next find the slope of the graph at these two points by differentiating equation (7) implicitly:

$$y - xy^2 + x^2 + 1 = 0$$

Use the product rule and the

$$\frac{d}{dx}y - \frac{d}{dx}xy^2 + \frac{d}{dx}x^2 + \frac{d}{dx}1 = \frac{d}{dx}0$$

chain rule for $\dfrac{d}{dx}xy^2$.

$$y' - (x \cdot 2yy' + y^2) + 2x = 0$$

$$y' - 2xyy' - y^2 + 2x = 0$$

Solve for y' by getting all
terms involving y' on one side.

$$y' - 2xyy' = y^2 - 2x$$

$$(1 - 2xy)y' = y^2 - 2x$$

$$y' = \frac{y^2 - 2x}{1 - 2xy}$$

Now find the slope at each point:

$$y'|_{(1,-1)} = \frac{(-1)^2 - 2(1)}{1 - 2(1)(-1)} = \frac{1 - 2}{1 + 2} = \frac{-1}{3} = -\frac{1}{3}$$

$$y'|_{(1,2)} = \frac{(2)^2 - 2(1)}{1 - 2(1)(2)} = \frac{4 - 2}{1 - 4} = \frac{2}{-3} = -\frac{2}{3}$$

Equation of tangent line at $(1, -1)$:   Equation of tangent line at $(1, 2)$:

$$y - y_1 = m(x - x_1)$$
$$y + 1 = -\tfrac{1}{3}(x - 1)$$
$$y + 1 = -\tfrac{1}{3}x + \tfrac{1}{3}$$
$$y = -\tfrac{1}{3}x - \tfrac{2}{3}$$

$$y - y_1 = m(x - x_1)$$
$$y - 2 = -\tfrac{2}{3}(x - 1)$$
$$y - 2 = -\tfrac{2}{3}x + \tfrac{2}{3}$$
$$y = -\tfrac{2}{3}x + \tfrac{8}{3}$$

Matched Problem 2   Repeat Example 2 for $x^2 + y^2 - xy - 7 = 0$ at $x = 1$.

EXAMPLE 3   **Differentiating Implicitly** Find x' for $x = x(t)$ defined implicitly by

$$t \ln x = xe^t - 1$$

and evaluate x' at $(t, x) = (0, 1)$.

SOLUTION   It is important to remember that x is the dependent variable and t is the independent variable. Therefore, we differentiate both sides of the equation with respect to t (using product and chain rules where appropriate) and then solve for x':

$$t \ln x = xe^t - 1 \qquad \text{Differentiate implicitly with respect to } t.$$

$$\frac{d}{dt}(t \ln x) = \frac{d}{dt}(xe^t) - \frac{d}{dt}1$$

$$t\frac{x'}{x} + \ln x = xe^t + x'e^t \qquad \text{Clear fractions.}$$

$$\boxed{x \cdot t\frac{x'}{x} + x \cdot \ln x = x \cdot xe^t + x \cdot e^t x'} \qquad x \neq 0$$

$$tx' + x \ln x = x^2e^t + xe^t x' \qquad \text{Solve for } x'.$$

$$tx' - xe'x' = x^2e^t - x \ln x \qquad \text{Factor out } x'.$$

$$(t - xe^t)x' = x^2e^t - x \ln x$$

$$x' = \frac{x^2e^t - x \ln x}{t - xe^t}$$

Now we evaluate x' at $(t, x) = (0, 1)$, as requested:

$$x'|_{(0,1)} = \frac{(1)^2e^0 - 1 \ln 1}{0 - 1e^0}$$

$$= \frac{1}{-1} = -1$$

Matched Problem 3 Find x' for $x = x(t)$ defined implicitly by

$$1 + x \ln t = te^x$$

and evaluate x' at $(t, x) = (1, 0)$.

Exercises 11-5

A

In Problems 1–4, find y' in two ways:

(A) *Differentiate the given equation implicitly and then solve for y'.*

(B) *Solve the given equation for y and then differentiate directly.*

1. $3x + 5y + 9 = 0$

2. $-2x + 6y - 4 = 0$

3. $3x^2 - 4y - 18 = 0$

4. $2x^3 + 5y - 2 = 0$

In Problems 5–22, use implicit differentiation to find y' and evaluate y' at the indicated point.

5. $y - 5x^2 + 3 = 0; (1, 2)$

6. $5x^3 - y - 1 = 0; (1, 4)$

7. $x^2 - y^3 - 3 = 0; (2, 1)$

8. $y^2 + x^3 + 4 = 0; (-2, 2)$

9. $y^2 + 2y + 3x = 0; (-1, 1)$

10. $y^2 - y - 4x = 0; (0, 1)$

B

11. $xy - 6 = 0; (2, 3)$

12. $3xy - 2x - 2 = 0; (2, 1)$

13. $2xy + y + 2 = 0; (-1, 2)$

14. $2y + xy - 1 = 0; (-1, 1)$

15. $x^2y - 3x^2 - 4 = 0; (2, 4)$

16. $2x^3y - x^3 + 5 = 0; (-1, 3)$

17. $e^y = x^2 + y^2; (1, 0)$

18. $x^2 - y = 4e^y; (2, 0)$

19. $x^3 - y = \ln y; (1, 1)$

20. $\ln y = 2y^2 - x; (2, 1)$

21. $x \ln y + 2y = 2x^3; (1, 1)$

22. $xe^y - y = x^2 - 2; (2, 0)$

In Problems 23 and 24, find x' for $x = x(t)$ defined implicitly by the given equation. Evaluate x' at the indicated point.

23. $x^2 - t^2x + t^3 + 11 = 0; (-2, 1)$

24. $x^3 - tx^2 - 4 = 0; (-3, -2)$

Problems 25 and 26 refer to the equation and graph shown in the figure.

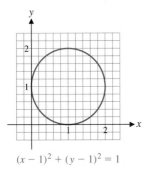

$(x - 1)^2 + (y - 1)^2 = 1$

Figure for 25 and 26

25. Use implicit differentiation to find the slopes of the tangent lines at the points on the graph where $x = 1.6$. Check your answers by visually estimating the slopes on the graph in the figure.

26. Find the slopes of the tangent lines at the points on the graph where $x = 0.2$. Check your answers by visually estimating the slopes on the graph in the figure.

In Problems 27–30, find the equation(s) of the tangent line(s) to the graphs of the indicated equations at the point(s) with the given value of x.

27. $xy - x - 4 = 0; x = 2$

28. $3x + xy + 1 = 0; x = -1$

29. $y^2 - xy - 6 = 0; x = 1$

30. $xy^2 - y - 2 = 0; x = 1$

31. If $xe^y = 1$, find y' in two ways, first by differentiating implicitly and then by solving for y explicitly in terms of x. Which method do you prefer? Explain.

32. Explain the difficulty that arises in solving $x^3 + y + xe^y = 1$ for y as an explicit function of x. Find the slope of the tangent line to the graph of the equation at the point $(0, 1)$.

C

In Problems 33–40, find y' and the slope of the tangent line to the graph of each equation at the indicated point.

33. $(1 + y)^3 + y = x + 7; (2, 1)$

34. $(y - 3)^4 - x = y; (-3, 4)$

35. $(x - 2y)^3 = 2y^2 - 3; (1, 1)$

36. $(2x - y)^4 - y^3 = 8; (-1, -2)$

37. $\sqrt{7 + y^2} - x^3 + 4 = 0; (2, 3)$

38. $6\sqrt{y^3 + 1} - 2x^{3/2} - 2 = 0; (4, 2)$

39. $\ln(xy) = y^2 - 1; (1, 1)$

40. $e^{xy} - 2x = y + 1; (0, 0)$

41. Find the equation(s) of the tangent line(s) at the point(s) on the graph of the equation

$$y^3 - xy - x^3 = 2$$

where $x = 1$. Round all approximate values to two decimal places.

42. Refer to the equation in Problem 41. Find the equation(s) of the tangent line(s) at the point(s) on the graph where $y = -1$. Round all approximate values to two decimal places.

Applications

For the demand equations in Problems 43–46, find the rate of change of p with respect to x by differentiating implicitly (x is the number of items that can be sold at a price of \$p).

43. $x = p^2 - 2p + 1,000$

44. $x = p^3 - 3p^2 + 200$

45. $x = \sqrt{10,000 - p^2}$

46. $x = \sqrt[3]{1,500 - p^3}$

47. Biophysics. In biophysics, the equation

$$(L + m)(V + n) = k$$

is called the *fundamental equation of muscle contraction*, where m, n, and k are constants and V is the velocity of the shortening of muscle fibers for a muscle subjected to a load L. Find dL/dV by implicit differentiation.

48. Biophysics. In Problem 47, find dV/dL by implicit differentiation.

49. Speed of sound. The speed of sound in air is given by the formula

$$v = k\sqrt{T}$$

where v is the velocity of sound, T is the temperature of the air, and k is a constant. Use implicit differentiation to find $\dfrac{dT}{dv}$.

50. Gravity. The equation

$$F = G\frac{m_1 m_2}{r^2}$$

is Newton's law of universal gravitation. G is a constant and F is the gravitational force between two objects having masses m_1 and m_2 that are a distance r from each other. Use implicit differentiation to find $\dfrac{dr}{dF}$. Assume that m_1 and m_2 are constant.

51. Speed of sound. Refer to Problem 49. Find $\dfrac{dv}{dT}$ and discuss the connection between $\dfrac{dv}{dT}$ and $\dfrac{dT}{dv}$.

52. Gravity. Refer to Problem 50. Find $\dfrac{dF}{dr}$ and discuss the connection between $\dfrac{dF}{dr}$ and $\dfrac{dr}{dF}$.

Answers to Matched Problems

1. $y' = -x/y$. When $x = 5, y = \pm 12$; thus, $y'|_{(5,12)} = -\frac{5}{12}$ and $y'|_{(5,-12)} = \frac{5}{12}$

2. $y' = \dfrac{y - 2x}{2y - x}$; $y = \frac{4}{5}x - \frac{14}{5}, y = \frac{1}{5}x + \frac{14}{5}$

3. $x' = \dfrac{te^x - x}{t \ln t - t^2 e^x}$; $x'|_{(1,0)} = -1$

11-6   Related Rates

Union workers are concerned that the rate at which wages are increasing is lagging behind the rate of increase in the company's profits. An automobile dealer wants to predict how badly an anticipated increase in interest rates will decrease his rate of sales. An investor is studying the connection between the rate of increase in the Dow Jones average and the rate of increase in the gross domestic product over the past 50 years.

In each of these situations, there are two quantities—wages and profits, for example—that are changing with respect to time. We would like to discover the precise relationship between the rates of increase (or decrease) of the two quantities. We begin our discussion of such *related rates* by considering familiar situations in which the two quantities are distances and the two rates are velocities.

EXAMPLE 1   **Related Rates and Motion**   A 26-foot ladder is placed against a wall (Fig. 1). If the top of the ladder is sliding down the wall at 2 feet per second, at what rate is the bottom of the ladder moving away from the wall when the bottom of the ladder is 10 feet away from the wall?

SOLUTION   Many people think that since the ladder is a constant length, the bottom of the ladder will move away from the wall at the rate that the top of the ladder is moving down the wall. This is not the case, however.

At any moment in time, let x be the distance of the bottom of the ladder from the wall and let y be the distance of the top of the ladder from the ground (see Fig. 1). Both x and y are changing with respect to time and can be thought of as functions of time; that is, $x = x(t)$ and $y = y(t)$. Furthermore, x and y are related by the Pythagorean relationship:

$$x^2 + y^2 = 26^2 \tag{1}$$

Differentiating equation (1) implicitly with respect to time t and using the chain rule where appropriate, we obtain

$$2x\frac{dx}{dt} + 2y\frac{dy}{dt} = 0 \tag{2}$$

The rates dx/dt and dy/dt are related by equation (2). This is a **related-rates problem**.

Our problem is to find dx/dt when $x = 10$ feet, given that $dy/dt = -2$ (y is decreasing at a constant rate of 2 feet per second). We have all the quantities we need in equation (2) to solve for dx/dt, except y. When $x = 10$, y can be found from equation (1):

$$10^2 + y^2 = 26^2$$

$$y = \sqrt{26^2 - 10^2} = 24 \text{ feet}$$

Substitute $dy/dt = -2$, $x = 10$, and $y = 24$ into (2). Then solve for dx/dt:

$$2(10)\frac{dx}{dt} + 2(24)(-2) = 0$$

$$\frac{dx}{dt} = \frac{-2(24)(-2)}{2(10)} = 4.8 \text{ feet per second}$$

The bottom of the ladder is moving away from the wall at a rate of 4.8 feet per second.

26 ft

y

x

Figure 1

CONCEPTUAL INSIGHT

In the solution to Example 1, we used equation (1) in two ways: first, to find an equation relating dy/dt and dx/dt, and second, to find the value of y when $x = 10$. These steps must be done in this order. Substituting $x = 10$ and then differentiating does not produce any useful results:

$$x^2 + y^2 = 26^2 \quad \text{Substituting 10 for x has the effect of}$$
$$100 + y^2 = 26^2 \quad \text{stopping the ladder.}$$
$$0 + 2yy' = 0 \quad \text{The rate of change of a stationary}$$
$$y' = 0 \quad \begin{array}{l}\text{object is always O, but that is not the}\\ \text{rate of change of the moving ladder.}\end{array}$$

Matched Problem 1 Again, a 26-foot ladder is placed against a wall (Fig. 1). If the bottom of the ladder is moving away from the wall at 3 feet per second, at what rate is the top moving down when the top of the ladder is 24 feet above ground?

EXPLORE & DISCUSS 1
(A) For which values of x and y in Example 1 is dx/dt equal to 2 (i.e., the same rate that the ladder is sliding down the wall)?

(B) When is dx/dt greater than 2? Less than 2?

DEFINITION Suggestions for Solving Related-Rates Problems

Step 1 Sketch a figure if helpful.

Step 2 Identify all relevant variables, including those whose rates are given and those whose rates are to be found.

Step 3 Express all given rates and rates to be found as derivatives.

Step 4 Find an equation connecting the variables identified in step 2.

Step 5 Implicitly differentiate the equation found in step 4, using the chain rule where appropriate, and substitute in all given values.

Step 6 Solve for the derivative that will give the unknown rate.

EXAMPLE 2 **Related Rates and Motion** Suppose that two motorboats leave from the same point at the same time. If one travels north at 15 miles per hour and the other travels east at 20 miles per hour, how fast will the distance between them be changing after 2 hours?

SOLUTION First, draw a picture, as shown in Figure 2.

All variables, x, y, and z, are changing with time. They can be considered as functions of time: $x = x(t)$, $y = y(t)$, and $z = z(t)$, given implicitly. It now makes sense to take derivatives of each variable with respect to time. From the Pythagorean theorem,

$$z^2 = x^2 + y^2 \qquad (3)$$

We also know that

$$\frac{dx}{dt} = 20 \text{ miles per hour} \qquad \text{and} \qquad \frac{dy}{dt} = 15 \text{ miles per hour}$$

Figure 2

We want to find dz/dt at the end of 2 hours—that is, when $x = 40$ miles and $y = 30$ miles. To do this, we differentiate both sides of equation (3) with respect to t and solve for dz/dt:

$$2z\frac{dz}{dt} = 2x\frac{dx}{dt} + 2y\frac{dy}{dt} \qquad (4)$$

We have everything we need except z. From equation (3), when $x = 40$ and $y = 30$, we find z to be 50. Substituting the known quantities into equation (4), we obtain

$$2(50)\frac{dz}{dt} = 2(40)(20) + 2(30)(15)$$

$$\frac{dz}{dt} = 25 \text{ miles per hour}$$

The boats will be separating at a rate of 25 miles per hour.

Matched Problem 2   Repeat Example 2 for the same situation at the end of 3 hours.

EXAMPLE 3   **Related Rates and Motion** Suppose that a point is moving along the graph of $x^2 + y^2 = 25$ (Fig. 3). When the point is at $(-3, 4)$, its x coordinate is increasing at the rate of 0.4 unit per second. How fast is the y coordinate changing at that moment?

SOLUTION   Since both x and y are changing with respect to time, we can consider each as a function of time, namely,

$$x = x(t) \qquad \text{and} \qquad y = y(t)$$

but restricted so that

$$x^2 + y^2 = 25 \qquad (5)$$

We want to find dy/dt, given $x = -3$, $y = 4$, and $dx/dt = 0.4$. Implicitly differentiating both sides of equation (5) with respect to t, we have

$$x^2 + y^2 = 25$$

$$2x\frac{dx}{dt} + 2y\frac{dy}{dt} = 0 \qquad \text{Divide both sides by 2.}$$

$$x\frac{dx}{dt} + y\frac{dy}{dt} = 0 \qquad \text{Substitute } x = -3, y = 4, \text{ and } dx/dt = 0.4, \text{ and solve for } dy/dt.$$

$$(-3)(0.4) + 4\frac{dy}{dt} = 0$$

$$\frac{dy}{dt} = 0.3 \text{ unit per second}$$

$x^2 + y^2 = 25$

Figure 3

Matched Problem 3   A point is moving on the graph of $y^3 = x^2$. When the point is at $(-8, 4)$, its y coordinate is decreasing by 2 units per second. How fast is the x coordinate changing at that moment?

EXAMPLE 4   **Related Rates and Business** Suppose that for a company manufacturing flash drives, the cost, revenue, and profit equations are given by

$$C = 5,000 + 2x \qquad \text{Cost equation}$$

$$R = 10x - 0.001x^2 \qquad \text{Revenue equation}$$

$$P = R - C \qquad \text{Profit equation}$$

where the production output in 1 week is x flash drives. If production is increasing at the rate of 500 flash drives per week when production is 2,000 flash drives, find the rate of increase in

(A) Cost   (B) Revenue   (C) Profit

SOLUTION If production x is a function of time (it must be, since it is changing with respect to time), then C, R, and P must also be functions of time. These functions are given implicitly (rather than explicitly). Letting t represent time in weeks, we differentiate both sides of each of the preceding three equations with respect to t and then substitute $x = 2,000$ and $dx/dt = 500$ to find the desired rates.

(A) $C = 5,000 + 2x$ Think: $C = C(t)$ and $x = x(t)$.

$$\frac{dC}{dt} = \frac{d}{dt}(5,000) + \frac{d}{dt}(2x) \quad \text{Differentiate both sides with respect to } t.$$

$$\frac{dC}{dt} = 0 + 2\frac{dx}{dt} = 2\frac{dx}{dt}$$

Since $dx/dt = 500$ when $x = 2,000$,

$$\frac{dC}{dt} = 2(500) = \$1,000 \text{ per week}$$

Cost is increasing at a rate of \$1,000 per week.

(B) $R = 10x - 0.001x^2$

$$\frac{dR}{dt} = \frac{d}{dt}(10x) - \frac{d}{dt}0.001x^2$$

$$\frac{dR}{dt} = 10\frac{dx}{dt} - 0.002x\frac{dx}{dt}$$

$$\frac{dR}{dt} = (10 - 0.002x)\frac{dx}{dt}$$

Since $dx/dt = 500$ when $x = 2,000$,

$$\frac{dR}{dt} = [10 - 0.002(2,000)](500) = \$3,000 \text{ per week}$$

Revenue is increasing at a rate of \$3,000 per week.

(C) $P = R - C$

$$\frac{dP}{dt} = \frac{dR}{dt} - \frac{dC}{dt} \qquad \text{Results from parts (A) and (B)}$$
$$= \$3,000 - \$1,000$$
$$= \$2,000 \text{ per week}$$

Profit is increasing at a rate of \$2,000 per week.

Matched Problem 4 Repeat Example 4 for a production level of 6,000 flash drives per week.

Exercises 11-6

A

In Problems 1–6, assume that $x = x(t)$ and $y = y(t)$. Find the indicated rate, given the other information.

1. $y = x^2 + 2$; $dx/dt = 3$ when $x = 5$; find dy/dt

2. $y = x^3 - 3$; $dx/dt = -2$ when $x = 2$; find dy/dt

3. $x^2 + y^2 = 1$; $dy/dt = -4$ when $x = -0.6$ and $y = 0.8$; find dx/dt

4. $x^2 + y^2 = 4$; $dy/dt = 5$ when $x = 1.2$ and $y = -1.6$; find dx/dt

5. $x^2 + 3xy + y^2 = 11$; $dx/dt = 2$ when $x = 1$ and $y = 2$; find dy/dt

6. $x^2 - 2xy - y^2 = 7$; $dy/dt = -1$ when $x = 2$ and $y = -1$; find dx/dt

B

7. A point is moving on the graph of $xy = 36$. When the point is at $(4, 9)$, its x coordinate is increasing by 4 units per second. How fast is the y coordinate changing at that moment?

8. A point is moving on the graph of $4x^2 + 9y^2 = 36$. When the point is at $(3, 0)$, its y coordinate is decreasing by 2 units per second. How fast is its x coordinate changing at that moment?

9. A boat is being pulled toward a dock as shown in the figure. If the rope is being pulled in at 3 feet per second, how fast is the distance between the dock and the boat decreasing when it is 30 feet from the dock?

Rope

4 ft

Figure for 9 and 10

10. Refer to Problem 9. Suppose that the distance between the boat and the dock is decreasing by 3.05 feet per second. How fast is the rope being pulled in when the boat is 10 feet from the dock?

11. A rock thrown into a still pond causes a circular ripple. If the radius of the ripple is increasing by 2 feet per second, how fast is the area changing when the radius is 10 feet? [Use $A = \pi R^2$, $\pi \approx 3.14$.]

12. Refer to Problem 11. How fast is the circumference of a circular ripple changing when the radius is 10 feet? [Use $C = 2\pi R$, $\pi \approx 3.14$.]

13. The radius of a spherical balloon is increasing at the rate of 3 centimeters per minute. How fast is the volume changing when the radius is 10 centimeters? [Use $V = \frac{4}{3}\pi R^3$, $\pi \approx 3.14$.]

14. Refer to Problem 13. How fast is the surface area of the sphere increasing when the radius is 10 centimeters? [Use $S = 4\pi R^2$, $\pi \approx 3.14$.]

15. Boyle's law for enclosed gases states that if the volume is kept constant, the pressure P and temperature T are related by the equation

$$\frac{P}{T} = k$$

where k is a constant. If the temperature is increasing at 3 kelvins per hour, what is the rate of change of pressure when the temperature is 250 kelvins and the pressure is 500 pounds per square inch?

16. Boyle's law for enclosed gases states that if the temperature is kept constant, the pressure P and volume V of a gas are related by the equation

$$VP = k$$

where k is a constant. If the volume is decreasing by 5 cubic inches per second, what is the rate of change of pressure when the volume is 1,000 cubic inches and the pressure is 40 pounds per square inch?

17. A 10-foot ladder is placed against a vertical wall. Suppose that the bottom of the ladder slides away from the wall at a constant rate of 3 feet per second. How fast is the top of the ladder sliding down the wall (negative rate) when the bottom is 6 feet from the wall? [*Hint:* Use the Pythagorean theorem, $a^2 + b^2 = c^2$, where c is the length of the hypotenuse of a right triangle and a and b are the lengths of the two shorter sides.]

18. A weather balloon is rising vertically at the rate of 5 meters per second. An observer is standing on the ground 300 meters from where the balloon was released. At what rate is the distance between the observer and the balloon changing when the balloon is 400 meters high?

C

19. A streetlight is on top of a 20-foot pole. A person who is 5 feet tall walks away from the pole at the rate of 5 feet per second. At what rate is the tip of the person's shadow moving away from the pole when he is 20 feet from the pole?

20. Refer to Problem 19. At what rate is the person's shadow growing when he is 20 feet from the pole?

21. Helium is pumped into a spherical balloon at a constant rate of 4 cubic feet per second. How fast is the radius increasing after 1 minute? After 2 minutes? Is there any time at which the radius is increasing at a rate of 100 feet per second? Explain.

22. A point is moving along the x axis at a constant rate of 5 units per second. At which point is its distance from $(0, 1)$ increasing at a rate of 2 units per second? At 4 units per second? At 5 units per second? At 10 units per second? Explain.

23. A point is moving on the graph of $y = e^x + x + 1$ in such a way that its x coordinate is always increasing at a rate of 3 units per second. How fast is the y coordinate changing when the point crosses the x axis?

24. A point is moving on the graph of $x^3 + y^2 = 1$ in such a way that its y coordinate is always increasing at a rate of 2 units per second. At which point(s) is the x coordinate increasing at a rate of 1 unit per second?

Applications

25. Cost, revenue, and profit rates. Suppose that for a company manufacturing calculators, the cost, revenue, and profit equations are given by

$$C = 90,000 + 30x \qquad R = 300x - \frac{x^2}{30}$$

$$P = R - C$$

where the production output in 1 week is x calculators. If production is increasing at a rate of 500 calculators per week when production output is 6,000 calculators, find the rate of increase (decrease) in

(A) Cost (B) Revenue (C) Profit

26. Cost, revenue, and profit rates. Repeat Problem 25 for

$$C = 72,000 + 60x \qquad R = 200x - \frac{x^2}{30}$$

$$P = R - C$$

where production is increasing at a rate of 500 calculators per week at a production level of 1,500 calculators.

27. Advertising. A retail store estimates that weekly sales s and weekly advertising costs x (both in dollars) are related by

$$s = 60,000 - 40,000e^{-0.0005x}$$

The current weekly advertising costs are $2,000, and these costs are increasing at the rate of $300 per week. Find the current rate of change of sales.

28. Advertising. Repeat Problem 27 for

$$s = 50,000 - 20,000e^{-0.0004x}$$

29. Price–demand. The price p (in dollars) and demand x for a product are related by

$$2x^2 + 5xp + 50p^2 = 80,000$$

(A) If the price is increasing at a rate of $2 per month when the price is $30, find the rate of change of the demand.

(B) If the demand is decreasing at a rate of 6 units per month when the demand is 150 units, find the rate of change of the price.

30. Price–demand. Repeat Problem 29 for

$$x^2 + 2xp + 25p^2 = 74,500$$

31. Pollution. An oil tanker aground on a reef is forming a circular oil slick about 0.1 foot thick (see the figure). To estimate the rate dV/dt (in cubic feet per minute) at which the oil is leaking from the tanker, it was found that the radius of the slick was increasing at 0.32 foot per minute ($dR/dt = 0.32$) when the radius R was 500 feet. Find dV/dt, using $\pi \approx 3.14$.

Figure for 31

32. Learning. A person who is new on an assembly line performs an operation in T minutes after x performances of the operation, as given by

$$T = 6\left(1 + \frac{1}{\sqrt{x}}\right)$$

If $dx/dt = 6$ operations per hours, where t is time in hours, find dT/dt after 36 performances of the operation.

Answers to Matched Problems

1. $dy/dt = -1.25$ ft/sec
2. $dz/dt = 25$ mi/hr
3. $dx/dt = 6$ units/sec
4. (A) $dC/dt = \$1,000/$wk
   (B) $dR/dt = -\$1,000/$wk
   (C) $dP/dt = -\$2,000/$wk

11-7 Elasticity of Demand

- Relative Rate of Change
- Elasticity of Demand

When will a price increase lead to an increase in revenue? To answer this question and study relationships among price, demand, and revenue, economists use the notion of *elasticity of demand*. In this section, we define the concepts of *relative rate of change*, *percentage rate of change*, and *elasticity of demand*.

Relative Rate of Change

EXPLORE & DISCUSS 1

A broker is trying to sell you two stocks: Biotech and Comstat. The broker estimates that Biotech's earnings will increase $2 per year over the next several years, while Comstat's earnings will increase only $1 per year. Is this sufficient information for you to choose between the two stocks? What other information might you request from the broker to help you decide?

Interpreting rates of change is a fundamental application of calculus. In Explore & Discuss 1, Biotech's earnings are increasing at twice the rate of Comstat's, but that does not automatically make Biotech the better buy. The obvious information that is missing is the cost of each stock. If Biotech costs $100 a share and Comstat costs $25 share, then which stock is the better buy? To answer this question, we introduce two new concepts: *relative rate of change* and *percentage rate of change*.

DEFINITION Relative and Percentage Rates of Change

The **relative rate of change** of a function $f(x)$ is $\dfrac{f'(x)}{f(x)}$.

The **percentage rate of change** is $100 \times \dfrac{f'(x)}{f(x)}$.

Because

$$\frac{d}{dx}\ln f(x) = \frac{f'(x)}{f(x)}$$

the relative rate of change of $f(x)$ is the derivative of the logarithm of $f(x)$. This is also referred to as the **logarithmic derivative** of $f(x)$. Returning to Explore & Discuss 1, we can now write

	Relative rate of change		Percentage rate of change
Biotech	$\dfrac{2}{100} = 0.02$	or	2%
Comstat	$\dfrac{1}{25} = 0.04$	or	4%

EXAMPLE 1 **Percentage Rate of Change** Table 1 lists the GDP (gross domestic product expressed in billions of 2005 dollars) and U.S. population from 2000 to 2008. A model for the GDP is

$$f(t) = 280t + 11{,}147$$

where t is years since 2000. Find and graph the percentage rate of change of $f(t)$ for $0 \le t \le 8$.

Table 1

Year	Real GDP (billions of 2005 dollars)	Population (in millions)
2000	$11,226	282.2
2002	$11,553	287.7
2004	$12,264	292.9
2006	$12,976	298.4
2008	$13,312	304.1

SOLUTION If $p(t)$ is the percentage rate of change of $f(t)$, then

$$p(t) = 100 \times \frac{d}{dx}\ln(280t + 11{,}147)$$

$$= \frac{28{,}000}{280t + 11{,}147}$$

The graph of $p(t)$ is shown in Figure 1 (graphing details omitted). Notice that $p(t)$ is decreasing, even though the GDP is increasing.

Figure 1

Matched Problem 1 A model for the population data in Table 1 is

$$f(t) = 2.7t + 282$$

where t is years since 2000. Find and graph $p(t)$, the percentage rate of change of $f(t)$ for $0 \le t \le 8$.

Elasticity of Demand

Economists use logarithmic derivatives and relative rates of change to study the relationship among price changes, demand, and revenue. Suppose the price $\$p$ and the demand x for a certain product are related by the price–demand equation

$$x + 500p = 10{,}000 \qquad (1)$$

In problems involving revenue, cost, and profit, it is customary to use the demand equation to express price as a function of demand. Since we want to know the effects that changes in price have on demand, it is more convenient to express demand as a function of price. Solving (1) for x, we have

$$x = 10{,}000 - 500p$$

$$= 500(20 - p) \quad \textit{Demand as a function of price}$$

or

$$x = f(p) = 500(20 - p) \qquad 0 \le p \le 20 \qquad (2)$$

Since x and p both represent nonnegative quantities, we must restrict p so that $0 \le p \le 20$. For most products, demand is assumed to be a decreasing function of price. That is, price increases result in lower demand, and price decreases result in higher demand (see Figure 2).

Figure 2

Economists use the *elasticity of demand* to study the relationship between changes in price and changes in demand. The **elasticity of demand** is the negative of the ratio of the relative rate of change of demand to the relative rate of change of price. If price and demand are related by a price–demand equation of the form $x = f(p)$, then the elasticity of demand can be expressed as

$$-\frac{\text{relative rate of change of demand}}{\text{relative rate of change of price}} = -\frac{\dfrac{d}{dp}\ln f(p)}{\dfrac{d}{dp}\ln p}$$

$$= -\frac{\dfrac{f'(p)}{f(p)}}{\dfrac{1}{p}}$$

$$= -\frac{pf'(p)}{f(p)}$$

THEOREM 1   Elasticity of Demand

If price and demand are related by $x = f(p)$, then the elasticity of demand is given by

$$E(p) = -\frac{pf'(p)}{f(p)}$$

CONCEPTUAL INSIGHT

Since p and $f(p)$ are nonnegative and $f'(p)$ is negative (remember, demand is usually a decreasing function of price), $E(p)$ is nonnegative. This is why elasticity of demand is defined as the negative of a ratio.

The next example illustrates interpretations of the elasticity of demand.

EXAMPLE 2   **Elasticity of Demand**   Find $E(p)$ for the price–demand equation

$$x = f(p) = 500(20 - p)$$

Find and interpret each of the following:

(A) $E(4)$ (B) $E(16)$ (C) $E(10)$

SOLUTION $E(p) = -\dfrac{pf'(p)}{f(p)} = -\dfrac{p(-500)}{500(20 - p)} = \dfrac{p}{20 - p}$

In order to interpret values of $E(p)$, we must recall the definition of elasticity:

$$E(p) = -\frac{\text{relative rate of change of demand}}{\text{relative rate of change of price}}$$

or

$$-\left(\begin{array}{c}\text{relative rate of}\\\text{change of demand}\end{array}\right) \approx E(p)\left(\begin{array}{c}\text{relative rate of}\\\text{change of price}\end{array}\right)$$

(A) $E(4) = \frac{4}{16} = 0.25 < 1$. If the \$4 price changes by 10%, then the demand will change by approximately $0.25(10\%) = 2.5\%$.

(B) $E(16) = \frac{16}{4} = 4 > 1$. If the \$16 price changes by 10%, then the demand will change by approximately $4(10\%) = 40\%$.

(C) $E(10) = \frac{10}{10} = 1$. If the \$10 price changes by 10%, then the demand will also change by approximately 10%.

CONCEPTUAL INSIGHT

Do not be concerned with the omission of any negative signs in these interpretations. We already know that if price increases, then demand decreases, and vice versa (Fig. 2 on page 605). $E(p)$ is a measure of *how much* the demand changes for a given change in price.

Matched Problem 2   Find $E(p)$ for the price–demand equation

$$x = f(p) = 1,000(40 - p)$$

Find and interpret each of the following:

(A) $E(8)$ (B) $E(30)$ (C) $E(20)$

The three cases illustrated in the solution to Example 2 are referred to as **inelastic demand, elastic demand**, and **unit elasticity**, as indicated in Table 2.

Table 2

E(p)	Demand	Interpretation
$0 < E(p) < 1$	Inelastic	Demand is not sensitive to changes in price. A change in price produces a smaller change in demand.
$E(p) > 1$	Elastic	Demand is sensitive to changes in price. A change in price produces a larger change in demand.
$E(p) = 1$	Unit	A change in price produces the same change in demand.

Now we want to see how revenue and elasticity are related. We have used the following model for revenue many times before:

$$\text{Revenue} = (\text{demand}) \times (\text{price})$$

Since we are looking for a connection between $E(p)$ and revenue, we will use a price–demand equation written in the form $x = f(p)$, where x is demand and p is price.

$$R(p) = xp = pf(p) \qquad \text{Revenue as a function of price}$$
$$R'(p) = pf'(p) + f(p)$$
$$= f(p)\left[\frac{pf'(p)}{f(p)} + 1\right] \qquad E(p) = -\frac{pf'(p)}{f(p)}$$
$$= f(p)[1 - E(p)]$$

Since $x = f(p) > 0$, it follows that $R'(p)$ and $[1 - E(p)]$ always have the same sign (see Table 3).

Table 3   Revenue and Elasticity of Demand

All Are True or All Are False	**All Are True or All Are False**
$R'(p) > 0$	$R'(p) < 0$
$E(p) < 1$	$E(p) > 1$
Demand is inelastic	Demand is elastic

These facts are interpreted in the following summary and in Figure 3:

SUMMARY   Revenue and Elasticity of Demand

When demand is inelastic,

A price increase will increase revenue.
A price decrease will decrease revenue.

When demand is elastic,

A price increase will decrease revenue.
A price decrease will increase revenue.

CONCEPTUAL INSIGHT

We know that a price increase will decrease demand at all price levels (Fig. 2). As Figure 3 illustrates, the effects of a price increase on revenue depends on the price level. If demand is elastic, then a price increase decreases revenue. If demand is inelastic, then a price increase increases revenue.

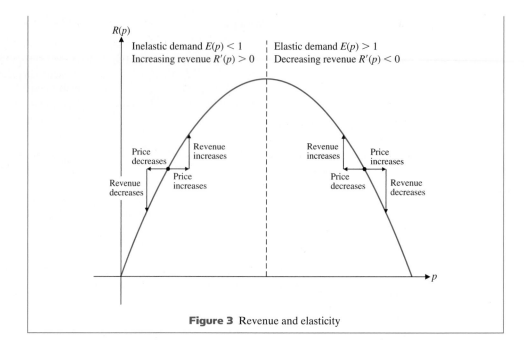

Figure 3 Revenue and elasticity

EXAMPLE 3   **Elasticity and Revenue**   A manufacturer of sunglasses currently sells one type for $15 a pair. The price p and the demand x for these glasses are related by

$$x = f(p) = 9{,}500 - 250p$$

If the current price is increased, will revenue increase or decrease?

SOLUTION
$$E(p) = -\frac{pf'(p)}{f(p)}$$

$$= -\frac{p(-250)}{9{,}500 - 250p}$$

$$= \frac{p}{38 - p}$$

$$E(15) = \frac{15}{23} \approx 0.65$$

At the $15 price level, demand is inelastic and a price increase will increase revenue.

Matched Problem 3   Repeat Example 3 if the current price for sunglasses is $21 a pair.

Exercises 11-7

A

In Problems 1–6, find the relative rate of change of f(x).

1. $f(x) = 35x - 0.4x^2$

2. $f(x) = 60x - 1.2x^2$

3. $f(x) = 7 + 4e^{-x}$

4. $f(x) = 15 - 3e^{-0.5x}$

5. $f(x) = 12 + 5 \ln x$

6. $f(x) = 25 - 2 \ln x$

In Problems 7–16, find the relative rate of change of f(x) at the indicated value of x. Round to three decimal places.

7. $f(x) = 45; x = 100$

8. $f(x) = 580; x = 300$

9. $f(x) = 420 - 5x; x = 25$

10. $f(x) = 500 - 6x; x = 40$

11. $f(x) = 420 - 5x; x = 55$

12. $f(x) = 500 - 6x; x = 75$

13. $f(x) = 4x^2 - \ln x; x = 2$

14. $f(x) = 9x - 5 \ln x; x = 3$

15. $f(x) = 4x^2 - \ln x; x = 5$

16. $f(x) = 9x - 5 \ln x; x = 7$

In Problems 17–24, find the percentage rate of change of f(x) at the indicated value of x. Round to the nearest tenth of a percent.

17. $f(x) = 225 + 65x; x = 5$

18. $f(x) = 75 + 110x; x = 4$

19. $f(x) = 225 + 65x; x = 15$

20. $f(x) = 75 + 110x; x = 16$

21. $f(x) = 5,100 - 3x^2; x = 35$

22. $f(x) = 3,000 - 8x^2; x = 12$

23. $f(x) = 5,100 - 3x^2; x = 41$

24. $f(x) = 3,000 - 8x^2; x = 18$

In Problems 25–30, use the price–demand equation to find E(p), the elasticity of demand.

25. $x = f(p) = 25,000 - 450p$

26. $x = f(p) = 10,000 - 190p$

27. $x = f(p) = 4,800 - 4p^2$

28. $x = f(p) = 8,400 - 7p^2$

29. $x = f(p) = 98 - 0.6e^p$

30. $x = f(p) = 160 - 35 \ln p$

B

In Problems 31–34, use the price–demand equation to determine whether demand is elastic, is inelastic, or has unit elasticity at the indicated values of p.

31. $x = f(p) = 12,000 - 10p^2$
(A) $p = 10$ (B) $p = 20$
(C) $p = 30$

32. $x = f(p) = 1,875 - p^2$
(A) $p = 15$ (B) $p = 25$
(C) $p = 40$

33. $x = f(p) = 950 - 2p - 0.1p^2$
(A) $p = 30$ (B) $p = 50$
(C) $p = 70$

34. $x = f(p) = 875 - p - 0.05p^2$
(A) $p = 50$ (B) $p = 70$
(C) $p = 100$

35. Given the price–demand equation

$$p + 0.005x = 30$$

(A) Express the demand x as a function of the price p.
(B) Find the elasticity of demand, $E(p)$.
(C) What is the elasticity of demand when $p = \$10$? If this price is increased by 10%, what is the approximate change in demand?
(D) What is the elasticity of demand when $p = \$25$? If this price is increased by 10%, what is the approximate change in demand?
(E) What is the elasticity of demand when $p = \$15$? If this price is increased by 10%, what is the approximate change in demand?

36. Given the price–demand equation

$$p + 0.01x = 50$$

(A) Express the demand x as a function of the price p.
(B) Find the elasticity of demand, $E(p)$.
(C) What is the elasticity of demand when $p = \$10$? If this price is decreased by 5%, what is the approximate change in demand?
(D) What is the elasticity of demand when $p = \$45$? If this price is decreased by 5%, what is the approximate change in demand?
(E) What is the elasticity of demand when $p = \$25$? If this price is decreased by 5%, what is the approximate change in demand?

37. Given the price–demand equation

$$0.02x + p = 60$$

(A) Express the demand x as a function of the price p.
(B) Express the revenue R as a function of the price p.
(C) Find the elasticity of demand, $E(p)$.
(D) For which values of p is demand elastic? Inelastic?
(E) For which values of p is revenue increasing? Decreasing?
(F) If $p = \$10$ and the price is decreased, will revenue increase or decrease?
(G) If $p = \$40$ and the price is decreased, will revenue increase or decrease?

38. Repeat Problem 37 for the price–demand equation

$$0.025x + p = 50$$

In Problems 39–46, use the price–demand equation to find the values of p for which demand is elastic and the values for which demand is inelastic. Assume that price and demand are both positive.

39. $x = f(p) = 210 - 30p$

40. $x = f(p) = 480 - 8p$

41. $x = f(p) = 3,125 - 5p^2$

42. $x = f(p) = 2,400 - 6p^2$

43. $x = f(p) = \sqrt{144 - 2p}$

44. $x = f(p) = \sqrt{324 - 2p}$

45. $x = f(p) = \sqrt{2,500 - 2p^2}$

46. $x = f(p) = \sqrt{3,600 - 2p^2}$

In Problems 47–52, use the demand equation to find the revenue function. Sketch the graph of the revenue function, and indicate the regions of inelastic and elastic demand on the graph.

47. $x = f(p) = 20(10 - p)$

48. $x = f(p) = 10(16 - p)$

49. $x = f(p) = 40(p - 15)^2$

50. $x = f(p) = 10(p - 9)^2$

51. $x = f(p) = 30 - 10\sqrt{p}$

52. $x = f(p) = 30 - 5\sqrt{p}$

C

If a price–demand equation is solved for p, then price is expressed as $p = g(x)$ and x becomes the independent variable. In this case, it can be shown that the elasticity of demand is given by

$$E(x) = -\frac{g(x)}{xg'(x)}$$

In Problems 53–56, use the price–demand equation to find E(x) at the indicated value of x.

53. $p = g(x) = 50 - 0.1x, x = 200$

54. $p = g(x) = 30 - 0.05x, x = 400$

55. $p = g(x) = 50 - 2\sqrt{x}, x = 400$

56. $p = g(x) = 20 - \sqrt{x}, x = 100$

In Problems 57–60, use the price–demand equation to find the values of x for which demand is elastic and for which demand is inelastic.

57. $p = g(x) = 180 - 0.3x$

58. $p = g(x) = 640 - 0.4x$

59. $p = g(x) = 90 - 0.1x^2$

60. $p = g(x) = 540 - 0.2x^2$

61. Find $E(p)$ for $x = f(p) = Ap^{-k}$, where A and k are positive constants.

62. Find $E(p)$ for $x = f(p) = Ae^{-kp}$, where A and k are positive constants.

Applications

63. **Rate of change of cost.** A fast-food restaurant can produce a hamburger for $2.50. If the restaurant's daily sales are increasing at the rate of 30 hamburgers per day, how fast is its daily cost for hamburgers increasing?

64. **Rate of change of cost.** The fast-food restaurant in Problem 63 can produce an order of fries for $0.80. If the restaurant's daily sales are increasing at the rate of 45 orders of fries per day, how fast is its daily cost for fries increasing?

65. **Revenue and elasticity.** The price–demand equation for hamburgers at a fast-food restaurant is

$$x + 400p = 3,000$$

Currently, the price of a hamburger is $3.00. If the price is increased by 10%, will revenue increase or decrease?

66. **Revenue and elasticity.** Refer to Problem 65. If the current price of a hamburger is $4.00, will a 10% price increase cause revenue to increase or decrease?

67. **Revenue and elasticity.** The price–demand equation for an order of fries at a fast-food restaurant is

$$x + 1,000p = 2,500$$

Currently, the price of an order of fries is $0.99. If the price is decreased by 10%, will revenue increase or decrease?

68. **Revenue and elasticity.** Refer to Problem 67. If the current price of an order of fries is $1.29, will a 10% price decrease cause revenue to increase or decrease?

69. **Maximum revenue.** Refer to Problem 65. What price will maximize the revenue from selling hamburgers?

70. **Maximum revenue.** Refer to Problem 67. What price will maximize the revenue from selling fries?

71. **Population growth.** A model for Canada's population growth (Table 4) is

$$f(t) = 0.31t + 18.5$$

where t is years since 1960. Find and graph the percentage rate of change of $f(t)$ for $0 \le t \le 50$.

72. **Population growth.** A model for Mexico's population growth (Table 4) is

Table 4	Population Growth	
Year	Canada (millions)	Mexico (millions)
1960	18	39
1970	22	53
1980	25	68
1990	28	85
2000	31	100
2010	34	112

$$f(t) = 1.49t + 38.8$$

where t is years since 1960. Find and graph the percentage rate of change of $f(t)$ for $0 \le t \le 50$.

73. **Crime.** A model for the number of robberies in the United States (Table 5) is

$$r(t) = 9.7 - 2.7 \ln t$$

where t is years since 1990. Find the relative rate of change for robberies in 2008.

Table 5	Number of Victimizations per 1,000 Population Age 12 and Over	
	Robbery	Aggravated Assault
1995	5.4	9.5
1997	4.3	8.6
1999	3.6	6.7
2001	2.8	5.3
2003	2.5	4.6
2005	2.6	4.3

74. **Crime.** A model for the number of assaults in the United States (Table 5) is

$$a(t) = 18.2 - 5.2 \ln t$$

where t is years since 1990. Find the relative rate of change for assaults in 2008.

Answers to Matched Problems

1. $p(t) = \dfrac{270}{2.7t + 282}$

2. $E(p) = \dfrac{p}{40 - p}$

(A) $E(8) = 0.25$; demand is inelastic.

(B) $E(30) = 3$; demand is elastic.

(C) $E(20) = 1$; demand has unit elasticity.

3. $E(21) = \dfrac{21}{17} \approx 1.2$; demand is elastic. Increasing price will decrease revenue.

Chapter 11 Review

Important Terms, Symbols, and Concepts

11-1 The Constant e and Continuous Compound Interest

EXAMPLES

- The number e is defined as

$$\lim_{x \to \infty}\left(1 + \frac{1}{n}\right)^{n} = \lim_{x \to 0}(1 + s)^{1/s} = 2.718\ 281\ 828\ 459\ldots$$

- If a principal P is invested at an annual rate r (expressed as a decimal) compounded continuously, then the amount A in the account at the end of t years is given by the **compound interest formula**

$$A = Pe^{rt}$$

Ex. 1, p. 561
Ex. 2, p. 561
Ex. 3, p. 562
Ex. 4, p. 562

11-2 Derivatives of Exponential and Logarithmic Functions

- For $b > 0, b \neq 1$,

$$\frac{d}{dx}e^{x} = e^{x} \qquad \frac{d}{dx}b^{x} = b^{x}\ln b$$

$$\frac{d}{dx}\ln x = \frac{1}{x} \qquad \frac{d}{dx}\log_{b} x = \frac{1}{\ln b}\frac{1}{x}$$

- The **change-of-base formulas** allow conversion from base e to any base $b, b > 0, b \neq 1$:

$$b^{x} = e^{x\ln b} \qquad \log_{b} x = \frac{\ln x}{\ln b}$$

Ex. 1, p. 566
Ex. 2, p. 568
Ex. 3, p. 570
Ex. 4, p. 570
Ex. 5, p. 571

11-3 Derivatives of Products and Quotients

- Product rule. If $y = f(x) = F(x)\,S(x)$, then $f'(x) = F(x)S'(x) + S(x)F'(x)$, provided that both $F'(x)$ and $S'(x)$ exist.

- Quotient rule. If $y = f(x) = \dfrac{T(x)}{B(x)}$, then $f'(x) = \dfrac{B(x)\,T'(x) - T(x)\,B'(x)}{[B(x)]^{2}}$ provided that both $T'(x)$ and $B'(x)$ exist.

Ex. 1, p. 574
Ex. 2, p. 575
Ex. 3, p. 575
Ex. 4, p. 577
Ex. 5, p. 578
Ex. 6, p. 578

11-4 The Chain Rule

- A function m is a **composite** of functions f and g if $m(x) = f[g(x)]$.
- The **chain rule** gives a formula for the derivative of the composite function $m(x) = f[g(x)]$:

$$m'(x) = f'[g(x)]g'(x)$$

- A special case of the chain rule is called the **general power rule:**

$$\frac{d}{dx}[f(x)]^{n} = n[f(x)]^{n-1}f'(x)$$

- Other special cases of the chain rule are the following **general derivative rules:**

$$\frac{d}{dx}\ln[f(x)] = \frac{1}{f(x)}f'(x)$$

$$\frac{d}{dx}e^{f(x)} = e^{f(x)}f'(x)$$

Ex. 1, p. 582
Ex. 2, p. 582
Ex. 4, p. 586
Ex. 5, p. 587
Ex. 3, p. 584

Ex. 6, p. 588

11-5 Implicit Differentiation

- If $y = y(x)$ is a function defined by the equation $F(x, y) = 0$, then we use **implicit differentiation** to find an equation in x, y, and y'.

Ex. 1, p. 593
Ex. 2, p. 594
Ex. 3, p. 595

11-6 Related Rates

- If x and y represent quantities that are changing with respect to time and are related by the equation $F(x, y) = 0$, then implicit differentiation produces an equation that relates x, y, dy/dt, and dx/dt. Problems of this type are called **related-rates problems**.
- Suggestions for solving related-rates problems are given on page 599.

Ex. 1, p. 598
Ex. 2, p. 599
Ex. 3, p. 600

11-7 Elasticity of Demand

- The **relative rate of change**, or the **logarithmic derivative**, of a function $f(x)$ is $f'(x)/f(x)$, and the **percentage rate of change** is $100 \times [f'(x)/f(x)]$.
- If price and demand are related by $x = f(p)$, then the **elasticity of demand** is given by

$$E(p) = -\frac{pf'(p)}{f(p)} = -\frac{\text{relative rate of change of demand}}{\text{relative rate of change of price}}$$

Ex. 1, p. 604

Ex. 2, p. 606

- **Demand is inelastic** if $0 < E(p) < 1$. (Demand is not sensitive to changes in price; a change in price produces a smaller change in demand.) **Demand is elastic** if $E(p) > 1$. (Demand is sensitive to changes in price; a change in price produces a larger change in demand.) **Demand has unit elasticity** if $E(p) = 1$. (A change in price produces the same change in demand.)
- If $R(p) = pf(p)$ is the revenue function, then $R'(p)$ and $[1 - E(p)]$ always have the same sign.

Ex. 3, p. 608

Review Exercises

Work through all the problems in this chapter review, and check your answers in the back of the book. Answers to all review problems are there, along with section numbers in italics to indicate where each type of problem is discussed. Where weaknesses show up, review appropriate sections of the text.

A

1. Use a calculator to evaluate $A = 2{,}000e^{0.09t}$ to the nearest cent for $t = 5, 10$, and 20.

Find the indicated derivatives in Problems 2–4.

2. $\dfrac{d}{dx}(2 \ln x + 3e^x)$ 3. $\dfrac{d}{dx}e^{2x-3}$

4. y' for $y = \ln(2x + 7)$

5. Let $y = \ln u$ and $u = 3 + e^x$.
   (A) Express y in terms of x.
   (B) Use the chain rule to find dy/dx, and then express dy/dx in terms of x.

6. Find y' for $y = y(x)$ defined implicity by the equation $2y^2 - 3x^3 - 5 = 0$, and evaluate at $(x, y) = (1, 2)$.

7. For $y = 3x^2 - 5$, where $x = x(t)$ and $y = y(t)$, find dy/dt if $dx/dt = 3$ when $x = 12$.

8. Given the demand equation $25p + x = 1{,}000$,
   (A) Express the demand x as a function of the price p.
   (B) Find the elasticity of demand, $E(p)$.
   (C) Find $E(15)$ and interpret.
   (D) Express the revenue function as a function of price p.
   (E) If $p = \$25$, what is the effect of a price cut on revenue?

B

9. Find the slope of the line tangent to $y = 100e^{-0.1x}$ when $x = 0$.

 10. Use a calculator and a table of values to investigate

$$\lim_{n \to \infty} \left(1 + \frac{2}{n}\right)^n$$

Do you think the limit exists? If so, what do you think it is?

Find the indicated derivatives in Problems 11–16.

11. $\dfrac{d}{dz}[(\ln z)^7 + \ln z^7]$ 12. $\dfrac{d}{dx}(x^6 \ln x)$

13. $\dfrac{d}{dx}\dfrac{e^x}{x^6}$ 14. y' for $y = \ln(2x^3 - 3x)$

15. $f'(x)$ for $f(x) = e^{x^3 - x^2}$ 16. dy/dx for $y = e^{-2x} \ln 5x$

17. Find the equation of the line tangent to the graph of $y = f(x) = 1 + e^{-x}$ at $x = 0$. At $x = -1$.

18. Find y' for $y = y(x)$ defined implicitly by the equation $x^2 - 3xy + 4y^2 = 23$, and find the slope of the graph at $(-1, 2)$.

19. Find x' for $x = x(t)$ defined implicitly by $x^3 - 2t^2x + 8 = 0$, and evaluate at $(t, x) = (-2, 2)$.

20. Find y' for $y = y(x)$ defined implicitly by $x - y^2 = e^y$, and evaluate at $(1, 0)$.

21. Find y' for $y = y(x)$ defined implicitly by $\ln y = x^2 - y^2$, and evaluate at $(1, 1)$.

22. A point is moving on the graph of $y^2 - 4x^2 = 12$ so that its x coordinate is decreasing by 2 units per second when $(x, y) = (1, 4)$. Find the rate of change of the y coordinate.

23. A 17-foot ladder is placed against a wall. If the foot of the ladder is pushed toward the wall at 0.5 foot per second, how fast is the top of the ladder rising when the foot is 8 feet from the wall?

24. Water is leaking onto a floor. The resulting circular pool has an area that is increasing at the rate of 24 square inches per minute. How fast is the radius R of the pool increasing when the radius is 12 inches? $[A = \pi R^2]$

C

25. Find the values of p for which demand is elastic and the values for which demand is inelastic if the price–demand equation is

$$x = f(p) = 20(p - 15)^2 \qquad 0 \le p \le 15$$

26. Graph the revenue function and indicate the regions of inelastic and elastic demand of the graph if the price–demand equation is

$$x = f(p) = 5(20 - p) \qquad 0 \le p \le 20$$

27. Let $y = w^3$, $w = \ln u$, and $u = 4 - e^x$.

(A) Express y in terms of x.

(B) Use the chain rule to find dy/dx, and then express dy/dx in terms of x.

Find the indicated derivatives in Problems 28–30.

28. y' for $y = 5^{x^2 - 1}$

29. $\dfrac{d}{dx} \log_5(x^2 - x)$ **30.** $\dfrac{d}{dx} \sqrt{\ln(x^2 + x)}$

31. Find y' for $y = y(x)$ defined implicitly by the equation $e^{xy} = x^2 + y + 1$, and evaluate at $(0, 0)$.

32. A rock thrown into a still pond causes a circular ripple. The radius is increasing at a constant rate of 3 feet per second. Show that the area does not increase at a constant rate. When is the rate of increase of the area the smallest? The largest? Explain.

33. A point moves along the graph of $y = x^3$ in such a way that its y coordinate is increasing at a constant rate of 5 units per second. Does the x coordinate ever increase at a faster rate than the y coordinate? Explain.

Applications

34. Doubling time. How long will it take money to double if it is invested at 5% interest compounded

(A) Annually?   (B) Continuously?

35. Continuous compound interest. If $100 is invested at 10% interest compounded continuously, then the amount (in dollars) at the end of t years is given by

$$A = 100e^{0.1t}$$

Find $A'(t)$, $A'(1)$, and $A'(10)$.

36. Marginal analysis. The price–demand equation for 14-cubic-foot refrigerators at an appliance store is

$$p(x) = 1,000e^{-0.02x}$$

where x is the monthly demand and p is the price in dollars. Find the marginal revenue equation.

37. Demand equation. Given the demand equation

$$x = \sqrt{5,000 - 2p^3}$$

find the rate of change of p with respect to x by implicit differentiation (x is the number of items that can be sold at a price of p per item).

38. Rate of change of revenue. A company is manufacturing kayaks and can sell all that it manufactures. The revenue (in dollars) is given by

$$R = 750x - \frac{x^2}{30}$$

where the production output in 1 day is x kayaks. If production is increasing at 3 kayaks per day when production is 40 kayaks per day, find the rate of increase in revenue.

39. Revenue and elasticity. The price–demand equation for home-delivered large pizzas is

$$p = 38.2 - 0.002x$$

where x is the number of pizzas delivered weekly. The current price of one pizza is $21. In order to generate additional revenue from the sale of large pizzas, would you recommend a price increase or a price decrease? Explain.

40. Average income. A model for the average income per household before taxes are paid is

$$f(t) = 1,700t + 20,500$$

where t is years since 1980. Find the relative rate of change of household income in 2015.

41. Drug concentration. The drug concentration in the bloodstream t hours after injection is given approximately by

$$C(t) = 5e^{-0.3t}$$

where $C(t)$ is concentration in milligrams per milliliter. What is the rate of change of concentration after 1 hour? After 5 hours?

42. Wound healing. A circular wound on an arm is healing at the rate of 45 square millimeters per day (the area of the wound is decreasing at this rate). How fast is the radius R of the wound decreasing when $R = 15$ millimeters? $[A = \pi R^2]$

43. Psychology: learning. In a computer assembly plant, a new employee, on the average, is able to assemble

$$N(t) = 10(1 - e^{-0.4t})$$

units after t days of on-the-job training.

(A) What is the rate of learning after 1 day? After 5 days?

(B) Find the number of days (to the nearest day) after which the rate of learning is less than 0.25 unit per day.

44. Learning. A new worker on the production line performs an operation in T minutes after x performances of the operation, as given by

$$T = 2\left(1 + \frac{1}{x^{3/2}}\right)$$

If, after performing the operation 9 times, the rate of improvement is $dx/dt = 3$ operations per hour, find the rate of improvement in time dT/dt in performing each operation.

> **THEOREM 1 Increasing and Decreasing Functions**
> For the interval (a, b),
>
> | $f'(x)$ | $f(x)$ | Graph of f | Examples |
> |---------|--------|--------------|----------|
> | $+$ | Increases ↗ | Rises ↗ | 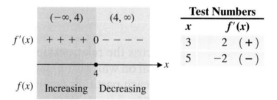 |
> | $-$ | Decreases ↘ | Falls ↘ | |

EXAMPLE 1 **Finding Intervals on Which a Function Is Increasing or Decreasing** Given the function $f(x) = 8x - x^2$,

(A) Which values of x correspond to horizontal tangent lines?

(B) For which values of x is $f(x)$ increasing? Decreasing?

(C) Sketch a graph of f. Add any horizontal tangent lines.

SOLUTION

(A) $f'(x) = 8 - 2x = 0$

$$x = 4$$

So, a horizontal tangent line exists at $x = 4$ only.

(B) We will construct a sign chart for $f'(x)$ to determine which values of x make $f'(x) > 0$ and which values make $f'(x) < 0$. Recall from Section 10-2 that the partition numbers for a function are the points where the function is 0 or discontinuous. When constructing a sign chart for $f'(x)$, we must locate all points where $f'(x) = 0$ or $f'(x)$ is discontinuous. From part (A), we know that $f'(x) = 8 - 2x = 0$ at $x = 4$. Since $f'(x) = 8 - 2x$ is a polynomial, it is continuous for all x. So, 4 is the only partition number. We construct a sign chart for the intervals $(-\infty, 4)$ and $(4, \infty)$, using test numbers 3 and 5:

	$(-\infty, 4)$	$(4, \infty)$	**Test Numbers**	
			x	$f'(x)$
$f'(x)$	$+ + + +$ 0	$- - - -$	3	2 $(+)$
		→x	5	-2 $(-)$
	4			
$f(x)$	Increasing	Decreasing		

Therefore, $f(x)$ is increasing on $(-\infty, 4)$ and decreasing on $(4, \infty)$.

x	$f(x)$
0	0
2	12
4	16
6	12
8	0

Matched Problem 1 Repeat Example 1 for $f(x) = x^2 - 6x + 10$.

As Example 1 illustrates, the construction of a sign chart will play an important role in using the derivative to analyze and sketch the graph of a function f. The partition numbers for f' are central to the construction of these sign charts and also to the analysis of the graph of $y = f(x)$. We already know that if $f'(c) = 0$, then the graph of $y = f(x)$ will have a horizontal tangent line at $x = c$. But the partition numbers for f' also include the numbers c such that $f'(c)$ does not exist.* There are two possibilities at this type of number: (1) $f(c)$ does not exist; or (2) $f(c)$ exists but the slope of the tangent line at $x = c$ is undefined.

DEFINITION   Critical Values

The values of x in the domain of f where $f'(x) = 0$ or where $f'(x)$ does not exist are called the **critical values** of f.

CONCEPTUAL INSIGHT

The critical values of f are always in the domain of f and are also partition numbers for f', but f' may have partition numbers that are not critical values.

If f is a polynomial, then both the partition numbers for f' and the critical values of f are the solutions of $f'(x) = 0$.

EXAMPLE 2   **Partition Numbers and Critical Values** Find the critical values of f, the intervals on which f is increasing, and those on which f is decreasing, for $f(x) = 1 + x^3$.

SOLUTION   Begin by finding the partition number for $f'(x)$:

$$f'(x) = 3x^2 = 0, \quad \text{only at } x = 0$$

The partition number 0 is in the domain of f, so 0 is the only critical value of f. The sign chart for $f'(x) = 3x^2$ (partition number is 0) is

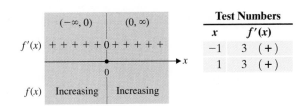

	$(-\infty, 0)$	$(0, \infty)$	**Test Numbers**	
			x	$f'(x)$
$f'(x)$	$+ + + + + 0 + + + + +$		-1	3 $(+)$
			1	3 $(+)$
$f(x)$	Increasing	Increasing		

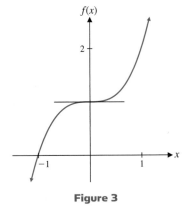

$f(x)$

Figure 3

The sign chart indicates that $f(x)$ is increasing on $(-\infty, 0)$ and $(0, \infty)$. Since f is continuous at $x = 0$, it follows that $f(x)$ is increasing for all x. The graph of f is shown in Figure 3.

Matched Problem 2   Find the critical values of f, the intervals on which f is increasing, and those on which f is decreasing, for $f(x) = 1 - x^3$.

EXAMPLE 3   **Partition Numbers and Critical Values** Find the critical values of f, the intervals on which f is increasing, and those on which f is decreasing, for $f(x) = (1 - x)^{1/3}$.

SOLUTION
$$f'(x) = -\frac{1}{3}(1 - x)^{-2/3} = \frac{-1}{3(1 - x)^{2/3}}$$

---

*We are assuming that $f'(c)$ does not exist at any point of discontinuity of f'. There do exist functions f such that f' is discontinuous at $x = c$, yet $f'(c)$ exists. However, we do not consider such functions in this book.

To find partition numbers for f', we note that f' is continuous for all x, except for values of x for which the denominator is 0; that is, $f'(1)$ does not exist and f' is discontinuous at $x = 1$. Since the numerator is the constant -1, $f'(x) \neq 0$ for any value of x. Thus, $x = 1$ is the only partition number for f'. Since 1 is in the domain of f, $x = 1$ is also the only critical value of f. When constructing the sign chart for f' we use the abbreviation ND to note the fact that $f'(x)$ is *not defined* at $x = 1$.

The sign chart for $f'(x) = -1/[3(1 - x)^{2/3}]$ (partition number is 1) is as follows:

f(x)

Figure 4

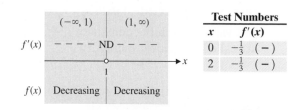

The sign chart indicates that f is decreasing on $(-\infty, 1)$ and $(1, \infty)$. Since f is continuous at $x = 1$, it follows that $f(x)$ is decreasing for all x. **A continuous function can be decreasing (or increasing) on an interval containing values of x where $f'(x)$ does not exist.** The graph of f is shown in Figure 4. Notice that the undefined derivative at $x = 1$ results in a vertical tangent line at $x = 1$. **A vertical tangent will occur at $x = c$ if f is continuous at $x = c$ and if $|f'(x)|$ becomes larger and larger as x approaches c.**

Matched Problem 3   Find the critical values of f, the intervals on which f is increasing, and those on which f is decreasing, for $f(x) = (1 + x)^{1/3}$.

EXAMPLE 4   **Partition Numbers and Critical Values**   Find the critical values of f, the intervals on which f is increasing, and those on which f is decreasing, for $f(x) = \dfrac{1}{x - 2}$.

SOLUTION

$$f(x) = \frac{1}{x - 2} = (x - 2)^{-1}$$
$$f'(x) = -(x - 2)^{-2} = \frac{-1}{(x - 2)^2}$$

To find the partition numbers for f', note that $f'(x) \neq 0$ for any x and f' is not defined at $x = 2$. Thus, $x = 2$ is the only partition number for f'. However, $x = 2$ is *not* in the domain of f. Consequently, $x = 2$ is not a critical value of f. This function has no critical values.

The sign chart for $f'(x) = -1/(x - 2)^2$ (partition number is 2) is as follows:

f(x)

Figure 5

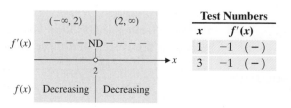

Therefore, f is decreasing on $(-\infty, 2)$ and $(2, \infty)$. The graph of f is shown in Figure 5.

Matched Problem 4 Find the critical values for f, the intervals on which f is increasing, and those on which f is decreasing, for $f(x) = \dfrac{1}{x}$.

EXAMPLE 5 **Partition Numbers and Critical Values** Find the critical values of f, the intervals on which f is increasing, and those on which f is decreasing, for $f(x) = 8 \ln x - x^2$.

SOLUTION The natural logarithm function $\ln x$ is defined on $(0, \infty)$, or $x > 0$, so $f(x)$ is defined only for $x > 0$.

$$f(x) = 8 \ln x - x^2, x > 0$$

$$f'(x) = \frac{8}{x} - 2x \qquad \text{\textit{Find a common denominator.}}$$

$$= \frac{8}{x} - \frac{2x^2}{x} \qquad \text{\textit{Subtract numerators.}}$$

$$= \frac{8 - 2x^2}{x} \qquad \text{\textit{Factor numerator.}}$$

$$= \frac{2(2 - x)(2 + x)}{x}, \quad x > 0$$

Note that $f'(x) = 0$ at -2 and at 2, and $f'(x)$ is discontinuous at 0. These are the partition numbers for $f'(x)$. Since the domain of f is $(0, \infty)$, 0 and -2 are not critical values. The remaining partition number, 2, is the only critical value for $f(x)$.

The sign chart for $f'(x) = \dfrac{2(2 - x)(2 + x)}{x}, x > 0$ (partition number is 2), is as follows:

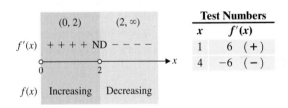

	(0, 2)	(2, ∞)
$f'(x)$	+ + + +	ND − − − −
$f(x)$	Increasing	Decreasing

Test Numbers	
x	$f'(x)$
1	6 (+)
4	−6 (−)

Therefore, f is increasing on $(0, 2)$ and decreasing on $(2, \infty)$. The graph of f is shown in Figure 6.

Figure 6

Matched Problem 5 Find the critical values of f, the intervals on which f is increasing, and those on which f is decreasing, for $f(x) = 5 \ln x - x$.

CONCEPTUAL INSIGHT

Examples 4 and 5 illustrate two important ideas:

1. Do not assume that all partition numbers for the derivative f' are critical values of the function f. To be a critical value, a partition number must also be in the domain of f.

2. The values for which a function is increasing or decreasing must always be expressed in terms of open intervals that are subsets of the domain of the function.

Local Extrema

When the graph of a continuous function changes from rising to falling, a high point, or *local maximum*, occurs. When the graph changes from falling to rising, a low point, or *local minimum*, occurs. In Figure 7, high points occur at c_3 and c_6, and low points occur at c_2 and c_4. In general, we call $f(c)$ a **local maximum** if there exists an interval (m, n) containing c such that

$$f(x) \leq f(c) \qquad \text{for all } x \text{ in } (m, n)$$

Note that this inequality need hold only for values of x near c, which is why we use the term *local*.

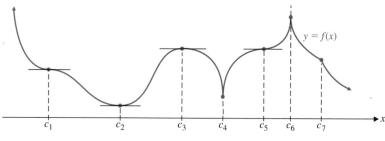

Figure 7

The quantity $f(c)$ is called a **local minimum** if there exists an interval (m, n) containing c such that

$$f(x) \geq f(c) \qquad \text{for all } x \text{ in } (m, n)$$

The quantity $f(c)$ is called a **local extremum** if it is either a local maximum or a local minimum. A point on a graph where a local extremum occurs is also called a **turning point**. In Figure 7 we see that local maxima occur at c_3 and c_6, local minima occur at c_2 and c_4, and all four values produce local extrema. Also, the local maximum $f(c_3)$ is not the highest point on the graph in Figure 7. Later in this chapter, we consider the problem of finding the highest and lowest points on a graph, or absolute extrema. For now, we are concerned only with locating *local* extrema.

EXAMPLE 6 **Analyzing a Graph** Use the graph of f in Figure 8 to find the intervals on which f is increasing, those on which f is decreasing, any local maxima, and any local minima.

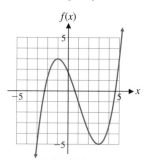

Figure 8

SOLUTION The function f is increasing (the graph is rising) on $(-\infty, -1)$ and on $(3, \infty)$ and is decreasing (the graph is falling) on $(-1, 3)$. Because the graph changes from rising to falling at $x = -1$, $f(-1) = 3$ is a local maximum. Because the graph changes from falling to rising at $x = 3$, $f(3) = -5$ is a local minimum.

Matched Problem 6   Use the graph of g in Figure 9 to find the intervals on which g is increasing, those on which g is decreasing, any local maxima, and any local minima.

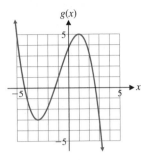

Figure 9

How can we locate local maxima and minima if we are given the equation of a function and not its graph? The key is to examine the critical values of the function. The local extrema of the function f in Figure 7 occur either at points where the derivative is 0 (c_2 and c_3) or at points where the derivative does not exist (c_4 and c_6). In other words, local extrema occur only at critical values of f. Theorem 2 shows that this is true in general.

THEOREM 2   Existence of Local Extrema

If f is continuous on the interval (a, b), c is a number in (a, b), and $f(c)$ is a local extremum, then either $f'(c) = 0$ or $f'(c)$ does not exist (is not defined).

Theorem 2 states that a local extremum can occur only at a critical value, but it does not imply that every critical value produces a local extremum. In Figure 7, c_1 and c_5 are critical values (the slope is 0), but the function does not have a local maximum or local minimum at either of these values.

Our strategy for finding local extrema is now clear: We find all critical values of f and test each one to see if it produces a local maximum, a local minimum, or neither.

First-Derivative Test

If $f'(x)$ exists on both sides of a critical value c, the sign of $f'(x)$ can be used to determine whether the point $(c, f(c))$ is a local maximum, a local minimum, or neither. The various possibilities are summarized in the following box and are illustrated in Figure 10:

PROCEDURE   First-Derivative Test for Local Extrema

Let c be a critical value of f [$f(c)$ is defined and either $f'(c) = 0$ or $f'(c)$ is not defined]. Construct a sign chart for $f'(x)$ close to and on either side of c.

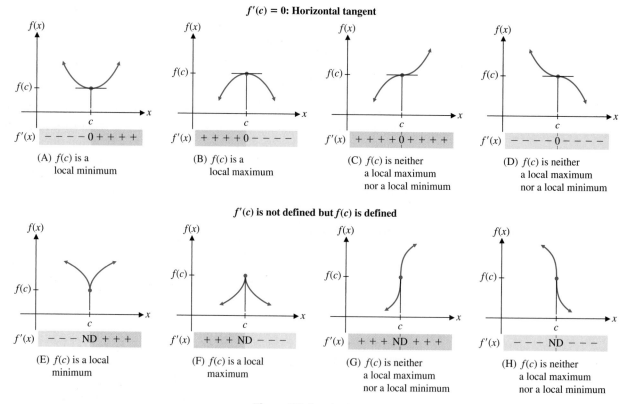

Figure 10 Local extrema

EXAMPLE 7 **Locating Local Extrema** Given $f(x) = x^3 - 6x^2 + 9x + 1$,

(A) Find the critical values of f.

(B) Find the local maxima and minima.

(C) Sketch the graph of f.

SOLUTION (A) Find all numbers x in the domain of f where $f'(x) = 0$ or $f'(x)$ does not exist.

$$f'(x) = 3x^2 - 12x + 9 = 0$$
$$3(x^2 - 4x + 3) = 0$$
$$3(x - 1)(x - 3) = 0$$
$$x = 1 \quad \text{or} \quad x = 3$$

$f'(x)$ exists for all x; the critical values are $x = 1$ and $x = 3$.

(B) The easiest way to apply the first-derivative test for local maxima and minima is to construct a sign chart for $f'(x)$ for all x. Partition numbers for $f'(x)$ are $x = 1$ and $x = 3$ (which also happen to be critical values of f).

Sign chart for $f'(x) = 3(x - 1)(x - 3)$:

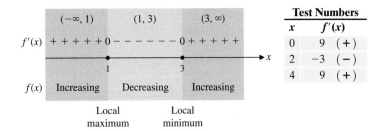

The sign chart indicates that f increases on $(-\infty, 1)$, has a local maximum at $x = 1$, decreases on $(1, 3)$, has a local minimum at $x = 3$, and increases on $(3, \infty)$. These facts are summarized in the following table:

x	$f'(x)$	$f(x)$	Graph of f
$(-\infty, 1)$	$+$	Increasing	Rising
$x = 1$	0	Local maximum	Horizontal tangent
$(1, 3)$	$-$	Decreasing	Falling
$x = 3$	0	Local minimum	Horizontal tangent
$(3, \infty)$	$+$	Increasing	Rising

(C) We sketch a graph of f, using the information from part (B) and point-by-point plotting.

x	$f(x)$
0	1
1	5
2	3
3	1
4	5

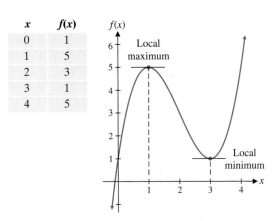

Matched Problem 7 Given $f(x) = x^3 - 9x^2 + 24x - 10$,

(A) Find the critical values of f.

(B) Find the local maxima and minima.

(C) Sketch a graph of f.

How can you tell if you have found all the local extrema of a function? In general, this can be a difficult question to answer. However, in the case of a polynomial function, there is an easily determined upper limit on the number of local extrema. Since the local extrema are the x intercepts of the derivative, this limit is a consequence of the number of x intercepts of a polynomial. The relevant information is summarized in the following theorem, which is stated without proof:

THEOREM 3 Intercepts and Local Extrema of Polynomial Functions

If $f(x) = a_n x^n + a_{n-1} x^{n-1} + \cdots + a_1 x + a_0$, $a_n \neq 0$, is an nth-degree polynomial, then f has at most n x intercepts and at most $n - 1$ local extrema.

Theorem 3 does not guarantee that every nth-degree polynomial has exactly $n - 1$ local extrema; it says only that there can never be more than $n - 1$ local extrema. For example, the third-degree polynomial in Example 7 has two local extrema, while the third-degree polynomial in Example 2 does not have any.

Economics Applications

In addition to providing information for hand-sketching graphs, the derivative is an important tool for analyzing graphs and discussing the interplay between a function and its rate of change. The next two examples illustrate this process in the context of economics applications.

EXAMPLE 8 **Agricultural Exports and Imports** Over the past few decades, the United States has exported more agricultural products than it has imported, maintaining a positive balance of trade in this area. However, the trade balance fluctuated considerably during that period. The graph in Figure 11 approximates the rate of change of the balance of trade over a 15-year period, where $B(t)$ is the balance of trade (in billions of dollars) and t is time (in years).

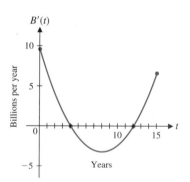

Figure 11 Rate of change of the balance of trade

✎ (A) Write a brief description of the graph of $y = B(t)$, including a discussion of any local extrema.

(B) Sketch a possible graph of $y = B(t)$.

SOLUTION (A) The graph of the derivative $y = B'(t)$ contains the same essential information as a sign chart. That is, we see that $B'(t)$ is positive on $(0, 4)$, 0 at $t = 4$, negative on $(4, 12)$, 0 at $t = 12$, and positive on $(12, 15)$. The trade balance increases for the first 4 years to a local maximum, decreases for the next 8 years to a local minimum, and then increases for the final 3 years.

(B) Without additional information concerning the actual values of $y = B(t)$, we cannot produce an accurate graph. However, we can sketch a possible graph that illustrates the important features, as shown in Figure 12. The absence of a scale on the vertical axis is a consequence of the lack of information about the values of $B(t)$.

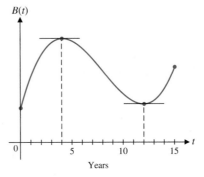

Figure 12 Balance of trade

Matched Problem 8 The graph in Figure 13 approximates the rate of change of the U.S. share of the total world production of motor vehicles over a 20-year period, where $S(t)$ is the U.S. share (as a percentage) and t is time (in years).

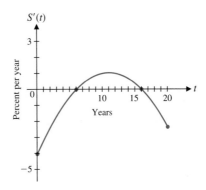

Figure 13

✎(A) Write a brief description of the graph of $y = S(t)$, including a discussion of any local extrema.

(B) Sketch a possible graph of $y = S(t)$.

EXAMPLE 9 **Revenue Analysis** The graph of the total revenue $R(x)$ (in dollars) from the sale of x bookcases is shown in Figure 14.

✎(A) Write a brief description of the graph of the marginal revenue function $y = R'(x)$, including a discussion of any x intercepts.

(B) Sketch a possible graph of $y = R'(x)$.

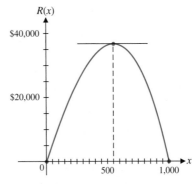

Figure 14 Revenue

SOLUTION   (A) The graph of $y = R(x)$ indicates that $R(x)$ increases on $(0, 550)$, has a local maximum at $x = 550$, and decreases on $(550, 1,000)$. Consequently, the marginal revenue function $R'(x)$ must be positive on $(0, 550)$, 0 at $x = 550$, and negative on $(550, 1,000)$.

(B) A possible graph of $y = R'(x)$ illustrating the information summarized in part (A) is shown in Figure 15.

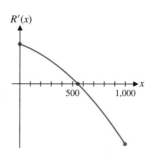

Figure 15 Marginal revenue

Matched Problem 9   The graph of the total revenue $R(x)$ (in dollars) from the sale of x desks is shown in Figure 16.

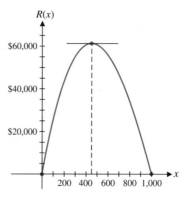

Figure 16

(A) Write a brief description of the graph of the marginal revenue function $y = R'(x)$, including a discussion of any x intercepts.

(B) Sketch a possible graph of $y = R'(x)$.

Comparing Examples 8 and 9, we see that we were able to obtain more information about the function from the graph of its derivative (Example 8) than we were when the process was reversed (Example 9). In the next section, we introduce some ideas that will help us obtain additional information about the derivative from the graph of the function.

Exercises 12-1

A

Problems 1–8 refer to the following graph of $y = f(x)$:

1. Identify the intervals on which $f(x)$ is increasing.

2. Identify the intervals on which $f(x)$ is decreasing.

3. Identify the intervals on which $f'(x) < 0$.

4. Identify the intervals on which $f'(x) > 0$.

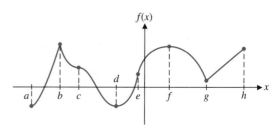

Figure for 1–8

5. Identify the x coordinates of the points where $f'(x) = 0$.

6. Identify the x coordinates of the points where $f'(x)$ does not exist.

7. Identify the x coordinates of the points where $f(x)$ has a local maximum.

8. Identify the x coordinates of the points where $f(x)$ has a local minimum.

In Problems 9 and 10, f(x) is continuous on $(-\infty, \infty)$ and has critical values at x = a, b, c, and d. Use the sign chart for f'(x) to determine whether f has a local maximum, a local minimum, or neither at each critical value.

9.

10.

In Problems 11–18, match the graph of f with one of the sign charts a–h in the figure.

11.

12.

13.

14.

15.

16.

17.

18.

(a)

(b)

(c)

(d)

(e)

(f)

(g)

(h)

Figure for 11–18

B

In Problems 19–26, find (A) f'(x), (B) the critical values of f, and (C) the partition numbers for f'.

19. $f(x) = x^3 - 12x + 8$

20. $f(x) = x^3 - 27x + 30$

21. $f(x) = (x + 5)^{1/3}$

22. $f(x) = (x - 9)^{2/3}$

23. $f(x) = \dfrac{6}{x+2}$

24. $f(x) = \dfrac{5}{x-4}$

25. $f(x) = |x|$

26. $f(x) = |x+3|$

In Problems 27–40, find the intervals on which $f(x)$ is increasing, the intervals on which $f(x)$ is decreasing, and the local extrema.

27. $f(x) = 2x^2 - 4x$

28. $f(x) = -3x^2 - 12x$

29. $f(x) = -2x^2 - 16x - 25$

30. $f(x) = -3x^2 + 12x - 5$

31. $f(x) = x^3 + 4x - 5$

32. $f(x) = -x^3 - 4x + 8$

33. $f(x) = 2x^3 - 3x^2 - 36x$

34. $f(x) = -2x^3 + 3x^2 + 120x$

35. $f(x) = 3x^4 - 4x^3 + 5$

36. $f(x) = x^4 + 2x^3 + 5$

37. $f(x) = (x-1)e^{-x}$

38. $f(x) = x \ln x - x$

39. $f(x) = 4x^{1/3} - x^{2/3}$

40. $f(x) = (x^2 - 9)^{2/3}$

In Problems 41–46, use a graphing calculator to approximate the critical values of $f(x)$ to two decimal places. Find the intervals on which $f(x)$ is increasing, the intervals on which $f(x)$ is decreasing, and the local extrema.

41. $f(x) = x^4 - 4x^3 + 9x$

42. $f(x) = x^4 + 5x^3 - 15x$

43. $f(x) = x \ln x - (x-2)^3$

44. $f(x) = e^{-x} - 3x^2$

45. $f(x) = e^x - 2x^2$

46. $f(x) = \dfrac{\ln x}{x} - 5x + x^2$

In Problems 47–54, find the intervals on which $f(x)$ is increasing and the intervals on which $f(x)$ is decreasing. Then sketch the graph. Add horizontal tangent lines.

47. $f(x) = 4 + 8x - x^2$

48. $f(x) = 2x^2 - 8x + 9$

49. $f(x) = x^3 - 3x + 1$

50. $f(x) = x^3 - 12x + 2$

51. $f(x) = 10 - 12x + 6x^2 - x^3$

52. $f(x) = x^3 + 3x^2 + 3x$

53. $f(x) = x^4 - 18x^2$

54. $f(x) = -x^4 + 50x^2$

In Problems 55–62, $f(x)$ is continuous on $(-\infty, \infty)$. Use the given information to sketch the graph of f.

55.

x	-2	-1	0	1	2
$f(x)$	-1	1	2	3	1

56.

x	-2	-1	0	1	2
$f(x)$	1	3	2	1	-1

57.

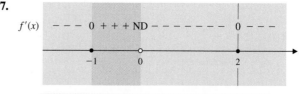

x	-2	-1	0	2	4
$f(x)$	2	1	2	1	0

58.

x	-2	-1	0	2	3
$f(x)$	-3	0	2	-1	0

59. $f(-2) = 4, f(0) = 0, f(2) = -4;$

$f'(-2) = 0, f'(0) = 0, f'(2) = 0;$

$f'(x) > 0$ on $(-\infty, -2)$ and $(2, \infty)$;

$f'(x) < 0$ on $(-2, 0)$ and $(0, 2)$

60. $f(-2) = -1, f(0) = 0, f(2) = 1;$

$f'(-2) = 0, f'(2) = 0;$

$f'(x) > 0$ on $(-\infty, -2), (-2, 2),$ and $(2, \infty)$

61. $f(-1) = 2, f(0) = 0, f(1) = -2;$

$f'(-1) = 0, f'(1) = 0, f'(0)$ is not defined;

$f'(x) > 0$ on $(-\infty, -1)$ and $(1, \infty)$;

$f'(x) < 0$ on $(-1, 0)$ and $(0, 1)$

62. $f(-1) = 2, f(0) = 0, f(1) = 2;$

$f'(-1) = 0, f'(1) = 0, f'(0)$ is not defined;

$f'(x) > 0$ on $(-\infty, -1)$ and $(0, 1)$;

$f'(x) < 0$ on $(-1, 0)$ and $(1, \infty)$

Problems 63–68 involve functions f_1–f_6 and their derivatives, g_1–g_6. Use the graphs shown in figures (A) and (B) to match each function f_i with its derivative g_j.

63. f_1 **64.** f_2 **65.** f_3

66. f_4 **67.** f_5 **68.** f_6

Figure (A) for 63–68

Figure (B) for 63–68

In Problems 69–74, use the given graph of $y = f'(x)$ to find the intervals on which f is increasing, the intervals on which f is decreasing, and the local extrema. Sketch a possible graph of $y = f(x)$.

69.   **70.**

71.   **72.**

73.   **74.**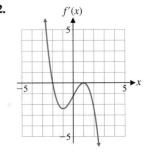

In Problems 75–78, use the given graph of $y = f(x)$ to find the intervals on which $f'(x) > 0$, the intervals on which $f'(x) < 0$, and the values of x for which $f'(x) = 0$. Sketch a possible graph of $y = f'(x)$.

75.   **76.**

77.

78.

C

In Problems 79–86, find the critical values, the intervals on which f(x) is increasing, the intervals on which f(x) is decreasing, and the local extrema. Do not graph.

79. $f(x) = x + \dfrac{4}{x}$

80. $f(x) = \dfrac{9}{x} + x$

81. $f(x) = 1 + \dfrac{1}{x} + \dfrac{1}{x^2}$

82. $f(x) = 3 - \dfrac{4}{x} - \dfrac{2}{x^2}$

83. $f(x) = \dfrac{x^2}{x - 2}$

84. $f(x) = \dfrac{x^2}{x + 1}$

85. $f(x) = x^4(x - 6)^2$

86. $f(x) = x^3(x - 5)^2$

87. Let $f(x) = x^3 + kx$, where k is a constant. Discuss the number of local extrema and the shape of the graph of f if
(A) $k > 0$ (B) $k < 0$ (C) $k = 0$

88. Let $f(x) = x^4 + kx^2$, where k is a constant. Discuss the number of local extrema and the shape of the graph of f if
(A) $k > 0$ (B) $k < 0$ (C) $k = 0$

Applications

89. Profit analysis. The graph of the total profit $P(x)$ (in dollars) from the sale of x cordless electric screwdrivers is shown in the figure.

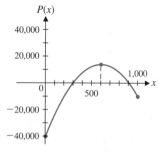

Figure for 89

(A) Write a brief description of the graph of the marginal profit function $y = P'(x)$, including a discussion of any x intercepts.

(B) Sketch a possible graph of $y = P'(x)$.

90. Revenue analysis. The graph of the total revenue $R(x)$ (in dollars) from the sale of x cordless electric screwdrivers is shown in the figure.

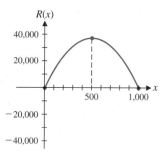

Figure for 90

(A) Write a brief description of the graph of the marginal revenue function $y = R'(x)$, including a discussion of any x intercepts.

(B) Sketch a possible graph of $y = R'(x)$.

91. Price analysis. The figure approximates the rate of change of the price of bacon over a 70-month period, where $B(t)$ is the price of a pound of sliced bacon (in dollars) and t is time (in months).

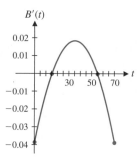

Figure for 91

(A) Write a brief description of the graph of $y = B(t)$, including a discussion of any local extrema.

(B) Sketch a possible graph of $y = B(t)$.

92. Price analysis. The figure approximates the rate of change of the price of eggs over a 70-month period, where $E(t)$ is the price of a dozen eggs (in dollars) and t is time (in months).

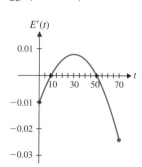

Figure for 92

(A) Write a brief description of the graph of $y = E(t)$, including a discussion of any local extrema.

(B) Sketch a possible graph of $y = E(t)$.

93. Average cost. A manufacturer incurs the following costs in producing x water ski vests in one day, for $0 < x < 150$: fixed costs, $320; unit production cost, $20 per vest; equipment maintenance and repairs, $0.05x^2$ dollars. So, the cost of manufacturing x vests in one day is given by

$$C(x) = 0.05x^2 + 20x + 320 \qquad 0 < x < 150$$

(A) What is the average cost $\overline{C}(x)$ per vest if x vests are produced in one day?

(B) Find the critical values of $\overline{C}(x)$, the intervals on which the average cost per vest is decreasing, the intervals on which the average cost per vest is increasing, and the local extrema. Do not graph.

94. Average cost. A manufacturer incurs the following costs in producing x rain jackets in one day for $0 < x < 200$: fixed costs, $450; unit production cost, $30 per jacket; equipment maintenance and repairs, $0.08x^2$ dollars.

(A) What is the average cost $\overline{C}(x)$ per jacket if x jackets are produced in one day?

(B) Find the critical values of $\overline{C}(x)$, the intervals on which the average cost per jacket is decreasing, the intervals on which the average cost per jacket is increasing, and the local extrema. Do not graph.

95. Marginal analysis. Show that profit will be increasing over production intervals (a, b) for which marginal revenue is greater than marginal cost. [*Hint:* $P(x) = R(x) - C(x)$]

96. Marginal analysis. Show that profit will be decreasing over production intervals (a, b) for which marginal revenue is less than marginal cost.

97. Medicine. A drug is injected into the bloodstream of a patient through the right arm. The drug concentration in the bloodstream of the left arm t hours after the injection is approximated by

$$C(t) = \frac{0.28t}{t^2 + 4} \qquad 0 < t < 24$$

Find the critical values of $C(t)$, the intervals on which the drug concentration is increasing, the intervals on which the concentration of the drug is decreasing, and the local extrema. Do not graph.

98. Medicine. The concentration $C(t)$, in milligrams per cubic centimeter, of a particular drug in a patient's bloodstream is given by

$$C(t) = \frac{0.3t}{t^2 + 6t + 9} \qquad 0 < t < 12$$

where t is the number of hours after the drug is taken orally. Find the critical values of $C(t)$, the intervals on which the drug concentration is increasing, the intervals on which the drug concentration is decreasing, and the local extrema. Do not graph.

1. (A) Horizontal tangent line at $x = 3$.

(B) Decreasing on $(-\infty, 3)$; increasing on $(3, \infty)$

(C) $f(x)$

2. Partition number: $x = 0$; critical value: $x = 0$; decreasing for all x

3. Partition number: $x = -1$; critical value: $x = -1$; increasing for all x

4. Partition number: $x = 0$; no critical values; decreasing on $(-\infty, 0)$ and $(0, \infty)$

5. Partition number: $x = 5$; critical value: $x = 5$; increasing on $(0, 5)$; decreasing on $(5, \infty)$

6. Increasing on $(-3, 1)$; decreasing on $(-\infty, -3)$ and $(1, \infty)$; local maximum at $x = 1$; local minimum at $x = -3$

7. (A) Critical values: $x = 2, x = 4$

(B) Local maximum at $x = 2$; local minimum at $x = 4$

(C) $f(x)$

8. (A) The U.S. share of the world market decreases for 6 years to a local minimum, increases for the next 10 years to a local maximum, and then decreases for the final 4 years.

(B) $S(t)$

9. (A) The marginal revenue is positive on $(0, 450)$, 0 at $x = 450$, and negative on $(450, 1{,}000)$.

(B) $R'(x)$

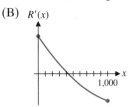

12-2 Second Derivative and Graphs

In Section 12-1, we saw that the derivative can be used when a graph is rising and falling. Now we want to see what the *second derivative* (the derivative of the derivative) can tell us about the shape of a graph.

Using Concavity as a Graphing Tool

Consider the functions

$$f(x) = x^2 \quad \text{and} \quad g(x) = \sqrt{x}$$

for x in the interval $(0, \infty)$. Since

$$f'(x) = 2x > 0 \quad \text{for } 0 < x < \infty$$

and

$$g'(x) = \frac{1}{2\sqrt{x}} > 0 \quad \text{for } 0 < x < \infty$$

both functions are increasing on $(0, \infty)$.

EXPLORE & DISCUSS 1

(A) Discuss the difference in the shapes of the graphs of f and g shown in Figure 1.

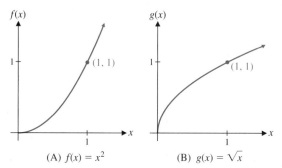

(A) $f(x) = x^2$ (B) $g(x) = \sqrt{x}$

Figure 1

(B) Complete the following table, and discuss the relationship between the values of the derivatives of f and g and the shapes of their graphs:

x	0.25	0.5	0.75	1
$f'(x)$				
$g'(x)$				

We use the term *concave upward* to describe a graph that opens upward and *concave downward* to describe a graph that opens downward. Thus, the graph of f in Figure 1A is concave upward, and the graph of g in Figure 1B is concave downward. Finding a mathematical formulation of concavity will help us sketch and analyze graphs.

We examine the slopes of f and g at various points on their graphs (see Fig. 2) and make two observations about each graph:

1. Looking at the graph of f in Figure 2A, we see that $f'(x)$ (the slope of the tangent line) is *increasing* and that the graph lies *above* each tangent line;

2. Looking at Figure 2B, we see that $g'(x)$ is *decreasing* and that the graph lies *below* each tangent line.

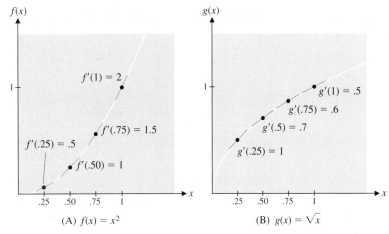

Figure 2

With these ideas in mind, we can state the general definition of concavity.

DEFINITION   Concavity

The graph of a function f is **concave upward** on the interval (a, b) if $f'(x)$ is *increasing* on (a, b) and is **concave downward** on the interval (a, b) if $f'(x)$ is *decreasing* on (a, b).

Geometrically, the graph is concave upward on (a, b) if it lies above its tangent lines in (a, b) and is concave downward on (a, b) if it lies below its tangent lines in (a, b).

How can we determine when $f'(x)$ is increasing or decreasing? In Section 12-1, we used the derivative to determine when a function is increasing or decreasing. To determine when the function $f'(x)$ is increasing or decreasing, we use the derivative of $f'(x)$. The derivative of the derivative of a function is called the *second derivative* of the function. Various notations for the second derivative are given in the following box:

NOTATION   Second Derivative

For $y = f(x)$, the **second derivative** of f, provided that it exists, is

$$f''(x) = \frac{d}{dx}f'(x)$$

Other notations for $f''(x)$ are

$$\frac{d^2y}{dx^2} \quad \text{and} \quad y''$$

Returning to the functions f and g discussed at the beginning of this section, we have

$$f(x) = x^2 \qquad\qquad g(x) = \sqrt{x} = x^{1/2}$$

$$f'(x) = 2x \qquad\qquad g'(x) = \frac{1}{2}x^{-1/2} = \frac{1}{2\sqrt{x}}$$

$$f''(x) = \frac{d}{dx}2x = 2 \qquad g''(x) = \frac{d}{dx}\frac{1}{2}x^{-1/2} = -\frac{1}{4}x^{-3/2} = -\frac{1}{4\sqrt{x^3}}$$

For $x > 0$, we see that $f''(x) > 0$; so, $f'(x)$ is increasing, and the graph of f is concave upward (see Fig. 2A). For $x > 0$, we also see that $g''(x) < 0$; so, $g'(x)$ is decreasing, and the graph of g is concave downward (see Fig. 2B). These ideas are summarized in the following box:

SUMMARY   Concavity

For the interval (a, b),

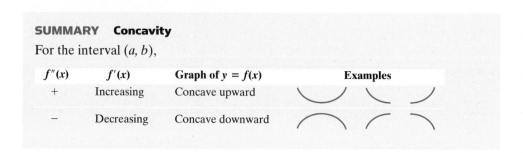

$f''(x)$	$f'(x)$	Graph of $y = f(x)$	Examples
+	Increasing	Concave upward	
−	Decreasing	Concave downward	

CONCEPTUAL INSIGHT

Be careful not to confuse concavity with falling and rising. A graph that is concave upward on an interval may be falling, rising, or both falling and rising on that interval. A similar statement holds for a graph that is concave downward. See Figure 3.

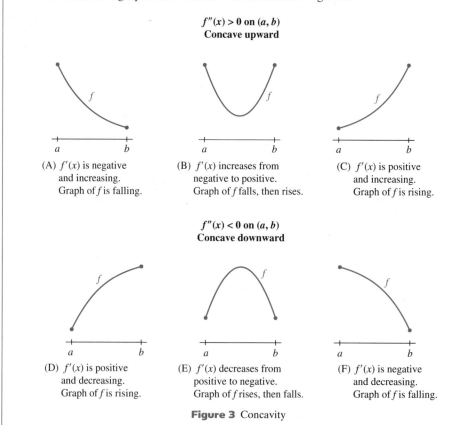

$f''(x) > 0$ on (a, b)
Concave upward

(A) $f'(x)$ is negative and increasing. Graph of f is falling.

(B) $f'(x)$ increases from negative to positive. Graph of f falls, then rises.

(C) $f'(x)$ is positive and increasing. Graph of f is rising.

$f''(x) < 0$ on (a, b)
Concave downward

(D) $f'(x)$ is positive and decreasing. Graph of f is rising.

(E) $f'(x)$ decreases from positive to negative. Graph of f rises, then falls.

(F) $f'(x)$ is negative and decreasing. Graph of f is falling.

Figure 3 Concavity

EXAMPLE 1   **Concavity of Graphs**   Determine the intervals on which the graph of each function is concave upward and the intervals on which it is concave downward. Sketch a graph of each function.

(A) $f(x) = e^x$ (B) $g(x) = \ln x$ (C) $h(x) = x^3$

SOLUTION   (A) $f(x) = e^x$

$$f'(x) = e^x$$

$$f''(x) = e^x$$

Since $f''(x) > 0$ on $(-\infty, \infty)$, the graph of $f(x) = e^x$ [Fig. 4(A)] is concave upward on $(-\infty, \infty)$.

(B) $g(x) = \ln x$

$$g'(x) = \frac{1}{x}$$

$$g''(x) = -\frac{1}{x^2}$$

The domain of $g(x) = \ln x$ is $(0, \infty)$ and $g''(x) < 0$ on this interval, so the graph of $g(x) = \ln x$ [Fig. 4(B)] is concave downward on $(0, \infty)$.

(C) $h(x) = x^3$

$$h'(x) = 3x^2$$

$$h''(x) = 6x$$

Since $h''(x) < 0$ when $x < 0$ and $h''(x) > 0$ when $x > 0$, the graph of $h(x) = x^3$ [Fig. 4(C)] is concave downward on $(-\infty, 0)$ and concave upward on $(0, \infty)$.

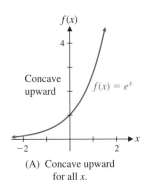

(A) Concave upward
for all x.

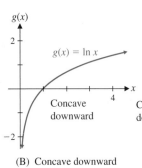

(B) Concave downward
for $x > 0$.

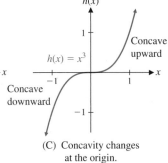

(C) Concavity changes
at the origin.

Figure 4

Matched Problem 1   Determine the intervals on which the graph of each function is concave upward and the intervals on which it is cancave downward. Sketch a graph of each function.

(A) $f(x) = -e^{-x}$ (B) $g(x) = \ln \frac{1}{x}$ (C) $h(x) = x^{1/3}$

Refer to Example 1. The graphs of $f(x) = e^x$ and $g(x) = \ln x$ never change concavity. But the graph of $h(x) = x^3$ changes concavity at $(0, 0)$. This point is called an *inflection point*.

Finding Inflection Points

An **inflection point** is a point on the graph of the function where the concavity changes (from upward to downward or from downward to upward). For the concavity to change at a point, $f''(x)$ must change sign at that point. But in Section 10-2, we saw that the partition numbers* identify the points where a function can change sign.

THEOREM 1   Inflection Points

If $y = f(x)$ is continuous on (a, b) and has an inflection point at $x = c$, then either $f''(c) = 0$ or $f''(c)$ does not exist.

---

*As we did with the first derivative, we assume that if f'' is discontinuous at c, then $f''(c)$ does not exist.

Note that inflection points can occur only at partition numbers of f'', but not every partition number of f'' produces an inflection point. Two additional requirements must be satisfied for an inflection point to occur:

A partition number c for f'' produces an inflection point for the graph of f only if

1. $f''(x)$ changes sign at c and

2. c is in the domain of f.

Figure 5 illustrates several typical cases.

If $f'(c)$ exists and $f''(x)$ changes sign at $x = c$, then the tangent line at an inflection point $(c, f(c))$ will always lie below the graph on the side that is concave upward and above the graph on the side that is concave downward (see Fig. 5A, B, and C).

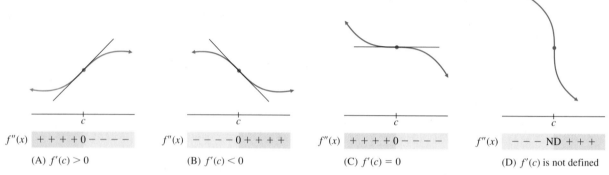

$f''(x)$ $+ + + + 0 - - - -$	$f''(x)$ $- - - - 0 + + + +$	$f''(x)$ $+ + + + 0 - - - -$	$f''(x)$ $- - -$ ND $+ + +$
(A) $f'(c) > 0$	(B) $f'(c) < 0$	(C) $f'(c) = 0$	(D) $f'(c)$ is not defined

Figure 5 Inflection points

EXAMPLE 2   **Locating Inflection Points**   Find the inflection point(s) of

$$f(x) = x^3 - 6x^2 + 9x + 1$$

SOLUTION   Since inflection points occur at values of x where $f''(x)$ changes sign, we construct a sign chart for $f''(x)$.

$$f(x) = x^3 - 6x^2 + 9x + 1$$
$$f'(x) = 3x^2 - 12x + 9$$
$$f''(x) = 6x - 12 = 6(x - 2)$$

The sign chart for $f''(x) = 6(x - 2)$ (partition number is 2) is as follows:

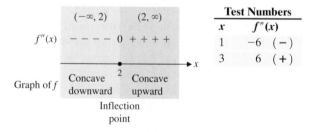

From the sign chart, we see that the graph of f has an inflection point at $x = 2$. That is, the point

$$(2, f(2)) = (2, 3) \qquad f(2) = 2^3 - 6 \cdot 2^2 + 9 \cdot 2 + 1 = 3$$

is an inflection point on the graph of f.

Matched Problem 2   Find the inflection point(s) of

$$f(x) = x^3 - 9x^2 + 24x - 10$$

EXAMPLE 3   **Locating Inflection Points**   Find the inflection point(s) of
$$f(x) = \ln(x^2 - 4x + 5)$$

SOLUTION   First we find the domain of f. Since $\ln x$ is defined only for $x > 0$, f is defined only for

$$x^2 - 4x + 5 > 0 \qquad \textit{Use completing the square (Section 2-3).}$$
$$(x - 2)^2 + 1 > 0 \qquad \textit{True for all x.}$$

So the domain of f is $(-\infty, \infty)$. Now we find $f''(x)$ and construct a sign chart for it.

$$f(x) = \ln(x^2 - 4x + 5)$$

$$f'(x) = \frac{2x - 4}{x^2 - 4x + 5}$$

$$f''(x) = \frac{(x^2 - 4x + 5)(2x - 4)' - (2x - 4)(x^2 - 4x + 5)'}{(x^2 - 4x + 5)^2}$$

$$= \frac{(x^2 - 4x + 5)2 - (2x - 4)(2x - 4)}{(x^2 - 4x + 5)^2}$$

$$= \frac{2x^2 - 8x + 10 - 4x^2 + 16x - 16}{(x^2 - 4x + 5)^2}$$

$$= \frac{-2x^2 + 8x - 6}{(x^2 - 4x + 5)^2}$$

$$= \frac{-2(x - 1)(x - 3)}{(x^2 - 4x + 5)^2}$$

The partition numbers for $f''(x)$ are $x = 1$ and $x = 3$.
Sign chart for $f''(x)$:

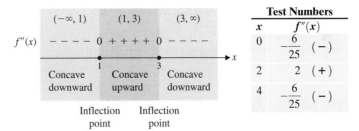

The sign chart shows that the graph of f has inflection points at $x = 1$ and $x = 3$.

Matched Problem 3   Find the inflection point(s) of
$$f(x) = \ln(x^2 - 2x + 5)$$

CONCEPTUAL INSIGHT

It is important to remember that the partition numbers for f'' are only *candidates* for inflection points. The function f must be defined at $x = c$, and the second derivative must change sign at $x = c$ in order for the graph to have an inflection point at $x = c$. For example, consider

$$f(x) = x^4 \qquad g(x) = \frac{1}{x}$$

$$f'(x) = 4x^3 \qquad g'(x) = -\frac{1}{x^2}$$

$$f''(x) = 12x^2 \qquad g''(x) = \frac{2}{x^3}$$

In each case, $x = 0$ is a partition number for the second derivative, but neither the graph of $f(x)$ nor the graph of $g(x)$ has an inflection point at $x = 0$. Function f does not have an inflection point at $x = 0$ because $f''(x)$ does not change sign at $x = 0$ (see Fig. 6A). Function g does not have an inflection point at $x = 0$ because $g(0)$ is not defined (see Fig. 6B).

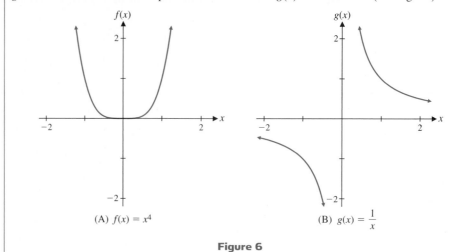

(A) $f(x) = x^4$ (B) $g(x) = \dfrac{1}{x}$

Figure 6

Analyzing Graphs

In the next example, we combine increasing/decreasing properties with concavity properties to analyze the graph of a function.

EXAMPLE 4   **Analyzing a Graph**   Figure 7 shows the graph of the derivative of a function f. Use this graph to discuss the graph of f. Include a sketch of a possible graph of f.

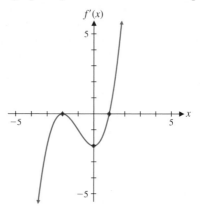

Figure 7

SOLUTION   The sign of the derivative determines where the original function is increasing and decreasing, and the increasing/decreasing properties of the derivative determine the concavity of the original function. The relevant information obtained from the graph of f' is summarized in Table 1, and a possible graph of f is shown in Figure 8.

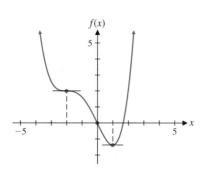

Figure 8

Table 1

x	$f'(x)$ (Fig. 7)	$f(x)$ (Fig. 8)
$-\infty < x < -2$	Negative and increasing	Decreasing and concave upward
$x = -2$	Local maximum	Inflection point
$-2 < x < 0$	Negative and decreasing	Decreasing and concave downward
$x = 0$	Local minimum	Inflection point
$0 < x < 1$	Negative and increasing	Decreasing and concave upward
$x = 1$	x intercept	Local minimum
$1 < x < \infty$	Positive and increasing	Increasing and concave upward

Matched Problem 4   Figure 9 shows the graph of the derivative of a function f. Use this graph to discuss the graph of f. Include a sketch of a possible graph of f.

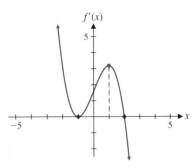

Figure 9

Curve Sketching

Graphing calculators and computers produce the graph of a function by plotting many points. However, important points on a plot many be difficult to identify. Using information gained from the function $f(x)$ and its derivatives, and plotting the important points—intercepts, local extrema, and inflection points—we can sketch by hand a very good representation of the graph of $f(x)$. This graphing process is called **curve sketching**.

PROCEDURE   Graphing Strategy (First Version)*

Step 1   *Analyze f(x)*. Find the domain and the intercepts. The x intercepts are the solutions of $f(x) = 0$, and the y intercept is $f(0)$.

Step 2   *Analyze f'(x)*. Find the partition numbers for, and critical values of, $f'(x)$. Construct a sign chart for $f'(x)$, determine the intervals on which f is increasing and decreasing, and find local maxima and minima.

Step 3   *Analyze f''(x)*. Find the partition numbers for $f''(x)$. Construct a sign chart for $f''(x)$, determine the intervals on which the graph of f is concave upward and concave downward, and find inflection points.

Step 4   *Sketch the graph of f*. Locate intercepts, local maxima and minima, and inflection points. Sketch in what you know from steps 1–3. Plot additional points as needed and complete the sketch.

EXAMPLE 5   **Using the Graphing Strategy**   Follow the graphing strategy and analyze the function

$$f(x) = x^4 - 2x^3$$

State all the pertinent information and sketch the graph of f.

SOLUTION   **Step 1**   *Analyze f(x)*. Since f is a polynomial, its domain is $(-\infty. \infty)$.

x intercept: $f(x) = 0$

$$x^4 - 2x^3 = 0$$

$$x^3(x - 2) = 0$$

$$x = 0, 2$$

y intercept: $f(0) = 0$

---

*We will modify this summary in Section 12-4 to include additional information about the graph of f.

Step 2 *Analyze $f'(x)$.* $f'(x) = 4x^3 - 6x^2 = 4x^2(x - \frac{3}{2})$

Critical values of $f(x)$: 0 and $\frac{3}{2}$

Partition numbers for $f'(x)$: 0 and $\frac{3}{2}$

Sign chart for $f'(x)$:

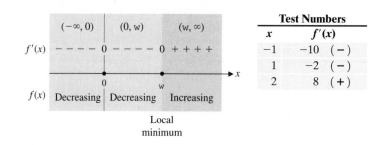

So $f(x)$ is decreasing on $(-\infty, \frac{3}{2})$, is increasing on $(\frac{3}{2}, \infty)$, and has a local minimum at $x = \frac{3}{2}$.

Step 3 *Analyze $f''(x)$.* $f''(x) = 12x^2 - 12x = 12x(x - 1)$

Partition numbers for $f''(x)$: 0 and 1

Sign chart for $f''(x)$:

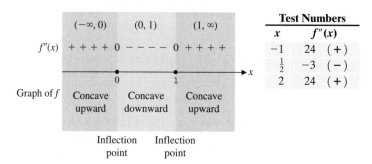

So the graph of f is concave upward on $(-\infty, 0)$ and $(1, \infty)$, is concave downward on $(0, 1)$, and has inflection points at $x = 0$ and $x = 1$.

Step 4 *Sketch the graph of f.*

Test Numbers	
x	$f(x)$
0	0
1	-1
$\frac{3}{2}$	$-\frac{27}{16}$
2	0

Matched Problem 5 Follow the graphing strategy and analyze the function $f(x) = x^4 + 4x^3$. State all the pertinent information and sketch the graph of f.

CONCEPTUAL INSIGHT

Refer to the solution of Example 5. Combining the sign charts for $f'(x)$ and $f''(x)$ (Fig. 10) partitions the real-number line into intervals on which neither $f'(x)$ nor $f''(x)$ changes sign. On each of these intervals, the graph of $f(x)$ must have one of four basic shapes (see also Fig. 3, parts A, C, D, and F on page 634). This reduces sketching the graph of a function to plotting the points identified in the graphing strategy and connecting them with one of the basic shapes.

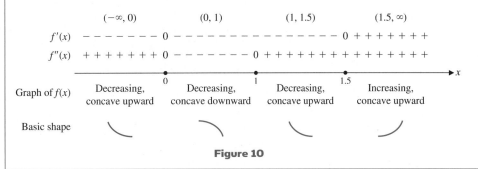

Figure 10

EXAMPLE 6   **Using the Graphing Strategy** Follow the graphing strategy and analyze the function

$$f(x) = 3x^{5/3} - 20x$$

State all the pertinent information and sketch the graph of f. Round any decimal values to two decimal places.

SOLUTION   **Step 1** *Analyze f(x).* $f(x) = 3x^{5/3} - 20x$

Since x^p is defined for any x and any positive p, the domain of f is $(-\infty, \infty)$.

x intercepts: Solve $f(x) = 0$

$$3x^{5/3} - 20x = 0$$

$$3x\left(x^{2/3} - \frac{20}{3}\right) = 0 \qquad (a^2 - b^2) = (a - b)(a + b)$$

$$3x\left(x^{1/3} - \sqrt{\frac{20}{3}}\right)\left(x^{1/3} + \sqrt{\frac{20}{3}}\right) = 0$$

The x intercepts of f are

$$x = 0, \quad x = \left(\sqrt{\frac{20}{3}}\right)^3 \approx 17.21, \quad x = \left(-\sqrt{\frac{20}{3}}\right)^3 \approx -17.21$$

y intercept: $f(0) = 0$.

Step 2 Analyze $f'(x)$.

$$f'(x) = 5x^{2/3} - 20$$

$$= 5(x^{2/3} - 4) \qquad\qquad \text{Again, } a^2 - b^2 = (a - b)(a + b)$$

$$= 5(x^{1/3} - 2)(x^{1/3} + 2)$$

Critical values of f: $x = 2^3 = 8$ and $x = (-2)^3 = -8$.
Partition numbers for f: $-8, 8$
Sign chart for $f'(x)$:

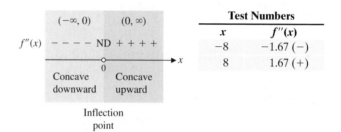

		Test Numbers
	x	**f′(x)**
	−12	6.21 (+)
	0	−20 (−)
	12	6.21 (+)

So f is increasing on $(-\infty, -8)$ and $(8, \infty)$ and decreasing on $(-8, 8)$. Therefore, $f(-8)$ is a local maximum, and $f(8)$ is a local minimum.

Step 3 *Analyze f″(x).*

$$f'(x) = 5x^{2/3} - 20$$

$$f''(x) = \frac{10}{3}x^{-1/3} = \frac{10}{3x^{1/3}}$$

Partition number for f'': 0

Sign chart for $f''(x)$:

	Test Numbers	
	x	**f″(x)**
	−8	−1.67 (−)
	8	1.67 (+)

So f is concave downward on $(-\infty, 0)$, is concave upward on $(0, \infty)$, and has an inflection point at $x = 0$.

Step 4 *Sketch the graph of f.*

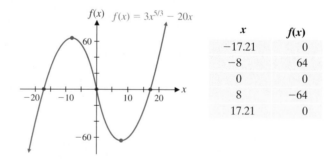

x	**f(x)**
−17.21	0
−8	64
0	0
8	−64
17.21	0

Matched Problem 6   Follow the graphing strategy and analyze the function $f(x) = 3x^{2/3} - x$. State all the pertinent information and sketch the graph of f. Round any decimal values to two decimal places.

Point of Diminishing Returns

If a company decides to increase spending on advertising, it would expect sales to increase. At first, sales will increase at an increasing rate and then increase at a decreasing rate. The value of x where the rate of change of sales goes from increasing to decreasing is called the **point of diminishing returns**. This is also the point where the rate of change has a maximum value. Money spent after this point may increase sales but at a lower rate.

EXAMPLE 7 **Maximum Rate of Change** Currently, a discount appliance store is selling 200 large-screen television sets monthly. If the store invests x thousand in an advertising campaign, the ad company estimates that sales will increase to

$$N(x) = 3x^3 - 0.25x^4 + 200 \qquad 0 \le x \le 9$$

When is the rate of change of sales increasing and when is it decreasing? What is the point of diminishing returns and the maximum rate of change of sales? Graph N and N' on the same coordinate system.

SOLUTION The rate of change of sales with respect to advertising expenditures is

$$N'(x) = 9x^2 - x^3 = x^2(9 - x)$$

To determine when $N'(x)$ is increasing and decreasing, we find $N''(x)$, the derivative of $N'(x)$:

$$N''(x) = 18x - 3x^2 = 3x(6 - x)$$

The information obtained by analyzing the signs of $N'(x)$ and $N''(x)$ is summarized in Table 2 (sign charts are omitted).

Table 2

x	$N''(x)$	$N'(x)$	$N'(x)$	$N(x)$
$0 < x < 6$	+	+	Increasing	Increasing, concave upward
$x = 6$	0	+	Local maximum	Inflection point
$6 < x < 9$	−	+	Decreasing	Increasing, concave downward

Examining Table 2, we see that $N'(x)$ is increasing on $(0, 6)$ and decreasing on $(6, 9)$. The point of diminishing returns is $x = 6$ and the maximum rate of change is $N'(6) = 108$. Note that $N'(x)$ has a local maximum and $N(x)$ has an inflection point at $x = 6$.

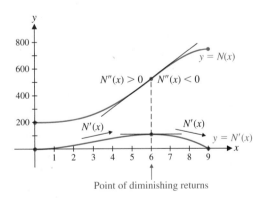

Matched Problem 7 Repeat Example 7 for

$$N(x) = 4x^3 - 0.25x^4 + 500 \qquad 0 \le x \le 12$$

Exercises 12-2

A

1. Use the graph of $y = f(x)$ to identify
   (A) Intervals on which the graph of f is concave upward
   (B) Intervals on which the graph of f is concave downward
   (C) Intervals on which $f''(x) < 0$
   (D) Intervals on which $f''(x) > 0$
   (E) Intervals on which $f'(x)$ is increasing
   (F) Intervals on which $f'(x)$ is decreasing
   (G) The x coordinates of inflection points
   (H) The x coordinates of local extrema for $f'(x)$

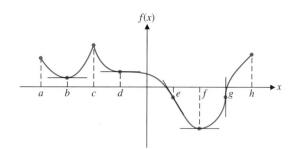

Figure for 1

2. Use the graph of $y = g(x)$ to identify
   (A) Intervals on which the graph of g is concave upward
   (B) Intervals on which the graph of g is concave downward
   (C) Intervals on which $g''(x) < 0$
   (D) Intervals on which $g''(x) > 0$
   (E) Intervals on which $g'(x)$ is increasing
   (F) Intervals on which $g'(x)$ is decreasing
   (G) The x coordinates of inflection points
   (H) The x coordinates of local extrema for $g'(x)$

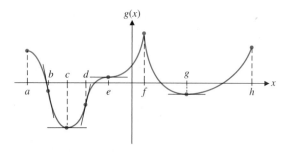

Figure for 2

In Problems 3–6, match the indicated conditions with one of the graphs (A)–(D) shown in the figure.

3. $f'(x) > 0$ and $f''(x) > 0$ on (a, b)

4. $f'(x) > 0$ and $f''(x) < 0$ on (a, b)

5. $f'(x) < 0$ and $f''(x) > 0$ on (a, b)

6. $f'(x) < 0$ and $f''(x) < 0$ on (a, b)

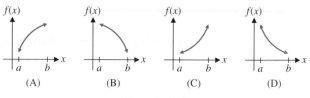

Figure for 3–6

In Problems 7–18, find the indicated derivative for each function.

7. $f''(x)$ for $f(x) = 2x^3 - 4x^2 + 5x - 6$

8. $g''(x)$ for $g(x) = -x^3 + 2x^2 - 3x + 9$

9. $h''(x)$ for $h(x) = 2x^{-1} - 3x^{-2}$

10. $k''(x)$ for $k(x) = -6x^{-2} + 12x^{-3}$

11. d^2y/dx^2 for $y = x^2 - 18x^{1/2}$

12. d^2y/dx^2 for $y = x^3 - 24x^{1/3}$

13. y'' for $y = (x^2 + 9)^4$

14. y'' for $y = (x^2 - 16)^5$

15. $f''(x)$ for $f(x) = e^{-x^2}$

16. $f''(x)$ for $f(x) = xe^{-x}$

17. y'' for $y = \dfrac{\ln x}{x^2}$

18. y'' for $y = x^2 \ln x$

In Problems 19–24, find the x and y coordinates of all inflection points.

19. $f(x) = x^3 + 30x^2$

20. $f(x) = x^3 - 24x^2$

21. $f(x) = x^{5/3} + 2$

22. $f(x) = 5 - x^{4/3}$

23. $f(x) = 1 + x + x^{2/5}$

24. $f(x) = x^{3/5} - 6x + 7$

In Problems 25–34, find the intervals on which the graph of f is concave upward, the intervals on which the graph of f is concave downward, and the inflection points.

25. $f(x) = x^4 + 6x^2$

26. $f(x) = x^4 + 6x$

27. $f(x) = x^3 - 4x^2 + 5x - 2$

28. $f(x) = -x^3 - 5x^2 + 4x - 3$

29. $f(x) = -x^4 + 12x^3 - 12x + 24$

30. $f(x) = x^4 - 2x^3 - 36x + 12$

31. $f(x) = \ln(x^2 - 2x + 10)$

32. $f(x) = \ln(x^2 + 6x + 13)$

33. $f(x) = 8e^x - e^{2x}$

34. $f(x) = e^{3x} - 9e^x$

In Problems 35–42, f(x) is continuous on $(-\infty, \infty)$. Use the given information to sketch the graph of f.

35.

x	-4	-2	-1	0	2	4
f(x)	0	3	1.5	0	-1	-3

36.

x	-4	-2	-1	0	2	4
f(x)	0	-2	-1	0	1	3

37.

x	-3	0	1	2	4	5
f(x)	-4	0	2	1	-1	0

38.

x	-4	-2	0	2	4	6
f(x)	0	3	0	-2	0	3

39. $f(0) = 2, f(1) = 0, f(2) = -2$;

$f'(0) = 0, f'(2) = 0$;

$f'(x) > 0$ on $(-\infty, 0)$ and $(2, \infty)$;

$f'(x) < 0$ on $(0, 2)$;

$f''(1) = 0$;

$f''(x) > 0$ on $(1, \infty)$;

$f''(x) < 0$ on $(-\infty, 1)$

40. $f(-2) = -2, f(0) = 1, f(2) = 4$;

$f'(-2) = 0, f'(2) = 0$;

$f'(x) > 0$ on $(-2, 2)$;

$f'(x) < 0$ on $(-\infty, -2)$ and $(2, \infty)$;

$f''(0) = 0$;

$f''(x) > 0$ on $(-\infty, 0)$;

$f''(x) < 0$ on $(0, \infty)$

41. $f(-1) = 0, f(0) = -2, f(1) = 0$;

$f'(0) = 0, f'(-1)$ and $f'(1)$ are not defined;

$f'(x) > 0$ on $(0, 1)$ and $(1, \infty)$;

$f'(x) < 0$ on $(-\infty, -1)$ and $(-1, 0)$;

$f''(-1)$ and $f''(1)$ are not defined;

$f''(x) > 0$ on $(-1, 1)$;

$f''(x) < 0$ on $(-\infty, -1)$ and $(1, \infty)$

42. $f(0) = -2, f(1) = 0, f(2) = 4$;

$f'(0) = 0, f'(2) = 0, f'(1)$ is not defined;

$f'(x) > 0$ on $(0, 1)$ and $(1, 2)$;

$f'(x) < 0$ on $(-\infty, 0)$ and $(2, \infty)$;

$f''(1)$ is not defined;

$f''(x) > 0$ on $(-\infty, 1)$;

$f''(x) < 0$ on $(1, \infty)$

B

In Problems 43–64, summarize the pertinent information obtained by applying the graphing strategy and sketch the graph of $y = f(x)$.

43. $f(x) = (x - 2)(x^2 - 4x - 8)$

44. $f(x) = (x - 3)(x^2 - 6x - 3)$

45. $f(x) = (x + 1)(x^2 - x + 2)$

46. $f(x) = (1 - x)(x^2 + x + 4)$

47. $f(x) = -0.25x^4 + x^3$

48. $f(x) = 0.25x^4 - 2x^3$

49. $f(x) = 16x(x - 1)^3$

50. $f(x) = -4x(x + 2)^3$

51. $f(x) = (x^2 + 3)(9 - x^2)$

52. $f(x) = (x^2 + 3)(x^2 - 1)$

53. $f(x) = (x^2 - 4)^2$

54. $f(x) = (x^2 - 1)(x^2 - 5)$

55. $f(x) = 2x^6 - 3x^5$

56. $f(x) = 3x^5 - 5x^4$

57. $f(x) = 1 - e^{-x}$

58. $f(x) = 2 - 3e^{-2x}$

59. $f(x) = e^{0.5x} + 4e^{-0.5x}$

60. $f(x) = 2e^{0.5x} + e^{-0.5x}$

61. $f(x) = -4 + 2\ln x$

62. $f(x) = 5 - 3 \ln x$

63. $f(x) = \ln(x + 4) - 2$

64. $f(x) = 1 - \ln(x - 3)$

In Problems 65–68, use the graph of $y = f'(x)$ to discuss the graph of $y = f(x)$. Organize your conclusions in a table (see Example 4), and sketch a possible graph of $y = f(x)$.

65.

66.

67.

68.

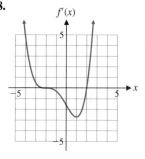

In Problems 69–76, apply steps 1–3 of the graphing strategy to $f(x)$. Use a graphing calculator to approximate (to two decimal places) x intercepts, critical values, and x coordinates of inflection points. Summarize all the pertinent information.

69. $f(x) = x^4 - 5x^3 + 3x^2 + 8x - 5$

70. $f(x) = x^4 + 2x^3 - 5x^2 - 4x + 4$

71. $f(x) = x^4 - 21x^3 + 100x^2 + 20x + 100$

72. $f(x) = x^4 - 12x^3 + 28x^2 + 76x - 50$

73. $f(x) = -x^4 - x^3 + 2x^2 - 2x + 3$

74. $f(x) = -x^4 + x^3 + x^2 + 6$

75. $f(x) = 0.1x^5 + 0.3x^4 - 4x^3 - 5x^2 + 40x + 30$

76. $f(x) = x^5 + 4x^4 - 7x^3 - 20x^2 + 20x - 20$

C

In Problems 77–80, assume that f is a polynomial.

77. Explain how you can locate inflection points for the graph of $y = f(x)$ by examining the graph of $y = f'(x)$.

78. Explain how you can determine where $f'(x)$ is increasing or decreasing by examining the graph of $y = f(x)$.

79. Explain how you can locate local maxima and minima for the graph of $y = f'(x)$ by examining the graph of $y = f(x)$.

80. Explain how you can locate local maxima and minima for the graph of $y = f(x)$ by examining the graph of $y = f'(x)$.

Applications

81. Inflation. One commonly used measure of inflation is the annual rate of change of the Consumer Price Index (CPI). A TV news story says that the rate of change of inflation for consumer prices is increasing. What does this say about the shape of the graph of the CPI?

82. Inflation. Another commonly used measure of inflation is the annual rate of change of the Producer Price Index (PPI). A government report states that the rate of change of inflation for producer prices is decreasing. What does this say about the shape of the graph of the PPI?

83. Cost analysis. A company manufactures a variety of camp stoves at different locations. The total cost $C(x)$ (in dollars) of producing x camp stoves per week at plant A is shown in the figure. Discuss the graph of the marginal cost function $C'(x)$ and interpret the graph of $C'(x)$ in terms of the efficiency of the production process at this plant.

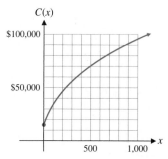

Figure for 83   Production costs at plant A

84. Cost analysis. The company in Problem 83 produces the same camp stove at another plant. The total cost $C(x)$ (in dollars) of producing x camp stoves per week at plant B is shown in the figure. Discuss the graph of the marginal cost function $C'(x)$ and interpret the graph of $C'(x)$ in terms of the efficiency of the production process at plant B. Compare the production processes at the two plants.

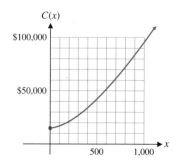

Figure for 84   Production costs at plant B

85. Revenue. The marketing research department of a computer company used a large city to test market the firm's new laptop. The department found that the relationship between price p (dollars per unit) and the demand x (units per week) was given approximately by

$$p = 1,296 - 0.12x^2 \qquad 0 < x < 80$$

So, weekly revenue can be approximated by

$$R(x) = xp = 1,296x - 0.12x^3 \qquad 0 < x < 80$$

(A) Find the local extrema for the revenue function.

(B) On which intervals is the graph of the revenue function concave upward? Concave downward?

86. Profit. Suppose that the cost equation for the company in Problem 85 is

$$C(x) = 830 + 396x$$

(A) Find the local extrema for the profit function.

(B) On which intervals is the graph of the profit function concave upward? Concave downward?

87. Revenue. A dairy is planning to introduce and promote a new line of organic ice cream. After test marketing the new line in a large city, the marketing research department found that the demand in that city is given approximately by

$$p = 10e^{-x} \qquad 0 \le x \le 5$$

where x thousand quarts were sold per week at a price of $\$p$ each.

(A) Find the local extrema for the revenue function.

(B) On which intervals is the graph of the revenue function concave upward? Concave downward?

88. Revenue. A national food service runs food concessions for sporting events throughout the country. The company's marketing research department chose a particular football stadium to test market a new jumbo hot dog. It was found that the demand for the new hot dog is given approximately by

$$p = 8 - 2 \ln x \qquad 5 \le x \le 50$$

where x is the number of hot dogs (in thousands) that can be sold during one game at a price of $\$p$.

(A) Find the local extrema for the revenue function.

(B) On which intervals is the graph of the revenue function concave upward? Concave downward?

89. Production: point of diminishing returns. A T-shirt manufacturer is planning to expand its workforce. It estimates that the number of T-shirts produced by hiring x new workers is given by

$$T(x) = -0.25x^4 + 5x^3 \qquad 0 \le x \le 15$$

When is the rate of change of T-shirt production increasing and when is it decreasing? What is the point of diminishing returns and the maximum rate of change of T-shirt production? Graph T and T' on the same coordinate system.

90. Production: point of diminishing returns. A baseball cap manufacturer is planning to expand its workforce. It estimates that the number of baseball caps produced by hiring x new workers is given by

$$T(x) = -0.25x^4 + 6x^3 \qquad 0 \le x \le 18$$

When is the rate of change of baseball cap production increasing and when is it decreasing? What is the point of diminishing returns and the maximum rate of change of

baseball cap production? Graph T and T' on the same coordinate system.

91. Advertising: point of diminishing returns. A company estimates that it will sell $N(x)$ units of a product after spending $\$x$ thousand on advertising, as given by

$$N(x) = -0.25x^4 + 23x^3 - 540x^2 + 80,000 \qquad 24 \le x \le 45$$

When is the rate of change of sales increasing and when is it decreasing? What is the point of diminishing returns and the maximum rate of change of sales? Graph N and N' on the same coordinate system.

92. Advertising: point of diminishing returns. A company estimates that it will sell $N(x)$ units of a product after spending $\$x$ thousand on advertising, as given by

$$N(x) = -0.25x^4 + 13x^3 - 180x^2 + 10,000 \qquad 15 \le x \le 24$$

When is the rate of change of sales increasing and when is it decreasing? What is the point of diminishing returns and the maximum rate of change of sales? Graph N and N' on the same coordinate system.

93. Advertising. An automobile dealer uses TV advertising to promote car sales. On the basis of past records, the dealer arrived at the following data, where x is the number of ads placed monthly and y is the number of cars sold that month:

Number of Ads	Number of Cars
x	y
10	325
12	339
20	417
30	546
35	615
40	682
50	795

(A) Enter the data in a graphing calculator and find a cubic regression equation for the number of cars sold monthly as a function of the number of ads.

(B) How many ads should the dealer place each month to maximize the rate of change of sales with respect to the number of ads, and how many cars can the dealer expect to sell with this number of ads? Round answers to the nearest integer.

94. Advertising. A sporting goods chain places TV ads to promote golf club sales. The marketing director used past records to determine the following data, where x is the number of ads placed monthly and y is the number of golf clubs sold that month.

Number of Ads	Number of Golf Clubs
x	y
10	345
14	488
20	746
30	1,228
40	1,671
50	1,955

(A) Enter the data in a graphing calculator and find a cubic regression equation for the number of golf clubs sold monthly as a function of the number of ads.

(B) How many ads should the store manager place each month to maximize the rate of change of sales with respect to the number of ads, and how many golf clubs can the manager expect to sell with this number of ads? Round answers to the nearest integer.

95. Population growth: bacteria. A drug that stimulates reproduction is introduced into a colony of bacteria. After t minutes, the number of bacteria is given approximately by

$$N(t) = 1,000 + 30t^2 - t^3 \qquad 0 \le t \le 20$$

(A) When is the rate of growth, $N'(t)$, increasing? Decreasing?

(B) Find the inflection points for the graph of N.

(C) Sketch the graphs of N and N' on the same coordinate system.

(D) What is the maximum rate of growth?

96. Drug sensitivity. One hour after x milligrams of a particular drug are given to a person, the change in body temperature $T(x)$, in degrees Fahrenheit, is given by

$$T(x) = x^2 \left(1 - \frac{x}{9}\right) \qquad 0 \le x \le 6$$

The rate $T'(x)$ at which $T(x)$ changes with respect to the size of the dosage x is called the *sensitivity* of the body to the dosage.

(A) When is $T'(x)$ increasing? Decreasing?

(B) Where does the graph of T have inflection points?

(C) Sketch the graphs of T and T' on the same coordinate system.

(D) What is the maximum value of $T'(x)$?

97. Learning. The time T (in minutes) it takes a person to learn a list of length n is

$$T(n) = 0.08n^3 - 1.2n^2 + 6n \qquad n \ge 0$$

(A) When is the rate of change of T with respect to the length of the list increasing? Decreasing?

(B) Where does the graph of T have inflection points?

(C) Graph T and T' on the same coordinate system.

(D) What is the minimum value of $T'(n)$?

Answers to Matched Problems

1. (A) Concave downward on $(-\infty, \infty)$

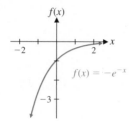

(B) Concave upward on $(0, \infty)$

(C) Concave upward on $(-\infty, 0)$ and concave downward on $(0, \infty)$

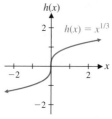

2. The only inflection point is $(3, f(3)) = (3, 8)$.

3. The inflection points are
$(-1, f(-1)) = (-1, \ln 8)$ and $(3, f(3)) = (3, \ln 8)$.

4.

x	$f'(x)$	$f(x)$
$-\infty < x < -1$	Positive and decreasing	Increasing and concave downward
$x = -1$	Local minimum	Inflection point
$-1 < x < 1$	Positive and increasing	Increasing and concave upward
$x = 1$	Local maximum	Inflection point
$1 < x < 2$	Positive and decreasing	Increasing and concave downward
$x = 2$	x intercept	Local maximum
$2 < x < \infty$	Negative and decreasing	Decreasing and concave downward

5. x intercepts: $-4, 0$; y intercept: $f(0) = 0$

Decreasing on $(-\infty, -3)$; increasing on $(-3, \infty)$; local minimum at $x = -3$

Concave upward on $(-\infty, -2)$ and $(0, \infty)$; concave downward on $(-2, 0)$

Inflection points at $x = -2$ and $x = 0$

x	$f(x)$
-4	0
-3	-27
-2	-16
0	0

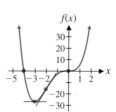

6. x intercepts: $0, 27$; y intercept: $f(0) = 0$

Decreasing on $(-\infty, 0)$ and $(8, \infty)$; increasing on $(0, 8)$; local minimum: $f(0) = 0$; local maximum: $f(8) = 4$

Concave downward on $(-\infty, 0)$ and $(0, \infty)$; no inflection points

x	$f(x)$
0	0
8	4
27	0

7. $N'(x)$ is increasing on $(0, 8)$ and decreasing on $(8, 12)$. The point of diminishing returns is $x = 8$ and the maximum rate of change is $N'(8) = 256$.

Point of diminishing returns

12-3 L'Hôpital's Rule

- Introduction
- L'Hôpital's Rule and the Indeterminate Form 0/0
- One-Sided Limits and Limits at ∞
- L'Hôpital's Rule and the Indeterminate Form ∞/∞

Introduction

The ability to evaluate a wide variety of different types of limits is one of the skills that are necessary to apply the techniques of calculus successfully. Limits play a fundamental role in the development of the derivative and are an important graphing tool. In order to deal effectively with graphs, we need to develop some more methods for evaluating limits.

In this section, we discuss a powerful technique for evaluating limits of quotients called *L'Hôpital's rule*. The rule is named after the French mathematician Marquis de L'Hôpital (1661–1704). To use L'Hôpital's rule, it is necessary to be familiar with the limit properties of some basic functions. Figure 1 reviews some limits involving powers of x that were discussed earlier.

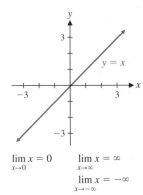

$$\lim_{x \to 0} x = 0 \qquad \lim_{x \to \infty} x = \infty$$
$$\lim_{x \to -\infty} x = -\infty$$

(A) $y = x$

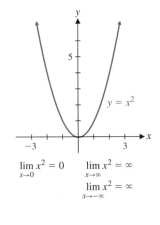

$$\lim_{x \to 0} x^2 = 0 \qquad \lim_{x \to \infty} x^2 = \infty$$
$$\lim_{x \to -\infty} x^2 = \infty$$

(B) $y = x^2$

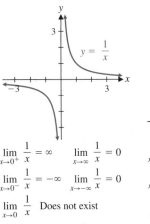

$$\lim_{x \to 0^+} \frac{1}{x} = \infty \qquad \lim_{x \to \infty} \frac{1}{x} = 0$$
$$\lim_{x \to 0^-} \frac{1}{x} = -\infty \qquad \lim_{x \to -\infty} \frac{1}{x} = 0$$
$$\lim_{x \to 0} \frac{1}{x} \quad \text{Does not exist}$$

(C) $y = \dfrac{1}{x}$

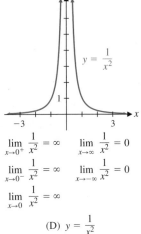

$$\lim_{x \to 0^+} \frac{1}{x^2} = \infty \qquad \lim_{x \to \infty} \frac{1}{x^2} = 0$$
$$\lim_{x \to 0^-} \frac{1}{x^2} = \infty \qquad \lim_{x \to -\infty} \frac{1}{x^2} = 0$$
$$\lim_{x \to 0} \frac{1}{x^2} = \infty$$

(D) $y = \dfrac{1}{x^2}$

Figure 1 Limits involving powers of x

The limits in Figure 1 are easily extended to functions of the form $f(x) = (x - c)^n$ and $g(x) = 1/(x - c)^n$. In general, if n is an odd integer, then limits involving $(x - c)^n$ or $1/(x - c)^n$ as x approaches c (or $\pm\infty$) behave, respectively, like the limits of x and $1/x$ as x approaches 0 (or $\pm\infty$). If n is an even integer, then limits involving these expressions behave, respectively, like the limits of x^2 and $1/x^2$ as x approaches 0 (or $\pm\infty$).

EXAMPLE 1 **Limits Involving Powers of** $x - c$

(A) $\lim\limits_{x \to 2} \dfrac{5}{(x - 2)^4} = \infty$ Compare with $\lim\limits_{x \to 0} \dfrac{1}{x^2}$ in Figure 1.

(B) $\lim\limits_{x \to -1^-} \dfrac{4}{(x + 1)^3} = -\infty$ Compare with $\lim\limits_{x \to 0^-} \dfrac{1}{x}$ in Figure 1.

(C) $\lim\limits_{x \to \infty} \dfrac{4}{(x - 9)^6} = 0$ Compare with $\lim\limits_{x \to 0^-} \dfrac{1}{x^2}$ in Figure 1.

(D) $\lim\limits_{x \to -\infty} 3x^3 = -\infty$ Compare with $\lim\limits_{x \to -\infty} x$ in Figure 1.

Matched Problem 1   Evaluate each limit.

(A) $\lim\limits_{x \to 3^+} \dfrac{7}{(x - 3)^5}$ (B) $\lim\limits_{x \to -4} \dfrac{6}{(x + 4)^6}$

(C) $\lim\limits_{x \to -\infty} \dfrac{3}{(x + 2)^3}$ (D) $\lim\limits_{x \to \infty} 5x^4$

Figure 2 reviews limits of exponential and logarithmic functions.
The limits in Figure 2 also generalize to other simple exponential and logarithmic forms.

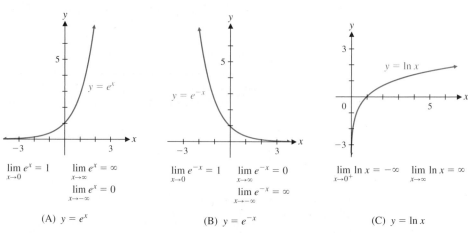

$\lim\limits_{x \to 0} e^x = 1$ $\lim\limits_{x \to \infty} e^x = \infty$ $\lim\limits_{x \to 0} e^{-x} = 1$ $\lim\limits_{x \to \infty} e^{-x} = 0$ $\lim\limits_{x \to 0^+} \ln x = -\infty$ $\lim\limits_{x \to \infty} \ln x = \infty$

$\lim\limits_{x \to -\infty} e^x = 0$ $\lim\limits_{x \to -\infty} e^{-x} = \infty$

       (A) $y = e^x$ (B) $y = e^{-x}$ (C) $y = \ln x$

Figure 2 Limits involving exponential and logarithmic functions

EXAMPLE 2 **Limits Involving Exponential and Logarithmic Forms**

(A) $\lim\limits_{x \to \infty} 2e^{3x} = \infty$ Compare with $\lim\limits_{x \to \infty} e^x$ in Figure 2.

(B) $\lim\limits_{x \to \infty} 4e^{-5x} = 0$ Compare with $\lim\limits_{x \to \infty} e^{-x}$ in Figure 2.

(C) $\lim\limits_{x \to \infty} \ln(x + 4) = \infty$ Compare with $\lim\limits_{x \to \infty} \ln x$ in Figure 2.

(D) $\lim\limits_{x \to 2^+} \ln(x - 2) = -\infty$ Compare with $\lim\limits_{x \to \infty^+} \ln x$ in Figure 2.

Matched Problem 2   Evaluate each limit.

(A) $\lim\limits_{x \to -\infty} 2e^{-6x}$

(B) $\lim\limits_{x \to -\infty} 3e^{2x}$

(C) $\lim\limits_{x \to -4^+} \ln(x + 4)$

(D) $\lim\limits_{x \to \infty} \ln(x - 10)$

Now that we have reviewed the limit properties of some basic functions, we are ready to consider the main topic of this section: L'Hôpital's rule.

L'Hôpital's Rule and the Indeterminate Form 0/0

Recall that the limit

$$\lim_{x \to c} \frac{f(x)}{g(x)}$$

is a 0/0 indeterminate form if

$$\lim_{x \to c} f(x) = 0 \quad \text{and} \quad \lim_{x \to c} g(x) = 0$$

The quotient property for limits in Section 10-1 does not apply since $\lim\limits_{x \to c} g(x) = 0$.

If we are dealing with a 0/0 indeterminate form, the limit may or may not exist, and we cannot tell which is true without further investigation.

Each of the following is a 0/0 indeterminate form:

$$\lim_{x \to 2} \frac{x^2 - 4}{x - 2} \quad \text{and} \quad \lim_{x \to 1} \frac{e^x - e}{x - 1}$$

The first limit can be evaluated by performing some algebraic simplifications, such as

$$\lim_{x \to 2} \frac{x^2 - 4}{x - 2} = \lim_{x \to 2} \frac{(x - 2)(x + 2)}{x - 2} = \lim_{x \to 2}(x + 2) = 4$$

The second cannot. Instead, we turn to the powerful **L'Hôpital's rule**, which we now state without proof. This rule can be used whenever a limit is a 0/0 indeterminate form.

THEOREM 1   L'Hôpital's Rule for 0/0 Indeterminate Forms: Version 1

For c a real number,
if $\lim\limits_{x \to c} f(x) = 0$ and $\lim\limits_{x \to c} g(x) = 0$, then

$$\lim_{x \to c} \frac{f(x)}{g(x)} = \lim_{x \to c} \frac{f'(x)}{g'(x)}$$

provided that the second limit exists or is $+\infty$ or $-\infty$.

EXAMPLE 3   **L'Hôpital's Rule**   Evaluate $\lim\limits_{x \to 1} \dfrac{e^x - e}{x - 1}$.

SOLUTION   **Step 1** *Check to see if L'Hôpital's rule applies:*

$$\lim_{x \to 1}(e^x - e) = e^1 - e = 0 \quad \text{and} \quad \lim_{x \to 1}(x - 1) = 1 - 1 = 0$$

L'Hôpital's rule does apply.

Step 2 *Apply L'Hôpital's rule:*

O/O form

$$\lim_{x \to 1} \frac{e^x - e}{x - 1} = \lim_{x \to 1} \frac{\frac{d}{dx}(e^x - e)}{\frac{d}{dx}(x - 1)}$$
  Apply L'Hôpital's rule.

$$= \lim_{x \to 1} \frac{e^x}{1}$$
  e^x *is continuous at x = 1.*

$$= \frac{e^1}{1} = e$$

Matched Problem 3 Evaluate $\displaystyle\lim_{x \to 4} \frac{e^x - e^4}{x - 4}$.

CONCEPTUAL INSIGHT

In L'Hôpital's rule, the symbol $f'(x)/g'(x)$ represents the derivative of $f(x)$ divided by the derivative of $g(x)$, not the derivative of the quotient $f(x)/g(x)$.

When applying L'Hôpital's rule to a 0/0 indeterminate form, be certain that you differentiate the numerator and denominator separately.

Figure 3

The functions

$$y_1 = \frac{e^x - e}{x - 1} \quad \text{and} \quad y_2 = \frac{e^x}{1}$$

of Example 3 are different functions (see Fig. 3), but both functions have the same limit e as x approaches 1. Although y_1 is undefined at $x = 1$, the graph of y_1 provides a check of the answer to Example 3.

EXAMPLE 4 **L'Hôpital's Rule** Evaluate $\displaystyle\lim_{x \to 0} \frac{\ln(1 + x^2)}{x^4}$.

SOLUTION **Step 1** *Check to see if L'Hôpital's rule applies:*

$$\lim_{x \to 0} \ln(1 + x^2) = \ln 1 = 0 \quad \text{and} \quad \lim_{x \to 0} x^4 = 0$$

L'Hôpital's rule does apply.

Step 2 *Apply L'Hôpital's rule:*

O/O form

$$\lim_{x \to 0} \frac{\ln(1 + x^2)}{x^4} = \lim_{x \to 0} \frac{\frac{dx}{dx}\ln(1 + x^2)}{\frac{d}{dx}x^4}$$
  Apply L'Hôpital's rule.

$$\lim_{x \to 0} \frac{\ln(1 + x^2)}{x^4} = \lim_{x \to 0} \frac{\frac{2x}{1 + x^2}}{4x^3}$$
  Multiply numerator and denominator by 1/4x³.

$$= \lim_{x \to 0} \frac{\frac{2x}{1 + x^2} \cdot \frac{1}{4x^3}}{4x^3 \cdot \frac{1}{4x^3}}$$
  Simplify.

$$= \lim_{x \to 0} \frac{1}{2x^2(1 + x^2)}$$

Apply Theorem 1 in Section 10-3 and compare with Fig. 1(D).

$$= \infty$$

Matched Problem 4   Evaluate $\lim\limits_{x \to 1} \dfrac{\ln x}{(x - 1)^3}$.

EXAMPLE 5   **L'Hôpital's Rule May Not Be Applicable** Evaluate $\lim\limits_{x \to 1} \dfrac{\ln x}{x}$.

SOLUTION   **Step 1** *Check to see if L'Hôpital's rule applies:*

$$\lim_{x \to 1} \ln x = \ln 1 = 0, \qquad \text{but} \qquad \lim_{x \to 1} x = 1 \neq 0$$

L'Hôpital's rule does not apply.

Step 2 *Evaluate by another method.* The quotient property for limits from Section 10-1 does apply, and we have

$$\lim_{x \to 1} \frac{\ln x}{x} = \frac{\lim\limits_{x \to 1} \ln x}{\lim\limits_{x \to 1} x} = \frac{\ln 1}{1} = \frac{0}{1} = 0$$

Note that applying L'Hôpital's rule would give us an incorrect result:

$$\lim_{x \to 1} \frac{\ln x}{x} \neq \lim_{x \to 1} \frac{\dfrac{d}{dx} \ln x}{\dfrac{d}{dx} x} = \lim_{x \to 1} \frac{1/x}{1} = 1$$

Matched Problem 5   Evaluate $\lim\limits_{x \to 0} \dfrac{x}{e^{-x}}$.

CONCEPTUAL INSIGHT

As Example 5 illustrates, all limits involving quotients are not 0/0 indeterminate forms.

You must always check to see if L'Hôpital's rule applies before you use it.

EXAMPLE 6   **Repeated Application of L'Hôpital's Rule** Evaluate

$$\lim_{x \to 0} \frac{x^2}{e^x - 1 - x}$$

SOLUTION   **Step 1** *Check to see if L'Hôpital's rule applies:*

$$\lim_{x \to 0} x^2 = 0 \qquad \text{and} \qquad \lim_{x \to 0}(e^x - 1 - x) = 0$$

L'Hôpital's rule does apply.

Step 2 Apply L'Hôpital's rule:

0/0 form

$$\lim_{x \to 0} \frac{x^2}{e^x - 1 - x} = \lim_{x \to 0} \frac{\dfrac{d}{dx} x^2}{\dfrac{d}{dx}(e^x - 1 - x)} = \lim_{x \to 0} \frac{2x}{e^x - 1}$$

Since $\lim_{x \to 0} 2x = 0$ and $\lim_{x \to 0}(e^x - 1) = 0$, the new limit obtained is also a 0/0 indeterminate form, and L'Hôpital's rule can be applied again.

Step 3 *Apply L'Hôpital's rule again:*

$$\lim_{x \to 0} \frac{2x}{e^x - 1} = \lim_{x \to 0} \frac{\frac{d}{dx} 2x}{\frac{d}{dx}(e^x - 1)} = \lim_{x \to 0} \frac{2}{e^x} = \frac{2}{e^0} = 2$$

0/0 form

Therefore,

$$\lim_{x \to 0} \frac{x^2}{e^x - 1 - x} = \lim_{x \to 0} \frac{2x}{e^x - 1} = \lim_{x \to 0} \frac{2x}{e^x} = 2$$

Matched Problem 6 Evaluate $\displaystyle\lim_{x \to 0} \frac{e^{2x} - 1 - 2x}{x^2}$

One-Sided Limits and Limits at ∞

In addition to examining the limit as x approaches c, we have discussed one-sided limits and limits at ∞ in Chapter 10. L'Hôpital's rule is valid in these cases also.

THEOREM 2 **L'Hôpital's Rule for 0/0 Indeterminate Forms: Version 2 (for one-sided limits and limits at infinity)**

The first version of L'Hôpital's rule (Theorem 1) remains valid if the symbol $x \to c$ is replaced everywhere it occurs with one of the following symbols:

$$x \to c^+ \qquad x \to c^- \qquad x \to \infty \qquad x \to -\infty$$

For example, if $\displaystyle\lim_{x \to \infty} f(x) = 0$ and $\displaystyle\lim_{x \to \infty} g(x) = 0$, then

$$\lim_{x \to \infty} \frac{f(x)}{g(x)} = \lim_{x \to \infty} \frac{f'(x)}{g'(x)}$$

provided that the second limit exists or is $+\infty$ or $-\infty$. Similar rules can be written for $x \to c^+$, $x \to c^-$, and $x \to -\infty$.

EXAMPLE 7 **L'Hôpital's Rule for One-Sided Limits** Evaluate $\displaystyle\lim_{x \to 1^+} \frac{\ln x}{(x - 1)^2}$.

SOLUTION **Step 1** *Check to see if L'Hôpital's rule applies:*

$$\lim_{x \to 1^+} \ln x = 0 \qquad \text{and} \qquad \lim_{x \to 1^+} (x - 1)^2 = 0$$

L'Hôpital's rule does apply.

Step 2 *Apply L'Hôpital's rule:*

$$\lim_{x \to 1^+} \frac{\ln x}{(x - 1)^2} = \lim_{x \to 1^+} \frac{\frac{d}{dx}(\ln x)}{\frac{d}{dx}(x - 1)^2} \qquad \text{Apply L'Hôpital's rule.}$$

0/0 form

$$= \lim_{x \to 1^+} \frac{1/x}{2(x - 1)} \qquad \text{Simplify.}$$

$$= \lim_{x \to 1^+} \frac{1}{2x(x - 1)}$$

$$= \infty$$

The limit as $x \to 1^+$ is ∞ because $1/2x(x-1)$ has a vertical asymptote at $x = 1$ (Theorem 1, Section 10-3) and $x(x-1) > 0$ for $x > 1$.

Matched Problem 7   Evaluate $\lim\limits_{x \to 1^-} \dfrac{\ln x}{(x-1)^2}$.

EXAMPLE 8   **L'Hôpital's Rule for Limits at Infinity**   Evaluate $\lim\limits_{x \to \infty} \dfrac{\ln(1 + e^{-x})}{e^{-x}}$.

SOLUTION   **Step 1** *Check to see if L'Hôpital's rule applies:*

$$\lim_{x \to \infty} \ln(1 + e^{-x}) = \ln(1 + 0) = \ln 1 = 0 \text{ and } \lim_{x \to \infty} e^{-x} = 0$$

L'Hôpital's rule does apply.

Step 2 *Apply L'Hôpital's rule:*

$$\underset{0/0 \text{ form}}{\lim_{x \to \infty} \frac{\ln(1 + e^{-x})}{e^{-x}}} = \lim_{x \to \infty} \frac{\dfrac{d}{dx}[\ln(1 + e^{-x})]}{\dfrac{d}{dx} e^{-x}} \qquad \text{Apply L'Hôpital's rule.}$$

$$= \lim_{x \to \infty} \frac{-e^{-x}/(1 + e^{-x})}{-e^{-x}} \qquad \begin{array}{l}\text{Multiply numerator and}\\\text{denominator by } -e^x.\end{array}$$

$$\lim_{x \to \infty} \frac{\ln(1 + e^{-x})}{e^{-x}} = \lim_{x \to \infty} \frac{1}{1 + e^{-x}} \qquad \lim_{x \to \infty} e^{-x} = 0$$

$$= \frac{1}{1 + 0} = 1$$

Matched Problem 8   Evaluate $\lim\limits_{x \to -\infty} \dfrac{\ln(1 + 2e^x)}{e^x}$.

L'Hôpital's Rule and the Indeterminate Form ∞/∞

In Section 10-3, we discussed techniques for evaluating limits of rational functions such as

$$\lim_{x \to \infty} \frac{2x^2}{x^3 + 3} \qquad \lim_{x \to \infty} \frac{4x^3}{2x^2 + 5} \qquad \lim_{x \to \infty} \frac{3x^3}{5x^3 + 6} \qquad (1)$$

Each of these limits is an ∞/∞ *indeterminate form*. In general, if $\lim_{x \to c} f(x) = \pm\infty$ and $\lim_{x \to c} g(x) = \pm\infty$, then

$$\lim_{x \to c} \frac{f(x)}{g(x)}$$

is called an ∞/∞ **indeterminate form**. Furthermore, $x \to c$ can be replaced in all three limits above with $x \to c^+$, $x \to c^-$, $x \to \infty$, or $x \to -\infty$. It can be shown that L'Hôpital's rule also applies to these ∞/∞ indeterminate forms.

THEOREM 3   L'Hôpital's Rule for the Indeterminate Form ∞/∞: Version 3
Versions 1 and 2 of L'Hôpital's rule for the indeterminate form $0/0$ are also valid if the limit of f and the limit of g are both infinite; that is, both $+\infty$ and $-\infty$ are permissible for either limit.

For example, if $\lim_{x \to c^+} f(x) = \infty$ and $\lim_{x \to c^+} g(x) = -\infty$, then L'Hôpital's rule can be applied to $\lim_{x \to c^+} [f(x)/g(x)]$.

> **EXPLORE & DISCUSS 1**
>
> Evaluate each of the limits in (1) in two ways:
> 1. Use Theorem 4 in Section 10-3.
> 2. Use L'Hôpital's rule.
>
> Given a choice, which method would you choose? Why?

EXAMPLE 9   **L'Hôpital's Rule for the Indeterminate Form ∞/∞**   Evaluate $\lim_{x \to \infty} \dfrac{\ln x}{x^2}$.

SOLUTION   **Step 1** *Check to see if L'Hôpital's rule applies:*

$$\lim_{x \to \infty} \ln x = \infty \qquad \text{and} \qquad \lim_{x \to \infty} x^2 = \infty$$

L'Hôpital's rule does apply.

Step 2 *Apply L'Hôpital's rule:*

$$\overset{\infty/\infty \text{ form}}{\lim_{x \to \infty} \frac{\ln x}{x^2}} = \lim_{x \to \infty} \frac{\dfrac{d}{dx}(\ln x)}{\dfrac{d}{dx} x^2} \qquad \text{Apply L'Hôpital's rule.}$$

$$= \lim_{x \to \infty} \frac{1/x}{2x} \qquad \text{Simplify.}$$

$$\lim_{x \to \infty} \frac{\ln x}{x^2} = \lim_{x \to \infty} \frac{1}{2x^2} \qquad \text{See Figure 1(D).}$$

$$= 0$$

Matched Problem 9   Evaluate $\lim_{x \to \infty} \dfrac{\ln x}{x}$.

EXAMPLE 10   **L'Hôpital's Rule for the Indeterminate Form ∞/∞**   Evaluate $\lim_{x \to \infty} \dfrac{e^x}{x^2}$.

SOLUTION   **Step 1** *Check to see if L'Hôpital's rule applies:*

$$\lim_{x \to \infty} e^x = \infty \qquad \text{and} \qquad \lim_{x \to \infty} x^2 = \infty$$

L'Hôpital's rule does apply.

Step 2 *Apply L'Hôpital's rule:*

$$\overset{\infty/\infty \text{ form}}{\lim_{x \to \infty} \frac{e^x}{x^2}} = \lim_{x \to \infty} \frac{\dfrac{d}{dx} e^x}{\dfrac{d}{dx} x^2} = \lim_{x \to \infty} \frac{e^x}{2x}$$

Since $\lim_{x \to \infty} e^x = \infty$ and $\lim_{x \to \infty} 2x = \infty$, this limit is an ∞/∞ indeterminate form and L'Hôpital's rule can be applied again.

Step 3 *Apply L'Hôpital's rule again:*

$$\overset{\infty/\infty \text{ form}}{\lim_{x \to \infty} \frac{e^x}{2x}} = \lim_{x \to \infty} \frac{\dfrac{d}{dx} e^x}{\dfrac{d}{dx} 2x} = \lim_{x \to \infty} \frac{e^x}{2} = \infty$$

Therefore,

$$\lim_{x\to\infty}\frac{e^x}{x^2} = \lim_{x\to\infty}\frac{e^x}{2x} = \lim_{x\to\infty}\frac{e^x}{2} = \infty$$

Matched Problem 10 Evaluate $\lim\limits_{x\to\infty}\dfrac{e^{2x}}{x^2}$.

CONCEPTUAL INSIGHT

The three versions of L'Hôpital's rule cover a multitude of limits—far too many to remember case by case. Instead, we suggest you use the following pattern, common to all versions, as a memory aid:

1. All versions involve three limits: $\lim f(x)/g(x)$, $\lim f(x)$, and $\lim g(x)$.

2. The independent variable x must behave the same way in all three limits. The acceptable behaviors are $x \to c$, $x \to c^+$, $x \to c^-$, $x \to \infty$, or $x \to -\infty$.

3. The form of $\lim f(x)/g(x)$ must be $\dfrac{0}{0}$ or $\dfrac{\pm\infty}{\pm\infty}$ and both $\lim f(x)$ and $\lim g(x)$ must approach 0 or both must approach $\pm\infty$.

Exercises 12-3

A

Use L'Hôpital's rule to find each limit in Problems 1–14.

1. $\lim\limits_{x\to2}\dfrac{x^4 - 16}{x^3 - 8}$

2. $\lim\limits_{x\to1}\dfrac{x^6 - 1}{x^5 - 1}$

3. $\lim\limits_{x\to2}\dfrac{x^2 + x - 6}{x^2 + 6x - 16}$

4. $\lim\limits_{x\to4}\dfrac{x^2 - 8x + 16}{x^2 - 5x + 4}$

5. $\lim\limits_{x\to0}\dfrac{e^x - 1}{x}$

6. $\lim\limits_{x\to1}\dfrac{\ln x}{x - 1}$

7. $\lim\limits_{x\to0}\dfrac{\ln(1 + 4x)}{x}$

8. $\lim\limits_{x\to0}\dfrac{e^{2x} - 1}{x}$

9. $\lim\limits_{x\to\infty}\dfrac{2x^2 + 7}{5x^3 + 9}$

10. $\lim\limits_{x\to\infty}\dfrac{3x^4 + 6}{2x^2 + 5}$

11. $\lim\limits_{x\to\infty}\dfrac{e^{3x}}{x}$

12. $\lim\limits_{x\to\infty}\dfrac{x}{e^{4x}}$

13. $\lim\limits_{x\to\infty}\dfrac{x^2}{\ln x}$

14. $\lim\limits_{x\to\infty}\dfrac{\ln x}{x^4}$

✎ *In Problems 15–18, explain why L'Hôpital's rule does not apply. If the limit exists, find it by other means.*

15. $\lim\limits_{x\to1}\dfrac{x^2 + 5x + 4}{x^3 + 1}$

16. $\lim\limits_{x\to\infty}\dfrac{e^{-x}}{\ln x}$

17. $\lim\limits_{x\to2}\dfrac{x + 2}{(x - 2)^4}$

18. $\lim\limits_{x\to-3}\dfrac{x^2}{(x + 3)^5}$

In Problems 19–22, the limit can be found in two ways. Use L'Hôpital's rule to find the limit and check your answer using an algebraic simplification.

19. $\lim\limits_{x\to-4}\dfrac{x + 4}{x^2 - 16}$

20. $\lim\limits_{x\to5}\dfrac{x - 5}{x^2 - 25}$

21. $\lim\limits_{x\to9}\dfrac{x^2 - x - 72}{x - 9}$

22. $\lim\limits_{x\to7}\dfrac{x - 7}{x^2 + 6x - 91}$

B

Find each limit in Problems 23–46. Note that L'Hôpital's rule does not apply to every problem, and some problems will require more than one application of L'Hôpital's rule.

23. $\lim\limits_{x\to0}\dfrac{e^{4x} + 1 - 4x}{x^2}$

24. $\lim\limits_{x\to0}\dfrac{3x + 1 - e^{3x}}{x^2}$

25. $\lim\limits_{x\to2}\dfrac{\ln(x - 1)}{x - 1}$

26. $\lim\limits_{x\to-1}\dfrac{\ln(x + 2)}{x + 2}$

27. $\lim\limits_{x\to0^+}\dfrac{\ln(1 + x^2)}{x^3}$

28. $\lim\limits_{x\to0^-}\dfrac{\ln(1 + 2x)}{x^2}$

29. $\lim\limits_{x\to0^+}\dfrac{\ln(1 + \sqrt{x})}{x}$

30. $\lim\limits_{x\to0^+}\dfrac{\ln(1 + x)}{\sqrt{x}}$

31. $\lim\limits_{x\to-2}\dfrac{x^2 + 2x + 1}{x^2 + x + 1}$

32. $\lim\limits_{x\to1}\dfrac{2x^3 - 3x^2 + 1}{x^3 - 3x + 2}$

33. $\lim\limits_{x\to-1}\dfrac{x^3 + x^2 - x - 1}{x^3 + 4x^2 + 5x + 2}$

34. $\lim\limits_{x\to3}\dfrac{x^3 + 3x^2 - x - 3}{x^2 + 6x + 9}$

35. $\lim\limits_{x\to2^-}\dfrac{x^3 - 12x + 16}{x^3 - 6x^2 + 12x - 8}$

36. $\lim\limits_{x\to1^+}\dfrac{x^3 + x^2 - x + 1}{x^3 + 3x^2 + 3x - 1}$

37. $\lim\limits_{x\to\infty}\dfrac{3x^2 + 5x}{4x^3 + 7}$

38. $\lim\limits_{x\to\infty}\dfrac{4x^2 + 9x}{5x^2 + 8}$

39. $\lim\limits_{x \to \infty} \dfrac{x^2}{e^{2x}}$

40. $\lim\limits_{x \to \infty} \dfrac{e^{3x}}{x^3}$

41. $\lim\limits_{x \to \infty} \dfrac{1 + e^{-x}}{1 + x^2}$

42. $\lim\limits_{x \to -\infty} \dfrac{1 + e^{-x}}{1 + x^2}$

43. $\lim\limits_{x \to \infty} \dfrac{e^{-x}}{\ln(1 + 4e^{-x})}$

44. $\lim\limits_{x \to \infty} \dfrac{\ln(1 + 2e^{-x})}{\ln(1 + e^{-x})}$

45. $\lim\limits_{x \to 0} \dfrac{e^x - e^{-x} - 2x}{x^3}$

46. $\lim\limits_{x \to 0} \dfrac{e^{2x} - 1 - 2x - 2x^2}{x^3}$

53. $\lim\limits_{x \to \infty} \dfrac{\sqrt{1 + x^2}}{x}$

54. $\lim\limits_{x \to -\infty} \dfrac{x}{\sqrt{4 + x^2}}$

55. $\lim\limits_{x \to -\infty} \dfrac{\sqrt[3]{x^3 + 1}}{x}$

56. $\lim\limits_{x \to \infty} \dfrac{x^2}{\sqrt[3]{(x^3 + 1)^2}}$

C

47. Find $\lim\limits_{x \to 0^+} (x \ln x)$.

[*Hint*: Write $x \ln x = (\ln x)/x^{-1}$.]

48. Find $\lim\limits_{x \to 0^+} (\sqrt{x} \ln x)$.

[*Hint*: Write $\sqrt{x} \ln x = (\ln x)/x^{-1/2}$.]

In Problems 49–52, n is a positive integer. Find each limit.

49. $\lim\limits_{x \to \infty} \dfrac{\ln x}{x^n}$

50. $\lim\limits_{x \to \infty} \dfrac{x^n}{\ln x}$

51. $\lim\limits_{x \to \infty} \dfrac{e^x}{x^n}$

52. $\lim\limits_{x \to \infty} \dfrac{x^n}{e^x}$

In Problems 53–56, show that the repeated application of L'Hôpital's rule does not lead to a solution. Then use algebraic manipulation to evaluate each limit. [Hint: If $x > 0$ and $n > 0$, then $\sqrt[n]{x^n} = x$.]

Answers to Matched Problems

1. (A) ∞
   (B) ∞
   (C) 0
   (D) ∞

2. (A) ∞
   (B) 0
   (C) $-\infty$
   (D) ∞

| **3.** e^4 | **4.** ∞ | **5.** 0 | **6.** 2 |
| **7.** $-\infty$ | **8.** 2 | **9.** 0 | **10.** ∞ |

12-4 Curve-Sketching Techniques

- Modifying the Graphing Strategy
- Using the Graphing Strategy
- Modeling Average Cost

When we summarized the graphing strategy in Section 12-2, we omitted one important topic: asymptotes. Polynomial functions do not have any asymptotes. Asymptotes of rational functions were discussed in Section 10-3, but what about all the other functions, such as logarithmic and exponential functions? Since investigating asymptotes always involves limits, we can now use L'Hôpital's rule (Section 12-3) as a tool for finding asymptotes of many different types of functions.

Modifying the Graphing Strategy

The first version of the graphing strategy in Section 12-2 made no mention of asymptotes. Including information about asymptotes produces the following (and final) version of the graphing strategy.

PROCEDURE Graphing Strategy (Final Version)

Step 1 *Analyze $f(x)$.*

(A) Find the domain of f.

(B) Find the intercepts.

(C) Find asymptotes.

Step 2 *Analyze $f'(x)$.* Find the partition numbers for, and critical values of, $f'(x)$. Construct a sign chart for $f'(x)$, determine the intervals on which f is increasing and decreasing, and find local maxima and minima.

Step 3 *Analyze $f''(x)$.* Find the partition numbers of $f''(x)$. Construct a sign chart for $f''(x)$, determine the intervals on which the graph of f is concave upward and concave downward, and find inflection points.

Step 4 *Sketch the graph of f.* Draw asymptotes and locate intercepts, local maxima and minima, and inflection points. Sketch in what you know from steps 1–3. Plot additional points as needed and complete the sketch.

Using the Graphing Strategy

We will illustrate the graphing strategy with several examples. From now on, you should always use the final version of the graphing strategy. If a function does not have any asymptotes, simply state this fact.

EXAMPLE 1 **Using the Graphing Strategy** Use the graphing strategy to analyze the function $f(x) = (x - 1)/(x - 2)$. State all the pertinent information and sketch the graph of f.

SOLUTION **Step 1** *Analyze $f(x)$.* $f(x) = \dfrac{x - 1}{x - 2}$

(A) Domain: All real x, except $x = 2$

(B) y intercept: $f(0) = \dfrac{0 - 1}{0 - 2} = \dfrac{1}{2}$

x intercepts: Since a fraction is 0 when its numerator is 0 and its denominator is not 0, the x intercept is $x = 1$.

(C) Horizontal asymptote: $\dfrac{a_m x^m}{b_n x^n} = \dfrac{x}{x} = 1$

So the line $y = 1$ is a horizontal asymptote.

Vertical asymptote: The denominator is 0 for $x = 2$, and the numerator is not 0 for this value. Therefore, the line $x = 2$ is a vertical asymptote.

Step 2 *Analyze $f'(x)$.* $f'(x) = \dfrac{(x - 2)(1) - (x - 1)(1)}{(x - 2)^2} = \dfrac{-1}{(x - 2)^2}$

Critical values of $f(x)$:   None

Partition number for $f'(x)$: $x = 2$

Sign chart for $f'(x)$:

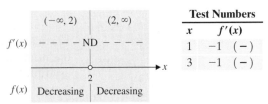

So $f(x)$ is decreasing on $(-\infty, 2)$ and $(2, \infty)$. There are no local extrema.

Step 3 *Analyze $f''(x)$.* $f''(x) = \dfrac{2}{(x - 2)^3}$

Partition number for $f''(x)$: $x = 2$

Sign chart for $f''(x)$:

	$(-\infty, 2)$	$(2, \infty)$
$f''(x)$	$- - - -$ ND	$+ + +$

Test Numbers

x	$f''(x)$
1	-2 $(-)$
3	2 $(+)$

Graph of f: Concave downward | Concave upward

The graph of f is concave downward on $(-\infty, 2)$ and concave upward on $(2, \infty)$. Since $f(2)$ is not defined, there is no inflection point at $x = 2$, even though $f''(x)$ changes sign at $x = 2$.

Step 4 *Sketch the graph of f.* Insert intercepts and asymptotes, and plot a few additional points (for functions with asymptotes, plotting additional points is often helpful). Then sketch the graph.

x	$f(x)$
-2	$\frac{3}{4}$
0	$\frac{1}{2}$
1	0
$\frac{3}{2}$	-1
$\frac{5}{2}$	3
3	2
4	$\frac{3}{2}$

Matched Problem 1 Follow the graphing strategy and analyze the function $f(x) = 2x/(1 - x)$. State all the pertinent information and sketch the graph of f.

EXAMPLE 2 **Using the Graphing Strategy** Use the graphing strategy to analyze the function

$$g(x) = \frac{2x - 1}{x^2}$$

State all pertinent information and sketch the graph of g.

SOLUTION **Step 1** *Analyze $g(x)$.*

(A) Domain: All real x, except $x = 0$

(B) x intercept: $x = \dfrac{1}{2} = 0.5$

y intercept: Since 0 is not in the domain of g, there is no y intercept.

(C) Horizontal asymptote: $y = 0$ (the x axis)

Vertical asymptote: The denominator of $g(x)$ is 0 at $x = 0$ and the numerator is not. So the line $x = 0$ (the y axis) is a vertical asymptote.

Step 2 *Analyze $g'(x)$.*

$$g(x) = \frac{2x - 1}{x^2} = \frac{2}{x} - \frac{1}{x^2} = 2x^{-1} - x^{-2}$$

$$g'(x) = -2x^{-2} + 2x^{-3} = -\frac{2}{x^2} + \frac{2}{x^3} = \frac{-2x + 2}{x^3}$$

$$= \frac{2(1 - x)}{x^3}$$

Critical values of $g(x)$: $x = 1$

Partition numbers for $g'(x)$: $x = 0, x = 1$

Sign chart for $g'(x)$:

	$(-\infty, 0)$	$(0, 1)$	$(1, \infty)$
$g'(x)$	$- - - -$ ND	$+ + + +$ 0	$- - - -$

0 (open circle)   1 (closed dot) x

Function $f(x)$ is decreasing on $(-\infty, 0)$ and $(1, \infty)$, is increasing on $(0, 1)$, and has a local maximum at $x = 1$.

Step 3 *Analyze $g''(x)$.*

$$g'(x) = -2x^{-2} + 2x^{-3}$$

$$g''(x) = 4x^{-3} - 6x^{-4} = \frac{4}{x^3} - \frac{6}{x^4} = \frac{4x - 6}{x^4} = \frac{2(2x - 3)}{x^4}$$

Partition numbers for $g''(x)$: $x = 0, x = \dfrac{3}{2} = 1.5$

Sign chart for $g''(x)$:

	$(-\infty, 0)$	$(0, 1.5)$	$(1.5, \infty)$
$g''(x)$	$- - - -$ ND	$- - - - - -$ 0	$+ + + +$

0 (open circle)   1.5 (closed dot) x

Function $g(x)$ is concave downward on $(-\infty, 0)$ and $(0, 1.5)$, is concave upward on $(1.5, \infty)$, and has an inflection point at $x = 1.5$.

Step 4 *Sketch the graph of g.* Plot key points, note that the coordinate axes are asymptotes, and sketch the graph.

x	$g(x)$
-10	-0.21
-1	-3
0.5	0
1	1
1.5	0.89
10	0.19

Matched Problem 2   Use the graphing strategy to analyze the function

$$h(x) = \frac{4x + 3}{x^2}$$

State all pertinent information and sketch the graph of h.

EXAMPLE 3   **Graphing Strategy** Follow the steps of the graphing strategy and analyze the function $f(x) = xe^x$. State all the pertinent information and sketch the graph of f.

SOLUTION   **Step 1** Analyze $f(x)$: $f(x) = xe^x$.

(A) Domain: All real numbers

(B) y intercept: $f(0) = 0$

x intercept: $xe^x = 0$ for $x = 0$ only, since $e^x > 0$ for all x.

(C) Vertical asymptotes: None

Horizontal asymptotes: We use tables to determine the nature of the graph of f as $x \to \infty$ and $x \to -\infty$:

x	1	5	10	$\to \infty$
$f(x)$	2.72	742.07	220,264.66	$\to \infty$

x	-1	-5	-10	$\to -\infty$
$f(x)$	-0.37	-0.03	$-0.000\,45$	$\to 0$

Step 2 *Analyze $f'(x)$:*

$$f'(x) = x\frac{d}{dx}e^x + e^x\frac{d}{dx}x$$

$$= xe^x + e^x = e^x(x+1)$$

Critical value of $f(x)$: -1

Partition number for $f'(x)$: -1

Sign chart for $f'(x)$:

<table>
<tr><th></th><th>$(-\infty, -1)$</th><th>$(-1, \infty)$</th><th colspan="2">Test Numbers</th></tr>
<tr><td></td><td></td><td></td><td>x</td><td>$f'(x)$</td></tr>
<tr><td>$f'(x)$</td><td>$----$</td><td>$0 ++++$</td><td>-2</td><td>$-e^{-2}$ $(-)$</td></tr>
<tr><td></td><td></td><td>-1</td><td>0</td><td>1 $(+)$</td></tr>
<tr><td>$f(x)$</td><td>Decreasing</td><td>Increasing</td><td></td><td></td></tr>
</table>

So $f(x)$ decreases on $(-\infty, -1)$, has a local minimum at $x = -1$, and increases on $(-1, \infty)$.

Step 3 *Analyze $f''(x)$:*

$$f''(x) = e^x\frac{d}{dx}(x+1) + (x+1)\frac{d}{dx}e^x$$

$$= e^x + (x+1)e^x = e^x(x+2)$$

Sign chart for $f''(x)$ (partition number is -2):

<table>
<tr><th></th><th>$(-\infty, -2)$</th><th>$(-2, \infty)$</th><th colspan="2">Test Numbers</th></tr>
<tr><td></td><td></td><td></td><td>x</td><td>$f''(x)$</td></tr>
<tr><td>$f''(x)$</td><td>$----$</td><td>$0 ++++$</td><td>-3</td><td>$-e^{-3}$ $(-)$</td></tr>
<tr><td></td><td></td><td>-2</td><td>-1</td><td>e^{-1} $(+)$</td></tr>
<tr><td>Graph of f</td><td>Concave downward</td><td>Concave upward</td><td></td><td></td></tr>
<tr><td></td><td colspan="2" align="center">Inflection point</td><td></td><td></td></tr>
</table>

The graph of f is concave downward on $(-\infty, -2)$, has an inflection point at $x = -2$, and is concave upward on $(-2, \infty)$.

Step 4 *Sketch the graph of f, using the information from steps 1 to 3:*

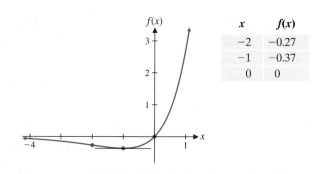

x	$f(x)$
-2	-0.27
-1	-0.37
0	0

Matched Problem 3   Analyze the function $f(x) = xe^{-0.5x}$. State all the pertinent information and sketch the graph of f.

EXPLORE & DISCUSS 1   Refer to the discussion of vertical asymptotes in the solution of Example 3. We used tables of values to estimate limits at infinity and determine horizontal asymptotes. In some cases, the functions involved in these limits can be written in a form that allows us to use L'Hôpital's rule.

$$\begin{aligned}
&\qquad\qquad\qquad -\infty \cdot 0 \text{ form}\\
\lim_{x \to -\infty} f(x) &= \lim_{x \to -\infty} xe^x \qquad \text{Rewrite as a fraction.}\\[1mm]
&\qquad\qquad\qquad -\infty/\infty \text{ form}\\
&= \lim_{x \to -\infty} \frac{x}{e^{-x}} \qquad \text{Apply L'Hôpital's rule.}\\[2mm]
&= \lim_{x \to -\infty} \frac{1}{-e^{-x}} \qquad \text{Simplify.}\\[2mm]
&= \lim_{x \to -\infty} (-e^x) \qquad \text{Property of } e^x\\[2mm]
&= 0
\end{aligned}$$

Use algebraic manipulation and L'Hôpital's rule to verify the value of each of the following limits:

(A) $\lim\limits_{x \to \infty} xe^{-0.5x} = 0$

(B) $\lim\limits_{x \to 0^+} x^2(\ln x - 0.5) = 0$

(C) $\lim\limits_{x \to 0^+} x \ln x = 0$

EXAMPLE 4   **Graphing Strategy** Let $f(x) = x^2 \ln x - 0.5x^2$. Follow the steps in the graphing strategy and analyze this function. State all the pertinent information and sketch the graph of f.

SOLUTION   **Step 1** *Analyze* $f(x)$: $f(x) = x^2 \ln x - 0.5x^2 = x^2(\ln x - 0.5)$.

(A) Domain: $(0, \infty)$

(B) y intercept: None [$f(0)$ is not defined.]

  x intercept: Solve $x^2(\ln x - 0.5) = 0$

  $\ln x - 0.5 = 0 \qquad$ or $\qquad x^2 = 0 \qquad$ Discard, since 0 is not in the domain of f.

  $\ln x = 0.5 \quad$ In $x = a$ if and only if $x = e^a$.

  $x = e^{0.5} \quad x$ intercept

(C) Asymptotes: None. The following tables suggest the nature of the graph as $x \to 0^+$ and as $x \to \infty$:

x	0.1	0.01	0.001	$\to 0^+$	See Explore &
$f(x)$	−0.0280	−0.00051	−0.00007	$\to 0$	Discuss 1(B).

x	10	100	1,000	$\to \infty$
$f(x)$	180	41,000	6,400,000	$\to \infty$

Step 2 *Analyze* $f'(x)$:

$$f'(x) = x^2 \frac{d}{dx} \ln x + (\ln x) \frac{d}{dx} x^2 - 0.5 \frac{d}{dx} x^2$$

$$= x^2 \frac{1}{x} + (\ln x)\, 2x - 0.5(2x)$$

$$= x + 2x \ln x - x$$

$$= 2x \ln x$$

Critical value of $f(x)$: 1

Partition number for $f'(x)$: 1

Sign chart for $f'(x)$:

	(0, 1)	(1, ∞)
	$- - - -\ 0\ + + + +$	

Decreasing   Increasing

Test Numbers		
x	$f'(x)$	
0.5	-0.2983	$(-)$
2	0.7726	$(+)$

The function $f(x)$ decreases on $(0, 1)$, has a local minimum at $x = 1$, and increases on $(1, \infty)$.

Step 3 *Analyze* $f''(x)$:

$$f''(x) = 2x \frac{d}{dx}(\ln x) + (\ln x) \frac{d}{dx}(2x)$$

$$= 2x \frac{1}{x} + (\ln x)\, 2$$

$$= 2 + 2 \ln x = 0$$

$$2 \ln x = -2$$

$$\ln x = -1$$

$$x = e^{-1} \approx 0.3679$$

Sign chart for $f'(x)$ (partition number is e^{-1}):

	$(0, e^{-1})$	(e^{-1}, ∞)
	$- - - -\ 0\ + + + +$	

Concave   Concave
downward   upward

Test Numbers		
x	$f'(x)$	
0.2	-1.2189	$(-)$
1	2	$(+)$

The graph of $f(x)$ is concave downward on $(0, e^{-1})$, has an inflection point at $x = e^{-1}$, and is concave upward on (e^{-1}, ∞).

Step 4 *Sketch the graph of f, using the information from steps 1 to 3:*

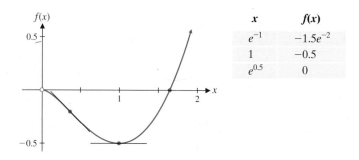

x	$f(x)$
e^{-1}	$-1.5e^{-2}$
1	-0.5
$e^{0.5}$	0

Matched Problem 4   Analyze the function $f(x) = x \ln x$. State all pertinent information and sketch the graph of f.

Modeling Average Cost

EXAMPLE 5   **Average Cost**   Given the cost function $C(x) = 5,000 + 0.5x^2$, where x is the number of items produced, use the graphing strategy to analyze the graph of the average cost function. State all the pertinent information and sketch the graph of the average cost function. Find the marginal cost function and graph it on the same set of coordinate axes.

SOLUTION   The average cost function is

$$\overline{C}(x) = \frac{5,000 + 0.5x^2}{x} = \frac{5,000}{x} + 0.5x$$

Step 1   *Analyze $\overline{C}(x)$.*

(A)   Domain: Since negative values of x do not make sense and $\overline{C}(0)$ is not defined, the domain is the set of positive real numbers.

(B)   Intercepts: None

(C)   Horizontal asymptote: $\dfrac{a_m x^m}{b_n x^n} = \dfrac{0.5x^2}{x} = 0.5x$

So there is no horizontal asymptote.

Vertical asymptote: The line $x = 0$ is a vertical asymptote since the denominator is 0 and the numerator is not 0 for $x = 0$.

Oblique asymptotes: If a graph approaches a line that is neither horizontal nor vertical as x approaches ∞ or $-\infty$, then that line is called an **oblique asymptote**. If x is a large positive number, then $5,000/x$ is very small and

$$\overline{C}(x) = \frac{5,000}{x} + 0.5x \approx 0.5x$$

That is,

$$\lim_{x \to \infty} \left[\overline{C}(x) - 0.5x \right] = \lim_{x \to \infty} \frac{5,000}{x} = 0$$

This implies that the graph of $y = \overline{C}(x)$ approaches the line $y = 0.5x$ as x approaches ∞. That line is an oblique asymptote for the graph of $y = \overline{C}(x)$.*

Step 2   *Analyze $\overline{C}'(x)$.*

$$\overline{C}'(x) = -\frac{5,000}{x^2} + 0.5$$

$$= \frac{0.5x^2 - 5,000}{x^2}$$

$$= \frac{0.5(x - 100)(x + 100)}{x^2}$$

---

*If $f(x) = n(x)/d(x)$ is a rational function for which the degree of $n(x)$ is 1 more than the degree of $d(x)$, then we can use polynomial long division to write $f(x) = mx + b + r(x)/d(x)$, where the degree of $r(x)$ is less than the degree of $d(x)$. The line $y = mx + b$ is then an oblique asymptote for the graph of $y = f(x)$.

7. Domain: All real x, except $x = -1$;

    $f(-3) = 2, f(-2) = 3, f(0) = -1, f(1) = 0$;

    $f'(x) > 0$ on $(-\infty, -1)$ and $(-1, \infty)$;

    $f''(x) > 0$ on $(-\infty, -1)$; $f''(x) < 0$ on $(-1, \infty)$;

    vertical asymptote: $x = -1$;

    horizontal asymptote: $y = 1$

8. Domain: All real x, except $x = 1$;

    $f(0) = -2, f(2) = 0$;

    $f'(x) < 0$ on $(-\infty, 1)$ and $(1, \infty)$;

    $f''(x) < 0$ on $(-\infty, 1)$;

    $f''(x) > 0$ on $(1, \infty)$;

    vertical asymptote: $x = 1$;

    horizontal asymptote: $y = -1$

9. Domain: All real x, except $x = -2$ and $x = 2$;

    $f(-3) = -1, f(0) = 0, f(3) = 1$;

    $f'(x) < 0$ on $(-\infty, -2)$ and $(2, \infty)$;

    $f'(x) > 0$ on $(-2, 2)$;

    $f''(x) < 0$ on $(-\infty, -2)$ and $(-2, 0)$;

    $f''(x) > 0$ on $(0, 2)$ and $(2, \infty)$;

    vertical asymptotes: $x = -2$ and $x = 2$;

    horizontal asymptote: $y = 0$

10. Domain: All real x, except $x = -1$ and $x = 1$;

    $f(-2) = 1, f(0) = 0, f(2) = 1$;

    $f'(x) > 0$ on $(-\infty, -1)$ and $(0, 1)$;

    $f'(x) < 0$ on $(-1, 0)$ and $(1, \infty)$;

    $f''(x) > 0$ on $(-\infty, -1), (-1, 1)$, and $(1, \infty)$;

    vertical asymptotes: $x = -1$ and $x = 1$;

    horizontal asymptote: $y = 0$

In Problems 11–16, find the domain and intercepts.

11. $f(x) = \sqrt{x + 4}$

12. $f(x) = \sqrt{x + 25}$

13. $f(x) = 75 - 5x$

14. $f(x) = 4x + 52$

15. $f(x) = \dfrac{95}{x - 5}$

16. $f(x) = \dfrac{102}{x + 3}$

In Problems 17–56, summarize the pertinent information obtained by applying the graphing strategy and sketch the graph of $y = f(x)$.

17. $f(x) = \dfrac{x + 3}{x - 3}$ 18. $f(x) = \dfrac{2x - 4}{x + 2}$

19. $f(x) = \dfrac{x}{x - 2}$ 20. $f(x) = \dfrac{2 + x}{3 - x}$

21. $f(x) = 5 + 5e^{-0.1x}$ 22. $f(x) = 3 + 7e^{-0.2x}$

23. $f(x) = 5xe^{-0.2x}$ 24. $f(x) = 10xe^{-0.1x}$

25. $f(x) = \ln(1 - x)$ 26. $f(x) = \ln(2x + 4)$

27. $f(x) = x - \ln x$ 28. $f(x) = \ln(x^2 + 4)$

29. $f(x) = \dfrac{x}{x^2 - 4}$ 30. $f(x) = \dfrac{1}{x^2 - 4}$

31. $f(x) = \dfrac{1}{1 + x^2}$ 32. $f(x) = \dfrac{x^2}{1 + x^2}$

33. $f(x) = \dfrac{2x}{1 - x^2}$ 34. $f(x) = \dfrac{2x}{x^2 - 9}$

35. $f(x) = \dfrac{-5x}{(x - 1)^2}$ 36. $f(x) = \dfrac{x}{(x - 2)^2}$

37. $f(x) = \dfrac{x^2 + x - 2}{x^2}$ 38. $f(x) = \dfrac{x^2 - 5x - 6}{x^2}$

39. $f(x) = \dfrac{x^2}{x - 1}$ 40. $f(x) = \dfrac{x^2}{2 + x}$

41. $f(x) = \dfrac{3x^2 + 2}{x^2 - 9}$ 42. $f(x) = \dfrac{2x^2 + 5}{4 - x^2}$

43. $f(x) = \dfrac{x^3}{x - 2}$ 44. $f(x) = \dfrac{x^3}{4 - x}$

45. $f(x) = (3 - x)e^x$ 46. $f(x) = (x - 2)e^x$

47. $f(x) = e^{-0.5x^2}$ 48. $f(x) = e^{-2x^2}$

49. $f(x) = x^2 \ln x$ 50. $f(x) = \dfrac{\ln x}{x}$

51. $f(x) = (\ln x)^2$ 52. $f(x) = \dfrac{x}{\ln x}$

53. $f(x) = \dfrac{1}{x^2 + 2x - 8}$ 54. $f(x) = \dfrac{1}{3 - 2x - x^2}$

55. $f(x) = \dfrac{x^3}{3 - x^2}$ 56. $f(x) = \dfrac{x^3}{x^2 - 12}$

In Problems 57–64, show that the line $y = x$ is an oblique asymptote for the graph of $y = f(x)$, summarize all pertinent information obtained by applying the graphing strategy, and sketch the graph of $y = f(x)$.

57. $f(x) = x + \dfrac{4}{x}$ 58. $f(x) = x - \dfrac{9}{x}$

59. $f(x) = x - \dfrac{4}{x^2}$ 60. $f(x) = x + \dfrac{32}{x^2}$

61. $f(x) = x - \dfrac{9}{x^3}$ 62. $f(x) = x + \dfrac{27}{x^3}$

63. $f(x) = x + \dfrac{1}{x} + \dfrac{4}{x^3}$ 64. $f(x) = x - \dfrac{16}{x^3}$

In Problems 65–72, summarize all pertinent information obtained by applying the graphing strategy, and sketch the graph of y = f(x). [Note: These rational functions are not reduced to lowest terms.]

65. $f(x) = \dfrac{x^2 + x - 6}{x^2 - 6x + 8}$

66. $f(x) = \dfrac{x^2 + x - 6}{x^2 - x - 12}$

67. $f(x) = \dfrac{2x^2 + x - 15}{x^2 - 9}$

68. $f(x) = \dfrac{2x^2 + 11x + 14}{x^2 - 4}$

69. $f(x) = \dfrac{x^3 - 5x^2 + 6x}{x^2 - x - 2}$

70. $f(x) = \dfrac{x^3 - 5x^2 - 6x}{x^2 + 3x + 2}$

71. $f(x) = \dfrac{x^2 + x - 2}{x^2 - 2x + 1}$

72. $f(x) = \dfrac{x^2 + x - 2}{x^2 + 4x + 4}$

Applications

73. Revenue. The marketing research department for a computer company used a large city to test market the firm's new laptop. The department found that the relationship between price p (dollars per unit) and demand x (units sold per week) was given approximately by

$$p = 1,296 - 0.12x^2 \qquad 0 \le x \le 80$$

So, weekly revenue can be approximated by

$$R(x) = xp = 1,296x - 0.12x^3 \qquad 0 \le x \le 80$$

Graph the revenue function R.

74. Profit. Suppose that the cost function $C(x)$ (in dollars) for the company in Problem 73 is

$$C(x) = 830 + 396x$$

(A) Write an equation for the profit $P(x)$.

(B) Graph the profit function P.

75. Pollution. In Silicon Valley, a number of computer firms were found to be contaminating underground water supplies with toxic chemicals stored in leaking underground containers. A water quality control agency ordered the companies to take immediate corrective action and contribute to a monetary pool for the testing and cleanup of the underground contamination. Suppose that the required monetary pool (in millions of dollars) is given by

$$P(x) = \frac{2x}{1 - x} \qquad 0 \le x < 1$$

where x is the percentage (expressed as a decimal fraction) of the total contaminant removed.

(A) Where is $P(x)$ increasing? Decreasing?

(B) Where is the graph of P concave upward? Downward?

(C) Find any horizontal and vertical asymptotes.

(D) Find the x and y intercepts.

(E) Sketch a graph of P.

76. Employee training. A company producing dive watches has established that, on average, a new employee can assemble $N(t)$ dive watches per day after t days of on-the-job training, as given by

$$N(t) = \frac{100t}{t + 9} \qquad t \ge 0$$

(A) Where is $N(t)$ increasing? Decreasing?

(B) Where is the graph of N concave upward? Downward?

(C) Find any horizontal and vertical asymptotes.

(D) Find the intercepts.

(E) Sketch a graph of N.

77. Replacement time. An outboard motor has an initial price of $3,200. A service contract costs $300 for the first year and increases $100 per year thereafter. The total cost of the outboard motor (in dollars) after n years is given by

$$C(n) = 3,200 + 250n + 50n^2 \qquad n \ge 1$$

(A) Write an expression for the average cost per year, $\overline{C}(n)$, for n years.

(B) Graph the average cost function found in part (A).

(C) When is the average cost per year minimum? (This time is frequently referred to as the **replacement time** for this piece of equipment.)

78. Construction costs. The management of a manufacturing plant wishes to add a fenced-in rectangular storage yard of 20,000 square feet, using a building as one side of the yard (see the figure). If x is the distance (in feet) from the building to the fence, show that the length of the fence required for the yard is given by

$$L(x) = 2x + \frac{20,000}{x} \qquad x > 0$$

Storage yard

x

Figure for 78

(A) Graph L.

(B) What are the dimensions of the rectangle requiring the least amount of fencing?

79. Average and marginal costs. The total daily cost (in dollars) of producing x mountain bikes is given by

$$C(x) = 1,000 + 5x + 0.1x^2$$

(A) Sketch the graphs of the average cost function and the marginal cost function on the same set of coordinate axes. Include any oblique asymptotes.

(B) Find the minimum average cost.

80. Average and marginal costs. The total daily cost (in dollars) of producing x city bikes is given by

$$C(x) = 500 + 2x + 0.2x^2$$

(A) Sketch the graphs of the average cost function and the marginal cost function on the same set of coordinate axes. Include any oblique asymptotes.

(B) Find the minimum average cost.

81. Minimizing average costs. The table gives the total daily costs y (in dollars) of producing x pepperoni pizzas at various production levels.

Number of Pizzas	Total Costs
x	y
50	395
100	475
150	640
200	910
250	1,140
300	1,450

(A) Enter the data into a graphing calculator and find a quadratic regression equation for the total costs.

(B) Use the regression equation from part (A) to find the minimum average cost (to the nearest cent) and the corresponding production level (to the nearest integer).

82. Minimizing average costs. The table gives the total daily costs y (in dollars) of producing x deluxe pizzas at various production levels.

Number of Pizzas	Total Costs
x	y
50	595
100	755
150	1,110
200	1,380
250	1,875
300	2,410

(A) Enter the data into a graphing calculator and find a quadratic regression equation for the total costs.

(B) Use the regression equation from part (A) to find the minimum average cost (to the nearest cent) and the corresponding production level (to the nearest integer).

83. Medicine. A drug is injected into the bloodstream of a patient through her right arm. The drug concentration in the bloodstream of the left arm t hours after the injection is given by

$$C(t) = \frac{0.14t}{t^2 + 1}$$

Graph C.

84. Physiology. In a study on the speed of muscle contraction in frogs under various loads, researchers found that the speed of contraction decreases with increasing loads. More precisely, they found that the relationship between speed of contraction, S (in centimeters per second), and load w (in grams) is given approximately by

$$S(w) = \frac{26 + 0.06w}{w} \qquad w \geq 5$$

Graph S.

85. Psychology: retention. Each student in a psychology class is given one day to memorize the same list of 30 special characters. The lists are turned in at the end of the day, and for each succeeding day for 30 days, each student is asked to turn in a list of as many of the symbols as can be recalled. Averages are taken, and it is found that

$$N(t) = \frac{5t + 20}{t} \qquad t \geq 1$$

provides a good approximation of the average number $N(t)$ of symbols retained after t days. Graph N.

Answers to Matched Problems

1. Domain: All real x, except $x = 1$
y intercept: $f(0) = 0$; x intercept: 0
Horizontal asymptote: $y = -2$;
vertical asymptote: $x = 1$
Increasing on $(-\infty, 1)$ and $(1, \infty)$
Concave upward on $(-\infty, 1)$; concave downward on $(1, \infty)$

x	$f(x)$
-1	-1
0	0
$\frac{1}{2}$	2
$\frac{3}{2}$	-6
2	-4
5	$-\frac{5}{2}$

2. Domain: All real x, except $x = 0$

x intercept: $= -\frac{3}{4} = -0.75$

$h(0)$ is not defined
Vertical asymptote: $x = 0$ (the y axis)
Horizontal asymptote: $y = 0$ (the x axis)
Increasing on $(-1.5, 0)$
Decreasing on $(-\infty, -1.5)$ and $(0, \infty)$
Local minimum at $x = 1.5$
Concave upward on $(-2.25, 0)$ and $(0, \infty)$
Concave downward on $(-\infty, -2.25)$
Inflection point at $x = -2.25$

x	$h(x)$
-10	-0.37
-2.25	-1.19
-1.5	-1.33
-0.75	0
2	2.75
10	0.43

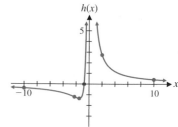

3. Domain: $(-\infty, \infty)$
y intercept: $f(0) = 0$
x intercept: $x = 0$
Horizontal asymptote: $y = 0$ (the x axis)
Increasing on $(-\infty, 2)$
Decreasing on $(2, \infty)$
Local maximum at $x = 2$
Concave downward on $(-\infty, 4)$
Concave upward on $(4, \infty)$
Inflection point at $x = 4$

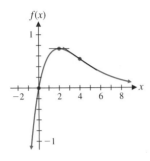

4. Domain: $(0, \infty)$
y intercept: None [$f(0)$ is not defined]
x intercept: $x = 1$
Increasing on (e^{-1}, ∞)
Decreasing on $(0, e^{-1})$
Local minimum at $x = e^{-1} \approx 0.368$
Concave upward on $(0, \infty)$

x	5	10	100	$\to \infty$
$f(x)$	8.05	23.03	460.52	$\to \infty$

x	0.1	0.01	0.001	0.000 1	$\to 0$
$f(x)$	-0.23	-0.046	$-0.006\ 9$	$-0.000\ 92$	$\to 0$

5. (A) Domain: $(0, \infty)$
Intercepts: None
Vertical asymptote: $x = 0$; oblique asymptote: $y = 0.25x$
Decreasing on $(0, 80)$; increasing on $(80, \infty)$; local minimum at $x = 80$
Concave upward on $(0, \infty)$

(B) Minimum average cost is 40 at $x = 80$.

12-5   Absolute Maxima and Minima

- Absolute Maxima and Minima
- Second Derivative and Extrema

Now we will consider one of the most important applications of the derivative: finding the absolute maximum or minimum value of a function. An economist may be interested in the price or production level of a commodity that will bring a maximum profit; a doctor may be interested in the time it takes for a drug to reach its maximum concentration in the bloodstream after an injection; and a city planner might be interested in the location of heavy industry in a city in order to produce minimum pollution in residential and business areas. In this section, we develop the procedures needed to find the absolute maximum and absolute minimum values of a function.

Absolute Maxima and Minima

Recall that $f(c)$ is a local maximum value if $f(x) \leq f(c)$ for x near c and a local minimum value if $f(x) \geq f(c)$ for x near c. Now we are interested in finding the largest and the smallest values of $f(x)$ throughout its domain.

DEFINITION **Absolute Maxima and Minima**

If $f(c) \geq f(x)$ for all x in the domain of f, then $f(c)$ is called the **absolute maximum value** of f.

If $f(c) \leq f(x)$ for all x in the domain of f, then $f(c)$ is called the **absolute minimum value** of f.

Figure 1 illustrates some typical examples.

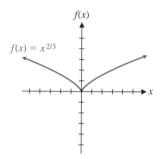

(A) No absolute maximum or minimum
One local maximum at $x = -2$
One local minimum at $x = 2$

(B) Absolute maximum at $x = 0$
No absolute minimum

(C) Absolute minimum at $x = 0$
No absolute maximum

Figure 1

CONCEPTUAL INSIGHT

If $f(c)$ is the absolute maximum value of a function f, then $f(c)$ is obviously a "value" of f. It is common practice to omit "value" and to refer to $f(c)$ as the **absolute maximum** of f. In either usage, note that c is a value of x in the domain of f where the absolute maximum occurs. It is incorrect to refer to c as the absolute maximum. Collectively, the absolute maximum and the absolute minimum are referred to as **absolute extrema**.

In many applications, the domain of a function is restricted because of practical or physical considerations. If the domain is restricted to some closed interval, as is often the case, then Theorem 1 applies.

THEOREM 1 **Extreme Value Theorem**

A function f that is continuous on a closed interval $[a, b]$ has both an absolute maximum value and an absolute minimum value on that interval.

It is important to understand that the absolute maximum and minimum values depend on both the function f and the interval $[a, b]$. Figure 2 illustrates four cases.

In all four cases illustrated in Figure 2, the absolute maximum value and absolute minimum value occur at a critical value or an endpoint. This property is generalized in Theorem 2. Note that both the absolute maximum value and the absolute minimum value are unique, but each can occur at more than one point in the interval (Fig. 2D).

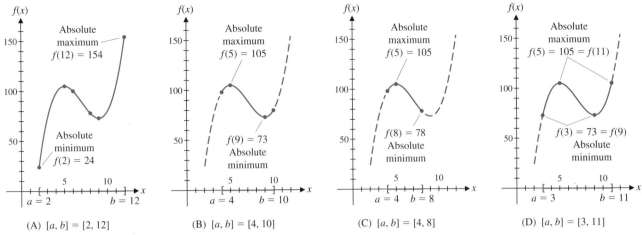

(A) $[a, b] = [2, 12]$ (B) $[a, b] = [4, 10]$ (C) $[a, b] = [4, 8]$ (D) $[a, b] = [3, 11]$

Figure 2 Absolute extrema for $f(x) = x^3 - 21x^2 + 135x - 170$ for various closed intervals

---

THEOREM 2   Locating Absolute Extrema

Absolute extrema (if they exist) must always occur at critical values or at endpoints.

To find the absolute maximum or minimum value of a continuous function on a closed interval, we simply identify the endpoints and critical values in the interval, evaluate the function at each, and then choose the largest and smallest values out of this group.

PROCEDURE   Finding Absolute Extrema on a Closed Interval

Step 1   Check to make certain that f is continuous over $[a, b]$.

Step 2   Find the critical values in the interval (a, b).

Step 3   Evaluate f at the endpoints a and b and at the critical values found in step 2.

Step 4   The absolute maximum $f(x)$ on $[a, b]$ is the largest value found in step 3.

Step 5   The absolute minimum $f(x)$ on $[a, b]$ is the smallest value found in step 3.

EXAMPLE 1   **Finding Absolute Extrema** Find the absolute maximum and absolute minimum values of

$$f(x) = x^3 + 3x^2 - 9x - 7$$

on each of the following intervals:

(A) $[-6, 4]$ (B) $[-4, 2]$ (C) $[-2, 2]$

SOLUTION   (A) The function is continuous for all values of x.

$$f'(x) = 3x^2 + 6x - 9 = 3(x - 1)(x + 3)$$

So, $x = -3$ and $x = 1$ are critical values in the interval $(-6, 4)$. Evaluate f at the endpoints and critical values $(-6, -3, 1,$ and $4)$, and choose the maximum and minimum from these:

$$f(-6) = -61 \quad \text{Absolute minimum}$$

$$f(-3) = 20$$

$$f(1) = -12$$

$$f(4) = 69 \quad \text{Absolute maximum}$$

(B) Interval: $[-4, 2]$

x	$f(x)$	
−4	13	
−3	20	Absolute maximum
1	−12	Absolute minimum
2	−5	

(C) Interval: $[-2, 2]$

x	$f(x)$	
−2	15	Absolute maximum
1	−12	Absolute minimum
2	−5	

The critical value $x = -3$ is not included in this table, because it is not in the interval $[-2, 2]$.

Matched Problem 1 Find the absolute maximum and absolute minimum values of

$$f(x) = x^3 - 12x$$

on each of the following intervals:
(A) $[-5, 5]$ (B) $[-3, 3]$ (C) $[-3, 1]$

Now, suppose that we want to find the absolute maximum or minimum value of a function that is continuous on an interval that is not closed. Since Theorem 1 no longer applies, we cannot be certain that the absolute maximum or minimum value exists. Figure 3 illustrates several ways that functions can fail to have absolute extrema.

In general, the best procedure to follow in searching for absolute extrema on an interval that is not of the form $[a, b]$ is to sketch a graph of the function. However, many applications can be solved with a new tool that does not require any graphing.

Second Derivative and Extrema

The second derivative can be used to classify the local extrema of a function. Suppose that f is a function satisfying $f'(c) = 0$ and $f''(c) > 0$. First, note that if $f''(c) > 0$, then it follows from the properties of limits* that $f''(x) > 0$ in some

*Actually, we are assuming that $f''(x)$ is continuous in an interval containing c. It is unlikely that we will encounter a function for which $f''(c)$ exists but $f''(x)$ is not continuous in an interval containing c.

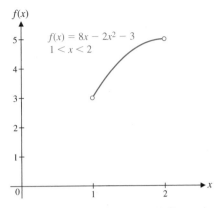

(A) No absolute extrema on $(-\infty, \infty)$:
    $-1 < f(x) < 1$ for all x
    $[f(x) \neq 1$ or -1 for any $x]$

(B) No absolute extrema on $(1, 2)$:
    $3 < f(x) < 5$ for $x \in (1, 2)$
    $[f(x) \neq 3$ or 5 for any $x \in (1, 2)]$

(C) No absolute extrema on $(-1, 1)$:
    Graph has vertical asymptotes
    at $x = -1$ and $x = 1$

Figure 3 Functions with no absolute extrema

interval (m, n) containing c. Thus, the graph of f must be concave upward in this interval. But this implies that $f'(x)$ is increasing in the interval. Since $f'(c) = 0$, $f'(x)$ must change from negative to positive at $x = c$, and $f(c)$ is a local minimum (see Fig. 4). Reasoning in the same fashion, we conclude that if $f'(c) = 0$ and $f''(c) < 0$, then $f(c)$ is a local maximum. Of course, it is possible that both $f'(c) = 0$ and $f''(c) = 0$. In this case, the second derivative cannot be used to determine the shape of the graph around $x = c$; $f(c)$ may be a local minimum, a local maximum, or neither.

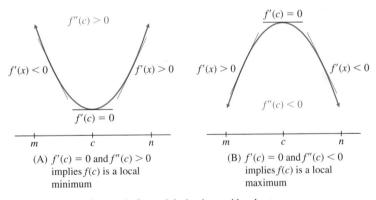

(A) $f'(c) = 0$ and $f''(c) > 0$
    implies $f(c)$ is a local
    minimum

(B) $f'(c) = 0$ and $f''(c) < 0$
    implies $f(c)$ is a local
    maximum

Figure 4 Second derivative and local extrema

The sign of the second derivative provides a simple test for identifying local maxima and minima. This test is most useful when we do not want to draw the graph of the function. If we are interested in drawing the graph and have already constructed the sign chart for $f'(x)$, then the first-derivative test can be used to identify the local extrema.

RESULT Second-Derivative Test

Let c be a critical value of $f(x)$.

$f'(c)$	$f''(c)$	Graph of f is:	$f(c)$	Example
0	+	Concave upward	Local minimum	$\smile$
0	−	Concave downward	Local maximum	$\frown$
0	0	?	Test does not apply	

EXAMPLE 2 **Testing Local Extrema** Find the local maxima and minima for each function. Use the second-derivative test when it applies.

(A) $f(x) = x^3 - 6x^2 + 9x + 1$

(B) $f(x) = xe^{-0.2x}$

(C) $f(x) = \frac{1}{6}x^6 - 4x^5 + 25x^4$

SOLUTION (A) Take first and second derivatives and find critical values:

$$f(x) = x^3 - 6x^2 + 9x + 1$$

$$f'(x) = 3x^2 - 12x + 9 = 3(x - 1)(x - 3)$$

$$f''(x) = 6x - 12 = 6(x - 2)$$

Critical values are $x = 1$ and $x = 3$.

$$f''(1) = -6 < 0 \qquad \text{\textit{f has a local maximum at x = 1.}}$$

$$f''(3) = 6 > 0 \qquad \text{\textit{f has a local minimum at x = 3.}}$$

(B) $$f(x) = xe^{-0.2x}$$

$$f'(x) = e^{-0.2x} + xe^{-0.2x}(-0.2)$$

$$= e^{-0.2x}(1 - 0.2x)$$

$$f''(x) = e^{-0.2x}(-0.2)(1 - 0.2x) + e^{-0.2x}(-0.2)$$

$$= e^{-0.2x}(0.04x - 0.4)$$

Critical value: $x = 1/0.2 = 5$

$f''(5) = e^{-1}(-0.2) < 0$

f has a local maximum at $x = 5$.

(C) $$f(x) = \frac{1}{6}x^6 - 4x^5 + 25x^4$$

$$f'(x) = x^5 - 20x^4 + 100x^3 = x^3(x - 10)^2$$

$$f''(x) = 5x^4 - 80x^3 + 300x^2$$

Critical values are $x = 0$ and $x = 10$.

$$f''(0) = 0 \qquad \text{\textit{The second-derivative test fails at both critical values, so}}$$

$$f''(10) = 0 \qquad \text{\textit{the first-derivative test must be used.}}$$

Sign chart for $f'(x) = x^3(x - 10)^2$ (partition numbers are 0 and 10):

	Test Numbers	
x	$f'(x)$	
-1	-121	$(-)$
1	81	$(+)$
11	$1,331$	$(+)$

From the chart, we see that $f(x)$ has a local minimum at $x = 0$ and does not have a local extremum at $x = 10$.

Matched Problem 2 Find the local maxima and minima for each function. Use the second-derivative test when it applies.

(A) $f(x) = x^3 - 9x^2 + 24x - 10$

(B) $f(x) = e^x - 5x$

(C) $f(x) = 10x^6 - 24x^5 + 15x^4$

CONCEPTUAL INSIGHT

The second-derivative test does not apply if $f''(c) = 0$ or if $f''(c)$ is not defined. As Example 2C illustrates, if $f''(c) = 0$, then $f(c)$ may or may not be a local extremum. Some other method, such as the first-derivative test, must be used when $f''(c) = 0$ or $f''(c)$ does not exist.

The solution of many optimization problems involves searching for an absolute extremum. If the function in question has only one critical value, then the second-derivative test not only classifies the local extremum but also guarantees that the local extremum is, in fact, the absolute extremum.

THEOREM 3   Second-Derivative Test for Absolute Extremum

Let f be continuous on an interval I with only one critical value c in I.

If $f'(c) = 0$ and $f''(c) > 0$, then $f(c)$ is the absolute minimum of f on I.

If $f'(c) = 0$ and $f''(c) < 0$, then $f(c)$ is the absolute maximum of f on I.

Since the second-derivative test cannot be applied when $f''(c) = 0$ or $f''(c)$ does not exist, Theorem 3 makes no mention of these cases.

EXAMPLE 3   **Finding an Absolute Extremum on an Open Interval** Find the absolute minimum value of each function on $(0, \infty)$.

(A) $f(x) = x + \dfrac{4}{x}$

(B) $f(x) = (\ln x)^2 - 3 \ln x$

SOLUTION   (A) $f(x) = x + \dfrac{4}{x}$

$$f'(x) = 1 - \frac{4}{x^2} = \frac{x^2 - 4}{x^2} = \frac{(x - 2)(x + 2)}{x^2} \qquad \text{Critical values are } x = -2 \text{ and } x = 2.$$

$$f''(x) = \frac{8}{x^3}$$

The only critical value in the interval $(0, \infty)$ is $x = 2$. Since $f''(2) = 1 > 0$, $f(2) = 4$ is the absolute minimum value of f on $(0, \infty)$.

(B) $f(x) = (\ln x)^2 - 3 \ln x$

$$f'(x) = (2 \ln x)\frac{1}{x} - \frac{3}{x} = \frac{2 \ln x - 3}{x} \qquad \text{Critical value is } x = e^{3/2}.$$

$$f''(x) = \frac{x\dfrac{2}{x} - (2 \ln x - 3)}{x^2} = \frac{5 - 2 \ln x}{x^2}$$

The only critical value in the interval $(0, \infty)$ is $x = e^{3/2}$. Since $f''(e^{3/2}) = 2/e^3 > 0$, $f(e^{3/2}) = -2.25$ is the absolute minimum value of f on $(0, \infty)$.

Matched Problem 3   Find the absolute maximum value of each function on $(0, \infty)$.

(A) $f(x) = 12 - x - \dfrac{5}{x}$ (B) $f(x) = 5 \ln x - x$

Exercises 12-5

A

Problems 1–10 refer to the graph of $y = f(x)$ shown here. Find the absolute minimum and the absolute maximum over the indicated interval.

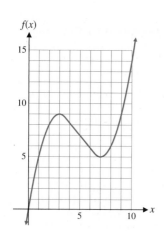

Figure for 1–10

1. $[0, 10]$ **2.** $[2, 8]$ **3.** $[0, 8]$ **4.** $[2, 10]$

5. $[1, 10]$ **6.** $[0, 9]$ **7.** $[1, 9]$ **8.** $[0, 2]$

9. $[2, 5]$ **10.** $[5, 8]$

In Problems 11–16, find the absolute maximum and absolute minimum of each function on the given interval.

11. $f(x) = 4x + 9$ on $[2, 3]$ **12.** $f(x) = -3x + 20$ on $[-2, 6]$

13. $f(x) = e^{-x}$ on $[-1, 1]$ **14.** $f(x) = \ln x$ on $[1, 2]$

15. $f(x) = 9 - x^2$ on $[-4, 4]$

16. $f(x) = x^2 - 6x + 7$ on $[0, 10]$

In Problems 17–32, find the absolute maximum and minimum, if either exists, for each function.

17. $f(x) = x^2 - 2x + 3$ **18.** $f(x) = x^2 + 4x - 3$

19. $f(x) = -x^2 - 6x + 9$ **20.** $f(x) = -x^2 + 2x + 4$

21. $f(x) = x^3 + x$ **22.** $f(x) = -x^3 - 2x$

23. $f(x) = 8x^3 - 2x^4$ **24.** $f(x) = x^4 - 4x^3$

25. $f(x) = x + \dfrac{16}{x}$ **26.** $f(x) = x + \dfrac{25}{x}$

27. $f(x) = \dfrac{x^2}{x^2 + 1}$ **28.** $f(x) = \dfrac{1}{x^2 + 1}$

29. $f(x) = \dfrac{2x}{x^2 + 1}$ **30.** $f(x) = \dfrac{-8x}{x^2 + 4}$

31. $f(x) = \dfrac{x^2 - 1}{x^2 + 1}$ **32.** $f(x) = \dfrac{9 - x^2}{x^2 + 4}$

B

In Problems 33–56, find the indicated extremum of each function on the given interval.

33. Absolute minimum value on $[0, \infty)$ for
$$f(x) = 2x^2 - 8x + 6$$

34. Absolute maximum value on $[0, \infty)$ for
$$f(x) = 6x - x^2 + 4$$

35. Absolute maximum value on $[0, \infty)$ for
$$f(x) = 3x^2 - x^3$$

36. Absolute minimum value on $[0, \infty)$ for
$$f(x) = x^3 - 6x^2$$

37. Absolute minimum value on $[0, \infty)$ for
$$f(x) = (x + 4)(x - 2)^2$$

38. Absolute minimum value on $[0, \infty)$ for
$$f(x) = (2 - x)(x + 1)^2$$

39. Absolute maximum value on $(0, \infty)$ for
$$f(x) = 2x^4 - 8x^3$$

40. Absolute maximum value on $(0, \infty)$ for
$$f(x) = 4x^3 - 8x^4$$

41. Absolute maximum value on $(0, \infty)$ for
$$f(x) = 20 - 3x - \dfrac{12}{x}$$

42. Absolute minimum value on $(0, \infty)$ for
$$f(x) = 4 + x + \dfrac{9}{x}$$

43. Absolute maximum value on $(0, \infty)$ for
$$f(x) = 10 + 2x + \dfrac{64}{x^2}$$

44. Absolute maximum value on $(0, \infty)$ for
$$f(x) = 20 - 4x - \dfrac{250}{x^2}$$

45. Absolute minimum value on $(0, \infty)$ for

$$f(x) = x + \frac{1}{x} + \frac{30}{x^3}$$

46. Absolute minimum value on $(0, \infty)$ for

$$f(x) = 2x + \frac{5}{x} + \frac{4}{x^3}$$

47. Absolute minimum value on $(0, \infty)$ for

$$f(x) = \frac{e^x}{x^2}$$

48. Absolute maximum value on $(0, \infty)$ for

$$f(x) = \frac{x^4}{e^x}$$

49. Absolute maximum value on $(0, \infty)$ for

$$f(x) = \frac{x^3}{e^x}$$

50. Absolute minimum value on $(0, \infty)$ for

$$f(x) = \frac{e^x}{x}$$

51. Absolute maximum value on $(0, \infty)$ for

$$f(x) = 5x - 2x \ln x$$

52. Absolute minimum value on $(0, \infty)$ for

$$f(x) = 4x \ln x - 7x$$

53. Absolute maximum value on $(0, \infty)$ for

$$f(x) = x^2(3 - \ln x)$$

54. Absolute minimum value on $(0, \infty)$ for

$$f(x) = x^3(\ln x - 2)$$

55. Absolute maximum value on $(0, \infty)$ for

$$f(x) = \ln(xe^{-x})$$

56. Absolute maximum value on $(0, \infty)$ for

$$f(x) = \ln(x^2 e^{-x})$$

In Problems 57–62, find the absolute maximum and minimum, if either exists, for each function on the indicated intervals.

57. $f(x) = x^3 - 6x^2 + 9x - 6$
  (A) $[-1, 5]$ (B) $[-1, 3]$ (C) $[2, 5]$

58. $f(x) = 2x^3 - 3x^2 - 12x + 24$
  (A) $[-3, 4]$ (B) $[-2, 3]$ (C) $[-2, 1]$

59. $f(x) = (x - 1)(x - 5)^3 + 1$
  (A) $[0, 3]$ (B) $[1, 7]$ (C) $[3, 6]$

60. $f(x) = x^4 - 8x^2 + 16$
  (A) $[-1, 3]$ (B) $[0, 2]$ (C) $[-3, 4]$

61. $f(x) = x^4 - 4x^3 + 5$
  (A) $[-1, 2]$ (B) $[0, 4]$ (C) $[-1, 1]$

62. $f(x) = x^4 - 18x^2 + 32$
  (A) $[-4, 4]$ (B) $[-1, 1]$ (C) $[1, 3]$

In Problems 63–70, describe the graph of f at the given point relative to the existence of a local maximum or minimum with one of the following phrases: "Local maximum," "Local minimum," "Neither," or "Unable to determine from the given information." Assume that f(x) is continuous on $(-\infty, \infty)$.

63. $(2, f(2))$ if $f'(2) = 0$ and $f''(2) > 0$

64. $(4, f(4))$ if $f'(4) = 1$ and $f''(4) < 0$

65. $(-3, f(-3))$ if $f'(-3) = 0$ and $f''(-3) = 0$

66. $(-1, f(-1))$ if $f'(-1) = 0$ and $f''(-1) < 0$

67. $(6, f(6))$ if $f'(6) = 1$ and $f''(6)$ does not exist

68. $(5, f(5))$ if $f'(5) = 0$ and $f''(5)$ does not exist

69. $(-2, f(-2))$ if $f'(-2) = 0$ and $f''(-2) < 0$

70. $(1, f(1))$ if $f'(1) = 0$ and $f''(1) > 0$

Answers to Matched Problems

1. (A) Absolute maximum: $f(5) = 65$; absolute minimum: $f(-5) = -65$
  (B) Absolute maximum: $f(-2) = 16$; absolute minimum: $f(2) = -16$
  (C) Absolute maximum: $f(-2) = 16$; absolute minimum: $f(1) = -11$

2. (A) $f(2)$ is a local maximum; $f(4)$ is a local minimum.
  (B) $f(\ln 5) = 5 - 5 \ln 5$ is a local minimum.
  (C) $f(0)$ is a local minimum; there is no local extremum at $x = 1$.

3. (A) $f(\sqrt{5}) = 12 - 2\sqrt{5}$ (B) $f(5) = 5 \ln 5 - 5$

12-6 Optimization

- Area and Perimeter
- Maximizing Revenue and Profit
- Inventory Control

Now we can use calculus to solve **optimization problems**—problems that involve finding the absolute maximum value or the absolute minimum value of a function. As you work through this section, note that the statement of the problem does not usually include the function to be optimized. Often, it is your responsibility to find the function and then to find its absolute extremum.

Area and Perimeter

The techniques used to solve optimization problems are best illustrated through examples.

EXAMPLE 1   **Maximizing Area** A homeowner has $320 to spend on building a fence around a rectangular garden. Three sides of the fence will be constructed with wire fencing at a cost of $2 per linear foot. The fourth side will be constructed with wood fencing at a cost of $6 per linear foot. Find the dimensions and the area of the largest garden that can be enclosed with $320 worth of fencing.

SOLUTION   To begin, we draw a figure (Fig. 1), introduce variables, and look for relationships among the variables.

Since we don't know the dimensions of the garden, the lengths of fencing are represented by the variables x and y. The costs of the fencing materials are fixed and are represented by constants.

Now we look for relationships among the variables. The area of the garden is

$$A = xy$$

while the cost of the fencing is

$$C = 2y + 2x + 2y + 6x$$
$$= 8x + 4y$$

Figure 1

The problem states that the homeowner has $320 to spend on fencing. We assume that enclosing the largest area will use all the money available for fencing. The problem has now been reduced to

Maximize $A = xy$ subject to $8x + 4y = 320$

Before we can use calculus to find the maximum area A, we must express A as a function of a single variable. We use the cost equation to eliminate one of the variables in the area expression (we choose to eliminate y—either will work).

$$8x + 4y = 320$$
$$4y = 320 - 8x$$
$$y = 80 - 2x$$
$$A = xy = x(80 - 2x) = 80x - 2x^2$$

Now we consider the permissible values of x. Because x is one of the dimensions of a rectangle, x must satisfy

$$x \geq 0 \quad \text{Length is always nonnegative.}$$

And because $y = 80 - 2x$ is also a dimension of a rectangle, y must satisfy

$$y = 80 - 2x \geq 0 \quad \text{Width is always nonnegative.}$$
$$80 \geq 2x$$
$$40 \geq x \quad \text{or} \quad x \leq 40$$

We summarize the preceding discussion by stating the following model for this optimization problem:

Maximize $A(x) = 80x - 2x^2$ for $0 \leq x \leq 40$

Next, we find any critical values of A:

$$A'(x) = 80 - 4x = 0$$
$$80 = 4x$$
$$x = \frac{80}{4} = 20 \quad \text{Critical value}$$

Table 1

x	$A(x)$
0	0
20	800
40	0

Since $A(x)$ is continuous on $[0, 40]$, the absolute maximum value of A, if it exists, must occur at a critical value or an endpoint. Evaluating A at these values (Table 1), we see that the maximum area is 800 when

$$x = 20 \quad \text{and} \quad y = 80 - 2(20) = 40$$

Finally, we must answer the questions posed in the problem. The dimensions of the garden with the maximum area of 800 square feet are 20 feet by 40 feet, with one 20-foot side of wood fencing.

Matched Problem 1 Repeat Example 1 if the wood fencing costs $8 per linear foot and all other information remains the same.

We summarize the steps in the solution of Example 1 in the following box:

PROCEDURE Strategy for Solving Optimization Problems

Step 1 Introduce variables, look for relationships among the variables, and construct a mathematical model of the form

Maximize (or minimize) $f(x)$ on the interval I

Step 2 Find the critical values of $f(x)$.

Step 3 Use the procedures developed in Section 12-5 to find the absolute maximum (or minimum) value of $f(x)$ on the interval I and the value(s) of x where this occurs.

Step 4 Use the solution to the mathematical model to answer all the questions asked in the problem.

EXAMPLE 2 **Minimizing Perimeter** Refer to Example 1. The homeowner judges that an area of 800 square feet for the garden is too small and decides to increase the area to 1,250 square feet. What is the minimum cost of building a fence that will enclose a garden with an area of 1,250 square feet? What are the dimensions of this garden? Assume that the cost of fencing remains unchanged.

SOLUTION Refer to Figure 1 and the solution of Example 1. This time we want to minimize the cost of the fencing that will enclose 1,250 square feet. The problem can be expressed as

Minimize $\quad C = 8x + 4y \quad$ subject to $\quad xy = 1{,}250$

Since x and y represent distances, we know that $x \geq 0$ and $y \geq 0$. But neither variable can equal 0 because their product must be 1,250.

$$xy = 1{,}250 \qquad \textit{Solve the area equation for y.}$$

$$y = \frac{1{,}250}{x}$$

$$C(x) = 8x + 4\frac{1{,}250}{x} \qquad \textit{Substitute for y in the cost equation.}$$

$$= 8x + \frac{5{,}000}{x} \qquad x > 0$$

The model for this problem is

$$\text{Minimize } C(x) = 8x + \frac{5,000}{x} \quad \text{for } x > 0$$

$$= 8x + 5,000x^{-1}$$

$$C'(x) = 8 - 5,000x^{-2}$$

$$= 8 - \frac{5,000}{x^2} = 0$$

$$8 = \frac{5,000}{x^2}$$

$$x^2 = \frac{5,000}{8} = 625$$

$$x = \sqrt{625} = 25 \quad \textit{The negative square root is discarded, since } x > 0.$$

We use the second derivative to determine the behavior at $x = 25$.

$$\boxed{C'(x) = 8 - 5,000x^{-2}}$$

$$C''(x) = 0 + 10,000x^{-3} = \frac{10,000}{x^3}$$

$$C''(25) = \frac{10,000}{25^3} = 0.64 > 0$$

The second-derivative test shows that $C(x)$ has a local minimum at $x = 25$, and since $x = 25$ is the only critical value of $x > 0$, then $C(25)$ must be the absolute minimum value of $C(x)$ for $x > 0$. When $x = 25$, the cost is

$$C(25) = 8(25) + \frac{5,000}{25} = 200 + 200 = \$400$$

and

$$y = \frac{1,250}{25} = 50$$

The minimal cost for enclosing a 1,250-square-foot garden is $400, and the dimensions are 25 feet by 50 feet, with one 25-foot side of wood fencing.

Matched Problem 2 Repeat Example 2 if the homeowner wants to enclose an 1,800-square-foot garden and all other data remain unchanged.

CONCEPTUAL INSIGHT

The restrictions on the variables in the solutions of Examples 1 and 2 are typical of problems involving areas or perimeters (or the cost of the perimeter):

$$8x + 4y = 320 \quad \textit{Cost of fencing (Example 1)}$$

$$xy = 1,250 \quad \textit{Area of garden (Example 2)}$$

The equation in Example 1 restricts the values of x to

$$0 \leq x \leq 40 \quad \text{or} \quad [0, 40]$$

The endpoints are included in the interval for our convenience (a closed interval is easier to work with than an open one). The area function is defined at each endpoint, so it does no harm to include them.

The equation in Example 2 restricts the values of x to

$$x > 0 \quad \text{or} \quad (0, \infty)$$

Neither endpoint can be included in this interval. We cannot include 0 because the area is not defined when $x = 0$, and we can never include ∞ as an endpoint. Remember, ∞ is not a number; it is a symbol that indicates the interval is unbounded.

Maximizing Revenue and Profit

EXAMPLE 3 **Maximizing Revenue** An office supply company sells x permanent markers per year at $\$p$ per marker. The price–demand equation for these markers is $p = 10 - 0.001x$. What price should the company charge for the markers to maximize revenue? What is the maximum revenue?

SOLUTION

$$\text{Revenue} = \text{price} \times \text{demand}$$

$$R(x) = (10 - 0.001x)x$$

$$= 10x - 0.001x^2$$

Both price and demand must be nonnegative, so

$$x \geq 0 \quad \text{and} \quad p = 10 - 0.001x \geq 0$$

$$10 \geq 0.001x$$

$$10,000 \geq x$$

The mathematical model for this problem is

$$\text{Maximize} \quad R(x) = 10x - 0.001x^2 \quad 0 \leq x \leq 10,000$$

$$R'(x) = 10 - 0.002x$$

$$10 - 0.002x = 0$$

$$10 = 0.002x$$

$$x = \frac{10}{0.002} = 5,000 \qquad \text{Critical value}$$

Use the second-derivative test for absolute extrema:

$$R''(x) = -0.002 < 0 \quad \text{for all } x$$

$$\text{Max} \quad R(x) = R(5,000) = \$25,000$$

When the demand is $x = 5,000$, the price is

$$10 - 0.001(5,000) = \$5 \quad p = 10 - 0.001x$$

The company will realize a maximum revenue of $\$25,000$ when the price of a marker is $\$5$.

Matched Problem 3 An office supply company sells x heavy-duty paper shredders per year at $\$p$ per shredder. The price–demand equation for these shredders is

$$p = 300 - \frac{x}{30}$$

What price should the company charge for the shredders to maximize revenue? What is the maximum revenue?

EXAMPLE 4 **Maximizing Profit** The total annual cost of manufacturing x permanent markers for the office supply company in Example 3 is

$$C(x) = 5{,}000 + 2x$$

What is the company's maximum profit? What should the company charge for each marker, and how many markers should be produced?

SOLUTION Using the revenue model in Example 3, we have

$$\text{Profit} = \text{Revenue} - \text{Cost}$$

$$
\begin{aligned}
P(x) &= R(x) - C(x) \\
&= 10x - 0.001x^2 - 5{,}000 - 2x \\
&= 8x - 0.001x^2 - 5{,}000
\end{aligned}
$$

The mathematical model for profit is

$$\text{Maximize} \quad P(x) = 8x - 0.001x^2 - 5{,}000 \qquad 0 \le x \le 10{,}000$$

The restrictions on x come from the revenue model in Example 3.

$$P'(x) = 8 - 0.002x = 0$$

$$8 = 0.002x$$

$$x = \frac{8}{0.002} = 4{,}000 \quad \textit{Critical value}$$

$$P''(x) = -0.002 < 0 \quad \text{for all } x$$

Since $x = 4{,}000$ is the only critical value and $P''(x) < 0$,

$$\text{Max } P(x) = P(4{,}000) = \$11{,}000$$

Using the price–demand equation from Example 3 with $x = 4{,}000$, we find that

$$p = 10 - 0.001(4{,}000) = \$6 \quad \textit{p = 10 - 0.001x}$$

A maximum profit of \$11,000 is realized when 4,000 markers are manufactured annually and sold for \$6 each.

The results in Examples 3 and 4 are illustrated in Figure 2.

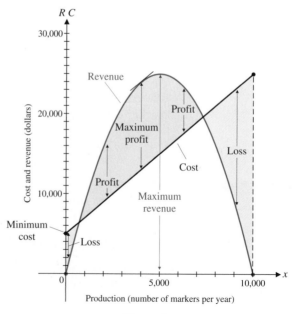

Figure 2

CONCEPTUAL INSIGHT

In Figure 2, notice that the maximum revenue and the maximum profit occur at different production levels. The maximum profit occurs when

$$P'(x) = R'(x) - C'(x) = 0$$

that is, when the marginal revenue is equal to the marginal cost. Notice that the slopes of the revenue function and the cost function are the same at this production level.

Matched Problem 4 The annual cost of manufacturing x paper shredders for the office supply company in Matched Problem 3 is $C(x) = 90,000 + 30x$. What is the company's maximum profit? What should it charge for each shredder, and how many shredders should it produce?

EXAMPLE 5 **Maximizing Profit** The government decides to tax the company in Example 4 $2 for each marker produced. Taking into account this additional cost, how many markers should the company manufacture each week to maximize its weekly profit? What is the maximum weekly profit? How much should the company charge for the markers to realize the maximum weekly profit?

SOLUTION The tax of $2 per unit changes the company's cost equation:

$$C(x) = \text{original cost} + \text{tax}$$

$$= 5,000 + 2x + 2x$$

$$= 5,000 + 4x$$

The new profit function is

$$P(x) = R(x) - C(x)$$

$$= 10x - 0.001x^2 - 5,000 - 4x$$

$$= 6x - 0.001x^2 - 5,000$$

So, we must solve the following equation:

$$\text{Maximize} \quad P(x) = 6x - 0.001x^2 - 5,000 \qquad 0 \le x \le 10,000$$

$$P'(x) = 6 - 0.002x$$

$$6 - 0.002x = 0$$

$$x = 3,000 \qquad \textit{Critical value}$$

$$P''(x) = -0.002 < 0 \quad \text{for all } x$$

$$\text{Max } P(x) = P(3,000) = \$4,000$$

Using the price–demand equation (Example 3) with $x = 3,000$, we find that

$$p = 10 - 0.001(3,000) = \$7 \quad p = 10 - 0.001x$$

The company's maximum profit is $4,000 when 3,000 markers are produced and sold weekly at a price of $7.

Even though the tax caused the company's cost to increase by $2 per marker, the price that the company should charge to maximize its profit increases by only $1. The company must absorb the other $1, with a resulting decrease of $7,000 in maximum profit.

Matched Problem 5 The government decides to tax the office supply company in Matched Problem 4 $20 for each shredder produced. Taking into account this additional cost, how many shredders should the company manufacture each week to maximize its weekly profit? What is the maximum weekly profit? How much should the company charge for the shredders to realize the maximum weekly profit?

EXAMPLE 6 **Maximizing Revenue** When a management training company prices its seminar on management techniques at $400 per person, 1,000 people will attend the seminar. The company estimates that for each $5 reduction in price, an additional 20 people will attend the seminar. How much should the company charge for the seminar in order to maximize its revenue? What is the maximum revenue?

SOLUTION Let x represent the number of $5 price reductions.

$$400 - 5x = \text{price per customer}$$

$$1{,}000 + 20x = \text{number of customers}$$

$$\text{Revenue} = (\text{price per customer})(\text{number of customers})$$

$$R(x) = (400 - 5x) \times (1{,}000 + 20x)$$

Since price cannot be negative, we have

$$400 - 5x \geq 0$$

$$400 \geq 5x$$

$$80 \geq x \qquad \text{or} \qquad x \leq 80$$

A negative value of x would result in a price increase. Since the problem is stated in terms of price reductions, we must restrict x so that $x \geq 0$. Putting all this together, we have the following model:

$$\text{Maximize} \quad R(x) = (400 - 5x)(1{,}000 + 20x) \quad \text{for } 0 \leq x \leq 80$$

$$R(x) = 400{,}000 + 3{,}000x - 100x^2$$

$$R'(x) = 3{,}000 - 200x = 0$$

$$3{,}000 = 200x$$

$$x = 15 \quad \textit{Critical value}$$

Since $R(x)$ is continuous on the interval $[0, 80]$, we can determine the behavior of the graph by constructing a table. Table 2 shows that $R(15) = \$422{,}500$ is the absolute maximum revenue. The price of attending the seminar at $x = 15$ is $400 - 5(15) = \$325$. The company should charge $325 for the seminar in order to receive a maximum revenue of $422,500.

Table 2

x	$R(x)$
0	400,000
15	422,500
80	0

Matched Problem 6 A walnut grower estimates from past records that if 20 trees are planted per acre, then each tree will average 60 pounds of nuts per year. If, for each additional tree planted per acre, the average yield per tree drops 2 pounds, then how many trees should be planted to maximize the yield per acre? What is the maximum yield?

EXAMPLE 7 **Maximizing Revenue** After additional analysis, the management training company in Example 6 decides that its estimate of attendance was too high. Its new estimate is that only 10 additional people will attend the seminar for each $5 decrease in price. All other information remains the same. How much should the company charge for the seminar now in order to maximize revenue? What is the new maximum revenue?

SOLUTION Under the new assumption, the model becomes

$$\text{Maximize} \quad R(x) = (400 - 5x)(1,000 + 10x) \quad 0 \le x \le 80$$

$$= 400,000 - 1,000x - 50x^2$$

$$R'(x) = -1,000 - 100x = 0$$

$$-1,000 = 100x$$

$$x = -10 \quad \text{Critical value}$$

Table 3

x	R(x)
0	400,000
80	0

Note that $x = -10$ is not in the interval $[0, 80]$. Since $R(x)$ is continuous on $[0, 80]$, we can use a table to find the absolute maximum revenue. Table 3 shows that the maximum revenue is $R(0) = \$400,000$. The company should leave the price at \$400. Any \$5 decreases in price will lower the revenue.

Matched Problem 7 After further analysis, the walnut grower in Matched Problem 6 determines that each additional tree planted will reduce the average yield by 4 pounds. All other information remains the same. How many additional trees per acre should the grower plant now in order to maximize the yield? What is the new maximum yield?

CONCEPTUAL INSIGHT

The solution in Example 7 is called an **endpoint solution** because the optimal value occurs at the endpoint of an interval rather than at a critical value in the interior of the interval. It is always important to verify that the optimal value has been found.

Inventory Control

EXAMPLE 8 **Inventory Control** A multimedia company anticipates that there will be a demand for 20,000 copies of a certain DVD during the next year. It costs the company \$0.50 to store a DVD for one year. Each time it must make additional DVDs, it costs \$200 to set up the equipment. How many DVDs should the company make during each production run to minimize its total storage and setup costs?

SOLUTION This type of problem is called an **inventory control problem**. One of the basic assumptions made in such problems is that the demand is uniform. For example, if there are 250 working days in a year, then the daily demand would be $20,000 \div 250 = 80$ DVDs. The company could decide to produce all 20,000 DVDs at the beginning of the year. This would certainly minimize the setup costs but would result in very large storage costs. At the other extreme, the company could produce 80 DVDs each day. This would minimize the storage costs but would result in very large setup costs. Somewhere between these two extremes is the optimal solution that will minimize the total storage and setup costs. Let

$$x = \text{number of DVDs manufactured during each production run}$$

$$y = \text{number of production runs}$$

It is easy to see that the total setup cost for the year is $200y$, but what is the total storage cost? If the demand is uniform, then the number of DVDs in storage between production runs will decrease from x to 0, and the average number in storage each day is $x/2$. This result is illustrated in Figure 3.

Since it costs \$0.50 to store a DVD for one year, the total storage cost is $0.5(x/2) = 0.25x$ and the total cost is

$$\text{total cost} = \text{setup cost} + \text{storage cost}$$

$$C = 200y + 0.25x$$

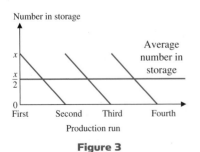

Figure 3

In order to write the total cost C as a function of one variable, we must find a relationship between x and y. If the company produces x DVDs in each of y production runs, then the total number of DVDs produced is xy.

$$xy = 20{,}000$$

$$y = \frac{20{,}000}{x}$$

Certainly, x must be at least 1 and cannot exceed 20,000. We must solve the following equation:

$$\text{Minimize} \quad C(x) = 200\left(\frac{20{,}000}{x}\right) + 0.25x \qquad 1 \le x \le 20{,}000$$

$$C(x) = \frac{4{,}000{,}000}{x} + 0.25x$$

$$C'(x) = -\frac{4{,}000{,}000}{x^2} + 0.25$$

$$-\frac{4{,}000{,}000}{x^2} + 0.25 = 0$$

$$x^2 = \frac{4{,}000{,}000}{0.25}$$

$$x^2 = 16{,}000{,}000 \qquad -4{,}000 \text{ is not a critical value, since}$$

$$x = 4{,}000 \qquad\qquad 1 \le x \le 20{,}000.$$

$$C''(x) = \frac{8{,}000{,}000}{x^3} > 0 \qquad \text{for } x \in (1, 20{,}000)$$

Therefore,

$$\text{Min } C(x) = C(4{,}000) = 2{,}000$$

$$y = \frac{20{,}000}{4{,}000} = 5$$

The company will minimize its total cost by making 4,000 DVDs five times during the year.

Matched Problem 8   Repeat Example 8 if it costs $250 to set up a production run and $0.40 to store a DVD for one year.

Exercises 12-6

Preliminary word problems:

1. Find two numbers whose sum is 15 and whose product is a maximum.

2. Find two numbers whose sum is 21 and whose product is a maximum.

3. Find two numbers whose difference is 15 and whose product is a minimum.

4. Find two numbers whose difference is 21 and whose product is a minimum.

5. Find two positive numbers whose product is 15 and whose sum is a minimum.

6. Find two positive numbers whose product is 21 and whose sum is a minimum.

7. Find the dimensions of a rectangle with an area of 200 square feet that has the minimum perimeter.

8. Find the dimensions of a rectangle with an area of 108 square feet that has the minimum perimeter.

9. Find the dimensions of a rectangle with a perimeter of 148 feet that has the maximum area.

10. Find the dimensions of a rectangle with a perimeter of 76 feet that has the maximum area.

11. **Maximum revenue and profit.** A company manufactures and sells x videophones per week. The weekly price–demand and cost equations are, respectively,

$$p = 500 - 0.5x \quad \text{and} \quad C(x) = 20,000 + 135x$$

(A) What price should the company charge for the phones, and how many phones should be produced to maximize the weekly revenue? What is the maximum weekly revenue?

(B) What is the maximum weekly profit? How much should the company charge for the phones, and how many phones should be produced to realize the maximum weekly profit?

12. **Maximum revenue and profit.** A company manufactures and sells x digital cameras per week. The weekly price–demand and cost equations are, respectively,

$$p = 400 - 0.4x \quad \text{and} \quad C(x) = 2,000 + 160x$$

(A) What price should the company charge for the cameras, and how many cameras should be produced to maximize the weekly revenue? What is the maximum revenue?

(B) What is the maximum weekly profit? How much should the company charge for the cameras, and how many cameras should be produced to realize the maximum weekly profit?

13. **Maximum revenue and profit.** A company manufactures and sells x television sets per month. The monthly cost and price–demand equations are

$$C(x) = 72,000 + 60x$$

$$p = 200 - \frac{x}{30} \qquad 0 \le x \le 6,000$$

(A) Find the maximum revenue.

(B) Find the maximum profit, the production level that will realize the maximum profit, and the price the company should charge for each television set.

(C) If the government decides to tax the company $5 for each set it produces, how many sets should the company manufacture each month to maximize its profit? What is the maximum profit? What should the company charge for each set?

14. **Maximum revenue and profit.** Repeat Problem 13 for

$$C(x) = 60,000 + 60x$$

$$p = 200 - \frac{x}{50} \qquad 0 \le x \le 10,000$$

15. **Maximum profit.** The following table contains price–demand and total cost data for the production of extreme-cold sleeping bags, where p is the wholesale price (in dollars) of a sleeping bag for an annual demand of x sleeping bags and C is the total cost (in dollars) of producing x sleeping bags:

(A) Find a quadratic regression equation for the price–demand data, using x as the independent variable.

x	p	C
950	240	130,000
1,200	210	150,000
1,800	160	180,000
2,050	120	190,000

(B) Find a linear regression equation for the cost data, using x as the independent variable.

(C) What is the maximum profit? What is the wholesale price per extreme-cold sleeping bag that should be charged to realize the maximum profit? Round answers to the nearest dollar.

16. **Maximum profit.** The following table contains price–demand and total cost data for the production of regular sleeping bags, where p is the wholesale price (in dollars) of a sleeping bag for an annual demand of x sleeping bags and C is the total cost (in dollars) of producing x sleeping bags:

x	p	C
2,300	98	145,000
3,300	84	170,000
4,500	67	190,000
5,200	51	210,000

(A) Find a quadratic regression equation for the price–demand data, using x as the independent variable.

(B) Find a linear regression equation for the cost data, using x as the independent variable.

(C) What is the maximum profit? What is the wholesale price per regular sleeping bag that should be charged to realize the maximum profit? Round answers to the nearest dollar.

17. **Maximum revenue.** A deli sells 640 sandwiches per day at a price of $8 each.

(A) A market survey shows that for every $0.10 reduction in price, 40 more sandwiches will be sold. How much should the deli charge for a sandwich in order to maximize revenue?

(B) A different market survey shows that for every $0.20 reduction in the original $8 price, 15 more sandwiches will be sold. Now how much should the deli charge for a sandwich in order to maximize revenue?

18. **Maximum revenue.** A university student center sells 1,600 cups of coffee per day at a price of $2.40.

(A) A market survey shows that for every $0.05 reduction in price, 50 more cups of coffee will be sold. How much should the student center charge for a cup of coffee in order to maximize revenue?

(B) A different market survey shows that for every $0.10 reduction in the original $2.40 price, 60 more cups of coffee will be sold. Now how much should the student center charge for a cup of coffee in order to maximize revenue?

19. **Car rental.** A car rental agency rents 200 cars per day at a rate of $30 per day. For each $1 increase in rate, 5 fewer cars are rented. At what rate should the cars be rented to produce the maximum income? What is the maximum income?

20. **Rental income.** A 300-room hotel in Las Vegas is filled to capacity every night at $80 a room. For each $1 increase in rent, 3 fewer rooms are rented. If each rented room costs $10 to service per day, how much should the management charge for each room to maximize gross profit? What is the maximum gross profit?

21. **Agriculture.** A commercial cherry grower estimates from past records that if 30 trees are planted per acre, then each tree will yield an average of 50 pounds of cherries per season. If, for each additional tree planted per acre (up to 20), the average yield per tree is reduced by 1 pound, how many trees should be planted per acre to obtain the maximum yield per acre? What is the maximum yield?

22. **Agriculture.** A commercial pear grower must decide on the optimum time to have fruit picked and sold. If the pears are picked now, they will bring 30¢ per pound, with each tree yielding an average of 60 pounds of salable pears. If the average yield per tree increases 6 pounds per tree per week for the next 4 weeks, but the price drops 2¢ per pound per week, when should the pears be picked to realize the maximum return per tree? What is the maximum return?

23. **Manufacturing.** A candy box is to be made out of a piece of cardboard that measures 8 by 12 inches. Squares of equal size will be cut out of each corner, and then the ends and sides will be folded up to form a rectangular box. What size square should be cut from each corner to obtain a maximum volume?

24. **Packaging.** A parcel delivery service will deliver a package only if the length plus girth (distance around) does not exceed 108 inches.

    (A) Find the dimensions of a rectangular box with square ends that satisfies the delivery service's restriction and has maximum volume. What is the maximum volume?

    (B) Find the dimensions (radius and height) of a cylindrical container that meets the delivery service's requirement and has maximum volume. What is the maximum volume?

Figure for 24

25. **Construction costs.** A fence is to be built to enclose a rectangular area of 800 square feet. The fence along three sides is to be made of material that costs $6 per foot. The material for the fourth side costs $18 per foot. Find the dimensions of the rectangle that will allow for the most economical fence to be built.

26. **Construction costs.** The owner of a retail lumber store wants to construct a fence to enclose an outdoor storage area adjacent to the store, using all of the store as part of one side of the area (see the figure). Find the dimensions that will enclose the largest area if

    (A) 240 feet of fencing material are used.

    (B) 400 feet of fencing material are used.

Figure for 26

27. **Inventory control.** A paint manufacturer has a uniform annual demand for 16,000 cans of automobile primer. It costs $4 to store one can of paint for one year and $500 to set up the plant for production of the primer. How many times a year should the company produce this primer in order to minimize the total storage and setup costs?

28. **Inventory control.** A pharmacy has a uniform annual demand for 200 bottles of a certain antibiotic. It costs $10 to store one bottle for one year and $40 to place an order. How many times during the year should the pharmacy order the antibiotic in order to minimize the total storage and reorder costs?

29. **Inventory control.** A publishing company sells 50,000 copies of a certain book each year. It costs the company $1 to store a book for one year. Each time that it prints additional copies, it costs the company $1,000 to set up the presses. How many books should the company produce during each printing in order to minimize its total storage and setup costs?

30. **Operational costs.** The cost per hour for fuel to run a train is $v^2/4$ dollars, where v is the speed of the train in miles per hour. (Note that the cost goes up as the square of the speed.) Other costs, including labor, are $300 per hour. How fast should the train travel on a 360-mile trip to minimize the total cost for the trip?

31. **Construction costs.** A freshwater pipeline is to be run from a source on the edge of a lake to a small resort community on an island 5 miles offshore, as indicated in the figure.

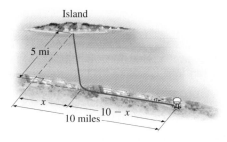

Figure for 31

(A) If it costs 1.4 times as much to lay the pipe in the lake as it does on land, what should x be (in miles) to minimize the total cost of the project?

(B) If it costs only 1.1 times as much to lay the pipe in the lake as it does on land, what should x be to minimize the total cost of the project? [*Note:* Compare with Problem 34.]

32. Drug concentration. The concentration $C(t)$, in milligrams per cubic centimeter, of a particular drug in a patient's bloodstream is given by

$$C(t) = \frac{0.16t}{t^2 + 4t + 4}$$

where t is the number of hours after the drug is taken. How many hours after the drug is taken will the concentration be maximum? What is the maximum concentration?

33. Bacteria control. A lake used for recreational swimming is treated periodically to control harmful bacteria growth. Suppose that t days after a treatment, the concentration of bacteria per cubic centimeter is given by

$$C(t) = 30t^2 - 240t + 500 \qquad 0 \le t \le 8$$

How many days after a treatment will the concentration be minimal? What is the minimum concentration?

34. Bird flights. Some birds tend to avoid flights over large bodies of water during daylight hours. Suppose that an adult bird with this tendency is taken from its nesting area on the edge of a large lake to an island 5 miles offshore and is then released (see the figure).

Figure for 34

(A) If it takes 1.4 times as much energy to fly over water as land, how far up the shore (x, in miles) should the bird head to minimize the total energy expended in returning to the nesting area?

(B) If it takes only 1.1 times as much energy to fly over water as land, how far up the shore should the bird head to minimize the total energy expended in returning to the nesting area? [*Note:* Compare with Problem 31.]

35. Botany. If it is known from past experiments that the height (in feet) of a certain plant after t months is given approximately by

$$H(t) = 4t^{1/2} - 2t \qquad 0 \le t \le 2$$

then how long, on average, will it take a plant to reach its maximum height? What is the maximum height?

36. Pollution. Two heavily industrial areas are located 10 miles apart, as shown in the figure. If the concentration of partic-

ulate matter (in parts per million) decreases as the reciprocal of the square of the distance from the source, and if area A_1 emits eight times the particulate matter as A_2, then the concentration of particulate matter at any point between the two areas is given by

$$C(x) = \frac{8k}{x^2} + \frac{k}{(10 - x)^2} \qquad 0.5 \le x \le 9.5, \quad k > 0$$

How far from A_1 will the concentration of particulate matter between the two areas be at a minimum?

Figure for 36

37. Politics. In a newly incorporated city, it is estimated that the voting population (in thousands) will increase according to

$$N(t) = 30 + 12t^2 - t^3 \qquad 0 \le t \le 8$$

where t is time in years. When will the rate of increase be most rapid?

38. Learning. A large grocery chain found that, on average, a checker can recall $P\%$ of a given price list x hours after starting work, as given approximately by

$$P(x) = 96x - 24x^2 \qquad 0 \le x \le 3$$

At what time x does the checker recall a maximum percentage? What is the maximum?

Answers to Matched Problems

1. The dimensions of the garden with the maximum area of 640 square feet are 16 feet by 40 feet, with one 16-foot side with wood fencing.

2. The minimal cost for enclosing a 1,800-square-foot garden is $480, and the dimensions are 30 feet by 60 feet, with one 30-foot side with wood fencing.

3. The company will realize a maximum revenue of $675,000 when the price of a shredder is $150.

4. A maximum profit of $456,750 is realized when 4,050 shredders are manufactured annually and sold for $165 each.

5. A maximum profit of $378,750 is realized when 3,075 shredders are manufactured annually and sold for $175 each.

6. The maximum yield is 1,250 pounds per acre when 5 additional trees are planted on each acre.

7. The maximum yield is 1,200 pounds when no additional trees are planted.

8. The company should produce 5,000 DVDs four times a year.

Chapter 12   Review

Important Terms, Symbols, and Concepts

12-1 First Derivative and Graphs

- **Increasing and decreasing properties** of a function can be determined by examining a sign chart for the derivative.
- A number c is a **partition number** for $f'(x)$ if $f'(c) = 0$ or $f'(x)$ is discontinuous at c. If c is also in the domain of $f(x)$, then c is a **critical value.**
- Increasing and decreasing properties and **local extrema** for $f(x)$ can be determined by examining the graph of $f'(x)$.
- The **first-derivative test** is used to locate extrema of a function.

12-2 Second Derivative and Graphs

- The **second derivative** of a function f can be used to determine the concavity of the graph of f.
- **Inflection points** on a graph are points where the concavity changes.
- The concavity of the graph of $f(x)$ can also be determined by an examination of the graph of $f'(x)$.
- A **graphing strategy** is used to organize the information obtained from the first and second derivatives.

12-3 L'Hôpital's Rule

- Limits at infinity and infinite limits involving powers of $x - c$, e^x, and ln x are reviewed.
- The first version of **L'Hôpital's rule** applies to limits involving the indeterminate form $0/0$ as $x \rightarrow c$.
- You must always check that L'Hôpital's rule applies.
- L'Hôpital's rule can be applied more than once.
- L'Hôpital's rule applies to one-sided limits and limits at infinity.
- L'Hôpital's rule applies to limits involving the indeterminate form ∞/∞.

12-4 Curve-Sketching Techniques

- The graphing strategy first used in Section 12-2 is expanded to include horizontal and vertical asymptotes.
- If $f(x) = n(x)/d(x)$ is a rational function with the degree of $n(x)$ 1 more than the degree of $d(x)$, then the graph of $f(x)$ has an **oblique asymptote** of the form $y = mx + b$.

12-5 Absolute Maxima and Minima

- The steps involved in finding the **absolute maximum and absolute minimum** values of a continuous function on a closed interval are listed in a procedure.
- The **second-derivative test for local extrema** can be used to test critical values, but it does not work in all cases.
- If a function is continuous on an interval I and has only one critical value in I, then the **second-derivative test for absolute extrema** can be used to find the absolute extrema, but it not does work in all cases.

12-6 Optimization

- The methods used to solve **optimization problems** are summarized and illustrated by examples.

Review Exercises

Work through all the problems in this chapter review, and check your answers in the back of the book. Answers to all review problems are there, along with section numbers in italics to indicate where each type of problem is discussed. Where weaknesses show up, review appropriate sections in the text.

A

Problems 1–8 refer to the following graph of $y = f(x)$. Identify the points or intervals on the x axis that produce the indicated behavior.

1. $f(x)$ is increasing.   **2.** $f'(x) < 0$

3. The graph of f is concave downward.

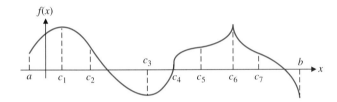

Figure for 1–8

4. Local minima   **5.** Absolute maxima

6. $f'(x)$ appears to be 0.   **7.** $f'(x)$ does not exist.

8. Inflection points

In Problems 9 and 10, use the given information to sketch the graph of f. Assume that f is continuous on its domain and that all intercepts are included in the information given.

9. Domain: All real x

x	-3	-2	-1	0	2	3
$f(x)$	0	3	2	0	-3	0

$f'(x)$ + + + 0 — — — — — — — — 0 — — — ND + + +
              -2 0   2

$f''(x)$ — — — — — — — — — — 0 + + + 0 — — — ND — — —
                                 -1 0   2

10. Domain: All real x

$f(-2) = 1, f(0) = 0, f(2) = 1;$

$f'(0) = 0; f'(x) < 0$ on $(-\infty, 0);$

$f'(x) > 0$ on $(0, \infty);$

$f''(-2) = 0, f''(2) = 0;$

$f''(x) < 0$ on $(-\infty, -2)$ and $(2, \infty);$

$f''(x) > 0$ on $(-2, 2);$

$\lim_{x \to -\infty} f(x) = 2; \lim_{x \to \infty} f(x) = 2$

11. Find $f''(x)$ for $f(x) = x^4 + 5x^3.$

12. Find y'' for $y = 3x + \dfrac{4}{x}.$

In Problems 13 and 14, find the domain and intercepts.

13. $f(x) = \dfrac{5 + x}{4 - x}$ **14.** $f(x) = \ln(x + 2)$

In Problems 15 and 16, find the horizontal and vertical asymptotes.

15. $f(x) = \dfrac{x + 3}{x^2 - 4}$ **16.** $f(x) = \dfrac{2x - 7}{3x + 10}$

In Problems 17 and 18, find the x and y coordinates of all inflection points.

17. $f(x) = x^4 - 12x^2$ **18.** $f(x) = (2x + 1)^{1/3} - 6$

In Problems 19 and 20, find (A) $f'(x)$, (B) the critical values of f, and (C) the partition numbers for f'.

19. $f(x) = x^{1/5}$ **20.** $f(x) = x^{-1/5}$

In Problems 21–30, summarize all the pertinent information obtained by applying the final version of the graphing strategy (Section 12–4) to f, and sketch the graph of f.

21. $f(x) = x^3 - 18x^2 + 81x$ **22.** $f(x) = (x + 4)(x - 2)^2$

23. $f(x) = 8x^3 - 2x^4$ **24.** $f(x) = (x - 1)^3(x + 3)$

25. $f(x) = \dfrac{3x}{x + 2}$ **26.** $f(x) = \dfrac{x^2}{x^2 + 27}$

27. $f(x) = \dfrac{x}{(x + 2)^2}$ **28.** $f(x) = \dfrac{x^3}{x^2 + 3}$

29. $f(x) = 5 - 5e^{-x}$ **30.** $f(x) = x^3 \ln x$

Find each limit in Problems 31–40.

31. $\lim\limits_{x \to 0} \dfrac{e^{3x} - 1}{x}$ **32.** $\lim\limits_{x \to 2} \dfrac{x^2 - 5x + 6}{x^2 + x - 6}$

33. $\lim\limits_{x \to 0^-} \dfrac{\ln(1 + x)}{x^2}$ **34.** $\lim\limits_{x \to 0} \dfrac{\ln(1 + x)}{1 + x}$

35. $\lim\limits_{x \to \infty} \dfrac{e^{4x}}{x^2}$ **36.** $\lim\limits_{x \to 0} \dfrac{e^x + e^{-x} - 2}{x^2}$

37. $\lim\limits_{x \to 0^+} \dfrac{\sqrt{1 + x} - 1}{\sqrt{x}}$ **38.** $\lim\limits_{x \to \infty} \dfrac{\ln x}{x^5}$

39. $\lim\limits_{x \to \infty} \dfrac{\ln(1 + 6x)}{\ln(1 + 3x)}$ **40.** $\lim\limits_{x \to 0} \dfrac{\ln(1 + 6x)}{\ln(1 + 3x)}$

41. Use the graph of $y = f'(x)$ shown here to discuss the graph of $y = f(x)$. Organize your conclusions in a table (see Example 4, Section 12-2). Sketch a possible graph of $y = f(x)$.

59.

60.

61.

62.

63

64

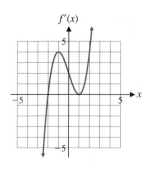

Figure for 41 and 42

42. Refer to the above graph of $y = f'(x)$. Which of the following could be the graph of $y = f''(x)$?

(A)

(B)

(C)

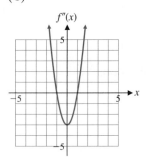

43. Use the second-derivative test to find any local extrema for

$$f(x) = x^3 - 6x^2 - 15x + 12$$

44. Find the absolute maximum and absolute minimum, if either exists, for

$$y = f(x) = x^3 - 12x + 12 \qquad -3 \le x \le 5$$

45. Find the absolute minimum, if it exists, for

$$y = f(x) = x^2 + \frac{16}{x^2} \qquad x > 0$$

46. Find the absolute maximum value, if it exists, for

$$f(x) = 11x - 2x \ln x \qquad x > 0$$

47. Find the absolute maximum value, if it exists, for

$$f(x) = 10xe^{-2x} \qquad x > 0$$

48. Let $y = f(x)$ be a polynomial function with local minima at $x = a$ and $x = b, a < b$. Must f have at least one local maximum between a and b? Justify your answer.

49. The derivative of $f(x) = x^{-1}$ is $f'(x) = -x^{-2}$. Since $f'(x) < 0$ for $x \ne 0$, is it correct to say that $f(x)$ is decreasing for all x except $x = 0$? Explain.

50. Discuss the difference between a partition number for $f'(x)$ and a critical value of $f(x)$, and illustrate with examples.

C

51. Find the absolute maximum for $f'(x)$ if

$$f(x) = 6x^2 - x^3 + 8$$

Graph f and f' on the same coordinate system for $0 \le x \le 4$.

52. Find two positive numbers whose product is 400 and whose sum is a minimum. What is the minimum sum?

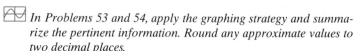 *In Problems 53 and 54, apply the graphing strategy and summarize the pertinent information. Round any approximate values to two decimal places.*

53. $f(x) = x^4 + x^3 - 4x^2 - 3x + 4$

54. $f(x) = 0.25x^4 - 5x^3 + 31x^2 - 70x$

55. Find the absolute maximum value, if it exists, for

$$f(x) = 3x - x^2 + e^{-x} x > 0$$

56. Find the absolute maximum value, if it exists, for

$$f(x) = \frac{\ln x}{e^x} x > 0$$

Applications

57. Price analysis. The graph in the figure approximates the rate of change of the price of tomatoes over a 60-month period, where $p(t)$ is the price of a pound of tomatoes and t is time (in months).

(A) Write a brief description of the graph of $y = p(t)$, including a discussion of local extrema and inflection points.

(B) Sketch a possible graph of $y = p(t)$.

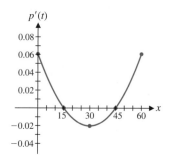

Figure for 57

58. Maximum revenue and profit. A company manufactures and sells x e-book readers per month. The monthly cost and price–demand equations are, respectively,

$$C(x) = 350x + 50,000$$

$$p = 500 - 0.025x \qquad 0 \le x \le 20,000$$

(A) Find the maximum revenue.

(B) How many readers should the company manufacture each month to maximize its profit? What is the maximum monthly profit? How much should the company charge for each reader?

(C) If the government decides to tax the company $20 for each reader it produces, how many readers should the company manufacture each month to maximize its profit? What is the maximum monthly profit? How much should the company charge for each reader?

59. Construction. A fence is to be built to enclose a rectangular area. The fence along three sides is to be made of material that costs $5 per foot. The material for the fourth side costs $15 per foot.

(A) If the area is 5,000 square feet, find the dimensions of the rectangle that will allow for the most economical fence.

(B) If $3,000 is available for the fencing, find the dimensions of the rectangle that will enclose the most area.

60. Rental income. A 200-room hotel in Reno is filled to capacity every night at a rate of $40 per room. For each $1 increase in the nightly rate, 4 fewer rooms are rented. If each rented room costs $8 a day to service, how much should the management charge per room in order to maximize gross profit? What is the maximum gross profit?

61. Inventory control. A computer store sells 7,200 boxes of storage disks annually. It costs the store $0.20 to store a box of disks for one year. Each time it reorders disks, the store must pay a $5.00 service charge for processing the order. How many times during the year should the store order disks to minimize the total storage and reorder costs?

62. Average cost. The total cost of producing x dorm refrigerators per day is given by

$$C(x) = 4,000 + 10x + 0.1x^2$$

Find the minimum average cost. Graph the average cost and the marginal cost functions on the same coordinate system. Include any oblique asymptotes.

63. Average cost. The cost of producing x wheeled picnic coolers is given by

$$C(x) = 200 + 50x - 50 \ln x \qquad x \geq 1$$

Find the minimum average cost.

64. Marginal analysis. The price–demand equation for a GPS device is

$$p(x) = 1,000e^{-0.02x}$$

where x is the monthly demand and p is the price in dollars. Find the production level and price per unit that produce the maximum revenue. What is the maximum revenue?

65. Maximum revenue. Graph the revenue function from Problem 64 for $0 \leq x \leq 100$.

66. Maximum profit. Refer to Problem 64. If the GPS devices cost the store $220 each, find the price (to the nearest cent) that maximizes the profit. What is the maximum profit (to the nearest dollar)?

67. Maximum profit. The data in the table show the daily demand x for cream puffs at a state fair at various price levels p. If it costs $1 to make a cream puff, use logarithmic regression ($p = a + b \ln x$) to find the price (to the nearest cent) that maximizes profit.

Demand x	Price per Cream Puff($) p
3,125	1.99
3,879	1.89
5,263	1.79
5,792	1.69
6,748	1.59
8,120	1.49

68. Construction costs. The ceiling supports in a new discount department store are 12 feet apart. Lights are to be hung from these supports by chains in the shape of a "Y." If the lights are 10 feet below the ceiling, what is the shortest length of chain that can be used to support these lights?

69. Average cost. The table gives the total daily cost y (in dollars) of producing x dozen chocolate chip cookies at various production levels.

Dozens of Cookies x	Total Cost y
50	119
100	187
150	248
200	382
250	505
300	695

(A) Enter the data into a graphing calculator and find a quadratic regression equation for the total cost.

(B) Use the regression equation from part (A) to find the minimum average cost (to the nearest cent) and the corresponding production level (to the nearest integer).

70. Advertising—point of diminishing returns. A company estimates that it will sell $N(x)$ units of a product after spending $x thousand on advertising, as given by

$$N(x) = -0.25x^4 + 11x^3 - 108x^2 + 3{,}000$$
$$9 \le x \le 24$$

When is the rate of change of sales increasing and when is it decreasing? What is the point of diminishing returns and the maximum rate of change of sales? Graph N and N' on the same coordinate system.

71. Advertising. A chain of appliance stores uses TV ads to promote its HDTV sales. Analyzing past records produced the data in the following table, where x is the number of ads placed monthly and y is the number of HDTVs sold that month:

Number of Ads x	Number of HDTVs y
10	271
20	427
25	526
30	629
45	887
48	917

(A) Enter the data into a graphing calculator, set the calculator to display two decimal places, and find a cubic regression equation for the number of HDTVs sold monthly as a function of the number of ads.

(B) How many ads should be placed each month to maximize the rate of change of sales with respect to the number of ads, and how many HDTVs can be expected to be sold with that number of ads? Round answers to the nearest integer.

72. Bacteria control. If t days after a treatment the bacteria count per cubic centimeter in a body of water is given by

$$C(t) = 20t^2 - 120t + 800 \qquad 0 \le t \le 9$$

then in how many days will the count be a minimum?

73. Politics. In a new suburb, it is estimated that the number of registered voters will grow according to

$$N = 10 + 6t^2 - t^3 \qquad 0 \le t \le 5$$

where t is time in years and N is in thousands. When will the rate of increase be a maximum?

Integration

Introduction

In the preceding three chapters, we studied the *derivative* and its applications. In Chapter 13, we introduce the *integral*, the second key concept of calculus. The integral can be used to calculate areas, volumes, the index of income concentration, and consumers' surplus. At first glance, the integral may appear to be unrelated to the derivative. There is, however, a close connection between these two concepts, which is made precise by the *fundamental theorem of calculus* (Section 13-5). We consider many applications of integrals and differential equations in Chapter 13. See, for example, Problem 67 in Section 13-3, which explores how the age of an archeological site or artifact can be estimated.

13-1 Antiderivatives and Indefinite Integrals

Many operations in mathematics have reverses—addition and subtraction, multiplication and division, powers and roots. We now know how to find the derivatives of many functions. The reverse operation, *antidifferentiation* (the reconstruction of a function from its derivative), will receive our attention in this and the next two sections.

Antiderivatives

A function F is an **antiderivative** of a function f if $F'(x) = f(x)$.

The function $F(x) = \dfrac{x^3}{3}$ is an antiderivative of the function $f(x) = x^2$ because

$$\frac{d}{dx}\left(\frac{x^3}{3}\right) = x^2$$

However, $F(x)$ is not the only antiderivative of x^2. Note also that

$$\frac{d}{dx}\left(\frac{x^3}{3} + 2\right) = x^2 \qquad \frac{d}{dx}\left(\frac{x^3}{3} - \pi\right) = x^2 \qquad \frac{d}{dx}\left(\frac{x^3}{3} + \sqrt{5}\right) = x^2$$

Therefore,

$$\frac{x^3}{3} + 2 \qquad \frac{x^3}{3} - \pi \qquad \frac{x^3}{3} + \sqrt{5}$$

are also antiderivatives of x^2 because each has x^2 as a derivative. In fact, it appears that

$$\frac{x^3}{3} + C \qquad \text{for any real number } C$$

is an antiderivative of x^2 because

$$\frac{d}{dx}\left(\frac{x^3}{3} + C\right) = x^2$$

Antidifferentiation of a given function does not give a unique function, but an entire family of functions.

Does the expression

$$\frac{x^3}{3} + C \qquad \text{with } C \text{ any real number}$$

include all antiderivatives of x^2? Theorem 1 (stated without proof) indicates that the answer is yes.

THEOREM 1 Antiderivatives
If the derivatives of two functions are equal on an open interval (a, b), then the functions differ by at most a constant. Symbolically, if F and G are differentiable functions on the interval (a, b) and $F'(x) = G'(x)$ for all x in (a, b), then $F(x) = G(x) + k$ for some constant k.

CONCEPTUAL INSIGHT

Suppose that $F(x)$ is an antiderivative of $f(x)$. If $G(x)$ is any other antiderivative of $f(x)$, then by Theorem 1, the graph of $G(x)$ is a vertical translation of the graph of $F(x)$ (see Section 2-2).

EXAMPLE 1 **A Family of Antiderivatives** Note that

$$\frac{d}{dx}\left(\frac{x^2}{2}\right) = x$$

(A) Find all antiderivatives of $f(x) = x$.

(B) Graph the antiderivative of $f(x) = x$ that passes through the point $(0, 0)$; through the point $(0, 1)$; through the point $(0, 2)$.

(C) How are the graphs of the three antiderivatives in part (B) related?

SOLUTION (A) By Theorem 1, any antiderivative of $f(x)$ has the form

$$F(x) = \frac{x^2}{2} + k$$

where k is a real number.

(B) Because $F(0) = (0^2/2) + k = k$, the functions

$$F_0(x) = \frac{x^2}{2}, \quad F_1(x) = \frac{x^2}{2} + 1, \quad \text{and} \quad F_2(x) = \frac{x^2}{2} + 2$$

pass through the points $(0, 0)$, $(0, 1)$, and $(0, 2)$, respectively (see Fig. 1).

(C) The graphs of the three antiderivatives are vertical translations of each other.

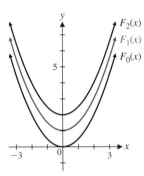

Figure 1

Matched Problem 1 Note that

$$\frac{d}{dx}(x^3) = 3x^2$$

(A) Find all antiderivatives of $f(x) = 3x^2$.

(B) Graph the antiderivative of $f(x) = 3x^2$ that passes through the point $(0, 0)$; through the point $(0, 1)$; through the point $(0, 2)$.

(C) How are the graphs of the three antiderivatives in part (B) related?

Indefinite Integrals: Formulas and Properties

Theorem 1 states that if the derivatives of two functions are equal, then the functions differ by at most a constant. We use the symbol

$$\int f(x)\, dx$$

called the **indefinite integral**, to represent the family of all antiderivatives of $f(x)$, and we write

$$\int f(x)\, dx = F(x) + C \qquad \text{if} \qquad F'(x) = f(x)$$

The symbol $\int$ is called an **integral sign**, and the function $f(x)$ is called the **integrand**. The symbol dx indicates that the antidifferentiation is performed with respect to the variable x. (We will have more to say about the symbols $\int$ and dx later in the chapter.) The arbitrary constant C is called the **constant of integration**. Referring to the preceding discussion, we can write

$$\int x^2\, dx = \frac{x^3}{3} + C \qquad \text{since} \qquad \frac{d}{dx}\left(\frac{x^3}{3} + C\right) = x^2$$

Of course, variables other than x can be used in indefinite integrals. For example,

$$\int t^2 \, dt = \frac{t^3}{3} + C \qquad \text{since} \qquad \frac{d}{dt}\left(\frac{t^3}{3} + C\right) = t^2$$

or

$$\int u^2 \, du = \frac{u^3}{3} + C \qquad \text{since} \qquad \frac{d}{du}\left(\frac{u^3}{3} + C\right) = u^2$$

The fact that indefinite integration and differentiation are reverse operations, except for the addition of the constant of integration, can be expressed symbolically as

$$\frac{d}{dx}\left[\int f(x) \, dx\right] = f(x) \qquad \text{\textit{The derivative of the indefinite integral of f(x) is f(x).}}$$

and

$$\int F'(x) \, dx = F(x) + C \qquad \text{\textit{The indefinite integral of the derivative of F(x) is F(x) + C.}}$$

We can develop formulas for the indefinite integrals of certain basic functions from the formulas for derivatives in Chapters 10 and 11.

FORMULAS **Indefinite Integrals of Basic Functions**

For C a constant,

1. $\displaystyle\int x^n \, dx = \frac{x^{n+1}}{n+1} + C, \qquad n \neq -1$

2. $\displaystyle\int e^x \, dx = e^x + C$

3. $\displaystyle\int \frac{1}{x} \, dx = \ln|x| + C, \qquad x \neq 0$

To justify each formula, show that the derivative of the right-hand side is the integrand of the left-hand side (see Problems 77–80 in Exercise 13-1). Note that formula 1 does not give the antiderivative of x^{-1} (because $x^{n+1}/(n+1)$ is undefined when $n = -1$), but formula 3 does.

EXPLORE & DISCUSS 1

Formulas 1, 2, and 3 do *not* provide a formula for the indefinite integral of the function $\ln x$. Show that if $x > 0$, then

$$\int \ln x \, dx = x \ln x - x + C$$

by differentiating the right-hand side.

We can obtain properties of the indefinite integral from derivative properties that were established in Chapter 10.

PROPERTIES **Indefinite Integrals**

For k a constant,

4. $\displaystyle\int k f(x) \, dx = k \int f(x) \, dx$

5. $\displaystyle\int [f(x) \pm g(x)] \, dx = \int f(x) \, dx \pm \int g(x) \, dx$

Property 4 states that

The indefinite integral of a constant times a function is the constant times the indefinite integral of the function.

Property 5 states that

The indefinite integral of the sum of two functions is the sum of the indefinite integrals, and the indefinite integral of the difference of two functions is the difference of the indefinite integrals.

To establish property 4, let F be a function such that $F'(x) = f(x)$. Then

$$k \int f(x)\, dx = k \int F'(x)\, dx = k[F(x) + C_1] = kF(x) + kC_1$$

and since $[kF(x)]' = kF'(x) = kf(x)$, we have

$$\int kf(x)\, dx = \int kF'(x)\, dx = kF(x) + C_2$$

But $kF(x) + kC_1$ and $kF(x) + C_2$ describe the same set of functions, because C_1 and C_2 are arbitrary real numbers. Property 4 is established. Property 5 can be established in a similar manner (see Problems 81 and 82 in Exercise 13-1).

⚠ **CAUTION** Property 4 states that **a constant factor can be moved across an integral sign. A variable factor cannot be moved across an integral sign:**

CONSTANT FACTOR	VARIABLE FACTOR
$\int 5x^{1/2}\, dx = 5 \int x^{1/2}\, dx$	$\int x x^{1/2}\, dx \neq x \int x^{1/2}\, dx$

Indefinite integral formulas and properties can be used together to find indefinite integrals for many frequently encountered functions. If $n = 0$, then formula 1 gives

$$\int dx = x + C$$

Therefore, by property 4,

$$\int k\, dx = k(x + C) = kx + kC$$

Because kC is a constant, we replace it with a single symbol that denotes an arbitrary constant (usually C), and write

$$\int k\, dx = kx + C$$

In words,

The indefinite integral of a constant function with value k is $kx + C$.

Similarly, using property 5 and then formulas 2 and 3, we obtain

$$\int \left(e^x + \frac{1}{x} \right) dx = \int e^x\, dx + \int \frac{1}{x}\, dx$$

$$= e^x + C_1 + \ln|x| + C_2$$

Because $C_1 + C_2$ is a constant, we replace it with the symbol C and write

$$\int \left(e^x + \frac{1}{x} \right) dx = e^x + \ln|x| + C$$

EXAMPLE 2 **Using Indefinite Integral Properties and Formulas**

(A) $\int 5\,dx = 5x + C$

(B) $\int 9e^x\,dx = 9\int e^x\,dx = 9e^x + C$

(C) $\int 5t^7\,dt = 5\int t^7\,dt = 5\dfrac{t^8}{8} + C = \dfrac{5}{8}t^8 + C$

(D) $\int (4x^3 + 2x - 1)\,dx = \int 4x^3\,dx + \int 2x\,dx - \int dx$

$\qquad\qquad\qquad\qquad = 4\int x^3\,dx + 2\int x\,dx - \int dx$

$\qquad\qquad\qquad\qquad = \dfrac{4x^4}{4} + \dfrac{2x^2}{2} - x + C$

$\qquad\qquad\qquad\qquad = x^4 + x^2 - x + C$

Property 4 can be extended to the sum and difference of an arbitrary number of functions.

(E) $\int \left(2e^x + \dfrac{3}{x}\right)dx = 2\int e^x\,dx + 3\int \dfrac{1}{x}\,dx$

$\qquad\qquad\qquad\qquad = 2e^x + 3\ln|x| + C$

To check any of the results in Example 2, we differentiate the final result to obtain the integrand in the original indefinite integral. When you evaluate an indefinite integral, do not forget to include the arbitrary constant C.

Matched Problem 2 Find each indefinite integral:

(A) $\int 2\,dx$ (B) $\int 16e^t\,dt$

(C) $\int 3x^4\,dx$ (D) $\int (2x^5 - 3x^2 + 1)\,dx$

(E) $\int \left(\dfrac{5}{x} - 4e^x\right)dx$

EXAMPLE 3 **Using Indefinite Integral Properties and Formulas**

(A) $\int \dfrac{4}{x^3}\,dx = \int 4x^{-3}\,dx = \dfrac{4x^{-3+1}}{-3+1} + C = -2x^{-2} + C$

(B) $\int 5\sqrt[3]{u^2}\,du = 5\int u^{2/3}\,du = 5\dfrac{u^{(2/3)+1}}{\frac{2}{3}+1} + C$

$\qquad\qquad\qquad\qquad = 5\dfrac{u^{5/3}}{\frac{5}{3}} + C = 3u^{5/3} + C$

(C) $\int \dfrac{x^3 - 3}{x^2}\,dx = \int \left(\dfrac{x^3}{x^2} - \dfrac{3}{x^2}\right)dx$

$\qquad\qquad\qquad = \int (x - 3x^{-2})\,dx$

$\qquad\qquad\qquad = \int x\,dx - 3\int x^{-2}\,dx$

$\qquad\qquad\qquad = \dfrac{x^{1+1}}{1+1} - 3\dfrac{x^{-2+1}}{-2+1} + C$

$\qquad\qquad\qquad = \tfrac{1}{2}x^2 + 3x^{-1} + C$

(D) $\displaystyle\int\left(\frac{2}{\sqrt[3]{x}}-6\sqrt{x}\right)dx=\int(2x^{-1/3}-6x^{1/2})\,dx$

$$=2\int x^{-1/3}\,dx-6\int x^{1/2}\,dx$$

$$=2\frac{x^{(-1/3)+1}}{-\frac{1}{3}+1}-6\frac{x^{(1/2)+1}}{\frac{1}{2}+1}+C$$

$$=2\frac{x^{2/3}}{\frac{2}{3}}-6\frac{x^{3/2}}{\frac{3}{2}}+C$$

$$=3x^{2/3}-4x^{3/2}+C$$

(E) $\displaystyle\int x(x^2+2)\,dx=\int(x^3+2x)\,dx=\frac{x^4}{4}+x^2+C$

Matched Problem 3   Find each indefinite integral:

(A) $\displaystyle\int\left(2x^{2/3}-\frac{3}{x^4}\right)dx$

(B) $\displaystyle\int 4\sqrt[5]{w^3}\,dw$

(C) $\displaystyle\int\frac{x^4-8x^3}{x^2}\,dx$

(D) $\displaystyle\int\left(8\sqrt[3]{x}-\frac{6}{\sqrt{x}}\right)dx$

(E) $\displaystyle\int(x^2-2)(x+3)\,dx$

⚠ **CAUTION**

1. Note from Example 3(E) that

$$\int x(x^2+2)\,dx\neq\frac{x^2}{2}\left(\frac{x^3}{3}+2x\right)+C$$

In general, the **indefinite integral of a product is not the product of the indefinite integrals.** (This is expected because the derivative of a product is not the product of the derivatives.)

2.
$$\int e^x\,dx\neq\frac{e^{x+1}}{x+1}+C$$

The power rule applies only to power functions of the form x^n, where the exponent n is a real constant not equal to -1 and the base x is the variable. The function e^x is an exponential function with variable exponent x and constant base e. The correct form is

$$\int e^x\,dx=e^x+C$$

3. Not all elementary functions have elementary antiderivatives. It is impossible, for example, to give a formula for the antiderivative of $f(x)=e^{x^2}$ in terms of elementary functions. Nevertheless, finding such a formula, when it exists, can markedly simplify the solution of certain problems.

Applications

Let's consider some applications of the indefinite integral.

EXAMPLE 4   **Curves** Find the equation of the curve that passes through $(2, 5)$ if the slope of the curve is given by $dy/dx = 2x$ at any point x.

SOLUTION   We want to find a function $y = f(x)$ such that

$$\frac{dy}{dx} = 2x \qquad (1)$$

and

$$y = 5 \qquad \text{when} \qquad x = 2 \qquad (2)$$

If $dy/dx = 2x$, then

$$y = \int 2x\, dx \qquad (3)$$

$$= x^2 + C$$

Since $y = 5$ when $x = 2$, we determine the *particular value of C* so that

$$5 = 2^2 + C$$

So $C = 1$, and

$$y = x^2 + 1$$

is the *particular antiderivative* out of all those possible from equation (3) that satisfies both equations (1) and (2) (see Fig. 2).

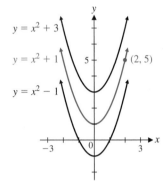

$y = x^2 + 3$
$y = x^2 + 1$
$y = x^2 - 1$

Figure 2 $y = x^2 + C$

Matched Problem 4   Find the equation of the curve that passes through $(2, 6)$ if the slope of the curve is given by $dy/dx = 3x^2$ at any point x.

In certain situations, it is easier to determine the rate at which something happens than to determine how much of it has happened in a given length of time (for example, population growth rates, business growth rates, the rate of healing of a wound, rates of learning or forgetting). If a rate function (derivative) is given and we know the value of the dependent variable for a given value of the independent variable, then we can often find the original function by integration.

EXAMPLE 5   **Cost Function** If the marginal cost of producing x units of a commodity is given by

$$C'(x) = 0.3x^2 + 2x$$

and the fixed cost is \$2,000, find the cost function $C(x)$ and the cost of producing 20 units.

SOLUTION   Recall that marginal cost is the derivative of the cost function and that fixed cost is cost at a zero production level. So we want to find $C(x)$, given

$$C'(x) = 0.3x^2 + 2x \qquad C(0) = 2,000$$

We find the indefinite integral of $0.3x^2 + 2x$ and determine the arbitrary integration constant using $C(0) = 2,000$:

$$C'(x) = 0.3x^2 + 2x$$

$$C(x) = \int (0.3x^2 + 2x)\, dx$$

$$= 0.1x^3 + x^2 + K \qquad \text{Since } C \text{ represents the cost, we use } K \text{ for the constant of integration.}$$

But

$$C(0) = (0.1)0^3 + 0^2 + K = 2,000$$

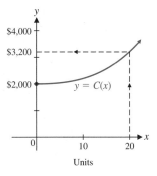

Figure 3

So $K = 2,000$, and the cost function is

$$C(x) = 0.1x^3 + x^2 + 2,000$$

We now find $C(20)$, the cost of producing 20 units:

$$C(20) = (0.1)20^3 + 20^2 + 2,000$$

$$= \$3,200$$

See Figure 3 for a geometric representation.

Matched Problem 5   Find the revenue function $R(x)$ when the marginal revenue is

$$R'(x) = 400 - 0.4x$$

and no revenue results at a zero production level. What is the revenue at a production level of 1,000 units?

EXAMPLE 6   **Advertising** A satellite radio station is launching an aggressive advertising campaign in order to increase the number of daily listeners. The station currently has 27,000 daily listeners, and management expects the number of daily listeners, $S(t)$, to grow at the rate of

$$S'(t) = 60t^{1/2}$$

listeners per day, where t is the number of days since the campaign began. How long should the campaign last if the station wants the number of daily listeners to grow to 41,000?

SOLUTION   We must solve the equation $S(t) = 41,000$ for t, given that

$$S'(t) = 60t^{1/2} \qquad \text{and} \qquad S(0) = 27,000$$

First, we use integration to find $S(t)$:

$$\int S(t) = 60t^{1/2}\, dt$$

$$= 60\frac{t^{3/2}}{\frac{3}{2}} + C$$

$$= 40t^{3/2} + C$$

Since

$$S(0) = 40(0)^{3/2} + C = 27,000$$

we have $C = 27,000$ and

$$S(t) = 40t^{3/2} + 27,000$$

Now we solve the equation $S(t) = 41,000$ for t:

$$40t^{3/2} + 27,000 = 41,000$$

$$40t^{3/2} = 14,000$$

$$t^{3/2} = 350$$

$$t = 350^{2/3} \qquad \text{Use a calculator.}$$

$$= 49.664\,419\ldots$$

The advertising campaign should last approximately 50 days.

Matched Problem 6 There are 64,000 subscribers to an online fashion magazine. Due to competition from a new magazine, the number $C(t)$ of subscribers is expected to decrease at the rate of

$$C'(t) = -600t^{1/3}$$

subscribers per month, where t is the time in months since the new magazine began publication. How long will it take until the number of subscribers to the online fashion magazine drops to 46,000?

Exercises 13-1

A

In Problems 1–16, find each indefinite integral. Check by differentiating.

1. $\int 7 \, dx$

2. $\int 10 \, dx$

3. $\int 8x \, dx$

4. $\int 14x \, dx$

5. $\int 9x^2 \, dx$

6. $\int 15x^2 \, dx$

7. $\int x^5 \, dx$

8. $\int x^8 \, dx$

9. $\int x^{-3} \, dx$

10. $\int x^{-4} \, dx$

11. $\int 10x^{3/2} \, dx$

12. $\int 8x^{1/3} \, dx$

13. $\int \frac{3}{z} \, dz$

14. $\int \frac{7}{z} \, dz$

15. $\int 16e^u \, du$

16. $\int 5e^u \, du$

In Problems 17–24, find all the antiderivatives for each derivative.

17. $\frac{dy}{dx} = 200x^4$

18. $\frac{dx}{dt} = 42t^5$

19. $\frac{dP}{dx} = 24 - 6x$

20. $\frac{dy}{dx} = 3x^2 - 4x^3$

21. $\frac{dy}{dx} = e^x + 3$

22. $\frac{dy}{dx} = x - e^x$

23. $\frac{dx}{dt} = 5t^{-1} + 1$

24. $\frac{du}{dv} = \frac{4}{v} + \frac{v}{4}$

B

In Problems 25–30, discuss the validity of each statement. If the statement is always true, explain why. If not, give a counterexample.

25. The constant function $f(x) = \pi$ is an antiderivative of the constant function $k(x) = 0$.

26. The constant function $k(x) = 0$ is an antiderivative of the constant function $f(x) = \pi$.

27. If n is an integer, then $x^{n+1}/(n + 1)$ is an antiderivative of x^n.

28. The constant function $k(x) = 0$ is an antiderivative of itself.

29. The function $h(x) = 5e^x$ is an antiderivative of itself.

30. The constant function $g(x) = 5e^\pi$ is an antiderivative of itself.

In Problems 31–34, could the three graphs in each figure be antiderivatives of the same function? Explain.

31.

32.

33.

34.

In Problems 35–50, find each indefinite integral. (Check by differentiation.)

35. $\int 5x(1 - x) \, dx$

36. $\int x^2(1 + x^3) \, dx$

37. $\int \frac{du}{\sqrt{u}}$

38. $\int \frac{dt}{\sqrt[3]{t}}$

39. $\int \frac{dx}{4x^3}$

40. $\int \frac{6 \, dm}{m^2}$

41. $\int \dfrac{4+u}{u}\,du$

42. $\int \dfrac{1-y^2}{3y}\,dy$

43. $\int (5e^z + 4)\,dz$

44. $\int \dfrac{e^t - t}{2}\,dt$

45. $\int \left(3x^2 - \dfrac{2}{x^2} \right)dx$

46. $\int \left(4x^3 + \dfrac{2}{x^3} \right)dx$

47. $\int \left(3\sqrt{x} + \dfrac{2}{\sqrt{x}} \right)dx$

48. $\int \left(\dfrac{2}{\sqrt[3]{x}} - \sqrt[3]{x^2} \right)dx$

49. $\int \dfrac{e^x - 3x}{4}\,dx$

50. $\int \dfrac{e^x - 3x^2}{2}\,dx$

In Problems 51–58, find the particular antiderivative of each derivative that satisfies the given condition.

51. $C'(x) = 6x^2 - 4x;\ C(0) = 3{,}000$

52. $R'(x) = 600 - 0.6x;\ R(0) = 0$

53. $\dfrac{dx}{dt} = \dfrac{20}{\sqrt{t}};\ x(1) = 40$

54. $\dfrac{dR}{dt} = \dfrac{100}{t^2};\ R(1) = 400$

55. $\dfrac{dy}{dx} = 2x^{-2} + 3x^{-1} - 1;\ y(1) = 0$

56. $\dfrac{dy}{dx} = 3x^{-1} + x^{-2};\ y(1) = 1$

57. $\dfrac{dx}{dt} = 4e^t - 2;\ x(0) = 1$

58. $\dfrac{dy}{dt} = 5e^t - 4;\ y(0) = -1$

59. Find the equation of the curve that passes through $(2, 3)$ if its slope is given by
$$\frac{dy}{dx} = 4x - 3$$
for each x.

60. Find the equation of the curve that passes through $(1, 3)$ if its slope is given by
$$\frac{dy}{dx} = 12x^2 - 12x$$
for each x.

[C]

In Problems 61–66, find each indefinite integral.

61. $\int \dfrac{2x^4 - x}{x^3}\,dx$

62. $\int \dfrac{x^{-1} - x^4}{x^2}\,dx$

63. $\int \dfrac{x^5 - 2x}{x^4}\,dx$

64. $\int \dfrac{1 - 3x^4}{x^2}\,dx$

65. $\int \dfrac{x^2 e^x - 2x}{x^2}\,dx$

66. $\int \dfrac{1 - xe^x}{x}\,dx$

In Problems 67–72, find the particular antiderivative of each derivative that satisfies the given condition.

67. $\dfrac{dM}{dt} = \dfrac{t^2 - 1}{t^2};\ M(4) = 5$

68. $\dfrac{dR}{dx} = \dfrac{1 - x^4}{x^3};\ R(1) = 4$

69. $\dfrac{dy}{dx} = \dfrac{5x + 2}{\sqrt[3]{x}};\ y(1) = 0$

70. $\dfrac{dx}{dt} = \dfrac{\sqrt{t^3} - t}{\sqrt{t^3}};\ x(9) = 4$

71. $p'(x) = -\dfrac{10}{x^2};\ p(1) = 20$

72. $p'(x) = \dfrac{10}{x^3};\ p(1) = 15$

In Problems 73–76, find the derivative or indefinite integral as indicated.

73. $\dfrac{d}{dx}\left(\int x^3\,dx \right)$

74. $\dfrac{d}{dt}\left(\int \dfrac{\ln t}{t}\,dt \right)$

75. $\int \dfrac{d}{dx}(x^4 + 3x^2 + 1)\,dx$

76. $\int \dfrac{d}{du}(e^{u^2})\,du$

77. Use differentiation to justify the formula
$$\int x^n\,dx = \frac{x^{n+1}}{n+1} + C$$
provided that $n \neq -1$.

78. Use differentiation to justify the formula
$$\int e^x\,dx = e^x + C$$

79. Assuming that $x > 0$, use differentiation to justify the formula
$$\int \frac{1}{x}\,dx = \ln|x| + C$$

80. Assuming that $x < 0$, use differentiation to justify the formula
$$\int \frac{1}{x}\,dx = \ln|x| + C$$

81. Show that the indefinite integral of the sum of two functions is the sum of the indefinite integrals.

[*Hint:* Assume that $\int f(x)\,dx = F(x) + C_1$ and $\int g(x)\,dx = G(x) + C_2$. Using differentiation, show that $F(x) + C_1 + G(x) + C_2$ is the indefinite integral of the function $s(x) = f(x) + g(x)$.]

82. Show that the indefinite integral of the difference of two functions is the difference of the indefinite integrals.

Applications

83. Cost function. The marginal average cost of producing x sports watches is given by

$$\overline{C}'(x) = -\frac{1,000}{x^2} \qquad \overline{C}(100) = 25$$

where $\overline{C}(x)$ is the average cost in dollars. Find the average cost function and the cost function. What are the fixed costs?

84. Renewable energy. In 2007, U.S. consumption of renewable energy was 6.8 quadrillion Btu (or 6.8×10^{15} Btu). Since the 1960s, consumption has been growing at a rate (in quadrillion Btu's per year) given by

$$f'(t) = 0.004t + 0.062$$

where t is years after 1960. Find $f(t)$ and estimate U.S. consumption of renewable energy in 2020.

85. Production costs. The graph of the marginal cost function from the production of x thousand bottles of sunscreen per month [where cost $C(x)$ is in thousands of dollars per month] is given in the figure.

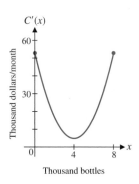

Figure for 85

(A) Using the graph shown, describe the shape of the graph of the cost function $C(x)$ as x increases from 0 to 8,000 bottles per month.

(B) Given the equation of the marginal cost function,

$$C'(x) = 3x^2 - 24x + 53$$

find the cost function if monthly fixed costs at 0 output are $30,000. What is the cost of manufacturing 4,000 bottles per month? 8,000 bottles per month?

(C) Graph the cost function for $0 \le x \le 8$. [Check the shape of the graph relative to the analysis in part (A).]

(D) Why do you think that the graph of the cost function is steeper at both ends than in the middle?

86. Revenue. The graph of the marginal revenue function from the sale of x sports watches is given in the figure.

(A) Using the graph shown, describe the shape of the graph of the revenue function $R(x)$ as x increases from 0 to 1,000.

(B) Find the equation of the marginal revenue function (the linear function shown in the figure).

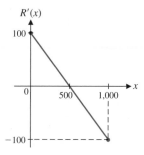

Figure for 86

(C) Find the equation of the revenue function that satisfies $R(0) = 0$. Graph the revenue function over the interval $[0, 1,000]$. [Check the shape of the graph relative to the analysis in part (A).]

(D) Find the price–demand equation and determine the price when the demand is 700 units.

87. Sales analysis. Monthly sales of an SUV model are expected to decline at the rate of

$$S'(t) = -24t^{1/3}$$

SUVs per month, where t is time in months and $S(t)$ is the number of SUVs sold each month. The company plans to stop manufacturing this model when monthly sales reach 300 SUVs. If monthly sales now ($t = 0$) are 1,200 SUVs, find $S(t)$. How long will the company continue to manufacture this model?

88. Sales analysis. The rate of change of the monthly sales of a newly released football game is given by

$$S'(t) = 500t^{1/4} \qquad S(0) = 0$$

where t is the number of months since the game was released and $S(t)$ is the number of games sold each month. Find $S(t)$. When will monthly sales reach 20,000 games?

89. Sales analysis. Repeat Problem 87 if $S'(t) = -24t^{1/3} - 70$ and all other information remains the same. Use a graphing calculator to approximate the solution of the equation $S(t) = 800$ to two decimal places.

90. Sales analysis. Repeat Problem 88 if $S'(t) = 500t^{1/4} + 300$ and all other information remains the same. Use a graphing calculator to approximate the solution of the equation $S(t) = 20,000$ to two decimal places.

91. Labor costs. A defense contractor is starting production on a new missile control system. On the basis of data collected during the assembly of the first 16 control systems, the production manager obtained the following function describing the rate of labor use:

$$g(x) = 2,400x^{-1/2}$$

$g(x)$ is the number of labor-hours required to assemble the xth unit of the control system. For example, after assembly of 16 units, the rate of assembly is 600 labor-hours per unit, and after assembly of 25 units, the rate of assembly is 480 labor-hours per unit. The more units assembled, the more efficient the process. If 19,200 labor-hours are required to assemble of the first 16 units, how many labor-hours $L(x)$ will be required to assemble the first x units? The first 25 units?

92. Labor costs. If the rate of labor use in Problem 91 is

$$g(x) = 2,000x^{-1/3}$$

and if the first 8 control units require 12,000 labor-hours, how many labor-hours, $L(x)$, will be required for the first x control units? The first 27 control units?

93. Weight–height. For an average person, the rate of change of weight W (in pounds) with respect to height h (in inches) is given approximately by

$$\frac{dW}{dh} = 0.0015h^2$$

Find $W(h)$ if $W(60) = 108$ pounds. Find the weight of an average person who is 5 feet, 10 inches, tall.

94. Wound healing. The area A of a healing wound changes at a rate given approximately by

$$\frac{dA}{dt} = -4t^{-3} \qquad 1 \le t \le 10$$

where t is time in days and $A(1) = 2$ square centimeters. What will the area of the wound be in 10 days?

95. Urban growth. The rate of growth of the population $N(t)$ of a new city t years after its incorporation is estimated to be

$$\frac{dN}{dt} = 400 + 600\sqrt{t} \qquad 0 \le t \le 9$$

If the population was 5,000 at the time of incorporation, find the population 9 years later.

96. Learning. A college language class was chosen for an experiment in learning. Using a list of 50 words, the experiment involved measuring the rate of vocabulary memorization at different times during a continuous 5-hour study session. It was found that the average rate of learning for the entire class was inversely proportional to the time spent studying and was given approximately by

$$V'(t) = \frac{15}{t} \qquad 1 \le t \le 5$$

If the average number of words memorized after 1 hour of study was 15 words, what was the average number of words memorized after t hours of study for $1 \le t \le 5$? After 4 hours of study? Round answer to the nearest whole number.

Answers to Matched Problems

1. (A) $x^3 + C$

    (B)

    (C) The graphs are vertical translations of each other.

2. (A) $2x + C$

    (B) $16e^t + C$

    (C) $\frac{3}{5}x^5 + C$

    (D) $\frac{1}{3}x^6 - x^3 + x + C$

    (E) $5\ln|x| - 4e^x + C$

3. (A) $\frac{6}{5}x^{5/3} + x^{-3} + C$

    (B) $\frac{5}{2}w^{8/5} + C$

    (C) $\frac{1}{3}x^3 - 4x^2 + C$

    (D) $6x^{4/3} - 12x^{1/2} + C$

    (E) $\frac{1}{4}x^4 + x^3 - x^2 - 6x + C$

4. $y = x^3 - 2$

5. $R(x) = 400x - 0.2x^2$; $R(1,000) = \$200,000$

6. $t = (40)^{3/4} \approx 16$ mo

13-2   Integration by Substitution

- Reversing the Chain Rule
- Integration by Substitution
- Additional Substitution Techniques
- Application

Many of the indefinite integral formulas introduced in the preceding section are based on corresponding derivative formulas studied earlier. We now consider indefinite integral formulas and procedures based on the chain rule for differentiation.

Reversing the Chain Rule

Recall the chain rule:

$$\frac{d}{dx} f[g(x)] = f'[g(x)]g'(x)$$

The expression on the right is formed from the expression on the left by taking the derivative of the outside function f and multiplying it by the derivative of the inside function g. If we recognize an integrand as a chain-rule form $f'[g(x)]g'(x)$, we can easily find an antiderivative and its indefinite integral:

$$\int f'[g(x)]g'(x)\,dx = f[g(x)] + C \tag{1}$$

We are interested in finding the indefinite integral

$$\int 3x^2 e^{x^3-1}\,dx \tag{2}$$

The integrand appears to be the chain-rule form $e^{g(x)}g'(x)$, which is the derivative of $e^{g(x)}$. Since

$$\frac{d}{dx}e^{x^3-1} = 3x^2 e^{x^3-1}$$

it follows that

$$\int 3x^2 e^{x^3-1}\,dx = e^{x^3-1} + C \tag{3}$$

How does the following indefinite integral differ from integral (2)?

$$\int x^2 e^{x^3-1}\,dx \tag{4}$$

It is missing the constant factor 3. That is, $x^2 e^{x^3-1}$ is within a constant factor of being the derivative of e^{x^3-1}. But because a constant factor can be moved across the integral sign, this causes us little trouble in finding the indefinite integral of $x^2 e^{x^3-1}$. We introduce the constant factor 3 and at the same time multiply by $\frac{1}{3}$ and move the $\frac{1}{3}$ factor outside the integral sign. This is equivalent to multiplying the integrand in integral (4) by 1:

$$\int x^2 e^{x^3-1}\,dx = \int \frac{3}{3}x^2 e^{x^3-1}\,dx \tag{5}$$

$$= \frac{1}{3}\int 3x^2 e^{x^3-1}\,dx = \frac{1}{3}e^{x^3-1} + C$$

The derivative of the rightmost side of equation (5) is the integrand of the indefinite integral (4). Check this.

How does the following indefinite integral differ from integral (2)?

$$\int 3x e^{x^3-1}\,dx \tag{6}$$

It is missing a variable factor x. This is more serious. As tempting as it might be, we *cannot* adjust integral (6) by introducing the variable factor x and moving $1/x$ outside the integral sign, as we did with the constant 3 in equation (5).

⚠️ **CAUTION** A constant factor can be moved across an integral sign, but a variable factor cannot.

There is nothing wrong with educated guessing when you are looking for an antiderivative of a given function. You have only to check the result by differentiation. If you are right, you go on your way; if you are wrong, you simply try another approach.

In Section 11-4, we saw that the chain rule extends the derivative formulas for x^n, e^x, and $\ln x$ to derivative formulas for $[f(x)]^n$, $e^{f(x)}$, and $\ln [f(x)]$. The chain rule can also be used to extend the indefinite integral formulas discussed in Section 13-1. Some general formulas are summarized in the following box:

FORMULAS   General Indefinite Integral Formulas

1. $\int [f(x)]^n f'(x)\, dx = \dfrac{[f(x)]^{n+1}}{n+1} + C, n \neq -1$

2. $\int e^{f(x)} f'(x)\, dx = e^{f(x)} + C$

3. $\int \dfrac{1}{f(x)} f'(x)\, dx = \ln|f(x)| + C$

We can verify each formula by using the chain rule to show that the derivative of the function on the right is the integrand on the left. For example,

$$\frac{d}{dx}[e^{f(x)} + C] = e^{f(x)} f'(x)$$

verifies formula 2.

EXAMPLE 1   **Reversing the Chain Rule**

(A) $\int (3x + 4)^{10}(3)\, dx = \dfrac{(3x + 4)^{11}}{11} + C$ Formula 1 with f(x) = 3x + 4 and f'(x) = 3

Check:

$$\frac{d}{dx}\frac{(3x + 4)^{11}}{11} = 11\frac{(3x + 4)^{10}}{11}\frac{d}{dx}(3x + 4) = (3x + 4)^{10}(3)$$

(B) $\int e^{x^2}(2x)\, dx = e^{x^2} + C$ Formula 2 with f(x) = x^2 and f'(x) = 2x

Check:

$$\frac{d}{dx}e^{x^2} = e^{x^2}\frac{d}{dx}x^2 = e^{x^2}(2x)$$

(C) $\int \dfrac{1}{1 + x^3}3x^2\, dx = \ln|1 + x^3| + C$ Formula 3 with f(x) = 1 + x^3 and f'(x) = $3x^2$

Check:

$$\frac{d}{dx}\ln|1 + x^3| = \frac{1}{1 + x^3}\frac{d}{dx}(1 + x^3) = \frac{1}{1 + x^3}3x^2$$

Matched Problem 1   Find each indefinite integral.

(A) $\int (2x^3 - 3)^{20}(6x^2)\, dx$ (B) $\int e^{5x}(5)\, dx$

(C) $\int \dfrac{1}{4 + x^2}2x\, dx$

Integration by Substitution

The key step in using formulas 1, 2, and 3 is recognizing the form of the integrand. Some people find it difficult to identify $f(x)$ and $f'(x)$ in these formulas and prefer to use a *substitution* to simplify the integrand. The *method of substitution*, which we now discuss, becomes increasingly useful as one progresses in studies of integration.

We start by introducing the idea of the *differential*. We represented the derivative by the symbol dy/dx taken as a whole. We now define dy and dx as two separate quantities with the property that their ratio is still equal to $f'(x)$:

DEFINITION Differentials

If $y = f(x)$ defines a differentiable function, then

1. The **differential dx** of the independent variable x is an arbitrary real number.

2. The **differential dy** of the dependent variable y is defined as the product of $f'(x)$ and dx:

$$dy = f'(x)\,dx$$

Differentials involve mathematical subtleties that are treated carefully in advanced mathematics courses. Here, we are interested in them mainly as a bookkeeping device to aid in the process of finding indefinite integrals. We can always check an indefinite integral by differentiating.

EXAMPLE 2   **Differentials**

(A) If $y = f(x) = x^2$, then

$$dy \boxed{= f'(x)\,dx} = 2x\,dx$$

(B) If $u = g(x) = e^{3x}$, then

$$du \boxed{= g'(x)\,dx} = 3e^{3x}\,dx$$

(C) If $w = h(t) = \ln(4 + 5t)$, then

$$dw \boxed{= h'(t)\,dt} = \frac{5}{4 + 5t}dt$$

Matched Problem 2   (A) Find dy for $y = f(x) = x^3$.

(B) Find du for $u = h(x) = \ln(2 + x^2)$.

(C) Find dv for $v = g(t) = e^{-5t}$.

The **method of substitution** is developed through Examples 3–6.

EXAMPLE 3   **Using Substitution** Find $\int (x^2 + 2x + 5)^5(2x + 2)\,dx$.

SOLUTION   If

$$u = x^2 + 2x + 5$$

then the differential of u is

$$du = (2x + 2)\,dx$$

Notice that du is one of the factors in the integrand. Substitute u for $x^2 + 2x + 5$ and du for $(2x + 2)\,dx$ to obtain

$$\int (x^2 + 2x + 5)^5(2x + 2)\,dx = \int u^5\,du$$

$$= \frac{u^6}{6} + C$$

$$= \frac{1}{6}(x^2 + 2x + 5)^6 + C \quad \text{Since } u = x^2 + 2x + 5$$

Check:

$$\frac{d}{dx}\frac{1}{6}(x^2 + 2x + 5)^6 = \frac{1}{6}(6)(x^2 + 2x + 5)^5\frac{d}{dx}(x^2 + 2x + 5)$$

$$= (x^2 + 2x + 5)^5(2x + 2)$$

Matched Problem 3   Find $\int(x^2 - 3x + 7)^4(2x - 3)\,dx$ by substitution.

The substitution method is also called the **change-of-variable method** since u replaces the variable x in the process. Substituting $u = f(x)$ and $du = f'(x)\,dx$ in formulas 1, 2, and 3 produces the general indefinite integral formulas 4, 5, and 6:

FORMULAS   General Indefinite Integral Formulas

4. $\displaystyle\int u^n\,du = \frac{u^{n+1}}{n + 1} + C, \qquad n \neq -1$

5. $\displaystyle\int e^u\,du = e^u + C$

6. $\displaystyle\int \frac{1}{u}\,du = \ln|u| + C$

These formulas are valid if u is an independent variable, or if u is a function of another variable and du is the differential of u with respect to that variable.

The substitution method for evaluating certain indefinite integrals is outlined as follows:

PROCEDURE   Integration by Substitution

Step 1   Select a substitution that appears to simplify the integrand. In particular, try to select u so that du is a factor in the integrand.

Step 2   Express the integrand entirely in terms of u and du, completely eliminating the original variable and its differential.

Step 3   Evaluate the new integral if possible.

Step 4   Express the antiderivative found in step 3 in terms of the original variable.

EXAMPLE 4   **Using Substitution**   Use a substitution to find each indefinite integral.

(A) $\displaystyle\int(3x + 4)^6(3)\,dx$

(B) $\displaystyle\int e^{t^2}(2t)\,dt$

(A) In Figure 1A (or a copy), draw tangent line segments for a solution curve of differential equation (1) that passes through $(-3, -1)$, $(0, -2)$, and $(2, -3)$.

(B) In Figure 1B (or a copy), sketch an approximate graph of the solution curve that passes through the three points given in part (A). Repeat the tangent line segments first.

(C) What type of function, of all the elementary functions discussed in the first two chapters, appears to be a solution of differential equation (1)?

In Explore & Discuss 1, if you guessed that all solutions of equation (1) are exponential functions, you are to be congratulated. We now show that

$$y = Ce^{0.2x} \qquad (2)$$

is a solution of equation (1) for any real number C. We substitute $y = Ce^{0.2x}$ into equation (1) to see if the left side is equal to the right side for all real x:

$$\frac{dy}{dx} = 0.2y$$

Left side: $\quad \dfrac{dy}{dx} = \dfrac{d}{dx}(Ce^{0.2x}) = 0.2Ce^{0.2x}$

Right side: $\quad 0.2y = 0.2Ce^{0.2x}$

So equation (2) is a solution of equation (1) for C any real number. Which values of C will produce solution curves that pass through $(0, 2)$ and $(0, -2)$, respectively? Substituting the coordinates of each point into equation (2) and solving for C, we obtain

$$y = 2e^{0.2x} \qquad \text{and} \qquad y = -2e^{0.2x} \qquad (3)$$

The graphs of equations (3) are shown in Figure 3, and they confirm the results shown in Figure 1B.

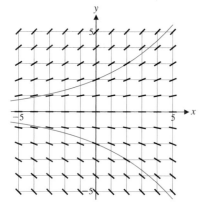

Figure 3

CONCEPTUAL INSIGHT

For a complicated first-order differential equation, say,

$$\frac{dy}{dx} = \frac{3 + \sqrt{xy}}{x^2 - 5y^4}$$

it may be impossible to find a formula analogous to (2) for its solutions. Nevertheless, it is routine to evaluate the right-hand side at each point in a grid. The resulting slope field provides a graphical representation of the solutions of the differential equation.

Drawing slope fields by hand is not a task for human beings: A 20-by-20 grid would require drawing 400 tangent line segments! Repetitive tasks of this type are what computers are for. A few problems in Exercise 13-3 involve interpreting slope fields, not drawing them.

Continuous Compound Interest Revisited

Let P be the initial amount of money deposited in an account, and let A be the amount in the account at any time t. Instead of assuming that the money in the account earns a particular rate of interest, suppose we say that the rate of growth of the amount of money in the account at any time t is proportional to the amount present at that time. Since dA/dt is the rate of growth of A with respect to t, we have

$$\frac{dA}{dt} = rA \qquad A(0) = P \qquad A, P > 0 \qquad (4)$$

where r is an appropriate constant. We would like to find a function $A = A(t)$ that satisfies these conditions. Multiplying both sides of equation (4) by $1/A$, we obtain

$$\frac{1}{A}\frac{dA}{dt} = r$$

Now we integrate each side with respect to t:

$$\int \frac{1}{A}\frac{dA}{dt}\,dt = \int r\,dt \qquad \frac{dA}{dt}dt = A'(t)dt = dA$$

$$\int \frac{1}{A}\,dA = \int r\,dt$$

$$\ln|A| = rt + C \qquad |A| = A, \text{ since } A > 0$$

$$\ln A = rt + C$$

We convert this last equation into the equivalent exponential form

$$A = e^{rt+C} \qquad \textit{Definition of logarithmic function:}$$
$$\qquad\qquad\qquad y = \ln x \text{ if and only if } x = e^y$$

$$= e^C e^{rt} \qquad \textit{Property of exponents: } b^m b^n = b^{m+n}$$

Since $A(0) = P$, we evaluate $A(t) = e^C e^{rt}$ at $t = 0$ and set the result equal to P:

$$A(0) = e^C e^0 = e^C = P$$

Hence, $e^C = P$, and we can rewrite $A = e^C e^{rt}$ in the form

$$A = Pe^{rt}$$

This is the same continuous compound interest formula obtained in Section 12-1, where the principal P is invested at an annual nominal rate r compounded continuously for t years.

Exponential Growth Law

In general, if the rate of change of a quantity Q with respect to time is proportional to the amount of Q present and $Q(0) = Q_0$, then, proceeding in exactly the same way as we just did, we obtain the following theorem:

THEOREM 1   Exponential Growth Law

If $\dfrac{dQ}{dt} = rQ$ and $Q(0) = Q_0$, then $Q = Q_0 e^{rt}$,

where

Q_0 = amount of Q at $t = 0$
r = relative growth rate (expressed as a decimal)
t = time
Q = quantity at time t

The constant r in the exponential growth law is called the **relative growth rate**. If the relative growth rate is $r = 0.02$, then the quantity Q is growing at a rate $dQ/dt = 0.02Q$ (that is, 2% of the quantity Q per unit of time t). Note the distinction between the relative growth rate r and the rate of growth dQ/dt of the quantity Q. If $r < 0$, then $dQ/dt < 0$ and Q is decreasing. This type of growth is called **exponential decay**.

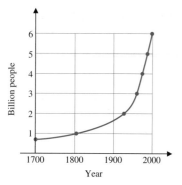

Figure 4 World population growth

Once we know that the rate of growth is proportional to the amount present, we recognize exponential growth and can use Theorem 1 without solving the differential equation each time. The exponential growth law applies not only to money invested at interest compounded continuously, but also to many other types of problems— population growth, radioactive decay, the depletion of a natural resource, and so on.

Population Growth, Radioactive Decay, and Learning

The world population passed 1 billion in 1804, 2 billion in 1927, 3 billion in 1960, 4 billion in 1974, 5 billion in 1987, and 6 billion in 1999, as illustrated in Figure 4. **Population growth** over certain periods often can be approximated by the exponential growth law of Theorem 1.

EXAMPLE 1 **Population Growth** India had a population of about 1.2 billion in 2010 ($t = 0$). Let P represent the population (in billions) t years after 2010, and assume a growth rate of 1.5% compounded continuously.

(A) Find an equation that represents India's population growth after 2010, assuming that the 1.5% growth rate continues.

(B) What is the estimated population (to the nearest tenth of a billion) of India in the year 2030?

(C) Graph the equation found in part (A) from 2000 to 2030.

SOLUTION (A) The exponential growth law applies, and we have

$$\frac{dP}{dt} = 0.015P \qquad P(0) = 1.2$$

Therefore,

$$P = 1.2e^{0.015t} \tag{5}$$

(B) Using equation (5), we can estimate the population in India in 2030 ($t = 20$):

$$P = 1.2e^{0.015(20)} = 1.6 \text{ billion people}$$

(C) The graph is shown in Figure 5.

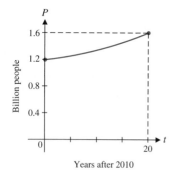

Figure 5 Population of India

Matched Problem 1 Assuming the same continuous compound growth rate as in Example 1, what will India's population be (to the nearest tenth of a billion) in the year 2020?

EXAMPLE 2 **Population Growth** If the exponential growth law applies to Canada's population growth, at what continuous compound growth rate will the population double over the next 100 years?

SOLUTION We must find r, given that $P = 2P_0$ and $t = 100$:

$$P = P_0e^{rt}$$
$$2P_0 = P_0e^{100r}$$
$$2 = e^{100r}$$
$$100r = \ln 2 \qquad \text{\textit{Take the natural logarithm}}$$
$$\qquad\qquad\qquad \text{\textit{of both sides and reverse}}$$
$$\qquad\qquad\qquad \text{\textit{the equation.}}$$
$$r = \frac{\ln 2}{100}$$
$$\approx 0.0069 \quad \text{or} \quad 0.69\%$$

Matched Problem 2   If the exponential growth law applies to population growth in Nigeria, find the doubling time (to the nearest year) of the population if it grows at 2.1% per year compounded continuously.

We now turn to another type of exponential growth: **radioactive decay**. In 1946, Willard Libby (who later received a Nobel Prize in chemistry) found that as long as a plant or animal is alive, radioactive carbon-14 is maintained at a constant level in its tissues. Once the plant or animal is dead, however, the radioactive carbon-14 diminishes by radioactive decay at a rate proportional to the amount present.

$$\frac{dQ}{dt} = rQ \qquad Q(0) = Q_0$$

This is another example of the exponential growth law. The continuous compound rate of decay for radioactive carbon-14 is 0.000 123 8, so $r = -0.000\ 123\ 8$, since decay implies a negative continuous compound growth rate.

EXAMPLE 3   **Archaeology** A human bone fragment was found at an archaeological site in Africa. If 10% of the original amount of radioactive carbon-14 was present, estimate the age of the bone (to the nearest 100 years).

SOLUTION   By the exponential growth law for

$$\frac{dQ}{dt} = -0.000\ 123\ 8Q \qquad Q(0) = Q_0$$

we have

$$Q = Q_0 e^{-0.0001238t}$$

We must find t so that $Q = 0.1Q_0$ (since the amount of carbon-14 present now is 10% of the amount Q_0 present at the death of the person).

$$0.1Q_0 = Q_0 e^{-0.0001238t}$$

$$0.1 = e^{-0.0001238t}$$

$$\ln 0.1 = \ln e^{-0.0001238t}$$

$$t = \frac{\ln 0.1}{-0.000\ 123\ 8} \approx 18{,}600 \text{ years}$$

Figure 6 $y_1 = e^{-0.0001238x}$; $y_2 = 0.1$

See Figure 6 for a graphical solution to Example 3.

Matched Problem 3   Estimate the age of the bone in Example 3 (to the nearest 100 years) if 50% of the original amount of carbon-14 is present.

In learning certain skills, such as typing and swimming, one often assumes that there is a maximum skill attainable—say, M—and the rate of improvement is proportional to the difference between what has been achieved y and the maximum attainable M. Mathematically,

$$\frac{dy}{dt} = k(M - y) \qquad y(0) = 0$$

We solve this type of problem with the same technique used to obtain the exponential growth law. First, multiply both sides of the first equation by $1/(M - y)$ to get

$$\frac{1}{M - y}\frac{dy}{dt} = k$$

and then integrate each side with respect to t:

$$\int \frac{1}{M-y} \frac{dy}{dt} dt = \int k \, dt$$

$$-\int \frac{1}{M-y} \left(-\frac{dy}{dt} \right) dt = \int k \, dt \qquad \text{Substitute } u = M - y \text{ and}$$

$$-\int \frac{1}{u} du = \int k \, dt \qquad du = -dy = -\frac{dy}{dt} dt.$$

$$-\ln|u| = kt + C \qquad \text{Substitute } M - y, \text{ which is } > 0, \text{ for } u.$$

$$-\ln(M-y) = kt + C \qquad \text{Multiply both sides by } -1.$$

$$\ln(M-y) = -kt - C$$

Change this last equation to an equivalent exponential form:

$$M - y = e^{-kt-C}$$

$$M - y = e^{-C} e^{-kt}$$

$$y = M - e^{-C} e^{-kt}$$

Now, $y(0) = 0$; hence,

$$y(0) = M - e^{-C} e^0 = 0$$

Solving for e^{-C}, we obtain

$$e^{-C} = M$$

and our final solution is

$$y = M - Me^{-kt} = M(1 - e^{-kt})$$

EXAMPLE 4   **Learning** For a particular person learning to swim, the distance y (in feet) that the person is able to swim in 1 minute after t hours of practice is given approximately by

$$y = 50(1 - e^{-0.04t})$$

What is the rate of improvement (to two decimal places) after 10 hours of practice?

SOLUTION

$$y = 50 - 50e^{-0.04t}$$

$$y'(t) = 2e^{-0.04t}$$

$$y'(10) = 2e^{-0.04(10)} \approx 1.34 \text{ feet per hour of practice}$$

Matched Problem 4   In Example 4, what is the rate of improvement (to two decimal places) after 50 hours of practice?

Comparison of Exponential Growth Phenomena

The graphs and equations given in Table 1 compare several widely used growth models. These models are divided into two groups: unlimited growth and limited growth. Following each equation and graph is a short (and necessarily incomplete) list of areas in which the models are used.

Table 1   Exponential Growth

Description	Model	Solution	Graph	Uses
Unlimited growth: Rate of growth is proportional to the amount present	$\dfrac{dy}{dt} = ky$ $k, t > 0$ $y(0) = c$	$y = ce^{kt}$		• Short-term population growth (people, bacteria, etc.) • Growth of money at continuous compound interest • Price–supply curves
Exponential decay: Rate of growth is proportional to the amount present	$\dfrac{dy}{dt} = -ky$ $k, t > 0$ $y(0) = c$	$y = ce^{-kt}$		• Depletion of natural resources • Radioactive decay • Absorption of light in water • Price–demand curves • Atmospheric pressure (t is altitude)
Limited growth: Rate of growth is proportional to the difference between the amount present and a fixed limit	$\dfrac{dy}{dt} = k(M - y)$ $k, t > 0$ $y(0) = 0$	$y = M(1 - e^{-kt})$		• Sales fads (for example, skateboards) • Depreciation of equipment • Company growth • Learning
Logistic growth: Rate of growth is proportional to the amount present and to the difference between the amount present and a fixed limit	$\dfrac{dy}{dt} = ky(M - y)$ $k, t > 0$ $y(0) = \dfrac{M}{1 + c}$	$y = \dfrac{M}{1 + ce^{-kMt}}$		• Long-term population growth • Epidemics • Sales of new products • Spread of a rumor • Company growth

Exercises 13-3

A

In Problems 1–12, find the general or particular solution, as indicated, for each differential equation.

1. $\dfrac{dy}{dx} = 6x$ **2.** $\dfrac{dy}{dx} = 3x^{-2}$

3. $\dfrac{dy}{dx} = \dfrac{7}{x}$ **4.** $\dfrac{dy}{dx} = e^{0.1x}$

5. $\dfrac{dy}{dx} = e^{0.02x}$ **6.** $\dfrac{dy}{dx} = 8x^{-1}$

7. $\dfrac{dy}{dx} = x^2 - x;\ y(0) = 0$ **8.** $\dfrac{dy}{dx} = \sqrt{x};\ y(0) = 0$

9. $\dfrac{dy}{dx} = -2xe^{-x^2};\ y(0) = 3$ **10.** $\dfrac{dy}{dx} = e^{x-3};\ y(3) = -5$

11. $\dfrac{dy}{dx} = \dfrac{2}{1 + x};\ y(0) = 5$ **12.** $\dfrac{dy}{dx} = \dfrac{1}{4(3 - x)};\ y(0) = 1$

B

Problems 13–18 refer to the following slope fields:

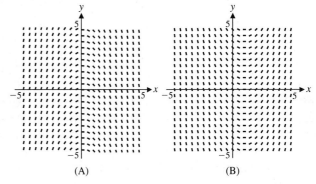

(A)   (B)

Figure for 13–18

13. Which slope field is associated with the differential equation $dy/dx = x - 1$? Briefly justify your answer.

14. Which slope field is associated with the differential equation $dy/dx = -x$? Briefly justify your answer.

15. Solve the differential equation $dy/dx = x - 1$ and find the particular solution that passes through $(0, -2)$.

16. Solve the differential equation $dy/dx = -x$ and find the particular solution that passes through $(0, 3)$.

17. Graph the particular solution found in Problem 15 in the appropriate figure A or B (or a copy).

18. Graph the particular solution found in Problem 16 in the appropriate figure A or B (or a copy).

In Problems 19–26, find the general or particular solution, as indicated, for each differential equation.

19. $\dfrac{dy}{dt} = 2y$ **20.** $\dfrac{dy}{dt} = -3y$

21. $\dfrac{dy}{dx} = -0.5y;\ y(0) = 100$

22. $\dfrac{dy}{dx} = 0.1y;\ y(0) = -2.5$

23. $\dfrac{dx}{dt} = -5x$ **24.** $\dfrac{dx}{dt} = 4t$

25. $\dfrac{dx}{dt} = -5t$ **26.** $\dfrac{dx}{dt} = 4x$

C

Problems 27–34 refer to the following slope fields:

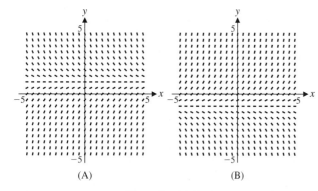

(A)   (B)

Figure for 27–34

27. Which slope field is associated with the differential equation $dy/dx = 1 - y$? Briefly justify your answer.

28. Which slope field is associated with the differential equation $dy/dx = y + 1$? Briefly justify your answer.

29. Show that $y = 1 - Ce^{-x}$ is a solution of the differential equation $dy/dx = 1 - y$ for any real number C. Find the particular solution that passes through $(0, 0)$.

30. Show that $y = Ce^{x} - 1$ is a solution of the differential equation $dy/dx = y + 1$ for any real number C. Find the particular solution that passes through $(0, 0)$.

31. Graph the particular solution found in Problem 29 in the appropriate figure, Figure A or Figure B (or a copy).

32. Graph the particular solution found in Problem 30 in the appropriate figure A or B (or a copy).

33. Use a graphing calculator to graph $y = 1 - Ce^{-x}$ for $C = -2, -1, 1$, and 2, for $-5 \le x \le 5$, $-5 \le y \le 5$, all in the same viewing window. Observe how the solution curves go with the flow of the tangent line segments in the corresponding slope field shown in figure A or figure B.

34. Use a graphing calculator to graph $y = Ce^{x} - 1$ for $C = -2, -1, 1$, and 2, for $-5 \le x \le 5$, $-5 \le y \le 5$, all in the same viewing window. Observe how the solution curves go with the flow of the tangent line segments in the corresponding slope field shown in figure A or figure B.

35. Show that $y = \sqrt{C - x^2}$ is a solution of the differential equation $dy/dx = -x/y$ for any positive real number C. Find the particular solution that passes through $(3, 4)$.

36. Show that $y = \sqrt{x^2 + C}$ is a solution of the differential equation $dy/dx = x/y$ for any real number C. Find the particular solution that passes through $(-6, 7)$.

37. Show that $y = Cx$ is a solution of the differential equation $dy/dx = y/x$ for any real number C. Find the particular solution that passes through $(-8, 24)$.

38. Show that $y = C/x$ is a solution of the differential equation $dy/dx = -y/x$ for any real number C. Find the particular solution that passes through $(2, 5)$.

39. Show that $y = 1/(1 + ce^{-t})$ is a solution of the differential equation $dy/dt = y(1 - y)$ for any real number c. Find the particular solution that passes through $(0, -1)$.

40. Show that $y = 2/(1 + ce^{-6t})$ is a solution of the differential equation $dy/dt = 3y(2 - y)$ for any real number c. Find the particular solution that passes through $(0, 1)$.

In Problems 41–48, use a graphing calculator to graph the given examples of the various cases in Table 1 on page 727.

41. Unlimited growth:

$y = 1{,}000e^{0.08t}$
$0 \le t \le 15$
$0 \le y \le 3{,}500$

42. Unlimited growth:

$y = 5{,}250e^{0.12t}$
$0 \le t \le 10$
$0 \le y \le 20{,}000$

43. Exponential decay:

$p = 100e^{-0.05x}$
$0 \le x \le 30$
$0 \le p \le 100$

44. Exponential decay:

$p = 1{,}000e^{-0.08x}$
$0 \le x \le 40$
$0 \le p \le 1{,}000$

45. Limited growth:

$N = 100(1 - e^{-0.05t})$
$0 \le t \le 100$
$0 \le N \le 100$

46. Limited growth:

$$N = 1,000(1 - e^{-0.07t})$$
$$0 \le t \le 70$$
$$0 \le N \le 1,000$$

47. Logistic growth:

$$N = \frac{1,000}{1 + 999e^{-0.4t}}$$
$$0 \le t \le 40$$
$$0 \le N \le 1,000$$

48. Logistic growth:

$$N = \frac{400}{1 + 99e^{-0.4t}}$$
$$0 \le t \le 30$$
$$0 \le N \le 400$$

49. Show that the rate of logistic growth, $dy/dt = ky(M - y)$, has its maximum value when $y = M/2$.

50. Find the value of t for which the logistic function

$$y = \frac{M}{1 + ce^{-kMt}}$$

is equal to $M/2$.

51. Let $Q(t)$ denote the population of the world at time t. In 1999, the world population was 6.0 billion and increasing at 1.3% per year; in 2009, it was 6.8 billion and increasing at 1.2% per year. In which year, 1999 or 2009, was dQ/dt (the rate of growth of Q with respect to t) greater? Explain.

52. Refer to Problem 51. Explain why the world population function $Q(t)$ does not satisfy an exponential growth law.

Applications

53. **Continuous compound interest.** Find the amount A in an account after t years if

$$\frac{dA}{dt} = 0.03A \qquad \text{and} \qquad A(0) = 1,000$$

54. **Continuous compound interest.** Find the amount A in an account after t years if

$$\frac{dA}{dt} = 0.02A \qquad \text{and} \qquad A(0) = 5,250$$

55. **Continuous compound interest.** Find the amount A in an account after t years if

$$\frac{dA}{dt} = rA \qquad A(0) = 8,000 \qquad A(2) = 8,260.14$$

56. **Continuous compound interest.** Find the amount A in an account after t years if

$$\frac{dA}{dt} = rA \qquad A(0) = 5,000 \qquad A(5) = 5,581.39$$

57. **Price–demand.** The marginal price dp/dx at x units of demand per week is proportional to the price p. There is no weekly demand at a price of $100 per unit $[p(0) = 100]$, and there is a weekly demand of 5 units at a price of $77.88 per unit $[p(5) = 77.88]$.

(A) Find the price–demand equation.

(B) At a demand of 10 units per week, what is the price?

(C) Graph the price–demand equation for $0 \le x \le 25$.

58. **Price–supply.** The marginal price dp/dx at x units of supply per day is proportional to the price p. There is no supply at a price of $10 per unit $[p(0) = 10]$, and there is a daily supply of 50 units at a price of $12.84 per unit $[p(50) = 12.84]$.

(A) Find the price–supply equation.

(B) At a supply of 100 units per day, what is the price?

(C) Graph the price–supply equation for $0 \le x \le 250$.

59. **Advertising.** A company is trying to expose a new product to as many people as possible through TV ads. Suppose that the rate of exposure to new people is proportional to the number of those who have not seen the product out of L possible viewers. No one is aware of the product at the start of the campaign, and after 10 days, 40% of L are aware of the product. Mathematically,

$$\frac{dN}{dt} = k(L - N) \quad N(0) = 0 \quad N(10) = 0.4L$$

(A) Solve the differential equation.

(B) What percent of L will have been exposed after 5 days of the campaign?

(C) How many days will it take to expose 80% of L?

(D) Graph the solution found in part (A) for $0 \le t \le 90$.

60. **Advertising.** Suppose that the differential equation for Problem 59 is

$$\frac{dN}{dt} = k(L - N) \quad N(0) = 0 \quad N(10) = 0.1L$$

(A) Explain what the equation $N(10) = 0.1L$ means.

(B) Solve the differential equation.

(C) How many days will it take to expose 50% of L?

(D) Graph the solution found in part (B) for $0 \le t \le 300$.

61. **Biology.** For relatively clear bodies of water, the intensity of light is reduced according to

$$\frac{dI}{dx} = -kI \qquad I(0) = I_0$$

where I is the intensity of light at x feet below the surface. For the Sargasso Sea off the West Indies, $k = 0.00942$. Find I in terms of x, and find the depth at which the light is reduced to half of that at the surface.

62. **Blood pressure.** Under certain assumptions, the blood pressure P in the largest artery in the human body (the aorta) changes between beats with respect to time t according to

$$\frac{dP}{dt} = -aP \qquad P(0) = P_0$$

where a is a constant. Find $P = P(t)$ that satisfies both conditions.

63. **Drug concentration.** A single injection of a drug is administered to a patient. The amount Q in the body then decreases at a rate proportional to the amount present. For a particular drug, the rate is 4% per hour. Thus,

$$\frac{dQ}{dt} = -0.04Q \qquad Q(0) = Q_0$$

where t is time in hours.

(A) If the initial injection is 3 milliliters [$Q(0) = 3$], find $Q = Q(t)$ satisfying both conditions.

(B) How many milliliters (to two decimal places) are in the body after 10 hours?

(C) How many hours (to two decimal places) will it take for only 1 milliliter of the drug to be left in the body?

(D) Graph the solution found in part (A).

64. Simple epidemic. A community of 1,000 people is homogeneously mixed. One person who has just returned from another community has influenza. Assume that the home community has not had influenza shots and all are susceptible. One mathematical model assumes that influenza tends to spread at a rate in direct proportion to the number N who have the disease and to the number $1,000 - N$ who have not yet contracted the disease. Mathematically,

$$\frac{dN}{dt} = kN(1,000 - N) \qquad N(0) = 1$$

where N is the number of people who have contracted influenza after t days. For $k = 0.0004$, $N(t)$ is given by

$$N(t) = \frac{1,000}{1 + 999e^{-0.4t}}$$

(A) How many people have contracted influenza after 10 days? After 20 days?

(B) How many days will it take until half the community has contracted influenza?

(C) Find $\lim_{t \to \infty} N(t)$.

(D) Graph $N = N(t)$ for $0 \le t \le 30$.

65. Nuclear accident. One of the dangerous radioactive isotopes detected after the Chernobyl nuclear disaster in 1986 was cesium-137. If 93.3% of the cesium-137 emitted during the disaster was still present 3 years later, find the continuous compound rate of decay of this isotope.

66. Insecticides. Many countries have banned the use of the insecticide DDT because of its long-term adverse effects. Five years after a particular country stopped using DDT, the amount of DDT in the ecosystem had declined to 75% of the amount present at the time of the ban. Find the continuous compound rate of decay of DDT.

67. Archaeology. A skull found in an ancient tomb has 5% of the original amount of radioactive carbon-14 present. Estimate the age of the skull. (See Example 3.)

68. Learning. For a person learning to type, the number N of words per minute that the person could type after t hours of practice was given by

$$N = 100(1 - e^{-0.02t})$$

What is the rate of improvement after 10 hours of practice? After 40 hours of practice?

69. Small-group analysis. In a study on small-group dynamics, sociologists found that when 10 members of a discussion group were ranked according to the number of times each participated, the number $N(k)$ of times that the kth-ranked person participated was given by

$$N(k) = N_1 e^{-0.11(k-1)} \qquad 1 \le k \le 10$$

where N_1 is the number of times that the first-ranked person participated in the discussion. If $N_1 = 180$, in a discussion group of 10 people, estimate how many times the sixth-ranked person participated. How about the 10th-ranked person?

70. Perception. The Weber–Fechner law concerns a person's sensed perception of various strengths of stimulation involving weights, sound, light, shock, taste, and so on. One form of the law states that the rate of change of sensed sensation S with respect to stimulus R is inversely proportional to the strength of the stimulus R. So

$$\frac{dS}{dR} = \frac{k}{R}$$

where k is a constant. If we let R_0 be the threshold level at which the stimulus R can be detected (the least amount of sound, light, weight, and so on, that can be detected), then

$$S(R_0) = 0$$

Find a function S in terms of R that satisfies these conditions.

71. Rumor propagation. Sociologists have found that a rumor tends to spread at a rate in direct proportion to the number x who have heard it and to the number $P - x$ who have not, where P is the total population. If a resident of a 400-student dormitory hears a rumor that there is a case of TB on campus, then $P = 400$ and

$$\frac{dx}{dt} = 0.001x(400 - x) \qquad x(0) = 1$$

where t is time (in minutes). From these conditions, it can be shown that

$$x(t) = \frac{400}{1 + 399e^{-0.4t}}$$

(A) How many people have heard the rumor after 5 minutes? after 20 minutes?

(B) Find $\lim_{t \to \infty} x(t)$.

(C) Graph $x = x(t)$ for $0 \le t \le 30$.

72. Rumor propagation. In Problem 71, how long (to the nearest minute) will it take for half of the group of 400 to have heard the rumor?

Answers to Matched Problems

1. 1.4 billion people
2. 33 yr
3. 5,600 yr
4. 0.27 ft/hr

13-4   The Definite Integral

The first three sections of this chapter focused on the *indefinite integral*. In this section, we introduce the *definite integral*. The definite integral is used to compute areas, probabilities, average values of functions, future values of continuous income streams, and many other quantities. Initially, the concept of the definite integral may seem unrelated to the notion of the indefinite integral. There is, however, a close connection between the two integrals. The fundamental theorem of calculus, discussed in Section 13-5, makes that connection precise.

Approximating Areas by Left and Right Sums

How do we find the shaded area in Figure 1? That is, how do we find the area bounded by the graph of $f(x) = 0.25x^2 + 1$, the x axis, and the vertical lines $x = 1$ and $x = 5$? [This cumbersome description is usually shortened to "the area under the graph of $f(x) = 0.25x^2 + 1$ from $x = 1$ to $x = 5$."] Our standard geometric area formulas do not apply directly, but the formula for the area of a rectangle can be used indirectly. To see how, we look at a method of approximating the area under the graph by using rectangles. This method will give us any accuracy desired, which is quite different from finding the area exactly. Our first area approximation is made by dividing the interval $[1, 5]$ on the x axis into four equal parts, each of length

$$\Delta x = \frac{5 - 1}{4} = 1^*$$

We then place a **left rectangle** on each subinterval, that is, a rectangle whose base is the subinterval and whose height is the value of the function at the left endpoint of the subinterval (see Fig. 2).

Summing the areas of the left rectangles in Figure 2 results in a **left sum** of four rectangles, denoted by L_4, as follows:

$$L_4 = f(1) \cdot 1 + f(2) \cdot 1 + f(3) \cdot 1 + f(4) \cdot 1$$
$$= 1.25 + 2.00 + 3.25 + 5 = 11.5$$

From Figure 3, since $f(x)$ is increasing, we see that the left sum L_4 underestimates the area, and we can write

$$11.5 = L_4 < \text{Area}$$

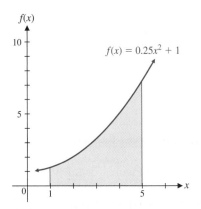

Figure 1 What is the shaded area?

Figure 2 Left rectangles

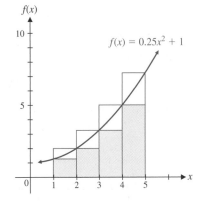

Figure 3 Left and right rectangles

---

*It is customary to denote the length of the subintervals by Δx, which is read "delta x," since Δ is the Greek capital letter delta.

EXPLORE & DISCUSS 1

If $f(x)$ were decreasing over the interval $[1, 5]$, would the left sum L_4 over- or under-estimate the actual area under the curve? Explain.

Similarly, we use the right endpoint of each subinterval to find the height of the **right rectangle** placed on top of it. Superimposing right rectangles on top of Figure 2, we get Figure 3.

Summing the areas of the right rectangles in Figure 3 results in a **right sum** of four rectangles, denoted by R_4, as follows (compare R_4 with L_4 and note that R_4 can be obtained from L_4 by deleting one rectangular area and adding one more):

$$R_4 = f(2) \cdot 1 + f(3) \cdot 1 + f(4) \cdot 1 + f(5) \cdot 1$$
$$= 2.00 + 3.25 + 5.00 + 7.25 = 17.5$$

From Figure 3, since $f(x)$ is increasing, we see that the right sum R_4 overestimates the area, and we conclude that the actual area is between 11.5 and 17.5. That is,

$$11.5 = L_4 < \text{Area} < R_4 = 17.5$$

EXPLORE & DISCUSS 2

If $f(x)$ in Figure 3 were decreasing over the interval $[1, 5]$, would the right sum R_4 overestimate or underestimate the actual area under the curve? Explain.

The first approximation of the area under the curve in Figure 1 is fairly coarse, but the method outlined can be continued with increasingly accurate results by dividing the interval $[1, 5]$ into more and more subintervals of equal horizontal length. Of course, this is not a job for hand calculation, but a job that computers are designed to do.* Figure 4 shows left- and right-rectangle approximations for 16 equal subdivisions.

For this case,

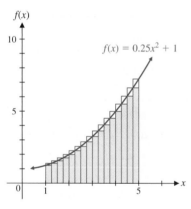

$f(x) = 0.25x^2 + 1$

Figure 4

$$\Delta x = \frac{5 - 1}{16} = 0.25$$

$$L_{16} = f(1) \cdot \Delta x + f(1.25) \cdot \Delta x + \cdots + f(4.75) \cdot \Delta x$$
$$= 13.59$$

$$R_{16} = f(1.25) \cdot \Delta x + f(1.50) \cdot \Delta x + \cdots + f(5) \cdot \Delta x$$
$$= 15.09$$

Thus, we now know that the area under the curve is between 13.59 and 15.09. That is,

$$13.59 = L_{16} < \text{Area} < R_{16} = 15.09$$

For 100 equal subdivisions, computer calculations give us

$$14.214 = L_{100} < \text{Area} < R_{100} = 14.454$$

The **error in an approximation** is the absolute value of the difference between the approximation and the actual value. In general, neither the actual value nor the error in an approximation is known. However, it is often possible to calculate an **error bound**—a positive number such that the error is guaranteed to be less than or equal to that number.

The error in the approximation of the area under the graph of f from $x = 1$ to $x = 5$ by the left sum L_{16} (or the right sum R_{16}) is less than the sum of the areas of the small rectangles in Figure 4. By stacking those rectangles (see Fig. 5), we see that

$$\text{Error} = |\text{Area} - L_{16}| < |f(5) - f(1)| \cdot \Delta x = 1.5$$

Therefore, 1.5 is an error bound for the approximation of the area under f by L_{16}. We can apply the same stacking argument to any positive function that is increasing on $[a, b]$ or decreasing on $[a, b]$, to obtain the error bound in Theorem 1.

---

*The computer software that accompanies this book will perform these calculations (see the preface).

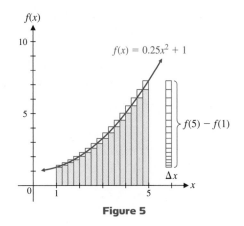

Figure 5

THEOREM 1   Error Bounds for Approximations of Area by Left or Right Sums

If $f(x) > 0$ and is either increasing on $[a, b]$ or decreasing on $[a, b]$, then

$$|f(b) - f(a)| \cdot \frac{b - a}{n}$$

is an error bound for the approximation of the area between the graph of f and the x axis, from $x = a$ to $x = b$, by L_n or R_n.

Because the error bound of Theorem 1 approaches 0 as $n \to \infty$, it can be shown that left and right sums, for certain functions, approach the same limit as $n \to \infty$.

THEOREM 2   Limits of Left and Right Sums

If $f(x) > 0$ and is either increasing on $[a, b]$ or decreasing on $[a, b]$, then its left and right sums approach the same real number as $n \to \infty$.

The number approached as $n \to \infty$ by the left and right sums in Theorem 2 is the area between the graph of f and the x axis from $x = a$ to $x = b$.

EXAMPLE 1   **Approximating Areas** Given the function $f(x) = 9 - 0.25x^2$, we want to approximate the area under $y = f(x)$ from $x = 2$ to $x = 5$.

(A) Graph the function over the interval $[0, 6]$. Then draw left and right rectangles for the interval $[2, 5]$ with $n = 6$.

(B) Calculate L_6, R_6, and error bounds for each.

(C) How large should n be in order for the approximation of the area by L_n or R_n to be within 0.05 of the true value?

SOLUTION   (A) $\Delta x = 0.5$:

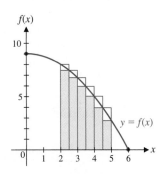

(B) $L_6 = f(2) \cdot \Delta x + f(2.5) \cdot \Delta x + f(3) \cdot \Delta x + f(3.5) \cdot \Delta x + f(4) \cdot \Delta x$

$\qquad + f(4.5) \cdot \Delta x = 18.53$

$\qquad R_6 = f(2.5) \cdot \Delta x + f(3) \cdot \Delta x + f(3.5) \cdot \Delta x + f(4) \cdot \Delta x$

$\qquad + f(4.5) \cdot \Delta x + f(5) \cdot \Delta x = 15.91$

The error bound for L_6 and R_6 is

$$\text{error} \le |f(5) - f(2)|\frac{5 - 2}{6} = |2.75 - 8|(0.5) = 2.625$$

(C)   For L_n and R_n, find n such that error ≤ 0.05:

$$|f(b) - f(a)|\frac{b - a}{n} \le 0.05$$

$$|2.75 - 8|\frac{3}{n} \le 0.05$$

$$|-5.25|\frac{3}{n} \le 0.05$$

$$15.75 \le 0.05n$$

$$n \ge \frac{15.75}{0.05} = 315$$

Matched Problem 1   Given the function $f(x) = 8 - 0.5x^2$, we want to approximate the area under $y = f(x)$ from $x = 1$ to $x = 3$.

(A)   Graph the function over the interval $[0, 4]$. Then draw left and right rectangles for the interval $[1, 3]$ with $n = 4$.

(B)   Calculate L_4, R_4, and error bounds for each.

(C)   How large should n be in order for the approximation of the area by L_n or R_n to be within 0.5 of the true value?

CONCEPTUAL INSIGHT

Note from Example 1(C) that a relatively large value of n ($n = 315$) is required to approximate the area by L_n or R_n to within 0.05. In other words, 315 rectangles must be used, and 315 terms must be summed, to guarantee that the error does not exceed 0.05. We can obtain a more efficient approximation of the area (fewer terms are summed to achieve a given accuracy) by replacing rectangles with trapezoids. The resulting **trapezoidal rule**, and other methods for approximating areas, are discussed in Group Activity 1 in this book's Web site.

The Definite Integral as a Limit of Sums

Left and right sums are special cases of more general sums, called *Riemann sums* [named after the German mathematician Georg Riemann (1826–1866)], that are used to approximate areas by means of rectangles.

Let f be a function defined on the interval $[a, b]$. We partition $[a, b]$ into n subintervals of equal length $\Delta x = (b - a)/n$ with endpoints

$$a = x_0 < x_1 < x_2 < \cdots < x_n = b$$

Then, using **summation notation** (see Appendix B-1), we have

Left sum: $L_n = f(x_0)\Delta x + f(x_1)\Delta x + \cdots + f(x_{n-1})\Delta x = \displaystyle\sum_{k=1}^{n} f(x_{k-1})\Delta x$

Right sum: $R_n = f(x_1)\Delta x + f(x_2)\Delta x + \cdots + f(x_n)\Delta x = \sum_{k=1}^{n} f(x_k)\Delta x$

Riemann sum: $S_n = f(c_1)\Delta x + f(c_2)\Delta x + \cdots + f(c_n)\Delta x = \sum_{k=1}^{n} f(c_k)\Delta x$

In a **Riemann sum,*** each c_k is required to belong to the subinterval $[x_{k-1}, x_k]$. Left and right sums are the special cases of Riemann sums in which c_k is the left endpoint or right endpoint, respectively, of the subinterval. If $f(x) > 0$, then each term of a Riemann sum S_n represents the area of a rectangle having height $f(c_k)$ and width Δx (see Fig. 6). If $f(x)$ has both positive and negative values, then some terms of S_n represent areas of rectangles, and others represent the negatives of areas of rectangles, depending on the sign of $f(c_k)$ (see Fig. 7).

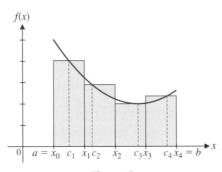

Figure 6   **Figure 7**

EXAMPLE 2   **Riemann Sums**   Consider the function $f(x) = 15 - x^2$ on $[1, 5]$. Partition the interval $[1, 5]$ into four subintervals of equal length. For each subinterval $[x_{k-1}, x_k]$, let c_k be the midpoint. Calculate the corresponding Riemann sum S_4. (Riemann sums for which the c_k are the midpoints of the subintervals are called **midpoint sums**.)

SOLUTION
$$\Delta x = \frac{5-1}{4} = 1$$
$$S_4 = f(c_1) \cdot \Delta x + f(c_2) \cdot \Delta x + f(c_3) \cdot \Delta x + f(c_4) \cdot \Delta x$$
$$= f(1.5) \cdot 1 + f(2.5) \cdot 1 + f(3.5) \cdot 1 + f(4.5) \cdot 1$$
$$= 12.75 + 8.75 + 2.75 - 5.25 = 19$$

Matched Problem 2   Consider the function $f(x) = x^2 - 2x - 10$ on $[2, 8]$. Partition the interval $[2, 8]$ into three subintervals of equal length. For each subinterval $[x_{k-1}, x_k]$, let c_k be the midpoint. Calculate the corresponding Riemann sum S_3.

By analyzing properties of a continuous function on a closed interval, it can be shown that the conclusion of Theorem 2 is valid if f is continuous. In that case, not just left and right sums, but Riemann sums, have the same limit as $n \to \infty$.

THEOREM 3   Limit of Riemann Sums
If f is a continuous function on $[a, b]$, then the Riemann sums for f on $[a, b]$ approach a real number limit I as $n \to \infty$.[†]

---

*The term *Riemann sum* is often applied to more general sums in which the subintervals $[x_{k-1}, x_k]$ are not required to have the same length. Such sums are not considered in this book.

[†]The precise meaning of this limit statement is as follows: For each $e > 0$, there exists some $d > 0$ such that $|S_n - I| < e$ whenever S_n is a Riemann sum for f on $[a, b]$ for which $\Delta x < d$.

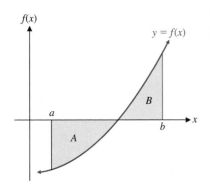

Figure 8 $\displaystyle\int_a^b f(x)\,dx = -A + B$

> **DEFINITION** **Definite Integral**
>
> Let f be a continuous function on $[a, b]$. The limit I of Riemann sums for f on $[a, b]$, guaranteed to exist by Theorem 2, is called the **definite integral** of f from a to b and is denoted as
>
> $$\int_a^b f(x)\,dx$$
>
> The **integrand** is $f(x)$, the **lower limit of integration** is a, and the **upper limit of integration** is b.

Because area is a positive quantity, the definite integral has the following geometric interpretation:

$$\int_a^b f(x)\,dx$$

represents the cumulative sum of the signed areas between the graph of f and the x axis from $x = a$ to $x = b$, where the areas above the x axis are counted positively and the areas below the x axis are counted negatively (see Fig. 8, where A and B are the actual areas of the indicated regions).

EXAMPLE 3 **Definite Integrals** Calculate the definite integrals by referring to Figure 9.

(A) $\displaystyle\int_a^b f(x)\,dx$

(B) $\displaystyle\int_a^c f(x)\,dx$

(C) $\displaystyle\int_b^c f(x)\,dx$

Area $A = 2.33$
Area $B = 10.67$
Area $C = 5.63$

Figure 9

SOLUTION (A) $\displaystyle\int_a^b f(x)\,dx = -2.33 + 10.67 = 8.34$

(B) $\displaystyle\int_a^c f(x)\,dx = -2.33 + 10.67 - 5.63 = 2.71$

(C) $\displaystyle\int_b^c f(x)\,dx = -5.63$

Matched Problem 3 Referring to the figure for Example 3, calculate the definite integrals.

(A) $\displaystyle\int_a^0 f(x)\,dx$ (B) $\displaystyle\int_0^c f(x)\,dx$ (C) $\displaystyle\int_0^b f(x)\,dx$

Properties of the Definite Integral

Because the definite integral is defined as the limit of Riemann sums, many properties of sums are also properties of the definite integral. Note that Properties 3 and 4 are similar to the indefinite integral properties given in Section 13-1.

PROPERTIES **Properties of Definite Integrals**

1. $\displaystyle\int_a^a f(x)\,dx = 0$

2. $\displaystyle\int_a^b f(x)\,dx = -\int_b^a f(x)\,dx$

3. $\displaystyle\int_a^b kf(x)\,dx = k\int_a^b f(x)\,dx$, k a constant

4. $\displaystyle\int_a^b [f(x) \pm g(x)]\,dx = \int_a^b f(x)\,dx \pm \int_a^b g(x)\,dx$

5. $\displaystyle\int_a^b f(x)\,dx = \int_a^c f(x)\,dx + \int_c^b f(x)\,dx$

EXAMPLE 4   **Using Properties of the Definite Integral** If

$$\int_0^2 x\,dx = 2 \qquad \int_0^2 x^2\,dx = \frac{8}{3} \qquad \int_2^3 x^2\,dx = \frac{19}{3}$$

then

(A) $\displaystyle\int_0^2 12x^2\,dx = 12\int_0^2 x^2\,dx = 12\left(\frac{8}{3}\right) = 32$

(B) $\displaystyle\int_0^2 (2x - 6x^2)\,dx = 2\int_0^2 x\,dx - 6\int_0^2 x^2\,dx = 2(2) - 6\left(\frac{8}{3}\right) = -12$

(C) $\displaystyle\int_3^2 x^2\,dx = -\int_2^3 x^2\,dx = -\frac{19}{3}$

(D) $\displaystyle\int_5^5 3x^2\,dx = 0$

(E) $\displaystyle\int_0^3 3x^2\,dx = 3\int_0^2 x^2\,dx + 3\int_2^3 x^2\,dx = 3\left(\frac{8}{3}\right) + 3\left(\frac{19}{3}\right) = 27$

Matched Problem 4   Using the same integral values given in Example 4, find

(A) $\displaystyle\int_2^3 6x^2\,dx$ (B) $\displaystyle\int_0^2 (9x^2 - 4x)\,dx$ (C) $\displaystyle\int_2^0 3x\,dx$

(D) $\displaystyle\int_{-2}^{-2} 3x\,dx$ (E) $\displaystyle\int_0^3 12x^2\,dx$

Exercises 13-4

A

Problems 1–4 refer to the rectangles A, B, C, D, and E in the following figure.

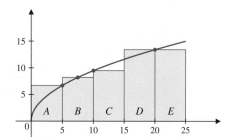

1. Which rectangles are left rectangles?

2. Which rectangles are right rectangles?

3. Which rectangles are neither left nor right rectangles?

4. Which rectangles are both left and right rectangles?

Problems 5–8 refer to the rectangles F, G, H, I, and J in the following figure.

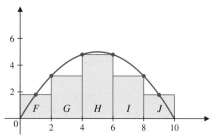

Figure for 5–8

5. Which rectangles are right rectangles?

6. Which rectangles are left rectangles?

7. Which rectangles are both left and right rectangles?

8. Which rectangles are neither left nor right rectangles?

Problems 9–16 involve estimating the area under the curves in Figures A–D from $x = 1$ to $x = 4$. For each figure, divide the interval $[1, 4]$ into three equal subintervals.

9. Draw in left and right rectangles for Figures A and B.

10. Draw in left and right rectangles for Figures C and D.

11. Using the results of Problem 9, compute L_3 and R_3 for Figure A and for Figure B.

12. Using the results of Problem 10, compute L_3 and R_3 for Figure C and for Figure D.

13. Replace the question marks with L_3 and R_3 as appropriate. Explain your choice.

$$? \leq \int_1^4 f(x)\, dx \leq ? \qquad ? \leq \int_1^4 g(x)\, dx \leq ?$$

(A)

(B)

(C)

(D)

Figure for 9–16

14. Replace the question marks with L_3 and R_3 as appropriate. Explain your choice.

$$? \leq \int_1^4 u(x)\, dx \leq ? \qquad ? \leq \int_1^4 v(x)\, dx \leq ?$$

15. Compute error bounds for L_3 and R_3 found in Problem 11 for both figures.

16. Compute error bounds for L_3 and R_3 found in Problem 12 for both figures.

In Problems 17–20, calculate the indicated Riemann sum S_n for the function $f(x) = 25 - 3x^2$.

17. Partition $[-2, 8]$ into five subintervals of equal length, and for each subinterval $[x_{k-1}, x_k]$, let $c_k = (x_{k-1} + x_k)/2$.

18. Partition $[0, 12]$ into four subintervals of equal length, and for each subinterval $[x_{k-1}, x_k]$, let $c_k = (x_{k-1} + 2x_k)/3$.

19. Partition $[0, 12]$ into four subintervals of equal length, and for each subinterval $[x_{k-1}, x_k]$, let $c_k = (2x_{k-1} + x_k)/3$.

20. Partition $[-5, 5]$ into five subintervals of equal length, and for each subinterval $[x_{k-1}, x_k]$, let $c_k = (x_{k-1} + x_k)/2$.

In Problems 21–24, calculate the indicated Riemann sum S_n for the function $f(x) = x^2 - 5x - 6$.

21. Partition $[0, 3]$ into three subintervals of equal length, and let $c_1 = 0.7$, $c_2 = 1.8$, and $c_3 = 2.4$.

22. Partition $[0, 3]$ into three subintervals of equal length, and let $c_1 = 0.2$, $c_2 = 1.5$, and $c_3 = 2.8$.

23. Partition $[1, 7]$ into six subintervals of equal length, and let $c_1 = 1, c_2 = 3, c_3 = 3, c_4 = 5, c_5 = 5$, and $c_6 = 7$.

24. Partition $[1, 7]$ into six subintervals of equal length, and let $c_1 = 2, c_2 = 2, c_3 = 4, c_4 = 4, c_5 = 6$, and $c_6 = 6$.

In Problems 25–36, calculate the definite integral by referring to the figure with the indicated areas.

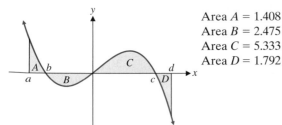

Area A = 1.408
Area B = 2.475
Area C = 5.333
Area D = 1.792

Figure for 25–36

25. $\int_b^0 f(x)\, dx$

26. $\int_0^c f(x)\, dx$

27. $\int_a^c f(x)\, dx$

28. $\int_b^d f(x)\, dx$

29. $\int_a^d f(x)\, dx$

30. $\int_0^d f(x)\, dx$

31. $\int_c^0 f(x)\, dx$

32. $\int_d^a f(x)\, dx$

33. $\int_0^a f(x)\, dx$

34. $\int_c^a f(x)\, dx$

35. $\int_d^b f(x)\, dx$

36. $\int_c^b f(x)\, dx$

In Problems 37–48, calculate the definite integral, given that

$$\int_1^4 x\, dx = 7.5 \qquad \int_1^4 x^2\, dx = 21 \qquad \int_4^5 x^2\, dx = \frac{61}{3}$$

37. $\int_1^4 2x\, dx$

38. $\int_1^4 3x^2\, dx$

39. $\int_1^4 (5x + x^2)\, dx$

40. $\int_1^4 (7x - 2x^2)\, dx$

41. $\int_1^4 (x^2 - 10x)\, dx$

42. $\int_1^4 (4x^2 - 9x)\, dx$

43. $\int_1^5 6x^2\, dx$

44. $\int_1^5 -4x^2\, dx$

45. $\int_4^4 (7x - 2)^2\, dx$

46. $\int_5^5 (10 - 7x + x^2)\, dx$

47. $\int_5^4 9x^2\, dx$

48. $\int_4^1 x(1 - x)\, dx$

✎ **B**

In Problems 49–54, discuss the validity of each statement. If the statement is always true, explain why. If it is not always true, give a counterexample.

49. If $\int_a^b f(x)\, dx = 0$, then $f(x) = 0$ for all x in $[a, b]$.

50. If $f(x) = 0$ for all x in $[a, b]$, then $\int_a^b f(x)\, dx = 0$.

51. If $f(x) = 2x$ on $[0, 10]$, then there is a positive integer n for which the left sum L_n equals the exact area under the graph of f from $x = 0$ to $x = 10$.

52. If $f(x) = 2x$ on $[0, 10]$ and n is a positive integer, then there is some Riemann sum S_n that equals the exact area under the graph of f from $x = 0$ to $x = 10$.

53. If the area under the graph of f on $[a, b]$ is equal to both the left sum L_n and the right sum R_n for some positive integer n, then f is constant on $[a, b]$.

54. If f is a decreasing function on $[a, b]$, then the area under the graph of f is greater than the left sum L_n and less than the right sum R_n, for any positive integer n.

Problems 55 and 56 refer to the following figure showing two parcels of land along a river:

Figure for 55 and 56

55. You want to purchase both parcels of land shown in the figure and make a quick check on their combined area. There is no equation for the river frontage, so you use the average of the left and right sums of rectangles covering the area. The 1,000-foot baseline is divided into 10 equal parts. At the end of each subinterval, a measurement is made from the baseline to the river, and the results are tabulated. Let x be the distance from the left end of the baseline and let $h(x)$ be the distance from the baseline to the river at x. Use L_{10} to estimate the combined area of both parcels, and calculate an error bound for this estimate. How many subdivisions of the baseline would be required so that the error incurred in using L_n would not exceed 2,500 square feet?

x	0	100	200	300	400	500
$h(x)$	0	183	235	245	260	286

x	600	700	800	900	1,000
$h(x)$	322	388	453	489	500

56. Refer to Problem 55. Use R_{10} to estimate the combined area of both parcels, and calculate an error bound for this estimate. How many subdivisions of the baseline would be required so that the error incurred in using R_n would not exceed 1,000 square feet?

30. Graph the two particular solutions found in Problem 29 in the slope field shown (or a copy).

31. Use a graphing calculator to graph, in the same viewing window, graphs of $y = Cx^2$ for $C = -2, -1, 1,$ and 2 for $-5 \le x \le 5$ and $-5 \le y \le 5$.

Find each integral in Problems 32–42.

32. $\int_{-1}^{1} \sqrt{1 + x}\, dx$

33. $\int_{-1}^{0} x^2(x^3 + 2)^{-2}\, dx$

34. $\int 5e^{-t}\, dt$

35. $\int_{1}^{e} \frac{1 + t^2}{t}\, dt$

36. $\int xe^{3x^2}\, dx$

37. $\int_{-3}^{1} \frac{1}{\sqrt{2 - x}}\, dx$

38. $\int_{0}^{3} \frac{x}{1 + x^2}\, dx$

39. $\int_{0}^{3} \frac{x}{(1 + x^2)^2}\, dx$

40. $\int x^3(2x^4 + 5)^5\, dx$

41. $\int \frac{e^{-x}}{e^{-x} + 3}\, dx$

42. $\int \frac{e^x}{(e^x + 2)^2}\, dx$

43. Find a function $y = f(x)$ that satisfies both conditions:

$$\frac{dy}{dx} = 3x^{-1} - x^{-2} \qquad f(1) = 5$$

44. Find the equation of the curve that passes through $(2, 10)$ if its slope is given by

$$\frac{dy}{dx} = 6x + 1$$

for each x.

45. (A) Find the average value of $f(x) = 3\sqrt{x}$ over the interval $[1, 9]$.

(B) Graph $f(x) = 3\sqrt{x}$ and its average over the interval $[1, 9]$ in the same coordinate system.

C

Find each integral in Problems 46–50.

46. $\int \frac{(\ln x)^2}{x}\, dx$

47. $\int x(x^3 - 1)^2\, dx$

48. $\int \frac{x}{\sqrt{6 - x}}\, dx$

49. $\int_{0}^{7} x\sqrt{16 - x}\, dx$

50. $\int_{1}^{1} (x + 1)^9\, dx$

51. Find a function $y = f(x)$ that satisfies both conditions:

$$\frac{dy}{dx} = 9x^2 e^{x^3} \qquad f(0) = 2$$

52. Solve the differential equation

$$\frac{dN}{dt} = 0.06N \qquad N(0) = 800 \qquad N > 0$$

Graph Problems 53–56 on a graphing calculator, and identify each curve as unlimited growth, exponential decay, limited growth, or logistic growth:

53. $N = 50(1 - e^{-0.07t}); 0 \le t \le 80, 0 \le N \le 60$

54. $p = 500e^{-0.03x}; 0 \le x \le 100, 0 \le p \le 500$

55. $A = 200e^{0.08t}; 0 \le t \le 20, 0 \le A \le 1,000$

56. $N = \dfrac{100}{1 + 9e^{-0.3t}}; 0 \le t \le 25, 0 \le N \le 100$

Use a numerical integration routine to evaluate each definite integral in Problems 57–59 (to three decimal places).

57. $\int_{-0.5}^{0.6} \frac{1}{\sqrt{1 - x^2}}\, dx$

58. $\int_{-2}^{3} x^2 e^x\, dx$

59. $\int_{0.5}^{2.5} \frac{\ln x}{x^2}\, dx$

Applications

60. Cost. A company manufactures downhill skis. The research department produced the marginal cost graph shown in the accompanying figure, where $C'(x)$ is in dollars and x is the number of pairs of skis produced per week. Estimate the increase in cost going from a production level of 200 to 600 pairs of skis per week. Use left and right sums over two equal subintervals. Replace the question marks with the values of L_2 and R_2 as appropriate:

$$? \le \int_{200}^{600} C'(x)\, dx \le ?$$

Figure for 60

61. Cost. Assuming that the marginal cost function in Problem 60 is linear, find its equation and write a definite integral that represents the increase in costs going from a production level of 200 to 600 pairs of skis per week. Evaluate the definite integral.

62. Profit and production. The weekly marginal profit for an output of x units is given approximately by

$$P'(x) = 150 - \frac{x}{10} \qquad 0 \le x \le 40$$

What is the total change in profit for a change in production from 10 units per week to 40 units? Set up a definite integral and evaluate it.

63. Profit function. If the marginal profit for producing x units per day is given by

$$P'(x) = 100 - 0.02x \qquad P(0) = 0$$

where $P(x)$ is the profit in dollars, find the profit function P and the profit on 10 units of production per day.

64. Resource depletion. An oil well starts out producing oil at the rate of 60,000 barrels of oil per year, but the production rate is expected to decrease by 4,000 barrels per year. Thus, if $P(t)$ is the total production (in thousands of barrels) in t years, then

$$P'(t) = f(t) = 60 - 4t \qquad 0 \le t \le 15$$

Write a definite integral that will give the total production after 15 years of operation, and evaluate the integral.

65. Inventory. Suppose that the inventory of a certain item t months after the first of the year is given approximately by

$$I(t) = 10 + 36t - 3t^2 \qquad 0 \le t \le 12$$

What is the average inventory for the second quarter of the year?

66. Price–supply. Given the price–supply function

$$p = S(x) = 8(e^{0.05x} - 1)$$

find the average price (in dollars) over the supply interval [40, 50].

67. Useful life. The total accumulated costs C(t) and revenues $R(t)$ (in thousands of dollars), respectively, for a coal mine satisfy

$$C'(t) = 3 \qquad \text{and} \qquad R'(t) = 20e^{-0.1t}$$

where t is the number of years that the mine has been in operation. Find the useful life of the mine, to the nearest year. What is the total profit accumulated during the useful life of the mine?

68. Marketing. The market research department for an automobile company estimates that sales (in millions of dollars) of a new electric car will increase at the monthly rate of

$$S'(t) = 4e^{-0.08t} \qquad 0 \le t \le 24$$

t months after the introduction of the car. What will be the total sales $S(t)$ t months after the car is introduced if we assume that there were 0 sales at the time the car entered the marketplace? What are the estimated total sales during the first 12 months after the introduction of the car? How long will it take for the total sales to reach $40 million?

69. Wound healing. The area of a healing skin wound changes at a rate given approximately by

$$\frac{dA}{dt} = -5t^{-2} \qquad 1 \le t \le 5$$

where t is time in days and $A(1) = 5$ square centimeters. What will be the area of the wound in 5 days?

70. Pollution. An environmental protection agency estimates that the rate of seepage of toxic chemicals from a waste dump (in gallons per year) is given by

$$R(t) = \frac{1,000}{(1 + t)^2}$$

where t is the time in years since the discovery of the seepage. Find the total amount of toxic chemicals that seep from the dump during the first 4 years of its discovery.

71. Population. The population of Mexico was 111 million in 2009 and was growing at a rate of 1.13% per year, compounded continuously.

(A) Assuming that the population continues to grow at this rate, estimate the population of Mexico in the year 2025.

(B) At the growth rate indicated, how long will it take the population of Mexico to double?

72. Archaeology. The continuous compound rate of decay for carbon-14 is $r = -0.000\,123\,8$. A piece of animal bone found at an archaeological site contains 4% of the original amount of carbon-14. Estimate the age of the bone.

73. Learning. An average student enrolled in a typing class progressed at a rate of $N'(t) = 7e^{-0.1t}$ words per minute t weeks after enrolling in a 15-week course. If a student could type 25 words per minute at the beginning of the course, how many words per minute $N(t)$ would the student be expected to type t weeks into the course? After completing the course?

Additional Integration Topics

14

Introduction

In Chapter 14 we explore additional applications and techniques of integration. We use the integral to find probabilities and to calculate several quantities that are important in business and economics: the total income and future value produced by a continuous income stream, consumers' and producers' surplus, and the Gini index of income concentration. The Gini index is a single number that measures the equality of a country's income distribution (see Problems 87 and 88, for example, in Section 14-1).

14-1 Area Between Curves

- Area Between Two Curves
- Application: Income Distribution

In Chapter 13, we found that the definite integral $\int_a^b f(x)\, dx$ represents the sum of the signed areas between the graph of $y = f(x)$ and the x axis from $x = a$ to $x = b$, where the areas above the x axis are counted positively and the areas below the x axis are counted negatively (see Fig. 1). In this section, we are interested in using the definite integral to find the actual area between a curve and the x axis or the actual area between two curves. These areas are always nonnegative quantities—**area measure is never negative**.

Area Between Two Curves

Consider the area bounded by $y = f(x)$ and $y = g(x)$, where $f(x) \geq g(x) \geq 0$, for $a \leq x \leq b$, as shown in Figure 2.

$$\begin{pmatrix} \text{Area } A \text{ between} \\ f(x) \text{ and } g(x) \end{pmatrix} = \begin{pmatrix} \text{area} \\ \text{under } f(x) \end{pmatrix} - \begin{pmatrix} \text{area} \\ \text{under } g(x) \end{pmatrix} \quad \text{Areas are from } x = a \text{ to } x = b \text{ above the } x \text{ axis.}$$

$$= \int_a^b f(x)\, dx - \int_a^b g(x)\, dx \quad \text{Use definite integral property 4 (Section 13-4).}$$

$$= \int_a^b [f(x) - g(x)]\, dx$$

It can be shown that the preceding result does not require $f(x)$ or $g(x)$ to remain positive over the interval $[a, b]$. A more general result is stated in the following box:

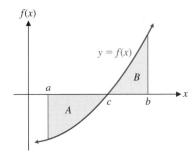

Figure 1 $\int_a^b f(x)\, dx = -A + B$

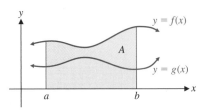

Figure 2

THEOREM 1 Area Between Two Curves

If f and g are continuous and $f(x) \geq g(x)$ over the interval $[a, b]$, then the area bounded by $y = f(x)$ and $y = g(x)$ for $a \leq x \leq b$ is given exactly by

$$A = \int_a^b [f(x) - g(x)]\, dx$$

CONCEPTUAL INSIGHT

Theorem 1 requires the graph of f to be *above* (or equal to) the graph of g throughout $[a, b]$, but f and g can be either positive, negative, or 0. In Section 13-4, we considered the special cases of Theorem 1 in which (1) f is positive and g is the zero function on $[a, b]$; and (2) f is the zero function and g is negative on $[a, b]$:

Special case 1. If f is continuous and positive over $[a, b]$, then the area bounded by the graph of f and the x axis for $a \leq x \leq b$ is given exactly by

$$\int_a^b f(x)\, dx$$

Special case 2. If g is continuous and negative over $[a, b]$, then the area bounded by the graph of g and the x axis for $a \leq x \leq b$ is given exactly by

$$\int_a^b -g(x)\, dx$$

EXAMPLE 1 **Area Between a Curve and the x Axis** Find the area bounded by $f(x) = 6x - x^2$ and $y = 0$ for $1 \le x \le 4$.

SOLUTION We sketch a graph of the region first (Fig. 3). The solution of every area problem should begin with a sketch. Since $f(x) \ge 0$ on $[1, 4]$,

$$A = \int_1^4 (6x - x^2)\, dx = \left(3x^2 - \frac{x^3}{3}\right)\Big|_1^4$$

$$= \left[3(4)^2 - \frac{(4)^3}{3}\right] - \left[3(1)^2 - \frac{(1)^3}{3}\right]$$

$$= 48 - \frac{64}{3} - 3 + \frac{1}{3}$$

$$= 48 - 21 - 3$$

$$= 24$$

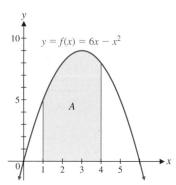

Figure 3

Matched Problem 1 Find the area bounded by $f(x) = x^2 + 1$ and $y = 0$ for $-1 \le x \le 3$.

EXAMPLE 2 **Area Between a Curve and the x Axis** Find the area between the graph of $f(x) = x^2 - 2x$ and the x axis over the indicated intervals:

(A) $[1, 2]$ (B) $[-1, 1]$

SOLUTION We begin by sketching the graph of f, as shown in Figure 4.

(A) From the graph, we see that $f(x) \le 0$ for $1 \le x \le 2$, so we integrate $-f(x)$:

$$A_1 = \int_1^2 [-f(x)]\, dx$$

$$= \int_1^2 (2x - x^2)\, dx$$

$$= \left(x^2 - \frac{x^3}{3}\right)\Big|_1^2$$

$$= \left[(2)^2 - \frac{(2)^3}{3}\right] - \left[(1)^2 - \frac{(1)^3}{3}\right]$$

$$= 4 - \frac{8}{3} - 1 + \frac{1}{3} \quad = \frac{2}{3} \approx 0.667$$

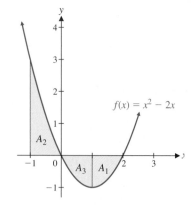

Figure 4

(B) Since the graph shows that $f(x) \ge 0$ on $[-1, 0]$ and $f(x) \le 0$ on $[0, 1]$, the computation of this area will require two integrals:

$$A = A_2 + A_3$$

$$= \int_{-1}^0 f(x)\, dx + \int_0^1 [-f(x)]\, dx$$

$$= \int_{-1}^0 (x^2 - 2x)\, dx + \int_0^1 (2x - x^2)\, dx$$

$$= \left(\frac{x^3}{3} - x^2\right)\Big|_{-1}^0 + \left(x^2 - \frac{x^3}{3}\right)\Big|_0^1$$

$$= \frac{4}{3} + \frac{2}{3} \quad = 2$$

Matched Problem 2   Find the area between the graph of $f(x) = x^2 - 9$ and the x axis over the indicated intervals:

(A) $[0, 2]$ (B) $[2, 4]$

EXAMPLE 3   **Area Between Two Curves** Find the area bounded by the graphs of $f(x) = \frac{1}{2}x + 3$, $g(x) = -x^2 + 1$, $x = -2$, and $x = 1$.

SOLUTION   We first sketch the area (Fig. 5) and then set up and evaluate an appropriate definite integral. We observe from the graph that $f(x) \geq g(x)$ for $-2 \leq x \leq 1$, so

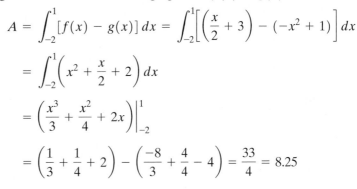

$$A = \int_{-2}^{1} [f(x) - g(x)]\, dx = \int_{-2}^{1}\left[\left(\frac{x}{2} + 3\right) - (-x^2 + 1)\right] dx$$

$$= \int_{-2}^{1}\left(x^2 + \frac{x}{2} + 2\right) dx$$

$$= \left(\frac{x^3}{3} + \frac{x^2}{4} + 2x\right)\Big|_{-2}^{1}$$

$$= \left(\frac{1}{3} + \frac{1}{4} + 2\right) - \left(\frac{-8}{3} + \frac{4}{4} - 4\right) = \frac{33}{4} = 8.25$$

Figure 5

Matched Problem 3   Find the area bounded by $f(x) = x^2 - 1$, $g(x) = -\frac{1}{2}x - 3$, $x = -1$, and $x = 2$.

EXAMPLE 4   **Area Between Two Curves** Find the area bounded by $f(x) = 5 - x^2$ and $g(x) = 2 - 2x$.

SOLUTION   First, graph f and g on the same coordinate system, as shown in Figure 6. Since the statement of the problem does not include any limits on the values of x, we must determine the appropriate values from the graph. The graph of f is a parabola and the graph of g is a line. The area bounded by these two graphs extends from the intersection point on the left to the intersection point on the right. To find these intersection points, we solve the equation $f(x) = g(x)$ for x:

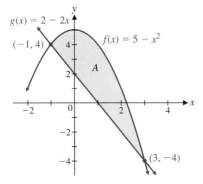

$$f(x) = g(x)$$

$$5 - x^2 = 2 - 2x$$

$$x^2 - 2x - 3 = 0$$

$$x = -1, 3$$

You should check these values in the original equations. (Note that the area between the graphs for $x < -1$ is unbounded on the left, and the area between the graphs for $x > 3$ is unbounded on the right.) Figure 6 shows that $f(x) \geq g(x)$ over the interval $[-1, 3]$, so we have

Figure 6

$$A = \int_{-1}^{3} [f(x) - g(x)]\, dx = \int_{-1}^{3} [5 - x^2 - (2 - 2x)]\, dx$$

$$= \int_{-1}^{3} (3 + 2x - x^2)\, dx$$

$$= \left(3x + x^2 - \frac{x^3}{3}\right)\Big|_{-1}^{3}$$

$$= \left[3(3) + (3)^2 - \frac{(3)^3}{3}\right] - \left[3(-1) + (-1)^2 - \frac{(-1)^3}{3}\right] = \frac{32}{3} \approx 10.667$$

Matched Problem 4   Find the area bounded by $f(x) = 6 - x^2$ and $g(x) = x$.

EXAMPLE 5   **Area Between Two Curves** Find the area bounded by $f(x) = x^2 - x$ and $g(x) = 2x$ for $-2 \le x \le 3$.

SOLUTION   The graphs of f and g are shown in Figure 7. Examining the graph, we see that $f(x) \ge g(x)$ on the interval $[-2, 0]$, but $g(x) \ge f(x)$ on the interval $[0, 3]$. Thus, two integrals are required to compute this area:

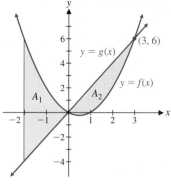

Figure 7

$$A_1 = \int_{-2}^{0} [f(x) - g(x)] \, dx \quad f(x) \ge g(x) \text{ on } [-2, 0]$$

$$= \int_{-2}^{0} [x^2 - x - 2x] \, dx$$

$$= \int_{-2}^{0} (x^2 - 3x) \, dx$$

$$= \left(\frac{x^3}{3} - \frac{3}{2}x^2 \right) \Big|_{-2}^{0}$$

$$= (0) - \left[\frac{(-2)^3}{3} - \frac{3}{2}(-2)^2 \right] = \frac{26}{3} \approx 8.667$$

$$A_2 = \int_{0}^{3} [g(x) - f(x)] \, dx \quad g(x) \ge f(x) \text{ on } [0, 3]$$

$$= \int_{0}^{3} [2x - (x^2 - x)] \, dx$$

$$= \int_{0}^{3} (3x - x^2) \, dx$$

$$= \left(\frac{3}{2}x^2 - \frac{x^3}{3} \right) \Big|_{0}^{3}$$

$$= \left[\frac{3}{2}(3)^2 - \frac{(3)^3}{3} \right] - (0) = \frac{9}{2} = 4.5$$

The total area between the two graphs is

$$A = A_1 + A_2 = \tfrac{26}{3} + \tfrac{9}{2} = \tfrac{79}{6} \approx 13.167$$

Matched Problem 5   Find the area bounded by $f(x) = 2x^2$ and $g(x) = 4 - 2x$ for $-2 \le x \le 2$.

EXAMPLE 6   **Computing Areas with a Numerical Integration Routine** Find the area (to three decimal places) bounded by $f(x) = e^{-x^2}$ and $g(x) = x^2 - 1$.

SOLUTION   First, we use a graphing calculator to graph the functions f and g and find their intersection points (see Fig. 8A). We see that the graph of f is bell shaped and the graph of g is a parabola. We note that $f(x) \ge g(x)$ on the interval $[-1.131, 1.131]$ and compute the area A by a numerical integration routine (see Fig. 8B):

$$A = \int_{-1.131}^{1.131} \left[e^{-x^2} - (x^2 - 1) \right] \, dx = 2.876$$

Figure 8

Matched Problem 6 Find the area (to three decimal places) bounded by the graphs of $f(x) = x^2 \ln x$ and $g(x) = 3x - 3$.

Application: Income Distribution

The U.S. Census Bureau compiles and analyzes a great deal of data having to do with the distribution of income among families in the United States. For 2006, the Bureau reported that the lowest 20% of families received 3% of all family income and the top 20% received 50%. Table 1 and Figure 9 give a detailed picture of the distribution of family income in 2006.

The graph of $y = f(x)$ in Figure 9 is called a **Lorenz curve** and is generally found by using *regression analysis,* a technique for fitting a function to a data set over a given interval. The variable **x represents the cumulative percentage of families at or below a given income level,** and **y represents the cumulative percentage of total family income received.** For example, data point (0.40, 0.12) in Table 1 indicates that the bottom 40% of families (those with incomes under $38,000) received 12% of the total income for all families in 2006, data point (0.60, 0.27) indicates that the bottom 60% of families received 27% of the total income for all families that year, and so on.

Table 1	Family Income Distribution in the United States, 2006	
Income Level	**x**	**y**
Under $20,000	0.20	0.03
Under $38,000	0.40	0.12
Under $60,000	0.60	0.27
Under $97,000	0.80	0.49

Source: U.S. Census Bureau

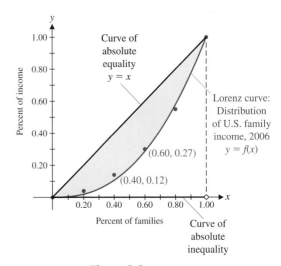

Figure 9 Lorenz curve

Absolute equality of income would occur if the area between the Lorenz curve and $y = x$ were 0. In this case, the Lorenz curve would be $y = x$ and all families would receive equal shares of the total income. That is, 5% of the families would receive 5% of the income, 20% of the families would receive 20% of the income, 65% of the families would receive 65% of the income, and so on. The maximum possible area between a Lorenz curve and $y = x$ is $\frac{1}{2}$, the area of the triangle below $y = x$. In this case, we would have **absolute inequality**: All the income would be in the hands of one family and the rest would have none. In actuality, Lorenz curves lie between these two extremes. But as the shaded area increases, the greater is the inequality of income distribution.

We use a single number, the **Gini index** [named after the Italian sociologist Corrado Gini (1884–1965)], to measure income concentration. The Gini index is the ratio of two areas: the area between $y = x$ and the Lorenz curve, and the area between $y = x$ and the x axis, from $x = 0$ to $x = 1$. The first area equals $\int_0^1 [x - f(x)]\, dx$ and the second (triangular) area equals $\frac{1}{2}$, giving the following definition:

DEFINITION Gini Index of Income Concentration

If $y = f(x)$ is the equation of a Lorenz curve, then

$$\textbf{Gini index} = 2 \int_0^1 [x - f(x)]\, dx$$

The Gini index is always a number between 0 and 1:

A Gini index of 0 indicates absolute equality—all people share equally in the income. A Gini index of 1 indicates absolute inequality—one person has all the income and the rest have none.

The closer the index is to 0, the closer the income is to being equally distributed. The closer the index is to 1, the closer the income is to being concentrated in a few hands. The Gini index of income concentration is used to compare income distributions at various points in time, between different groups of people, before and after taxes are paid, between different countries, and so on.

EXAMPLE 7 **Distribution of Income** The Lorenz curve for the distribution of income in a certain country in 2010 is given by $f(x) = x^{2.6}$. Economists predict that the Lorenz curve for the country in the year 2025 will be given by $g(x) = x^{1.8}$. Find the Gini index of income concentration for each curve, and interpret the results.

SOLUTION The Lorenz curves are shown in Figure 10.

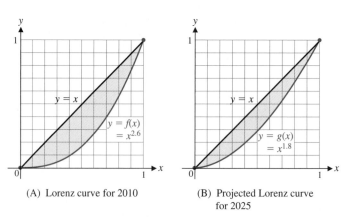

(A) Lorenz curve for 2010

(B) Projected Lorenz curve for 2025

Figure 10

The Gini index in 2010 is (see Fig. 10A)

$$2 \int_0^1 [x - f(x)]\, dx = 2 \int_0^1 [x - x^{2.6}]\, dx = 2 \left(\frac{1}{2} x^2 - \frac{1}{3.6} x^{3.6} \right) \Big|_0^1$$

$$= 2 \left(\frac{1}{2} - \frac{1}{3.6} \right) \approx 0.444$$

The projected Gini index in 2025 is (see Fig. 10B)

$$2 \int_0^1 [x - g(x)]\, dx = 2 \int_0^1 [x - x^{1.8}]\, dx = 2\left(\frac{1}{2}x^2 - \frac{1}{2.8}x^{2.8}\right)\Bigg|_0^1$$

$$= 2\left(\frac{1}{2} - \frac{1}{2.8}\right) \approx 0.286$$

If this projection is correct, the Gini index will decrease, and income will be more equally distributed in the year 2025 than in 2010.

Matched Problem 7   Repeat Example 7 if the projected Lorenz curve in the year 2025 is given by $g(x) = x^{3.8}$.

EXPLORE & DISCUSS 1   Do you agree or disagree with each of the following statements (explain your answers by referring to the data in Table 2):

(A) In countries with a low Gini index, there is little incentive for individuals to strive for success, and therefore productivity is low.

(B) In countries with a high Gini index, it is almost impossible to rise out of poverty, and therefore productivity is low.

Table 2

Country	Gini Index	Per Capita Gross Domestic Product
Brazil	0.57	$8,402
China	0.47	6,757
France	0.33	30,386
Germany	0.28	29,461
Japan	0.25	31,267
Jordan	0.39	5,530
Mexico	0.46	10,751
Russia	0.40	10,845
Sweden	0.25	32,525
United States	0.41	41,890

Source: The World Bank

Exercises 14-1

A

Problems 1–6 refer to Figures A–D on page 766. Set up definite integrals in Problems 1–4 that represent the indicated shaded area.

1. Shaded area in Figure B

2. Shaded area in Figure A

3. Shaded area in Figure C

4. Shaded area in Figure D

5. Explain why $\int_a^b h(x)\, dx$ does not represent the area between the graph of $y = h(x)$ and the x axis from $x = a$ to $x = b$ in Figure C.

6. Explain why $\int_a^b [-h(x)]\, dx$ represents the area between the graph of $y = h(x)$ and the x axis from $x = a$ to $x = b$ in Figure C.

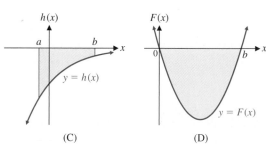

Figures for 1–6

24. $y = 3x + 6; y = \frac{1}{2}x + 1; 8 \leq x \leq 10$

25. $y = -4x + 1; y = \frac{3}{2}x + 1; 0 \leq x \leq 4$

26. $y = -2x - 3; y = x - 3; 0 \leq x \leq 20$

Problems 27–36 refer to Figures A and B. Set up definite integrals in Problems 27–34 that represent the indicated shaded areas over the given intervals.

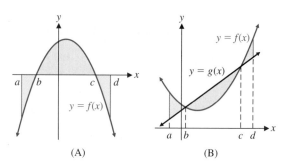

Figures for 27–34

In Problems 7–20, find the area bounded by the graphs of the indicated equations over the given interval. Compute answers to three decimal places.

7. $y = x + 4; y = 0; 0 \leq x \leq 4$

8. $y = -x + 10; y = 0; -2 \leq x \leq 2$

9. $y = x^2 - 20; y = 0; -3 \leq x \leq 0$

10. $y = x^2 + 2; y = 0; 0 \leq x \leq 3$

11. $y = -x^2 + 10; y = 0; -3 \leq x \leq 3$

12. $y = -2x^2; y = 0; -6 \leq x \leq 0$

13. $y = x^3 + 1; y = 0; 0 \leq x \leq 2$

14. $y = -x^3 + 3; y = 0; -2 \leq x \leq 1$

15. $y = x(1 - x); y = 0; -1 \leq x \leq 0$

16. $y = -x(3 - x); y = 0; 1 \leq x \leq 2$

17. $y = -e^x; y = 0; -1 \leq x \leq 1$

18. $y = e^x; y = 0; 0 \leq x \leq 1$

19. $y = \frac{1}{x}; y = 0; 1 \leq x \leq e$

20. $y = -\frac{1}{x}; y = 0; -1 \leq x \leq -\frac{1}{e}$

B

In Problems 21–26, use a definite integral to find the area bounded by the graphs of the indicated equations over the given interval. Then check your answer by finding the area without using a definite integral. [Hint: Partition the region into triangles and/or rectangles].

21. $y = x; y = -2; 0 \leq x \leq 3$

22. $y = -x; y = 8; 0 \leq x \leq 5$

23. $y = 2x + 3; y = x - 1; 4 \leq x \leq 6$

27. Over interval $[a, b]$ in Figure A

28. Over interval $[c, d]$ in Figure A

29. Over interval $[b, d]$ in Figure A

30. Over interval $[a, c]$ in Figure A

31. Over interval $[c, d]$ in Figure B

32. Over interval $[a, b]$ in Figure B

33. Over interval $[a, c]$ in Figure B

34. Over interval $[b, d]$ in Figure B

35. Referring to Figure B, explain how you would use definite integrals and the functions f and g to find the area bounded by the two functions from $x = a$ to $x = d$.

36. Referring to Figure A, explain how you would use definite integrals to find the area between the graph of $y = f(x)$ and the x axis from $x = a$ to $x = d$.

In Problems 37–52, find the area bounded by the graphs of the indicated equations over the given intervals (when stated). Compute answers to three decimal places.

37. $y = -x; y = 0; -2 \leq x \leq 1$

38. $y = -x + 1; y = 0; -1 \leq x \leq 2$

39. $y = x^2 - 4; y = 0; 0 \leq x \leq 3$

40. $y = 4 - x^2; y = 0; 0 \leq x \leq 4$

41. $y = x^2 - 3x; y = 0; -2 \leq x \leq 2$

42. $y = -x^2 - 2x; y = 0; -2 \leq x \leq 1$

43. $y = -2x + 8; y = 12; -1 \leq x \leq 2$

44. $y = 2x + 6; y = 3; -1 \leq x \leq 2$

45. $y = 3x^2; y = 12$

46. $y = x^2; y = 9$

47. $y = 4 - x^2; y = -5$

48. $y = x^2 - 1; y = 3$

49. $y = x^2 + 1; y = 2x - 2; -1 \le x \le 2$

50. $y = x^2 - 1; y = x - 2; -2 \le x \le 1$

51. $y = e^{0.5x}; y = -\dfrac{1}{x}; 1 \le x \le 2$

52. $y = \dfrac{1}{x}; y = -e^x; 0.5 \le x \le 1$

In Problems 53–58, set up a definite integral that represents the area bounded by the graphs of the indicated equations over the given interval. Find the areas to three decimal places. [Hint: A circle of radius r, with center at the origin, has equation $x^2 + y^2 = r^2$ and area πr^2].

53. $y = \sqrt{9 - x^2}; y = 0; -3 \le x \le 3$

54. $y = \sqrt{25 - x^2}; y = 0; -5 \le x \le 5$

55. $y = -\sqrt{16 - x^2}; y = 0; 0 \le x \le 4$

56. $y = -\sqrt{36 - x^2}; y = 0; -6 \le x \le 0$

57. $y = -\sqrt{4 - x^2}; y = \sqrt{4 - x^2}; -2 \le x \le 2$

58. $y = -\sqrt{100 - x^2}; y = \sqrt{100 - x^2}; -10 \le x \le 10$

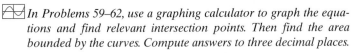 *In Problems 59–62, use a graphing calculator to graph the equations and find relevant intersection points. Then find the area bounded by the curves. Compute answers to three decimal places.*

59. $y = 3 - 5x - 2x^2; y = 2x^2 + 3x - 2$

60. $y = 3 - 2x^2; y = 2x^2 - 4x$

61. $y = -0.5x + 2.25; y = \dfrac{1}{x}$

62. $y = x - 4.25; y = -\dfrac{1}{x}$

C

In Problems 63–68, find the area bounded by the graphs of the indicated equations over the given intervals (when stated). Compute answers to three decimal places.

63. $y = e^x; y = e^{-x}; 0 \le x \le 4$

64. $y = e^x; y = -e^{-x}; 1 \le x \le 2$

65. $y = x^3; y = 4x$

66. $y = x^3 + 1; y = x + 1$

67. $y = x^3 - 3x^2 - 9x + 12; y = x + 12$

68. $y = x^3 - 6x^2 + 9x; y = x$

In Problems 69–74, use a graphing calculator to graph the equations and find relevant intersection points. Then find the area bounded by the curves. Compute answers to three decimal places.

69. $y = x^3 - x^2 + 2; y = -x^3 + 8x - 2$

70. $y = 2x^3 + 2x^2 - x; y = -2x^3 - 2x^2 + 2x$

71. $y = e^{-x}; y = 3 - 2x$

72. $y = 2 - (x + 1)^2; y = e^{x+1}$

73. $y = e^x; y = 5x - x^3$

74. $y = 2 - e^x; y = x^3 + 3x^2$

In Problems 75–78, use a numerical integration routine on a graphing calculator to find the area bounded by the graphs of the indicated equations over the given interval (when stated). Compute answers to three decimal places.

75. $y = e^{-x}; y = \sqrt{\ln x}; 2 \le x \le 5$

76. $y = x^2 + 3x + 1; y = e^{e^x}; -3 \le x \le 0$

77. $y = e^{x^2}; y = x + 2$

78. $y = \ln(\ln x); y = 0.01x$

Applications

In the applications that follow, it is helpful to sketch graphs to get a clearer understanding of each problem and to interpret results. A graphing calculator will prove useful if you have one, but it is not necessary.

79. Oil production. Using production and geological data, the management of an oil company estimates that oil will be pumped from a producing field at a rate given by

$$R(t) = \frac{100}{t + 10} + 10 \qquad 0 \le t \le 15$$

where $R(t)$ is the rate of production (in thousands of barrels per year) t years after pumping begins. Find the area between the graph of R and the t axis over the interval [5, 10] and interpret the results.

80. Oil production. In Problem 79, if the rate is found to be

$$R(t) = \frac{100t}{t^2 + 25} + 4 \qquad 0 \le t \le 25$$

then find the area between the graph of R and the t axis over the interval [5, 15] and interpret the results.

81. Useful life. An amusement company maintains records for each video game it installs in an arcade. Suppose that $C(t)$ and $R(t)$ represent the total accumulated costs and revenues (in thousands of dollars), respectively, t years after a particular game has been installed. If

$$C'(t) = 2 \quad \text{and} \quad R'(t) = 9e^{-0.3t}$$

then find the area between the graphs of C' and R' over the interval on the t axis from 0 to the useful life of the game and interpret the results.

82. Useful life. Repeat Problem 81 if

$$C'(t) = 2t \quad \text{and} \quad R'(t) = 5te^{-0.1t^2}$$

83. Income distribution. In a study on the effects of World War II on the U.S. economy, an economist used data from the U.S. Census Bureau to produce the following Lorenz curves for the distribution of U.S. income in 1935 and in 1947:

$$f(x) = x^{2.4} \quad \text{Lorenz curve for 1935}$$

$$g(x) = x^{1.6} \quad \text{Lorenz curve for 1947}$$

Find the Gini index of income concentration for each Lorenz curve and interpret the results.

84. Income distribution. Using data from the U.S. Census Bureau, an economist produced the following Lorenz curves for the distribution of U.S. income in 1962 and in 1972:

$$f(x) = \tfrac{3}{10}x + \tfrac{7}{10}x^2 \quad \text{Lorenz curve for 1962}$$
$$g(x) = \tfrac{1}{2}x + \tfrac{1}{2}x^2 \quad \text{Lorenz curve for 1972}$$

Find the Gini index of income concentration for each Lorenz curve and interpret the results.

85. Distribution of wealth. Lorenz curves also can provide a relative measure of the distribution of a country's total assets. Using data in a report by the U.S. Congressional Joint Economic Committee, an economist produced the following Lorenz curves for the distribution of total U.S. assets in 1963 and in 1983:

$$f(x) = x^{10} \quad \text{Lorenz curve for 1963}$$
$$g(x) = x^{12} \quad \text{Lorenz curve for 1983}$$

Find the Gini index of income concentration for each Lorenz curve and interpret the results.

86. Income distribution. The government of a small country is planning sweeping changes in the tax structure in order to provide a more equitable distribution of income. The Lorenz curves for the current income distribution and for the projected income distribution after enactment of the tax changes are as follows:

$$f(x) = x^{2.3} \qquad \text{Current Lorenz curve}$$
$$g(x) = 0.4x + 0.6x^2 \qquad \text{Projected Lorenz curve after changes in tax laws}$$

Find the Gini index of income concentration for each Lorenz curve. Will the proposed changes provide a more equitable income distribution? Explain.

87. Distribution of wealth. The data in the following table describe the distribution of wealth in a country:

x	0	0.20	0.40	0.60	0.80	1
y	0	0.12	0.31	0.54	0.78	1

(A) Use quadratic regression to find the equation of a Lorenz curve for the data.

(B) Use the regression equation and a numerical integration routine to approximate the Gini index of income concentration.

88. Distribution of wealth. Refer to Problem 87.

(A) Use cubic regression to find the equation of a Lorenz curve for the data.

(B) Use the cubic regression equation you found in Part (A) and a numerical integration routine to approximate the Gini index of income concentration.

89. Biology. A yeast culture is growing at a rate of $W'(t) = 0.3e^{0.1t}$ grams per hour. Find the area between the graph of W' and the t axis over the interval $[0, 10]$ and interpret the results.

90. Natural resource depletion. The instantaneous rate of change in demand for U.S. lumber since 1970 ($t = 0$), in billions of cubic feet per year, is given by

$$Q'(t) = 12 + 0.006t^2 \qquad 0 \le t \le 50$$

Find the area between the graph of Q' and the t axis over the interval $[15, 20]$, and interpret the results.

91. Learning. A college language class was chosen for a learning experiment. Using a list of 50 words, the experiment measured the rate of vocabulary memorization at different times during a continuous 5-hour study session. The average rate of learning for the entire class was inversely proportional to the time spent studying and was given approximately by

$$V'(t) = \frac{15}{t} \qquad 1 \le t \le 5$$

Find the area between the graph of V' and the t axis over the interval $[2, 4]$, and interpret the results.

92. Learning. Repeat Problem 91 if $V'(t) = 13/t^{1/2}$ and the interval is changed to $[1, 4]$.

Answers to Matched Problems

1. $A = \int_{-1}^{3} (x^2 + 1)\, dx = \frac{40}{3} \approx 13.333$

2. (A) $A = \int_{0}^{2} (9 - x^2)\, dx = \frac{46}{3} \approx 15.333$

   (B) $A = \int_{2}^{3} (9 - x^2)\, dx + \int_{3}^{4} (x^2 - 9)\, dx = 6$

3. $A = \int_{-1}^{2} \left[(x^2 - 1) - \left(-\frac{x}{2} - 3\right) \right] dx = \frac{39}{4} = 9.75$

4. $A = \int_{-3}^{2} [(6 - x^2) - x]\, dx = \frac{125}{6} \approx 20.833$

5. $A = \int_{-2}^{1} [(4 - 2x) - 2x^2]\, dx + \int_{1}^{2} [2x^2 - (4 - 2x)]\, dx = \frac{38}{3} \approx 12.667$

6. 0.443

7. Gini index of income concentration ≈ 0.583; income will be less equally distributed in 2025.

14-2   Applications in Business and Economics

- Probability Density Functions
- Continuous Income Stream
- Future Value of a Continuous Income Stream
- Consumers' and Producers' Surplus

This section contains important applications of the definite integral to business and economics. Included are three independent topics: probability density functions, continuous income streams, and consumers' and producers' surplus. Any of the three may be covered in any order as time and interests dictate.

Probability Density Functions

We now take a brief, informal look at the use of the definite integral to determine probabilities. A more formal treatment of the subject requires the use of the special "improper" integral form $\int_{-\infty}^{\infty} f(x)\, dx$, which we will not discuss.

Suppose that an experiment is designed in such a way that any real number x on the interval $[c, d]$ is a possible outcome. For example, x may represent an IQ score, the height of a person in inches, or the life of a lightbulb in hours. Technically, we refer to x as a *continuous random variable*.

In certain situations, we can find a function f with x as an independent variable such that the function f can be used to determine the probability that the outcome x of an experiment will be in the interval $[c, d]$. Such a function, called a **probability density function**, must satisfy the following three conditions (see Fig. 1):

1. $f(x) \geq 0$ for all real x.

2. The area under the graph of $f(x)$ over the interval $(-\infty, \infty)$ is exactly 1.

3. If $[c, d]$ is a subinterval of $(-\infty, \infty)$, then

$$\text{Probability } (c \leq x \leq d) = \int_{c}^{d} f(x)\, dx$$

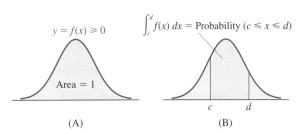

Figure 1 Probability density function

EXAMPLE 1   **Duration of Telephone Calls** Suppose that the length of telephone calls (in minutes) is a continuous random variable with the probability density function shown in Figure 2:

$$f(t) = \begin{cases} \frac{1}{4}e^{-t/4} & \text{if } t \geq 0 \\ 0 & \text{otherwise} \end{cases}$$

(A) Determine the probability that a call selected at random will last between 2 and 3 minutes.

(B) Find b (to two decimal places) so that the probability of a call selected at random lasting between 2 and b minutes is .5.

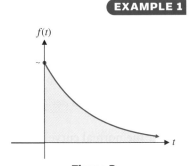

Figure 2

SOLUTION   (A) Probability $(2 \leq t \leq 3) = \displaystyle\int_{2}^{3} \frac{1}{4}e^{-t/4}\, dt$

$$= (-e^{-t/4})\big|_{2}^{3}$$

$$= -e^{-3/4} + e^{-1/2} \approx .13$$

Matched Problem 2   Referring to Example 2, find the total income produced (to the nearest dollar) during the second 5 years of operation.

In reality, income from a vending machine is not usually received as a single payment at the end of each year, even though the rate is given as a yearly rate. Income is usually collected on a daily or weekly basis. In problems of this type, it is convenient to assume that income is actually received in a **continuous stream**; that is, we assume that the rate at which income is received is a continuous function of time. The rate of change is called the **rate of flow** of the continuous income stream. In general, we have the following definition:

DEFINITION   Total Income for a Continuous Income Stream

If $f(t)$ is the rate of flow of a continuous income stream, then the **total income** produced during the period from $t = a$ to $t = b$ is

$$\text{Total income} = \int_a^b f(t)\,dt$$

Future Value of a Continuous Income Stream

In Section 11-1, we discussed the continuous compound interest formula

$$A = Pe^{rt}$$

where P is the principal (or present value), A is the amount (or future value), r is the annual rate of continuous compounding (expressed as a decimal), and t is time in years. For example, if money is worth 12% compounded continuously, then the future value of a $10,000 investment in 5 years is (to the nearest dollar)

$$A = 10,000e^{0.12(5)} = \$18,221$$

We want to apply the future value concept to the income produced by a continuous income stream. Suppose that $f(t)$ is the rate of flow of a continuous income stream, and the income produced by this continuous income stream is invested as soon as it is received at a rate r, compounded continuously. We already know how to find the total income produced after T years, but how can we find the total of the income produced and the interest earned by this income? Since the income is received in a continuous flow, we cannot just use the formula $A = Pe^{rt}$. This formula is valid only for a single deposit P, not for a continuous flow of income. Instead, we use a Riemann sum approach that will allow us to apply the formula $A = Pe^{rt}$ repeatedly. To begin, we divide the time interval $[0, T]$ into n equal subintervals of length Δt and choose an arbitrary point c_k in each subinterval, as shown in Figure 6.

The total income produced during the period from $t = t_{k-1}$ to $t = t_k$ is equal to the area under the graph of $f(t)$ over this subinterval and is approximately equal to $f(c_k)\,\Delta t$, the area of the shaded rectangle in Figure 6. The income received during this period will earn interest for approximately $T - c_k$ years. So, from the future-value formula $A = Pe^{rt}$ with $P = f(c_k)\,\Delta t$ and $t = T - c_k$, the future value of the income produced during the period from $t = t_{k-1}$ to $t = t_k$ is approximately equal to

$$f(c_k)\,\Delta t\,e^{(T - c_k)r}$$

The total of these approximate future values over n subintervals is then

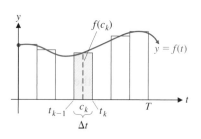

Figure 6

$$f(c_1) \, \Delta t \, e^{(T-c_1)r} + f(c_2) \, \Delta t \, e^{(T-c_2)r} + \cdots + f(c_n) \, \Delta t \, e^{(T-c_n)r} = \sum_{k=1}^{n} f(c_k) e^{r(T-c_k)} \, \Delta t$$

This equation has the form of a Riemann sum, the limit of which is a definite integral. (See the definition of the definite integral in Section 13-4.) Therefore, the *future value FV* of the income produced by the continuous income stream is given by

$$FV = \int_0^T f(t) e^{r(T-t)} \, dt$$

Since r and T are constants, we also can write

$$FV = \int_0^T f(t) e^{rT} e^{-rt} \, dt = e^{rT} \int_0^T f(t) e^{-rt} \, dt \qquad (1)$$

This last form is preferable, since the integral is usually easier to evaluate than the first form.

DEFINITION **Future Value of a Continuous Income Stream**

If $f(t)$ is the rate of flow of a continuous income stream, $0 \le t \le T$, and if the income is continuously invested at a rate r, compounded continuously, then the **future value FV** at the end of T years is given by

$$FV = \int_0^T f(t) e^{r(T-t)} \, dt = e^{rT} \int_0^T f(t) e^{-rt} \, dt$$

The future value of a continuous income stream is the total value of all money produced by the continuous income stream (income and interest) at the end of T years.

We return to the trust that your aunt set up for you. Suppose that the $2,000 per year you receive from the trust is invested as soon as it is received at 8%, compounded continuously. We consider the trust income to be a continuous income stream with a flow rate of $2,000 per year. What is its future value (to the nearest dollar) by the end of the 10th year? Using the definite integral for future value from the preceding box, we have

$$FV = e^{rT} \int_0^T f(t) e^{-rt} \, dt$$

$$FV = e^{0.08(10)} \int_0^{10} 2{,}000 e^{-0.08t} \, dt \qquad r = 0.08, \, T = 10, \, f(t) = 2{,}000$$

$$= 2{,}000 e^{0.8} \int_0^{10} e^{-0.08t} \, dt$$

$$= 2{,}000 e^{0.8} \left[\frac{e^{-0.08t}}{-0.08} \right]\Bigg|_0^{10}$$

$$= 2{,}000 e^{0.8} [-12.5 e^{-0.8} + 12.5] = \$30{,}639$$

At the end of 10 years, you will have received $30,639, including interest. How much is interest? Since you received $20,000 in income from the trust, the interest is the difference between the future value and income. So,

$$\$30{,}639 - \$20{,}000 = \$10{,}639$$

is the interest earned by the income received from the trust over the 10-year period.

EXAMPLE 3 **Future Value of a Continuous Income Stream** Using the continuous income rate of flow for the vending machine in Example 2, namely,

$$f(t) = 5,000e^{0.04t}$$

find the future value of this income stream at 12%, compounded continuously for 5 years, and find the total interest earned. Compute answers to the nearest dollar.

SOLUTION Using the formula

$$FV = e^{rT} \int_0^T f(t)e^{-rt} \, dt$$

with $r = 0.12$, $T = 5$, and $f(t) = 5,000e^{0.04t}$, we have

$$FV = e^{0.12(5)} \int_0^5 5,000e^{0.04t}e^{-0.12t} \, dt$$

$$= 5,000e^{0.6} \int_0^5 e^{-0.08t} \, dt$$

$$= 5,000e^{0.6} \left(\frac{e^{-0.08t}}{-0.08} \right) \Big|_0^5$$

$$= 5,000e^{0.6}(-12.5e^{-0.4} + 12.5)$$

$$= \$37,545 \quad \text{Rounded to the nearest dollar}$$

The future value of the income stream at 12% compounded continuously at the end of 5 years is $37,545.

In Example 2, we saw that the total income produced by this vending machine over a 5-year period was $27,675. The difference between future value and income is interest. So,

$$\$37,545 - \$27,675 = \$9,870$$

is the interest earned by the income produced by the vending machine during the 5-year period.

Matched Problem 3 Repeat Example 3 if the interest rate is 9%, compounded continuously.

Consumers' and Producers' Surplus

Let $p = D(x)$ be the price–demand equation for a product, where x is the number of units of the product that consumers will purchase at a price of $\$p$ per unit. Suppose that $\bar{p}$, is the current price and $\bar{x}$ is the number of units that can be sold at that price. Then the price–demand curve in Figure 7 shows that if the price is higher than $\bar{p}$, the demand x is less than $\bar{x}$, but some consumers are still willing to pay the higher price. Consumers who are willing to pay more than $\bar{p}$, but who are still able to buy the product at $\bar{p}$, have saved money. We want to determine the total amount saved by all the consumers who are willing to pay a price higher than $\bar{p}$ for the product.

To do this, consider the interval $[c_k, c_k + \Delta x]$, where $c_k + \Delta x < \bar{x}$. If the price remained constant over that interval, the savings on each unit would be the difference between $D(c_k)$, the price consumers are willing to pay, and $\bar{p}$, the price they actually pay. Since Δx represents the number of units purchased by consumers over the interval, the total savings to consumers over this interval is approximately equal to

$$[D(c_k) - \bar{p}] \, \Delta x \quad \text{(savings per unit)} \times \text{(number of units)}$$

Figure 7

which is the area of the shaded rectangle shown in Figure 7. If we divide the interval $[0, \overline{x}]$ into n equal subintervals, then the total savings to consumers is approximately equal to

$$[D(c_1) - \overline{p}] \Delta x + [D(c_2) - \overline{p}] \Delta x + \cdots + [D(c_n) - \overline{p}] \Delta x = \sum_{k=1}^{n} [D(c_k) - \overline{p}] \Delta x$$

which we recognize as a Riemann sum for the integral

$$\int_0^{\overline{x}} [D(x) - \overline{p}] \, dx$$

We define the *consumers' surplus* to be this integral.

DEFINITION Consumers' Surplus

If $(\overline{x}, \overline{p})$ is a point on the graph of the price–demand equation $p = D(x)$ for a particular product, then the **consumers' surplus CS** at a price level of $\overline{p}$ is

$$CS = \int_0^{\overline{x}} [D(x) - \overline{p}] \, dx$$

which is the area between $p = \overline{p}$ and $p = D(x)$ from $x = 0$ to $x = \overline{x}$, as shown in Figure 8.

The consumers' surplus represents the total savings to consumers who are willing to pay more than $\overline{p}$ for the product but are still able to buy the product for $\overline{p}$.

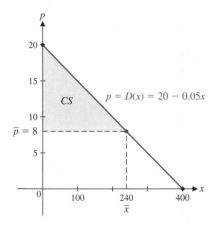

Figure 8

EXAMPLE 4 **Consumers' Surplus** Find the consumers' surplus at a price level of $8 for the price–demand equation

$$p = D(x) = 20 - 0.05x$$

SOLUTION **Step 1** Find $\overline{x}$, the demand when the price is $\overline{p} = 8$:

$$\overline{p} = 20 - 0.05\overline{x}$$
$$8 = 20 - 0.05\overline{x}$$
$$0.05\overline{x} = 12$$
$$\overline{x} = 240$$

Step 2 Sketch a graph, as shown in Figure 9.

Step 3 Find the consumers' surplus (the shaded area in the graph):

$$CS = \int_0^{\overline{x}} [D(x) - \overline{p}] \, dx$$
$$= \int_0^{240} (20 - 0.05x - 8) \, dx$$
$$= \int_0^{240} (12 - 0.05x) \, dx$$
$$= (12x - 0.025x^2)\big|_0^{240}$$
$$= 2{,}880 - 1{,}440 = \$1{,}440$$

The total savings to consumers who are willing to pay a higher price for the product is $1,440.

Figure 9

Matched Problem 4 Repeat Example 4 for a price level of $4.

If $p = S(x)$ is the price–supply equation for a product, $\overline{p}$ is the current price, and $\overline{x}$ is the current supply, then some suppliers are still willing to supply some units at a lower price than $\overline{p}$. The additional money that these suppliers gain from the higher price is called the *producers' surplus* and can be expressed in terms of a definite integral (proceeding as we did for the consumers' surplus).

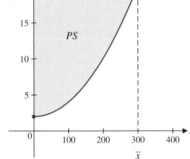

Figure 10

DEFINITION Producers' Surplus

If $(\overline{x}, \overline{p})$ is a point on the graph of the price–supply equation $p = S(x)$, then the **producers' surplus PS** at a price level of $\overline{p}$ is

$$PS = \int_0^{\overline{x}} [\overline{p} - S(x)] \, dx$$

which is the area between $p = \overline{p}$ and $p = S(x)$ from $x = 0$ to $x = \overline{x}$, as shown in Figure 10.

The producers' surplus represents the total gain to producers who are willing to supply units at a lower price than $\overline{p}$ but are still able to supply units at $\overline{p}$.

EXAMPLE 5   **Producers' Surplus** Find the producers' surplus at a price level of $20 for the price–supply equation

$$p = S(x) = 2 + 0.0002x^2$$

SOLUTION   **Step 1** Find $\overline{x}$, the supply when the price is $\overline{p} = 20$:

$$\overline{p} = 2 + 0.0002\overline{x}^2$$
$$20 = 2 + 0.0002\overline{x}^2$$
$$0.0002\overline{x}^2 = 18$$
$$\overline{x}^2 = 90{,}000$$
$$\overline{x} = 300 \qquad \textit{There is only one solution, since } \overline{x} \geq 0.$$

Step 2 Sketch a graph, as shown in Figure 11.

Step 3 Find the producers' surplus (the shaded area in the graph):

$$PS = \int_0^{\overline{x}} [\overline{p} - S(x)] \, dx = \int_0^{300} [20 - (2 + 0.0002x^2)] \, dx$$
$$= \int_0^{300} (18 - 0.0002x^2) \, dx = \left(18x - 0.0002\frac{x^3}{3} \right)\Big|_0^{300}$$
$$= 5{,}400 - 1{,}800 = \$3{,}600$$

The total gain to producers who are willing to supply units at a lower price is $3,600.

Figure 11

Matched Problem 5   Repeat Example 5 for a price level of $4.

In a free competitive market, the price of a product is determined by the relationship between supply and demand. If $p = D(x)$ and $p = S(x)$ are the price–demand and price–supply equations, respectively, for a product and if $(\overline{x}, \overline{p})$ is the point of intersection of these equations, then $\overline{p}$ is called the **equilibrium price** and $\overline{x}$ is called the **equilibrium quantity**. If the price stabilizes at the equilibrium price $\overline{p}$, then this is the price level that will determine both the consumers' surplus and the producers' surplus.

EXAMPLE 6   **Equilibrium Price and Consumers' and Producers' Surplus** Find the equilibrium price and then find the consumers' surplus and producers' surplus at the equilibrium price level, if

$$p = D(x) = 20 - 0.05x \qquad \text{and} \qquad p = S(x) = 2 + 0.0002x^2$$

SOLUTION   **Step 1** Find the equilibrium point. Set $D(x)$ equal to $S(x)$ and solve:

$$D(x) = S(x)$$
$$20 - 0.05x = 2 + 0.0002x^2$$
$$0.0002x^2 + 0.05x - 18 = 0$$
$$x^2 + 250x - 90{,}000 = 0$$
$$x = 200, \, -450$$

Since x cannot be negative, the only solution is $x = 200$. The equilibrium price can be determined by using $D(x)$ or $S(x)$. We will use both to check our work:

$$\overline{p} = D(200) \qquad\qquad \overline{p} = S(200)$$
$$= 20 - 0.05(200) = 10 \qquad = 2 + 0.0002(200)^2 = 10$$

The equilibrium price is $\overline{p} = 10$, and the equilibrium quantity is $\overline{x} = 200$.

Step 2 Sketch a graph, as shown in Figure 12.

Step 3 Find the consumers' surplus:

$$CS = \int_0^{\overline{x}} [D(x) - \overline{p}] \, dx = \int_0^{200} (20 - 0.05x - 10) \, dx$$

$$= \int_0^{200} (10 - 0.05x) \, dx$$

$$= (10x - 0.025x^2)\big|_0^{200}$$

$$= 2{,}000 - 1{,}000 = \$1{,}000$$

Step 4 Find the producers' surplus:

$$PS = \int_0^{\overline{x}} [\overline{p} - S(x)] \, dx$$

$$= \int_0^{200} [10 - (2 + 0.0002x^2)] \, dx$$

$$= \int_0^{200} (8 - 0.0002x^2) \, dx$$

$$= \left(8x - 0.0002\frac{x^3}{3}\right)\Big|_0^{200}$$

$$= 1{,}600 - \tfrac{1{,}600}{3} \approx \$1{,}067 \qquad\qquad \textit{Rounded to the nearest dollar}$$

Figure 12

(A)

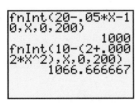

(B)

Figure 13

A graphing calculator offers an alternative approach to finding the equilibrium point for Example 6 (Fig. 13A). A numerical integration command can then be used to find the consumers' and producers' surplus (Fig. 13B).

Matched Problem 6   Repeat Example 6 for

$$p = D(x) = 25 - 0.001x^2 \qquad \text{and} \qquad p = S(x) = 5 + 0.1x$$

Exercises 14-2

A

In Problems 1–10, evaluate each definite integral to two decimal places.

1. $\int_0^1 e^{-2t} \, dt$

2. $\int_1^3 e^{-t} \, dt$

3. $\int_0^2 e^{4(2-t)} \, dt$

4. $\int_0^1 e^{3(1-t)} \, dt$

5. $\int_0^8 e^{0.06(8-t)} \, dt$

6. $\int_1^{10} e^{0.07(10-t)} \, dt$

7. $\int_0^{20} e^{0.08t} e^{0.12(20-t)} \, dt$

8. $\int_0^{15} e^{0.05t} e^{0.06(15-t)} \, dt$

9. $\int_0^{30} 500 \, e^{0.02t} e^{0.09(30-t)} \, dt$

10. $\int_0^{25} 900 \, e^{0.03t} e^{0.04(25-t)} \, dt$

B

In Problems 11 and 12, explain which of (A), (B), and (C) are equal before evaluating the expressions. Then evaluate each expression to two decimal places.

11. (A) $\int_0^8 e^{0.07(8-t)} \, dt$

(B) $\int_0^8 (e^{0.56} - e^{0.07t}) \, dt$

(C) $e^{0.56} \int_0^8 e^{-0.07t} \, dt$

12. (A) $\int_0^{10} 2,000 e^{0.05t} e^{0.12(10-t)} \, dt$

(B) $2,000 e^{1.2} \int_0^{10} e^{-0.07t} \, dt$

(C) $2,000 e^{0.05} \int_0^{10} e^{0.12(10-t)} \, dt$

Applications

Unless stated to the contrary, compute all monetary answers to the nearest dollar.

13. The life expectancy (in years) of a microwave oven is a continuous random variable with probability density function

$$f(x) = \begin{cases} 2/(x+2)^2 & \text{if } x \geq 0 \\ 0 & \text{otherwise} \end{cases}$$

(A) Find the probability that a randomly selected microwave oven lasts at most 6 years.

(B) Find the probability that a randomly selected microwave oven lasts from 6 to 12 years.

(C) Graph $y = f(x)$ for $[0, 12]$ and show the shaded region for part (A).

14. The shelf life (in years) of a laser pointer battery is a continuous random variable with probability density function

$$f(x) = \begin{cases} 1/(x+1)^2 & \text{if } x \geq 0 \\ 0 & \text{otherwise} \end{cases}$$

(A) Find the probability that a randomly selected laser pointer battery has a shelf life of 3 years or less.

(B) Find the probability that a randomly selected laser pointer battery has a shelf life of from 3 to 9 years.

(C) Graph $y = f(x)$ for $[0, 10]$ and show the shaded region for part (A).

15. In Problem 13, find d so that the probability of a randomly selected microwave oven lasting d years or less is .8.

16. In Problem 14, find d so that the probability of a randomly selected laser pointer battery lasting d years or less is .5.

17. A manufacturer guarantees a product for 1 year. The time to failure of the product after it is sold is given by the probability density function

$$f(t) = \begin{cases} .01e^{-.01t} & \text{if } t \geq 0 \\ 0 & \text{otherwise} \end{cases}$$

where t is time in months. What is the probability that a buyer chosen at random will have a product failure

(A) During the warranty period?

(B) During the second year after purchase?

18. In a certain city, the daily use of water (in hundreds of gallons) per household is a continuous random variable with probability density function

$$f(x) = \begin{cases} .15e^{-.15x} & \text{if } x \geq 0 \\ 0 & \text{otherwise} \end{cases}$$

Find the probability that a household chosen at random will use

(A) At most 400 gallons of water per day

(B) Between 300 and 600 gallons of water per day

19. In Problem 17, what is the probability that the product will last at least 1 year? [*Hint:* Recall that the total area under the probability density function curve is 1.]

20. In Problem 18, what is the probability that a household will use more than 400 gallons of water per day? [See the hint in Problem 19.]

21. Find the total income produced by a continuous income stream in the first 5 years if the rate of flow is $f(t) = 2,500$.

22. Find the total income produced by a continuous income stream in the first 10 years if the rate of flow is $f(t) = 3,000$.

23. Interpret the results of Problem 21 with both a graph and a description of the graph.

24. Interpret the results of Problem 22 with both a graph and a description of the graph.

25. Find the total income produced by a continuous income stream in the first 3 years if the rate of flow is $f(t) = 400e^{0.05t}$.

26. Find the total income produced by a continuous income stream in the first 2 years if the rate of flow is $f(t) = 600e^{0.06t}$.

27. Interpret the results of Problem 25 with both a graph and a description of the graph.

28. Interpret the results of Problem 26 with both a graph and a description of the graph.

29. Starting at age 25, you deposit $2,000 a year into an IRA account. Treat the yearly deposits into the account as a continuous income stream. If money in the account earns 5%, compounded continuously, how much will be in the account 40 years later, when you retire at age 65? How much of the final amount is interest?

30. Suppose in Problem 29 that you start the IRA deposits at age 30, but the account earns 6%, compounded continuously. Treat the yearly deposits into the account as a continuous income stream. How much will be in the account 35 years later when you retire at age 65? How much of the final amount is interest?

31. Find the future value at 3.25% interest, compounded continuously for 4 years, of the continuous income stream with rate of flow $f(t) = 1,650e^{-0.02t}$.

32. Find the future value, at 2.95% interest, compounded continuously for 6 years, of the continuous income stream with rate of flow $f(t) = 2,000e^{0.06t}$.

33. Compute the interest earned in Problem 31.

34. Compute the interest earned in Problem 32.

35. An investor is presented with a choice of two investments: an established clothing store and a new computer store. Each choice requires the same initial investment and each produces a continuous income stream of 4%, compounded continuously. The rate of flow of income from the clothing store is $f(t) = 12,000$, and the rate of flow of income from the computer store is expected to be $g(t) = 10,000e^{0.05t}$. Compare the future values of these investments to determine which is the better choice over the next 5 years.

36. Refer to Problem 35. Which investment is the better choice over the next 10 years?

37. An investor has $10,000 to invest in either a bond that matures in 5 years or a business that will produce a continuous stream of income over the next 5 years with rate of flow $f(t) = 2,150$. If both the bond and the continuous income stream earn 3.75%, compounded continuously, which is the better investment?

38. Refer to Problem 37. Which is the better investment if the rate of the income from the business is $f(t) = 2,250$?

39. A business is planning to purchase a piece of equipment that will produce a continuous stream of income for 8 years with rate of flow $f(t) = 9,000$. If the continuous income stream earns 6.95%, compounded continuously, what single deposit into an account earning the same interest rate will produce the same future value as the continuous income stream? (This deposit is called the **present value** of the continuous income stream.)

40. Refer to Problem 39. Find the present value of a continuous income stream at 7.65%, compounded continuously for 12 years, if the rate of flow is $f(t) = 1,000e^{0.03t}$.

41. Find the future value at a rate r, compounded continuously for T years, of a continuous income stream with rate of flow $f(t) = k$, where k is a constant.

42. Find the future value at a rate r, compounded continuously for T years, of a continuous income stream with rate of flow $f(t) = ke^{ct}$, where c and k are constants, $c \neq r$.

43. Find the consumers' surplus at a price level of $\bar{p} = \$150$ for the price–demand equation

$$p = D(x) = 400 - 0.05x$$

44. Find the consumers' surplus at a price level of $\bar{p} = \$120$ for the price–demand equation

$$p = D(x) = 200 - 0.02x$$

45. Interpret the results of Problem 43 with both a graph and a description of the graph.

46. Interpret the results of Problem 44 with both a graph and a description of the graph.

47. Find the producers' surplus at a price level of $\bar{p} = \$67$ for the price–supply equation

$$p = S(x) = 10 + 0.1x + 0.0003x^2$$

48. Find the producers' surplus at a price level of $\bar{p} = \$55$ for the price–supply equation

$$p = S(x) = 15 + 0.1x + 0.003x^2$$

49. Interpret the results of Problem 47 with both a graph and a description of the graph.

50. Interpret the results of Problem 48 with both a graph and a description of the graph.

In Problems 51–58, find the consumers' surplus and the producers' surplus at the equilibrium price level for the given price–demand and price–supply equations. Include a graph that identifies the consumers' surplus and the producers' surplus. Round all values to the nearest integer.

51. $p = D(x) = 50 - 0.1x; p = S(x) = 11 + 0.05x$

52. $p = D(x) = 25 - 0.004x^2; p = S(x) = 5 + 0.004x^2$

53. $p = D(x) = 80e^{-0.001x}; p = S(x) = 30e^{0.001x}$

54. $p = D(x) = 185e^{-0.005x}; p = S(x) = 25e^{0.005x}$

55. $p = D(x) = 80 - 0.04x; p = S(x) = 30e^{0.001x}$

56. $p = D(x) = 190 - 0.2x; p = S(x) = 25e^{0.005x}$

57. $p = D(x) = 80e^{-0.001x}; p = S(x) = 15 + 0.0001x^2$

58. $p = D(x) = 185e^{-0.005x}; p = S(x) = 20 + 0.002x^2$

Since the integrand involves the expression $\sqrt{25 - x^2}$, we examine formulas 29 to 31 in Table II and select formula 29 with $a^2 = 25$ and $a = 5$:

$$\int \frac{1}{u\sqrt{a^2 - u^2}}\,du = -\frac{1}{a}\ln\left|\frac{a + \sqrt{a^2 - u^2}}{u}\right| \qquad \text{Formula 29}$$

$$\int \frac{1}{x\sqrt{25 - x^2}}\,dx = -\frac{1}{5}\ln\left|\frac{5 + \sqrt{25 - x^2}}{x}\right| + C$$

So

$$\int_3^4 \frac{1}{x\sqrt{25 - x^2}}\,dx = -\frac{1}{5}\ln\left|\frac{5 + \sqrt{25 - x^2}}{x}\right|\Bigg|_3^4$$

$$= -\frac{1}{5}\ln\left|\frac{5 + 3}{4}\right| + \frac{1}{5}\ln\left|\frac{5 + 4}{3}\right|$$

$$= -\tfrac{1}{5}\ln 2 + \tfrac{1}{5}\ln 3 = \tfrac{1}{5}\ln 1.5 \approx 0.0811$$

Matched Problem 2 Evaluate $\displaystyle\int_6^8 \frac{1}{x^2\sqrt{100 - x^2}}\,dx.$

Substitution and Integral Tables

As Examples 1 and 2 illustrate, if the integral we want to evaluate can be made to match one in the table exactly, then evaluating the indefinite integral consists simply of substituting the correct values of the constants into the formula. But what happens if we cannot match an integral with one of the formulas in the table? In many cases, a substitution will change the given integral into one that corresponds to a table entry.

EXAMPLE 3 **Integration Using Substitution and Tables** Find $\displaystyle\int \frac{x^2}{\sqrt{16x^2 - 25}}\,dx.$

SOLUTION In order to relate this integral to one of the formulas involving $\sqrt{u^2 - a^2}$ (formulas 40 to 45 in Table II), we observe that if $u = 4x$, then

$$u^2 = 16x^2 \qquad \text{and} \qquad \sqrt{16x^2 - 25} = \sqrt{u^2 - 25}$$

So, we will use the substitution $u = 4x$ to change this integral into one that appears in the table:

$$\int \frac{x^2}{\sqrt{16x^2 - 25}}\,dx = \frac{1}{4}\int \frac{\frac{1}{16}u^2}{\sqrt{u^2 - 25}}\,du \qquad \begin{array}{l}\textit{Substitution:} \\ u = 4x,\ du = 4\ dx,\ x = \tfrac{1}{4}u\end{array}$$

$$= \frac{1}{64}\int \frac{u^2}{\sqrt{u^2 - 25}}\,du$$

This last integral can be evaluated with the aid of formula 44 in Table II with $a = 5$:

$$\int \frac{u^2}{\sqrt{u^2 - a^2}}\,du = \frac{1}{2}\left(u\sqrt{u^2 - a^2} + a^2\ln\left|u + \sqrt{u^2 - a^2}\right|\right) \qquad \text{Formula 44}$$

$$\int \frac{x^2}{\sqrt{16x^2 - 25}}\,dx = \frac{1}{64}\int \frac{u^2}{\sqrt{u^2 - 25}}\,du \qquad \textit{Use formula 44 with } a = 5.$$

$$= \tfrac{1}{128}\left(u\sqrt{u^2 - 25} + 25\ln\left|u + \sqrt{u^2 - 25}\right|\right) + C \quad \textit{Substitute } u = 4x.$$

$$= \tfrac{1}{128}\left(4x\sqrt{16x^2 - 25} + 25\ln\left|4x + \sqrt{16x^2 - 25}\right|\right) + C$$

Matched Problem 3   Find $\int \sqrt{9x^2 - 16}\, dx$.

EXAMPLE 4   **Integration Using Substitution and Tables** Find $\int \dfrac{x}{\sqrt{x^4 + 1}}\, dx$.

SOLUTION   None of the formulas in Table II involve fourth powers; however, if we let $u = x^2$, then

$$\sqrt{x^4 + 1} = \sqrt{u^2 + 1}$$

and this form does appear in formulas 32 to 39. Thus, we substitute $u = x^2$:

$$\int \frac{1}{\sqrt{x^4 + 1}}\, x\, dx = \frac{1}{2} \int \frac{1}{\sqrt{u^2 + 1}}\, du \qquad \begin{array}{l} \textit{Substitution:} \\ u = x^2,\, du = 2x\, dx \end{array}$$

We recognize the last integral as formula 36 with $a = 1$:

$$\int \frac{1}{\sqrt{u^2 + a^2}}\, du = \ln|u + \sqrt{u^2 + a^2}| \qquad \textit{Formula 36}$$

$$\int \frac{x}{\sqrt{x^4 + 1}}\, dx = \frac{1}{2} \int \frac{1}{\sqrt{u^2 + 1}}\, du \qquad \textit{Use formula 36 with } a = 1.$$

$$= \tfrac{1}{2}\ln|u + \sqrt{u^2 + 1}| + C \qquad \textit{Substitute } u = x^2.$$

$$= \tfrac{1}{2}\ln|x^2 + \sqrt{x^4 + 1}| + C$$

Matched Problem 4   Find $\int x\sqrt{x^4 + 1}\, dx$.

Reduction Formulas

EXAMPLE 5   **Using Reduction Formulas** Use Table II to find $\int x^2 e^{3x}\, dx$.

SOLUTION   Since the integrand involves the function e^{3x}, we examine formulas 46–48 and conclude that formula 47 can be used for this problem. Letting $u = x$, $n = 2$, and $a = 3$ in formula 47, we have

$$\int u^n e^{au}\, du = \frac{u^n e^{au}}{a} - \frac{n}{a} \int u^{n-1} e^{au}\, du \qquad \textit{Formula 47}$$

$$\int x^2 e^{3x}\, dx = \frac{x^2 e^{3x}}{3} - \frac{2}{3} \int x e^{3x}\, dx$$

Notice that the expression on the right still contains an integral, but the exponent of x has been reduced by 1. Formulas of this type are called **reduction formulas** and are designed to be applied repeatedly until an integral that can be evaluated is obtained. Applying formula 47 to $\int x e^{3x}\, dx$ with $n = 1$, we have

$$\int x^2 e^{3x}\, dx = \frac{x^2 e^{3x}}{3} - \frac{2}{3}\left(\frac{x e^{3x}}{3} - \frac{1}{3} \int e^{3x}\, dx \right)$$

$$= \frac{x^2 e^{3x}}{3} - \frac{2x e^{3x}}{9} + \frac{2}{9} \int e^{3x}\, dx$$

This last expression contains an integral that is easy to evaluate:

$$\int e^{3x}\, dx = \tfrac{1}{3} e^{3x}$$

After making a final substitution and adding a constant of integration, we have

$$\int x^2 e^{3x}\, dx = \frac{x^2 e^{3x}}{3} - \frac{2x e^{3x}}{9} + \frac{2}{27} e^{3x} + C$$

Matched Problem 5   Use Table II to find $\int (\ln x)^2 \, dx$.

Application

EXAMPLE 6   **Producers' Surplus** Find the producers' surplus at a price level of \$20 for the price–supply equation

$$p = S(x) = \frac{5x}{500 - x}$$

SOLUTION   **Step 1**   Find $\bar{x}$, the supply when the price is $\bar{p} = 20$:

$$\bar{p} = \frac{5\bar{x}}{500 - \bar{x}}$$

$$20 = \frac{5\bar{x}}{500 - \bar{x}}$$

$$10{,}000 - 20\bar{x} = 5\bar{x}$$

$$10{,}000 = 25\bar{x}$$

$$\bar{x} = 400$$

Step 2   Sketch a graph, as shown in Figure 1.

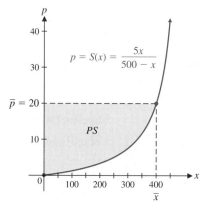

Figure 1

Step 3   Find the producers' surplus (the shaded area of the graph):

$$PS = \int_0^{\bar{x}} [\bar{p} - S(x)] \, dx$$

$$= \int_0^{400} \left(20 - \frac{5x}{500 - x}\right) dx$$

$$= \int_0^{400} \frac{10{,}000 - 25x}{500 - x} \, dx$$

Use formula 20 with $a = 10{,}000$, $b = -25$, $c = 500$, and $d = -1$:

$$\int \frac{a + bu}{c + du} \, du = \frac{bu}{d} + \frac{ad - bc}{d^2} \ln|c + du| \qquad \text{Formula 20}$$

$$PS = (25x + 2{,}500 \ln|500 - x|) \big|_0^{400}$$

$$= 10{,}000 + 2{,}500 \ln|100| - 2{,}500 \ln|500|$$

$$\approx \$5{,}976$$

Matched Problem 6   Find the consumers' surplus at a price level of \$10 for the price–demand equation

$$p = D(x) = \frac{20x - 8{,}000}{x - 500}$$

Exercises 14-4

A

Use Table II on pages 926–928 to find each indefinite integral in Problems 1–14.

1. $\int \dfrac{1}{x(1 + x)}\,dx$

2. $\int \dfrac{1}{x^2(1 + x)}\,dx$

3. $\int \dfrac{1}{(3 + x)^2(5 + 2x)}\,dx$

4. $\int \dfrac{x}{(5 + 2x)^2(2 + x)}\,dx$

5. $\int \dfrac{x}{\sqrt{16 + x}}\,dx$

6. $\int \dfrac{1}{x\sqrt{16 + x}}\,dx$

7. $\int \dfrac{1}{x\sqrt{1 - x^2}}\,dx$

8. $\int \dfrac{\sqrt{9 - x^2}}{x}\,dx$

9. $\int \dfrac{1}{x\sqrt{x^2 + 4}}\,dx$

10. $\int \dfrac{1}{x^2\sqrt{x^2 - 16}}\,dx$

11. $\int x^2 \ln x\,dx$

12. $\int x^3 \ln x\,dx$

13. $\int \dfrac{1}{1 + e^x}\,dx$

14. $\int \dfrac{1}{5 + 2e^{3x}}\,dx$

Evaluate each definite integral in Problems 15–20. Use Table II on pages 926–928 to find the antiderivative.

15. $\int_1^3 \dfrac{x^2}{3 + x}\,dx$

16. $\int_2^6 \dfrac{x}{(6 + x)^2}\,dx$

17. $\int_0^7 \dfrac{1}{(3 + x)(1 + x)}\,dx$

18. $\int_0^7 \dfrac{x}{(3 + x)(1 + x)}\,dx$

19. $\int_0^4 \dfrac{1}{\sqrt{x^2 + 9}}\,dx$

20. $\int_4^5 \sqrt{x^2 - 16}\,dx$

B

In Problems 21–32, use substitution techniques and Table II to find each indefinite integral.

21. $\int \dfrac{\sqrt{4x^2 + 1}}{x^2}\,dx$

22. $\int x^2\sqrt{9x^2 - 1}\,dx$

23. $\int \dfrac{x}{\sqrt{x^4 - 16}}\,dx$

24. $\int x\sqrt{x^4 - 16}\,dx$

25. $\int x^2\sqrt{x^6 + 4}\,dx$

26. $\int \dfrac{x^2}{\sqrt{x^6 + 4}}\,dx$

27. $\int \dfrac{1}{x^3\sqrt{4 - x^4}}\,dx$

28. $\int \dfrac{\sqrt{x^4 + 4}}{x}\,dx$

29. $\int \dfrac{e^x}{(2 + e^x)(3 + 4e^x)}\,dx$

30. $\int \dfrac{e^x}{(4 + e^x)^2(2 + e^x)}\,dx$

31. $\int \dfrac{\ln x}{x\sqrt{4 + \ln x}}\,dx$

32. $\int \dfrac{1}{x \ln x\sqrt{4 + \ln x}}\,dx$

C

In Problems 33–38, use Table II to find each indefinite integral.

33. $\int x^2 e^{5x}\,dx$

34. $\int x^2 e^{-4x}\,dx$

35. $\int x^3 e^{-x}\,dx$

36. $\int x^3 e^{2x}\,dx$

37. $\int (\ln x)^3\,dx$

38. $\int (\ln x)^4\,dx$

Problems 39–46 are mixed—some require the use of Table II, and others can be solved with techniques considered earlier.

39. $\int_3^5 x\sqrt{x^2 - 9}\,dx$

40. $\int_3^5 x^2\sqrt{x^2 - 9}\,dx$

41. $\int_2^4 \dfrac{1}{x^2 - 1}\,dx$

42. $\int_2^4 \dfrac{x}{(x^2 - 1)^2}\,dx$

43. $\displaystyle\int \frac{\ln x}{x^2}\,dx$

44. $\displaystyle\int \frac{(\ln x)^2}{x}\,dx$

45. $\displaystyle\int \frac{x}{\sqrt{x^2 - 1}}\,dx$

46. $\displaystyle\int \frac{x^2}{\sqrt{x^2 - 1}}\,dx$

 In Problems 47–50, find the area bounded by the graphs of $y = f(x)$ and $y = g(x)$ to two decimal places. Use a graphing calculator to approximate intersection points to two decimal places.

47. $f(x) = \dfrac{10}{\sqrt{x^2 + 1}}$; $g(x) = x^2 + 3x$

48. $f(x) = \sqrt{1 + x^2}$; $g(x) = 5x - x^2$

49. $f(x) = x\sqrt{4 + x}$; $g(x) = 1 + x$

50. $f(x) = \dfrac{x}{\sqrt{x + 4}}$; $g(x) = x - 2$

Applications

Use Table II to evaluate all integrals involved in any solutions of Problems 51–74.

51. Consumers' surplus. Find the consumers' surplus at a price level of $\bar{p} = \$15$ for the price–demand equation
$$p = D(x) = \frac{7{,}500 - 30x}{300 - x}$$

52. Producers' surplus. Find the producers' surplus at a price level of $\bar{p} = \$20$ for the price–supply equation
$$p = S(x) = \frac{10x}{300 - x}$$

53. Consumers' surplus. Graph the price–demand equation and the price-level equation $\bar{p} = 15$ of Problem 51 in the same coordinate system. What region represents the consumers' surplus?

54. Producers' surplus. Graph the price–supply equation and the price-level equation $\bar{p} = 20$ of Problem 52 in the same coordinate system. What region represents the producers' surplus?

55. Cost. A company manufactures downhill skis. It has fixed costs of $25,000 and a marginal cost given by
$$C'(x) = \frac{250 + 10x}{1 + 0.05x}$$
where $C(x)$ is the total cost at an output of x pairs of skis. Find the cost function $C(x)$ and determine the production level (to the nearest unit) that produces a cost of $150,000. What is the cost (to the nearest dollar) for a production level of 850 pairs of skis?

56. Cost. A company manufactures a portable DVD player. It has fixed costs of $11,000 per week and a marginal cost given by
$$C'(x) = \frac{65 + 20x}{1 + 0.4x}$$
where $C(x)$ is the total cost per week at an output of x players per week. Find the cost function $C(x)$ and determine the production level (to the nearest unit) that produces a cost of $52,000 per week. What is the cost (to the nearest dollar) for a production level of 700 players per week?

57. Continuous income stream. Find the future value at 4.4%, compounded continuously, for 10 years for the continuous income stream with rate of flow $f(t) = 50t^2$.

58. Continuous income stream. Find the interest earned at 3.7%, compounded continuously, for 5 years for the continuous income stream with rate of flow $f(t) = 200t$.

59. Income distribution. Find the Gini index of income concentration for the Lorenz curve with equation
$$y = \tfrac{1}{2}x\sqrt{1 + 3x}$$

60. Income distribution. Find the Gini index of income concentration for the Lorenz curve with equation
$$y = \tfrac{1}{2}x^2\sqrt{1 + 3x}$$

61. Income distribution. Graph $y = x$ and the Lorenz curve of Problem 59 over the interval $[0, 1]$. Discuss the effect of the area bounded by $y = x$ and the Lorenz curve getting smaller relative to the equitable distribution of income.

62. Income distribution. Graph $y = x$ and the Lorenz curve of Problem 60 over the interval $[0, 1]$. Discuss the effect of the area bounded by $y = x$ and the Lorenz curve getting larger relative to the equitable distribution of income.

63. Marketing. After test marketing a new high-fiber cereal, the market research department of a major food producer estimates that monthly sales (in millions of dollars) will grow at the monthly rate of
$$S'(t) = \frac{t^2}{(1 + t)^2}$$
t months after the cereal is introduced. If we assume 0 sales at the time the cereal is introduced, find $S(t)$, the total sales, t months after the cereal is introduced. Find the total sales during the first 2 years that the cereal is on the market.

64. Average price. At a discount department store, the price–demand equation for premium motor oil is given by
$$p = D(x) = \frac{50}{\sqrt{100 + 6x}}$$
where x is the number of cans of oil that can be sold at a price of $p. Find the average price over the demand interval $[50, 250]$.

65. Marketing. For the cereal of Problem 63, show the sales over the first 2 years geometrically, and describe the geometric representation.

66. Price–demand. For the motor oil of Problem 64, graph the price–demand equation and the line representing the average price in the same coordinate system over the interval [50, 250]. Describe how the areas under the two curves over the interval [50, 250] are related.

 67. Profit. The marginal profit for a small car agency that sells x cars per week is given by

$$P'(x) = x\sqrt{2 + 3x}$$

where $P(x)$ is the profit in dollars. The agency's profit on the sale of only 1 car per week is $-\$2,000$. Find the profit function and the number of cars that must be sold (to the nearest unit) to produce a profit of $13,000 per week. How much weekly profit (to the nearest dollar) will the agency have if 80 cars are sold per week?

 68. Revenue. The marginal revenue for a company that manufactures and sells x graphing calculators per week is given by

$$R'(x) = \frac{x}{\sqrt{1 + 2x}} \qquad R(0) = 0$$

where $R(x)$ is the revenue in dollars. Find the revenue function and the number of calculators that must be sold (to the nearest unit) to produce $10,000 in revenue per week. How much weekly revenue (to the nearest dollar) will the company have if 1,000 calculators are sold per week?

69. Pollution. An oil tanker is producing an oil slick that is radiating outward at a rate given approximately by

$$\frac{dR}{dt} = \frac{100}{\sqrt{t^2 + 9}} \qquad t \geq 0$$

where R is the radius (in feet) of the circular slick after t minutes. Find the radius of the slick after 4 minutes if the radius is 0 when $t = 0$.

70. Pollution. The concentration of particulate matter (in parts per million) during a 24-hour period is given approximately by

$$C(t) = t\sqrt{24 - t} \qquad 0 \leq t \leq 24$$

where t is time in hours. Find the average concentration during the period from $t = 0$ to $t = 24$.

71. Learning. A person learns N items at a rate given approximately by

$$N'(t) = \frac{60}{\sqrt{t^2 + 25}} \qquad t \geq 0$$

where t is the number of hours of continuous study. Determine the total number of items learned in the first 12 hours of continuous study.

72. Politics. The number of voters (in thousands) in a metropolitan area is given approximately by

$$f(t) = \frac{500}{2 + 3e^{-t}} \qquad t \geq 0$$

where t is time in years. Find the average number of voters during the period from $t = 0$ to $t = 10$.

73. Learning. Interpret Problem 71 geometrically. Describe the geometric interpretation.

74. Politics. For the voters of Problem 72, graph $y = f(t)$ and the line representing the average number of voters over the interval [0, 10] in the same coordinate system. Describe how the areas under the two curves over the interval [0, 10] are related.

Answers to Matched Problems

1. $\dfrac{1}{2}\left(\dfrac{1}{5 + 3x}\right) + \dfrac{1}{4}\ln\left|\dfrac{1 + x}{5 + 3x}\right| + C$

2. $\frac{7}{1,200} \approx 0.0058$

3. $\frac{1}{6}(3x\sqrt{9x^2 - 16} - 16\ln|3x + \sqrt{9x^2 - 16}|) + C$

4. $\frac{1}{4}(x^2\sqrt{x^4 + 1} + \ln|x^2 + \sqrt{x^4 + 1}|) + C$

5. $x(\ln x)^2 - 2x\ln x + 2x + C$

6. $3,000 + 2,000\ln 200 - 2,000\ln 500 \approx \$1,167$

Chapter 14   Review

Important Terms, Symbols, and Concepts

14-1 Area Between Curves

EXAMPLES

- If f and g are continuous and $f(x) \geq g(x)$ over the interval $[a, b]$, then the area bounded by $y = f(x)$ and $y = g(x)$ for $a \leq x \leq b$ is given exactly by

$$A = \int_a^b [f(x) - g(x)]\, dx$$

Ex. 1, p. 760
Ex. 2, p. 760
Ex. 3, p. 761
Ex. 4, p. 761

- A graphical representation of the distribution of income among a population can be found by plotting data points (x, y), where **x represents the cumulative percentage of families at or below a given income level** and **y represents the cumulative percentage of total family income received.** Regression analysis can be used to find a particular function $y = f(x)$, called a **Lorenz curve,** that best fits the data.

Ex. 5, p. 762
Ex. 6, p. 762

- A single number, the **Gini index,** measures income concentration:

$$\text{Gini index} = 2\int_0^1 [x - f(x)]\, dx$$

Ex. 7, p. 764

A Gini index of 0 indicates **absolute equality:** All families share equally in the income. A Gini index of 1 indicates **absolute inequality:** One family has all of the income and the rest have none.

14-2 Applications in Business and Economics

- *Probability Density Functions.* If any real number x in an interval is a possible outcome of an experiment, then x is said to be a **continuous random variable.** The probability distribution of a continuous random variable is described by a **probability density function** f that satisfies the following conditions:
  1. $f(x) \geq 0$ for all real x.
  2. The area under the graph of $f(x)$ over the interval $(-\infty, \infty)$ is exactly 1.
  3. If $[c, d]$ is a subinterval of $(-\infty, \infty)$, then

  Ex. 1, p. 769

  $$\text{Probability} \quad (c \leq x \leq d) = \int_c^d f(x) \, dx$$

- *Continuous Income Stream* If the rate at which income is received—its **rate of flow**—is a continuous function $f(t)$ of time, then the income is said to be a **continuous income stream.** The **total income** produced by a continuous income stream from $t = a$ to $t = b$ is

  Ex. 2, p. 771

  $$\text{Total income} = \int_a^b f(t) \, dt$$

  The **future value** of a continuous income stream that is invested at rate r, compounded continuously, for $0 \leq t \leq T$, is

  Ex. 3, p. 774

  $$FV = \int_0^T f(t) e^{r(T-t)} \, dt$$

- *Consumers' and Producers' Surplus* If $(\bar{x}, \bar{p})$ is a point on the graph of a price–demand equation $p = D(x)$, then the **consumers' surplus** at a price level of $\bar{p}$ is

  Ex. 4, p. 775

  $$CS = \int_0^{\bar{x}} [D(x) - \bar{p}] \, dx$$

  The consumers' surplus represents the total savings to consumers who are willing to pay more than $\bar{p}$ but are still able to buy the product for $\bar{p}$.

  Similarly, for a point $(\bar{x}, \bar{p})$ on the graph of a price–supply equation $p = S(x)$, the **producers' surplus** at a price level of $\bar{p}$ is

  Ex. 5, p. 776

  $$PS = \int_0^{\bar{x}} [\bar{p} - S(x)] \, dx$$

  The producers' surplus represents the total gain to producers who are willing to supply units at a lower price $\bar{p}$, but are still able to supply units at $\bar{p}$.

  If $(\bar{x}, \bar{p})$ is the intersection point of a price–demand equation $p = D(x)$ and a price–supply equation $p = S(x)$, then $\bar{p}$ is called the **equilibrium price** and $\bar{x}$ is called the **equilibrium quantity**.

  Ex. 6, p. 777

14-3 Integration by Parts

- Some indefinite integrals, but not all, can be found by means of the **integration-by-parts formula**

  Ex. 1, p. 781
  Ex. 2, p. 782
  Ex. 3, p. 783
  Ex. 4, p. 784

  $$\int u \, dv = uv - \int v \, du$$

- Select u and dv with the help of the guidelines in the summary on page 783.

14-4 Integration Using Tables

- A **table of integrals** is a list of integration formulas that can be used to find indefinite or definite integrals of frequently encountered functions. Such a list appears in Table II of Appendix C on pages 926–928.

  Ex. 1, p. 787
  Ex. 2, p. 787
  Ex. 3, p. 788
  Ex. 4, p. 789
  Ex. 5, p. 789
  Ex. 6, p. 790

Review Exercises

Work through all the problems in this chapter review and check your answers in the back of the book. Answers to all review problems are there, along with section numbers in italics to indicate where each type of problem is discussed. Where weaknesses show up, review appropriate sections of the text.

  Compute all numerical answers to three decimal places unless directed otherwise.

A

In Problems 1–3, set up definite integrals that represent the shaded areas in the figure over the indicated intervals.

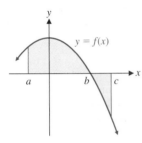

Figure for 1–3

1. Interval $[a, b]$

2. Interval $[b, c]$

3. Interval $[a, c]$

4. Sketch a graph of the area between the graphs of $y = \ln x$ and $y = 0$ over the interval $[0.5, e]$ and find the area.

In Problems 5–10, evaluate each integral.

5. $\int xe^{4x}\, dx$

6. $\int x \ln x\, dx$

7. $\int \dfrac{\ln x}{x}\, dx$

8. $\int \dfrac{x}{1 + x^2}\, dx$

9. $\int \dfrac{1}{x(1 + x)^2}\, dx$

10. $\int \dfrac{1}{x^2\sqrt{1 + x}}\, dx$

In Problems 11–16, find the area bounded by the graphs of the indicated equations over the given interval.

11. $y = 5 - 2x - 6x^2;\ y = 0,\ 1 \le x \le 2$

12. $y = 5x + 7;\ y = 12,\ -3 \le x \le 1$

13. $y = -x + 2;\ y = x^2 + 3,\ -1 \le x \le 4$

14. $y = \dfrac{1}{x};\ y = -e^{-x},\ 1 \le x \le 2$

15. $y = x;\ y = -x^3,\ -2 \le x \le 2$

16. $y = x^2;\ y = -x^4;\ -2 \le x \le 2$

B

In Problems 17–20, set up definite integrals that represent the shaded areas in the figure over the indicated intervals.

17. Interval $[a, b]$ **18.** Interval $[b, c]$

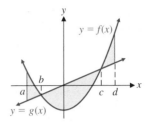

Figure for 17–20

19. Interval $[b, d]$ **20.** Interval $[a, d]$

21. Sketch a graph of the area bounded by the graphs of $y = x^2 - 6x + 9$ and $y = 9 - x$ and find the area.

In Problems 22–27, evaluate each integral.

22. $\int_0^1 xe^x\, dx$

23. $\int_0^3 \dfrac{x^2}{\sqrt{x^2 + 16}}\, dx$

24. $\int \sqrt{9x^2 - 49}\, dx$

25. $\int te^{-0.5t}\, dt$

26. $\int x^2 \ln x\, dx$

27. $\int \dfrac{1}{1 + 2e^x}\, dx$

28. Sketch a graph of the area bounded by the indicated graphs, and find the area. In part (B), approximate intersection points and area to two decimal places.
  (A) $y = x^3 - 6x^2 + 9x;\ y = x$
   (B) $y = x^3 - 6x^2 + 9x;\ y = x + 1$

C

In Problems 29–36, evaluate each integral.

29. $\int \dfrac{(\ln x)^2}{x}\, dx$

30. $\int x(\ln x)^2\, dx$

31. $\int \dfrac{x}{\sqrt{x^2 - 36}}\, dx$

32. $\int \dfrac{x}{\sqrt{x^4 - 36}}\, dx$

33. $\int_0^4 x \ln(10 - x)\, dx$

34. $\int (\ln x)^2\, dx$

35. $\int xe^{-2x^2}\, dx$

36. $\int x^2 e^{-2x}\, dx$

37. Use a numerical integration routine on a graphing calculator to find the area in the first quadrant that is below the graph of

$$y = \dfrac{6}{2 + 5e^{-x}}$$

and above the graph of $y = 0.2x + 1.6$.

Applications

38. Product warranty. A manufacturer warrants a product for parts and labor for 1 year and for parts only for a second year. The time to a failure of the product after it is sold is given by the probability density function

$$f(t) = \begin{cases} 0.21e^{-0.21t} & \text{if } t \ge 0 \\ 0 & \text{otherwise} \end{cases}$$

What is the probability that a buyer chosen at random will have a product failure

(A) During the first year of warranty?

(B) During the second year of warranty?

39. **Product warranty.** Graph the probability density function for Problem 38 over the interval [0, 3], interpret part (B) of Problem 38 geometrically and describe the geometric representation.

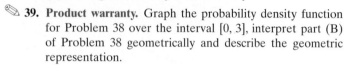

40. **Revenue function.** The weekly marginal revenue from the sale of x hair dryers is given by

$$R'(x) = 65 - 6\ln(x + 1) \qquad R(0) = 0$$

where $R(x)$ is the revenue in dollars. Find the revenue function and the production level (to the nearest unit) for a revenue of $20,000 per week. What is the weekly revenue (to the nearest dollar) at a production level of 1,000 hair dryers per week?

41. **Continuous income stream.** The rate of flow (in dollars per year) of a continuous income stream for a 5-year period is given by

$$f(t) = 2,500e^{0.05t} \qquad 0 \le t \le 5$$

(A) Graph $y = f(t)$ over [0, 5] and shade the area that represents the total income received from the end of the first year to the end of the fourth year.

(B) Find the total income received, to the nearest dollar, from the end of the first year to the end of the fourth year.

42. **Future value of a continuous income stream.** The continuous income stream in Problem 41 is invested at 4%, compounded continuously.

(A) Find the future value (to the nearest dollar) at the end of the 5-year period.

(B) Find the interest earned (to the nearest dollar) during the 5-year period.

43. **Income distribution.** An economist produced the following Lorenz curves for the current income distribution and the projected income distribution 10 years from now in a certain country:

$$f(x) = 0.1x + 0.9x^2 \qquad \textit{Current Lorenz curve}$$

$$g(x) = x^{1.5} \qquad \textit{Projected Lorenz curve}$$

(A) Graph $y = x$ and the current Lorenz curve on one set of coordinate axes for [0, 1] and graph $y = x$ and the projected Lorenz curve on another set of coordinate axes over the same interval.

(B) Looking at the areas bounded by the Lorenz curves and $y = x$, can you say that the income will be more or less equitably distributed 10 years from now?

(C) Compute the Gini index of income concentration (to one decimal place) for the current and projected curves. What can you say about the distribution of income 10 years from now? Is it more equitable or less?

44. **Consumers' and producers' surplus.** Find the consumers' surplus and the producers' surplus at the equilibrium price level for each pair of price–demand and price–supply equations. Include a graph that identifies the consumers' surplus and the producers' surplus. Round all values to the nearest integer.

(A) $p = D(x) = 70 - 0.2x$;

$p = S(x) = 13 + 0.0012x^2$

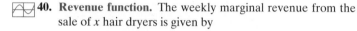 (B) $p = D(x) = 70 - 0.2x$; $p = S(x) = 13e^{0.006x}$

45. **Producers' surplus.** The accompanying table gives price–supply data for the sale of hogs at a livestock market, where x is the number of pounds (in thousands) and p is the price per pound (in cents):

Price–Supply	
x	$p = S(x)$
0	43.50
10	46.74
20	50.05
30	54.72
40	59.18

(A) Using quadratic regression to model the data, find the demand at a price of 52.50 cents per pound.

(B) Use a numerical integration routine to find the producers' surplus (to the nearest dollar) at a price level of 52.50 cents per pound.

46. **Drug assimilation.** The rate at which the body eliminates a certain drug (in milliliters per hour) is given by

$$R(t) = \frac{60t}{(t + 1)^2(t + 2)}$$

where t is the number of hours since the drug was administered. How much of the drug is eliminated during the first hour after it was administered? During the fourth hour?

47. With the aid of a graphing calculator, illustrate Problem 46 geometrically.

48. **Medicine.** For a particular doctor, the length of time (in hours) spent with a patient per office visit has the probability density function

$$f(t) = \begin{cases} \dfrac{\frac{4}{3}}{(t + 1)^2} & \text{if } 0 \le t \le 3 \\ 0 & \text{otherwise} \end{cases}$$

(A) What is the probability that this doctor will spend less than 1 hour with a randomly selected patient?

(B) What is the probability that this doctor will spend more than 1 hour with a randomly selected patient?

49. **Medicine.** Illustrate part (B) in Problem 48 geometrically. Describe the geometric interpretation.

50. **Politics.** The rate of change of the voting population of a city with respect to time t (in years) is estimated to be

$$N'(t) = \frac{100t}{(1 + t^2)^2}$$

where $N(t)$ is in thousands. If $N(0)$ is the current voting population, how much will this population increase during the next 3 years?

51. **Psychology.** Rats were trained to go through a maze by rewarding them with a food pellet upon successful completion of the run. After the seventh successful run, the probability density function for length of time (in minutes) until success on the eighth trial was given by

$$f(t) = \begin{cases} .5e^{-.5t} & \text{if } t \ge 0 \\ 0 & \text{otherwise} \end{cases}$$

What is the probability that a rat selected at random after seven successful runs will take 2 or more minutes to complete the eighth run successfully? [Recall that the area under a probability density function curve from $-\infty$ to ∞ is 1.]

Multivariable Calculus

Introduction

In previous chapters, we have applied the key concepts of calculus, the derivative and the integral, to functions with one independent variable. The graph of such a function is a curve in the plane. In Chapter 15, we extend the key concepts of calculus to functions with two independent variables. Graphs of such functions are surfaces in a three-dimensional coordinate system. We use functions with two independent variables to study how production depends on both labor and capital; how braking distance depends on both the weight and speed of a car; how resistance in a blood vessel depends on both its length and radius. In Section 15-5, we justify the method of least squares and use the method to construct linear models (see, for example, Problem 31 in Section 15-5 on global warming).

15-1   Functions of Several Variables

Functions of Two or More Independent Variables

In Section 2-1, we introduced the concept of a function with one independent variable. Now we broaden the concept to include functions with more than one independent variable.

A small manufacturing company produces a standard type of surfboard. If fixed costs are $500 per week and variable costs are $70 per board produced, the weekly cost function is given by

$$C(x) = 500 + 70x \tag{1}$$

where x is the number of boards produced per week. The cost function is a function of a single independent variable x. For each value of x from the domain of C, there exists exactly one value of $C(x)$ in the range of C.

Now, suppose that the company decides to add a high-performance competition board to its line. If the fixed costs for the competition board are $200 per week and the variable costs are $100 per board, then the cost function (1) must be modified to

$$C(x, y) = 700 + 70x + 100y \tag{2}$$

where $C(x, y)$ is the cost for a weekly output of x standard boards and y competition boards. Equation (2) is an example of a function with two independent variables x and y. Of course, as the company expands its product line even further, its weekly cost function must be modified to include more and more independent variables, one for each new product produced.

In general, an equation of the form

$$z = f(x, y)$$

describes a **function of two independent variables** if, for each permissible ordered pair (x, y), there is one and only one value of z determined by $f(x, y)$. The variables x and y are **independent variables**, and the variable z is a **dependent variable**. The set of all ordered pairs of permissible values of x and y is the **domain** of the function, and the set of all corresponding values $f(x, y)$ is the **range** of the function. Unless otherwise stated, we will assume that the domain of a function specified by an equation of the form $z = f(x, y)$ is the set of all ordered pairs of real numbers (x, y) such that $f(x, y)$ is also a real number. It should be noted, however, that certain conditions in practical problems often lead to further restrictions on the domain of a function.

We can similarly define functions of three independent variables, $w = f(x, y, z)$; of four independent variables, $u = f(w, x, y, z)$; and so on. In this chapter, we concern ourselves primarily with functions of two independent variables.

EXAMPLE 1   **Evaluating a Function of Two Independent Variables** For the cost function $C(x, y) = 700 + 70x + 100y$ described earlier, find $C(10, 5)$.

SOLUTION
$$C(10, 5) = 700 + 70(10) + 100(5)$$
$$= \$1,900$$

Matched Problem 1   Find $C(20, 10)$ for the cost function in Example 1.

EXAMPLE 2   **Evaluating a Function of Three Independent Variables** For the function $f(x, y, z) = 2x^2 - 3xy + 3z + 1$, find $f(3, 0, -1)$.

SOLUTION
$$f(3, 0, -1) = 2(3)^2 - 3(3)(0) + 3(-1) + 1$$
$$= 18 - 0 - 3 + 1 = 16$$

Matched Problem 2   Find $f(-2, 2, 3)$ for f in Example 2.

EXAMPLE 3   **Revenue, Cost, and Profit Functions** Suppose the surfboard company discussed earlier has determined that the demand equations for its two types of boards are given by

$$p = 210 - 4x + y$$
$$q = 300 + x - 12y$$

where p is the price of the standard board, q is the price of the competition board, x is the weekly demand for standard boards, and y is the weekly demand for competition boards.

(A) Find the weekly revenue function $R(x, y)$, and evaluate $R(20, 10)$.

(B) If the weekly cost function is

$$C(x, y) = 700 + 70x + 100y$$

find the weekly profit function $P(x, y)$ and evaluate $P(20, 10)$.

SOLUTION   (A)

$$\text{Revenue} = \begin{pmatrix} \text{demand for} \\ \text{standard} \\ \text{boards} \end{pmatrix} \times \begin{pmatrix} \text{price of a} \\ \text{standard} \\ \text{board} \end{pmatrix} + \begin{pmatrix} \text{demand for} \\ \text{competition} \\ \text{boards} \end{pmatrix} \times \begin{pmatrix} \text{price of a} \\ \text{competition} \\ \text{board} \end{pmatrix}$$

$$R(x, y) = xp + yq$$
$$= x(210 - 4x + y) + y(300 + x - 12y)$$
$$= 210x + 300y - 4x^2 + 2xy - 12y^2$$
$$R(20, 10) = 210(20) + 300(10) - 4(20)^2 + 2(20)(10) - 12(10)^2$$
$$= \$4,800$$

(B)   Profit = revenue − cost
$$P(x, y) = R(x, y) - C(x, y)$$
$$= 210x + 300y - 4x^2 + 2xy - 12y^2 - 700 - 70x - 100y$$
$$= 140x + 200y - 4x^2 + 2xy - 12y^2 - 700$$
$$P(20, 10) = 140(20) + 200(10) - 4(20)^2 + 2(20)(10) - 12(10)^2 - 700$$
$$= \$1,700$$

Matched Problem 3   Repeat Example 3 if the demand and cost equations are given by

$$p = 220 - 6x + y$$
$$q = 300 + 3x - 10y$$
$$C(x, y) = 40x + 80y + 1,000$$

Examples of Functions of Several Variables

A number of concepts can be considered as functions of two or more variables.

Area of a rectangle	$A(x, y) = xy$	A = area ▭ with sides x, y
Volume of a box	$V(x, y, z) = xyz$	V = volume
Volume of a right circular cylinder	$V(r, h) = \pi r^2 h$	
Simple interest	$A(P, r, t) = P(1 + rt)$	A = amount P = principal r = annual rate t = time in years
Compound interest	$A(P, r, t, n) = P\left(1 + \dfrac{r}{n}\right)^{nt}$	A = amount P = principal r = annual rate t = time in years n = number of compound periods per year
IQ	$Q(M, C) = \dfrac{M}{C}(100)$	Q = IQ = intelligence quotient M = MA = mental age C = CA = chronological age
Resistance for blood flow in a vessel (Poiseuille's law)	$R(L, r) = k\dfrac{L}{r^4}$	R = resistance L = length of vessel r = radius of vessel k = constant

EXAMPLE 4   **Package Design** A company uses a box with a square base and an open top for a bath assortment (see figure). If x is the length (in inches) of each side of the base and y is the height (in inches), find the total amount of material $M(x, y)$ required to construct one of these boxes, and evaluate $M(5, 10)$.

SOLUTION

$$\text{Area of base} = x^2$$
$$\text{Area of one side} = xy$$
$$\text{Total material} = (\text{area of base}) + 4(\text{area of one side})$$
$$M(x, y) = x^2 + 4xy$$
$$M(5, 10) = (5)^2 + 4(5)(10)$$
$$= 225 \text{ square inches}$$

Matched Problem 4   For the box in Example 4, find the volume $V(x, y)$ and evaluate $V(5, 10)$.

The next example concerns the **Cobb–Douglas production function**

$$f(x, y) = kx^m y^n$$

where k, m, and n are positive constants with $m + n = 1$. Economists use this function to describe the number of units $f(x, y)$ produced from the utilization of x units of labor and y units of capital (for equipment such as tools, machinery, buildings, and so on). Cobb–Douglas production functions are also used to describe the productivity of a single industry, of a group of industries producing the same product, or even of an entire country.

EXAMPLE 5 **Productivity** The productivity of a steel-manufacturing company is given approximately by the function

$$f(x, y) = 10x^{0.2}y^{0.8}$$

with the utilization of x units of labor and y units of capital. If the company uses 3,000 units of labor and 1,000 units of capital, how many units of steel will be produced?

SOLUTION The number of units of steel produced is given by

$$f(3,000, 1,000) = 10(3,000)^{0.2}(1,000)^{0.8} \quad \textit{Use a calculator.}$$

$$\approx 12,457 \text{ units}$$

Matched Problem 5 Refer to Example 5. Find the steel production if the company uses 1,000 units of labor and 2,000 units of capital.

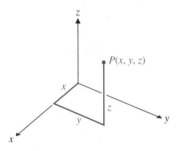

Figure 1 Rectangular coordinate system

Three-Dimensional Coordinate Systems

We now take a brief look at graphs of functions of two independent variables. Since functions of the form $z = f(x, y)$ involve two independent variables x and y, and one dependent variable z, we need a *three-dimensional coordinate system* for their graphs. A **three-dimensional coordinate system** is formed by three mutually perpendicular number lines intersecting at their origins (see Fig. 1). In such a system, every ordered **triplet of numbers (x, y, z)** can be associated with a unique point, and conversely.

EXAMPLE 6 **Three-Dimensional Coordinates** Locate $(-3, 5, 2)$ in a rectangular coordinate system.

SOLUTION

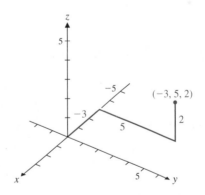

Matched Problem 6 Find the coordinates of the corners $A, C, G,$ and D of the rectangular box shown in the following figure.

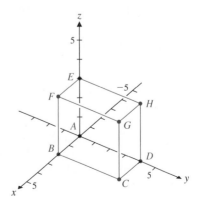

Imagine that you are facing the front of a classroom whose rectangular walls meet at right angles. Suppose that the point of intersection of the floor, front wall, and left-side wall is the origin of a three-dimensional coordinate system in which every point in the room has nonnegative coordinates. Then the plane $z = 0$ (or, equivalently, the xy plane) can be described as "the floor," and the plane $z = 2$ can be described as "the plane parallel to, but 2 units above, the floor." Give similar descriptions of the following planes:

(A) $x = 0$ (B) $x = 3$ (C) $y = 0$ (D) $y = 4$ (E) $x = -1$

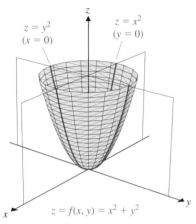

$z = y^2$
$(x = 0)$

$z = x^2$
$(y = 0)$

$z = f(x, y) = x^2 + y^2$

Figure 2 Paraboloid

What does the graph of $z = x^2 + y^2$ look like? If we let $x = 0$ and graph $z = 0^2 + y^2 = y^2$ in the yz plane, we obtain a parabola; if we let $y = 0$ and graph $z = x^2 + 0^2 = x^2$ in the xz plane, we obtain another parabola. The graph of $z = x^2 + y^2$ is either one of these parabolas rotated around the z axis (see Fig. 2). This cup-shaped figure is a *surface* and is called a **paraboloid**.

In general, the graph of any function of the form $z = f(x, y)$ is called a **surface**. The graph of such a function is the graph of all ordered triplets of numbers (x, y, z) that satisfy the equation. Graphing functions of two independent variables is a difficult task, and the general process will not be dealt with in this book. We present only a few simple graphs to suggest extensions of earlier geometric interpretations of the derivative and local maxima and minima to functions of two variables. Note that $z = f(x, y) = x^2 + y^2$ appears (see Fig. 2) to have a local minimum at $(x, y) = (0, 0)$. Figure 3 shows a local maximum at $(x, y) = (0, 0)$.

Figure 4 shows a point at $(x, y) = (0, 0)$, called a **saddle point**, that is neither a local minimum nor a local maximum. Note that if $x = 0$, the saddle point is a local minimum, and if $y = 0$, the saddle point is a local maximum. More will be said about local maxima and minima in Section 15-3.

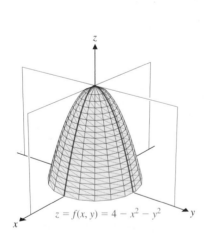

$z = f(x, y) = 4 - x^2 - y^2$

Figure 3 Local maximum:
$f(0, 0) = 4$

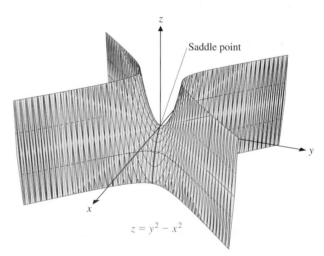

Saddle point

$z = y^2 - x^2$

Figure 4 Saddle point at $(0, 0, 0)$

Some graphing calculators are designed to draw graphs (like those of Figs. 2, 3, and 4) of functions of two independent variables. Others, such as the graphing calculator used for the displays in this book, are designed to draw graphs of functions of one independent variable. When using the latter type of calculator, we can graph cross sections produced by cutting surfaces with planes parallel to the xz plane or yz plane to gain insight into the graph of a function of two independent variables.

EXAMPLE 7 **Graphing Cross Sections**

(A) Describe the cross sections of $f(x, y) = 2x^2 + y^2$ in the planes $y = 0$, $y = 1$, $y = 2$, $y = 3$, and $y = 4$.

(B) Describe the cross sections of $f(x, y) = 2x^2 + y^2$ in the planes $x = 0$, $x = 1$, $x = 2$, $x = 3$, and $x = 4$.

SOLUTION (A) The cross section of $f(x, y) = 2x^2 + y^2$ produced by cutting it with the plane $y = 0$ is the graph of the function $f(x, 0) = 2x^2$ in this plane. We can examine the shape of this cross section by graphing $y_1 = 2x^2$ on a graphing calculator (Fig. 5). Similarly, the graphs of $y_2 = f(x, 1) = 2x^2 + 1$, $y_3 = f(x, 2) = 2x^2 + 4$, $y_4 = f(x, 3) = 2x^2 + 9$, and $y_5 = f(x, 4) = 2x^2 + 16$ show the shapes of the other four cross sections (see Fig. 5). Each of these is a parabola that opens upward. Note the correspondence between the graphs in Figure 5 and the actual cross sections of $f(x, y) = 2x^2 + y^2$ shown in Figure 6.

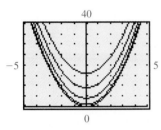

Figure 5

$y_1 = 2x^2$ $y_4 = 2x^2 + 9$

$y_2 = 2x^2 + 1$ $y_5 = 2x^2 + 16$

$y_3 = 2x^2 + 4$

Figure 6

Figure 7

$y_1 = x^2$ $y_4 = 18 + x^2$

$y_2 = 2 + x^2$ $y_5 = 32 + x^2$

$y_3 = 8 + x^2$

(B) The five cross sections are represented by the graphs of the functions $f(0, y) = y^2$, $f(1, y) = 2 + y^2$, $f(2, y) = 8 + y^2$, $f(3, y) = 18 + y^2$, and $f(4, y) = 32 + y^2$. These five functions are graphed in Figure 7. (Note that changing the name of the independent variable from y to x for graphing purposes does not affect the graph displayed.) Each of the five cross sections is a parabola that opens upward.

Matched Problem 7 (A) Describe the cross sections of $g(x, y) = y^2 - x^2$ in the planes $y = 0$, $y = 1$, $y = 2$, $y = 3$, and $y = 4$.

 (B) Describe the cross sections of $g(x, y) = y^2 - x^2$ in the planes $x = 0$, $x = 1$, $x = 2$, $x = 3$, and $x = 4$.

CONCEPTUAL INSIGHT

The graph of the *equation*

$$x^2 + y^2 + z^2 = 4 \tag{3}$$

is the graph of all ordered triplets of numbers (x, y, z) that satisfy the equation. The Pythagorean theorem can be used to show that the distance from the point (x, y, z) to the origin $(0, 0, 0)$ is equal to

$$\sqrt{x^2 + y^2 + z^2}$$

Therefore, the graph of (3) consists of all points that are at a distance 2 from the origin—that is, all points on the sphere of radius 2 and with center at the origin. Recall that a circle in the plane is *not* the graph of a function $y = f(x)$, because it fails the vertical-line test (Section 2-1). Similarly, a sphere is *not* the graph of a *function* $z = f(x, y)$ of two variables.

Exercises 15-1

A

In Problems 1–10, find the indicated values of the functions

$$f(x, y) = 2x + 7y - 5 \quad \text{and} \quad g(x, y) = \frac{88}{x^2 + 3y}$$

1. $f(4, -1)$

2. $f(0, 10)$

3. $f(8, 0)$

4. $f(5, 6)$

5. $g(1, 7)$

6. $g(-2, 0)$

7. $g(3, -3)$

8. $g(0, 0)$

9. $3f(-2, 2) + 5g(-2, 2)$

10. $2f(10, -4) - 7g(10, -4)$

In Problems 11–14, find the indicated values of

$$f(x, y, z) = 2x - 3y^2 + 5z^3 - 1$$

11. $f(0, 0, 0)$

12. $f(0, 0, 2)$

13. $f(6, -5, 0)$

14. $f(-10, 4, -3)$

B

In Problems 15–24, find the indicated value of the given function.

15. $P(13, 5)$ for $P(n, r) = \dfrac{n!}{(n - r)!}$

16. $C(13, 5)$ for $C(n, r) = \dfrac{n!}{r!(n - r)!}$

17. $V(4, 12)$ for $V(R, h) = \pi R^2 h$

18. $T(4, 12)$ for $T(R, h) = 2\pi R(R + h)$

19. $S(3, 10)$ for $S(R, h) = \pi R \sqrt{R^2 + h^2}$

20. $W(3, 10)$ for $W(R, h) = \dfrac{1}{3}\pi R^2 h$

21. $A(100, 0.06, 3)$ for $A(P, r, t) = P + Prt$

22. $A(10, 0.04, 3, 2)$ for $A(P, r, t, n) = P\left(1 + \dfrac{r}{n}\right)^{tn}$

23. $P(0.05, 12)$ for $P(r, T) = \displaystyle\int_0^T 4{,}000 e^{-rt}\, dt$

24. $F(0.07, 10)$ for $F(r, T) = \displaystyle\int_0^T 4{,}000 e^{r(T-t)}\, dt$

In Problems 25–30, find the indicated function f of a single variable.

25. $f(x) = G(x, 0)$ for $G(x, y) = x^2 + 3xy + y^2 - 7$

26. $f(y) = H(0, y)$ for $H(x, y) = x^2 - 5xy - y^2 + 2$

27. $f(y) = K(4, y)$ for $K(x, y) = 10xy + 3x - 2y + 8$

28. $f(x) = L(x, -2)$ for $L(x, y) = 25 - x + 5y - 6xy$

29. $f(y) = M(y, y)$ for $M(x, y) = x^2 y - 3xy^2 + 5$

30. $f(x) = N(x, 2x)$ for $N(x, y) = 3xy + x^2 - y^2 + 1$

31. Let $F(x, y) = 2x + 3y - 6$. Find all values of y such that $F(0, y) = 0$.

32. Let $F(x, y) = 5x - 4y + 12$. Find all values of x such that $F(x, 0) = 0$.

33. Let $F(x, y) = 2xy + 3x - 4y - 1$. Find all values of x such that $F(x, x) = 0$.

34. Let $F(x, y) = xy + 2x^2 + y^2 - 25$. Find all values of y such that $F(y, y) = 0$.

35. Let $F(x, y) = x^2 + e^x y - y^2$. Find all values of x such that $F(x, 2) = 0$.

36. Let $G(a, b, c) = a^3 + b^3 + c^3 - (ab + ac + bc) - 6$. Find all values of b such that $G(2, b, 1) = 0$.

C

37. For the function $f(x, y) = x^2 + 2y^2$, find

$$\frac{f(x + h, y) - f(x, y)}{h}$$

38. For the function $f(x, y) = x^2 + 2y^2$, find

$$\frac{f(x, y + k) - f(x, y)}{k}$$

39. For the function $f(x, y) = 2xy^2$, find

$$\frac{f(x + h, y) - f(x, y)}{h}$$

40. For the function $f(x, y) = 2xy^2$, find

$$\frac{f(x, y + k) - f(x, y)}{k}$$

41. Find the coordinates of E and F in the figure for Matched Problem 6 on page 801.

42. Find the coordinates of B and H in the figure for Matched Problem 6 on page 801.

In Problems 43–48, use a graphing calculator as necessary to explore the graphs of the indicated cross sections.

43. Let $f(x, y) = x^2$.

(A) Explain why the cross sections of the surface $z = f(x, y)$ produced by cutting it with planes parallel to $y = 0$ are parabolas.

(B) Describe the cross sections of the surface in the planes $x = 0$, $x = 1$, and $x = 2$.

(C) Describe the surface $z = f(x, y)$.

44. Let $f(x, y) = \sqrt{4 - y^2}$.

(A) Explain why the cross sections of the surface $z = f(x, y)$ produced by cutting it with planes parallel to $x = 0$ are semicircles of radius 2.

(B) Describe the cross sections of the surface in the planes $y = 0$, $y = 2$, and $y = 3$.

(C) Describe the surface $z = f(x, y)$.

45. Let $f(x, y) = \sqrt{36 - x^2 - y^2}$.

(A) Describe the cross sections of the surface $z = f(x, y)$ produced by cutting it with the planes $y = 1$, $y = 2$, $y = 3$, $y = 4$, and $y = 5$.

(B) Describe the cross sections of the surface in the planes $x = 0$, $x = 1$, $x = 2$, $x = 3$, $x = 4$, and $x = 5$.

(C) Describe the surface $z = f(x, y)$.

46. Let $f(x, y) = 100 + 10x + 25y - x^2 - 5y^2$.

(A) Describe the cross sections of the surface $z = f(x, y)$ produced by cutting it with the planes $y = 0$, $y = 1$, $y = 2$, and $y = 3$.

(B) Describe the cross sections of the surface in the planes $x = 0$, $x = 1$, $x = 2$, and $x = 3$.

(C) Describe the surface $z = f(x, y)$.

47. Let $f(x, y) = e^{-(x^2 + y^2)}$.

(A) Explain why $f(a, b) = f(c, d)$ whenever (a, b) and (c, d) are points on the same circle centered at the origin in the xy plane.

(B) Describe the cross sections of the surface $z = f(x, y)$ produced by cutting it with the planes $x = 0$, $y = 0$, and $x = y$.

(C) Describe the surface $z = f(x, y)$.

48. Let $f(x, y) = 4 - \sqrt{x^2 + y^2}$.

(A) Explain why $f(a, b) = f(c, d)$ whenever (a, b) and (c, d) are points on the same circle with center at the origin in the xy plane.

(B) Describe the cross sections of the surface $z = f(x, y)$ produced by cutting it with the planes $x = 0$, $y = 0$, and $x = y$.

(C) Describe the surface $z = f(x, y)$.

Applications

49. Cost function. A small manufacturing company produces two models of a surfboard: a standard model and a competition model. If the standard model is produced at a variable cost of \$210 each and the competition model at a variable cost of \$300 each, and if the total fixed costs per month are \$6,000, then the monthly cost function is given by

$$C(x, y) = 6,000 + 210x + 300y$$

where x and y are the numbers of standard and competition models produced per month, respectively. Find $C(20, 10)$, $C(50, 5)$, and $C(30, 30)$.

50. Advertising and sales. A company spends \$$x$ thousand per week on online advertising and \$$y$ thousand per week on TV advertising. Its weekly sales are found to be given by

$$S(x, y) = 5x^2 y^3$$

Find $S(3, 2)$ and $S(2, 3)$.

51. Revenue function. A supermarket sells two brands of coffee: brand A at \$$p$ per pound and brand B at \$$q$ per pound. The daily demand equations for brands A and B are, respectively,

$$x = 200 - 5p + 4q$$
$$y = 300 + 2p - 4q$$

(both in pounds). Find the daily revenue function $R(p, q)$. Evaluate $R(2, 3)$ and $R(3, 2)$.

52. Revenue, cost, and profit functions. A company manufactures 10- and 3-speed bicycles. The weekly demand and cost equations are

$$p = 230 - 9x + y$$
$$q = 130 + x - 4y$$
$$C(x, y) = 200 + 80x + 30y$$

where \$$p$ is the price of a 10-speed bicycle, \$$q$ is the price of a 3-speed bicycle, x is the weekly demand for 10-speed bicycles, y is the weekly demand for 3-speed bicycles, and $C(x, y)$ is the cost function. Find the weekly revenue function $R(x, y)$ and the weekly profit function $P(x, y)$. Evaluate $R(10, 15)$ and $P(10, 15)$.

53. Productivity. The Cobb–Douglas production function for a petroleum company is given by

$$f(x, y) = 20x^{0.4} y^{0.6}$$

where x is the utilization of labor and y is the utilization of capital. If the company uses 1,250 units of labor and 1,700 units of capital, how many units of petroleum will be produced?

54. Productivity. The petroleum company in Problem 53 is taken over by another company that decides to double both the units of labor and the units of capital utilized in the production of petroleum. Use the Cobb–Douglas production function given in Problem 53 to find the amount of petroleum that will be produced by this increased utilization of labor and capital. What is the effect on productivity of doubling both the units of labor and the units of capital?

55. Future value. At the end of each year, \$5,000 is invested into an IRA earning 3% compounded annually.

(A) How much will be in the account at the end of 30 years? Use the annuity formula

$$F(P, i, n) = P\frac{(1 + i)^n - 1}{i}$$

where

P = periodic payment
i = rate per period
n = number of payments (periods)
F = FV = future value

(B) Use graphical approximation methods to determine the rate of interest that would produce \$300,000 in the account at the end of 30 years.

56. Package design. The packaging department in a company has been asked to design a rectangular box with no top and a partition down the middle (see the figure on the next page). Let x, y, and z be the dimensions of the box (in inches).

Figure for 56

Figure for 59

(A) Find the total amount of material $M(x, y, z)$ used in constructing one of these boxes, and evaluate $M(10, 12, 6)$.

 (B) Suppose that the box will have a square base and a volume of 720 cubic inches. Use graphical approximation methods to determine the dimensions that require the least amount of material.

57. Marine biology. Using scuba-diving gear, a marine biologist estimates the time of a dive according to the equation

$$T(V, x) = \frac{33V}{x + 33}$$

where

T = time of dive in minutes
V = volume of air, at sea level pressure, compressed into tanks
x = depth of dive in feet

Find $T(70, 47)$ and $T(60, 27)$.

58. Blood flow. Poiseuille's law states that the resistance R for blood flowing in a blood vessel varies directly as the length L of the vessel and inversely as the fourth power of its radius r. Stated as an equation,

$$R(L, r) = k\frac{L}{r^4} \qquad k \text{ a constant}$$

Find $R(8, 1)$ and $R(4, 0.2)$.

59. Physical anthropology. Anthropologists use an index called the *cephalic index*. The cephalic index C varies directly as the width W of the head and inversely as the length L of the head (both viewed from the top). In terms of an equation,

$$C(W, L) = 100\frac{W}{L}$$

where

W = width in inches
L = length in inches

Find $C(6, 8)$ and $C(8.1, 9)$.

60. Safety research. Under ideal conditions, if a person driving a car slams on the brakes and skids to a stop, the length of the skid marks (in feet) is given by the formula

$$L(w, v) = kwv^2$$

where

k = constant
w = weight of car in pounds
v = speed of car in miles per hour

For $k = 0.000\ 013\ 3$, find $L(2,000, 40)$ and $L(3,000, 60)$.

61. Psychology. The intelligence quotient (IQ) is defined to be the ratio of mental age (MA), as determined by certain tests, to chronological age (CA), multiplied by 100. Stated as an equation,

$$Q(M, C) = \frac{M}{C} \cdot 100$$

where

Q = IQ M = MA C = CA

Find $Q(12, 10)$ and $Q(10, 12)$.

Answers to Matched Problems

1. $3,100

2. 30

3. (A) $R(x, y) = 220x + 300y - 6x^2 + 4xy - 10y^2$;
   $R(20, 10) = \$4,800$
   (B) $P(x, y) = 180x + 220y - 6x^2 + 4xy - 10y^2$
   $-1,000; P(20, 10) = \$2,200$

4. $V(x, y) = x^2y; V(5, 10) = 250$ in.^{3}

5. 17,411 units

6. $A(0, 0, 0); C(2, 4, 0); G(2, 4, 3); D(0, 4, 0)$

7. (A) Each cross section is a parabola that opens downward.
   (B) Each cross section is a parabola that opens upward.

15-2   Partial Derivatives

Partial Derivatives

We know how to differentiate many kinds of functions of one independent variable and how to interpret the derivatives that result. What about functions with two or more independent variables? Let's return to the surfboard example considered on page 798.

For the company producing only the standard board, the cost function was

$$C(x) = 500 + 70x$$

Differentiating with respect to x, we obtain the marginal cost function

$$C'(x) = 70$$

Since the marginal cost is constant, \$70 is the change in cost for a 1-unit increase in production at any output level.

For the company producing two types of boards—a standard model and a competition model—the cost function was

$$C(x, y) = 700 + 70x + 100y$$

Now suppose that we differentiate with respect to x, holding y fixed, and denote the resulting function by $C_x(x, y)$; or suppose we differentiate with respect to y, holding x fixed, and denote the resulting function by $C_y(x, y)$. Differentiating in this way, we obtain

$$C_x(x, y) = 70 \qquad C_y(x, y) = 100$$

Each of these functions is called a **partial derivative**, and, in this example, each represents marginal cost. The first is the change in cost due to a 1-unit increase in production of the standard board with the production of the competition model held fixed. The second is the change in cost due to a 1-unit increase in production of the competition board with the production of the standard board held fixed.

In general, if $z = f(x, y)$, then the **partial derivative of f with respect to x**, denoted $\partial z/\partial x$, f_x, or $f_x(x, y)$, is defined by

$$\frac{\partial z}{\partial x} = \lim_{h \to 0} \frac{f(x + h, y) - f(x, y)}{h}$$

provided that the limit exists. We recognize this formula as the ordinary derivative of f with respect to x, holding y constant. We can continue to use all the derivative rules and properties discussed in Chapters 10 to 12 and apply them to partial derivatives.

Similarly, the **partial derivative of f with respect to y**, denoted $\partial z/\partial y$, f_y, or $f_y(x, y)$, is defined by

$$\frac{\partial z}{\partial y} = \lim_{k \to 0} \frac{f(x, y + h) - f(x, y)}{k}$$

which is the ordinary derivative with respect to y, holding x constant.

Parallel definitions and interpretations hold for functions with three or more independent variables.

EXAMPLE 1   **Partial Derivatives** For $z = f(x, y) = 2x^2 - 3x^2y + 5y + 1$, find

(A) $\partial z/\partial x$ (B) $f_x(2, 3)$

SOLUTION   (A) $z = 2x^2 - 3x^2y + 5y + 1$

Differentiating with respect to x, holding y constant (that is, treating y as a constant), we obtain

$$\frac{\partial z}{\partial x} = 4x - 6xy$$

Figure 1 $y_1 = -7x^2 + 16$

(B) $f(x, y) = 2x^2 - 3x^2 y + 5y + 1$

First, differentiate with respect to x. From part (A), we have

$$f_x(x, y) = 4x - 6xy$$

Then evaluate this equation at $(2, 3)$:

$$f_x(2, 3) = 4(2) - 6(2)(3) = -28$$

In part 1(B), an alternative approach would be to substitute $y = 3$ into $f(x, y)$ and graph the function $f(x, 3) = -7x^2 + 16$, which represents the cross section of the surface $z = f(x, y)$ produced by cutting it with the plane $y = 3$. Then determine the slope of the tangent line when $x = 2$. Again, we conclude that $f_x(2, 3) = -28$ (see Fig. 1).

Matched Problem 1   For f in Example 1, find

(A) $\partial z / \partial y$ (B) $f_y(2, 3)$

EXAMPLE 2   **Partial Derivatives Using the Chain Rule**   For $z = f(x, y) = e^{x^2 + y^2}$, find

(A) $\partial z / \partial x$ (B) $f_y(2, 1)$

SOLUTION   (A) Using the chain rule [thinking of $z = e^u$, $u = u(x)$; y is held constant], we obtain

$$\frac{\partial z}{\partial x} = e^{x^2 + y^2} \frac{\partial (x^2 + y^2)}{\partial x}$$

$$= 2x e^{x^2 + y^2}$$

(B) $$f_y(x, y) = e^{x^2 + y^2} \frac{\partial (x^2 + y^2)}{\partial y} = 2y e^{x^2 + y^2}$$

$$f_y(2, 1) = 2(1) e^{(2)^2 + (1)^2}$$

$$= 2e^5$$

Matched Problem 2   For $z = f(x, y) = (x^2 + 2xy)^5$, find

(A) $\partial z / \partial y$ (B) $f_x(1, 0)$

EXAMPLE 3   **Profit**   The profit function for the surfboard company in Example 3 of Section 15-1 was

$$P(x, y) = 140x + 200y - 4x^2 + 2xy - 12y^2 - 700$$

Find $P_x(15, 10)$ and $P_x(30, 10)$, and interpret the results.

SOLUTION $$P_x(x, y) = 140 - 8x + 2y$$

$$P_x(15, 10) = 140 - 8(15) + 2(10) = 40$$

$$P_x(30, 10) = 140 - 8(30) + 2(10) = -80$$

At a production level of 15 standard and 10 competition boards per week, increasing the production of standard boards by 1 unit and holding the production of competition boards fixed at 10 will increase profit by approximately \$40. At a production level of 30 standard and 10 competition boards per week, increasing the production of standard boards by 1 unit and holding the production of competition boards fixed at 10 will decrease profit by approximately \$80.

Matched Problem 3 For the profit function in Example 3, find $P_y(25, 10)$ and $P_y(25, 15)$, and interpret the results.

EXAMPLE 4 **Productivity** The productivity of a major computer manufacturer is given approximately by the Cobb–Douglas production function

$$f(x, y) = 15x^{0.4}y^{0.6}$$

with the utilization of x units of labor and y units of capital. The partial derivative $f_x(x, y)$ represents the rate of change of productivity with respect to labor and is called the **marginal productivity of labor**. The partial derivative $f_y(x, y)$ represents the rate of change of productivity with respect to capital and is called the **marginal productivity of capital**. If the company is currently utilizing 4,000 units of labor and 2,500 units of capital, find the marginal productivity of labor and the marginal productivity of capital. For the greatest increase in productivity, should the management of the company encourage increased use of labor or increased use of capital?

SOLUTION

$$f_x(x, y) = 6x^{-0.6}y^{0.6}$$
$$f_x(4{,}000, 2{,}500) = 6(4{,}000)^{-0.6}(2{,}500)^{0.6}$$
$$\approx 4.53 \quad \text{Marginal productivity of labor}$$
$$f_y(x, y) = 9x^{0.4}y^{-0.4}$$
$$f_y(4{,}000, 2{,}500) = 9(4{,}000)^{0.4}(2{,}500)^{-0.4}$$
$$\approx 10.86 \quad \text{Marginal productivity of capital}$$

At the current level of utilization of 4,000 units of labor and 2,500 units of capital, each 1-unit increase in labor utilization (keeping capital utilization fixed at 2,500 units) will increase production by approximately 4.53 units, and each 1-unit increase in capital utilization (keeping labor utilization fixed at 4,000 units) will increase production by approximately 10.86 units. The management of the company should encourage increased use of capital.

Matched Problem 4 The productivity of an airplane-manufacturing company is given approximately by the Cobb–Douglas production function

$$f(x, y) = 40x^{0.3}y^{0.7}$$

(A) Find $f_x(x, y)$ and $f_y(x, y)$.

(B) If the company is currently using 1,500 units of labor and 4,500 units of capital, find the marginal productivity of labor and the marginal productivity of capital.

(C) For the greatest increase in productivity, should the management of the company encourage increased use of labor or increased use of capital?

Partial derivatives have simple geometric interpretations, as shown in Figure 2. If we hold x fixed at $x = a$, then $f_y(a, y)$ is the slope of the curve obtained by intersecting the surface $z = f(x, y)$ with the plane $x = a$. A similar interpretation is given to $f_x(x, b)$.

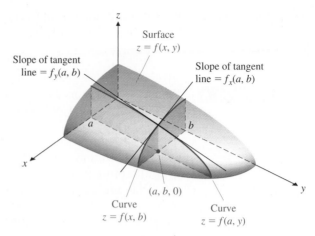

Figure 2

Second-Order Partial Derivatives

The function

$$z = f(x, y) = x^4 y^7$$

has two **first-order partial derivatives**:

$$\frac{\partial z}{\partial x} = f_x = f_x(x, y) = 4x^3 y^7 \quad \text{and} \quad \frac{\partial z}{\partial y} = f_y = f_y(x, y) = 7x^4 y^6$$

Each of these partial derivatives, in turn, has two partial derivatives called **second-order partial derivatives** of $z = f(x, y)$. Generalizing the various notations we have for first-order partial derivatives, we write the four second-order partial derivatives of $z = f(x, y) = x^4 y^7$ as

Equivalent notations

$$f_{xx} = f_{xx}(x, y) = \frac{\partial^2 z}{\partial x^2} = \frac{\partial}{\partial x}\left(\frac{\partial z}{\partial x}\right) = \frac{\partial}{\partial x}(4x^3 y^7) = 12x^2 y^7$$

$$f_{xy} = f_{xy}(x, y) = \frac{\partial^2 z}{\partial y\, \partial x} = \frac{\partial}{\partial y}\left(\frac{\partial z}{\partial x}\right) = \frac{\partial}{\partial y}(4x^3 y^7) = 28x^3 y^6$$

$$f_{yx} = f_{yx}(x, y) = \frac{\partial^2 z}{\partial x\, \partial y} = \frac{\partial}{\partial x}\left(\frac{\partial z}{\partial y}\right) = \frac{\partial}{\partial x}(7x^4 y^6) = 28x^3 y^6$$

$$f_{yy} = f_{yy}(x, y) = \frac{\partial^2 z}{\partial y^2} = \frac{\partial}{\partial y}\left(\frac{\partial z}{\partial y}\right) = \frac{\partial}{\partial y}(7x^4 y^6) = 42x^4 y^5$$

In the mixed partial derivative $\partial^2 z / \partial y\, \partial x = f_{xy}$, we started with $z = f(x, y)$ and first differentiated with respect to x (holding y constant). Then we differentiated with respect to y (holding x constant). In the other mixed partial derivative, $\partial^2 z / \partial x\, \partial y = f_{yx}$, the order of differentiation was reversed; however, the final result was the same—that is, $f_{xy} = f_{yx}$. Although it is possible to find functions for which $f_{xy} \neq f_{yx}$, such functions rarely occur in applications involving partial derivatives. For all the functions in this book, we will assume that $f_{xy} = f_{yx}$.

In general, we have the following definitions:

DEFINITION Second-Order Partial Derivatives

If $z = f(x, y)$, then

$$f_{xx} = f_{xx}(x, y) = \frac{\partial^2 z}{\partial x^2} = \frac{\partial}{\partial x}\left(\frac{\partial z}{\partial x}\right)$$

$$f_{xy} = f_{xy}(x, y) = \frac{\partial^2 z}{\partial y\,\partial x} = \frac{\partial}{\partial y}\left(\frac{\partial z}{\partial x}\right)$$

$$f_{yx} = f_{yx}(x, y) = \frac{\partial^2 z}{\partial x\,\partial y} = \frac{\partial}{\partial x}\left(\frac{\partial z}{\partial y}\right)$$

$$f_{yy} = f_{yy}(x, y) = \frac{\partial^2 z}{\partial y^2} = \frac{\partial}{\partial y}\left(\frac{\partial z}{\partial y}\right)$$

EXAMPLE 5 **Second-Order Partial Derivatives** For $z = f(x, y) = 3x^2 - 2xy^3 + 1$, find

(A) $\dfrac{\partial^2 z}{\partial x\,\partial y}, \dfrac{\partial^2 z}{\partial y\,\partial x}$ (B) $\dfrac{\partial^2 z}{\partial x^2}$ (C) $f_{yx}(2, 1)$

SOLUTION (A) First differentiate with respect to y and then with respect to x:

$$\frac{\partial z}{\partial y} = -6xy^2 \qquad \frac{\partial^2 z}{\partial x\,\partial y} = \frac{\partial}{\partial x}\left(\frac{\partial z}{\partial y}\right) = \frac{\partial}{\partial x}(-6xy^2) = -6y^2$$

Now differentiate with respect to x and then with respect to y:

$$\frac{\partial z}{\partial x} = 6x - 2y^3 \qquad \frac{\partial^2 z}{\partial y\,\partial x} = \frac{\partial}{\partial y}\left(\frac{\partial z}{\partial x}\right) = \frac{\partial}{\partial y}(6x - 2y^3) = -6y^2$$

(B) Differentiate with respect to x twice:

$$\frac{\partial z}{\partial x} = 6x - 2y^3 \qquad \frac{\partial^2 z}{\partial x^2} = \frac{\partial}{\partial x}\left(\frac{\partial z}{\partial x}\right) = 6$$

(C) First find $f_{yx}(x, y)$; then evaluate the resulting equation at $(2, 1)$. Again, remember that f_{yx} signifies differentiation first with respect to y and then with respect to x.

$$f_y(x, y) = -6xy^2 \qquad f_{yx}(x, y) = -6y^2$$

and

$$f_{yx}(2, 1) = -6(1)^2 = -6$$

Matched Problem 5 For $z = f(x, y) = x^3 y - 2y^4 + 3$, find

(A) $\dfrac{\partial^2 z}{\partial y\,\partial x}$ (B) $\dfrac{\partial^2 z}{\partial y^2}$

(C) $f_{xy}(2, 3)$ (D) $f_{yx}(2, 3)$

CONCEPTUAL INSIGHT

Although the mixed second-order partial derivatives f_{xy} and f_{yx} are equal for all functions considered in this book, it is a good idea to compute both of them, as in Example 5(A), as a check on your work. By contrast, the other two second-order partial derivatives, f_{xx} and f_{yy}, are generally not equal to each other. For example, for the function

$$f(x, y) = 3x^2 - 2xy^3 + 1$$

of Example 5,

$$f_{xx} = 6 \qquad \text{and} \qquad f_{yy} = -12xy$$

Exercises 15-2

A

In Problems 1–18, find the indicated first-order partial derivative for each function $z = f(x, y)$.

1. $f_x(x, y)$ if $f(x, y) = 4x - 3y + 6$

2. $f_x(x, y)$ if $f(x, y) = 7x + 8y - 2$

3. $f_y(x, y)$ if $f(x, y) = x^2 - 3xy + 2y^2$

4. $f_y(x, y)$ if $f(x, y) = 3x^2 + 2xy - 7y^2$

5. $\dfrac{\partial z}{\partial x}$ if $z = x^3 + 4x^2y + 2y^3$

6. $\dfrac{\partial z}{\partial y}$ if $z = 4x^2y - 5xy^2$

7. $\dfrac{\partial z}{\partial y}$ if $z = (5x + 2y)^{10}$

8. $\dfrac{\partial z}{\partial x}$ if $z = (2x - 3y)^8$

In Problems 9–16, find the indicated value.

9. $f_x(1, 3)$ if $f(x, y) = 5x^3y - 4xy^2$

10. $f_x(4, 1)$ if $f(x, y) = x^2y^2 - 5xy^3$

11. $f_y(1, 0)$ if $f(x, y) = 3xe^y$

12. $f_y(2, 4)$ if $f(x, y) = x^4 \ln y$

13. $f_y(2, 1)$ if $f(x, y) = e^{x^2} - 4y$

14. $f_y(3, 3)$ if $f(x, y) = e^{3x} - y^2$

15. $f_x(1, -1)$ if $f(x, y) = \dfrac{2xy}{1 + x^2y^2}$

16. $f_x(-1, 2)$ if $f(x, y) = \dfrac{x^2 - y^2}{1 + x^2}$

✎ In Problems 17–22, $M(x, y) = 68 + 0.3x - 0.8y$ gives the mileage (in mpg) of a new car as a function of tire pressure x (in psi) and speed (in mph). Find the indicated quantity (include the appropriate units) and explain what it means.

17. $M(32, 40)$

18. $M(22, 40)$

19. $M(32, 50)$

20. $M(22, 50)$

21. $M_x(32, 50)$

22. $M_y(32, 50)$

B

In Problems 23–34, find the indicated second-order partial derivative for each function $f(x, y)$.

23. $f_{xx}(x, y)$ if $f(x, y) = 6x - 5y + 3$

24. $f_{yx}(x, y)$ if $f(x, y) = -2x + y + 8$

25. $f_{xy}(x, y)$ if $f(x, y) = 4x^2 + 6y^2 - 10$

26. $f_{yy}(x, y)$ if $f(x, y) = x^2 + 9y^2 - 4$

27. $f_{xy}(x, y)$ if $f(x, y) = e^{xy^2}$

28. $f_{yx}(x, y)$ if $f(x, y) = e^{3x+2y}$

29. $f_{yy}(x, y)$ if $f(x, y) = \dfrac{\ln x}{y}$

30. $f_{xx}(x, y)$ if $f(x, y) = \dfrac{3 \ln x}{y^2}$

31. $f_{xx}(x, y)$ if $f(x, y) = (2x + y)^5$

32. $f_{yx}(x, y)$ if $f(x, y) = (3x - 8y)^6$

33. $f_{xy}(x, y)$ if $f(x, y) = (x^2 + y^4)^{10}$

34. $f_{yy}(x, y)$ if $f(x, y) = (1 + 2xy^2)^8$

In Problems 35–44, find the indicated function or value if $C(x, y) = 3x^2 + 10xy - 8y^2 + 4x - 15y - 120$.

35. $C_x(x, y)$

36. $C_y(x, y)$

37. $C_x(3, -2)$

38. $C_y(3, -2)$

39. $C_{xx}(x, y)$

40. $C_{yy}(x, y)$

41. $C_{xy}(x, y)$

42. $C_{yx}(x, y)$

43. $C_{xx}(3, -2)$

44. $C_{yy}(3, -2)$

In Problems 45–56, find the indicated function or value if $S(x, y) = x^3 \ln y + 4y^2e^x$.

45. $S_y(x, y)$

46. $S_x(x, y)$

47. $S_y(-1, 1)$

48. $S_x(-1, 1)$

49. $S_{yx}(x, y)$

50. $S_{xy}(x, y)$

51. $S_{yy}(x, y)$

52. $S_{xx}(x, y)$

53. $S_{yx}(-1, 1)$

54. $S_{xy}(-1, 1)$

55. $S_{yy}(-1, 1)$

56. $S_{xx}(-1, 1)$

In Problems 57–62, $S(T, r) = 50(T - 40)(5 - r)$ gives an ice cream shop's daily sales as a function of temperature T (in °F) and rain r (in inches). Find the indicated quantity (include the appropriate units) and explain what it means.

57. $S(60, 2)$ **58.** $S(80, 0)$

59. $S_r(90, 1)$ **60.** $S_T(90, 1)$

61. $S_{Tr}(90, 1)$ **62.** $S_{rT}(90, 1)$

63. (A) Let $f(x, y) = y^3 + 4y^2 - 5y + 3$. Show that $\partial f/\partial x = 0$.

    (B) Explain why there are an infinite number of functions $g(x, y)$ such that $\partial g/\partial x = 0$.

64. (A) Find an example of a function $f(x, y)$ such that $\partial f/\partial x = 3$ and $\partial f/\partial y = 2$.

    (B) How many such functions are there? Explain.

In Problems 65–70, find $f_{xx}(x, y), f_{xy}(x, y), f_{yx}(x, y),$ and $f_{yy}(x, y)$ for each function f.

65. $f(x, y) = x^2y^2 + x^3 + y$

66. $f(x, y) = x^3y^3 + x + y^2$

67. $f(x, y) = \dfrac{x}{y} - \dfrac{y}{x}$

68. $f(x, y) = \dfrac{x^2}{y} - \dfrac{y^2}{x}$

69. $f(x, y) = xe^{xy}$

70. $f(x, y) = x\ln(xy)$

C

71. For

$$P(x, y) = -x^2 + 2xy - 2y^2 - 4x + 12y - 5$$

find all values of x and y such that

$$P_x(x, y) = 0 \quad \text{and} \quad P_y(x, y) = 0$$

simultaneously.

72. For

$$C(x, y) = 2x^2 + 2xy + 3y^2 - 16x - 18y + 54$$

find all values of x and y such that

$$C_x(x, y) = 0 \quad \text{and} \quad C_y(x, y) = 0$$

simultaneously.

73. For

$$F(x, y) = x^3 - 2x^2y^2 - 2x - 4y + 10$$

find all values of x and y such that

$$F_x(x, y) = 0 \quad \text{and} \quad F_y(x, y) = 0$$

simultaneously.

74. For

$$G(x, y) = x^2 \ln y - 3x - 2y + 1$$

find all values of x and y such that

$$G_x(x, y) = 0 \quad \text{and} \quad G_y(x, y) = 0$$

simultaneously

75. Let $f(x, y) = 3x^2 + y^2 - 4x - 6y + 2$.

    (A) Find the minimum value of $f(x, y)$ when $y = 1$.

    (B) Explain why the answer to part (A) is not the minimum value of the function $f(x, y)$.

76. Let $f(x, y) = 5 - 2x + 4y - 3x^2 - y^2$.

    (A) Find the maximum value of $f(x, y)$ when $x = 2$.

    (B) Explain why the answer to part (A) is not the maximum value of the function $f(x, y)$.

77. Let $f(x, y) = 4 - x^4y + 3xy^2 + y^5$.

    (A) Use graphical approximation methods to find c (to three decimal places) such that $f(c, 2)$ is the maximum value of $f(x, y)$ when $y = 2$.

    (B) Find $f_x(c, 2)$ and $f_y(c, 2)$.

78. Let $f(x, y) = e^x + 2e^y + 3xy^2 + 1$.

    (A) Use graphical approximation methods to find d (to three decimal places) such that $f(1, d)$ is the minimum value of $f(x, y)$ when $x = 1$.

    (B) Find $f_x(1, d)$ and $f_y(1, d)$.

In Problems 79 and 80, show that the function f satisfies $f_{xx}(x, y) + f_{yy}(x, y) = 0$.

79. $f(x, y) = \ln(x^2 + y^2)$

80. $f(x, y) = x^3 - 3xy^2$

81. For $f(x, y) = x^2 + 2y^2$, find

    (A) $\displaystyle\lim_{h \to 0} \dfrac{f(x + h, y) - f(x, y)}{h}$

    (B) $\displaystyle\lim_{k \to 0} \dfrac{f(x, y + k) - f(x, y)}{k}$

82. For $f(x, y) = 2xy^2$, find

    (A) $\displaystyle\lim_{h \to 0} \dfrac{f(x + h, y) - f(x, y)}{h}$

    (B) $\displaystyle\lim_{k \to 0} \dfrac{f(x, y + k) - f(x, y)}{k}$

Applications

83. Profit function. A firm produces two types of calculators each week, x of type A and y of type B. The weekly revenue and cost functions (in dollars) are

$$R(x, y) = 80x + 90y + 0.04xy - 0.05x^2 - 0.05y^2$$

$$C(x, y) = 8x + 6y + 20{,}000$$

Find $P_x(1{,}200, 1{,}800)$ and $P_y(1{,}200, 1{,}800)$, and interpret the results.

84. Advertising and sales. A company spends $\$x$ per week on online advertising and $\$y$ per week on TV advertising. Its weekly sales were found to be given by

$$S(x, y) = 10x^{0.4}y^{0.8}$$

Find $S_x(3{,}000, 2{,}000)$ and $S_y(3{,}000, 2{,}000)$, and interpret the results.

85. **Demand equations.** A supermarket sells two brands of coffee: brand A at $\$p$ per pound and brand B at $\$q$ per pound. The daily demands x and y (in pounds) for brands A and B, respectively, are given by

$$x = 200 - 5p + 4q$$

$$y = 300 + 2p - 4q$$

Find $\partial x/\partial p$ and $\partial y/\partial p$, and interpret the results.

86. **Revenue and profit functions.** A company manufactures 10- and 3-speed bicycles. The weekly demand and cost functions are

$$p = 230 - 9x + y$$

$$q = 130 + x - 4y$$

$$C(x, y) = 200 + 80x + 30y$$

where $\$p$ is the price of a 10-speed bicycle, $\$q$ is the price of a 3-speed bicycle, x is the weekly demand for 10-speed bicycles, y is the weekly demand for 3-speed bicycles, and $C(x, y)$ is the cost function. Find $R_x(10, 5)$ and $P_x(10, 5)$, and interpret the results.

87. **Productivity.** The productivity of a certain third-world country is given approximately by the function

$$f(x, y) = 10x^{0.75}y^{0.25}$$

with the utilization of x units of labor and y units of capital.

(A) Find $f_x(x, y)$ and $f_y(x, y)$.

(B) If the country is now using 600 units of labor and 100 units of capital, find the marginal productivity of labor and the marginal productivity of capital.

(C) For the greatest increase in the country's productivity, should the government encourage increased use of labor or increased use of capital?

88. **Productivity.** The productivity of an automobile-manufacturing company is given approximately by the function

$$f(x, y) = 50\sqrt{xy} = 50x^{0.5}y^{0.5}$$

with the utilization of x units of labor and y units of capital.

(A) Find $f_x(x, y)$ and $f_y(x, y)$.

(B) If the company is now using 250 units of labor and 125 units of capital, find the marginal productivity of labor and the marginal productivity of capital.

(C) For the greatest increase in the company's productivity, should the management encourage increased use of labor or increased use of capital?

Problems 89–92 refer to the following: If a decrease in demand for one product results in an increase in demand for another product, the two products are said to be **competitive**, *or* **substitute**, **products**. *(Real whipping cream and imitation whipping cream are examples of competitive, or substitute, products.) If a decrease in demand for one product results in a decrease in demand for another product, the two products are said to be* **complementary products**. *(Fishing boats and outboard motors are examples of complementary products.) Partial derivatives can be used to test whether two products are competitive, complementary, or neither. We start with demand functions for two*

products such that the demand for either depends on the prices for both:

$$x = f(p, q) \quad \text{Demand function for product } A$$

$$y = g(p, q) \quad \text{Demand function for product } B$$

The variables x and y represent the number of units demanded of products A and B, respectively, at a price p for 1 unit of product A and a price q for 1 unit of product B. Normally, if the price of A increases while the price of B is held constant, then the demand for A will decrease; that is, $f_p(p, q) < 0$. Then, if A and B are competitive products, the demand for B will increase; that is, $g_p(p, q) > 0$. Similarly, if the price of B increases while the price of A is held constant, the demand for B will decrease; that is, $g_q(p, q) < 0$. Then, if A and B are competitive products, the demand for A will increase; that is, $f_q(p, q) > 0$. Reasoning similarly for complementary products, we arrive at the following test:

Test for Competitive and Complementary Products

Partial Derivatives		Products A and B
$f_q(p, q) > 0$ and	$g_p(p, q) > 0$	Competitive (substitute)
$f_q(p, q) < 0$ and	$g_p(p, q) < 0$	Complementary
$f_q(p, q) \geq 0$ and	$g_p(p, q) \leq 0$	Neither
$f_q(p, q) \leq 0$ and	$g_p(p, q) \geq 0$	Neither

Use this test in Problems 89–92 to determine whether the indicated products are competitive, complementary, or neither.

89. **Product demand.** The weekly demand equations for the sale of butter and margarine in a supermarket are

$$x = f(p, q) = 8{,}000 - 0.09p^2 + 0.08q^2 \quad \text{Butter}$$

$$y = g(p, q) = 15{,}000 + 0.04p^2 - 0.3q^2 \quad \text{Margarine}$$

90. **Product demand.** The daily demand equations for the sale of brand A coffee and brand B coffee in a supermarket are

$$x = f(p, q) = 200 - 5p + 4q \quad \text{Brand } A \text{ coffee}$$

$$y = g(p, q) = 300 + 2p - 4q \quad \text{Brand } B \text{ coffee}$$

91. **Product demand.** The monthly demand equations for the sale of skis and ski boots in a sporting goods store are

$$x = f(p, q) = 800 - 0.004p^2 - 0.003q^2 \quad \text{Skis}$$

$$y = g(p, q) = 600 - 0.003p^2 - 0.002q^2 \quad \text{Ski boots}$$

92. **Product demand.** The monthly demand equations for the sale of tennis rackets and tennis balls in a sporting goods store are

$$x = f(p, q) = 500 - 0.5p - q^2 \quad \text{Tennis rackets}$$

$$y = g(p, q) = 10{,}000 - 8p - 100q^2 \quad \text{Tennis balls (cans)}$$

93. **Medicine.** The following empirical formula relates the surface area A (in square inches) of an average human body to its weight w (in pounds) and its height h (in inches):

$$A = f(w, h) = 15.64w^{0.425}h^{0.725}$$

(A) Find $f_w(w, h)$ and $f_h(w, h)$.

(B) For a 65-pound child who is 57 inches tall, find $f_w(65, 57)$ and $f_h(65, 57)$, and interpret the results.

94. Blood flow. Poiseuille's law states that the resistance R for blood flowing in a blood vessel varies directly as the length L of the vessel and inversely as the fourth power of its radius r. Stated as an equation,

$$R(L, r) = k\frac{L}{r^4} \qquad k \text{ a constant}$$

Find $R_L(4, 0.2)$ and $R_r(4, 0.2)$, and interpret the results.

95. Physical anthropology. Anthropologists use the cephalic index C, which varies directly as the width W of the head and inversely as the length L of the head (both viewed from the top). In terms of an equation,

$$C(W, L) = 100\frac{W}{L}$$

where

$$W = \text{width in inches} \qquad L = \text{length in inches}$$

Find $C_W(6, 8)$ and $C_L(6, 8)$, and interpret the results.

Figure for 95

96. Safety research. Under ideal conditions, if a person driving a car slams on the brakes and skids to a stop, the length of the skid marks (in feet) is given by the formula

$$L(w, v) = kwv^2$$

where

$$k = \text{constant}$$
$$w = \text{weight of car in pounds}$$
$$v = \text{speed of car in miles per hour}$$

For $k = 0.000\,013\,3$, find $L_w(2,500, 60)$ and $L_v(2,500, 60)$, and interpret the results.

Answers to Matched Problems

1. (A) $\partial z/\partial y = -3x^2 + 5$
   (B) $f_y(2, 3) = -7$

2. (A) $10x(x^2 + 2xy)^4$
   (B) 10

3. $P_y(25, 10) = 10$: At a production level of $x = 25$ and $y = 10$, increasing y by 1 unit and holding x fixed at 25 will increase profit by approximately \$10; $P_y(25, 15) = -110$: At a production level of $x = 25$ and $y = 15$, increasing y by 1 unit and holding x fixed at 25 will decrease profit by approximately \$110

4. (A) $f_x(x, y) = 12x^{-0.7}y^{0.7}; f_y(x, y) = 28x^{0.3}y^{-0.3}$
   (B) Marginal productivity of labor ≈ 25.89; marginal productivity of capital ≈ 20.14
   (C) Labor

5. (A) $3x^2$ (B) $-24y^2$
   (C) 12 (D) 12

15-3 Maxima and Minima

We are now ready to undertake a brief, but useful, analysis of local maxima and minima for functions of the type $z = f(x, y)$. We will extend the second-derivative test developed for functions of a single independent variable. We assume that all second-order partial derivatives exist for the function f in some circular region in the xy plane. This guarantees that the surface $z = f(x, y)$ has no sharp points, breaks, or ruptures. In other words, we are dealing only with smooth surfaces with no edges (like the edge of a box), breaks (like an earthquake fault), or sharp points (like the bottom point of a golf tee). (See Figure 1.)

Figure 1

In addition, we will not concern ourselves with boundary points or absolute maxima–minima theory. Despite these restrictions, the procedure we will describe will help us solve a large number of useful problems.

What does it mean for $f(a, b)$ to be a local maximum or a local minimum? We say that $f(a, b)$ **is a local maximum** if there exists a circular region in the domain of f with (a, b) as the center, such that

$$f(a, b) \geq f(x, y)$$

for all (x, y) in the region. Similarly, we say that $f(a, b)$ **is a local minimum** if there exists a circular region in the domain of f with (a, b) as the center, such that

$$f(a, b) \leq f(x, y)$$

for all (x, y) in the region. Figure 2A illustrates a local maximum, Figure 2B a local minimum, and Figure 2C a **saddle point**, which is neither a local maximum nor a local minimum.

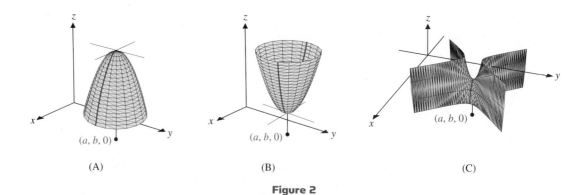

(A)   (B)   (C)

Figure 2

What happens to $f_x(a, b)$ and $f_y(a, b)$ if $f(a, b)$ is a local minimum or a local maximum and the partial derivatives of f exist in a circular region containing (a, b)? Figure 2 suggests that $f_x(a, b) = 0$ and $f_y(a, b) = 0$, since the tangent lines to the given curves are horizontal. Theorem 1 indicates that our intuitive reasoning is correct.

THEOREM 1   Local Extrema and Partial Derivatives

Let $f(a, b)$ be a local extremum (a local maximum or a local minimum) for the function f. If both f_x and f_y exist at (a, b), then

$$f_x(a, b) = 0 \quad \text{and} \quad f_y(a, b) = 0 \tag{1}$$

The converse of this theorem is false. If $f_x(a, b) = 0$ and $f_y(a, b) = 0$, then $f(a, b)$ may or may not be a local extremum; for example, the point $(a, b, f(a, b))$ may be a saddle point (see Fig. 2C).

Theorem 1 gives us *necessary* (but not *sufficient*) conditions for $f(a, b)$ to be a local extremum. We find all points (a, b) such that $f_x(a, b) = 0$ and $f_y(a, b) = 0$ and test these further to determine whether $f(a, b)$ is a local extremum or a saddle point. Points (a, b) such that conditions (1) hold are called **critical points**.

EXPLORE & DISCUSS 1

(A) Let $f(x, y) = y^2 + 1$. Explain why $f(x, y)$ has a local minimum at every point on the x axis. Verify that every point on the x axis is a critical point. Explain why the graph of $z = f(x, y)$ could be described as a trough.

(B) Let $g(x, y) = x^3$. Show that every point on the y axis is a critical point. Explain why no point on the y axis is a local extremum. Explain why the graph of $z = g(x, y)$ could be described as a slide.

The next theorem, using second-derivative tests, gives us *sufficient* conditions for a critical point to produce a local extremum or a saddle point.

THEOREM 2   Second-Derivative Test for Local Extrema

If

1. $z = f(x, y)$
2. $f_x(a, b) = 0$ and $f_y(a, b) = 0$ [(a, b) is a critical point]
3. All second-order partial derivatives of f exist in some circular region containing (a, b) as center.
4. $A = f_{xx}(a, b),\quad B = f_{xy}(a, b),\quad C = f_{yy}(a, b)$

Then

Case 1.   If $AC - B^2 > 0$ and $A < 0$, then $f(a, b)$ is a local maximum.

Case 2.   If $AC - B^2 > 0$ and $A > 0$, then $f(a, b)$ is a local minimum.

Case 3.   If $AC - B^2 < 0$, then f has a saddle point at (a, b).

Case 4.   If $AC - B^2 = 0$, the test fails.

CONCEPTUAL INSIGHT

The condition $A = f_{xx}(a, b) < 0$ in case 1 of Theorem 2 is analogous to the condition $f''(c) < 0$ in the second-derivative test for a function of one variable (Section 12-5), which implies that the function is concave downward and therefore has a local maximum. Similarly, the condition $A = f_{xx}(a, b) > 0$ in case 2 is analogous to the condition $f''(c) > 0$ in the earlier second-derivative test, which implies that the function is concave upward and therefore has a local minimum.

To illustrate the use of Theorem 2, we find the local extremum for a very simple function whose solution is almost obvious: $z = f(x, y) = x^2 + y^2 + 2$. From the function f itself and its graph (Fig. 3), it is clear that a local minimum is found at $(0, 0)$. Let us see how Theorem 2 confirms this observation.

Step 1   Find critical points: Find (x, y) such that $f_x(x, y) = 0$ and $f_y(x, y) = 0$ simultaneously:

$$f_x(x, y) = 2x = 0 \qquad f_y(x, y) = 2y = 0$$
$$x = 0 \qquad\qquad\quad y = 0$$

The only critical point is $(a, b) = (0, 0)$.

Step 2   Compute $A = f_{xx}(0, 0)$, $B = f_{xy}(0, 0)$, and $C = f_{yy}(0, 0)$:

$$f_{xx}(x, y) = 2; \qquad \text{so,} \qquad A = f_{xx}(0, 0) = 2$$
$$f_{xy}(x, y) = 0; \qquad \text{so,} \qquad B = f_{xy}(0, 0) = 0$$
$$f_{yy}(x, y) = 2; \qquad \text{so,} \qquad C = f_{yy}(0, 0) = 2$$

Step 3   Evaluate $AC - B^2$ and try to classify the critical point $(0, 0)$ by using Theorem 2:

$$AC - B^2 = (2)(2) - (0)^2 = 4 > 0 \qquad \text{and} \qquad A = 2 > 0$$

Therefore, case 2 in Theorem 2 holds. That is, $f(0, 0) = 2$ is a local minimum.

We will now use Theorem 2 to analyze extrema without the aid of graphs.

Figure 3

EXAMPLE 1   **Finding Local Extrema** Use Theorem 2 to find local extrema of

$$f(x, y) = -x^2 - y^2 + 6x + 8y - 21$$

SOLUTION   **Step 1**   Find critical points: Find (x, y) such that $f_x(x, y) = 0$ and $f_y(x, y) = 0$ simultaneously:

$$f_x(x, y) = -2x + 6 = 0 \qquad f_y(x, y) = -2y + 8 = 0$$
$$x = 3 \qquad\qquad\qquad y = 4$$

The only critical point is $(a, b) = (3, 4)$.

Step 2   Compute $A = f_{xx}(3, 4)$, $B = f_{xy}(3, 4)$, and $C = f_{yy}(3, 4)$:

$$f_{xx}(x, y) = -2; \qquad \text{so,} \qquad A = f_{xx}(3, 4) = -2$$
$$f_{xy}(x, y) = 0; \qquad \text{so,} \qquad B = f_{xy}(3, 4) = 0$$
$$f_{yy}(x, y) = -2; \qquad \text{so,} \qquad C = f_{yy}(3, 4) = -2$$

Step 3   Evaluate $AC - B^2$ and try to classify the critical point $(3, 4)$ by using Theorem 2:

$$AC - B^2 = (-2)(-2) - (0)^2 = 4 > 0 \qquad \text{and} \qquad A = -2 < 0$$

Therefore, case 1 in Theorem 2 holds, and $f(3, 4) = 4$ is a local maximum.

Matched Problem 1   Use Theorem 2 to find local extrema of

$$f(x, y) = x^2 + y^2 - 10x - 2y + 36$$

EXAMPLE 2   **Finding Local Extrema: Multiple Critical Points** Use Theorem 2 to find local extrema of

$$f(x, y) = x^3 + y^3 - 6xy$$

SOLUTION   **Step 1**   Find critical points of $f(x, y) = x^3 + y^3 - 6xy$:

$$f_x(x, y) = 3x^2 - 6y = 0 \qquad\qquad \textit{Solve for y.}$$
$$6y = 3x^2$$
$$y = \tfrac{1}{2}x^2 \qquad\qquad\qquad\qquad\qquad (2)$$
$$f_y(x, y) = 3y^2 - 6x = 0$$
$$3y^2 = 6x \qquad\qquad \textit{Use equation (2) to eliminate y.}$$
$$3(\tfrac{1}{2}x^2)^2 = 6x$$
$$\tfrac{3}{4}x^4 = 6x \qquad\qquad \textit{Solve for x.}$$
$$3x^4 - 24x = 0$$
$$3x(x^3 - 8) = 0$$
$$x = 0 \qquad \text{or} \qquad x = 2$$
$$y = 0 \qquad\qquad y = \tfrac{1}{2}(2)^2 = 2$$

The critical points are $(0, 0)$ and $(2, 2)$.

Since there are two critical points, steps 2 and 3 must be performed twice.

Test (0, 0)   **Step 2**   Compute $A = f_{xx}(0, 0)$, $B = f_{xy}(0, 0)$, and $C = f_{yy}(0, 0)$:

$$f_{xx}(x, y) = 6x; \qquad \text{so,} \qquad A = f_{xx}(0, 0) = 0$$

$$f_{xy}(x, y) = -6; \qquad \text{so,} \qquad B = f_{xy}(0, 0) = -6$$

$$f_{yy}(x, y) = 6y; \qquad \text{so,} \qquad C = f_{yy}(0, 0) = 0$$

Step 3 Evaluate $AC - B^2$ and try to classify the critical point $(0, 0)$ by using Theorem 2:

$$AC - B^2 = (0)(0) - (-6)^2 = -36 < 0$$

Therefore, case 3 in Theorem 2 applies. That is, f has a saddle point at $(0, 0)$. Now we will consider the second critical point, $(2, 2)$:

Test (2, 2) **Step 2** Compute $A = f_{xx}(2, 2)$, $B = f_{xy}(2, 2)$, and $C = f_{yy}(2, 2)$:

$$f_{xx}(x, y) = 6x; \qquad \text{so,} \qquad A = f_{xx}(2, 2) = 12$$

$$f_{xy}(x, y) = -6; \qquad \text{so,} \qquad B = f_{xy}(2, 2) = -6$$

$$f_{yy}(x, y) = 6y; \qquad \text{so,} \qquad C = f_{yy}(2, 2) = 12$$

Step 3 Evaluate $AC - B^2$ and try to classify the critical point $(2, 2)$ by using Theorem 2:

$$AC - B^2 = (12)(12) - (-6)^2 = 108 > 0 \qquad \text{and} \qquad A = 12 > 0$$

So, case 2 in Theorem 2 applies, and $f(2, 2) = -8$ is a local minimum.

Our conclusions in Example 2 may be confirmed geometrically by graphing cross sections of the function f. The cross sections of f in the planes $y = 0$, $x = 0$, $y = x$, and $y = -x$ [each of these planes contains $(0, 0)$] are represented by the graphs of the functions $f(x, 0) = x^3$, $f(0, y) = y^3$, $f(x, x) = 2x^3 - 6x^2$, and $f(x, -x) = 6x^2$, respectively, as shown in Figure 4A (note that the first two functions have the same graph). The cross sections of f in the planes $y = 2$, $x = 2$, $y = x$, and $y = 4 - x$ [each of these planes contains $(2, 2)$] are represented by the graphs of $f(x, 2) = x^3 - 12x + 8$, $f(2, y) = y^3 - 12y + 8$, $f(x, x) = 2x^3 - 6x^2$, and $f(x, 4 - x) = x^3 + (4 - x)^3 + 6x^2 - 24x$, respectively, as shown in Figure 4B (the first two functions have the same graph). Figure 4B illustrates the fact that since f has a local minimum at $(2, 2)$, each of the cross sections of f through $(2, 2)$ has a local minimum of -8 at $(2, 2)$. Figure 4A, by contrast, indicates that some cross sections of f through $(0, 0)$ have a local minimum, some a local maximum, and some neither one, at $(0, 0)$.

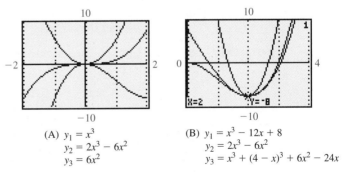

(A) $y_1 = x^3$
$y_2 = 2x^3 - 6x^2$
$y_3 = 6x^2$

(B) $y_1 = x^3 - 12x + 8$
$y_2 = 2x^3 - 6x^2$
$y_3 = x^3 + (4 - x)^3 + 6x^2 - 24x$

Figure 4

Matched Problem 2   Use Theorem 2 to find local extrema for $f(x, y) = x^3 + y^2 - 6xy$.

EXAMPLE 3 **Profit** Suppose that the surfboard company discussed earlier has developed the yearly profit equation

$$P(x, y) = -22x^2 + 22xy - 11y^2 + 110x - 44y - 23$$

where x is the number (in thousands) of standard surfboards produced per year, y is the number (in thousands) of competition surfboards produced per year, and P is profit (in thousands of dollars). How many of each type of board should be produced per year to realize a maximum profit? What is the maximum profit?

SOLUTION **Step 1** Find critical points:

$$P_x(x, y) = -44x + 22y + 110 = 0$$

$$P_y(x, y) = 22x - 22y - 44 = 0$$

Solving this system, we obtain $(3, 1)$ as the only critical point.

Step 2 Compute $A = P_{xx}(3, 1)$, $B = P_{xy}(3, 1)$, and $C = P_{yy}(3, 1)$:

$$P_{xx}(x, y) = -44; \quad \text{so,} \quad A = P_{xx}(3, 1) = -44$$

$$P_{xy}(x, y) = 22; \quad \text{so,} \quad B = P_{xy}(3, 1) = 22$$

$$P_{yy}(x, y) = -22; \quad \text{so,} \quad C = P_{yy}(3, 1) = -22$$

Step 3 Evaluate $AC - B^2$ and try to classify the critical point $(3, 1)$ by using Theorem 2:

$$AC - B^2 = (-44)(-22) - 22^2 = 484 > 0 \quad \text{and} \quad A = -44 < 0$$

Therefore, case 1 in Theorem 2 applies. That is, $P(3, 1) = 120$ is a local maximum. A maximum profit of $120,000 is obtained by producing and selling 3,000 standard boards and 1,000 competition boards per year.

Matched Problem 3 Repeat Example 3 with

$$P(x, y) = -66x^2 + 132xy - 99y^2 + 132x - 66y - 19$$

EXAMPLE 4 **Package Design** The packaging department in a company is to design a rectangular box with no top and a partition down the middle. The box must have a volume of 48 cubic inches. Find the dimensions that will minimize the amount of material used to construct the box.

SOLUTION Refer to Figure 5. The amount of material used in constructing this box is

$$\begin{array}{c} \text{Front,} \quad \text{Sides,} \\ \text{Base} \quad \text{back} \quad \text{partition} \\ M = xy + 2xz + 3yz \end{array} \qquad (3)$$

The volume of the box is

$$V = xyz = 48 \qquad (4)$$

Since Theorem 2 applies only to functions with two independent variables, we must use equation (4) to eliminate one of the variables in equation (3):

$$M = xy + 2xz + 3yz \qquad \text{Substitute } z = 48/xy.$$

$$= xy + 2x\left(\frac{48}{xy}\right) + 3y\left(\frac{48}{xy}\right)$$

$$= xy + \frac{96}{y} + \frac{144}{x}$$

Figure 5

So, we must find the minimum value of

$$M(x, y) = xy + \frac{96}{y} + \frac{144}{x} \qquad x > 0 \qquad \text{and} \qquad y > 0$$

Step 1 Find critical points:

$$M_x(x, y) = y - \frac{144}{x^2} = 0$$

$$y = \frac{144}{x^2} \tag{5}$$

$$M_y(x, y) = x - \frac{96}{y^2} = 0$$

$$x = \frac{96}{y^2} \qquad\qquad \textit{Solve for } y^2.$$

$$y^2 = \frac{96}{x} \qquad\qquad \textit{Use equation (5) to eliminate } y \textit{ and solve for x.}$$

$$\left(\frac{144}{x^2}\right)^2 = \frac{96}{x}$$

$$\frac{20{,}736}{x^4} = \frac{96}{x} \qquad\qquad \textit{Multiply both sides by } x^4/96 \textit{ (recall that x > 0).}$$

$$x^3 = \frac{20{,}736}{96} = 216 \qquad\qquad \textit{Use equation (5) to find y.}$$

$$x = 6$$

$$y = \frac{144}{36} = 4$$

Therefore, $(6, 4)$ is the only critical point.

Step 2 Compute $A = M_{xx}(6, 4)$, $B = M_{xy}(6, 4)$, and $C = M_{yy}(6, 4)$:

$$M_{xx}(x, y) = \frac{288}{x^3}; \qquad \text{so,} \qquad A = M_{xx}(6, 4) = \tfrac{288}{216} = \tfrac{4}{3}$$

$$M_{xy}(x, y) = 1; \qquad \text{so,} \qquad B = M_{xy}(6, 4) = 1$$

$$M_{yy}(x, y) = \frac{192}{y^3}; \qquad \text{so,} \qquad C = M_{yy}(6, 4) = \tfrac{192}{64} = 3$$

Step 3 Evaluate $AC - B^2$ and try to classify the critical point $(6, 4)$ by using Theorem 2:

$$AC - B^2 = \left(\tfrac{4}{3}\right)(3) - (1)^2 = 3 > 0 \qquad \text{and} \qquad A = \tfrac{4}{3} > 0$$

Case 2 in Theorem 2 applies, and $M(x, y)$ has a local minimum at $(6, 4)$. If $x = 6$ and $y = 4$, then

$$z = \frac{48}{xy} = \frac{48}{(6)(4)} = 2$$

The dimensions that will require the minimum amount of material are 6 inches by 4 inches by 2 inches (see Fig. 6).

2 inches

4 inches

6 inches

Figure 6

Matched Problem 4 If the box in Example 4 must have a volume of 384 cubic inches, find the dimensions that will require the least amount of material.

Exercises 15-3

A

✎ *In Problems 1–4, find $f_x(x, y)$ and $f_y(x, y)$, and explain, using Theorem 1, why $f(x, y)$ has no local extrema.*

1. $f(x, y) = 4x + 5y - 6$

2. $f(x, y) = 10 - 2x - 3y + x^2$

3. $f(x, y) = 3.7 - 1.2x + 6.8y + 0.2y^3 + x^4$

4. $f(x, y) = x^3 - y^2 + 7x + 3y + 1$

Use Theorem 2 to find local extrema in Problems 5–24.

5. $f(x, y) = 6 - x^2 - 4x - y^2$

6. $f(x, y) = 3 - x^2 - y^2 + 6y$

7. $f(x, y) = x^2 + y^2 + 2x - 6y + 14$

8. $f(x, y) = x^2 + y^2 - 4x + 6y + 23$

B

9. $f(x, y) = xy + 2x - 3y - 2$

10. $f(x, y) = x^2 - y^2 + 2x + 6y - 4$

11. $f(x, y) = -3x^2 + 2xy - 2y^2 + 14x + 2y + 10$

12. $f(x, y) = -x^2 + xy - 2y^2 + x + 10y - 5$

13. $f(x, y) = 2x^2 - 2xy + 3y^2 - 4x - 8y + 20$

14. $f(x, y) = 2x^2 - xy + y^2 - x - 5y + 8$

C

15. $f(x, y) = e^{xy}$

16. $f(x, y) = x^2y - xy^2$

17. $f(x, y) = x^3 + y^3 - 3xy$

18. $f(x, y) = 2y^3 - 6xy - x^2$

19. $f(x, y) = 2x^4 + y^2 - 12xy$

20. $f(x, y) = 16xy - x^4 - 2y^2$

21. $f(x, y) = x^3 - 3xy^2 + 6y^2$

22. $f(x, y) = 2x^2 - 2x^2y + 6y^3$

23. $f(x, y) = y^3 + 2x^2y^2 - 3x - 2y + 8$

24. $f(x, y) = x \ln y + x^2 - 4x - 5y + 3$

✎ **25.** Explain why $f(x, y) = x^2$ has an infinite number of local extrema.

✎ **26.** (A) Find the local extrema of the functions $f(x, y) = x + y, g(x, y) = x^2 + y^2$, and $h(x, y) = x^3 + y^3$.

(B) Discuss the local extrema of the function $k(x, y) = x^n + y^n$, where n is a positive integer.

27. (A) Show that $(0, 0)$ is a critical point of the function $f(x, y) = x^4e^y + x^2y^4 + 1$, but that the second-derivative test for local extrema fails.

(B) Use cross sections, as in Example 2, to decide whether f has a local maximum, a local minimum, or a saddle point at $(0, 0)$.

28. (A) Show that $(0, 0)$ is a critical point of the function $g(x, y) = e^{xy^2} + x^2y^3 + 2$, but that the second-derivative test for local extrema fails.

(B) Use cross sections, as in Example 2, to decide whether g has a local maximum, a local minimum, or a saddle point at $(0, 0)$.

Applications

29. Product mix for maximum profit. A firm produces two types of earphones per year: x thousand of type A and y thousand of type B. If the revenue and cost equations for the year are (in millions of dollars)

$$R(x, y) = 2x + 3y$$

$$C(x, y) = x^2 - 2xy + 2y^2 + 6x - 9y + 5$$

determine how many of each type of earphone should be produced per year to maximize profit. What is the maximum profit?

30. Automation–labor mix for minimum cost. The annual labor and automated equipment cost (in millions of dollars) for a company's production of HDTV's is given by

$$C(x, y) = 2x^2 + 2xy + 3y^2 - 16x - 18y + 54$$

where x is the amount spent per year on labor and y is the amount spent per year on automated equipment (both in millions of dollars). Determine how much should be spent on each per year to minimize this cost. What is the minimum cost?

31. Maximizing profit. A store sells two brands of camping chairs. The store pays $60 for each brand A chair and $80 for each brand B chair. The research department has estimated the weekly demand equations for these two competitive products to be

$x = 260 - 3p + q$ *Demand equation for brand A*

$y = 180 + p - 2q$ *Demand equation for brand B*

where p is the selling price for brand A and q is the selling price for brand B.

(A) Determine the demands x and y when $p = \$100$ and $q = \$120$; when $p = \$110$ and $q = \$110$.

(B) How should the store price each chair to maximize weekly profits? What is the maximum weekly profit? [*Hint:* $C = 60x + 80y, R = px + qy$, and $P = R - C$.]

32. Maximizing profit. A store sells two brands of laptop sleeves. The store pays $25 for each brand A sleeve and $30 for each brand B sleeve. A consulting firm has estimated the daily demand equations for these two competitive products to be

$x = 130 - 4p + q$ *Demand equation for brand A*

$y = 115 + 2p - 3q$ *Demand equation for brand B*

where p is the selling price for brand A and q is the selling price for brand B.

(A) Determine the demands x and y when $p = \$40$ and $q = \$50$; when $p = \$45$ and $q = \$55$.

(B) How should the store price each brand of sleeve to maximize daily profits? What is the maximum daily profit? [*Hint:* $C = 25x + 30y$, $R = px + qy$, and $P = R - C$.]

33. Minimizing cost. A satellite TV station is to be located at $P(x, y)$ so that the sum of the squares of the distances from P to the three towns A, B, and C is a minimum (see the figure). Find the coordinates of P, the location that will minimize the cost of providing satellite TV for all three towns.

Figure for 33

34. Minimizing cost. Repeat Problem 33, replacing the coordinates of B with $B(6, 9)$ and the coordinates of C with $C(9, 0)$.

35. Minimum material. A rectangular box with no top and two parallel partitions (see the figure) must hold a volume of 64 cubic inches. Find the dimensions that will require the least amount of material.

Figure for 35

36. Minimum material. A rectangular box with no top and two intersecting partitions (see the figure) must hold a volume of 72 cubic inches. Find the dimensions that will require the least amount of material.

Figure for 36

37. Maximum volume. A mailing service states that a rectangular package cannot have the sum of its length and girth exceed 120 inches (see the figure). What are the dimensions of the largest (in volume) mailing carton that can be constructed to meet these restrictions?

Figure for 37

38. Maximum shipping volume. A shipping box is to be reinforced with steel bands in all three directions, as shown in the figure. A total of 150 inches of steel tape is to be used, with 6 inches of waste because of a 2-inch overlap in each direction. Find the dimensions of the box with maximum volume that can be taped as described.

Figure for 38

Answers to Matched Problems

1. $f(5, 1) = 10$ is a local minimum

2. f has a saddle point at $(0, 0)$; $f(6, 18) = -108$ is a local minimum

3. Local maximum for $x = 2$ and $y = 1$; $P(2, 1) = 80$; a maximum profit of $80,000 is obtained by producing and selling 2,000 standard boards and 1,000 competition boards

4. 12 in. by 8 in. by 4 in.

15-4 Maxima and Minima Using Lagrange Multipliers

- Functions of Two Independent Variables
- Functions of Three Independent Variables

Existing fence

Figure 1

Functions of Two Independent Variables

We now consider a powerful method of solving a certain class of maxima–minima problems. Joseph Louis Lagrange (1736–1813), an eighteenth-century French mathematician, discovered this method, called the **method of Lagrange multipliers**. We introduce the method through an example.

A rancher wants to construct two feeding pens of the same size along an existing fence (see Fig. 1). If the rancher has 720 feet of fencing materials available, how long should x and y be in order to obtain the maximum total area? What is the maximum area?

The total area is given by

$$f(x, y) = xy$$

which can be made as large as we like, provided that there are no restrictions on x and y. But there are restrictions on x and y, since we have only 720 feet of fencing. The variables x and y must be chosen so that

$$3x + y = 720$$

This restriction on x and y, called a **constraint**, leads to the following maxima–minima problem:

$$\text{Maximize} \quad f(x, y) = xy \tag{1}$$

$$\text{subject to} \quad 3x + y = 720, \quad \text{or} \quad 3x + y - 720 = 0 \tag{2}$$

This problem is one of a general class of problems of the form

$$\text{Maximize (or minimize)} \quad z = f(x, y) \tag{3}$$

$$\text{subject to} \quad g(x, y) = 0 \tag{4}$$

Of course, we could try to solve equation (4) for y in terms of x, or for x in terms of y, then substitute the result into equation (3), and use methods developed in Section 5-5 for functions of a single variable. But what if equation (4) is more complicated than equation (2), and solving for one variable in terms of the other is either very difficult or impossible? In the method of Lagrange multipliers, we will work with $g(x, y)$ directly and avoid solving equation (4) for one variable in terms of the other. In addition, the method generalizes to functions of arbitrarily many variables subject to one or more constraints.

Now to the method: We form a new function F, using functions f and g in equations (3) and (4), as follows:

$$F(x, y, \lambda) = f(x, y) + \lambda g(x, y) \tag{5}$$

Here, λ (the Greek lowercase letter lambda) is called a **Lagrange multiplier**. Theorem 1 gives the basis for the method.

THEOREM 1 Method of Lagrange Multipliers for Functions of Two Variables
Any local maxima or minima of the function $z = f(x, y)$ subject to the constraint $g(x, y) = 0$ will be among those points (x_0, y_0) for which (x_0, y_0, λ_0) is a solution of the system

$$F_x(x, y, \lambda) = 0$$

$$F_y(x, y, \lambda) = 0$$

$$F_\lambda(x, y, \lambda) = 0$$

where $F(x, y, \lambda) = f(x, y) + \lambda g(x, y)$, provided that all the partial derivatives exist.

We now use the method of Lagrange multipliers to solve the fence problem.

Step 1   Formulate the problem in the form of equations (3) and (4):

$$\text{Maximize} \quad f(x, y) = xy$$

$$\text{subject to} \quad g(x, y) = 3x + y - 720 = 0$$

Step 2   Form the function F, introducing the Lagrange multiplier λ:

$$F(x, y, \lambda) = f(x, y) + \lambda g(x, y)$$

$$= xy + \lambda(3x + y - 720)$$

Step 3   Solve the system $F_x = 0$, $F_y = 0$, $F_\lambda = 0$ (the solutions are **critical points** of F):

$$F_x = y + 3\lambda = 0$$

$$F_y = x + \lambda = 0$$

$$F_\lambda = 3x + y - 720 = 0$$

From the first two equations, we see that

$$y = -3\lambda$$

$$x = -\lambda$$

Substitute these values for x and y into the third equation and solve for λ:

$$-3\lambda - 3\lambda = 720$$

$$-6\lambda = 720$$

$$\lambda = -120$$

So,

$$y = -3(-120) = 360 \text{ feet}$$

$$x = -(-120) = 120 \text{ feet}$$

and $(x_0, y_0, \lambda_0) = (120, 360, -120)$ is the only critical point of F.

Step 4   According to Theorem 1, if the function $f(x, y)$, subject to the constraint $g(x, y) = 0$, has a local maximum or minimum, that maximum or minimum must occur at $x = 120$, $y = 360$. Although it is possible to develop a test similar to Theorem 2 in Section 15-3 to determine the nature of this local extremum, we will not do so. [Note that Theorem 2 cannot be applied to $f(x, y)$ at $(120, 360)$, since this point is not a critical point of the unconstrained function $f(x, y)$.] We simply assume that the maximum value of $f(x, y)$ must occur for $x = 120$, $y = 360$.

$$\text{Max } f(x, y) = f(120, 360)$$

$$= (120)(360) = 43{,}200 \text{ square feet}$$

The key steps in applying the method of Lagrange multipliers are as follows:

PROCEDURE   Method of Lagrange Multipliers: Key Steps

Step 1   Write the problem in the form

$$\text{Maximize (or minimize)} \quad z = f(x, y)$$

$$\text{subject to} \quad g(x, y) = 0$$

Step 2   Form the function F:

$$F(x, y, \lambda) = f(x, y) + \lambda g(x, y)$$

Step 3 Find the critical points of F; that is, solve the system

$$F_x(x, y, \lambda) = 0$$
$$F_y(x, y, \lambda) = 0$$
$$F_\lambda(x, y, \lambda) = 0$$

Step 4 If (x_0, y_0, λ_0) is the only critical point of F, we assume that (x_0, y_0) will always produce the solution to the problems we consider. If F has more than one critical point, we evaluate $z = f(x, y)$ at (x_0, y_0) for each critical point (x_0, y_0, λ_0) of F. For the problems we consider, we assume that the largest of these values is the maximum value of $f(x, y)$, subject to the constraint $g(x, y) = 0$, and the smallest is the minimum value of $f(x, y)$, subject to the constraint $g(x, y) = 0$.

EXAMPLE 1 **Minimization Subject to a Constraint** Minimize $f(x, y) = x^2 + y^2$ subject to $x + y = 10$.

SOLUTION **Step 1**

$$\text{Minimize} \quad f(x, y) = x^2 + y^2$$

$$\text{subject to} \quad g(x, y) = x + y - 10 = 0$$

Step 2

$$F(x, y, \lambda) = x^2 + y^2 + \lambda(x + y - 10)$$

Step 3

$$F_x = 2x + \lambda = 0$$
$$F_y = 2y + \lambda = 0$$
$$F_\lambda = x + y - 10 = 0$$

From the first two equations, $x = -\lambda/2$ and $y = -\lambda/2$. Substituting these values into the third equation, we obtain

$$-\frac{\lambda}{2} - \frac{\lambda}{2} = 10$$

$$-\lambda = 10$$

$$\lambda = -10$$

The only critical point is $(x_0, y_0, \lambda_0) = (5, 5, -10)$.

Step 4 Since $(5, 5, -10)$ is the only critical point of F, we conclude that (see step 4 in the box)

$$\text{Min } f(x, y) = f(5, 5) = (5)^2 + (5)^2 = 50$$

Since $g(x, y)$ in Example 1 has a relatively simple form, an alternative to the method of Lagrange multipliers is to solve $g(x, y) = 0$ for y and then substitute into $f(x, y)$ to obtain the function $h(x) = f(x, 10 - x) = x^2 + (10 - x)^2$ in the single variable x. Then we minimize h (see Fig. 2). From Figure 2, we conclude that Min $f(x, y) = f(5, 5) = 50$. This technique depends on being able to solve the constraint for one of the two variables and so is not always available as an alternative to the method of Lagrange multipliers.

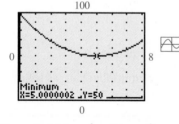

Figure 2 $h(x) = x^2 + (10 - x)^2$

Matched Problem 1 Maximize $f(x, y) = 25 - x^2 - y^2$ subject to $x + y = 4$.

Figures 3 and 4 illustrate the results obtained in Example 1 and Matched Problem 1, respectively.

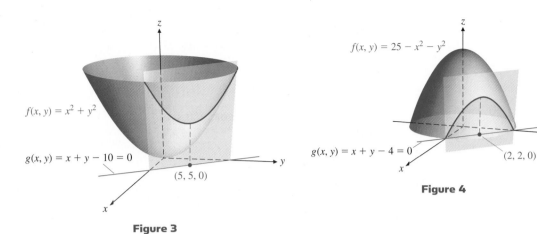

Figure 3

Figure 4

| EXPLORE & DISCUSS 1 |

Consider the problem of minimizing $f(x, y) = 3x^2 + 5y^2$ subject to the constraint $g(x, y) = 2x + 3y - 6 = 0$.

(A) Compute the value of $f(x, y)$ when x and y are integers, $0 \le x \le 3$, $0 \le y \le 2$. Record your answers in the empty boxes next to the points (x, y) in Figure 5.

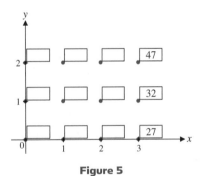

Figure 5

(B) Graph the constraint $g(x, y) = 0$.

(C) Estimate the minimum value of f on the basis of your graph and the computations from part (A).

(D) Use the method of Lagrange multipliers to solve the minimization problem.

EXAMPLE 2   **Productivity** The Cobb–Douglas production function for a new product is given by

$$N(x, y) = 16x^{0.25}y^{0.75}$$

where x is the number of units of labor and y is the number of units of capital required to produce $N(x, y)$ units of the product. Each unit of labor costs \$50 and each unit of capital costs \$100. If \$500,000 has been budgeted for the production of this product, how should that amount be allocated between labor and capital in order to maximize production? What is the maximum number of units that can be produced?

SOLUTION   The total cost of using x units of labor and y units of capital is $50x + 100y$. Thus, the constraint imposed by the \$500,000 budget is

$$50x + 100y = 500,000$$

Step 1   Maximize $N(x, y) = 16x^{0.25}y^{0.75}$

subject to $g(x, y) = 50x + 100y - 500,000 = 0$

Step 2 $$F(x, y, \lambda) = 16x^{0.25}y^{0.75} + \lambda(50x + 100y - 500{,}000)$$

Step 3 $$F_x = 4x^{-0.75}y^{0.75} + 50\lambda = 0$$

$$F_y = 12x^{0.25}y^{-0.25} + 100\lambda = 0$$

$$F_\lambda = 50x + 100y - 500{,}000 = 0$$

From the first two equations,

$$\lambda = -\tfrac{2}{25}x^{-0.75}y^{0.75} \quad \text{and} \quad \lambda = -\tfrac{3}{25}x^{0.25}y^{-0.25}$$

Therefore,

$$-\tfrac{2}{25}x^{-0.75}y^{0.75} = -\tfrac{3}{25}x^{0.25}y^{-0.25} \quad \text{Multiply both sides by } x^{0.75}\,y^{0.25}.$$

$$-\tfrac{2}{25}y = -\tfrac{3}{25}x \qquad \text{(We can assume that } x \neq 0 \text{ and } y \neq 0.)$$

$$y = \tfrac{3}{2}x$$

Now substitute for y in the third equation and solve for x:

$$50x + 100\left(\tfrac{3}{2}x\right) - 500{,}000 = 0$$

$$200x = 500{,}000$$

$$x = 2{,}500$$

So,

$$y = \tfrac{3}{2}(2{,}500) = 3{,}750$$

and

$$\lambda = -\tfrac{2}{25}(2{,}500)^{-0.75}(3{,}750)^{0.75} \approx -0.1084$$

The only critical point of F is $(2{,}500, 3{,}750, -0.1084)$.

Step 4 Since F has only one critical point, we conclude that maximum productivity occurs when 2,500 units of labor and 3,750 units of capital are used (see step 4 in the method of Lagrange multipliers).

$$\text{Max } N(x, y) = N(2{,}500, 3{,}750)$$

$$= 16(2{,}500)^{0.25}(3{,}750)^{0.75}$$

$$\approx 54{,}216 \text{ units}$$

The negative of the value of the Lagrange multiplier found in step 3 is called the **marginal productivity of money** and gives the approximate increase in production for each additional dollar spent on production. In Example 2, increasing the production budget from $500,000 to $600,000 would result in an approximate increase in production of

$$0.1084(100{,}000) = 10{,}840 \text{ units}$$

Note that simplifying the constraint equation

$$50x + 100y - 500{,}000 = 0$$

to

$$x + 2y - 10{,}000 = 0$$

before forming the function $F(x, y, \lambda)$ would make it difficult to interpret $-\lambda$ correctly. **In marginal productivity problems, the constraint equation should not be simplified.**

Matched Problem 2 The Cobb–Douglas production function for a new product is given by

$$N(x, y) = 20x^{0.5}y^{0.5}$$

where x is the number of units of labor and y is the number of units of capital required to produce $N(x, y)$ units of the product. Each unit of labor costs \$40 and each unit of capital costs \$120.

(A) If \$300,000 has been budgeted for the production of this product, how should that amount be allocated in order to maximize production? What is the maximum production?

(B) Find the marginal productivity of money in this case, and estimate the increase in production if an additional \$40,000 is budgeted for production.

EXPLORE & DISCUSS 2

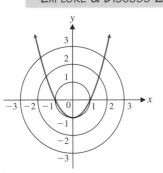

Figure 6

Consider the problem of maximizing $f(x, y) = 4 - x^2 - y^2$ subject to the constraint $g(x, y) = y - x^2 + 1 = 0$.

(A) Explain why $f(x, y) = 3$ whenever (x, y) is a point on the circle of radius 1 centered at the origin. What is the value of $f(x, y)$ when (x, y) is a point on the circle of radius 2 centered at the origin? On the circle of radius 3 centered at the origin? (See Fig. 6.)

(B) Explain why some points on the parabola $y - x^2 + 1 = 0$ lie inside the circle $x^2 + y^2 = 1$.

(C) In light of part (B), would you guess that the maximum value of $f(x, y)$ subject to the constraint is greater than 3? Explain.

(D) Use Lagrange multipliers to solve the maximization problem.

Functions of Three Independent Variables

The method of Lagrange multipliers can be extended to functions with arbitrarily many independent variables with one or more constraints. We now state a theorem for functions with three independent variables and one constraint, and we consider an example that demonstrates the advantage of the method of Lagrange multipliers over the method used in Section 15-3.

THEOREM 2 Method of Lagrange Multipliers for Functions of Three Variables

Any local maxima or minima of the function $w = f(x, y, z)$, subject to the constraint $g(x, y, z) = 0$, will be among the set of points (x_0, y_0, z_0) for which $(x_0, y_0, z_0, \lambda_0)$ is a solution of the system

$$F_x(x, y, z, \lambda) = 0$$

$$F_y(x, y, z, \lambda) = 0$$

$$F_z(x, y, z, \lambda) = 0$$

$$F_\lambda(x, y, z, \lambda) = 0$$

where $F(x, y, z, \lambda) = f(x, y, z) + \lambda g(x, y, z)$, provided that all the partial derivatives exist.

EXAMPLE 3 **Package Design** A rectangular box with an open top and one partition is to be constructed from 162 square inches of cardboard (Fig. 7). Find the dimensions that result in a box with the largest possible volume.

SOLUTION We must maximize

$$V(x, y, z) = xyz$$

subject to the constraint that the amount of material used is 162 square inches. So x, y, and z must satisfy

$$xy + 2xz + 3yz = 162$$

Figure 7

Step 1 Maximize $V(x, y, z) = xyz$
subject to $g(x, y, z) = xy + 2xz + 3yz - 162 = 0$

Step 2 $F(x, y, z, \lambda) = xyz + \lambda(xy + 2xz + 3yz - 162)$

Step 3 $F_x = yz + \lambda(y + 2z) = 0$

$$F_y = xz + \lambda(x + 3z) = 0$$

$$F_z = xy + \lambda(2x + 3y) = 0$$

$$F_\lambda = xy + 2xz + 3yz - 162 = 0$$

From the first two equations, we can write

$$\lambda = \frac{-yz}{y + 2z} \qquad \lambda = \frac{-xz}{x + 3z}$$

Eliminating λ, we have

$$\frac{-yz}{y + 2z} = \frac{-xz}{x + 3z}$$

$$-xyz - 3yz^2 = -xyz - 2xz^2$$

$$3yz^2 = 2xz^2 \qquad \textit{We can assume that } z \neq 0.$$

$$3y = 2x$$

$$x = \tfrac{3}{2}y$$

From the second and third equations,

$$\lambda = \frac{-xz}{x + 3z} \qquad \lambda = \frac{-xy}{2x + 3y}$$

Eliminating λ, we have

$$\frac{-xz}{x + 3z} = \frac{-xy}{2x + 3y}$$

$$-2x^2z - 3xyz = -x^2y - 3xyz$$

$$2x^2z = x^2y \qquad \textit{We can assume that } x \neq 0.$$

$$2z = y$$

$$z = \tfrac{1}{2}y$$

Substituting $x = \tfrac{3}{2}y$ and $z = \tfrac{1}{2}y$ into the fourth equation, we have

$$\left(\tfrac{3}{2}y\right)y + 2\left(\tfrac{3}{2}y\right)\left(\tfrac{1}{2}y\right) + 3y\left(\tfrac{1}{2}y\right) - 162 = 0$$

$$\tfrac{3}{2}y^2 + \tfrac{3}{2}y^2 + \tfrac{3}{2}y^2 = 162$$

$$y^2 = 36 \qquad \textit{We can assume that } y > 0.$$

$$y = 6$$

$$x = \tfrac{3}{2}(6) = 9 \qquad \textit{Using } x = \tfrac{3}{2}y$$

$$z = \tfrac{1}{2}(6) = 3 \qquad \textit{Using } z = \tfrac{1}{2}y$$

and finally,

Figure 8

3 inches

6 inches

9 inches

$$\lambda = \frac{-(6)(3)}{6 + 2(3)} = -\frac{3}{2} \quad \text{Using } \lambda = \frac{-yz}{y + 2z}$$

The only critical point of F with x, y, and z all positive is $(9, 6, 3, -\frac{3}{2})$.

Step 4   The box with the maximum volume has dimensions 9 inches by 6 inches by 3 inches (see Fig. 8).

Matched Problem 3   A box of the same type as in Example 3 is to be constructed from 288 square inches of cardboard. Find the dimensions that result in a box with the largest possible volume.

CONCEPTUAL INSIGHT

An alternative to the method of Lagrange multipliers would be to solve Example 3 by means of Theorem 2 (the second-derivative test for local extrema) in Section 15-3. That approach involves solving the material constraint for one of the variables, say, z:

$$z = \frac{162 - xy}{2x + 3y}$$

Then we would eliminate z in the volume function to obtain a function of two variables:

$$V(x, y) = xy \frac{162 - xy}{2x + 3y}$$

The method of Lagrange multipliers allows us to avoid the formidable tasks of calculating the partial derivatives of V and finding the critical points of V in order to apply Theorem 2.

Exercises 15-4

A

Use the method of Lagrange multipliers in Problems 1–4.

1. Maximize $f(x, y) = 2xy$

   subject to $x + y = 6$

2. Minimize $f(x, y) = 6xy$

   subject to $y - x = 6$

3. Minimize $f(x, y) = x^2 + y^2$

   subject to $3x + 4y = 25$

4. Maximize $f(x, y) = 25 - x^2 - y^2$

   subject to $2x + y = 10$

B

In Problems 5 and 6, use Theorem 1 to explain why no maxima or minima exist.

5. Minimize $f(x, y) = 4y - 3x$

   subject to $2x + 5y = 3$

6. Maximize $f(x, y) = 6x + 5y + 24$

   subject to $3x + 2y = 4$

Use the method of Lagrange multipliers in Problems 7–16.

7. Find the maximum and minimum of $f(x, y) = 2xy$ subject to $x^2 + y^2 = 18$.

8. Find the maximum and minimum of $f(x, y) = x^2 - y^2$ subject to $x^2 + y^2 = 25$.

9. Maximize the product of two numbers if their sum must be 10.

10. Minimize the product of two numbers if their difference must be 10.

C

11. Minimize $f(x, y, z) = x^2 + y^2 + z^2$

   subject to $2x - y + 3z = -28$

12. Maximize $f(x, y, z) = xyz$

   subject to $2x + y + 2z = 120$

13. Maximize and minimize $f(x, y, z) = x + y + z$

   subject to $x^2 + y^2 + z^2 = 12$

14. Maximize and minimize $f(x, y, z) = 2x + 4y + 4z$

   subject to $x^2 + y^2 + z^2 = 9$

15. Maximize $f(x, y) = y + xy^2$

subject to $x + y^2 = 1$

16. Maximize and minimize $f(x, y) = x + e^y$

subject to $x^2 + y^2 = 1$

In Problems 17 and 18, use Theorem 1 to explain why no maxima or minima exist.

17. Maximize $f(x, y) = e^x + 3e^y$

subject to $x - 2y = 6$

18. Minimize $f(x, y) = x^3 + 2y^3$

subject to $6x - 2y = 1$

19. Consider the problem of maximizing $f(x, y)$ subject to $g(x, y) = 0$, where $g(x, y) = y - 5$. Explain how the maximization problem can be solved without using the method of Lagrange multipliers.

20. Consider the problem of minimizing $f(x, y)$ subject to $g(x, y) = 0$, where $g(x, y) = 4x - y + 3$. Explain how the minimization problem can be solved without using the method of Lagrange multipliers.

21. Consider the problem of maximizing $f(x, y) = e^{-(x^2+y^2)}$ subject to the constraint $g(x, y) = x^2 + y - 1 = 0$.

(A) Solve the constraint equation for y, and then substitute into $f(x, y)$ to obtain a function $h(x)$ of the single variable x. Solve the original maximization problem by maximizing h (round answers to three decimal places).

(B) Confirm your answer by the method of Lagrange multipliers.

22. Consider the problem of minimizing

$$f(x, y) = x^2 + 2y^2$$

subject to the constraint $g(x, y) = ye^{x^2} - 1 = 0$.

(A) Solve the constraint equation for y, and then substitute into $f(x, y)$ to obtain a function $h(x)$ of the single variable x. Solve the original minimization problem by minimizing h (round answers to three decimal places).

(B) Confirm your answer by the method of Lagrange multipliers.

Applications

23. Budgeting for least cost. A manufacturing company produces two models of an HDTV per week, x units of model A and y units of model B at a cost (in dollars) of

$$C(x, y) = 6x^2 + 12y^2$$

If it is necessary (because of shipping considerations) that

$$x + y = 90$$

how many of each type of set should be manufactured per week to minimize cost? What is the minimum cost?

24. Budgeting for maximum production. A manufacturing firm has budgeted $60,000 per month for labor and materi-

als. If x thousand is spent on labor and y thousand is spent on materials, and if the monthly output (in units) is given by

$$N(x, y) = 4xy - 8x$$

then how should the $60,000 be allocated to labor and materials in order to maximize N? What is the maximum N?

25. Productivity. A consulting firm for a manufacturing company arrived at the following Cobb–Douglas production function for a particular product:

$$N(x, y) = 50x^{0.8}y^{0.2}$$

In this equation, x is the number of units of labor and y is the number of units of capital required to produce $N(x, y)$ units of the product. Each unit of labor costs $40 and each unit of capital costs $80.

(A) If $400,000 is budgeted for production of the product, determine how that amount should be allocated to maximize production, and find the maximum production.

(B) Find the marginal productivity of money in this case, and estimate the increase in production if an additional $50,000 is budgeted for the production of the product.

26. Productivity. The research department of a manufacturing company arrived at the following Cobb–Douglas production function for a particular product:

$$N(x, y) = 10x^{0.6}y^{0.4}$$

In this equation, x is the number of units of labor and y is the number of units of capital required to produce $N(x, y)$ units of the product. Each unit of labor costs $30 and each unit of capital costs $60.

(A) If $300,000 is budgeted for production of the product, determine how that amount should be allocated to maximize production, and find the maximum production.

(B) Find the marginal productivity of money in this case, and estimate the increase in production if an additional $80,000 is budgeted for the production of the product.

27. Maximum volume. A rectangular box with no top and two intersecting partitions is to be constructed from 192 square inches of cardboard (see the figure). Find the dimensions that will maximize the volume.

Figure for 27

28. Maximum volume. A mailing service states that a rectangular package shall have the sum of its length and girth not to exceed 120 inches (see the figure). What are the dimensions of the largest (in volume) mailing carton that can be constructed to meet these restrictions?

Figure for 28

29. Agriculture. Three pens of the same size are to be built along an existing fence (see the figure). If 400 feet of fencing is available, what length should x and y be to produce the maximum total area? What is the maximum area?

Figure for 29

30. Diet and minimum cost. A group of guinea pigs is to receive 25,600 calories per week. Two available foods produce $200xy$ calories for a mixture of x kilograms of type M food and y kilograms of type N food. If type M costs \$1 per kilogram and type N costs \$2 per kilogram, how much of each type of food should be used to minimize weekly food costs? What is the minimum cost?

Note: $x \geq 0$, $y \geq 0$

Answers to Matched Problems

1. Max $f(x, y) = f(2, 2) = 17$ (see Fig. 4)

2. (A) 3,750 units of labor and 1,250 units of capital;
   Max $N(x, y) = N(3{,}750, 1{,}250) \approx 43{,}301$ units

   (B) Marginal productivity of money ≈ 0.1443; increase in production $\approx 5{,}774$ units

3. 12 in. by 8 in. by 4 in.

15-5 Method of Least Squares

- Least Squares Approximation
- Applications

Least Squares Approximation

Regression analysis is the process of fitting an elementary function to a set of data points by the **method of least squares**. The mechanics of using regression techniques were introduced in Chapter 1. Now, using the optimization techniques of Section 15-3, we can develop and explain the mathematical foundation of the method of least squares. We begin with **linear regression**, the process of finding the equation of the line that is the "best" approximation to a set of data points.

Suppose that a manufacturer wants to approximate the cost function for a product. The value of the cost function has been determined for certain levels of production, as listed in Table 1. Although these points do not all lie on a line (see Fig. 1),

Table 1	
Number of Units	**Cost**
x *(hundreds)*	y *(thousand \$)*
2	4
5	6
6	7
9	8

Figure 1

they are very close to being linear. The manufacturer would like to approximate the cost function by a linear function—that is, determine values a and b so that the line

$$y = ax + b$$

is, in some sense, the "best" approximation to the cost function.

What do we mean by "best"? Since the line $y = ax + b$ will not go through all four points, it is reasonable to examine the differences between the y coordinates of the points listed in the table and the y coordinates of the corresponding points on the line. Each of these differences is called the **residual** at that point (see Fig. 2). For example, at $x = 2$, the point from Table 1 is $(2, 4)$ and the point on the line is $(2, 2a + b)$, so the residual is

$$4 - (2a + b) = 4 - 2a - b$$

All the residuals are listed in Table 2.

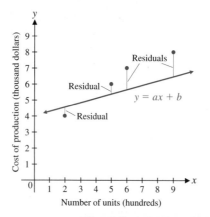

Figure 2

Table 2			
x	**y**	**ax + b**	**Residual**
2	4	$2a + b$	$4 - 2a - b$
5	6	$5a + b$	$6 - 5a - b$
6	7	$6a + b$	$7 - 6a - b$
9	8	$9a + b$	$8 - 9a - b$

Our criterion for the "best" approximation is the following: Determine the values of a and b that *minimize the sum of the squares* of the residuals. The resulting line is called the **least squares line**, or the **regression line**. To this end, we minimize

$$F(a, b) = (4 - 2a - b)^2 + (6 - 5a - b)^2 + (7 - 6a - b)^2 + (8 - 9a - b)^2$$

Step 1   Find critical points:

$$F_a(a, b) = 2(4 - 2a - b)(-2) + 2(6 - 5a - b)(-5)$$
$$+ 2(7 - 6a - b)(-6) + 2(8 - 9a - b)(-9)$$
$$= -304 + 292a + 44b = 0$$

$$F_b(a, b) = 2(4 - 2a - b)(-1) + 2(6 - 5a - b)(-1)$$
$$+ 2(7 - 6a - b)(-1) + 2(8 - 9a - b)(-1)$$
$$= -50 + 44a + 8b = 0$$

After dividing each equation by 2, we solve the system

$$146a + 22b = 152$$
$$22a + 4b = 25$$

obtaining $(a, b) = (0.58, 3.06)$ as the only critical point.

Step 2   Compute $A = F_{aa}(a, b)$, $B = F_{ab}(a, b)$, and $C = F_{bb}(a, b)$:

$$F_{aa}(a, b) = 292; \quad \text{so,} \quad A = F_{aa}(0.58, 3.06) = 292$$

$$F_{ab}(a, b) = 44; \quad \text{so,} \quad B = F_{ab}(0.58, 3.06) = 44$$

$$F_{bb}(a, b) = 8; \quad \text{so,} \quad C = F_{bb}(0.58, 3.06) = 8$$

Step 3 Evaluate $AC - B^2$ and try to classify the critical point (a, b) by using Theorem 2 in Section 15-3:

$$AC - B^2 = (292)(8) - (44)^2 = 400 > 0 \qquad \text{and} \qquad A = 292 > 0$$

Therefore, case 2 in Theorem 2 applies, and $F(a, b)$ has a local minimum at the critical point $(0.58, 3.06)$.

So, the least squares line for the given data is

$$y = 0.58x + 3.06 \qquad \text{\textsl{Least squares line}}$$

The sum of the squares of the residuals is minimized for this choice of a and b (see Fig. 3).

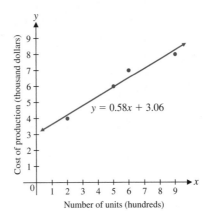

Figure 3

This linear function can now be used by the manufacturer to estimate any of the quantities normally associated with the cost function—such as costs, marginal costs, average costs, and so on. For example, the cost of producing 2,000 units is approximately

$$y = (0.58)(20) + 3.06 = 14.66, \qquad \text{or} \qquad \$14,660$$

The marginal cost function is

$$\frac{dy}{dx} = 0.58$$

The average cost function is

$$\bar{y} = \frac{0.58x + 3.06}{x}$$

In general, if we are given a set of n points $(x_1, y_1), (x_2, y_2), \ldots, (x_n, y_n)$, we want to determine the line $y = ax + b$ for which the sum of the squares of the residuals is minimized. Using summation notation, we find that the sum of the squares of the residuals is given by

$$F(a, b) = \sum_{k=1}^{n}(y_k - ax_k - b)^2$$

Note that in this expression the variables are a and b, and the x_k and y_k are all known values. To minimize $F(a, b)$, we thus compute the partial derivatives with respect to a and b and set them equal to 0:

$$F_b(a, b) = \sum_{k=1}^{n}2(y_k - ax_k - b)(-x_k) = 0$$

$$F_b(a, b) = \sum_{k=1}^{n}2(y_k - ax_k - b)(-1) = 0$$

Dividing each equation by 2 and simplifying, we see that the coefficients a and b of the least squares line $y = ax + b$ must satisfy the following system of *normal equations:*

$$\left(\sum_{k=1}^{n} x_k^2\right)a + \left(\sum_{k=1}^{n} x_k\right)b = \sum_{k=1}^{n} x_k y_k$$

$$\left(\sum_{k=1}^{n} x_k\right)a + nb = \sum_{k=1}^{n} y_k$$

Solving this system for a and b produces the formulas given in Theorem 1.

THEOREM 1   Least Squares Approximation

For a set of n points $(x_1, y_1), (x_2, y_2), \ldots, (x_n, y_n)$, the coefficients of the least squares line $y = ax + b$ are the solutions of the system of **normal equations**

$$\left(\sum_{k=1}^{n} x_k^2\right)a + \left(\sum_{k=1}^{n} x_k\right)b = \sum_{k=1}^{n} x_k y_k \tag{1}$$

$$\left(\sum_{k=1}^{n} x_k\right)a + nb = \sum_{k=1}^{n} y_k$$

and are given by the formulas

$$a = \frac{n\left(\sum_{k=1}^{n} x_k y_k\right) - \left(\sum_{k=1}^{n} x_k\right)\left(\sum_{k=1}^{n} y_k\right)}{n\left(\sum_{k=1}^{n} x_k^2\right) - \left(\sum_{k=1}^{n} x_k\right)^2} \tag{2}$$

$$b = \frac{\sum_{k=1}^{n} y_k - a\left(\sum_{k=1}^{n} x_k\right)}{n} \tag{3}$$

Now we return to the data in Table 1 and tabulate the sums required for the normal equations and their solution in Table 3.

The normal equations (1) are then

$$146a + 22b = 152$$

$$22a + 4b = 25$$

The solution of the normal equations given by equations (2) and (3) is

$$a = \frac{4(152) - (22)(25)}{4(146) - (22)^2} = 0.58$$

$$b = \frac{25 - 0.58(22)}{4} = 3.06$$

Table 3

	x_k	y_k	$x_k y_k$	x_k^2
	2	4	8	4
	5	6	30	25
	6	7	42	36
	9	8	72	81
Totals	22	25	152	146

Compare these results with step 1 on page 834. Note that Table 3 provides a convenient format for the computation of step 1.

Many graphing calculators have a linear regression feature that solves the system of normal equations obtained by setting the partial derivatives of the sum of squares of the residuals equal to 0. Therefore, in practice, we simply enter the given data points and use the linear regression feature to determine the line $y = ax + b$ that best fits the data (see Fig. 4). There is no need to compute partial derivatives or even to tabulate sums (as in Table 3).

8.4

1.3   9.7

3.6

(A)   (B)   (C) $y_1 = 0.58x + 3.06$

Figure 4

EXPLORE & DISCUSS 1

(A) Plot the four points $(0, 0), (0, 1), (10, 0)$, and $(10, 1)$. Which line would you guess "best" fits these four points? Use formulas (2) and (3) to test your conjecture.

(B) Plot the four points $(0, 0), (0, 10), (1, 0)$ and $(1, 10)$. Which line would you guess "best" fits these four points? Use formulas (2) and (3) to test your conjecture.

(C) If either of your conjectures was wrong, explain how your reasoning was mistaken.

CONCEPTUAL INSIGHT

Formula (2) for a is undefined if the denominator equals 0. When can this happen? Suppose $n = 3$. Then

$$n\left(\sum_{k=1}^{n} x_k^2\right) - \left(\sum_{k=1}^{n} x_k\right)^2$$

$$= 3\left(x_1^2 + x_2^2 + x_3^2\right) - (x_1 + x_2 + x_3)^2$$
$$= 3\left(x_1^2 + x_2^2 + x_3^2\right) - \left(x_1^2 + x_2^2 + x_3^2 + 2x_1x_2 + 2x_1x_3 + 2x_2x_3\right)$$
$$= 2\left(x_1^2 + x_2^2 + x_3^2\right) - (2x_1x_2 + 2x_1x_3 + 2x_2x_3)$$
$$= \left(x_1^2 + x_2^2\right) + \left(x_1^2 + x_3^2\right) + \left(x_2^2 + x_3^2\right) - (2x_1x_2 + 2x_1x_3 + 2x_2x_3)$$
$$= \left(x_1^2 - 2x_1x_2 + x_2^2\right) + \left(x_1^2 - 2x_1x_3 + x_3^2\right) + \left(x_2^2 - 2x_2x_3 + x_3^2\right)$$
$$= (x_1 - x_2)^2 + (x_1 - x_3)^2 + (x_2 - x_3)^2$$

and the last expression is equal to 0 if and only if $x_1 = x_2 = x_3$ (i.e., if and only if the three points all lie on the same vertical line). A similar algebraic manipulation works for any integer $n > 1$, showing that, in formula (2) for a, the denominator equals 0 if and only if all n points lie on the same vertical line.

The method of least squares can also be applied to find the quadratic equation $y = ax^2 + bx + c$ that best fits a set of data points. In this case, the sum of the squares of the residuals is a function of three variables:

$$F(a, b, c) = \sum_{k=1}^{n}\left(y_k - ax_k^2 - bx_k - c\right)^2$$

There are now three partial derivatives to compute and set equal to 0:

$$F_a(a, b, c) = \sum_{k=1}^{n} 2\left(y_k - ax_k^2 - bx_k - c\right)\left(-x_k^2\right) = 0$$

$$F_b(a, b, c) = \sum_{k=1}^{n} 2\left(y_k - ax_k^2 - bx_k - c\right)(-x_k) = 0$$

$$F_c(a, b, c) = \sum_{k=1}^{n} 2\left(y_k - ax_k^2 - bx_k - c\right)(-1) = 0$$

The resulting set of three linear equations in the three variables a, b, and c is called the *set of normal equations for quadratic regression*.

 A quadratic regression feature on a calculator is designed to solve such normal equations after the given set of points has been entered. Figure 5 illustrates the computation for the data of Table 1.

(A) (B) (C) $y_1 = -0.0417x^2 + 1.0383x + 2.06$

Figure 5

EXPLORE & DISCUSS 2

(A) Use the graphs in Figures 4 and 5 to predict which technique, linear regression or quadratic regression, yields the smaller sum of squares of the residuals for the data of Table 1. Explain.

 (B) Confirm your prediction by computing the sum of squares of the residuals in each case.

The method of least squares can also be applied to other regression equations—for example, cubic, quartic, logarithmic, exponential, and power regression models. Details are explored in some of the exercises at the end of this section.

Applications

EXAMPLE 1 **Exam Scores** Table 4 lists the midterm and final examination scores of 10 students in a calculus course.

Table 4			
Midterm	**Final**	**Midterm**	**Final**
49	61	78	77
53	47	83	81
67	72	85	79
71	76	91	93
74	68	99	99

(A) Use formulas (1), (2), and (3) to find the normal equations and the least squares line for the data given in Table 4.

 (B) Use the linear regression feature on a graphing calculator to find and graph the least squares line.

(C) Use the least squares line to predict the final examination score of a student who scored 95 on the midterm examination.

SOLUTION (A) Table 5 shows a convenient way to compute all the sums in the formulas for a and b.

Table 5

	x_k	y_k	$x_k y_k$	x_k^2
	49	61	2,989	2,401
	53	47	2,491	2,809
	67	72	4,824	4,489
	71	76	5,396	5,041
	74	68	5,032	5,476
	78	77	6,006	6,084
	83	81	6,723	6,889
	85	79	6,715	7,225
	91	93	8,463	8,281
	99	99	9,801	9,801
Totals	750	753	58,440	58,496

From the last line in Table 5, we have

$$\sum_{k=1}^{10} x_k = 750 \qquad \sum_{k=1}^{10} y_k = 753 \qquad \sum_{k=1}^{10} x_k y_k = 58,440 \qquad \sum_{k=1}^{10} x_k^2 = 58,496$$

and the normal equations are

$$58,496a + 750b = 58,440$$
$$750a + 10b = 753$$

Using formulas (2) and (3), we obtain

$$a = \frac{10(58,440) - (750)(753)}{10(58,496) - (750)^2} = \frac{19,650}{22,460} \approx 0.875$$

$$b = \frac{753 - 0.875(750)}{10} = 9.675$$

The least squares line is given (approximately) by

$$y = 0.875x + 9.675$$

(B) We enter the data and use the linear regression feature, as shown in Figure 6. [The discrepancy between values of a and b in the preceding calculations and those in Figure 6B is due to rounding in part (A).]

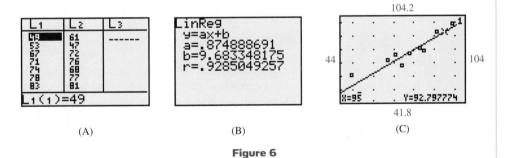

(A)   (B)   (C)

Figure 6

(C) If $x = 95$, then $y = 0.875(95) + 9.675 \approx 92.8$ is the predicted score on the final exam. This is also indicated in Figure 6C. If we assume that the exam score must be an integer, then we would predict a score of 93.

Matched Problem 1   Repeat Example 1 for the scores listed in Table 6.

Table 6			
Midterm	**Final**	**Midterm**	**Final**
54	50	84	80
60	66	88	95
75	80	89	85
76	68	97	94
78	71	99	86

EXAMPLE 2

Energy Consumption The use of fuel oil for home heating in the United States has declined steadily for several decades. Table 7 lists the percentage of occupied housing units in the United States that were heated by fuel oil for various years between 1960 and 2000. Use the data in the table and linear regression to estimate the percentage of occupied housing units in the United States that were heated by fuel oil in the year 2005.

Table 7	Occupied Housing Units Heated by Fuel Oil		
Year	**Percent**	**Year**	**Percent**
1960	32.4	1990	13.2
1970	26.0	2000	9.0
1980	18.1		

SOLUTION   We enter the data, with $x = 0$ representing 1960, $x = 10$ representing 1970, and so on, and use linear regression as shown in Figure 7.

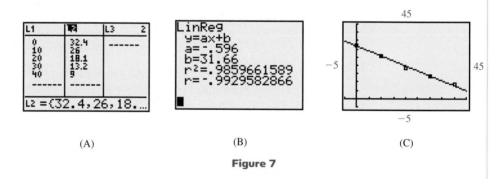

| (A) | (B) | (C) |

Figure 7

Figure 7 indicates that the least squares line is $y = -0.596x + 31.66$. To estimate the percentage of occupied housing units heated by fuel oil in the year 2005 (corresponding to $x = 45$), we substitute $x = 45$ in the equation of the least squares line: $-0.596(45) + 31.66 = 4.84$. The estimated percentage for 2005 is 4.84%.

Matched Problem 2

In 1950, coal was still a major source of fuel for home energy consumption, and the percentage of occupied housing units heated by fuel oil was only 22.1%. Add the data for 1950 to the data for Example 2, and compute the new least squares line and the new estimate for the percentage of occupied housing units heated by fuel oil in the year 2005. Discuss the discrepancy between the two estimates. (As in Example 2, let $x = 0$ represent 1960.)

Exercises 15-5

A

In Problems 1–6, find the least squares line. Graph the data and the least squares line.

1.	x	y
	1	1
	2	3
	3	4
	4	3

2.	x	y
	1	−2
	2	−1
	3	3
	4	5

3.	x	y
	1	8
	2	5
	3	4
	4	0

4.	x	y
	1	20
	2	14
	3	11
	4	3

5.	x	y
	1	3
	2	4
	3	5
	4	6

6.	x	y
	1	2
	2	3
	3	3
	4	2

B

In Problems 7–14, find the least squares line and use it to estimate y for the indicated value of x. Round answers to two decimal places.

7.	x	y
	1	3
	2	1
	2	2
	3	0

Estimate y when x = 2.5.

8.	x	y
	1	0
	3	1
	3	6
	3	4

Estimate y when x = 3.

9.	x	y
	0	10
	5	22
	10	31
	15	46
	20	51

Estimate y when x = 25.

10.	x	y
	−5	60
	0	50
	5	30
	10	20
	15	15

Estimate y when x = 20.

11.	x	y
	−1	14
	1	12
	3	8
	5	6
	7	5

Estimate y when x = 2.

12.	x	y
	2	−4
	6	0
	10	8
	14	12
	18	14

Estimate y when x = 15.

13.	x	y	x	y
	0.5	25	9.5	12
	2	22	11	11
	3.5	21	12.5	8
	5	21	14	5
	6.5	18	15.5	1

Estimate y when x = 8.

14.	x	y	x	y
	0	−15	12	11
	2	−9	14	13
	4	−7	16	19
	6	−7	18	25
	8	−1	20	33

Estimate y when x = 10.

C

15. To find the coefficients of the parabola

$$y = ax^2 + bx + c$$

that is the "best" fit to the points $(1, 2)$, $(2, 1)$, $(3, 1)$, and $(4, 3)$, minimize the sum of the squares of the residuals

$$F(a, b, c) = (a + b + c - 2)^2$$
$$+ (4a + 2b + c - 1)^2$$
$$+ (9a + 3b + c - 1)^2$$
$$+ (16a + 4b + c - 3)^2$$

by solving the system of normal equations

$$F_a(a, b, c) = 0 \qquad F_b(a, b, c) = 0 \qquad F_c(a, b, c) = 0$$

for a, b, and c. Graph the points and the parabola.

16. Repeat Problem 15 for the points $(-1, -2)$, $(0, 1)$, $(1, 2)$, and $(2, 0)$.

Problems 17 and 18 refer to the system of normal equations and the formulas for a and b given on page 836.

17. Verify formulas (2) and (3) by solving the system of normal equations (1) for a and b.

18. If

$$\bar{x} = \frac{1}{n}\sum_{k=1}^{n} x_k \qquad \text{and} \qquad \bar{y} = \frac{1}{n}\sum_{k=1}^{n} y_k$$

are the averages of the x and y coordinates, respectively, show that the point $(\bar{x}, \bar{y})$ satisfies the equation of the least squares line, $y = ax + b$.

19. (A) Suppose that $n = 5$ and the x coordinates of the data points $(x_1, y_1), (x_2, y_2), \ldots, (x_n, y_n)$ are $-2, -1, 0, 1, 2$. Show that system (1) in the text implies that

$$a = \frac{\sum x_k y_k}{\sum x_k^2}$$

and that b is equal to the average of the values of y_k.

(B) Show that the conclusion of part (A) holds whenever the average of the x coordinates of the data points is 0.

20. (A) Give an example of a set of six data points such that half of the points lie above the least squares line and half lie below.

(B) Give an example of a set of six data points such that just one of the points lies above the least squares line and five lie below.

21. (A) Find the linear and quadratic functions that best fit the data points $(0, 1.3), (1, 0.6), (2, 1.5), (3, 3.6)$, and $(4, 7.4)$. Round coefficients to two decimal places.

(B) Which of the two functions best fits the data? Explain.

22. (A) Find the linear, quadratic, and logarithmic functions that best fit the data points $(1, 3.2), (2, 4.2), (3, 4.7), (4, 5.0)$, and $(5, 5.3)$. (Round coefficients to two decimal places.)

(B) Which of the three functions best fits the data? Explain.

23. Describe the normal equations for cubic regression. How many equations are there? What are the variables? What techniques could be used to solve the equations?

24. Describe the normal equations for quartic regression. How many equations are there? What are the variables? What techniques could be used to solve the equations?

Applications

25. **Crime rate.** Data on U.S. property crimes (in number of crimes per 100,000 population) are given in the table for the years 2001 through 2006.

U.S. Property Crime Rates	
Year	Rate
2001	3,658
2002	3,631
2003	3,591
2004	3,514
2005	3,432
2006	3,335

(A) Find the least squares line for the data, using $x = 0$ for 2000.

(B) Use the least squares line to predict the property crime rate in 2016.

26. **Cable TV revenue.** Data for cable TV revenue are given in the table for the years 2003 through 2007.

Cable TV Revenue	
Year	Millions of dollars
2003	53,991
2004	59,428
2005	65,041
2006	71,843
2007	78,886

(A) Find the least squares line for the data, using $x = 0$ for 2000.

(B) Use the least squares line to predict cable TV revenue in 2017.

27. **Maximizing profit.** The market research department for a drugstore chain chose two summer resort areas to test market a new sunscreen lotion packaged in 4-ounce plastic bottles. After a summer of varying the selling price and recording the monthly demand, the research department arrived at the following demand table, where y is the number of bottles purchased per month (in thousands) at x dollars per bottle:

x	y
5.0	2.0
5.5	1.8
6.0	1.4
6.5	1.2
7.0	1.1

(A) Use the method of least squares to find a demand equation.

(B) If each bottle of sunscreen costs the drugstore chain $4, how should the sunscreen be priced to achieve a maximum monthly profit? [*Hint:* Use the result of part (A), with $C = 4y$, $R = xy$, and $P = R - C$.]

28. **Maximizing profit.** A market research consultant for a supermarket chain chose a large city to test market a new brand of mixed nuts packaged in 8-ounce cans. After a year of varying the selling price and recording the monthly demand, the consultant arrived at the following demand table, where y is the number of cans purchased per month (in thousands) at x dollars per can:

x	y
4.0	4.2
4.5	3.5
5.0	2.7
5.5	1.5
6.0	0.7

(A) Use the method of least squares to find a demand equation.

(B) If each can of nuts costs the supermarket chain $3, how should the nuts be priced to achieve a maximum monthly profit?

29. **Olympic Games.** The table gives the winning heights in the pole vault in the Olympic Games from 1980 to 2008.

Olympic Pole Vault Winning Height	
Year	Height (ft)
1980	18.96
1984	18.85
1988	19.35
1992	19.02
1996	19.42
2000	19.35
2004	19.52
2008	19.56

(A) Use a graphing calculator to find the least squares line for the data, letting $x = 0$ for 1980.

(B) Estimate the winning height in the pole vault in the Olympic Games of 2020.

30. **Biology.** In biology, there is an approximate rule, called the *bioclimatic rule for temperate climates*. This rule states that in spring and early summer, periodic phenomena such as the blossoming of flowers, the appearance of insects, and the

ripening of fruit usually come about 4 days later for each 500 feet of altitude. Stated as a formula, the rule becomes

$$d = 8h \qquad 0 \le h \le 4$$

where d is the change in days and h is the altitude (in thousands of feet). To test this rule, an experiment was set up to record the difference in blossoming times of the same type of apple tree at different altitudes. A summary of the results is given in the following table:

h	d
0	0
1	7
2	18
3	28
4	33

(A) Use the method of least squares to find a linear equation relating h and d. Does the bioclimatic rule $d = 8h$ appear to be approximately correct?

(B) How much longer will it take this type of apple tree to blossom at 3.5 thousand feet than at sea level? [Use the linear equation found in part (A).]

 31. Global warming. Average global temperatures from 1885 to 2005 are given in the table.

Average Global Temperatures			
Year	**°F**	**Year**	**°F**
1885	56.65	1955	57.06
1895	56.64	1965	57.05
1905	56.52	1975	57.04
1915	56.57	1985	57.36
1925	56.74	1995	57.64
1935	57.00	2005	58.59
1945	57.13		

(A) Find the least squares line for the data, using $x = 0$ for 1885.

(B) Use the least squares line to estimate the average global temperature in 2085.

 32. Air pollution. Data for emissions of sulfur dioxide in the United States from selected years from 1972 to 2007 are given in the table.

Emissions of Sulfur Dioxide in the United States			
Year	**Million Short Tons**	**Year**	**Million Short Tons**
1972	30.4	1992	22.1
1977	28.6	1997	18.8
1982	23.2	2002	15.4
1987	22.2	2007	12.4

(A) Find the least squares line for the data, using $x = 0$ for 1972.

(B) Use the least squares line to estimate the emissions of sulfur dioxide in the United States in 2017.

Answers to Matched Problems

1. (A) $y = 0.85x + 9.47$

(B)

(C) 90.3

2. $y = -0.37x + 25.75; 9.1\%$

15-6 Double Integrals over Rectangular Regions

Introduction

We have generalized the concept of differentiation to functions with two or more independent variables. How can we do the same with integration, and how can we interpret the results? Let's look first at the operation of antidifferentiation. We can antidifferentiate a function of two or more variables with respect to one of the variables by treating all the other variables as though they were constants. Thus, this operation is the reverse operation of partial differentiation, just as ordinary antidifferentiation is the reverse operation of ordinary differentiation. We write $\int f(x, y) \, dx$ to indicate that we are to antidifferentiate $f(x, y)$ with respect to x, holding y fixed; we write $\int f(x, y) \, dy$ to indicate that we are to antidifferentiate $f(x, y)$ with respect to y, holding x fixed.

EXAMPLE 1 **Partial Antidifferentiation** Evaluate:

(A) $\displaystyle\int (6xy^2 + 3x^2)\, dy$ (B) $\displaystyle\int (6xy^2 + 3x^2)\, dx$

SOLUTION (A) Treating x as a constant and using the properties of antidifferentiation from Section 13-1, we have

$$\int (6xy^2 + 3x^2)\, dy = \int 6xy^2\, dy + \int 3x^2\, dy$$

The dy tells us that we are looking for the antiderivative of $6xy^2 + 3x^2$ with respect to y only, holding x constant.

$$= 6x\int y^2\, dy + 3x^2\int dy$$

$$= 6x\left(\frac{y^3}{3}\right) + 3x^2(y) + C(x)$$

$$= 2xy^3 + 3x^2y + C(x)$$

Note that the constant of integration can be *any function of x alone* since for any such function,

$$\frac{\partial}{\partial y}C(x) = 0$$

Check:

We can verify that our answer is correct by using partial differentiation:

$$\frac{\partial}{\partial y}[2xy^3 + 3x^2y + C(x)] = 6xy^2 + 3x^2 + 0$$

$$= 6xy^2 + 3x^2$$

(B) We treat y as a constant:

$$\int (6xy^2 + 3x^2)\, dx = \int 6xy^2\, dx + \int 3x^2\, dx$$

$$= 6y^2\int x\, dx + 3\int x^2\, dx$$

$$= 6y^2\left(\frac{x^2}{2}\right) + 3\left(\frac{x^3}{3}\right) + E(y)$$

$$= 3x^2y^2 + x^3 + E(y)$$

The antiderivative contains an arbitrary function $E(y)$ of y alone.

Check:

$$\frac{\partial}{\partial x}[3x^2y^2 + x^3 + E(y)] = 6xy^2 + 3x^2 + 0$$

$$= 6xy^2 + 3x^2$$

Matched Problem 1 Evaluate (A) $\displaystyle\int (4xy + 12x^2y^3)\, dy$ (B) $\displaystyle\int (4xy + 12x^2y^3)\, dx$

Now that we have extended the concept of antidifferentiation to functions with two variables, we also can evaluate definite integrals of the form

$$\int_a^b f(x, y)\, dx \qquad \text{or} \qquad \int_c^d f(x, y)\, dy$$

EXAMPLE 2   **Evaluating a Partial Antiderivative**   Evaluate, substituting the limits of integration in y if dy is used and in x if dx is used:

(A) $\displaystyle\int_0^2 (6xy^2 + 3x^2)\, dy$

(B) $\displaystyle\int_0^1 (6xy^2 + 3x^2)\, dx$

SOLUTION   (A)   From Example 1A, we know that

$$\int (6xy^2 + 3x^2)\, dy = 2xy^3 + 3x^2y + C(x)$$

According to properties of the definite integral for a function of one variable, we can use any antiderivative to evaluate the definite integral. Thus, choosing $C(x) = 0$, we have

$$\int_0^2 (6xy^2 + 3x^2)\, dy = (2xy^3 + 3x^2y)\big|_{y=0}^{y=2}$$

$$= [2x(2)^3 + 3x^2(2)] - [2x(0)^3 + 3x^2(0)]$$

$$= 16x + 6x^2$$

(B)   From Example 1B, we know that

$$\int (6xy^2 + 3x^2)\, dx = 3x^2y^2 + x^3 + E(y)$$

Choosing $E(y) = 0$, we have

$$\int_0^1 (6xy^2 + 3x^2)\, dx = (3x^2y^2 + x^3)\big|_{x=0}^{x=1}$$

$$= [3y^2(1)^2 + (1)^3] - [3y^2(0)^2 + (0)^3]$$

$$= 3y^2 + 1$$

Matched Problem 2   Evaluate:

(A) $\displaystyle\int_0^1 (4xy + 12x^2y^3)\, dy$

(B) $\displaystyle\int_0^3 (4xy + 12x^2y^3)\, dx$

Integrating and evaluating a definite integral with integrand $f(x, y)$ with respect to y produces a function of x alone (or a constant). Likewise, integrating and evaluating a definite integral with integrand $f(x, y)$ with respect to x produces a function of y alone (or a constant). Each of these results, involving at most one variable, can now be used as an integrand in a second definite integral.

EXAMPLE 3   **Evaluating Integrals**   Evaluate:

(A) $\displaystyle\int_0^1 \left[\int_0^2 (6xy^2 + 3x^2)\, dy \right] dx$

(B) $\displaystyle\int_0^2 \left[\int_0^1 (6xy^2 + 3x^2)\, dx \right] dy$

SOLUTION   (A)   Example 2A showed that

$$\int_0^2 (6xy^2 + 3x^2)\, dy = 16x + 6x^2$$

Therefore,

$$\int_0^1 \left[\int_0^2 (6xy^2 + 3x^2)\, dy \right] dx = \int_0^1 (16x + 6x^2)\, dx$$

$$= (8x^2 + 2x^3)\big|_{x=0}^{x=1}$$

$$= [8(1)^2 + 2(1)^3] - [8(0)^2 + 2(0)^3] = 10$$

(B) Example 2B showed that

$$\int_0^1 (6xy^2 + 3x^2)\, dx = 3y^2 + 1$$

Therefore,

$$\int_0^2 \left[\int_0^1 (6xy^2 + 3x^2)\, dx \right] dy = \int_0^2 (3y^2 + 1)\, dy$$
$$= (y^3 + y)\big|_{y=0}^{y=2}$$
$$= [(2)^3 + 2] - [(0)^3 + 0] = 10$$

Figure 1

A numerical integration command can be used as an alternative to the fundamental theorem of calculus to evaluate the last integrals in Examples 3A and 3B, $\int_0^1 (16x + 6x^2)\, dx$ and $\int_0^2 (3y^2 + 1)\, dy$, since the integrand in each case is a function of a single variable (see Fig. 1).

Matched Problem 3 Evaluate

(A) $\displaystyle\int_0^3 \left[\int_0^1 (4xy + 12x^2y^3)\, dy \right] dx$ (B) $\displaystyle\int_0^1 \left[\int_0^3 (4xy + 12x^2y^3)\, dx \right] dy$

Definition of the Double Integral

Notice that the answers in Examples 3A and 3B are identical. This is not an accident. In fact, it is this property that enables us to define the *double integral*, as follows:

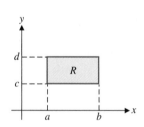

> **DEFINITION Double Integral**
>
> The **double integral** of a function $f(x, y)$ over a rectangle
> $$R = \{(x, y) | a \le x \le b,\ c \le y \le d\}$$
> is
> $$\iint\limits_R f(x, y)\, dA = \int_a^b \left[\int_c^d f(x, y)\, dy \right] dx$$
> $$= \int_c^d \left[\int_a^b f(x, y)\, dx \right] dy$$

In the double integral $\iint_R f(x, y)\, dA$, $f(x, y)$ is called the **integrand**, and R is called the **region of integration**. The expression dA indicates that this is an integral over a two-dimensional region. The integrals

$$\int_a^b \left[\int_c^d f(x, y)\, dy \right] dx \quad \text{and} \quad \int_c^d \left[\int_a^b f(x, y)\, dx \right] dy$$

are referred to as **iterated integrals** (the brackets are often omitted), and the order in which dx and dy are written indicates the order of integration. This is not the most general definition of the double integral over a rectangular region; however, it is equivalent to the general definition for all the functions we will consider.

EXAMPLE 4   **Evaluating a Double Integral**   Evaluate

$$\iint\limits_R (x + y)\, dA \qquad \text{over} \qquad R = \{(x, y)|1 \le x \le 3, \quad -1 \le y \le 2\}$$

Figure 2

SOLUTION   Region R is illustrated in Figure 2. We can choose either order of iteration. As a check, we will evaluate the integral both ways:

$$\iint\limits_R (x + y)\, dA = \int_1^3 \int_{-1}^2 (x + y)\, dy\, dx$$

$$= \int_1^3 \left[\left(xy + \frac{y^2}{2}\right)\Big|_{y=-1}^{y=2}\right] dx$$

$$= \int_1^3 \left[(2x + 2) - \left(-x + \tfrac{1}{2}\right)\right] dx$$

$$= \int_1^3 \left(3x + \tfrac{3}{2}\right) dx$$

$$= \left(\tfrac{3}{2}x^2 + \tfrac{3}{2}x\right)\Big|_{x=1}^{x=3}$$

$$= \left(\tfrac{27}{2} + \tfrac{9}{2}\right) - \left(\tfrac{3}{2} + \tfrac{3}{2}\right) = 18 - 3 = 15$$

$$\iint\limits_R (x + y)\, dA = \int_{-1}^2 \int_1^3 (x + y)\, dx\, dy$$

$$= \int_{-1}^2 \left[\left(\frac{x^2}{2} + xy\right)\Big|_{x=1}^{x=3}\right] dy$$

$$= \int_{-1}^2 \left[\left(\tfrac{9}{2} + 3y\right) - \left(\tfrac{1}{2} + y\right)\right] dy$$

$$= \int_{-1}^2 (4 + 2y)\, dy$$

$$= (4y + y^2)\big|_{y=-1}^{y=2}$$

$$= (8 + 4) - (-4 + 1) = 12 - (-3) = 15$$

Matched Problem 4   Evaluate

$$\iint\limits_R (2x - y)\, dA \qquad \text{over} \qquad R = \{(x, y)|-1 \le x \le 5, \quad 2 \le y \le 4\}$$

both ways.

EXAMPLE 5   **Double Integral of an Exponential Function**   Evaluate

$$\iint\limits_R 2xe^{x^2+y}\, dA \qquad \text{over} \qquad R = \{(x, y)|0 \le x \le 1, \quad -1 \le y \le 1\}$$

Figure 3

SOLUTION   Region R is illustrated in Figure 3.

$$\iint\limits_R 2xe^{x^2+y}\, dA = \int_{-1}^1 \int_0^1 2xe^{x^2+y}\, dx\, dy$$

$$= \int_{-1}^1 \left[(e^{x^2+y})\Big|_{x=0}^{x=1}\right] dy$$

$$= \int_{-1}^1 (e^{1+y} - e^y)\, dy$$

$$= (e^{1+y} - e^y)|_{y=-1}^{y=1}$$
$$= (e^2 - e) - (e^0 - e^{-1})$$
$$= e^2 - e - 1 + e^{-1}$$

Matched Problem 5   Evaluate $\displaystyle\iint_R \frac{x}{y^2} e^{x/y}\, dA$ over $R = \{(x, y)|0 \le x \le 1, \ 1 \le y \le 2\}$.

Average Value over Rectangular Regions

In Section 13-5, the average value of a function $f(x)$ over an interval $[a, b]$ was defined as

$$\frac{1}{b - a}\int_a^b f(x)\, dx$$

This definition is easily extended to functions of two variables over rectangular regions as follows (notice that the denominator $(b - a)(d - c)$ is simply the area of the rectangle R):

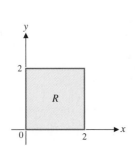

> **DEFINITION** **Average Value over Rectangular Regions**
> The **average value** of the function $f(x, y)$ over the rectangle
> $$R = \{(x, y)|a \le x \le b, \ c \le y \le d\}$$
> is
> $$\frac{1}{(b - a)(d - c)}\iint_R f(x, y)\, dA$$

EXAMPLE 6   **Average Value** Find the average value of $f(x, y) = 4 - \frac{1}{2}x - \frac{1}{2}y$ over the rectangle $R = \{(x, y)|0 \le x \le 2, \ 0 \le y \le 2\}$.

SOLUTION   Region R is illustrated in Figure 4. We have

$$\frac{1}{(b - a)(d - c)}\iint_R f(x, y)\, dA = \frac{1}{(2 - 0)(2 - 0)}\iint_R \left(4 - \frac{1}{2}x - \frac{1}{2}y\right) dA$$

$$= \frac{1}{4}\int_0^2 \int_0^2 \left(4 - \frac{1}{2}x - \frac{1}{2}y\right) dy\, dx$$

$$= \frac{1}{4}\int_0^2 \left[\left(4y - \frac{1}{2}xy - \frac{1}{4}y^2\right)\Big|_{y=0}^{y=2}\right] dx$$

$$= \frac{1}{4}\int_0^2 (7 - x)\, dx$$

$$= \frac{1}{4}\left(7x - \frac{1}{2}x^2\right)\Big|_{x=0}^{x=2}$$

$$= \frac{1}{4}(12) = 3$$

Figure 5 illustrates the surface $z = f(x, y)$, and our calculations show that 3 is the average of the z values over the region R.

Figure 4

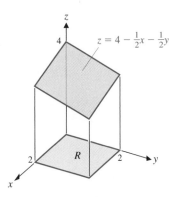

Figure 5

Matched Problem 6 Find the average value of $f(x, y) = x + 2y$ over the rectangle

$$R = \{(x, y)|0 \le x \le 2, \quad 0 \le y \le 1\}$$

EXPLORE & DISCUSS 1

(A) Which of the functions $f(x, y) = 4 - x^2 - y^2$ and $g(x, y) = 4 - x - y$ would you guess has the greater average value over the rectangle $R = \{(x, y)|0 \le x \le 1, \quad 0 \le y \le 1\}$? Explain.

(B) Use double integrals to check the correctness of your guess in part (A).

Volume and Double Integrals

One application of the definite integral of a function with one variable is the calculation of areas, so it is not surprising that the definite integral of a function of two variables can be used to calculate volumes of solids.

THEOREM 1 Volume under a Surface

If $f(x, y) \ge 0$ over a rectangle $R = \{(x, y)|a \le x \le b, \quad c \le y \le d\}$, then the volume of the solid formed by graphing f over the rectangle R is given by

$$V = \iint_R f(x, y) \, dA$$

EXAMPLE 7 **Volume** Find the volume of the solid under the graph of $f(x, y) = 1 + x^2 + y^2$ over the rectangle $R = \{(x, y)|0 \le x \le 1, \quad 0 \le y \le 1\}$.

SOLUTION Figure 6 shows the region R, and Figure 7 illustrates the volume under consideration.

$$V = \iint_R (1 + x^2 + y^2) \, dA$$

$$= \int_0^1 \int_0^1 (1 + x^2 + y^2) \, dx \, dy$$

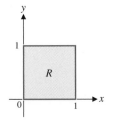

Figure 6

$$= \int_0^1 \left[\left(x + \tfrac{1}{3}x^3 + xy^2 \right) \Big|_{x=0}^{x=1} \right] dy$$

$$= \int_0^1 \left(\tfrac{4}{3} + y^2 \right) dy$$

$$= \left(\tfrac{4}{3}y + \tfrac{1}{3}y^3 \right) \Big|_{y=0}^{y=1} = \tfrac{5}{3} \text{ cubic units}$$

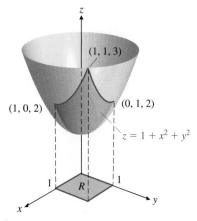

Figure 7

Matched Problem 7   Find the volume of the solid under the graph of $f(x, y) = 1 + x + y$ over the rectangle $R = \{(x, y) | 0 \le x \le 1, \; 0 \le y \le 2\}$.

CONCEPTUAL INSIGHT

Double integrals can be defined over regions that are more general than rectangles. For example, let $R > 0$. Then the function $f(x, y) = \sqrt{R^2 - (x^2 + y^2)}$ can be integrated over the circular region $C = \{(x, y) | x^2 + y^2 \le R^2\}$. In fact, it can be shown that

$$\iint\limits_C \sqrt{R^2 - (x^2 + y^2)} \, dx \, dy = \frac{2\pi R^3}{3}$$

Because $x^2 + y^2 + z^2 = R^2$ is the equation of a sphere of radius R centered at the origin, the double integral over C represents the volume of the upper hemisphere. Therefore, the volume of a sphere of radius R is given by

$$V = \frac{4\pi R^3}{3} \qquad \textit{Volume of sphere of radius R}$$

Double integrals can also be used to obtain volume formulas for other geometric figures (see Table 1, Appendix C).

Exercises 15-6

A

In Problems 1–8, find each antiderivative. Then use the antiderivative to evaluate the definite integral.

1. (A) $\displaystyle\int 12x^2y^3 \, dy$ (B) $\displaystyle\int_0^1 12x^2y^3 \, dy$

2. (A) $\displaystyle\int 12x^2y^3 \, dx$ (B) $\displaystyle\int_{-1}^2 12x^2y^3 \, dx$

3. (A) $\displaystyle\int (4x + 6y + 5) \, dx$

(B) $\displaystyle\int_{-2}^3 (4x + 6y + 5) \, dx$

4. (A) $\displaystyle\int (4x + 6y + 5) \, dy$

(B) $\displaystyle\int_1^4 (4x + 6y + 5) \, dy$

5. (A) $\displaystyle\int \frac{x}{\sqrt{y + x^2}}\,dx$ (B) $\displaystyle\int_0^2 \frac{x}{\sqrt{y + x^2}}\,dx$

6. (A) $\displaystyle\int \frac{x}{\sqrt{y + x^2}}\,dy$ (B) $\displaystyle\int_1^5 \frac{x}{\sqrt{y + x^2}}\,dy$

7. (A) $\displaystyle\int \frac{\ln x}{xy}\,dy$ (B) $\displaystyle\int_1^{e^2} \frac{\ln x}{xy}\,dy$

8. (A) $\displaystyle\int \frac{\ln x}{xy}\,dx$ (B) $\displaystyle\int_1^{e} \frac{\ln x}{xy}\,dx$

B

In Problems 9–16, evaluate each iterated integral. (See the indicated problem for the evaluation of the inner integral.)

9. $\displaystyle\int_{-1}^2 \int_0^1 12x^2 y^3 \, dy \, dx$

(See Problem 1.)

10. $\displaystyle\int_0^1 \int_{-1}^2 12x^2 y^3 \, dx \, dy$

(See Problem 2.)

11. $\displaystyle\int_1^4 \int_{-2}^3 (4x + 6y + 5) \, dx \, dy$

(See Problem 3.)

12. $\displaystyle\int_{-2}^3 \int_1^4 (4x + 6y + 5) \, dy \, dx$

(See Problem 4.)

13. $\displaystyle\int_1^5 \int_0^2 \frac{x}{\sqrt{y + x^2}}\,dx \, dy$

(See Problem 5.)

14. $\displaystyle\int_0^2 \int_1^5 \frac{x}{\sqrt{y + x^2}}\,dy \, dx$

(See Problem 6.)

15. $\displaystyle\int_1^e \int_1^{e^2} \frac{\ln x}{xy}\,dy \, dx$

(See Problem 7.)

16. $\displaystyle\int_1^{e^2} \int_1^e \frac{\ln x}{xy}\,dx \, dy$

(See Problem 8.)

Use both orders of iteration to evaluate each double integral in Problems 17–20.

17. $\displaystyle\iint_R xy \, dA; R = \{(x, y)|0 \le x \le 2, \ 0 \le y \le 4\}$

18. $\displaystyle\iint_R \sqrt{xy} \, dA; R = \{(x, y)|1 \le x \le 4, \ 1 \le y \le 9\}$

19. $\displaystyle\iint_R (x + y)^5 \, dA; R = \{(x, y)|-1 \le x \le 1, \ 1 \le y \le 2\}$

20. $\displaystyle\iint_R xe^y \, dA; R = \{(x, y)|-2 \le x \le 3, \ 0 \le y \le 2\}$

In Problems 21–24, find the average value of each function over the given rectangle.

21. $f(x, y) = (x + y)^2;$

$R = \{(x, y)|1 \le x \le 5, \ -1 \le y \le 1\}$

22. $f(x, y) = x^2 + y^2;$

$R = \{(x, y)|-1 \le x \le 2, \ 1 \le y \le 4\}$

23. $f(x, y) = x/y; R = \{(x, y)|1 \le x \le 4, \ 2 \le y \le 7\}$

24. $f(x, y) = x^2 y^3;$

$R = \{(x, y)|-1 \le x \le 1, \ 0 \le y \le 2\}$

In Problems 25–28, find the volume of the solid under the graph of each function over the given rectangle.

25. $f(x, y) = 2 - x^2 - y^2;$

$R = \{(x, y)|0 \le x \le 1, \ 0 \le y \le 1\}$

26. $f(x, y) = 5 - x;$

$R = \{(x, y)|0 \le x \le 5, \ 0 \le y \le 5\}$

27. $f(x, y) = 4 - y^2;$

$R = \{(x, y)|0 \le x \le 2, \ 0 \le y \le 2\}$

28. $f(x, y) = e^{-x-y};$

$R = \{(x, y)|0 \le x \le 1, \ 0 \le y \le 1\}$

C

Evaluate each double integral in Problems 29–32. Select the order of integration carefully; each problem is easy to do one way and difficult the other.

29. $\displaystyle\iint_R xe^{xy} \, dA; R = \{(x, y)|0 \le x \le 1, \ 1 \le y \le 2\}$

30. $\displaystyle\iint_R xye^{x^2 y} \, dA; R = \{(x, y)|0 \le x \le 1, \ 1 \le y \le 2\}$

31. $\displaystyle\iint_R \frac{2y + 3xy^2}{1 + x^2} \, dA;$

$R = \{(x, y)|0 \le x \le 1, \ -1 \le y \le 1\}$

32. $\displaystyle\iint_R \frac{2x + 2y}{1 + 4y + y^2} \, dA;$

$R = \{(x, y)|1 \le x \le 3, \ 0 \le y \le 1\}$

33. Show that $\int_0^2 \int_0^2 (1 - y) \, dx \, dy = 0$. Does the double integral represent the volume of a solid? Explain.

34. (A) Find the average values of the functions $f(x, y) = x + y$, $g(x, y) = x^2 + y^2$, and $h(x, y) = x^3 + y^3$ over the rectangle

$R = \{(x, y)|0 \le x \le 1, \ 0 \le y \le 1\}$

(B) Does the average value of $k(x, y) = x^n + y^n$ over the rectangle

$R_1 = \{(x, y)|0 \le x \le 1, \ 0 \le y \le 1\}$

increase or decrease as n increases? Explain.

(C) Does the average value of $k(x, y) = x^n + y^n$ over the rectangle

$R_2 = \{(x, y)|0 \le x \le 2, \ 0 \le y \le 2\}$

increase or decrease as n increases? Explain.

35. Let $f(x, y) = x^3 + y^2 - e^{-x} - 1$.

    (A) Find the average value of $f(x, y)$ over the rectangle
    $R = \{(x, y)| -2 \le x \le 2, \ -2 \le y \le 2\}$.

    (B) Graph the set of all points (x, y) in R for which
    $f(x, y) = 0$.

    (C) For which points (x, y) in R is $f(x, y)$ greater than 0?
    Less than 0? Explain.

36. Find the dimensions of the square S centered at the origin
    for which the average value of $f(x, y) = x^2 e^y$ over S is
    equal to 100.

Applications

37. **Multiplier principle.** Suppose that Congress enacts a one-
    time-only 10% tax rebate that is expected to infuse $\$y$ bil-
    lion, $5 \le y \le 7$, into the economy. If every person and
    every corporation is expected to spend a proportion
    $x, 0.6 \le x \le 0.8$, of each dollar received, then, by the
    multiplier principle in economics, the total amount of
    spending S (in billions of dollars) generated by this tax re-
    bate is given by

    $$S(x, y) = \frac{y}{1 - x}$$

    What is the average total amount of spending for the indi-
    cated ranges of the values of x and y? Set up a double inte-
    gral and evaluate it.

38. **Multiplier principle.** Repeat Problem 37 if $6 \le y \le 10$ and
    $0.7 \le x \le 0.9$.

39. **Cobb–Douglas production function.** If an industry invests
    x thousand labor-hours, $10 \le x \le 20$, and $\$y$ million,
    $1 \le y \le 2$, in the production of N thousand units of a cer-
    tain item, then N is given by

    $$N(x, y) = x^{0.75} y^{0.25}$$

    What is the average number of units produced for the indi-
    cated ranges of x and y? Set up a double integral and evalu-
    ate it.

40. **Cobb–Douglas production function.** Repeat Problem 39
    for

    $$N(x, y) = x^{0.5} y^{0.5}$$

    where $10 \le x \le 30$ and $1 \le y \le 3$.

41. **Population distribution.** In order to study the population
    distribution of a certain species of insect, a biologist has
    constructed an artificial habitat in the shape of a rectangle
    16 feet long and 12 feet wide. The only food available to the
    insects in this habitat is located at its center. The biologist
    has determined that the concentration C of insects per
    square foot at a point d units from the food supply (see the
    figure) is given approximately by

    $$C = 10 - \tfrac{1}{10} d^2$$

What is the average concentration of insects throughout the
habitat? Express C as a function of x and y, set up a double
integral, and evaluate it.

Figure for 41

42. **Population distribution.** Repeat Problem 41 for a square
    habitat that measures 12 feet on each side, where the insect
    concentration is given by

    $$C = 8 - \tfrac{1}{10} d^2$$

43. **Pollution.** A heavy industrial plant located in the center of
    a small town emits particulate matter into the atmosphere.
    Suppose that the concentration of particulate matter (in
    parts per million) at a point d miles from the plant (see the
    figure) is given by

    $$C = 100 - 15d^2$$

    If the boundaries of the town form a rectangle 4 miles long
    and 2 miles wide, what is the average concentration of par-
    ticulate matter throughout the town? Express C as a func-
    tion of x and y, set up a double integral, and evaluate it.

Figure for 43

44. **Pollution.** Repeat Problem 43 if the boundaries of the town
    form a rectangle 8 miles long and 4 miles wide and the con-
    centration of particulate matter is given by

    $$C = 100 - 3d^2$$

45. **Safety research.** Under ideal conditions, if a person driving
    a car slams on the brakes and skids to a stop, the length of
    the skid marks (in feet) is given by the formula

    $$L = 0.000\ 013\ 3xy^2$$

    where x is the weight of the car (in pounds) and y is the
    speed of the car (in miles per hour). What is the average
    length of the skid marks for cars weighing between 2,000
    and 3,000 pounds and traveling at speeds between 50 and 60
    miles per hour? Set up a double integral and evaluate it.

46. **Safety research.** Repeat Problem 45 for cars weighing be-
    tween 2,000 and 2,500 pounds and traveling at speeds be-
    tween 40 and 50 miles per hour.

47. Psychology. The intelligence quotient Q for a person with mental age x and chronological age y is given by

$$Q(x, y) = 100\frac{x}{y}$$

In a group of sixth-graders, the mental age varies between 8 and 16 years and the chronological age varies between 10 and 12 years. What is the average intelligence quotient for this group? Set up a double integral and evaluate it.

48. Psychology. Repeat Problem 47 for a group with mental ages between 6 and 14 years and chronological ages between 8 and 10 years.

15-7   Double Integrals over More General Regions

- Regular Regions
- Double Integrals over Regular Regions
- Reversing the Order of Integration
- Volume and Double Integrals

In this section, we extend the concept of double integration discussed in Section 15-6 to nonrectangular regions. We begin with an example and some new terminology.

Regular Regions

Let R be the region graphed in Figure 1. We can describe R with the following inequalities:

$$R = \{(x, y) \mid x \le y \le 6x - x^2, \ 0 \le x \le 5\}$$

The region R can be viewed as a union of vertical line segments. For each x in the interval $[0, 5]$, the line segment from the point $(x, g(x))$ to the point $(x, f(x))$ lies in the region R. Any region that can be covered by vertical line segments in this manner is called a *regular x region*.

Now consider the region S in Figure 2. It can be described with the following inequalities:

$$S = \{(x, y) \mid y^2 \le x \le y + 2, \ -1 \le y \le 2\}$$

The region S can be viewed as a union of horizontal line segments going from the graph of $h(y) = y^2$ to the graph of $k(y) = y + 2$ on the interval $[-1, 2]$. Regions that can be described in this manner are called *regular y regions*.

In general, *regular regions* are defined as follows:

Figure 1

Figure 2

DEFINITION   Regular Regions

A region R in the xy plane is a **regular x region** if there exist functions $f(x)$ and $g(x)$ and numbers a and b such that

$$R = \{(x, y) \mid g(x) \le y \le f(x), \ a \le x \le b\}$$

A region R is a **regular y region** if there exist functions $h(y)$ and $k(y)$ and numbers c and d such that

$$R = \{(x, y) \mid h(y) \le x \le k(y), \ c \le y \le d\}$$

See Figure 3 for a geometric interpretation.

CONCEPTUAL INSIGHT

If, for some region R, there is a horizontal line that has a nonempty intersection I with R, and if I is neither a closed interval nor a point, then R is *not* a regular y region. Similarly, if, for some region R, there is a vertical line that has a nonempty intersection I with R, and if I is neither a closed interval nor a point, then R is *not* a regular x region (see Fig. 3).

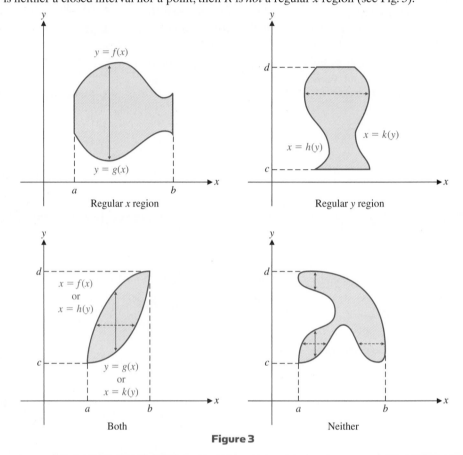

Figure 3

EXAMPLE 1   **Describing a Regular x Region** The region R is bounded by the graphs of $y = 4 - x^2$ and $y = x - 2$, $x \geq 0$, and the y axis. Graph R and use set notation and double inequalities to describe R as a regular x region.

SOLUTION   As the solid line in the following figure indicates, R can be covered by vertical line segments that go from the graph of $y = x - 2$ to the graph of $y = 4 - x^2$. So, R is a regular x region. In terms of set notation and double inequalities, we can write

$$R = \{(x, y) \mid x - 2 \leq y \leq 4 - x^2, \ 0 \leq x \leq 2\}$$

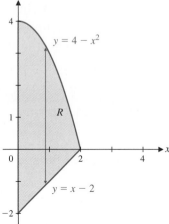

CONCEPTUAL INSIGHT

The region R of Example 1 is also a regular y region, since $R = \{(x, y) | 0 \le x \le k(y),\ -2 \le y \le 4\}$, where

$$k(y) = \begin{cases} 2 + y & \text{if } -2 \le y \le 0 \\ \sqrt{4 - y} & \text{if } 0 \le y \le 4 \end{cases}$$

But because $k(y)$ is piecewise defined, this description is more complicated than the description of R in Example 1 as a regular x region.

Matched Problem 1   Describe the region R bounded by the graphs of $x = 6 - y$ and $x = y^2$, $y \ge 0$, and the x axis as a regular y region.

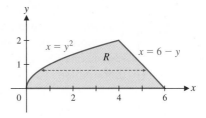

EXAMPLE 2   **Describing Regular Regions** The region R is bounded by the graphs of $x + y^2 = 9$ and $x + 3y = 9$. Graph R and describe R as a regular x region, a regular y region, both, or neither. Represent R in set notation and with double inequalities.

SOLUTION

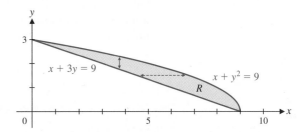

Region R can be covered by vertical line segments that go from the graph of $x + 3y = 9$ to the graph of $x + y^2 = 9$. Thus, R is a regular x region. In order to describe R with inequalities, we must solve each equation for y in terms of x:

$$\begin{array}{ll} x + 3y = 9 & x + y^2 = 9 \\ 3y = 9 - x & y^2 = 9 - x \\ y = 3 - \tfrac{1}{3}x & y = \sqrt{9 - x} \end{array}$$

We use the positive square root, since the graph is in the first quadrant.

So,

$$R = \{(x, y) | 3 - \tfrac{1}{3}x \le y \le \sqrt{9 - x},\ 0 \le x \le 9\}$$

Since region R also can be covered by horizontal line segments (see the dashed line in the preceding figure) that go from the graph of $x + 3y = 9$ to the graph of $x + y^2 = 9$, it is a regular y region. Now we must solve each equation for x in terms of y:

$$\begin{array}{ll} x + 3y = 9 & x + y^2 = 9 \\ x = 9 - 3y & x = 9 - y^2 \end{array}$$

Therefore,

$$R = \{(x, y) | 9 - 3y \le x \le 9 - y^2,\ 0 \le y \le 3\}$$

Matched Problem 2   Repeat Example 2 for the region bounded by the graphs of $2y - x = 4$ and $y^2 - x = 4$, as shown in the following figure:

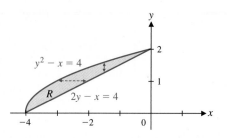

EXPLORE & DISCUSS 1

A E I O U

Consider the vowels A, E, I, O, U, written in block letters as shown in the margin, to be regions of the plane. One of the vowels is a regular x region, but not a regular y region; one is a regular y region, but not a regular x region; one is both; two are neither. Explain.

Double Integrals over Regular Regions

Now we want to extend the definition of double integration to include regular x regions and regular y regions. The order of integration now depends on the nature of the region R. If R is a regular x region, we integrate with respect to y first, while if R is a regular y region, we integrate with respect to x first.

> **Note that the variable limits of integration (when present) are always on the inner integral, and the constant limits of integration are always on the outer integral.**

DEFINITION Double Integration over Regular Regions

Regular x Region

If $R = \{(x, y) \mid g(x) \le y \le f(x), \quad a \le x \le b\}$, then

$$\iint\limits_{R} F(x, y)\, dA = \int_a^b \left[\int_{g(x)}^{f(x)} F(x, y)\, dy \right] dx$$

Regular y Region

If $R = \{(x, y) \mid h(y) \le x \le k(y), \quad c \le y \le d\}$, then

$$\iint\limits_{R} F(x, y)\, dA = \int_c^d \left[\int_{h(y)}^{k(y)} F(x, y)\, dx \right] dy$$

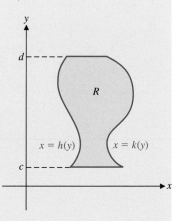

EXAMPLE 3 **Evaluating a Double Integral** Evaluate $\iint\limits_R 2xy\,dA$, where R is the region bounded by the graphs of $y = -x$ and $y = x^2$, $x \geq 0$, and the graph of $x = 1$.

SOLUTION From the graph, we can see that R is a regular x region described by

$$R = \{(x, y)\,|-x \leq y \leq x^2, \ \ 0 \leq x \leq 1\}$$

$$\iint\limits_R 2xy\,dA = \int_0^1 \left[\int_{-x}^{x^2} 2xy\,dy\right] dx$$

$$= \int_0^1 \left[xy^2\Big|_{y=-x}^{y=x^2}\right] dx$$

$$= \int_0^1 \left[x(x^2)^2 - x(-x)^2\right] dx$$

$$= \int_0^1 (x^5 - x^3)\,dx$$

$$= \left(\frac{x^6}{6} - \frac{x^4}{4}\right)\Big|_{x=0}^{x=1}$$

$$= \left(\tfrac{1}{6} - \tfrac{1}{4}\right) - (0 - 0) = -\tfrac{1}{12}$$

Matched Problem 3 Evaluate $\iint\limits_R 3xy^2\,dA$, where R is the region in Example 3.

EXAMPLE 4 **Evaluating a Double Integral** Evaluate $\iint\limits_R (2x + y)\,dA$, where R is the region bounded by the graphs of $y = \sqrt{x}$, $x + y = 2$, and $y = 0$.

SOLUTION From the graph, we can see that R is a regular y region. After solving each equation for x, we can write

$$R = \{(x, y)\,|\,y^2 \leq x \leq 2 - y, \ \ 0 \leq y \leq 1\}$$

$$\iint\limits_R (2x + y)\,dA = \int_0^1 \left[\int_{y^2}^{2-y} (2x + y)\,dx\right] dy$$

$$= \int_0^1 \left[(x^2 + yx)\Big|_{x=y^2}^{x=2-y}\right] dy$$

$$= \int_0^1 \{[(2 - y)^2 + y(2 - y)] - [(y^2)^2 + y(y^2)]\}\,dy$$

$$= \int_0^1 (4 - 2y - y^3 - y^4)\,dy$$

$$= \left(4y - y^2 - \tfrac{1}{4}y^4 - \tfrac{1}{5}y^5\right)\Big|_{y=0}^{y=1}$$

$$= \left(4 - 1 - \tfrac{1}{4} - \tfrac{1}{5}\right) - 0 = \tfrac{51}{20}$$

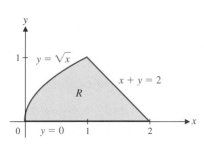

Matched Problem 4   Evaluate $\iint\limits_{R} (y - 4x)\,dA$, where R is the region in Example 4.

EXAMPLE 5   **Evaluating a Double Integral** The region R is bounded by the graphs of $y = \sqrt{x}$ and $y = \frac{1}{2}x$. Evaluate $\iint\limits_{R} 4xy^3\,dA$ two different ways.

SOLUTION   Region R is both a regular x region and a regular y region:

$$R = \{(x, y)\,|\,\tfrac{1}{2}x \le y \le \sqrt{x},\ \ 0 \le x \le 4\} \qquad \text{Regular } x \text{ region}$$

$$R = \{(x, y)\,|\,y^2 \le x \le 2y,\ \ 0 \le y \le 2\} \qquad \text{Regular } y \text{ region}$$

Using the first representation (a regular x region), we obtain

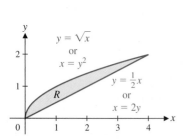

$$\iint\limits_{R} 4xy^3\,dA = \int_0^4 \left[\int_{x/2}^{\sqrt{x}} 4xy^3\,dy \right] dx$$

$$= \int_0^4 \left[xy^4 \Big|_{y=x/2}^{y=\sqrt{x}} \right] dx$$

$$= \int_0^4 \left[x(\sqrt{x})^4 - x(\tfrac{1}{2}x)^4 \right] dx$$

$$= \int_0^4 \left(x^3 - \tfrac{1}{16}x^5 \right) dx$$

$$= \left(\tfrac{1}{4}x^4 - \tfrac{1}{96}x^6 \right) \Big|_{x=0}^{x=4}$$

$$= \left(64 - \tfrac{128}{3} \right) - 0 = \tfrac{64}{3}$$

Using the second representation (a regular y region), we obtain

$$\iint\limits_{R} 4xy^3\,dA = \int_0^2 \left[\int_{y^2}^{2y} 4xy^3\,dx \right] dy$$

$$= \int_0^2 \left[2x^2y^3 \Big|_{x=y^2}^{x=2y} \right] dy$$

$$= \int_0^2 \left[2(2y)^2y^3 - 2(y^2)^2y^3 \right] dy$$

$$= \int_0^2 \left(8y^5 - 2y^7 \right) dy$$

$$= \left(\tfrac{4}{3}y^6 - \tfrac{1}{4}y^8 \right) \Big|_{y=0}^{y=2}$$

$$= \left(\tfrac{256}{3} - 64 \right) - 0 = \tfrac{64}{3}$$

Matched Problem 5   The region R is bounded by the graphs of $y = x$ and $y = \frac{1}{2}x^2$. Evaluate $\iint\limits_{R} 4xy^3\,dA$ two different ways.

Reversing the Order of Integration

Example 5 shows that

$$\iint\limits_{R} 4xy^3 \, dA = \int_0^4 \left[\int_{x/2}^{\sqrt{x}} 4xy^3 \, dy \right] dx = \int_0^2 \left[\int_{y^2}^{2y} 4xy^3 \, dx \right] dy$$

In general, if R is both a regular x region and a regular y region, then the two iterated integrals are equal. In rectangular regions, reversing the order of integration in an iterated integral was a simple matter. As Example 5 illustrates, the process is more complicated in nonrectangular regions. The next example illustrates how to start with an iterated integral and reverse the order of integration. Since we are interested in the reversal process and not in the value of either integral, the integrand will not be specified.

EXAMPLE 6   **Reversing the Order of Integration** Reverse the order of integration in

$$\int_1^3 \left[\int_0^{x-1} f(x, y) \, dy \right] dx$$

SOLUTION   The order of integration indicates that the region of integration is a regular x region:

$$R = \{(x, y) | 0 \le y \le x - 1, \ 1 \le x \le 3\}$$

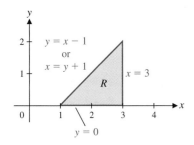

Graph region R to determine whether it is also a regular y region. The graph shows that R is also a regular y region, and we can write

$$R = \{(x, y) | y + 1 \le x \le 3, \ 0 \le y \le 2\}$$
$$\int_1^3 \left[\int_0^{x-1} f(x, y) \, dy \right] dx = \int_0^2 \left[\int_{y+1}^3 f(x, y) \, dx \right] dy$$

Matched Problem 6   Reverse the order of integration in $\int_2^4 \left[\int_0^{4-x} f(x, y) \, dy \right] dx$.

EXPLORE & DISCUSS 2   Explain the difficulty in evaluating $\int_0^2 \int_{x^2}^4 xe^{y^2} \, dy \, dx$ and how it can be overcome by reversing the order of integration.

Volume and Double Integrals

In Section 15-6, we used the double integral to calculate the volume of a solid with a rectangular base. In general, if a solid can be described by the graph of a positive function $f(x, y)$ over a regular region R (not necessarily a rectangle), then the double integral of the function f over the region R still represents the volume of the corresponding solid.

EXAMPLE 7   **Volume** The region R is bounded by the graphs of $x + y = 1$, $y = 0$, and $x = 0$. Find the volume of the solid under the graph of $z = 1 - x - y$ over the region R.

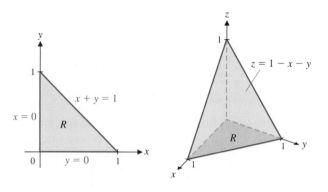

SOLUTION   The graph of R shows that R is both a regular x region and a regular y region. We choose to use the regular x region:

$$R = \{(x, y)|0 \le y \le 1 - x, \ \ 0 \le x \le 1\}$$

The volume of the solid is

$$
\begin{aligned}
V = \iint\limits_{R} (1 - x - y)\, dA &= \int_{0}^{1} \left[\int_{0}^{1-x} (1 - x - y)\, dy \right] dx \\
&= \int_{0}^{1} \left[\left(y - xy - \tfrac{1}{2}y^2 \right) \Big|_{y=0}^{y=1-x} \right] dx \\
&= \int_{0}^{1} \left[(1 - x) - x(1 - x) - \tfrac{1}{2}(1 - x)^2 \right] dx \\
&= \int_{0}^{1} \left(\tfrac{1}{2} - x + \tfrac{1}{2}x^2 \right) dx \\
&= \left(\tfrac{1}{2}x - \tfrac{1}{2}x^2 + \tfrac{1}{6}x^3 \right) \Big|_{x=0}^{x=1} \\
&= \left(\tfrac{1}{2} - \tfrac{1}{2} + \tfrac{1}{6} \right) - 0 = \tfrac{1}{6}
\end{aligned}
$$

Matched Problem 7   The region R is bounded by the graphs of $y + 2x = 2$, $y = 0$, and $x = 0$. Find the volume of the solid under the graph of $z = 2 - 2x - y$ over the region R. [*Hint*: Sketch the region first; the solid does not have to be sketched.]

Exercises 15-7

A

In Problems 1–6, graph the region R bounded by the graphs of the equations. Use set notation and double inequalities to describe R as a regular x region and a regular y region in Problems 1 and 2, and as a regular x region or a regular y region, whichever is simpler, in Problems 3–6.

1. $y = 4 - x^2, y = 0, 0 \le x \le 2$

2. $y = x^2, y = 9, 0 \le x \le 3$

3. $y = x^3, y = 12 - 2x, x = 0$

4. $y = 5 - x, y = 1 + x, y = 0$

5. $y^2 = 2x, y = x - 4$

6. $y = 4 + 3x - x^2, x + y = 4$

Evaluate each integral in Problems 7–10.

7. $\int_{0}^{1} \int_{0}^{x} (x + y)\, dy\, dx$

8. $\int_{0}^{2} \int_{0}^{y} xy\, dx\, dy$

9. $\int_{0}^{1} \int_{y^3}^{\sqrt{y}} (2x + y)\, dx\, dy$

10. $\int_{1}^{4} \int_{x}^{x^2} (x^2 + 2y)\, dy\, dx$

B

✎ *In Problems 11–14, give a verbal description of the region R and determine whether R is a regular x region, a regular y region, both, or neither.*

11. $R = \{(x, y)\,|\,|x| \le 2,\ \ |y| \le 3\}$

12. $R = \{(x, y)\,|\,1 \le x^2 + y^2 \le 4\}$

13. $R = \{(x, y)\,|\,x^2 + y^2 \ge 1,\ \ |x| \le 2,\ \ 0 \le y \le 2\}$

14. $R = \{(x, y)\,|\,|x| + |y| \le 1\}$

In Problems 15–20, use the description of the region R to evaluate the indicated integral.

15. $\displaystyle\iint\limits_{R} (x^2 + y^2)\, dA;$

$R = \{(x, y)\,|\,0 \le y \le 2x,\ \ 0 \le x \le 2\}$

16. $\displaystyle\iint\limits_{R} 2x^2 y\, dA;$

$R = \{(x, y)\,|\,0 \le y \le 9 - x^2,\ \ -3 \le x \le 3\}$

17. $\displaystyle\iint\limits_{R} (x + y - 2)^3\, dA;$

$R = \{(x, y)\,|\,0 \le x \le y + 2,\ \ 0 \le y \le 1\}$

18. $\displaystyle\iint\limits_{R} (2x + 3y)\, dA;$

$R = \{(x, y)\,|\,y^2 - 4 \le x \le 4 - 2y,\ \ 0 \le y \le 2\}$

19. $\displaystyle\iint\limits_{R} e^{x+y}\, dA;$

$R = \{(x, y)\,|-x \le y \le x,\ \ 0 \le x \le 2\}$

20. $\displaystyle\iint\limits_{R} \frac{x}{\sqrt{x^2 + y^2}}\, dA;$

$R = \{(x, y)\,|\,0 \le x \le \sqrt{4y - y^2},\ \ 0 \le y \le 2\}$

In Problems 21–26, graph the region R bounded by the graphs of the indicated equations. Describe R in set notation with double inequalities, and evaluate the indicated integral.

21. $y = x + 1,\ y = 0,\ x = 0,\ x = 1;$

$\displaystyle\iint\limits_{R} \sqrt{1 + x + y}\, dA$

22. $y = x^2,\ \ y = \sqrt{x}\,;\ \ \displaystyle\iint\limits_{R} 12xy\, dA$

23. $y = 4x - x^2,\ \ y = 0;\ \displaystyle\iint\limits_{R} \sqrt{y + x^2}\, dA$

24. $x = 1 + 3y,\ \ x = 1 - y,\ \ y = 1;$

$\displaystyle\iint\limits_{R} (x + y + 1)^3\, dA$

25. $y = 1 - \sqrt{x},\ y = 1 + \sqrt{x},\ x = 4;$

$\displaystyle\iint\limits_{R} x(y - 1)^2\, dA$

26. $y = \tfrac{1}{2}x,\ y = 6 - x,\ \ y = 1;\ \ \displaystyle\iint\limits_{R} \frac{1}{x + y}\, dA$

In Problems 27–32, evaluate each integral. Graph the region of integration, reverse the order of integration, and then evaluate the integral with the order reversed.

27. $\displaystyle\int_0^3 \int_0^{3-x} (x + 2y)\, dy\, dx$

28. $\displaystyle\int_0^2 \int_0^{y} (y - x)^4\, dx\, dy$

29. $\displaystyle\int_0^1 \int_0^{1-x^2} x\sqrt{y}\, dy\, dx$

30. $\displaystyle\int_0^2 \int_{x^3}^{4x} (1 + 2y)\, dy\, dx$

31. $\displaystyle\int_0^4 \int_{x/4}^{\sqrt{x}/2} x\, dy\, dx$

32. $\displaystyle\int_0^4 \int_{y^2/4}^{2\sqrt{y}} (1 + 2xy)\, dx\, dy$

In Problems 33–36, find the volume of the solid under the graph of f (x, y) over the region R bounded by the graphs of the indicated equations. Sketch the region R; the solid does not have to be sketched.

33. $f(x, y) = 4 - x - y;\ R$ is the region bounded by the graphs of $x + y = 4,\ y = 0,\ x = 0$

34. $f(x, y) = (x - y)^2;\ R$ is the region bounded by the graphs of $y = x,\ y = 2,\ x = 0$

35. $f(x, y) = 4;\ R$ is the region bounded by the graphs of $y = 1 - x^2$ and $y = 0$ for $0 \le x \le 1$

36. $f(x, y) = 4xy;\ R$ is the region bounded by the graphs of $y = \sqrt{1 - x^2}$ and $y = 0$ for $0 \le x \le 1$

C

In Problems 37–40, reverse the order of integration for each integral. Evaluate the integral with the order reversed. Do not attempt to evaluate the integral in the original form.

37. $\displaystyle\int_0^2 \int_{x^2}^4 \frac{4x}{1 + y^2}\, dy\, dx$

38. $\displaystyle\int_0^1 \int_y^1 \sqrt{1 - x^2}\, dx\, dy$

39. $\displaystyle\int_0^1 \int_{y^2}^1 4ye^{x^2}\, dx\, dy$

40. $\displaystyle\int_0^4 \int_{\sqrt{x}}^2 \sqrt{3x + y^2}\, dy\, dx$

▱ *In Problems 41–46, use a graphing calculator to graph the region R bounded by the graphs of the indicated equations. Use approximation techniques to find intersection points correct to two decimal places. Describe R in set notation with double inequalities, and evaluate the indicated integral correct to two decimal places.*

41. $y = 1 + \sqrt{x},\quad y = x^2,\quad x = 0;\ \ \displaystyle\iint\limits_{R} x\, dA$

42. $y = 1 + \sqrt[3]{x},\ y = x,\ x = 0;\ \displaystyle\iint\limits_{R} x\, dA$

43. $y = \sqrt[3]{x},\ y = 1 - x,\ y = 0;\ \displaystyle\iint\limits_{R} 24xy\, dA$

44. $y = x^3,\ y = 1 - x,\ y = 0;\ \displaystyle\iint\limits_{R} 48xy\, dA$

45. $y = e^{-x}$, $y = 3 - x$; $\displaystyle\iint\limits_{R} 4y\, dA$

46. $y = e^{x}$, $y = 2 + x$; $\displaystyle\iint\limits_{R} 8y\, dA$

3. $\frac{13}{40}$

4. $-\frac{77}{20}$

5. $\frac{16}{3}$

6. $\int_0^2 \int_2^{4-y} f(x, y)\, dx\, dy$

7. $\frac{2}{3}$

Answers to Matched Problems

1. $R = \{(x, y)|y^2 \le x \le 6 - y, \ 0 \le y \le 2\}$

2. R is both a regular x region and a regular y region:

$R = \{(x, y) \mid \frac{1}{2}x + 2 \le y \le \sqrt{x + 4}, \ -4 \le x \le 0\}$

$R = \{(x, y)|y^2 - 4 \le x \le 2y - 4, \ 0 \le y \le 2\}$

Chapter 15 Review

Important Terms, Symbols, and Concepts

15-1 Functions of Several Variables

EXAMPLES

- An equation of the form $z = f(x, y)$ describes a **function of two independent variables** if, for each permissible ordered pair (x, y), there is one and only one value of z determined by $f(x, y)$. The variables x and y are **independent variables**, and z is a **dependent variable**. The set of all ordered pairs of permissible values of x and y is the **domain** of the function, and the set of all corresponding values $f(x, y)$ is the **range**. Functions of more than two independent variables are defined similarly.

Ex. 1, p. 798
Ex. 2, p. 799
Ex. 3, p. 799
Ex. 4, p. 800
Ex. 5, p. 801
Ex. 6, p. 801
Ex. 7, p. 803

- The graph of $z = f(x, y)$ consists of all triples (x, y, z) in a **three-dimensional coordinate system** that satisfy the equation. The graphs of the functions $z = f(x, y) = x^2 + y^2$ and $z = g(x, y) = x^2 - y^2$, for example, are **surfaces**; the first has a local minimum, and the second has a **saddle point**, at $(0, 0)$.

15-2 Partial Derivatives

- If $z = f(x, y)$, then the **partial derivative of f with respect to x**, denoted as $\partial z/\partial x$, f_x, or $f_x(x, y)$, is

Ex. 1, p. 807
Ex. 2, p. 808
Ex. 3, p. 808
Ex. 4, p. 809

$$\frac{\partial z}{\partial x} = \lim_{h \to 0} \frac{f(x + h, y) - f(x, y)}{h}$$

Similarly, the **partial derivative of f with respect to y**, denoted as $\partial z/\partial y$, f_y, or $f_y(x, y)$, is

$$\frac{\partial z}{\partial y} = \lim_{k \to 0} \frac{f(x, y + k) - f(x, y)}{k}$$

The partial derivatives $\partial z/\partial x$ and $\partial z/\partial y$ are said to be **first-order partial derivatives**.

- There are four **second-order partial derivatives** of $z = f(x, y)$:

Ex. 5, p. 811

$$f_{xx} = f_{xx}(x, y) = \frac{\partial^2 z}{\partial x^2} = \frac{\partial}{\partial x}\left(\frac{\partial z}{\partial x}\right)$$

$$f_{xy} = f_{xy}(x, y) = \frac{\partial^2 z}{\partial y\, \partial x} = \frac{\partial}{\partial y}\left(\frac{\partial z}{\partial x}\right)$$

$$f_{yx} = f_{yx}(x, y) = \frac{\partial^2 z}{\partial x\, \partial y} = \frac{\partial}{\partial x}\left(\frac{\partial z}{\partial y}\right)$$

$$f_{yy} = f_{yy}(x, y) = \frac{\partial^2 z}{\partial y^2} = \frac{\partial}{\partial y}\left(\frac{\partial z}{\partial y}\right)$$

15-3 Maxima and Minima

- If $f(a, b) \ge f(x, y)$ for all (x, y) in a circular region in the domain of f with (a, b) as center, then $f(a, b)$ is a **local maximum**. If $f(a, b) \le f(x, y)$ for all (x, y) in such a region, then $f(a, b)$ is a **local minimum**.

Ex. 1, p. 818
Ex. 2, p. 818
Ex. 3, p. 820
Ex. 4, p. 820

- If a function $f(x, y)$ has a local maximum or minimum at the point (a, b), and f_x and f_y exist at (a, b), then both first-order partial derivatives equal 0 at (a, b) [Theorem 1, p. 816].

- The second-derivative test for local extrema (Theorem 2, p. 817) gives conditions on the first- and second-order partial derivatives of $f(x, y)$, which guarantee that $f(a, b)$ is a local maximum, local minimum, or saddle point.

15-4 Maxima and Minima Using Lagrange Multipliers

- The **method of Lagrange multipliers** can be used to find local extrema of a function $z = f(x, y)$ subject to the constraint $g(x, y) = 0$. A procedure that lists the key steps in the method is given on page 825.
- The method of Lagrange multipliers can be extended to functions with arbitrarily many independent variables with one or more constraints (see Theorem 1, p. 824, and Theorem 2, p. 829, for the method when there are two and three independent variables, respectively).

Ex. 1, p. 826
Ex. 2, p. 827
Ex. 3, p. 829

15-5 Method of Least Squares

- **Linear regression** is the process of fitting a line $y = ax + b$ to a set of data points $(x_1, y_1), (x_2, y_2), \ldots, (x_n, y_n)$ by using the **method of least squares**.

Ex. 1, p. 838

- We minimize $F(a, b) = \displaystyle\sum_{k=1}^{n} (y_k - ax_k - b)^2$, the **sum of the squares of the residuals**, by computing the first-order partial derivatives of F and setting them equal to 0. Solving for a and b gives the formulas

$$a = \frac{n\left(\displaystyle\sum_{k=1}^{n} x_k y_k\right) - \left(\displaystyle\sum_{k=1}^{n} x_k\right)\left(\displaystyle\sum_{k=1}^{n} y_k\right)}{n\left(\displaystyle\sum_{k=1}^{n} x_k^2\right) - \left(\displaystyle\sum_{k=1}^{n} x_k\right)^2}$$

$$b = \frac{\displaystyle\sum_{k=1}^{n} y_k - a\left(\displaystyle\sum_{k=1}^{n} x_k\right)}{n}$$

- Graphing calculators have built-in routines to calculate linear—as well as quadratic, cubic, quartic, logarithmic, exponential, power, and trigonometric—regression equations.

Ex. 2, p. 840

15-6 Double Integrals over Rectangular Regions

- The **double integral** of a function $f(x, y)$ over a rectangle

$$R = \{(x, y)\,|\,a \le x \le b,\ \ c \le y \le d\}$$

is

Ex. 1, p. 844
Ex. 2, p. 845
Ex. 3, p. 845
Ex. 4, p. 847
Ex. 5, p. 847

$$\iint\limits_{R} f(x, y)\, dA = \int_a^b \left[\int_c^d f(x, y)\, dy \right] dx$$

$$= \int_c^d \left[\int_a^b f(x, y)\, dx \right] dy$$

- In the double integral $\iint_R f(x, y)\, dA$, $f(x, y)$ is called the **integrand** and R is called the **region of integration.** The expression dA indicates that this is an integral over a two-dimensional region. The integrals

$$\int_a^b \left[\int_c^d f(x, y)\, dy \right] dx \qquad \text{and} \qquad \int_c^d \left[\int_a^b f(x, y)\, dx \right] dy$$

are referred to as **iterated integrals** (the brackets are often omitted), and the order in which dx and dy are written indicates the order of integration.

- The **average value** of the function $f(x, y)$ over the rectangle

$$R = \{(x, y)\,|\,a \le x \le b,\ \ c \le y \le d\}$$

is

Ex. 6, p. 848

$$\frac{1}{(b - a)(d - c)} \iint\limits_{R} f(x, y)\, dA$$

- If $f(x, y) \ge 0$ over a rectangle $R = \{(x, y)\,|\,a \le x \le b, c \le y \le d\}$, then the volume of the solid formed by graphing f over the rectangle R is given by

Ex. 7, p. 849

$$V = \iint\limits_{R} f(x, y)\, dA$$

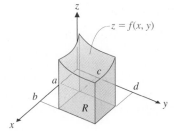

15-7 Double Integrals over More General Regions

- A region R in the xy plane is a **regular x region** if there exist functions $f(x)$ and $g(x)$ and numbers a and b such that
$$R = \{(x, y) \mid g(x) \le y \le f(x), \quad a \le x \le b\}$$
Ex. 1, p. 854

- A region R in the xy plane is a **regular y region** if there exist functions $h(y)$ and $k(y)$ and numbers c and d such that
$$R = \{(x, y) \mid h(y) \le x \le k(y), \quad c \le y \le d\}$$
Ex. 2, p. 855

- The double integral of a function $F(x, y)$ over a regular x region $R = \{(x, y) \mid g(x) \le y \le f(x), a \le x \le b\}$ is
$$\iint\limits_{R} F(x, y) \, dA = \int_a^b \left[\int_{g(x)}^{f(x)} F(x, y) \, dy \right] dx$$
Ex. 3, p. 857
Ex. 4, p. 857
Ex. 5, p. 858
Ex. 6, p. 859
Ex. 7, p. 860

- The double integral of a function $F(x, y)$ over a regular y region $R = \{(x, y) \mid h(y) \le x \le k(y), c \le y \le d\}$ is
$$\iint\limits_{R} F(x, y) \, dA = \int_c^d \left[\int_{h(y)}^{k(y)} F(x, y) \, dx \right] dy$$

Review Exercises

Work through all the problems in this chapter review and check your answers in the back of the book. Answers to all review problems are there, along with section numbers in italics to indicate where each type of problem is discussed. Where weaknesses show up, review appropriate sections of the text.

A

1. For $f(x, y) = 2{,}000 + 40x + 70y$, find $f(5, 10)$, $f_x(x, y)$, and $f_y(x, y)$.

2. For $z = x^3 y^2$, find $\partial^2 z/\partial x^2$ and $\partial^2 z/\partial x \, \partial y$.

3. Evaluate $\int (6xy^2 + 4y) \, dy$.

4. Evaluate $\int (6xy^2 + 4y) \, dx$.

5. Evaluate $\int_0^1 \int_0^1 4xy \, dy \, dx$.

6. For $f(x, y) = 6 + 5x - 2y + 3x^2 + x^3$, find $f_x(x, y)$, and $f_y(x, y)$, and explain why $f(x, y)$ has no local extrema.

B

7. For $f(x, y) = 3x^2 - 2xy + y^2 - 2x + 3y - 7$, find $f(2, 3)$, $f_y(x, y)$, and $f_y(2, 3)$.

8. For $f(x, y) = -4x^2 + 4xy - 3y^2 + 4x + 10y + 81$, find $[f_{xx}(2, 3)][f_{yy}(2, 3)] - [f_{xy}(2, 3)]^2$.

9. If $f(x, y) = x + 3y$ and $g(x, y) = x^2 + y^2 - 10$, find the critical points of $F(x, y, \lambda) = f(x, y) + \lambda g(x, y)$.

10. Use the least squares line for the data in the following table to estimate y when $x = 10$.

x	y
2	12
4	10
6	7
8	3

11. For $R = \{(x, y) \mid -1 \le x \le 1, \ 1 \le y \le 2\}$, evaluate the following in two ways:
$$\iint\limits_{R} (4x + 6y) \, dA$$

12. For $R = \{(x, y) \mid \sqrt{y} \le x \le 1, \ 0 \le y \le 1\}$, evaluate
$$\iint\limits_{R} (6x + y) \, dA$$

C

13. For $f(x, y) = e^{x^2 + 2y}$, find f_x, f_y, and f_{xy}.

14. For $f(x, y) = (x^2 + y^2)^5$, find f_x and f_{xy}.

15. Find all critical points and test for extrema for
$$f(x, y) = x^3 - 12x + y^2 - 6y$$

16. Use Lagrange multipliers to maximize $f(x, y) = xy$ subject to $2x + 3y = 24$.

17. Use Lagrange multipliers to minimize $f(x, y, z) = x^2 + y^2 + z^2$ subject to $2x + y + 2z = 9$.

18. Find the least squares line for the data in the following table.

x	y	x	y
10	50	60	80
20	45	70	85
30	50	80	90
40	55	90	90
50	65	100	110

19. Find the average value of $f(x, y) = x^{2/3} y^{1/3}$ over the rectangle
$$R = \{(x, y) \mid -8 \le x \le 8, \ 0 \le y \le 27\}$$

20. Find the volume of the solid under the graph of $z = 3x^2 + 3y^2$ over the rectangle
$$R = \{(x, y) \mid 0 \le x \le 1, \ -1 \le y \le 1\}$$

21. Without doing any computation, predict the average value of $f(x, y) = x + y$ over the rectangle $R = \{(x, y) \mid -10 \le x \le 10, \ -10 \le y \le 10\}$. Then check the correctness of your prediction by evaluating a double integral.

22. (A) Find the dimensions of the square S centered at the origin such that the average value of

$$f(x, y) = \frac{e^x}{y + 10}$$

over S is equal to 5.

 (B) Is there a square centered at the origin over which

$$f(x, y) = \frac{e^x}{y + 10}$$

has average value 0.05? Explain.

23. Explain why the function $f(x, y) = 4x^3 - 5y^3$, subject to the constraint $3x + 2y = 7$, has no maxima or minima.

24. Find the volume of the solid under the graph of $F(x, y) = 60x^2y$ over the region R bounded by the graph of $x + y = 1$ and the coordinate axes.

Applications

25. Maximizing profit. A company produces x units of product A and y units of product B (both in hundreds per month). The monthly profit equation (in thousands of dollars) is given by

$$P(x, y) = -4x^2 + 4xy - 3y^2 + 4x + 10y + 81$$

(A) Find $P_x(1, 3)$ and interpret the results.

(B) How many of each product should be produced each month to maximize profit? What is the maximum profit?

26. Minimizing material. A rectangular box with no top and six compartments (see the figure) is to have a volume of 96 cubic inches. Find the dimensions that will require the least amount of material.

Figure for 26

27. Profit. A company's annual profits (in millions of dollars) over a 5-year period are given in the following table. Use the least squares line to estimate the profit for the sixth year.

Year	Profit
1	2
2	2.5
3	3.1
4	4.2
5	4.3

28. Productivity. The Cobb–Douglas production function for a product is

$$N(x, y) = 10x^{0.8}y^{0.2}$$

where x is the number of units of labor and y is the number of units of capital required to produce N units of the product.

(A) Find the marginal productivity of labor and the marginal productivity of capital at $x = 40$ and $y = 50$. For the greatest increase in productivity, should management encourage increased use of labor or increased use of capital?

(B) If each unit of labor costs \$100, each unit of capital costs \$50, and \$10,000 is budgeted for production of this product, use the method of Lagrange multipliers to determine the allocations of labor and capital that will maximize the number of units produced and find the maximum production. Find the marginal productivity of money and approximate the increase in production that would result from an increase of \$2,000 in the amount budgeted for production.

(C) If $50 \leq x \leq 100$ and $20 \leq y \leq 40$, find the average number of units produced. Set up a double integral, and evaluate it.

29. Marine biology. The function used for timing dives with scuba gear is

$$T(V, x) = \frac{33V}{x + 33}$$

where T is the time of the dive in minutes, V is the volume of air (in cubic feet, at sea-level pressure) compressed into tanks, and x is the depth of the dive in feet. Find $T_x(70, 17)$ and interpret the results.

30. Pollution. A heavy industrial plant located in the center of a small town emits particulate matter into the atmosphere. Suppose that the concentration of particulate matter (in parts per million) at a point d miles from the plant is given by

$$C = 100 - 24d^2$$

If the boundaries of the town form a square 4 miles long and 4 miles wide, what is the average concentration of particulate matter throughout the town? Express C as a function of x and y, and set up a double integral and evaluate it.

31. Sociology. A sociologist found that the number n of long-distance telephone calls between two cities during a given period varied (approximately) jointly as the populations P_1 and P_2 of the two cities and varied inversely as the distance d between the cities. An equation for a period of 1 week is

$$n(P_1, P_2, d) = 0.001\frac{P_1P_2}{d}$$

Find $n(100,000, 50,000, 100)$.

32. Education. At the beginning of the semester, students in a foreign language course take a proficiency exam. The same exam is given at the end of the semester. The results for 5 students are shown in the following table. Use the least squares line to estimate the second exam score of a student who scored 40 on the first exam.

First Exam	Second Exam
30	60
50	75
60	80
70	85
90	90

33. Population density. The following table gives the U.S. population per square mile for the years 1900–2000:

U.S. Population Density

Year	Population (per Square Mile)	Year	Population (per Square Mile)
1900	25.6	1960	50.6
1910	31.0	1970	57.4
1920	35.6	1980	64.0
1930	41.2	1990	70.4
1940	44.2	2000	77.8
1950	50.7		

(A) Find the least squares line for the data, using $x = 0$ for 1900.

(B) Use the least squares line to estimate the population density in the United States in the year 2020.

(C) Now use quadratic regression and exponential regression to obtain the estimate of part (B).

34. Life expectancy. The following table gives life expectancies for males and females in a sample of Central and South American countries:

Life Expectancies for Central and South American Countries

Males	Females	Males	Females
62.30	67.50	70.15	74.10
68.05	75.05	62.93	66.58
72.40	77.04	68.43	74.88
63.39	67.59	66.68	72.80
55.11	59.43		

(A) Find the least squares line for the data.

(B) Use the least squares line to estimate the life expectancy of a female in a Central or South American country in which the life expectancy for males is 60 years.

(C) Now use quadratic regression and logarithmic regression to obtain the estimate of part (B).

APPENDIX A Basic Algebra Review

Appendix A reviews some important basic algebra concepts usually studied in earlier courses. The material may be studied systematically before beginning the rest of the book or reviewed as needed.

A-1 Real Numbers

- Set of Real Numbers
- Real Number Line
- Basic Real Number Properties
- Further Properties
- Fraction Properties

The rules for manipulating and reasoning with symbols in algebra depend, in large measure, on properties of the real numbers. In this section we look at some of the important properties of this number system. To make our discussions here and elsewhere in the book clearer and more precise, we occasionally make use of simple *set* concepts and notation.

Set of Real Numbers

Informally, a **real number** is any number that has a decimal representation. Table 1 describes the set of real numbers and some of its important subsets. Figure 1 illustrates how these sets of numbers are related.

The set of integers contains all the natural numbers and something else—their negatives and 0. The set of rational numbers contains all the integers and something else—noninteger ratios of integers. And the set of real numbers contains all the rational numbers and something else—irrational numbers.

Table 1 Set of Real Numbers

Symbol	Name	Description	Examples
N	Natural numbers	Counting numbers (also called positive integers)	$1, 2, 3, \ldots$
Z	Integers	Natural numbers, their negatives, and 0	$\ldots, -2, -1, 0, 1, 2, \ldots$
Q	Rational numbers	Numbers that can be represented as a/b, where a and b are integers and $b \neq 0$; decimal representations are repeating or terminating	$-4, 0, 1, 25, \frac{-3}{5}, \frac{2}{3}, 3.67, -0.33\bar{3}, 5.272\,7\overline{27}$*
I	Irrational numbers	Numbers that can be represented as nonrepeating and nonterminating decimal numbers	$\sqrt{2}, \pi, \sqrt[3]{7}, 1.414\,213\ldots, 2.718\,281\,82\ldots$
R	Real numbers	Rational and irrational numbers	

*The overbar indicates that the number (or block of numbers) repeats indefinitely. The space after every third digit is used to help keep track of the number of decimal places.

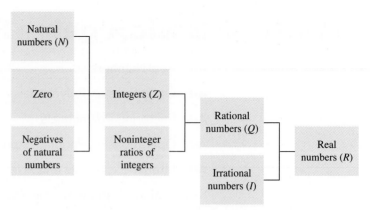

Figure 1 Real numbers and important subsets

Real Number Line

A one-to-one correspondence exists between the set of real numbers and the set of points on a line. That is, each real number corresponds to exactly one point, and each point corresponds to exactly one real number. A line with a real number associated with each point, and vice versa, as shown in Figure 2, is called a **real number line**, or simply a **real line**. Each number associated with a point is called the coordinate of the point.

Figure 2 Real number line

The point with coordinate 0 is called the **origin**. The arrow on the right end of the line indicates a positive direction. The coordinates of all points to the right of the origin are called positive **real numbers**, and those to the left of the origin are called **negative real numbers**. The real number 0 is neither positive nor negative.

Basic Real Number Properties

We now take a look at some of the basic properties of the real number system that enable us to convert algebraic expressions into *equivalent forms*.

SUMMARY   Basic Properties of the Set of Real Numbers

Let a, b, and c be arbitrary elements in the set of real numbers R.

Addition Properties

Associative: $(a + b) + c = a + (b + c)$

Commutative: $a + b = b + a$

Identity: 0 is the additive identity; that is, $0 + a = a + 0 = a$ for all a in R, and 0 is the only element in R with this property.

Inverse: For each a in R, $-a$, is its unique additive inverse; that is, $a + (-a) = (-a) + a = 0$ and $-a$ is the only element in R relative to a with this property.

Multiplication Properties

Associative: $(ab)c = a(bc)$

Commutative: $ab = ba$

Identity: 1 is the multiplicative identity; that is, $(1)a = a(1) = a$ for all a in R, and 1 is the only element in R with this property.

Inverse: For each a in R, $a \neq 0$, $1/a$ is its unique multiplicative inverse; that is, $a(1/a) = (1/a)a = 1$, and $1/a$ is the only element in R relative to a with this property.

Distributive Properties

$$a(b + c) = ab + ac \qquad (a + b)c = ac + bc$$

You are already familiar with the **commutative properties** for addition and multiplication. They indicate that the order in which the addition or multiplication of two numbers is performed does not matter. For example,

$$7 + 2 = 2 + 7 \quad \text{and} \quad 3 \cdot 5 = 5 \cdot 3$$

Is there a commutative property relative to subtraction or division? That is, does $a - b = b - a$ or does $a \div b = b \div a$ for all real numbers a and b (division by 0 excluded)? The answer is no, since, for example,

$$8 - 6 \neq 6 - 8 \quad \text{and} \quad 10 \div 5 \neq 5 \div 10$$

When computing

$$3 + 2 + 6 \quad \text{or} \quad 3 \cdot 2 \cdot 6$$

why don't we need parentheses to indicate which two numbers are to be added or multiplied first? The answer is to be found in the **associative properties**. These properties allow us to write

$$(3 + 2) + 6 = 3 + (2 + 6) \quad \text{and} \quad (3 \cdot 2) \cdot 6 = 3 \cdot (2 \cdot 6)$$

so it does not matter how we group numbers relative to either operation. Is there an associative property for subtraction or division? The answer is no, since, for example,

$$(12 - 6) - 2 \neq 12 - (6 - 2) \quad \text{and} \quad (12 \div 6) \div 2 \neq 12 \div (6 \div 2)$$

Evaluate each side of each equation to see why.

What number added to a given number will give that number back again? What number times a given number will give that number back again? The answers are 0 and 1, respectively. Because of this, 0 and 1 are called the **identity elements** for the real numbers. Hence, for any real numbers a and b,

$$0 + 5 = 5 \quad \text{and} \quad (a + b) + 0 = a + b$$
$$1 \cdot 4 = 4 \quad \text{and} \quad (a + b) \cdot 1 = a + b$$

We now consider **inverses**. For each real number a, there is a unique real number $-a$ such that $a + (-a) = 0$. The number $-a$ is called the **additive inverse** of a, or the **negative** of a. For example, the additive inverse (or negative) of 7 is -7, since $7 + (-7) = 0$. The additive inverse (or negative) of -7 is $-(-7) = 7$, since $-7 + [-(-7)] = 0$.

CONCEPTUAL INSIGHT

Do not confuse negation with the sign of a number. If a is a real number, $-a$ is the negative of a and may be positive or negative. Specifically, if a is negative, then $-a$ is positive and if a is positive, then $-a$ is negative.

For each nonzero real number a, there is a unique real number $1/a$ such that $a(1/a) = 1$. The number $1/a$ is called the **multiplicative inverse** of a, or the **reciprocal** of a. For example, the multiplicative inverse (or reciprocal) of 4 is $\frac{1}{4}$, since $4\left(\frac{1}{4}\right) = 1$. (Also note that 4 is the multiplicative inverse of $\frac{1}{4}$.) The number 0 has no multiplicative inverse.

We now turn to the **distributive properties**, which involve both multiplication and addition. Consider the following two computations:

$$5(3 + 4) = 5 \cdot 7 = 35 \qquad 5 \cdot 3 + 5 \cdot 4 = 15 + 20 = 35$$

Thus,

$$5(3 + 4) = 5 \cdot 3 + 5 \cdot 4$$

and we say that multiplication by 5 *distributes* over the sum $(3 + 4)$. In general, **multiplication distributes over addition** in the real number system. Two more illustrations are

$$9(m + n) = 9m + 9n \qquad (7 + 2)u = 7u + 2u$$

EXAMPLE 1 **Real Number Properties** State the real number property that justifies the indicated statement.

Statement	Property Illustrated
(A) $x(y + z) = (y + z)x$	Commutative $(\cdot)$
(B) $5(2y) = (5 \cdot 2)y$	Associative $(\cdot)$
(C) $2 + (y + 7) = 2 + (7 + y)$	Commutative $(+)$
(D) $4z + 6z = (4 + 6)z$	Distributive
(E) If $m + n = 0$, then $n = -m$.	Inverse $(+)$

Matched Problem 1 State the real number property that justifies the indicated statement.

(A) $8 + (3 + y) = (8 + 3) + y$

(B) $(x + y) + z = z + (x + y)$

(C) $(a + b)(x + y) = a(x + y) + b(x + y)$

(D) $5xy + 0 = 5xy$

(E) If $xy = 1$, $x \neq 0$, then $y = 1/x$.

Further Properties

Subtraction and *division* can be defined in terms of addition and multiplication, respectively:

DEFINITION **Subtraction and Division**

For all real numbers a and b,

Subtraction: $\qquad a - b = a + (-b) \qquad 7 - (-5) = 7 + [-(-5)]$
$$= 7 + 5 = 12$$

Division: $\qquad a \div b = a\left(\dfrac{1}{b}\right), b \neq 0 \qquad 9 \div 4 = 9\left(\dfrac{1}{4}\right) = \dfrac{9}{4}$

To subtract b from a, add the negative (the additive inverse) of b to a. To divide a by b, multiply a by the reciprocal (the multiplicative inverse) of b. Note that division by 0 is not defined, since 0 does not have a reciprocal. **0 can never be used as a divisor!**

The following properties of negatives can be proved using the preceding assumed properties and definitions.

THEOREM 1 **Negative Properties**

For all real numbers a and b,

1. $-(-a) = a$

2. $(-a)b = -(ab)$
   $\qquad = a(-b) = -ab$

3. $(-a)(-b) = ab$

4. $(-1)a = -a$

5. $\dfrac{-a}{b} = -\dfrac{a}{b} = \dfrac{a}{-b}, b \neq 0$

6. $\dfrac{-a}{-b} = -\dfrac{-a}{b} = -\dfrac{a}{-b} = \dfrac{a}{b}, b \neq 0$

We now state two important properties involving 0.

THEOREM 2 **Zero Properties**

For all real numbers a and b,

1. $a \cdot 0 = 0 \qquad 0 \cdot 0 = 0 \qquad (-35)(0) = 0$

2. $ab = 0$ if and only if $\quad a = 0 \quad$ or $\quad b = 0$
   If $(3x + 2)(x - 7) = 0$, then either $3x + 2 = 0$ or $x - 7 = 0$.

Fraction Properties

Recall that the quotient $a \div b$ $(b \neq 0)$ written in the form a/b is called a **fraction**. The quantity a is called the **numerator**, and the quantity b is called the **denominator**.

THEOREM 3 Fraction Properties

For all real numbers a, b, c, d, and k (division by 0 excluded):

1. $\dfrac{a}{b} = \dfrac{c}{d}$ if and only if $ad = bc$ $\dfrac{4}{6} = \dfrac{6}{9}$ since $4 \cdot 9 = 6 \cdot 6$

2. $\dfrac{ka}{kb} = \dfrac{a}{b}$ 3. $\dfrac{a}{b} \cdot \dfrac{c}{d} = \dfrac{ac}{bd}$ 4. $\dfrac{a}{b} \div \dfrac{c}{d} = \dfrac{a}{b} \cdot \dfrac{d}{c}$

    $\dfrac{7 \cdot 3}{7 \cdot 5} = \dfrac{3}{5}$ $\dfrac{3}{5} \cdot \dfrac{7}{8} = \dfrac{3 \cdot 7}{5 \cdot 8}$ $\dfrac{2}{3} \div \dfrac{5}{7} = \dfrac{2}{3} \cdot \dfrac{7}{5}$

5. $\dfrac{a}{b} + \dfrac{c}{b} = \dfrac{a + c}{b}$ 6. $\dfrac{a}{b} - \dfrac{c}{b} = \dfrac{a - c}{b}$ 7. $\dfrac{a}{b} + \dfrac{c}{d} = \dfrac{ad + bc}{bd}$

    $\dfrac{3}{6} + \dfrac{5}{6} = \dfrac{3 + 5}{6}$ $\dfrac{7}{8} - \dfrac{3}{8} = \dfrac{7 - 3}{8}$ $\dfrac{2}{3} + \dfrac{3}{5} = \dfrac{2 \cdot 5 + 3 \cdot 3}{3 \cdot 5}$

Exercises A-1

All variables represent real numbers.

A

In Problems 1–6, replace each question mark with an appropriate expression that will illustrate the use of the indicated real number property.

1. Commutative property $(\cdot)$: $uv = ?$

2. Commutative property $(+)$: $x + 7 = ?$

3. Associative property $(+)$: $3 + (7 + y) = ?$

4. Associative property $(\cdot)$: $x(yz) = ?$

5. Identity property $(\cdot)$: $1(u + v) = ?$

6. Identity property $(+)$: $0 + 9m = ?$

In Problems 7–26, indicate true (T) or false (F).

7. $5(8m) = (5 \cdot 8)m$

8. $a + cb = a + bc$

9. $5x + 7x = (5 + 7)x$

10. $uv(w + x) = uvw + uvx$

11. $-2(-a)(2x - y) = 2a(-4x + y)$

12. $8 \div (-5) = 8\left(\dfrac{1}{-5}\right)$

13. $(x + 3) + 2x = 2x + (x + 3)$

14. $\dfrac{x}{3y} \div \dfrac{5y}{x} = \dfrac{15y^2}{x^2}$

15. $\dfrac{2x}{-(x + 3)} = -\dfrac{2x}{x + 3}$

16. $-\dfrac{2x}{-(x - 3)} = \dfrac{2x}{x - 3}$

17. $(-3)\left(\dfrac{1}{-3}\right) = 1$

18. $(-0.5) + (0.5) = 0$

19. $-x^2 y^2 = (-1)x^2 y^2$

20. $[-(x + 2)](-x) = (x + 2)x$

21. $\dfrac{a}{b} + \dfrac{c}{d} = \dfrac{a + c}{b + d}$

22. $\dfrac{k}{k + b} = \dfrac{1}{1 + b}$

23. $(x + 8)(x + 6) = (x + 8)x + (x + 8)6$

24. $u(u - 2v) + v(u - 2v) = (u + v)(u - 2v)$

25. If $(x - 2)(2x + 3) = 0$, then either $x - 2 = 0$ or $2x + 3 = 0$.

26. If either $x - 2 = 0$ or $2x + 3 = 0$, then $(x - 2)(2x + 3) = 0$.

B

27. If $uv = 1$, does either u or v have to be 1? Explain.

28. If $uv = 0$, does either u or v have to be 0? Explain.

29. Indicate whether the following are true (T) or false (F):

   (A) All integers are natural numbers.

   (B) All rational numbers are real numbers.

   (C) All natural numbers are rational numbers.

30. Indicate whether the following are true (T) or false (F):

   (A) All natural numbers are integers.

   (B) All real numbers are irrational.

   (C) All rational numbers are real numbers.

31. Give an example of a real number that is not a rational number.

32. Give an example of a rational number that is not an integer.

33. Given the sets of numbers N (natural numbers), Z (integers), Q (rational numbers), and R (real numbers), indicate to which set(s) each of the following numbers belongs:

(A) 8   (B) $\sqrt{2}$ (C) -1.414 (D) $\frac{-5}{2}$

34. Given the sets of numbers N, Z, Q, and R (see Problem 33), indicate to which set(s) each of the following numbers belongs:

(A) -3 (B) 3.14   (C) π (D) $\frac{2}{3}$

35. Indicate true (T) or false (F), and for each false statement find real number replacements for a, b, and c that will provide a counterexample. For all real numbers a, b, and c,

(A) $a(b - c) = ab - c$

(B) $(a - b) - c = a - (b - c)$

(C) $a(bc) = (ab)c$

(D) $(a \div b) \div c = a \div (b \div c)$

36. Indicate true (T) or false (F), and for each false statement find real number replacements for a and b that will provide a counterexample. For all real numbers a and b,

(A) $a + b = b + a$

(B) $a - b = b - a$

(C) $ab = ba$

(D) $a \div b = b \div a$

C

37. If $c = 0.151\,515\ldots$, then $100c = 15.151\,5\ldots$ and

$$100c - c = 15.151\,5\ldots - 0.151\,515\ldots$$
$$99c = 15$$
$$c = \tfrac{15}{99} = \tfrac{5}{33}$$

Proceeding similarly, convert the repeating decimal $0.090\,909\ldots$ into a fraction. (All repeating decimals are rational numbers, and all rational numbers have repeating decimal representations.)

38. Repeat Problem 37 for $0.181\,818\ldots$.

Use a calculator to express each number in Problems 39 and 40 as a decimal to the capacity of your calculator. Observe the repeating decimal representation of the rational numbers and the nonrepeating decimal representation of the irrational numbers.

39. (A) $\frac{13}{6}$ (B) $\sqrt{21}$ (C) $\frac{7}{16}$ (D) $\frac{29}{111}$

40. (A) $\frac{8}{9}$ (B) $\frac{3}{11}$ (C) $\sqrt{5}$ (D) $\frac{11}{8}$

Answers to Matched Problems

1. (A) Associative (+)

(B) Commutative (+)

(C) Distributive

(D) Identity (+)

(E) Inverse (·)

A-2 Operations on Polynomials

- Natural Number Exponents
- Polynomials
- Combining Like Terms
- Addition and Subtraction
- Multiplication
- Combined Operations

This section covers basic operations on *polynomials*. Our discussion starts with a brief review of natural number exponents. Integer and rational exponents and their properties will be discussed in detail in subsequent sections. (Natural numbers, integers, and rational numbers are important parts of the real number system; see Table 1 and Figure 1 in Appendix A-1.)

Natural Number Exponents

We define a **natural number exponent** as follows:

> **DEFINITION Natural Number Exponent**
>
> For n a natural number and b any real number,
>
> $$b^n = b \cdot b \cdot \cdots \cdot b \qquad n \text{ factors of } b$$
> $$3^5 = 3 \cdot 3 \cdot 3 \cdot 3 \cdot 3 \qquad 5 \text{ factors of } 3$$
>
> where n is called the exponent and b is called the **base**.

Along with this definition, we state the **first property of exponents**:

> **THEOREM 1   First Property of Exponents**
> For any natural numbers m and n, and any real number b:
> $$b^m b^n = b^{m+n} \quad (2t^4)(5t^3) \boxed{= 2 \cdot 5t^{4+3}} = 10t^7$$

Polynomials

Algebraic expressions are formed by using constants and variables and the algebraic operations of addition, subtraction, multiplication, division, raising to powers, and taking roots. Special types of algebraic expressions are called *polynomials*. A **polynomial in one variable** x is constructed by adding or subtracting constants and terms of the form ax^n, where a is a real number and n is a natural number. A **polynomial in two variables** x and y is constructed by adding and subtracting constants and terms of the form $ax^m y^n$, where a is a real number and m and n are natural numbers. Polynomials in three and more variables are defined in a similar manner.

Polynomials		Not Polynomials	
8	0	$\dfrac{1}{x}$	$\dfrac{x-y}{x^2+y^2}$
$3x^3 - 6x + 7$	$6x + 3$		
$2x^2 - 7xy - 8y^2$	$9y^3 + 4y^2 - y + 4$	$\sqrt{x^3 - 2x}$	$2x^{-2} - 3x^{-1}$
$2x - 3y + 2$	$u^5 - 3u^3v^2 + 2uv^4 - v^4$		

Polynomial forms are encountered frequently in mathematics. For the efficient study of polynomials, it is useful to classify them according to their *degree*. If a term in a polynomial has only one variable as a factor, then the **degree of the term** is the power of the variable. If two or more variables are present in a term as factors, then the **degree of the term** is the sum of the powers of the variables. The **degree of a polynomial** is the degree of the nonzero term with the highest degree in the polynomial. Any nonzero constant is defined to be a **polynomial of degree 0**. The number 0 is also a polynomial but is not assigned a degree.

EXAMPLE 1

Degree

(A) The degree of the first term in $5x^3 + \sqrt{3}x - \frac{1}{2}$ is 3, the degree of the second term is 1, the degree of the third term is 0, and the degree of the whole polynomial is 3 (the same as the degree of the term with the highest degree).

(B) The degree of the first term in $8u^3v^2 - \sqrt{7}uv^2$ is 5, the degree of the second term is 3, and the degree of the whole polynomial is 5.

Matched Problem 1

(A) Given the polynomial $6x^5 + 7x^3 - 2$, what is the degree of the first term? The second term? The third term? The whole polynomial?

(B) Given the polynomial $2u^4v^2 - 5uv^3$, what is the degree of the first term? The second term? The whole polynomial?

In addition to classifying polynomials by degree, we also call a single-term polynomial a **monomial**, a two-term polynomial a **binomial**, and a three-term polynomial a **trinomial**.

Combining Like Terms

The concept of *coefficient* plays a central role in the process of combining *like terms*. A constant in a term of a polynomial, including the sign that precedes it, is called the **numerical coefficient**, or simply, the **coefficient**, of the term. If a constant does not appear, or only a $+$ sign appears, the coefficient is understood to be 1. If only a $-$ sign appears, the coefficient is understood to be -1. Given the polynomial

$$5x^4 - x^3 - 3x^2 + x - 7 \quad \boxed{= 5x^4 + (-1)x^3 + (-3)x^2 + 1x + (-7)}$$

the coefficient of the first term is 5, the coefficient of the second term is -1, the coefficient of the third term is -3, the coefficient of the fourth term is 1, and the coefficient of the fifth term is -7.

The following distributive properties are fundamental to the process of combining *like terms*.

THEOREM 2 Distributive Properties of Real Numbers

1. $a(b + c) = (b + c)a = ab + ac$
2. $a(b - c) = (b - c)a = ab - ac$
3. $a(b + c + \cdots + f) = ab + ac + \cdots + af$

Two terms in a polynomial are called **like terms** if they have exactly the same variable factors to the same powers. The numerical coefficients may or may not be the same. Since constant terms involve no variables, all constant terms are like terms. If a polynomial contains two or more like terms, these terms can be combined into a single term by making use of distributive properties. The following example illustrates the reasoning behind the process:

$$3x^2y - 5xy^2 + x^2y - 2x^2y \quad \begin{aligned} &= 3x^2y + x^2y - 2x^2y - 5xy^2 \\ &= (3x^2y + 1x^2y - 2x^2y) - 5xy^2 \\ &= (3 + 1 - 2)x^2y - 5xy^2 \\ &= 2x^2y - 5xy^2 \end{aligned}$$

Note the use of distributive properties.

Free use is made of the real number properties discussed in Appendix A-1.

How can we simplify expressions such as $4(x - 2y) - 3(2x - 7y)$? We clear the expression of parentheses using distributive properties, and combine like terms:

$$\begin{aligned} 4(x - 2y) - 3(2x - 7y) &= 4x - 8y - 6x + 21y \\ &= -2x + 13y \end{aligned}$$

EXAMPLE 2 **Removing Parentheses** Remove parentheses and simplify:

(A) $2(3x^2 - 2x + 5) + (x^2 + 3x - 7) \quad \begin{aligned} &= 2(3x^2 - 2x + 5) + 1(x^2 + 3x - 7) \\ &= 6x^2 - 4x + 10 + x^2 + 3x - 7 \\ &= 7x^2 - x + 3 \end{aligned}$

(B) $(x^3 - 2x - 6) - (2x^3 - x^2 + 2x - 3)$

$$\begin{aligned} &= 1(x^3 - 2x - 6) + (-1)(2x^3 - x^2 + 2x - 3) \quad \text{Be careful with the} \\ & \qquad\qquad\qquad\qquad\qquad\qquad\qquad\qquad\qquad\qquad\quad \text{sign here} \\ &= x^3 - 2x - 6 - 2x^3 + x^2 - 2x + 3 \\ &= -x^3 + x^2 - 4x - 3 \end{aligned}$$

(C) $[3x^2 - (2x + 1)] - (x^2 - 1) = [3x^2 - 2x - 1] - (x^2 - 1)$ Remove inner
$$\begin{aligned} &= 3x^2 - 2x - 1 - x^2 + 1 \qquad \text{parentheses} \\ &= 2x^2 - 2x \qquad\qquad\qquad\qquad \text{first.} \end{aligned}$$

Matched Problem 2 Remove parentheses and simplify:

(A) $3(u^2 - 2v^2) + (u^2 + 5v^2)$

(B) $(m^3 - 3m^2 + m - 1) - (2m^3 - m + 3)$

(C) $(x^3 - 2) - [2x^3 - (3x + 4)]$

Addition and Subtraction

Addition and subtraction of polynomials can be thought of in terms of removing parentheses and combining like terms, as illustrated in Example 2. Horizontal and vertical arrangements are illustrated in the next two examples. You should be able to work either way, letting the situation dictate your choice.

EXAMPLE 3   **Adding Polynomials**   Add horizontally and vertically:

$$x^4 - 3x^3 + x^2, \quad -x^3 - 2x^2 + 3x, \quad \text{and} \quad 3x^2 - 4x - 5$$

SOLUTION   Add horizontally:

$$(x^4 - 3x^3 + x^2) + (-x^3 - 2x^2 + 3x) + (3x^2 - 4x - 5)$$
$$= x^4 - 3x^3 + x^2 - x^3 - 2x^2 + 3x + 3x^2 - 4x - 5$$
$$= x^4 - 4x^3 + 2x^2 - x - 5$$

Or vertically, by lining up like terms and adding their coefficients:

$$
\begin{array}{r}
x^4 - 3x^3 + x^2 \\
- x^3 - 2x^2 + 3x \\
3x^2 - 4x - 5\\
\hline
x^4 - 4x^3 + 2x^2 - x - 5
\end{array}
$$

Matched Problem 3   Add horizontally and vertically:

$$3x^4 - 2x^3 - 4x^2, \quad x^3 - 2x^2 - 5x, \quad \text{and} \quad x^2 + 7x - 2$$

EXAMPLE 4   **Subtracting Polynomials**   Subtract $4x^2 - 3x + 5$ from $x^2 - 8$, both horizontally and vertically.

SOLUTION

$$
\begin{aligned}
(x^2 - 8) - (4x^2 - 3x + 5) \qquad &\text{or} \qquad \\
= x^2 - 8 - 4x^2 + 3x - 5 \qquad & \\
= -3x^2 + 3x - 13 \qquad &
\end{aligned}
$$

$$
\begin{array}{r}
x^2 - 8\\
-4x^2 + 3x - 5 \quad \leftarrow \text{Change signs and add.}\\
\hline
-3x^2 + 3x - 13
\end{array}
$$

Matched Problem 4   Subtract $2x^2 - 5x + 4$ from $5x^2 - 6$, both horizontally and vertically.

Multiplication

Multiplication of algebraic expressions involves the extensive use of distributive properties for real numbers, as well as other real number properties.

EXAMPLE 5   **Multiplying Polynomials**   Multiply: $(2x - 3)(3x^2 - 2x + 3)$

SOLUTION

$$(2x - 3)(3x^2 - 2x + 3) \boxed{= 2x(3x^2 - 2x + 3) - 3(3x^2 - 2x + 3)}$$
$$= 6x^3 - 4x^2 + 6x - 9x^2 + 6x - 9$$
$$= 6x^3 - 13x^2 + 12x - 9$$

Or, using a vertical arrangement,

$$
\begin{array}{r}
3x^2 - 2x + 3\\
2x - 3\\
\hline
6x^3 - 4x^2 + 6x\\
- 9x^2 + 6x - 9\\
\hline
6x^3 - 13x^2 + 12x - 9
\end{array}
$$

Matched Problem 5   Multiply: $(2x - 3)(2x^2 + 3x - 2)$

Thus, to multiply two polynomials, multiply each term of one by each term of the other, and combine like terms.

Products of binomial factors occur frequently, so it is useful to develop procedures that will enable us to write down their products by inspection. To find the product $(2x - 1)(3x + 2)$, we proceed as follows:

$$(2x - 1)(3x + 2) \quad = 6x^2 + 4x - 3x - 2$$

The inner and outer products are like terms, so combine into a single term.

$$= 6x^2 + x - 2$$

To speed the process, we do the step in the dashed box mentally.

Products of certain binomial factors occur so frequently that it is useful to learn formulas for their products. The following formulas are easily verified by multiplying the factors on the left.

THEOREM 3   Special Products

1. $(a - b)(a + b) = a^2 - b^2$
2. $(a + b)^2 = a^2 + 2ab + b^2$
3. $(a - b)^2 = a^2 - 2ab + b^2$

EXAMPLE 6   **Special Products** Multiply mentally, where possible.

(A) $(2x - 3y)(5x + 2y)$ (B) $(3a - 2b)(3a + 2b)$

(C) $(5x - 3)^2$ (D) $(m + 2n)^3$

SOLUTION   (A) $(2x - 3y)(5x + 2y) = 10x^2 + 4xy - 15xy - 6y^2$

$$= 10x^2 - 11xy - 6y^2$$

(B) $(3a - 2b)(3a + 2b) = (3a)^2 - (2b)^2$

$$= 9a^2 - 4b^2$$

(C) $(5x - 3)^2 = (5x)^2 - 2(5x)(3) + 3^2$

$$= 25x^2 - 30x + 9$$

(D) $(m + 2n)^3 = (m + 2n)^2(m + 2n)$

$$= (m^2 + 4mn + 4n^2)(m + 2n)$$

$$= m^2(m + 2n) + 4mn(m + 2n) + 4n^2(m + 2n)$$

$$= m^3 + 2m^2n + 4m^2n + 8mn^2 + 4mn^2 + 8n^3$$

$$= m^3 + 6m^2n + 12mn^2 + 8n^3$$

Matched Problem 6   Multiply mentally, where possible.

(A) $(4u - 3v)(2u + v)$

(B) $(2xy + 3)(2xy - 3)$

(C) $(m + 4n)(m - 4n)$

(D) $(2u - 3v)^2$

(E) $(2x - y)^3$

Combined Operations

We complete this section by considering several examples that use all the operations just discussed. Note that in simplifying, we usually remove grouping symbols starting from the inside. That is, we remove parentheses ( ) first, then brackets [ ], and finally braces { }, if present. Also,

DEFINITION Order of Operations

Multiplication and division precede addition and subtraction, and taking powers precedes multiplication and division.

$$2 \cdot 3 + 4 = 6 + 4 = 10, \quad \text{not} \quad 2 \cdot 7 = 14$$

$$\frac{10^2}{2} = \frac{100}{2} = 50, \quad \text{not} \quad 5^2 = 25$$

EXAMPLE 7   **Combined Operations** Perform the indicated operations and simplify:

(A) $3x - \{5 - 3[x - x(3 - x)]\} = 3x - \{5 - 3[x - 3x + x^2]\}$
$$= 3x - \{5 - 3x + 9x - 3x^2\}$$
$$= 3x - 5 + 3x - 9x + 3x^2$$
$$= 3x^2 - 3x - 5$$

(B) $(x - 2y)(2x + 3y) - (2x + y)^2 = 2x^2 - xy - 6y^2 - (4x^2 + 4xy + y^2)$
$$= 2x^2 - xy - 6y^2 - 4x^2 - 4xy - y^2$$
$$= -2x^2 - 5xy - 7y^2$$

Matched Problem 7   Perform the indicated operations and simplify:

(A) $2t - \{7 - 2[t - t(4 + t)]\}$

(B) $(u - 3v)^2 - (2u - v)(2u + v)$

Exercises A-2

A

Problems 1–8 refer to the following polynomials:

(A) $2x - 3$ (B) $2x^2 - x + 2$ (C) $x^3 + 2x^2 - x + 3$

1. What is the degree of (C)?

2. What is the degree of (A)?

3. Add (B) and (C).

4. Add (A) and (B).

5. Subtract (B) from (C).

6. Subtract (A) from (B).

7. Multiply (B) and (C).

8. Multiply (A) and (C).

In Problems 9–30, perform the indicated operations and simplify.

9. $2(u - 1) - (3u + 2) - 2(2u - 3)$

10. $2(x - 1) + 3(2x - 3) - (4x - 5)$

11. $4a - 2a[5 - 3(a + 2)]$

12. $2y - 3y[4 - 2(y - 1)]$

13. $(a + b)(a - b)$

14. $(m - n)(m + n)$

15. $(3x - 5)(2x + 1)$

16. $(4t - 3)(t - 2)$

17. $(2x - 3y)(x + 2y)$

18. $(3x + 2y)(x - 3y)$

19. $(3y + 2)(3y - 2)$

20. $(2m - 7)(2m + 7)$

21. $-(2x - 3)^2$

22. $-(5 - 3x)^2$

23. $(4m + 3n)(4m - 3n)$

24. $(3x - 2y)(3x + 2y)$

25. $(3u + 4v)^2$

26. $(4x - y)^2$

27. $(a - b)(a^2 + ab + b^2)$

28. $(a + b)(a^2 - ab + b^2)$

29. $[(x - y) + 3z][(x - y) - 3z]$

30. $[a - (2b - c)][a + (2b - c)]$

B

In Problems 31–44, perform the indicated operations and simplify.

31. $m - \{m - [m - (m - 1)]\}$

32. $2x - 3\{x + 2[x - (x + 5)] + 1\}$

33. $(x^2 - 2xy + y^2)(x^2 + 2xy + y^2)$

34. $(3x - 2y)^2(2x + 5y)$

35. $(5a - 2b)^2 - (2b + 5a)^2$

36. $(2x - 1)^2 - (3x + 2)(3x - 2)$

37. $(m - 2)^2 - (m - 2)(m + 2)$

38. $(x - 3)(x + 3) - (x - 3)^2$

39. $(x - 2y)(2x + y) - (x + 2y)(2x - y)$

40. $(3m + n)(m - 3n) - (m + 3n)(3m - n)$

41. $(u + v)^3$

42. $(x - y)^3$

43. $(x - 2y)^3$

44. $(2m - n)^3$

45. Subtract the sum of the last two polynomials from the sum of the first two: $2x^2 - 4xy + y^2, 3xy - y^2,$ $x^2 - 2xy - y^2, -x^2 + 3xy - 2y^2$

46. Subtract the sum of the first two polynomials from the sum of the last two: $3m^2 - 2m + 5, 4m^2 - m, 3m^2 - 3m - 2,$ $m^3 + m^2 + 2$

C

In Problems 47–50, perform the indicated operations and simplify.

47. $[(2x - 1)^2 - x(3x + 1)]^2$

48. $[5x(3x + 1) - 5(2x - 1)^2]^2$

49. $2\{(x - 3)(x^2 - 2x + 1) - x[3 - x(x - 2)]\}$

50. $-3x\{x[x - x(2 - x)] - (x + 2)(x^2 - 3)\}$

51. If you are given two polynomials, one of degree m and the other of degree n, where m is greater than n, what is the degree of their product?

52. What is the degree of the sum of the two polynomials in Problem 51?

53. How does the answer to Problem 51 change if the two polynomials can have the same degree?

54. How does the answer to Problem 52 change if the two polynomials can have the same degree?

55. Show by example that, in general, $(a + b)^2 \neq a^2 + b^2$. Discuss possible conditions on a and b that would make this a valid equation.

56. Show by example that, in general, $(a - b)^2 \neq a^2 - b^2$. Discuss possible conditions on a and b that would make this a valid equation.

Applications

57. Investment. You have $10,000 to invest, part at 9% and the rest at 12%. If x is the amount invested at 9%, write an algebraic expression that represents the total annual income from both investments. Simplify the expression.

58. Investment. A person has $100,000 to invest. If x are invested in a money market account yielding 7% and twice that amount in certificates of deposit yielding 9%, and if the rest is invested in high-grade bonds yielding 11%, write an algebraic expression that represents the total annual income from all three investments. Simplify the expression.

59. Gross receipts. Four thousand tickets are to be sold for a musical show. If x tickets are to be sold for $20 each and three times that number for $30 each, and if the rest are sold for $50 each, write an algebraic expression that represents the gross receipts from ticket sales, assuming all tickets are sold. Simplify the expression.

60. Gross receipts. Six thousand tickets are to be sold for a concert, some for $20 each and the rest for $35 each. If x is the number of $20 tickets sold, write an algebraic expression that represents the gross receipts from ticket sales, assuming all tickets are sold. Simplify the expression.

61. Nutrition. Food mix A contains 2% fat, and food mix B contains 6% fat. A 10-kilogram diet mix of foods A and B is formed. If x kilograms of food A are used, write an algebraic expression that represents the total number of kilograms of fat in the final food mix. Simplify the expression.

62. Nutrition. Each ounce of food M contains 8 units of calcium, and each ounce of food N contains 5 units of calcium. A 160-ounce diet mix is formed using foods M and N. If x is the number of ounces of food M used, write an algebraic expression that represents the total number of units of calcium in the diet mix. Simplify the expression.

Answers to Matched Problems

1. (A) $5, 3, 0, 5$ (B) $6, 4, 6$

2. (A) $4u^2 - v^2$
    (B) $-m^3 - 3m^2 + 2m - 4$
    (C) $-x^3 + 3x + 2$

3. $3x^4 - x^3 - 5x^2 + 2x - 2$

4. $3x^2 + 5x - 10$

5. $4x^3 - 13x + 6$

6. (A) $8u^2 - 2uv - 3v^2$
    (B) $4x^2y^2 - 9$
    (C) $m^2 - 16n^2$
    (D) $4u^2 - 12uv + 9v^2$
    (E) $8x^3 - 12x^2y + 6xy^2 - y^3$

7. (A) $-2t^2 - 4t - 7$ (B) $-3u^2 - 6uv + 10v^2$

A-3 Factoring Polynomials

A polynomial is written in factored form if it is written as the product of two or more polynomials. The following polynomials are written in factored form:

$$4x^2y - 6xy^2 = 2xy(2x - 3y) \qquad 2x^3 - 8x = 2x(x - 2)(x + 2)$$
$$x^2 - x - 6 = (x - 3)(x + 2) \qquad 5m^2 + 20 = 5(m^2 + 4)$$

Unless stated to the contrary, we will limit our discussion of factoring polynomials to polynomials with integer coefficients.

A polynomial with integer coefficients is said to be **factored completely** if each factor cannot be expressed as the product of two or more polynomials with integer coefficients, other than itself or 1. All the polynomials above, as we will see by the conclusion of this section, are factored completely.

Writing polynomials in completely factored form is often a difficult task. But accomplishing it can lead to the simplification of certain algebraic expressions and to the solution of certain types of equations and inequalities. The distributive properties for real numbers are central to the factoring process.

Common Factors

Generally, a first step in any factoring procedure is to factor out all factors common to all terms.

EXAMPLE 1 **Common Factors** Factor out all factors common to all terms.

(A) $3x^3y - 6x^2y^2 - 3xy^3$

(B) $3y(2y + 5) + 2(2y + 5)$

SOLUTION (A) $3x^3y - 6x^2y^2 - 3xy^3 \boxed{= (3xy)x^2 - (3xy)2xy - (3xy)y^2}$

$$= 3xy(x^2 - 2xy - y^2)$$

(B) $3y(2y + 5) + 2(2y + 5) \boxed{= 3y(2y + 5) + 2(2y + 5)}$

$$= (3y + 2)(2y + 5)$$

Matched Problem 1 Factor out all factors common to all terms.

(A) $2x^3y - 8x^2y^2 - 6xy^3$ \qquad (B) $2x(3x - 2) - 7(3x - 2)$

Factoring by Grouping

Occasionally, polynomials can be factored by grouping terms in such a way that we obtain results that look like Example 1B. We can then complete the factoring following the steps used in that example. This process will prove useful in the next subsection, where an efficient method is developed for factoring a second-degree polynomial as the product of two first-degree polynomials, if such factors exist.

EXAMPLE 2 **Factoring by Grouping** Factor by grouping.

(A) $3x^2 - 3x - x + 1$

(B) $4x^2 - 2xy - 6xy + 3y^2$

(C) $y^2 + xz + xy + yz$

SOLUTION (A) $3x^2 - 3x - x + 1$

$$= (3x^2 - 3x) - (x - 1)$$

$$= 3x(x - 1) - (x - 1)$$

$$= (x - 1)(3x - 1)$$

Group the first two and the last two terms. Factor out any common factors from each group. The common factor $(x - 1)$ can be taken out, and the factoring is complete.

(B) $4x^2 - 2xy - 6xy + 3y^2 = (4x^2 - 2xy) - (6xy - 3y^2)$
$$= 2x(2x - y) - 3y(2x - y)$$
$$= (2x - y)(2x - 3y)$$

(C) If, as in parts (A) and (B), we group the first two terms and the last two terms of $y^2 + xz + xy + yz$, no common factor can be taken out of each group to complete the factoring. However, if the two middle terms are reversed, we can proceed as before:

$$y^2 + xz + xy + yz = y^2 + xy + xz + yz$$
$$= (y^2 + xy) + (xz + yz)$$
$$= y(y + x) + z(x + y)$$
$$= y(x + y) + z(x + y)$$
$$= (x + y)(y + z)$$

Matched Problem 2 Factor by grouping.

(A) $6x^2 + 2x + 9x + 3$ (B) $2u^2 + 6uv - 3uv - 9v^2$

(C) $ac + bd + bc + ad$

Factoring Second-Degree Polynomials

We now turn our attention to factoring second-degree polynomials of the form

$$2x^2 - 5x - 3 \quad \text{and} \quad 2x^2 + 3xy - 2y^2$$

into the product of two first-degree polynomials with integer coefficients. Since many second-degree polynomials with integer coefficients cannot be factored in this way, it would be useful to know ahead of time that the factors we are seeking actually exist. The factoring approach we use, involving the *ac test*, determines at the beginning whether first-degree factors with integer coefficients do exist. Then, if they exist, the test provides a simple method for finding them.

THEOREM 1 *ac* **Test for Factorability**

If in polynomials of the form

$$ax^2 + bx + c \quad \text{or} \quad ax^2 + bxy + cy^2 \qquad (1)$$

the product ac has two integer factors p and q whose sum is the coefficient b of the middle term; that is, if integers p and q exist so that

$$pq = ac \quad \text{and} \quad p + q = b \qquad (2)$$

then the polynomials have first-degree factors with integer coefficients. If no integers p and q exist that satisfy equations (2), then the polynomials in equations (1) will not have first-degree factors with integer coefficients.

If integers p and q exist that satisfy equations (2) in the *ac* test, the factoring always can be completed as follows: Using $b = p + q$, split the middle terms in equations (1) to obtain

$$ax^2 + bx + c = ax^2 + px + qx + c$$
$$ax^2 + bxy + cy^2 = ax^2 + pxy + qxy + cy^2$$

Complete the factoring by grouping the first two terms and the last two terms as in Example 2. This process always works, and it does not matter if the two middle terms on the right are interchanged.

Several examples should make the process clear. After a little practice, you will perform many of the steps mentally and will find the process fast and efficient.

EXAMPLE 3 **Factoring Second-Degree Polynomials** Factor, if possible, using integer coefficients.

(A) $4x^2 - 4x - 3$

(B) $2x^2 - 3x - 4$

(C) $6x^2 - 25xy + 4y^2$

SOLUTION (A) $4x^2 - 4x - 3$

Step 1 Use the *ac* test to test for factorability. Comparing $4x^2 - 4x - 3$ with $ax^2 + bx + c$, we see that $a = 4, b = -4$, and $c = -3$. Multiply *a* and *c* to obtain

$$ac = (4)(-3) = -12$$

List all pairs of integers whose product is -12, as shown in the margin. These are called **factor pairs** of -12. Then try to find a factor pair that sums to $b = -4$, the coefficient of the middle term in $4x^2 - 4x - 3$. (In practice, this part of Step 1 is often done mentally and can be done rather quickly.) Notice that the factor pair 2 and -6 sums to -4. By the *ac* test, $4x^2 - 4x - 3$ has first-degree factors with integer coefficients.

pq
$(1)(-12)$
$(-1)(12)$
$(2)(-6)$
$(-2)(6)$
$(3)(-4)$
$(-3)(4)$

All factor pairs of $-12 = ac$

Step 2 Split the middle term, using $b = p + q$, and complete the factoring by grouping. Using $-4 = 2 + (-6)$, we split the middle term in $4x^2 - 4x - 3$ and complete the factoring by grouping:

$$4x^2 - 4x - 3 = 4x^2 + 2x - 6x - 3$$
$$= (4x^2 + 2x) - (6x + 3)$$
$$= 2x(2x + 1) - 3(2x + 1)$$
$$= (2x + 1)(2x - 3)$$

The result can be checked by multiplying the two factors to obtain the original polynomial.

(B) $2x^2 - 3x - 4$

Step 1 Use the *ac* test to test for factorability:

$$ac = (2)(-4) = -8$$

pq
$(-1)(8)$
$(1)(-8)$
$(-2)(4)$
$(2)(-4)$

All factor pairs of $-8 = ac$

Does -8 have a factor pair whose sum is -3? None of the factor pairs listed in the margin sums to $-3 = b$, the coefficient of the middle term in $2x^2 - 3x - 4$. According to the *ac* test, we can conclude that $2x^2 - 3x - 4$ does not have first-degree factors with integer coefficients, and we say that the polynomial is **not factorable**.

(C) $6x^2 - 25xy + 4y^2$

Step 1 Use the *ac* test to test for factorability:

$$ac = (6)(4) = 24$$

Mentally checking through the factor pairs of 24, keeping in mind that their sum must be $-25 = b$, we see that if $p = -1$ and $q = -24$, then

$$pq = (-1)(-24) = 24 = ac$$

and

$$p + q = (-1) + (-24) = -25 = b$$

So the polynomial is factorable.

Step 2 Split the middle term, using $b = p + q$, and complete the factoring by grouping. Using $-25 = (-1) + (-24)$, we split the middle term in $6x^2 - 25xy + 4y^2$ and complete the factoring by grouping:

$$6x^2 - 25xy + 4y^2 = 6x^2 - xy - 24xy + 4y^2$$
$$= (6x^2 - xy) - (24xy - 4y^2)$$
$$= x(6x - y) - 4y(6x - y)$$
$$= (6x - y)(x - 4y)$$

The check is left to the reader.

Matched Problem 3   Factor, if possible, using integer coefficients.

(A) $2x^2 + 11x - 6$ (B) $4x^2 + 11x - 6$ (C) $6x^2 + 5xy - 4y^2$

Special Factoring Formulas

The factoring formulas listed in the following box will enable us to factor certain polynomial forms that occur frequently. These formulas can be established by multiplying the factors on the right.

THEOREM 2   Special Factoring Formulas

Perfect square:	1. $u^2 + 2uv + v^2 = (u + v)^2$
Perfect square:	2. $u^2 - 2uv + v^2 = (u - v)^2$
Difference of squares:	3. $u^2 - v^2 = (u - v)(u + v)$
Difference of cubes:	4. $u^3 - v^3 = (u - v)(u^2 + uv + v^2)$
Sum of cubes:	5. $u^3 + v^3 = (u + v)(u^2 - uv + v^2)$

⚠ **CAUTION** Notice that $u^2 + v^2$ is not included in the list of special factoring formulas. In fact,

$$u^2 + v^2 \neq (au + bv)(cu + dv)$$

for any choice of real number coefficients $a, b, c,$ and d.

EXAMPLE 4   **Factoring** Factor completely.

(A) $4m^2 - 12mn + 9n^2$ (B) $x^2 - 16y^2$ (C) $z^3 - 1$
(D) $m^3 + n^3$ (E) $a^2 - 4(b + 2)^2$

SOLUTION   (A) $4m^2 - 12mn + 9n^2 = (2m - 3n)^2$

(B) $x^2 - 16y^2 = x^2 - (4y)^2 = (x - 4y)(x + 4y)$

(C) $z^3 - 1 = (z - 1)(z^2 + z + 1)$ Use the ac test to verify that $z^2 + z + 1$ cannot be factored.

(D) $m^3 + n^3 = (m + n)(m^2 - mn + n^2)$ Use the ac test to verify that $m^2 - mn + n^2$ cannot be factored.

(E) $a^2 - 4(b + 2)^2 = [a - 2(b + 2)][a + 2(b + 2)]$

Matched Problem 4   Factor completely:

(A) $x^2 + 6xy + 9y^2$ (B) $9x^2 - 4y^2$ (C) $8m^3 - 1$
(D) $x^3 + y^3z^3$ (E) $9(m - 3)^2 - 4n^2$

Combined Factoring Techniques

We complete this section by considering several factoring problems that involve combinations of the preceding techniques.

> **PROCEDURE Factoring Polynomials**
>
> **Step 1** Take out any factors common to all terms.
>
> **Step 2** Use any of the special formulas listed in Theorem 2 that are applicable.
>
> **Step 3** Apply the *ac* test to any remaining second-degree polynomial factors.
>
> **Note:** It may be necessary to perform some of these steps more than once. Furthermore, the order of applying these steps can vary.

EXAMPLE 5 **Combined Factoring Techniques** Factor completely.

(A) $3x^3 - 48x$ (B) $3u^4 - 3u^3v - 9u^2v^2$

(C) $3m^4 - 24mn^3$ (D) $3x^4 - 5x^2 + 2$

SOLUTION (A) $3x^3 - 48x = 3x(x^2 - 16) = 3x(x - 4)(x + 4)$

(B) $3u^4 - 3u^3v - 9u^2v^2 = 3u^2(u^2 - uv - 3v^2)$

(C) $3m^4 - 24mn^3 = 3m(m^3 - 8n^3) = 3m(m - 2n)(m^2 + 2mn + 4n^2)$

(D) $3x^4 - 5x^2 + 2 = (3x^2 - 2)(x^2 - 1) = (3x^2 - 2)(x - 1)(x + 1)$

Matched Problem 5 Factor completely.

(A) $18x^3 - 8x$ (B) $4m^3n - 2m^2n^2 + 2mn^3$

(C) $2t^4 - 16t$ (D) $2y^4 - 5y^2 - 12$

Exercises A-3

A

In Problems 1–8, factor out all factors common to all terms.

1. $6m^4 - 9m^3 - 3m^2$ **2.** $6x^4 - 8x^3 - 2x^2$

3. $8u^3v - 6u^2v^2 + 4uv^3$ **4.** $10x^3y + 20x^2y^2 - 15xy^3$

5. $7m(2m - 3) + 5(2m - 3)$ **6.** $5x(x + 1) - 3(x + 1)$

7. $4ab(2c + d) - (2c + d)$

8. $12a(b - 2c) - 15b(b - 2c)$

In Problems 9–18, factor by grouping.

9. $2x^2 - x + 4x - 2$ **10.** $x^2 - 3x + 2x - 6$

11. $3y^2 - 3y + 2y - 2$ **12.** $2x^2 - x + 6x - 3$

13. $2x^2 + 8x - x - 4$ **14.** $6x^2 + 9x - 2x - 3$

15. $wy - wz + xy - xz$ **16.** $ac + ad + bc + bd$

17. $am - 3bm + 2na - 6bn$ **18.** $ab + 6 + 2a + 3b$

B

In Problems 19–56, factor completely. If a polynomial cannot be factored, say so.

19. $3y^2 - y - 2$ **20.** $2x^2 + 5x - 3$

21. $u^2 - 2uv - 15v^2$ **22.** $x^2 - 4xy - 12y^2$

23. $m^2 - 6m - 3$ **24.** $x^2 + x - 4$

25. $w^2x^2 - y^2$ **26.** $25m^2 - 16n^2$

27. $9m^2 - 6mn + n^2$ **28.** $x^2 + 10xy + 25y^2$

29. $y^2 + 16$ **30.** $u^2 + 81$

31. $4z^2 - 28z + 48$ **32.** $6x^2 + 48x + 72$

33. $2x^4 - 24x^3 + 40x^2$ **34.** $2y^3 - 22y^2 + 48y$

35. $4xy^2 - 12xy + 9x$ **36.** $16x^2y - 8xy + y$

37. $6m^2 - mn - 12n^2$ **38.** $6s^2 + 7st - 3t^2$

39. $4u^3v - uv^3$ **40.** $x^3y - 9xy^3$

41. $2x^3 - 2x^2 + 8x$ **42.** $3m^3 - 6m^2 + 15m$

43. $8x^3 - 27y^3$ **44.** $5x^3 + 40y^3$

45. $x^4y + 8xy$ **46.** $8a^3 - 1$

C

47. $(x + 2)^2 - 9y^2$ **48.** $(a - b)^2 - 4(c - d)^2$

49. $5u^2 + 4uv - 2v^2$ **50.** $3x^2 - 2xy - 4y^2$

51. $6(x - y)^2 + 23(x - y) - 4$

52. $4(A + B)^2 - 5(A + B) - 6$

53. $y^4 - 3y^2 - 4$

54. $m^4 - n^4$

55. $15y(x - y)^3 + 12x(x - y)^2$

56. $15x^2(3x - 1)^4 + 60x^3(3x - 1)^3$

In Problems 57–60, discuss the validity of each statement. If the statement is true, explain why. If not, give a counterexample.

57. If n is a positive integer greater than 1, then $u^n - v^n$ can be factored.

58. If m and n are positive integers and $m \neq n$, then $u^m - v^n$ is not factorable.

59. If n is a positive integer greater than 1, then $u^n + v^n$ can be factored.

60. If k is a positive integer, then $u^{2k+1} + v^{2k+1}$ can be factored.

Answers to Matched Problems

1. (A) $2xy(x^2 - 4xy - 3y^2)$ (B) $(2x - 7)(3x - 2)$

2. (A) $(3x + 1)(2x + 3)$

   (B) $(u + 3v)(2u - 3v)$

   (C) $(a + b)(c + d)$

3. (A) $(2x - 1)(x + 6)$

   (B) Not factorable

   (C) $(3x + 4y)(2x - y)$

4. (A) $(x + 3y)^2$

   (B) $(3x - 2y)(3x + 2y)$

   (C) $(2m - 1)(4m^2 + 2m + 1)$

   (D) $(x + yz)(x^2 - xyz + y^2z^2)$

   (E) $[3(m - 3) - 2n][3(m - 3) + 2n]$

5. (A) $2x(3x - 2)(3x + 2)$

   (B) $2mn(2m^2 - mn + n^2)$

   (C) $2t(t - 2)(t^2 + 2t + 4)$

   (D) $(2y^2 + 3)(y - 2)(y + 2)$

A-4 Operations on Rational Expressions

- Reducing to Lowest Terms
- Multiplication and Division
- Addition and Subtraction
- Compound Fractions

We now turn our attention to fractional forms. A quotient of two algebraic expressions (division by 0 excluded) is called a **fractional expression**. If both the numerator and the denominator are polynomials, the fractional expression is called a **rational expression**. Some examples of rational expressions are

$$\frac{1}{x^3 + 2x} \qquad \frac{5}{x} \qquad \frac{x + 7}{3x^2 - 5x + 1} \qquad \frac{x^2 - 2x + 4}{1}$$

In this section, we discuss basic operations on rational expressions. Since variables represent real numbers in the rational expressions we will consider, the properties of real number fractions summarized in Appendix A-1 will play a central role.

> **AGREEMENT**   **Variable Restriction**
> Even though not always explicitly stated, we always assume that variables are restricted so that division by 0 is excluded.

For example, given the rational expression

$$\frac{2x + 5}{x(x + 2)(x - 3)}$$

the variable x is understood to be restricted from being 0, -2, or 3, since these values would cause the denominator to be 0.

Reducing to Lowest Terms

Central to the process of reducing rational expressions to *lowest terms* is the *fundamental property of fractions*, which we restate here for convenient reference:

> **THEOREM 1**   **Fundamental Property of Fractions**
> If a, b, and k are real numbers with $b, k \neq 0$, then
> $$\frac{ka}{kb} = \frac{a}{b} \qquad \frac{5 \cdot 2}{5 \cdot 7} = \frac{2}{7} \qquad \frac{x(x + 4)}{2(x + 4)} = \frac{x}{2}, \quad x \neq -4$$

Using this property from left to right to eliminate all common factors from the numerator and the denominator of a given fraction is referred to as **reducing a fraction to lowest terms**. We are actually dividing the numerator and denominator by the same nonzero common factor.

Using the property from right to left—that is, multiplying the numerator and denominator by the same nonzero factor—is referred to as **raising a fraction to higher terms**. We will use the property in both directions in the material that follows.

EXAMPLE 1 **Reducing to Lowest Terms** Reduce each rational expression to lowest terms.

(A) $\dfrac{6x^2 + x - 1}{2x^2 - x - 1} = \dfrac{(2x + 1)(3x - 1)}{(2x + 1)(x - 1)}$ *Factor numerator and denominator completely.*

$= \dfrac{3x - 1}{x - 1}$ *Divide numerator and denominator by the common factor $(2x + 1)$.*

(B) $\dfrac{x^4 - 8x}{3x^3 - 2x^2 - 8x} = \dfrac{x(x - 2)(x^2 + 2x + 4)}{x(x - 2)(3x + 4)}$

$= \dfrac{x^2 + 2x + 4}{3x + 4}$

Matched Problem 1 Reduce each rational expression to lowest terms.

(A) $\dfrac{x^2 - 6x + 9}{x^2 - 9}$ (B) $\dfrac{x^3 - 1}{x^2 - 1}$

CONCEPTUAL INSIGHT

Using Theorem 1 to divide the numerator and denominator of a fraction by a common factor is often referred to as **canceling**. This operation can be denoted by drawing a slanted line through each common factor and writing any remaining factors above or below the common factor. Canceling is often incorrectly applied to individual terms in the numerator or denominator, instead of to common factors. For example,

$$\frac{14 - 5}{2} = \frac{9}{2}$$ *Theorem 1 does not apply. There are no common factors in the numerator.*

$$\frac{14 - 5}{2} \neq \frac{\overset{7}{\cancel{14}} - 5}{\underset{1}{\cancel{2}}} = 2$$ *Incorrect use of Theorem 1. To cancel 2 in the denominator, 2 must be a factor of each term in the numerator.*

Multiplication and Division

Since we are restricting variable replacements to real numbers, multiplication and division of rational expressions follow the rules for multiplying and dividing real number fractions summarized in Appendix A-1.

THEOREM 2 Multiplication and Division

If $a, b, c,$ and d are real numbers, then

1. $\dfrac{a}{b} \cdot \dfrac{c}{d} = \dfrac{ac}{bd},$ $b, d \neq 0$ $\qquad \dfrac{3}{5} \cdot \dfrac{x}{x + 5} = \dfrac{3x}{5(x + 5)}$

2. $\dfrac{a}{b} \div \dfrac{c}{d} = \dfrac{a}{b} \cdot \dfrac{d}{c},$ $b, c, d \neq 0$ $\qquad \dfrac{3}{5} \div \dfrac{x}{x + 5} = \dfrac{3}{5} \cdot \dfrac{x + 5}{x}$

EXAMPLE 2 **Multiplication and Division** Perform the indicated operations and reduce to lowest terms.

(A) $\dfrac{10x^3y}{3xy + 9y} \cdot \dfrac{x^2 - 9}{4x^2 - 12x}$ *Factor numerators and denominators. Then divide any numerator and any denominator with a like common factor.*

$$= \dfrac{\overset{5x^2}{\overset{\cancel{10x^3y}}{}}}{\underset{3 \cdot 1}{\cancel{3y}(x + 3)}} \cdot \dfrac{\overset{1 \cdot 1}{\cancel{(x - 3)}\cancel{(x + 3)}}}{\underset{2 \cdot 1}{\cancel{4x}(x - 3)}}$$

$$= \dfrac{5x^2}{6}$$

(B) $\dfrac{4 - 2x}{4} \div (x - 2) = \dfrac{\overset{1}{2(2 - x)}}{\underset{2}{4}} \cdot \dfrac{1}{x - 2}$ $x - 2 = \dfrac{x - 2}{1}$

$$= \dfrac{2 - x}{2(x - 2)} = \dfrac{\overset{-1}{-\cancel{(x - 2)}}}{\underset{1}{2\cancel{(x - 2)}}}$$ *$b - a = -(a - b)$, a useful change in some problems*

$$= -\dfrac{1}{2}$$

Matched Problem 2 Perform the indicated operations and reduce to lowest terms.

(A) $\dfrac{12x^2y^3}{2xy^2 + 6xy} \cdot \dfrac{y^2 + 6y + 9}{3y^3 + 9y^2}$ (B) $(4 - x) \div \dfrac{x^2 - 16}{5}$

Addition and Subtraction

Again, because we are restricting variable replacements to real numbers, addition and subtraction of rational expressions follow the rules for adding and subtracting real number fractions.

THEOREM 3 **Addition and Subtraction**

For a, b, and c real numbers,

1. $\dfrac{a}{b} + \dfrac{c}{b} = \dfrac{a + c}{b}, \quad b \neq 0$ $\dfrac{x}{x + 5} + \dfrac{8}{x + 5} = \dfrac{x + 8}{x + 5}$

2. $\dfrac{a}{b} - \dfrac{c}{b} = \dfrac{a - c}{b}, \quad b \neq 0$ $\dfrac{x}{3x^2y^2} - \dfrac{x + 7}{3x^2y^2} = \dfrac{x - (x + 7)}{3x^2y^2}$

We add rational expressions with the same denominators by adding or subtracting their numerators and placing the result over the common denominator. If the denominators are not the same, we raise the fractions to higher terms, using the fundamental property of fractions to obtain common denominators, and then proceed as described.

Even though any common denominator will do, our work will be simplified if the *least common denominator (LCD)* is used. Often, the LCD is obvious, but if it is not, the steps in the next box describe how to find it.

PROCEDURE   Least Common Denominator

The least common denominator (LCD) of two or more rational expressions is found as follows:

  1. Factor each denominator completely, including integer factors.

  2. Identify each different factor from all the denominators.

  3. Form a product using each different factor to the highest power that occurs in any one denominator. This product is the LCD.

EXAMPLE 3   **Addition and Subtraction** Combine into a single fraction and reduce to lowest terms.

(A) $\dfrac{3}{10} + \dfrac{5}{6} - \dfrac{11}{45}$ (B) $\dfrac{4}{9x} - \dfrac{5x}{6y^2} + 1$ (C) $\dfrac{1}{x-1} - \dfrac{1}{x} - \dfrac{2}{x^2-1}$

SOLUTION   (A) To find the LCD, factor each denominator completely:

$$\left.\begin{array}{l} 10 = 2 \cdot 5 \\ 6 = 2 \cdot 3 \\ 45 = 3^2 \cdot 5 \end{array}\right\} \quad LCD = 2 \cdot 3^2 \cdot 5 = 90$$

Now use the fundamental property of fractions to make each denominator 90:

$$\frac{3}{10} + \frac{5}{6} - \frac{11}{45} = \frac{\mathbf{9} \cdot 3}{\mathbf{9} \cdot 10} + \frac{\mathbf{15} \cdot 5}{\mathbf{15} \cdot 6} - \frac{\mathbf{2} \cdot 11}{\mathbf{2} \cdot 45}$$

$$= \frac{27}{90} + \frac{75}{90} - \frac{22}{90}$$

$$= \frac{27 + 75 - 22}{90} = \frac{80}{90} = \frac{8}{9}$$

(B) $\left.\begin{array}{l} 9x = 3^2 x \\ 6y^2 = 2 \cdot 3 y^2 \end{array}\right\} \quad LCD = 2 \cdot 3^2 xy^2 = 18xy^2$

$$\frac{4}{9x} - \frac{5x}{6y^2} + 1 = \frac{2y^2 \cdot 4}{2y^2 \cdot 9x} - \frac{3x \cdot 5x}{3x \cdot 6y^2} + \frac{18xy^2}{18xy^2}$$

$$= \frac{8y^2 - 15x^2 + 18xy^2}{18xy^2}$$

(C) $\dfrac{1}{x-1} - \dfrac{1}{x} - \dfrac{2}{x^2-1}$

$$= \frac{1}{x-1} - \frac{1}{x} - \frac{2}{(x-1)(x+1)} \qquad LCD = x(x-1)(x+1)$$

$$= \frac{x(x+1) - (x-1)(x+1) - 2x}{x(x-1)(x+1)}$$

$$= \frac{x^2 + x - x^2 + 1 - 2x}{x(x-1)(x+1)}$$

$$= \frac{1-x}{x(x-1)(x+1)}$$

$$= \frac{\overset{-1}{\cancel{-(x-1)}}}{x\underset{1}{\cancel{(x-1)}}(x+1)} = \frac{-1}{x(x+1)}$$

Matched Problem 3 Combine into a single fraction and reduce to lowest terms.

(A) $\dfrac{5}{28} - \dfrac{1}{10} + \dfrac{6}{35}$

(B) $\dfrac{1}{4x^2} - \dfrac{2x+1}{3x^3} + \dfrac{3}{12x}$

(C) $\dfrac{2}{x^2 - 4x + 4} + \dfrac{1}{x} - \dfrac{1}{x-2}$

Compound Fractions

A fractional expression with fractions in its numerator, denominator, or both is called a **compound fraction**. It is often necessary to represent a compound fraction as a **simple fraction**—that is (in all cases we will consider), as the quotient of two polynomials. The process does not involve any new concepts. It is a matter of applying old concepts and processes in the correct sequence.

EXAMPLE 4 **Simplifying Compound Fractions** Express as a simple fraction reduced to lowest terms:

(A) $\dfrac{\dfrac{1}{5+h} - \dfrac{1}{5}}{h}$

(B) $\dfrac{\dfrac{y}{x^2} - \dfrac{x}{y^2}}{\dfrac{y}{x} - \dfrac{x}{y}}$

SOLUTION We will simplify the expressions in parts (A) and (B) using two different methods—each is suited to the particular type of problem.

(A) We simplify this expression by combining the numerator into a single fraction and using division of rational forms.

$$\dfrac{\dfrac{1}{5+h} - \dfrac{1}{5}}{h} = \left[\dfrac{1}{5+h} - \dfrac{1}{5}\right] \div \dfrac{h}{1}$$

$$= \dfrac{5 - 5 - h}{5(5+h)} \cdot \dfrac{1}{h}$$

$$= \dfrac{-h}{5(5+h)h} = \dfrac{-1}{5(5+h)}$$

(B) The method used here makes effective use of the fundamental property of fractions in the form

$$\dfrac{a}{b} = \dfrac{ka}{kb} \qquad b, k \neq 0$$

Multiply the numerator and denominator by the LCD of all fractions in the numerator and denominator—in this case, $x^2 y^2$:

$$\dfrac{x^2 y^2 \left(\dfrac{y}{x^2} - \dfrac{x}{y^2}\right)}{x^2 y^2 \left(\dfrac{y}{x} - \dfrac{x}{y}\right)} = \dfrac{x^2 y^2 \dfrac{y}{x^2} - x^2 y^2 \dfrac{x}{y^2}}{x^2 y^2 \dfrac{y}{x} - x^2 y^2 \dfrac{x}{y}} = \dfrac{y^3 - x^3}{xy^3 - x^3 y}$$

$$= \dfrac{\overset{1}{\cancel{(y-x)}}(y^2 + xy + x^2)}{xy\underset{1}{\cancel{(y-x)}}(y+x)}$$

$$= \dfrac{y^2 + xy + x^2}{xy(y+x)} \quad \text{or} \quad \dfrac{x^2 + xy + y^2}{xy(x+y)}$$

Matched Problem 4   Express as a simple fraction reduced to lowest terms:

(A) $\dfrac{\dfrac{1}{2+h} - \dfrac{1}{2}}{h}$ (B) $\dfrac{\dfrac{a}{b} - \dfrac{b}{a}}{\dfrac{a}{b} + 2 + \dfrac{b}{a}}$

Exercises A-4

A

In Problems 1–18, perform the indicated operations and reduce answers to lowest terms.

1. $\dfrac{d^5}{3a} \div \left(\dfrac{d^2}{6a^2} \cdot \dfrac{a}{4d^3}\right)$ 2. $\left(\dfrac{d^5}{3a} \div \dfrac{d^2}{6a^2}\right) \cdot \dfrac{a}{4d^3}$

3. $\dfrac{x^2}{12} + \dfrac{x}{18} - \dfrac{1}{30}$ 4. $\dfrac{2y}{18} - \dfrac{-1}{28} - \dfrac{y}{42}$

5. $\dfrac{4m-3}{18m^3} + \dfrac{3}{4m} - \dfrac{2m-1}{6m^2}$ 6. $\dfrac{3x+8}{4x^2} - \dfrac{2x-1}{x^3} - \dfrac{5}{8x}$

7. $\dfrac{x^2-9}{x^2-3x} \div (x^2 - x - 12)$ 8. $\dfrac{2x^2+7x+3}{4x^2-1} \div (x+3)$

9. $\dfrac{2}{x} - \dfrac{1}{x-3}$ 10. $\dfrac{5}{m-2} - \dfrac{3}{2m+1}$

11. $\dfrac{2}{(x+1)^2} - \dfrac{5}{x^2-x-2}$ 12. $\dfrac{3}{x^2-5x+6} - \dfrac{5}{(x-2)^2}$

13. $\dfrac{x+1}{x-1} - 1$ 14. $m - 3 - \dfrac{m-1}{m-2}$

15. $\dfrac{3}{a-1} - \dfrac{2}{1-a}$ 16. $\dfrac{5}{x-3} - \dfrac{2}{3-x}$

17. $\dfrac{2x}{x^2-16} - \dfrac{x-4}{x^2+4x}$ 18. $\dfrac{m+2}{m^2-2m} - \dfrac{m}{m^2-4}$

B

In Problems 19–30, perform the indicated operations and reduce answers to lowest terms. Represent any compound fractions as simple fractions reduced to lowest terms.

19. $\dfrac{x^2}{x^2+2x+1} + \dfrac{x-1}{3x+3} - \dfrac{1}{6}$

20. $\dfrac{y}{y^2-y-2} - \dfrac{1}{y^2+5y-14} - \dfrac{2}{y^2+8y+7}$

21. $\dfrac{1 - \dfrac{x}{y}}{2 - \dfrac{y}{x}}$ 22. $\dfrac{2}{5 - \dfrac{3}{4x+1}}$

23. $\dfrac{c+2}{5c-5} - \dfrac{c-2}{3c-3} + \dfrac{c}{1-c}$

24. $\dfrac{x+7}{ax-bx} + \dfrac{y+9}{by-ay}$

25. $\dfrac{1 + \dfrac{3}{x}}{x - \dfrac{9}{x}}$ 26. $\dfrac{1 - \dfrac{y^2}{x^2}}{1 - \dfrac{y}{x}}$

27. $\dfrac{\dfrac{1}{2(x+h)} - \dfrac{1}{2x}}{h}$ 28. $\dfrac{\dfrac{1}{x+h} - \dfrac{1}{x}}{h}$

29. $\dfrac{\dfrac{x}{y} - 2 + \dfrac{y}{x}}{\dfrac{x}{y} - \dfrac{y}{x}}$ 30. $\dfrac{1 + \dfrac{2}{x} - \dfrac{15}{x^2}}{1 + \dfrac{4}{x} - \dfrac{5}{x^2}}$

✎ In Problems 31–38, imagine that the indicated "solutions" were given to you by a student whom you were tutoring in this class.

(A) Is the solution correct? If the solution is incorrect, explain what is wrong and how it can be corrected.

(B) Show a correct solution for each incorrect solution.

31. $\dfrac{x^2+4x+3}{x+3} = \dfrac{x^2+4x}{x} = x + 4$

32. $\dfrac{x^2-3x-4}{x-4} = \dfrac{x^2-3x}{x} = x - 3$

33. $\dfrac{(x+h)^2 - x^2}{h} = (x+1)^2 - x^2 = 2x + 1$

34. $\dfrac{(x+h)^3 - x^3}{h} = (x+1)^3 - x^3 = 3x^2 + 3x + 1$

35. $\dfrac{x^2-3x}{x^2-2x-3} + x - 3 = \dfrac{x^2-3x+x-3}{x^2-2x-3} = 1$

36. $\dfrac{2}{x-1} - \dfrac{x+3}{x^2-1} = \dfrac{2x+2-x-3}{x^2-1} = \dfrac{1}{x+1}$

37. $\dfrac{2x^2}{x^2-4} - \dfrac{x}{x-2} = \dfrac{2x^2-x^2-2x}{x^2-4} = \dfrac{x}{x+2}$

38. $x + \dfrac{x-2}{x^2-3x+2} = \dfrac{x+x-2}{x^2-3x+2} = \dfrac{2}{x-2}$

C

Represent the compound fractions in Problems 39–42 as simple fractions reduced to lowest terms.

39. $\dfrac{\dfrac{1}{3(x+h)^2} - \dfrac{1}{3x^2}}{h}$

40. $\dfrac{\dfrac{1}{(x+h)^2} - \dfrac{1}{x^2}}{h}$

41. $x - \dfrac{2}{1 - \dfrac{1}{x}}$

42. $2 - \dfrac{1}{1 - \dfrac{2}{a+2}}$

A-5   Integer Exponents and Scientific Notation

- Integer Exponents
- Scientific Notation

We now review basic operations on integer exponents and scientific notation.

Integer Exponents

DEFINITION Integer Exponents

For *n* an integer and *a* a real number:

1. For *n* a positive integer,
$$a^n = a \cdot a \cdot \, \cdots \, \cdot a \qquad n \text{ factors of } a \qquad 5^4 = 5 \cdot 5 \cdot 5 \cdot 5$$

2. For $n = 0$,
$$a^0 = 1 \qquad a \neq 0 \qquad 12^0 = 1$$
$$0^0 \text{ is not defined.}$$

3. For *n* a negative integer,
$$a^n = \frac{1}{a^{-n}} \qquad a \neq 0 \qquad a^{-3} = \frac{1}{a^{-(-3)}} = \frac{1}{a^3}$$

[If *n* is negative, then $(-n)$ is positive.]
Note: It can be shown that for *all* integers *n*,
$$a^{-n} = \frac{1}{a^n} \quad \text{and} \quad a^n = \frac{1}{a^{-n}} \qquad a \neq 0 \qquad a^5 = \frac{1}{a^{-5}}, \quad a^{-5} = \frac{1}{a^5}$$

The following properties are very useful in working with integer exponents.

THEOREM 1   Exponent Properties
For *n* and *m* integers and *a* and *b* real numbers,

1. $a^m a^n = a^{m+n}$ $a^8 a^{-3} = a^{8+(-3)} = a^5$

2. $(a^n)^m = a^{mn}$ $(a^{-2})^3 = a^{3(-2)} = a^{-6}$

3. $(ab)^m = a^m b^m$ $(ab)^{-2} = a^{-2} b^{-2}$

4. $\left(\dfrac{a}{b}\right)^m = \dfrac{a^m}{b^m} \qquad b \neq 0$ $\left(\dfrac{a}{b}\right)^5 = \dfrac{a^5}{b^5}$

5. $\dfrac{a^m}{a^n} = a^{m-n} = \dfrac{1}{a^{n-m}} \qquad a \neq 0$ $\dfrac{a^{-3}}{a^7} = \dfrac{1}{a^{7-(-3)}} = \dfrac{1}{a^{10}}$

Exponents are frequently encountered in algebraic applications. You should sharpen your skills in using exponents by reviewing the preceding basic definitions and properties and the examples that follow.

EXAMPLE 1 **Simplifying Exponent Forms** Simplify, and express the answers using positive exponents only.

(A) $(2x^3)(3x^5) \boxed{= 2 \cdot 3x^{3+5}} = 6x^8$

(B) $x^5 x^{-9} = x^{-4} = \dfrac{1}{x^4}$

(C) $\dfrac{x^5}{x^7} \boxed{= x^{5-7}} = x^{-2} = \dfrac{1}{x^2}$ or $\dfrac{x^5}{x^7} = \boxed{\dfrac{1}{x^{7-5}}} = \dfrac{1}{x^2}$

(D) $\dfrac{x^{-3}}{y^{-4}} = \dfrac{y^4}{x^3}$

(E) $(u^{-3}v^2)^{-2} \boxed{= (u^{-3})^{-2}(v^2)^{-2}} = u^6 v^{-4} = \dfrac{u^6}{v^4}$

(F) $\left(\dfrac{y^{-5}}{y^{-2}}\right)^{-2} = \boxed{\dfrac{(y^{-5})^{-2}}{(y^{-2})^{-2}}} = \dfrac{y^{10}}{y^4} = y^6$

(G) $\dfrac{4m^{-3}n^{-5}}{6m^{-4}n^3} \boxed{= \dfrac{2m^{-3-(-4)}}{3n^{3-(-5)}}} = \dfrac{2m}{3n^8}$

Matched Problem 1 Simplify, and express the answers using positive exponents only.

(A) $(3y^4)(2y^3)$ (B) $m^2 m^{-6}$ (C) $(u^3 v^{-2})^{-2}$

(C) $\left(\dfrac{y^{-6}}{y^{-2}}\right)^{-1}$ (D) $\dfrac{8x^{-2}y^{-4}}{6x^{-5}y^2}$

EXAMPLE 2 **Converting to a Simple Fraction** Write $\dfrac{1-x}{x^{-1}-1}$ as a simple fraction with positive exponents.

SOLUTION First note that

$$\frac{1-x}{x^{-1}-1} \neq \frac{x(1-x)}{-1} \qquad \text{A common error}$$

The original expression is a complex fraction, and we proceed to simplify it as follows:

$$\frac{1-x}{x^{-1}-1} = \frac{1-x}{\dfrac{1}{x}-1} \qquad \text{Multiply numerator and denominator by } x \text{ to clear internal fractions.}$$

$$= \frac{x(1-x)}{x\left(\dfrac{1}{x}-1\right)}$$

$$= \frac{x(1-x)}{1-x} = x$$

Matched Problem 2 Write $\dfrac{1+x^{-1}}{1-x^{-2}}$ as a simple fraction with positive exponents.

Scientific Notation

In the real world, one often encounters very large and very small numbers. For example,

- The public debt in the United States in 2008, to the nearest billion dollars, was

$$\$10,025,000,000,000$$

- The world population in the year 2025, to the nearest million, is projected to be

$$7,947,000,000$$

- The sound intensity of a normal conversation is

$$0.000\ 000\ 000\ 316 \text{ watt per square centimeter*}$$

It is generally troublesome to write and work with numbers of this type in standard decimal form. The first and last example cannot even be entered into many calculators as they are written. But with exponents defined for all integers, we can now express any finite decimal form as the product of a number between 1 and 10 and an integer power of 10, that is, in the form

$$a \times 10^n \qquad 1 \le a < 10, \quad a \text{ in decimal form}, \quad n \text{ an integer}$$

A number expressed in this form is said to be in **scientific notation**. The following are some examples of numbers in standard decimal notation and in scientific notation:

DECIMAL AND SCIENTIFIC NOTATION

$7 = 7 \times 10^0$	$0.5 = 5 \times 10^{-1}$
$67 = 6.7 \times 10$	$0.45 = 4.5 \times 10^{-1}$
$580 = 5.8 \times 10^2$	$0.0032 = 3.2 \times 10^{-3}$
$43,000 = 4.3 \times 10^4$	$0.000\ 045 = 4.5 \times 10^{-5}$
$73,400,000 = 7.34 \times 10^7$	$0.000\ 000\ 391 = 3.91 \times 10^{-7}$

Note that the power of 10 used corresponds to the number of places we move the decimal to form a number between 1 and 10. The power is positive if the decimal is moved to the left and negative if it is moved to the right. Positive exponents are associated with numbers greater than or equal to 10; negative exponents are associated with positive numbers less than 1; and a zero exponent is associated with a number that is 1 or greater, but less than 10.

EXAMPLE 3 **Scientific Notation**

(A) Write each number in scientific notation:

$$7,320,000 \qquad \text{and} \qquad 0.000\ 000\ 54$$

(B) Write each number in standard decimal form:

$$4.32 \times 10^6 \qquad \text{and} \qquad 4.32 \times 10^{-5}$$

SOLUTION

(A) $\quad 7,320,000 = 7.320\ 000. \times 10^6 = 7.32 \times 10^6$

6 places left
Positive exponent

$\quad 0.000\ 000\ 54 = 0.000\ 000\ 5.4 \times 10^{-7} = 5.4 \times 10^{-7}$

7 places right
Negative exponent

---

*We write 0.000 000 000 316 in place of 0.000000000316, because it is then easier to keep track of the number of decimal places. We follow this convention when there are more than five decimal places to the right of the decimal.

(B) $4.32 \times 10^6 = 4,320,000$

6 places right

Positive exponent 6

$4.32 \times 10^{-5} = \dfrac{4.32}{10^5} = 0.000\ 043\ 2$

5 places left

Negative exponent −5

Matched Problem 3   (A) Write each number in scientific notation: 47,100; 2,443,000,000; 1.45

(B) Write each number in standard decimal form: 3.07×10^8; 5.98×10^{-6}

Exercises A-5

A

In Problems 1–14, simplify and express answers using positive exponents only. Variables are restricted to avoid division by 0.

1. $2x^{-9}$

2. $3y^{-5}$

3. $\dfrac{3}{2w^{-7}}$

4. $\dfrac{5}{4x^{-9}}$

5. $2x^{-8}x^5$

6. $3c^{-9}c^4$

7. $\dfrac{w^{-8}}{w^{-3}}$

8. $\dfrac{m^{-11}}{m^{-5}}$

9. $(2a^{-3})^2$

10. $7d^{-4}d^4$

11. $(a^{-3})^2$

12. $(5b^{-2})^2$

13. $(2x^4)^{-3}$

14. $(a^{-3}b^4)^{-3}$

In Problems 15–20, write each number in scientific notation.

15. 82,300,000,000

16. 5,380,000

17. 0.783

18. 0.019

19. 0.000 034

20. 0.000 000 007 832

In Problems 21–28, write each number in standard decimal notation.

21. 4×10^4

22. 9×10^6

23. 7×10^{-3}

24. 2×10^{-5}

25. 6.171×10^7

26. 3.044×10^3

27. 8.08×10^{-4}

28. 1.13×10^{-2}

B

In Problems 29–38, simplify and express answers using positive exponents only.

29. $(22 + 31)^0$

30. $(2x^3y^4)^0$

31. $\dfrac{10^{-3} \cdot 10^4}{10^{-11} \cdot 10^{-2}}$

32. $\dfrac{10^{-17} \cdot 10^{-5}}{10^{-3} \cdot 10^{-14}}$

33. $(5x^2y^{-3})^{-2}$

34. $(2m^{-3}n^2)^{-3}$

35. $\left(\dfrac{-5}{2x^3}\right)^{-2}$

36. $\left(\dfrac{2a}{3b^2}\right)^{-3}$

37. $\dfrac{8x^{-3}y^{-1}}{6x^2y^{-4}}$

38. $\dfrac{9m^{-4}n^3}{12m^{-1}n^{-1}}$

In Problems 39–42, write each expression in the form $ax^p + bx^q$ or $ax^p + bx^q + cx^r$, where a, b, and c are real numbers and p, q, and r are integers. For example,

$$\dfrac{2x^4 - 3x^2 + 1}{2x^3} = \dfrac{2x^4}{2x^3} - \dfrac{3x^2}{2x^3} + \dfrac{1}{2x^3} = x - \dfrac{3}{2}x^{-1} + \dfrac{1}{2}x^{-3}$$

39. $\dfrac{7x^5 - x^2}{4x^5}$

40. $\dfrac{5x^3 - 2}{3x^2}$

41. $\dfrac{5x^4 - 3x^2 + 8}{2x^2}$

42. $\dfrac{2x^3 - 3x^2 + x}{2x^2}$

Write each expression in Problems 43–46 with positive exponents only, and as a single fraction reduced to lowest terms.

43. $\dfrac{3x^2(x - 1)^2 - 2x^3(x - 1)}{(x - 1)^4}$

44. $\dfrac{5x^4(x + 3)^2 - 2x^5(x + 3)}{(x + 3)^4}$

45. $2x^{-2}(x - 1) - 2x^{-3}(x - 1)^2$

46. $2x(x + 3)^{-1} - x^2(x + 3)^{-2}$

In Problems 47–50, convert each number to scientific notation and simplify. Express the answer in both scientific notation and in standard decimal form.

47. $\dfrac{9,600,000,000}{(1,600,000)(0.000\ 000\ 25)}$

48. $\dfrac{(60,000)(0.000\ 003)}{(0.0004)(1,500,000)}$

49. $\dfrac{(1,250,000)(0.000\ 38)}{0.0152}$

50. $\dfrac{(0.000\ 000\ 82)(230,000)}{(625,000)(0.0082)}$

51. What is the result of entering 2^{3^2} on a calculator?

52. Refer to Problem 51. What is the difference between $2^{(3^2)}$ and $(2^3)^2$? Which agrees with the value of 2^{3^2} obtained with a calculator?

53. If $n = 0$, then property 1 in Theorem 1 implies that $a^m a^0 = a^{m+0} = a^m$. Explain how this helps motivate the definition of a^0.

54. If $m = -n$, then property 1 in Theorem 1 implies that $a^{-n}a^n = a^0 = 1$. Explain how this helps motivate the definition of a^{-n}.

Write the fractions in Problems 55–58 as simple fractions reduced to lowest terms.

55. $\dfrac{u + v}{u^{-1} + v^{-1}}$

56. $\dfrac{x^{-2} - y^{-2}}{x^{-1} + y^{-1}}$

57. $\dfrac{b^{-2} - c^{-2}}{b^{-3} - c^{-3}}$

58. $\dfrac{xy^{-2} - yx^{-2}}{y^{-1} - x^{-1}}$

Applications

Problems 59 and 60 refer to Table 1.

Table 1 U.S. Public Debt, Interest on Debt, and Population

Year	Public Debt ($)	Interest on Debt ($)	Population
2000	5,674,000,000,000	362,000,000,000	281,000,000
2008	10,025,000,000,000	451,000,000,000	304,000,000

59. Public debt. Carry out the following computations using scientific notation, and write final answers in standard decimal form.

(A) What was the per capita debt in 2008 (to the nearest dollar)?

(B) What was the per capita interest paid on the debt in 2008 (to the nearest dollar)?

(C) What was the percentage interest paid on the debt in 2008 (to two decimal places)?

60. Public debt. Carry out the following computations using scientific notation, and write final answers in standard decimal form.

(A) What was the per capita debt in 2000 (to the nearest dollar)?

(B) What was the per capita interest paid on the debt in 2000 (to the nearest dollar)?

(C) What was the percentage interest paid on the debt in 2000 (to two decimal places)?

Air pollution. *Air quality standards establish maximum amounts of pollutants considered acceptable in the air. The amounts are frequently given in parts per million (ppm). A standard of 30 ppm also can be expressed as follows:*

$$30 \text{ ppm} = \frac{30}{1{,}000{,}000} = \frac{3 \times 10}{10^6}$$
$$= 3 \times 10^{-5} = 0.000\,03 = 0.003\%$$

In Problems 61 and 62, express the given standard:

(A) In scientific notation

(B) In standard decimal notation

(C) As a percent

61. 9 ppm, the standard for carbon monoxide, when averaged over a period of 8 hours

62. 0.03 ppm, the standard for sulfur oxides, when averaged over a year

63. Crime. In 2008, the United States had a violent crime rate of 466 per 100,000 people and a population of 304 million people. How many violent crimes occurred that year? Compute the answer using scientific notation and convert the answer to standard decimal form (to the nearest thousand).

64. Population density. The United States had a 2008 population of 304 million people and a land area of 3,539,000 square miles. What was the population density? Compute the answer using scientific notation and convert the answer to standard decimal form (to one decimal place).

Answers to Matched Problems

1. (A) $6y^7$ (B) $\dfrac{1}{m^4}$ (C) $\dfrac{v^4}{u^6}$ (D) y^4 (E) $\dfrac{4x^3}{3y^6}$

2. $\dfrac{x}{x - 1}$

3. (A) 4.7×10^4; 2.443×10^9; 1.45×10^0

    (B) 307,000,000; 0.000 005 98

A-6   Rational Exponents and Radicals

- *n*th Roots of Real Numbers
- Rational Exponents and Radicals
- Properties of Radicals

Square roots may now be generalized to *n*th roots, and the meaning of exponent may be generalized to include all rational numbers.

*n*th Roots of Real Numbers

Consider a square of side r with area 36 square inches. We can write

$$r^2 = 36$$

and conclude that side r is a number whose square is 36. We say that r is a **square root** of b if $r^2 = b$. Similarly, we say that r is a **cube root** of b if $r^3 = b$. And, in general,

DEFINITION *n*th Root

For any natural number *n*,

$$r \text{ is an } \textbf{\textit{n}th root} \text{ of } b \text{ if } r^n = b$$

So 4 is a square root of 16, since $4^2 = 16$; -2 is a cube root of -8, since $(-2)^3 = -8$. Since $(-4)^2 = 16$, we see that -4 is also a square root of 16. It can be shown that any positive number has two real square roots, two real 4th roots, and, in general, two real *n*th roots if *n* is even. Negative numbers have no real square roots, no real 4th roots, and, in general, no real *n*th roots if *n* is even. The reason is that no real number raised to an even power can be negative. For odd roots, the situation is simpler. Every real number has exactly one real cube root, one real 5th root, and, in general, one real nth root if *n* is odd.

Additional roots can be considered in the *complex number system*. In this book, we restrict our interest to *real roots of real numbers*, and *root* will always be interpreted to mean "real root."

Rational Exponents and Radicals

We now turn to the question of what symbols to use to represent *n*th roots. For *n* a natural number greater than 1, we use

$$b^{1/n} \quad \text{or} \quad \sqrt[n]{b}$$

to represent a **real *n*th root of *b***. The exponent form is motivated by the fact that $(b^{1/n})^n = b$ if exponent laws are to continue to hold for rational exponents. The other form is called an **_n_th root radical**. In the expression below, the symbol $\sqrt{}$ is called a **radical**, *n* is the **index** of the radical, and *b* is the **radicand**:

$$\text{Index} \longrightarrow \overset{\text{Radical}}{\sqrt[n]{b}} $$
$$\underset{\text{Radicand}}{} $$

When the index is 2, it is usually omitted. That is, when dealing with square roots, we simply use $\sqrt{b}$ rather than $\sqrt[2]{b}$. If there are two real *n*th roots, both $b^{1/n}$ and $\sqrt[n]{b}$ denote the positive root, called the **principal *n*th root**.

EXAMPLE 1   **Finding *n*th Roots** Evaluate each of the following:

(A) $4^{1/2}$ and $\sqrt{4}$ (B) $-4^{1/2}$ and $-\sqrt{4}$ (C) $(-4)^{1/2}$ and $\sqrt{-4}$
(D) $8^{1/3}$ and $\sqrt[3]{8}$ (E) $(-8)^{1/3}$ and $\sqrt[3]{-8}$ (F) $-8^{1/3}$ and $-\sqrt[3]{8}$

SOLUTION   (A) $4^{1/2} = \sqrt{4} = 2$ $(\sqrt{4} \neq \pm 2)$ (B) $-4^{1/2} = -\sqrt{4} = -2$
(C) $(-4)^{1/2}$ and $\sqrt{-4}$ are not real numbers
(D) $8^{1/3} = \sqrt[3]{8} = 2$ (E) $(-8)^{1/3} = \sqrt[3]{-8} = -2$
(F) $-8^{1/3} = -\sqrt[3]{8} = -2$

Matched Problem 1   Evaluate each of the following:

(A) $16^{1/2}$ (B) $-\sqrt{16}$ (C) $\sqrt[3]{-27}$ (D) $(-9)^{1/2}$ (E) $(\sqrt[4]{81})^3$

⚠ **CAUTION** The symbol $\sqrt{4}$ represents the single number 2, not ± 2. Do not confuse $\sqrt{4}$ with the solutions of the equation $x^2 = 4$, which are usually written in the form $x = \pm\sqrt{4} = \pm 2$.

We now define b^r for any rational number $r = m/n$.

DEFINITION Rational Exponents

If m and n are natural numbers without common prime factors, b is a real number, and b is nonnegative when n is even, then

$$b^{m/n} = \begin{cases} (b^{1/n})^m = (\sqrt[n]{b})^m & 8^{2/3} = (8^{1/3})^2 = (\sqrt[3]{8})^2 = 2^2 = 4 \\ (b^m)^{1/n} = \sqrt[n]{b^m} & 8^{2/3} = (8^2)^{1/3} = \sqrt[3]{8^2} = \sqrt[3]{64} = 4 \end{cases}$$

and

$$b^{-m/n} = \frac{1}{b^{m/n}} \quad b \neq 0 \qquad 8^{-2/3} = \frac{1}{8^{2/3}} = \frac{1}{4}$$

Note that the two definitions of $b^{m/n}$ are equivalent under the indicated restrictions on $m, n,$ and b.

CONCEPTUAL INSIGHT

All the properties for integer exponents listed in Theorem 1 in Section A-5 also hold for rational exponents, provided that b is nonnegative when n is even. This restriction on b is necessary to avoid nonreal results. For example,

$$(-4)^{3/2} = \sqrt{(-4)^3} = \sqrt{-64} \qquad \text{Not a real number}$$

To avoid nonreal results, all variables in the remainder of this discussion represent positive real numbers.

EXAMPLE 2 **From Rational Exponent Form to Radical Form and Vice Versa** Change rational exponent form to radical form.

(A) $x^{1/7} = \sqrt[7]{x}$

(B) $(3u^2v^3)^{3/5} = \sqrt[5]{(3u^2v^3)^3}$ or $(\sqrt[5]{3u^2v^3})^3$ The first is usually preferred.

(C) $y^{-2/3} = \dfrac{1}{y^{2/3}} = \dfrac{1}{\sqrt[3]{y^2}}$ or $\sqrt[3]{y^{-2}}$ or $\sqrt[3]{\dfrac{1}{y^2}}$

Change radical form to rational exponent form.

(D) $\sqrt[5]{6} = 6^{1/5}$ (E) $-\sqrt[3]{x^2} = -x^{2/3}$

(F) $\sqrt{x^2 + y^2} = (x^2 + y^2)^{1/2}$ Note that $(x^2 + y^2)^{1/2} \neq x + y$. Why?

Matched Problem 2 Convert to radical form.

(A) $u^{1/5}$ (B) $(6x^2y^5)^{2/9}$ (C) $(3xy)^{-3/5}$

Convert to rational exponent form.

(D) $\sqrt[4]{9u}$ (E) $-\sqrt{(2x)^4}$ (F) $\sqrt[3]{x^3 + y^3}$

EXAMPLE 3 **Working with Rational Exponents** Simplify each and express answers using positive exponents only. If rational exponents appear in final answers, convert to radical form.

(A) $(3x^{1/3})(2x^{1/2}) = 6x^{1/3+1/2} = 6x^{5/6} = 6\sqrt[6]{x^5}$

(B) $(-8)^{5/3} = [(-8)^{1/3}]^5 = (-2)^5 = -32$

(C) $(2x^{1/3}y^{-2/3})^3 = 8xy^{-2} = \dfrac{8x}{y^2}$

(D) $\left(\dfrac{4x^{1/3}}{x^{1/2}}\right)^{1/2} = \dfrac{4^{1/2}x^{1/6}}{x^{1/4}} = \dfrac{2}{x^{1/4-1/6}} = \dfrac{2}{x^{1/12}} = \dfrac{2}{\sqrt[12]{x}}$

Matched Problem 3   Simplify each and express answers using positive exponents only. If rational exponents appear in final answers, convert to radical form.

(A) $9^{3/2}$ (B) $(-27)^{4/3}$ (C) $(5y^{1/4})(2y^{1/3})$ (D) $(2x^{-3/4}y^{1/4})^4$

(E) $\left(\dfrac{8x^{1/2}}{x^{2/3}}\right)^{1/3}$

EXAMPLE 4   **Working with Rational Exponents** Multiply, and express answers using positive exponents only.

(A) $3y^{2/3}(2y^{1/3} - y^2)$ (B) $(2u^{1/2} + v^{1/2})(u^{1/2} - 3v^{1/2})$

SOLUTION   (A) $3y^{2/3}(2y^{1/3} - y^2) = 6y^{2/3+1/3} - 3y^{2/3+2}$

$$= 6y - 3y^{8/3}$$

(B) $(2u^{1/2} + v^{1/2})(u^{1/2} - 3v^{1/2}) = 2u - 5u^{1/2}v^{1/2} - 3v$

Matched Problem 4   Multiply, and express answers using positive exponents only.

(A) $2c^{1/4}(5c^3 - c^{3/4})$ (B) $(7x^{1/2} - y^{1/2})(2x^{1/2} + 3y^{1/2})$

EXAMPLE 5   **Working with Rational Exponents** Write the following expression in the form $ax^p + bx^q$, where a and b are real numbers and p and q are rational numbers:

$$\frac{2\sqrt{x} - 3\sqrt[3]{x^2}}{2\sqrt[3]{x}}$$

SOLUTION $\dfrac{2\sqrt{x} - 3\sqrt[3]{x^2}}{2\sqrt[3]{x}} = \dfrac{2x^{1/2} - 3x^{2/3}}{2x^{1/3}}$ *Change to rational exponent form.*

$$= \frac{2x^{1/2}}{2x^{1/3}} - \frac{3x^{2/3}}{2x^{1/3}}$$ *Separate into two fractions.*

$$= x^{1/6} - 1.5x^{1/3}$$

Matched Problem 5   Write the following expression in the form $ax^p + bx^q$, where a and b are real numbers and p and q are rational numbers:

$$\frac{5\sqrt[3]{x} - 4\sqrt{x}}{2\sqrt{x^3}}$$

Properties of Radicals

Changing or simplifying radical expressions is aided by several properties of radicals that follow directly from the properties of exponents considered earlier.

THEOREM 1   **Properties of Radicals**

If c, n, and m are natural numbers greater than or equal to 2, and if x and y are positive real numbers, then

1. $\sqrt[n]{x^n} = x$ $\qquad \sqrt[3]{x^3} = x$

2. $\sqrt[n]{xy} = \sqrt[n]{x}\sqrt[n]{y}$ $\quad \sqrt[5]{xy} = \sqrt[5]{x}\,\sqrt[5]{y}$.

3. $\sqrt[n]{\dfrac{x}{y}} = \dfrac{\sqrt[n]{x}}{\sqrt[n]{y}}$ $\quad \sqrt[4]{\dfrac{x}{y}} = \dfrac{\sqrt[4]{x}}{\sqrt[4]{y}}$

EXAMPLE 6   **Applying Properties of Radicals** Simplify using properties of radicals.

(A) $\sqrt[4]{(3x^4y^3)^4}$ (B) $\sqrt[4]{8}\sqrt[4]{2}$ (C) $\sqrt[3]{\dfrac{xy}{27}}$

SOLUTION   (A) $\sqrt[4]{(3x^4y^3)^4} = 3x^4y^3$ Property 1

(B) $\sqrt[4]{8}\sqrt[4]{2} = \sqrt[4]{16} = \sqrt[4]{2^4} = 2$ Properties 2 and 1

(C) $\sqrt[3]{\dfrac{xy}{27}} = \dfrac{\sqrt[3]{xy}}{\sqrt[3]{27}} = \dfrac{\sqrt[3]{xy}}{3}$ or $\dfrac{1}{3}\sqrt[3]{xy}$ Properties 3 and 1

Matched Problem 6   Simplify using properties of radicals.

(A) $\sqrt[7]{(x^3 + y^3)^7}$ (B) $\sqrt[3]{8y^3}$ (C) $\dfrac{\sqrt[3]{16x^4y}}{\sqrt[3]{2xy}}$

What is the best form for a radical expression? There are many answers, depending on what use we wish to make of the expression. In deriving certain formulas, it is sometimes useful to clear either a denominator or a numerator of radicals. The process is referred to as **rationalizing** the denominator or numerator. Examples 7 and 8 illustrate the rationalizing process.

EXAMPLE 7   **Rationalizing Denominators** Rationalize each denominator.

(A) $\dfrac{6x}{\sqrt{2x}}$ (B) $\dfrac{6}{\sqrt{7} - \sqrt{5}}$ (C) $\dfrac{x - 4}{\sqrt{x} + 2}$

SOLUTION   (A) $\dfrac{6x}{\sqrt{2x}} = \dfrac{6x}{\sqrt{2x}} \cdot \dfrac{\sqrt{2x}}{\sqrt{2x}} = \dfrac{6x\sqrt{2x}}{2x} = 3\sqrt{2x}$

(B) $\dfrac{6}{\sqrt{7} - \sqrt{5}} = \dfrac{6}{\sqrt{7} - \sqrt{5}} \cdot \dfrac{\sqrt{7} + \sqrt{5}}{\sqrt{7} + \sqrt{5}}$

$= \dfrac{6(\sqrt{7} + \sqrt{5})}{2} = 3(\sqrt{7} + \sqrt{5})$

(C) $\dfrac{x - 4}{\sqrt{x} + 2} = \dfrac{x - 4}{\sqrt{x} + 2} \cdot \dfrac{\sqrt{x} - 2}{\sqrt{x} - 2}$

$= \dfrac{(x - 4)(\sqrt{x} - 2)}{x - 4} = \sqrt{x} - 2$

Matched Problem 7   Rationalize each denominator.

(A) $\dfrac{12ab^2}{\sqrt{3ab}}$ (B) $\dfrac{9}{\sqrt{6} + \sqrt{3}}$ (C) $\dfrac{x^2 - y^2}{\sqrt{x} - \sqrt{y}}$

EXAMPLE 8   **Rationalizing Numerators** Rationalize each numerator.

(A) $\dfrac{\sqrt{2}}{2\sqrt{3}}$ (B) $\dfrac{3 + \sqrt{m}}{9 - m}$ (C) $\dfrac{\sqrt{2 + h} - \sqrt{2}}{h}$

SOLUTION   (A) $\dfrac{\sqrt{2}}{2\sqrt{3}} = \dfrac{\sqrt{2}}{2\sqrt{3}} \cdot \dfrac{\sqrt{2}}{\sqrt{2}} = \dfrac{2}{2\sqrt{6}} = \dfrac{1}{\sqrt{6}}$

(B) $\dfrac{3 + \sqrt{m}}{9 - m} = \dfrac{3 + \sqrt{m}}{9 - m} \cdot \dfrac{3 - \sqrt{m}}{3 - \sqrt{m}} = \dfrac{9 - m}{(9 - m)(3 - \sqrt{m})} = \dfrac{1}{3 - \sqrt{m}}$

(C) $\dfrac{\sqrt{2 + h} - \sqrt{2}}{h} = \dfrac{\sqrt{2 + h} - \sqrt{2}}{h} \cdot \dfrac{\sqrt{2 + h} + \sqrt{2}}{\sqrt{2 + h} + \sqrt{2}}$

$= \dfrac{h}{h(\sqrt{2 + h} + \sqrt{2})} = \dfrac{1}{\sqrt{2 + h} + \sqrt{2}}$

Matched Problem 8 Rationalize each numerator.

(A) $\dfrac{\sqrt{3}}{3\sqrt{2}}$ (B) $\dfrac{2 - \sqrt{n}}{4 - n}$ (C) $\dfrac{\sqrt{3 + h} - \sqrt{3}}{h}$

Exercises A-6

A

Change each expression in Problems 1–6 to radical form. Do not simplify.

1. $6x^{3/5}$ **2.** $7y^{2/5}$ **3.** $(32x^2y^3)^{3/5}$

4. $(7x^2y)^{5/7}$ **5.** $(x^2 + y^2)^{1/2}$ **6.** $x^{1/2} + y^{1/2}$

Change each expression in Problems 7–12 to rational exponent form. Do not simplify.

7. $5\sqrt[4]{x^3}$ **8.** $7m\sqrt[5]{n^2}$ **9.** $\sqrt[5]{(2x^2y)^3}$

10. $\sqrt{(8x^4y)^3}$ **11.** $\sqrt[3]{x} + \sqrt[3]{y}$ **12.** $\sqrt[3]{x^2 + y^3}$

In Problems 13–24, find rational number representations for each, if they exist.

13. $25^{1/2}$ **14.** $64^{1/3}$ **15.** $16^{3/2}$

16. $16^{3/4}$ **17.** $-49^{1/2}$ **18.** $(-49)^{1/2}$

19. $-64^{2/3}$ **20.** $(-64)^{2/3}$ **21.** $\left(\dfrac{4}{25}\right)^{3/2}$

22. $\left(\dfrac{8}{27}\right)^{2/3}$ **23.** $9^{-3/2}$ **24.** $8^{-2/3}$

In Problems 25–34, simplify each expression and write answers using positive exponents only. All variables represent positive real numbers.

25. $x^{4/5}x^{-2/5}$ **26.** $y^{-3/7}y^{4/7}$ **27.** $\dfrac{m^{2/3}}{m^{-1/3}}$

28. $\dfrac{x^{1/4}}{x^{3/4}}$ **29.** $(8x^3y^{-6})^{1/3}$ **30.** $(4u^{-2}v^4)^{1/2}$

31. $\left(\dfrac{4x^{-2}}{y^4}\right)^{-1/2}$ **32.** $\left(\dfrac{w^4}{9x^{-2}}\right)^{-1/2}$ **33.** $\dfrac{(8x)^{-1/3}}{12x^{1/4}}$

34. $\dfrac{6a^{3/4}}{15a^{-1/3}}$

Simplify each expression in Problems 35–40 using properties of radicals. All variables represent positive real numbers.

35. $\sqrt[5]{(2x + 3)^5}$ **36.** $\sqrt[3]{(7 + 2y)^3}$

37. $\sqrt{6x}\sqrt{15x^3}\sqrt{30x^7}$ **38.** $\sqrt[5]{16a^4}\sqrt[5]{4a^2}\sqrt[5]{8a^3}$

39. $\dfrac{\sqrt{6x}\sqrt{10}}{\sqrt{15x}}$ **40.** $\dfrac{\sqrt{8}\sqrt{12y}}{\sqrt{6y}}$

B

In Problems 41–48, multiply, and express answers using positive exponents only.

41. $3x^{3/4}(4x^{1/4} - 2x^8)$

42. $2m^{1/3}(3m^{2/3} - m^6)$

43. $(3u^{1/2} - v^{1/2})(u^{1/2} - 4v^{1/2})$

44. $(a^{1/2} + 2b^{1/2})(a^{1/2} - 3b^{1/2})$

45. $(6m^{1/2} + n^{-1/2})(6m - n^{-1/2})$

46. $(2x - 3y^{1/3})(2x^{1/3} + 1)$

47. $(3x^{1/2} - y^{1/2})^2$

48. $(x^{1/2} + 2y^{1/2})^2$

Write each expression in Problems 49–54 in the form $ax^p + bx^q$, where a and b are real numbers and p and q are rational numbers.

49. $\dfrac{\sqrt[3]{x^2} + 2}{2\sqrt[3]{x}}$ **50.** $\dfrac{12\sqrt{x} - 3}{4\sqrt{x}}$ **51.** $\dfrac{2\sqrt[4]{x^3} + \sqrt[3]{x}}{3x}$

52. $\dfrac{3\sqrt[3]{x^2} + \sqrt{x}}{5x}$ **53.** $\dfrac{2\sqrt[3]{x} - \sqrt{x}}{4\sqrt{x}}$ **54.** $\dfrac{x^2 - 4\sqrt{x}}{2\sqrt[3]{x}}$

Rationalize the denominators in Problems 55–60.

55. $\dfrac{12mn^2}{\sqrt{3mn}}$ **56.** $\dfrac{14x^2}{\sqrt{7x}}$ **57.** $\dfrac{2(x + 3)}{\sqrt{x} - 2}$

58. $\dfrac{3(x + 1)}{\sqrt{x} + 4}$ **59.** $\dfrac{7(x - y)^2}{\sqrt{x} - \sqrt{y}}$ **60.** $\dfrac{3a - 3b}{\sqrt{a} + \sqrt{b}}$

Rationalize the numerators in Problems 61–66.

61. $\dfrac{\sqrt{5xy}}{5x^2y^2}$ **62.** $\dfrac{\sqrt{3mn}}{3mn}$

63. $\dfrac{\sqrt{x + h} - \sqrt{x}}{h}$ **64.** $\dfrac{\sqrt{2(a + h)} - \sqrt{2a}}{h}$

65. $\dfrac{\sqrt{t} - \sqrt{x}}{t^2 - x^2}$ **66.** $\dfrac{\sqrt{x} - \sqrt{y}}{\sqrt{x} + \sqrt{y}}$

Problems 67–70 illustrate common errors involving rational exponents. In each case, find numerical examples that show that the left side is not always equal to the right side.

67. $(x + y)^{1/2} \neq x^{1/2} + y^{1/2}$ **68.** $(x^3 + y^3)^{1/3} \neq x + y$

69. $(x + y)^{1/3} \neq \dfrac{1}{(x + y)^3}$ **70.** $(x + y)^{-1/2} \neq \dfrac{1}{(x + y)^2}$

C

In Problems 71–82, discuss the validity of each statement. If the statement is true, explain why. If not, give a counterexample.

71. $\sqrt{x^2} = x$ for all real numbers x

72. $\sqrt{x^2} = |x|$ for all real numbers x

73. $\sqrt[3]{x^3} = |x|$ for all real numbers x

74. $\sqrt[3]{x^3} = x$ for all real numbers x

75. If $r < 0$, then r has no cube roots.

76. If $r < 0$, then r has no square roots.

77. If $r > 0$, then r has two square roots.

78. If $r > 0$, then r has three cube roots.

79. The fourth roots of 100 are $\sqrt{10}$ and $-\sqrt{10}$.

80. The square roots of $2\sqrt{6} - 5$ are $\sqrt{3} - \sqrt{2}$ and $\sqrt{2} - \sqrt{3}$.

81. $\sqrt{355 - 60\sqrt{35}} = 5\sqrt{7} - 6\sqrt{5}$

82. $\sqrt[3]{7 - 5\sqrt{2}} = 1 - \sqrt{2}$

In Problems 83–88, simplify by writing each expression as a simple or single fraction reduced to lowest terms and without negative exponents.

83. $-\frac{1}{2}(x - 2)(x + 3)^{-3/2} + (x + 3)^{-1/2}$

84. $2(x - 2)^{-1/2} - \frac{1}{2}(2x + 3)(x - 2)^{-3/2}$

85. $\dfrac{(x - 1)^{1/2} - x\left(\frac{1}{2}\right)(x - 1)^{-1/2}}{x - 1}$

86. $\dfrac{(2x - 1)^{1/2} - (x + 2)\left(\frac{1}{2}\right)(2x - 1)^{-1/2}(2)}{2x - 1}$

87. $\dfrac{(x + 2)^{2/3} - x\left(\frac{2}{3}\right)(x + 2)^{-1/3}}{(x + 2)^{4/3}}$

88. $\dfrac{2(3x - 1)^{1/3} - (2x + 1)\left(\frac{1}{3}\right)(3x - 1)^{-2/3}(3)}{(3x - 1)^{2/3}}$

In Problems 89–94, evaluate using a calculator. (Refer to the instruction book for your calculator to see how exponential forms are evaluated.)

89. $22^{3/2}$ **90.** $15^{5/4}$ **91.** $827^{-3/8}$

92. $103^{-3/4}$ **93.** $37.09^{7/3}$ **94.** $2.876^{8/5}$

In Problems 95 and 96, evaluate each expression on a calculator and determine which pairs have the same value. Verify these results algebraically.

95. (A) $\sqrt{3} + \sqrt{5}$ (B) $\sqrt{2 + \sqrt{3}} + \sqrt{2 - \sqrt{3}}$
(C) $1 + \sqrt{3}$ (D) $\sqrt[3]{10 + 6\sqrt{3}}$
(E) $\sqrt{8 + \sqrt{60}}$ (F) $\sqrt{6}$

96. (A) $2\sqrt[3]{2} + \sqrt{5}$ (B) $\sqrt{8}$
(C) $\sqrt{3} + \sqrt{7}$ (D) $\sqrt{3 + \sqrt{8}} + \sqrt{3 - \sqrt{8}}$
(E) $\sqrt{10 + \sqrt{84}}$ (F) $1 + \sqrt{5}$

Answers to Matched Problems

1. (A) 4 (B) -4
(C) -3 (D) Not a real number (E) 27
2. (A) $\sqrt[5]{u}$ (B) $\sqrt[9]{(6x^2 y^5)^2}$ or $\left(\sqrt[9]{6x^2 y^5}\right)^2$
(C) $1/\sqrt[5]{(3xy)^3}$ (D) $(9u)^{1/4}$ (E) $-(2x)^{4/7}$
(F) $(x^3 + y^3)^{1/3}$ (not $x + y$)
3. (A) 27 (B) 81
(C) $10y^{7/12} = 10\sqrt[12]{y^7}$ (D) $16y/x^3$
(E) $2/x^{1/18} = 2/\sqrt[18]{x}$
4. (A) $10c^{13/4} - 2c$ (B) $14x + 19x^{1/2}y^{1/2} - 3y$
5. $2.5x^{-7/6} - 2x^{-1}$
6. (A) $x^3 + y^3$ (B) $2y$ (C) $2x$
7. (A) $4b\sqrt{3ab}$
(B) $3(\sqrt{6} - \sqrt{3})$
(C) $(x + y)(\sqrt{x} + \sqrt{y})$
8. (A) $\dfrac{1}{\sqrt{6}}$ (B) $\dfrac{1}{2 + \sqrt{n}}$ (C) $\dfrac{1}{\sqrt{3 + h} + \sqrt{3}}$

A-7 Quadratic Equations

- Solution by Square Root
- Solution by Factoring
- Quadratic Formula
- Quadratic Formula and Factoring
- Application: Supply and Demand

In this section we consider equations involving second-degree polynomials.

DEFINITION Quadratic Equation

A **quadratic equation** in one variable is any equation that can be written in the form

$$ax^2 + bx + c = 0 \qquad a \neq 0 \qquad \text{Standard form}$$

where x is a variable and a, b, and c are constants.

The equations

$$5x^2 - 3x + 7 = 0 \quad \text{and} \quad 18 = 32t^2 - 12t$$

are both quadratic equations, since they are either in the standard form or can be transformed into this form.

We restrict our review to finding real solutions to quadratic equations.

Solution by Square Root

The easiest type of quadratic equation to solve is the special form where the first-degree term is missing:

$$ax^2 + c = 0 \quad a \neq 0$$

The method of solution of this special form makes direct use of the square-root property:

THEOREM 1   Square-Root Property
If $a^2 = b$, then $a = \pm\sqrt{b}$.

EXAMPLE 1   **Square-Root Method** Use the square-root property to solve each equation.

(A) $x^2 - 7 = 0$ (B) $2x^2 - 10 = 0$

(C) $3x^2 + 27 = 0$ (D) $(x - 8)^2 = 9$

SOLUTION   (A) $x^2 - 7 = 0$

$\qquad\qquad x^2 = 7$ *What real number squared is 7?*

$\qquad\qquad x = \pm\sqrt{7}$ *Short for $\sqrt{7}$ and $-\sqrt{7}$*

(B) $2x^2 - 10 = 0$

$\qquad\qquad 2x^2 = 10$

$\qquad\qquad x^2 = 5$ *What real number squared is 5?*

$\qquad\qquad x = \pm\sqrt{5}$

(C) $3x^2 + 27 = 0$

$\qquad\qquad 3x^2 = -27$

$\qquad\qquad x^2 = -9$ *What real number squared is -9?*

No real solution, since no real number squared is negative.

(D) $(x - 8)^2 = 9$

$\qquad\qquad x - 8 = \pm\sqrt{9}$

$\qquad\qquad x - 8 = \pm 3$

$\qquad\qquad x = 8 \pm 3 = 5 \quad \text{or} \quad 11$

Matched Problem 1   Use the square-root property to solve each equation.

(A) $x^2 - 6 = 0$ (B) $3x^2 - 12 = 0$

(C) $x^2 + 4 = 0$ (D) $(x + 5)^2 = 1$

Solution by Factoring

If the left side of a quadratic equation when written in standard form can be factored, the equation can be solved very quickly. The method of solution by factoring rests on a basic property of real numbers, first mentioned in Section A-1.

CONCEPTUAL INSIGHT

Theorem 2 in Section A-1 states that if a and b are real numbers, then $ab = 0$ if and only if $a = 0$ or $b = 0$. To see that this property is useful for solving quadratic equations, consider the following:

$$x^2 - 4x + 3 = 0 \qquad (1)$$
$$(x - 1)(x - 3) = 0$$
$$x - 1 = 0 \quad \text{or} \quad x - 3 = 0$$
$$x = 1 \quad \text{or} \quad x = 3$$

You should check these solutions in equation (1).

If one side of the equation is not 0, then this method cannot be used. For example, consider

$$x^2 - 4x + 3 = 8 \qquad (2)$$
$$(x - 1)(x - 3) = 8$$
$$x - 1 \neq 8 \quad \text{or} \quad x - 3 \neq 8 \qquad ab = 8 \text{ does not imply}$$
$$\qquad\qquad\qquad\qquad\qquad\qquad\qquad that\ a = 8\ or\ b = 8.$$
$$x = 9 \quad \text{or} \quad x = 11$$

Verify that neither $x = 9$ nor $x = 11$ is a solution for equation (2).

EXAMPLE 2   **Factoring Method** Solve by factoring using integer coefficients, if possible.

(A) $3x^2 - 6x - 24 = 0$ (B) $3y^2 = 2y$ (C) $x^2 - 2x - 1 = 0$

SOLUTION   (A) $3x^2 - 6x - 24 = 0$ Divide both sides by 3, since 3 is a factor of each coefficient.

$$x^2 - 2x - 8 = 0 \quad \text{Factor the left side, if possible.}$$
$$(x - 4)(x + 2) = 0$$
$$x - 4 = 0 \quad \text{or} \quad x + 2 = 0$$
$$x = 4 \quad \text{or} \quad x = -2$$

(B)
$$3y^2 = 2y$$
$$3y^2 - 2y = 0 \quad \text{We lose the solution } y = 0 \text{ if both sides are divided}$$
$$y(3y - 2) = 0 \quad \text{by } y\ (3y^2 = 2y \text{ and } 3y = 2 \text{ are not equivalent).}$$
$$y = 0 \quad \text{or} \quad 3y - 2 = 0$$
$$3y = 2$$
$$y = \tfrac{2}{3}$$

(C) $x^2 - 2x - 1 = 0$

This equation cannot be factored using integer coefficients. We will solve this type of equation by another method, considered below.

Matched Problem 2   Solve by factoring using integer coefficients, if possible.

(A) $2x^2 + 4x - 30 = 0$ (B) $2x^2 = 3x$ (C) $2x^2 - 8x + 3 = 0$

Note that an equation such as $x^2 = 25$ can be solved by either the square-root or the factoring method, and the results are the same (as they should be). Solve this equation both ways and compare.

Also, note that the factoring method can be extended to higher-degree polynomial equations. Consider the following:

$$x^3 - x = 0$$
$$x(x^2 - 1) = 0$$
$$x(x - 1)(x + 1) = 0$$
$$x = 0 \quad \text{or} \quad x - 1 = 0 \quad \text{or} \quad x + 1 = 0$$
$$\text{Solution: } x = 0, 1, -1$$

Check these solutions in the original equation.

The factoring and square-root methods are fast and easy to use when they apply. However, there are quadratic equations that look simple but cannot be solved by either method. For example, as was noted in Example 2C, the polynomial in

$$x^2 - 2x - 1 = 0$$

cannot be factored using integer coefficients. This brings us to the well-known and widely used *quadratic formula*.

Quadratic Formula

There is a method called *completing the square* that will work for all quadratic equations. After briefly reviewing this method, we will use it to develop the quadratic formula, which can be used to solve any quadratic equation.

The method of **completing the square** is based on the process of transforming a quadratic equation in standard form,

$$ax^2 + bx + c = 0$$

into the form

$$(x + A)^2 = B$$

where A and B are constants. Then, this last equation can be solved easily (if it has a real solution) by the square-root method discussed above.

Consider the equation from Example 2C:

$$x^2 - 2x - 1 = 0 \tag{3}$$

Since the left side does not factor using integer coefficients, we add 1 to each side to remove the constant term from the left side:

$$x^2 - 2x = 1 \tag{4}$$

Now we try to find a number that we can add to each side to make the left side a square of a first-degree polynomial. Note the following square of a binomial:

$$(x + m)^2 = x^2 + 2mx + m^2$$

We see that the third term on the right is the square of one-half the coefficient of x in the second term on the right. To complete the square in equation (4), we add the square of one-half the coefficient of x, $\left(-\frac{2}{2}\right)^2 = 1$, to each side. (This rule works only when the coefficient of x^2 is 1, that is, $a = 1$.) Thus,

$$x^2 - 2x + \mathbf{1} = 1 + \mathbf{1}$$

The left side is the square of $x - 1$, and we write

$$(x - 1)^2 = 2$$

What number squared is 2?

$$x - 1 = \pm\sqrt{2}$$
$$x = 1 \pm \sqrt{2}$$

And equation (3) is solved!

Let us try the method on the general quadratic equation

$$ax^2 + bx + c = 0 \qquad a \neq 0 \tag{5}$$

and solve it once and for all for x in terms of the coefficients a, b, and c. We start by multiplying both sides of equation (5) by $1/a$ to obtain

$$x^2 + \frac{b}{a}x + \frac{c}{a} = 0$$

Add $-c/a$ to both sides:

$$x^2 + \frac{b}{a}x = -\frac{c}{a}$$

Now we complete the square on the left side by adding the square of one-half the coefficient of x, that is, $(b/2a)^2 = b^2/4a^2$, to each side:

$$x^2 + \frac{b}{a}x + \frac{b^2}{4a^2} = \frac{b^2}{4a^2} - \frac{c}{a}$$

Writing the left side as a square and combining the right side into a single fraction, we obtain

$$\left(x + \frac{b}{2a}\right)^2 = \frac{b^2 - 4ac}{4a^2}$$

Now we solve by the square-root method:

$$x + \frac{b}{2a} = \pm\sqrt{\frac{b^2 - 4ac}{4a^2}}$$

$$x = -\frac{b}{2a} \pm \frac{\sqrt{b^2 - 4ac}}{2a} \qquad \text{Since } \pm\sqrt{4a^2} = \pm 2a \text{ for any real number } a$$

When this is written as a single fraction, it becomes the **quadratic formula**:

Quadratic Formula
If $ax^2 + bx + c = 0$, $a \neq 0$, then

$$x = \frac{-b \pm \sqrt{b^2 - 4ac}}{2a}$$

This formula is generally used to solve quadratic equations when the square-root or factoring methods do not work. The quantity $b^2 - 4ac$ under the radical is called the **discriminant**, and it gives us the useful information about solutions listed in Table 1.

Table 1	
$b^2 - 4ac$	$ax^2 + bx + c = 0$
Positive	Two real solutions
Zero	One real solution
Negative	No real solutions

EXAMPLE 3   **Quadratic Formula Method** Solve $x^2 - 2x - 1 = 0$ using the quadratic formula.

SOLUTION $x^2 - 2x - 1 = 0$

$$x = \frac{-b \pm \sqrt{b^2 - 4ac}}{2a} \qquad a = 1, b = -2, c = -1$$

$$= \frac{-(-2) \pm \sqrt{(-2)^2 - 4(1)(-1)}}{2(1)}$$

$$= \frac{2 \pm \sqrt{8}}{2} = \frac{2 \pm 2\sqrt{2}}{2} = 1 \pm \sqrt{2} \approx -0.414 \quad \text{or} \quad 2.414$$

CHECK $x^2 - 2x - 1 = 0$
When $x = 1 + \sqrt{2}$,

$$(1 + \sqrt{2})^2 - 2(1 + \sqrt{2}) - 1 = 1 + 2\sqrt{2} + 2 - 2 - 2\sqrt{2} - 1 = 0$$

When $x = 1 - \sqrt{2}$,

$$(1 - \sqrt{2})^2 - 2(1 - \sqrt{2}) - 1 = 1 - 2\sqrt{2} + 2 - 2 + 2\sqrt{2} - 1 = 0$$

Matched Problem 3   Solve $2x^2 - 4x - 3 = 0$ using the quadratic formula.

If we try to solve $x^2 - 6x + 11 = 0$ using the quadratic formula, we obtain

$$x = \frac{6 \pm \sqrt{-8}}{2}$$

which is not a real number. (Why?)

Quadratic Formula and Factoring

As in Section A-3, we restrict our interest in factoring to polynomials with integer coefficients. If a polynomial cannot be factored as a product of lower-degree polynomials with integer coefficients, we say that the polynomial is **not factorable in the integers**.

How can you factor the quadratic polynomial $x^2 - 13x - 2{,}310$? We start by solving the corresponding quadratic equation using the quadratic formula:

$$x^2 - 13x - 2{,}310 = 0$$

$$x = \frac{-(-13) \pm \sqrt{(-13)^2 - 4(1)(-2{,}310)}}{2}$$

$$x = \frac{-(-13) \pm \sqrt{9{,}409}}{2}$$

$$= \frac{13 \pm 97}{2} = 55 \quad \text{or} \quad -42$$

Now we write

$$x^2 - 13x - 2{,}310 = [x - 55][x - (-42)] = (x - 55)(x + 42)$$

Multiplying the two factors on the right produces the second-degree polynomial on the left.

What is behind this procedure? The following two theorems justify and generalize the process:

THEOREM 2   Factorability Theorem

A second-degree polynomial, $ax^2 + bx + c$, with integer coefficients can be expressed as the <u>product</u> of two first-degree polynomials with integer coefficients if and only if $\sqrt{b^2 - 4ac}$ is an integer.

THEOREM 3   Factor Theorem

If r_1 and r_2 are solutions to the second-degree equation $ax^2 + bx + c = 0$, then

$$ax^2 + bx + c = a(x - r_1)(x - r_2)$$

EXAMPLE 4   **Factoring with the Aid of the Discriminant** Factor, if possible, using integer coefficients.

(A) $4x^2 - 65x + 264$ 　　　　　　　　　 (B) $2x^2 - 33x - 306$

SOLUTION   (A) $4x^2 - 65x + 264$

Step 1 Test for factorability:

$$\sqrt{b^2 - 4ac} = \sqrt{(-65)^2 - 4(4)(264)} = 1$$

Since the result is an integer, the polynomial has first-degree factors with integer coefficients.

Step 2   Factor, using the factor theorem. Find the solutions to the corresponding quadratic equation using the quadratic formula:

$$4x^2 - 65x + 264 = 0 \quad \text{From step 1}$$

$$x = \frac{-(-65) \pm 1}{2 \cdot 4} = \frac{33}{4} \quad \text{or} \quad 8$$

Thus,

$$4x^2 - 65x + 264 = 4\left(x - \frac{33}{4}\right)(x - 8)$$
$$= (4x - 33)(x - 8)$$

(B) $2x^2 - 33x - 306$

Step 1   Test for factorability:

$$\sqrt{b^2 - 4ac} = \sqrt{(-33)^2 - 4(2)(-306)} = \sqrt{3{,}537}$$

Since $\sqrt{3{,}537}$ is not an integer, the polynomial is not factorable in the integers.

Matched Problem 4   Factor, if possible, using integer coefficients.

(A) $3x^2 - 28x - 464$ (B) $9x^2 + 320x - 144$

Application: Supply and Demand

Supply-and-demand analysis is a very important part of business and economics. In general, producers are willing to supply more of an item as the price of an item increases and less of an item as the price decreases. Similarly, buyers are willing to buy less of an item as the price increases, and more of an item as the price decreases. We have a dynamic situation where the price, supply, and demand fluctuate until a price is reached at which the supply is equal to the demand. In economic theory, this point is called the **equilibrium point**. If the price increases from this point, the supply will increase and the demand will decrease; if the price decreases from this point, the supply will decrease and the demand will increase.

EXAMPLE 5   **Supply and Demand**   At a large summer beach resort, the weekly supply-and-demand equations for folding beach chairs are

$$p = \frac{x}{140} + \frac{3}{4} \qquad \text{Supply equation}$$
$$p = \frac{5{,}670}{x} \qquad \text{Demand equation}$$

The supply equation indicates that the supplier is willing to sell x units at a price of p dollars per unit. The demand equation indicates that consumers are willing to buy x units at a price of p dollars per unit. How many units are required for supply to equal demand? At what price will supply equal demand?

SOLUTION   Set the right side of the supply equation equal to the right side of the demand equation and solve for x.

$$\frac{x}{140} + \frac{3}{4} = \frac{5{,}670}{x} \qquad \text{Multiply by 140x, the LCD.}$$
$$x^2 + 105x = 793{,}800 \qquad \text{Write in standard form.}$$
$$x^2 + 105x - 793{,}800 = 0 \qquad \text{Use the quadratic formula.}$$
$$x = \frac{-105 \pm \sqrt{105^2 - 4(1)(-793{,}800)}}{2}$$
$$x = 840 \text{ units}$$

The negative root is discarded since a negative number of units cannot be produced or sold. Substitute $x = 840$ back into either the supply equation or the demand equation to find the equilibrium price (we use the demand equation).

$$p = \frac{5{,}670}{x} = \frac{5{,}670}{840} = \$6.75$$

At a price of \$6.75 the supplier is willing to supply 840 chairs and consumers are willing to buy 840 chairs during a week.

Matched Problem 5   Repeat Example 5 if near the end of summer, the supply-and-demand equations are

$$p = \frac{x}{80} - \frac{1}{20} \qquad \text{Supply equation}$$
$$p = \frac{1{,}264}{x} \qquad \text{Demand equation}$$

Exercises A-7

Find only real solutions in the problems below. If there are no real solutions, say so.

A

Solve Problems 1–4 by the square-root method.

1. $2x^2 - 22 = 0$

2. $3m^2 - 21 = 0$

3. $(3x - 1)^2 = 25$

4. $(2x + 1)^2 = 16$

Solve Problems 5–8 by factoring.

5. $2u^2 - 8u - 24 = 0$

6. $3x^2 - 18x + 15 = 0$

7. $x^2 = 2x$

8. $n^2 = 3n$

Solve Problems 9–12 by using the quadratic formula.

9. $x^2 - 6x - 3 = 0$

10. $m^2 + 8m + 3 = 0$

11. $3u^2 + 12u + 6 = 0$

12. $2x^2 - 20x - 6 = 0$

B

Solve Problems 13–30 by using any method.

13. $\dfrac{2x^2}{3} = 5x$

14. $x^2 = -\dfrac{3}{4}x$

15. $4u^2 - 9 = 0$

16. $9y^2 - 25 = 0$

17. $8x^2 + 20x = 12$

18. $9x^2 - 6 = 15x$

19. $x^2 = 1 - x$

20. $m^2 = 1 - 3m$

21. $2x^2 = 6x - 3$

22. $2x^2 = 4x - 1$

23. $y^2 - 4y = -8$

24. $x^2 - 2x = -3$

25. $(2x + 3)^2 = 11$

26. $(5x - 2)^2 = 7$

27. $\dfrac{3}{p} = p$

28. $x - \dfrac{7}{x} = 0$

29. $2 - \dfrac{2}{m^2} = \dfrac{3}{m}$

30. $2 + \dfrac{5}{u} = \dfrac{3}{u^2}$

In Problems 31–38, factor, if possible, as the product of two first-degree polynomials with integer coefficients. Use the quadratic formula and the factor theorem.

31. $x^2 + 40x - 84$

32. $x^2 - 28x - 128$

33. $x^2 - 32x + 144$

34. $x^2 + 52x + 208$

35. $2x^2 + 15x - 108$

36. $3x^2 - 32x - 140$

37. $4x^2 + 241x - 434$

38. $6x^2 - 427x - 360$

C

39. Solve $A = P(1 + r)^2$ for r in terms of A and P; that is, isolate r on the left side of the equation (with coefficient 1) and end up with an algebraic expression on the right side involving A and P but not r. Write the answer using positive square roots only.

40. Solve $x^2 + 3mx - 3n = 0$ for x in terms of m and n.

41. Consider the quadratic equation

$$x^2 + 4x + c = 0$$

where c is a real number. Discuss the relationship between the values of c and the three types of roots listed in Table 1 on page 904.

42. Consider the quadratic equation

$$x^2 - 2x + c = 0$$

where c is a real number. Discuss the relationship between the values of c and the three types of roots listed in Table 1 on page 904.

Applications

43. Supply and demand. A company wholesales shampoo in a particular city. Their marketing research department established the following weekly supply-and-demand equations:

$$p = \frac{x}{450} + \frac{1}{2} \qquad \text{Supply equation}$$

$$p = \frac{6,300}{x} \qquad \text{Demand equation}$$

How many units are required for supply to equal demand? At what price per bottle will supply equal demand?

44. Supply and demand. An importer sells an automatic camera to outlets in a large city. During the summer, the weekly supply-and-demand equations are

$$p = \frac{x}{6} + 9 \qquad \text{Supply equation}$$

$$p = \frac{24,840}{x} \qquad \text{Demand equation}$$

How many units are required for supply to equal demand? At what price will supply equal demand?

45. Interest rate. If P dollars are invested at $100r$ percent compounded annually, at the end of 2 years it will grow to $A = P(1 + r)^2$. At what interest rate will $484 grow to $625 in 2 years? (*Note:* If $A = 625$ and $P = 484$ find r.)

46. Interest rate. Using the formula in Problem 45, determine the interest rate that will make $1,000 grow to $1,210 in 2 years.

47. Ecology. To measure the velocity v (in feet per second) of a stream, we position a hollow L-shaped tube with one end under the water pointing upstream and the other end pointing straight up a couple of feet out of the water. The water will then be pushed up the tube a certain distance h (in feet) above the surface of the stream. Physicists have shown that $v^2 = 64h$. Approximately how fast is a stream flowing if $h = 1$ foot? If $h = 0.5$ foot?

48. Safety research. It is of considerable importance to know the least number of feet d in which a car can be stopped, including reaction time of the driver, at various speeds v (in miles per hour). Safety research has produced the formula $d = 0.044v^2 + 1.1v$. If it took a car 550 feet to stop, estimate the car's speed at the moment the stopping process was started.

Answers to Matched Problems

1. (A) $\pm\sqrt{6}$ (B) ± 2

    (C) No real solution   (D) $-6, -4$

2. (A) $-5, 3$ (B) $0, \frac{3}{2}$

    (C) Cannot be factored using integer coefficients

3. $(2 \pm \sqrt{10})/2$

4. (A) Cannot be factored using integer coefficients

    (B) $(9x - 4)(x + 36)$

5. 320 chairs at $3.95 each

APPENDIX B Special Topics

B-1 Sequences, Series, and Summation Notation

- Sequences
- Series and Summation Notation

If someone asked you to list all natural numbers that are perfect squares, you might begin by writing

$$1, 4, 9, 16, 25, 36$$

But you would soon realize that it is impossible to actually list all the perfect squares, since there are an infinite number of them. However, you could represent this collection of numbers in several different ways. One common method is to write

$$1, 4, 9, \ldots, n^2, \ldots \quad n \in N$$

where N is the set of natural numbers. A list of numbers such as this is generally called a *sequence*.

Sequences

Consider the function f given by

$$f(n) = 2n + 1 \tag{1}$$

where the domain of f is the set of natural numbers N. Note that

$$f(1) = 3, \quad f(2) = 5, \quad f(3) = 7, \quad \ldots$$

The function f is an example of a sequence. In general, a **sequence** is a function with domain a set of successive integers. Instead of the standard function notation used in equation (1), sequences are usually defined in terms of a special notation.

The range value $f(n)$ is usually symbolized more compactly with a symbol such as a_n. Thus, in place of equation (1), we write

$$a_n = 2n + 1$$

and the domain is understood to be the set of natural numbers unless something is said to the contrary or the context indicates otherwise. The elements in the range are called **terms of the sequence**; a_1 is the first term, a_2 is the second term, and a_n is the **nth term**, or **general term**.

$$a_1 = 2(1) + 1 = 3 \qquad \text{First term}$$
$$a_2 = 2(2) + 1 = 5 \qquad \text{Second term}$$
$$a_3 = 2(3) + 1 = 7 \qquad \text{Third term}$$
$$\vdots$$
$$a_n = 2n + 1 \qquad \text{General term}$$

The ordered list of elements

$$3, 5, 7, \ldots, 2n + 1, \ldots$$

obtained by writing the terms of the sequence in their natural order with respect to the domain values is often informally referred to as a sequence. A sequence also may be represented in the abbreviated form $\{a_n\}$, where a symbol for the nth term is written within braces. For example, we could refer to the sequence $3, 5, 7, \ldots, 2n + 1, \ldots$ as the sequence $\{2n + 1\}$.

If the domain of a sequence is a finite set of successive integers, then the sequence is called a **finite sequence**. If the domain is an infinite set of successive integers, then the sequence is called an **infinite sequence.** The sequence $\{2n + 1\}$ discussed above is an infinite sequence.

EXAMPLE 1   **Writing the Terms of a Sequence** Write the first four terms of each sequence:

(A) $a_n = 3n - 2$ (B) $\left\{\dfrac{(-1)^n}{n}\right\}$

SOLUTION   (A) $1, 4, 7, 10$ (B) $-1, \dfrac{1}{2}, \dfrac{-1}{3}, \dfrac{1}{4}$

Matched Problem 1   Write the first four terms of each sequence:

(A) $a_n = -n + 3$ (B) $\left\{\dfrac{(-1)^n}{2^n}\right\}$

Now that we have seen how to use the general term to find the first few terms in a sequence, we consider the reverse problem. That is, can a sequence be defined just by listing the first three or four terms of the sequence? And can we then use these initial terms to find a formula for the nth term? In general, without other information, the answer to the first question is no. Many different sequences may start off with the same terms. Simply listing the first three terms (or any other finite number of terms) does not specify a particular sequence.

What about the second question? That is, given a few terms, can we find the general formula for at least one sequence whose first few terms agree with the given terms? The answer to this question is a qualified yes. If we can observe a simple pattern in the given terms, we usually can construct a general term that will produce that pattern. The next example illustrates this approach.

EXAMPLE 2   **Finding the General Term of a Sequence** Find the general term of a sequence whose first four terms are

(A) $3, 4, 5, 6, \ldots$ (B) $5, -25, 125, -625, \ldots$

SOLUTION   (A) Since these terms are consecutive integers, one solution is $a_n = n, n \geq 3$. If we want the domain of the sequence to be all natural numbers, another solution is $b_n = n + 2$.

(B) Each of these terms can be written as the product of a power of 5 and a power of -1:

$$5 = (-1)^0 5^1 = a_1$$
$$-25 = (-1)^1 5^2 = a_2$$
$$125 = (-1)^2 5^3 = a_3$$
$$-625 = (-1)^3 5^4 = a_4$$

If we choose the domain to be all natural numbers, a solution is

$$a_n = (-1)^{n-1} 5^n$$

Matched Problem 2   Find the general term of a sequence whose first four terms are

(A) $3, 6, 9, 12, \ldots$ (B) $1, -2, 4, -8, \ldots$

In general, there is usually more than one way of representing the nth term of a given sequence (see the solution of Example 2A). However, unless something is stated to the contrary, we assume that the domain of the sequence is the set of natural numbers N.

Series and Summation Notation

If $a_1, a_2, a_3, \ldots, a_n, \ldots$ is a sequence, the expression

$$a_1 + a_2 + a_3 + \cdots + a_n + \cdots$$

is called a **series**. If the sequence is finite, the corresponding series is a **finite series**. If the sequence is infinite, the corresponding series is an **infinite series**. We consider only finite series in this section. For example,

$$1, 3, 5, 7, 9 \qquad \textit{Finite sequence}$$
$$1 + 3 + 5 + 7 + 9 \qquad \textit{Finite series}$$

Notice that we can easily evaluate this series by adding the five terms:

$$1 + 3 + 5 + 7 + 9 = 25$$

Series are often represented in a compact form called **summation notation**. Consider the following examples:

$$\sum_{k=3}^{6} k^2 = 3^2 + 4^2 + 5^2 + 6^2$$

$$= 9 + 16 + 25 + 36 = 86$$

$$\sum_{k=0}^{2} (4k + 1) = (4 \cdot 0 + 1) + (4 \cdot 1 + 1) + (4 \cdot 2 + 1)$$

$$= 1 + 5 + 9 = 15$$

In each case, the terms of the series on the right are obtained from the expression on the left by successively replacing the **summing index k** with integers, starting with the number indicated below the **summation sign** Σ and ending with the number that appears above Σ. The summing index may be represented by letters other than k and may start at any integer and end at any integer greater than or equal to the starting integer. If we are given the finite sequence

$$\frac{1}{2}, \frac{1}{4}, \frac{1}{8}, \ldots, \frac{1}{2^n}$$

the corresponding series is

$$\frac{1}{2} + \frac{1}{4} + \frac{1}{8} + \cdots + \frac{1}{2^n} = \sum_{j=1}^{n} \frac{1}{2^j}$$

where we have used j for the summing index.

EXAMPLE 3   **Summation Notation**   Write

$$\sum_{k=1}^{5} \frac{k}{k^2 + 1}$$

without summation notation. Do not evaluate the sum.

SOLUTION $$\sum_{k=1}^{5} \frac{k}{k^2 + 1} = \frac{1}{1^2 + 1} + \frac{2}{2^2 + 1} + \frac{3}{3^2 + 1} + \frac{4}{4^2 + 1} + \frac{5}{5^2 + 1}$$

$$= \frac{1}{2} + \frac{2}{5} + \frac{3}{10} + \frac{4}{17} + \frac{5}{26}$$

Matched Problem 3   Write

$$\sum_{k=1}^{5} \frac{k + 1}{k}$$

without summation notation. Do not evaluate the sum.

If the terms of a series are alternately positive and negative, we call the series an **alternating series**. The next example deals with the representation of such a series.

EXAMPLE 4   **Summation Notation** Write the alternating series

$$\frac{1}{2} - \frac{1}{4} + \frac{1}{6} - \frac{1}{8} + \frac{1}{10} - \frac{1}{12}$$

using summation notation with

(A) The summing index k starting at 1

(B) The summing index j starting at 0

SOLUTION   (A) $(-1)^{k+1}$ provides the alternation of sign, and $1/(2k)$ provides the other part of each term. So, we can write

$$\frac{1}{2} - \frac{1}{4} + \frac{1}{6} - \frac{1}{8} + \frac{1}{10} - \frac{1}{12} = \sum_{k=1}^{6} \frac{(-1)^{k+1}}{2k}$$

(B) $(-1)^j$ provides the alternation of sign, and $1/[2(j+1)]$ provides the other part of each term. So, we can write

$$\frac{1}{2} - \frac{1}{4} + \frac{1}{6} - \frac{1}{8} + \frac{1}{10} - \frac{1}{12} = \sum_{j=0}^{5} \frac{(-1)^j}{2(j+1)}$$

Matched Problem 4   Write the alternating series

$$1 - \frac{1}{3} + \frac{1}{9} - \frac{1}{27} + \frac{1}{81}$$

using summation notation with

(A) The summing index k starting at 1

(B) The summing index j starting at 0

Summation notation provides a compact notation for the sum of any list of numbers, even if the numbers are not generated by a formula. For example, suppose that the results of an examination taken by a class of 10 students are given in the following list:

$$87, 77, 95, 83, 86, 73, 95, 68, 75, 86$$

If we let $a_1, a_2, a_3, \ldots, a_{10}$ represent these 10 scores, then the average test score is given by

$$\frac{1}{10} \sum_{k=1}^{10} a_k = \frac{1}{10}(87 + 77 + 95 + 83 + 86 + 73 + 95 + 68 + 75 + 86)$$

$$= \frac{1}{10}(825) = 82.5$$

More generally, in statistics, the **arithmetic mean** $\bar{a}$ of a list of n numbers $a_1, a_2, \ldots, a_n$ is defined as

$$\bar{a} = \frac{1}{n} \sum_{k=1}^{n} a_k$$

EXAMPLE 5   **Arithmetic Mean** Find the arithmetic mean of $3, 5, 4, 7, 4, 2, 3$, and 6.

SOLUTION $\bar{a} = \frac{1}{8} \sum_{k=1}^{8} a_k = \frac{1}{8}(3 + 5 + 4 + 7 + 4 + 2 + 3 + 6) = \frac{1}{8}(34) = 4.25$

Matched Problem 5   Find the arithmetic mean of $9, 3, 8, 4, 3$, and 6.

Exercises B-1

A

Write the first four terms for each sequence in Problems 1–6.

1. $a_n = 2n + 3$

2. $a_n = 4n - 3$

3. $a_n = \dfrac{n + 2}{n + 1}$

4. $a_n = \dfrac{2n + 1}{2n}$

5. $a_n = (-3)^{n+1}$

6. $a_n = \left(-\frac{1}{4}\right)^{n-1}$

7. Write the 10th term of the sequence in Problem 1.

8. Write the 15th term of the sequence in Problem 2.

9. Write the 99th term of the sequence in Problem 3.

10. Write the 200th term of the sequence in Problem 4.

In Problems 11–16, write each series in expanded form without summation notation, and evaluate.

11. $\displaystyle\sum_{k=1}^{6} k$

12. $\displaystyle\sum_{k=1}^{5} k^2$

13. $\displaystyle\sum_{k=4}^{7} (2k - 3)$

14. $\displaystyle\sum_{k=0}^{4} (-2)^k$

15. $\displaystyle\sum_{k=0}^{3} \dfrac{1}{10^k}$

16. $\displaystyle\sum_{k=1}^{4} \dfrac{1}{2^k}$

Find the arithmetic mean of each list of numbers in Problems 17–20.

17. $5, 4, 2, 1,$ and 6

18. $7, 9, 9, 2,$ and 4

19. $96, 65, 82, 74, 91, 88, 87, 91, 77,$ and 74

20. $100, 62, 95, 91, 82, 87, 70, 75, 87,$ and 82

B

Write the first five terms of each sequence in Problems 21–26.

21. $a_n = \dfrac{(-1)^{n+1}}{2^n}$

22. $a_n = (-1)^n (n - 1)^2$

23. $a_n = n[1 + (-1)^n]$

24. $a_n = \dfrac{1 - (-1)^n}{n}$

25. $a_n = \left(-\dfrac{3}{2}\right)^{n-1}$

26. $a_n = \left(-\dfrac{1}{2}\right)^{n+1}$

In Problems 27–42, find the general term of a sequence whose first four terms agree with the given terms.

27. $-2, -1, 0, 1, \ldots$

28. $4, 5, 6, 7, \ldots$

29. $4, 8, 12, 16, \ldots$

30. $-3, -6, -9, -12, \ldots$

31. $\frac{1}{2}, \frac{3}{4}, \frac{5}{6}, \frac{7}{8}, \ldots$

32. $\frac{1}{2}, \frac{2}{3}, \frac{3}{4}, \frac{4}{5}, \ldots$

33. $1, -2, 3, -4, \ldots$

34. $-2, 4, -8, 16, \ldots$

35. $1, -3, 5, -7, \ldots$

36. $3, -6, 9, -12, \ldots$

37. $1, \frac{2}{5}, \frac{4}{25}, \frac{8}{125}, \ldots$

38. $\frac{4}{3}, \frac{16}{9}, \frac{64}{27}, \frac{256}{81}, \ldots$

39. $x, x^2, x^3, x^4, \ldots$

40. $1, 2x, 3x^2, 4x^3, \ldots$

41. $x, -x^3, x^5, -x^7, \ldots$

42. $x, \dfrac{x^2}{2}, \dfrac{x^3}{3}, \dfrac{x^4}{4}, \ldots$

Write each series in Problems 43–50 in expanded form without summation notation. Do not evaluate.

43. $\displaystyle\sum_{k=1}^{5} (-1)^{k+1} (2k - 1)^2$

44. $\displaystyle\sum_{k=1}^{4} \dfrac{(-2)^{k+1}}{2k + 1}$

45. $\displaystyle\sum_{k=2}^{5} \dfrac{2^k}{2k + 3}$

46. $\displaystyle\sum_{k=3}^{7} \dfrac{(-1)^k}{k^2 - k}$

47. $\displaystyle\sum_{k=1}^{5} x^{k-1}$

48. $\displaystyle\sum_{k=1}^{3} \dfrac{1}{k} x^{k+1}$

49. $\displaystyle\sum_{k=0}^{4} \dfrac{(-1)^k x^{2k+1}}{2k + 1}$

50. $\displaystyle\sum_{k=0}^{4} \dfrac{(-1)^k x^{2k}}{2k + 2}$

Write each series in Problems 51–54 using summation notation with

(A) The summing index k starting at $k = 1$

(B) The summing index j starting at $j = 0$

51. $2 + 3 + 4 + 5 + 6$

52. $1^2 + 2^2 + 3^2 + 4^2$

53. $1 - \frac{1}{2} + \frac{1}{3} - \frac{1}{4}$

54. $1 - \frac{1}{3} + \frac{1}{5} - \frac{1}{7} + \frac{1}{9}$

Write each series in Problems 55–58 using summation notation with the summing index k starting at $k = 1$.

55. $2 + \dfrac{3}{2} + \dfrac{4}{3} + \cdots + \dfrac{n + 1}{n}$

56. $1 + \dfrac{1}{2^2} + \dfrac{1}{3^2} + \cdots + \dfrac{1}{n^2}$

57. $\dfrac{1}{2} - \dfrac{1}{4} + \dfrac{1}{8} - \cdots + \dfrac{(-1)^{n+1}}{2^n}$

58. $1 - 4 + 9 - \cdots + (-1)^{n+1} n^2$

C

In Problems 59–62, discuss the validity of each statement. If the statement is true, explain why. If not, give a counterexample.

59. For each positive integer n, the sum of the series
$1 + \dfrac{1}{2} + \dfrac{1}{3} + \cdots + \dfrac{1}{n}$ is less than 4.

60. For each positive integer n, the sum of the series
$\dfrac{1}{2} + \dfrac{1}{4} + \dfrac{1}{8} + \cdots + \dfrac{1}{2^n}$ is less than 1.

61. For each positive integer n, the sum of the series
$\dfrac{1}{2} - \dfrac{1}{4} + \dfrac{1}{8} - \cdots + \dfrac{(-1)^{n+1}}{2^n}$ is greater than or equal to $\dfrac{1}{4}$.

62. For each positive integer n, the sum of the series
$1 - \dfrac{1}{2} + \dfrac{1}{3} - \dfrac{1}{4} + \cdots + \dfrac{(-1)^{n+1}}{n}$ is greater than or equal to $\dfrac{1}{2}$.

Some sequences are defined by a **recursion formula**—*that is, a formula that defines each term of the sequence in terms of one or more of the preceding terms. For example, if $\{a_n\}$ is defined by*

$$a_1 = 1 \quad and \quad a_n = 2a_{n-1} + 1 \quad for\ n \geq 2$$

then

$$a_2 = 2a_1 + 1 = 2 \cdot 1 + 1 = 3$$
$$a_3 = 2a_2 + 1 = 2 \cdot 3 + 1 = 7$$
$$a_4 = 2a_3 + 1 = 2 \cdot 7 + 1 = 15$$

and so on. In Problems 63–66, write the first five terms of each sequence.

63. $a_1 = 2$ and $a_n = 3a_{n-1} + 2$ for $n \geq 2$

64. $a_1 = 3$ and $a_n = 2a_{n-1} - 2$ for $n \geq 2$

65. $a_1 = 1$ and $a_n = 2a_{n-1}$ for $n \geq 2$

66. $a_1 = 1$ and $a_n = -\frac{1}{3}a_{n-1}$ for $n \geq 2$

If A is a positive real number, the terms of the sequence defined by

$$a_1 = \frac{A}{2} \quad and \quad a_n = \frac{1}{2}\left(a_{n-1} + \frac{A}{a_{n-1}}\right) \quad for\ n \geq 2$$

can be used to approximate $\sqrt{A}$ to any decimal place accuracy desired. In Problems 67 and 68, compute the first four terms of this sequence for the indicated value of A, and compare the fourth term with the value of $\sqrt{A}$ obtained from a calculator.

67. $A = 2$ **68.** $A = 6$

69. The sequence defined recursively by $a_1 = 1$, $a_2 = 1$, $a_n = a_{n-1} + a_{n-2}$ for $n \geq 3$ is called the *Fibonacci sequence*. Find the first ten terms of the Fibonacci sequence.

70. The sequence defined by $b_n = \frac{\sqrt{5}}{5}\left(\frac{1 + \sqrt{5}}{2}\right)^n$ is related to the Fibonacci sequence. Find the first ten terms (to three decimal places) of the sequence $\{b_n\}$ and describe the relationship.

Answers to Matched Problems

1. (A) $2, 1, 0, -1$ (B) $\frac{-1}{2}, \frac{1}{4}, \frac{-1}{8}, \frac{1}{16}$

2. (A) $a_n = 3n$ (B) $a_n = (-2)^{n-1}$

3. $2 + \frac{3}{2} + \frac{4}{3} + \frac{5}{4} + \frac{6}{5}$

4. (A) $\sum_{k=1}^{5} \frac{(-1)^{k-1}}{3^{k-1}}$ (B) $\sum_{j=0}^{4} \frac{(-1)^j}{3^j}$

5. 5.5

B-2 Arithmetic and Geometric Sequences

- Arithmetic and Geometric Sequences
- *n*th-Term Formulas
- Sum Formulas for Finite Arithmetic Series
- Sum Formulas for Finite Geometric Series
- Sum Formula for Infinite Geometric Series
- Applications

For most sequences, it is difficult to sum an arbitrary number of terms of the sequence without adding term by term. But particular types of sequences—*arithmetic sequences* and *geometric sequences*—have certain properties that lead to convenient and useful formulas for the sums of the corresponding *arithmetic series* and *geometric series*.

Arithmetic and Geometric Sequences

The sequence $5, 7, 9, 11, 13, \ldots, 5 + 2(n - 1), \ldots$, where each term after the first is obtained by adding 2 to the preceding term, is an example of an arithmetic sequence. The sequence $5, 10, 20, 40, 80, \ldots, 5(2)^{n-1}, \ldots$, where each term after the first is obtained by multiplying the preceding term by 2, is an example of a geometric sequence.

DEFINITION Arithmetic Sequence

A sequence of numbers

$$a_1, a_2, a_3, \ldots, a_n, \ldots$$

is called an **arithmetic sequence** if there is a constant d, called the **common difference**, such that

$$a_n - a_{n-1} = d$$

That is,

$$a_n = a_{n-1} + d \quad \text{for every } n > 1$$

> **DEFINITION Geometric Sequence**
>
> A sequence of numbers
>
> $$a_1, a_2, a_3, \ldots, a_n, \ldots$$
>
> is called a **geometric sequence** if there exists a nonzero constant r, called a **common ratio**, such that
>
> $$\frac{a_n}{a_{n-1}} = r$$
>
> That is,
>
> $$a_n = r a_{n-1} \quad \text{for every } n > 1$$

EXAMPLE 1 **Recognizing Arithmetic and Geometric Sequences** Which of the following can be the first four terms of an arithmetic sequence? Of a geometric sequence?

(A) $1, 2, 3, 5, \ldots$ (B) $-1, 3, -9, 27, \ldots$

(C) $3, 3, 3, 3, \ldots$ (D) $10, 8.5, 7, 5.5, \ldots$

SOLUTION (A) Since $2 - 1 \neq 5 - 3$, there is no common difference, so the sequence is not an arithmetic sequence. Since $2/1 \neq 3/2$, there is no common ratio, so the sequence is not geometric either.

(B) The sequence is geometric with common ratio -3. It is not arithmetic.

(C) The sequence is arithmetic with common difference 0, and is also geometric with common ratio 1.

(D) The sequence is arithmetic with common difference -1.5. It is not geometric.

Matched Problem 1 Which of the following can be the first four terms of an arithmetic sequence? Of a geometric sequence?

(A) $8, 2, 0.5, 0.125, \ldots$ (B) $-7, -2, 3, 8, \ldots$ (C) $1, 5, 25, 100, \ldots$

nth-Term Formulas

If $\{a_n\}$ is an arithmetic sequence with common difference d, then

$$a_2 = a_1 + d$$
$$a_3 = a_2 + d = a_1 + 2d$$
$$a_4 = a_3 + d = a_1 + 3d$$

This suggests that

> **THEOREM 1** n**th Term of an Arithmetic Sequence**
>
> $$a_n = a_1 + (n - 1)d \qquad \text{for all } n > 1 \tag{1}$$

Similarly, if $\{a_n\}$ is a geometric sequence with common ratio r, then

$$a_2 = a_1 r$$
$$a_3 = a_2 r = a_1 r^2$$
$$a_4 = a_3 r = a_1 r^3$$

This suggests that

> **THEOREM 2** *n*th Term of a Geometric Sequence
>
> $$a_n = a_1 r^{n-1} \quad \text{for all } n > 1 \tag{2}$$

EXAMPLE 2 **Finding Terms in Arithmetic and Geometric Sequences**

(A) If the 1st and 10th terms of an arithmetic sequence are 3 and 30, respectively, find the 40th term of the sequence.

(B) If the 1st and 10th terms of a geometric sequence are 3 and 30, find the 40th term to three decimal places.

SOLUTION

(A) First use formula (1) with $a_1 = 3$ and $a_{10} = 30$ to find d:

$$a_n = a_1 + (n - 1)d$$
$$a_{10} = a_1 + (10 - 1)d$$
$$30 = 3 + 9d$$
$$d = 3$$

Now find a_{40}:

$$a_{40} = 3 + 39 \cdot 3 = 120$$

(B) First use formula (2) with $a_1 = 3$ and $a_{10} = 30$ to find r:

$$a_n = a_1 r^{n-1}$$
$$a_{10} = a_1 r^{10-1}$$
$$30 = 3r^9$$
$$r^9 = 10$$
$$r = 10^{1/9}$$

Now find a_{40}:

$$a_{40} = 3(10^{1/9})^{39} = 3(10^{39/9}) = 64{,}633.041$$

Matched Problem 2

(A) If the 1st and 15th terms of an arithmetic sequence are -5 and 23, respectively, find the 73rd term of the sequence.

(B) Find the 8th term of the geometric sequence

$$\frac{1}{64}, \frac{-1}{32}, \frac{1}{16}, \dots$$

Sum Formulas for Finite Arithmetic Series

If $a_1, a_2, a_3, \dots, a_n$ is a finite arithmetic sequence, then the corresponding series $a_1 + a_2 + a_3 + \cdots + a_n$ is called a *finite arithmetic series*. We will derive two simple and very useful formulas for the sum of a finite arithmetic series. Let d be the common difference of the arithmetic sequence $a_1, a_2, a_3, \dots, a_n$ and let S_n denote the sum of the series $a_1 + a_2 + a_3 + \cdots + a_n$. Then

$$S_n = a_1 + (a_1 + d) + \cdots + [a_1 + (n - 2)d] + [a_1 + (n - 1)d]$$

Reversing the order of the sum, we obtain

$$S_n = [a_1 + (n - 1)d] + [a_1 + (n - 2)d] + \cdots + (a_1 + d) + a_1$$

Something interesting happens if we combine these last two equations by addition (adding corresponding terms on the right sides):

$$2S_n = [2a_1 + (n - 1)d] + [2a_1 + (n - 1)d] + \cdots + [2a_1 + (n - 1)d] + [2a_1 + (n - 1)d]$$

All the terms on the right side are the same, and there are n of them. Thus,

$$2S_n = n[2a_1 + (n - 1)d]$$

and we have the following general formula:

THEOREM 3   Sum of a Finite Arithmetic Series: First Form

$$S_n = \frac{n}{2}[2a_1 + (n - 1)d] \tag{3}$$

Replacing

$$[a_1 + (n - 1)d] \quad \text{in} \quad \frac{n}{2}[a_1 + a_1 + (n - 1)d]$$

by a_n from equation (1), we obtain a second useful formula for the sum:

THEOREM 4   Sum of a Finite Arithmetic Series: Second Form

$$S_n = \frac{n}{2}(a_1 + a_n) \tag{4}$$

EXAMPLE 3   **Finding a Sum** Find the sum of the first 30 terms in the arithmetic sequence:

$$3, 8, 13, 18, \ldots$$

SOLUTION   Use formula (3) with $n = 30$, $a_1 = 3$, and $d = 5$:

$$S_{30} = \frac{30}{2}[2 \cdot 3 + (30 - 1)5] = 2{,}265$$

Matched Problem 3   Find the sum of the first 40 terms in the arithmetic sequence:

$$15, 13, 11, 9, \ldots$$

EXAMPLE 4   **Finding a Sum** Find the sum of all the even numbers between 31 and 87.

SOLUTION   First, find n using equation (1):

$$a_n = a_1 + (n - 1)d$$
$$86 = 32 + (n - 1)2$$
$$n = 28$$

Now find S_{28} using formula (4):

$$S_n = \frac{n}{2}(a_1 + a_n)$$

$$S_{28} = \frac{28}{2}(32 + 86) = 1{,}652$$

Matched Problem 4   Find the sum of all the odd numbers between 24 and 208.

Sum Formulas for Finite Geometric Series

If $a_1, a_2, a_3, \ldots, a_n$ is a finite geometric sequence, then the corresponding series $a_1 + a_2 + a_3 + \cdots + a_n$ is called a *finite geometric series.* As with arithmetic series, we can derive two simple and very useful formulas for the sum of a finite geometric series. Let r be the common ratio of the geometric sequence and let S_n denote the sum of the series $a_1 + a_2 + a_3 + \cdots + a_n$. Then

$$S_n = a_1 + a_1 r + a_1 r^2 + \cdots + a_1 r^{n-2} + a_1 r^{n-1}$$

If we multiply both sides by r, we obtain

$$rS_n = a_1 r + a_1 r^2 + a_1 r^3 + \cdots + a_1 r^{n-1} + a_1 r^n$$

Now combine these last two equations by subtraction to obtain

$$rS_n - S_n = (a_1 r + a_1 r^2 + a_1 r^3 + \cdots + a_1 r^{n-1} + a_1 r^n) - (a_1 + a_1 r + a_1 r^2 + \cdots + a_1 r^{n-2} + a_1 r^{n-1})$$
$$(r - 1)S_n = a_1 r^n - a_1$$

Notice how many terms drop out on the right side. Solving for S_n, we have

---

THEOREM 5   Sum of a Finite Geometric Series: First Form

$$S_n = \frac{a_1(r^n - 1)}{r - 1} \qquad r \neq 1 \tag{5}$$

Since $a_n = a_1 r^{n-1}$, or $ra_n = a_1 r^n$, formula (5) also can be written in the form

---

THEOREM 6   Sum of a Finite Geometric Series: Second Form

$$S_n = \frac{ra_n - a_1}{r - 1} \qquad r \neq 1 \tag{6}$$

EXAMPLE 5   **Finding a Sum** Find the sum (to 2 decimal places) of the first ten terms of the geometric sequence:

$$1, 1.05, 1.05^2, \ldots$$

SOLUTION   Use formula (5) with $a_1 = 1$, $r = 1.05$, and $n = 10$:

$$S_n = \frac{a_1(r^n - 1)}{r - 1}$$
$$S_{10} = \frac{1(1.05^{10} - 1)}{1.05 - 1}$$
$$\approx \frac{0.6289}{0.05} \approx 12.58$$

Matched Problem 5   Find the sum of the first eight terms of the geometric sequence:

$$100, 100(1.08), 100(1.08)^2, \ldots$$

Sum Formula for Infinite Geometric Series

Given a geometric series, what happens to the sum S_n of the first n terms as n increases without stopping? To answer this question, let us write formula (5) in the form

$$S_n = \frac{a_1 r^n}{r - 1} - \frac{a_1}{r - 1}$$

It is possible to show that if $-1 < r < 1$, then r^n will approach 0 as n increases. The first term above will approach 0 and S_n can be made as close as we please to the second term, $-a_1/(r - 1)$ [which can be written as $a_1/(1 - r)$], by taking n sufficiently large. So, if the common ratio r is between -1 and 1, we conclude that the sum of an infinite geometric series is

> **THEOREM 7 Sum of an Infinite Geometric Series**
> $$S_\infty = \frac{a_1}{1 - r} \qquad -1 < r < 1 \qquad\qquad (7)$$

If $r \le -1$ or $r \ge 1$, then an infinite geometric series has no sum.

Applications

EXAMPLE 6 **Loan Repayment** A person borrows $3,600 and agrees to repay the loan in monthly installments over 3 years. The agreement is to pay 1% of the unpaid balance each month for using the money and $100 each month to reduce the loan. What is the total cost of the loan over the 3 years?

SOLUTION Let us look at the problem relative to a time line:

The total cost of the loan is

$$1 + 2 + \cdots + 34 + 35 + 36$$

The terms form a finite arithmetic series with $n = 36$, $a_1 = 1$, and $a_{36} = 36$, so we can use formula (4):

$$S_n = \frac{n}{2}(a_1 + a_n)$$

$$S_{36} = \frac{36}{2}(1 + 36) = \$666$$

We conclude that the total cost of the loan over 3 years is $666.

Matched Problem 6 Repeat Example 6 with a loan of $6,000 over 5 years.

EXAMPLE 7 **Economy Stimulation** The government has decided on a tax rebate program to stimulate the economy. Suppose that you receive $1,200 and you spend 80% of this, and each of the people who receive what you spend also spend 80% of what they receive, and this process continues without end. According to the **multiplier principle** in economics, the effect of your $1,200 tax rebate on the economy is multiplied many times. What is the total amount spent if the process continues as indicated?

SOLUTION We need to find the sum of an infinite geometric series with the first amount spent being $a_1 = (0.8)(\$1,200) = \$960$ and $r = 0.8$. Using formula (7), we obtain

$$S_\infty = \frac{a_1}{1 - r}$$

$$= \frac{\$960}{1 - 0.8} = \$4,800$$

Assuming the process continues as indicated, we would expect the $1,200 tax rebate to result in about $4,800 of spending.

Matched Problem 7 Repeat Example 7 with a tax rebate of $2,000.

Exercises B-2

A

In Problems 1 and 2, determine whether the indicated sequence can be the first three terms of an arithmetic or geometric sequence, and, if so, find the common difference or common ratio and the next two terms of the sequence.

1. (A) $-11, -16, -21, \ldots$ (B) $2, -4, 8, \ldots$

    (C) $1, 4, 9, \ldots$ (D) $\frac{1}{2}, \frac{1}{6}, \frac{1}{18}, \ldots$

2. (A) $5, 20, 100, \ldots$ (B) $-5, -5, -5, \ldots$

    (C) $7, 6.5, 6, \ldots$ (D) $512, 256, 128, \ldots$

B

In Problems 3–8, determine whether the finite series is arithmetic, geometric, both, or neither. If the series is arithmetic or geometric, find its sum.

3. $\displaystyle\sum_{k=1}^{101} (-1)^{k+1}$ **4.** $\displaystyle\sum_{k=1}^{200} 3$

5. $1 + \dfrac{1}{2} + \dfrac{1}{3} + \cdots + \dfrac{1}{50}$

6. $3 - 9 + 27 - \cdots - 3^{20}$

7. $5 + 4.9 + 4.8 + \cdots + 0.1$

8. $1 - \dfrac{1}{4} + \dfrac{1}{9} - \cdots - \dfrac{1}{100^2}$

Let $a_1, a_2, a_3, \ldots, a_n, \ldots$ be an arithmetic sequence. In Problems 9–14, find the indicated quantities.

9. $a_1 = 7; d = 4; a_2 = ?; a_3 = ?$

10. $a_1 = -2; d = -3; a_2 = ?; a_3 = ?$

11. $a_1 = 2; d = 4; a_{21} = ?; S_{31} = ?$

12. $a_1 = 8; d = -10; a_{15} = ?; S_{23} = ?$

13. $a_1 = 18; a_{20} = 75; S_{20} = ?$

14. $a_1 = 203; a_{30} = 261; S_{30} = ?$

Let $a_1, a_2, a_3, \ldots, a_n, \ldots$ be a geometric sequence. In Problems 15–24, find the indicated quantities.

15. $a_1 = 3; r = -2; a_2 = ?; a_3 = ?; a_4 = ?$

16. $a_1 = 32; r = -\frac{1}{2}; a_2 = ?; a_3 = ?; a_4 = ?$

17. $a_1 = 1; a_7 = 729; r = -3; S_7 = ?$

18. $a_1 = 3; a_7 = 2{,}187; r = 3; S_7 = ?$

19. $a_1 = 100; r = 1.08; a_{10} = ?$

20. $a_1 = 240; r = 1.06; a_{12} = ?$

21. $a_1 = 100; a_9 = 200; r = ?$

22. $a_1 = 100; a_{10} = 300; r = ?$

23. $a_1 = 500; r = 0.6; S_{10} = ?; S_\infty = ?$

24. $a_1 = 8{,}000; r = 0.4; S_{10} = ?; S_\infty = ?$

25. $S_{41} = \displaystyle\sum_{k=1}^{41} (3k + 3) = ?$ **26.** $S_{50} = \displaystyle\sum_{k=1}^{50} (2k - 3) = ?$

27. $S_8 = \displaystyle\sum_{k=1}^{8} (-2)^{k-1} = ?$ **28.** $S_8 = \displaystyle\sum_{k=1}^{8} 2^k = ?$

29. Find the sum of all the odd integers between 12 and 68.

30. Find the sum of all the even integers between 23 and 97.

31. Find the sum of each infinite geometric sequence (if it exists).

    (A) $2, 4, 8, \ldots$ (B) $2, -\frac{1}{2}, \frac{1}{8}, \ldots$

32. Repeat Problem 31 for:

    (A) $16, 4, 1, \ldots$ (B) $1, -3, 9, \ldots$

C

33. Find $f(1) + f(2) + f(3) + \cdots + f(50)$ if $f(x) = 2x - 3$.

34. Find $g(1) + g(2) + g(3) + \cdots + g(100)$ if $g(t) = 18 - 3t$.

35. Find $f(1) + f(2) + \cdots + f(10)$ if $f(x) = \left(\frac{1}{2}\right)^x$.

36. Find $g(1) + g(2) + \cdots + g(10)$ if $g(x) = 2^x$.

37. Show that the sum of the first n odd positive integers is n^2, using appropriate formulas from this section.

38. Show that the sum of the first n even positive integers is $n + n^2$, using formulas in this section.

39. If $r = 1$, neither the first form nor the second form for the sum of a finite geometric series is valid. Find a formula for the sum of a finite geometric series if $r = 1$.

40. If all of the terms of an infinite geometric series are less than 1, could the sum be greater than 1,000? Explain.

41. Does there exist a finite arithmetic series with $a_1 = 1$ and $a_n = 1.1$ that has sum equal to 100? Explain.

42. Does there exist a finite arithmetic series with $a_1 = 1$ and $a_n = 1.1$ that has sum equal to 105? Explain.

43. Does there exist an infinite geometric series with $a_1 = 10$ that has sum equal to 6? Explain.

44. Does there exist an infinite geometric series with $a_1 = 10$ that has sum equal to 5? Explain.

Applications

45. Loan repayment. If you borrow \$4,800 and repay the loan by paying \$200 per month to reduce the loan and 1% of the unpaid balance each month for the use of the money, what is the total cost of the loan over 24 months?

46. Loan repayment. If you borrow \$5,400 and repay the loan by paying \$300 per month to reduce the loan and 1.5% of the unpaid balance each month for the use of the money, what is the total cost of the loan over 18 months?

47. Economy stimulation. The government, through a subsidy program, distributes \$5,000,000. If we assume that each person or agency spends 70% of what is received, and 70% of this is spent, and so on, how much total increase in spending results from this government action? (Let $a_1 = \$3,500,000$.)

48. Economy stimulation. Due to reduced taxes, a person has an extra $1,200 in spendable income. If we assume that the person spends 65% of this on consumer goods, and the producers of these goods in turn spend 65% on consumer goods, and that this process continues indefinitely, what is the total amount spent (to the nearest dollar) on consumer goods?

49. Compound interest. If $1,000 is invested at 5% compounded annually, the amount A present after n years forms a geometric sequence with common ratio $1 + 0.05 = 1.05$. Use a geometric sequence formula to find the amount A in the account (to the nearest cent) after 10 years. After 20 years. (*Hint*: Use a time line.)

50. Compound interest. If $\$P$ is invested at $100r\%$ compounded annually, the amount A present after n years forms a geometric sequence with common ratio $1 + r$. Write a

formula for the amount present after n years. (*Hint*: Use a time line.)

Answers to Matched Problems

1. (A) The sequence is geometric with $r = \frac{1}{4}$. It is not arithmetic.

  (B) The sequence is arithmetic with $d = 5$. It is not geometric.

  (C) The sequence is neither arithmetic nor geometric.

2. (A) 139 (B) -2

3. -960 **4.** 10,672

5. 1,063.66   **6.** $1,830

7. $8,000

B-3 Binomial Theorem

- Factorial
- Development of the Binomial Theorem

The binomial form

$$(a + b)^n$$

where n is a natural number, appears more frequently than you might expect. The coefficients in the expansion play an important role in probability studies. The *binomial formula*, which we will derive informally, enables us to expand $(a + b)^n$ directly for n any natural number. Since the formula involves *factorials*, we digress for a moment here to introduce this important concept.

Factorial

For n a natural number, *n factorial*, denoted by $n!$, is the product of the first n natural numbers. **Zero factorial** is defined to be 1. That is,

---

DEFINITION n Factorial

$$n! = n \cdot (n - 1) \cdot \cdots \cdot 2 \cdot 1$$
$$1! = 1$$
$$0! = 1$$

It is also useful to note that $n!$ can be defined recursively.

DEFINITION n Factorial—Recursive Definition
$$n! = n \cdot (n - 1)! \qquad n \geq 1$$

EXAMPLE 1 **Factorial Forms** Evaluate.

(A) $5! = 5 \cdot 4 \cdot 3 \cdot 2 \cdot 1 = 120$

(B) $\dfrac{8!}{7!} = \dfrac{8 \cdot 7!}{7!} = 8$

(C) $\dfrac{10!}{7!} = \dfrac{10 \cdot 9 \cdot 8 \cdot 7!}{7!} = 720$

Matched Problem 1   Evaluate.

(A) $4!$ (B) $\dfrac{7!}{6!}$ (C) $\dfrac{8!}{5!}$

The following formula involving factorials has applications in many areas of mathematics and statistics. We will use this formula to provide a more concise form for the expressions encountered later in this discussion.

THEOREM 1   **For n and r integers satisfying $0 \leq r \leq n$,**

$$C_{n,r} = \frac{n!}{r!(n-r)!}$$

EXAMPLE 2   Evaluating $C_{n,r}$

(A) $C_{9,2} = \dfrac{9!}{2!(9-2)!} = \dfrac{9!}{2!7!} = \dfrac{9 \cdot 8 \cdot 7!}{2 \cdot 7!} = 36$

(B) $C_{5,5} = \dfrac{5!}{5!(5-5)!} = \dfrac{5!}{5!0!} = \dfrac{5!}{5!} = 1$

Matched Problem 2   Find

(A) $C_{5,2}$ (B) $C_{6,0}$

Development of the Binomial Theorem

Let us expand $(a + b)^n$ for several values of n to see if we can observe a pattern that leads to a general formula for the expansion for any natural number n:

$$(a + b)^1 = a + b$$
$$(a + b)^2 = a^2 + 2ab + b^2$$
$$(a + b)^3 = a^3 + 3a^2b + 3ab^2 + b^3$$
$$(a + b)^4 = a^4 + 4a^3b + 6a^2b^2 + 4ab^3 + b^4$$
$$(a + b)^5 = a^5 + 5a^4b + 10a^3b^2 + 10a^2b^3 + 5ab^4 + b^5$$

CONCEPTUAL INSIGHT

1. The expansion of $(a + b)^n$ has $(n + 1)$ terms.
2. The power of a decreases by 1 for each term as we move from left to right.
3. The power of b increases by 1 for each term as we move from left to right.
4. In each term, the sum of the powers of a and b always equals n.
5. Starting with a given term, we can get the coefficient of the next term by multiplying the coefficient of the given term by the exponent of a and dividing by the number that represents the position of the term in the series of terms. For example, in the expansion of $(a + b)^4$ above, the coefficient of the third term is found from the second term by multiplying 4 and 3, and then dividing by 2 [that is, the coefficient of the third term $= (4 \cdot 3)/2 = 6$].

We now postulate these same properties for the general case:

$$(a + b)^n = a^n + \frac{n}{1}a^{n-1}b + \frac{n(n-1)}{1 \cdot 2}a^{n-2}b^2 + \frac{n(n-1)(n-2)}{1 \cdot 2 \cdot 3}a^{n-3}b^3 + \cdots + b^n$$

$$= \frac{n!}{0!(n-0)!}a^n + \frac{n!}{1!(n-1)!}a^{n-1}b + \frac{n!}{2!(n-2)!}a^{n-2}b^2 + \frac{n!}{3!(n-3)!}a^{n-3}b^3 + \cdots + \frac{n!}{n!(n-n)!}b^n$$

$$= C_{n,0}a^n + C_{n,1}a^{n-1}b + C_{n,2}a^{n-2}b^2 + C_{n,3}a^{n-3}b^3 + \cdots + C_{n,n}b^n$$

And we are led to the formula in the binomial theorem:

> **THEOREM 2 Binomial Theorem**
> For all natural numbers n,
> $$(a + b)^n = C_{n,0}a^n + C_{n,1}a^{n-1}b + C_{n,2}a^{n-2}b^2 + C_{n,3}a^{n-3}b^3 + \cdots + C_{n,n}b^n$$

EXAMPLE 3 **Using the Binomial Theorem** Use the binomial theorem to expand $(u + v)^6$.

SOLUTION
$$(u + v)^6 = C_{6,0}u^6 + C_{6,1}u^5v + C_{6,2}u^4v^2 + C_{6,3}u^3v^3 + C_{6,4}u^2v^4 + C_{6,5}uv^5 + C_{6,6}v^6$$
$$= u^6 + 6u^5v + 15u^4v^2 + 20u^3v^3 + 15u^2v^4 + 6uv^5 + v^6$$

Matched Problem 3 Use the binomial theorem to expand $(x + 2)^5$.

EXAMPLE 4 **Using the Binomial Theorem** Use the binomial theorem to find the sixth term in the expansion of $(x - 1)^{18}$.

SOLUTION $\text{Sixth term} = C_{18,5}x^{13}(-1)^5 = \dfrac{18!}{5!(18 - 5)!}x^{13}(-1)$
$$= -8,568x^{13}$$

Matched Problem 4 Use the binomial theorem to find the fourth term in the expansion of $(x - 2)^{20}$.

Exercises B-3

A

In Problems 1–20, evaluate each expression.

1. $6!$ **2.** $7!$ **3.** $\dfrac{10!}{9!}$

4. $\dfrac{20!}{19!}$ **5.** $\dfrac{12!}{9!}$ **6.** $\dfrac{10!}{6!}$

7. $\dfrac{5!}{2!3!}$ **8.** $\dfrac{7!}{3!4!}$ **9.** $\dfrac{6!}{5!(6-5)!}$

10. $\dfrac{7!}{4!(7-4)!}$ **11.** $\dfrac{20!}{3!17!}$ **12.** $\dfrac{52!}{50!2!}$

B

13. $C_{5,3}$ **14.** $C_{7,3}$ **15.** $C_{6,5}$ **16.** $C_{7,4}$

17. $C_{5,0}$ **18.** $C_{5,5}$ **19.** $C_{18,15}$ **20.** $C_{18,3}$

Expand each expression in Problems 21–26 using the binomial theorem.

21. $(a + b)^4$ **22.** $(m + n)^5$

23. $(x - 1)^6$ **24.** $(u - 2)^5$

25. $(2a - b)^5$ **26.** $(x - 2y)^5$

Find the indicated term in each expansion in Problems 27–32.

27. $(x - 1)^{18}$; 5th term **28.** $(x - 3)^{20}$; 3rd term

29. $(p + q)^{15}$; 7th term **30.** $(p + q)^{15}$; 13th term

31. $(2x + y)^{12}$; 11th term **32.** $(2x + y)^{12}$; 3rd term

C

33. Show that $C_{n,0} = C_{n,n}$ for $n \geq 0$.

34. Show that $C_{n,r} = C_{n,n-r}$ for $n \geq r \geq 0$.

35. The triangle next is called **Pascal's triangle**. Can you guess what the next two rows at the bottom are? Compare these numbers with the coefficients of binomial expansions.

$$
\begin{array}{ccccccccc}
 & & & & 1 & & & & \\
 & & & 1 & & 1 & & & \\
 & & 1 & & 2 & & 1 & & \\
 & 1 & & 3 & & 3 & & 1 & \\
1 & & 4 & & 6 & & 4 & & 1 \\
\end{array}
$$

36. Explain why the sum of the entries in each row of Pascal's triangle is a power of 2. (*Hint:* Let $a = b = 1$ in the binomial theorem.)

37. Explain why the alternating sum of the entries in each row of Pascal's triangle (e.g., $1 - 4 + 6 - 4 + 1$) is equal to 0.

38. Show that $C_{n,r} = \dfrac{n - r + 1}{r}C_{n,r-1}$ for $n \geq r \geq 1$.

39. Show that $C_{n,r-1} + C_{n,r} = C_{n+1,r}$ for $n \geq r \geq 1$.

Answers to Matched Problems

1. (A) 24 (B) 7 (C) 336

2. (A) 10 (B) 1

3. $x^5 + 10x^4 + 40x^3 + 80x^2 + 80x + 32$

4. $-9,120x^{17}$

APPENDIX C Tables

Table I Basic Geometric Formulas

1. **Similar Triangles**

   (A) Two triangles are similar if two angles of one triangle have the same measure as two angles of the other.

   (B) If two triangles are similar, their corresponding sides are proportional:

   $$\frac{a}{a'} = \frac{b}{b'} = \frac{c}{c'}$$

2. **Pythagorean Theorem**

   $$c^2 = a^2 + b^2$$

3. **Rectangle**

   $A = ab$ Area

   $P = 2a + 2b$ Perimeter

4. **Parallelogram**

   h = height

   $A = ah = ab \sin\theta$ Area

   $P = 2a + 2b$ Perimeter

5. **Triangle**

   h = height

   $A = \frac{1}{2}hc$ Area

   $P = a + b + c$ Perimeter

   $s = \frac{1}{2}(a + b + c)$ Semiperimeter

   $A = \sqrt{s(s - a)(s - b)(s - c)}$ Area: Heron's formula

6. **Trapezoid**

   Base a is parallel to base b.

   h = height

   $A = \frac{1}{2}(a + b)h$ Area

7. **Circle**

   R = radius

   D = diameter

   $D = 2R$

   $A = \pi R^2 = \frac{1}{4}\pi D^2$ Area

   $C = 2\pi R = \pi D$ Circumference

   $\dfrac{C}{D} = \pi$ For all circles

   $\pi \approx 3.14159$

8. **Rectangular Solid**

   $V = abc$ Volume

   $T = 2ab + 2ac + 2bc$ Total surface area

Table I   (continued)

9. Right Circular Cylinder

R = radius of base

h = height

$V = \pi R^2 h$ Volume

$S = 2\pi R h$ Lateral surface area

$T = 2\pi R(R + h)$ Total surface area

10. Right Circular Cone

R = radius of base

h = height

s = slant height

$V = \frac{1}{3}\pi R^2 h$ Volume

$S = \pi R s = \pi R\sqrt{R^2 + h^2}$ Lateral surface area

$T = \pi R(R + s) = \pi R(R + \sqrt{R^2 + h^2})$ Total surface area

11. Sphere

R = radius

D = diameter

$D = 2R$

$V = \frac{4}{3}\pi R^3 = \frac{1}{6}\pi D^3$ Volume

$S = 4\pi R^2 = \pi D^2$ Surface area

Table II Integration Formulas

[*Note:* The constant of integration is omitted for each integral, but must be included in any particular application of a formula. The variable u is the variable of integration; all other symbols represent constants.]

Integrals Involving u^n

1. $\int u^n \, du = \dfrac{u^{n+1}}{n+1}, \quad n \neq -1$

2. $\int u^{-1} \, du = \int \dfrac{1}{u} \, du = \ln|u|$

Integrals Involving $a + bu, a \neq 0$ and $b \neq 0$

3. $\int \dfrac{1}{a+bu} \, du = \dfrac{1}{b} \ln|a+bu|$

4. $\int \dfrac{u}{a+bu} \, du = \dfrac{u}{b} - \dfrac{a}{b^2} \ln|a+bu|$

5. $\int \dfrac{u^2}{a+bu} \, du = \dfrac{(a+bu)^2}{2b^3} - \dfrac{2a(a+bu)}{b^3} + \dfrac{a^2}{b^3} \ln|a+bu|$

6. $\int \dfrac{u}{(a+bu)^2} \, du = \dfrac{1}{b^2} \left(\ln|a+bu| + \dfrac{a}{a+bu} \right)$

7. $\int \dfrac{u^2}{(a+bu)^2} \, du = \dfrac{(a+bu)}{b^3} - \dfrac{a^2}{b^3(a+bu)} - \dfrac{2a}{b^3} \ln|a+bu|$

8. $\int u(a+bu)^n \, du = \dfrac{(a+bu)^{n+2}}{(n+2)b^2} - \dfrac{a(a+bu)^{n+1}}{(n+1)b^2}, \quad n \neq -1, -2$

9. $\int \dfrac{1}{u(a+bu)} \, du = \dfrac{1}{a} \ln \left| \dfrac{u}{a+bu} \right|$

10. $\int \dfrac{1}{u^2(a+bu)} \, du = -\dfrac{1}{au} + \dfrac{b}{a^2} \ln \left| \dfrac{a+bu}{u} \right|$

11. $\int \dfrac{1}{u(a+bu)^2} \, du = \dfrac{1}{a(a+bu)} + \dfrac{1}{a^2} \ln \left| \dfrac{u}{a+bu} \right|$

12. $\int \dfrac{1}{u^2(a+bu)^2} \, du = -\dfrac{a+2bu}{a^2u(a+bu)} + \dfrac{2b}{a^3} \ln \left| \dfrac{a+bu}{u} \right|$

Integrals Involving $a^2 - u^2, a > 0$

13. $\int \dfrac{1}{u^2-a^2} \, du = \dfrac{1}{2a} \ln \left| \dfrac{u-a}{u+a} \right|$

14. $\int \dfrac{1}{a^2-u^2} \, du = \dfrac{1}{2a} \ln \left| \dfrac{u+a}{u-a} \right|$

Integrals Involving $(a + bu)$ and $(c + du), b \neq 0, d \neq 0,$ and $ad - bc \neq 0$

15. $\int \dfrac{1}{(a+bu)(c+du)} \, du = \dfrac{1}{ad-bc} \ln \left| \dfrac{c+du}{a+bu} \right|$

16. $\int \dfrac{u}{(a+bu)(c+du)} \, du = \dfrac{1}{ad-bc} \left(\dfrac{a}{b} \ln|a+bu| - \dfrac{c}{d} \ln|c+du| \right)$

17. $\int \dfrac{u^2}{(a+bu)(c+du)} \, du = \dfrac{1}{bd}u - \dfrac{1}{ad-bc} \left(\dfrac{a^2}{b^2} \ln|a+bu| - \dfrac{c^2}{d^2} \ln|c+du| \right)$

18. $\int \dfrac{1}{(a+bu)^2(c+du)} \, du = \dfrac{1}{ad-bc} \dfrac{1}{a+bu} + \dfrac{d}{(ad-bc)^2} \ln \left| \dfrac{c+du}{a+bu} \right|$

19. $\int \dfrac{u}{(a+bu)^2(c+du)} \, du = -\dfrac{a}{b(ad-bc)} \dfrac{1}{a+bu} - \dfrac{c}{(ad-bc)^2} \ln \left| \dfrac{c+du}{a+bu} \right|$

20. $\int \dfrac{a+bu}{c+du} \, du = \dfrac{bu}{d} + \dfrac{ad-bc}{d^2} \ln|c+du|$

Table II   (continued)

Integrals Involving $\sqrt{a + bu}, a \neq 0$ and $b \neq 0$

21. $\displaystyle\int \sqrt{a + bu}\, du = \frac{2\sqrt{(a + bu)^3}}{3b}$

22. $\displaystyle\int u\sqrt{a + bu}\, du = \frac{2(3bu - 2a)}{15b^2}\sqrt{(a + bu)^3}$

23. $\displaystyle\int u^2\sqrt{a + bu}\, du = \frac{2(15b^2u^2 - 12abu + 8a^2)}{105b^3}\sqrt{(a + bu)^3}$

24. $\displaystyle\int \frac{1}{\sqrt{a + bu}}\, du = \frac{2\sqrt{a + bu}}{b}$

25. $\displaystyle\int \frac{u}{\sqrt{a + bu}}\, du = \frac{2(bu - 2a)}{3b^2}\sqrt{a + bu}$

26. $\displaystyle\int \frac{u^2}{\sqrt{a + bu}}\, du = \frac{2(3b^2u^2 - 4abu + 8a^2)}{15b^3}\sqrt{a + bu}$

27. $\displaystyle\int \frac{1}{u\sqrt{a + bu}}\, du = \frac{1}{\sqrt{a}}\ln\left|\frac{\sqrt{a + bu} - \sqrt{a}}{\sqrt{a + bu} + \sqrt{a}}\right|, \quad a > 0$

28. $\displaystyle\int \frac{1}{u^2\sqrt{a + bu}}\, du = -\frac{\sqrt{a + bu}}{au} - \frac{b}{2a\sqrt{a}}\ln\left|\frac{\sqrt{a + bu} - \sqrt{a}}{\sqrt{a + bu} + \sqrt{a}}\right|, \quad a > 0$

Integrals Involving $\sqrt{a^2 - u^2}, a > 0$

29. $\displaystyle\int \frac{1}{u\sqrt{a^2 - u^2}}\, du = -\frac{1}{a}\ln\left|\frac{a + \sqrt{a^2 - u^2}}{u}\right|$

30. $\displaystyle\int \frac{1}{u^2\sqrt{a^2 - u^2}}\, du = -\frac{\sqrt{a^2 - u^2}}{a^2 u}$

31. $\displaystyle\int \frac{\sqrt{a^2 - u^2}}{u}\, du = \sqrt{a^2 - u^2} - a\ln\left|\frac{a + \sqrt{a^2 - u^2}}{u}\right|$

Integrals Involving $\sqrt{u^2 + a^2}, a > 0$

32. $\displaystyle\int \sqrt{u^2 + a^2}\, du = \frac{1}{2}\left(u\sqrt{u^2 + a^2} + a^2\ln|u + \sqrt{u^2 + a^2}|\right)$

33. $\displaystyle\int u^2\sqrt{u^2 + a^2}\, du = \frac{1}{8}\left[u(2u^2 + a^2)\sqrt{u^2 + a^2} - a^4\ln|u + \sqrt{u^2 + a^2}|\right]$

34. $\displaystyle\int \frac{\sqrt{u^2 + a^2}}{u}\, du = \sqrt{u^2 + a^2} - a\ln\left|\frac{a + \sqrt{u^2 + a^2}}{u}\right|$

35. $\displaystyle\int \frac{\sqrt{u^2 + a^2}}{u^2}\, du = -\frac{\sqrt{u^2 + a^2}}{u} + \ln|u + \sqrt{u^2 + a^2}|$

36. $\displaystyle\int \frac{1}{\sqrt{u^2 + a^2}}\, du = \ln|u + \sqrt{u^2 + a^2}|$

37. $\displaystyle\int \frac{1}{u\sqrt{u^2 + a^2}}\, du = \frac{1}{a}\ln\left|\frac{u}{a + \sqrt{u^2 + a^2}}\right|$

38. $\displaystyle\int \frac{u^2}{\sqrt{u^2 + a^2}}\, du = \frac{1}{2}\left(u\sqrt{u^2 + a^2} - a^2\ln|u + \sqrt{u^2 + a^2}|\right)$

39. $\displaystyle\int \frac{1}{u^2\sqrt{u^2 + a^2}}\, du = -\frac{\sqrt{u^2 + a^2}}{a^2 u}$

(continued)

Table II (continued)

Integrals Involving $\sqrt{u^2 - a^2}, a > 0$

40. $\displaystyle\int \sqrt{u^2 - a^2}\, du = \frac{1}{2}(u\sqrt{u^2 - a^2} - a^2 \ln|u + \sqrt{u^2 - a^2}|)$

41. $\displaystyle\int u^2\sqrt{u^2 - a^2}\, du = \frac{1}{8}[u(2u^2 - a^2)\sqrt{u^2 - a^2} - a^4 \ln|u + \sqrt{u^2 - a^2}|]$

42. $\displaystyle\int \frac{\sqrt{u^2 - a^2}}{u^2}\, du = -\frac{\sqrt{u^2 - a^2}}{u} + \ln|u + \sqrt{u^2 - a^2}|$

43. $\displaystyle\int \frac{1}{\sqrt{u^2 - a^2}}\, du = \ln|u + \sqrt{u^2 - a^2}|$

44. $\displaystyle\int \frac{u^2}{\sqrt{u^2 - a^2}}\, du = \frac{1}{2}(u\sqrt{u^2 - a^2} + a^2 \ln|u + \sqrt{u^2 - a^2}|)$

45. $\displaystyle\int \frac{1}{u^2\sqrt{u^2 - a^2}}\, du = \frac{\sqrt{u^2 - a^2}}{a^2 u}$

Integrals Involving $e^{au}, a \neq 0$

46. $\displaystyle\int e^{au}\, du = \frac{e^{au}}{a}$

47. $\displaystyle\int u^n e^{au}\, du = \frac{u^n e^{au}}{a} - \frac{n}{a}\int u^{n-1} e^{au}\, du$

48. $\displaystyle\int \frac{1}{c + d e^{au}}\, du = \frac{u}{c} - \frac{1}{ac}\ln|c + d e^{au}|, \quad c \neq 0$

Integrals Involving $\ln u$

49. $\displaystyle\int \ln u\, du = u \ln u - u$

50. $\displaystyle\int \frac{\ln u}{u}\, du = \frac{1}{2}(\ln u)^2$

51. $\displaystyle\int u^n \ln u\, du = \frac{u^{n+1}}{n+1}\ln u - \frac{u^{n+1}}{(n+1)^2}, \quad n \neq -1$

52. $\displaystyle\int (\ln u)^n\, du = u(\ln u)^n - n\int (\ln u)^{n-1}\, du$

Integrals Involving Trigonometric Functions of $au, a \neq 0$

53. $\displaystyle\int \sin au\, du = -\frac{1}{a}\cos au$

54. $\displaystyle\int \cos au\, du = \frac{1}{a}\sin au$

55. $\displaystyle\int \tan au\, du = -\frac{1}{a}\ln|\cos au|$

56. $\displaystyle\int \cot au\, du = \frac{1}{a}\ln|\sin au|$

57. $\displaystyle\int \sec au\, du = \frac{1}{a}\ln|\sec au + \tan au|$

58. $\displaystyle\int \csc au\, du = \frac{1}{a}\ln|\csc au - \cot au|$

59. $\displaystyle\int (\sin au)^2\, du = \frac{u}{2} - \frac{1}{4a}\sin 2au$

60. $\displaystyle\int (\cos au)^2\, du = \frac{u}{2} + \frac{1}{4a}\sin 2au$

61. $\displaystyle\int (\sin au)^n\, du = -\frac{1}{an}(\sin au)^{n-1}\cos au + \frac{n-1}{n}\int (\sin au)^{n-2}\, du, \quad n \neq 0$

62. $\displaystyle\int (\cos au)^n\, du = \frac{1}{an}\sin au(\cos au)^{n-1} + \frac{n-1}{n}\int (\cos au)^{n-2}\, du, \quad n \neq 0$

ANSWERS

Diagnostic Algebra Test

1. (A) $(y + z)x$ (B) $(2 + x) + y$ (C) $2x + 3x$ *(A-1)*   **2.** $x^3 - 3x^2 + 4x + 8$ *(A-2)*   **3.** $x^3 + 3x^2 - 2x + 12$ *(A-2)*

4. $-3x^5 + 2x^3 - 24x^2 + 16$ *(A-2)*   **5.** (A) 1   (B) 1   (C) 2   (D) 3 *(A-2)*   **6.** (A) 3   (B) 1   (C) -3 (D) 1 *(A-2)*

7. $14x^2 - 30x$ *(A-2)*   **8.** $6x^2 - 5xy - 4y^2$ *(A-2)*   **9.** $4a^2 - 12ab + 9b^2$ *(A-2)*   **10.** $4xy - 2y^2$ *(A-2)*

11. $9x^6 - 12x^3y + 4y^2$ *(A-2)*   **12.** $x^3 - 6x^2y + 12xy^2 - 8y^3$ *(A-2)*   **13.** (A) 4.065×10^{12} (B) 7.3×10^{-3} *(A-5)*

14. (A) 255,000,000   (B) 0.000 406 *(A-5)*   **15.** (A) T   (B) F *(A-1)*   **16.** 0 and -3 are two examples of infinitely many. *(A-1)*

17. $6x^5y^{15}$ *(A-5)*   **18.** $3u^4/v^2$ *(A-5)*   **19.** 6×10^2 *(A-5)*   **20.** x^6/y^4 *(A-5)*   **21.** $u^{7/3}$ *(A-6)*   **22.** $3a^2/b$ *(A-6)*   **23.** $\frac{5}{9}$ *(A-5)*

24. $x + 2x^{1/2}y^{1/2} + y$ *(A-6)*   **25.** $6x + 7x^{1/2}y^{1/2} - 3y$ *(A-6)*   **26.** $(3x - 1)(4x + 3)$ *(A-3)*   **27.** $(4x - 3y)(2x - 3y)$ *(A-3)*

28. Not factorable relative to the integers *(A-3)*   **29.** $3n(2n - 5)(n + 1)$ *(A-3)*   **30.** $(x - y)(7x - y)$ *(A-3)*

31. $3x(2x + 1)(2 - x)$ *(A-3)*   **32.** $\dfrac{12a^3b - 40b^2 - 5a}{30a^3b^2}$ *(A-4)*   **33.** $\dfrac{7x - 4}{6x(x - 4)}$ *(A-4)*   **34.** $\dfrac{-8(x + 2)}{x(x - 4)(x + 4)}$ *(A-4)*

35. $2x + y$ *(A-4)*   **36.** $\dfrac{-1}{7(7 + h)}$ *(A-4)*   **37.** $\dfrac{xy}{y - x}$ *(A-6)*

38. (A) Subtraction   (B) Commutative (+)   (C) Distributive   (D) Associative ($\cdot$)   (E) Negatives   (F) Identity (+) *(A-1)*

39. $6x^{2/5} - 7(x - 1)^{3/4}$ *(A-6)*   **40.** $2\sqrt{x} - 3\sqrt[3]{x^2}$ *(A-6)*   **41.** $2 - \frac{3}{2}x^{-1/2}$ *(A-6)*   **42.** $\sqrt{3x}$ *(A-6)*   **43.** $\sqrt{x} + \sqrt{5}$ *(A-6)*

44. $\dfrac{1}{\sqrt{x - 5}}$ *(A-6)*   **45.** $\dfrac{1}{\sqrt{u + h} + \sqrt{u}}$ **46.** $x = 0, 5$ *(A-7)*   **47.** $x = \pm\sqrt{7}$ *(A-7)*   **48.** $x = -4, 5$ *(A-7)*   **49.** $x = 1, \frac{1}{6}$ *(A-7)*

Chapter 1

Exercises 1–1

1. $m = 5$ **3.** $x < -\dfrac{7}{2}$ **5.** $x \leq 4$ **7.** $x < -3$ or $(-\infty, -3)$ **9.** $-1 \leq x \leq 2$

or $[-1, 2]$ **11.** $x = -\dfrac{3}{2}$ **13.** $y < -\dfrac{15}{2}$ **15.** $u = -\dfrac{3}{4}$ **17.** $x = 10$ **19.** $y \geq 3$ **21.** $x = 36$

23. $m < \dfrac{36}{7}$ **25.** $3 \leq x < 7$ or $[3, 7)$ **27.** $-20 \leq C \leq 20$ or $[-20, 20]$

29. $y = \dfrac{3}{4}x - 3$ **31.** $y = -(A/B)x + (C/B) = (-Ax + C)/B$ **33.** $C = \dfrac{5}{9}(F - 32)$

35. $-2 < x \leq 1$ or $(-2, 1]$ **37.** (A) and (C): $a > 0$ and $b > 0$, or $a < 0$ and $b < 0$ (B) and (D): $a > 0$

and $b < 0$, or $a < 0$ and $b > 0$ **39.** Negative   **41.** True   **43.** False   **45.** True   **47.** 4,500 \$35 tickets and 5,000 \$55 tickets
49. \$180,000 in Fund A and \$320,000 in Fund B   **51.** \$14,943   **53.** (A) \$420   (B) \$55   **55.** 34 rounds   **57.** \$32,000   **59.** 5,851
books   **61.** (B) 6,180 books   (C) At least \$11.50   **63.** 5,000   **65.** 12.6 yr   **67.** 66.7% to 100%

Exercises 1–2

1. (D)   **3.** (C)   **5.**

7.

9. Slope $= 5$; y intercept $= -7$ **11.** Slope $= -\dfrac{5}{2}$; y intercept $= -9$ **13.** Slope $= \dfrac{1}{4}$; y intercept $= \dfrac{2}{3}$ **15.** $y = 2x + 1$

17. $y = -\dfrac{1}{3}x + 6$ **19.** x intercept: -1; y intercept: -2; $y = -2x - 2$ **21.** x intercept: -3; y intercept: 1; $y = x/3 + 1$

23.

25.

27.

29. -4 **31.** $-\dfrac{3}{5}$ **33.** 2

35.

37.

39.

(B) x intercept: 3.5; y intercept: -4.2

(C)

(D) x intercept: 3.5; y intercept: -4.2

41. $x = 4, y = -3$ **43.** $x = -1.5, y = -3.5$ **45.** $y = -4x + 5$

47. $y = \dfrac{3}{2}x + 1$ **49.** $y = 4.6$ **51.** (A) $m = \dfrac{2}{3}$ (B) $-2x + 3y = 11$ (C) $y = \dfrac{2}{3}x + \dfrac{11}{3}$ **53.** (A) $m = -\dfrac{5}{4}$

(B) $5x + 4y = -14$ (C) $y = -\dfrac{5}{4}x - \dfrac{7}{2}$ **55.** (A) Not defined   (B) $x = 5$ (C) None   **57.** (A) $m = 0$ (B) $y = 5$ (C) $y = 5$

59. The graphs have the same
y intercept, $(0, 2)$.

61. $C = 124 + 0.12x$; 1,050 donuts

63. (A) $C = 75x + 1,647$

(B)

(C) The y intercept, \$1,647, is the
fixed cost and the slope, \$75, is
the cost per club.

65. (A) $R = 1.4C - 7$
(B) \$137

67. (A) $V = -7,500t + 157,000$
(B) \$112,000
(C) During the 12th year
(D)

69. (A) $T = -1.84x + 212$
(B) $205.56°F$
(C) 6,522 ft
(D)

71. (A) $T = 70 - 3.6A$
(B) 10,000 ft

73. (A) $N = -0.0075t + 2.76$
(B) 2.46 persons

75. (A) $f = -0.5t + 21$
(B) 2022

77. (A) $p = 0.000225x + 0.5925$
(B) $p = -0.0009x + 9.39$
(C) $(7,820, 2.352)$
(D)

79. (A) $s = \dfrac{2}{5}w$
(B) 8 in
(C) 9 lb

81. (A) $y = 0.5x + 9$
(B) $y = 0.3x + 9$
(C)

(D) A: 39%; B: 27%

Exercises 1–3

1. (A) $w = 49 + 1.7h$ (B) The rate of change of weight with respect to height is 1.7 kg/in.   (C) 55.8 kg   (D) 5′6.5″
3. (A) $p = 0.44\overline{5}d + 14.7$ (B) The rate of change of pressure with respect to depth is $0.44\overline{5}$ lb/in.² per foot.   (C) 37 lb/in.²
(D) 99 ft   **5.** (A) $a = 2,880 - 24t$ (B) -24 ft/sec   (C) 24 ft/sec   **7.** $s = 0.6t + 331$; the rate of change of the speed of sound with
respect to temperature is 0.6 m/s per °C.

9. (A)

(B) The rate of change of fossil fuel production is -0.3% per year.
(C) 74.1% of total production
(D) 2034

11. (A)

(B) 2023

13. (A)

(B) 16,200,000
(C) Undergraduate enrollment is increasing at a rate of 170,000 students per year.

15. (A)

(B) 1,110,000
(C) 986,000

17. (A)

(B) $650 billion

19. (A)

(B) $2°F$
(C) 22.75%

21. (A) The rate of change of height with respect to Dbh is 1.37 ft/in. (B) Height increases by approximately 1.37 ft. (C) 18 ft (D) 20 in **23.** (A) The monthly price is increasing at a rate of $1.84 per year. (B) $67.22 **25.** (A) Male enrollment is increasing at a rate of 50,000 students per year; female enrollment is increasing at a rate of 170,000 students per year. (B) Male: 7.7 million; female: 12.2 million (C) 2023 **27.** Men: $y = -0.094x + 50.107$; women: $y = -0.076x + 55.512$; no **29.** Supply: $y = 0.2x + 0.87$; demand: $y = -0.15x + 3.5$; equilibrium price = $2.37

Chapter 1 Review Exercises

1. $x = 2.8$ *(1-1)* **2.** $x = 2$ *(1-1)* **3.** $y = 1.8 - 0.4x$ *(1-1)* **4.** $x = \dfrac{4}{3}y + \dfrac{7}{3}$ *(1-1)*

5. $y < \dfrac{13}{4}$ or $\left(-\infty, \dfrac{13}{4}\right)$ 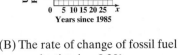 *(1-1)* **6.** $1 \le x < 3$ or $[1, 3)$ *(1-1)*

7. $x \ge \dfrac{9}{2}$ or $\left[\dfrac{9}{2}, \infty\right)$ ⟶ *(1-1)* **8.** *(1-2)*

9. $2x + 3y = 12$ *(1-2)* **10.** x intercept $= 9$; y intercept $= -6$; slope $= \dfrac{2}{3}$ *(1-2)*

11. $y = -\dfrac{2}{3}x + 6$ *(1-2)* **12.** Vertical line: $x = -6$; horizontal line: $y = 5$ *(1-2)*

13. (A) $y = -\dfrac{2}{3}x$ (B) $y = 3$ *(1-2)* **14.** (A) $3x + 2y = 1$ (B) $y = 5$ (C) $x = -2$ *(1-2)* **15.** $x = \dfrac{25}{2}$ *(1-1)*

16. $u = 36$ *(1-1)* **17.** $x = \dfrac{30}{11}$ *(1-1)* **18.** $x = 21$ *(1-1)* **19.** $x = 4$ *(1-1)* **20.** $x < 4$ or $(-\infty, 4)$ *(1-1)* ⟵

21. $x \ge 1$ or $[1, \infty)$ *(1-1)* ⟶ **22.** $x < -\dfrac{143}{17}$ or $\left(-\infty, -\dfrac{143}{17}\right)$ ⟵ *(1-1)*

23. $1 < x \le 4$ or $(1, 4]$ ⟶ *(1-1)* **24.** $\dfrac{3}{8} \le x \le \dfrac{7}{8}$ or $\left[\dfrac{3}{8}, \dfrac{7}{8}\right]$ ⟶ *(1-1)*

25. *(1-2)* **26.** The graph of $x = -3$ is a vertical line with x intercept -3, and the graph of $y = 2$ is a horizontal line with y intercept 2. *(1-2)*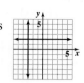

27. (A) An oblique line through the origin with slope $-3/4$ (B) A vertical line with x intercept $-4/3$ (C) The x axis (D) An oblique line with x intercept 12 and y intercept 9 *(1-2)* **28.** $\dfrac{2A - bh}{h}$ *(1-1)* **29.** $\dfrac{S - P}{St}$ *(1-1)* **30.** $a < 0$ and b any real number *(1-1)* **31.** Less than *(1-1)* **32.** The graphs appear to be perpendicular to each other. (It can be shown that if the slopes of two slant lines are the negative reciprocals of each other, then the two lines are perpendicular.) *(1-2)* **33.** \$75,000 *(1-1)* **34.** 9,375 CDs *(1-1)* **35.** (A) $m = 132 - 0.6x$ (B) $M = 187 - 0.85x$ (C) Between 120 and 170 beats per minute (D) Between 102 and 144.5 beats per minute *(1-3)* **36.** (A) $V = 224,000 - 15,500t$ (B) \$38,000 *(1-2)* **37.** (A) $R = 1.6C$ (B) \$192 (C) \$110 (D) The slope is 1.6. This is the rate of change of retail price with respect to cost. *(1-2)* **38.** \$400; \$800 *(1-1)* **39.** Demand: $p = 5.24 - 0.00125x$; 1,560 bottles *(1-2)* **40.** (A) (B) $-30°F$ (C) 45% *(1-3)*

41. (A) The dropout rate is decreasing at a rate of 0.164 percentage points per year. (B) (C) 2016 *(1-3)*

42. (A) The CPI is increasing at a rate of 4.66 units per year. (B) 264.5 *(1-3)* **43.** (A) The rate of change of tree height with respect to Dbh is 0.74. (B) Tree height increases by about 0.74 ft. (C) 21 ft (D) 16 in. *(1-3)*

Chapter 2

Exercises 2–1

1. **3.** **5.** **7.**

9. A function **11.** Not a function
13. A function **15.** A function **17.** Not a function
19. A function **21.** Linear **23.** Neither
25. Constant **27.** Linear

29. **31.** **33.** **35.** **37.** (image of graph)

39. $y = 0$ **41.** $y = 4$ **43.** $x = -5, 0, 4$ **45.** $x = -6$ **47.** 7 **49.** 48 **51.** 25 **53.** 22 **55.** All real numbers
57. All real numbers except -4 **59.** $x \leq 7$ **61.** A function with domain R **63.** Not a function; for example, when $x = 1$, $y = \pm 3$
65. A function with domain all real numbers except $x = 4$ **67.** Not a function; for example, when $x = 4$, $y = \pm 3$
69. $4x^2 - 1$ **71.** $x^2 - 6x + 8$ **73.** $15 + 8h + h^2$ **75.** $8h + h^2$ **77.** (A) $4x + 4h - 3$ (B) $4h$ (C) 4
79. (A) $4x^2 + 8xh + 4h^2 - 7x - 7h + 6$ (B) $8xh + 4h^2 - 7h$ (C) $8x + 4h - 7$ **81.** (A) $20x + 20h - x^2 - 2xh - h^2$
(B) $20h - 2xh - h^2$ (C) $20 - 2x - h$ **83.** $P(w) = 2w + \dfrac{50}{w}, w > 0$ **85.** $A(l) = l(50 - l), 0 < l < 50$

87. (A)

(B) \$54, \$42

89. (A) $R(x) = (75 - 3x)x$, $1 \leq x \leq 20$

(B)

x	$R(x)$
1	72
4	252
8	408
12	468
16	432
20	300

(C)

91. (A) $P(x) = 59x - 3x^2 - 125$, $1 \leq x \leq 20$

(B)

x	$P(x)$
1	-69
4	63
8	155
12	151
16	51
20	-145

(C) (image of graph)

93. (A) $V(x) = x(8 - 2x)(12 - 2x)$
(B) $0 < x < 4$
(C)

x	$V(x)$
1	60
2	64
3	36

(D)

95. (A) The graph indicates that there is a value of x near 2 that will produce a volume of 65.
(B) The table shows $x = 1.9$ to one decimal place:

x	1.8	1.9	2
$V(x)$	66.5	65.4	64

(C) $x = 1.93$ to two decimal places

97. $v = \dfrac{75 - w}{15 + w}$; 1.9032 cm/sec

Exercises 2-2

1. Domain: all real numbers; range: $[3, \infty)$ **3.** Domain: all real numbers; range: $(-\infty, 0]$ **5.** Domain: $[0, \infty)$; range: $[-10, \infty)$

7. Domain: all real numbers; range: all real numbers

9.

11.

13.

15.

17.

19.

21. The graph of $g(x) = -|x + 3|$ is the graph of $y = |x|$ reflected in the x axis and shifted 3 units to the left.

23. The graph of $f(x) = (x - 4)^2 - 3$ is the graph of $y = x^2$ shifted 4 units to the right and 3 units down.

25. The graph of $f(x) = 7 - \sqrt{x}$ is the graph of $y = \sqrt{x}$ reflected in the x axis and shifted 7 units up.

27. The graph of $h(x) = -3|x|$ is the graph of $y = |x|$ reflected in the x axis and vertically expanded by a factor of 3.

29. The graph of the basic function $y = x^2$ is shifted 2 units to the left and 3 units down. Equation: $y = (x + 2)^2 - 3$.

31. The graph of the basic function $y = x^2$ is reflected in the x axis and shifted 3 units to the right and 2 units up. Equation: $y = 2 - (x - 3)^2$.

33. The graph of the basic function $y = \sqrt{x}$ is reflected in the x axis and shifted 4 units up. Equation: $y = 4 - \sqrt{x}$.

35. The graph of the basic function $y = x^3$ is shifted 2 units to the left and 1 unit down. Equation: $y = (x + 2)^3 - 1$.

37. $g(x) = \sqrt{x - 2} - 3$

39. $g(x) = -|x + 3|$

41. $g(x) = -(x - 2)^3 - 1$

43.

45.

47.

49. The graph of the basic function $y = |x|$ is reflected in the x axis and vertically contracted by a factor of 0.5. Equation: $y = -0.5|x|$.

51. The graph of the basic function $y = x^2$ is reflected in the x axis and vertically expanded by a factor of 2. Equation: $y = -2x^2$.

53. The graph of the basic function $y = \sqrt[3]{x}$ is reflected in the x axis and vertically expanded by a factor of 3. Equation: $y = -3\sqrt[3]{x}$.

55. Reversing the order does not change the result.
57. Reversing the order can change the result.
59. Reversing the order can change the result.

61. (A) The graph of the basic function $y = \sqrt{x}$ is reflected in the x axis, vertically expanded by a factor of 4, and shifted up 115 units.

(B)

63. (A) The graph of the basic function is vertically contracted by a factor of 0.000 48 and shifted right 500 units and up 60,000 units.

(B)

65. (A) $S(x) = \begin{cases} 8.5 + 0.065x & \text{if } 0 \leq x \leq 700 \\ -9 + 0.09x & \text{if } x > 700 \end{cases}$

(B)

67. (A) $T(x) = \begin{cases} 0.035x & \text{if } 0 \leq x \leq 30,000 \\ 0.0625x - 825 & \text{if } 30,000 < x \leq 60,000 \\ 0.0645x - 945 & \text{if } x > 60,000 \end{cases}$

(B)

(C) $1,675; $3,570

69. (A) The graph of the basic function is vertically expanded by a factor of 5.5 and shifted down 220 units.

(B)

71. (A) The graph of the basic function is vertically expanded by a factor of 7.08.

(B)

Exercises 2–3

1. $(x - 2)^2 - 1$ **3.** $-(x - 3)^2 + 5$ **5.** The graph of $f(x)$ is the graph of $y = x^2$ shifted right 2 units and down 1 unit.

7. The graph of $m(x)$ is the graph of $y = x^2$ reflected in the x axis, then shifted right 3 units and up 5 units.

9. (A) m (B) g (C) f (D) n

11. (A) x intercepts: $1, 3$; y intercept: -3 (B) Vertex: $(2, 1)$ (C) Maximum: 1   (D) Range: $y \leq 1$ or $(-\infty, 1]$

13. (A) x intercepts: $-3, -1$; y intercept: 3 (B) Vertex: $(-2, -1)$ (C) Minimum: -1 (D) Range: $y \geq -1$ or $[-1, \infty)$

15. (A) x intercepts: $3 \pm \sqrt{2}$; y intercept: -7 (B) Vertex: $(3, 2)$ (C) Maximum: 2   (D) Range: $y \leq 2$ or $(-\infty, 2]$

17. (A) x intercepts: $-1 \pm \sqrt{2}$; y intercept: -1 (B) Vertex: $(-1, -2)$ (C) Minimum: -2 (D) Range: $y \geq -2$ or $[-2, \infty)$

19. $y = -[x - (-2)]^2 + 5$ or $y = -(x + 2)^2 + 5$ **21.** $y = (x - 1)^2 - 3$

23. Vertex form: $(x - 4)^2 - 4$ (A) x intercepts: $2, 6$; y intercept: 12 (B) Vertex: $(4, -4)$ (C) Minimum: -4
(D) Range: $y \geq -4$ or $[-4, \infty)$

25. Vertex form: $-4(x - 2)^2 + 1$ (A) x intercepts: $1.5, 2.5$; y intercept: -15 (B) Vertex: $(2, 1)$ (C) Maximum: 1
(D) Range: $y \leq 1$ or $(-\infty, 1]$

27. Vertex form: $0.5(x - 2)^2 + 3$ (A) x intercepts: none; y intercept: 5 (B) Vertex: $(2, 3)$ (C) Minimum: 3
(D) Range: $y \geq 3$ or $[3, \infty)$

29. (A) $-4.87, 8.21$ (B) $-3.44, 6.78$ (C) No solution   **31.** 651.0417

33. $g(x) = 0.25(x - 3)^2 - 9.25$ (A) x intercepts: $-3.08, 9.08$; y intercept: -7 (B) Vertex: $(3, -9.25)$
(C) Minimum: -9.25 (D) Range: $y \geq -9.25$ or $[-9.25, \infty)$

35. $f(x) = -0.12(x - 4)^2 + 3.12$ (A) x intercepts: $-1.1, 9.1$; y intercept: 1.2 (B) Vertex: $(4, 3.12)$ (C) Maximum: 3.12
(D) Range: $y \leq 3.12$ or $(-\infty, 3.12]$

37. $x = -5.37, 0.37$ **39.** $-1.37 < x < 2.16$ **41.** $x \leq -0.74$ or $x \geq 4.19$

43. Axis: $x = 2$; vertex: $(2, 4)$; range: $y \geq 4$ or $[4, \infty)$; no x intercepts

45. (A)

(B) $1.64, 7.61$
(C) $1.64 < x < 7.61$
(D) $0 \leq x < 1.64$ or $7.61 < x \leq 10$

47. (A)

(B) $1.10, 5.57$
(C) $1.10 < x < 5.57$
(D) $0 \leq x < 1.10$ or $5.57 < x \leq 8$

57. (A)

x	28	30	32	34	36
Mileage	45	52	55	51	47
$f(x)$	45.3	51.8	54.2	52.4	46.5

(B)

(C) $f(31) = 53.50$ thousand miles;
$f(35) = 49.95$ thousand miles

61. (A)

(B) 12.5 (12,500,000 chips); $468,750,000
(C) $37.50

63. (A)

(B) 2,415,000 chips and 17,251,000 chips
(C) Loss: $1 \leq x < 2.415$ or $17.251 < x \leq 20$; profit: $2.415 < x < 17.251$

65. (A) $P(x) = 59x - 3x^2 - 125$

(C) Intercepts and break-even points: 2,415,000 chips and 17,251,000 chips

(E) Maximum profit is $165,083,000 at a production level of 9,833,000 chips. This is much smaller than the maximum revenue of $468,750,000.

67. $x = 0.14$ cm

69. 10.6 mph

Exercises 2–4

1. (A) 1 (B) −3/5 (C) 3 **3.** (A) 2 (B) 3,−3 (C) −9 **5.** (A) 3 (B) −3, 2, 5 (C) 30 **7.** (A) 2 (B) −4/3, 9/2 (C) −36

9. (A) 6 (B) None (C) 1 **11.** (A) 4 (B) Negative **13.** (A) 5 (B) Negative **15.** (A) 1 (B) Negative

17. (A) 6 (B) Positive **19.** 10 **21.** 1

23. (A) x intercept: −2; y intercept: −1
(B) Domain: all real numbers except 2
(C) Vertical asymptote: $x = 2$; horizontal asymptote: $y = 1$
(D)

(E)

25. (A) x intercept: 0; y intercept: 0
(B) Domain: all real numbers except −2
(C) Vertical asymptote: $x = -2$;
horizontal asymptote: $y = 3$
(D)

(E)

27. (A) x intercept: 2; y intercept: −1
(B) Domain: all real numbers except 4
(C) Vertical asymptote: $x = 4$; horizontal asymptote: $y = -2$

(D)

(E)

29. (A)

$y = 2x^4$

$y = 2x^4 - 5x^2 + x + 2$

(B)

$y = 2x^4$

$y = 2x^4 - 5x^2 + x + 2$

31. (A)

$y = -x^5$

$y = -x^5 + 4x^3 - 4x + 1$

(B)

$y = -x^5$

$y = -x^5 + 4x^3 - 4x + 1$

33. $y = \dfrac{5}{6}$ **35.** $y = \dfrac{1}{4}$ **37.** $y = 0$ **39.** None **41.** $x = -1, x = 1, x = -3, x = 3$ **43.** $x = 5$ **45.** $x = -6, x = 6$

47. (A) x intercept: 0; y intercept: 0
(B) Vertical asymptotes: $x = -2, x = 3$;
horizontal asymptote: $y = 2$
(C)

(D)

49. (A) x intercept: $\pm\sqrt{3}$; y intercept: $-\dfrac{2}{3}$
(B) Vertical asymptotes: $x = -3, x = 3$;
horizontal asymptote: $y = -2$
(C)

(D)

51. (A) x intercept: 0; y intercept: 0   (B) Vertical asymptotes: $x = -3$, $x = 2$; horizontal asymptote: $y = 0$

(C)   (D)   **53.** $f(x) = x^2 - x - 2$ **55.** $f(x) = 4x - x^3$

57. (A) $C(x) = 180x + 200$ (B) $\overline{C}(x) = \dfrac{180x + 200}{x}$ **59.** (A) $\overline{C}(n) = \dfrac{2{,}500 + 175n + 25n^2}{n}$ (C) 10 yr; \$675.00 per year

(C) 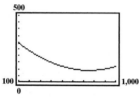   (D) \$180 per board   (D) 10 yr; \$675.00 per year

(B)

61. (A) $\overline{C}(x) = \dfrac{0.00048(x - 500)^3 + 60{,}000}{x}$ **63.** (A)   **65.** (A) 0.06 cm/sec

(B)

(B)

(B) 8.9 lb

(C) 750 cases per month; \$90 per case

67. (A)   (B) 8.4

Exercises 2–5

1. (A) k (B) g (C) h (D) f

3.   **5.**   **7.**   **9.**

11. The graph of g is the graph of f reflected in the x axis.

13. The graph of g is the graph of f shifted 1 unit to the left.

15. The graph of g is the graph of f shifted 1 unit up.

17. The graph of g is the graph of f vertically expanded by a factor of 2 and shifted to the left 2 units.

19. (A)   (B)   (C)   (D)   **21.**   **23.**

25.   **27.** $a = 1, -1$ **29.** $x = 1$ **39.**   **41.**

31. $x = -1, 6$ **33.** $x = 3$

35. $x = 3$ **37.** $x = -3, 0$

43. \$16,064.07

45. (A) \$2,633.56   (B) \$7,079.54

47. \$10,706

49. (A) \$10,553.57   (B) \$10,507.42   (C) \$10,525.03

51. N approaches 2 as t increases without bound.

53. (A) \$10,411,000

(B) The model gives an average salary of \$1,710,000 in 2000. Inclusion of the data for 2000 gives an annual salary of \$10,721,000 in 2020.

55. (A) 10%   (B) 1%

57. (A) $P = 6.8e^{0.0114t}$
(B) 2020: 7.7 billion; 2030: 8.6 billion

59. (A) 28,652,000

Exercises 2–6

1. $27 = 3^3$ **3.** $10^0 = 1$ **5.** $8 = 4^{3/2}$ **7.** $\log_7 49 = 2$ **9.** $\log_4 8 = \frac{3}{2}$ **11.** $\log_b A = u$ **13.** 0 **15.** 1 **17.** -3 **19.** 3
21. $\log_b P - \log_b Q$ **23.** $5 \log_b L$ **25.** q^p **27.** $x = 9$ **29.** $y = 2$ **31.** $b = 10$ **33.** $x = 2$ **35.** False **37.** True **39.** True
41. False **43.** $x = 2$ **45.** $x = 8$ **47.** $x = 7$ **49.** No solution

51.

53. The graph of $y = \log_2(x - 2)$ is the graph of $y = \log_2 x$ shifted to the right 2 units.
55. Domain: $(-1, \infty)$; range: all real numbers
57. (A) 3.547 43 (B) $-2.160\,32$ (C) 5.626 29 (D) $-3.197\,04$
59. (A) 13.4431 (B) 0.0089 (C) 16.0595 (D) 0.1514
61. 1.0792 **63.** 1.4595 **65.** 18.3559

67. Increasing: $(0, \infty)$

69. Decreasing: $(0, 1]$
Increasing: $[1, \infty)$

71. Increasing: $(-2, \infty)$

73. Increasing: $(0, \infty)$

75. Because $b^0 = 1$ for any permissible base $b (b > 0, b \neq 1)$.
77. $x > \sqrt{x} > \ln x$ for $1 < x \leq 16$
79. 4 yr **81.** 9.87 yr; 9.80 yr
83. 7.51 yr

85. (A) 5,373

(B) 7,220

89. 160.1 bushels/acre

91. 887 yr

Chapter 2 Review Exercises

1. *(2-1)*

2. *(2-1)*

3. *(2-1)*

4. (A) Not a function (B) A function (C) A function (D) Not a function *(2-1)*
5. (A) -2 (B) -8 (C) 0 (D) Not defined *(2-1)*
6. $v = \ln u$ *(2-6)* **7.** $y = \log x$ *(2-6)*
8. $M = e^N$ *(2-6)* **9.** $u = 10^v$ *(2-6)*
10. $x = 9$ *(2-6)* **11.** $x = 6$ *(2-6)* **12.** $x = 4$ *(2-6)*
13. $x = 2.157$ *(2-6)* **14.** $x = 13.128$ *(2-6)*
15. $x = 1,273.503$ *(2-6)* **16.** $x = 0.318$ *(2-6)*

17. (A) $y = 4$ (B) $x = 0$ (C) $y = 1$ (D) $x = -1$ or 1 (E) $y = -2$ (F) $x = -5$ or 5 *(2-1)*
18. (A)

(B)

(C)

(D)

(2-2)

19. $f(x) = -(x - 2)^2 + 4$. The graph of $f(x)$ is the graph of $y = x^2$ reflected in the x axis, then shifted right 2 units and up 4 units. *(2-2)*
20. (A) g (B) m (C) n (D) f *(2-2, 2-3)* **21.** (A) x intercepts: $-4, 0$; y intercept: 0 (B) Vertex: $(-2, -4)$
(C) Minimum: -4 (D) Range: $y \geq -4$ or $[-4, \infty)$ *(2-3)* **22.** Quadratic *(2-3)* **23.** Linear *(2-1)* **24.** None *(2-1, 2-3)*
25. Constant *(2-1)* **26.** $x = 8$ *(2-6)* **27.** $x = 3$ *(2-6)* **28.** $x = 3$ *(2-5)* **29.** $x = -1, 3$ *(2-5)* **30.** $x = 0, \frac{3}{2}$ *(2-5)*
31. $x = -2$ *(2-6)* **32.** $x = \frac{1}{2}$ *(2-6)* **33.** $x = 27$ *(2-6)* **34.** $x = 13.3113$ *(2-6)* **35.** $x = 158.7552$ *(2-6)*
36. $x = 0.0097$ *(2-6)* **37.** $x = 1.4359$ *(2-6)* **38.** $x = 1.4650$ *(2-6)* **39.** $x = 92.1034$ *(2-6)* **40.** $x = 9.0065$ *(2-6)*
41. $x = 2.1081$ *(2-6)* **42.** (A) All real numbers except $x = -2$ and 3 (B) $x < 5$ *(2-1)*
43. Vertex form: $4\left(x + \frac{1}{2}\right)^2 - 4$; x intercepts: $-\frac{3}{2}$ and $\frac{1}{2}$; y intercept: -3; vertex: $\left(-\frac{1}{2}, -4\right)$; minimum: -4;
range: $y \geq -4$ or $[-4, \infty)$ *(2-3)* **44.** $(-1.54, -0.79); (0.69, 0.99)$ *(2-5, 2-6)*

45. *(2-1)*

46. *(2-1)*

47. 6 *(2-1)*   **48.** −19 *(2-1)*   **49.** $10x − 4$ *(2-1)*   **50.** $21 − 5x$ *(2-1)*
51. (A) −1   (B) $−1 − 2h$ (C) $−2h$ (D) −2 *(2-1)*
52. (A) $a^2 − 3a + 1$ (B) $a^2 + 2ah + h^2 − 3a − 3h + 1$
   (C) $2ah + h^2 − 3h$ (D) $2a + h − 3$ *(2-1)*
53. The graph of function m is the graph of $y = |x|$ reflected in the x axis and shifted to the right
   4 units. *(2-2)*
54. The graph of function g is the graph of $y = x^3$ vertically contracted by a factor of 0.3 and shifted
   up 3 units. *(2-2)*
55. The graph of $y = x^2$ is vertically expanded by a factor of 2, reflected in the x axis, and shifted to
   the left 3 units. Equation: $y = −2(x + 3)^2$ *(2-2)*

56. $f(x) = 2\sqrt{x + 3} − 1$ *(2-2)*   **57.** $y = 0$ *(2-4)*   **58.** $y = \dfrac{3}{4}$ *(2-4)*   **59.** None *(2-4)*   **60.** $x = −10, x = 10$ *(2-4)*

61. $x = −2$ *(2-4)*   **62.** True *(2-3)*   **63.** False *(2-3)*   **64.** False *(2-3)*   **65.** True *(2-4)*
66. True *(2-5)*   **67.** True *(2-3)*   **68.**   *(2-2)*   **69.**   *(2-2)*

70. $y = −(x − 4)^2 + 3$ *(2-2, 2-3)*
71. $f(x) = −0.4(x − 4)^2 + 7.6$ (A) x intercepts: −0.4, 8.4; y intercept: 1.2
   (B) Vertex: (4.0, 7.6)   (C) Maximum: 7.6   (D) Range: $y ≤ 7.6$ or $(−∞, 7.6]$ *(2-3)*

72.

(A) x intercepts: −0.4, 8.4; y intercept: 1.2
(B) Vertex: (4.0, 7.6)   (C) Maximum: 7.6
(D) Range: $y ≤ 7.6$ or $(−∞, 7.6]$ *(2-3)*

73. $\log 10^\pi = \pi$ and $10^{\log \sqrt{2}} = \sqrt{2}$; $\ln e^\pi = \pi$ and $e^{\ln \sqrt{2}} = \sqrt{2}$ *(2-6)*
74. $x = 2$ *(2-6)*   **75.** $x = 2$ *(2-6)*   **76.** $x = 1$ *(2-6)*   **77.** $x = 300$ *(2-6)*
78. $y = ce^{-5t}$ *(2-6)*
79. If $\log_1 x = y$, then $1^y = x$; that is, $1 = x$ for all positive real numbers x, which is
   not possible. *(2-6)*
80. The graph of $y = \sqrt[3]{x}$ is vertically expanded by a factor of 2, reflected in the x
   axis, and shifted 1 unit left and 1 unit down. Equation: $y = −2\sqrt[3]{x + 1} − 1$. *(2-2)*
81. $G(x) = 0.3(x + 2)^2 − 8.1$ (A) x intercepts: −7.2, 3.2; y intercept: −6.9
   (B) Vertex: (−2, −8.1)   (C) Minimum: −8.1   (D) Range: $y ≥ −8.1$ or $[−8.1, ∞)$
   (2-3)

82.

(A) x intercepts: −7.2, 3.2; y intercept: −6.9   (B) Vertex: (−2, −8.1)   (C) Minimum: −8.1
(D) Range: $y ≥ −8.1$ or $[−8.1, ∞)$ *(2-3)*

83. (A) $S(x) = \begin{cases} 3 & \text{if } 0 ≤ x ≤ 20 \\ 0.057x + 1.86 & \text{if } 20 < x ≤ 200 \\ 0.0346x + 6.34 & \text{if } 200 < x ≤ 1{,}000 \\ 0.0217x + 19.24 & \text{if } x > 1{,}000 \end{cases}$

(B) $S(x)$

(2-2)

84. \$6,521.89 *(2-5)*   **85.** \$6,362.50 *(2-5)*   **86.** 201 months ($≈$16.7 years) *(2-5)*   **87.** 9.38 yr *(2-5)*
88. (A)

(B) $R = C$ for $x = 4.686$ thousand units (4,686 units) and for $x = 27.314$ thousand units
   (27,314 units); $R < C$ for $1 ≤ x < 4.686$ or $27.314 < x ≤ 40$; $R > C$ for $4.686 < x < 27.314$.
(C) Maximum revenue is 500 thousand dollars (\$500,000). This occurs at an output of 20 thousand
   units (20,000 units). At this output, the wholesale price is $p(20) = \$25$. *(2-3)*

89. (A) $P(x) = R(x) − C(x) = x(50 − 1.25x) − (160 + 10x)$

(B) $P = 0$ for $x = 4.686$ thousand units (4,686 units) and for $x = 27.314$ thousand units
   (27,314 units); $P < 0$ for $1 ≤ x < 4.686$ or $27.314 < x ≤ 40$; $P > 0$ for
   $4.686 < x < 27.314$.
(C) Maximum profit is 160 thousand dollars (\$160,000). This occurs at an output of 16 thousand
   units (16,000 units). At this output, the wholesale price is $p(16) = \$30$. *(2-3)*

90. (A) $A(x) = -\frac{3}{2}x^2 + 420x$

(B) Domain: $0 \le x \le 280$

(C)

(D) There are two solutions to the equation $A(x) = 25,000$, one near 90 and another near 190.

(E) 86 ft; 194 ft

(F) Maximum combined area is 29,400 ft². This occurs for $x = 140$ ft and $y = 105$ ft. *(2-3)*

91. (A) 2,833 sets   (B) 4,836

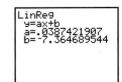

(D) Equilibrium price: $131.59; equilibrium quantity: 3,587 cookware sets *(2-3)*

92. (A)   (B) 1,806 *(2-4)*

93. (A) $N = 2^{2t}$ or $N = 4^t$ (B) 15 days *(2-5)*   **94.** $k = 0.009\ 42$; 489 ft *(2-6)*

95. (A) 5,569,000 *(2-6)*   **96.** 23.1 yr *(2-5)*   **97.** (A) $931 billion   (B) 2018 *(2-5)*

Chapter 3

Exercises 3–1

1. 0.03   **3.** 10.5%   **5.** 0.0475   **7.** 21%   **9.** $\frac{1}{3}$ yr   **11.** $\frac{2}{3}$ yr   **13.** $\frac{3}{13}$ yr   **15.** $\frac{1}{2}$ yr   **17.** $42   **19.** $1,800   **21.** 0.12 or 12%

23. $\frac{1}{2}$ yr   **25.** $4,612.50   **27.** $875   **29.** 0.36 or 36%   **31.** 1 yr   **33.** $r = I/Pt$ **35.** $P = A/(1 + rt)$ **37.** $t = \dfrac{A - P}{Pr}$

39. The graphs are linear, all with y intercept $1,000; their slopes are 40, 80, and 120, respectively.   **41.** $45   **43.** $9.23

45. $7,647.20   **47.** 8.1%   **49.** 18%   **51.** $1,604.40; 20.88%   **53.** 4.298%   **55.** $992.38   **57.** 5.396%   **59.** 6.986%   **61.** 12.085%

63. 109.895%   **65.** 87.158%

Exercises 3–2

1. $A = \$5,983.40$ **3.** $P = \$4,245.07$ **5.** $3,125.79   **7.** $2,958.11   **9.** 2.5 yr   **11.** 6.789%

13. 0.75% per month   **15.** 0.04% per day   **17.** 1.2% per quarter   **19.** 4.74%   **21.** 3.6%   **23.** 4.2%

25. (A) $126.25; $26.25   (B) $126.90; $26.90   (C) $127.05; $27.05   **27.** (A) $5,524.71   (B) $6,104.48   **29.** $12,175.69

31. All three graphs are increasing, curve upward, and have the same y intercept; the greater the interest rate, the greater the increase. The amounts at the end of 8 years are $1,376.40, $1,892.46, and $2,599.27, respectively.

33.

Period	Interest	Amount
0		$1,000.00
1	$97.50	$1,097.50
2	$107.01	$1,204.51
3	$117.44	$1,321.95
4	$128.89	$1,450.84
5	$141.46	$1,592.29
6	$155.25	$1,747.54

35. (A) $7,440.94   (B) $5,536.76   **37.** (A) $19,084.49   (B) $11,121.45

39. (A) 3.97%   (B) 2.32%   **41.** (A) 5.28%   (B) 5.27%   **43.** $11\frac{2}{3}$ yr

45. 3.75 yr   **47.** $n \approx 12$ **49.** (A) $7\frac{1}{4}$ yr   (B) 6 yr   **51.** (A) 7.7 yr   (B) 6.3 yr

53. $65,068.44   **55.** $282,222.44   **57.** $19.78 per ft² per mo   **59.** 41 yr

61. 9% compounded monthly, since its APY is 9.38%; the APY of 9.3% compounded annually is 9.3%

63. (A) In 2016, 240 years after the signing, it would be worth $130,392.50.

(B) If interest were compounded monthly, daily, or continuously, it would be worth $132,744.98, $133,903.45, or $133,943.08, respectively.

(C)

65. 9.664%   **67.** 2 yr, 10 mo   **69.** $163,295.21

71. 3,615 days; 8.453 yr

73.

Years	Exact Rate	Rule of 72
6	12.2	12.0
7	10.4	10.3
8	9.1	9.0
9	8.0	8.0
10	7.2	7.2
11	6.5	6.5
12	5.9	6.0

75. 14 quarters
77. To maximize earnings, choose 10% simple interest for investments lasting fewer than 11 years and 7% compound interest otherwise.
79. 6.58% **81.** 7.020% **83.** $15,843.80 **85.** 4.526%
87. (A) 4.404% (B) 4.446% (C) 4.448% **89.** 13.44% **91.** 17.62%

Exercises 3–3

1. $i = 0.02; n = 80$ **3.** $i = 0.0375; n = 24$ **5.** $i = 0.0075; n = 48$ **7.** $i = 0.0595; n = 12$ **9.** $FV = \$13,435.19$

11. $PMT = \$310.62$ **13.** $n = 17$ **15.** $i = 0.09$ **19.** $n = \dfrac{\ln\left(1 + i\,\dfrac{FV}{PMT}\right)}{\ln(1 + i)}$ **21.** Value: $84,895.40; interest: $24,895.40

23. $20,931.01 **25.** $667.43 **27.** $763.39

29.

Period	Amount	Interest	Balance
1	$1,000.00	$ 0.00	$1,000.00
2	$1,000.00	$ 83.20	$2,083.20
3	$1,000.00	$173.32	$3,256.52
4	$1,000.00	$270.94	$4,527.46
5	$1,000.00	$376.69	$5,904.15

31. First year: $33.56; second year: $109.64; third year: $190.41
33. $111,050.77 **35.** $1,308.75 **37.** (A) 4.755% (B) $189.56
39. 33 months **41.** 7.77% **43.** 7.13%
45. After 11 quarterly payments

Exercises 3–4

1. $i = 0.006; n = 48$ **3.** $i = 0.02475; n = 40$ **5.** $i = 0.02525; n = 32$ **7.** $i = 0.0548; n = 9$ **9.** $PV = \$3,458.41$
11. $PMT = \$586.01$ **13.** $n = 29$ **15.** $i = 0.029$ **21.** $35,693.18 **23.** $11,241.81; $1,358.19 **25.** $69.58; $839.84
27. For 0% financing, the monthly payments should be $129.58, not $179. If a loan of $9,330 is amortized in 72 payments of $179, the rate is 11.29% compounded monthly.
29. The monthly payments with 0% financing are $455. If you take the rebate, the monthly payments are $434.24. You should choose the rebate.
31. $314.72; $17,319.68

33.

Payment Number	Payment	Interest	Unpaid Balance Reduction	Unpaid Balance
0				$5,000.00
1	$ 706.29	$140.00	$ 566.29	4,433.71
2	706.29	124.14	582.15	3,851.56
3	706.29	107.84	598.45	3,253.11
4	706.29	91.09	615.20	2,637.91
5	706.29	73.86	632.43	2,005.48
6	706.29	56.15	650.14	1,355.34
7	706.29	37.95	668.34	687.00
8	706.24	19.24	687.00	0.00
Totals	$5,650.27	$650.27	$5,000.00	

35. First year: $466.05; second year: $294.93; third year: $107.82
37. $97,929.78; $116,070.22 **39.** $143.85/mo; $904.80
41. Monthly payment: $908.99
 (A) $125,862 (B) $81,507 (C) $46,905
43. (A) Monthly payment: $1,015.68; interest: $114,763
 (B) 197 months; interest saved: $23,499
45. (A) 157 (B) 243
 (C) The withdrawals continue forever.
47. (A) Monthly withdrawals: $1,229.66; total interest: $185,338.80
 (B) Monthly deposits: $162.65
49. $65,584 **51.** $34,692

53. All three graphs are decreasing, curve downward, and have the same x intercept; the unpaid balances are always in the ratio 2:3:4. The monthly payments are $402.31, $603.47, and $804.62, with total interest amounting to $94,831.60, $142,249.20, and $189,663.20, respectively.
55. 14.45% **57.** 10.21%

Chapter 3 Review Exercises

1. $A = \$104.50$ (3-1) **2.** $P = \$800$ (3-1) **3.** $t = 0.75$ yr, or 9 mo (3-1) **4.** $r = 6\%$ (3-1) **5.** $A = \$1,393.68$ (3-2)
6. $P = \$3,193.50$ (3-2) **7.** $A = \$5,824.92$ (3-2) **8.** $P = \$22,612.86$ (3-2) **9.** $FV = \$69,770.03$ (3-3) **10.** $PMT = \$115.00$ (3-3)
11. $PV = \$33,944.27$ (3-4) **12.** $PMT = \$166.07$ (3-4) **13.** $n \approx 16$ (3-2) **14.** $n \approx 41$ (3-3) **15.** $3,350.00; $350.00 (3-1)
16. $19,654.42 (3-2) **17.** $12,944.67 (3-2)

18. (A)

Period	Interest	Amount
0		$400.00
1	$21.60	$421.60
2	$22.77	$444.37
3	$24.00	$468.36
4	$25.29	$493.65

(3-2)

(B)

Period	Interest	Payment	Balance
1		$100.00	$100.00
2	$ 5.40	$100.00	$205.40
3	$11.09	$100.00	$316.49
4	$17.09	$100.00	$433.58

(3-3)

19. To maximize earnings, choose 13% simple interest for investments lasting less than 9 years and 9% compound interest for investments lasting 9 years or more. *(3-2)*
20. $164,402 *(3-2)* **21.** 7.833% *(3-2)*
22. 9% compounded quarterly, since its effective rate is 9.31%, while the effective rate of 9.25% compounded annually is 9.25% *(3-2)*
23. $25,861.65; $6,661.65 *(3-3)* **24.** $11.64 *(3-1)* **25.** $29,354 *(3-2)* **26.** $18,021 *(3-2)* **27.** 15% *(3-1)*
28. The monthly payments with 0% financing are $450. If you take the rebate, the monthly payments are $426.66. You should choose the rebate. *(3-4)*
29. (A) 6.432% (B) 6.449% *(3-2)* **30.** 2 yr, 3 mo *(3-2)* **31.** 139 mo; 93 mo *(3-2)* **32.** (A) $571,499 (B) $1,973,277 *(3-3)*
33. 10.45% *(3-2)* **34.** (A) 174% (B) 65.71% *(3-1)* **35.** $725.89 *(3-3)* **36.** (A) $140,945.57 (B) $789.65 (C) $136,828 *(3-3, 3-4)*
37. $102.99; $943.52 *(3-4)* **38.** $576.48 *(3-3)* **39.** 3,374 days; 10 yr *(3-2)* **40.** $175.28; $2,516.80 *(3-4)* **41.** $13,418.78 *(3-2)*
42. 5 yr, 10 mo *(3-3)* **43.** 18 yr *(3-4)* **44.** 28.8% *(3-1)*

45.

Payment Number	Payment	Interest	Unpaid Balance Reduction	Unpaid Balance
0				$1,000.00
1	$265.82	$25.00	$ 240.82	759.18
2	265.82	18.98	246.84	512.34
3	265.82	12.81	253.01	259.33
4	265.81	6.48	259.33	0.00
Totals	$1,063.27	$63.27	$1,000.00	

(3-4)

46. 28 months *(3-3)*
47. $55,347.48; $185,830.24 *(3-3)*
48. 6.30% *(3-2)* **49.** 6.33% *(3-1)*
50. 44 deposits *(3-3)*
51. (A) $1,189.52 (B) $72,963.07
  (C) $7,237.31 *(3-4)*

52. The certificate would be worth $53,394.30 when the 360th payment is made. By reducing the principal the loan would be paid off in 252 months. If the monthly payment were then invested at 7% compounded monthly, it would be worth $67,234.20 at the time of the 360th payment. *(3-2, 3-3, 3-4)*
53. The lower rate would save $12,247.20 in interest payments. *(3-4)* **54.** $3,807.59 *(3-2)* **55.** 5.79% *(3-2)*
56. $4,844.96 *(3-1)* **57.** $6,697.11 *(3-4)* **58.** 7.24% *(3-2)* **59.** (A) $398,807 (B) $374,204 *(3-3)*
60. $15,577.64 *(3-2)* **61.** (A) 30 yr: $569.26; 15 yr: $749.82 (B) 30 yr: $69,707.99; 15 yr: $37,260.74 *(3-4)*
62. $20,516 *(3-4)* **63.** 33.52% *(3-4)* **64.** (A) 10.74% (B) 15 yr; 40 yr *(3-3)*

Chapter 4

Exercises 4-1

1. (B); no solution **3.** (A); $x = -3, y = 1$ **5.** $x = 2, y = 4$ **7.** No solution (parallel lines) **9.** $x = 4, y = 5$
11. $x = 1, y = 4$ **13.** $u = 2, v = -3$ **15.** $m = 8, n = 6$ **17.** $x = 1, y = -5$ **19.** No solution (inconsistent) **21.** $x = -\frac{4}{3}, y = 1$
23. Infinitely many solutions (dependent) **25.** $x = \frac{4}{7}, y = \frac{3}{7}$ **27.** $x = 7, y = 3$ **29.** $x = \frac{4}{5}, y = -\frac{2}{3}$ **31.** $x = 0, y = 0$
33. $x = 14, y = 5$ **35.** Price tends to come down. **41.** $(-14, -37)$ **43.** No solution **45.** $(4.176, -1.235)$ **47.** $(-3.310, -2.241)$

49.

51.

53.

55. (A) $(20, -24)$
  (B) $(-4, 6)$
  (C) No solution

57. (A) Supply: 143 T-shirts; demand: 647 T-shirts
  (B) Supply: 857 T-shirts; demand: 353 T-shirts
  (C) Equilibrium price = $6.50;
  equilibrium quantity = 500 T-shirts
  (D)

59. (A) $p = 1.5x + 1.95$
  (B) $p = -1.5x + 7.8$
  (C) Equilibrium price: $4.875; equilibrium quantity: 1.95 billion bushels
  (D)

61. (A) 120 mowers
  (B)

63. (A) $C = 24,000 + 7.45x; R = 19.95x$
  (B) 1,920
  (C)

65. Base price = $17.95; surcharge = $2.45/lb
67. 5,720 lb robust blend; 6,160 lb mild blend
69. Mix *A*: 80 g; mix *B*: 60 g
71. Operate the Mexico plant for 75 hours and the Taiwan plant for 50 hours.
73. (A) $a = 196, b = -16$
  (B) 196 ft
  (C) 3.5 sec
75. 40 sec, 24 sec, 120 mi

77. (A)

  (B) $d = 141$ cm (approx.)
  (C) Vacillate

Exercises 4-2

1. A is 2×3; C is 1×3 **3.** C **5.** B **7.** $a_{12} = -4$; $a_{23} = -5$ **9.** $-1, 8, 0$ **11.** (A) 2×4 (B) 1 (C) $e_{23} = 7$; $f_{12} = -6$

13. $\begin{bmatrix} 4 & -6 & | & -8 \\ 1 & -3 & | & 2 \end{bmatrix}$ **15.** $\begin{bmatrix} -4 & 12 & | & -8 \\ 4 & -6 & | & -8 \end{bmatrix}$ **17.** $\begin{bmatrix} 1 & -3 & | & 2 \\ 8 & -12 & | & -16 \end{bmatrix}$ **19.** $\begin{bmatrix} 1 & -3 & | & 2 \\ 0 & 6 & | & -16 \end{bmatrix}$ **21.** $\begin{bmatrix} 1 & -3 & | & 2 \\ 2 & 0 & | & -12 \end{bmatrix}$

23. $\begin{bmatrix} 1 & -3 & | & 2 \\ 3 & -3 & | & -10 \end{bmatrix}$ **25.** $\frac{1}{3}R_2 \to R_2$ **27.** $6R_1 + R_2 \to R_2$ **29.** $\frac{1}{3}R_2 + R_1 \to R_1$ **31.** $R_1 \leftrightarrow R_2$

33. $\{(6, 6)\}$ **35.** $\left\{\left(\frac{2}{3}t - 1, t\right) \middle| t \text{ is any real number}\right\}$

37. $x_1 = 3$, $x_2 = 2$; each pair of lines has the same intersection point.

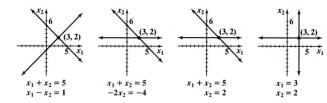

39. $x_1 = -4$, $x_2 = 6$ **41.** No solution **43.** $x_1 = 2t + 15$, $x_2 = t$ for any real number t **45.** $x_1 = 3$, $x_2 = 1$ **47.** $x_1 = 2$, $x_2 = 1$
49. $x_1 = 2$, $x_2 = 4$ **51.** No solution **53.** $x_1 = 1$, $x_2 = 4$ **55.** Infinitely many solutions: $x_2 = s$, $x_1 = 2s - 3$ for any real number s
57. Infinitely many solutions; $x_2 = s$, $x_1 = \frac{1}{2}s + \frac{1}{2}$ for any real number s **59.** $x_1 = -1$, $x_2 = 3$ **61.** No solution
63. Infinitely many solutions: $x_2 = t$, $x_1 = \frac{3}{2}t + 2$ for any real number t **65.** $x_1 = 2$, $x_2 = -1$ **67.** $x_1 = 2$, $x_2 = -1$
69. $x_1 = 1.1$, $x_2 = 0.3$ **71.** $x_1 = -23.125$, $x_2 = 7.8125$ **73.** $x_1 = 3.225$, $x_2 = -6.9375$

Exercises 4-3

1. Reduced form **3.** Not reduced form; $R_2 \leftrightarrow R_3$ **5.** Not reduced form; $\frac{1}{3}R_2 \to R_2$ **7.** Reduced form
9. Not reduced form; $2R_2 + R_1 \to R_1$ **11.** $x_1 = -2$, $x_2 = 3$, $x_3 = 0$ **13.** $x_1 = 2t + 3$, $x_2 = -t - 5$, $x_3 = t$ for t any real number
15. No solution **17.** $x_1 = 3t + 5$, $x_2 = -2t - 7$, $x_3 = t$ for t any real number
19. $x_1 = 2s + 3t - 5$, $x_2 = s$, $x_3 = -3t + 2$, $x_4 = t$ for s and t any real numbers. **21.** 11 **23.** 13, 17, 19 **25.** False **27.** True

29. False **31.** $\begin{bmatrix} 1 & 0 & | & -7 \\ 0 & 1 & | & 3 \end{bmatrix}$ **33.** $\begin{bmatrix} 1 & 0 & -1 & | & 23 \\ 0 & 1 & 2 & | & -7 \end{bmatrix}$ **35.** $\begin{bmatrix} 1 & 0 & 0 & | & -5 \\ 0 & 1 & 0 & | & 4 \\ 0 & 0 & 1 & | & -2 \end{bmatrix}$ **37.** $\begin{bmatrix} 1 & 0 & 2 & | & -\frac{5}{3} \\ 0 & 1 & -2 & | & \frac{1}{3} \\ 0 & 0 & 0 & | & 0 \end{bmatrix}$ **39.** $x_1 = -2$, $x_2 = 3$, $x_3 = 1$
41. $x_1 = 0$, $x_2 = -2$, $x_3 = 2$

43. $x_1 = 2t + 3$, $x_2 = t - 2$, $x_3 = t$ for t any real number **45.** $x_1 = 1$, $x_2 = 2$ **47.** No solution
49. $x_1 = t - 1$, $x_2 = 2t + 2$, $x_3 = t$ for t any real number **51.** $x_1 = -2s + t + 1$, $x_2 = s$, $x_3 = t$ for s and t any real numbers
53. No solution
55. (A) Dependent system with two parameters and an infinite number of solutions   (B) Dependent system with one parameter and
an infinite number of solutions   (C) Independent system with a unique solution   (D) Impossible
57. $x_1 = 2s - 3t + 3$, $x_2 = s + 2t + 2$, $x_3 = s$, $x_4 = t$ for s and t any real numbers **59.** $x_1 = -0.5$, $x_2 = 0.2$, $x_3 = 0.3$, $x_4 = -0.4$
61. $x_1 = 2s - 1.5t + 1$, $x_2 = s$, $x_3 = -t + 1.5$, $x_4 = 0.5t - 0.5$, $x_5 = t$ for s and t any real numbers **63.** $a = 2$, $b = -4$, $c = -7$
65. (A) $x_1 =$ number of one-person boats   (B) $0.5x_1 + x_2 + 1.5x_3 = 380$ (C) $0.5x_1 + x_2 = 380$
   $x_2 =$ number of two-person boats $0.6x_1 + 0.9x_2 + 1.2x_3 = 330$ $0.6x_1 + 0.9x_2 = 330$
   $x_3 =$ number of four-person boats $t - 80$ one-person boats, $420 - 2t$ $0.2x_1 + 0.3x_2 = 120$
   $0.5x_1 + x_2 + 1.5x_3 = 380$ two-person boats, and t four-person   There is no production schedule
   $0.6x_1 + 0.9x_2 + 1.2x_3 = 330$ boats, where t is an integer satisfying   that will use all the labor-hours in
   $0.2x_1 + 0.3x_2 + 0.5x_3 = 120$ $80 \le t \le 210$ all departments.
   20 one-person boats, 220 two-person
   boats, and 100 four-person boats

67. x_1 = number of 8,000-gal tank cars
x_2 = number of 16,000-gal tank cars
x_3 = number of 24,000-gal tank cars
$$x_1 + x_2 + x_3 = 24$$
$$8{,}000x_1 + 16{,}000x_2 + 24{,}000x_3 = 520{,}000$$
$t - 17$ 8,000-gal tank cars,
$41 - 2t$ 16,000-gal tank cars, and t 24,000-gal tank cars, where $t = 17, 18, 19,$ or 20

69. The minimum monthly cost is \$24,100 when 7 16,000-gallon and 17 24,000-gallon tank cars are leased.

71. x_1 = federal income tax
x_2 = state income tax
x_3 = local income tax
$$x_1 + 0.5x_2 + 0.5x_3 = 3{,}825{,}000$$
$$0.2x_1 + x_2 + 0.2x_3 = 1{,}530{,}000$$
$$0.1x_1 + 0.1x_2 + x_3 = 765{,}000$$
Tax liability is 57.65%.

73. x_1 = taxable income of company A
x_2 = taxable income of company B
x_3 = taxable income of company C
x_4 = taxable income of company D
$$x_1 - 0.08x_2 - 0.03x_3 - 0.07x_4 = 2.272$$
$$-0.12x_1 + x_2 - 0.11x_3 - 0.13x_4 = 2.106$$
$$-0.11x_1 - 0.09x_2 + x_3 - 0.08x_4 = 2.736$$
$$-0.06x_1 - 0.02x_2 - 0.14x_3 + x_4 = 3.168$$
Taxable incomes are \$2,927,000 for company A, \$3,372,000 for company B, \$3,675,000 for company C, and \$3,926,000 for company D.

75. (A) x_1 = number of ounces of food A
x_2 = number of ounces of food B
x_3 = number of ounces of food C
$$30x_1 + 10x_2 + 20x_3 = 340$$
$$10x_1 + 10x_2 + 20x_3 = 180$$
$$10x_1 + 30x_2 + 20x_3 = 220$$
8 oz of food A, 2 oz of food B, and 4 oz of food C
(B) $$30x_1 + 10x_2 = 340$$
$$10x_1 + 10x_2 = 180$$
$$10x_1 + 30x_2 = 220$$
There is no combination that will meet all the requirements.
(C) $$30x_1 + 10x_2 + 20x_3 = 340$$
$$10x_1 + 10x_2 + 20x_3 = 180$$
8 oz of food A, $10 - 2t$ oz of food B, and t oz of food C, where $0 \le t \le 5$

77. x_1 = number of barrels of mix A
x_2 = number of barrels of mix B
x_3 = number of barrels of mix C
x_4 = number of barrels of mix D
$$30x_1 + 30x_2 + 30x_3 + 60x_4 = 900$$
$$50x_1 + 75x_2 + 25x_3 + 25x_4 = 750$$
$$30x_1 + 20x_2 + 20x_3 + 50x_4 = 700$$
$10 - t$ barrels of mix A, $t - 5$ barrels of mix B, $25 - 2t$ barrels of mix C, and t barrels of mix D, where t is an integer satisfying $5 \le t \le 10$

79. 0 barrels of mix A, 5 barrels of mix B, 5 barrels of mix C, and 10 barrels of mix D
81. $y = 0.01x^2 + x + 75$, 450 million
83. $y = 0.004x^2 + 0.06x + 77.6$; 1995–2000: 79.4 years; 2000–2005: 80.4 years

85.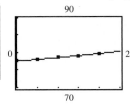

87. x_1 = number of hours for company A
x_2 = number of hours for company B
$$30x_1 + 20x_2 = 600$$
$$10x_1 + 20x_2 = 400$$
Company A: 10 hr; company B: 15 hr

89. (A) 6th St. and Washington Ave.: $x_1 + x_2 = 1{,}200$; 6th St. and Lincoln Ave.: $x_2 + x_3 = 1{,}000$; 5th St. and Lincoln Ave.: $x_3 + x_4 = 1{,}300$
(B) $x_1 = 1{,}500 - t$, $x_2 = t - 300$, $x_3 = 1{,}300 - t$, and $x_4 = t$, where $300 \le t \le 1{,}300$
(C) 1,300; 300
(D) Washington Ave.: 500; 6th St.: 700; Lincoln Ave.: 300

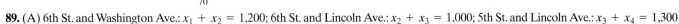

Exercises 4-4

1. $\begin{bmatrix} -1 & 0 \\ 5 & -3 \end{bmatrix}$ **3.** Not defined **5.** $\begin{bmatrix} 5 & -7 \\ -5 & 2 \\ 0 & 4 \end{bmatrix}$ **7.** $\begin{bmatrix} 5 & -10 & 0 & 20 \\ -15 & 10 & -5 & 30 \end{bmatrix}$ **9.** $\begin{bmatrix} 5 \\ -3 \end{bmatrix}$ **11.** $\begin{bmatrix} 2 & 4 \\ 1 & -5 \end{bmatrix}$ **13.** $\begin{bmatrix} 1 & -5 \\ -2 & -4 \end{bmatrix}$

15. $\begin{bmatrix} 5 & 10 \\ 15 & 20 \end{bmatrix}$ **17.** $\begin{bmatrix} 5 & 10 \\ 15 & 20 \end{bmatrix}$ **19.** $\begin{bmatrix} 7 & 9 \\ 0 & 0 \end{bmatrix}$ **21.** $\begin{bmatrix} 0 & 3 \\ 0 & 7 \end{bmatrix}$ **23.** $[-7]$ **25.** $\begin{bmatrix} -15 & 6 \\ -20 & 8 \end{bmatrix}$ **27.** $[11]$ **29.** $\begin{bmatrix} 3 & -2 & -4 \\ 6 & -4 & -8 \\ -9 & 6 & 12 \end{bmatrix}$

31. $\begin{bmatrix} -12 & 12 & 18 \\ 20 & -18 & -6 \end{bmatrix}$ **33.** Not defined **35.** $\begin{bmatrix} 11 & 2 \\ 4 & 27 \end{bmatrix}$ **37.** $\begin{bmatrix} 6 & 4 \\ 0 & -3 \end{bmatrix}$ **39.** $\begin{bmatrix} -1.3 & -0.7 \\ -0.2 & -0.5 \\ 0.1 & 1.1 \end{bmatrix}$ **41.** $\begin{bmatrix} -66 & 69 & 39 \\ 92 & -18 & -36 \end{bmatrix}$

43. Not defined **45.** $\begin{bmatrix} -18 & 48 \\ 54 & -34 \end{bmatrix}$ **47.** $\begin{bmatrix} -26 & -15 & -25 \\ -4 & -18 & 4 \\ 2 & 43 & -19 \end{bmatrix}$ **49.** $AB = \begin{bmatrix} 0 & 0 \\ 0 & 0 \end{bmatrix}$, $BA = \begin{bmatrix} a^2 + ab & a^2 + ab \\ -a^2 - ab & -a^2 - ab \end{bmatrix}$

51. $\begin{bmatrix} 0 & 0 \\ 0 & 0 \end{bmatrix}$ **53.** B^n approaches $\begin{bmatrix} 0.25 & 0.75 \\ 0.25 & 0.75 \end{bmatrix}$; AB^n approaches $[0.25 \ \ 0.75]$ **55.** $a = -1, b = 1, c = 3, d = -5$

57. $a = 3, b = 4, c = 1, d = 2$ **59.** False **61.** True **63.** (A) True (B) True (C) True (D) True **65.**

	Guitar	Banjo	
	\$51.50	\$40.50	Materials
	\$87.00	\$120.00	Labor

67.

	Basic car	Air	AM/FM radio	Cruise control
Model A	$2,937	$459	$200	$118
Model B	$2,864	$201	$88	$52
Model C	$2,171	$417	$177	$101

69. (A) $19.84 (B) $38.19
(C) MN gives the labor costs at each plant.
(D)

$$MN = \begin{bmatrix} \$19.84 & \$16.90 \\ \$31.49 & \$26.81 \\ \$44.87 & \$38.19 \end{bmatrix} \begin{matrix} \text{One-person boat} \\ \text{Two-person boat} \\ \text{Four-person boat} \end{matrix}$$

with column headers MA, VA.

71. (A) 70 g
(B) 30 g
(C) MN gives the amount (in grams) of protein, carbohydrate, and fat in 20 oz of each mix.
(D)

$$MN = \begin{bmatrix} 70 & 60 & 50 \\ 380 & 360 & 340 \\ 50 & 40 & 30 \end{bmatrix} \begin{matrix} \text{Protein} \\ \text{Carbohydrate} \\ \text{Fat} \end{matrix}$$

with column headers Mix X, Mix Y, Mix Z.

73. (A) $9,950 (B) $16,400 (C) NM gives the total cost per town.
(D)

$$NM = \begin{bmatrix} \$9,950 \\ \$16,400 \end{bmatrix} \begin{matrix} \text{Berkeley} \\ \text{Oakland} \end{matrix}$$

(E)
$$[1 \quad 1]N = [3,000 \quad 1,300 \quad 13,000]$$
with column headers Telephone call, House call, Letter.

(F)
$$N\begin{bmatrix} 1 \\ 1 \\ 1 \end{bmatrix} = \begin{bmatrix} 6,500 \\ 10,800 \end{bmatrix} \begin{matrix} \text{Berkeley} \\ \text{Oakland} \end{matrix}$$
with column header Total contacts.

Exercises 4-5

1. (A) $\begin{bmatrix} 2 & -3 \\ 0 & 0 \end{bmatrix}$ (B) $\begin{bmatrix} 2 & 0 \\ 4 & 0 \end{bmatrix}$ **3.** (A) $\begin{bmatrix} 0 & 0 \\ 4 & 5 \end{bmatrix}$ (B) $\begin{bmatrix} 0 & -3 \\ 0 & 5 \end{bmatrix}$ **5.** (A) $\begin{bmatrix} 2 & -3 \\ 4 & 5 \end{bmatrix}$ (B) $\begin{bmatrix} 2 & -3 \\ 4 & 5 \end{bmatrix}$ **7.** $\begin{bmatrix} -2 & 1 & 3 \\ 2 & 4 & -2 \\ 5 & 1 & 0 \end{bmatrix}$

9. $\begin{bmatrix} -2 & 1 & 3 \\ 2 & 4 & -2 \\ 5 & 1 & 0 \end{bmatrix}$ **11.** Yes **13.** No **15.** Yes **17.** No **19.** Yes **31.** $\begin{bmatrix} -1 & 0 \\ -3 & 1 \end{bmatrix}$ **33.** $\begin{bmatrix} 3 & -2 \\ -1 & 1 \end{bmatrix}$ **35.** $\begin{bmatrix} 7 & -3 \\ -2 & 1 \end{bmatrix}$

37. $\begin{bmatrix} -5 & -12 & 3 \\ -2 & -4 & 1 \\ 2 & 5 & -1 \end{bmatrix}$ **39.** $\begin{bmatrix} 6 & -2 & -1 \\ -5 & 2 & 1 \\ -3 & 1 & 1 \end{bmatrix}$ **41.** $\begin{bmatrix} -2 & -3 \\ 3 & 4 \end{bmatrix}$ **43.** Does not exist **45.** $\begin{bmatrix} 1.5 & -0.5 \\ -2 & 1 \end{bmatrix}$ **47.** $\begin{bmatrix} \frac{1}{2} & 0 \\ 0 & \frac{1}{2} \end{bmatrix}$

49. $\begin{bmatrix} \frac{1}{3} & 0 \\ 0 & -\frac{1}{5} \end{bmatrix}$ **51.** $\begin{bmatrix} \frac{1}{4} & 0 & 0 \\ 0 & \frac{1}{2} & 0 \\ 0 & 0 & -\frac{1}{8} \end{bmatrix}$ **53.** $\begin{bmatrix} 1 & 2 & 2 \\ -2 & -3 & -4 \\ -1 & -2 & -1 \end{bmatrix}$ **55.** Does not exist **57.** $\begin{bmatrix} -3 & -2 & 1.5 \\ 4 & 3 & -2 \\ 3 & 2 & -1.25 \end{bmatrix}$

59. $\begin{bmatrix} -1.75 & -0.375 & 0.5 \\ -5.5 & -1.25 & 1 \\ 0.5 & 0.25 & 0 \end{bmatrix}$ **63.** M^{-1} exists if and only if all the elements on the main diagonal are nonzero.
65. $A^{-1} = A; A^2 = I$ **67.** $A^{-1} = A; A^2 = I$ **69.** 36 44 5 5 61 82 14 14 25 37 49 64 36 54 47 66 43 62

71. GONE WITH THE WIND **73.** 27 19 55 9 35 50 114 74 70 69 23 19 48 18 62 36 69 72 42 72 52 78 79 56 70 5 19 29 0 24
75. THE GREATEST SHOW ON EARTH

Exercises 4-6

1. $3x_1 + x_2 = 5$
$\quad 2x_1 - x_2 = -4$

3. $-3x_1 + x_2 = 3$
$\quad 2x_1 + x_3 = -4$
$\quad -x_1 + 3x_2 - 2x_3 = 2$

5. $\begin{bmatrix} 3 & -4 \\ 2 & 1 \end{bmatrix}\begin{bmatrix} x_1 \\ x_2 \end{bmatrix} = \begin{bmatrix} 1 \\ 5 \end{bmatrix}$

7. $\begin{bmatrix} 1 & -3 & 2 \\ -2 & 3 & 0 \\ 1 & 1 & 4 \end{bmatrix}\begin{bmatrix} x_1 \\ x_2 \\ x_3 \end{bmatrix} = \begin{bmatrix} -3 \\ 1 \\ -2 \end{bmatrix}$

9. $x_1 = -8, x_2 = 2$ **11.** $x_1 = 0, x_2 = 4$ **13.** $x_1 = 3, x_2 = -2$ **15.** $x_1 = 11, x_2 = 4$ **17.** $x_1 = 4, x_2 = 1$ **19.** $x_1 = 9.5, x_2 = -6$
21. No solution **23.** (A) $x_1 = -3, x_2 = 2$ (B) $x_1 = -1, x_2 = 2$ (C) $x_1 = -8, x_2 = 3$
25. (A) $x_1 = 17, x_2 = -5$ (B) $x_1 = 7, x_2 = -2$ (C) $x_1 = 24, x_2 = -7$
27. (A) $x_1 = 1, x_2 = 0, x_3 = 0$ (B) $x_1 = -7, x_2 = -2, x_3 = 3$ (C) $x_1 = 17, x_2 = 5, x_3 = -7$
29. (A) $x_1 = 8, x_2 = -6, x_3 = -2$ (B) $x_1 = -6, x_2 = 6, x_3 = 2$ (C) $x_1 = 20, x_2 = -16, x_3 = -10$ **31.** $X = A^{-1}B$ **33.** $X = BA^{-1}$
35. $X = A^{-1}BA$ **37.** $x_1 = 2t + 2.5, x_2 = t, t$ any real number **39.** No solution
41. $x_1 = 13t + 3, x_2 = 8t + 1, x_3 = t, t$ any real number **43.** $X = (A - B)^{-1}C$ **45.** $X = (A + I)^{-1}C$
47. $X = (A + B)^{-1}(C + D)$ **49.** (A) $x_1 = 1, x_2 = 0$ (B) $x_1 = -2,000, x_2 = 1,000$ (C) $x_1 = 2,001, x_2 = -1,000$
51. $x_1 = 18.2, x_2 = 27.9, x_3 = -15.2$ **53.** $x_1 = 24, x_2 = 5, x_3 = -2, x_4 = 15$
55. (A) Concert 1: 7,500 $25 tickets, 2,500 $35 tickets
 Concert 2: 5,000 $25 tickets, 5,000 $35 tickets
 Concert 3: 2,500 $25 tickets, 7,500 $35 tickets
(B) No
(C) $250,000 + 10t, 0 \le t \le 10,000$

57. $x_1 = $ number of hours plant A operates
 $x_2 = $ number of hours plant B operates
 $10x_1 + 8x_2 = k_1$ Number of car frames produced
 $5x_1 + 8x_2 = k_2$ Number of truck frames produced

 Order 1: 280 hr at plant A and 25 hr at plant B
 Order 2: 160 hr at plant A and 150 hr at plant B
 Order 3: 80 hr at plant A and 225 hr at plant B

59. x_1 = president's bonus
$\quad$ x_2 = executive vice-president's bonus
$\quad$ x_3 = associate vice-president's bonus
$\quad$ x_4 = assistant vice-president's bonus
$\qquad x_1 + 0.03x_2 + 0.03x_3 + 0.03x_4 = 60{,}000$
$\quad 0.025x_1 + \quad x_2 + 0.025x_3 + 0.025x_4 = 50{,}000$
$\quad 0.02x_1 + 0.02x_2 + \quad x_3 + 0.02x_4 = 40{,}000$
$\quad 0.015x_1 + 0.015x_2 + 0.015x_3 + \quad x_4 = 30{,}000$
President: \$56,600; executive vice-president: \$47,000; associate
vice-president: \$37,400; assistant vice-president: \$27,900

61. (A) x_1 = number of ounces of mix A
$\qquad x_2$ = number of ounces of mix B
$\qquad 0.20x_1 + 0.14x_2 = k_1$ *Protein*
$\qquad 0.04x_1 + 0.03x_2 = k_2$ *Fat*
$\qquad$ Diet 1: 50 oz mix A and 500 oz mix B
$\qquad$ Diet 2: 450 oz mix A and 0 oz mix B
$\qquad$ Diet 3: 150 oz mix A and 500 oz mix B
$\quad$ (B) No

Exercises 4-7

1. 40¢ from A; 20¢ from E **3.** $\begin{bmatrix} 0.6 & -0.2 \\ -0.2 & 0.9 \end{bmatrix}; \begin{bmatrix} 1.8 & 0.4 \\ 0.4 & 1.2 \end{bmatrix}$ **5.** $X = \begin{bmatrix} x_1 \\ x_2 \end{bmatrix} = \begin{bmatrix} 16.4 \\ 9.2 \end{bmatrix}$

7. 20¢ from A; 10¢ from B; 10¢ from E **11.** Agriculture: \$18 billion; building: \$15.6 billion; energy: \$22.4 billion

13. $\begin{bmatrix} 1.4 & 0.4 \\ 0.6 & 1.6 \end{bmatrix}; \begin{bmatrix} 24 \\ 46 \end{bmatrix}$ **15.** $I - M$ is singular; X does not exist. **17.** $\begin{bmatrix} 1.58 & 0.24 & 0.58 \\ 0.4 & 1.2 & 0.4 \\ 0.22 & 0.16 & 1.22 \end{bmatrix}; \begin{bmatrix} 38.6 \\ 18 \\ 17.4 \end{bmatrix}$

19. (A) Agriculture: \$80 million; manufacturing: \$64 million
$\quad$ (B) The final demand for agriculture increases to \$54 million and the final demand for manufacturing decreases to \$38 million.

21. $\begin{bmatrix} 0.25 & 0.1 \\ 0.25 & 0.3 \end{bmatrix}$ **23.** The total output of the energy sector should be 75% of the total output of the mining sector.

25. Each element should be between 0 and 1, inclusive. **27.** Coal: \$28 billion; steel: \$26 billion
29. Agriculture: \$148 million; tourism: \$146 million
31. Agriculture: \$40.1 billion; manufacturing: \$29.4 billion; energy: \$34.4 billion
33. Year 1: agriculture: \$65 billion; energy: \$83 billion; labor: \$71 billion; manufacturing: \$88 billion
$\quad$ Year 2: agriculture: \$81 billion; energy: \$97 billion; labor: \$83 billion; manufacturing: \$99 billion
$\quad$ Year 3: agriculture: \$117 billion; energy: \$124 billion; labor: \$106 billion; manufacturing: \$120 billion

Chapter 4 Review Exercises

1. $x = 4, y = 4$ *(4-1)* **2.** $x = 4, y = 4$ *(4-1)*
3. (A) Not in reduced form; $R_1 \leftrightarrow R_2$ (B) Not in reduced form; $\frac{1}{3}R_2 \rightarrow R_2$ (C) Reduced form
$\quad$ (D) Not in reduced form; $(-1)R_2 + R_1 \rightarrow R_1$ *(4-3)*
4. (A) $2 \times 5, 3 \times 2$ (B) $a_{24} = 3, a_{15} = 2, b_{31} = -1, b_{22} = 4$ (C) AB is not defined; BA is defined *(4-2, 4-4)*
5. (A) $x_1 = 8, x_2 = 2$ (B) $x_1 = -15.5, x_2 = 23.5$ *(4-6)* **6.** $\begin{bmatrix} 3 & 3 \\ 4 & 2 \end{bmatrix}$ *(4-4)* **7.** Not defined *(4-4)* **8.** $\begin{bmatrix} -3 & 0 \\ 1 & -1 \end{bmatrix}$ *(4-4)*

9. $\begin{bmatrix} 4 & 3 \\ 7 & 4 \end{bmatrix}$ *(4-4)* **10.** Not defined *(4-4)* **11.** $\begin{bmatrix} 5 \\ 5 \end{bmatrix}$ *(4-4)* **12.** $\begin{bmatrix} 2 & 3 \\ 4 & 6 \end{bmatrix}$ *(4-4)* **13.** $[8]$ *(4-4)* **14.** Not defined *(4-4)*

15. $\begin{bmatrix} -2 & 3 \\ 3 & -4 \end{bmatrix}$ *(4-5)* **16.** $x_1 = 9, x_2 = -11$ *(4-1)* **17.** $x_1 = 9, x_2 = -11$ *(4-2)*

18. $x_1 = 9, x_2 = -11$; $x_1 = 16, x_2 = -19$; $x_1 = -2, x_2 = 4$ *(4-6)* **19.** Not defined *(4-4)* **20.** $\begin{bmatrix} 10 & -8 \\ 4 & 6 \end{bmatrix}$ *(4-4)*

21. $\begin{bmatrix} -2 & 8 \\ 8 & 6 \end{bmatrix}$ *(4-4)* **22.** $\begin{bmatrix} -2 & -1 & -3 \\ 4 & 2 & 6 \\ 6 & 3 & 9 \end{bmatrix}$ *(4-4)* **23.** $[9]$ *(4-4)* **24.** $\begin{bmatrix} 10 & -5 & 1 \\ -1 & -4 & -5 \\ 1 & -7 & -2 \end{bmatrix}$ *(4-4)* **25.** $\begin{bmatrix} -\frac{5}{2} & 2 & -\frac{1}{2} \\ 1 & -1 & 1 \\ \frac{1}{2} & 0 & -\frac{1}{2} \end{bmatrix}$ *(4-5)*

26. (A) $x_1 = 2, x_2 = 1, x_3 = -1$
$\quad$ (B) $x_1 = -5t - 12, x_2 = 3t + 7, x_3 = t$
$\qquad$ for t any real number
$\quad$ (C) $x_1 = -2t + 5, x_2 = t + 3, x_3 = t$
$\qquad$ for t any real number *(4-3)*

27. $x_1 = 2, x_2 = 1, x_3 = -1$; $x_1 = 1, x_2 = -2, x_3 = 1$; $x_1 = -1, x_2 = 2, x_3 = -2$ *(4-6)*
28. The system has an infinite number of solutions for $k = 3$ and a unique solution for any other value of k. *(4-3)*
29. $(I - M)^{-1} = \begin{bmatrix} 1.4 & 0.3 \\ 0.8 & 1.6 \end{bmatrix}$; $X = \begin{bmatrix} 48 \\ 56 \end{bmatrix}$ *(4-7)* **30.** $\begin{bmatrix} 0.3 & 0.4 \\ 0.15 & 0.2 \end{bmatrix}$ *(4-7)*

31. $I - M$ is singular; X does not exist. *(4-5)* **32.** $x = 3.46, y = 1.69$ *(4-1)*
33. $\begin{bmatrix} -0.9 & -0.1 & 5 \\ 0.8 & 0.2 & -4 \\ 0.1 & -0.1 & 0 \end{bmatrix}$ *(4-5)* **34.** $x_1 = 1{,}400, x_2 = 3{,}200, x_3 = 2{,}400$ *(4-6)*
$\qquad \qquad \qquad \qquad$ **35.** $x_1 = 1{,}400, x_2 = 3{,}200, x_3 = 2{,}400$ *(4-3)*
36. $(I - M)^{-1} = \begin{bmatrix} 1.3 & 0.4 & 0.7 \\ 0.2 & 1.6 & 0.3 \\ 0.1 & 0.8 & 1.4 \end{bmatrix}$; $X = \begin{bmatrix} 81 \\ 49 \\ 62 \end{bmatrix}$ *(4-7)*

37. (A) Unique solution

(B) Either no solution or an infinite number of solutions *(4-6)*

39. (B) is the only correct solution. *(4-6)*

41. x_1 = number of tons of Voisey's Bay ore

x_2 = number of tons of Hawk Ridge ore

$0.02x_1 + 0.03x_2 = 6$

$0.04x_1 + 0.02x_2 = 8$

$x_1 = 150$ tons of Voisey's Bay ore

$x_2 = 100$ tons of Hawk Ridge ore *(4-3)*

42. (A) $\begin{bmatrix} x_1 \\ x_2 \end{bmatrix} = \begin{bmatrix} -25 & 37.5 \\ 50 & -25 \end{bmatrix}\begin{bmatrix} 6 \\ 8 \end{bmatrix} = \begin{bmatrix} 150 \\ 100 \end{bmatrix}$

$x_1 = 150$ tons of Voisey's Bay ore

$x_2 = 100$ tons of Hawk Ridge ore

43. (A) x_1 = number of 3,000-ft^3 hoppers

x_2 = number of 4,500-ft^3 hoppers

x_3 = number of 6,000-ft^3 hoppers

$x_1 + \quad x_2 + \quad x_3 = 20$

$3{,}000x_1 + 4{,}500x_2 + 6{,}000x_3 = 108{,}000$

$x_1 = t - 12$ 3,000-ft^3 hoppers

$x_2 = 32 - 2t$ 4,500-ft^3 hoppers

$x_3 = t$ 6,000-ft^3 hoppers

where $t = 12, 13, 14, 15,$ or 16

(B) The minimum monthly cost is \$5,700 when 8 4,500-ft^3 and 12 6,000-ft^3 hoppers are leased. *(4-3)*

45. (A) \$6.35

(B) Elements in *MN* give the total labor costs for each calculator at each plant.

(C)

$MN = \begin{bmatrix} \$3.65 & \$3.00 \\ \$6.35 & \$5.20 \end{bmatrix} \begin{matrix} \text{Model A} \\ \text{Model B} \end{matrix}$ *(4-4)*

with column headers CA   TX

49. x_1 = number of \$8 tickets

x_2 = number of \$12 tickets

x_3 = number of \$20 tickets

$x_1 + \quad x_2 + \quad x_3 = 25{,}000$

$8x_1 + 12x_2 + 20x_3 = k_1$ Return requested

$x_1 \qquad - \quad x_3 = 0$

50. $x_1 + \quad x_2 + \quad x_3 = 25{,}000$

$8x_1 + 12x_2 + 20x_3 = k_1$ Return requested

Concert 1: $2t - 5{,}000$ \$8 tickets, $30{,}000 - 3t$ \$12 tickets, and t \$20 tickets, where t is an integer satisfying $2{,}500 \le t \le 10{,}000$

Concert 2: $2t - 7{,}500$ \$8 tickets, $32{,}500 - 3t$ \$12 tickets, and t \$20 tickets, where t is an integer satisfying $3{,}750 \le t \le 10{,}833$

Concert 3: $2t - 10{,}000$ \$8 tickets, $35{,}000 - 3t$ \$12 tickets, and t \$20 tickets, where t is an integer satisfying $5{,}000 \le t \le 11{,}666$ *(4-3)*

51. (A) Agriculture: \$80 billion; fabrication: \$60 billion

(B) Agriculture: \$135 billion; fabrication: \$145 billion *(4-7)*

38. (A) Unique solution

(B) No solution

(C) Infinite number of solutions *(4-3)*

40. (A) $C = 243{,}000 + 22.45x$; $R = 59.95x$

(B) $x = 6{,}480$ machines; $R = C = \$388{,}476$

(C) Profit occurs if $x > 6{,}480$; loss occurs if $x < 6{,}480$. *(4-1)*

(B) $\begin{bmatrix} x_1 \\ x_2 \end{bmatrix} = \begin{bmatrix} -25 & 37.5 \\ 50 & -25 \end{bmatrix}\begin{bmatrix} 7.5 \\ 7 \end{bmatrix} = \begin{bmatrix} 75 \\ 200 \end{bmatrix}$

$x_1 = 75$ tons of Voisey's Bay ore

$x_2 = 200$ tons of Hawk Ridge ore *(4-6)*

44. (A) Elements in *MN* give the cost of materials for each alloy from each supplier.

(B)

$MN = \begin{bmatrix} \$7{,}620 & \$7{,}530 \\ \$13{,}880 & \$13{,}930 \end{bmatrix} \begin{matrix} \text{Alloy 1} \\ \text{Alloy 2} \end{matrix}$

with column headers Supplier A   Supplier B

(C)

$[1\ 1]MN = [\$21{,}500 \quad \$21{,}460]$ Total material costs *(4-4)*

with column headers Supplier A   Supplier B

46. x_1 = amount invested at 5%

x_2 = amount invested at 10%

$x_1 + \quad x_2 = 5{,}000$

$0.05x_1 + 0.1x_2 = \quad 400$

\$2,000 at 5%, \$3,000 at 10% *(4-3)*

47. \$2,000 at 5% and \$3,000 at 10% *(4-6)*

48. No to both. The annual yield must be between \$250 and \$500 inclusive. *(4-6)*

Concert 1: 5000 \$8 tickets, 15,000 \$12 tickets, and 5,000 \$20 tickets

Concert 2: 7,500 \$8 tickets, 10,000 \$12 tickets, and 7,500 \$20 tickets

Concert 3: 10,000 \$8 tickets, 5,000 \$12 tickets, and 10,000 \$20 tickets *(4-6)*

52. GRAPHING UTILITY *(4-5)*

53. (A) 1st & Elm: $x_1 + x_4 = 1{,}300$

2nd & Elm: $x_1 - x_2 = \quad 400$

2nd & Oak: $x_2 + x_3 = \quad 700$

1st & Oak: $x_3 - x_4 = -200$

(B) $x_1 = 1{,}300 - t$, $x_2 = 900 - t$, $x_3 = t - 200$, $x_4 = t$, where $200 \le t \le 900$

(C) 900; 200 (D) Elm St.: 800; 2nd St.: 400; Oak St.: 300 *(4-3)*

Chapter 5

Exercises 5–1

1.   **3.**   **5.**   **7.**   **9.**

11. (A)   (B)   **13.** (A)   (B)

15. Let h = number of overtime hours; $h < 20$ **17.** Let s = annual salary; $s \geq \$65{,}000$

19. Let a = number of freshmen admitted; $a \leq 1{,}700$ **21.** $2x + 3y = -6$; $2x + 3y \geq -6$ **23.** $y = 3$; $y < 3$

25. $4x - 5y = 0$; $4x - 5y \geq 0$ **27.** Let x = enrollment in finite mathematics; let y = enrollment in calculus; $x + y < 300$

29. Let x = revenue; y = cost; $x \leq y - 20{,}000$

31. Let x = number of grams of saturated fat; let y = number of grams of unsaturated fat; $x > 3y$

33.   **35.**   **37.**   **39.**

41. The solution set is the empty set and has no graph.

43. Let x = number of acres planted with corn. Let y = number of acres planted with soybeans. $40x + 32y \leq 5{,}000$, $x \geq 0$, $y \geq 0$

45. Let x = number of pounds of brand A.
Let y = number of pounds of brand B.
(A) $0.26x + 0.16y \geq 120$, $x \geq 0$, $y \geq 0$ (B) $0.03x + 0.08y \leq 28$, $x \geq 0$, $y \geq 0$

47. Let x = number of pounds of the standard blend.
Let y = number of pounds of the deluxe blend.
$0.3x + 0.09y \geq 0.20(x + y)$, $x \geq 0$, $y \geq 0$

49. Let x = number of weeks Plant A is operated.
Let y = number of weeks Plant B is operated.
$10x + 8y \geq 400$, $x \geq 0$, $y \geq 0$

53. Let x = number of regular mattresses cut per day.
Let y = number of king mattresses cut per day
$5x + 6y \leq 3{,}000$, $x \geq 0$, $y \geq 0$

51. Let x = number of radio spots.
Let y = number of television spots.
$200x + 800y \leq 10{,}000$, $x \geq 0$, $y \geq 0$

Exercises 5–2

1. IV **3.** I **5.**

7.

9. IV; $(8, 0), (18, 0), (6, 4)$ **11.** I; $(0, 16), (6, 4), (18, 0)$

13. Bounded

15. Bounded

17. Unbounded

19. Bounded

21. Unbounded

23. Bounded

25. Empty

27. Unbounded

29. Bounded

31. Bounded

33. (A) $3x + 4y = 36$ and $3x + 2y = 30$ intersect at $(8, 3)$;
  $3x + 4y = 36$ and $x = 0$ intersect at $(0, 9)$;
  $3x + 4y = 36$ and $y = 0$ intersect at $(12, 0)$;
  $3x + 2y = 30$ and $x = 0$ intersect at $(0, 15)$;
  $3x + 2y = 30$ and $y = 0$ intersect at $(10, 0)$;
  $x = 0$ and $y = 0$ intersect at $(0, 0)$

(B) $(8, 3), (0, 9), (10, 0), (0, 0)$

35. $6x + 4y \leq 108$
  $x + y \leq 24$
  $x \geq 0$
  $y \geq 0$

37. (A) All production schedules in the feasible region that are on the graph of $50x + 60y = 1{,}100$ will result in a profit of $1,100.

(B) There are many possible choices. For example, producing 5 trick skis and 15 slalom skis will produce a profit of $1,150. All the production schedules in the feasible region that are on the graph of $50x + 60y = 1{,}150$ will result in a profit of $1,150.

39. $20x + 10y \geq 460$
  $30x + 30y \geq 960$
  $5x + 10y \geq 220$
  $x \geq 0$
  $y \geq 0$

41. $10x + 20y \leq 800$
  $20x + 10y \leq 640$
  $x \geq 0$
  $y \geq 0$

Exercises 5–3

1. Max $P = 16$ at $x = 7$ and $y = 9$

3. Max $P = 84$ at $x = 7$ and $y = 9$, at $x = 0$ and $y = 12$, and at every point on the line segment joining the preceding two points.

5. Min $C = 32$ at $x = 0$ and $y = 8$ **7.** Min $C = 36$ at $x = 4$ and $y = 3$ **9.** Max $P = 30$ at $x = 4$ and $y = 2$

11. Min $z = 14$ at $x = 4$ and $y = 2$; no max **13.** Max $P = 260$ at $x = 2$ and $y = 5$ **15.** Min $z = 140$ at $x = 14$ and $y = 0$; no max

17. Min $P = 20$ at $x = 0$ and $y = 2$; Max $P = 150$ at $x = 5$ and $y = 0$ **19.** Feasible region empty; no optimal solutions

21. Min $P = 140$ at $x = 3$ and $y = 8$; Max $P = 260$ at $x = 8$ and $y = 10$, at $x = 12$ and $y = 2$, or at any point on the line segment from $(8, 10)$ to $(12, 2)$ **23.** Max $P = 26{,}000$ at $x = 400$ and $y = 600$ **25.** Max $P = 5{,}507$ at $x = 6.62$ and $y = 4.25$

27. Max $z = 2$ at $x = 4$ and $y = 2$; Min z does not exist **29.** (A) $2a < b$ (B) $\frac{1}{3}a < b < 2a$ (C) $b < \frac{1}{3}a$ (D) $b = 2a$ (E) $b = \frac{1}{3}a$

31. (A) Let: x = number of trick skis
  y = number of slalom skis produced per day.
  Maximize $P = 40x + 30y$
  subject to $6x + 4y \leq 108$
  $x + y \leq 24$
  $x \geq 0, y \geq 0$
  Max profit = $780 when 6 trick skis and 18 slalom skis are produced.

(B) Max profit decreases to $720 when 18 trick skis and no slalom skis are produced.

(C) Max profit increases to $1,080 when no trick skis and 24 slalom skis are produced.

33. (A) Let x = number of days to operate plant A
$\quad\quad\quad y$ = number of days to operate plant B
$\quad\quad$ Minimize $C = 1000x + 900y$
$\quad\quad$ subject to $20x + 25y \geq 200$
$\quad\quad\quad\quad\quad\quad 60x + 50y \geq 500$
$\quad\quad\quad\quad\quad\quad\quad x \geq 0, y \geq 0$
$\quad\quad$ Plant A: 5 days; Plant B: 4 days; min cost $8,600
$\quad$ (B) Plant A: 10 days; Plant B: 0 days; min cost $6,000
$\quad$ (C) Plant A: 0 days; Plant B: 10 days; min cost $8,000

35. Let x = number of buses
$\quad\quad y$ = number of vans
$\quad$ Minimize $C = 1,200x + 100y$
$\quad$ subject to $40x + 8y \geq 400$
$\quad\quad\quad\quad\quad\quad 3x + \ y \leq \ 36$
$\quad\quad\quad\quad\quad\quad\ x \geq 0, y \geq 0$
$\quad$ 7 buses, 15 vans; min cost $9,900

37. Let x = amount invested in the CD
$\quad\quad y$ = amount invested in the mutual fund
$\quad$ Maximize $P = 0.05x + 0.09y$
$\quad$ subject to $x + y \leq 60,000$
$\quad\quad\quad\quad\quad\quad\quad y \geq 10,000$
$\quad\quad\quad\quad\quad\quad\quad x \geq 2y$
$\quad\quad\quad\quad\quad\quad\ x, y \geq 0$
$40,000 in the CD and $20,000 in the mutual fund;
max return is $3,800

39. (A) Let x = number of gallons produced by the old process
$\quad\quad\quad y$ = number of gallons produced by the new process
$\quad\quad$ Maximize $P = 60x + 20y$
$\quad\quad$ subject to $20x + \ 5y \leq 16,000$
$\quad\quad\quad\quad\quad\quad\quad 40x + 20y \leq 30,000$
$\quad\quad\quad\quad\quad\quad\quad\quad x \geq 0, y \geq 0$
$\quad\quad$ Max P = $450 when 750 gal are produced using the old
$\quad\quad$ process exclusively.
$\quad$ (B) Max P = $380 when 400 gal are produced using the old
$\quad\quad\quad$ process and 700 gal are produced using the new process.
$\quad$ (C) Max P = $288 when 1,440 gal are produced using the
$\quad\quad\quad$ new process exclusively.

41. (A) Let x = number of bags of brand A
$\quad\quad\quad y$ = number of bags of brand B
$\quad\quad$ Maximize $N = 8x + 3y$
$\quad\quad$ subject to $4x + 4y \geq 1,000$
$\quad\quad\quad\quad\quad\quad 2x + \ y \leq 400$
$\quad\quad\quad\quad\quad\quad\ x \geq 0, y \geq 0$
$\quad\quad$ 150 bags brand A, 100 bags brand B;
$\quad\quad$ max nitrogen 1,500 lb
$\quad$ (B) 0 bags brand A, 250 bags brand B;
$\quad\quad\quad$ min nitrogen 750 lb

43. Let x = number of cubic yards of mix A
$\quad\quad y$ = number of cubic yards of mix B
$\quad$ Minimize $C = 30x + 35y$
$\quad$ subject to $20x + 10y \geq 460$
$\quad\quad\quad\quad\quad\quad 30x + 30y \geq 960$
$\quad\quad\quad\quad\quad\quad\ 5x + 10y \geq 220$
$\quad\quad\quad\quad\quad\quad\ x \geq 0, y \geq 0$
$\quad$ 20 yd³A, 12 yd³B; $1,020

45. Let x = number of mice used
$\quad\quad y$ = number of rats used
$\quad$ Maximize $P = x + y$
$\quad$ subject to $10x + 20y \leq 800$
$\quad\quad\quad\quad\quad\quad 20x + 10y \leq 640$
$\quad\quad\quad\quad\quad\quad\ x \geq 0, y \geq 0$
$\quad$ 48; 16 mice, 32 rats

Chapter 5 Review Exercises

1. *(5-1)*   **2.** *(5-1)*   **3.** Bounded *(5-2)* **4.** Unbounded *(5-2)* **5.** Bounded *(5-2)* **6.** Unbounded *(5-2)*

7. $2x - 3y = 12; 2x - 3y \leq 12$ *(5-1)*
8. $4x + y = 8; 4x + y \geq 8$ *(5-1)*
9. Max P = 24 at $x = 0$ and $y = 4$ *(5-3)*
10. Min C = 40 at $x = 0$ and $y = 20$ *(5-3)*
11. Max P = 26 at $x = 2$ and $y = 5$ *(5-3)*
12. Min C = 51 at $x = 3$ and $y = 9$ *(5-3)*
13. Max P = 36 at $x = 8$ and $y = 6$ *(5-3)*

14. Let x = the number of calculator boards. *(5-1)*
$\quad$ Let y = the number of toaster boards
$\quad$ (A) $4x + 3y \leq 300, x \geq 0, y \geq 0$ (B) $2x + y \leq 120, x \geq 0, y \geq 0$

15. (A) Let x = number of regular sails
$\quad\quad\quad y$ = number of competition sails
$\quad\quad$ Maximize $P = 100x + 200y$
$\quad\quad$ subject to $2x + \ 3y \leq 150$
$\quad\quad\quad\quad\quad\quad 4x + 10y \leq 380$
$\quad\quad\quad\quad\quad\quad\quad x, y \geq 0$
$\quad\quad$ Max P = $8,500 when 45 regular and 20 competition
$\quad\quad$ sails are produced.
$\quad$ (B) Max profit increases to $9,880 when 38 competition and
$\quad\quad\quad$ no regular sails are produced.
$\quad$ (C) Max profit decreases to $7,500 when no competition and
$\quad\quad\quad$ 75 regular sails are produced. *(5-3)*

16. (A) Let x = number of grams of mix A
$\quad\quad\quad y$ = number of grams of mix B
$\quad\quad$ Minimize $C = 0.04x + 0.09y$
$\quad\quad$ subject to $2x + 5y \geq \ 850$
$\quad\quad\quad\quad\quad\quad 2x + 4y \geq \ 800$
$\quad\quad\quad\quad\quad\quad 4x + 5y \geq 1,150$
$\quad\quad\quad\quad\quad\quad\quad x, y \geq 0$
$\quad\quad$ Min C = $16.50 when 300 g mix A and 50 g mix B are
$\quad\quad$ used.
$\quad$ (B) The minimum cost decreases to $13.00 when 100 g mix A
$\quad\quad\quad$ and 150 g mix B are used.
$\quad$ (C) The minimum cost increases to $17.00 when 425 g mix A
$\quad\quad\quad$ and no mix B are used. *(5-3)*

Chapter 6

Exercises 6-1

1. (A) 2   (B) 2 basic and 3 nonbasic variables   (C) 2 linear equations with 2 variables
3. (A) 5   (B) 4   (C) 5 basic and 4 nonbasic variables   (D) 5 linear equations with 5 variables
5.

	Nonbasic	Basic	Feasible?
(A)	x_1, x_2	s_1, s_2	Yes
(B)	x_1, s_1	x_2, s_2	Yes
(C)	x_1, s_2	x_2, s_1	No
(D)	x_2, s_1	x_1, s_2	No
(E)	x_2, s_2	x_1, s_1	Yes
(F)	s_1, s_2	x_1, x_2	Yes

7.

	x_1	x_2	s_1	s_2	Feasible?
(A)	0	0	50	40	Yes
(B)	0	50	0	−60	No
(C)	0	20	30	0	Yes
(D)	25	0	0	15	Yes
(E)	40	0	−30	0	No
(F)	20	10	0	0	Yes

9.

$$x_1 + x_2 + s_1 = 16$$
$$2x_1 + x_2 + s_2 = 20$$

x_1	x_2	s_1	s_2	Intersection Point	Feasible?
0	0	16	20	O	Yes
0	16	0	4	A	Yes
0	20	−4	0	B	No
16	0	0	−12	E	No
10	0	6	0	D	Yes
4	12	0	0	C	Yes

11.

x_1	x_2	s_1	s_2	s_3	Intersection Point	Feasible?
0	0	22	12	20	O	Yes
0	22	0	−10	−24	C	No
0	12	10	0	−4	B	No
0	10	12	2	0	A	Yes
11	0	0	1	9	G	Yes
12	0	−2	0	8	H	No
20	0	−18	−8	0	I	No
10	2	0	0	6	F	Yes
8	6	0	−2	0	E	No
4	8	6	0	0	D	Yes

$$2x_1 + x_2 + s_1 = 22$$
$$x_1 + x_2 + s_2 = 12$$
$$x_1 + 2x_2 + s_3 = 20$$

Exercises 6-2

1. (A) Basic: x_2, s_1, P; nonbasic: x_1, s_2 (B) $x_1 = 0, x_2 = 12, s_1 = 15, s_2 = 0, P = 50$ (C) Additional pivot required
3. (A) Basic: x_2, x_3, s_3, P; nonbasic: x_1, s_1, s_2 (B) $x_1 = 0, x_2 = 15, x_3 = 5, s_1 = 0, s_2 = 0, s_3 = 12, P = 45$ (C) No optimal solution

5.

Enter ↓

$$
\begin{array}{c}
\\
\text{Exit} \to \ s_1 \\
s_2 \\
P
\end{array}
\left[
\begin{array}{ccccc|c}
x_1 & x_2 & s_1 & s_2 & P & \\
① & 4 & 1 & 0 & 0 & 4 \\
3 & 5 & 0 & 1 & 0 & 24 \\
\hline
-8 & -5 & 0 & 0 & 1 & 0
\end{array}
\right]
$$

$$
\begin{array}{c}
x_1 \\
\sim s_2 \\
P
\end{array}
\left[
\begin{array}{ccccc|c}
1 & 4 & 1 & 0 & 0 & 4 \\
0 & -7 & -3 & 1 & 0 & 12 \\
\hline
0 & 27 & 8 & 0 & 1 & 32
\end{array}
\right]
$$

7.

Enter ↓

$$
\begin{array}{c}
\\
\text{Exit} \to \ x_2 \\
s_2 \\
s_3 \\
P
\end{array}
\left[
\begin{array}{cccccc|c}
x_1 & x_2 & s_1 & s_2 & s_3 & P & \\
② & 1 & 1 & 0 & 0 & 0 & 4 \\
3 & 0 & 1 & 1 & 0 & 0 & 8 \\
0 & 0 & 2 & 0 & 1 & 0 & 2 \\
\hline
-4 & 0 & -3 & 0 & 0 & 1 & 5
\end{array}
\right]
$$

$$
\begin{array}{c}
x_1 \\
\sim s_2 \\
s_3 \\
P
\end{array}
\left[
\begin{array}{cccccc|c}
1 & \frac{1}{2} & \frac{1}{2} & 0 & 0 & 0 & 2 \\
0 & -\frac{3}{2} & -\frac{1}{2} & 1 & 0 & 0 & 2 \\
0 & 0 & 2 & 0 & 1 & 0 & 2 \\
\hline
0 & 2 & -1 & 0 & 0 & 1 & 13
\end{array}
\right]
$$

9. (A)
$$2x_1 + x_2 + s_1 = 10$$
$$x_1 + 3x_2 + s_2 = 10$$
$$-15x_1 - 10x_2 + P = 0$$
$$x_1, x_2, s_1, s_2 \geq 0$$

(B)

Enter ↓

$$
\begin{array}{c}
\\
\text{Exit} \to \ s_1 \\
s_2 \\
P
\end{array}
\left[
\begin{array}{ccccc|c}
x_1 & x_2 & s_1 & s_2 & P & \\
② & 1 & 1 & 0 & 0 & 10 \\
1 & 3 & 0 & 1 & 0 & 10 \\
\hline
-15 & -10 & 0 & 0 & 1 & 0
\end{array}
\right]
$$

(C) Max $P = 80$ at $x_1 = 4$ and $x_2 = 2$

11. (A)
$$2x_1 + x_2 + s_1 = 10$$
$$x_1 + 3x_2 + s_2 = 10$$
$$-30x_1 - x_2 + P = 0$$
$$x_1, x_2, s_1, s_2 \geq 0$$

(B)

Enter ↓

$$
\begin{array}{c}
\\
\text{Exit} \to \ s_1 \\
s_2 \\
P
\end{array}
\left[
\begin{array}{ccccc|c}
x_1 & x_2 & s_1 & s_2 & P & \\
② & 1 & 1 & 0 & 0 & 10 \\
1 & 3 & 0 & 1 & 0 & 10 \\
\hline
-30 & -1 & 0 & 0 & 1 & 0
\end{array}
\right]
$$

(C) Max $P = 150$ at $x_1 = 5$ and $x_2 = 0$

13. Max $P = 260$ at $x_1 = 2$ and $x_2 = 5$

15. No optimal solution exists.

17. Max $P = 7$ at $x_1 = 3$ and $x_2 = 5$

19. Max $P = 58$ at $x_1 = 12$, $x_2 = 0$, and $x_3 = 2$

21. Max $P = 17$ at $x_1 = 4$, $x_2 = 3$, and $x_3 = 0$

23. Max $P = 22$ at $x_1 = 1$, $x_2 = 6$, and $x_3 = 0$

25. Max $P = 26,000$ at $x_1 = 400$ and $x_2 = 600$

27. Max $P = 450$ at $x_1 = 0$, $x_2 = 180$, and $x_3 = 30$

29. Max $P = 88$ at $x_1 = 24$ and $x_2 = 8$

31. No solution   **33.** Choosing either column produces the same optimal solution: max $P = 13$ at $x_1 = 3$ and $x_2 = 10$.

35. Choosing column 1: max $P = 60$ at $x_1 = 12$, $x_2 = 8$, and $x_3 = 0$. Choosing column 2: max $P = 60$ at $x_1 = 0$, $x_2 = 20$, and $x_3 = 0$.

37. Let $x_1 =$ number of A components

$x_2 =$ number of B components

$x_3 =$ number of C components

Maximize $P = 7x_1 + 8x_2 + 10x_3$

subject to $2x_1 + 3x_2 + 2x_3 \le 1,000$

$x_1 + x_2 + 2x_3 \le 800$

$x_1, x_2, x_3 \ge 0$

200 A components, 0 B components, and 300 C components; max profit is \$4,400

39. Let $x_1 =$ amount invested in government bonds

$x_2 =$ amount invested in mutual funds

$x_3 =$ amount invested in money market funds

Maximize $P = 0.08x_1 + 0.13x_2 + 0.15x_3$

subject to $x_1 + x_2 + x_3 \le 100,000$

$-x_1 + x_2 + x_3 \le 0$

$x_1, x_2, x_3 \ge 0$

\$50,000 in government bonds, \$0 in mutual funds, and \$50,000 in money market funds; max return is \$11,500

41. Let $x_1 =$ number of ads placed in daytime shows

$x_2 =$ number of ads placed in prime-time shows

$x_3 =$ number of ads placed in late-night shows

Maximize $P = 14,000x_1 + 24,000x_2 + 18,000x_3$

subject to $x_1 + x_2 + x_3 \le 15$

$1,000x_1 + 2,000x_2 + 1,500x_3 \le 20,000$

$x_1, x_2, x_3 \ge 0$

10 daytime ads, 5 prime-time ads, and 0 late-night ads; max number of potential customers is 260,000

43. Let $x_1 =$ number of colonial houses

$x_2 =$ number of split-level houses

$x_3 =$ number of ranch houses

Maximize $P = 20,000x_1 + 18,000x_2 + 24,000x_3$

subject to $\frac{1}{2}x_1 + \frac{1}{2}x_2 + x_3 \le 30$

$60,000x_1 + 60,000x_2 + 80,000x_3 \le 3,200,000$

$4,000x_1 + 3,000x_2 + 4,000x_3 \le 180,000$

$x_1, x_2, x_3 \ge 0$

20 colonial, 20 split-level, and 10 ranch houses; max profit is \$1,000,000

45. The model is the same as the model for Problem 43 except that $P = 17,000x_1 + 18,000x_2 + 24,000x_3$.

0 colonial, 40 split-level, and 10 ranch houses; max profit is \$960,000; 20,000 labor-hours are not used

47. The model is the same as the model for Problem 43 except that $P = 25,000x_1 + 18,000x_2 + 24,000x_3$.

45 colonial, 0 split-level, and 0 ranch houses; max profit is \$1,125,000; 7.5 acres of land and \$500,000 of capital are not used

49. Let $x_1 =$ number of grams of food A

$x_2 =$ number of grams of food B

$x_3 =$ number of grams of food C

Maximize $P = 3x_1 + 4x_2 + 5x_3$

subject to $x_1 + 3x_2 + 2x_3 \le 30$

$2x_1 + x_2 + 2x_3 \le 24$

$x_1, x_2, x_3 \ge 0$

0 g food A, 3 g food B, and 10.5 g food C; max protein is 64.5 units

51. Let $x_1 =$ number of undergraduate students

$x_2 =$ number of graduate students

$x_3 =$ number of faculty members

Maximize $P = 18x_1 + 25x_2 + 30x_3$

subject to $x_1 + x_2 + x_3 \le 20$

$100x_1 + 150x_2 + 200x_3 \le 3,200$

$x_1, x_2, x_3 \ge 0$

0 undergraduate students, 16 graduate students, and 4 faculty members; max number of interviews is 520

Exercises 6-3

1. $\begin{bmatrix} -5 \\ 0 \\ 3 \\ -1 \\ 8 \end{bmatrix}$ **3.** $\begin{bmatrix} 1 & -2 & 0 & 4 \end{bmatrix}$ **5.** $\begin{bmatrix} 2 & 5 \\ 1 & 2 \\ -6 & 0 \\ 0 & 1 \\ -1 & 3 \end{bmatrix}$ **7.** $\begin{bmatrix} 1 & 0 & 8 & 4 \\ 2 & 2 & 0 & -1 \\ -1 & -7 & 1 & 3 \end{bmatrix}$

9. (A) Maximize $P = 4y_1 + 5y_2$

subject to $y_1 + 2y_2 \le 8$

$3y_1 + y_2 \le 9$

$y_1, y_2 \ge 0$

(B) $y_1 + 2y_2 + x_1 \qquad\qquad = 8$

$3y_1 + y_2 \qquad + x_2 \qquad = 9$

$-4y_1 - 5y_2 \qquad\qquad + P = 0$

(C)

$$\begin{array}{c} \begin{array}{ccccc} y_1 & y_2 & x_1 & x_2 & P \end{array} \\ \left[\begin{array}{ccccc|c} 1 & 2 & 1 & 0 & 0 & 8 \\ 3 & 1 & 0 & 1 & 0 & 9 \\ \hline -4 & -5 & 0 & 0 & 1 & 0 \end{array}\right] \end{array}$$

11. (A) Max $P = 121$ at $y_1 = 3$ and $y_2 = 5$ (B) Min $C = 121$ at $x_1 = 1$ and $x_2 = 2$

13. (A) Maximize $P = 13y_1 + 12y_2$
subject to $4y_1 + 3y_2 \leq 9$
$y_1 + y_2 \leq 2$
$y_1, y_2 \geq 0$
(B) Min $C = 26$ at $x_1 = 0$ and $x_2 = 13$

15. (A) Maximize $P = 15y_1 + 8y_2$
subject to $2y_1 + y_2 \leq 7$
$3y_1 + 2y_2 \leq 12$
$y_1, y_2 \geq 0$
(B) Min $C = 54$ at $x_1 = 6$ and $x_2 = 1$

17. (A) Maximize $P = 8y_1 + 4y_2$
subject to $2y_1 - 2y_2 \leq 11$
$y_1 + 3y_2 \leq 4$
$y_1, y_2 \geq 0$
(B) Min $C = 32$ at $x_1 = 0$ and $x_2 = 8$

19. (A) Maximize $P = 6y_1 + 4y_2$
subject to $-3y_1 + y_2 \leq 7$
$y_1 - 2y_2 \leq 9$
$y_1, y_2 \geq 0$
(B) No optimal solution exists.

21. Min $C = 24$ at $x_1 = 8$ and $x_2 = 0$

23. Min $C = 20$ at $x_1 = 0$ and $x_2 = 4$
25. Min $C = 140$ at $x_1 = 14$ and $x_2 = 0$
27. Min $C = 44$ at $x_1 = 6$ and $x_2 = 2$
29. Min $C = 43$ at $x_1 = 0$, $x_2 = 1$, and $x_3 = 3$
31. No optimal solution exists.
33. 2 variables and 4 problem constraints

35. 2 constraints and any number of variables
37. No; the dual problem is not a standard maximization problem.
39. Yes; multiply both sides of the inequality by -1.

41. Min $C = 44$ at $x_1 = 0$, $x_2 = 3$, and $x_3 = 5$ **43.** Min $C = 166$ at $x_1 = 0$, $x_2 = 12$, $x_3 = 20$, and $x_4 = 3$

45. Let x_1 = number of hours the Cedarburg plant is operated
x_2 = number of hours the Grafton plant is operated
x_3 = number of hours the West Bend plant is operated

Minimize $C = 70x_1 + 75x_2 + 90x_3$
subject to $20x_1 + 10x_2 + 20x_3 \geq 300$
$10x_1 + 20x_2 + 20x_3 \geq 200$
$x_1, x_2, x_3 \geq 0$

Cedarburg plant 10 hr per day, West Bend plant 5 hr per day, Grafton plant not used; min cost is \$1,150
47. The model is the same as the model for Problem 45 except that the second constraint (deluxe ice cream) is
$10x_1 + 20x_2 + 20x_3 \geq 300$.
West Bend plant 15 hr per day, Cedarburg and Grafton plants not used; min cost is \$1,350
49. The model is the same as the model for Problem 45 except that the second constraint (deluxe ice cream) is
$10x_1 + 20x_2 + 20x_3 \geq 400$.
Grafton plant 10 hr per day, West Bend plant 10 hr per day, Cedarburg plant not used; min cost is \$1,650
51. Let x_1 = number of ounces of food L
x_2 = number of ounces of food M
x_3 = number of ounces of food N

Minimize $C = 20x_1 + 24x_2 + 18x_3$
subject to $20x_1 + 10x_2 + 10x_3 \geq 300$
$10x_1 + 10x_2 + 10x_3 \geq 200$
$10x_1 + 15x_2 + 10x_3 \geq 240$
$x_1, x_2, x_3 \geq 0$

10 oz L, 8 oz M, 2 oz N; min cholesterol intake is 428 units
53. Let x_1 = number of students bused from North Division to Central
x_2 = number of students bused from North Division to Washington
x_3 = number of students bused from South Division to Central
x_4 = number of students bused from South Division to Washington

Minimize $C = 5x_1 + 2x_2 + 3x_3 + 4x_4$
subject to $x_1 + x_2 \geq 300$
$x_3 + x_4 \geq 500$
$x_1 + x_3 \leq 400$
$x_2 + x_4 \leq 500$
$x_1, x_2, x_3, x_4 \geq 0$

300 students bused from North Division to Washington, 400 from South Division to Central, and 100 from South Division to Washington; min cost is \$2,200

Exercises 6–4

1. (A) Maximize $P = 5x_1 + 2x_2 - Ma_1$
subject to $x_1 + 2x_2 + s_1 = 12$
$x_1 + x_2 - s_2 + a_1 = 4$
$x_1, x_2, s_1, s_2, a_1 \geq 0$

(B)

x_1	x_2	s_1	s_2	a_1	P	
1	2	1	0	0	0	12
1	1	0	-1	1	0	4
$-M-5$	$-M-2$	0	M	0	1	$-4M$

(C) $x_1 = 12$, $x_2 = 0$, $s_1 = 0$, $s_2 = 8$, $a_1 = 0$, $P = 60$ (D) Max $P = 60$ at $x_1 = 12$ and $x_2 = 0$

3. (A) Maximize $P = 3x_1 + 5x_2 - Ma_1$
subject to $2x_1 + x_2 + s_1 = 8$
$x_1 + x_2 + a_1 = 6$
$x_1, x_2, s_1, a_1 \geq 0$

(B)

x_1	x_2	s_1	a_1	P	
2	1	1	0	0	8
1	1	0	1	0	6
$-M-3$	$-M-5$	0	0	1	$-6M$

(C) $x_1 = 0$, $x_2 = 6$, $s_1 = 2$, $a_1 = 0$, $P = 30$ (D) Max $P = 30$ at $x_1 = 0$ and $x_2 = 6$

5. (A) Maximize $P = 4x_1 + 3x_2 - Ma_1$
subject to $-x_1 + 2x_2 + s_1 = 2$
$x_1 + x_2 - s_2 + a_1 = 4$
$x_1, x_2, s_1, s_2, a_1 \geq 0$

(B)

x_1	x_2	s_1	s_2	a_1	P	
-1	2	1	0	0	0	2
1	1	0	-1	1	0	4
$-M-4$	$-M-3$	0	M	0	1	$-4M$

(C) No optimal solution exists. (D) No optimal solution exists.

7. (A) Maximize $P = 5x_1 + 10x_2 - Ma_1$
subject to $x_1 + x_2 + s_1 = 3$
$2x_1 + 3x_2 - s_2 + a_1 = 12$
$x_1, x_2, s_1, s_2, a_1 \geq 0$

(B)

x_1	x_2	s_1	s_2	a_1	P	
1	1	1	0	0	0	3
2	3	0	-1	1	0	12
$-2M-5$	$-3M-10$	0	M	0	1	$-12M$

(C) $x_1 = 0$, $x_2 = 3$, $s_1 = 0$, $s_2 = 0$, $a_1 = 3$, $P = -3M + 30$ (D) No optimal solution exists.

9. Min $P = 1$ at $x_1 = 3$ and $x_2 = 5$; max $P = 16$ at $x_1 = 8$ and $x_2 = 0$ **11.** Max $P = 44$ at $x_1 = 2$ and $x_2 = 8$
13. No optimal solution exists. **15.** Min $C = -9$ at $x_1 = 0$, $x_2 = \frac{7}{4}$, and $x_3 = \frac{3}{4}$ **17.** Max $P = 32$ at $x_1 = 0$, $x_2 = 4$, and $x_3 = 2$
19. Max $P = 65$ at $x_1 = \frac{35}{2}$, $x_2 = 0$, and $x_3 = \frac{15}{2}$ **21.** Max $P = 120$ at $x_1 = 20$, $x_2 = 0$, and $x_3 = 20$
23. Problem 5: unbounded feasible region: Problem 7: empty feasible region:

25. Min $C = -30$ at $x_1 = 0$, $x_2 = \frac{3}{4}$, and $x_3 = 0$
27. Max $P = 17$ at $x_1 = \frac{49}{5}$, $x_2 = 0$, and $x_3 = \frac{22}{5}$
29. Min $C = \frac{135}{2}$ at $x_1 = \frac{15}{4}$, $x_2 = \frac{3}{4}$, and $x_3 = 0$
31. Max $P = 372$ at $x_1 = 28$, $x_2 = 4$, and $x_3 = 0$

33. Let x_1 = number of ads placed in the *Sentinel*
$\qquad x_2$ = number of ads placed in the *Journal*
$\qquad x_3$ = number of ads placed in the *Tribune*
Minimize $C = 200x_1 + 200x_2 + 100x_3$
subject to $\quad x_1 + \quad x_2 + \quad x_3 \le \quad 10$
$\qquad\qquad 2{,}000x_1 + 500x_2 + 1{,}500x_3 \ge 16{,}000$
$\qquad\qquad\qquad\qquad\qquad x_1, x_2, x_3 \ge 0$
2 ads in the *Sentinel*, 0 ads in the *Journal*, 8 ads in the *Tribune*;
min cost is $1,200

35. Let x_1 = number of bottles of brand A
$\qquad x_2$ = number of bottles of brand B
$\qquad x_3$ = number of bottles of brand C
Minimize $C = 0.6x_1 + 0.4x_2 + 0.9x_3$
subject to $\quad 10x_1 + 10x_2 + 20x_3 \ge 100$
$\qquad\qquad 2x_1 + \quad 3x_2 + \quad 4x_3 \le \quad 24$
$\qquad\qquad\qquad\qquad x_1, x_2, x_3 \ge 0$
0 bottles of A, 4 bottles of B, 3 bottles of C;
min cost is $4.30

37. Let x_1 = number of cubic yards of mix A
$\qquad x_2$ = number of cubic yards of mix B
$\qquad x_3$ = number of cubic yards of mix C
Maximize $P = 12x_1 + 16x_2 + 8x_3$
subject to $\quad 12x_1 + 8x_2 + 16x_3 \le 700$
$\qquad\qquad 16x_1 + 8x_2 + 16x_3 \ge 800$
$\qquad\qquad\qquad\qquad x_1, x_2, x_3 \ge 0$
25 yd^3 A, 50 yd^3 B, 0 yd^3 C; max is 1,100 lb

39. Let x_1 = number of car frames produced at the
$\qquad\qquad$ Milwaukee plant
$\qquad x_2$ = number of truck frames produced at the
$\qquad\qquad$ Milwaukee plant
$\qquad x_3$ = number of car frames produced at the
$\qquad\qquad$ Racine plant
$\qquad x_4$ = number of truck frames produced at the
$\qquad\qquad$ Racine plant
Maximize $P = 50x_1 + 70x_2 + 50x_3 + 70x_4$
subject to $\quad x_1 \qquad + \quad x_3 \qquad\quad \le \quad 250$
$\qquad\qquad\qquad x_2 \qquad + \quad x_4 \le \quad 350$
$\qquad\qquad x_1 + \quad x_2 \qquad\qquad\quad \le \quad 300$
$\qquad\qquad\qquad\qquad x_3 + \quad x_4 \le \quad 200$
$\qquad\quad 150x_1 + 200x_2 \qquad\qquad \le 50{,}000$
$\qquad\qquad\qquad\quad 135x_3 + 180x_4 \le 35{,}000$
$\qquad\qquad\qquad\qquad x_1, x_2, x_3, x_4 \ge 0$

41. Let x_1 = number of barrels of A used in regular gasoline
$\qquad x_2$ = number of barrels of A used in premium gasoline
$\qquad x_3$ = numbers of barrels of B used in regular gasoline
$\qquad x_4$ = number of barrels of B used in premium gasoline
$\qquad x_5$ = numbers of barrels of C used in regular gasoline
$\qquad x_6$ = numbers of barrels of C used in premium gasoline
Maximize $P = 10x_1 + 18x_2 + 8x_3 + 16x_4 + 4x_5 + 12x_6$
subject to $\qquad x_1 + \quad x_2 \qquad\qquad\qquad\qquad \le 40{,}000$
$\qquad\qquad\qquad\qquad x_3 + \quad x_4 \qquad\qquad \le 25{,}000$
$\qquad\qquad\qquad\qquad\qquad\qquad x_5 + \quad x_6 \le 15{,}000$
$\qquad\qquad x_1 \qquad + \quad x_3 \qquad + \quad x_5 \qquad \ge 30{,}000$
$\qquad\qquad\qquad x_2 \qquad + \quad x_4 \qquad + \quad x_6 \ge 25{,}000$
$\qquad -5x_1 \qquad + 5x_3 \qquad + 15x_5 \qquad \ge 0$
$\qquad\qquad -15x_2 \qquad - 5x_4 \qquad + 5x_6 \ge 0$
$\qquad\qquad\qquad\qquad x_1, x_2, x_3, x_4, x_5, x_6 \ge 0$

43. Let x_1 = percentage invested in high-tech funds
$\qquad x_2$ = percentage invested in global funds
$\qquad x_3$ = percentage invested in corporate bonds
$\qquad x_4$ = percentage invested in municipal bonds
$\qquad x_5$ = percentage invested in CDs
Maximize $P = 0.11x_1 + 0.1x_2 + 0.09x_3 + 0.08x_4 + 0.05x_5$
subject to $\quad x_1 + \quad x_2 + \quad x_3 + \quad x_4 + x_5 = 1$
$\qquad\quad 2.7x_1 + 1.8x_2 + 1.2x_3 + 0.5x_4 \qquad\quad \le 1.8$
$\qquad\qquad\qquad\qquad\qquad\qquad\qquad x_5 \ge 0.2$
$\qquad\qquad\qquad\qquad x_1, x_2, x_3, x_4, x_5 \ge 0$

45. Let x_1 = number of ounces of food L
$\qquad x_2$ = number of ounces of food M
$\qquad x_3$ = number of ounces of food N
Minimize $C = 0.4x_1 + 0.6x_2 + 0.8x_3$
subject to $\quad 30x_1 + 10x_2 + 30x_3 \ge 400$
$\qquad\qquad 10x_1 + 10x_2 + 10x_3 \ge 200$
$\qquad\qquad 10x_1 + 30x_2 + 20x_3 \ge 300$
$\qquad\qquad\; 8x_1 + \quad 4x_2 + \quad 6x_3 \le 150$
$\qquad\qquad 60x_1 + 40x_2 + 50x_3 \le 900$
$\qquad\qquad\qquad\qquad x_1, x_2, x_3 \ge 0$

47. Let x_1 = number of students from town A enrolled in school I

x_2 = number of students from town A enrolled in school II

x_3 = number of students from town B enrolled in school I

x_4 = number of students from town B enrolled in school II

x_5 = number of students from town C enrolled in school I

x_6 = number of students from town C enrolled in school II

Minimize $\quad C = 4x_1 + 8x_2 + 6x_3 + 4x_4 + 3x_5 + 9x_6$

subject to $\quad x_1 + x_2 \qquad\qquad\qquad\qquad\quad = 500$

$x_3 + x_4 \qquad\qquad\quad = 1{,}200$

$x_5 + x_6 = 1{,}800$

$x_1 \quad + x_3 \quad\quad + x_5 \qquad\quad \le 2{,}000$

$x_2 \quad + x_4 \quad\quad + x_6 \le 2{,}000$

$x_1 \quad + x_3 \quad\quad + x_5 \qquad\quad \ge 1{,}400$

$x_2 \quad + x_4 \quad\quad + x_6 \ge 1{,}400$

$x_1 \qquad\qquad\qquad\qquad\qquad\quad \le 300$

$x_2 \qquad\qquad\qquad\qquad\quad \le 300$

$x_3 \qquad\qquad\qquad\quad \le 720$

$x_4 \qquad\qquad\quad \le 720$

$x_5 \qquad\quad \le 1{,}080$

$x_6 \le 1{,}080$

$x_1, x_2, x_3, x_4, x_5, x_6 \ge 0$

Chapter 6 Review Exercises

1. $2x_1 + x_2 + s_1 \qquad = 8$
$x_1 + 2x_2 \qquad + s_2 = 10$ *(6-1)*

2. 2 basic and 2 nonbasic variables *(6-1)*

3.

x_1	x_2	s_1	s_2	Feasible?
0	0	8	10	Yes
0	8	0	−6	No
0	5	3	0	Yes
4	0	0	6	Yes
10	0	−12	0	No
2	4	0	0	Yes

(6-1)

4.

Enter
↓

$$\begin{array}{c} \\ \text{Exit} \to \begin{array}{c} s_1 \\ s_2 \\ P \end{array} \end{array} \begin{array}{c} x_1 \quad x_2 \quad s_1 \quad s_2 \quad P \\ \left[\begin{array}{ccccc|c} ② & 1 & 1 & 0 & 0 & 8 \\ 1 & 2 & 0 & 1 & 0 & 10 \\ \hline -6 & -2 & 0 & 0 & 1 & 0 \end{array}\right] \end{array}$$ *(6-2)*

5. Max $P = 24$ at $x_1 = 4$ and $x_2 = 0$ *(6-2)*

6. Basic variables: x_2, s_2, s_3, P; nonbasic variables: x_1, x_3, s_1

Enter
↓

$$\begin{array}{c} \\ \\ \text{Exit} \to \\ \\ \end{array} \begin{array}{c} x_2 \\ s_2 \\ s_3 \\ P \end{array} \begin{array}{c} x_1 \quad x_2 \quad x_3 \quad s_1 \quad s_2 \quad s_3 \quad P \\ \left[\begin{array}{ccccccc|c} 2 & 1 & 3 & -1 & 0 & 0 & 0 & 20 \\ 3 & 0 & 4 & 1 & 1 & 0 & 0 & 30 \\ ② & 0 & 5 & 2 & 0 & 1 & 0 & 10 \\ \hline -8 & 0 & -5 & 3 & 0 & 0 & 1 & 50 \end{array}\right] \end{array} \sim \begin{array}{c} x_2 \\ s_2 \\ x_1 \\ P \end{array} \begin{array}{c} x_1 \quad x_2 \quad x_3 \quad s_1 \quad s_2 \quad s_3 \quad P \\ \left[\begin{array}{ccccccc|c} 0 & 1 & -2 & -3 & 0 & -1 & 0 & 10 \\ 0 & 0 & -\frac{7}{2} & -2 & 1 & -\frac{3}{2} & 0 & 15 \\ 1 & 0 & \frac{5}{2} & 1 & 0 & \frac{1}{2} & 0 & 5 \\ \hline 0 & 0 & 15 & 11 & 0 & 4 & 1 & 90 \end{array}\right] \end{array}$$ *(6-2)*

7. (A) $x_1 = 0, x_2 = 2, s_1 = 0, s_2 = 5, P = 12$; additional pivoting required
(B) $x_1 = 0, x_2 = 0, s_1 = 0, s_2 = 7, P = 22$; no optimal solution exists
(C) $x_1 = 6, x_2 = 0, s_1 = 15, s_2 = 0, P = 10$; optimal solution *(6-2)*

8. Maximize $\quad P = 15y_1 + 20y_2$
subject to $\quad y_1 + 2y_2 \le 5$
$3y_1 + y_2 \le 2$
$y_1, y_2 \ge 0$ *(6-3)*

9. $\quad y_1 + 2y_2 + x_1 \qquad\qquad = 5$
$3y_1 + y_2 \qquad + x_2 \qquad = 2$
$-15y_1 - 20y_2 \qquad\qquad + P = 0$ *(6-3)*

10.
$$\begin{array}{c} y_1 \quad y_2 \quad x_1 \quad x_2 \quad P \\ \left[\begin{array}{ccccc|c} 1 & 2 & 1 & 0 & 0 & 5 \\ 3 & 1 & 0 & 1 & 0 & 2 \\ \hline -15 & -20 & 0 & 0 & 1 & 0 \end{array}\right] \end{array}$$ *(6-3)*

11. Max $P = 40$ at $y_1 = 0$ and $y_2 = 2$ *(6-2)*
12. Min $C = 40$ at $x_1 = 0$ and $x_2 = 20$ *(6-3)*
13. Max $P = 26$ at $x_1 = 2$ and $x_2 = 5$ *(6-2)*

14. Maximize $\quad P = 10y_1 + 15y_2 + 3y_3$
subject to $\quad y_1 + y_2 \qquad \le 3$
$y_1 + 2y_2 + y_3 \le 8$
$y_1, y_2, y_3 \ge 0$ *(6-3)*

15. Min $C = 51$ at $x_1 = 9$ and $x_2 = 3$ *(6-3)*
16. No optimal solution exists. *(6-2)*
17. Max $P = 23$ at $x_1 = 4, x_2 = 1$, and $x_3 = 0$ *(6-2)*

18. (A) Modified problem:
Maximize $\quad P = x_1 + 3x_2 - Ma_1$
subject to $\quad x_1 + x_2 - s_1 + a_1 \qquad = 6$
$x_1 + 2x_2 \qquad\qquad + s_2 = 8$
$x_1, x_2, s_1, s_2, a_1 \ge 0$

(B) Preliminary simplex tableau:

$$\begin{array}{c} x_1 \quad x_2 \quad s_1 \quad a_1 \quad s_2 \quad P \\ \left[\begin{array}{cccccc|c} 1 & 1 & -1 & 1 & 0 & 0 & 6 \\ 1 & 2 & 0 & 0 & 1 & 0 & 8 \\ \hline -1 & -3 & 0 & M & 0 & 1 & 0 \end{array}\right] \end{array}$$

Initial simplex tableau:

$$\begin{array}{c} x_1 \qquad x_2 \qquad s_1 \quad a_1 \quad s_2 \quad P \\ \left[\begin{array}{cccccc|c} 1 & 1 & -1 & 1 & 0 & 0 & 6 \\ 1 & 2 & 0 & 0 & 1 & 0 & 8 \\ \hline -M-1 & -M-3 & M & 0 & 0 & 1 & -6M \end{array}\right] \end{array}$$

(C) $x_1 = 4, x_2 = 2, s_1 = 0, a_1 = 0, s_2 = 0, P = 10$

(D) Since $a_1 = 0$, the optimal solution to the original problem is Max $P = 10$ at $x_1 = 4$ and $x_2 = 2$ *(6-4)*

19. (A) Modified problem:

Maximize $P = x_1 + x_2 - Ma_1$

subject to $x_1 + x_2 - s_1 + a_1 \qquad = 5$

$\qquad\quad x_1 + 2x_2 \qquad\quad + s_2 = 4$

$\qquad\qquad x_1, x_2, s_1, s_2, a_1 \geq 0$

(B) Preliminary simplex tableau:

$$\begin{array}{cccccc|c}
x_1 & x_2 & s_1 & a_1 & s_2 & P & \\
\hline
1 & 1 & -1 & 1 & 0 & 0 & 5 \\
1 & 2 & 0 & 0 & 1 & 0 & 4 \\
\hline
-1 & -1 & 0 & M & 0 & 1 & 0
\end{array}$$

Initial simplex tableau:

$$\begin{array}{cccccc|c}
x_1 & x_2 & s_1 & a_1 & s_2 & P & \\
\hline
1 & 1 & -1 & 1 & 0 & 0 & 5 \\
1 & 2 & 0 & 0 & 1 & 0 & 4 \\
\hline
-M-1 & -M-1 & M & 0 & 0 & 1 & -5M
\end{array}$$

(C) $x_1 = 4$, $x_2 = 0$, $s_1 = 0$, $s_2 = 0$, $a_1 = 1$, $P = -M + 4$ (D) Since $a_1 \neq 0$, the original problem has no optimal solution. *(6-4)*

20. Maximize $P = 2x_1 + 3x_2 + x_3 - Ma_1 - Ma_2$

subject to $\quad x_1 - 3x_2 + x_3 + s_1 \qquad\qquad\qquad = 7$

$\qquad\quad x_1 + x_2 - 2x_3 \qquad - s_2 + a_1 \qquad = 2$

$\qquad\quad 3x_1 + 2x_2 - x_3 \qquad\qquad\qquad + a_2 = 4$

$\qquad\qquad x_1, x_2, x_3, s_1, s_2, a_1, a_2 \geq 0$ *(6-4)*

21. The basic simplex method with slack variables solves standard maximization problems involving $\leq$ constraints with non-negative constants on the right side. *(6-2)*

22. The dual method solves minimization problems with positive coefficients in the objective function. *(6-3)*

23. The big M method solves any linear programming problem. *(6-4)*

24. Max $P = 36$ at $x_1 = 6$, $x_2 = 8$ *(6-2)*

25. Min $C = 15$ at $x_1 = 3$ and $x_2 = 3$ *(6-3)*

26. Min $C = 15$ at $x_1 = 3$ and $x_2 = 3$ *(6-4)*

27. Min $C = 9,960$ at $x_1 = 0$, $x_2 = 240$, $x_3 = 400$, and $x_4 = 60$ *(6-3)*

28. (A) Let x_1 = amount invested in oil stock

$\qquad x_2$ = amount invested in steel stock

$\qquad x_3$ = amount invested in government bonds

Maximize $\quad P = 0.12x_1 + 0.09x_2 + 0.05x_3$

subject to $\quad x_1 + x_2 + x_3 \leq 150,000$

$\qquad\qquad x_1 \qquad\qquad \leq 50,000$

$\qquad\qquad x_1 + x_2 - x_3 \leq 25,000$

$\qquad\qquad x_1, x_2, x_3 \geq 0$

Max return is $12,500 when $50,000 is invested in oil stock, $37,500 is invested in steel stock, and $62,500 in government bonds.

(B) Max return is $13,625 when $87,500 is invested in steel stock and $62,500 in government bonds. *(6-2)*

29. (A) Let x_1 = number of regular chairs

$\qquad x_2$ = number of rocking chairs

$\qquad x_3$ = number of chaise lounges

Maximize $\quad P = 17x_1 + 24x_2 + 31x_3$

subject to $\quad x_1 + 2x_2 + 3x_3 \leq 2,500$

$\qquad\qquad 2x_1 + 2x_2 + 4x_3 \leq 3,000$

$\qquad\qquad 3x_1 + 3x_2 + 2x_3 \leq 3,500$

$\qquad\qquad x_1, x_2, x_3 \geq 0$

Max $P = \$30,000$ when 250 regular chairs, 750 rocking chairs, and 250 chaise lounges are produced.

(B) Maximum profit increases to $32,750 when 1,000 regular chairs, 0 rocking chairs, and 250 chaise lounges are produced.

(C) Maximum profit decreases to $28,750 when 125 regular chairs, 625 rocking chairs, and 375 chaise lounges are produced. *(6-2)*

30. Let x_1 = number of motors shipped from factory A to plant X

$\quad x_2$ = number of motors shipped from factory A to plant Y

$\quad x_3$ = number of motors shipped from factory B to plant X

$\quad x_4$ = number of motors shipped from factory B to plant Y

Minimize $\quad C = 5x_1 + 8x_2 + 9x_3 + 7x_4$

subject to $\quad x_1 + x_2 \qquad\qquad \leq 1,500$

$\qquad\qquad\qquad x_3 + x_4 \leq 1,000$

$\qquad\qquad x_1 \quad + x_3 \qquad \geq 900$

$\qquad\qquad\quad x_2 + \qquad x_4 \geq 1,200$

$\qquad\qquad x_1, x_2, x_3, x_4 \geq 0$

Min $C = \$13,100$ when 900 motors are shipped from factory A to plant X, 200 motors are shipped from factory A to plant Y, and 1,000 motors are shipped from factory B to plant Y *(6-3)*

31. Let x_1 = number of pounds of long-grain rice used in brand A

$\qquad x_2$ = number of pounds of long-grain rice used in brand B

$\qquad x_3$ = number of pounds of wild rice used in brand A

$\qquad x_4$ = number of pounds of wild rice used in brand B

Maximize $\quad P = 0.8x_1 + 0.5x_2 - 1.9x_3 - 2.2x_4$

subject to $\quad 0.1x_1 \qquad\quad - 0.9x_3 \qquad\qquad \leq \quad 0$

$\qquad\qquad\quad 0.05x_2 \qquad\quad - 0.95x_4 \leq \quad 0$

$\qquad\qquad x_1 + \quad x_2 \qquad\qquad\qquad \leq 8,000$

$\qquad\qquad\qquad\qquad x_3 + \quad x_4 \leq \quad 500$

$\qquad\qquad x_1, x_2, x_3, x_4 \geq 0$

Max profit is $3,350 when 1,350 lb long-grain rice and 150 lb wild rice are used to produce 1,500 lb brand A, and 6,650 lb long-grain rice and 350 lb wild rice are used to produce 7,000 lb brand B. *(6-2)*

Chapter 7

Exercises 7–1

1. $10 \cdot 12$ is not less than $9 \cdot 13$; true   **3.** $11 \cdot 11 = 121$ and $10 \cdot 12 < 9 \cdot 13$; false   **5.** If $10 \cdot 12 < 9 \cdot 13$, then $11 \cdot 11 = 121$; true
7. If $2^9 + 2^8 + 2^7 > 987$, then $9 \cdot 10^2 + 8 \cdot 10 + 7 = 987$; true   **9.** $2^9 + 2^8 + 2^7 > 987$ or $9 \cdot 10^2 + 8 \cdot 10 + 7 = 987$; true
11. If $9 \cdot 10^2 + 8 \cdot 10 + 7$ is not equal to 987, then $2^9 + 2^8 + 2^7$ is not greater than 987; true   **13.** Disjunction; true
15. Conditional; false   **17.** Negation; false   **19.** Conjunction; true
21. Converse: If triangle ABC is equiangular, then triangle ABC is equilateral. Contrapositive: If triangle ABC is not equiangular, then triangle ABC is not equilateral.
23. Converse: If $f(x)$ is an increasing function, then $f(x)$ is a linear function with positive slope. Contrapositive: If $f(x)$ is not an increasing function, then $f(x)$ is not a linear function with positive slope.
25. Converse: If n is an integer that is a multiple of 2 and a multiple of 4, then n is an integer that is a multiple of 8. Contrapositive: If n is an integer that is not a multiple of 2 or not a multiple of 4, then n is an integer that is not a multiple of 8.

27.

p	q	$\neg p \wedge q$	Contingency
T	T	F	
T	F	F	
F	T	T	
F	F	F	

29.

p	q	$\neg p \to q$	Contingency
T	T	T	
T	F	T	
F	T	T	
F	F	F	

31.

p	q	$q \wedge (p \vee q)$	Contingency
T	T	T	
T	F	F	
F	T	T	
F	F	F	

33.

p	q	$p \vee (p \to q)$	Tautology
T	T	T	
T	F	T	
F	T	T	
F	F	T	

35.

p	q	$p \to (p \wedge q)$	Contingency
T	T	T	
T	F	F	
F	T	T	
F	F	T	

37.

p	q	$(p \to q) \to \neg p$	Contingency
T	T	F	
T	F	T	
F	T	T	
F	F	T	

39.

p	q	$\neg p \to (p \vee q)$	Contingency
T	T	T	
T	F	T	
F	T	T	
F	F	F	

41.

p	q	$q \to (\neg p \wedge q)$	Contingency
T	T	F	
T	F	T	
F	T	T	
F	F	T	

43.

p	q	$(\neg p \wedge q) \wedge (q \to p)$	Contradiction
T	T	F	
T	F	F	
F	T	F	
F	F	F	

45.

p	q	$p \vee q$
T	T	T
T	F	T
F	T	T
F	F	F

47.

p	q	$\neg p \wedge q$	$p \vee q$
T	T	F	T
T	F	F	T
F	T	T	T
F	F	F	F

49.

p	q	$\neg p \to (q \wedge \neg q)$
T	T	T
T	F	T
F	T	F
F	F	F

51.

p	q	$\neg p \to (p \vee q)$	$p \vee q$
T	T	T	T
T	F	T	T
F	T	T	T
F	F	F	F

53.

p	q	$q \wedge (p \vee q)$	$q \vee (p \wedge q)$
T	T	T	T
T	F	F	F
F	T	T	T
F	F	F	F

55.

p	q	$p \vee (p \to q)$	$p \to (p \vee q)$
T	T	T	T
T	F	T	T
F	T	T	T
F	F	T	T

57. $p \to \neg q \equiv \neg p \vee \neg q$ By (4)
$\equiv \neg(p \wedge q)$ By (6)
59. $\neg(p \to q) \equiv \neg(\neg p \vee q)$ By (4)
$\equiv \neg(\neg p) \wedge \neg q$ By (5)
$\equiv p \wedge \neg q$ By (1)
61. Yes   **63.** No

Exercises 7–2

1. T   **3.** T   **5.** T   **7.** F   **9.** $\{2, 3\}$ **11.** $\{1, 2, 3, 4\}$ **13.** $\{1, 4, 7, 10, 13\}$ **15.** $\varnothing$ **17.** $\{5, -5\}$ **19.** $\{-3\}$ **21.** $\{1, 3, 5, 7, 9\}$
23. $A' = \{1, 5\}$ **25.** 40   **27.** 60   **29.** 60   **31.** 20   **33.** 95   **35.** 40   **37.** (A) $\{1, 2, 3, 4, 6\}$ (B) $\{1, 2, 3, 4, 6\}$
39. $\{1, 2, 3, 4, 6\}$ **41.** Finite   **43.** Infinite   **45.** Finite   **47.** Infinite   **49.** Finite   **51.** Disjoint   **53.** Not disjoint
55. True   **57.** False   **59.** False   **61.** False   **63.** False   **65.** (A) 2   (B) 4   (C) 8   (D) 16   **67.** 800   **69.** 200   **71.** 200
73. 800   **75.** 200   **77.** 200   **79.** 6   **81.** A+, AB+   **83.** A−, A+, B+, AB−, AB+, O+   **85.** O+, O−   **87.** B−, B+

Exercises 7–3

1. 115   **3.** 300
5. 165   **7.** 210
9. 95   **11.** 260

13. (A) 4 ways:

COIN 1 OUTCOME	COIN 2 OUTCOME	COMBINED OUTCOMES
H	H	(H, H)
	T	(H, T)
T	H	(T, H)
	T	(T, T)

(B) $2 \cdot 2 = 4$ ways

15. (A) 12 combined outcomes:

Start → H → 1, 2, 3, 4, 5, 6; T → 1, 2, 3, 4, 5, 6

(B) $2 \cdot 6 = 12$ combined outcomes

17. (A) 9   (B) 18   **19.** (A) 8   (B) 144
21. $n(A \cap B') = 60, n(A \cap B) = 20, n(A' \cap B) = 30, n(A' \cap B') = 90$
23. $n(A \cap B') = 5, n(A \cap B) = 20, n(A' \cap B) = 35, n(A' \cap B') = 40$
25. $n(A \cap B') = 15, n(A \cap B) = 70, n(A' \cap B) = 40, n(A' \cap B') = 25$

27.

	A	A'	Totals
B	30	60	90
B'	40	70	110
Totals	70	130	200

29.

	A	A'	Totals
B	20	35	55
B'	25	20	45
Totals	45	55	100

31.

	A	A'	Totals
B	58	8	66
B'	17	7	24
Totals	75	15	90

33. (A) True   (B) False   **35.** $5 \cdot 3 \cdot 4 \cdot 2 = 120$
37. $6 \cdot 5 \cdot 4 \cdot 3 = 360; 6 \cdot 6 \cdot 6 \cdot 6 = 1{,}296;$
$6 \cdot 5 \cdot 5 \cdot 5 = 750$
39. $10 \cdot 9 \cdot 8 \cdot 7 \cdot 6 = 30{,}240; 10 \cdot 10 \cdot 10 \cdot 10 \cdot 10 = 100{,}000; 10 \cdot 9 \cdot 9 \cdot 9 \cdot 9 = 65{,}610$

41. $26 \cdot 26 \cdot 26 \cdot 10 \cdot 10 \cdot 10 = 17{,}576{,}000; 26 \cdot 25 \cdot 24 \cdot 10 \cdot 9 \cdot 8 = 11{,}232{,}000$ **53.** (A) 6 combined outcomes: (B) $3 \cdot 2 = 6$
43. No, the same 8 combined choices are available either way.   **45.** z
47. x and z **49.** 14   **51.** 14

Start → H → A, P; M → A, P; L → A, P

55. 12   **57.** (A) 1,010   (B) 190   (C) 270   **65.** 2,905
59. 1,570   **61.** (A) 102,000   (B) 689,000   (C) 1,470,000   (D) 1,372,000
63. (A) 12 classifications: (B) $2 \cdot 2 \cdot 3 = 12$

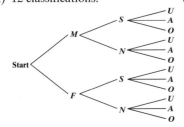

Start → M → S → U, A, O; N → U, A, O; F → S → U, A, O; N → U, A, O

Exercises 7–4

1. 5,040   **3.** 39,916,800   **5.** 840   **7.** 1,680   **9.** 70   **11.** 249,500   **13.** 3,991,680   **15.** 792   **17.** 0.0026   **19.** 0.2228   **21.** $n(n - 1)$
23. $n(n + 1)/2$ **25.** Permutation   **27.** Combination   **29.** Neither   **31.** $P_{10,3} = 10 \cdot 9 \cdot 8 = 720$ **33.** $C_{7,3} = 35; P_{7,3} = 210$
35. The factorial function $x!$ grows much faster than the exponential function 3^x, which in turn grows much faster than the cubic function x^3.
37. $C_{13,5} = 1{,}287$ **39.** $C_{13,5}C_{13,2} = 100{,}386$ **41.** $C_{8,3}C_{10,4}C_{7,2} = 246{,}960$
43. The numbers are the same read up or down, since $C_{n,r} = C_{n,n-r}$.   **45.** True   **47.** False   **49.** True
51. (A) $C_{8,2} = 28$ (B) $C_{8,3} = 56$ (C) $C_{8,4} = 70$ **53.** $P_{5,2} = 20; P_{5,3} = 60; P_{5,4} = 120; P_{5,5} = 120$
55. (A) $P_{8,5} = 6{,}720$ (B) $C_{8,5} = 56$ (C) $2 \cdot C_{6,4} = 30$ **57.** For many calculators $k = 69$, but your calculator may be different.
59. $C_{24,12} = 2{,}704{,}156$ **61.** (A) $C_{24,3} = 2{,}024$ (B) $C_{19,3} = 969$ **63.** (A) $C_{30,10} = 30{,}045{,}015$ (B) $C_{8,2}C_{12,5}C_{10,3} = 2{,}661{,}120$
65. (A) $C_{6,3}C_{5,2} = 200$ (B) $C_{6,4}C_{5,1} = 75$ (C) $C_{6,5} = 6$ (D) $C_{11,5} = 462$ (E) $C_{6,4}C_{5,1} + C_{6,5} = 81$ **67.** 336; 512
69. $P_{4,2} = 12$

Chapter 7 Review Exercises

1. 3^4 is not less than 4^3; true *(7-1)*   2. 2^3 is less than 3^2 or 3^4 is less than 4^3; true *(7-1)*
3. 2^3 is less than 3^2 and 3^4 is less than 4^3; false *(7-1)*   4. If 2^3 is less than 3^2, then 3^4 is less than 4^3; false *(7-1)*
5. If 3^4 is less than 4^3, then 2^3 is less than 3^2; true *(7-1)*   6. If 3^4 is not less than 4^3, then 2^3 is not less than 3^2; false *(7-1)*
7. T *(7-2)* 8. F *(7-2)* 9. T *(7-2)* 10. F *(7-2)* 11. Conditional; true *(7-1)* 12. Disjunction; false *(7-1)*
13. Conjunction; false *(7-1)* 14. Negation; true *(7-1)*
15. Converse: If the square matrix A does not have an inverse, then the square matrix A has a row of zeros. Contrapositive: If the square matrix A has an inverse, then the square matrix A does not have a row of zeros. *(7-1)*
16. Converse: If the square matrix A has an inverse, then the square matrix A is an identity matrix. Contrapositive: If the square matrix A does not have an inverse, then the square matrix A is not an identity matrix. *(7-1)*
17. $\{1, 2, 3, 4, 5\}$ *(7-2)* 18. $\{2, 3, 4\}$ *(7-2)* 19. $\varnothing$ *(7-2)*
20. (A) 12 combined outcomes: 21. (A) 65 (B) 75 (C) 35 (D) 105 (E) 150 (F) 85 (G) 115 (H) 45 *(7-3)*
    (B) $6 \cdot 2 = 12$ *(7-3)*   22. 39,916,800 *(7-4)* 23. 24 *(7-4)* 24. 3,628,080 *(7-4)* 25. 360,360 *(7-4)* 26. 3,003 *(7-4)*
    27. 56 *(7-4)* 28. 6720 *(7-4)*
    29. $6 \cdot 5 \cdot 4 \cdot 3 \cdot 2 \cdot 1 = 720$ *(7-3)* 30. $P_{6,6} = 6! = 720$ *(7-4)*

31.

p	q	$(p \to q) \land (q \to p)$	Contingency
T	T	T	
T	F	F	
F	T	F	
F	F	T	*(7-1)*

32.

p	q	$p \lor (q \to p)$	Contingency
T	T	T	
T	F	T	
F	T	F	
F	F	T	*(7-1)*

33.

p	q	$(p \lor \neg p) \to (q \land \neg q)$	Contradiction
T	T	F	
T	F	F	
F	T	F	
F	F	F	*(7-1)*

34.

p	q	$\neg q \land (p \to q)$	Contingency
T	T	F	
T	F	F	
F	T	F	
F	F	T	*(7-1)*

35.

p	q	$\neg p \to (p \to q)$	Tautology
T	T	T	
T	F	T	
F	T	T	
F	F	T	*(7-1)*

36.

p	q	$\neg(p \lor \neg q)$	Contingency
T	T	F	
T	F	F	
F	T	T	
F	F	F	*(7-1)*

37. Infinite *(7-2)* 38. Finite *(7-2)* 39. Infinite *(7-2)*
40. Infinite *(7-2)* 41. Disjoint *(7-2)* 42. Not disjoint *(7-2)*
43. Disjoint *(7-2)*
44. 5 children, 15 grandchildren, and 30 great grandchildren, for a total of 50 descendants *(7-3, 7-4)*

45. 336; 512; 392 *(7-3)* 46. (A) $P_{6,3} = 120$ (B) $C_{5,2} = 10$ *(7-4)* 47. $C_{25,12} = C_{25,13} = 5,200,300$ *(7-4)*
48. $N_1 \cdot N_2 \cdot N_3$ *(7-3)* 49. $\{-1, 0, 1\}$ *(7-2)* 50. $\{1, 2, 3, 4\}$ *(7-2, 7-4)* 51. $\{1, 4, 9, 16, 25, 36, 49\}$ *(7-2)*
52. (A) $P_{10,3} = 720$ (B) $P_{6,3} = 120$ (C) $C_{10,3} = 120$ *(7-3, 7-4)* 53. 33 *(7-3)* 54. x *(7-3)*
55. $x, z,$ and w *(7-3)* 56. True *(7-4)* 57. False *(7-4)* 58. True *(7-4)*

59.

p	q	$p \land q$
T	T	T
T	F	F
F	T	F
F	F	F

(7-1)

60.

p	q	$p \to q$
T	T	T
T	F	F
F	T	T
F	F	T

(7-1)

61.

p	q	$\neg p \to (q \land \neg q)$
T	T	T
T	F	T
F	T	F
F	F	F

(7-1)

62.

p	q	$p \lor q$	$\neg p \to q$
T	T	T	T
T	F	T	T
F	T	T	T
F	F	F	F

(7-1)

63.

p	q	$p \land (p \to q)$
T	T	T
T	F	F
F	T	F
F	F	F

(7-1)

64.

p	q	$\neg(p \land \neg q)$	$p \to q$
T	T	T	T
T	F	F	F
F	T	T	T
F	F	T	T

(7-1)

65. $2^5 = 32$; 6 *(7-3)* 66. Yes, it is both if $r = 0$ or $r = 1$. *(7-4)*
67. 120 *(7-3)* 68. (A) 610 (B) 390 (C) 270 *(7-3)*
69. $C_{40,6} = 3,838,380$ *(7-4)* 70. (A) $67! \approx 3.647 \times 10^{94}$ *(7-4)*

Chapter 8

Exercises 8–1

1. Occurrence of E is certain.   **3.** $\frac{1}{3}$ **5.** $\frac{1}{4}$ **7.** 0   **9.** 1   **11.** $\frac{1}{4}$ **13.** $\frac{1}{2}$ **15.** $\frac{1}{52}$ **17.** $\frac{4}{13}$ **19.** 0   **21.** $\frac{1}{2}$
23. (A) Reject; no probability can be negative   (B) Reject; $P(J) + P(G) + P(P) + P(S) \neq 1$ (C) Acceptable
25. $P(J) + P(P) = .56$ **27.** $\frac{1}{8}$ **29.** $1/P_{10,3} \approx .0014$ **31.** $C_{26,5}/C_{52,5} \approx .025$ **33.** $C_{12,5}/C_{52,5} \approx .000\,305$
35. $S = \{$All days in a year, 365, excluding leap year$\}$; $\frac{1}{365}$, assuming each day is as likely as any other day for a person to be born
37. $1/P_{5,5} = 1/5! = .008\,33$ **39.** $\frac{1}{36}$ **41.** $\frac{5}{36}$ **43.** $\frac{1}{6}$ **45.** $\frac{7}{9}$ **47.** 0   **49.** $\frac{1}{3}$ **51.** $\frac{2}{9}$ **53.** $\frac{2}{3}$ **55.** $\frac{1}{4}$ **57.** $\frac{1}{4}$ **59.** $\frac{3}{4}$ **61.** No   **63.** Yes
65. Yes   **67.** (A) Yes   (B) Yes, because we would expect, on average, 20 heads in 40 flips; $P(H) = \frac{37}{40} = .925$; $P(T) = \frac{3}{40} = .075$
69. $\frac{1}{9}$ **71.** $\frac{1}{3}$ **73.** $\frac{1}{9}$ **75.** $\frac{4}{9}$ **77.** $C_{16,5}/C_{52,5} \approx .001\,68$ **79.** $48/C_{52,5} \approx .000\,018\,5$ **81.** $4/C_{52,5} \approx .000\,001\,5$
83. $C_{4,2}C_{4,3}/C_{52,5} \approx .000\,009$ **85.** (A) $\frac{7}{50} = .14$ (B) $\frac{1}{6} \approx .167$ (C) Answer depends on results of simulation.
87. (A) Represent the outcomes H and T by 1 and 2, respectively, and select 500 random integers from the integers 1 and 2.
   (B) Answer depends on results of simulation.   (C) Each is $\frac{1}{2} = .5$
89. (A) $1/P_{12,4} \approx .000\,084$ (B) $1/12^4 \approx .000\,048$
91. (A) $C_{6,3}C_{5,2}/C_{11,5} \approx .433$ (B) $C_{6,4}C_{5,1}/C_{11,5} \approx .162$ (C) $C_{6,5}/C_{11,5} \approx .013$ (D) $(C_{6,4}C_{5,1} + C_{6,5})/C_{11,5} \approx .175$
93. (A) $1/P_{8,3} \approx .0030$ (B) $1/8^3 \approx .0020$
95. (A) $C_{6,2}/C_{11,2} \approx .273$ (B) $(C_{5,3} + C_{6,1}C_{5,2})/C_{11,3} \approx .424$

Exercises 8–2

1. .39   **3.** .86   **5.** .26   **7.** $\frac{1}{4}$ **9.** $\frac{10}{13}$ **11.** $\frac{3}{52}$ **13.** $\frac{11}{26}$ **15.** $\frac{5}{26}$ **17.** $\frac{43}{52}$ **19.** (1); .44   **21.** (2); .48   **23.** (2); .6   **25.** .49   **27.** $\frac{5}{18}$
29. $\frac{11}{36}$ **31.** (A) $\frac{3}{5}; \frac{5}{3}$ (B) $\frac{1}{3}; \frac{3}{1}$ (C) $\frac{2}{3}; \frac{3}{2}$ (D) $\frac{11}{9}; \frac{9}{11}$ **33.** (A) $\frac{3}{11}$ (B) $\frac{11}{18}$ (C) $\frac{4}{5}$ or .8   (D) .49   **35.** False   **37.** False   **39.** True
41. 1:1   **43.** 7:1   **45.** 2:1   **47.** 1:2   **49.** (A) $\frac{1}{8}$ (B) \$8   **51.** (A) $.31; \frac{31}{69}$ (B) $.6; \frac{3}{2}$ **53.** $\frac{11}{26}; \frac{11}{15}$ **55.** $\frac{7}{13}; \frac{7}{6}$ **57.** .78   **59.** $\frac{250}{1,000} = .25$
61. Either events A, B, and C are mutually exclusive, or events A and B are not mutually exclusive and the other pairs of events are mutually exclusive.
63. There are fewer calculator steps, and, in addition, 365! produces an overflow error on many calculators, while $P_{365,n}$ does not produce an overflow error for many values of n.
65. $P(E) = 1 - \dfrac{12!}{(12 - n)!\,12^n}$
69. (A) $\frac{10}{50} + \frac{10}{50} = \frac{20}{50} = .4$ (B) $\frac{6}{36} + \frac{5}{36} = \frac{11}{36} \approx .306$ (C) Answer depends on results of simulation.
71. (A) $P(C \cup S) = P(C) + P(S) - P(C \cap S) = .45 + .75 - .35 = .85$ (B) $P(C' \cap S') = .15$
73. (A) $P(M_1 \cup A) = P(M_1) + P(A) - P(M_1 \cap A) = .2 + .3 - .05 = .45$
   (B) $P[(M_2 \cap A') \cup (M_3 \cap A')] = P(M_2 \cap A') + P(M_3 \cap A') = .2 + .35 = .55$
75. .83   **77.** $P(A \cap S) = \frac{50}{1,000} = .05$ **79.** (A) $P(U \cup N) = .22; \frac{11}{39}$ (B) $P[(D \cap A) \cup (R \cap A)] = .3; \frac{7}{3}$

Exercises 8–3

1. .10   **3.** .03   **5.** .3   **7.** .1   **9.** .35   **11.** 0   **13.** Dependent   **15.** Independent   **17.** Dependent   **19.** Dependent
21. (A) $\frac{1}{2}$ (B) $2\left(\frac{1}{2}\right)^8 \approx .00781$ **23.** (A) $\frac{1}{4}$ (B) Dependent   **25.** (A) .18   (B) .26
27. (A) Independent and not mutually exclusive   (B) Dependent and mutually exclusive.   **29.** $\left(\frac{1}{2}\right)\left(\frac{1}{2}\right) = \frac{1}{4}; \frac{1}{2} + \frac{1}{2} - \frac{1}{4} = \frac{3}{4}$
31. (A) $\left(\frac{1}{4}\right)\left(\frac{13}{51}\right) \approx .0637$ (B) $\left(\frac{1}{4}\right)\left(\frac{1}{4}\right) = .0625$ **33.** (A) $\frac{3}{13}$ (B) Independent   **35.** (A) Dependent   (B) Independent

37. (A)   (B)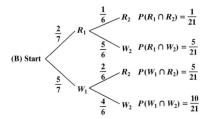

39. (A) $\frac{24}{49}$ (B) $\frac{11}{21}$ **41.** False   **43.** True   **45.** False   **47.** True   **49.** $\frac{5}{18}$ **51.** (A) .167   (B) .25   (C) .25
59. (A)

	H	S	B	Totals
Y	.400	.180	.020	.600
N	.150	.120	.130	.400
Totals	.550	.300	.150	1.000

(B) $P(Y|H) = \dfrac{.400}{.550} \approx .727$ (C) $P(Y|B) = \dfrac{.020}{.150} \approx .133$
(D) $P(S) = .300$; $P(S|Y) = .300$ (E) $P(H) = .550$; $P(H|Y) \approx .667$
(F) $P(B \cap N) = .130$ (G) Yes   (H) No   (I) No

61. (A) .167   (B) .25   (C) .25

63. (A)

	C	**C'**	**Totals**
R	.06	.44	.50
R'	.02	.48	.50
Totals	.08	.92	1.00

(B) Dependent
(C) $P(C|R) = .12$ and $P(C) = .08$; since $P(C|R) > P(C)$, the red dye should be banned.
(D) $P(C|R) = .04$ and $P(C) = .08$; since $P(C|R) < P(C)$, the red dye should not be banned, since it appears to prevent cancer.

65. (A)

	A	**B**	**C**	**Totals**
F	.130	.286	.104	.520
F'	.120	.264	.096	.480
Totals	.250	.550	.200	1.000

(B) $P(A|F) = \dfrac{.130}{.520} = .250$; $P(A|F') = \dfrac{.120}{.480} = .250$
(C) $P(C|F) = \dfrac{.104}{.520} = .200$; $P(C|F') = \dfrac{.096}{.480} = .200$
(D) $P(A) = .250$ (E) $P(B) = .550$; $P(B|F') = .550$
(F) $P(F \cap C) = .104$
(G) No; A, B, and C are independent of F and F'.

Exercises 8-4

1. $(.6)(.8) = .48$ **3.** $(.6)(.8) + (.4)(.3) = .60$ **5.** .80 **7.** .417 **9.** .375 **11.** .108 **13.** .568 **15.** .324 **17.** .125 **19.** .50 **21.** .375
25. .25 **27.** .333 **29.** .50 **31.** .745 **35.** (A) True (B) True
37. .235 **39.** $\frac{1}{3}$ **41.** .581 **43.** .052 **47.** .913; .226 **49.** .091; .545; .364
51. .667; .000 412 **53.** .231; .036 **55.** .941; .0588

23.

Exercises 8-5

1. $E(X) = -.1$
3. Probability distribution:

x_i	0	1	2
p_i	$\frac{1}{4}$	$\frac{1}{2}$	$\frac{1}{4}$

$E(X) = 1$

5. Payoff table:

x_i	\$1	$-\$1$
p_i	$\frac{1}{2}$	$\frac{1}{2}$

$E(X) = 0$; game is fair

7. Payoff table:

x_i	$-\$3$	$-\$2$	$-\$1$	\$0	\$1	\$2
p_i	$\frac{1}{6}$	$\frac{1}{6}$	$\frac{1}{6}$	$\frac{1}{6}$	$\frac{1}{6}$	$\frac{1}{6}$

$E(X) = -50¢$; game is not fair

9. $-\$0.50$ **11.** $-\$0.036$; \$0.036 **13.** \$40. Let $x =$ amount you should lose if a 6 turns up. Set up a payoff table; then set the expected value of the game equal to zero and solve for x. **15.** Win \$1 **17.** $-\$0.154$ **19.** \$2.75 **21.** A_2; \$210

23. Payoff table:

x_i	\$35	$-\$1$
p_i	$\frac{1}{38}$	$\frac{37}{38}$

$E(X) = -5.26¢$

25. .002

27. Payoff table:

x_i	\$499	\$99	\$19	\$4	$-\$1$
p_i	.0002	.0006	.001	.004	.9942

$E(X) = -80¢$

29. (A)

x_i	0	1	2
p_i	$\frac{7}{15}$	$\frac{7}{15}$	$\frac{1}{15}$

(B) .60

31. (A)

x_i	$-\$5$	\$195	\$395	\$595
p_i	.985	.0149	.000 059 9	.000 000 06

(B) $E(X) \approx -\$2$

33. (A) $-\$92$
(B) The value per game is $\dfrac{-\$92}{200} = -\$0.46$, compared with an expected value of $-\$0.0526$.
(C) The simulated gain or loss depends on the results of the simulation; the expected loss is \$26.32.

35. \$36.27
37. Payoff table:

x_i	\$4,850	$-\$150$
p_i	.01	.99

$E(X) = -\$100$

39. Site A, with $E(X) = \$3.6$ million **41.** 1.54
43. For A_1, $E(X) = \$4$, and for A_2, $E(X) = \$4.80$; A_2 is better

Chapter 8 Review Exercises

1. $C_{13,5}/C_{52,5} \approx .0005$ *(8-1)* **2.** $1/P_{15,2} \approx .0048$ *(8-1)* **3.** $1/P_{10,3} \approx .0014$; $1/C_{10,3} \approx .0083$ *(8-1)* **4.** .05 *(8-1)*
5. Payoff table:

x_i	$-\$2$	$-\$1$	\$0	\$1	\$2
p_i	$\frac{1}{5}$	$\frac{1}{5}$	$\frac{1}{5}$	$\frac{1}{5}$	$\frac{1}{5}$

$E(X) = 0$; game is fair *(8-5)*

6. (A) .7 (B) .6 *(8-2)* **7.** $P(R \cup G) = .8$; odds for $R \cup G$ are 8 to 2 *(8-2)*
8. $\frac{5}{11} \approx .455$ *(8-2)* **9.** .27 *(8-3)* **10.** .20 *(8-3)* **11.** .02 *(8-3)* **12.** .03 *(8-3)*
13. .15 *(8-3)* **14.** .1304 *(8-3)* **15.** .1 *(8-3)* **16.** No, since $P(T|Z) \neq P(T)$ *(8-3)*
17. Yes, since $P(S \cap X) = P(S)P(X)$ *(8-3)* **18.** .4 *(8-3)* **19.** .2 *(8-3)*
20. .3 *(8-3)* **21.** .08 *(8-3)* **22.** .18 *(8-3)* **23.** .26 *(8-3)* **24.** .31 *(8-4)* **25.** .43 *(8-4)*

26. (A) $\frac{5}{16}$ (B) $\frac{1}{4}$
(C) As the sample in part (A) increases in size, approximate empirical probabilities should approach the theoretical probabilities. *(8-1)*

27. No *(8-1)*   **28.** Yes *(8-1)*

29. Payoff table:

x_i	\$5	−\$4	\$2
p_i	.25	.5	.25

$E(X) = -25¢$; game is not fair *(8-5)*

30. (A) $\frac{1}{3}$ (B) $\frac{2}{9}$ *(8-3)*   **31.** (A) $\frac{2}{13}$; 2 to 11;   (B) $\frac{4}{13}$; 4 to 9;   (C) $\frac{12}{13}$; 12 to 1 *(8-2)*

32. (A) 1 to 8   (B) \$8 *(8-2)*

33. (A) $P(2\ heads) = .21, P(1\ head) = .48, P(0\ heads) = .31$

(B) $P(2\ heads) = .25, P(1\ head) = .50, P(0\ heads) = .25$

(C) 2 heads, 250; 1 head, 500; 0 heads, 250 *(8-1, 8-5)*

34. $\frac{1}{2}$; since the coin has no memory, the 10th toss is independent of the preceding 9 tosses. *(8-3)*

35. (A)

x_i	2	3	4	5	6	7	8	9	10	11	12
p_i	$\frac{1}{36}$	$\frac{2}{36}$	$\frac{3}{36}$	$\frac{4}{36}$	$\frac{5}{36}$	$\frac{6}{36}$	$\frac{5}{36}$	$\frac{4}{36}$	$\frac{3}{36}$	$\frac{2}{36}$	$\frac{1}{36}$

(B) $E(X) = 7$ *(8-5)*

36. $A = \{(1, 3), (2, 2), (3, 1), (2, 6), (3, 5), (4, 4), (5, 3), (6, 2), (6, 6)\}$;

$B = \{(1, 5), (2, 4), (3, 3), (4, 2), (5, 1), (6, 6)\}$; $P(A) = \frac{1}{4}$; $P(B) = \frac{1}{6}$; $P(A \cap B) = \frac{1}{36}$; $P(A \cup B) = \frac{7}{18}$ *(8-2)*

37. (1) Probability of an event cannot be negative; (2) sum of probabilities of simple events must be 1; (3) probability of an event cannot be greater than 1. *(8-1)*

38.

	A	A'	**Totals**
B	15	30	45
B'	35	20	55
Totals	50	50	100

(8-2)

39. (A) .6   (B) $\frac{5}{6}$ *(8-3)*   **40.** (A) $\frac{1}{13}$ (B) Independent *(8-3)*

41. (A) $\frac{6}{25}$ (B) $\frac{3}{10}$ *(8-3)*   **42.** Part (B) *(8-3)*   **43.** (A) 1.2   (B) 1.2 *(8-5)*

44. (A) $\frac{3}{5}$ (B) $\frac{1}{3}$ (C) $\frac{7}{15}$ (D) $\frac{9}{14}$ (E) $\frac{5}{8}$ (F) $\frac{3}{10}$ *(8-3, 8-4)*

45. No *(8-3)*   **46.** (A) $C_{13,5}/C_{52,5}$ (B) $C_{13,3} \cdot C_{13,2}/C_{52,5}$ *(8-1)*

47. $C_{8,2}/C_{10,4} = \frac{2}{15}$ *(8-1)*

48. Events S and H are mutually exclusive. Hence, $P(S \cap H) = 0$, while $P(S) \neq 0$ and $P(H) \neq 0$. Therefore, $P(S \cap H) \neq P(S)P(H)$, which implies S and H are dependent. *(8-3)*

49. (A) $\frac{9}{50} = .18$ (B) $\frac{9}{36} = .25$

(C) The empirical probability depends on the results of the simulation; the theoretical probability is $\frac{5}{36} \approx .139$. *(8-1)*

50. The empirical probability depends on the results of the simulation; the theoretical probability is $\frac{2}{52} \approx .038$. *(8-3)*

51. False *(8-2)*   **52.** True *(8-2)*   **53.** False *(8-3)*   **54.** False *(8-2)*   **55.** True *(8-3)*   **56.** False *(8-2)*

57. (A) .350   (B) $\frac{3}{8} = .375$ (C) 375 *(8-1)*   **58.** −.0172; .0172; no *(8-5)*   **59.** $1 - C_{7,3}/C_{10,3} = \frac{17}{24}$ *(8-1)*

60. $\frac{12}{51} \approx .235$ *(8-3)*   **61.** $\frac{12}{51} \approx .235$ *(8-3)*

62. (A)

x_i	2	3	4	5	6
p_i	$\frac{9}{36}$	$\frac{12}{36}$	$\frac{10}{36}$	$\frac{4}{36}$	$\frac{1}{36}$

(B) $E(X) = \frac{10}{3}$ *(8-5)*

63. $E(X) \approx -\$0.167$; no; $\$(10/3) \approx \$3.33$ *(8-5)*

64. (A) $\frac{1}{4}$; 1 to 3   (B) \$3 *(8-2, 8-4)*

65. $1 - 10!/(5!10^5) \approx .70$ *(8-2)*

66. $P(A|B) = P(B|A)$ if and only if $P(A) = P(B)$ or $P(A \cap B) = 0$. *(8-3)*

67. (A) .8   (B) .2   (C) .5 *(8-2)*   **68.** $P(A \cap P) = P(A)P(P|A) = .34$ *(8-3)*

69. (A) $P(A) = .290; P(B) = .290; P(A \cap B) = .100; P(A|B) = .345; P(B|A) = .345$

(B) No, since $P(A \cap B) \neq P(A)P(B)$.

(C) $P(C) = .880; P(D) = .120; P(C \cap D) = 0; P(C|D) = 0; P(D|C) = 0$

(D) Yes, since $C \cap D = \emptyset$; dependent, since $P(C \cap D) = 0$ and $P(C)P(D) \neq 0$ *(8-3)*

70. Plan A: $E(X) = \$7.6$ million; plan B: $E(X) = \$7.8$ million; plan B *(8-5)*

71. Payoff table:

x_i	\$1,830	−\$170
p_i	.08	.92

$E(X) = -\$10$ *(8-5)*

72. $1 - (C_{10,4}/C_{12,4}) \approx .576$ *(8-2)*

73. (A)

x_i	0	1	2
p_i	$\frac{12}{22}$	$\frac{9}{22}$	$\frac{1}{22}$

(B) $E(X) = \frac{1}{2}$ *(8-5)*

74. .955 *(8-4)*

75. $\frac{6}{7} \approx .857$ *(8-4)*

Chapter 9

Exercises 9-1

1. $S_1 = [.8 \quad .2]$; the probability of being in state A after one trial is .8, and the probability of being in state B after one trial is .2.

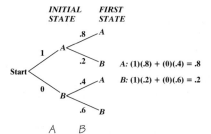

3. $S_1 = [.6 \quad .4]$; the probability of being in state A after one trial is .6, and the probability of being in state B after one trial is .4.

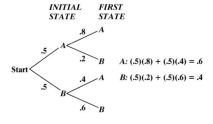

5. $S_2 = [.72 \quad .28]$; the probability of being in state A after two trials is .72, and the probability of being in state B after two trials is .28.

7. $S_2 = [.64 \quad .36]$; the probability of being in state A after two trials is .64, and the probability of being in state B after two trials is .36.
9. $S_1 = [.86 \quad .14]$ **11.** $S_1 = [.72 \quad .28]$ **13.** $S_2 = [.728 \quad .272]$ **15.** $S_2 = [.756 \quad .244]$ **17.** Yes **19.** No **21.** No **23.** Yes

25.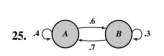
$$\begin{array}{c} \\ A \\ B \end{array}\begin{array}{cc} A & B \\ \begin{bmatrix} .4 & .6 \\ .7 & .3 \end{bmatrix} \end{array}$$

27. No

29.
$$\begin{array}{c} \\ A \\ B \\ C \end{array}\begin{array}{ccc} A & B & C \\ \begin{bmatrix} .1 & .4 & .5 \\ .5 & .2 & .3 \\ .7 & .2 & .1 \end{bmatrix} \end{array}$$

31. $a = .5, b = .6, c = .7$ **33.** $a = .7, b = 1, c = .2$ **35.** No

37.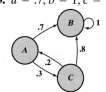
$$\begin{array}{c} \\ A \\ B \end{array}\begin{array}{cc} A & B \\ \begin{bmatrix} .3 & .7 \\ .9 & .1 \end{bmatrix} \end{array}$$

39.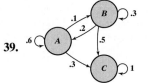
$$\begin{array}{c} \\ A \\ B \\ C \end{array}\begin{array}{ccc} A & B & C \\ \begin{bmatrix} .6 & .1 & .3 \\ .2 & .3 & .5 \\ 0 & 0 & 1 \end{bmatrix} \end{array}$$

41. .35 **43.** .212 **45.** $S_2 = [.43 \quad .35 \quad .22]$; the probabilities of going from state A to states A, B, and C in two trials

47. $S_3 = [.212 \quad .298 \quad .49]$; the probabilities of going from state C to states A, B, and C in three trials **49.** $n = 9$

51. $P^4 = \begin{array}{c} A \\ B \end{array}\begin{array}{cc} A & B \\ \begin{bmatrix} .4375 & .5625 \\ .375 & .625 \end{bmatrix} \end{array}$; $S_4 = [.425 \quad .575]$ **53.** $P^4 = \begin{array}{c} A \\ B \\ C \end{array}\begin{array}{ccc} A & B & C \\ \begin{bmatrix} .36 & .16 & .48 \\ .6 & 0 & .4 \\ .4 & .24 & .36 \end{bmatrix} \end{array}$; $S_4 = [.452 \quad .152 \quad .396]$

57. False
59. True
61. False

63. (A) $\begin{array}{c} A \\ B \\ C \\ D \end{array}\begin{array}{cccc} A & B & C & D \\ \begin{bmatrix} .0154 & .3534 & .0153 & .6159 \\ 0 & 1 & 0 & 0 \\ .0102 & .2962 & .0103 & .6833 \\ 0 & 0 & 0 & 1 \end{bmatrix} \end{array}$ (B) .6159 (C) .2962 (D) 0

67. (A) $[.25 \quad .75]$ (B) $[.25 \quad .75]$
(C) $[.25 \quad .75]$ (D) $[.25 \quad .75]$
(E) The state matrices appear to approach the same matrix, $S = [.25 \quad .75]$, regardless of the values in the initial-state matrix.

69. $Q = \begin{bmatrix} .25 & .75 \\ .25 & .75 \end{bmatrix}$; the rows of Q are the same as the matrix S from Problem 67

71. (A) R = rain, R' = no rain

(B) $\begin{array}{c} R \\ R' \end{array}\begin{array}{cc} R & R' \\ \begin{bmatrix} .4 & .6 \\ .06 & .94 \end{bmatrix} \end{array}$ (C) Saturday: .196;
Sunday: .12664

73. (A)

(B) $\begin{array}{c} X \\ X' \end{array}\begin{array}{cc} X & X' \\ \begin{bmatrix} .8 & .2 \\ .2 & .8 \end{bmatrix} \end{array}$ (C) 32%; 39.2%

75. (A) N = National Property, U = United Family,
O = other companies

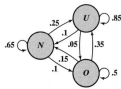

(B) $\begin{array}{c} N \\ U \\ O \end{array}\begin{array}{ccc} N & U & O \\ \begin{bmatrix} .65 & .25 & .1 \\ .1 & .85 & .05 \\ .15 & .35 & .5 \end{bmatrix} \end{array}$

(C) 38.5%; 32% (D) 45%; 53.65%

77. (A) B = beginning agent, I = intermediate agent,
T = terminated agent, Q = qualified agent

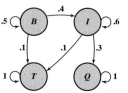

(B) $\begin{array}{c} B \\ I \\ T \\ Q \end{array}\begin{array}{cccc} B & I & T & Q \\ \begin{bmatrix} .5 & .4 & .1 & 0 \\ 0 & .6 & .1 & .3 \\ 0 & 0 & 1 & 0 \\ 0 & 0 & 0 & 1 \end{bmatrix} \end{array}$ (C) .12; .3612

79. (A) $\begin{array}{c} HMO \\ PPO \\ FFS \end{array}\begin{array}{ccc} HMO & PPO & FFS \\ \begin{bmatrix} .8 & .15 & .05 \\ .2 & .7 & .1 \\ .25 & .3 & .45 \end{bmatrix} \end{array}$

(B) HMO: 34.75%; PPO: 37%; FFS: 28.25%
(C) HMO: 42.2625%; PPO: 39.5875%; FFS: 18.15%

81. (A) $\begin{array}{c} H \\ R \end{array}\begin{array}{cc} H & R \\ \begin{bmatrix} .924 & .076 \\ .108 & .892 \end{bmatrix} \end{array}$

(B) 40.5%
(C) 46.6%

Exercises 9-2

1. Yes **3.** No **5.** No **7.** Yes **9.** No **11.** Yes **13.** No

15. $S = [.4 \quad .6]; \overline{P} = \begin{bmatrix} .4 & .6 \\ .4 & .6 \end{bmatrix}$ **17.** $S = [.375 \quad .625]; \overline{P} = \begin{bmatrix} .375 & .625 \\ .375 & .625 \end{bmatrix}$ **19.** $S = [.3 \quad .5 \quad .2]; \overline{P} = \begin{bmatrix} .3 & .5 & .2 \\ .3 & .5 & .2 \\ .3 & .5 & .2 \end{bmatrix}$

21. $S = [.6 \quad .24 \quad .16]; \overline{P} = \begin{bmatrix} .6 & .24 & .16 \\ .6 & .24 & .16 \\ .6 & .24 & .16 \end{bmatrix}$ **23.** False **25.** True **27.** False **29.** $S = [.3553 \quad .6447]$ **31.** $S = [.3636 \quad .4091 \quad .2273]$

33. (A)

(B) $\begin{array}{c} \\ \text{Red} \\ \text{Blue} \end{array} \begin{matrix} \text{Red} & \text{Blue} \\ \begin{bmatrix} .4 & .6 \\ .2 & .8 \end{bmatrix} \end{matrix}$ (C) $[.25 \quad .75]$; in the long run, the red urn will be selected 25% of the time and the blue urn 75% of the time.

35. (A) The state matrices alternate between $[.2 \quad .8]$ and $[.8 \quad .2]$; so they do not approach any one matrix.
  (B) The state matrices are all equal to S_0, so S_0 is a stationary matrix.
  (C) The powers of P alternate between P and I (the 2×2 identity); so they do not approach a limiting matrix.
  (D) Parts (B) and (C) of Theorem 1 are not valid for this matrix. Since P is not regular, this is not a contradiction.
37. (A) Since P is not regular, it may have more than one stationary matrix.   (B) $[.5 \quad 0 \quad .5]$ is another stationary matrix.
  (C) P has an infinite number of stationary matrices.

39. $\overline{P} = \begin{bmatrix} 1 & 0 & 0 \\ .25 & 0 & .75 \\ 0 & 0 & 1 \end{bmatrix}$; each row of $\overline{P}$ is a stationary matrix for P.

41. (A) .39; .3; .284; .277
  (B) Each entry of the second column of P^{k+1} is the product of a row of P and the second column of P^k. Each entry of the latter is $\leq M_k$, so the product is $\leq M_k$.

43. 72.5%
45. (A) $S_1 = [.512 \quad .488]; S_2 = [.568 \quad .432]; S_3 = [.609 \quad .391]$

(B)

Year	Data (%)	Model (%)
1970	43.3	43.3
1980	51.5	51.2
1990	57.5	56.8
2000	59.8	60.9

(C) 71.4%

47. GTT: 25%; NCJ: 25%; Dash: 50%
49. Poor: 20%; satisfactory: 40%; preferred: 40% **51.** 51%
53. Stationary matrix $= [.25 \quad .50 \quad .25]$
55. (A) $[.25 \quad .75]$ (B) 42.5%; 51.25%
  (C) 60% rapid transit; 40% automobile

57. (A) $S_1 = [.334 \quad .666]; S_2 = [.343 \quad .657]; S_3 = [.347 \quad .653]$

(B)

Year	Data (%)	Model (%)
1970	30.9	30.9
1980	33.3	33.4
1990	34.4	34.3
2000	35.6	34.7

(C) 35%

Exercises 9-3

1. B, C **3.** No absorbing states **5.** A, D **7.** B is an absorbing state; absorbing chain
9. C is an absorbing state; not an absorbing chain **11.** No **13.** Yes **15.** Yes **17.** No **19.** Yes

21. $\begin{array}{c} \\ B \\ A \\ C \end{array} \begin{matrix} \begin{matrix} B & A & C \end{matrix} \\ \begin{bmatrix} 1 & 0 & 0 \\ .5 & .2 & .3 \\ .1 & .5 & .4 \end{bmatrix} \end{matrix}$ **23.** $\begin{array}{c} \\ B \\ D \\ A \\ C \end{array} \begin{matrix} \begin{matrix} B & D & A & C \end{matrix} \\ \begin{bmatrix} 1 & 0 & 0 & 0 \\ 0 & 1 & 0 & 0 \\ .4 & .1 & .3 & .2 \\ .4 & .3 & 0 & .3 \end{bmatrix} \end{matrix}$ **25.** $\begin{array}{c} \\ C \\ A \\ B \end{array} \begin{matrix} \begin{matrix} C & A & B \end{matrix} \\ \begin{bmatrix} 1 & 0 & 0 \\ .5 & .2 & .3 \\ 0 & 1 & 0 \end{bmatrix} \end{matrix}$ **27.** $\begin{array}{c} \\ B \\ D \\ A \\ C \end{array} \begin{matrix} \begin{matrix} B & D & A & C \end{matrix} \\ \begin{bmatrix} 1 & 0 & 0 & 0 \\ 0 & 1 & 0 & 0 \\ .2 & .4 & .1 & .3 \\ .2 & .1 & .5 & .2 \end{bmatrix} \end{matrix}$

29. $\overline{P} = \begin{array}{c} \\ A \\ B \\ C \end{array} \begin{matrix} \begin{matrix} A & B & C \end{matrix} \\ \begin{bmatrix} 1 & 0 & 0 \\ 0 & 1 & 0 \\ .2 & .8 & 0 \end{bmatrix} \end{matrix}$; $P(C \text{ to } A) = .2; P(C \text{ to } B) = .8$. It will take an average of 2 trials to go from C to either A or B.

31. $\overline{P} = \begin{array}{c} \\ A \\ B \\ C \end{array} \begin{matrix} \begin{matrix} A & B & C \end{matrix} \\ \begin{bmatrix} 1 & 0 & 0 \\ 1 & 0 & 0 \\ 1 & 0 & 0 \end{bmatrix} \end{matrix}$; $P(B \text{ to } A) = 1; P(C \text{ to } A) = 1$. It will take an average of 4 trials to go from B to A, and an average of 3 trials to go from C to A.

33. $\overline{P} = \begin{array}{c} \\ A \\ B \\ C \\ D \end{array} \begin{matrix} \begin{matrix} A & B & C & D \end{matrix} \\ \begin{bmatrix} 1 & 0 & 0 & 0 \\ 0 & 1 & 0 & 0 \\ .36 & .64 & 0 & 0 \\ .44 & .56 & 0 & 0 \end{bmatrix} \end{matrix}$; $P(C \text{ to } A) = .36; P(C \text{ to } B) = .64; P(D \text{ to } A) = .44; P(D \text{ to } B) = .56$. It will take an average of 3.2 trials to go from C to either A or B, and an average of 2.8 trials to go from D to either A or B.

35. (A) $[.2 \quad .8 \quad 0]$ (B) $[.26 \quad .74 \quad 0]$ **37.** (A) $[1 \quad 0 \quad 0]$ (B) $[1 \quad 0 \quad 0]$
39. (A) $[.44 \quad .56 \quad 0 \quad 0]$ (B) $[.36 \quad .64 \quad 0 \quad 0]$ (C) $[.408 \quad .592 \quad 0 \quad 0]$ (D) $[.384 \quad .616 \quad 0 \quad 0]$
41. False **43.** False **45.** True **47.** False

49.
$$\begin{array}{c} \\ A \\ B \\ C \\ D \end{array}\begin{array}{cccc} A & B & C & D \\ \left[\begin{array}{cccc} 1 & 0 & 0 & 0 \\ 0 & 1 & 0 & 0 \\ .6375 & .3625 & 0 & 0 \\ .7375 & .2625 & 0 & 0 \end{array}\right]\end{array}$$

51.
$$\begin{array}{c} \\ A \\ B \\ C \\ D \\ E \end{array}\begin{array}{ccccc} A & B & C & D & E \\ \left[\begin{array}{ccccc} 1 & 0 & 0 & 0 & 0 \\ 0 & 1 & 0 & 0 & 0 \\ .0875 & .9125 & 0 & 0 & 0 \\ .1875 & .8125 & 0 & 0 & 0 \\ .4375 & .5625 & 0 & 0 & 0 \end{array}\right]\end{array}$$

53.
$$\begin{array}{c} \\ A \\ B \\ C \\ D \end{array}\begin{array}{cccc} A & B & C & D \\ \left[\begin{array}{cccc} 0 & .52 & 0 & .48 \\ 0 & 1 & 0 & 0 \\ 0 & .36 & 0 & .64 \\ 0 & 0 & 0 & 1 \end{array}\right]\end{array}$$

59. (A) .370; .297; .227; .132; .045 (B) For large k, all entries of Q^k are close to 0.
61. (A) 75% (B) 12.5% (C) 7.5 months
63. (A) Company A: 30%, company B: 15%, company C: 55% (B) 5 yr
65. (A) 91.52% (B) 4.96% (C) 6.32 days **67.** (A) .375 (B) 1.75 exits

Chapter 9 Review Exercises

1. $S_1 = \begin{array}{cc} A & B \\ [.32 & .68] \end{array}$; $S_2 = \begin{array}{cc} A & B \\ [.328 & .672] \end{array}$. The probability of being in state A after one trial is .32 and after two trials is .328; the probability of being in state B after one trial is .68 and after two trials is .672. *(9-1)*

2. State A is absorbing; chain is absorbing. *(9-2, 9-3)* **3.** No absorbing states; chain is regular. *(9-2, 9-3)*
4. No absorbing states; chain is neither. *(9-2, 9-3)* **5.** States B and C are absorbing; chain is absorbing. *(9-2, 9-3)*
6. States A and B are absorbing; chain is neither. *(9-2, 9-3)*

7.
$$\begin{array}{c} \\ A \\ B \\ C \end{array}\begin{array}{ccc} A & B & C \\ \left[\begin{array}{ccc} 0 & 1 & 0 \\ .1 & 0 & .9 \\ 0 & 1 & 0 \end{array}\right]\end{array}$$; no absorbing states; chain is neither. *(9-1, 9-2, 9-3)*

8.
$$\begin{array}{c} \\ A \\ B \\ C \end{array}\begin{array}{ccc} A & B & C \\ \left[\begin{array}{ccc} 0 & 1 & 0 \\ .1 & .2 & .7 \\ 0 & 0 & 1 \end{array}\right]\end{array}$$; C is absorbing; chain is absorbing. *(9-1, 9-2, 9-3)*

9.
$$\begin{array}{c} \\ A \\ B \\ C \end{array}\begin{array}{ccc} A & B & C \\ \left[\begin{array}{ccc} 0 & 0 & 1 \\ .1 & .2 & .7 \\ 0 & 1 & 0 \end{array}\right]\end{array}$$; no absorbing states; chain is regular. *(9-1, 9-2, 9-3)*

10.
$$\begin{array}{c} \\ A \\ B \\ C \\ D \end{array}\begin{array}{cccc} A & B & C & D \\ \left[\begin{array}{cccc} .3 & .2 & 0 & .5 \\ 0 & 1 & 0 & 0 \\ 0 & 0 & .2 & .8 \\ 0 & 0 & .3 & .7 \end{array}\right]\end{array}$$; B is absorbing; chain is neither. *(9-1, 9-2, 9-3)*

11.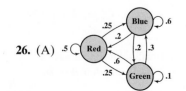
$$\begin{array}{c} \\ A \\ B \\ C \end{array}\begin{array}{ccc} A & B & C \\ \left[\begin{array}{ccc} .3 & .2 & .5 \\ .8 & 0 & .2 \\ .1 & .3 & .6 \end{array}\right]\end{array}$$ *(9-1)* **12.** (A) .3 (B) .675 *(9-1)* **13.** $S = \begin{array}{cc} A & B \\ [.25 & .75] \end{array}$; $\overline{P} = \begin{array}{c} \\ A \\ B \end{array}\begin{array}{cc} A & B \\ \left[\begin{array}{cc} .25 & .75 \\ .25 & .75 \end{array}\right]\end{array}$ *(9-2)*

14. $S = \begin{array}{ccc} A & B & C \\ [.4 & .48 & .12] \end{array}$; $\overline{P} = \begin{array}{c} \\ A \\ B \\ C \end{array}\begin{array}{ccc} A & B & C \\ \left[\begin{array}{ccc} .4 & .48 & .12 \\ .4 & .48 & .12 \\ .4 & .48 & .12 \end{array}\right]\end{array}$ *(9-2)* **15.** $\begin{array}{c} \\ A \\ B \\ C \end{array}\begin{array}{ccc} A & B & C \\ \left[\begin{array}{ccc} 1 & 0 & 0 \\ 0 & 1 & 0 \\ .75 & .25 & 0 \end{array}\right]\end{array}$; $P(C \text{ to } A) = .75$; $P(C \text{ to } B) = .25$. It takes an average of 2.5 trials to go from C to an absorbing state. *(9-3)*

16.
$$\begin{array}{c} \\ A \\ B \\ C \\ D \end{array}\begin{array}{cccc} A & B & C & D \\ \left[\begin{array}{cccc} 1 & 0 & 0 & 0 \\ 0 & 1 & 0 & 0 \\ .2 & .8 & 0 & 0 \\ .3 & .7 & 0 & 0 \end{array}\right]\end{array}$$; $P(C \text{ to } A) = .2$; $P(C \text{ to } B) = .8$; $P(D \text{ to } A) = .3$; $P(D \text{ to } B) = .7$. It takes an average of 2 trials to go from C to an absorbing state and an average of 3 trials to go from D to an absorbing state. *(9-3)*.

21.
$$\begin{array}{c} \\ B \\ D \\ A \\ C \end{array}\begin{array}{cccc} B & D & A & C \\ \left[\begin{array}{cccc} 1 & 0 & 0 & 0 \\ 0 & 1 & 0 & 0 \\ .1 & .1 & .6 & .2 \\ .2 & .2 & .3 & .3 \end{array}\right]\end{array}$$ *(9-3)*

22. (A) $\begin{array}{ccc} A & B & C \\ [.1 & .4 & .5] \end{array}$ (B) $\begin{array}{ccc} A & B & C \\ [.1 & .4 & .5] \end{array}$ *(9-3)* **23.** (A) $\begin{array}{ccc} A & B & C \\ [.25 & .75 & 0] \end{array}$ (B) $\begin{array}{ccc} A & B & C \\ [.55 & .45 & 0] \end{array}$ *(9-3)*

24. No. Each row of P would contain a 0 and a 1, but none of the four matrices with this property is regular. *(9-2)*

25. Yes; for example, $P = \left[\begin{array}{ccc} 0 & 0 & 1 \\ 0 & 0 & 1 \\ .2 & .3 & .5 \end{array}\right]$ is regular. *(9-2)*

26. (A) diagram (B) $\begin{array}{c} \\ R \\ B \\ G \end{array}\begin{array}{ccc} R & B & G \\ \left[\begin{array}{ccc} .5 & .25 & .25 \\ .2 & .6 & .2 \\ .6 & .3 & .1 \end{array}\right]\end{array}$ (D) $\begin{array}{c} \\ R \\ B \\ G \end{array}\begin{array}{ccc} R & B & G \\ \left[\begin{array}{ccc} .4 & .4 & .2 \\ .4 & .4 & .2 \\ .4 & .4 & .2 \end{array}\right]\end{array}$ In the long run, the red urn will be selected 40% of the time, the blue urn 40% of the time, and the green urn 20% of the time. *(9-2)*
(C) Regular

27. (A)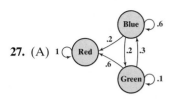
(B) $\begin{array}{c} \\ R \\ B \\ G \end{array} \begin{array}{ccc} R & B & G \\ \left[\begin{array}{ccc} 1 & 0 & 0 \\ .2 & .6 & .2 \\ .6 & .3 & .1 \end{array}\right] \end{array}$
(C) Absorbing
(D) $\begin{array}{c} \\ R \\ B \\ G \end{array} \begin{array}{ccc} R & B & G \\ \left[\begin{array}{ccc} 1 & 0 & 0 \\ 1 & 0 & 0 \\ 1 & 0 & 0 \end{array}\right] \end{array}$
Once the red urn is selected, the blue and green urns will never be selected again. It will take an average of 3.67 trials to reach the red urn from the blue urn and an average of 2.33 trials to reach the red urn from the green urn. *(9-3)*

29. No such chain exists. *(9-2, 9-3)*   **30.** No such chain exists. *(9-2, 9-3)*   **31.** No such chain exists. *(9-2)*

32. $S = \begin{bmatrix} 1 & 0 & 0 \end{bmatrix}$ and $S' = \begin{bmatrix} 0 & 1 & 0 \end{bmatrix}$ are both stationary matrices for $P = \begin{array}{c} \\ A \\ B \\ C \end{array} \begin{array}{ccc} A & B & C \\ \left[\begin{array}{ccc} 1 & 0 & 0 \\ 0 & 1 & 0 \\ .6 & .3 & .1 \end{array}\right] \end{array}$ *(9-3)*   **33.** $P = \begin{array}{c} \\ A \\ B \end{array} \begin{array}{cc} A & B \\ \left[\begin{array}{cc} 0 & 1 \\ 1 & 0 \end{array}\right] \end{array}$ *(9-2, 9-3)*

34. No such chain exists. *(9-2)*   **35.** No such chain exists. *(9-3)*   **36.** No limiting matrix *(9-2, 9-3)*

37. $P = \begin{array}{c} \\ A \\ B \\ C \\ D \end{array} \begin{array}{cccc} A & B & C & D \\ \left[\begin{array}{cccc} .392 & .163 & .134 & .311 \\ .392 & .163 & .134 & .311 \\ .392 & .163 & .134 & .311 \\ .392 & .163 & .134 & .311 \end{array}\right] \end{array}$ *(9-2)*

38. (A)
(B) $\begin{array}{c} \\ X \\ X' \end{array} \begin{array}{cc} X & X' \\ \left[\begin{array}{cc} .7 & .3 \\ .5 & .5 \end{array}\right] \end{array}$ (C) $\begin{array}{cc} X & X' \\ \begin{bmatrix} .2 & .8 \end{bmatrix} \end{array}$

(D) $\begin{array}{cc} X & X' \\ \begin{bmatrix} .54 & .46 \end{bmatrix} \end{array}$; 54% of the consumers will purchase brand X on the next purchase.

(E) $\begin{array}{cc} X & X' \\ \begin{bmatrix} .625 & .375 \end{bmatrix} \end{array}$ (F) 62.5% *(9-2)*

39. (A) Brand A: 24%, brand B: 32%, brand C: 44%   (B) 4 yr *(9-3)*

40. (A) $S_1 = \begin{bmatrix} .48 & .52 \end{bmatrix}$; $S_2 = \begin{bmatrix} .66 & .34 \end{bmatrix}$

(B)

Year	Data (%)	Model (%)
1995	14	14
2000	49	48
2005	68	66

(C) 89% *(9-2)*

41. (A) 63.75%
(B) 15%
(C) 8.75 yr *(9-3)*

42. $\overline{P} = \begin{array}{c} \\ Red \\ Pink \\ White \end{array} \begin{array}{ccc} Red & Pink & White \\ \left[\begin{array}{ccc} 1 & 0 & 0 \\ 1 & 0 & 0 \\ 1 & 0 & 0 \end{array}\right] \end{array}$ *(9-3)*

43. (A) $S_1 = \begin{bmatrix} .244 & .756 \end{bmatrix}$; $S_2 = \begin{bmatrix} .203 & .797 \end{bmatrix}$

(B)

Year	Data (%)	Model (%)
1985	30.1	30.1
1995	24.7	24.4
2005	20.9	20.3

(C) 10.3% *(9-2)*

Chapter 10

Exercises 10-1

1. 2   **3.** 1.25   **5.** (A) 2   (B) 2   (C) 2   (D) 2   **7.** (A) 1   (B) 2   (C) Does not exist   (D) 2   (E) No   **9.** 2   **11.** 0.5
13. (A) 1   (B) 2   (C) Does not exist   (D) Does not exist   (E) No   **15.** (A) 1   (B) 1   (C) 1   (D) 3   (E) Yes
17. (A) -2 (B) -2 (C) -2 (D) 1   (E) Yes   **19.** (A) 2   (B) 2   (C) 2   (D) Does not exist   (E) Yes

21. 12   **23.** 1   **25.** -4 **27.** -1.5 **29.** 3   **31.** 15   **33.** -6 **35.** $\dfrac{7}{5}$ **37.** 3

39.
41.
43. (A) 1   (B) 1   (C) 1   (D) 1
45. (A) 2   (B) 1   (C) Does not exist   (D) Does not exist
47. (A) -6 (B) Does not exist   (C) 6
49. (A) 1   (B) -1 (C) Does not exist   (D) Does not exist
51. (A) Does not exist   (B) $\dfrac{1}{2}$ (C) $\dfrac{1}{4}$ **53.** (A) -5 (B) -3 (C) 0

55. (A) 0   (B) -1 (C) Does not exist   **57.** (A) 1   (B) $\dfrac{1}{3}$ (C) $\dfrac{3}{4}$ **59.** False   **61.** True   **63.** False   **65.** 3   **67.** 4

69. (A) $\lim_{x\to 1^-} f(x) = 2$ (B) $\lim_{x\to 1^-} f(x) = 3$ (C) $m = 1.5$ (D) The graph in (A) is broken when it jumps from (1, 2) up to (1, 3). The graph in (B) is also broken when it jumps down from (1, 3) to (1, 2). The graph in (C) is one continuous piece, with no breaks or jumps.
$\lim_{x\to 1^+} f(x) = 3$ $\lim_{x\to 1^+} f(x) = 2$

71. $2a$ **73.** $1/(2\sqrt{a})$ **75.** (A) $F(x) = \begin{cases} 0.99 & \text{if } 0 < x \le 20 \\ 0.07x - 0.41 & \text{if } x \ge 20 \end{cases}$ (B)   (C) All 3 limits are 0.99.

79. (A) $D(x) = \begin{cases} x & \text{if } 0 \le x < 300 \\ 0.97x & \text{if } 300 \le x < 1{,}000 \\ 0.95x & \text{if } 1{,}000 \le x < 3{,}000 \\ 0.93x & \text{if } 3{,}000 \le x < 5{,}000 \\ 0.9x & \text{if } x \ge 5{,}000 \end{cases}$

(B) $\lim\limits_{x\to 1{,}000} D(x)$ does not exist because

$\lim\limits_{x\to 1{,}000^-} D(x) = 970$ and $\lim\limits_{x\to 1{,}000^+} D(x) = 950$;

$\lim\limits_{x\to 3{,}000} D(x)$ does not exist because

$\lim\limits_{x\to 3{,}000^-} D(x) = 2{,}850$ and $\lim\limits_{x\to 3{,}000^+} D(x) = 2{,}790$

81. $F(x) = \begin{cases} 20x & \text{if } 0 < x \le 4{,}000 \\ 80{,}000 & \text{if } x \ge 4{,}000 \end{cases}$

$\lim\limits_{x\to 4{,}000} F(x) = 80{,}000$; $\lim\limits_{x\to 8{,}000} F(x) = 80{,}000$

83. $\lim\limits_{x\to 5} f(x)$ does not exist; $\lim\limits_{x\to 10} f(x) = 0$;

$\lim\limits_{x\to 5} g(x) = 0$; $\lim\limits_{x\to 10} g(x) = 1$

Exercises 10-2

1. -2 **3.** $-\infty$ **5.** Does not exist **7.** 0 **9. (A)** $-\infty$ **(B)** ∞ **(C)** Does not exist
11. (A) ∞ **(B)** ∞ **(C)** ∞ **13. (A)** 3 **(B)** 3 **(C)** 3 **15. (A)** $-\infty$ **(B)** ∞ **(C)** Does not exist
17. (A) ∞ **(B)** $-\infty$ **19. (A)** $-\infty$ **(B)** $-\infty$ **21.** $\lim\limits_{x\to -3^-} f(x) = -\infty$; $\lim\limits_{x\to -3^+} f(x) = \infty$; $x = -3$ is a vertical asymptote
23. $\lim\limits_{x\to -2^-} h(x) = \infty$; $\lim\limits_{x\to -2^+} h(x) = -\infty$; $\lim\limits_{x\to 2^-} h(x) = -\infty$; $\lim\limits_{x\to 2^+} h(x) = \infty$; $x = -2$ and $x = 2$ are vertical asymptotes
25. No zeros of denominator; no vertical asymptotes
27. $\lim\limits_{x\to 1^-} H(x) = -\infty$; $\lim\limits_{x\to 1^+} H(x) = \infty$; $\lim\limits_{x\to 3} H(x) = 2$; $x = 1$ is a vertical asymptote
29. $\lim\limits_{x\to 0} T(x) = -\infty$; $\lim\limits_{x\to 4} T(x) = \infty$; $x = 0$ and $x = 4$ are vertical asymptotes

31. (A) $\dfrac{47}{41} \approx 1.146$ **(B)** $\dfrac{407}{491} \approx 0.829$ **(C)** $\dfrac{4}{5} = 0.8$ **33. (A)** $\dfrac{2{,}011}{138} \approx 14.572$ **(B)** $\dfrac{12{,}511}{348} \approx 35.951$ **(C)** ∞

35. (A) $-\dfrac{8{,}568}{46{,}653} \approx -0.184$ **(B)** $-\dfrac{143{,}136}{1{,}492{,}989} \approx 0.096$ **(C)** 0 **37. (A)** $-\dfrac{7{,}010}{996} \approx -7.038$ **(B)** $-\dfrac{56{,}010}{7{,}996} \approx -7.005$ **(C)** -7

39. Horizontal asymptote: $y = 2$; vertical asymptote: $x = -2$ **41.** Horizontal asymptote: $y = 1$; vertical asymptotes: $x = -1$ and $x = 1$
43. No horizontal asymptotes; no vertical asymptotes **45.** Horizontal asymptote: $y = 0$; no vertical asymptotes
47. No horizontal asymptotes; vertical asymptote: $x = 3$
49. Horizontal asymptote: $y = 2$; vertical asymptotes: $x = -1$ and $x = 2$
51. Horizontal asymptote: $y = 2$; vertical asymptote: $x = -1$
53. False **55.** False **57.** True **59.** If $n \ge 1$ and $a_n > 0$, then the limit is ∞. If $n \ge 1$ and $a_n < 0$, then the limit is $-\infty$.
61. $\lim\limits_{x\to\infty} f(x) = \infty$; $\lim\limits_{x\to -\infty} f(x) = \infty$ **63.** $\lim\limits_{x\to\infty} f(x) = \infty$; $\lim\limits_{x\to -\infty} f(x) = -\infty$ **65.** $\lim\limits_{x\to\infty} f(x) = \infty$; $\lim\limits_{x\to -\infty} f(x) = -\infty$
67. $\lim\limits_{x\to\infty} f(x) = -\infty$; $\lim\limits_{x\to -\infty} f(x) = -\infty$

69. (A) $C(x) = 180x + 200$

(B) $\overline{C}(x) = \dfrac{180x + 200}{x}$

(C)

(D) \$180 per board

71. (A) $C_e(x) = 950 + 56x$; $\overline{C}_e(x) = \dfrac{950}{x} + 56$

(B) $C_c(x) = 900 + 66x$; $\overline{C}_c(x) = \dfrac{900}{x} + 66$

(C) At $x = 5$ years
(D) At $x = 5$ years
(E) $\lim\limits_{x\to\infty} \overline{C}_e(x) = 56$; $\lim\limits_{x\to\infty} \overline{C}_c(x) = 66$

73. The long-term drug concentration is 5 mg/ml.
75. (A) \$18 million
(B) \$38 million
(C) $\lim\limits_{x\to 1^-} P(x) = \infty$

77. (C) $V_{\max} = 4$, $K_M = 20$

(D) $v(s) = \dfrac{4s}{20 + s}$

(E) $v = \dfrac{12}{7}$ when $s = 15$; $s = 60$ when $v = 3$

79. (A) $C_{\max} = 18$, $M = 150$

(B) $C(T) = \dfrac{18T}{150 + T}$
(C) $C = 14.4$ when $T = 600$ K; $T = 300$ K when $C = 12$

Exercises 10-3

1. f is continuous at $x = 1$, since $\lim_{x \to 1} f(x) = f(1)$.

3. f is discontinuous at $x = 1$, since $\lim_{x \to 1} f(x) \neq f(1)$.

5. f is discontinuous at $x = 1$, since $\lim_{x \to 1} f(x)$ does not exist.

7. 1.9   **9.** 0.9   **11.** (A) 2   (B) 1   (C) Does not exist   (D) 1   (E) No   **13.** (A) 1   (B) 1   (C) 1   (D) 3   (E) No
15. 0.9   **17.** 2.05   **19.** (A) 1   (B) 1   (C) 1   (D) 3   (E) No   **21.** (A) 2   (B) −1   (C) Does not exist   (D) 2   (E) No

23. All x **25.** All x, except $x = -2$ **27.** All x, except $x = -4$ and $x = 1$ **29.** All x **31.** All x, except $x = \pm\dfrac{3}{2}$

33. (A)

(B) 1   (C) 2   (D) No   (E) All integers
35. $-3 < x < 4$; $(-3, 4)$ **37.** $x < 3$ or $x > 7$; $(-\infty, 3) \cup (7, \infty)$
39. $x < -2$ or $0 < x < 2$; $(-\infty, -2) \cup (0, 2)$ **41.** $-5 < x < 0$ or $x > 3$; $(-5, 0) \cup (3, \infty)$
43. (A) $(-4, -2) \cup (0, 2) \cup (4, \infty)$ (B) $(-\infty, -4) \cup (-2, 0) \cup (2, 4)$
45. (A) $(-\infty, -2.5308) \cup (-0.7198, \infty)$ (B) $(-2.5308, -0.7198)$
47. (A) $(-\infty, -2.1451) \cup (-1, -0.5240) \cup (1, 2.6691)$
(B) $(-2.1451, -1) \cup (-0.5240, 1) \cup (2.6691, \infty)$

49. $[6, \infty)$ **51.** $(-\infty, \infty)$ **53.** $(-\infty, -3] \cup [3, \infty)$ **55.** $(-\infty, \infty)$

57. Since $\lim_{x \to 1^-} f(x) = 2$ and $\lim_{x \to 1^+} f(x) = 4$, $\lim_{x \to 1} f(x)$ does not exist and f is not continuous at $x = 1$.

59. This function is continuous for all x.

61. Since $\lim_{x \to 0} f(x) = 0$ and $f(0) = 1$, $\lim_{x \to 0} f(x) \neq f(0)$ and f is not continuous at $x = 0$.

63. (A) Yes   (B) No   (C) Yes   (D) No   (E) Yes   **65.** True   **67.** False   **69.** True
71. x intercepts: $x = -5, 2$ **73.** x intercepts: $x = -6, -1, 4$ **75.** No, but this does not contradict Theorem 2, since f is discontinuous at $x = 1$.

77. (A) $P(x) = \begin{cases} 0.44 & \text{if } 0 < x \leq 1 \\ 0.61 & \text{if } 1 < x \leq 2 \\ 0.78 & \text{if } 2 < x \leq 3 \\ 0.95 & \text{if } 3 < x \leq 3.5 \end{cases}$ (B)

(C) Yes; no

81. (A) $S(x) = \begin{cases} 5 + 0.63x & \text{if } 0 \leq x \leq 50 \\ 14 + 0.45x & \text{if } 50 < x \end{cases}$

(B)

(C) Yes

83. (A)

(B) $\lim_{s \to 10,000} E(s) = \$1,000$; $E(10,000) = \$1,000$
(C) $\lim_{s \to 20,000} E(s)$ does not exist; $E(20,000) = \$2,000$
(D) Yes; no

85. (A) t_2, t_3, t_4, t_6, t_7 (B) $\lim_{t \to t_5} N(t) = 7$; $N(t_5) = 7$ (C) $\lim_{t \to t_3} N(t)$ does not exist; $N(t_3) = 4$

Exercises 10-4

1. (A) -3; slope of the secant line through $(1, f(1))$ and $(2, f(2))$
(B) $-2 - h$; slope of the secant line through $(1, f(1))$ and $(1 + h, f(1 + h))$
(C) -2; slope of the tangent line at $(1, f(1))$
3. (A) 15   (B) 15   (C) $6 + 3h$ (D) 6   (E) 6   (F) 6   (G) $y = 6x - 3$
5. $f'(x) = 0$; $f'(1) = 0, f'(2) = 0, f'(3) = 0$ **7.** $f'(x) = 3$; $f'(1) = 3, f'(2) = 3, f'(3) = 3$
9. $f'(x) = -6x$; $f'(1) = -6, f'(2) = -12, f'(3) = -18$ **11.** $f'(x) = 2x + 6$; $f'(1) = 8, f'(2) = 10, f'(3) = 12$
13. $f'(x) = 4x - 7$; $f'(1) = -3, f'(2) = 1, f'(3) = 5$ **15.** $f'(x) = -2x + 4$; $f'(1) = 2, f'(2) = 0, f'(3) = -2$

17. $f'(x) = 6x^2$; $f'(1) = 6$, $f'(2) = 24$, $f'(3) = 54$ **19.** $f'(x) = -\dfrac{4}{x^2}$; $f'(1) = -4$, $f'(2) = -1$, $f'(3) = -\dfrac{4}{9}$

21. $f'(x) = \dfrac{3}{2\sqrt{x}}$; $f'(1) = \dfrac{3}{2}$, $f'(2) = \dfrac{3}{2\sqrt{2}}$ or $\dfrac{3\sqrt{2}}{4}$, $f'(3) = \dfrac{3}{2\sqrt{3}}$ or $\dfrac{\sqrt{3}}{2}$

23. $f'(x) = \dfrac{5}{\sqrt{x+5}}$; $f'(1) = \dfrac{5}{\sqrt{6}}$ or $\dfrac{5\sqrt{6}}{6}$, $f'(2) = \dfrac{5}{\sqrt{7}}$ or $\dfrac{5\sqrt{7}}{7}$, $f'(3) = \dfrac{5}{2\sqrt{2}}$ or $\dfrac{5\sqrt{2}}{4}$

25. $f'(x) = \dfrac{6}{(x+2)^2}$; $f'(1) = \dfrac{2}{3}$, $f'(2) = \dfrac{3}{8}$, $f'(3) = \dfrac{6}{25}$

27. (A) 5   (B) $3 + h$ (C) 3   (D) $y = 3x - 1$ **29.** (A) 5 m/s   (B) $3 + h$ m/s   (C) 3 m/s

31. Yes   **33.** No   **35.** Yes   **37.** Yes

39. (A) $f'(x) = 2x - 4$ (B) $-4, 0, 4$ **41.** $v = f'(x) = 8x - 2$; 6 ft/s, 22 ft/s, 38 ft/s

(C)

43. (A) The graphs of g and h are vertical translations of the graph of f. All three functions should have the same derivative.

(B) $2x$

45. True

47. False

49. False

51. f is nondifferentiable at $x = 1$ **53.** f is differentiable for all real numbers   **55.** No   **57.** No   **59.** $f'(0) = 0$ **61.** 6 s; 192 ft/s

63. (A) \$8.75

(B) $R'(x) = 60 - 0.05x$

(C) $R(1,000) = 35,000$; $R'(1,000) = 10$; At a production level of 1,000 car seats, the revenue is \$35,000 and is increasing at the rate of \$10 per seat.

65. (A) $S'(t) = 1/\sqrt{t + 10}$

(B) $S(15) = 10$; $S'(15) = 0.2$. After 15 months, the total sales are \$10 million and are increasing at the rate of \$0.2 million, or \$200,000, per month.

(C) The estimated total sales are \$10.2 million after 16 months and \$10.4 million after 17 months.

67. (A) $p'(t) = 328t + 161$

(B) $p(10) = 30,336$; $p'(10) = 413.4$; In 2015, 30,336 metric tons of tungsten are consumed and this quantity is increasing at the rate of 3,441 metric tons per year.

69. (A)

(B) $R(20) = 1,403.5$ billion kilowatts, $R'(20) = -10.7$ billion kilowatts. In 2020, 1,403.5 billion kilowatts will be sold and the amount sold is decreasing at the rate of 10.7 billion kilowatts per year.

71. (A) $P'(t) = 12 - 2t$

(B) $P(3) = 107$; $P'(3) = 6$. After 3 hours, the ozone level is 107 ppb and is increasing at the rate of 6 ppb per hour.

Exercises 10-5

1. 0   **3.** $9x^8$ **5.** $3x^2$ **7.** $-4x^{-5}$ **9.** $\dfrac{8}{3}x^{5/3}$ **11.** $-\dfrac{10}{x^{11}}$ **13.** $10x$ **15.** $2.8x^6$ **17.** $\dfrac{x^2}{6}$ **19.** 12   **21.** 2   **23.** 9   **25.** 2   **27.** $4t - 3$

29. $-10x^{-3} - 9x^{-2}$ **31.** $1.5u^{-0.7} - 8.8u^{1.2}$ **33.** $0.5 - 3.3t^2$ **35.** $-\dfrac{8}{5}x^{-5}$ **37.** $3x + \dfrac{14}{5}x^{-3}$ **39.** $-\dfrac{20}{9}w^{-5} + \dfrac{5}{3}w^{-2/3}$

41. $2u^{-1/3} - \dfrac{5}{3}u^{-2/3}$ **43.** $-\dfrac{9}{5}t^{-8/5} + 3t^{-3/2}$ **45.** $-\dfrac{1}{3}x^{-4/3}$ **47.** $-0.6x^{-3/2} + 6.4x^{-3} + 1$

49. (A) $f'(x) = 6 - 2x$ (B) $f'(2) = 2$; $f'(4) = -2$ (C) $y = 2x + 4$; $y = -2x + 16$ (D) $x = 3$

51. (A) $f'(x) = 12x^3 - 12x$ (B) $f'(2) = 72$; $f'(4) = 720$ (C) $y = 72x - 127$; $y = 720x - 2,215$ (D) $x = -1, 0, 1$

53. (A) $v = f'(x) = 176 - 32x$ (B) $f'(0) = 176$ ft/s; $f'(3) = 80$ ft/s   (C) 5.5 s

55. (A) $v = f'(x) = 3x^2 - 18x + 15$ (B) $f'(0) = 15$ ft/s; $f'(3) = -12$ ft/s   (C) $x = 1$ s, $x = 5$ s

57. $f'(x) = 2x - 3 - 2x^{-1/2} = 2x - 3 - \dfrac{2}{x^{1/2}}$; $x = 2.1777$ **59.** $f'(x) = 4\sqrt[3]{x} - 3x - 3$; $x = -2.9018$

61. $f'(x) = 0.2x^3 + 0.3x^2 - 3x - 1.6$; $x = -4.4607, -0.5159, 3.4765$

63. $f'(x) = 0.8x^3 - 9.36x^2 + 32.5x - 28.25$; $x = 1.3050$

69. $8x - 4$ **71.** $-20x^{-2}$ **73.** $-\dfrac{1}{4}x^{-2} + \dfrac{2}{3}x^{-3}$ **75.** True   **77.** False   **79.** True

81. (A) $S'(t) = 0.09t^2 + t + 2$

(B) $S(5) = 29.25$, $S'(5) = 9.25$. After 5 months, sales are \$29.25 million and are increasing at the rate of \$9.25 million per month.

(C) $S(10) = 103$, $S'(10) = 21$. After 10 months, sales are \$103 million and are increasing at the rate of \$21 million per month.

83. (A) $N'(x) = 3,780/x^2$
  (B) $N'(10) = 37.8$. At the \$10,000 level of advertising, sales are increasing at the rate of 37.8 boats per \$1,000 spent on advertising.
  $N'(20) = 9.45$. At the \$20,000 level of advertising, sales are increasing at the rate of 9.45 boats per \$1,000 spent on advertising.

85. (A)

(B) In 2016, 55.7% of male high-school graduates enroll in college and the percentage is decreasing at the rate of 1.9% per year.

87. (A) -1.37 beats/min
  (B) -0.58 beat/min

89. (A) 25 items/h
  (B) 8.33 items/h

Exercises 10-6

1. $\Delta x = 3; \Delta y = 45; \Delta y/\Delta x = 15$ **3.** 12 **5.** 12 **7.** $dy = (24x - 3x^2)\, dx$ **9.** $dy = \left(2x - \dfrac{x^2}{3}\right) dx$ **11.** $dy = -\dfrac{295}{x^{3/2}}\, dx$

13. (A) $12 + 3\Delta x$ (B) 12 **15.** $dy = (8x + 4)\, dx$ **17.** $dy = (1 - 9x^{-2})\, dx$ **19.** $dy = 1.4; \Delta y = 1.44$

21. $dy = -3; \Delta y = -3\frac{1}{3}$ **23.** 120 in.^{3}

25. (A) $\Delta y = \Delta x + (\Delta x)^2; dy = \Delta x$
  (B) 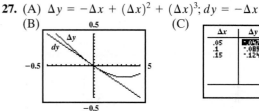 (C)

27. (A) $\Delta y = -\Delta x + (\Delta x)^2 + (\Delta x)^3; dy = -\Delta x$
  (B) (C)

29. True **31.** False **33.** $dy = \left(\dfrac{2}{3}x^{-1/3} - \dfrac{10}{3}x^{2/3}\right) dx$ **35.** $dy = 3.9; \Delta y = 3.83$ **37.** 40-unit increase; 20-unit increase

39. $-\$2.50; \$1.25$ **41.** -1.37/min; -0.58/min **43.** 1.26 mm^2 **45.** 3 wpm

47. (A) 2,100 increase (B) 4,800 increase (C) 2,100 increase

Exercises 10-7

1. $C'(x) = 0.8$ **3.** $C'(x) = 4.6 - 0.02x$ **5.** $R'(x) = 4 - 0.02x$ **7.** $R'(x) = 12 - 0.08x$ **9.** $P'(x) = 3.2 - 0.02x$

11. $P'(x) = 7.4 - 0.06x$ **13.** $\overline{C}(x) = 1.1 + \dfrac{145}{x}$ **15.** $\overline{C}'(x) = -\dfrac{145}{x^2}$ **17.** $P(x) = 3.9x - 0.02x^2 - 145$

19. $\overline{P}(x) = 3.9 - 0.02x - \dfrac{145}{x}$ **21.** True **23.** False **25.** (A) \$29.50 (B) \$30

27. (A) \$420
  (B) $\overline{C}'(500) = -0.24$. At a production level of 500 frames, average cost is decreasing at the rate of 24¢ per frame.
  (C) Approximately \$419.76

29. (A) \$14.70 (B) \$15

31. (A) $P'(450) = 0.5$. At a production level of 450 cassettes, profit is increasing at the rate of 50¢ per cassette.
  (B) $P'(750) = -2.5$. At a production level of 750 cassettes, profit is decreasing at the rate of \$2.50 per cassette.

33. (A) \$13.50
  (B) $\overline{P}'(50) = \$0.27$. At a production level of 50 mowers, the average profit per mower is increasing at the rate of \$0.27 per mower.
  (C) Approximately \$13.77

35. (A) $p = 100 - 0.025x$, domain: $0 \le x \le 4,000$
  (B) $R(x) = 100x - 0.025x^2$, domain: $0 \le x \le 4,000$
  (C) $R'(1,600) = 20$. At a production level of 1,600 radios, revenue is increasing at the rate of \$20 per radio.
  (D) $R'(2,500) = -25$. At a production level of 2,500 radios, revenue is decreasing at the rate of \$25 per radio.

37. (A) $p = 200 - \frac{1}{30}x$, domain: $0 \le x \le 6,000$
  (B) $C'(x) = 60$
  (C) $R(x) = 200x - (x^2/30)$, domain: $0 \le x \le 6,000$
  (D) $R'(x) = 200 - (x/15)$
  (E) $R'(1,500) = 100$. At a production level of 1,500 saws, revenue is increasing at the rate of \$100 per saw.
  $R'(4,500) = -100$. At a production level of 4,500 saws, revenue is decreasing at the rate of \$100 per saw.

(F) Break-even points: (600, 108,000) and (3,600, 288,000)

39. (A) $p = 20 - 0.02x$, domain: $0 \le x \le 1,000$
(B) $R(x) = 20x - 0.02x^2$, domain: $0 \le x \le 1,000$
(C) $C(x) = 4x + 1,400$

41. (A) $x = 500$
(B) $P(x) = 176x - 0.2x^2 - 21,900$
(C) $x = 440$
(D) Break-even points: (150, 25,500) and (730, 39,420);
x intercepts for $P(x)$: $x = 150$ and $x = 730$

45. (A)

(G) $P(x) = -(x^2/30) + 140x - 72,000$
(H) $P'(x) = -(x/15) + 140$
(I) $P'(1,500) = 40$. At a production level of 1,500 saws, profit is increasing at the rate of $40 per saw.
$P'(3,000) = -60$. At a production level of 3,000 saws, profit is decreasing at the rate of $60 per saw.

(D) Break-even points: (100, 1,800) and (700, 4,200)
(E) $P(x) = 16x - 0.02x^2 - 1,400$
(F) $P'(250) = 6$. At a production level of 250 toasters, profit is increasing at the rate of $6 per toaster. $P'(475) = -3$. At a production level of 475 toasters, profit is decreasing at the rate of $3 per toaster.

43. (A) $R(x) = 20x - x^{3/2}$
(B) Break-even points: (44, 588), (258, 1,016)

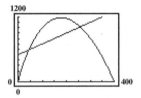

(B) Fixed costs $\approx$ \$721,680
Variable costs $\approx$ \$121

(C) (713, 807,703), (5,423, 1,376,227)
(D) $254 \le p \le \$1,133$

Chapter 10 Review Exercises

1. (A) 16 (B) 8 (C) 8 (D) 4 (E) 4 (F) 4 *(10-2)* **2.** $f'(x) = -3$ *(10-2)* **3.** (A) 22 (B) 8 (C) 2 (D) -5 *(10-1)*
4. 1.5 *(10-1)* **5.** 3.5 *(10-1)* **6.** 3.75 *(10-1)* **7.** 3.75 *(10-1)* **8.** (A) 1 (B) 1 (C) 1 (D) 1 *(10-1)*
9. (A) 2 (B) 3 (C) Does not exist (D) 3 *(10-1)* **10.** (A) 4 (B) 4 (C) 4 (D) Does not exist *(10-1)*
11. (A) Does not exist (B) 3 (C) No *(10-3)* **12.** (A) 2 (B) Not defined (C) No *(10-3)*
13. (A) 1 (B) 1 (C) Yes *(10-3)* **14.** 5 *(10-2)* **15.** 5 *(10-2)* **16.** ∞ *(10-2)* **17.** $-\infty$ *(10-2)* **18.** 0 *(10-1)* **19.** 0 *(10-1)*
20. 0 *(10-1)* **21.** Vertical asymptote: $x = 2$ *(10-3)* **22.** Horizontal asymptote: $y = 5$ *(10-2)* **23.** $x = 2$ **24.** $f'(x) = 10x$ *(10-4)*

25. (A) -3 (B) 6 (C) -2 (D) 3 (E) -11 *(10-5)* **26.** $x^2 - 10x$ *(10-5)* **27.** $x^{-1/2} - 3 = \dfrac{1}{x^{1/2}} - 3$ *(10-5)* **28.** 0 *(10-5)*

29. $-\dfrac{3}{2}x^{-2} + \dfrac{15}{4}x^2 = \dfrac{-3}{2x^2} + \dfrac{15x^2}{4}$ *(10-5)* **30.** $-2x^{-5} + x^3 = \dfrac{-2}{x^5} + x^3$ *(10-5)* **31.** $f'(x) = 12x^3 + 9x^2 - 2$ *(10-5)*

32. $\Delta x = 2, \Delta y = 10, \Delta y/\Delta x = 5$ *(10-6)* **33.** 5 *(10-6)* **34.** 6 *(10-6)* **35.** $\Delta y = 0.64; dy = 0.6$ *(10-6)*

36. (A) 4 (B) 6 (C) Does not exist (D) 6 (E) No *(10-3)* **37.** (A) 3 (B) 3 (C) 3 (D) 3 (E) Yes *(10-3)*
38. (A) $(8, \infty)$ (B) $[0, 8]$ *(10-3)* **39.** $(-3, 4)$ *(10-3)* **40.** $(-3, 0) \cup (5, \infty)$ *(10-3)* **41.** $(-2.3429, -0.4707) \cup (1.8136, \infty)$ *(10-3)*

42. (A) 3 (B) $2 + 0.5h$ (C) 2 *(10-4)* **43.** $-x^{-4} + 10x^{-3}$ *(10-4)* **44.** $\dfrac{3}{4}x^{-1/2} - \dfrac{5}{6}x^{-3/2} = \dfrac{3}{4\sqrt{x}} - \dfrac{5}{6\sqrt{x^3}}$ *(10-5)*

45. $0.6x^{-2/3} - 0.3x^{-4/3} = \dfrac{0.6}{x^{2/3}} - \dfrac{0.3}{x^{4/3}}$ *(10-4)* **46.** $-\dfrac{3}{5}(-3)x^{-4} = \dfrac{9}{5x^4}$ *(10-5)* **47.** (A) $m = f'(1) = 2$ (B) $y = 2x + 3$ *(10-4, 10-5)*
48. $x = 5$ *(10-4)* **49.** $x = -5, x = 3$ *(10-5)* **50.** $x = -1.3401, 0.5771, 2.2630$ *(10-4)* **51.** ±2.4824 *(10-5)*
52. (A) $v = f'(x) = 16x - 4$ (B) 44 ft/sec *(10-5)* **53.** (A) $v = f'(x) = -10x + 16$ (B) $x = 1.6$ sec *(10-5)*

54. (A) The graph of *g* is the graph of *f* shifted 4 units to the right, and the graph of *h* is the graph of *f* shifted 3 units to the left:

(B) The graph of *g′* is the graph of *f′* shifted 4 units to the right, and the graph of *h′* is the graph of *f′* shifted 3 units to the left:

55. $(-\infty, \infty)$ *(10-3)* **56.** $(-\infty, 2) \cup (2, \infty)$ *(10-3)* **57.** $(-\infty, -4) \cup (-4, 1) \cup (1, \infty)$ *(10-3)* **58.** $(-\infty, \infty)$ *(10-3)*

59. $[-2, 2]$ *(10-3)* **60.** (A) -1 (B) Does not exist (C) $-\dfrac{2}{3}$ *(10-1)* **61.** (A) $\dfrac{1}{2}$ (B) 0 (C) Does not exist *(10-1)*

62. (A) -1 (B) 1 (C) Does not exist *(10-1)* **63.** (A) $-\dfrac{1}{6}$ (B) Does not exist (C) $-\dfrac{1}{3}$ *(10-1)*

64. (A) 0 (B) -1 (C) Does not exist *(10-1)* **65.** (A) $\dfrac{2}{3}$ (B) $\dfrac{2}{3}$ (C) Does not exist *(10-2)*

66. (A) ∞ (B) $-\infty$ (C) ∞ *(10-3)* **67.** (A) 0 (B) 0 (C) Does not exist *(10-2)* **68.** 4 *(10-1)* **69.** $\dfrac{-1}{(x+2)^2}$ *(10-1)*

70. $2x - 1$ *(10-4)* **71.** $1/(2\sqrt{x})$ *(10-4)* **72.** Yes *(10-4)* **73.** No *(10-4)* **74.** No *(10-4)* **75.** No *(10-4)* **76.** Yes *(10-4)* **77.** Yes *(10-4)*

78. Horizontal asymptote: $y = 5$; vertical asymptote: $x = 7$ *(10-2)* **79.** Horizontal asymptote: $y = 0$; vertical asymptote: $x = 4$ *(10-2)* **80.** No horizontal asymptotes; vertical asymptote: $x = 3$ *(10-2)*

81. Horizontal asymptotes: $y = 1$; vertical asymptotes: $x = -2, x = 1$ *(10-2)* **82.** Horizontal asymptote: $y = 1$; vertical asymptotes: $x = -1, x = 1$ *(10-2)*

83. The domain of $f'(x)$ is all real numbers except $x = 0$. At $x = 0$, the graph of $y = f(x)$ is smooth, but it has a vertical tangent. *(10-4)*

84. (A) $\lim_{x \to 1^-} f(x) = 1; \lim_{x \to 1^+} f(x) = -1$ (B) $\lim_{x \to 1^-} f(x) = -1; \lim_{x \to 1^+} f(x) = 1$ (C) $m = 1$

(D) The graphs in (A) and (B) have discontinuities at $x = 1$; the graph in (C) does not. *(10-2)*

85. (A) 1 (B) -1 (C) Does not exist (D) No *(10-4)*

86. (A) $S(x) = \begin{cases} 7.47 + 0.4x & \text{if } 0 \le x \le 90 \\ 24.786 + 0.2076x & \text{if } 90 < x \end{cases}$

(B)

(C) Yes *(10-2)*

87. (A) $179.90 (B) $180 *(10-7)*

88. (A) $C(100) = 9{,}500; C'(100) = 50$. At a production level of 100 bicycles, the total cost is $9,500, and cost is increasing at the rate of $50 per bicycle.

(B) $\overline{C}(100) = 95; \overline{C}'(100) = -0.45$. At a production level of 100 bicycles, the average cost is $95, and average cost is decreasing at a rate of $0.45 per bicycle. *(10-7)*

89. The approximate cost of producing the 201st printer is greater than that of the 601st printer. Since these marginal costs are decreasing, the manufacturing process is becoming more efficient. *(10-7)*

90. (A) $C'(x) = 2; \overline{C}(x) = 2 + \dfrac{9{,}000}{x}; \overline{C}'(x) = \dfrac{-9{,}000}{x^2}$

(B) $R(x) = xp = 25x - 0.01x^2; R'(x) = 25 - 0.02x; \overline{R}(x) = 25 - 0.01x; \overline{R}'(x) = -0.01$

(C) $P(x) = R(x) - C(x) = 23x - 0.01x^2 - 9{,}000; P'(x) = 23 - 0.02x;$
$\overline{P}(x) = 23 - 0.01x - \dfrac{9{,}000}{x}; \overline{P}'(x) = -0.01 + \dfrac{9{,}000}{x^2}$

(D) $(500, 10{,}000)$ and $(1{,}800, 12{,}600)$

(E) $P'(1{,}000) = 3$. Profit is increasing at the rate of $3 per umbrella.
$P'(1{,}150) = 0$. Profit is flat.
$P'(1{,}400) = -5$. Profit is decreasing at the rate of $5 per umbrella.

(F)

91. (A) 8 (B) 20 *(10-5)*

92. $N(9) = 27; N'(t) = 3.5$; After 9 months, 27,000 pools have been sold and the total sales are increasing at the rate of 3,500 pools per month. *(10-5)*

93. (A)

```
CubicReg
y=ax³+bx²+cx+d
a=.001225
b=-.0819285714
c=1.564642857
d=12.08428571
```

(B) $N(50) = 38.6$; $N'(50) = 2.6$. In 2010, natural gas consumption is 38.6 trillion cubic feet and is increasing at the rate of 2.6 trillion cubic feet per year *(10-4)*

94. (A)

```
LinReg
y=ax+b
a=-.0384180791
b=13.59887006
r=-.9897782666
```

(B) Fixed costs: \$484.21; variable costs per kringle: \$2.11

```
LinReg
y=ax+b
a=2.107344633
b=484.2090395
r=.9939318704
```

(C) $(51, 591.15), (248, 1,007.62)$ (D) \$4.07 $< p <$ \$11.64 *(10-7)*

95. $C'(10) = -1$; $C'(100) = -0.001$ *(10-5)*

96. $F(4) = 98.16$; $F'(4) = -0.32$; After 4 hours the patient's temperature is 98.16°F and is decreasing at the rate of 0.32°F per hour. *(10-5)*

97. (A) 10 items/h   (B) 5 items/h *(10-5)*

98. (A)

(B) $C(T) = \dfrac{12T}{150 + T}$

(C) $C = 9.6$ at $T = 600$ K, $T = 750$ K when $C = 10$ *(10-3)*

Chapter 11

Exercises 11-1

1. \$1,221.40; \$1,648.72; \$2,225.54

3.

$\$15,000$ $A = 6,000e^{0.1t}$

5. 11.55   **7.** 10.99   **9.** 0.14

11.

n	$[1 + (1/n)]^n$
10	2.593 74
100	2.704 81
1,000	2.716 92
10,000	2.718 15
100,000	2.718 27
1,000,000	2.718 28
10,000,000	2.718 28
↓	↓
∞	$e = 2.718\ 281\ 828\ 459\ldots$

13. $\lim_{n\to\infty}(1 + n)^{1/n} = 1$

15.

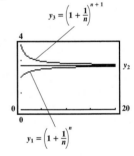

17. (A) \$15,143.71   (B) 14.16 yr
19. \$11,890.41
21. 8.11%
23. (A)

$10,000$

(B) $\lim_{t\to\infty}10,000e^{-0.08t} = 0$

25. 17.33 yr   **27.** 8.66%   **29.** 7.3 yr

31. (A)
$$A = Pe^{rt}$$
$$2P = Pe^{rt}$$
$$2 = e^{rt}$$
$$rt = \ln 2$$
$$t = \frac{\ln 2}{r}$$

(B)

$t = \frac{\ln 2}{r}$

Although r could be any positive number, the restrictions on r are reasonable in the sense that most investments would be expected to earn a return of between 2% and 30%.

(C) The doubling times (in years) are 13.86, 6.93, 4.62, 3.47, 2.77, and 2.31, respectively.

33. $t = -(\ln 0.5)/0.000\ 433\ 2 \approx 1,600$ yr   **35.** $r = (\ln 0.5)/30 \approx -0.0231$ **37.** 53.3 yr   **39.** 1.39%

Exercises 11-2

1. $5e^x + 3$ **3.** $-\dfrac{2}{x} + 2x$ **5.** $3x^2 - 6e^x$ **7.** $e^x + 1 - \dfrac{1}{x}$ **9.** $\dfrac{3}{x}$ **11.** $5 - \dfrac{5}{x}$ **13.** $\dfrac{2}{x} + 4e^x$ **15.** $f'(x) = \dfrac{1}{x}$; $y = x + 2$

17. $f'(x) = 3e^x$; $y = 3x + 3$ **19.** $f'(x) = \dfrac{3}{x}$; $y = \dfrac{3}{e^x}$ **21.** $f'(x) = e^x$; $y = ex + 2$ **23.** Yes; yes   **25.** No; no

27. $f(x) = 10x + \ln 10 + \ln x$; $f'(x) = 10 + \dfrac{1}{x}$ **29.** $f(x) = \ln 4 - 3\ln x$; $f'(x) = -\dfrac{3}{x}$ **31.** $\dfrac{1}{x \ln 2}$ **33.** $3^x \ln 3$

35. $2 - \dfrac{1}{x \ln 10}$ **37.** $1 + 10^x \ln 10$ **39.** $\dfrac{3}{x} + \dfrac{2}{x \ln 3}$ **41.** $2^x \ln 2$ **43.** $(-0.82, 0.44), (1.43, 4.18), (8.61, 5503.66)$

45. $(0.49, 0.49)$ **47.** $(3.65, 1.30), (332, 105.11, 12.71)$ **51.** $28,447/yr; $18,664/yr; $11,021/yr

53. $A'(t) = 5,000(\ln 4)4^t$; $A'(1) = 27,726$ bacteria/hr (rate of change at the end of the first hour); $A'(5) = 7,097,827$ bacteria/hr (rate of change at the end of the fifth hour)

55. At the 40-lb weight level, blood pressure would increase at the rate of 0.44 mm of mercury per pound of weight gain. At the 90-lb weight level, blood pressure would increase at the rate of 0.19 mm of mercury per pound of weight gain.

57. $dR/dS = k/S$

Exercises 11-3

1. $2x^3(2x) + (x^2 - 2)(6x^2) = 10x^4 - 12x^2$ **3.** $(x - 3)(2) + (2x - 1)(1) = 4x - 7$

5. $\dfrac{(x - 3)(1) - x(1)}{(x - 3)^2} = \dfrac{-3}{(x - 3)^2}$ **7.** $\dfrac{(x - 2)(2) - (2x + 3)(1)}{(x - 2)^2} = \dfrac{-7}{(x - 2)^2}$

9. $3xe^x + 3e^x = 3(x + 1)e^x$ **11.** $x^3\left(\dfrac{1}{x}\right) + 3x^2 \ln x = x^2(1 + 3 \ln x)$

13. $(x^2 + 1)(2) + (2x - 3)(2x) = 6x^2 - 6x + 2$ **15.** $(0.4x + 2)(0.5) + (0.5x - 5)(0.4) = 0.4x - 1$

17. $\dfrac{(2x - 3)(2x) - (x^2 + 1)(2)}{(2x - 3)^2} = \dfrac{2x^2 - 6x - 2}{(2x - 3)^2}$ **19.** $(x^2 + 2)2x + (x^2 - 3)2x = 4x^3 - 2x$

21. $\dfrac{(x^2 - 3)2x - (x^2 + 2)2x}{(x^2 - 3)^2} = \dfrac{-10x}{(x^2 - 3)^2}$ **23.** $\dfrac{(x^2 + 1)e^x - e^x(2x)}{(x^2 + 1)^2} = \dfrac{(x - 1)^2 e^x}{(x^2 + 1)^2}$

25. $\dfrac{(1 + x)\left(\dfrac{1}{x}\right) - \ln x}{(1 + x)^2} = \dfrac{1 + x - x \ln x}{x(1 + x)^2}$ **27.** $xf'(x) + f(x)$ **29.** $x^3 f'(x) + 3x^2 f(x)$ **31.** $\dfrac{x^2 f'(x) - 2xf(x)}{x^4}$

33. $\dfrac{f(x) - xf'(x)}{[f(x)]^2}$ **35.** $e^x f'(x) + f(x)e^x = e^x[f'(x) + f(x)]$ **37.** $\dfrac{f(x)\left(\dfrac{1}{x}\right) - (\ln x)f'(x)}{f(x)^2} = \dfrac{f(x) - (x \ln x)f'(x)}{x f(x)^2}$

39. $(2x + 1)(2x - 3) + (x^2 - 3x)(2) = 6x^2 - 10x - 3$ **41.** $(2.5t - t^2)(4) + (4t + 1.4)(2.5 - 2t) = -12t^2 + 17.2t + 3.5$

43. $\dfrac{(x^2 + 2x)(5) - (5x - 3)(2x + 2)}{(x^2 + 2x)^2} = \dfrac{-5x^2 + 6x + 6}{(x^2 + 2x)^2}$ **45.** $\dfrac{(w^2 - 1)(2w - 3) - (w^2 - 3w + 1)(2w)}{(w^2 - 1)^2} = \dfrac{3w^2 - 4w + 3}{(w^2 - 1)^2}$

47. $(1 + x - x^2)e^x + e^x(1 - 2x) = (2 - x - x^2)e^x$ **49.** $f'(x) = (1 + 3x)(-2) + (5 - 2x)(3); y = -11x + 29$

51. $f'(x) = \dfrac{(3x - 4)(1) - (x - 8)(3)}{(3x - 4)^2}; y = 5x - 13$ **53.** $f'(x) = \dfrac{2^x - x(2^x \ln 2)}{2^{2x}}; y = \left(\dfrac{1 - 2 \ln 2}{4}\right)x + \ln 2$

55. $f'(x) = (2x - 15)(2x) + (x^2 + 18)(2) = 6(x - 2)(x - 3); x = 2, x = 3$

57. $f'(x) = \dfrac{(x^2 + 1)(1) - x(2x)}{(x^2 + 1)^2} = \dfrac{1 - x^2}{(x^2 + 1)^2}; x = -1, x = 1$ **59.** $7x^6 - 3x^2$ **61.** $-27x^{-4} = -\dfrac{27}{x^4}$

63. $(w + 1)2^w \ln 2 + 2^w = [(w + 1) \ln 2 + 1]2^w$ **65.** $\dfrac{(4x^2 + 5x - 1)(6x - 2) - (3x^2 - 2x + 3)(8x + 5)}{(4x^2 + 5x - 1)^2} = \dfrac{23x^2 - 30x - 13}{(4x^2 + 5x - 1)^2}$

67. $9x^{1/3}(3x^2) + (x^3 + 5)(3x^{-2/3}) = \dfrac{30x^3 + 15}{x^{2/3}}$ **69.** $\dfrac{(1 + x^2)\dfrac{1}{x \ln 2} - 2x \log_2 x}{(1 + x^2)^2} = \dfrac{1 + x^2 - 2x^2 \ln x}{x(1 + x^2)^2 \ln 2}$

71. $\dfrac{(x^2 - 3)(2x^{-2/3}) - 6x^{1/3}(2x)}{(x^2 - 3)^2} = \dfrac{-10x^2 - 6}{(x^2 - 3)^2 x^{2/3}}$ **73.** $g'(t) = \dfrac{(3t^2 - 1)(0.2) - (0.2t)(6t)}{(3t^2 - 1)^2} = \dfrac{-0.6t^2 - 0.2}{(3t^2 - 1)^2}$

75. $(20x)\dfrac{1}{x \ln 10} + 20 \log x = \dfrac{20(1 + \ln x)}{\ln 10}$ **77.** $x^{-2/3}(3x^2 - 4x) + (x^3 - 2x^2)\left(-\dfrac{2}{3}x^{-5/3}\right) = -\dfrac{8}{3}x^{1/3} + \dfrac{7}{3}x^{4/3}$

79. $\dfrac{(x^2 + 1)[(2x^2 - 1)(2x) + (x^2 + 3)(4x)] - (2x^2 - 1)(x^2 + 3)(2x)}{(x^2 + 1)^2} = \dfrac{4x^5 + 8x^3 + 16x}{(x^2 + 1)^2}$

81. $\dfrac{e^t(1 + \ln t) - (t \ln t)e^t}{e^{2t}} = \dfrac{1 + \ln t - t \ln t}{e^t}$

83. (A) $S'(t) = \dfrac{(t^2 + 50)(180t) - 90t^2(2t)}{(t^2 + 50)^2} = \dfrac{9,000t}{(t^2 + 50)^2}$

(B) $S(10) = 60; S'(10) = 4$. After 10 months, the total sales are 60,000 DVDs and sales are increasing at the rate of 4,000 DVDs per month.

(C) Approximately 64,000 DVDs

85. (A) $\dfrac{dx}{dp} = \dfrac{(0.1p + 1)(0) - 4{,}000(0.1)}{(0.1p + 1)^2} = \dfrac{-400}{(0.1p + 1)^2}$

(B) $x = 800$; $dx/dp = -16$. At a price level of \$40, the demand is 800 DVD players per week and demand is decreasing at the rate of 16 players per dollar.

(C) Approximately 784 DVD players

87. (A) $C'(t) = \dfrac{(t^2 + 1)(0.14) - 0.14t(2t)}{(t^2 + 1)^2} = \dfrac{0.14 - 0.14t^2}{(t^2 + 1)^2}$

(B) $C'(0.5) = 0.0672$. After 0.5 h, concentration is increasing at the rate of 0.0672 mg/cm^3 per hour.
$C'(3) = -0.0112$. After 3 h, concentration is decreasing at the rate of 0.0112 mg/cm^3 per hour.

89. (A) $N'(x) = \dfrac{(x + 32)(100) - (100x + 200)}{(x + 32)^2} = \dfrac{3{,}000}{(x + 32)^2}$

(B) $N'(4) = 2.31$; $N'(68) = 0.30$

Exercises 11-4

1. $(3x^2 + 2)^3$ **3.** e^{-x^2} **5.** $y = u^4; u = 3x^2 - x + 5$ **7.** $y = e^u; u = 1 + x + x^2$ **9.** 3   **11.** $(-4x)$
13. $2x$ **15.** $4x^3$ **17.** $2(x + 3)$ **19.** $6(2x + 5)^2$ **21.** $-8(5 - 2x)^3$ **23.** $5(4 + 0.2x)^4(0.2) = (4 + 0.2x)^4$ **25.** $30x(3x^2 + 5)^4$

27. $5e^x$ **29.** $5e^{5x}$ **31.** $-18e^{-6x}$ **33.** $(2x - 5)^{-1/2} = \dfrac{1}{(2x - 5)^{1/2}}$ **35.** $-8x^3(x^4 + 1)^{-3} = \dfrac{-8x^3}{(x^4 + 1)^3}$ **37.** $-\dfrac{2}{x}$ **39.** $\dfrac{6x}{1 + x^2}$

41. $\dfrac{3(1 + \ln x)^2}{x}$ **43.** $f'(x) = 6(2x - 1)^2; y = 6x - 5; x = \frac{1}{2}$ **45.** $f'(x) = 2(4x - 3)^{-1/2} = \dfrac{2}{(4x - 3)^{1/2}}; y = \dfrac{2}{3}x + 1$; none

47. $f'(x) = 10(x - 2)e^{x^2 - 4x + 1}; y = -20ex + 5e; x = 2$ **49.** $12(x^2 - 2)^3(2x) = 24x(x^2 - 2)^3$

51. $-6(t^2 + 3t)^{-4}(2t + 3) = \dfrac{-6(2t + 3)}{(t^2 + 3t)^4}$ **53.** $\dfrac{1}{2}(w^2 + 8)^{-1/2}(2w) = \dfrac{w}{\sqrt{w^2 + 8}}$ **55.** $12xe^{3x} + 4e^{3x} = 4(3x + 1)e^{3x}$

57. $\dfrac{x^3\left(\dfrac{1}{1 + x}\right) - 3x^2 \ln(1 + x)}{x^6} = \dfrac{x - 3(1 + x) \ln(1 + x)}{x^4(1 + x)}$ **59.** $6te^{3(t^2 + 1)}$ **61.** $\dfrac{3x}{x^2 + 3}$

63. $-5(w^3 + 4)^{-6}(3w^2) = \dfrac{-15w^2}{(w^3 + 4)^6}$ **65.** $f'(x) = (4 - x)^3 - 3x(4 - x)^2 = 4(4 - x)^2(1 - x); y = -16x + 48$

67. $f'(x) = \dfrac{(2x - 5)^3 - 6x(2x - 5)^2}{(2x - 5)^6} = \dfrac{-4x - 5}{(2x - 5)^4}; y = -17x + 54$ **69.** $f'(x) = \dfrac{1}{2x\sqrt{\ln x}}; y = \dfrac{1}{2e^x} + \dfrac{1}{2}$

71. $f'(x) = 2x(x - 5)^3 + 3x^2(x - 5)^2 = 5x(x - 5)^2(x - 2); x = 0, 2, 5$

73. $f'(x) = \dfrac{(2x + 5)^2 - 4x(2x + 5)}{(2x + 5)^4} = \dfrac{5 - 2x}{(2x + 5)^3}; x = \frac{5}{2}$

75. $f'(x) = (x^2 - 8x + 20)^{-1/2}(x - 4) = \dfrac{x - 4}{(x^2 - 8x + 20)^{1/2}}; x = 4$ **77.** No; yes

79. $18x^2(x^2 + 1)^2 + 3(x^2 + 1)^3 = 3(x^2 + 1)^2(7x^2 + 1)$ **81.** $\dfrac{24x^5(x^3 - 7)^3 - (x^3 - 7)^4 6x^2}{4x^6} = \dfrac{3(x^3 - 7)^3(3x^3 + 7)}{2x^4}$

83. $\dfrac{1}{\ln 2}\left(\dfrac{6x}{3x^2 - 1}\right)$ **85.** $(2x + 1)(10^{x^2 + x})(\ln 10)$ **87.** $\dfrac{12x^2 + 5}{(4x^3 + 5x + 7)\ln 3}$ **89.** $2^{x^3 - x^2 + 4x + 1}(3x^2 - 2x + 4)\ln 2$

91. (A) $C'(x) = (2x + 16)^{-1/2} = \dfrac{1}{(2x + 16)^{1/2}}$

(B) $C'(24) = \frac{1}{8}$, or \$12.50. At a production level of 24 cell phones, total cost is increasing at the rate of \$12.50 per cell phone and the cost of producing the 25th cell phone is approximately \$12.50.
$C'(42) = \frac{1}{10}$, or \$10.00. At a production level of 42 cell phones, total cost is increasing at the rate of \$10.00 per cell phone and the cost of producing the 43rd cell phone is approximately \$10.00.

93. (A) $\dfrac{dx}{dp} = 40(p + 25)^{-1/2} = \dfrac{40}{(p + 25)^{1/2}}$ **(B)** $x = 400$ and $dx/dp = 4$. At a price of \$75, the supply is 400 bicycle helmets per week and supply is increasing at the rate of 4 bicycle helmets per dollar.

95. (A) After 1 hr, the concentration is decreasing at the rate of 1.60 mg/mL per hour; after 4 hr, the concentration is decreasing at the rate of 0.08 mg/mL per hour.

(B)

97. 2.27 mm of mercury/yr; 0.81 mm of mercury/yr; 0.41 mm of mercury/yr
99. (A) $f'(n) = n(n-2)^{-1/2} + 2(n-2)^{1/2}$

  (B) $f'(11) = \frac{29}{3} \approx 9.67$. When the list contains 11 items, the learning time is increasing at the rate of 9.67 min per item.
  $f'(27) = \frac{77}{5} = 15.4$. When the list contains 27 items, the learning time is increasing at the rate of 15.4 min per item.

Exercises 11-5

1. $y' = -\frac{3}{5}$ **3.** $y' = \frac{3x}{2}$ **5.** $y' = 10x; 10$ **7.** $y' = \frac{2x}{3y^2}; \frac{4}{3}$ **9.** $y' = -\frac{3}{2y+2}; -\frac{3}{4}$ **11.** $y' = -\frac{y}{x}; -\frac{3}{2}$

13. $y' = -\frac{2y}{2x+1}; 4$ **15.** $y' = \frac{6-2y}{x}; -1$ **17.** $y' = \frac{2x}{e^y - 2y}; 2$ **19.** $y' = \frac{3x^2 y}{y+1}; \frac{3}{2}$ **21.** $y' = \frac{6x^2 y - y \ln y}{x + 2y}; 2$

23. $x' = \frac{2tx - 3t^2}{2x - t^2}; 8$ **25.** $y'|_{(1.6, 1.8)} = -\frac{3}{4}; y'|_{(1.6, 0.2)} = \frac{3}{4}$ **27.** $y = -x + 5$ **29.** $y = \frac{2}{5}x - \frac{12}{5}; y = \frac{3}{5}x + \frac{12}{5}$

31. $y' = -\frac{1}{x}$ **33.** $y' = \frac{1}{3(1+y)^2 + 1}; \frac{1}{13}$ **35.** $y' = \frac{3(x-2y)^2}{6(x-2y)^2 + 4y}; \frac{3}{10}$ **37.** $y' = \frac{3x^2(7 + y^2)^{1/2}}{y}; 16$

39. $y' = \frac{y}{2xy^2 - x}; 1$ **41.** $y = 0.63x + 1.04$ **43.** $p' = \frac{1}{2p - 2}$ **45.** $p' = -\frac{\sqrt{10{,}000 - p^2}}{p}$

47. $\frac{dL}{dV} = \frac{-(L+m)}{V+n}$ **49.** $\frac{dT}{dv} = \frac{2}{k}\sqrt{T}$ **51.** $\frac{dv}{dT} = \frac{k}{2\sqrt{T}}$

Exercises 11-6

1. 30 **3.** $-\frac{16}{3}$ **5.** $-\frac{16}{7}$ **7.** Decreasing at 9 units/sec **9.** Approx. -3.03 ft/sec **11.** $dA/dt \approx 126$ ft²/sec
13. 3,768 cm³/min **15.** 6 lb/in.²/hr **17.** $-\frac{9}{4}$ ft/sec **19.** $\frac{20}{3}$ ft/sec **21.** 0.0214 ft/sec; 0.0135 ft/sec; yes, at $t = 0.000\,19$ sec
23. 3.835 units/sec **25.** (A) $dC/dt = \$15{,}000$/wk (B) $dR/dt = -\$50{,}000$/wk (C) $dP/dt = -\$65{,}000$/wk
27. $ds/dt = \$2{,}207$/wk **29.** (A) $dx/dt = -12.73$ units/month (B) $dp/dt = \$1.53$/month **31.** Approximately 100 ft³/min

Exercises 11-7

1. $\frac{35 - 0.8x}{35x - 0.4x^2}$ **3.** $-\frac{4e^{-x}}{7 + 4e^x}$ **5.** $\frac{5}{x(12 + 5\ln x)}$ **7.** 0 **9.** -0.017 **11.** -0.034 **13.** 1.013 **15.** 0.405 **17.** 11.8%

19. 5.4% **21.** -14.7% **23.** -431.6% **25.** $E(p) = \frac{450p}{25{,}000 - 450p}$ **27.** $E(p) = \frac{8p^2}{4{,}800 - 4p^2}$ **29.** $E(p) = \frac{0.6pe^p}{98 - 0.6e^p}$

31. (A) Inelastic (B) Unit elasticity (C) Elastic **33.** (A) Inelastic (B) Unit elasticity (C) Elastic

35. (A) $x = 6{,}000 - 200p$ $0 \le p \le 30$ **37.** (A) $x = 3{,}000 - 50p$ $0 \le p \le 60$ **39.** Elastic on $(3.5, 7)$;
  (B) $E(p) = \frac{p}{30 - p}$ (B) $R(p) = 3{,}000p - 50p^2$ inelastic on $(0, 3.5)$
  (C) $E(10) = 0.5$; 5% decrease   (C) $E(p) = \frac{p}{60 - p}$ **41.** Elastic on $(25/\sqrt{3}, 25)$;
  (D) $E(25) = 5$; 50% decrease   (D) Elastic on $(30, 60)$; inelastic on $(0, 30)$ inelastic on $(0, 25/\sqrt{3})$
  (E) $E(15) = 1$; 10% decrease   (E) Increasing on $(0, 30)$; decreasing on $(30, 60)$ **43.** Elastic on $(48, 72)$;
               (F) Decrease   inelastic on $(0, 48)$
               (G) Increase   **45.** Elastic on $(25, 25\sqrt{2})$;
                   inelastic on $(0, 25)$

47. $R(p) = 20p(10 - p)$ **49.** $R(p) = 40p(p - 15)^2$ **51.** $R(p) = 30p - 10p\sqrt{p}$ **53.** $\frac{3}{2}$ **55.** $\frac{1}{2}$

57. Elastic on $(0, 300)$;
  inelastic on $(300, 600)$

59. Elastic on $(0, 10\sqrt{3})$;
  inelastic on $(10\sqrt{3}, 30)$

61. k

63. \$75 per day

65. Increase **67.** Decrease **69.** \$3.75 **71.** $p(t) = \frac{31}{0.31t + 18.5}$ **73.** -0.08

Chapter 11 Review Exercises

1. $3,136.62$; $4,919.21$; $12,099.29$ *(11-1)*   **2.** $\dfrac{2}{x} + 3e^x$ *(11-2)*   **3.** $2e^{2x-3}$ *(11-4)*   **4.** $\dfrac{2}{2x+7}$ *(11-4)*

5. (A) $y = \ln(3 + e^x)$ (B) $\dfrac{dy}{dx} = \dfrac{e^x}{3 + e^x}$ *(11-4)*   **6.** $y' = \dfrac{9x^2}{4y}; \dfrac{9}{8}$ *(11-5)*   **7.** $dy/dt = 216$ *(11-6)*

8. (A) $x = 1,000 - 25p$ (B) $\dfrac{p}{40 - p}$ (C) 0.6; demand is inelastic and insensitive to small changes in price.

 (D) $1,000p - 25p^2$ (E) Revenue increases *(11-7)*

9. -10 *(11-2)*   **10.** $\lim\limits_{n \to \infty} \left(1 + \dfrac{2}{n}\right)^n = e^2 \approx 7.389\,06$ *(11-1)*   **11.** $\dfrac{7[(\ln z)^6 + 1]}{z}$ *(11-4)*   **12.** $x^5(1 + 6\ln x)$ *(11-3)*   **13.** $\dfrac{e^x(x - 6)}{x^7}$ *(11-3)*

14. $\dfrac{6x^2 - 3}{2x^3 - 3x}$ *(11-4)*   **15.** $(3x^2 - 2x)e^{x^3 - x^2}$ *(11-4)*   **16.** $\dfrac{1 - 2x\ln 5x}{xe^{2x}}$ *(11-4)*   **17.** $y = -x + 2$; $y = -ex + 1$ *(11-4)*

18. $y' = \dfrac{3y - 2x}{8y - 3x}; \dfrac{8}{19}$ *(11-5)*   **19.** $x' = \dfrac{4tx}{3x^2 - 2t^2}; -4$ *(11-5)*   **20.** $y' = \dfrac{1}{e^y + 2y}; 1$ *(11-5)*   **21.** $y' = \dfrac{2xy}{1 + 2y^2}; \dfrac{2}{3}$ *(11-5)*

22. $dy/dt = -2$ units/sec *(11-6)*   **23.** 0.27 ft/sec *(11-6)*   **24.** $dR/dt = 1/\pi \approx 0.318$ in./min *(11-6)*
25. Elastic for $5 < p < 15$; inelastic for $0 < p < 5$ *(11-7)*

26.

(11-7)

27. (A) $y = [\ln(4 - e^x)]^3$ (B) $\dfrac{dy}{dx} = \dfrac{-3e^x[\ln(4 - e^x)]^2}{4 - e^x}$ *(11-4)*

28. $2x(5^{x^2-1})(\ln 5)$ *(11-4)*   **29.** $\left(\dfrac{1}{\ln 5}\right)\dfrac{2x - 1}{x^2 - x}$ *(11-4)*

30. $\dfrac{2x + 1}{2(x^2 + x)\sqrt{\ln(x^2 + x)}}$ *(11-4)*   **31.** $y' = \dfrac{2x - e^{xy}y}{xe^{xy} - 1}; 0$ *(11-5)*

32. The rate of increase of area is proportional to the radius R, so the rate is smallest when $R = 0$, and has no largest value. *(11-6)*

33. Yes, for $-\sqrt{3}/3 < x < \sqrt{3}/3$ *(11-6)*   **34.** (A) 15 yr   (B) 13.9 yr *(11-1)*
35. $A'(t) = 10e^{0.1t}$; $A'(1) = 11.05$/yr; $A'(10) = 27.18$/yr *(11-1)*   **36.** $R'(x) = (1,000 - 20x)e^{-0.02x}$ *(11-4)*

37. $p' = \dfrac{-(5,000 - 2p^3)^{1/2}}{3p^2}$ *(11-5)*   **38.** $dR/dt = 2,242$/day *(11-6)*   **39.** Decrease price *(11-7)*   **40.** 0.02125 *(11-7)*

41. -1.111 mg/mL per hour; -0.335 mg/mL per hour *(11-4)*   **42.** $dR/dt = -3/(2\pi)$; approx. 0.477 mm/day *(11-6)*
43. (A) Increasing at the rate of 2.68 units/day at the end of 1 day of training; increasing at the rate of 0.54 unit/day after 5 days of training
 (B) 7 days *(11-4)*
44. $dT/dt = -1/27 \approx -0.037$ min/operation hour *(11-6)*

Chapter 12

Exercises 12-1

1. (a, b); (d, f); (g, h) **3.** (b, c); (c, d); (f, g) **5.** c, d, f **7.** b, f
9. Local maximum at $x = a$; local minimum at $x = c$; no local extrema at $x = b$ and $x = d$ **11.** e **13.** d **15.** f

17. c **19.** (A) $f'(x) = 3x^2 - 12$ (B) $-2, 2$ (C) $-2, 2$ **21.** (A) $f'(x) = \dfrac{1}{3}(x + 5)^{-2/3}$ (B) -5 (C) -5

23. (A) $f'(x) = -\dfrac{6}{(x + 2)^2}$ (B) None   (C) -2 **25.** (A) $f'(x) = \begin{cases} -1 \text{ if } x < 0 \\ 1 \text{ if } x > 0 \end{cases}$ (B) 0   (C) 0
27. Decreasing on $(-\infty, 1)$; increasing on $(1, \infty)$; $f(1) = -2$ is a local minimum
29. Increasing on $(-\infty, -4)$; decreasing on $(-4, \infty)$; $f(-4) = 7$ is a local maximum
31. Increasing for all x; no local extrema
33. Increasing on $(-\infty, -2)$ and $(3, \infty)$; decreasing on $(-2, 3)$; $f(-2) = 44$ is a local maximum, $f(3) = -81$ is a local minimum
35. Decreasing on $(-\infty, 1)$; increasing on $(1, \infty)$; $f(1) = 4$ is a local minimum
37. Increasing on $(-\infty, 2)$; decreasing on $(2, \infty)$; $f(2) = e^{-2} \approx 0.135$ is a local maximum
39. Increasing on $(-\infty, 8)$; decreasing on $(8, \infty)$; $f(8) = 4$ is a local maximum
41. Critical values: $x = -0.77, 1.08, 2.69$; decreasing on $(-\infty, -0.77)$ and $(1.08, 2.69)$; increasing on $(-0.77, 1.08)$ and $(2.69, \infty)$; local minima at $x = -0.77$ and $x = 2.69$; local maximum at $x = 1.08$
43. Critical values: $x = 1.34, 2.82$; decreasing on $(0, 1.34)$ and $(2.82, \infty)$; increasing on $(1.34, 2.82)$; local minimum at $x = 1.34$; and local maximum at $x = 2.82$
45. Critical values: $0.36, 2.15$; increasing on $(-\infty, 0.36)$ and $(2.15, \infty)$; decreasing on $(0.36, 2.15)$; local maximum at $x = 0.36$; local minimum at $x = 2.15$

47. Increasing on $(-\infty, 4)$
Decreasing on $(4, \infty)$
Horizontal tangent at $x = 4$

49. Increasing on $(-\infty, -1), (1, \infty)$
Decreasing on $(-1, 1)$
Horizontal tangents at $x = -1, 1$

51. Decreasing for all x
Horizontal tangent at $x = 2$

53. Decreasing on $(-\infty, -3)$ and $(0, 3)$;
increasing on $(-3, 0)$ and $(3, \infty)$
Horizontal tangents at $x = -3, 0, 3$

55.

57.

59.

61.

63. g_4
65. g_6
67. g_2

69. Increasing on $(-1, 2)$; decreasing on
$(-\infty, -1)$ and $(2, \infty)$; local minimum
at $x = -1$; local maximum at $x = 2$

71. Increasing on $(-1, 2)$ and $(2, \infty)$;
decreasing on $(-\infty, -1)$; local
minimum at $x = -1$

73. Increasing on $(-2, 0)$ and $(3, \infty)$;
decreasing on $(-\infty, -2)$ and $(0, 3)$;
local minima at $x = -2$ and $x = 3$;
local maximum at $x = 0$

75. $f'(x) > 0$ on $(-\infty, -1)$
and $(3, \infty)$; $f'(x) < 0$ on
$(-1, 3)$; $f'(x) = 0$ at
$x = -1$ and $x = 3$

77. $f'(x) > 0$ on $(-2, 1)$ and
$(3, \infty)$; $f'(x) < 0$ on $(-\infty, -2)$
and $(1, 3)$; $f'(x) = 0$ at
$x = -2, x = 1$, and $x = 3$

79. Critical values: $x = -2, x = 2$; increasing on $(-\infty, -2)$ and $(2, \infty)$; decreasing on $(-2, 0)$ and $(0, 2)$; local maximum at $x = -2$;
local minimum at $x = 2$

81. Critical value: $x = -2$; increasing on $(-2, 0)$; decreasing on $(-\infty, -2)$ and $(0, \infty)$; local minimum at $x = -2$

83. Critical values: $x = 0, x = 4$; increasing on $(-\infty, 0)$ and $(4, \infty)$; decreasing on $(0, 2)$ and $(2, 4)$; local maximum at $x = 0$; local
minimum at $x = 4$

85. Critical values: $x = 0, x = 4, x = 6$; increasing on $(0, 4)$ and $(6, \infty)$; decreasing on $(-\infty, 0)$ and $(4, 6)$; local maximum at $x = 4$;
local minima at $x = 0$ and $x = 6$

87. (A) There are no critical values and no local extrema. The function is increasing for all x.
    (B) There are two critical values, $x = \pm\sqrt{-k/3}$. The function increases on $(-\infty, -\sqrt{-k/3})$ to a local maximum at
       $x = -\sqrt{-k/3}$, decreases on $(-\sqrt{-k/3}, \sqrt{-k/3})$ to a local minimum at $x = \sqrt{-k/3}$, and increases on $(\sqrt{-k/3}, \infty)$.
    (C) The only critical value is $x = 0$. There are no local extrema. The function is increasing for all x.

89. (A) The marginal profit is positive on $(0, 600)$, 0 at
       $x = 600$, and negative on $(600, 1,000)$.
    (B)

91. (A) The price decreases for the first 15 months to a local
       minimum, increases for the next 40 months to a local
       maximum, and then decreases for the remaining 15 months.
    (B)

93. (A) $\overline{C}(x) = 0.05x + 20 + \dfrac{320}{x}$

    (B) Critical value: $x = 80$; decreasing for $0 < x < 80$; increasing for $80 < x < 150$; local minimum at $x = 80$

95. $P(x)$ is increasing over (a, b) if $P'(x) = R'(x) - C'(x) > 0$ over (a, b); that is, if $R'(x) > C'(x)$ over (a, b).

97. Critical value: $t = 2$; increasing on $(0, 2)$; decreasing on $(2, 24)$; $C(2) = 0.07$ is a local maximum.

Exercises 12-2

1. (A) $(a, c), (c, d), (e, g)$ (B) $(d, e), (g, h)$ (C) $(d, e), (g, h)$ (D) $(a, c), (c, d), (e, g)$ (E) $(a, c), (c, d), (e, g)$ (F) $(d, e), (g, h)$
(G) d, e, g (H) d, e, g **3.** (C) **5.** (D) **7.** $12x - 8$ **9.** $4x^{-3} - 18x^{-4}$
11. $2 + \dfrac{9}{2}x^{-3/2}$ **13.** $8(x^2 + 9)^3 + 48x^2(x^2 + 9)^2 = 8(x^2 + 9)^2(7x^2 + 9)$

15. $-2e^{-x^2} + 4x^2e^{-x^2} = 2e^{-x^2}(2x^2 - 1)$ **17.** $\dfrac{x^3\left(-\dfrac{2}{x}\right) - (1 - 2\ln x)3x^2}{x^6} = \dfrac{6\ln x - 5}{x^4}$ **19.** $(-10, 2{,}000)$ **21.** $(0, 2)$ **23.** None

25. Concave upward for all x; no inflection points
27. Concave downward on $\left(-\infty, \frac{4}{3}\right)$; concave upward on $\left(\frac{4}{3}, \infty\right)$; inflection point at $x = \frac{4}{3}$
29. Concave downward on $(-\infty, 0)$ and $(6, \infty)$; concave upward on $(0, 6)$; inflection points at $x = 0$ and $x = 6$
31. Concave upward on $(-2, 4)$; concave downward on $(-\infty, -2)$ and $(4, \infty)$; inflection points at $x = -2$ and $x = 4$
33. Concave upward on $(-\infty, \ln 2)$; concave downward on $(\ln 2, \infty)$; inflection point at $x = \ln 2$

35.   **37.**   **39.**   **41.**

43. Domain: All real numbers
y intercept: 16; x intercepts: $2 - 2\sqrt{3}, 2, 2 + 2\sqrt{3}$
Increasing on $(-\infty, 0)$ and $(4, \infty)$
Decreasing on $(0, 4)$
Local maximum at $x = 0$, local minimum at $x = 4$
Concave downward on $(-\infty, 2)$
Concave upward on $(2, \infty)$
Inflection point at $x = 2$

45. Domain: All real numbers
y intercept: 2; x intercept: -1
Increasing on $(-\infty, \infty)$
Concave downward on $(-\infty, 0)$
Concave upward on $(0, \infty)$
Inflection point at $x = 0$

47. Domain: All real numbers
y intercept: 0; x intercepts: 0, 4
Increasing on $(-\infty, 3)$
Decreasing on $(3, \infty)$
Local maximum at $x = 3$
Concave upward on $(0, 2)$
Concave downward on $(-\infty, 0)$ and $(2, \infty)$
Inflection points at $x = 0$ and $x = 2$

49. Domain: All real numbers
y intercept: 0; x intercepts: 0, 1
Increasing on $(0.25, \infty)$
Decreasing on $(-\infty, 0.25)$
Local minimum at $x = 0.25$
Concave upward on $(-\infty, 0.5)$ and $(1, \infty)$
Concave downward on $(0.5, 1)$
Inflection points at $x = 0.5$ and $x = 1$

51. Domain: All real numbers
y intercept: 27; x intercepts: $-3, 3$
Increasing on $(-\infty, -\sqrt{3})$ and $(0, \sqrt{3})$
Decreasing on $(-\sqrt{3}, 0)$ and $(\sqrt{3}, \infty)$
Local maxima at $x = -\sqrt{3}$ and $x = \sqrt{3}$
Local minimum at $x = 0$
Concave upward on $(-1, 1)$
Concave downward on $(-\infty, -1)$ and $(1, \infty)$
Inflection points at $x = -1$ and $x = 1$

53. Domain: All real numbers
y intercept: 16; x intercepts: $-2, 2$
Decreasing on $(-\infty, -2)$ and $(0, 2)$
Increasing on $(-2, 0)$ and $(2, \infty)$
Local minima at $x = -2$ and $x = 2$
Local maximum at $x = 0$
Concave upward on $\left(-\infty, -2\sqrt{3}/3\right)$ and $\left(2\sqrt{3}/3, \infty\right)$
Concave downward on $\left(-2\sqrt{3}/3, 2\sqrt{3}/3\right)$
Inflection points at $x = -2\sqrt{3}/3$ and $x = 2\sqrt{3}/3$

55. Domain: All real numbers
y intercept: 0; x intercepts: 0, 1.5
Decreasing on $(-\infty, 0)$ and $(0, 1.25)$
Increasing on $(1.25, \infty)$
Local minimum at $x = 1.25$
Concave upward on $(-\infty, 0)$ and $(1, \infty)$
Concave downward on $(0, 1)$
Inflection points at $x = 0$ and $x = 1$

57. Domain: All real numbers
y intercept: 0; x intercept: 0
Increasing on $(-\infty, \infty)$
Concave downward on $(-\infty, \infty)$

59. Domain: All real numbers
 y intercept: 5
 Decreasing on $(-\infty, \ln 4)$
 Increasing on $(\ln 4, \infty)$
 Local minimum at $x = \ln 4$
 Concave upward on $(-\infty, \infty)$

61. Domain: $(0, \infty)$
 x intercept: e^2
 Increasing on $(-\infty, \infty)$
 Concave downward on $(-\infty, \infty)$

63. Domain: $(-4, \infty)$
 x intercept: $e^2 - 4$
 Increasing on $(-4, \infty)$
 Concave downward on $(-4, \infty)$

65.

x	$f'(x)$	$f(x)$
$-\infty < x < -1$	Positive and decreasing	Increasing and concave downward
$x = -1$	*x* intercept	Local maximum
$-1 < x < 0$	Negative and decreasing	Decreasing and concave downward
$x = 0$	Local minimum	Inflection point
$0 < x < 2$	Negative and increasing	Decreasing and concave upward
$x = 2$	Local maximum	Inflection point
$2 < x < \infty$	Negative and decreasing	Decreasing and concave downward

67.

x	$f'(x)$	$f(x)$
$-\infty < x < -2$	Negative and increasing	Decreasing and concave upward
$x = -2$	Local maximum	Inflection point
$-2 < x < 0$	Negative and decreasing	Decreasing and concave downward
$x = 0$	Local minimum	Inflection point
$0 < x < 2$	Negative and increasing	Decreasing and concave upward
$x = 2$	Local maximum	Inflection point
$2 < x < \infty$	Negative and decreasing	Decreasing and concave downward

69. Domain: All real numbers
 x intercepts: $-1.18, 0.61, 1.87, 3.71$
 y intercept: -5
 Decreasing on $(-\infty, -0.53)$ and $(1.24, 3.04)$
 Increasing on $(-0.53, 1.24)$ and $(3.04, \infty)$
 Local minima at $x = -0.53$ and $x = 3.04$
 Local maximum at $x = 1.24$
 Concave upward on $(-\infty, 0.22)$ and $(2.28, \infty)$
 Concave downward on $(0.22, 2.28)$
 Inflection points at $x = 0.22$ and $x = 2.28$

71. Domain: All real numbers
 y intercept: 100; *x* intercepts: 8.01, 13.36
 Increasing on $(-0.10, 4.57)$ and $(11.28, \infty)$
 Decreasing on $(-\infty, -0.10)$ and $(4.57, 11.28)$
 Local maximum at $x = 4.57$
 Local minima at $x = -0.10$ and $x = 11.28$
 Concave upward on $(-\infty, 1.95)$ and $(8.55, \infty)$
 Concave downward on $(1.95, 8.55)$
 Inflection points at $x = 1.95$ and $x = 8.55$

73. Domain: All real numbers
 x intercepts: $-2.40, 1.16$; *y* intercept: 3
 Increasing on $(-\infty, -1.58)$
 Decreasing on $(-1.58, \infty)$
 Local maximum at $x = -1.58$
 Concave downward on $(-\infty, -0.88)$ and $(0.38, \infty)$
 Concave upward on $(-0.88, 0.38)$
 Inflection points at $x = -0.88$ and $x = 0.38$

75. Domain: All real numbers
 x intercepts: $-6.68, -3.64, -0.72$; *y* intercept: 30
 Decreasing on $(-5.59, -2.27)$ and $(1.65, 3.82)$
 Increasing on $(-\infty, -5.59)$, $(-2.27, 1.65)$, and $(3.82, \infty)$
 Local minima at $x = -2.27$ and $x = 3.82$
 Local maxima at $x = -5.59$ and $x = 1.65$
 Concave upward on $(-4.31, -0.40)$ and $(2.91, \infty)$
 Concave downward on $(-\infty, -4.31)$ and $(-0.40, 2.91)$
 Inflection points at $x = -4.31$, $x = -0.40$, and $x = 2.91$

77. If $f'(x)$ has a local extremum at $x = c$, then $f'(x)$ must change from increasing to decreasing or from decreasing to increasing at $x = c$. The graph of $y = f(x)$ must change concavity at $x = c$, and there must be an inflection point at $x = c$.

79. If there is an inflection point on the graph of $y = f(x)$ at $x = c$, then $f(x)$ must change concavity at $x = c$. Consequently, $f'(x)$ must change from increasing to decreasing or from decreasing to increasing at $x = c$, and $x = c$ is a local extremum for $f'(x)$.

81. The graph of the CPI is concave upward.

83. The graph of $y = C'(x)$ is positive and decreasing. Since marginal costs are decreasing, the production process is becoming more efficient as production increases.

85. (A) Local maximum at $x = 60$
(B) Concave downward on the whole interval $(0, 80)$

87. (A) Local maximum at $x = 1$
(B) Concave downward on $(-\infty, 2)$;
concave upward on $(2, \infty)$

89. Increasing on $(0, 10)$; decreasing on $(10, 15)$; point of diminishing returns is $x = 10$, max $T'(x) = T'(10) = 500$

91. Increasing on $(24, 36)$; decreasing on $(36, 45)$; point of diminishing returns is $x = 36$, max $N'(x) = N'(36) = 3{,}888$

93. (A)

(B) 32 ads to sell 574 cars per month

95. (A) Increasing on $(0, 10)$;
decreasing on $(10, 20)$
(B) Inflection point at $t = 10$
(C)

(D) $N'(10) = 300$

97. (A) Increasing on $(5, \infty)$;
decreasing on $(0, 5)$
(B) Inflection point at $n = 5$
(C)

(D) $T'(5) = 0$

Exercises 12-3

1. $\frac{8}{3}$ **3.** $\frac{1}{2}$ **5.** 1   **7.** 4   **9.** 0   **11.** ∞ **13.** ∞ **15.** 5   **17.** ∞ **19.** $-\frac{1}{8}$ **21.** 17   **23.** 8   **25.** 0   **27.** ∞ **29.** ∞ **31.** $\frac{1}{3}$
33. -2 **35.** $-\infty$ **37.** 0   **39.** 0   **41.** 0   **43.** $\frac{1}{4}$ **45.** $\frac{1}{3}$ **47.** 0   **49.** 0   **51.** ∞ **53.** 1   **55.** 1

Exercises 12-4

1. (A) $(-\infty, b), (0, e), (e, g)$ (B) $(b, d), (d, 0), (g, \infty)$ (C) $(b, d), (d, 0), (g, \infty)$ (D) $(-\infty, b), (0, e), (e, g)$ (E) $x = 0$
(F) $x = b, x = g$ (G) $(-\infty, a), (d, e), (h, \infty)$ (H) $(a, d), (e, h)$ (I) $(a, d), (e, h)$ (J) $(-\infty, a), (d, e), (h, \infty)$
(K) $x = a, x = h$ (L) $y = L$ (M) $x = d, x = e$

3.

5.

7.

9.

11. Domain: $[-4, \infty)$ y intercept: 2; x intercept: -4 **13.** Domain: All real numbers y intercept: 75; x intercept: 15
15. Domain: All real numbers, except 5 y intercept: -19
17. Domain: All real numbers, except 3
y intercept: -1; x intercept: -3
Horizontal asymptote: $y = 1$
Vertical asymptote: $x = 3$
Decreasing on $(-\infty, 3)$ and $(3, \infty)$
Concave upward on $(3, \infty)$
Concave downward on $(-\infty, 3)$

19. Domain: All real numbers, except 2
y intercept: 0; x intercept: 0
Horizontal asymptote: $y = 1$
Vertical asymptote: $x = 2$
Decreasing on $(-\infty, 2)$ and $(2, \infty)$
Concave downward on $(-\infty, 2)$
Concave upward on $(2, \infty)$

21. Domain: $(-\infty, \infty)$
y intercept: 10
Horizontal asymptote: $y = 5$
Decreasing on $(-\infty, \infty)$
Concave upward on $(-\infty, \infty)$

23. Domain: $(-\infty, \infty)$
y intercept: 0; x intercept: 0
Horizontal asymptote: $y = 0$
Increasing on $(-\infty, 5)$
Decreasing on $(5, \infty)$
Local maximum at $x = 5$
Concave upward on $(10, \infty)$
Concave downward on $(-\infty, 10)$
Inflection point at $x = 10$

25. Domain: $(-\infty, 1)$
y intercept: 0; x intercept: 0
Vertical asymptote: $x = 1$
Decreasing on $(-\infty, 1)$
Concave downward on $(-\infty, 1)$

27. Domain: $(0, \infty)$
Vertical asymptote: $x = 0$
Increasing on $(1, \infty)$
Decreasing on $(0, 1)$
Local minimum at $x = 1$
Concave upward on $(0, \infty)$

29. Domain: All real numbers, except ± 2
y intercept: 0; x intercept: 0
Horizontal asymptote: $y = 0$
Vertical asymptotes: $x = -2, x = 2$
Decreasing on $(-\infty, -2), (-2, 2)$,
and $(2, \infty)$
Concave upward on $(-2, 0)$ and $(2, \infty)$
Concave downward on $(-\infty, -2)$ and $(0, 2)$
Inflection point at $x = 0$

31. Domain: All real numbers
y intercept: 1
Horizontal asymptote: $y = 0$
Increasing on $(-\infty, 0)$
Decreasing on $(0, \infty)$
Local maximum at $x = 0$
Concave upward on $(-\infty, -\sqrt{3}/3)$ and $(\sqrt{3}/3, \infty)$
Concave downward on $(-\sqrt{3}/3, \sqrt{3}/3)$
Inflection points at $x = -\sqrt{3}/3$ and $x = \sqrt{3}/3$

33. Domain: All real numbers except -1 and 1
y intercept: 0; x intercept: 0
Horizontal asymptote: $y = 0$
Vertical asymptote: $x = -1$ and $x = 1$
Increasing on $(-\infty, -1), (-1, 1)$, and $(1, \infty)$
Concave upward on $(-\infty, -1)$ and $(0, 1)$
Concave downward on $(-1, 0)$ and $(1, \infty)$
Inflection point at $x = 0$

35. Domain: All real numbers except 1
y intercept: 0; x intercept: 0
Horizontal asymptote: $y = 0$
Vertical asymptote: $x = 1$
Increasing on $(-\infty, -1)$ and $(1, \infty)$
Decreasing on $(-1, 1)$
Local maximum at $x = -1$
Concave upward on $(-\infty, -2)$
Concave downward on $(-2, 1)$ and $(1, \infty)$
Inflection point at $x = -2$

37. Domain: All real numbers except 0
Horizontal asymptote: $y = 1$
Vertical asymptote: $x = 0$
Increasing on $(0, 4)$
Decreasing on $(-\infty, 0)$ and $(4, \infty)$
Local maximum at $x = 4$
Concave upward on $(6, \infty)$
Concave downward on $(-\infty, 0)$ and $(0, 6)$
Inflection point at $x = 6$

39. Domain: All real numbers except 1
y intercept: 0; x intercept: 0
Vertical asymptote: $x = 1$
Increasing on $(-\infty, 0)$ and $(2, \infty)$
Decreasing on $(0, 1)$ and $(1, 2)$
Local maximum at $x = 0$
Local minimum at $x = 2$
Concave upward on $(1, \infty)$
Concave downward on $(-\infty, 1)$

41. Domain: All real numbers except $-3, 3$
y intercept: $-\frac{2}{9}$
Horizontal asymptote: $y = 3$
Vertical asymptotes: $x = -3, x = 3$
Increasing on $(-\infty, -3)$ and $(-3, 0)$
Decreasing on $(0, 3)$ and $(3, \infty)$
Local maximum at $x = 0$
Concave upward on $(-\infty, -3)$ and $(3, \infty)$
Concave downward on $(-3, 3)$

43. Domain: All real numbers except 2
y intercept: 0; x intercept: 0
Vertical asymptote: $x = 2$
Increasing on $(3, \infty)$
Decreasing on $(-\infty, 2)$ and $(2, 3)$
Local minimum at $x = 3$
Concave upward on $(-\infty, 0)$ and $(2, \infty)$
Concave downward on $(0, 2)$
Inflection point at $x = 0$

45. Domain: All real numbers
y intercept: 3; x intercept: 3
Horizontal asymptote: $y = 0$
Increasing on $(-\infty, 2)$
Decreasing on $(2, \infty)$
Local maximum at $x = 2$
Concave upward on $(-\infty, 1)$
Concave downward on $(1, \infty)$
Inflection point at $x = 1$

47. Domain: $(-\infty, \infty)$
y intercept: 1
Horizontal asymptote: $y = 0$
Increasing on $(-\infty, 0)$
Decreasing on $(0, \infty)$
Local maximum at $x = 0$
Concave upward on $(-\infty, -1)$ and $(1, \infty)$
Concave downward on $(-1, 1)$
Inflection points at $x = -1$ and $x = 1$

49. Domain: $(0, \infty)$
x intercept: 1
Increasing on $(e^{-1/2}, \infty)$
Decreasing on $(0, e^{-1/2})$
Local minimum at $x = e^{-1/2}$
Concave upward on $(e^{-3/2}, \infty)$
Concave downward on $(0, e^{-3/2})$
Inflection point at $x = e^{-3/2}$

51. Domain: $(0, \infty)$
x intercept: 1
Vertical asymptote: $x = 0$
Increasing on $(1, \infty)$
Decreasing on $(0, 1)$
Local minimum at $x = 1$
Concave upward on $(0, e)$
Concave downward on (e, ∞)
Inflection point at $x = e$

53. Domain: All real numbers except $-4, 2$
y intercept: $-1/8$
Horizontal asymptote: $y = 0$
Vertical asymptote: $x = -4, x = 2$
Increasing on $(-\infty, -4)$ and $(-4, -1)$
Decreasing on $(-1, 2)$ and $(2, \infty)$
Local maximum at $x = -1$
Concave upward on $(-\infty, -4)$ and $(2, \infty)$
Concave downward on $(-4, 2)$

55. Domain: All real numbers except $-\sqrt{3}, \sqrt{3}$
y intercept: 0; x intercept: 0
Vertical asymptote: $x = -\sqrt{3}, x = \sqrt{3}$
Increasing on $(-3, -\sqrt{3}), (-\sqrt{3}, \sqrt{3})$, and $(\sqrt{3}, 3)$
Decreasing on $(-\infty, -3)$ and $(3, \infty)$
Local maximum at $x = 3$
Local minimum at $x = -3$
Concave upward on $(-\infty, -\sqrt{3})$ and $(0, \sqrt{3})$
Concave downward on $(-\sqrt{3}, 0)$ and $(\sqrt{3}, \infty)$
Inflection point at $x = 0$

57. Domain: All real numbers except 0
Vertical asymptote: $x = 0$
Oblique asymptote: $y = x$
Increasing on $(-\infty, -2)$ and $(2, \infty)$
Decreasing on $(-2, 0)$ and $(0, 2)$
Local maximum at $x = -2$
Local minimum at $x = 2$
Concave upward on $(0, \infty)$
Concave downward on $(-\infty, 0)$

59. Domain: All real numbers except 0
x intercept: $\sqrt[3]{4}$
Vertical asymptote: $x = 0$
Oblique asymptote: $y = x$
Increasing on $(-\infty, -2)$ and $(0, \infty)$
Local maximum at $x = -2$
Decreasing on $(-2, 0)$
Concave downward on $(-\infty, 0)$ and $(0, \infty)$

61. Domain: All real numbers except 0
x intercepts: $-\sqrt{3}, \sqrt{3}$
Vertical asymptote: $x = 0$
Oblique asymptote: $y = x$
Increasing on $(-\infty, 0)$ and $(0, \infty)$
Concave upward on $(-\infty, 0)$
Concave downward on $(0, \infty)$

63. Domain: All real numbers except 0
Vertical asymptote: $x = 0$
Oblique asymptote: $y = x$
Increasing on $(-\infty, -2)$ and $(2, \infty)$
Decreasing on $(-2, 0)$ and $(0, 2)$
Local maximum at $x = -2$
Local minimum at $x = 2$
Concave upward on $(0, \infty)$
Concave downward on $(-\infty, 0)$

65. Domain: All real numbers except $2, 4$
y intercept: $-3/4$; x intercept: -3
Vertical asymptote: $x = 4$
Horizontal asymptote: $y = 1$
Decreasing on $(-\infty, 2), (2, 4)$, and $(4, \infty)$
Concave upward on $(4, \infty)$
Concave downward on $(-\infty, 2)$ and $(2, 4)$

67. Domain: All real numbers except $-3, 3$
y intercept: $5/3$; x intercept: 2.5
Vertical asymptote: $x = 3$
Horizontal asymptote: $y = 2$
Decreasing on $(-\infty, -3), (-3, 3)$, and $(3, \infty)$
Concave upward on $(3, \infty)$
Concave downward on $(-\infty, -3)$ and $(-3, 3)$

69. Domain: All real numbers except $-1, 2$
y intercept: 0; x intercepts: $0, 3$
Vertical asymptote: $x = -1$
Increasing on $(-\infty, -3), (1, 2)$, and $(2, \infty)$
Decreasing on $(-3, -1)$ and $(-1, 1)$
Local maximum at $x = -3$
Local minimum at $x = 1$
Concave upward on $(-1, 2)$ and $(2, \infty)$
Concave downward on $(-\infty, -1)$

71. Domain: All real numbers except 1
y intercept: -2; x intercept: -2
Vertical asymptote: $x = 1$
Horizontal asymptote: $y = 1$
Decreasing on $(-\infty, 1)$ and $(1, \infty)$
Concave upward on $(1, \infty)$
Concave downward on $(-\infty, 1)$

73.

75. (A) Increasing on $(0, 1)$
(B) Concave upward on $(0, 1)$
(C) $x = 1$ is a vertical asymptote
(D) The origin is both an x and a y intercept
(E)

77. (A) $\overline{C}(n) = \dfrac{3,200}{n} + 250 + 50n$

(B)

(C) 8 yr

79. (A)

(B) 25 at $x = 100$

81. (A)

(B) Minimum average cost is $4.35 when 177 pizzas are produced daily.

83.

85.

Exercises 12-5

1. Min $f(x) = f(0) = 0$; Max $f(x) = f(10) = 14$ **3.** Min $f(x) = f(0) = 0$; Max $f(x) = f(3) = 9$
5. Min $f(x) = f(1) = f(7) = 5$; Max $f(x) = f(10) = 14$ **7.** Min $f(x) = f(1) = f(7) = 5$; Max $f(x) = f(3) = f(9) = 9$
9. Min $f(x) = f(5) = 7$; Max $f(x) = f(3) = 9$ **11.** Max $f(x) = f(3) = 21$; Min $f(x) = f(2) = 17$
13. Max $f(x) = f(-1) = e \approx 2.718$; Min $f(x) = e^{-1} \approx 0.368$ **15.** Max $f(x) = f(0) = 9$; Min $f(x) = f(\pm 4) = -7$
17. Min $f(x) = f(1) = 2$; no maximum   **19.** Max $f(x) = f(-3) = 18$; no minimum   **21.** No absolute extrema
23. Max $f(x) = f(3) = 54$; no minimum   **25.** No absolute extrema   **27.** Min $f(x) = f(0) = 0$; no maximum
29. Max $f(x) = f(1) = 1$; Min $f(x) = f(-1) = -1$ **31.** Min $f(x) = f(0) = -1$, no maximum   **33.** Min $f(x) = f(2) = -2$
35. Max $f(x) = f(2) = 4$ **37.** Min $f(x) = f(2) = 0$ **39.** No maximum   **41.** Max $f(x) = f(2) = 8$
43. Min $f(x) = f(4) = 22$ **45.** Min $f(x) = f(\sqrt{10}) = 14/\sqrt{10}$ **47.** Min $f(x) = f(2) = \dfrac{e^2}{4} \approx 1.847$
49. Min $f(x) = f(3) = \dfrac{27}{e^3} \approx 1.344$ **51.** Max $f(x) = f(e^{1.5}) = 2e^{1.5} \approx 8.963$
53. Min $f(x) = f(e^{2.5}) = \dfrac{e^5}{2} \approx 74.207$ **55.** Max $f(x) = f(1) = -1$
57. (A) Max $f(x) = f(5) = 14$; Min $f(x) = f(-1) = -22$ (B) Max $f(x) = f(1) = -2$; Min $f(x) = f(-1) = -22$
      (C) Max $f(x) = f(5) = 14$; Min $f(x) = f(3) = -6$
59. (A) Max $f(x) = f(0) = 126$; Min $f(x) = f(2) = -26$ (B) Max $f(x) = f(7) = 49$; Min $f(x) = f(2) = -26$
      (C) Max $f(x) = f(6) = 6$; Min $f(x) = f(3) = -15$
61. (A) Max $f(x) = f(-1) = 10$; Min $f(x) = f(2) = -11$ (B) Max $f(x) = f(0) = f(4) = 5$; Min $f(x) = f(3) = -22$
      (C) Max $f(x) = f(-1) = 10$; Min $f(x) = f(1) = 2$
63. Local minimum   **65.** Unable to determine   **67.** Neither   **69.** Local maximum

Exercises 12-6

1. 7.5 and 7.5   **3.** 7.5 and -7.5 **5.** $\sqrt{15}$ and $\sqrt{15}$ **7.** $10\sqrt{2}$ ft by $10\sqrt{2}$ ft   **9.** 37 ft by 37 ft
11. (A) Maximum revenue is $125,000 when 500 phones are produced and sold for $250 each.
    (B) Maximum profit is $46,612.50 when 365 phones are produced and sold for $317.50 each.
13. (A) Max $R(x) = R(3,000) = \$300,000$
    (B) Maximum profit is $75,000 when 2,100 sets are manufactured and sold for $130 each.
    (C) Maximum profit is $64,687.50 when 2,025 sets are manufactured and sold for $132.50 each.
15. (A)   (B) 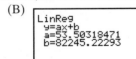   (C) The maximum profit is $118,996 when the price per sleeping bag is $195.

17. (A) $4.80   (B) $8   **19.** $35; $6,125   **21.** 40 trees; 1,600 lb   **23.** $(10 - 2\sqrt{7})/3 = 1.57$ in. squares
25. 20 ft by 40 ft (with the expensive side being one of the short sides)   **27.** 8 production runs per year
29. 10,000 books in 5 printings   **31.** (A) $x = 5.1$ mi   (B) $x = 10$ mi   **33.** 4 days; 20 bacteria/cm^3
35. 1 month; 2 ft   **37.** 4 yr from now

Chapter 12 Review Exercises

1. $(a, c_1), (c_3, c_6)$ *(12-1, 12-2)*   **2.** $(c_1, c_3), (c_6, b)$ *(12-1, 12-2)*   **3.** $(a, c_2), (c_4, c_5), (c_7, b)$ *(12-1, 12-2)*   **4.** c_3 *(12-1)*
5. c_1, c_6 *(12-1)*   **6.** c_1, c_3, c_5 *(12-1)*   **7.** c_4, c_6 *(12-1)*   **8.** c_2, c_4, c_5, c_7 *(12-2)*   **11.** $f''(x) = 12x^2 + 30x$ *(12-2)*
9. *(12-2)*   **10.** *(12-2)*   **12.** $y'' = 8/x^3$ *(12-2)*
13. Domain: All real numbers, except 4
      y intercept: $\frac{5}{4}$; x intercept: -5 *(12-2)*
14. Domain: $(-2, \infty)$
      y intercept: ln 2; x intercept: -1 *(12-2)*

15. Horizontal asymptote: $y = 0$;
Vertical asymptotes: $x = -2$, $x = 2$ *(12-4)*

16. Horizontal asymptote: $y = \frac{2}{3}$;
Vertical asymptote: $x = -\frac{10}{3}$ *(12-4)*

17. $(-\sqrt{2}, -20), (\sqrt{2}, -20)$ *(12-2)* **18.** $(-\frac{1}{2}, -6)$ *(12-2)* **19.** (A) $f'(x) = \frac{1}{5}x^{-1/5}$ (B) 0 (C) 0 *(12-1)*

20. (A) $f'(x) = -\frac{1}{5}x^{-6/5}$ (B) None (C) 0 *(12-1)*

21. Domain: All real numbers
y intercept: 0; x intercepts: 0, 9
Increasing on $(-\infty, 3)$ and $(9, \infty)$
Decreasing on $(3, 9)$
Local maximum at $x = 3$
Local minimum at $x = 9$
Concave upward on $(6, \infty)$
Concave downward on $(-\infty, 6)$
Inflection point at $x = 6$ *(12-4)*

22. Domain: All real numbers
y intercept: 16; x intercepts: -4, 2
Increasing on $(-\infty, -2)$ and $(2, \infty)$
Decreasing on $(-2, 2)$
Local maximum at $x = -2$
Local minimum at $x = 2$
Concave upward on $(0, \infty)$
Concave downward on $(-\infty, 0)$
Inflection point at $x = 0$ *(12-4)*

23. Domain: All real numbers
y intercept: 0; x intercepts: 0, 4
Increasing on $(-\infty, 3)$
Decreasing on $(3, \infty)$
Local maximum at $x = 3$
Concave upward on $(0, 2)$
Concave downward on $(-\infty, 0)$ and $(2, \infty)$
Inflection points at $x = 0$ and $x = 2$ *(12-4)*

24. Domain: all real numbers
y intercept: -3; x intercepts: -3, 1
No vertical or horizontal asymptotes
Increasing on $(-2, \infty)$
Decreasing on $(-\infty, -2)$
Local minimum at $x = -2$
Concave upward on $(-\infty, -1)$ and $(1, \infty)$
Concave downward on $(-1, 1)$
Inflection points at $x = -1$ and $x = 1$ *(12-4)*

25. Domain: All real numbers, except -2
y intercept: 0; x intercept: 0
Horizontal asymptote: $y = 3$
Vertical asymptote: $x = -2$
Increasing on $(-\infty, -2)$ and $(-2, \infty)$
Concave upward on $(-\infty, -2)$
Concave downward on $(-2, \infty)$ *(12-4)*

26. Domain: All real numbers
y intercept: 0; x intercept: 0
Horizontal asymptote: $y = 1$
Increasing on $(0, \infty)$
Decreasing on $(-\infty, 0)$
Local minimum at $x = 0$
Concave upward on $(-3, 3)$
Concave downward on $(-\infty, -3)$ and $(3, \infty)$
Inflection points at $x = -3, 3$ *(12-4)*

27. Domain: All real numbers except $x = -2$
y intercept: 0; x intercept: 0
Horizontal asymptote: $y = 0$
Vertical asymptote: $x = -2$
Increasing on $(-2, 2)$
Decreasing on $(-\infty, -2)$ and $(2, \infty)$
Local maximum at $x = 2$
Concave upward on $(4, \infty)$
Concave downward on $(-\infty, -2)$ and $(-2, 4)$
Inflection point at $x = 4$ *(12-4)*

28. Domain: All real numbers
y intercept: 0; x intercept: 0
Increasing on $(-\infty, \infty)$
Concave upward on $(-\infty, -3)$ and $(0, 3)$
Concave downward on $(-3, 0)$ and $(3, \infty)$
Inflection points at $x = -3, 0, 3$ *(12-4)*

29. Domain: All real numbers
y intercept: 0; x intercept: 0
Horizontal asymptote: $y = 5$
Increasing on $(-\infty, \infty)$
Concave downward on $(-\infty, \infty)$

30. Domain: $(0, \infty)$
x intercept: 1
Increasing on $(e^{-1/3}, \infty)$
Decreasing on $(0, e^{-1/3})$
Local minimum at $x = e^{-1/3}$
Concave upward on $(e^{-5/6}, \infty)$
Concave downward on $(0, e^{-5/6})$
Inflection point at $x = e^{-5/6}$

31. 3 *(12-3)* **32.** $-\frac{1}{5}$ *(12-3)* **33.** $-\infty$ *(12-3)* **34.** 0 *(12-3)* **35.** 0 *(12-3)*
36. 1 *(12-3)* **37.** 0 *(12-3)* **38.** 0 *(12-3)* **39.** 1 *(12-3)* **40.** 2 *(12-3)*

41.

x	$f'(x)$	$f(x)$
$-\infty < x < -2$	Negative and increasing	Decreasing and concave upward
$x = -2$	x intercept	Local minimum
$-2 < x < -1$	Positive and increasing	Increasing and concave upward
$x = -1$	Local maximum	Inflection point
$-1 < x < 1$	Positive and decreasing	Increasing and concave downward
$x = 1$	Local minimum	Inflection point
$1 < x < \infty$	Positive and increasing	Increasing and concave upward

42. (C) *(12-2)*   **43.** Local maximum at $x = -1$; local minimum at $x = 5$ *(12-5)*

44. Min $f(x) = f(2) = -4$; Max $f(x) = f(5) = 77$ *(12-5)*   **45.** Min $f(x) = f(2) = 8$ *(12-5)*

46. Max $f(x) = f(e^{4.5}) = 2e^{4.5} \approx 180.03$ *(12-5)*   **47.** Max $f(x) = f(0.5) = 5e^{-1} \approx 1.84$ *(12-5)*

48. Yes. Since f is continuous on $[a, b]$, f has an absolute maximum on $[a, b]$. But each endpoint is a local minimum; hence, the absolute maximum must occur between a and b. *(12-5)*

49. No, increasing/decreasing properties apply to intervals in the domain of f. It is correct to say that $f(x)$ is decreasing on $(-\infty, 0)$ and $(0, \infty)$. *(12-1)*

50. A critical value for $f(x)$ is a partition number for $f'(x)$ that is also in the domain of f. For example, if $f(x) = x^{-1}$, then 0 is a partition number for $f'(x) = -x^{-2}$, but 0 is not a critical value for $f(x)$ since 0 is not in the domain of f. *(12-1)*

51. Max $f'(x) = f'(2) = 12$ *(12-2, 12-5)*

52. Each number is 20; minimum sum is 40 *(12-6)*

53. Domain: All real numbers
x intercepts: 0.79, 1.64; y intercept: 4
Increasing on $(-1.68, -0.35)$ and $(1.28, \infty)$
Decreasing on $(-\infty, -1.68)$ and $(-0.35, 1.28)$
Local minima at $x = -1.68$ and $x = 1.28$
Local maximum at $x = -0.35$
Concave downward on $(-1.10, 0.60)$
Concave upward on $(-\infty, -1.10)$ and $(0.60, \infty)$
Inflection points at $x = -1.10$ and $x = 0.60$ *(12-4)*

54. Domain: All real numbers
x intercepts; 0, 11.10; y intercept: 0
Increasing on $(1.87, 4.19)$ and $(8.94, \infty)$
Decreasing on $(-\infty, 1.87)$ and $(4.19, 8.94)$
Local maximum at $x = 4.19$
Local minima at $x = 1.87$ and $x = 8.94$
Concave upward on $(-\infty, 2.92)$ and $(7.08, \infty)$
Concave downward on $(2.92, 7.08)$
Inflection points at $x = 2.92$ and $x = 7.08$ *(12-4)*

55. Max $f(x) = f(1.373) = 2.487$ *(12-5)*
56. Max $f(x) = f(1.763) = 0.097$ *(12-5)*

57. (A) For the first 15 months, the graph of the price is increasing and concave downward, with a local maximum at $t = 15$. For the next 15 months, the graph of the price is decreasing and concave downward, with an inflection point at $t = 30$. For the next 15 months, the graph of the price is decreasing and concave upward, with a local minimum at $t = 45$. For the remaining 15 months, the graph of the price is increasing and concave upward.

(B)

(12-2)

58. (A) Max $R(x) = R(10,000) = \$2,500,000$
(B) Maximum profit is \$175,000 when 3,000 readers are manufactured and sold for \$425 each.
(C) Maximum profit is \$119,000 when 2,600 readers are manufactured and sold for \$435 each. *(12-6)*

59. (A) The expensive side is 50 ft; the other side is 100 ft.
(B) The expensive side is 75 ft; the other side is 150 ft. *(12-6)*

60. \$49; \$6,724 *(12-6)*   **61.** 12 orders/yr *(12-6)*   **62.** Min $\overline{C}(x) = \overline{C}(200) = 50$

63. Min $\overline{C}(x) = \overline{C}(e^5) \approx \$49.66$ *(12-4)*   **64.** A maximum revenue of \$18,394 is realized at a production level of 50 units at \$367.88 each. *(12-6)*

65.

66. \$549.15; \$9,864 *(12-6)*
67. \$1.52 *(12-6)*
68. 20.39 feet *(12-6)*
69. (A)

```
QuadReg
y=ax²+bx+c
a=.0061285714
b=.1224285714
c=102.2
```

(B) Min $\overline{C}(x) = \overline{C}(129) = \$1.71$ *(12-4)*

70. Increasing on $(0, 18)$; decreasing on $(18, 24)$; point of diminishing returns is $x = 18$, max $N'(x) = N'(18) = 972$ *(12-2)*

71. (A)
```
CubicReg
  y=ax³+bx²+cx+d
  a=-.01
  b=.83
  c=-2.3
  d=221
```

(B) 28 ads to sell 588 refrigerators per month *(12-2)*

72. 3 days *(12-1)*

73. 2 yr from now *(12-1)*

Chapter 13

Exercises 13-1

1. $7x + C$ **3.** $4x^2 + C$ **5.** $3x^3 + C$ **7.** $(x^6/6) + C$ **9.** $(-x^{-2}/2) + C$ **11.** $4x^{5/2} + C$ **13.** $3 \ln|z| + C$ **15.** $16e^u + C$
17. $y = 40x^5 + C$ **19.** $P = 24x - 3x^2 + C$ **21.** $y = e^x + 3x + C$ **23.** $x = 5 \ln|t| + t + C$ **25.** True   **27.** False   **29.** True
31. No, since one graph cannot be obtained from another by a vertical translation.
33. Yes, since one graph can be obtained from another by a vertical translation.
35. $(5x^2/2) - (5x^3/3) + C$ **37.** $2\sqrt{u} + C$ **39.** $-(x^{-2}/8) + C$ **41.** $4 \ln|u| + u + C$ **43.** $5e^z + 4z + C$
45. $x^3 + 2x^{-1} + C$ **47.** $2x^{3/2} + 4x^{1/2} + C$ **49.** $(e^x/4) - (3x^2/8) + C$ **51.** $C(x) = 2x^3 - 2x^2 + 3,000$
53. $x = 40\sqrt{t}$ **55.** $y = -2x^{-1} + 3 \ln|x| - x + 3$ **57.** $x = 4e^t - 2t - 3$ **59.** $y = 2x^2 - 3x + 1$ **61.** $x^2 + x^{-1} + C$
63. $\frac{1}{2}x^2 + x^{-2} + C$ **65.** $e^x - 2 \ln|x| + C$ **67.** $M = t + t^{-1} + \frac{3}{4}$ **69.** $y = 3x^{5/3} + 3x^{2/3} - 6$

71. $p(x) = 10x^{-1} + 10$ **73.** x^3 **75.** $x^4 + 3x^2 + C$ **83.** $\overline{C}(x) = 15 + \dfrac{1,000}{x}$; $C(x) = 15x + 1,000$; $C(0) = \$1,000$

85. (A) The cost function increases from 0 to 8, is concave downward from 0 to 4, and is concave upward from 4 to 8. There is an inflection point at $x = 4$.
(B) $C(x) = x^3 - 12x^2 + 53x + 30$; $C(4) = \$114,000$; $C(8) = \$198,000$
(C)

(D) Manufacturing plants are often inefficient at low and high levels of production.

87. $S(t) = 1,200 - 18t^{4/3}$; $50^{3/4} \approx 19$ mo
89. $S(t) = 1,200 - 18t^{4/3} - 70t$; $t \approx 4.05$ mo
91. $L(x) = 4,800x^{1/2}$; 24,000 labor-hours
93. $W(h) = 0.0005h^3$; 171.5 lb
95. 19,400

Exercises 13-2

1. $\frac{1}{3}(3x + 5)^3 + C$ **3.** $\frac{1}{6}(x^2 - 1)^6 + C$ **5.** $-\frac{1}{2}(5x^3 + 1)^{-2} + C$ **7.** $e^{5x} + C$ **9.** $\ln|1 + x^2| + C$ **11.** $\frac{2}{3}(1 + x^4)^{3/2} + C$
13. $\frac{1}{11}(x + 3)^{11} + C$ **15.** $-\frac{1}{6}(6t - 7)^{-1} + C$ **17.** $\frac{1}{12}(t^2 + 1)^6 + C$ **19.** $\frac{1}{2}e^{x^2} + C$ **21.** $\frac{1}{5}\ln|5x + 4| + C$
23. $-e^{1-t} + C$ **25.** $-\frac{1}{18}(3t^2 + 1)^{-3} + C$ **27.** $\frac{2}{5}(x + 4)^{5/2} - \frac{8}{3}(x + 4)^{3/2} + C$ **29.** $\frac{2}{3}(x - 3)^{3/2} + 6(x - 3)^{1/2} + C$
31. $\frac{1}{11}(x - 4)^{11} + \frac{2}{5}(x - 4)^{10} + C$ **33.** $\frac{1}{8}(1 + e^{2x})^4 + C$ **35.** $\frac{1}{2}\ln|4 + 2x + x^2| + C$ **37.** $\frac{1}{2}(5x + 3)^2 + C$
39. $\frac{1}{2}(x^2 - 1)^2 + C$ **41.** $\frac{1}{5}(x^5)^5 + C$ **49.** $\frac{1}{9}(3x^2 + 7)^{3/2} + C$ **51.** $\frac{1}{8}x^8 + \frac{4}{5}x^5 + 2x^2 + C$ **53.** $\frac{1}{9}(x^3 + 2)^3 + C$
55. $\frac{1}{4}(2x^4 + 3)^{1/2} + C$ **57.** $\frac{1}{4}(\ln x)^4 + C$ **59.** $e^{-1/x} + C$ **61.** $x = \frac{1}{3}(t^3 + 5)^7 + C$ **63.** $y = 3(t^2 - 4)^{1/2} + C$
65. $p = -(e^x - e^{-x})^{-1} + C$ **67.** $p(x) = \dfrac{2,000}{3x + 50} + 4$; 250 bottles   **69.** $C(x) = 12x + 500 \ln(x + 1) + 2,000$; $\overline{C}(1,000) = \$17.45$
71. (A) $S(t) = 10t + 100e^{-0.1t} - 100$, $0 \le t \le 24$ **(B)** \$50 million   **(C)** 18.41 mo
73. $Q(t) = 100 \ln(t + 1) + 5t$, $0 \le t \le 20$; 275 thousand barrels   **75.** $W(t) = 2e^{0.1t}$; 4.45 g
77. (A) $-1,000$ bacteria/mL per day   **(B)** $N(t) = 5,000 - 1,000 \ln(1 + t^2)$; 385 bacteria/mL   **(C)** 7.32 days
79. $N(t) = 100 - 60e^{-0.1t}$, $0 \le t \le 15$; 87 words/min
81. $E(t) = 12,000 - 10,000 (t + 1)^{-1/2}$; 9,500 students

Exercises 13-3

1. $y = 3x^2 + C$ **3.** $y = 7 \ln|x| + C$ **5.** $y = 50e^{0.02x} + C$ **7.** $y = \dfrac{x^3}{3} - \dfrac{x^2}{2}$ **9.** $y = e^{-x^2} + 2$
11. $y = 2 \ln|1 + x| + 5$
13. Figure B. When $x = 1$, the slope $dy/dx = 1 - 1 = 0$ for any y. When $x = 0$, the slope $dy/dx = 0 - 1 = -1$ for any y. Both are consistent with the slope field shown in Figure B.
15. $y = \dfrac{x^2}{2} - x + C$; $y = \dfrac{x^2}{2} - x - 2$

17.

19. $y = Ce^{2t}$ **21.** $y = 100e^{-0.5x}$ **23.** $x = Ce^{-5t}$ **25.** $x = -(5t^2/2) + C$

27. Figure A. When $y = 1$, the slope $dy/dx = 1 - 1 = 0$ for any x. When $y = 2$, the slope $dy/dx = 1 - 2 = -1$ for any x. Both are consistent with the slope field shown in Figure A.

29. $y = 1 - e^{-x}$

31.

33.

35. $y = \sqrt{25 - x^2}$ **37.** $y = -3x$ **39.** $y = 1/(1 - 2e^{-t})$

41.

43.

45.

47.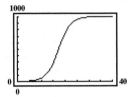

49. Apply the second-derivative test to $f(y) = ky(M - y)$. **51.** 2009 **53.** $A = 1{,}000e^{0.03t}$ **55.** $A = 8{,}000e^{0.016t}$

57. (A) $p(x) = 100e^{-0.05x}$
(B) $60.65 per unit
(C)

59. (A) $N = L(1 - e^{-0.051t})$
(B) 22.5%
(C) 32 days
(D)

61. $I = I_0e^{-0.00942x}$; $x \approx 74$ ft
63. (A) $Q = 3e^{-0.04t}$ (B) $Q(10) = 2.01$ mL
(C) 27.47 hr
(D)

65. 0.023 117 **67.** Approx. 24,200 yr **69.** 104 times; 67 times
71. (A) 7 people; 353 people (B) 400
(C)

Exercises 13-4

1. C, E **3.** B **5.** H, I **7.** H
9.

11. Figure A: $L_3 = 13$, $R_3 = 20$; Figure B: $L_3 = 14$, $R_3 = 7$
13. $L_3 \le \int_1^4 f(x)\, dx \le R_3$; $R_3 \le \int_1^4 g(x)\, dx \le L_3$; since $f(x)$ is increasing, L_3 underestimates the area and R_3 overestimates the area; since $g(x)$ is decreasing, the reverse is true.
15. In both figures, the error bound for L_3 and R_3 is 7.
17. $S_5 = -260$ **19.** $S_4 = -1{,}194$ **21.** $S_3 = -33.01$ **23.** $S_6 = -38$ **25.** -2.475
27. 4.266 **29.** 2.474 **31.** -5.333 **33.** 1.067 **35.** -1.066 **37.** 15 **39.** 58.5

41. -54 **43.** 248 **45.** 0 **47.** -183 **49.** False **51.** False **53.** False
55. $L_{10} = 286{,}100$ ft^2; error bound is 50,000 ft^2; $n \ge 200$
57. $L_6 = -3.53$, $R_6 = -0.91$; error bound for L_6 and R_6 is 2.63. Geometrically, the definite integral over the interval [2, 5] is the sum of the areas between the curve and the x axis from $x = 2$ to $x = 5$, with the areas below the x axis counted negatively and those above the x axis counted positively.
59. Increasing on $(-\infty, 0]$; decreasing on $[0, \infty)$
61. Increasing on $[-1, 0]$ and $[1, \infty)$; decreasing on $(-\infty, -1]$ and $[0, 1]$ **63.** $n \ge 22$ **65.** $n \ge 104$
67. $L_3 = 2{,}580$, $R_3 = 3{,}900$; error bound for L_3 and R_3 is 1,320
69. (A) $L_5 = 3.72$; $R_5 = 3.37$ (B) $R_5 = 3.37 \le \int_0^5 A'(t)\, dt \le 3.72 = L_5$
71. $L_3 = 114$, $R_3 = 102$; error bound for L_3 and R_3 is 12

Exercises 13-5

1. (A) $F(15) - F(10) = 375$
(B)

3. (A) $F(15) - F(10) = 85$
(B)

5. 40 **7.** 72 **9.** 46.5 **11.** $e - 1 \approx 1.718$
13. $\ln 2 \approx 0.693$ **15.** 0 **17.** 48 **19.** -48
21. -10.25 **23.** 0 **25.** -2 **27.** 14
29. $5^6 = 15{,}625$ **31.** $\ln 4 \approx 1.386$
33. $20(e^{0.25} - e^{-0.5}) \approx 13.550$ **35.** $\frac{1}{2}$
37. $\frac{1}{2}(1 - e^{-1}) \approx 0.316$ **39.** 0

41. (A) Average $f(x) = 250$
(B)
$f(x) = 500 - 50x$

43. (A) Average $f(t) = 2$
(B)
$f(t) = 3t^2 - 2t$

45. (A) Average $f(x) = \frac{45}{28} \approx 1.61$
(B)
$f(x) = \sqrt[3]{x}$

47. (A) Average $f(x) = 2(1 - e^{-2}) \approx 1.73$
(B)
$f(x) = 4e^{-0.2x}$

49. $\frac{1}{6}(15^{3/2} - 5^{3/2}) \approx 7.819$ **51.** $\frac{1}{2}(\ln 2 - \ln 3) \approx -0.203$ **53.** 0

55. 4.566 **57.** 2.214 **61.** $\int_{300}^{900} \left(500 - \frac{x}{3}\right) dx = \$180{,}000$

63. $\int_0^5 500(t - 12)\, dt = -\$23{,}750$; $\int_5^{10} 500(t - 12)\, dt = -\$11{,}250$

65. (A)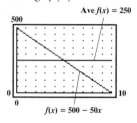
(B) 6,505

67. Useful life $= \sqrt{\ln 55} \approx 2$ yr; total
profit $= \frac{51}{22} - \frac{5}{2}e^{-4} \approx 2.272$ or $\$2{,}272$
69. (A) $\$420$ (B) $\$135{,}000$

71. (A)
(B) $\$100{,}505$

73. $50e^{0.6} - 50e^{0.4} - 10 \approx \$6.51$
75. 4,800 labor-hours
77. (A) $I = -200t + 600$
(B) $\frac{1}{3}\int_0^3 (-200t + 600)\, dt = 300$
79. $100 \ln 11 + 50 \approx 290$ thousand barrels;
$100 \ln 21 - 100 \ln 11 + 50 \approx 115$ thousand barrels

81. $2e^{0.8} - 2 \approx 2.45$ g; $2e^{1.6} - 2e^{0.8} \approx 5.45$ g **83.** $10°C$
85. $0.6 \ln 2 + 0.1 \approx 0.516$; $(4.2 \ln 625 + 2.4 - 4.2 \ln 49)/24 \approx 0.546$

Chapter 13 Review Exercises

1. $3x^2 + 3x + C$ *(13-1)* **2.** 50 *(13-5)* **3.** -207 *(13-5)* **4.** $-\frac{1}{8}(1 - t^2)^4 + C$ *(13-2)* **5.** $\ln|u| + \frac{1}{4}u^4 + C$ *(13-1)*
6. 0.216 *(13-5)* **7.** e^{-x^2} *(13-1)* **8.** $\sqrt{4 + 5x} + C$ *(13-1)* **9.** $y = f(x) = x^3 - 2x + 4$ *(13-3)*

10. (A) $2x^4 - 2x^2 - x + C$ (B) $e^t - 4\ln|t| + C$ *(13-1)* **11.** $R_2 = 72$; error bound for R_2 is 48 *(13-4)*

12. $\int_1^5 (x^2 + 1)\, dx = \frac{136}{3} \approx 45.33$; actual error is $\frac{80}{3} \approx 26.67$ *(13-5)* **13.** $L_4 = 30.8$ *(13-4)*

14. 7 *(13-5)* **15.** Width $= 2 - (-1) = 3$; height $=$ average $f(x) = 7$ *(13-5)* **16.** $S_4 = 368$ *(13-4)* **17.** $S_5 = 906$ *(13-4)*
18. -10 *(13-4)* **19.** 0.4 *(13-4)* **20.** 1.4 *(13-4)* **21.** 0 *(13-4)* **22.** 0.4 *(13-4)* **23.** 2 *(13-4)* **24.** -2 *(13-4)*
25. -0.4 *(13-4)* **26.** (A) 1;1 (B) 4;4 *(13-3)*
27. $dy/dx = (2y)/x$; the slopes computed in Problem 26A are compatible with the slope field shown. *(13-3)*
29. $y = \frac{1}{4}x^2$; $y = -\frac{1}{4}x^2$ *(13-3)*

30. *(13-3)*

31. *(13-3)*

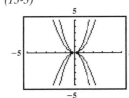

32. $\frac{2}{3}(2)^{3/2} \approx 1.886$ *(13-5)*   **33.** $\frac{1}{6} \approx 0.167$ *(13-5)*

34. $-5e^{-t} + C$ *(13-1)*   **35.** $\frac{1}{2}(1 + e^2)$ *(13-1)*

36. $\frac{1}{6}e^{3x^2} + C$ *(13-2)*   **37.** $2(\sqrt{5} - 1) \approx 2.472$ *(13-5)*

38. $\frac{1}{2}\ln 10 \approx 1.151$ *(13-5)*   **39.** 0.45 *(13-5)*

40. $\frac{1}{48}(2x^4 + 5)^6 + C$ *(13-2)*   **41.** $-\ln(e^{-x} + 3) + C$ *(13-2)*

42. $-(e^x + 2)^{-1} + C$ *(13-2)*

43. $y = f(x) = 3\ln|x| + x^{-1} + 4$ *(13-2, 13-3)*   **44.** $y = 3x^2 + x - 4$ *(13-3)*

45. (A) Average $f(x) = 6.5$

(B)

46. $\frac{1}{3}(\ln x)^3 + C$ *(13-2)*

47. $\frac{1}{8}x^8 - \frac{2}{5}x^5 + \frac{1}{2}x^2 + C$ *(13-2)*

48. $\frac{2}{3}(6 - x)^{3/2} - 12(6 - x)^{1/2} + C$ *(13-2)*

49. $\frac{1,234}{15} \approx 82.267$ *(13-5)*

50. 0 *(13-5)*

51. $y = 3e^{x^3} - 1$ *(13-3)*

52. $N = 800e^{0.06t}$ *(13-3)*

53. Limited growth

(13-3)

54. Exponential decay

(13-3)

55. Unlimited growth

(13-3)

56. Logistic growth

(13-3)

57. 1.167 *(13-5)*   **58.** 99.074 *(13-5)*   **59.** -0.153 *(13-5)*   **60.** $L_2 = \$180,000;$ $R_2 = \$140,000;$ $\$140,000 \le \int_{200}^{600} C'(x)\, dx \le \$180,000$ *(13-4)*

61. $\int_{200}^{600}\left(600 - \frac{x}{2}\right) dx = \$160,000$ *(13-5)*   **62.** $\int_{10}^{40}\left(150 - \frac{x}{10}\right) dx = \$4,425$ *(13-5)*   **63.** $P(x) = 100x - 0.01x^2; P(10) = \$999$ *(13-3)*

64. $\int_{0}^{15}(60 - 4t)\, dt = 450$ thousand barrels *(13-5)*   **65.** 109 items *(13-5)*   **66.** $16e^{2.5} - 16e^2 - 8 \approx \$68.70$ *(13-5)*

67. Useful life $= 10\ln\frac{20}{3} \approx 19$ yr; total profit $= 143 - 200e^{-1.9} \approx 113.086$ or $\$113,086$ *(13-5)*

68. $S(t) = 50 - 50e^{-0.08t}; 50 - 50e^{-0.96} \approx \$31$ million; $-(\ln 0.2)/0.08 \approx 20$ mo *(13-3)*   **69.** 1 cm^2 *(13-3)*   **70.** 800 gal *(13-5)*

71. (A) 133 million   (B) About 61 years *(13-3)*   **72.** $\dfrac{-\ln 0.04}{0.000\,123\,8} \approx 26,000$ yr *(13-3)*

73. $N(t) = 95 - 70e^{-0.1t}; N(15) \approx 79$ words/min *(13-3)*

Chapter 14

Exercises 14-1

1. $\int_a^b g(x)\, dx$ **3.** $\int_a^b [-h(x)]\, dx$

5. Since the shaded region in Figure C is below the x axis, $h(x) \le 0$; so, $\int_a^b h(x)\, dx$ represents the negative of the area.

7. 24   **9.** 51   **11.** 42   **13.** 6   **15.** 0.833   **17.** 2.350   **19.** 1   **21.** 10.5   **23.** 18   **25.** 44

27. $\int_a^b [-f(x)]\, dx$ **29.** $\int_b^c f(x)\, dx + \int_c^d [-f(x)]\, dx$ **31.** $\int_c^d [f(x) - g(x)]\, dx$

33. $\int_a^b [f(x) - g(x)]\, dx + \int_b^c [g(x) - f(x)]\, dx$

35. Find the intersection points by solving $f(x) = g(x)$ on the interval $[a, d]$ to determine b and c. Then observe that $f(x) \ge g(x)$

over $[a, b], g(x) \ge f(x)$ over $[b, c]$, and $f(x) \ge g(x)$ over $[c, d]$.

Area $= \int_a^b [f(x) - g(x)]\, dx + \int_b^c [g(x) - f(x)]\, dx + \int_c^d [f(x) - g(x)]\, dx$.

37. 2.5   **39.** 7.667   **41.** 12   **43.** 15   **45.** 32   **47.** 36   **49.** 9   **51.** 2.832

53. $\int_{-3}^{3}\sqrt{9 - x^2}\, dx; 14.137$ **55.** $\int_0^4 \sqrt{16 - x^2}\, dx; 12.566$ **57.** $\int_{-2}^{2} 2\sqrt{9 - x^2}\, dx; 12.566$

59. 18   **61.** 1.858   **63.** 52.616   **65.** 8   **67.** 101.75   **69.** 17.979   **71.** 5.113   **73.** 8.290   **75.** 3.166   **77.** 1.385

79. Total production from the end of the fifth year to the end of the 10th year is $50 + 100\ln 20 - 100\ln 15 \approx 79$ thousand barrels.

81. Total profit over the 5-yr useful life of the game is $20 - 30e^{-1.5} \approx 13.306$, or $\$13,306$.

83. 1935: 0.412; 1947: 0.231; income was more equally distributed in 1947.
85. 1963: 0.818; 1983: 0.846; total assets were less equally distributed in 1983.
87. (A) $f(x) = 0.3125x^2 + 0.7175x - 0.015$ (B) 0.104
89. Total weight gain during the first 10 hr is $3e - 3 \approx 5.15$ g.
91. Average number of words learned from $t = 2$ hr to $t = 4$ hr is $15 \ln 4 - 15 \ln 2 \approx 10$.

Exercises 14-2

1. 0.43 **3.** 744.99 **5.** 10.27 **7.** 151.75 **9.** 93,268.66 **11.** (A) 10.72 (B) 3.28 (C) 10.72
13. (A) .75 (B) .11
(C)

15. 8 yr **17.** (A) .11 B) .10
19. $P(t \geq 12) = 1 - P(0 \leq t \leq 12) = .89$
21. $12,500
23. If $f(t)$ is the rate of flow of a continuous income stream, then the total income produced from 0 to 5 yr is the area under the graph of $y = f(t)$ from $t = 0$ to $t = 5$.

25. $8,000(e^{0.15} - 1) \approx \$1,295$
27. If $f(t)$ is the rate of flow of a continuous income stream, then the total income produced from 0 to 3 yr is the area under the graph of $y = f(t)$ from $t = 0$ to $t = 3$.

29. $255,562; $175,562 **31.** $6,779.52 **33.** $436.62
35. Clothing store: $66,420.83; computer store: $62,622.66; the clothing store is the better investment.
37. Bond: $12,062.30 business: $11,823.87; the bond is the better investment. **39.** $55,230
41. $\dfrac{k}{r}(e^{rT} - 1)$ **43.** $625,000

45. The shaded area is the consumers' surplus and represents the total savings to consumers who are willing to pay more than $150 for a product but are still able to buy the product for $150.

47. $9,900
49. The area of the region PS is the producers' surplus and represents the total gain to producers who are willing to supply units at a lower price than $67 but are still able to supply the product at $67.

51. $CS = \$3,380; PS = \$1,690$

53. $CS = \$6,980; PS = \$5,041$

55. $CS = \$7,810; PS = \$8,336$

57. $CS = \$8,544; PS = \$11,507$

59. (A) $\bar{x} = 21.457; \bar{p} = \$6.51$
(B) $CS = 1.774$ or $1,774; PS = 1.087$ or $1,087$

Exercises 14-3

1. $\frac{1}{3}xe^{3x} - \frac{1}{9}e^{3x} + C$ **3.** $\dfrac{x^3}{3}\ln x - \dfrac{x^3}{9} + C$ **5.** $u = x + 2$; $\dfrac{(x+2)(x+1)^6}{6} - \dfrac{(x+1)^7}{42} + C$ **7.** $-xe^{-x} - e^{-x} + C$
9. $\frac{1}{2}e^{x^2} + C$ **11.** $(xe^x - 4e^x)|_0^1 = -3e + 4 \approx -4.1548$ **13.** $(x \ln 2x - x)|_1^3 = (3 \ln 6 - 3) - (\ln 2 - 1) \approx 2.6821$
15. $\ln(x^2 + 1) + C$ **17.** $(\ln x)^2/2 + C$ **19.** $\frac{2}{3}x^{3/2}\ln x - \frac{4}{9}x^{3/2} + C$
21. $\dfrac{(x-3)(x+1)^3}{3} - \dfrac{(x+1)^4}{12} + C$ or $\dfrac{x^4}{4} - \dfrac{x^3}{3} - \dfrac{5x^2}{2} - 3x + C$

23. $\dfrac{(2x + 1)(x - 2)^3}{3} - \dfrac{(x - 2)^4}{6} + C$ or $\dfrac{x^4}{2} - \dfrac{7x^3}{3} + 2x^2 + 4x + C$

25. The integral represents the negative of the area between the graph of $y = (x - 3)e^x$ and the x axis from $x = 0$ to $x = 1$.

$y = (x - 3)e^x$

27. The integral represents the area between the graph of $y = \ln 2x$ and the x axis from $x = 1$ to $x = 3$.

$y = \ln 2x$

29. $(x^2 - 2x + 2)e^x + C$ **31.** $\dfrac{xe^{ax}}{a} - \dfrac{e^{ax}}{a^2} + C$ **33.** $\left(-\dfrac{\ln x}{x} - \dfrac{1}{x}\right)\Big|_1^e = -\dfrac{2}{e} + 1 \approx 0.2642$

35. $6 \ln 6 - 4 \ln 4 - 2 \approx 3.205$ **37.** $xe^{x-2} - e^{x-2} + C$ **39.** $\frac{1}{2}(1 + x^2) \ln(1 + x^2) - \frac{1}{2}(1 + x^2) + C$

41. $(1 + e^x) \ln(1 + e^x) - (1 + e^x) + C$ **43.** $x(\ln x)^2 - 2x \ln x + 2x + C$ **45.** $x(\ln x)^3 - 3x(\ln x)^2 + 6x \ln x - 6x + C$

47. 2 **49.** $\dfrac{1}{3}$ **51.** 1.56 **53.** 34.98 **55.** $\int_0^5 (2t - te^{-t})\, dt = \$24$ million

57. The total profit for the first 5 yr (in millions of dollars) is the same as the area under the marginal profit function, $P'(t) = 2t - te^{-t}$, from $t = 0$ to $t = 5$.

$P'(t) = 2t - te^{-t}$

59. $2,854.88 **61.** 0.264

63. The area bounded by $y = x$ and the Lorenz curve $y = xe^{x-1}$, divided by the area under the graph of $y = x$ from $x = 0$ to $x = 1$, is the Gini index of income concentration. The closer this index is to 0, the more equally distributed the income; the closer the index is to 1, the more concentrated the income in a few hands.

$y = x$

$y = xe^{x-1}$

65. $S(t) = 1,600 + 400e^{0.1t} - 40te^{0.1t}$; 15 mo **67.** \$977

69. The area bounded by the price–demand equation, $p = 9 - \ln(x + 4)$, and the price equation, $y = \bar{p} = 2.089$, from $x = 0$ to $x = \bar{x} = 1,000$, represents the consumers' surplus. This is the amount consumers who are willing to pay more than \$2,089 save.

71. 2.1388 ppm

73. $N(t) = -4te^{-0.25t} - 40e^{-0.25t} + 80$; 8 wk; 78 words/min

75. 20,980

$p = D(x)$

$\bar{p} = 2.089$ CS

2,000 x

$\bar{x} = 1,000$

Exercises 14-4

1. $\ln\left|\dfrac{x}{1 + x}\right| + C$ **3.** $\dfrac{1}{3 + x} + 2 \ln\left|\dfrac{5 + 2x}{3 + x}\right| + C$ **5.** $\dfrac{2(x - 32)}{3}\sqrt{16 + x} + C$ **7.** $-\ln\left|\dfrac{1 + \sqrt{1 - x^2}}{x}\right| + C$

9. $\dfrac{1}{2}\ln\left|\dfrac{x}{2 + \sqrt{x^2 + 4}}\right| + C$ **11.** $\frac{1}{3}x^3 \ln x - \frac{1}{9}x^3 + C$ **13.** $x - \ln|1 + e^x| + C$ **15.** $9 \ln\frac{3}{2} - 2 \approx 1.6492$

17. $\frac{1}{2}\ln\frac{12}{5} \approx 0.4377$ **19.** $\ln 3 \approx 1.0986$ **21.** $-\dfrac{\sqrt{4x^2 + 1}}{x} + 2 \ln|2x + \sqrt{4x^2 + 1}| + C$ **23.** $\frac{1}{2}\ln|x^2 + \sqrt{x^4 - 16}| + C$

25. $\frac{1}{6}(x^3\sqrt{x^6 + 4} + 4 \ln|x^3 + \sqrt{x^6 + 4}|) + C$ **27.** $-\dfrac{\sqrt{4 - x^4}}{8x^2} + C$ **29.** $\dfrac{1}{5}\ln\left|\dfrac{3 + 4e^x}{2 + e^x}\right| + C$ **31.** $\frac{2}{3}(\ln x - 8)\sqrt{4 + \ln x} + C$

33. $\frac{1}{5}x^2e^{5x} - \frac{2}{25}xe^{5x} + \frac{2}{125}e^{5x} + C$ **35.** $-x^3e^{-x} - 3x^2e^{-x} - 6xe^{-x} - 6e^{-x} + C$ **37.** $x(\ln x)^3 - 3x(\ln x)^2 + 6x \ln x - 6x + C$

39. $\frac{64}{3}$ **41.** $\frac{1}{2}\ln\frac{9}{5} \approx 0.2939$ **43.** $\dfrac{-1 - \ln x}{x} + C$ **45.** $\sqrt{x^2 - 1} + C$ **47.** 31.38 **49.** 5.48 **51.** $3,000 + 1,500 \ln\frac{1}{3} \approx \$1,352$

53.

$p = D(x)$

CS

$\bar{p} = 15$

250 x

$\bar{x} = 200$

55. $C(x) = 200x + 1,000 \ln(1 + 0.05x) + 25,000$; 608; \$198,773

57. \$18,673.95 **59.** 0.1407

61. As the area bounded by the two curves gets smaller, the Lorenz curve approaches $y = x$ and the distribution of income approaches perfect equality—all persons share equally in the income available.

$y = x$

Lorenz curve

75. (A) $-\frac{13}{3}$ (B) The function $f(0, y)$, for example, has values less than $-\frac{3}{13}$.

77. (A) $c = 1.145$ (B) $f_x(c, 2) = 0$; $f_y(c, 2) = 92.021$

79. $f_{xx}(x, y) + f_{yy}(x, y) = (2y^2 - 2x^2)/(x^2 + y^2)^2 + (2x^2 - 2y^2)/(x^2 + y^2)^2 = 0$

81. (A) $2x$ (B) $4y$

83. $P_x(1{,}200, 1{,}800) = 24$; profit will increase approx. \$24 per unit increase in production of type A calculators at the $(1{,}200, 1{,}800)$ output level; $P_y(1{,}200, 1{,}800) = -48$; profit will decrease approx. \$48 per unit increase in production of type B calculators at the $(1{,}200, 1{,}800)$ output level

85. $\partial x/\partial p = -5$: a \$1 increase in the price of brand A will decrease the demand for brand A by 5 lb at any price level (p, q); $\partial y/\partial p = 2$: a \$1 increase in the price of brand A will increase the demand for brand B by 2 lb at any price level (p, q)

87. (A) $f_x(x, y) = 7.5x^{-0.25}y^{0.25}$; $f_y(x, y) = 2.5x^{0.75}y^{-0.75}$

    (B) Marginal productivity of labor $= f_x(600, 100) \approx 4.79$; Marginal productivity of capital $= f_y(600, 100) \approx 9.58$

    (C) Capital

89. Competitive   **91.** Complementary

93. (A) $f_w(w, h) = 6.65w^{-0.575}h^{0.725}$; $f_h(w, h) = 11.34w^{0.425}h^{-0.275}$

    (B) $f_w(65, 57) = 11.31$: for a 65-lb child 57 in. tall, the rate of change in surface area is 11.31 in.^{2} for each pound gained in weight (height is held fixed); $f_h(65, 57) = 21.99$: for a child 57 in. tall, the rate of change in surface area is 21.99 in.^{2} for each inch gained in height (weight is held fixed)

95. $C_W(6, 8) = 12.5$: index increases approx. 12.5 units for a 1-in. increase in width of head (length held fixed) when $W = 6$ and $L = 8$; $C_L(6, 8) = -9.38$: index decreases approx. 9.38 units for a 1-in. increase in length (width held fixed) when $W = 6$ and $L = 8$.

Exercises 15-3

1. $f_x(x, y) = 4$; $f_y(x, y) = 5$; the functions $f_x(x, y)$ and $f_y(x, y)$ never have the value 0.

3. $f_x(x, y) = -1.2 + 4x^3$; $f_y(x, y) = 6.8 + 0.6y^2$; the function $f_y(x, y)$ never has the value 0.

5. $f(-2, 0) = 10$ is a local maximum.   **7.** $f(-1, 3) = 4$ is a local minimum.

9. f has a saddle point at $(3, -2)$.   **11.** $f(3, 2) = 33$ is a local maximum.

13. $f(2, 2) = 8$ is a local minimum.   **15.** f has a saddle point at $(0, 0)$.

17. f has a saddle point at $(0, 0)$; $f(1, 1) = -1$ is a local minimum.

19. f has a saddle point at $(0, 0)$; $f(3, 18) = -162$ and $f(-3, -18) = -162$ are local minima.

21. The test fails at $(0, 0)$; f has saddle points at $(2, 2)$ and $(2, -2)$.   **23.** f has a saddle point at $(0.614, -1.105)$.

25. $f(x, y)$ is nonnegative and equals 0 when $x = 0$, so f has a local minimum at each point of the y axis.

27. (B) Local minimum   **29.** 2,000 type A and 4,000 type B; Max $P = P(2, 4) = \$15$ million

31. (A) When $p = \$110$ and $q = \$120$, $x = 80$ and $y = 40$; when $p = \$110$ and $q = \$110$, $x = 40$ and $y = 70$

    (B) A maximum weekly profit of \$4,800 is realized for $p = \$100$ and $q = \$120$.

33. $P(x, y) = P(4, 2)$

35. 8 in. by 4 in. by 2 in.

37. 20 in. by 20 in. by 40 in.

Exercises 15-4

1. Max $f(x, y) = f(3, 3) = 18$ **3.** Min $f(x, y) = f(3, 4) = 25$

5. $F_x = -3 + 2\lambda = 0$ and $F_y = 4 + 5\lambda = 0$ have no simultaneous solution.

7. Max $f(x, y) = f(3, 3) = f(-3, -3) = 18$; Min $f(x, y) = f(3, -3) = f(-3, 3) = -18$

9. Maximum product is 25 when each number is 5.   **11.** Min $f(x, y, z) = f(-4, 2, -6) = 56$

13. Max $f(x, y, z) = f(2, 2, 2) = 6$; Min $f(x, y, z) = f(-2, -2, -2) = -6$

15. Max $f(x, y) = f(0.217, 0.885) = 1.055$ **17.** $F_x = e^x + \lambda = 0$ and $F_y = 3e^y - 2\lambda = 0$ have no simultaneous solution.

19. Maximize $f(x, 5)$, a function of just one independent variable.

21. (A) Max $f(x, y) = f(0.707, 0.5) = f(-0.707, 0.5) = 0.47$

23. 60 of model A and 30 of model B will yield a minimum cost of \$32,400 per week.

25. (A) 8,000 units of labor and 1,000 units of capital; Max $N(x, y) = N(8{,}000, 1{,}000) \approx 263{,}902$ units

    (B) Marginal productivity of money ≈ 0.6598; increase in production $\approx 32{,}990$ units

27. 8 in. by 8 in. by $\frac{8}{3}$ in.   **29.** $x = 50$ ft and $y = 200$ ft; maximum area is 10,000 ft^2

Exercises 15-5

1. $y = 0.7x + 1$ **3.** $y = -2.5x + 10.5$ **5.** $y = x + 2$

7. $y = -1.5x + 4.5$; $y = 0.75$ when $x = 2.5$

9. $y = 2.12x + 10.8$; $y = 63.8$ when $x = 25$

11. $y = -1.2x + 12.6$; $y = 10.2$ when $x = 2$

13. $y = -1.53x + 26.67$; $y = 14.4$ when $x = 8$

15. $y = 0.75x^2 - 3.45x + 4.75$ **21.** (A) $y = 1.52x - 0.16$; $y = 0.73x^2 - 1.39x + 1.30$ (B) The quadratic function

23. The normal equations form a system of 4 linear equations in the 4 variables a, b, c, and d, which can be solved by Gauss–Jordan elimination.

25. (A) $y = -65.4x + 3755.7$ (B) 2,709 crimes per 100,000 population

27. (A) $y = -0.48x + 4.38$ (B) \$6.56 per bottle

29. (A) $y = 0.0237x + 18.92$ (B) 19.87 ft

31. (A) $y = 0.0121x + 56.35$ (B) $58.77°F$

Exercises 15-6

1. (A) $3x^2y^4 + C(x)$ (B) $3x^2$ **3.** (A) $2x^2 + 6xy + 5x + E(y)$ (B) $35 + 30y$

5. (A) $\sqrt{y + x^2} + E(y)$ (B) $\sqrt{y + 4} - \sqrt{y}$ **7.** (A) $\dfrac{\ln x \ln y}{x} + C(x)$ (B) $\dfrac{2\ln x}{x}$

9. 9   **11.** 330   **13.** $(56 - 20\sqrt{5})/3$ **15.** 1   **17.** 16   **19.** 49   **21.** $\frac{1}{8}\int_1^5 \int_{-1}^1 (x + y)^2 \, dy \, dx = \frac{32}{3}$

23. $\frac{1}{15}\int_1^4 \int_2^7 (x/y) \, dy \, dx = \frac{1}{2}\ln\frac{7}{2} \approx 0.6264$ **25.** $\frac{4}{3}$ cubic units   **27.** $\frac{32}{3}$ cubic units   **29.** $\int_0^1 \int_1^2 xe^{xy} \, dy \, dx = \frac{1}{2} + \frac{1}{2}e^2 - e$

31. $\int_0^1 \int_{-1}^1 \dfrac{2y + 3xy^2}{1 + x^2} \, dy \, dx = \ln 2$

35. (A) $\frac{1}{3} + \frac{1}{4}e^{-2} - \frac{1}{4}e^2$

(B)

(C) Points to the right of the graph in part (B) are greater than 0; points to the left of the graph are less than 0.

37. $\dfrac{1}{0.4}\int_{0.6}^{0.8} \int_5^7 \dfrac{y}{1 - x} \, dy \, dx = 30 \ln 2 \approx \$20.8$ billion

39. $\frac{1}{10}\int_{10}^{20} \int_1^2 x^{0.75}y^{0.25} \, dy \, dx = \frac{8}{175}(2^{1.25} - 1)(20^{1.75} - 10^{1.75}) \approx 8.375$ or 8,375 units

41. $\frac{1}{192}\int_{-8}^8 \int_{-6}^6 [10 - \frac{1}{10}(x^2 + y^2)] \, dy \, dx = \frac{20}{3}$ insects/ft^2

43. $\frac{1}{8}\int_{-2}^2 \int_{-1}^1 [100 - 15(x^2 + y^2)] \, dy \, dx = 75$ ppm

45. $\frac{1}{10,000}\int_{2,000}^{3,000} \int_{50}^{60} 0.000\,013\,3xy^2 \, dy \, dx \approx 100.86$ ft

47. $\frac{1}{16}\int_8^{16} \int_{10}^{12} 100\dfrac{x}{y} \, dy \, dx = 600 \ln 1.2 \approx 109.4$

Exercises 15-7

1. $R = \{(x, y)|0 \le y \le 4 - x^2, 0 \le x \le 2\}$
$R = \{(x, y)|0 \le x \le \sqrt{4 - y}, 0 \le y \le 4\}$

3. R is a regular x region:
$R = \{(x, y)|x^3 \le y \le 12 - 2x, 0 \le x \le 2\}$

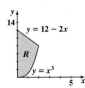

5. R is a regular y region:
$R = \{(x, y)|\frac{1}{2}y^2 \le x \le y + 4, -2 \le y \le 4\}$

7. $\frac{1}{2}$ **9.** $\frac{39}{70}$

11. R consists of the points on or inside the rectangle with corners $(\pm 2, \pm 3)$; both

13. R is the arch-shaped region consisting of the points on or inside the rectangle with corners $(\pm 2, 0)$ and $(\pm 2, 2)$ that are not inside the circle of radius 1 centered at the origin; regular x region

15. $\frac{56}{3}$ **17.** $-\frac{3}{4}$ **19.** $\frac{1}{2}e^4 - \frac{5}{2}$

21. $R = \{(x, y)|0 \le y \le x + 1, \ 0 \le x \le 1\}$
$\int_0^1 \int_0^{x+1} \sqrt{1 + x + y} \, dy \, dx = (68 - 24\sqrt{2})/15$

23. $R = \{(x, y)|0 \le y \le 4x - x^2, 0 \le x \le 4\}$
$\int_0^4 \int_0^{4x - x^2} \sqrt{y + x^2} \, dy \, dx = \frac{128}{5}$

25. $R = \{(x, y) \mid 1 - \sqrt{x} \le y \le 1 + \sqrt{x}, 0 \le x \le 4\}$

$\int_0^4 \int_{1-\sqrt{x}}^{1+\sqrt{x}} x(y - 1)^2 \, dy \, dx = \frac{512}{21}$

27. $\int_0^3 \int_0^{3-y} (x + 2y) \, dx \, dy = \frac{27}{2}$

29. $\int_0^1 \int_0^{\sqrt{1-y}} x\sqrt{y} \, dx \, dy = \frac{2}{15}$

31. $\int_0^1 \int_{4y^2}^{4y} x \, dx \, dy = \frac{16}{15}$

33. $\int_0^4 \int_0^{4-x} (4 - x - y) \, dy \, dx = \frac{32}{3}$

35. $\int_0^1 \int_0^{1-x^2} 4 \, dy \, dx = \frac{8}{3}$

37. $\int_0^4 \int_0^{\sqrt{y}} \frac{4x}{1 + y^2} \, dx \, dy = \ln 17$

39. $\int_0^1 \int_0^{\sqrt{x}} 4ye^{x^2} \, dy \, dx = e - 1$

41. $R = \{(x, y) \mid x^2 \le y \le 1 + \sqrt{x}, 0 \le x \le 1.49\}$

$\int_0^{1.49} \int_{x^2}^{1+\sqrt{x}} x \, dy \, dx \approx 0.96$

43. $R = \{(x, y) \mid y^3 \le x \le 1 - y, 0 \le y \le 0.68\}$

$\int_0^{0.68} \int_{y^3}^{1-y} 24xy \, dx \, dy \approx 0.83$

45. $R = \{(x, y) \mid e^{-x} \le y \le 3 - x, \quad -1.51 \le x \le 2.95\}$ Regular x region

$R = \{(x, y) \mid -\ln y \le x \le 3 - y, \quad 0.05 \le y \le 4.51\}$ Regular y region

$\int_{-1.51}^{2.95} \int_{e^{-x}}^{3-x} 4y \, dy \, dx = \int_{0.05}^{4.51} \int_{-\ln y}^{3-y} 4y \, dx \, dy \approx 40.67$

Chapter 15 Review Exercises

1. $f(5, 10) = 2,900; f_x(x, y) = 40; f_y(x, y) = 70$ *(15-1, 15-2)*   **2.** $\partial^2 z/\partial x^2 = 6xy^2; \partial^2 z/\partial x \, \partial y = 6x^2 y$ *(15-2)*

3. $2xy^3 + 2y^2 + C(x)$ *(15-6)*   **4.** $3x^2 y^2 + 4xy + E(y)$ *(15-6)*   **5.** 1 *(15-6)*

6. $f_x(x, y) = 5 + 6x + 3x^2; f_y(x, y) = -2$; the function $f_y(x, y)$ never has the value 0. *(15-3)*

7. $f(2, 3) = 7; f_y(x, y) = -2x + 2y + 3; f_y(2, 3) = 5$ *(15-1, 15-2)*   **8.** $(-8)(-6) - (4)^2 = 32$ *(15-2)*

9. $(1, 3, -\frac{1}{2}), (-1, -3, \frac{1}{2})$ *(15-4)*   **10.** $y = -1.5x + 15.5; y = 0.5$ when $x = 10$ *(15-5)*   **11.** 18 *(15-6)*   **12.** $\frac{8}{5}$ *(15-7)*

13. $f_x(x, y) = 2xe^{x^2+2y}; f_y(x, y) = 2e^{x^2+2y}; f_{xy}(x, y) = 4xe^{x^2+2y}$ *(15-2)*

14. $f_x(x, y) = 10x(x^2 + y^2)^4; f_{xy}(x, y) = 80xy(x^2 + y^2)^3$ *(15-2)*

15. $f(2, 3) = -25$ is a local minimum; f has a saddle point at $(-2, 3)$. *(15-3)*   **16.** Max $f(x, y) = f(6, 4) = 24$ *(15-4)*

17. Min $f(x, y, z) = f(2, 1, 2) = 9$ *(15-4)*   **18.** $y = \frac{116}{165}x + \frac{100}{3}$ *(15-5)*   **19.** $\frac{27}{5}$ *(15-6)*   **20.** 4 cubic units *(15-6)*

21. 0 *(15-6)*   **22.** (A) 12.56   (B) No *(15-6)*
23. $F_x = 12x^2 + 3\lambda = 0$, $F_y = -15y^2 + 2\lambda = 0$, and $F_\lambda = 3x + 2y - 7 = 0$ have no simultaneous solution. *(15-4)*   **24.** 1 *(15-7)*
25. (A) $P_x(1, 3) = 8$; profit will increase \$8,000 for a 100-unit increase in product A if the production of product B is held fixed at an output level of $(1, 3)$.
   (B) For 200 units of A and 300 units of B, $P(2, 3) = \$100$ thousand is a local maximum. *(15-2, 15-3)*
26. 8 in. by 6 in. by 2 in. *(15-3)*
27. $y = 0.63x + 1.33$; profit in sixth year is \$5.11 million *(15-4)*
28. (A) Marginal productivity of labor ≈ 8.37; marginal productivity of capital ≈ 1.67; management should encourage increased use of labor.
   (B) 80 units of labor and 40 units of capital; Max $N(x, y) = N(80, 40) \approx 696$ units; marginal productivity of money ≈ 0.0696; increase in production ≈ 139 units
   (C) $\dfrac{1}{1,000}\int_{50}^{100}\int_{20}^{40} 10x^{0.8}y^{0.2}\, dy\, dx = \dfrac{(40^{1.2} - 20^{1.2})(100^{1.8} - 50^{1.8})}{216} = 621$ items *(15-4)*
29. $T_x(70, 17) = -0.924$ min/ft increase in depth when $V = 70$ ft^3 and $x = 17$ ft *(15-2)*
30. $\frac{1}{16}\int_{-2}^{2}\int_{-2}^{2}[100 - 24(x^2 + y^2)]\, dy\, dx = 36$ ppm *(15-6)*   **31.** 50,000 *(15-1)*
32. $y = \frac{1}{2}x + 48$; $y = 68$ when $x = 40$ *(15-5)*
33. (A) $y = 0.4933x + 25.20$ (B) 84.40 people/mi^2 (C) 89.30 people/mi^2; 97.70 people/mi^2 *(15-5)*
34. (A) $y = 1.069x + 0.522$ (B) 64.68 yr   (C) 64.78 yr; 64.80 yr *(15-5)*

Appendix A

Exercises A-1

1. vu **3.** $(3 + 7) + y$ **5.** $u + v$ **7.** T   **9.** T   **11.** F   **13.** T   **15.** T   **17.** T   **19.** T   **21.** F   **23.** T   **25.** T   **27.** No
29. (A) F   (B) T   (C) T   **31.** $\sqrt{2}$ and π are two examples of infinitely many.   **33.** (A) N, Z, Q, R (B) R (C) Q, R (D) Q, R
35. (A) F, since, for example, $2(3 - 1) \neq 2 \cdot 3 - 1$ (B) F, since, for example, $(8 - 4) - 2 \neq 8 - (4 - 2)$
   (C) T   (D) F, since, for example, $(8 \div 4) \div 2 \neq 8 \div (4 \div 2)$.
37. $\frac{1}{11}$ **39.** (A) $2.166\,666\,666\ldots$ (B) $4.582\,575\,69\ldots$ (C) $0.437\,500\,000\ldots$ (D) $0.261\,261\,261\ldots$

Exercises A-2

1. 3   **3.** $x^3 + 4x^2 - 2x + 5$ **5.** $x^3 + 1$ **7.** $2x^5 + 3x^4 - 2x^3 + 11x^2 - 5x + 6$ **9.** $-5u + 2$ **11.** $6a^2 + 6a$ **13.** $a^2 - b^2$
15. $6x^2 - 7x - 5$ **17.** $2x^2 + xy - 6y^2$ **19.** $9y^2 - 4$ **21.** $-4x^2 + 12x - 9$ **23.** $16m^2 - 9n^2$ **25.** $9u^2 + 24uv + 16v^2$
27. $a^3 - b^3$ **29.** $x^2 - 2xy + y^2 - 9z^2$ **31.** 1   **33.** $x^4 - 2x^2y^2 + y^4$ **35.** $-40ab$ **37.** $-4m + 8$ **39.** $-6xy$
41. $u^3 + 3u^2v + 3uv^2 + v^3$ **43.** $x^3 - 6x^2y + 12xy^2 - 8y^3$ **45.** $2x^2 - 2xy + 3y^2$ **47.** $x^4 - 10x^3 + 27x^2 - 10x + 1$
49. $4x^3 - 14x^2 + 8x - 6$ **51.** $m + n$ **53.** No change   **55.** $(1 + 1)^2 \neq 1^2 + 1^2$; either a or b must be 0
57. $0.09x + 0.12(10,000 - x) = 1,200 - 0.03x$ **59.** $20x + 30(3x) + 50(4,000 - x - 3x) = 200,000 - 90x$
61. $0.02x + 0.06(10 - x) = 0.6 - 0.04x$

Exercises A-3

1. $3m^2(2m^2 - 3m - 1)$ **3.** $2uv(4u^2 - 3uv + 2v^2)$ **5.** $(7m + 5)(2m - 3)$ **7.** $(4ab - 1)(2c + d)$ **9.** $(2x - 1)(x + 2)$
11. $(y - 1)(3y + 2)$ **13.** $(x + 4)(2x - 1)$ **15.** $(w + x)(y - z)$ **17.** $(a - 3b)(m + 2n)$ **19.** $(3y + 2)(y - 1)$
21. $(u - 5v)(u + 3v)$ **23.** Not factorable   **25.** $(wx - y)(wx + y)$ **27.** $(3m - n)^2$ **29.** Not factorable   **31.** $4(z - 3)(z - 4)$
33. $2x^2(x - 2)(x - 10)$ **35.** $x(2y - 3)^2$ **37.** $(2m - 3n)(3m + 4n)$ **39.** $uv(2u - v)(2u + v)$ **41.** $2x(x^2 - x + 4)$
43. $(2x - 3y)(4x^2 + 6xy + 9y^2)$ **45.** $xy(x + 2)(x^2 - 2x + 4)$ **47.** $[(x + 2) - 3y][(x + 2) + 3y]$ **49.** Not factorable
51. $(6x - 6y - 1)(x - y + 4)$ **53.** $(y - 2)(y + 2)(y^2 + 1)$ **55.** $3(x - y)^2(5xy - 5y^2 + 4x)$ **57.** True   **59.** False

Exercises A-4

1. $8d^6$ **3.** $\dfrac{15x^2 + 10x - 6}{180}$ **5.** $\dfrac{15m^2 + 14m - 6}{36m^3}$ **7.** $\dfrac{1}{x(x - 4)}$ **9.** $\dfrac{x - 6}{x(x - 3)}$ **11.** $\dfrac{-3x - 9}{(x - 2)(x + 1)^2}$ **13.** $\dfrac{2}{x - 1}$ **15.** $\dfrac{5}{a - 1}$
17. $\dfrac{x^2 + 8x - 16}{x(x - 4)(x + 4)}$ **19.** $\dfrac{7x^2 - 2x - 3}{6(x + 1)^2}$ **21.** $\dfrac{x(y - x)}{y(2x - y)}$ **23.** $\dfrac{-17c + 16}{15(c - 1)}$ **25.** $\dfrac{1}{x - 3}$ **27.** $\dfrac{-1}{2x(x + h)}$ **29.** $\dfrac{x - y}{x + y}$
31. (A) Incorrect   (B) $x + 1$ **33.** (A) Incorrect   (B) $2x + h$ **35.** (A) Incorrect   (B) $\dfrac{x^2 - x - 3}{x + 1}$ **37.** (A) Correct
39. $\dfrac{-2x - h}{3(x + h)^2 x^2}$ **41.** $\dfrac{x(x - 3)}{x - 1}$

Exercises A-5

1. $2/x^9$ **3.** $3w^7/2$ **5.** $2/x^3$ **7.** $1/w^5$ **9.** $4/a^6$ **11.** $1/a^6$ **13.** $1/8x^{12}$ **15.** 8.23×10^{10} **17.** 7.83×10^{-1} **19.** 3.4×10^{-5}
21. 40,000   **23.** 0.007   **25.** 61,710,000   **27.** 0.000 808   **29.** 1   **31.** 10^{14} **33.** $y^6/25x^4$ **35.** $4x^6/25$ **37.** $4y^3/3x^5$

39. $\frac{7}{4} - \frac{1}{4}x^{-3}$ **41.** $\frac{5}{2}x^2 - \frac{3}{2} + 4x^{-2}$ **43.** $\frac{x^2(x-3)}{(x-1)^3}$ **45.** $\frac{2(x-1)}{x^3}$ **47.** 2.4×10^{10}; 24,000,000,000

49. 3.125×10^4; 31,250 **51.** 64 **55.** uv **57.** $\frac{bc(c+b)}{c^2 + bc + b^2}$ **59.** (A) \$32,977 (B) \$1,484 (C) 4.50%

61. (A) 9×10^{-6} (B) 0.000 009 (C) 0.0009% **63.** 1,417,000

Exercises A-6

1. $6\sqrt[5]{x^3}$ **3.** $\sqrt[5]{(32x^2y^3)^3}$ **5.** $\sqrt{x^2 + y^2}$ (not $x + y$) **7.** $5x^{3/4}$ **9.** $(2x^2y)^{3/5}$ **11.** $x^{1/3} + y^{1/3}$ **13.** 5 **15.** 64 **17.** -7 **19.** -16
21. $\frac{8}{125}$ **23.** $\frac{1}{27}$ **25.** $x^{2/5}$ **27.** m **29.** $2x/y^2$ **31.** $xy^2/2$ **33.** $1/(24x^{7/12})$ **35.** $2x + 3$ **37.** $30x^5\sqrt{3x}$ **39.** 2 **41.** $12x - 6x^{35/4}$
43. $3u - 13u^{1/2}v^{1/2} + 4v$ **45.** $36m^{3/2} - \frac{6m^{1/2}}{n^{1/2}} + \frac{6m}{n^{1/2}} - \frac{1}{n}$ **47.** $9x - 6x^{1/2}y^{1/2} + y$ **49.** $\frac{1}{2}x^{1/3} + x^{-1/3}$ **51.** $\frac{2}{3}x^{-1/4} + \frac{1}{3}x^{-2/3}$
53. $\frac{1}{2}x^{-1/6} - \frac{1}{4}$ **55.** $4n\sqrt{3mn}$ **57.** $\frac{2(x+3)\sqrt{x-2}}{x-2}$ **59.** $7(x-y)(\sqrt{x} + \sqrt{y})$ **61.** $\frac{1}{xy\sqrt{5xy}}$ **63.** $\frac{1}{\sqrt{x+h} + \sqrt{x}}$
65. $\frac{1}{(t+x)(\sqrt{t} + \sqrt{x})}$ **67.** $x = y = 1$ is one of many choices. **69.** $x = y = 1$ is one of many choices.
71. False **73.** False **75.** False **77.** True **79.** True **81.** False **83.** $\frac{x+8}{2(x+3)^{3/2}}$ **85.** $\frac{x-2}{2(x-1)^{3/2}}$ **87.** $\frac{x+6}{3(x+2)^{5/3}}$
89. 103.2 **91.** 0.0805 **93.** 4,588 **95.** (A) and (E); (B) and (F); (C) and (D)

Exercises A-7

1. $\pm\sqrt{11}$ **3.** $-\frac{4}{3}, 2$ **5.** $-2, 6$ **7.** $0, 2$ **9.** $3 \pm 2\sqrt{3}$ **11.** $-2 \pm \sqrt{2}$ **13.** $0, \frac{15}{2}$ **15.** $\pm\frac{3}{2}$ **17.** $\frac{1}{2}, -3$ **19.** $\left(-1 \pm \sqrt{5}\right)/2$
21. $\left(3 \pm \sqrt{3}\right)/2$ **23.** No real solution **25.** $\left(-3 \pm \sqrt{11}\right)/2$ **27.** $\pm\sqrt{3}$ **29.** $-\frac{1}{2}, 2$ **31.** $(x-2)(x+42)$
33. Not factorable in the integers **35.** $(2x-9)(x+12)$ **37.** $(4x-7)(x+62)$ **39.** $r = \sqrt{A/P} - 1$
41. If $c < 4$, there are two distinct real roots; if $c = 4$, there is one real double root; and if $c > 4$, there are no real roots.
43. 1,575 bottles at \$4 each **45.** 13.64% **47.** 8 ft/sec; $4\sqrt{2}$ or 5.66 ft/sec

Appendix B

Exercises B-1

1. 5, 7, 9, 11 **3.** $\frac{3}{2}, \frac{4}{3}, \frac{5}{4}, \frac{6}{5}$ **5.** 9, -27, 81, -243 **7.** 23 **9.** $\frac{101}{100}$ **11.** $1 + 2 + 3 + 4 + 5 + 6 = 21$ **13.** $5 + 7 + 9 + 11 = 32$
15. $1 + \frac{1}{10} + \frac{1}{100} + \frac{1}{1,000} = \frac{1,111}{1,000}$ **17.** 3.6 **19.** 82.5 **21.** $\frac{1}{2}, -\frac{1}{4}, \frac{1}{8}, -\frac{1}{16}, \frac{1}{32}$ **23.** 0, 4, 0, 8, 0 **25.** $1, -\frac{3}{2}, \frac{9}{4}, -\frac{27}{8}, \frac{81}{16}$ **27.** $a_n = n - 3$
29. $a_n = 4n$ **31.** $a_n = (2n-1)/2n$ **33.** $a_n = (-1)^{n+1}n$ **35.** $a_n = (-1)^{n+1}(2n-1)$ **37.** $a_n = \left(\frac{2}{5}\right)^{n-1}$ **39.** $a_n = x^n$
41. $a_n = (-1)^{n+1}x^{2n-1}$ **43.** $1 - 9 + 25 - 49 + 81$ **45.** $\frac{4}{7} + \frac{8}{9} + \frac{16}{11} + \frac{32}{13}$ **47.** $1 + x + x^2 + x^3 + x^4$ **49.** $x - \frac{x^3}{3} + \frac{x^5}{5} - \frac{x^7}{7} + \frac{x^9}{9}$
51. (A) $\sum_{k=1}^{5}(k+1)$ (B) $\sum_{j=0}^{4}(j+2)$ **53.** (A) $\sum_{k=1}^{4}\frac{(-1)^{k+1}}{k}$ (B) $\sum_{j=0}^{3}\frac{(-1)^j}{j+1}$ **55.** $\sum_{k=1}^{n}\frac{k+1}{k}$ **57.** $\sum_{k=1}^{n}\frac{(-1)^{k+1}}{2^k}$ **59.** False **61.** True
63. 2, 8, 26, 80, 242 **65.** 1, 2, 4, 8, 16 **67.** $1, \frac{3}{2}, \frac{17}{12}, \frac{577}{408}$; $a_4 = \frac{577}{408} \approx 1.414\ 216$, $\sqrt{2} \approx 1.414\ 214$ **69.** 1, 1, 2, 3, 5, 8, 13, 21, 34, 55

Exercises B-2

1. (A) Arithmetic, with $d = -5$; $-26, -31$ (B) Geometric, with $r = -2$; $-16, 32$ (C) Neither (D) Geometric, with $r = \frac{1}{3}$; $\frac{1}{54}, \frac{1}{162}$
3. Geometric; 1 **5.** Neither **7.** Arithmetic; 127.5 **9.** $a_2 = 11, a_3 = 15$ **11.** $a_{21} = 82, S_{31} = 1,922$ **13.** $S_{20} = 930$
15. $a_2 = -6, a_3 = 12, a_4 = -24$ **17.** $S_7 = 547$ **19.** $a_{10} = 199.90$ **21.** $r = 1.09$ or -1.09 **23.** $S_{10} = 1,242, S_\infty = 1,250$
25. 2,706 **27.** -85 **29.** 1,120 **31.** (A) Does not exist (B) $S_\infty = \frac{8}{5} = 1.6$ **33.** 2,400 **35.** 0.999
37. Use $a_1 = 1$ and $d = 2$ in $S_n = (n/2)[2a_1 + (n-1)d]$. **39.** $S_n = na_1$ **41.** No **43.** Yes
45. $\$48 + \$46 + \cdots + \$4 + \$2 = \$600$ **47.** About \$11,670,000 **49.** \$1,628.89; \$2,653.30

Exercises B-3

1. 720 **3.** 10 **5.** 1,320 **7.** 10 **9.** 6 **11.** 1,140 **13.** 10 **15.** 6 **17.** 1 **19.** 816
21. $C_{4,0}a^4 + C_{4,1}a^3b + C_{4,2}a^2b^2 + C_{4,3}ab^3 + C_{4,4}b^4 = a^4 + 4a^3b + 6a^2b^2 + 4ab^3 + b^4$ **23.** $x^6 - 6x^5 + 15x^4 - 20x^3 + 15x^2 - 6x + 1$
25. $32a^5 - 80a^4b + 80a^3b^2 - 40a^2b^3 + 10ab^4 - b^5$ **27.** $3,060x^{14}$ **29.** $5,005p^9q^6$ **31.** $264x^2y^{10}$
33. $C_{n,0} = \frac{n!}{0!\,n!} = 1$; $C_{n,n} = \frac{n!}{n!\,0!} = 1$ **35.** 1 5 10 10 5 1; 1 6 15 20 15 6 1

SUBJECT INDEX

Note: Page numbers followed by fn refer to footnotes.

A

Abscissa, 13, 39
Absolute equality of income, 763–764, 793
Absolute extrema, 672. *See also* Absolute maxima and minima
Absolute inequality of income, 763–764, 793
Absolute maxima and minima, 671–679, 692. *See also* Extrema
  extreme value theorem, 672
  locating absolute extrema, 673–674, 677
  optimization problems (*See* Optimization)
  second derivative and, 674–678
Absolute value, 60
Absolute value function, 59–60, 477
Absorbing chain, 455
Absorbing Markov chains, 453–467
  absorbing states, 454–456
  defined, 455, 468
  graphing calculator approximations, 462–463
  limiting matrix, 446, 457–463
  standard forms for, 456
Absorbing states, 454–456, 468
  and transition matrices, 454
Acceptable probability assignment, 377–378, 379, 427
Addition. *See also* Sum
  elimination by, 174–176
  of fractions, 871
  of matrices, 206–207
  of polynomials, 875
  of rational expressions, 886–888
Addition equality of matrices, 229
Addition principle, 348–349, 369
Addition properties
  of matrices, 206, 229
  of real numbers, 868–869
Algebra, compared to calculus, 474
Algebraic expressions, 873
Alternating series, 912
Amortization, 156–160
Amortization formula, 156, 166
Amortization schedules, 157–160, 166
Amortizing a debt, 156, 166
Amount (future value), 101, 127, 128, 164
Analytic geometry, fundamental theorem of, 13
And, 336, 345, 346, 386–387
Annual nominal rate, 133–134
Annual percentage yield (APY), 139–141, 165
Annuity
  defined, 145, 165
  future value of, 145–148, 165
  ordinary, 145–148, 154, 165
  present value of, 153–155, 165
Antiderivatives, 698–699, 742, 743, 753
Antidifferentiation, 698
  partial, 843–846
Applications. *See* Applications Index, pp. I13–I15.
Approximate empirical probability, 379, 427
Approximating areas by left and right sums, 731–734

Approximation, least squares, 833–838
Approximations using differentials, 538–540
APY (annual percentage yield), 139–141, 165
Area(s)
  approximating by left and right sums, 731–734
  formulas for geometric figures, 924–925
  as function of several variables, 800
  in fundamental theorem of calculus, 741–742
  optimization problems, 680–681
  between two curves, 759–768, 793
Arithmetic mean, 912
Arithmetic sequence, 914–916
Arithmetic series, 916–917
Artificial variable, 315–316, 318, 331
Associative properties
  of matrices, 206, 229
  of real numbers, 868–869
Asymptotes. *See* Horizontal asymptotes; Vertical asymptotes
Augmented coefficient matrix, 184, 245
Augmented matrix, 184
  finding inverse of square matrix, 221
  solving linear systems using, 185–189
Average cost, 547, 553, 665–666
Average profit, 547
Average rate of change, 28, 514, 552
Average revenue, 547
Average value, 747–749, 754
  of continuous function over [a, b], 747–748
  over rectangular regions, 848–849, 863
Average velocity, 515–516
Axis of parabola, 74–75

B

Balance sheet, 148, 165
Banker's year, 129fn
Base, change-of-base formulas, 112, 569fn, 611
Base 2, logarithmic function with, 107
Base e exponential functions, 98–99
Base e logarithms, 110, 565
Base of exponential function, 96, 872
Basic elementary functions, 59–60, 118
Basic feasible solutions, 281–283, 330
  for initial systems, 286
  and simplex method, 284
Basic solutions, 281–283, 330
  for initial systems, 286
Basic variables, 281–283, 288, 330
Bayes, Thomas, 413
Bayes' formula, 411–417, 428
Best approximation, 834
Best fit, 30, 39
Big M method, 279, 315–330, 331
  basics of, 315–318
  minimization by, 322–324
  procedure of, 318–322
Binomial, 873
Binomial formula, 921–922
Binomial theorem, 922–923
Bioclimatic rule for temperate climates, 842–843
Boiling point, 25
Boole, George, 334

Boundary line, half-planes, 251, 277
Bounded function, 91
Bounded solution regions, 261, 277
Box surface area, 5
Break-even analysis, 9–10, 51, 118
Break-even points, 78, 118, 545
British thermal unit (Btu), 511fn

C

Calculators. *See also* Graphing calculators
  permutations, 359
  truth tables, 339
Calculus
  compared to algebra, 474
  fundamental theorem of (*See* Fundamental theorem of calculus)
  multivariable (*See* Multivariable calculus)
Canceling, in fractions, 885
Cardano, Girolamo, 372
Card decks, 363–365
Cartesian coordinate system, 13, 39
Cautions, 114, 136, 141, 196, 230, 302, 406, 484, 548, 566, 701, 703, 710, 718, 882, 895
Cayle, Arthur, 208
Cephalic index, 806
Chain rule, 581–591, 611
  about, 585–588
  composite functions, 581–582, 585
  general derivative rules, 587–588
  general power rule, 581, 583–585
  partial derivatives using, 808
  reversing, 709–711
Chains. *See* Markov chains
Change in x or y, 536
Change-of-base formulas, 112, 569fn, 611
Change-of-variable method, 713, 753
Circle, 593–594, 924
Closed interval, 6
  continuous function on, 505
  finding absolute extrema on, 673–674
Cobb-Douglas production function, 800–801, 809, 827
Coefficients, 873
  augmented coefficient matrix, 184
  leading, 86
Column matrix, 183, 209
Combinations, 360–362, 369
  of n objects, taken r at a time, 360–361
  and permutations, 361–362
Combined properties of matrices, 229
Common difference, in arithmetic sequence, 914
Common factors, 879
Common logarithms, 110, 119, 567
Common ratio, in geometric sequence, 915
Commutative properties
  of matrices, 206, 211, 229
  of real numbers, 868–869
Competitive products, 814
Complement
  of events, 389–391, 427
  of set, 345, 368
Complementary products, 814
Completing the square, 73, 118, 903–904

INDEX OF APPLICATIONS

Life Sciences

A LIBRARY OF ELEMENTARY FUNCTIONS

BASIC FUNCTIONS

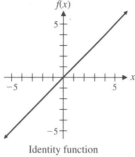

Identity function
$f(x) = x$

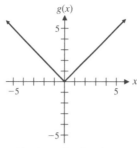

Absolute value function
$g(x) = |x|$

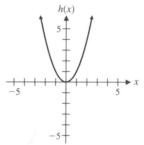

Square function
$h(x) = x^2$

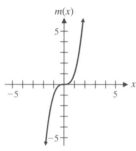

Cube function
$m(x) = x^3$

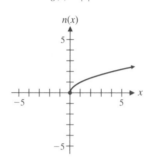

Square root function
$n(x) = \sqrt{x}$

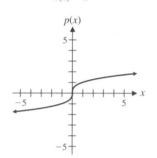

Cube root function
$p(x) = \sqrt[3]{x}$

LINEAR AND CONSTANT FUNCTIONS

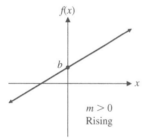

$m > 0$
Rising

Linear function
$f(x) = mx + b$

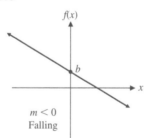

$m < 0$
Falling

Linear function
$f(x) = mx + b$

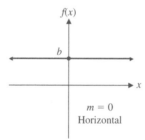

$m = 0$
Horizontal

Constant function
$f(x) = b$

QUADRATIC FUNCTIONS

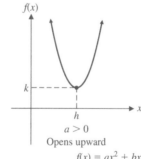

$a > 0$
Opens upward

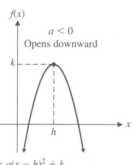

$a < 0$
Opens downward

$$f(x) = ax^2 + bx + c = a(x - h)^2 + k$$

EXPONENTIAL AND LOGARITHMIC FUNCTIONS

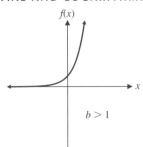

$b > 1$

Exponential function
$f(x) = b^x$

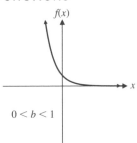

$0 < b < 1$

Exponential function
$f(x) = b^x$

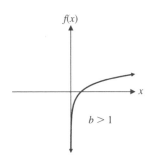

$b > 1$

Logarithmic function
$f(x) = \log_b x$

REPRESENTATIVE POLYNOMIAL FUNCTIONS (DEGREE > 2)

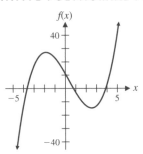

Third-degree polynomial
$f(x) = x^3 - x^2 - 14x + 11$

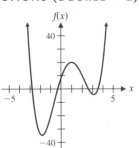

Fourth-degree polynomial
$f(x) = x^4 - 3x^3 - 9x^2 + 23x + 8$

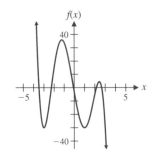

Fifth-degree polynomial
$f(x) = -x^5 - x^4 + 14x^3 + 6x^2 - 45x - 3$

REPRESENTATIVE RATIONAL FUNCTIONS

$f(x) = \dfrac{x - 3}{x - 2}$

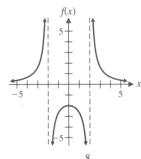

$f(x) = \dfrac{8}{x^2 - 4}$

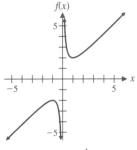

$f(x) = x + \dfrac{1}{x}$

GRAPH TRANSFORMATIONS

Vertical shift
$g(x) = f(x) + 2$
$h(x) = f(x) - 3$

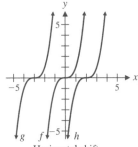

Horizontal shift
$g(x) = f(x + 3)$
$h(x) = f(x - 2)$

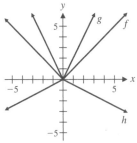

Stretch, shrink and reflection
$g(x) = 2f(x)$
$h(x) = -0.5f(x)$